LEGAL NURSE CONSULTING
PRINCIPLES AND PRACTICES

Legal Nurse Consulting Principles and Practices, Fourth Edition, provides foundational knowledge on the specialty nursing practice of legal nurse consulting. Legal nurse consulting is defined, and essential information about the practice is discussed (history, certification, scope and standards of practice, and ethical and liability considerations). The essentials of the law and medical records are explored. Analysis of the various types of legal cases on which legal nurse consultants work is provided, as are other practice areas for legal nurse consultants. The various roles and skills of legal nurse consultants are explored, and the textbook concludes with discussion of the ways in which legal cases are adjudicated.

This volume allows nurses to bridge the gap from their clinical experience to the unfamiliar territory of the legal world, with practical advice on topics including tactics for being cross-examined in the courtroom and investigative and analytical techniques for medical records. Individual chapters by subject-matter experts focus on the full range of legal, medical, and business issues that new or experienced legal nurse consultants and nurse experts will encounter in their work. A nuanced look at the realities and complexities of toxic torts, medical malpractice cases, civil rights in correctional health care, ERISA and HMO litigation, and other practice areas is offered.

Suitable for experienced nurses studying for certification as legal nurse consultants, and for expert witnesses, practitioners seeking to expand their current legal nurse roles, and other health care and legal practitioners.

Senior Editors:

Julie Dickinson, MBA, BSN, RN, LNCC®, is a Senior Claims Analyst at Allied World Assurance Company in Farmington, CT, where she handles healthcare professional liability claims. Prior to her current position, she worked for nearly 10 years as a legal nurse consultant at Fontaine Alissi, P.C., a defense law firm in Hartford, CT. After graduating as Valedictorian of the Washington Hospital (PA) School of Nursing Class of 1998, Julie earned a Bachelor of Science degree in Nursing in 2000 from Waynesburg College (PA) and was inducted into the Sigma

Theta Tau International Nursing Honor Society. In 2007, Julie graduated from Yale University (CT) as a member of the inaugural class of the Leadership in Healthcare MBA for Executives program. Julie was the founding president of the Connecticut Chapter of the American Association of Legal Nurse Consultants (AALNC), a past president of the AALNC, and a recipient of the AALNC's Distinguished Service Award. She is board-certified in legal nurse consulting and has lectured and published on numerous legal nursing topics.

Anne Meyer, BSN, RN, LNCC®, received her Bachelor of Science degree in Nursing from Marycrest College, Davenport (IA). She obtained board certification as a Legal Nurse Consultant Certified (LNCC®) in 2010. Anne brings over 30 years of professional nursing experience to her work as a consultant and expert witness. She has worked as a hospital staff and charge nurse in medical-surgical, cardiac, and critical care areas, Director of Nursing in both long-term care and a national home health infusion company, and implemented and facilitated a vestibular diagnostic and rehabilitation program for an outpatient rehabilitation company. She is currently President of Med-Law Connection, Inc., a legal nurse consulting firm established in 2005. As an experienced legal nurse consultant, Anne provides consulting and expert witness services to both plaintiff and defense attorneys, insurance companies and corporations covering the areas of medical malpractice and negligence, workers' compensation, personal injury, and long-term care. She is a member of the American Association of Legal Nurse Consultants (AALNC), served as chair of the American Legal Nurse Consultant Certification Board (ALNCCB®) for two years, and as an ALNCCB® board member for an additional four years. Anne has also been an item writer for the Legal Nurse Consultant Certified (LNCC®) examination and authored and edited learning modules for the AALNC online Legal Nurse Consulting course. She is a nurse educator and strong advocate for the nursing profession.

LEGAL NURSE CONSULTING
PRINCIPLES AND PRACTICES
Fourth Edition

Edited by

Julie Dickinson, MBA, BSN, RN, LNCC®
Anne Meyer, BSN, RN, LNCC®

Lead Associate Editors
Karen J. Huff, BSN, RN, LNCC®
Deborah A. Wipf, MS, APRN-GCNS, LNCC®
Elizabeth K. Zorn, RN, BSN, LNCC®

Associate Editors
Kathy G. Ferrell, RN, BS, LNCC®
Lisa Mancuso, BSN, RN, PCCN, CCRN, CLCP, LNCC®
Marjorie Berg Pugatch, MA, RN LNCC®, EMT-B
Joanne Walker, BSEd, RN
Karen Wilkinson, MN, ARNP

AALNC
AMERICAN ASSOCIATION OF
LEGAL NURSE CONSULTANTS

Routledge
Taylor & Francis Group

NEW YORK AND LONDON

AALNC

AMERICAN ASSOCIATION OF
LEGAL NURSE CONSULTANTS

Founded in 1989, the American Association of Legal Nurse Consultants (AALNC) is a not-for-profit membership organization dedicated to the professional enhancement and growth of registered nurses practicing in the specialty of legal nurse consulting and to the advancement of the nursing specialty. The AALNC is the gold standard for professionals with an interest in the legal nurse consulting arena, including novice and veteran legal nurse consultants. The AALNC provides networking opportunities, educational advancement, and professional development and supports certification through the American Legal Nurse Consultant Certification Board (ALNCCB®).

Additional information regarding the AALNC, the ALNCCB®, and their offerings can be found at:

Website: www.aalnc.org
Email: info@aalnc.org
Phone: (312) 321–5177

Fourth edition published 2020
by Routledge
52 Vanderbilt Avenue, New York, NY 10017

and by Routledge
2 Park Square, Milton Park, Abingdon, Oxon, OX14 4RN

Routledge is an imprint of the Taylor & Francis Group, an informa business

© 2020 Taylor & Francis

The right of Julie Dickinson and Anne Meyer to be identified as the authors of the editorial material, and of the authors for their individual chapters, has been asserted in accordance with sections 77 and 78 of the Copyright, Designs and Patents Act 1988.

First edition published by CRC Press 1998
Second edition published by CRC Press 2003
Third edition published by CRC Press 2010

Library of Congress Cataloging-in-Publication Data
Names: Dickinson, Julie, editor. | Meyer, Anne, editor.
Title: Legal nurse consulting : principles and practices / [edited by] Julie Dickinson & Anne Meyer.
Other titles: Legal nurse consulting principles.
Description: 4th edition. | Abingdon, Oxon [UK] ; New York, NY : Routledge, 2019.
Identifiers: LCCN 2019012219 (print) | LCCN 2019012879 (ebook) | ISBN 9780429283642 (Ebook) | ISBN 9780367246402 (hardback)
Subjects: LCSH: Nursing–Law and legislation–United States. | Nursing consultants–Legal status, laws, etc.–United States. | American Association of Legal Nurse Consultants.
Classification: LCC KF2915.N8 (ebook) | LCC KF2915.N8 L349 2019 (print) | DDC 344.7304/14–dc23
LC record available at https://lccn.loc.gov/2019012219

ISBN: 978-0-367-24640-2 (hbk)
ISBN: 978-0-429-28364-2 (ebk)

Typeset in Adobe Garamond
by Wearset Ltd, Boldon, Tyne and Wear

Contents

Karen J. Huff, BSN, RN, LNCC®; Tricia West, RN, BSN, MBA/HCM,
PHN, CHN; and Irene Kniss, RN, BSN, LNCC®; and Contributor:
Tracy Lynn Rodgers, RN, BSN, LNCC®, RN-CLTC, WCC, DWC

Joan Magnusson, BSN, RN, LNCC®; Elizabeth K. Zorn, RN, BSN, LNCC®;
and Julie Dickinson, MBA, BSN, RN, LNCC®

Tonia Aiken, RN, JD; Adam B. Kuenning, JD, LLM; Flynn P. Carey, JD;
Karen E. Evans, BSN, JD; Zakiya Sloley, JD; Grace Morse-McNelis,
BSN, JD

Corey G. Lorenz, Esq.

Peter I. Bergé, JD, MPA, PA-C Emeritus

Nikki Chuml, MSN/Ed, RNC-OB, PRN

Acknowledgments

The publication of this fourth edition textbook was achieved through the generosity of hundreds of volunteers. We are extremely grateful to these individuals for sharing their expertise and donating their time, as their collective contributions made this textbook possible.

The authors undertook the laborious process of updating or overhauling existing chapters and writing new chapters. They gave of their time and knowledge, without which this textbook could not exist. We also thank them for their patience throughout this lengthy project.

The Lead Associate Editors—Debbie Wipf, Beth Zorn, and Karen Huff—have been invaluable, and we are exceptionally grateful for them. They went above and beyond to ensure the quality of the chapters met the high standards set for this textbook. Their guidance, feedback, expertise, and perseverance have been extraordinary, and we cannot thank them enough.

The Associate Editors were instrumental in liaising with the authors, managing the chapters, editing the drafts, and keeping the project moving forward. They shared valuable ideas and suggestions for the project, and we are grateful for their vital contributions.

The peer reviewers were key to ensuring the chapter content was relevant, complete, and up-to-date. Their feedback ensured the textbook provided the necessary information to the readers.

We would like to extend our heartfelt thanks to the AALNC Board of Directors for entrusting us with this critical project. They backed our vision for the textbook, provided us with the resources to make it a reality, and encouraged and supported us along the way. Thank you for giving us this opportunity.

There are numerous other individuals who were essential to this project. Samantha Cook from the AALNC headquarters was indispensable. Her organizational skills, logistical support, and patience are unparalleled, and we could not have done this without her. Laura Harshberger, our project manager, provided considerable guidance, feedback, and publication expertise to us and this project. She was instrumental in helping us move the project to publication. We also wish to thank Mariann Cosby and Cheryl White for their significant contributions to this textbook. Their efforts provided the groundwork for this project.

We are also indebted to our families who provided never-ending encouragement, support, and patience throughout this project. Their sacrifices allowed us the freedom and time to see this project through, and we are so blessed and thankful for their love and support.

Lastly, we are grateful to have had the opportunity to serve together as Senior Editors of this textbook. We shared the same vision for this project, and our approach and leadership styles complemented each other perfectly. It was an honor to work together. We are proud to present this textbook to you, as it lays the foundation for the practice of legal nurse consulting.

Julie Dickinson, MBA, BSN, RN, LNCC®
Anne Meyer, BSN, RN, LNCC®
Senior Editors

Preface

Legal Nurse Consulting Principles and Practices, Fourth Edition, provides foundational information on the practice of legal nurse consulting. Legal nurse consultants (LNCs) apply their nursing education, training, and clinical experience to the evaluation of medically related issues in legal cases or claims. The more LNCs learn and understand the legal context in which this evaluation is performed, the more valuable their work products become to their clients and employers.

This textbook offers a general overview of the basic legal concepts and processes common to medical-legal cases, thereby providing a framework for legal nurse consulting practice. While some state-specific examples are used to illustrate these concepts and processes, it is outside the scope of this textbook to delve into the nuances of each state's laws and statutes. Therefore, it is imperative that LNCs gain an understanding of the relevant laws and statutes in the jurisdictions in which they work.

In addition to introducing nurses to these legal fundamentals and the practice of legal nurse consulting, this textbook is also a resource for experienced LNCs who are seeking to fine-tune their skills, expand into other legal nurse consulting practice areas, offer new services to their clients, enhance their value to existing clients or employers, or transition to a different practice setting.

The continuous evolution of legal nurse consultant practice and the legal arena necessitated an updated textbook to address these changes. This Fourth Edition also features a significant content adjustment and reorganization to allow readers to build their knowledge base as the textbook progresses from the essentials of legal nurse consulting and the law through the adjudication of medical-legal cases. Readers are introduced to the primary practice areas identified in the 2017 Legal Nurse Consultant Practice Analysis conducted by the American Legal Nurse Consultant Certification Board (ALNCCB®). The analysis of cases in these practice areas is a significant focus of the textbook, and effort was made to ensure the broad applicability of this content regardless of the specifics of the underlying case (e.g., the clinical specialty of the medical malpractice case or the type of accident in the personal injury case).

To achieve an even higher-quality benchmark for this widely used textbook, content experts were utilized during every step of the process. Each chapter was written by an author or authors with extensive expertise and experience in the topic and was carefully vetted by another content expert(s) through a double-blind peer review process.

It is because of this consideration and attention to the thoroughness and quality of the content that this textbook is used by the American Association of Legal Nurse Consultants (AALNC) and other providers of LNC education as the core for curriculum development. It is also used by the ALNCCB® and its volunteers as a resource in developing questions for the Legal Nurse Consultant Certified (LNCC®) examination. As such, *Legal Nurse Consulting Principles and Practices* is recognized as the pre-eminent resource on the practice of legal nurse consulting.

Julie Dickinson, MBA, BSN, RN, LNCC®
Anne Meyer, BSN, RN, LNCC®

About the Editors

Senior Editors

Julie Dickinson, MBA, BSN, RN, LNCC® is a Senior Claims Analyst at Allied World Assurance Company in Farmington, CT, where she handles healthcare professional liability claims. Prior to her current position, she worked for nearly 10 years as a legal nurse consultant at Fontaine Alissi, P.C., a defense law firm in Hartford, CT. After graduating as Valedictorian of the Washington Hospital (PA) School of Nursing Class of 1998, Julie earned a Bachelor of Science degree in Nursing in 2000 from Waynesburg College (PA) and was inducted into the Sigma Theta Tau International Nursing Honor Society. In 2007, Julie graduated from Yale University (CT) as a member of the inaugural class of the Leadership in Healthcare MBA for Executives program. Julie was the founding president of the Connecticut Chapter of the American Association of Legal Nurse Consultants (AALNC), a past president of the AALNC, and a recipient of the AALNC's Distinguished Service Award. She is board-certified in legal nurse consulting and has lectured and published on numerous legal nursing topics.

Anne Meyer, BSN, RN, LNCC® received her Bachelor of Science degree in Nursing from Marycrest College, Davenport (IA). She obtained board certification as a Legal Nurse Consultant Certified (LNCC®) in 2010. Anne brings over 30 years of professional nursing experience to her work as a consultant and expert witness. She has worked as a hospital staff and charge nurse in medical-surgical, cardiac, and critical care areas, Director of Nursing in both long-term care and a national home health infusion company, and implemented and facilitated a vestibular diagnostic and rehabilitation program for an outpatient rehabilitation company. She is currently President of Med-Law Connection, Inc., a legal nurse consulting firm established in 2005. As an experienced legal nurse consultant, Anne provides consulting and expert witness services to both plaintiff and defense attorneys, insurance companies and corporations covering the areas of medical malpractice and negligence, workers' compensation, personal injury, and long-term care. She is a member of the American Association of Legal Nurse Consultants (AALNC), served as chair of the American Legal Nurse Consultant Certification Board (ALNCCB®) for two years, and as an ALNCCB® board member for an additional four years. Anne has also been an item writer for the LNCC® examination and authored and edited learning modules for the AALNC online Legal Nurse Consulting course. She is a nurse educator and strong advocate for the nursing profession.

Lead Associate Editors

Karen J. Huff, BSN, RN, LNCC® is an in-house legal nurse consultant for Steptoe & Johnson, a defense firm in Charleston (WV). For over 20 years she has assisted attorneys with a variety of cases, primarily medical malpractice and long-term care litigation. She was the founding president of her local chapter and the WV Bar Association's LNC Section. After two terms on the Certification Board, she was elected to the American Association of Legal Nurse Consultants (AALNC) Board of Directors where she served as AALNC President in 2010.

Deborah A. Wipf, MS, APRN-GCNS, LNCC® has been a legal nurse consultant (LNC) since 1999, working for a law firm for 15 years and as an independent LNC. She has been a nurse for nearly 50 years with varied experiences that include medical-surgical, emergency, flight nursing and flight clinical coordinator (USAF, fixed-wing), intensive care, ambulatory care services, management and administrative duties/positions, military officer position (USAF 20 years). Her editing and writing experience includes position descriptions, policies and procedures, efficiency reports, and American Association of Legal Nurse Consultants (AALNC) projects, including "Growing Your Practice," *Principles and Practices*, Fourth Edition (Lead Associate Editor and co-author of two chapters), and authoring two e-books for the AALNC. Deborah has served as chairperson and/or member of numerous committees, including the AALNC's Scope and Standards of Practice revision (2016–2017; chairperson); the AALNC's Education Committee (2009–2011); quality/risk management, infection control, and pharmacy and therapeutics committees; and executive meetings.

Elizabeth K. Zorn, RN, BSN, LNCC® is a board certified legal nurse consultant with more than 30 years' experience in the legal field. She is a member of the American Association of Legal Nurse Consultants (AALNC) and The American Association for Justice. From 2010 to 2014, she served on the AALNC Board of Directors, including one year as president. Elizabeth has contributed to multiple AALNC educational resources including *Legal Nurse Consulting Principles and Practice* (three editions), the *Journal of Legal Nurse Consulting*, the Online Course, the Code of Ethics, Scope and Standards of Practice, and the LNCC® Review Course. She has presented at several AALNC forums and multiple AALNC webinars. Since 2006, she has served on numerous national AALNC committees. Elizabeth has mentored numerous LNC interns at her law firm and, in 2006, started LNCExchange, a national networking forum for LNCs. Elizabeth's extensive experience in the medical legal field has allowed her to develop an advanced level of knowledge and skills to assist attorneys at Faraci Lange, LLP in the screening and prosecution of medical malpractice, wrongful death, and personal injury claims.

Associate Editors

Kathy G. Ferrell, RN, BS, LNCC® has been a registered nurse for over 30 years and an independent legal nurse consultant since 2001. She graduated from Georgia Baptist Hospital School of Nursing in Atlanta, GA, where she obtained a nursing diploma. She then obtained a Bachelor of Science in Health Arts from the University of St. Francis in Joliet (IL). Her clinical experiences include medical/surgical and OB-GYN nursing, nursing education, and healthcare insurance. Kathy uses her unique knowledge and experiences to work with plaintiff and defense attorneys in cases involving medical malpractice, person injury, product liability, and insurance. She also serves as an expert witness in cases involving insurance and billing issues. Kathy has been a member of the American Association of Legal Nurse Consultants (AALNC) since 2006 and has served on various committees and the Board of Directors. She has authored several articles and educational products for the AALNC.

Lisa Mancuso, BSN, RN, PCCN, CCRN, CLCP, LNCC® has been a staff nurse in Boston since 1983. Her clinical focus is cardiology, nephrology, and progressive care nursing. She is a past recipient of the Massachusetts Nurses' Association Award for Excellence in Nursing Practice. In 2010, Lisa started Mancuso Medical Legal Consulting. She does "behind-the-scenes" consulting for medical malpractice, workers' compensation, and criminal cases. Lisa also provides expert witness testimony. In 2016, Lisa certified as a Life Care Planner and is busy expanding this aspect of her business. Lisa has been the chairperson of the American Association of Legal Nurse Consultants (AALNC)'s Online Educational and Professional Development Committee since 2017 and has enjoyed being an Associate Editor for *Principles and Practices*, Fourth Edition.

Marjorie Berg Pugatch, MA, RN, EMT-B, LNCC®, has been an LNC since 1998 with the defense firm of Lewis Johs Avallone Aviles with locations in New York City and Long Island. She joined the American Association of Legal Nurse Consultants (AALNC) in 1998 and has served the AALNC on many committees and in many capacities over the years. She obtained her LNCC® in 2007. She has authored journal articles and served as an author and associate editor to the Fourth Edition of the *Principles and Practices* textbook and has presented at previous forums, on the chapter level and in the webinar format for the AALNC. She has sat on the AALNC Board of Directors as a Director at Large since 2018.

Joanne Walker, BSEd, RN has been a nurse for over 40 years and has extensive clinical experience in the Perioperative area. She has worked as a legal nurse consultant (LNC) since 2007 and has testified as an expert witness at trial. She founded Clarity Medical Legal Consulting in 2009. Joanne's interest in Nursing Research has developed over her career, both in the operating room and as an LNC. Her goal is to de-mystify the science of research for other LNCs. Joanne is a member of several professional organizations, keeping up to date in clinical advances to retain her RN license and assist her clients with their research needs.

Karen Wilkinson, MN, ARNP, LNCC®, CNLCP® offers a broad 36-year expertise in all types of nursing. This includes 20 years as a nursing faculty member, being the author of numerous publications related to nursing practice, and having a paralegal degree.

Contributors

Tonia Aiken, RN, JD
Law Office of Tonia D. Aiken, RN, JD

Tracy Albee, BSN, RN, PHN, LNCC®,
CLCP, FIALCP
MediLegal, A Professional Nursing
Corporation

Rachael Arruda, BA, RN, LNCC®, CCM
StarLine

Marguerite Barbacci, BSN, RN,
MPH, LNCC®
Independent LNC

Patricia J. Bartzak, DNP, RN, CMSRN
Milford Regional Medical Center,
Milford, MA

Martha Heath Beach, MS, M.Ed., RN, CNS,
ARNP, CNP, CRC, CCM, CDMS, CLCP,
CNLCP®, CCRN, CNRN, CNOR, LNCC®,
CCNS, ACNP-BC
Law Nurse, LLC—President

Peter I. Bergé, JD, MPA, PA-C Emeritus
Medicolegal Consulting and Education

Kathleen P. Buckheit, MPH, BSN, RN,
CEN, COHN-S/CM, CCM, FAAOHN
NC OSHERC at UNC-Chapel Hill

Joahnna Evans Budge, BSN, RN,
CCRN, CLNC
Songer Evans Legal Nurse Experts

Rebecca Mendoza Saltiel Busch, MBA,
CCM, RN, CFE, CPC, CHS-IV, CRMA,
CICA, FIALCP, FHFMA
Medical Business Associates, Inc.

Kelly K. Campbell, RN, BSN, CP,
CLNC, CLCP
CARDINAL LifeCare Consulting

Elena Capella, EdD, RN, CNL,
CPHQ, LNCC®
University of San Francisco

Flynn P. Carey, JD
Mitchell Stein Carey Chapman, PC

Nikki Chuml, MSN/Ed, RNC-OB, PRN
Nikki Chuml Consulting

Mariann F. Cosby, DNP, MPA, RN, PHN,
CEN, NE-BC, LNCC®, CLCP, CCM, MSCC
MFC Consulting

Sean Dennin
Precise, Inc.

Julie Dickinson, MBA, BSN, RN, LNCC®
Allied World Assurance Company

Marian Ead, BSN, RN
Massachusetts Board of Registration in
Medicine

J. Thaddeus Eckenrode, Esq.
Eckenrode-Maupin, Attorneys at Law

Bruce Edens, MD
Kaiser Permanente

Deborah Enicke, RN, CEN, COS-C, HCS-D
Enicke and Associates, LLC

Karen E. Evans, BSN, JD
The Cochran Firm

Margaret M. Gallagher, RN, MSN, LNCC®, CLNC
Patient Care Executive Consulting, LLC

Vicki W. Garnett, RN, CCRC, LNCC®
Chesterfield, Virginia

William P. Gavin, Esq.
Gavin Law Firm LLC

Patricia Ann "Stormy" Green, RN, BSHS, RNFA
Green Legal Nurse Consultants

Sandra Higelin, MSN, RN, CNS, CWCN, CLNC
Sandra Higelin Nurse Consulting Services

Wendie A. Howland, MN, RN-BC, CRRN, CCM, CNLCP®, LNCC®
Howland Health Consulting

Karen J. Huff, BSN, RN, LNCC®
Steptoe & Johnson PLLC

Patricia W. Iyer, MSN, RN, LNCC®
President, LNC Academy

Todd A. Jennings, Esq.
Macfarlane Ferguson & McMullen

Katy Jones, MSN, RN
LNCtips.com

Moniaree Parker Jones, EdD, MSN, RN, CCM, COI
Samford University

Jennifer C. Jordan, Esq., MSCC, CMSP-F
Special Counsel to the Louisiana Association of Self Insured Employers

Irene Kniss, RN, BSN, LNCC®
Kniss & Spencer Legal Nurse Solutions

Adam B. Kuenning, JD, LLM
Erickson Sederstrom

Corey G. Lorenz, Esq.
Habush Habush & Rottier S.C.

Mark A. Love, Esq.
Selman Breitman LLP

Linda Luedtke, MSN, RN
MLCS, Inc.

Cynthia A. Maag, BA, RN, LNCC®
Eckenrode-Maupin

Joan Magnusson, BSN, RN, LNCC®
JKM Consulting LLC

Sharon K. McQuown, MSN, RN, LNCC®
Law Offices of Frank L. Branson PC

Anne Meyer, BSN, RN, LNCC®
Med-Law Connection, Inc.

Phyllis ZaiKaner Miller, RN
In house Medical Legal Analyst, Retired

Grace Morse-McNelis, BSN, JD
Sands Anderson, PC

Elizabeth Murray, BSN, RN, LNCC®
Elizabeth Murray Consulting, LLC

Andree Neddermeyer, RN, MBA, CPHRM, CSSGB
Nova Consulting

Stacy Newsome, MSN, RN, LNCC®
Stacy Newsome, LNCC®, LLC

Jennifer Oldham, BSN, RN, CEN, SANE-A
Christiana Care Health System

**Victoria Powell, RN, CCM, LNCC®,
CNLCP®, CLCP, CBIS, CEASII**
VP Medical Consulting, LLC

**Marjorie Berg Pugatch, MA, RN
LNCC®, EMT-B**
Lewis Johs Avallone Aviles

**Diane L. Reboy, MS, BSN, RN, LNCC®,
CNLCP®, CCDS**
DLR Associates

Annalese H. Reese, Esq.
Hall Booth Smith, P.C.

Paul K. Reese, Esq.
Steptoe & Johnson PLLC

**Rebecca A. Reier, BS, RN, CRNA
(Ret.), CCS-P**
Med-Econ, Inc.

**Tracy Lynn Rodgers, RN, BSN, LNCC®,
RN-CLTC, WCC, DWC**
First Choice Legal Nurse Consulting, LLC

**Leslie Schumacher, RN, CRRN, CCM,
LNCC®, CLCP, CNLCP®, MSCC, CMSP-F**
PlanPoint LLC

Noreen Sisko, PhD, RN
Cape Medical-Legal Consulting

Zakiya Sloley, JD
The Cochran Firm

**Anita Symonds, MS, BSN, RN, CFC, CFN,
SANE-A, SANE-P**
Christiana Care Health System

Kelly Tanner, BSN, RN, CCRN-A, CNLCP®
Tanner Legal Nurse Consulting, PLLC

Diane Trace Warlick, RN, JD
Nurse Attorney Institute, LLC

Cathy Weitzel, MSN, APRN
Wichita State University School of Nursing

**Tricia West, RN, BSN, MBA/HCM,
PHN, CHN**
P J West and Associates, Inc.

**Cheryl E. White, MSHL, BS, AS, RN,
LHRM, LNCC®, MSCC, DFSHRMPS**
Total Pain and Risk Consultants, LLC

Kari Williamson, BS, RN, LNCC®, CCM
CEO, MKC Medical Management

**Deborah A. Wipf, MS, APRN-
GCNS, LNCC®**
American Association of Legal Nurse
Consultants

Paula J. Yost, Esq., LPCA
Law Office of Paula J. Yost

Elizabeth K. Zorn, RN, BSN, LNCC®
Faraci Lange, LLP

Reviewers

Alice Adams, RN, LNCC®, MSCC, CNLCP®
Medical Case Consultants, LLC

Darla Adams, APRN-BC, MSN, HHCNS-BC, CHCE, C-AL, CFN
Darla Adams & Associates, LLC

Garrett Asher, JD, BSN, RN
Surber, Asher, Surber & Moushon, PLLC
Attorneys at Law

Kathleen C. Ashton, PhD, RN, ACNS-BC
Drexel University, Philadelphia, PA

Sarah Barnes, RN, DNP
California State University

Jane E. Barone, BS, RN, LNCC®
Medi-Law Solutions, LLC

Jennie Bergen, EdD, RNC-OB
Clayton State University

Kristen Bishop, MSN, RN, NE-BC, CPPS, OCN
PA Department of Health

Colleen M. Blinkoff, JD
Doran & Murphy, PLLC

Kelly K. Campbell RN, BSN, CP, CLNC, CLCP
CARDINAL LifeCare Consulting

Pamela Chambers, DNP, EJD, MSN, CRNA
Pamela Chambers Consulting

Rebecca Clay, RN, LNCC®, MSCC, CLCP, CMSP
MEDliable, LLC

Mindy Cohen, MSN, RN, LNCC®
Mindy Cohen & Associates

Marlene Garvis, JD, MSN
Marlene S. Garvis, LLC

Jane Grametbaur, RN, CCHP-A, CCHP-RN
Retired

Patricia Ann "Stormy" Green, RN, BSHS, RNFA
Green Legal Nurse Consultants

Kimberly A. Such Groteboer, BSN, RN, CHC, CDMS, QRC
Nursing Analysis & Review, LLC

Deborah J. Hafernick, BSN, RN
Hafernick Legal-Nurse Consulting

James Hanus, MHA, BSN, RN, OCN
McKesson Corp/US Oncology

Jane D. Heron, MBA, BSN, RN, LNCC®
Heron and Associates, LLC Medical Legal Consulting

Wendie A. Howland, MN, RN-BC, CRRN, CCM, CNLCP®, LNCC®
Howland Health Consulting

Genifer J. Johnson, DHA, MSN, RN
Palm Beach Vocational Institute

Tamara Karlin, RN, LNCC®
Hanover Insurance Group

Deana Kilmer, MBA, MSN, CRNP, FNP-CB, HNB-BC, CLCP, MSCC
DMK Medical Legal Consulting, LLC

William C. Krasner, Esq., RN, JD, MBA, BSN
Millville Rescue Squad

Julie A. Marlatt, MSN, RNC-NIC
MKC Medical Management

Cynthia Mascarenhas, RN, LNCC®
Legal Nurse Consulting Matters, LLC

Adam Mack McKinnon, Sr., BSN, RN, CCRN
McKinnon Legal Nurse Consulting

Veronica McMillan, JD, BSN
Mount Saint Mary College

Angela Renee Miller, RN
Garretson Resolution Group

Stacey A. Mitchell, DNP, RN, SANE-A, SANE-P, FAAN
Texas A&M University Health Science Center

Anita Beasley Ogle, BSN, RN, CCM, QRP
Anita Ogle & Associates

Jacqueline Olexy, JD, MSN, CCHP
Madison, Mroz, Steinman & Dekleva, PA

Rebecca Paley, BSN, RN
Independent Contractor

Deanna W. Parsons, RN, BSN, MBA, LNCC®, CPHRM, CPPS
Cabell Huntington Hospital, Inc.

Kimberly M. Pearson, MHA, MBA, RN, CCHP
Kimberly M. Pearson, Consultant

Maureen T. Power, RN, MPH, LNCC®
Farmers Insurance

Elizabeth Sassatelli, PhD, RN
University of Tampa

Jane Shufro, MS, BSN, RN, CPAN, LNCC®
Brigham and Women's Faulkner Hospital

Gerrie M. Springston, BSN, RN, LNCC®, CCM, CNLCP®
Vocational Diagnostics, Inc.

Wendy L. Votroubek, RN, MPH, LNC
Integrity Legal Nurse Consulting PDX

Annette H. Weisgarber, BSN, RN, LNCC®
Sanford Health

Julie Wescott, DNP, CNS, ACNS-BC, CNS-BC, CEN
Hourigan, Kluger & Quinn

Judy A. Young, MSN, MHL, RN, LNCC®
Florida Legal Nurse Experts, LLC

Section I

Essentials of Legal Nurse Consulting

Chapter 1

History, Entry into Practice, and Certification

Karen J. Huff, BSN, RN, LNCC®
Tricia West, RN, BSN, MBA/HCM, PHN, CHN
Irene Kniss, RN, BSN, LNCC®

Contributor:
Tracy Lynn Rodgers, RN, BSN, LNCC®, RN-CLTC, WCC, DWC

Contents

Objectives

- Describe the role of the American Association of Legal Nurse Consultants in developing, supporting, and promoting the nursing specialty practice of legal nurse consulting
- List the pros and cons of in-house and independent legal nurse consulting practice
- Define the qualities and traits of successful legal nurse consultants
- Explain the difference between certification and a certificate
- Identify the purpose of specialty nursing certification
- Describe how the LNCC® meets accreditation standards

Introduction

Legal nurse consulting is an exciting and unique specialty nursing practice that emerged in the early 1970s. This chapter details the history of legal nursing, including the founding of the American Association of Legal Nurse Consultants (AALNC) in 1989 and its major accomplishments over the next several decades. For nurses who are considering entry into legal nurse consultant practice, the pros and cons of working independently and in-house are explored, as are the necessary qualities, traits, skills, and education. The distinction between certification and a certificate of completion is explained and segues into a detailed discussion of the American Legal Nurse Consultant Certification Board (ALNCCB®) and the Legal Nurse Consultant Certified (LNCC®) credential. The LNCC® is the only certification in legal nurse consulting recognized by the AALNC and accredited by the Accreditation Board of Specialty Nursing Certification (ABSNC).

History

Early Legal Nurse Consultant Practice

It is difficult to determine exactly when nurses gained recognition as legal nurse consultants (LNCs) since attorneys have sought nurses to answer questions for many years regarding medical-legal matters. But at least since the early 1970s, nurses have been recognized as consultants to attorneys and have been compensated for their expertise and contributions. Nurses' earliest and most common experiences in the legal arena were as expert witnesses in nursing malpractice cases. During the 1980s, nursing malpractice litigation expanded along with medical malpractice. Courts began to recognize that nurses, rather than physicians, should define and evaluate the standards of nursing practice. Nurses became more interested and educated about the legal issues impacting health care, and it was clear to both nurses and attorneys that nurses were uniquely qualified to aid attorneys in their nursing malpractice cases. Attorneys sought nurses to review these cases and offer opinion testimony about nursing care, and thus the role of the nurse expert witness came to be essential for nursing malpractice cases.

During the same period, attorneys were searching for resources to help them understand medical records, medical literature, hospital policies and procedures, and medical testimony. Nurse consultants came to be valued as cost-effective alternatives to physician consultants, who were often unavailable due to their practice demands. Law firms began to employ nurses "behind-the-scenes" (i.e., not for expert witness testimony) and valued their expertise and input on a broader scope—not just in medical and nursing negligence cases but in personal injury and criminal cases as well. Since then, the scope of practice for LNCs has broadened considerably and includes the practice areas discussed below in Table 1.4 and in subsequent chapters of this textbook.

Formation of the Association

During the 1980s, nurses in California, Arizona, and Georgia, who were practicing as consultants to attorneys, formed local professional groups. Their goals were to educate the legal profession about the effectiveness of the nurse consultant as a liaison between the legal and medical communities and to provide a network for members to share expertise. Leaders from these three groups became the driving force for founding the national association. On July 29, 1989, a steering committee composed of these leaders met in San Diego and founded the American Association of Legal Nurse Consultants. From its inception, the AALNC was established as a nursing organization, rather than a legal organization. The founding members were passionate about distinguishing legal nurse consulting as a specialty practice of nursing, not of the law—a fundamental belief that continues to be important today.

The national steering committee was replaced as the decision-making body of the AALNC when the first board of directors was elected in March 1990. The AALNC's mission of promoting the professional advancement of registered nurses (RNs) consulting within the legal arena was inaugurated.

Definition of Legal Nurse Consulting

The AALNC defines legal nurse consulting as follows:

> The legal nurse consultant is a licensed registered nurse who performs a critical analysis of clinically related issues in a variety of settings in the legal arena.

Legal nurse consulting:

- Is the application of knowledge acquired during the course of professional nursing education, training, and clinical experience to the evaluation of standard of care, causation, damages and other clinically related issues in cases or claims
- Is the application of additional knowledge acquired through education and experience regarding applicable legal standards and/or strategy to the evaluation of cases or claims
- Involves critical analysis of healthcare records and medical literature, as well as relevant legal documents and other information pertinent to the evaluation and resolution of cases or claims
- Results in the development of case-specific work products and opinions for use by legal professionals or agencies handling cases or claims (AALNC, 2017, p. 4).

Major Contributions

Since its formation in 1989, the AALNC has made countless contributions to the specialty practice of legal nurse consulting. These contributions were made possible by the efforts of innumerable volunteers and were achieved through various means, including chapters, education, certification, publications, code of ethics, scope and standards of practice, position statements, and professional relationships.

Chapters

While the AALNC offered national membership benefits to nurses licensed in any state or territory of the United States, it was through the establishment of chartered chapters that the AALNC fostered membership growth, networking, and education at the local level. As more LNCs found it beneficial to attend in-person chapter meetings, the number of chapters grew and within one year (by 1990), there were nine chapters (Bogart, 1998). In more recent years, the option of "virtual" meetings became a reality, and many chapters began offering online meetings and educational programs to attract members. Several chapters have expanded their membership using these meeting tools.

Education

The AALNC offers numerous educational opportunities in live, online, print, and audio formats. These are designed to assist nurses at all levels of expertise in legal nurse consulting practice. Information regarding all of the AALNC's educational opportunities is available at the AALNC website (www.aalnc.org). The AALNC is accredited as a provider of continuing nursing education by the American Nurses Credentialing Center's (ANCC's) Commission on Accreditation. The AALNC Director of Programs and Education oversees the association's educational offerings and ensures that education provided by the association complies with ANCC standards.

ANNUAL EDUCATIONAL AND NETWORKING FORUM

The first annual AALNC educational conference was held in Phoenix, Arizona in 1990. Now known as the Educational and Networking Forum, this annual conference has been the major networking and educational opportunity for LNCs. The Forum offers cutting-edge clinical, legal, and practice topics and high-profile speakers as well as sessions for the less experienced LNC. It also includes the AALNC annual business meeting and provides for the transition of board members.

LEGAL NURSE CONSULTING PROFESSIONAL COURSE

The AALNC introduced its first online legal nurse consulting course in 2007. Developed by experienced LNC content experts, the Legal Nurse Consulting Professional Course provides learners with a convenient, self-paced, and cost-effective method of securing information needed to begin legal nurse consulting practice. Originally offered in eight modules, the online course underwent a significant revision when it was expanded to 17 modules, which were released over several years from 2015 to 2017 (Dickinson, 2015).

WEBINARS

In the summer of 2010, the AALNC launched its first webinar series for members and non-members (Huff, 2010a). Now offered on a variety of clinical, legal, and practice topics year-round, AALNC webinars are a convenient way to obtain continuing nursing education credits without incurring the cost of travel. The AALNC Online Educational and Professional Development Committee (formerly the Webinar Committee) oversees the selection of topics and speakers. Most webinars are recorded and available "on demand" for attendees who are unable to attend the "live" webinar. Currently, AALNC membership includes a certain number of free webinars per year as a benefit of membership. In addition, the AALNC Board of Directors periodically hosts a free webinar entitled "So You Want to Be an LNC" to educate nurses interested in becoming an LNC (Huff, 2011a). This webinar is also a useful resource for newer LNCs. The AALNC has also offered joint webinars with attorney and nursing organizations, which will be discussed later in this chapter.

LEGAL NURSE CONSULTANT CERTIFIED (LNCC®) REVIEW COURSE

In 2012, the AALNC launched the LNCC® Review Course to help LNCs prepare for the LNCC® exam. The course is based on the LNC Practice Analysis, and now includes 12 content webinars plus one webinar devoted to test-taking tips. These webinars may also be of interest to any LNC wishing to learn more about a particular area of legal nurse consulting practice. More information about the LNCC® Review Course can be found on the AALNC website at www.aalnc.org/page/lncc-review-course.

Certification

Recognizing the importance of nursing certification that incorporates experiential and educational requirements, the AALNC established the American Legal Nurse Consultant Certification Board (ALNCCB®) in 1997. The ALNCCB® developed the LNCC® certification program and credential, with the first exam given in 1998. The LNCC® is the only certification in legal nurse consulting that is endorsed by the AALNC and accredited by the ABSNC, formerly known as the Accreditation Council for the American Board of Nursing Specialties (ABNS). A more detailed discussion regarding the LNCC® program and credential is provided later in this chapter.

Publications

NEWSLETTERS

From its inception, the AALNC has provided a newsletter to its members. Initially called Network News, this communication tool has changed over the years and is now an electronic Member Update. This update is sent monthly via email to provide members with professional and organizational information. The *President's Blog* has also been used by the association's leadership to communicate with the membership. Additionally, a monthly education update is sent to the members summarizing upcoming webinars and other educational opportunities.

JOURNAL OF LEGAL NURSE CONSULTING

In January 1995, the AALNC issued the first edition of the *Journal of Legal Nurse Consulting* (*JLNC*), which is the official publication of the AALNC. It is a refereed journal providing articles of interest to nurses in the legal nurse consulting specialty. The JLNC is now digital and is available to members and non-members on the AALNC website.

LEGAL NURSE CONSULTING PRINCIPLES AND PRACTICES

The first edition of *Legal Nurse Consulting Principles and Practice* (Bogart, 1998) was published in 1998 as the AALNC's effort to provide a core curriculum for LNCs. It became the primary resource textbook for legal nurse consulting courses and for nurses who wished to learn more about this practice specialty through self-study. The core curriculum is also a key reference for the LNCC® exam. It is used by the ALNCCB® during exam development and also by LNCs studying to take the exam.

The second edition was published in 2003 (Iyer, 2003). With the publication of the third edition in 2010, the textbook expanded to two volumes: *Legal Nurse Consulting Principles* (Volume 1) and *Legal Nurse Consulting Practices* (Volume 2) (Peterson & Kopishke, 2010). This Fourth Edition is a continuation of the AALNC's ongoing effort to provide nurses with an authoritative reference regarding the practice of legal nurse consulting.

OTHER PROFESSIONAL RESOURCES

The AALNC also publishes a variety of other professional resources, such as reference cards on various relevant topics, the "Growing Your Practice" online resource, and "The Nurse Expert Witness: Guidelines for Practice" virtual booklet. Such resources are available for sale to assist LNCs in establishing and developing their businesses or practices. These materials are designed to give realistic and practical information to enhance the practitioner's knowledge and skills.

The AALNC's online resources include the LNC Locator®, which is designed to assist other professionals, including attorneys, with finding an LNC or nurse expert witness in a certain geographic area and/or with a certain clinical or legal nurse consulting background.

Code of Ethics and Scope and Standards of Practice

CODE OF ETHICS

The *Code of Ethics and Conduct with Interpretive Discussion* was originally adopted in April 1992 and subsequently revised in 2005, 2009, and 2015. The code provides guidelines for ethical performance and conduct in the practice of legal nurse consulting (AALNC, 2015). See Chapter 2 for more information on the AALNC's *Code of Ethics and Conduct.*

SCOPE AND STANDARDS OF PRACTICE FOR THE LNC

In its initial effort to develop a scope of practice and standards of practice for legal nurse consulting, the AALNC conducted a role delineation study in 1992. The survey document contained questions regarding professional activities to identify the essential knowledge and skills for legal nurse consulting practice. Following the analysis of the survey data provided by LNC members, the AALNC published the first edition of the *Scope of Practice for the Legal Nurse Consultant* in January 1994 (AALNC, 1994).

In 1995, the AALNC Board of Directors determined that, while LNCs need legal knowledge and skills, the nursing profession is the basis for the practice of legal nurse consulting. In October 1995, the AALNC published *Scope and Standards of Practice for the Legal Nurse Consultant* based on the nursing process model (AALNC, 2002).

In 2005, the AALNC began to collaborate with the American Nurses Association (ANA) to update these standards to reflect the evolving practice of legal nurse consulting and to further establish legal nurse consulting as a specialty practice of nursing. Work was completed in 2006 when the AALNC co-published *Legal Nurse Consulting: Scope and Standards of Practice* in collaboration with the ANA (AALNC & ANA, 2006). In 2010, a taskforce was formed to revise the 2006 Scope and Standards in accordance with the ANA's updated scope and standards of practice template for specialty nursing organizations. Work continued on this project for several years, and in 2016, the AALNC Board of Directors voted to self-publish the Scope and Standards. The final document entitled *Legal Nurse Consulting Scope and Standards of Practice* was published by the AALNC in 2017 and is available for purchase on the website (AALNC, 2017). See Chapter 2 for more information on the AALNC's *Legal Nurse Consulting Scope and Standards of Practice.*

Position Statements

The AALNC Board of Directors is responsible for developing and publishing position statements on topics related to legal nurse consulting. Over the years, several position statements have been published; some have been updated, and others have been retired. Current AALNC position statements include *Education and Certification in Legal Nurse Consulting* and *Providing Expert Nursing Testimony Regarding Nursing Negligence.* An additional position statement titled *Certification in Legal Nurse Consulting* is published by the ALNCCB® and endorsed by the AALNC.

In 2000, the AALNC published the position statement entitled *Education and Certification in Legal Nurse Consulting.* The purpose was to clarify the Association's position that legal nurse consulting education should build on nursing education and clinical experience; to recommend *Legal Nurse Consulting Principles and Practices* as the core curriculum for legal nurse consulting education; and to recognize and endorse the ALNCCB®'s LNCC® credential as the only certification in legal nurse consulting accredited by the ABSNC. See Appendix A for this position statement, which was updated in 2013 and 2016 (AALNC, 2016).

Recognizing that the profession of nursing is autonomous from the profession of medicine and other allied health disciplines and that nursing has the responsibility and knowledge to define its standards of practice, the AALNC published the position statement *Providing Expert Nursing Testimony* in 2006. It defines the AALNC's position that the only expert qualified to testify regarding nursing standards and on clinical and administrative nursing issues is a licensed RN. This position statement was updated in 2014 and is now titled *Providing Expert Nursing Testimony Regarding Nursing Negligence* (AALNC, 2014). See Appendix B.

In 2006, the ALNCCB® published a position statement on *Certification in Legal Nurse Consulting.* This position statement is endorsed by the AALNC and available on the website (ALNCCB®, 2006). See Appendix C.

The AALNC Board of Directors periodically reviews existing position statements to ensure their relevancy and to revise or retire as needed. See Table 1.1 for a list of current and retired position statements. Revision dates for the AALNC's Code of Ethics and Scope and Standards are also included.

Professional Relationships

NURSING ORGANIZATIONS ALLIANCE

In January 1994, the AALNC was seated as an affiliate member of the National Federation of Specialty Nursing Organizations (NFSNO). In November 1996, the AALNC became a regular participant in the Nursing Organization Liaison Forum (NOLF). By 2001, the NOLF and NFSNO, noting that both organizations were designed to achieve identical goals, merged to form one organization, the Nursing Organizations Alliance (NOA or The Alliance). The purpose of the NOA is to inspire and develop leaders in the community of nursing organizations (NOA, 2018a). The AALNC is a member of The Alliance. Delegates from member associations meet regularly to address issues of mutual concern across nursing specialties (NOA, 2018b).

LEGAL ORGANIZATIONS/BAR ASSOCIATIONS

The AALNC has long included as part of its mission the responsibility to increase awareness of the legal nurse consulting specialty practice among both the legal and nursing communities. In addition to ongoing efforts toward building relationships with other nursing organizations, the AALNC increased its focus on the legal community to enhance attorney awareness of the value of the LNC. The AALNC has made strides in collaborating with several attorney organizations, including Defense Research Institute (DRI) and the American Bar Association (ABA), and has

Table 1.1   AALNC's Code of Ethics, Scope & Standards, and Position Statements

Publication Name	Category	Original Date	Status
Code of Ethics and Conduct with Interpretive Discussion	Code of Ethics	1992	Revised in 2005, 2009, 2015
Legal Nurse Consulting Scope & Standards of Practice	Scope & Standards	1992	Revised in 1995, 2005, 2017
Role of the LNC as Distinct from the Role of the Paralegal and Legal Assistant	Position Statement	1999	Retired in 2012
Education and Certification in Legal Nurse Consulting	Position Statement	2000	Revised in 2013, 2016
The Specialty Practice of Legal Nurse Consulting 2005	Position Statement	2005	Retired in 2015
Licensure for Expert Witnesses	Position Statement	2006	Retired in 2013
Providing Expert Nursing Testimony Regarding Nursing Negligence	Position Statement	2006	Revised in 2014
Certification in Legal Nurse Consulting	Position Statement published by ALNCCB®	2006	Revised in 2008, 2011
Criminal Prosecution of Health Care Providers for Unintentional Human Error	Joint Position Statement with TAANA	2011	Retired in 2016

Note: Data on Code of Ethics from AALNC (2015), on Scope and Standards from AALNC (2017), on Role of the LNC position statement from AALNC (J. Dickinson, personal communication, August 9, 2016), on Education and Certification in Legal Nurse Consulting position statement from AALNC (S. Cook, personal communication, January 22, 2018), on Specialty Practice position statement from AALNC (J. Dickinson, personal communication, August 9, 2016), on Licensure for Expert Witnesses position statement from AALNC (J. Dickinson, personal communication, August 9, 2016), on Providing Expert Nursing Testimony position statement from AALNC (2014) (J. Dickinson, personal communication, August 9, 2016), on Certification in Legal Nurse Consulting position statement from ALNCCB® (2006) (K. Tamkus, personal communication, January 16, 2018), and on Criminal Prosecution position statement from AALNC (K. Dee, personal communication, August 7, 2017).

presented joint webinars with both (Huff, 2010b; Huff, 2011b). Several AALNC leaders have also served on attorney committees within these organizations to help raise awareness of the AALNC and legal nurse consulting.

Educating the legal community on legal nurse consulting continues to be one of the AALNC's strategic goals. In 2014, the Health Law Section of the ABA signed a Memo of Understanding (MOU) with the AALNC. The MOU outlines a common objective to educate legal and nursing professionals and a desire to collaborate on programs and initiatives that will benefit members of both organizations (ABA, 2014).

Entry into Practice

Becoming an LNC is an avenue for registered nurses who are interested in expanding their practice area by using their knowledge and experience in a non-traditional setting. In deciding whether to enter the specialty practice of legal nurse consulting, consideration should be given to the pros and cons of in-house and independent legal nurse consulting practices and to the qualities, traits, and skills of successful LNCs. Educational options and the distinction between certification and a certificate should also be understood.

Pros and Cons of Legal Nurse Consulting Practice

There are significant differences between in-house legal nurse consulting practice (in which the LNC is an employee of a law firm, a legal nurse consulting firm, etc.) and independent legal nurse consulting practice (in which the LNC is self-employed and contracted to work on a specific project for a particular case).

The pros of working as an in-house legal nurse consultant include:

■ Guaranteed salary
■ Regular pay check
■ Benefits package that typically includes:
  – Vacation time
  – Paid time off
  – 401k or 403b retirement plans
  – Health insurance and
  – Disability insurance
■ Team atmosphere
■ Working on a case from inception through adjudication
■ On-the-job experience under the tutelage of an attorney or another LNC
■ Regular work hours
■ Holidays and weekends off and
■ No overhead costs

The cons of working as an in-house legal nurse consultant include having set work hours with limited, if any, flexibility in the work schedule and receiving a flat salary regardless of the number of hours worked. If a nurse is hired as a firm's first LNC, there is no in-house LNC mentor available for training, but the nurse will have the unique opportunity to develop and mold the position. Depending on the size of the firm and the types of cases handled by the firm, in-house legal nurse consulting practice may also limit the LNC's exposure to different attorneys and types of legal cases.

The pros of working as an independent legal nurse consultant include:

■ Being part of a team or fully independent
■ Having autonomy
■ Setting one's own hourly rate
■ Billing by the hour (not a flat salary)
■ Having flexible hours
■ Taking time off when desired

- Having a flexible case load
- Experiencing tax benefits
- Having more creativity and latitude in decision-making
- Working from home (if desired)
- Experiencing variety in types of cases and
- Experiencing variety in attorney-clients (Carleo, 2017)

The cons of working as an independent legal nurse consultant include:

- Variable income
- No benefits package, typically (thus responsible for own insurance and retirement savings)
- No paid time off
- Responsibility for billing and collecting accounts receivable
- Responsibility for own taxes and accounting
- Overhead costs
- Nonbillable business management activities
- Work hours intruding on family time (possibly)
- The need for more self-discipline
- Limited interaction with colleagues (if fully independent) and
- The need for home office/dedicated space for confidential material (Carleo, 2017)

New independent LNCs frequently seek out mentoring or shadowing opportunities to work alongside an experienced LNC in independent practice, at a law firm, or in other settings. This can be very helpful but requires a time-intensive commitment from both the mentor and mentee to assure success from this mentoring process.

Independent LNCs may desire to perform only behind-the-scenes work, or they may wish to testify as an expert witness or an expert fact witness. Expert witnesses offer opinion testimony on the standard of care, causation, future healthcare needs, etc. If a nurse wishes to testify as an expert witness for nursing malpractice cases, the nurse must remain clinically active in the clinical practice area about which the nurse will testify. For example, an experienced labor and delivery nurse will need to remain clinically active in a labor and delivery unit to opine on the standard of care owed by a labor and delivery nurse. Expert fact witnesses testify about the facts in a case without offering opinion testimony about the healthcare issues (Costantini, Huff, & Mihalich, 2013). They educate the jury and judge about the case facts. See Chapters 31 and 32 for more information about expert witnesses and expert fact witnesses.

Successful entry into the specialty practice of legal nurse consulting, whether as an independent or in-house LNC, will require change. Prospective LNCs should weigh family obligations, personal relationships, and financial considerations. Possessing the qualities, traits, and skills necessary to succeed in legal nurse consulting practice will help make this transition smoother.

Qualities, Traits, and Skills

According to the AALNC, "the foundation of legal nurse consulting is nursing education and experience" (AALNC, 2017). Thus, legal nurse consultants are validly licensed registered nurses. It is this foundation of education and experience in the field of nursing that provides registered nurses the knowledge and capability to consult on medical-legal matters. Therefore, it is recommended that an entry-level LNC has, at a minimum, five years of clinical experience as a registered nurse.

Specific qualities, traits, and skills need to be in place to ensure success as an LNC, whether independent or in-house. Organizational and prioritization skills, in addition to professionalism, are integrated within the fundamentals of nursing education and training. These essential skills are necessary for the LNC as well, because LNCs juggle multiple cases in various stages of litigation and are assigned different tasks on different cases with different deadlines (AALNC, 2018). Attributes such as dependability, flexibility, good judgment, uncompromising ethical standards, problem-solving skills, and a positive attitude are also critical. To succeed, LNCs must demonstrate effective time-management skills and be prepared to do every job efficiently, cost effectively, and accurately (Costantini et al., 2013). Exceptional computer and research skills are also essential.

Independent LNCs need strong marketing, networking, sales, accounting, and other business and entrepreneurial skills to develop their consulting businesses. In-house LNCs need solid delegation and conflict-resolution skills, people skills, initiative, and foresight. Both independent and in-house LNCs must be politically savvy to navigate the organization or firm with whom they work. They must present a professional image and utilize leadership skills when collaborating with the legal team on a case. Legal nurse consultants must have a strong work ethic and the "ability to work independently with minimal supervision and direction" (AALNC, 2018). They must be willing to learn about the relevant laws and rules applicable to their cases (AALNC, 2018). See Chapters 29 and 30 for more information about in-house and independent LNCs.

Other qualities, traits, and skills of successful LNCs include drive, analytical skills, attention to detail, communication skills, and writing skills.

DRIVE

Drive, as a quality to building a successful independent or in-house legal nurse consulting practice, requires a significant amount of ambition, energy, and effort. This ambition is grounded in goal-oriented planning, a characteristic that every nurse uses in reaching objectives. Industry and hard work are the traits that support this quality, as are diligence and the thoroughness to see a task to completion with a watchful eye on meeting deadlines.

ANALYTICAL SKILLS

To succeed in this specialty practice, an LNC needs to have strong analytical skills. The analysis of medical records and other information is performed in the context of the allegations and applicable legal standards, and it focuses on critical details related to injuries, care and treatment of disease or injury conditions, timing of events, and completeness of information. The analytical LNC spots the missing records, the sequence of events that seems to be out of order, the defendant's deviations from the standard of care, the plaintiff's contributory negligence, details that do not seem right, etc. The role of the LNC often involves collecting and synthesizing data to reconstruct a series of events or determine what should have been done for an injured person. Attorneys rely on LNCs' clinical knowledge and experience and their ability to place data into a framework that helps the attorneys understand the medical information and focus on the critical case issues. The LNC must remember most attorneys do not have a clinical background and even those who are experienced in handling medical-legal tort claims still rely on the LNC's analytical skills to uncover the nuances in the case.

ATTENTION TO DETAIL

A keen sense of what is and is not relevant to a case is another trait that is important to a conscientious, successful LNC. Being detail-oriented when analyzing records and evaluating a case is more than just dotting all the i's and crossing all the t's to ensure that nothing essential is missed. Detail-oriented LNCs work through the minutiae of lengthy documents with an eye for the smallest items of importance. The ability to review each piece of evidence for its potential significance to a case is a valuable service that LNCs provide to their attorney-clients. Sifting through and clarifying the most significant details or themes of a case are invaluable to the attorney. Just as important is the LNC's identification of what is extraneous information and essentially a distraction in the case. One does not want to have an attorney waste time and money on facts or issues that are not germane to the underlying case and do not add anything to the claim. For example, the LNC might identify a breach in the standard of care. However, if that breach did not cause harm (i.e., if it does not have associated damages), it is irrelevant to the case.

COMMUNICATION SKILLS

It is important to be an active listener to show understanding and attentiveness when an attorney-client or the attorney's client relates details of a case. Concentrating on what is being said and, at the same time, perceiving body language that may or may not be contradictory are basic active listening skills honed by most nurses through years of clinical practice. The ability to accurately and succinctly document what is said and observed requires practice and is crucial in discriminating between critical and non-critical information. The LNC must parse out relevant details that are at issue. See Chapter 33 for more information on communicating with attorneys' clients.

Good teaching skills are essential for LNCs and expert witnesses. Whether teaching the attorney-clients and their staff, the attorney's client, or a judge and jury, the legal nurse consultant's or expert witness's teaching ability is paramount. The LNC and expert witness must reduce complex medical conditions, treatment, and outcomes to layman's terms, so all can understand and appreciate the importance of the information and how it fits into the case.

WRITING SKILLS

Decisive writing skills that provide the necessary breadth and depth of relevant information in a succinct manner are needed to be effective as an LNC. It is essential that the LNC's writing style presents information clearly and concisely. Written work products and other written communication (including emails) should be free of grammatical and spelling errors. When asked to prepare a written work product, it is imperative the LNC understand the purpose and intended audience of the document and then tailor the document to meet those needs. See Chapter 35 for more information on preparing written work products.

Aspiring LNCs should perform an honest, objective self-assessment to identify the qualities, traits, and skills they possess as well as those that would need to be strengthened. Honing these qualities, traits, and skills will improve the likelihood of the LNC's success. This effort is rewarded in the long run by adding proficiency and competency to the list of assets the legal nurse provides to the attorney or other client.

Education

Entering the specialty practice of legal nurse consulting does not require additional education in a formal program. However, many nurses seeking to transition to legal nurse consulting prefer formal training in their new venture. Of note, if the RN is seeking expert witness work, many attorneys do not want experts who have formal legal training, as nursing experts are retained solely for their clinical nursing expertise. The concern is that opposing counsel could paint the expert as being biased by asserting that the expert's opinions are not objective but, rather, are influenced by the expert's knowledge of legal standards. That, however, does not mean that such RNs cannot or should not seek to obtain additional information that will serve them in this specialty practice. Some nurse experts opt to maintain two separate curricula vitae—one for expert work (that lists only their clinical nursing information) and one for behind-the-scenes work (that includes their legal nurse consulting education).

There are many legal nurse consulting courses offered in a variety of settings. One is the AALNC's interactive Legal Nurse Consulting Professional Course. The 17 modules cover a variety of topics such as "Legal Fundamentals," "Medical Records Identification, Access, and Analysis," "Communication and Report Writing," and more. These modules may be accessed individually to fit one's needs, or in their entirety. These resources, and others of benefit to the novice as well as the experienced LNC, are available through the AALNC website.

Other education is available by proprietary schools, for-profit and non-profit businesses, universities, four-year colleges, and community colleges. This education is offered through traditional on-campus programs, tele-courses, and distance courses that may be print-based or online. Some courses culminate with a certificate of completion. Some universities offer post-graduate classes in legal nurse consulting, and a few offer a Master of Science in Nursing with a concentration in legal nurse consulting (AALNC, 2017).

In evaluating the merit of any course or program, the reputation and accreditation of the sponsoring institution should be considered, as well as the cost, format, and length of the program; its schedule; and the convenience of the location or online accessibility. Another consideration includes whether the program offers student placement in an externship with a law firm or a legal nurse consultant firm. If a local AALNC chapter is available, it is a valuable resource of information regarding availability of university-based programs and other options in the area.

Although legal education is available to nurses through legal assistant or paralegal education programs, it must be stressed that the education of paralegals and legal assistants is vastly different from the needs of the nurse practicing in the legal arena. The terms "paralegal" and "legal assistant" are sometimes used interchangeably in different parts of the country. According to the ABA, a legal assistant or paralegal is "a person qualified by education, training or work experience … employed by an attorney … who performs specifically delegated substantive legal work for which a lawyer is responsible" (ABA, 2008). The legal nurse consultant is distinct from the paralegal or legal assistant, because the foundation of legal nurse consulting is nursing education and experience (AALNC, 2017).

The primary focus of legal nurse consulting education is teaching nurses how to apply their nursing education and clinical experience to the analysis of legal cases.

> The AALNC maintains the position that legal nurse consulting education programs must be developed and presented as specialty nursing curricula by nurse educators in partnership with legal educators. The qualifications of the program directors and instructors should be considered when evaluating a program. In general, programs developed and taught by experienced nurse educators who are practicing LNCs are preferred, as these

instructors have current real-life experience and success in the medical-legal field (AALNC, 2016).

Certification versus Certificate

Legal nurse consultants beginning in this specialty practice are often confused by the number of different courses that advertise "certification" or certificates at the completion of the program and bestow their own "credentials." While education from any reputable source is helpful, it can be difficult for the new LNC to decipher which credentials have meaning to those in the medical-legal community. The differences between certification and certificate programs are outlined in Table 1.2. The only true board certification in legal nurse consulting is the LNCC® credential, which meets the rigorous standards of the ABSNC. The LNCC® is the only certification in legal nurse consulting that is endorsed by the AALNC. The LNCC® exam is based not only on knowledge of the specialty practice but also on experience as a practicing legal nurse consultant and requires 2,000 hours of legal nurse consulting experience prior to being eligible to sit for the exam.

Certification

The founding members of the AALNC have been credited for their long-range vision for the association and the specialty practice of legal nurse consulting. Some of the initial decisions made

Table 1.2   Certification versus Certificate Programs

Certification	*Certificate*
Results from an assessment process that recognizes an individual's knowledge, skills, and competency in a particular specialty	Results from an educational process
Typically requires professional experience	For newcomers and experienced professionals
Awarded by a third-party, standard-setting organization, typically not-for-profit	Awarded by the educational program or institution, often for profit
Indicates mastery/competency as measured against a defensible set of standards, usually by application or exam	Indicates completion of a course or series of courses with a specific focus (different from a degree-granting program)
Standards set through a defensible, industry-wide process (job analysis/role delineation) that results in an outline of required knowledge and skills	Course content determined by the specific provider or institution, not standardized
Typically results in credentials to be listed after one's name (LNCC®, ONC, CCRN)	Usually listed on a resume detailing education
Has ongoing requirements in order to maintain; holder must continue to demonstrate meeting the requirements	Demonstrates knowledge of course content at the end of a set period in time

Source: AALNC (2018).

by these founders had a lasting impact on the association and the specialty practice and ultimately led to the certification offered by the ALNCCB®. This section will discuss the purpose of nursing certification, the importance of accreditation, and key elements involved in developing the LNCC® exam.

Certification in a Nursing Specialty

Definition and Purpose

Professional certification in nursing is widely used to recognize a higher level of nursing skill and expertise within a specialty than is expected from nurses with the minimal qualifications required for entry into the practice setting. Nurses who achieve certification from an accredited certification program in their specialty are considered "board certified."

Standards for nursing professional certification programs vary, but three minimum components are generally required (ALNCCB®, 2018a):

1. Licensure as an RN
2. Eligibility criteria, which include experience in the specialty, such as clinical experience or a specified number of work hours using skills and knowledge unique to the specialty and
3. Identification and testing of a specialized body of knowledge that is distinctly different from the general practice of nursing

In legal nurse consulting, the only certification that meets these minimum requirements is the Legal Nurse Consultant Certified, designated as LNCC®. The LNCC® is the only certification in the specialty endorsed by the AALNC and accredited by the ABSNC, formerly known as the Accreditation Council of the American Board of Nursing Specialties. The LNCC® is comparable to other recognized nursing specialty credentials, such as Certified Critical Care Nurse (CCRN®) and Certified Emergency Nurse (CEN). Since LNCC® meets the definition of a credential as described above, LNCC® becomes part of the individual's professional title, as in Lucy Smith, BSN, RN, LNCC®.

Certification in Legal Nurse Consulting

Overview

The mission of the LNCC® program is to promote expertise and professionalism in the practice of legal nurse consulting by recognizing practitioners who have met defined qualifications and demonstrated knowledge on a certifying examination in the specialty. The certification program is not designed to determine who is qualified or who shall engage in legal nurse consulting, but rather to promote a level of expertise and professionalism by documenting individual performance as measured against a predetermined level of knowledge about legal nurse consulting.

Per the ALNCCB®, the objectives of the LNCC® program are to:

1. Identify legal nurse consultants who have met eligibility criteria and demonstrated a defined level of knowledge of the principles and practice of legal nurse consulting for employers, clients, the public, and members of other nursing specialties
2. Encourage legal nurse consultants to further their professional development by achieving and maintaining certification in the specialty and

3. Promote the recognition of legal nurse consulting as a specialty practice of nursing (ALNCCB®, 2018c)

History of the LNCC®

Once the founding members of AALNC, through their visionary leadership and long-range planning for the association, overcame challenges and laid the groundwork, the AALNC Board of Directors was ready to move forward with establishing a certification examination in the legal nurse consulting specialty. In 1997, a Certification Task Force was appointed to determine the scope of the program and to seek bids from testing companies.

The first Legal Nurse Consultant Certified examination was offered on October 24, 1998. The exam was originally offered every April and October in various cities around the country as well as at the AALNC annual education conferences. In October 2010, a computer-based testing model was developed, and the LNCC® examination is now offered electronically at over 300 computer-based testing sites twice each year—during a two-week period in the spring and fall of each year.

Setting the LNCC® Apart Through Accreditation

Early in the AALNC's research process, one of the goals for the development of the certification program was to meet the standards necessary for accreditation (Ehrlich, 1995; Janes, Bogart, Magnusson, Joos, & Beerman, 1998). The early certification committees identified the ABNS, now the ABSNC, as the accreditation body best qualified to give the certification program the credibility they sought.

The American Board of Nursing Specialties

The American Board of Nursing Specialties was incorporated in 1991 after a number of years of discussion and consensus-building within the nursing profession. Consensus-building discussions resulted in the development of 12 standards for nursing certification programs.

In 1996, the ABNS formed a task force to review and strengthen the original standards. In addition, a rationale section was added to each standard. The task force developed 17 revised standards which were adopted by consensus among members at the ABNS Assembly. In 1999, the ABNS Assembly revised the standards to delete the previous requirement for a BSN degree as an eligibility criterion for examination candidates.

Soon afterward, the ABNS restructured to create a membership organization with an autonomous accrediting body called the Accreditation Council. In 2007, the ABNS began a process for creating a separate, autonomous body to perform the accreditation function. In 2009, the ABNS Accreditation Council was renamed the Accreditation Board for Specialty Nursing Certification, and a separate corporation was established (ABSNC, 2019). The Accreditation Board for Specialty Nursing Certification currently has 18 standards that must be met in order to pass the stringent peer review process. These accreditation standards are listed in Table 1.3.

Initial Accreditation of the LNCC® Exam

The LNCC® program was awarded initial accreditation at the September 1999 ABNS meeting. The initial accreditation was attributed to the volunteer members of AALNC and ALNCCB®, as well as the testing professionals who were involved in creating a quality certification program.

Table 1.3 Accreditation Board for Speciality Nursing Certification (ABSNC) Standards: Promoting Excellence in Nursing Certification*

Standard 1   *Definition and Scope of Nursing Specialty*
The certification examination program is based on a distinct and well-defined field of nursing practice that subscribes to the overall purpose and functions of nursing. The nursing specialty is distinct from other nursing specialties and is national in scope. There is an identified need for the specialty and nurses who devote most of their practice to the specialty.

Standard 2   *Research Based Body of Knowledge*
A body of research based knowledge related to the nursing specialty exists. Mechanisms have been established for the support, review, and dissemination of research and knowledge in the specialty. Activities within the specialty contribute to the advancement of nursing science within the specialty.

Standard 3   *Organizational Autonomy*
The certifying organization is an entity with organizational autonomy governed in part or in whole by certified nursing members.

Standard 4   *Non-discrimination*
The certifying organization does not discriminate among candidates as to age, sex, race, religion, national origin, ethnicity, disability, marital status, sexual orientation, and gender identity.

Standard 5   *Public Representation*
The certifying organization includes at least one Public Member with full voting rights on its Board of Directors.

Standard 6   *Eligibility Criteria for Test Candidates*
The eligibility criteria for non-RN nursing team member certification include:
- Licensure or registration as required
- Education and/or experiential qualifications defined by the certifying organization

The eligibility criteria for specialty RN nursing certification include:
- Current RN licensure
- Educational and experiential qualifications as determined by the certifying organization

The eligibility criteria for advanced practice nursing certification include:
- RN licensure
- A minimum of a graduate degree in nursing or the appropriate equivalent, including content in the specific area of advanced specialty practice

The eligibility criteria for advanced practice registered nurse (APRN) certification include:
- RN licensure
- Completion of a graduate degree program in nursing or the appropriate equivalent (or post-master's or post-doctoral certificate program) from an accredited program in one of the four APRN roles across at least one of six APRN population foci as described in the 2008 Consensus Document
- Three separate courses in advanced pathophysiology across the life span, advanced health/physical assessment, and advanced pharmacology as part of graduate educational preparation
- A minimum of 500 clinical hours as part of graduate educational preparation

Standard 7	*Validity*
	The certifying organization has conducted validation studies to assure inferences made on the basis of test scores are appropriate and justified.
Standard 8	*Test Development*
	Certification examinations are constructed and evaluated using methods that are psychometrically sound and fair to all candidates.
Standard 9	*Reliability*
	The certifying organization assures test scores, including subscores, are sufficiently reliable for their intended uses.
Standard 10	*Test Administration*
	The certification examination is administered in a manner that minimizes construct-irrelevant variance and maintains examination security.
Standard 11	*Test Security*
	Procedures are in place to maximize the security of all certification examination materials.
Standard 12	*Standard Setting, Scaling, and Equating*
	The passing score for the certification examination is set in a manner that is fair to all candidates, using criterion-referenced methods and sound equating and scaling procedures.
Standard 13	*Recertification and Continuing Competence*
	The certifying organization has a recertification program in place that requires certificants to maintain current knowledge and to provide documentation showing how competence in the specialty is maintained and/or measured over time.
Standard 14	*Communications*
	The certifying organization provides information that clearly describes the certification and recertification process to candidates, certificants, and other stakeholders.
Standard 15	*Confidentiality and Security*
	The certifying organization protects confidential information about candidates and certificants.
Standard 16	*Appeals*
	The certifying organization has an appeal process available to candidates/certificants who have been denied recertification or access to an examination, or who have had certification revoked.
Standard 17	*Misrepresentation and Non-compliance*
	The certifying organization has a mechanism in place to respond to instances of misrepresentation and non-compliance with eligibility criteria or the certifying organization's policies; this mechanism includes reporting cases of misrepresentation and non-compliance to appropriate authorities.
Standard 18	*Quality Improvement*
	The certifying organization shall have an internal audit and management review system in place, including provisions for continuous corrective and preventive actions for quality improvement.

Note: * The ABSNC is the only accrediting body specifically for nursing-related certification programs. Nursing certification organizations may attain accreditation by demonstrating compliance with the 18 standards established by the ABSNC. The ABSNC is an approved accrediting agency for the National Council of State Boards of Nursing's Advanced Practice Registered Nurses (APRN) Certification Review Program.

Reaccreditation

Since the initial accreditation, the ALNCCB® has continued to ensure that the LNCC® program meets or exceeds the ABSNC accreditation standards as outlined in Table 1.3. This requires application for recertification every five years. The recertification process is difficult and requires the ALNCCB® to follow a calendar of yearly requirements to assure there is no lapse in the certification. The LNCC® is the only certification program in legal nurse consulting that has achieved ABSNC accreditation, a distinction that sets the LNCC® program apart from others.

The American Legal Nurse Consultant Certification Board

The ALNCCB® was established in September 1997 to provide an accredited examination and certification program (ALNCCB®, 2018c). The ALNCCB® also maintains membership status in the ABNS. As such, the ALNCCB® is invited to attend ABNS Assembly meetings where issues of interest to all nursing specialty certification organizations are discussed.

Autonomy

The Accreditation Board of Specialty Nursing Certification standard three requires that the certifying organization is an entity with organizational autonomy governed in part or in whole by certified nursing members. Based on this standard, the ALNCCB® has independent responsibility for the certification program. The ALNCCB® develops the certification budget, determines the eligibility criteria for the examination, audits applications for compliance with the criteria, sets fees, and sets criteria for certification renewal. The ALNCCB® is charged with the responsibility of maintaining an examination that is valid, reliable, and legally defensible. The AALNC and ALNCCB® share some resources while still maintaining separation of power. A Memorandum of Understanding approved by both boards defines this relationship (AALNC & ALNCCB®, n.d.).

Position Statement on Certification in Legal Nurse Consulting

As previously discussed, numerous certificate courses for legal nurse consulting are offered by for-profit companies in the marketplace. The ALNCCB® has published a position statement entitled "Certification in Legal Nurse Consulting" to clarify the distinction between "certificate" and "certification" and to identify the LNCC® credential as the gold standard in legal nurse consulting. A copy of this position statement can be found in Appendix C.

The LNCC® Practice Test

The LNCC® practice test, first published in 2001, was created by ALNCCB® in conjunction with a testing company. The test has 100 questions that meet the current exam blueprint (discussed below) and is designed to help the test-taker assess one's readiness to sit for the certification examination. In addition to the practice test, a number of products have been developed by the ALNCCB® to assist in preparation for the examination. These products are available for purchase on the AALNC website.

The LNCC® Exam

Necessary Expertise: Working with the Testing Company

The Accreditation Board of Specialty Nursing Certification standards 7 through 12 have detailed requirements for maintaining statistical validity, reliability, and security related to the certification examination (ABSNC, 2017b). To achieve this, the ALNCCB® depends on help from outside experts in the testing field.

The Standards for Educational and Psychological Testing, published jointly by the American Educational Research Association (AERA), the American Psychological Association (APA), and the National Council on Measurement in Education (NCME), offer guidance for developing valid and reliable examinations, including certification examinations. Standard 14.14 states: "The content domain to be covered by a credentialing test should be defined clearly and justified in terms of the importance of the content for credential-worthy performance in an occupation or profession" (AERA, APA, & NCME, 2014, p. 181).

The same standard also specifies that the knowledge and skills addressed in the certification examination should be those necessary to protect the public. In general, the standard states that the knowledge and skills contained in a core curriculum designed to train people for the profession are relevant. Thus, the AALNC's *Legal Nurse Consulting Principles and Practices* textbook is used as a primary resource for test development. In addition, the ALNCCB® adheres to guidelines of the Equal Employment Opportunity Commission and the standards set by ABSNC to ensure fairness to all test-takers and validity of test content.

Determining What to Test: Practice Analysis

A practice analysis provides the primary basis for defining the content domain of a certification examination. The first role delineation survey performed by the AALNC took place in 1992. Numerous surveys, with the assistance of expertise from vetted testing companies, were developed and mailed to determine the "blueprint" for the certification examination. Most recently, an LNC practice analysis was completed in 2016 and 2017, and from it, the 2018 LNCC® test matrix, as shown in Table 1.4, was developed.

The content areas covered by the exam continue to expand with each successive practice analysis, but the top five content areas have remained constant since the inception of the certification

Table 1.4   2018 LNCC® Test Blueprint

Content Area	% of Exam
Medical malpractice	19–23
Personal injury	12–14
Long term care litigation	8–10
Product liability	7–9
Toxic tort	5–7
Workers' compensation	6–9
Risk management	6–8
Life care planning	5–7
Regulatory compliance	5–8
Medicare set-aside	4–6

Source: American Legal Nurse Consultant Certification Board (2018b).

exam. This is exemplified in Table 1.5, which notes the evolution of the LNCC® certification test blueprint.

A practice analysis is completed approximately every five years to ensure that the certification examination remains a valid assessment of the knowledge and skills required for effective practice by legal nurse consultants. The practice analysis is important for due diligence in test development and is required by the standards of the ABSNC and other accrediting bodies.

Developing Test Items

The original and current examination questions, or "items," are designed to test the nurse's ability to apply legal nurse consulting knowledge in situations that simulate actual practice. The majority of items are in case study format, meaning the test-taker is presented with a passage describing a legal case followed by several questions relating to the case.

Originally, a group of 12 item writers were selected from the AALNC membership. These item writers were experienced practitioners in a wide range of practice settings from all regions of the country. All item writers were required to meet the eligibility requirements for the examination. The ALNCCB® Item Writing Panel was charged with the responsibility of developing new items as needed based on the exam blueprint. Over time, this item writing panel has evolved into a group of AALNC members who have completed applications to volunteer as item writers in their areas of expertise and have been selected by members of the ALNCCB® from the applicant pool.

In September of 2014, the ALNCCB® created a new volunteer role for an experienced LNCC® to act as a liaison between the testing vendor, the ALNCCB®, and the item writers. This role is intended to assist in meeting the needs of the item writers and to ensure that an adequate number of items for each practice area is available in the item bank. The goal is to keep enough items in the item bank to change the certification test at least every two years and to keep both the certification and practice tests current.

Each new item is reviewed by ALNCCB® members, experts from the testing company, and other item writers approved by the ALNCCB® to ensure that psychometric testing standards are met. Each individual item is coded by content area and scope of practice (ALNCCB®, 2018b). The highest portion of items on the certification exam are in the content areas of medical malpractice and personal injury, as noted in Table 1.5.

Validating Test Items

Initially, two pilot tests were developed. The pilot tests were offered to all LNCs attending the 1998 AALNC National Education Conference in Dallas, Texas. The pilot tests did not exclude LNCs who would not have met eligibility criteria, but a questionnaire included with the pilot tests revealed that most of the 217 LNCs who took the pilot tests would have met eligibility requirements. The superior performance by those who met eligibility requirements validated that the eligibility criteria did tend to identify those candidates who had reached the level of proficiency measured by the examination.

In accordance with ABSNC standards, the ALNCCB® regularly evaluates the validity of test items with the assistance of the testing company and in partnership with an independent psychometrician. Post-administration analysis has consistently found the examination to be psychometrically sound. Denoting that the questions are directly related to the roles of experienced LNCs as identified by the practice analysis, the majority of LNCs who meet eligibility criteria perform successfully on the examination.

Table 1.5 Evolution of the LNCC® Certification Test Blueprint 1998–2017

Content Areas	% in 1998	% in 2008	% in 2012	% in 2017
Medical malpractice	28 to 32	27 to 31	19 to 23	22 to 25
Personal injury	20 to 24	19 to 23	12 to 14	13 to 15
Long term care litigation/Elder law	1 to 3	3 to 6	8 to 10	12 to 14
Product liability/toxic tort	12 to 16	10 to 14	7 to 9 (Product liability only)	8 to 10 (Product liability only)
Toxic tort	–	–	5 to 7	5 to 7
Workers' compensation	12 to 16	12 to 16	6 to 9	10 to 12
Risk management	4 to 8	5 to 9	6 to 8	5 to 7
Life care planning	5 to 9	4 to 7	5 to 7	4 to 6
Regulatory compliance	–	–	5 to 8	5 to 8
Forensic/criminal	1 to 4	1 to 4	4 to 6	2 to 4
Administrative health law	1 to 4	4 to 8 (incl. regulatory compliance)	–	–
Civil rights	–	–	3 to 5	3 to 5
Employment discrimination (including ADA)	–	–	3 to 5	4 to 6
Medicare set-aside	–	–	4 to 6	2 to 4

Source: Data on 1998 and 2008 content areas from Peterson and Kopishke, 2010; data on 2012 content areas from Webb, 2012; and Data on 2017 content areas from Webb, 2017.

Eligibility Requirements and Recertification

Eligibility requirements to take the LNCC® examination include:

1. Current unrestricted licensure as an RN in the United States or its territories
2. A minimum of five years' experience practicing as an RN and
3. Evidence of 2,000 hours of legal nurse consulting experience within the past five years

Hours worked in a formal internship or practicum program can be counted toward the legal nurse consulting practice experience eligibility criterion as long as these internship or practicum hours are worked on active client cases and consist of activities that would generally be considered billable. These activities should fall under the content areas and scope of practice identified on the most current practice analysis. Internship and practicum hours can only be used toward a maximum of 10% of the practice hours submitted.

Certification is valid for five years (ALNCCB®, 2018a). Board-certified LNCs (LNCC®s) can renew their certification by meeting the eligibility criteria for recertification, which are:

1. Having a current, unrestricted RN license
2. Having evidence of 2,000 hours of legal nurse consulting practice during the five-year certification period and
3. Completing one of the following:
   a. Submitting 60 contact hours that meet published criteria and were earned over the five-year certification period, or
   b. Retaking and passing the LNCC® certification examination

The recertification application can be completed on the ALNCCB® website, and as of January 2018, all recertifications are due in October of the fifth year after the LNCC®'s initial certification or recertification (ALNCCB®, 2018d).

Protecting the Value of LNCC®

Nurses who achieve specialty certification want their credential to be meaningful to others. Indeed, the aim of specialty nursing certification and accreditation is to provide assurance to the public that the certification holder is proficient in the specialty practice at a level that exceeds the minimum requirements for entry into practice.

The ALNCCB® has taken a number of steps to assure that the value of the LNCC® designation signifies proficiency in the specialty practice. Both ALNCCB® and LNCC® are registered trademarks. No other organization or person may use LNCC® to designate certification as a legal nurse consultant. While it is not necessary to use the registered trademark symbol with the credential, its use may help distinguish the LNCC® from the ever-evolving list of entry-level certificates.

Accreditation by the ABSNC indicates that the LNCC® is comparable to other nursing specialty certifications with high standards and legally defensible programs. The ABSNC accreditation process includes a stringent third-party peer-review process of all applications submitted for accreditation.

The ALNCCB® performs ongoing review of the examination and the individual items and writes new items on a regular basis. Applications for examination and recertification are subject to audit by appointed members of the audit panel, which is under the supervision of the ALNCCB®.

Appeals related to examination and recertification applications are also under the supervision of the ALNCCB®.

Confidentiality regarding test content is a strict requirement for every member of the ALNCCB®, its staff, and contracted advisers. All examination candidates are required to read and sign a confidentiality statement.

Ultimately, the public should judge the value of the LNCC® credential. As in other nursing specialties, the process of proving the value of certification takes a great deal of time. A specialty practice as small as legal nurse consulting is at a greater disadvantage in this regard. The LNCC®'s employers and clients usually do not work with enough LNCs to make comparisons between those who have achieved the LNCC® credential and those who have not. Consumers, including the LNCC®'s employer's clients, may not even know of the LNCC®'s involvement in the case and have no way to judge the LNCC®'s impact on the case. The complexity of legal processes and the multitude of variables that affect case outcome make it difficult to measure any one individual's effect on a case.

To protect the value of the LNCC® credential, the ALNCCB® has developed a "Use of the LNCC® Credential Policy." This policy speaks directly to: (1) Use of the credential; (2) Eligibility criteria; (3) Irregular behavior; (4) Disciplinary action; (5) Trademark infringement and/or fraud; (6) Preliminary determination; (7) Disciplinary hearing; (8) Disciplinary action (after the hearing); (9) Notice; (10) Appeal; (11) Records; (12) Confidentiality; (13) Impartiality; (14) Reapplication; and (15) Revocation (ALNCCB®, 2011).

Education is needed to help consumers differentiate the LNCC® credential from other less meaningful "credentials." The AALNC recommends listing certificates and entry-level "certifications" in the education section of one's resume or curriculum vitae rather than adding initials to one's title that do not represent attainment of specialty nursing certification.

Research

Nursing Certification

In describing the purposes of nursing certification in patient care settings, Ann Cary, director of the International Program of Research on the Certified Nurse Workforce, states: "Ostensibly, [nursing certification] protects the public from unsafe and incompetent providers, gives consumers more choices in selecting healthcare providers, distinguishes among levels of care, and gives better trained providers a competitive advantage" (Cary, 2001, p. 44). While legal nurse consulting practice does not involve patient care, this statement can easily be adapted to describe the purpose and value of board certification in legal nurse consulting (LNCC®).

ABNS Value of Certification Study

In March of 2016, the ABNS hosted a national convening of more than 100 experts from the healthcare, academia, and professional certification industries on The Value of Certification: Building the Business Case for Certification. The Value of Certification convening developed actionable and measurable activities to support certification research that builds a business case for the value of certification across multiple stakeholders. The convening focused on the value of a multidisciplinary certified workforce, continuing competence, and the work of certified team members in team practice. The Value of Certification convening provided participating organizations with concrete ideas to implement and strategies to enable them to work together. The

ABSNC developed a statement that outlines the importance of accreditation with the ABSNC (ABSNC, 2017a).

At this 2016 national convening, the following research priorities were identified to define the value of certification:

■ Certification improves the recruitment and retention of qualified nurses, enhances their employability and potential job prospects
■ Certification is recognized validation of knowledge in the specialty
■ Certification improves organizational culture of healthcare delivery, job satisfaction, empowerment, and confidence and
■ Certification advances safety, improves processes of care, and improves quality of care

Future Trends

The ALNCCB® has the unique opportunity of being involved in developing a national research agenda by remaining a member of the ABNS. As noted, research related to the value of certification continues to be important.

Summary

The AALNC is widely known as the representative voice for LNCs. Through the efforts of its leaders, members, volunteers, and staff, the AALNC has focused on the development and continued growth of the specialty practice of legal nurse consulting since its inception. The practice of legal nurse consulting marries the fields of nursing and law. The intersection of these two professions has created opportunities for registered nurses to provide consultation to attorneys, insurance companies, and others who work on legal matters in which there are medical components. Nurses considering entry into legal nursing practice should carefully weigh the pros and cons of independent and in-house practice and conduct a self-assessment relative to the qualities, traits, and skills of successful LNCs. Once eligibility criteria are met, all LNCs are encouraged to seek LNCC® certification to validate their knowledge. As the only legal nursing certification in the nursing profession endorsed by the AALNC and accredited by the ABSNC, the LNCC® is the gold standard sought by experienced practitioners in the field.

References

Accreditation Board for Specialty Nursing Certification. (2017a). A commitment to quality and care: The importance of accreditation for certifying organizations and their members. Retrieved from https://absnc.org/sites/default/files/docs/2017/absnc_valueaccreditation.pdf.

Accreditation Board for Specialty Nursing Certification. (2017b). Promoting excellence in nursing certification: Accreditation standards. Retrieved from www.absnc.org/sites/default/files/docs/2017/absnc-standards-fact-sheet-080117.pdf.

Accreditation Board for Specialty Nursing Certification. (2019). About. Retrieved from www.absnc.org/about.

American Association of Legal Nurse Consultants. (1994). *Scope of practice for the legal nurse consultant.* Glenview, IL: AALNC.

American Association of Legal Nurse Consultants. (2002). *Scope and standards of practice for the legal nurse consultant.* Glenview, IL: AALNC.

American Association of Legal Nurse Consultants. (2014). Providing expert nursing testimony regarding nursing negligence. Retrieved from www.aalnc.org/d/do/258.

American Association of Legal Nurse Consultants. (2015). Code of ethics and conduct with interpretive discussion. Retrieved from www.aalnc.org/d/do/85.

American Association of Legal Nurse Consultants. (2016). Education and certification in legal nurse consulting. Retrieved from www.aalnc.org/page/position-statement-on-education-certification.

American Association of Legal Nurse Consultants. (2017). *Legal nurse consulting scope and standards of practice.* Retrieved from www.aalnc.org/page/aalnc-online-bookstore.

American Association of Legal Nurse Consultants. (2018). *Legal nurse consulting: A nursing specialty* (4th ed.). Retrieved from www.aalnc.org/d/do/424.

American Association of Legal Nurse Consultants, & American Legal Nurse Consultant Certification Board. (n.d.) Memo of understanding. In ALNCCB®'s Operating Guidelines.

American Association of Legal Nurse Consultants, & American Nurses Association. (2006). *Legal nurse consulting: Scope and standards of practice.* [Brochure]. Silver Spring, MD: NurseBooks.Org.

American Bar Association. (2008). Current ABA definition of legal assistant/paralegal. Retrieved from www.americanbar.org/groups/paralegals/resources/current_aba_definition_of_legal_assistant_paralegal.html.

American Bar Association. (2014). ABA signs memorandum of understanding with American Association of Legal Nurse Consultants. Retrieved from www.americanbar.org/news/abanews/aba-news-archives/2014/08/aba_signs_memorandum.html

American Education Research Association, American Psychological Association, & National Council on Measurement in Education. (2014). *Standards for educational and psychological testing.* Washington, DC: American Educational Research Association.

American Legal Nurse Consultant Certification Board. (2006). Certification in legal nurse consulting. Retrieved from https://lncc.aalnc.org/page/position-statement.

American Legal Nurse Consultant Certification Board. (2011). *ALNCCB® policy and procedure manual: Use of the LNCC® credential policy.* Chicago, IL: ALNCCB®.

American Legal Nurse Consultant Certification Board. (2018a). Eligibility criteria. Retrieved from http://lncc.aalnc.org/page/lncc-certification-faq.

American Legal Nurse Consultant Certification Board. (2018b). Examination, scope and content. Retrieved from http://lncc.aalnc.org/page/examination-scope-and-content.

American Legal Nurse Consultant Certification Board. (2018c). Mission and objectives. Retrieved from http://lncc.aalnc.org/page/mission-objectives.

American Legal Nurse Consultant Certification Board. (2018d). Recertification. Retrieved from http://lncc.aalnc.org/page/recertification.

Bogart, J. B. (Ed.). (1998). *Legal nurse consulting: Principles and practice.* Boca Raton, FL: CRC Press.

Carleo, S. (2017). Business principles and practices. In *AALNC Legal nurse consultant professional course* (module 13). Retrieved from www.aalnc.org/page/course-content.

Cary, A. H. (2001). Certified registered nurses: Results of the study of the certified workforce. *American Journal of Nursing, 101*(1), 44–52.

Costantini, P., Huff, K., & Mihalich, J. (2013). Introduction to legal nurse consulting. In *AALNC Legal nurse consultant professional course* (module 1). Retrieved from www.aalnc.org/page/course-content.

Dickinson. (2015, January 20). New online LNC course. [Web log post]. Retrieved from www.aalnc.org/p/bl/et/blogaid=5.

Ehrlich, C. J. (1995). Certification development. *Journal of Legal Nurse Consulting, 6,* 6.

Huff, K. (2010a, June 21). AALNC webinar series. [Web log post]. Retrieved from www.aalnc.org/p/bl/et/blogaid=52.

Huff, K. (2010b, October 8). AALNC announces joint webinar with DRI. [Web log post]. Retrieved from www.aalnc.org/p/bl/et/blogid=2&ym=201010.

Huff, K. (2011a, January 26). Free webinar—so you want to be an LNC. [Web log post]. Retrieved from www.aalnc.org/p/bl/et/blogid=2&ym=201101.

Huff, K. (2011b, March 29). AALNC announces webinar series with the American Bar Association. [Web log post]. Retrieved from www.aalnc.org/p/bl/et/blogid=2&ym=201103.

Iyer, P. (Ed.). (2003). *Legal nurse consulting: Principles and practice* (2nd ed.). Boca Raton, FL: CRC Press.

Janes, R., Bogart, J., Magnusson, J., Joos, B., & Beerman, J. (1998). The history and evolution of legal nurse consulting. In J. B. Bogart (Ed.), *Legal nurse consulting practices* (pp. 3–24). Boca Raton, FL: CRC Press.

Nursing Organizations Alliance. (2018a). About us. Retrieved from www.nursing-alliance.org/dnn/About-Us.

Nursing Organizations Alliance. (2018b). Member benefits. Retrieved from www.nursing-alliance.org/dnn/Join-Us.

Peterson, A., & Kopishke, L. (Eds.). (2010). *Legal nurse consulting practices* (3rd ed.). Boca Raton, FL: CRC Press.

Webb, L. C. (2012). Practice analysis report for legal nurse consultants prepared for the American Legal Nurse Consultant Certification Board (ALNCCB®) by testing consultant.

Webb, L. C. (2017). Practice analysis report for legal nurse consultants prepared for the American Legal Nurse Consultant Certification Board (ALNCCB®) by testing consultant.

Test Questions

1. The primary value of an LNC to an attorney comes from the LNC's
   A. Legal knowledge gained from educational courses
   B. Medical knowledge and computer skills
   C. Nursing knowledge and experience
   D. Research and organizational skills

2. According to AALNC, the definition of legal nurse consulting includes all of the following EXCEPT:
   A. The application of knowledge acquired during the course of professional nursing education, training, and clinical experience to the evaluation of standard of care, causation, damages and other clinically related issues in cases or claims
   B. The application of legal standards and analysis to a particular case or claim based on experience working with attorneys
   C. Critical analysis of healthcare records and medical literature, as well as relevant legal documents and other information pertinent to the evaluation and resolution of cases or claims
   D. The development of case-specific work products and opinions for use by legal professionals or agencies handling cases or claims

3. The pros of working as an independent legal nurse consultant include:
   A. Autonomy
   B. Flexible hours
   C. Greater variety of cases and attorney-clients
   D. All of the above

4. The qualities, traits, and skills of successful legal nurse consultants include:
   A. Analytical skills
   B. Attention to detail
   C. Communication skills
   D. Writing skills
   E. All of the above

5. Eligibility requirements to sit for a certification examination in a nursing specialty include all of the following EXCEPT:
   A. Experience as an RN
   B. Evidence of formal education in the specialty practice
   C. Current licensure as an RN
   D. Current practice in the specialty

6. Which tool should be used to determine the test specifications (blueprint) of a nursing specialty certification exam?
   A. Core curriculum
   B. Accreditation standards
   C. Practice analysis
   D. Post-examination statistical analysis

Answers: 1. C, 2. B, 3. D, 4. E, 5. B, 6. C

Appendix A: AALNC Position Statement on Education and Certification in Legal Nurse Consulting

Education and Certification in Legal Nurse Consulting

The legal nurse consultant's primary educational foundation is the theory and practice of professional nursing. Entry into the specialty requires at a minimum, completion of a formal nursing education program and active licensure as a registered nurse. Optimally, legal nurse consultants should have been licensed as a registered nurse for at least five years and have significant clinical experience in order to bring the most value to the legal nurse consulting role.

Legal nurse consulting is the analysis and evaluation of facts and testimony related to the delivery of nursing and other healthcare services. Legal nurses render informed opinions on the nature and cause of injuries and (in relation to) patient outcomes. The legal nurse consultant is a licensed registered nurse who performs a critical analysis of clinically related issues in a variety of settings in the legal arena. The nurse expert with a strong educational and experiential foundation is qualified to assess adherence to standards and guidelines of practice as applied to nursing practice.

The practice of legal nurse consulting predates any specialty organization, training program, or certification. While many legal nurse consultants have acquired knowledge of the legal system through such experience as consulting with attorneys and attending seminars, legal or paralegal education is not a prerequisite to the practice of legal nurse consulting. In the early days of the specialty, nurses became legal nurse consultants (LNCs) without the benefit of formal education, relying on their nursing expertise and informal guidance or "on the job training" from attorneys. Then as now, nurses entered the specialty with a variety of educational backgrounds and practical experiences in nursing. The nurses who founded the American Association of Legal Nurse Consultants in 1989 were already practicing as LNCs when they came together to share their experience and to promote the specialty by forming a professional association.

Education

While formal education in legal nurse consulting is not required to enter the field, there are universities, colleges, professional organizations, and businesses that offer legal nurse consulting courses that culminate with a certificate of completion. In addition, some universities have postgraduate classes in legal nurse consulting, and a few offer a Master of Science in Nursing with a concentration in legal nurse consulting. The American Association of Legal Nurse Consultants has developed and recommends incorporation of *Legal Nurse Consulting Practices*, a two-volume core curriculum, into educational programs for this nursing specialty (Peterson & Kopishke, 2010).

The legal nurse consultant should continually expand one's knowledge of pertinent clinical and legal topics (e.g., legal standards and strategy) and hone their technical skills (e.g., research and writing) which are used in the specialty practice. Continuing education is necessary to remain current in medical and legal issues, assures value for clients and employers, and to maintain licensure and specialty certification. In addition to the educational opportunities already described, the *Journal of Legal Nurse Consulting* and other publications (i.e., legal journals) serve as educational resources for legal nurse consultants from entry level to the most experienced in the field.

The AALNC maintains the position that legal nurse consulting education programs should be developed and presented as specialty nursing curricula by nurse educators in partnership with legal educators. The qualifications of the program directors and instructors should be considered when evaluating a program. In general, programs developed and taught by experienced nurse educators who are practicing LNCs are preferred. The growth of this specialty into new practice areas and the changes in both the legal and healthcare fields pose constant educational challenges for the legal nurse consultant.

Certification

Most LNC education programs offer a certificate that testifies to the completion of a course of study and, in some cases, to passing an examination on the course material. Some graduates of LNC certificate programs chose to include letters such as "LNC" after their names, along with their educational degrees and professional credentials. The AALNC does not endorse this practice. It is customary to list such certificates in the education section of a resume or curriculum vitae. These certificate programs should not be confused with the certification programs offered by nursing certification boards, which are commonly affiliated with professional nursing associations. Certification is a process that recognizes an individual's qualifications and demonstrated knowledge in a specialty. In 1997, the AALNC established the American Legal Nurse Consultant Certification Board (ALNCCB®) to administer the Legal Nurse Consultant Certified (LNCC®) program. The LNCC® certification program is accredited by the American Board of Nursing Specialties (ABNS).

The purpose of the LNCC® program is to promote a level of expertise and professionalism in legal nurse consulting. Legal nurse consultants must meet the eligibility requirements, which include consulting experience, and achieve a passing score on a multiple-choice examination to earn the LNCC® designation. As with many clinical nursing certification programs, the LNCC® credential is designed for those who have demonstrated experience and knowledge in the specialty.[1] Certification is an appropriate goal for those who are committed to a professional legal nurse consulting practice.

The AALNC supports the practice initiated by the American Nurses Association of listing one's credentials in the following order: highest educational degree, highest nursing degree if different, licensure, and professional certifications. "LNCC®" is the only legal nurse consulting credential recognized by AALNC and ABNS.

To the extent that legal education is provided to nurses by legal assistant or paralegal education programs, it should be considered separate from the education of paralegals and legal assistants because of the differences in their practice in the legal arena. The primary focus of legal nurse consulting education should be to build on nursing education and clinical experience and to prepare nurses to function in the legal arena. In evaluating a particular program, its mission and purpose should be compared to this standard.

Revised 2016
Revised 2013
Originally published 2000

Note

1 The LNCC® credential can be compared to recognized nursing credentials such as RNC; CCRN; CEN; CPN; and CRRN.

Appendix B: AALNC Position Statement: Providing Expert Nursing Testimony Regarding Nursing Negligence

Introduction

Nurses are uniquely prepared to perform a critical review and analysis of clinical nursing care and administrative nursing practice to provide the foundation for testifying on nursing negligence issues.

Background and Discussion

Nursing has evolved into a profession with a distinct body of knowledge, methodology, university-based education, specialized practice, standards of practice, board certifications, a societal contract, and an ethical code. The practice of nursing requires decision-making and skill based upon principles of the biological, physical, behavioral, and social sciences as well as evidence-based research related to functions such as identifying risk factors, providing specific interventions, and evaluating outcomes of care. Each state has a Board of Nursing that is the authorized state entity with the legal authority to regulate nursing practice. State legislature has set forth licensing and regulations for the nursing profession in their respective Nurse Practice Acts and Advanced Practice Nursing Acts. It is evident that, under these nursing acts, only a nurse would meet the qualifications for sitting for nursing licensure examination and, as such, be eligible for licensure and practice as a registered nurse.

It appears straightforward that, generally, the most qualified expert to render expert opinion testimony regarding standards of care would be a member of the same profession who practices in a substantially similar clinical specialty as the potential defendant in the case. The courts are now generally acknowledging that nurses possess specialized knowledge that physicians do not have unless they have been trained and practice as a nurse.

The Supreme Court of Illinois held that a board certified internal medicine physician was not competent to testify as to the standard of care of a nurse. Citing the Amicus Brief submitted by The American Association of Nurse Attorneys, *the court noted:*

> A physician who is not a nurse is no more qualified to offer expert opinion testimony as to the standard of care for nurses than a nurse would be to offer an opinion as to the physician standard of care. Certainly, nurses are not permitted to offer expert testimony against a physician based on their observances of physicians or their familiarity with the procedures involved. An operating room nurse, who stands shoulder to shoulder with surgeons every day, would not be permitted to testify as to the standard of care of a surgeon. An endoscopy nurse would not be permitted to testify as to the standard of care of a gastroenterologist performing a colonoscopy. A labor and delivery nurse would not be permitted to offer expert testimony as to the standard of care for an obstetrician or even a midwife. Such testimony would be, essentially, expert testimony as to the standard of medical care.
>
> (*Sullivan v. Edward Hospital*, 806 N.E. 2d 645 (Ill. 2004))

The AALNC supports nursing expert opinions with regard to all aspects of nursing negligence.

Conclusion

Nursing has the knowledge, experience, and responsibility to define its standards of practice and indeed has published these standards of care. Therefore, licensed registered nurses are the only competent professionals to address these standards of nursing practice in the litigation arena.

It is the position of the American Association of Legal Nurse Consultants that, when registered nursing standards need to be established through expert testimony, the expert shall be a licensed, registered nurse.

Additional References

Albee, T. (2007). The legal nurse consultant as a board of nursing expert witness. *Journal of Legal Nurse Consulting, 18*(1), 11–14.

American Association of Legal Nurse Consultants. (2006). Position statement: Providing expert nurse witness testimony. Retrieved from www.aalnc.org/images/EXPWit. pdf.=.

American Association of Legal Nurse Consultants. (AALNC). (Peterson & Kopishke, Eds.) (2010). *Legal nurse consulting practices.* (3rd ed.). Boca Raton, FL: CRC Press.

Amom, E. (2007). Expert witness testimony. *Clinics in Perinatology, 34,* 473–478.

Cohen, M., Rosen, L., & Barbacci, M. (2008). Past, present and future: The evolution of the nurse expert witness. *Journal of Legal Nurse Consulting, 19*(4), 3–8.

Lynch, V., & Duval, J. (2011). *Forensic nursing science* (2nd ed.). St. Louis, MO: Elsevier Mosby.

Peterson, A., & Kopishke, L.(Eds.). (2010). *Legal nurse consulting practices* (3rd ed.). Boca Raton, FL: CRC Press.

Sullivan v. Edward Hospital, No. 95409, 2004 WL 228956 (Ill. Feb 5, 2004) Amicus brief submitted to Illinois Supreme Court—Karen Butler, Esq American Association of Nurse Attorneys.

Approved by the American Association of Legal Nurse Consultants Board of Directors, January 2006
Revised and approved 2014

Appendix C: ALNCCB® Position Statement: Certification in Legal Nurse Consulting

Position Statement

Certification in Legal Nurse Consulting

SUMMARY

The purpose of this position statement is to define and clarify the role of certification for legal nurse consultants and to establish the Legal Nurse Consultant Certified (LNCC®) program[1] as the premier certification in this specialty.

INTRODUCTION

As a nursing specialty recognized by the American Nurses Association (ANA), it is vital that legal nurse consultants (LNCs) have a pathway to certification which incorporates experiential and educational requirements. The LNCC® program is the only certification examination in the field endorsed by the American Association of Legal Nurse Consultants (AALNC) and accredited by the Accreditation Board for Specialty Nursing Certification (ABSNC).

BACKGROUND & DISCUSSION

Established in 1997 by AALNC, the American Legal Nurse Consultant Certification Board (ALNCCB®) is responsible for developing and maintaining a certification program in legal nurse consulting.

As part of the decision to offer a high-quality certification program, ALNCCB® sought accreditation by an outside body and selected ABSNC as the most appropriate accreditor. ABSNC is an advocate for consumer protection, and is the only accrediting body specifically for nursing certification. ABSNC provides a peer-review mechanism that allows nursing certification organizations to obtain accreditation by demonstrating compliance with established ABSNC standards.

ALNCCB® maintains the only certification in legal nurse consulting accredited by ABSNC and endorsed by AALNC. The LNCC® program was initially accredited in 1999 and reaccredited in 2004 and 2009. Accreditation distinguishes the LNCC® Program within the field of legal nurse consulting and equates the LNCC® credential with credentials from other highly respected programs.

ALNCCB® endorses the definition of certification adopted by ABNS, now ABSNC:

> *Certification* is the formal recognition of the specialized knowledge, skills, and experience demonstrated by the achievement of standards identified by a nursing specialty to promote optimal health outcomes.
>
> (ABNS, 2005)

A certification program helps advance the profession, and is one of the required elements for recognition as a nursing specialty. AALNC achieved this milestone in 2006 when the ANA officially recognized legal nurse consulting as a specialty practice of nursing. AALNC, in collaboration with the ANA, published *Legal Nurse Consulting Scope and Standards of Practice*. In this document, the authors note:

> Participation in the specialty's certification process demonstrates a level of professionalism and commitment, and allows community recognition of those legal nurse consultants who have achieved a higher level of skill and expertise within the specialty.
>
> (ANA, 2006)

While RN licensure ensures entry-level competency, certification is the gold standard for demonstrating knowledge and experience in specialty practice. Similar to physician board certification, nursing specialty certification is not achieved at entry into practice. The ABNS/ABSNC Position Statement on the Value of Certification address the issue of certification as a standard beyond licensure, noting that:

> While state licensure provides the legal authority for an individual to practice professional nursing, private voluntary certification is obtained through individual specialty nursing certifying organizations and reflects achievement of a standard beyond licensure for specialty nursing practice.
>
> (ABNS, 2005)

The value of certification also extends to the public. According to ABNS:

> The increasingly complex patient/client needs within the current healthcare delivery system are best met when registered nurses, certified in specialty practice, provide nursing care.
>
> (ABNS, 2005)

This statement applies to traditional nursing roles as well as legal nurse consulting practice. Similar to certified nurses in other specialties, LNCC®s, by virtue of their knowledge and experience in the specialty, can more readily meet the needs of their client than the novice practitioner.

Certification is a commitment that begins at entry into the specialty and continues throughout a nurse's career. Although voluntary, certification allows nursing specialties—including Legal Nurse Consulting—to publicly acknowledge a member's level of experience, judgment, and knowledge. Legal nurse consultants should commit to building their competency in the field, with a goal of sitting for the LNCC® examination.

CONCLUSION

The LNCC® program is designed to promote a level of expertise and professionalism by documenting individual performance as measured against a predetermined level of knowledge in legal nurse consulting; however it is not intended to determine who is qualified or who shall engage in legal nurse consulting. The LNCC® credential allows the public to more readily identify legal nurse consultants who have demonstrated a high level of experience, expertise, and commitment to this specialty nursing practice.

Legal nurse consultants who wish to distinguish themselves in the profession should seek voluntary certification as an LNCC®. As the only practice-based certification program that meets national testing standards, the LNCC® is comparable to board certification in other nursing specialties. In addition to the personal satisfaction that comes with certification, LNCs who invest their time in achieving and maintaining LNCC® certification can be comfortable in the knowledge that they have achieved a credential that has met or exceeded ABNS/ABSNC requirements, and is the gold standard for certification in the specialty.

It is the position of the American Legal Nurse Consultant Certification Board that
1. Certification is an objective measure of professional knowledge. It demonstrates to the public that an individual has met national testing standards, and has achieved a level of expertise in the specialty.
2. Certification in Legal Nurse Consulting is based on experience and knowledge, and is not achieved at entry into the specialty.
3. The Legal Nurse Consultant Certified (LNCC®) is the premier certification credential for legal nurse consultants, which is the only legal nurse consultant certification program accredited by the Accreditation Board for Specialty Nursing Certification (ABSNC).

Note

1 The LNCC® program is the collective term for all components of the certification process, including policies related to test development, certification, and recertification.

References

American Board of Nursing Specialties. (March 5, 2005). A position statement on the value of specialty nursing certification. Retrieved July 11, 2006 from www.nursingcertification.org/position_statements.htm.

American Board of Nursing Specialties. (October, 10, 2010). Frequently asked questions about ABSNC accreditation. Retrieved December 8, 2011 from http://nursingcertification.org/pdf/10-19-10%20 Final%20FAQs.pdf.

American Nurses Association, & American Association of Legal Nurse Consultants. (2006). *Scope and standards of practice for legal nurse consultants*. Silver Spring, MD: Nursesbooks.org.

Approved by the American Legal Nurse Consultant Certification Board
November 2006
Amended December 2008
Amended December 2011

Chapter 2

Professionalism, Ethics, Scope and Standards of Practice

Joan Magnusson, BSN, RN, LNCC®
Elizabeth K. Zorn, RN, BSN, LNCC®
Julie Dickinson, MBA, BSN, RN, LNCC®

Contents

Objectives

- Compare the key elements that define a profession to the characteristics of the practice of nursing
- Describe the purpose of the AALNC Code of Ethics in legal nurse consulting
- Detail three areas of potential liability for legal nurse consultants and nurse experts
- Discuss the relationship of the specialty practice of legal nurse consulting to the nursing profession
- Discuss the rationale for standards of practice and professional performance in nursing
- Identify the six Standards of Practice used by legal nurse consultants as a process for completion of work and assignments
- Discuss how the application of the Standards of Professional Performance may enhance the legal nurse consultant's practice

Introduction

Since the inception of the specialty practice of legal nurse consulting and the term "legal nurse consultant" (LNC), there have been efforts to distinguish the identity of these nurses from others practicing in the nursing or legal professions. Both professions, other allied fields, and the public needed to understand the LNC's role as a participant in the legal arena. Just as important, LNCs needed guidelines to practice ethically and successfully within this specialty practice of nursing.

This chapter provides an overview of the use of a code of ethics and a scope and standards of practice in legal nurse consulting. These published guidelines can be used by LNCs to steer practice activities and roles and by consumers of service to develop job descriptions, contractual arrangements, protocols, and performance evaluations.

Professionalism in Nursing

Endeavors have been made to define a profession by identifying various common characteristics. The five elements generally accepted as attributes of a profession are:

- A systematic, unique body of theory obtained through a formal education followed by examination for entry into practice
- An authority to define the profession and autonomy in its practice
- A high status granted by society because of altruistic motivation and commitment to serve society
- A code of ethics governing the conduct of members and
- A professional culture that embodies specific values, norms and symbols (Fowler, 2013).

The attempt to apply these attributes to nursing as a profession has promoted recognition of inconsistencies and movement toward solutions, most notably in the areas of educational preparation and control over professional practice.

While the nursing profession may accept various degrees for entry into practice, the commonality is a formal delivery of education in the health sciences, with a focus on the nursing process, coupled with a minimum level of experience necessary to prepare one for licensure and practice.

The concept of autonomy in practice has been an area of challenge for nursing. However, changes in the healthcare system have actually propelled nurses into more autonomous roles (e.g., nurse practitioners, clinical specialists, and case managers) as cost-effective providers of healthcare services.

It is generally accepted that nurses provide a valued service based on altruistic motivation. The public assumes the title of "nurse" carries with it a certain level of expertise, caring, and commitment. They believe nurses provide essential services desired and needed by society. These assumptions, in part, set the legal precedent of professional duty. The increasing responsibility and authority of advanced practice nurses in public health maintenance and illness management further validates nursing as a profession.

Professionals have codes of ethics to help regulate their relationships with consumers and each other. Formal codes of ethics are usually based on a set of values and norms that represent the philosophy and practice of the profession. Professionals have strong values pertaining to their occupational identity. This identity impacts all aspects of the professional's attitude and behavior toward work and lifestyle. The values established by the profession become the rules of expected behavior among the members of the profession, with expectations of loyalty and adherence.

Today, nurses have many options for practice settings besides direct patient care. In those settings, nurses apply health science education and expertise in a wide variety of situations. Consumers are protected by nurses adhering to the scope of nursing practice, using the nursing process, and applying professional ethics and standards.

Nursing practice in the legal arena facilitates the efforts to identify and right a wrong, prevent future untoward events, and mitigate damages resulting from such events. For example, whether working with the plaintiff or defense in a professional negligence case, the LNC's goal is to defend the appropriate standard of care as defined by medical research and the law. The LNC healthcare risk manager uses root cause analysis to identify and correct system failures. The LNC insurance case manager analyzes and recommends treatment modalities to maximize recovery.

Ethics in the Nursing Profession

The American Nurses Association's (ANA's) Code of Ethics for Nurses with Interpretive Statements (ANA, 2015a) contains nine provisions which identify the responsibilities of nurses, while the interpretive statements provide guidance in their application. While the first three provisions speak to a nurse's obligations to a patient, the remainder are designed to be guidelines for all nurses regardless of their practice areas. Legal nurse consultants should apply these ethics to their practice and behavior in society.

Identifying and Handling Ethical Dilemmas in Legal Nurse Consulting

Ethical dilemmas may arise in legal nurse consulting practice, and LNCs and nurse experts must be able to promptly identify and handle them. The American Association of Legal Nurse Consultants (AALNC) has developed and promoted ethical standards for LNCs since 1992, publishing the current Code of Ethics and Conduct in 2015. This Code of Ethics and the *Legal Nurse Consulting: Scope and Standards of Practice* (AALNC, 2017) offer guidelines to identify, resolve, and prevent ethical issues for practicing LNCs and testifying experts. See Appendix A for the AALNC Code of Ethics and Conduct.

An example of an ethical dilemma would be if a town resident, who is a personal injury attorney, approaches an LNC, who volunteers for the town's Zoning Board of Appeals. The attorney privately requests facilitation of a zoning variance application the attorney has submitted to the board. In exchange, the attorney offers to contract the LNC to work on several cases. The LNC understands from the seventh ethical standard that this quid pro quo is unethical and declines the attorney's request.

Another example would be if an attorney calls a nurse to explain that a nursing expert has withdrawn from a case. The attorney gives the nurse an overview of the case, explains there are voluminous medical records and deposition transcripts, and asks the nurse to sign the prior expert's report to meet a looming disclosure deadline. The nurse expert understands that an expert must develop independent opinions through an objective review of the records. The nurse expert declines to sign another's work and offers to review the records independently.

Avoiding Liability in Legal Nurse Consulting

Nurse experts and LNCs generally have a low risk of professional liability. Risk factors include serving as a nurse expert, working independently, and full-time practice. Factors that mitigate liability risk are working behind the scenes (i.e., not serving as a testifying expert), in-house employment, and part-time work (Dickinson & Zorn, 2013).

Areas of Potential Liability

Any improper conduct that adversely impacts a client, a claim, or a party to a legal action could give rise to a professional liability claim. Legal nurse consultants and nurse experts should be mindful of the following most common areas of potential liability and implement measures to reduce potential liability exposure (Dickinson & Zorn, 2013).

CONFLICT OF INTEREST

Conflicts of interest involving LNC practice may be legal or personal (Dickinson & Zorn, 2013). Legal conflicts of interest affect attorneys and their cases. If a plaintiff attorney hired a nurse expert who works on the same unit where the care at issue occurred, defense counsel may file a motion to preclude the plaintiff attorney's continued representation of the client on the grounds that the nurse expert possesses information to which the plaintiff attorney would not ordinarily be entitled. Personal conflicts of interest affect an LNC's or nurse expert's ability to evaluate a case objectively (e.g., if a party to the claim is a family member or friend).

As set forth in AALNC's Code of Ethics (AALNC, 2015), "Relationships that may give an appearance of or create a conflict of interest will be considered and disclosed when practicing." Thus, prior to agreeing to work on a case, the LNC and nurse expert should always consider whether any potential or actual conflicts of interest may exist and, if so, discuss the details with the hiring attorney.

EVALUATING POTENTIAL CLAIMS WITHOUT ATTORNEY INVOLVEMENT

Persons contemplating a medical malpractice claim sometimes approach an LNC for an opinion regarding the merits of such a claim. However, in accordance with AALNC's Code of Ethics (AALNC, 2015), the LNC should always decline to evaluate a potential claim without an attorney being involved, as it could be construed as the unauthorized practice of law. The primary concern is that, if the statute of limitations or a notice requirement expires while the LNC is still evaluating the potential claim, the claim may be forever barred, thus exposing the LNC to a liability claim.

INSUFFICIENT QUALIFICATIONS OR EXPERT AFFIDAVIT

The rules related to expert witness qualifications and testimony are set forth in the Federal Rules of Evidence for federal court cases and in a state's evidentiary rules for state court cases. If an expert's qualifications, testimony, or expert affidavit or report does not meet the applicable evidentiary requirements, the judge may preclude the expert from testifying or preclude the specific testimony, affidavit, or report from being admitted into evidence, negatively impacting that side's case. Nurse experts should be mindful of the applicable requirements pertaining to expert witness qualifications and opinions and should work with the hiring attorney to ensure compliance with these rules.

In a notable case involving improper expert credentials, a malicious prosecution claim was brought against a nurse expert who signed an expert affidavit against an urologist. The malicious prosecution claim alleged bad faith, fraud, misrepresentation, and civil conspiracy (Dickinson, Zorn, & Burroughs, 2014). The attorney who hired the nurse expert was also sued. The nurse and the attorney should have known that evidentiary rules do not permit a nurse to opine as to the proper standard of care for an urologist. The case ultimately settled.

OPINING OUTSIDE ONE'S SCOPE OF EXPERTISE

The validity of expert opinions directly impacts case outcomes. Opining outside the scope of one's experience, knowledge, or expertise could adversely affect a case outcome, giving rise to potential liability. As set forth in AALNC's Code of Ethics (AALNC, 2015), "the legal nurse consultant does not purport to be competent in matters in which he or she has limited knowledge or experience." Thus, the nurse expert must only opine on those issues about which the nurse has significant knowledge and experience. For example, it is improper for a perioperative nurse to offer opinions on the standards of care for an emergency department nurse.

IMPROPER WITHDRAWAL AS AN EXPERT WITNESS

Withdrawing as an expert in a case without sufficient notice to the attorney could negatively impact the attorney's case if the attorney is unable to retain another qualified expert prior to the procedural deadlines. At the outset of the case assignment, it is critical that the nurse communicate with the attorney regarding willingness to serve as an expert witness should the nurse's review support the attorney's case. If, after review of all the medical records and other evidence, the nurse expert cannot support the case, the attorney should be notified as soon as possible. If the nurse expert's review was favorable but extenuating circumstances arose that prevent the nurse expert from continuing to work on the case, the attorney should be notified immediately, and every effort should be made to assist the attorney to find a qualified, available replacement so the attorney can still meet the procedural deadlines.

ADVICE AND WORK PRODUCT OF BEHIND-THE-SCENES LNCS

Ultimately, the attorney is responsible for evaluating the work product, research, and opinions of behind-the-scenes consultants. Even so, improper conduct by such consultants (such as incomplete medical literature research leading to a faulty recommendation on the merits of a case) has given rise to litigation, and thus these LNCs "still have exposure and are accountable for generating opinions and work products that are of the utmost quality" (Dickinson & Zorn, 2013).

FEE DISPUTES

Billing disputes related to professional services are the most common claims against LNCs and are sometimes related to the attorney's perception of the work quality. To avoid such disputes, it is essential to utilize a fee schedule and business contract and discuss its terms and conditions with the attorney at the outset (Dickinson & Zorn, 2013). In addition, the provision of excellent work that enhances the attorney's delivery of high-quality legal services lessens the likelihood of a billing dispute.

CONFIDENTIALITY VIOLATIONS

Breach of confidentiality or violation of privacy laws pertaining to protected health information may give rise to liability claims against the LNC and the hiring attorney (Dickinson & Zorn, 2013). As set forth in AALNC's Code of Ethics (AALNC, 2015), "the legal nurse consultant uses confidential materials with discretion and abides by applicable statutes, regulations, and professional codes of conduct that pertain to confidentiality."

Scope of Practice and Standards in the Nursing Profession

Defining Legal Nurse Consulting as a Specialty Practice of Nursing

The AALNC Board of Directors resolved in 1995 that the professional foundation of legal nurse consulting was the practice of nursing, not the practice of law. The LNC's value to the legal arena was one's nursing education and experience, rather than the knowledge of the law. By applying that foundation in a consulting capacity in the legal arena, AALNC defined legal nurse consulting as a new specialty practice of nursing. While knowledge of applicable laws and regulations can enhance the LNC's contributions, the primary value of the LNC is one's knowledge of healthcare systems and sciences.

Scope of Legal Nurse Consulting

One of the characteristics of a profession is the ability to define its own scope and standards of practice. The purpose of the scope is to describe the "who, what, where, when, why, and how" of the persons practicing in that profession. Standards are authoritative statements of the duties or responsibilities the professional should be able to perform competently. The ANA has long assumed the responsibility for developing and maintaining the Scope and Standards of Practice for the nursing profession. This document, in turn, serves as a template for the scope and standards of nursing specialty practice.

The Legal Nurse Consulting Scope of Practice (AALNC, 2017) identifies the LNC as a licensed registered nurse who:

- Applies knowledge acquired during the course of professional nursing education, training, and clinical experience to the evaluation of standard of care, causation, damages, and other clinically health related issues in cases or claims
- Applies additional knowledge acquired through education and experience regarding applicable legal standards and/or strategy to the evaluation of cases or claims
- Critically analyzes healthcare records, medical literature, relevant legal documents, and other information pertinent to the evaluation and resolution of cases or claims and
- Develops case-specific work products and opinions for use by legal professionals or agencies handling cases or claims

The LNC generally performs these activities in cases involving civil or criminal litigation or administrative actions. The most common areas of practice for the LNC continues to be medical malpractice and general liability involving personal injury or death. Other practice areas include long-term care/violation of resident rights, product liability, toxic tort, mass tort, healthcare risk management, life care planning, regulatory compliance, workers' compensation, forensics, and violation of civil or disability rights. More recently, LNC activities have expanded into areas of Medicare Set-Aside, Social Security disability, and medical billing fraud. The common factor is the need for a practitioner with knowledge and skills in evaluating evidence pertaining to quality or standard of care, cost of care, cause of physical/mental injury, treatment of injury, violation of rights specific to health and safety, and impact of disability.

Legal nurse consultant practice settings are defined as those venues in which LNCs provide the above services. Law firms remain the prominent consumer of LNC services. Legal nurse consultants are also hired by other agencies, companies, and institutions that handle liability or disability insurance claims, healthcare risk management, professional licensing issues, or medical products safety. Whether the employer hires the LNC as an in-house employee or an independent contractor often depends on the LNC's role. Law firms tend to hire nurses either as a behind-the-scenes LNC or as a testifying expert. The nurse expert is usually hired as an independent contractor on an as-needed basis. Whether law firms or companies prefer to hire behind-the-scenes LNCs as employees or independent contractors often depends on the employer's work load, job descriptions and responsibilities, desire for exclusivity, and extent of financial compensation and benefits.

Standards for Legal Nurse Consulting

The ANA Standards of Practice (ANA, 2015b) are based on the nursing process which consists of actions that are logical, interdependent, and sequential but cyclic: assessment, diagnosis, outcome identification and planning, implementation, and evaluation. All of these actions require critical thinking, the use of clinical experience, and the application of theory learned in a formal nursing education (ANA, 2015b).

Using the nursing process provides the LNC with a framework or consistent problem-solving approach for meeting the needs of a particular case, client, project, or role. In legal nurse consulting, the process includes needs assessment, issue identification, case outcome identification, case planning, implementation, and evaluation. (See Table 2.1.)

Consumers of legal nurse consulting services have the right to expect quality services and work products. The first six Standards in the Legal Nurse Consulting Standards of Practice (Appendix B) outline competencies the LNC performs to provide such services and work products. The LNC may apply these tools flexibly as applicable to the practice setting, practice role, and stage of

Table 2.1 Comparison of ANA's Standards of Professional Nursing Practice and the AALNC Standards of LNC Practice

Professional Nursing Practice Standards	LNC Practice Standards
Standard 1: Assessment The registered nurse collects pertinent data and information relative to the healthcare consumer's health or the situation.	**Assessment** The LNC identifies and collects comprehensive data pertinent to the assessment of a medical-legal case or claim.
Standard 2: Diagnosis The registered nurse analyzes the assessment data to determine actual or potential diagnoses, problems, and issues.	**Issue Identification** The LNC analyzes the collected data to determine the issues in a medical-legal case or claim.
Standard 3: Outcomes Identification The registered nurse identifies expected outcomes for a plan individualized to the healthcare consumer or the situation.	**Case Outcome Identification** The LNC participates in the identification of the optimal outcome for the medical-legal case or claim.
Standard 4: Planning The registered nurse develops a plan that prescribes strategies to attain expected, measurable outcomes.	**Case Planning** The LNC develops a work plan that contributes to optimal case outcome.
Standard 5. Implementation The registered nurse implements the identified plan. 5A. Coordination of care The registered nurse coordinates care delivery. 5B. Health teaching and health promotion. The registered nurse employs strategies to promote health and a safe environment.	**Implementation** The LNC implements the plan, participating in the legal process pertinent to resolution of the medical-legal case or claim.
Standard 6: Evaluation The registered nurse evaluates progress toward the attainment of goals and outcomes.	**Evaluation** The LNC evaluates progress toward attainment of optimal case outcome.

Note: Data for Professional Nursing Practice Standards from ANA (2015b) and for LNC Practice Standards from AALNC (2017).

litigation. The resulting standardized, systematic action plan results in economical use of time and energy, consistent work quality, and job satisfaction.

Standards 7–16 provide the LNC with guidelines for professional behavior in the specialty, providing the LNC with a roadmap to personal and professional growth. Taken together, the Standards define, direct, and offer a framework for legal nurse consulting practice to benefit consumers and the profession (AALNC, 2017).

Summary

Registered nurses possess the knowledge of science, healthcare theory, and clinical practice that makes them valued assets in a multitude of roles and settings as consultants to those handling medical-legal matters. The American Association of Legal Nurse Consultants' *Legal Nurse Consulting: Scope and Standards of Practice* (2017) and Code of Ethics and Conduct with Interpretive Statements (2015) create a foundation for quality LNC practice, including guidelines for ethical practice to reduce the risk of liability. Legal nurse consultants are encouraged to base their practices on these guidelines and standards according to their individual education, experience, and client needs.

References

American Association of Legal Nurse Consultants. (2015). Code of ethics and conduct with interpretive discussion. Retrieved from www.aalnc.org/d/do/85.

American Association of Legal Nurse Consultants. (2017). *Legal nurse consulting: Scope and standards of practice*. Retrieved from www.aalnc.org.

American Nurses Association. (2015a). *Code of ethics for nurses with interpretive statements*. Washington, DC: American Nurses Publishing.

American Nurses Association. (2015b). *Nursing: Scope and standards of practice*. Washington, DC: Nursesbooks.org.

Dickinson, J., & Zorn, E. (2013). Liability lessons for legal nurse consultants part one: An analysis of claims involving legal nurse consultants. *Journal of Legal Nursing Consulting, 24*(2), 4–9.

Dickinson, J., Zorn, E. & Burroughs, R. (2014). Liability lessons for legal nurse consultants part two: A case study with risk management strategies. *Journal of Legal Nurse Consulting, 25*(1), 4–6.

Fowler, M. (2013). *Guide to nursing's social policy statement: Understanding the profession*. Washington, DC: American Nurses Publishing.

Test Questions

1. The key element that *challenges* the premise that nursing is a profession is:
   A. Disagreement regarding ethical standards in nursing practice
   B. Nursing's failure to define its unique professional autonomy
   C. Lack of minimum requirement for university-based education
   D. Public perception that nursing is under the direction of physicians

2. When comparing the general nursing standards to the legal nurse consulting standards of practice, the standard most similar to Diagnosis is:
   A. Assessment findings
   B. Outcomes identification
   C. Issues identification
   D. Analysis results

3. Applying the AALNC Code of Ethics and Conduct can assist legal nurse consultants and nurse experts to:
   A. Identify ethical dilemmas
   B. Make practice decisions
   C. Evaluate their professional performance and behavior
   D. All of the above

4. Areas of potential liability in LNC practice include:
   A. Evaluating potential claims without attorney involvement
   B. Fee dispute
   C. Opining outside one's scope of expertise
   D. All of the above

5. Which one of the following is a Standard of Professional Performance
   A. Evaluation
   B. Leadership
   C. Records review
   D. Teaching

6. After reviewing the deposition testimony of one defendant, the LNC identified several new facts about deviations in care by another defendant. This is known as:
   A. Issues identification
   B. Outcomes identification
   C. Planning
   D. Evaluation

7. The independent LNC applies the Evaluation standard by:
   A. Showing a work product to other LNCs at an AALNC chapter meeting for feedback
   B. Sending holiday gifts to those clients who provided the most work opportunities
   C. Comparing one's annual income from LNC work to that of previous years
   D. Discussing work product effectiveness with the client after case resolution

Answers: 1. D, 2. C, 3. D, 4. D, 5. B 6. A, 7. D

Appendix A: Code of Ethics and Conduct with Interpretive Discussion

Preamble

The Code of Ethics and Conduct of the American Association of Legal Nurse Consultants (AALNC) establishes the ethical standard for the specialty practice and provides a guide for legal nurse consultants to use in ethical analysis and decision-making in their practice. It provides guidelines for the professional performance and behavior of legal nurse consultants. The esteem of this specialty practice of nursing results from the competence and integrity of its practitioners. Thus, AALNC sets forth this code to impart its ethical expectations for legal nurse consultants and to set the standards of accountability.

1. **The legal nurse consultant maintains professional nursing competence.** The legal nurse consultant is a Registered Nurse and maintains an active nursing license. The legal nurse consultant is knowledgeable about the current scope and standards of legal nursing practice and advocates for these standards.
2. **The legal nurse consultant uses informed judgment, objectivity and individual professional competence as criteria when accepting assignments.** The legal nurse consultant does not purport to be competent in matters in which he or she has limited knowledge or experience. Only services that meet high personal and professional standards are offered or rendered. The legal nurse consultant is accountable for his or her decisions and actions.
3. **The legal nurse consultant does not engage in activities that could be construed as the unauthorized practice of law**. The legal nurse consultant refrains from offering opinions that could be deemed legal opinions requiring a law license (e.g., opining directly to a potential plaintiff without an attorney being involved regarding whether a claim may have merit).
4. **The legal nurse consultant's work products and opinions are free from bias.** The legal nurse consultant does not discriminate against any person based on race, creed, color, age, gender, sexual orientation, national origin, social status or disability. The legal nurse consultant does not allow personal attitudes or individual differences to interfere with professional performance and practice. Financial and/or other relationships that may give an appearance of or create a conflict of interest will be considered and disclosed when practicing.
5. **The legal nurse consultant performs his or her work with the highest degree of integrity.** Integrity is exemplified by uprightness, honesty, and sincerity. The legal nurse consultant applies these attributes to the specialty practice. Integrity is a personal and sacred trust and the standard against which the legal nurse consultant must ultimately measure all actions and decisions. Honest errors and differences of opinion may occur, but deceit, poor judgment, and/or lack of principles are unacceptable.
6. **The legal nurse consultant respects and protects the privacy and confidentiality of the individuals involved in a medical-legal case or claim.** The legal nurse consultant uses confidential materials with discretion and abides by applicable statutes, regulations, and professional codes of conduct that pertain to confidentiality. The legal nurse consultant does not use any case information for personal gain.
7. **The legal nurse consultant maintains standards of personal conduct that reflect honorably upon the profession of nursing and the specialty practice of legal nurse consulting.**

The legal nurse consultant abides by all local, state and federal laws and other regulatory requirements. The legal nurse consultant who knowingly becomes involved in unethical or illegal activities prioritizes personal interest or personal gain over professional responsibility. Such activities jeopardize the public confidence and trust in the nursing profession and are unacceptable to the profession and to this specialty nursing practice.

8. **The legal nurse consultant integrates ethical considerations into his or her practice.** The legal nurse consultant works to achieve client goals while upholding the responsibility to provide accurate information, independent and sound opinions, and professional recommendations. The legal nurse consultant contributes to resolving ethical issues in practice; reports illegal, incompetent or impaired practice; and promotes respect for the judicial system.

Conclusion

By promulgating this Code of Ethics and Conduct, the American Association of Legal Nurse Consultants sets forth the level of professional behavior and conduct expected of legal nurse consultants. Each legal nurse consultant's personal commitment to this Code of Ethics and Conduct safeguards the continued honor and integrity of both the nursing profession and this specialty nursing practice.

For more information, contact:

American Association of Legal Nurse Consultants
Toll free: 877-402-2562
Web site: **www.aalnc.org**
Email: **info@aalnc.org**
Adopted and copyrighted © April 1992
Revised 2005, 2009, 2015
By the American Association of Legal Nurse Consultants

Appendix to the Code of Ethics and Conduct with Interpretive Discussion

Resources

Legal nurse consultants, as nurses, should acknowledge and be mindful of the American Nurses Association's *Code of Ethics for Nurses*.

As consultants in the legal arena, legal nurse consultants should acknowledge and be mindful of the applicable portions[1] of the American Bar Association's *Model Rules of Professional Conduct*.

1 The applicable portions are Rule 1.6c (maintaining the confidentiality of information), Rule 5.3 (the attorneys' responsibilities regarding non-lawyer assistants), and Rule 5.7b (unauthorized practice of law).

Note

1. The applicable portions are Rule 1.6c (maintaining the confidentiality of information), Rule 5.3 (the attorneys' responsibilities regarding non-lawyer assistants), and Rule 5.7b (unauthorized practice of law).

Appendix B: Legal Nurse Consulting: Standards of Practice and Professional Performance

Standard 1: Assessment

The LNC identifies and collects comprehensive data pertinent to the assessment of a medical-legal case or claim.

Competencies

The LNC:
  A. Identifies comprehensive, relevant data in a systematic and ongoing process to include potential conflicts of interest, statute of limitations, medical and non-medical records, knowledge gaps requiring research, and purpose and source of medical literature.
  B. Collects the identified data from parties and witnesses, medical records and literature, legal documents, expert witness opinions, and other sources, via interviews or processes consistent with federal or state laws, rules, or regulations.
  C. Collects data regarding testifying experts and defendant healthcare providers, including background research, licensure, accreditation, qualifications, prior testimony, publications, and reliance materials.
  D. Prioritizes data collection based on the procedural deadlines of the case or claim and the needs of the legal professional.
  E. Organizes data collected (e.g., medical records) in an appropriate manner.
  F. Applies ethical, legal, and HIPAA guidelines and policies to the collection, maintenance, use, and dissemination of information in a case or claim.
  G. Documents relevant data in a retrievable and appropriate format.

Standard 2: Issue Identification

The LNC analyzes the collected data to determine the issues in a medical-legal case or claim.

Competencies

The LNC:
  A. Derives case issues from the collected data, including identification of potential defendants, certificates of merit, complaints, petitions, records, and analysis of research findings.
  B. Validates identified issues with the legal professionals, healthcare providers, experts, and parties.
  C. Utilizes data to identify case strengths/weaknesses regarding liability, causation and damages, and their impact on potential case value.
  D. Recognizes the potential impact of personal attitudes, values, and beliefs on case analysis.
  E. Assesses parties, fact witnesses, and experts as witnesses and their likely impact on the case.
  F. Documents research findings.

Standard 3: Case Outcome Identification

The LNC participates in the identification of the optimal outcome for the medical-legal case or claim.

Competencies

The LNC:
- A. Contributes to analysis of case issues to identify optimal case outcome.
- B. Participates in ongoing case strategy discussions with legal professionals.
- C. Participates in ongoing discussions regarding risks of proceeding to trial versus case settlement.
- D. Documents expected outcomes in terms of probability versus possibility of reaching goals, when applicable.

Standard 4: Case Planning

The LNC develops a work plan that contributes to optimal case outcome.

Competencies

The LNC:
- A. Develops a plan based on the issues and needs of the case and client/attorney.
- B. Incorporates applicable procedural rules and deadlines into the plan to include statute of limitations.
- C. Considers the cost-benefit analysis of the components within the plan.
- D. Establishes work priorities within a given case and among all case projects.
- E. Incorporates a timeline for completion of projects.
- F. Utilizes the plan to provide direction to other members of the legal team.
- G. Provides for continuity and follow-up within the plan.
- H. Modifies the plan according to the legal professional's feedback and changes in case or claim status.
- I. Documents progress toward completion of plan.

Standard 5: Implementation

The LNC implements the plan, participating in the legal process pertinent to resolution of medical-legal case or claim.

Competencies

The LNC:
- A. Engages in appropriate and effective oral and written communication with the legal team, experts, and parties.
- B. Accommodates for barriers to effective communication.
- C. Partners with legal professionals, parties, and others as appropriate to implement the plan in a realistic and timely manner.
- D. Utilizes technology to implement, maximize access to, and optimize the effectiveness of the plan.
- E. Applies clinical and legal knowledge to extract relevant information from the medical literature, medical records, deposition testimony, and other sources when preparing case work products and discussing strategy.

F. Provides content relevant to case issues for the preparation of legal documents and correspondence.
G. Collaborates with legal professionals in mediation, arbitration, or trial preparation, to include preparation of witnesses and experts, and identifying appropriate exhibits and demonstrative evidence.
H. Serves as an effective nurse expert or fact witness.
I. Identifies the legal professional, client, witnesses' knowledge gap of the clinically-related issues in the case.
J. Educates the legal professional, parties, witnesses, and others regarding clinically-related issues on standards of care, causation, and injuries pertinent to the case.

Standard 6: Evaluation

The LNC evaluates progress toward attainment of optimal case outcome.

Competencies

The LNC:
A. Seeks feedback from the legal professional regarding ideas to improve the effectiveness of the work product and advice toward achieving optimal case outcome.
B. Incorporates new knowledge and strategies in LNC practice to optimize effectiveness and quality of work products.
C. Collaborates, as appropriate, with the parties, family members, legal professional, and others in the case evaluation process.
D. Evaluates the effectiveness of the case plan and the progress toward the optimal case outcome with the legal professional.

Standard 7: Ethics

The LNC practices ethically.

Competencies

The LNC:
A. Utilizes Guide to the Code of Ethics for Nurses with Interpretive Statements (ANA, 2015a), and the Code of Ethics and Conduct with Interpretive Discussion (AALNC, 2015) to guide professional activities.
B. Maintains client confidentiality.
C. Maintains a client-LNC relationship within appropriate professional role boundaries.
D. Questions decisions that may not be in the best interest of the legal professional's client.
E. Takes appropriate action regarding illegal or inappropriate behavior that arises in a case or claim.
F. Provides services in a manner that preserves and protects parties' autonomy, dignity, rights, values, and beliefs.

Standard 8: Education

The LNC attains knowledge and competence reflecting current specialty practice.

Competencies

The LNC:
  A. Demonstrates a commitment to lifelong learning through self-evaluation and inquiry to address learning and personal growth needs.
  B. Identifies learning needs based on medical-legal knowledge, the various roles the LNC may assume, and the trends and issues in the clinical and legal environments.
  C. Participates in formal and informal educational activities to develop, maintain, and expand professional skills and knowledge.
  D. Shares knowledge, educational experiences, and ideas with colleagues.
  E. Contributes to a practice environment conducive to the education of healthcare and legal professionals.
  F. Maintains professional records that provide evidence of competence and lifelong learning.

Standard 9: Practice and Research

The LNC integrates evidence and research into practice.

Competencies

The LNC:
  A. Contributes to the expansion of a research-based body of knowledge in the practice.
  B. Shares pertinent research findings with colleagues and peers.
  C. Applies research findings to practice, as appropriate.

Standard 10: Quality of Practice

The LNC participates in providing quality services.

Competencies

The LNC:
  A. Demonstrates an ongoing commitment to quality by consistently applying the nursing process.
  B. Uses creativity and innovation to enhance the practice.
  C. Participates in quality improvement of practice, to include:
    ■ Identifying aspects of practice important for delivery of quality services.
    ■ Formulating recommendations to improve practice services.
    ■ Implementing activities to enhance the quality of practice services.
    ■ Developing, implementing, and/or evaluating policies, procedures, and guidelines to improve the quality of practice services.
    ■ Analyzing factors related to quality and effectiveness of practice services.

Standard 11: Communication

The LNC communicates effectively in a variety of formats in all areas of practice.

Competencies

The LNC:
  A. Determines communication format preferences of legal professionals, clients, experts, and colleagues.
  B. Conveys information to the legal team and others in formats that promote accuracy, clarity, conciseness, completeness, and logic.
  C. Contributes own professional perspective in discussions with the legal team.
  D. Evaluates personal communication skills in encounters with legal professionals, clients, experts, and colleagues.
  E. Seeks continuous improvement of personal communication and conflict resolution skills.

Standard 12: Leadership

The LNC demonstrates leadership in the practice setting and the profession.

Competencies

The LNC:
  A. Oversees the delegated work performed by others as appropriate, while retaining account-ability for the quality of the work.
  B. Contributes to the identification, implementation, and evaluation of goals and strategies for resolving cases and claims.
  C. Mentors colleagues for the advancement of the specialty practice, the nursing profession and quality of LNC services.
  D. Treats colleagues with respect and dignity.
  E. Achieves trustworthiness among colleagues and clients.
  F. Develops effective communication and conflict resolution skills.
  G. Participates in professional associations.
  H. Seeks ways to advance legal nurse consulting autonomy and accountability within the applicable ethical guidelines.

Standard 13: Collaboration

The LNC collaborates with legal professionals and others in the conduct of the practice.

Competencies

The LNC:
  A. Partners with others to produce favorable outcomes through the sharing of knowledge regarding the case or claim, as appropriate.
  B. Communicates with the legal professionals and clients, as appropriate, regarding the legal nurse consultant's role in the provision of services provided on the case or claim.

C. Adheres to standards and applicable codes of conduct that govern behavior among colleagues to create a work environment that promotes cooperation, respect, and trust.
D. Engages in teamwork and consensus-building processes.

Standard 14: Professional Practice Evaluation

The LNC evaluates one's own practice in relation to professional practice standards and applicable rules and regulations.

Competencies

The LNC:
A. Obtains feedback regarding one's own practice and services from legal professionals and others, as appropriate.
B. Engages in self-evaluation of practice on a regular basis, identifying areas of strength as well as areas in which professional growth would be beneficial.
C. Takes action to achieve goals for professional growth identified during the evaluation process.
D. Interacts with colleagues to identify ways to enhance one's own practice or role performance.

Standard 15: Resource Utilization

The LNC utilizes appropriate resources to provide effective and financially-responsible services.

Competencies

The LNC:
A. Identifies available resources to provide quality services.
B. Considers the legal professional's needs, complexity of task, and costs when recommending resources.
C. Delegates work to legal team members, as appropriate.
D. Advocates for use of the latest technology that enhances specialty practice.

Standard 16: Environmental Health

The LNC practices in an environmentally-responsible manner.

Competencies

The LNC:
A. Attains knowledge of environmental health concepts.
B. Promotes a practice environment that reduces environmental waste.
C. Advocates for the judicious use of materials.

The full *Legal Nurse Consulting: Scope and Standards of Practice* is available for purchase at www. aalnc.org/page/aalnc-online-bookstore.

Section II

Essentials of the Law

Chapter 3

Legal Fundamentals

Tonia Aiken, RN, JD
Adam B. Kuenning, JD, LLM
Flynn P. Carey, JD
Karen E. Evans, BSN, JD
Zakiya Sloley, JD
Grace Morse-McNelis, BSN, JD

Contents

Objectives

- Discuss the sources and types of law
- Discuss the considerations when deciding whether to litigate a case in state or federal court
- Describe what makes potential evidence relevant to a case
- List the rules of civil procedure that pertain to initiating a lawsuit and engaging in pre-trial discovery
- Discuss two common legal doctrines

Introduction

Over the centuries, the law has evolved into a quagmire of rules, statutes, regulations, case law, codes, and opinions that, in many instances, vary from state to state, state court to federal court, and jurisdiction to jurisdiction. Laws serve to control and guide people and entities in relationships, unions, and interactions. Laws are also used to resolve conflicts involving people, corporations, countries, and states. Laws have evolved through the ages and have resulted in major changes in the way people live and work in a modern society. This chapter introduces the legal nurse consultant (LNC) to the law, court systems, evidentiary rules, procedural rules, and legal doctrines frequently encountered in medical-legal cases.

Sources of Laws

The word *law* originates from the Anglo-Saxon term *lagu*, meaning *that which is fixed*. There are several sources of laws that affect individuals, society, and the medical-legal arena. Sources of laws include constitutional law, statutory law, administrative law, and common law.

Constitutional Law

Constitutional law is a compilation of laws, principles, and amendments derived from the United States (U.S.) and state constitutions that govern and guide federal and state governments, corporations, society, and individuals. The constitutional laws and amendments guarantee individuals certain rights, such as the right to privacy, freedom of speech, and equal protection. The U.S. Constitution grants certain powers to the federal government and agencies and reserves powers for the states. The Constitution is the supreme law of the land and takes precedence over state and local laws. Constitutional law is the highest form of law in the United States. If not addressed in federal law, then the issue is "given" to the state government. In some instances, laws are codified (arranged by subject/area of law) at both the state and federal levels for different circumstances.

Federal and state governments have the constitutional authority to develop and create laws. In addition to creating laws, governments also have the ability to enforce the laws that have been established. Federal and state laws can be accessed at http://law.justia.com/.

Statutory Law

Statutory laws are laws enacted by federal, state, and local legislative bodies. Many healthcare providers, special interest groups, legal groups, attorneys, and lobbyists are involved in lobbying for certain bills or amendments to pass that will promote or protect their specific interests or special interest groups. An example of statutory law that every state has addressed is the law outlining the statute of limitations for filing a medical malpractice, wrongful death, or personal injury claim. Other examples of statutory laws related to health care include the reporting of elder and child abuse and communicable diseases.

Administrative Law

Administrative laws originate from administrative agencies that are under the arm of the executive branch of the government. For example, state boards of nursing are state administrative agencies. These agencies promulgate rules and regulations to guide nursing practice in the state and to enforce nurse practice acts. Such nursing board regulations are legally binding. The state boards for healthcare professionals conduct investigations and hearings to ensure enforcement of the practice acts. These administrative laws also detail the sanctions that can be imposed upon healthcare professionals if they are found to have violated their practice act.

The state's laws and the National Council of State Boards of Nursing are resources for identifying the acts considered to be healthcare professional practice violations in that specific state. The following are examples of violations that can affect a healthcare provider's license. (For more information on healthcare provider licensure investigations, see Chapter 25.)

- Practicing while using a diploma, license, renewal of license, or record illegally or fraudulently obtained, illegally signed, or unlawfully issued
- Practicing when the license has been revoked or suspended
- Practicing when the license has lapsed due to failure to renew
- Aiding or abetting a felon
- Using controlled substances or dangerous drugs or devices that may impair the ability to practice
- Diverting patient medications (e.g., narcotics)
- Presenting an illegal prescription
- Abusing drugs or alcohol
- Failing to follow the diversionary or recovering healthcare provider program
- Failing to exercise appropriate judgment and skills
- Falsifying documents
- Failing to intervene and follow orders
- Delegating care improperly
- Failing to disclose prior arrests or criminal convictions
- Unprofessional conduct
- Guilty of moral turpitude
- Gross negligence involving patient care or when carrying out licensed functions
- Incompetence in carrying out certified or licensed functions
- Practicing outside the scope of the license (e.g., a nurse practicing medicine without a medical license or a dental hygienist practicing dentistry without a dental license)
- Aiding unlicensed practice and
- Willfully employing an unlicensed person to perform licensed functions

For any LNC working on a matter involving the practice of any healthcare provider, it is necessary to have access to the statutes that regulate that practice.

Another example of administrative law is an attorney general's opinion. The attorney general may provide an opinion regarding a specific interpretation of a law that cannot be found in a statute or regulation. The opinion is based on statutory and common law principles.

Other examples of administrative agencies include the Social Security Administration (SSA), the Environmental Protection Agency (EPA), and the Occupational Safety and Health Administration (OSHA).

Common Law

Common law was developed in England. The king in his divine right decided disputes on a case-by-case basis. Common law is used by all states and the federal courts except for Louisiana. Louisiana is the only state that has adopted the Napoleonic Code, developed from a compilation of French, Spanish, and Roman civil law.

Common law is based on court decisions that originate from the judiciary branch of the government. Court cases that are resolved through the judicial process act as a data bank for those seeking information in various types of cases, whether personal injury, medical malpractice, workers' compensation, admiralty, bankruptcy, or domestic issues. Attorneys search for cases similar to the ones they are evaluating, mediating, arbitrating, settling, or trying. Common law interprets disputed legal issues, statutes, and regulations, and is created by the various courts.

Types of Law

The LNC may encounter cases involving criminal law, civil law, contract law, and tort law.

Criminal Law

Criminal law is created to provide guidance and protection to those injured by offenses against society. A criminal action by an individual is considered a criminal act against society as a whole, even if the act is directed solely at an individual. The criminal justice system was created to deter, punish, and rehabilitate persons who perform criminal acts. Criminal conduct can include forgery, burglary, murder, assault, battery, theft, rape, and false imprisonment. To prove guilt in a criminal action, the level of proof required is beyond a reasonable doubt. Remedies in criminal law usually involve fines and imprisonment of the guilty defendant.

Healthcare providers have been prosecuted in the criminal justice system, most often for Medicare and Medicaid fraud and abuse, drug diversion, nursing home patient abuse, failure to report elder or child abuse as required by statute, and sexual misconduct. (Both criminal and civil claims can be pursued against a healthcare provider for the same act or omission. The criminal action relates to the crime against society; the civil action relates to the injury incurred by an individual or entity.)

Civil Law

Civil law is law that applies to the rights of individuals or entities, whereas criminal law deals with offenses against the general public. Under civil law, the remedies for a person or entity involve money or compensation to make the plaintiff whole again. The amount of monetary compensation, or damages, is generally determined by a judge or jury following trial. Monetary remedies are common in personal injury, medical malpractice, and tort cases.

The other legal remedy (besides money) is an equitable remedy. Equitable remedies are ordered by the court and require the person to do something other than pay money for the violation. Examples include ordering an injunction which prevents a person from doing a specific action and ordering a specific performance which requires a person who has breached a contract to actually perform specific contract terms.

Contract Law

Contract law is an area of civil law that involves agreements between parties, individuals, and entities. The requirements for a contract to exist include:

1. Capacity to contract/competent parties (e.g., those who are not minors, mentally incompetent, or under the influence of drugs or alcohol)

2. Legality (i.e., the purpose of the contract must be lawful; a contract entered into for an illegal purpose is not legally binding)
3. Offer
4. Acceptance and
5. Consideration (i.e., the exchange of something of value between the parties to a contract)

A contract can be in oral or written form, depending on the subject matter and the reason for the contract. However, written contracts specifically outlining the details of the agreement, along with the payments and other terms agreed upon by the parties, are advisable in case a dispute arises later. Today, healthcare providers are faced with many situations that involve contracts, including employee/employer contracts and contracts with health maintenance organizations, vendors, other healthcare providers, and facilities. Contract litigation involves allegations of failure to perform, or a breach of, contractual duties.

Tort Law

Basics of Tort Law

Tort law is an area of civil law that encompasses negligence, personal injury, and medical malpractice claims. A tort is a wrongful act committed by some individual or entity that causes injury to another person or property. Remedies in tort law attempt to make the injured person "whole" again, usually with compensation in the form of a monetary award.

Negligence is a failure to act as an ordinary prudent or reasonable person would under similar circumstances. Professional negligence is the failure to act as a reasonably prudent similar professional would under similar circumstances. Professional negligence claims can involve attorneys, real estate agents, etc. Medical malpractice claims are professional negligence claims involving healthcare professionals. Professional negligence is different from ordinary negligence, because professionals are held to certain standards of care dictated by the profession. Ordinary negligence is conduct that involves undue risk of harm to someone caused by the failure to act as an ordinary prudent person would have acted. For example, a nursing assistant sees water on the floor in a patient's room but fails to mop up the water. The patient falls and breaks a hip, requiring surgery. This is ordinary negligence, because professional judgment and standards of care are not involved.

Examples of professional negligence allegations resulting from healthcare providers causing injury to the plaintiff include but are not limited to:

- Failure to timely or properly perform a surgery
- Failure to timely or properly perform a procedure, resulting in a retained foreign body (e.g., lap pad, hemostat, cotton ball, or needle)
- Failure to properly position a patient in surgery resulting in a paralyzed limb
- Failure to timely and properly render care and treatment
- Failure to timely perform blood work or recommend that blood work be done
- Failure to timely perform blood cultures or recommend blood cultures be done
- Failure to prevent or timely treat an infection
- Failure to timely and properly refer to the proper consultant or recommend a referral
- Negligently hiring healthcare providers who failed to provide timely and proper treatment
- Negligently hiring an employee, agent, or independent contractor who lacked the requisite skills for the job description and clearly breached standards of care

- Failure to properly perform an imaging study resulting in a delay in diagnosis
- Failure to properly read and interpret imaging studies
- Failure to properly compare previous imaging studies and report findings
- Failure to inform a patient of the limitations of an imaging study or test (e.g., that dense breasts might mask the earliest signs of tumors on supposedly "clean" mammograms)
- Failure to timely and properly diagnose cancer resulting in a more extensive and invasive cancer and necessitating more extensive surgery, severe disfigurement, chemotherapy, radiation, side effects, treatment, emotional distress, and mental anguish
- Failure to timely diagnose and treat cancer resulting in loss of chance of survival and an untimely death
- Failure to detect signs and symptoms of bleeding resulting in hemorrhaging and death
- Failure to provide a patient with a safe environment resulting in the patient's molestation
- Failure to prescribe the recommended medication resulting in further patient injury
- Failure to properly administer medication resulting in death
- Failure to timely and properly administer intravenous medication resulting in severe damage to the arm, loss of use of the arm, or loss of the arm
- Failure to properly monitor a restrained patient resulting in asphyxia, brain damage, and death and
- Failure to properly evaluate a limb in a cast, resulting in an infection and osteomyelitis

Typical causes of action (i.e., the specific legal claims for which a plaintiff is seeking compensation) arising from alleged negligent healthcare delivery include breach of contract (guaranteeing a specific medical result), negligence, insufficient informed consent or negligence in obtaining informed consent, confidentiality violation, and intentional misconduct.

Four elements of negligence must be established for there to be a viable medical malpractice claim:

1. A duty must be owed to the patient. This duty usually occurs when the healthcare provider accepts responsibility for the care and treatment of that patient.
2. There is a breach of duty or standard of care by the professional through an act of omission or commission. The standard of care for the specific healthcare profession/specialty and treatment rendered must be determined to see if there was a breach that caused injury to the patient/plaintiff.
3. Proximate cause or causal connection must be evident between the breach of duty and the harm or damages that have occurred to the patient/plaintiff.
4. Damages or injuries must be suffered by the patient/plaintiff. Damages or injuries can include (but are not limited to) pain and suffering; mental anguish; emotional distress; disfigurement; past, present, and future medical expenses; past, present, and future loss of wages; premature death; decreased life expectancy; loss of enjoyment of life; and loss of love, affection, and nurturance (loss of consortium). Some states also recognize damages for the loss of chance for survival due to misdiagnosis, late diagnosis, or failure to diagnose a condition such as cancer or hemorrhaging.

See Chapter 4 for more information on the four elements of proof in negligence claims.

The burden of proof in a medical malpractice claim (civil tort law) is met by a preponderance of the evidence, or more likely than not, which attributes 50.1% or more of fault to the defendant(s). The burden of proof is further discussed later in this chapter.

Some states award punitive damages in medical malpractice cases. Punitive awards are designed to punish the defendant and deter this type of behavior. Some states have made punitive damages available only in claims involving intentional malpractice or gross negligence. The LNC should check the specific state's laws and statutes to determine if punitive damages can be awarded.

Quasi-Intentional Torts

A *quasi-intentional* tort is a wrongdoing that involves speech (oral or written). The claim focuses on protection of an individual's interest in privacy, reputation, and freedom from unfounded legal action. In contrast to medical malpractice cases, quasi-intentional (and intentional) torts are not based on the negligence theory of law. These torts are intentional, in that the person or entity committing the tort (the tortfeasor) is reasonably certain that harm will result from the actions. If the defendant can establish a lack of intent, the defendant will likely be successful in defending against the claimed intentional tort.

For example, defamation (libel—written defamation and slander—oral defamation) is a quasi-intentional tort. Defamation is the false communication of information to a third party that in some way causes harm to the subject person (e.g., economic loss, loss of a promotion, loss of esteem/reputation in the community, etc.). The tort is that the tortfeasor *knew* the statement was false when making it. Truth is the defense of the tortfeasor's false statement.

Breach of confidentiality is another quasi-intentional tort. Healthcare providers must be especially cautious not to discuss a patient's healthcare information in common areas where such breaches can occur. The defense in a breach of confidentiality case may claim the defendant was not informed of the proper handling and usage of confidential information as it related to clients or patients.

Intentional Torts

Intentional torts include assault, battery, invasion of privacy, false imprisonment, trespass to land, and intentional infliction of emotional distress. Assault is an intentional act that causes fear or apprehension that a person will be touched in an injurious or offensive manner. Battery is the actual unpermitted touching. Medical battery is the unpermitted touching of a patient associated with the lack of informed consent to perform the procedure or treatment. Some states no longer recognize medical battery per se but have incorporated the cause into the informed consent law. For example, a patient gave an informed consent for a right foot amputation due to gangrene, but the surgeon actually amputates the left foot. In such a case, the patient may file a tort claim based on medical negligence as well as an intentional tort claim of medical battery for amputation of the wrong foot (Aiken, 2008).

Other intentional torts include the following:

■ Invasion of privacy, which occurs when a person's privacy right has been violated through public disclosure. Disclosure is such that a reasonable person would object to such an intrusion or disclosure. For example, the use of photographs (taken before and after plastic surgery) for an advertisement, without the patient's consent, is an example of an unauthorized disclosure. An important legislative act that focuses on protection of the patient's privacy is the Health Insurance Portability and Accountability Act of 1996 (HIPAA). This act establishes privacy and security standards to protect a patient's healthcare information.

In December 2000, the Department of Health and Human Services issued final regulations governing privacy of this information under HIPAA.

■ False imprisonment is the unlawful intentional confinement of a person through physical, chemical, or emotional restraints so that the person is conscious of being confined and is harmed by it. Areas of healthcare that are more likely to encounter such claims include emergency departments and psychiatric facilities. Following hospital restraint policies and documentation are the keys to protecting the healthcare provider from liability.

■ Trespass to land can be both an intentional tort and a negligent act that occurs when a person refuses to leave a place, places something on the property, or causes another person to enter the property of another without permission. An example is a patient who absolutely refuses to leave the hospital after being discharged.

■ Intentional infliction of emotional distress is the intentional invasion of a person's peace of mind by the defendant's outrageous behavior. Some states do not recognize a claim for intentional infliction of emotional distress, and others strictly limit its application. The conduct must be extreme and outrageous, intentional and reckless, and cause severe emotional distress and possibly bodily harm. For example, ulcers or headaches can be caused by severe emotional distress.

State and Federal Court Systems

State and Municipal Courts

Courts' functions are divided along geographical lines, level of responsibility, the types of injury for which relief is sought, and the identity of the plaintiff or the defendant who is involved in a potential suit. As individual states are empowered to create their own justice systems, there is significant variation among the names given to the state-level courts; however, the majority of states have developed some division between the various court functions.

Municipal, Justice, and City Courts

Cities and other municipalities generally are authorized to pass local laws or ordinances, and city courts are tasked with adjudicating those laws. City courts also adjudicate lower-level state law criminal violations and low-dollar value or "small claims" civil suits. (The federal court system has a similar specialty court called the Central Violation Bureau, which processes minor civil, criminal, and petty offense violations that occur on federal property.) While an LNC may not directly encounter cases that involve these lower courts, it is important to note healthcare professionals can be held to answer to their boards for alleged unprofessional conduct arising out of a municipal or low-level criminal violation.

State Trial Courts

State courts are where the majority of civil lawsuits and felony criminal offenses are litigated. State courts are established by the state constitution and laws of the state in which they sit. State courts are referred to as courts of *general jurisdiction*, because state courts have wide-ranging jurisdiction to hear any case with a connection to the state unless otherwise limited by the United States Constitution, Congress, or the federal courts. State courts typically adjudicate cases that involve parties within the state and issues involving state law, although many cases that involve a federal issue can be heard in state court. State trial courts also often act as a court of appeals for administrative law decisions, such as findings by boards of nursing or administrative hearing offices.

Above the state courts are typically one or two levels of appellate courts. These courts do not hold trials or engage in fact-finding about a case. Rather, they review the decisions and outcomes of the trial courts and determine if a decision or outcome complied with state law. As aforementioned, because each state is empowered to develop its own court system, there is variation in how the state courts are named and structured. For example, the Supreme Court of Arizona is the highest appellate court in Arizona, but the Supreme Court in New York is the trial court. Similarly, Colorado has a Court of Appeals and a Supreme Court that hear appeals, but Montana does not have an intermediate court of appeals—cases heard in the trial court are appealed directly to the Montana Supreme Court.

Federal Courts

Federal courts exist by operation of the United States Constitution and through laws passed by Congress establishing the District Court system and the Court of Appeals (known as the Circuit Court). Federal courts are referred to as courts of *limited jurisdiction*, because they are generally not permitted by law to hear cases that lack a connection to federal law or cases that Congress has not explicitly permitted the federal court to hear. The majority of litigation occurs in the District Court, which is the trial-court level of the federal court. On appeal, a case is transferred to one of the 13 Circuit Courts, based on the state or federal territory in which the District Court that heard the original case sits.

Federal courts have jurisdiction over cases involving questions of federal law. This type of jurisdiction is called "federal question jurisdiction." In addition, in order to ensure that an out-of-state defendant is treated fairly and not disadvantaged by litigating in a foreign state court, federal courts also have jurisdiction over such cases, called "diversity jurisdiction." Bringing a case in federal court involving a "federal question" or "diversity" of the parties is at the parties' discretion, as state courts can also hear these disputes. A defendant may have the ability to move a case from a state court to federal court, if certain requirements are met. Once a District Court obtains jurisdiction, it is generally empowered to decide any state law claims that are involved in the suit.

Some suits, however, *must* be filed in federal court, including cases in which the United States is a party or in which Congress has given federal court exclusive jurisdiction. For example, the Federal Tort Claims Act (FTCA), a federal law that allows plaintiffs to sue the United States government for damages (monetary payment) resulting from a tort injury, requires that suit be brought in federal court. A veteran wishing to bring a medical malpractice suit against a Veterans Affairs hospital or employee, for example, would file suit under the FTCA, as would a patient of a federal healthcare clinic. There are also specialty courts, such as Bankruptcy Courts, the United States Court of Federal Claims, and the federal Tax Court, which are granted exclusive jurisdiction to hear certain types of claims.

The Decision to Litigate in State or Federal Court

In preparing a case for suit, or when defending against a suit, where the litigation occurs can make a substantial difference in the strategy and outcome. State and federal courts can be physically located in the same city or county but may operate under different laws and rules. The decision to bring suit in state or federal court (or to move it from state to federal court) is a complex strategy decision. The LNC should be aware of the various factors that are evaluated when determining the appropriate court in which to bring or move a suit.

For example, there is a uniform rule of evidence that every federal court in the United States uses to determine whether an expert is qualified to testify and whether the tests or methods that an expert used are sufficiently reliable to present in trial. However, state courts are not bound by the federal court's evidentiary rule, and a particular state may have rules about experts that differ significantly from the federal court located in the same city. Similarly, federal rules of procedure impose a limit of 10 7-hour depositions in a case, unless permission is sought to exceed those limits. States vary on the number and length of depositions that are permitted.

The choice of whether to file in state or federal court is crucial and can greatly impact the scope and course of litigation and drastically change the outcome of a case. Some considerations include:

■ Whether any law requires bringing a case exclusively in state or federal court
■ Court congestion and the respective average length of suits in each court
■ Physical location of the state court versus the federal court
■ Historical monetary awards or relief given
■ Historical awards by the Court of attorneys' fees and costs to the successful party
■ Eligibility of the case to be decided by a judge or jury
■ Composition of the jury pool (registered voters, licensed drivers, taxpayers)
■ Rules of procedure or evidence that may help or hinder a case, including the scope of investigation or pre-trial "discovery" that is permitted
■ Philosophy or decision history of the judge or jury regarding the type of claim
■ Complexity of the filing process and
■ Barriers to entry to a court, including state or federal requirements that must be satisfied before litigating in a particular court

Substantive Law and Procedural Rules

Whether addressing a state healthcare professional board complaint involving unprofessional conduct, a malpractice lawsuit, or a claim for Veteran's benefits, for example, there are rules and laws that govern *what* constitutes a violation of the law, and there are also rules and laws that govern *how* to litigate that violation. Although specific analysis of these sets of rules and laws are outside the scope of this text, an LNC should be aware of the two overarching categories of law: substantive law (what) and procedural rules (how).

Substantive law refers to the laws that establish what is and is not permitted and the different rights and duties an individual or entity has to others. Statutes are the laws passed by the legislative body, such as a state or federal government. For example, a state law may explicitly define the rights of access a parent has to a child's medical records. Government agencies generally are given authority to draft regulations that pertain to the activities governed by the agency. Regulations are the rules that interpret and provide further guidance regarding how an agency will enforce the statutes that have been passed by the legislature. For example, a government agency may be empowered to set forth the specific documentation or qualifications a nurse must possess before applying to become an advanced practitioner. Substantive law is also developed through case law. For example, a jurisdiction may not have passed a statute defining what constitutes a contract; however, through the development of the law by way of prior court rulings, there will be a definition on which a litigant can rely.

Procedural rules establish the "ground rules" for litigation. There are a variety of sources of procedural law. Jurisdiction-specific Rules of Civil Procedure include rules concerning who can be sued in a particular court, what a complaint or lawsuit must contain, what kinds of investigation or pre-trial discovery is allowed, and time limits and deadlines for many of the activities that occur in litigation. In the professional discipline setting, acts regarding administrative procedures similarly set forth rules of procedure for administrative actions before a board or administrative agency. While there is a uniform set of rules for federal litigation, certain federal specialty courts have their own sets of rules that vary from the rules that govern more routine federal cases. Courts can also have "local rules," which modify or expand on the state-wide or federal rules of procedure.

An LNC must be conversant in the procedural rules that govern the litigation. While the rules are often focused on the process of litigating a case, failure to follow procedural rules can result in sanctions for the violating party, including dismissal of claims or the entire case. For LNCs who are involved in professional license defense or prosecution of board complaints, mastery of procedural rules is critical. A professional who fails to follow procedural rules may "waive" or give up a claim. Similarly, a board that fails to follow its own rules is subject to having its decision reversed or found to be invalid by a reviewing court. For more information on procedural rules, see the Federal Rules of Civil Procedure section later in this chapter and see Chapter 5. For more information on administrative actions involving healthcare professionals, see Chapter 25.

Litigating requires the use of both substantive laws and procedural rules. A case may be substantively strong, but if the procedures are not followed, the fact-finder (e.g., judge or jury) may never hear the strength of the claims because of a procedural shortcoming. Similarly, a litigant may strictly adhere to all procedural requirements but may, nevertheless, be unsuccessful in litigating a claim due to an inability to prove that a substantive law was violated. When evaluating a claim, the LNC and legal team should consider whether it is viable from both a substantive and procedural perspective.

Federal Rules of Civil Procedure

The primary role of an LNC is to analyze, evaluate, and provide informed opinions about the medical aspects of a legal case, thereby establishing the medical basis or defense of a case. While that remains the focus of the LNC's work, in order to bridge the gap between the medicine and the litigation process, the LNC must have a basic understanding of the legal process.

The legal framework is established by the rules of civil procedure and the written opinions of the judges who interpret them. The rules of civil procedure establish the roadmap that all civil cases traverse, from the initial complaint to resolution of the matter by settlement or trial. The Federal Rules of Civil Procedure (FRCP) prescribe how federal lawsuits are governed. The Federal Rules of Civil Procedure are to be "construed, administered, and employed by the court and the parties to secure the just, speedy, and inexpensive determination of every action and proceeding" (Fed. R. Civ. P. 1). They have been adopted in whole or in part by most states (*Bell Atlantic v. Twombly*, 2007; Tarpley, 2015).

The FRCP (or the equivalent state rules for state cases) of most importance to an LNC are those related to (1) initiation of a lawsuit and (2) pre-trial discovery of the facts and opinions known by the opposing party. Rules 3–12 relate to the initiation of a lawsuit and Rule 16 and Rules 26–37 relate to pre-trial discovery.

Initiation of a Lawsuit

Every civil action begins with a plaintiff, the person who files a complaint pursuant to Rule 3. The purpose of the complaint is to inform the defendant(s), the person(s) and entities being sued, and the court of the basis of the plaintiff's claim. Under Rule 8, the complaint need only contain a short and plain statement of the claim, a statement of the grounds for the court's jurisdiction, and a demand for the relief sought.

A summons must be served with a copy of the complaint. A summons is an order by a court requiring the presence of a person, usually a defendant, to defend a legal case. On or after filing the complaint, the plaintiff must present a summons to the court clerk for signature and seal. If the summons is properly completed, the clerk must sign, seal, and issue it to the plaintiff for service on the defendant(s). The complaint must then be properly sent to or "served" upon the defendant(s). This procedure is known as "service of process."

Service of process is the method by which courts assert their authority over the defendant(s), and Rule 4 governs service of process in federal court. It sets forth what content must be in the summons, identifies who may serve process, and specifies how and when service may be made. Under the FRCP 4(m), the plaintiff is responsible for serving the summons and complaint upon the defendant(s) within 90 days, or the plaintiff risks dismissal of the complaint.

Once service of process is completed, the defendant(s) is deemed to have notice of the claim(s), and the Federal Rules of Civil Procedure require that the defendant respond (Fed. R. Civ. P. 12(a)(1)). Rule 12 requires that a defendant either file an answer delineating its defenses to the claim or file a motion to dismiss the claim. Rule 12(b) lists seven key defenses utilized in motions to dismiss. They exist to expedite and simplify the pre-trial phase and to eliminate fatally flawed complaints. Defenses 12(b)(2)–(7) must be claimed immediately after service of the complaint; otherwise, the opportunity to assert them will be lost forever (Fed. R. Civ. P. 12(h)). The key defenses are:

- Rule 12(b)(1): Lack of subject-matter jurisdiction (wrong type of case for that court)
- Rule 12(b)(2): Lack of personal jurisdiction (wrong person)
- Rule 12(b)(3): Improper venue (wrong place)
- Rule 12(b)(4): Insufficient process (wrong summons or complaint)
- Rule 12(b)(5): Insufficient service of process (defective service of the summons or complaint)
- Rule 12(b)(6): Failure to state a claim upon which relief can be granted (does not state enough facts to show a violation of law or entitlement to a legal remedy) and
- Rule 12(b)(7): Failure to join a necessary party under Rule 19, Required Joinder of Parties (did not sue all of the persons necessary to resolve the dispute)

If the defendant does not file a motion to dismiss, or if the court denies the motion, the defendant must then file an answer which admits or denies the claims or states the defendant lacks sufficient information to admit or deny the claims. See Chapter 5 for more information on initiating lawsuits, including the LNC's role.

Pre-trial Discovery

After the complaint has been served and the defendant(s) has submitted an answer, all parties may engage in discovery or formal investigation. Rule 16, which "addresses pretrial conferences, pretrial orders, and the activities that courts may require as part of the pretrial case management process," governs the pretrial schedule by requiring the court to issue a scheduling order which limits the time to join parties, amend pleadings, complete discovery, and file motions (Gensler, 2019). It still leaves enough room, though, for individual judges to determine how to manage a particular case.

While Rule 16 manages the pre-trial schedule, Rule 26 provides the "foundation of discovery practice in federal court" (Gensler, 2019). Other rules, such as Rule 30, which covers depositions, and Rule 34, which covers requests for production, provide for particular discovery tools; but Rule 26 defines the "universe of information" that parties may seek by utilizing those tools (Gensler, 2019).

The goal of discovery is to gain knowledge about the adversary's case. It is used to avoid surprises at trial and to facilitate settlement. Rule 26(b)(1) establishes the scope of discovery and, according to the 2015 amendments to the rule, provides that "parties may obtain discovery regarding any non-privileged matter that is relevant to any party's claim or defense and proportional to the needs of the case..." When determining proportionality, considerations include the amount in controversy, a party's access to the information, a party's resources, and a determination as to whether the burden or expense of producing the discoverable information outweighs its benefit. Although information that is relevant to a party's claim or defense may not be admissible at trial, it can still be discoverable. Discoverable information includes the existence, description, nature, custody, condition, and location of any books, electronic data, documents, or other tangible things, and the identity and location of persons who have knowledge of any discoverable matter.

While proportionality serves as one limitation on the scope of discovery, there are other limitations, including Rule 26 protection of trial preparation materials (i.e., work product) and communications between attorneys and experts. In addition, Rule 26(c) allows parties to move for protective orders "against overzealous, abusive, or otherwise improper discovery" (Gensler, 2019). Despite the adversarial nature of litigation, Rule 26(f) requires that attorneys communicate early in the lawsuit to discuss their discovery needs and possible problems.

Under Rule 26, there are two types of witnesses: (1) the fact witness who has direct knowledge of the issues and (2) the expert witness who will use specialized education, training, experience and knowledge to assist the judge or jury to understand the evidence (Bell, 2013). However, these roles are often conjoined when a person, not retained or specifically employed to provide expert opinion testimony, has both personal knowledge of the facts of a case and expertise in the relevant field, thus establishing a hybrid witness (Fed. R. Civ. P. 26; Meckstroth, 2017). Common examples of a hybrid witness include a treating healthcare professional and the medical examiner who performed an autopsy in a death case (Bell, 2013; Rahman, 2016).

Rule 26(a)(2) governs the disclosure of expert witnesses, and subsection (a)(2)(B) requires that a detailed written report accompany disclosure when the witness is "retained or specifically employed" to provide expert testimony. A hybrid witness is not required to submit a detailed written report, but the hybrid witness must be disclosed with a summary of the expected testimony under Rule 26(a)(2)(C) (*Alfaro v. D. Las Vegas, Inc.*, 2016; Fed. R. Civ. P. Advisory Committee Notes, 2010; *Harvey v. District of Columbia*, 2015).

Key Discovery Tools Under the Federal Rules of Civil Procedure

Interrogatories: Rule 33

Interrogatories are lists of questions one party sends to another as part of the discovery process. Per Rule 33, the questions may relate to any matter not privileged that is relevant to the subject matter of the litigation. Once served, the responding party has up to 30 days to respond or object (Fed. R. Civ. P. 33(b)(2)). Interrogatory answers must be in writing and answered under oath. If information is withheld by the responding party, a proper explanation must be provided.

Requests for Production: Rule 34

Requests for production are requests for documents, electronically stored information, or other tangible items that would assist in establishing or refuting the facts asserted in the complaint. Like interrogatories, requests for production are made in writing and must be responded to within 30 days (Fed. R. Civ. P. 34(b)). Requests for production also "permit entry onto designated land or other property," so site visits may be requested to inspect the place where the injury occurred (Fed. R. Civ. P. 34(a)(2)).

Depositions: Rule 30

Under Rule 30, depositions are oral examinations, under oath, of any person a party believes has relevant information (Fed. R. Civ. P. 30). Therefore, unlike interrogatories, depositions are not limited to the plaintiff(s) and defendant(s). Witnesses and any other persons with information relevant to the matter may be deposed. Deposition testimony is similar to trial testimony in that the entire process is conducted under oath and recorded by a court reporter. The vast majority of civil cases never make it to trial, however, so depositions are the evidentiary basis for the resolution of most disputes (Cochran, 2012). Therefore, depositions are very important.

Obtaining information from institutional adversaries, as opposed to discrete individuals, can be extremely challenging as individual witnesses do not normally have access to all information known to the organization (Kosieradzki, 2016). Therefore, Rule 30(b)(6) exists to force institutions like hospitals, for example, to designate and prepare a representative who is able to speak to all of the information that an institution has on an identified topic.

Physical and Mental Examinations: Rule 35

A physical or mental examination may be requested by either party when the physical or mental state of a client is at issue (Fed. R. Civ. P. 35(a)). In practice, physical and mental examinations are usually limited to personal injury and paternity lawsuits, but they also arise in medical malpractice and disability lawsuits. They may be used to substantiate the cause of injury, provide a prognosis, or make recommendations for future treatment. The examination should be conducted by an impartial healthcare provider, one who has never been involved in the direct care of the client. However, because the party who requests the exam selects the healthcare provider who performs it, some providers may be biased toward the requesting (paying) party. The LNC may attend the exam as an observer. See Chapter 6 for more information on these medical examinations.

Subpoena: Rule 45

A subpoena is a discovery tool that requires a witness or non-party to appear or produce documents. It has the force and effect of a court order. There are two types of subpoenas. One is a subpoena *ad testificandum*, which requires that the person testify before a court or other legal authority. The other is a subpoena *duces tecum*, which requires that the person produce documents, materials, or other tangible evidence. Subpoenas may be issued by either a clerk of the court where the action is pending or an attorney licensed in the state.

Failure to Cooperate in Discovery: Rule 37

If a party fails to respond to discovery requests, then the party seeking the discovery may file a motion to compel with the court (Fed. R. Civ. P. 37(a)). If the court grants the motion to compel, then the party who objected or failed to respond must respond. If a party fails to comply once the court issues an order compelling discovery, the court may then sanction the party in various ways which include prohibiting the party's evidence at trial, dismissing the plaintiff's lawsuit, striking the defendant's defense to the lawsuit, and imposing financial sanctions (Fed. R. Civ. P. 37(b)).

See Chapter 5 for more information on the discovery process, including the LNC's role.

Federal Rules of Evidence

The Federal Rules of Evidence (the "Rules") govern what type of evidence may be considered by a judge and jury (each a "trier of fact") in the event of a trial. The Rules range from broad pronouncements relating to the admissibility of prior criminal convictions and the proper uses of character evidence to specific rules relating to admissibility of documents and how jurors can sometimes serve as witnesses.

The primary question addressed by the Rules is whether a statement, document, item, or witness testimony ("Evidence") is admissible. From a practical perspective, evidence is considered admissible if it is relevant, unless it is expressly excluded by another of the Rules. Evidence is relevant if "it has any tendency to make a fact more or less probable than it would be without the evidence[,] and the fact is of consequence in determining the action" (Fed. R. Evid. 401). If the Evidence is relevant, it is admissible pursuant to the Rules, and it may be admitted to the case for the triers of fact to consider in making their decision. If not, the Evidence may not be admitted, and the triers of fact will not have that Evidence to consider when reaching their decision.

It is important to note that numerous other federal and common law legal frameworks may be implicated when considering Evidence issues under the Rules. For example, HIPAA may hinder or prevent access to potentially admissible Evidence without a court order. In addition, whether and to what extent a medical professional may testify on an issue may implicate professional-patient relationship laws and guidelines.

A comprehensive review of the Rules is beyond the scope of this textbook. However, LNCs should be aware of several Rules with particular relevance to healthcare providers.

Hearsay

Hearsay is one of the more common Evidence issues. Hearsay is not admissible under the Rules unless one or more specific exceptions or exemptions apply. The Rules define hearsay as "a statement that: the declarant does not make while testifying at the current trial or hearing; and a party offers in evidence to prove the truth of the matter asserted in the statement" [Fed. R. Evid. 801(c)]. The definition is helpful but conceptually difficult for many professionals to apply. It is quite common for some to consider any verbal statement made by anyone to be a hearsay issue under the Rules. However, statements can be written, verbal, or non-verbal, and the Rule is only implicated if another party is trying to prove the truth of what was asserted in the statement. Restating the Rule with particular attention to the parties involved can be helpful. Hearsay is an out-of-court statement made by a person (the "Declarant"), which is being offered to the court by a separate party (the "Proponent"), to demonstrate the truth of the matter asserted in the statement by the Declarant (the "Hearsay Rule").

Statements for Purposes of Medical Treatment or Diagnosis

The Hearsay Rule contains an exception for statements made by a Declarant for purposes of medical diagnosis. The statement made by the Declarant must be for the purposes of medical diagnosis or treatment, and it must describe medical history, past or present symptoms or sensations, or the inception or general character of the cause of the Declarant's medical condition. These types of statements are often made by the Declarant to a nurse, doctor, or someone else who may use the information for medical diagnosis or treatment. Statements made for medical diagnosis are often relevant in lawsuits, as the statements can include present and past conditions as well as the cause of the conditions if the cause is relevant to diagnosis and treatment. This Hearsay Rule exception contemplates that these types of statements should generally be admissible for trier of fact's consideration.

For example, a patient visits a healthcare provider complaining of back pain and a headache. The patient tells the healthcare provider, "I felt this sudden back pain a couple hours ago, and I've developed a headache since then." The healthcare provider asked what happened, and the patient described trying to pry a 500-pound bale of compressed cardboard from the baler at work. Using this information, the healthcare provider diagnoses the patient's back pain and provides treatment (prescriptions) for muscle swelling and the headache. The patient is sent home and dies later that day from an aneurysm. The patient's spouse brings a lawsuit against the patient's employer seeking worker's compensation survivor benefits. The spouse (the Proponent in this example) wants the healthcare provider to testify about what the patient (the Declarant) told the healthcare provider. The spouse wants to use the patient's statements to the healthcare provider to prove the truth of the matter asserted, that the aneurysm that ultimately led to the patient's death was caused by an injury sustained at work. In this example, the patient's statements to the healthcare provider would likely be admissible under the Hearsay Rule exception for statements made for purposes of medical diagnosis or treatment. The healthcare provider would likely be allowed to testify about what the patient said, and the spouse would be able to use those statements to help establish to the trier of fact that the patient's death was caused by an injury sustained at work, which would allow the spouse access to worker's compensation survivor benefits.

Records

The Hearsay Rule also contains an exception for records kept in the course of a regularly conducted business activity. This includes medical records, provided that the record includes conditions, opinions, or diagnoses and was made at or near the time of the treatment or consultation. Continuing the above example, if the healthcare provider summarized the patient's assertion about the cause of the injury in the written notes of the medical record, the spouse may be able to use the healthcare provider's notes to argue that the patient's death was caused by an injury sustained at work.

Opinions

Medical professionals may be asked to provide formal medical opinions from time to time. For example, a medical professional may be asked to describe a patient's appearance and mannerisms in a pain and suffering case or offer an opinion as to whether a patient has reached maximum medical improvement in a personal injury case. An LNC should be familiar with the types of opinion testimony that a medical professional may be able to provide. Opinion testimony, particularly expert opinion testimony, can be quite persuasive depending on the type of case. Article VII of the Rules addresses opinions and expert testimony.

Lay Opinions

Any person can offer opinion testimony, provided that:

■ The person has opinions or inferences that are based on that person's perception
■ The opinion or inference would be helpful to a clear understanding of that person's testimony or of a fact at issue in the case and
■ The opinion or inference is not based on scientific, technical, or specialized knowledge

From a healthcare perspective, this may include a medical professional describing how someone looked to be distressed or in pain when the issue (or amount) of pain and suffering is disputed in a lawsuit.

Expert Opinions

Expert opinions are sometimes requested of medical professionals. As with lay opinions, these expert opinions must be helpful to the trier of fact. To be permitted to offer expert testimony and opinions, a medical professional must be qualified as an expert by knowledge, skill, experience, training, or education. Ultimately, the attorneys on either side of a lawsuit attempt to establish or discredit a professional's expertise. However, the final decision as to expertise is often made by the court.

Once a professional is established as an expert, the professional may offer opinions on complex issues, provided that:

■ The opinion is based on facts or data
■ The opinion is analyzed and evaluated utilizing reliable principles and methods and
■ The professional has applied the principles and methods reliably to the facts of the case

These expert opinions can even address the ultimate issue in a case (e.g., legal fault). However, there are limitations relating to mental state opinions. An expert cannot offer an opinion or inference regarding whether a defendant in a criminal case had a particular mental state or condition. For more information on the Rules, see Chapter 5.

Common Legal Doctrines and Concepts

Statute of Limitations

This is the time period within which a prospective plaintiff may bring a cause of action following the event giving rise to a potential claim. The governing period of time is set by statute. Each jurisdiction has statutory limitations periods for different types of lawsuits. For example, some jurisdictions provide for a five-year limitations period for actions based in contract violations and a two-year limitations period for personal injury lawsuits. Some of the relevant law surrounding statutes of limitations provide that a plaintiff's cause of action may not accrue until the plaintiff discovers the injury.

While it is the attorney's responsibility to determine exactly when a cause of action "arose" (and thus when the statutory limitations period began), it is very important for the LNC to be cognizant of the relevant statute of limitations period pertaining to the matter at hand. Plaintiff LNCs who are screening cases for merit need to identify, and alert the attorney to, a limitations period that is nearing its expiration. Defense LNCs may discover information showing the lawsuit was filed outside the statutory limitations period.

Burden of Proof

The burden of proof is the requirement that is placed on one of the parties to prove (or disprove) the merits of an argument or assertion. For example, in a medical malpractice case, the plaintiff asserting negligence bears the burden to prove that the defendant or defendants were negligent or fell below the standard of care and that the plaintiff was injured as a result of the negligence.

There are various burdens of proof, and one or more may apply to claims and defenses that arise during the litigation of a claim. Generally, in order to prevail in civil litigation, the plaintiff must prove the different elements of the case to a preponderance of the evidence. That is, it is more likely than not that the plaintiff's evidence supports the claims in comparison to evidence presented by the defendant to the contrary. In some instances, the law will impose a higher burden of clear and convincing evidence, which requires an elevated showing that the party with the burden has presented substantial evidence in support of its assertion. Examples of when this standard may be used include certain civil fraud cases, actions to terminate parental rights, and certain administrative law actions. The highest burden of proof, which requires proof beyond a reasonable doubt, is typically reserved for criminal proceedings. Under this standard, the government entity seeking to prove a defendant's guilt must show that there is no reasonable doubt of the defendant's guilt and must firmly convince the finders of fact of the defendant's guilt.

A detailed discussion of the burdens of proof and their application is beyond the scope of this text. However, the LNC should be aware of which burden of proof applies in a particular instance, understand which party bears the burden on a given issue, and develop sufficient evidence to meet the burden.

Res Ipsa Loquitur

Generally, a plaintiff must prove how negligence occurred and whose negligence caused the injury. However, there are some injuries that are extraordinary and do not normally occur unless someone was negligent. In those situations, the plaintiff's burden of proof is relaxed by the legal doctrine of *res ipsa loquitur*, which translates to "the thing speaks for itself."

Certain acts of negligence in medical litigation readily lend themselves to the application of this doctrine. For example, a patient who is injured when a surgical sponge is left inside the abdominal cavity may use *res ipsa loquitur*. Similarly, a patient who has had the wrong side of the body operated upon can invoke this doctrine. Even though the patient in either example may be unable to identify the specific circumstances that lead to the negligence, those acts of negligence would not have occurred without some member of the surgical team acting negligently.

To successfully assert this doctrine, plaintiff presents to the court that the injury *only* occurs when there is negligence. The plaintiff is relieved of having to identify (1) a specific defendant as the source of the negligent act and (2) the way in which the defendant or defendants acted negligently. Instead, the fact that the act occurred suffices, and the jury can infer that negligence occurred. Then, the burden of proof shifts to the defendant to disprove that the defendant acted negligently or to prove that the defendant was not the cause of the injury.

In order to utilize this doctrine, the plaintiff cannot bear any responsibility or control over the acts that lead to the injury, and the circumstances or instrumentality of the injury must have been exclusively within the control of the defendant or defendants.

Wrongful Birth/Life

These two legal theories of liability are similar but are brought by two different plaintiffs. In a wrongful birth action, the lawsuit is brought by the parent of a child born with some sort of birth defect, and allegations are made that there was negligent medical treatment on the part of health-care providers or a failure to provide advice that has deprived the parent of the opportunity to either avoid conceiving the child or timely terminate the pregnancy. Typically, these claims arise when there has been a failure to provide the parents with certain types of genetic testing or when a prenatal ultrasound was misread that evidenced severe birth defects. These claimants usually seek medical costs and expenses associated with caring for a child with a serious medical condition.

A wrongful life claim, on the other hand, is a lawsuit brought by a severely disabled child, but for similar reasons. Both types of lawsuits are emotionally challenging, very complex, and are not recognized in all jurisdictions. Indeed, 12 states do not allow wrongful birth claims at all.

In a sentinel Iowa case, *Plowman v. Fort Madison Community Hospital* (2017), the parents alleged that the defendant physicians failed to accurately interpret and communicate fetal abnormalities noted during a prenatal ultrasound. The parents claimed that, if they had been informed of the fetal abnormalities, they would have terminated the pregnancy. The child was born severely disabled. The parents sought to recover for the ordinary and extraordinary care associated with raising the child as well as for their emotional distress and lost income as a result of the child's life.

Loss of Consortium

This principle was introduced earlier in the chapter as one of the types of damages that is potentially recoverable in tort actions. The word "consortium" loosely means companionship or association. Legally, it is an expanded concept that deals with losses suffered by a spouse or partner, child, or other family member as a result of the death or disability of a person due to a negligent act. Each jurisdiction defines the specific scope of loss of consortium, but generally it includes things such as contributions of the injured/deceased to the household, care, companionship, advices, and affection. The damages are termed "non-economic" damages, meaning they do not have actual concrete money value that can be shown with documents, receipts, and the like. Instead, the jury ascribes the value based on the evidence presented about the length and closeness of the relationship(s). It is, simply put, a way to quantify a loss that cannot be valued with money alone.

In jurisdictions that recognize loss of consortium claims, these claims are typically "derivative" claims, meaning they originate from a primary claim. For example, if a person who sustained a debilitating stroke due to medical negligence brings a suit to recover for damages (the primary claim), the person's spouse/partner, and in some instances, child, may assert a separate cause of action for loss of consortium and would also be listed as a plaintiff. The success of a derivative claim is dependent on the viability of the primary claim; if the primary claim is dismissed or lost, so is the loss of consortium claim.

If a loss of consortium claim is permitted and asserted in the jurisdiction, the LNC will look at medical records for valuable clues to assist in either pursuing or defending against such a claim. Life expectancy of the injured becomes very relevant as well as co-morbid conditions. Further, illuminating the nature of the relationships between the injured/deceased and the beneficiaries is key in loss of consortium claims.

Ostensible Agency (Apparent Agency)

In general, the negligence of one person cannot be assigned or imputed to another person or entity. However, there are exceptions to this rule. Ostensible/apparent agency is one such tort doctrine that imposes liability upon one party for the breach of another due to the existence of a special legal relationship giving rise to such a duty.

To best understand this concept, one can first look at the inverse principle of "actual agency." This is what occurs when a principal actually empowers another to bind it legally. For example, a hospital may give a particular employee the right to sign legal documents that bind it. Apparent or ostensible agency occurs most often when an employer may be legally bound by, or legally responsible for, the acts of an employee (or apparent employee). The agency relationship exists typically only to the extent that it is reasonable for a third person dealing with the agent to believe the agent was authorized by the principal and the principal did nothing to correct that incorrect belief. For example, in a suit involving negligent care by an emergency medicine physician, the plaintiff may also name the hospital as a defendant under the doctrine of ostensible agency. Most patients do not realize that emergency medicine physicians may not be hospital employees; thus, these patients believe the physicians are agents of the hospital and, during the course of litigation, will attempt to establish that the hospital is responsible for the physicians' acts.

Respondeat Superior/*Vicarious Liability*

This is another exception to the rule outlined above, when negligence of one party can be assigned to another by virtue of a certain type of relationship. Generally, vicarious liability allows a plaintiff to hold a third party liable for the actions of a tortfeasor despite the fact that the third party is not guilty of any wrongdoing. The term *"respondeat superior,"* a Latin term, and therefore always written in italics, literally means "let the master answer." This common law doctrine essentially defines the liability of an employer for the acts of its employee, provided the employee was working within the scope of employment at the time the tort was committed. Of note, a plaintiff is more likely to bring a lawsuit against a larger entity (the company/employer) along with the actual tortfeasor. This is because the larger entity will likely have "deeper pockets" than an individual, and therefore, oftentimes, plaintiffs seek to establish a *respondeat superior* relationship (even if there is not a clear-cut employer/employee relationship available) in order to avail themselves of potential economic sources of recovery. Whether an employment relationship actually exists involves analysis of many factors including how the employee was paid, the employer's right to control the manner in which the employee performed the job, and the employer's right to dismiss the employee.

For example, in the Virginia case of *Majorana v. Crown Cent. Petroleum Corp.* (2000), the plaintiff alleged she was assaulted in a store by a store employee. The Virginia Supreme Court held that, when a plaintiff presents sufficient evidence to show the existence of an employer/employee relationship, the plaintiff has established a *prima facie* (at first sight) case triggering a presumption of liability on the part of the employer. The burden of proof then shifts to the employer, who may then rebut the presumption by showing that the employee departed from the scope of the employment relationship at the time the injurious act was committed.

Eggshell Plaintiff

This funny-sounding term has nothing to do with poultry, but the reference to the fragility of eggs is a good way to recall the meaning of this concept. Eggshells are delicate, weak, and easy to crack. The premise here is that the eggshell plaintiff may come to the table with a multitude of pre-existing issues, and this is something that has to be dealt with—the defense takes the plaintiff as found. For example, Ms. X was involved in a car accident which was caused by Mr. Y, who clearly ran a red light. The average person, one could conjecture, would only have suffered minor soft tissue injuries. It just so happens, though, that Ms. X was seven months pregnant and also had a prior cervical spine injury and fusion. This fender bender caused damage to Ms. X's fetus and significantly exacerbated her already delicate neck problems. The concept of "taking the plaintiff as found" means the defense cannot argue the plaintiff was different from the average person and, therefore, only average damages can be claimed. *Actual* damages and injuries must be evaluated, regardless of how "brittle" the plaintiff may have been before the injury occurred.

Failure to Mitigate Damages

This concept comes into play once an injury has been alleged and a claim for negligence has been brought. It is essentially a defense to overly inflated damages claims. The legal principle is as follows: although a person may have been injured at the hand of another, that person still has a responsibility to take reasonable measures to avoid further loss or injury and to minimize the extent of the injury. Under the rule of "mitigation of damages," a personal injury plaintiff can be denied the right to recover the portion of damages that could have been avoided (as found by the court or a jury). In other words, a plaintiff has an obligation to act in a way that an ordinary, reasonably prudent person would have acted in a similar situation.

For example, Mr. A alleges Dr. B failed to timely diagnose a stroke, which resulted in right hand weakness and aphasia. Mr. A's physicians referred him to physical rehabilitation, but Mr. A missed over 70% of his appointments. The medical records also reflect that he was non-compliant with his anticoagulant medication, and he suffered a second stroke as a result, causing additional neurological effects. Defendant Dr. B argues that Mr. A failed to mitigate his damages by not participating in the recommended rehabilitation and by refusing to take his anticoagulation medication.

Assumption of the Risk

This is an affirmative defense in tort law, meaning the party seeking to invoke the doctrine must raise the defense before it will be considered by the Court. Affirmative defenses can bar a plaintiff's right to recover. Essentially, assumption of risk means that a person knowingly engaged in an activity that was understood to be risky/dangerous, and therefore, any injury that resulted from voluntarily undertaking that activity was completely at the person's own hand. Typically, in order for a court to find that a plaintiff assumed the risk of a dangerous activity, the burden is on the defendant to prove the plaintiff knew of the dangers involved with that activity and then willingly engaged in the activity, notwithstanding the dangers.

Comparative and Contributory Negligence

Both of these legal concepts are ways in which a plaintiff's recovery may be limited in litigation if the plaintiff is found to be at fault. Like failure to mitigate damages and assumption of the risk, these legal doctrines are employed to reduce a plaintiff's damages award or act as a defense to liability altogether. They are best explained by example.

The doctrine of "comparative negligence," which is more common, allows the finder of fact to determine the plaintiff's own percentage of fault in the incident giving rise to the injuries. The total recovery amount will then be reduced by that percentage. For example, if a plaintiff was found to have suffered $1,000,000 in damages but was also found to be 10% responsible for an accident that gave rise to the injuries, the plaintiff's award would be $900,000 ($1,000,000 minus 10%, which is $100,000). Under this doctrine, damages are apportioned between at-fault parties based on their proportionate shares of fault.

In "contributory negligence" jurisdictions (currently Alabama, Maryland, North Carolina, Virginia, and the District of Columbia), if a plaintiff is found to be even 1% at fault for causing an injury-producing event, the plaintiff will recover nothing, despite the defendant being up to 99% at fault. A finding of any fault by the plaintiff in these jurisdictions is a total bar to recovery by the plaintiff.

Some jurisdictions follow a doctrine of modified comparative negligence, which apportions fault to the parties, limits recovery if the plaintiff was a marginal contributor to the injuries, and bars recovery if the plaintiff was the majority contributor to the injuries. If the plaintiff is found to be less than 50% or 51% at fault (depending on the specific jurisdiction's rules), the plaintiff recovers damages (less the percentage the plaintiff was at fault). If the plaintiff is found to be more than 50% or 51% at fault, recovery is completely barred. For example, if a plaintiff was found to have sustained $100,000 in damages and to have no fault, the plaintiff would recover the full $100,000. If the plaintiff was found to have been 25% at fault, the plaintiff would recover $75,000 ($100,000 minus 25%, which is $25,000). If the plaintiff was found to have been 51% at fault, the plaintiff would recover $0.

When assisting with a case review, it is important for the LNC to know which doctrine is followed by the jurisdiction in which the case is venued.

Stare Decisis

Stare decisis is a doctrine that promotes consistency and predictability in the justice system. *Stare decisis* is Latin for "to stand by decided matters." The doctrine instructs a court to decide legal issues in subsequent cases consistently with how it decided legal issues in previous cases. The doctrine also requires that lower courts adhere to decisions made by the higher courts as binding on the lower court. In other words, cases that have been decided set "precedent" for how subsequent cases will be decided.

When deciding on a course of action, individuals and entities responsible for risk management will often consider prior legal decisions by courts as part of their decision-making. Knowing this, courts work to promote consistency, predictability, and deliberate and incremental development of the law. Therefore, courts are reluctant to make decisions on legal issues contrary to what has already been decided, unless there is a compelling reason to do so. This is not to say a court is prohibited from re-evaluating legal precedent. However, the court will typically favor adhering to precedent over substantially changing the law. Compelling reasons to ignore precedent may include that the court decided a case incorrectly or that changes in society or the law have rendered a court's previous decision unworkable.

In cases in which the precedent is not favorable, the attorney may first attempt to develop arguments that the matter is distinguishable from existing precedent, and therefore compels a different outcome, before resorting to the more challenging approach of attempting to convince a court that it should disregard established precedent.

Res Judicata *and Collateral Estoppel*

The litigation process favors finality, and United States law has developed a series of doctrines to prevent cases from being re-litigated after a claim or issue has been resolved. Both *res judicata* and collateral estoppel are affirmative defenses. *Res judicata* (also known as "claim preclusion") is a legal doctrine that prevents a party from re-litigating the same claim after that claim has been decided on the merits. While the specific application of *res judicata* can vary from jurisdiction to jurisdiction, a party seeking to assert it must generally demonstrate: (1) the claim at issue was previously litigated; (2) the parties involved in the present litigation were the same parties in the previous assertion of the claim or at least share a common interest with the parties that litigated the claim previously; and (3) the previously litigated claim resolved with a final judgment on the merits.

Collateral estoppel is a related doctrine. Collateral estoppel is also known as "issue preclusion." This doctrine prevents a factual or legal issue from being re-litigated in another case or within the same case. Essentially, once a factual or legal issue has been decided by the court in relation to the litigants, that decision becomes the "law of the case" and will generally not be decided differently within the case without a compelling reason. Collateral estoppel can be used to prevent a party from changing its position on an issue that has already been fully litigated. Collateral estoppel requires showing that: (1) the issue was litigated on the merits in the previous case or proceeding; (2) the parties were given an opportunity to litigate the issue; (3) a decision on the issue and its merits was made; (4) the parties are the same or at least share a common interest.

Summary

Legal nurse consultants serve a vital role on the medical side of a legal team. Those who master a basic understanding of the law, court systems, evidentiary and procedural rules, and common legal doctrines have greater insight into the legal framework in which their work is conducted, thereby enhancing their value and their ability to assist the attorney in the presentation of a formidable case.

References

Aiken, T. D. (Ed.). (2008). *Legal, ethical and political issues in nursing* (2nd ed.). Philadelphia: F.A. Davis.

Alfaro v. D. Las Vegas, Inc., No. 2:15-CV-02190-MMD-PAL, 2016 WL 4473421, at *11 (D. Nev. Aug. 24, 2016).

Bell Atlantic Corp. v. Twombly, 550 U.S. 544 (2007). (Stevens, J. dissenting).

Bell, Stacey A. (2013, October 10). Litigation: The hybrid fact/expert witness is a trap for the unwary. Retrieved from http://web3.insidecounsel.com/2013/10/10/litigation-the-hybrid-fact-expert-witness-is-a-tra?slreturn=1527872856.

Cochran, IV, C. M. (2012, April 18). "But the examination still proceeds": A primer on surviving the difficult depositions. *ABA Sections of Litigation 2012 Section Annual Conference.* Retrieved from www.americanbar.org/content/dam/aba/administrative/litigation/materials/sac_2013_ut_the_examination_still_proceeds_primer.authcheckdam.pdf.

Federal Rule of Civil Procedure 1. Retrieved from www.law.cornell.edu/rules/frcp/rule_1.

Federal Rule of Civil Procedure 3. Retrieved from www.law.cornell.edu/rules/frcp/rule_3.

Federal Rule of Civil Procedure 4. Retrieved from www.law.cornell.edu/rules/frcp/rule_4.

Federal Rule of Civil Procedure 8. Retrieved from www.law.cornell.edu/rules/frcp/rule_8.

Federal Rule of Civil Procedure 12. Retrieved from www.law.cornell.edu/rules/frcp/rule_12.

Federal Rule of Civil Procedure 16. Retrieved from www.law.cornell.edu/rules/frcp/rule_16.

Federal Rule of Civil Procedure 19. Retrieved from www.law.cornell.edu/rules/frcp/rule_19.

Federal Rule of Civil Procedure 26. Retrieved from www.law.cornell.edu/rules/frcp/rule_26.

Federal Rule of Civil Procedure 30. Retrieved from www.law.cornell.edu/rules/frcp/rule_30.

Federal Rule of Civil Procedure 33. Retrieved from www.law.cornell.edu/rules/frcp/rule_33.

Federal Rule of Civil Procedure 34. Retrieved from www.law.cornell.edu/rules/frcp/rule_34.

Federal Rule of Civil Procedure 35. Retrieved from www.law.cornell.edu/rules/frcp/rule_35.

Federal Rule of Civil Procedure 37. Retrieved from www.law.cornell.edu/rules/frcp/rule_37.

Federal Rule of Civil Procedure 45. Retrieved from www.law.cornell.edu/rules/frcp/rule_45.

Federal Rule of Civil Procedure Committee Advisory Notes (2010).

Federal Rule of Evidence 401. Retrieved from www.law.cornell.edu/rules/fre/rule_401.

Federal Rule of Evidence 801. Retrieved from www.law.cornell.edu/rules/fre/rule_801.

Gensler, Steven S. (Ed.). (2019). *Federal rules of civil procedure: Rules and commentary.* St. Paul, MN: Thomson Reuters.

Harvey v. District of Columbia, 798 F.3d 1042 (D.C. Cir. 2015).

Kosieradzki, M. (2016). *30(b)(6) deposing corporations, organizations, and the government.* Portland, OR: Trial Guides.

Majorana v. Crown Cent. Petroleum Corp., 260 Va. 521 (2000).

Meckstroth, Max S. (2017, March 2). Seventh circuit explains disclosure of hybrid witnesses under Fed. R. Civ. P. 26(a)(2)(C).

Plowman v. Fort Madison Community Hosp., 896 N.W.2d 393, (2017).

Rahman, M. (2016, April 26). Mastering expert witness discovery: the ultimate guide. *expertinstitute.com.* Retrieved from www.theexpertinstitute.com/mastering-expert-witness-discovery-the-ultimate-guide/.

Tarpley, Philip A. (2015). The doctrine in the shadows: Reverse-Erie, its cases, its theories, and its future with plausibility pleading in Alaska. 32 *Alaska L. Rev.* 213.

Additional Reading

Algero, M. (1999). In defense of forum shopping: A realistic look at selecting a venue. *Nebraska Law Review, 78*(1), 79–112.

Aquilera-Sanchez v. Wal-Mart Stores, Inc., No. 95–61 (Starr Co. Tex. Dist. Ct.). *The National Law Journal,* October 18, 2001; In Touch … with LTLA, October 26, 2001.

Baicker-McKee, S., Janssen, W., & Corr, J. (2018). *Federal civil rules handbook.* Toronto: Thomson Reuters.

Conerly v. State of Louisiana, 690 So. 2d 980 (La. Ct. App. 1997).

Cruzan by Cruzan v. Dir., Missouri Dep't of Health, 497 U.S. 261 (1990).

Diversity of Citizenship; Amount in Controversy; Costs, 28 U.S.C. § 1332 (2012).

Federal Question, 28 U.S.C. § 1331 (2012).

Federal Rules of Civil Procedure: www.uscourts.gov/rules-policies/current-rules-practice-procedure/federal-rules-civil-procedure and www.law.cornell.edu/rules/frcp.

Federal Rules of Evidence: www.law.cornell.edu/rules/fre.

Federal Torts Claims Act, 28 U.S.C. §§ 1346(b), 2671–2680 (1946).

Ferrell, K. G. (Ed.). (2016). *Nurse's legal handbook* (6th ed.). Philadelphia: Wolters Kluwer.

Glannon, J. (2018). *Examples & explanations for civil procedure* (8th ed.). New York, NY: Wolters Kluwer.

Hebert v. Parker, 796 So. 2d 19 (La. Ct. App. 2001).

Iyer, P. (Ed.). (2011). *Nursing malpractice* (4th ed.). Tucson, AZ: Lawyers and Judges Publishing Company.

Laska, L. (Ed.). (2002a). Failure to pre-oxygenate patient. *Medical Malpractice Verdicts, Settlements and Experts*, January 3.

Laska, L. (Ed.). (2002b). Failure to diagnose bowel cancer leads to death. *Medical Malpractice Verdicts, Settlements and Experts*, January 13.

Laska, L. (Ed.). (2002c). Failure to provide adequate home nursing wound care for diabetic patient leads to partial amputation of foot. *Medical Malpractice Verdicts, Settlements and Experts*, January 20.

Laska, L. (Ed.). (2002d). Nurse administers near-lethal dose of Demerol in emergency room. *Medical Malpractice Verdicts, Settlements and Experts*, January 21.

Laska, L. (Ed.). (2002e). Ambulance driver fails to seat belt wheelchair-bound patient. *Medical Malpractice Verdicts, Settlements and Experts*, January 22.

Lincoln Property Co. v. Roche, 546 U.S. 81 (2005).

Mims v. Arrow, 565 U.S. 368 (2012).

O'Keefe, M. (2001). *Nursing practice and the law.* Philadelphia: F.A. Davis.

Olson v. Morris, 188 F.3d 1083, 1086 (9th Cir. 1999).

Owen Equipment & Erection Co. v. Kroger, 437 U.S. 365 (1978).

Payne v. Tennessee, 501 U.S. 808 (1991).

Supplemental Jurisdiction, 28 U.S.C. § 1367 (2012).

U.S. Const. Art. III § 2, cl. 1.

U.S. Const. Art. III, § 1.

United Mine Workers of America v. Gibbs, 383 U.S. 715 (1966).

United States Federal Courts, Management Statistics (2018). Retrieved from www.uscourts.gov/statistics-reports/analysis-reports/federal-court-management-statistics.

Webb, G. G. (2010). The law of falling objects: *Byrne v. Boadle* and the birth of *res ipsa loquitur.* 59 *Stan. L. Rev.* 1065.

Test Questions

1. Four sources of laws include all of the following EXCEPT:
   A. Constitutional law
   B. Administrative law
   C. Stationary law
   D. Common law
2. Which of the following statements about battery is true?
   A. It is a quasi-intentional tort
   B. It is unpermitted touching
   C. It is based on the *stare decisis* theory
   D. It is only a criminal offense
3. All of the following are intentional torts, EXCEPT:
   A. Battery
   B. Libel
   C. Assault
   D. False imprisonment
4. Which of the following statements about hearsay is true?
   A. It is a common procedural issue
   B. It is a statement made by the proponent
   C. Records kept in the course of a regularly conducted business activity would not be an exception to the hearsay rule
   D. A statement made for the purpose of medical diagnosis would be an exception to the hearsay rule
5. Legal doctrines employed to reduce or bar a plaintiff's damages award include all of the following EXCEPT:
   A. Causative negligence
   B. Comparative negligence
   C. Failure to mitigate damages
   D. Assumption of risk

Answers: 1. C, 2. B, 3. B, 4. D, 5. A

Chapter 4

Elements of Proof in Negligence Claims

Corey G. Lorenz, Esq.

Contents

Objectives

- Explain the concept of reasonable care
- Explain the various contexts in which a negligence cause of action can arise
- Identify the four elements of proof of a negligence claim
- Discuss each element of proof of negligence and what each entails

Introduction

A cause of action for negligence can arise in a variety of different legal claims. When asserting negligence, a person claims that another person failed to exercise reasonable care, that is, the level of care that a reasonable, prudent person would use in the circumstances. What constitutes reasonable care is determined by the type of legal claim at issue and the circumstances of each case. A person must ultimately establish four elements to succeed on a negligence cause of action:

1. Duty
2. Breach
3. Causation (factual cause and proximate cause) and
4. Damages

To summarize, a person asserting negligence has the burden of establishing that the opposing party had a duty to exercise reasonable care, the party breached that duty, and this breach caused injury.

This chapter will use the terms "plaintiff" and "defendant." A plaintiff is the party that initiates the legal action. A defendant is the party against whom that legal action is brought. It is most common that the plaintiff claims a defendant is negligent; however, as discussed in more detail later in this chapter, a defendant can also claim that a plaintiff was negligent. The elements of a negligence claim remain the same in both instances.

It is important to remember that jurisdictions adopt different versions of these general principles, and one must consult the applicable standards in the jurisdiction where the case lies. This chapter will discuss each of these four elements in depth, in broad terms that apply across various legal contexts.

Negligence Cause of Action

Negligence is based on the very simple principle that each person owes a duty to others to act reasonably and not create a risk of harm. This duty exists in all contexts, from day-to-day actions to professional obligations. The law requires that each person exercise *reasonable care* in all circumstances, and the failure to do so is negligence (Restatement (Third) of Torts, 2010).

Reasonable Care

The key question in a negligence claim is whether a person's conduct lacked *reasonable care*. "Reasonable care" will be defined by the context of the case and the facts and circumstances surrounding the claim. Primary factors to consider are:

1. The foreseeable likelihood that the person's conduct will result in harm
2. The foreseeable severity of such harm and
3. The burden of precautions to eliminate or reduce the risk of harm (Restatement (Third) of Torts, 2010)

In assessing these factors, the jury must decide (1) if a person should have known of the risk and severity of harm at the time of the conduct and (2) the feasibility of risk reduction or prevention. The jury makes this decision after both parties have presented all the evidence. These factors illustrate that determining reasonableness is truly a balancing test. Negligence is a fact-specific inquiry in which evidence must be presented on each of these variables to help juries determine whether the conduct at issue was reasonable in the circumstances. Examples of facts that may become relevant include a person's age, mental capacity, profession, and the facts surrounding the resulting harm. This is discussed in more detail within this chapter.

Both action and inaction can result in a failure to exercise reasonable care. A person can be negligent for doing something that a reasonable person would not do or for failing to do something that a reasonable person would do. For example, an automobile driver might be deemed negligent for running a red light and causing injury; in this example, the driver's action was unreasonable. A product manufacturer might be negligent for failing to take appropriate steps in the design of a product; in this example, the manufacturer's inaction was unreasonable. Both can serve as the basis for a negligence claim.

Scope of Legal Claims

Negligence can be claimed any time another person's action or inaction was unreasonable under the circumstances, when that conduct created a risk of harm to others, and when that conduct caused injury (Restatement (Third) of Torts, 2010). As such, negligence can be alleged in a wide variety of legal contexts.

For example, a plaintiff may claim professional negligence when a defendant fails to exercise the level of care required by that profession. This includes claims of medical malpractice, when it is alleged that a medical provider's action or inaction fell below the standard of care required of medical professionals in that field. A plaintiff may also claim negligence in a product liability matter related to a manufacturer's alleged failure to use reasonable care in the development or marketing of a specific product. Negligence can also arise in other personal injury matters. For instance, in an automobile accident, a person may assert that the other driver failed to exercise reasonable care in the operation of a motor vehicle. These all serve as examples, but negligence claims are not limited to these contexts. Indeed, negligence can be claimed across a broad spectrum of cases as warranted by the specific facts at hand.

Once a plaintiff claims negligence against a defendant, that defendant may assert that the plaintiff was also negligent. This is called "contributory negligence." The basis of this claim is that the plaintiff's own negligence contributed in some way to the alleged injury, and thus the defendant should not be solely liable for the injury that occurred. A defendant's negligent conduct creates a risk of harm to the plaintiff; a plaintiff is contributorily negligent when the conduct creates a risk of harm to oneself (Restatement (Third) of Torts, 2010). The effects of a contributory negligence claim and how it may impact a defendant's liability will be determined by the rules of the applicable jurisdiction. The elements of proof in a negligence cause of action, and the standard for establishing each element, are the same whether negligence is claimed against a plaintiff or a defendant.

Elements of Proof

Duty

The first element that must be established in a negligence claim is the existence of a duty. As outlined earlier in this chapter, all people have a duty to exercise reasonable care when their conduct creates a risk of physical harm. In other words, every person has a duty to exercise the care of a reasonable person to prevent others from becoming injured (Restatement (Third) of Torts, 2010). In most cases, at issue is this duty to exercise such reasonable care. In some instances, a more defined duty exists based on the type of legal claim and specific circumstances involved. The existence of a legal duty is a question of law determined by the court.

Each case involves different facts and actors, and those considerations may impact the scope of a party's duty. What is "reasonable" can only be assessed in the context of the facts at hand. A key example of this is a lay person's duty when acting in response to an emergency. In an emergent situation, it is plausible that a lay person does not have time to fully weigh all possible options and actions to determine what "reasonable care" is in those specific circumstances. On the other hand, in an emergency, healthcare professionals might have a heightened duty in certain situations, even to individuals who are not patients, due to their advanced education and training in a specific field. This illustrates that each factual scenario warrants consideration when defining the duty to exercise reasonable care.

Status of the Actor

To determine an actor's duty, it is also necessary to identify if that actor holds a certain *status* that must be considered. The first primary example of this is a person's age. In most jurisdictions, when a case involves a child actor, that child actor's duty is to exercise reasonable care of a person of the same age, intelligence, and experience (Restatement (Third) of Torts, 2010). In some jurisdictions, children below a certain age may not have any duty at all. The child's actions must also be put in context of the activity in question; if a child engages in a dangerous activity that is typically engaged in by adults, that child may be held to the standard of reasonable care of an adult in similar circumstances.

A second example of status is if the actor has any type of physical disability. If so, in most jurisdictions, an actor with a physical disability has a duty to act as a reasonably prudent person who has that same disability (Restatement (Third) of Torts, 2010).

A third example of an actor's status is whether the actor has a higher level of experience, knowledge, or skill than the average person in the area that is the subject of the claim (i.e., whether the negligence claim is brought against a person or entity that has specialized knowledge or expertise in the relevant field). If an actor has experience, knowledge, or skills exceeding most others, those circumstances may determine if the actor acted as a reasonably careful person (Restatement (Third) of Torts, 2010). (On the other hand, in most jurisdictions, below average knowledge or skill is not normally considered.) This type of scenario can arise in several different contexts, such as a claim against a pharmaceutical company related to the manufacture of a medical drug. Another example is an automobile accident in which the allegedly negligent actor traveled on the road in question multiple times per day. It can be argued that the actor has heightened, above average experience and knowledge of the road in question. In these circumstances, the actor's superior experience or knowledge may be relevant to determine what was required of that actor.

This can also arise in the context of medical negligence claims. When negligence is claimed against a medical professional, it is important to identify the pertinent experience and knowledge that professional has in the area that is the subject of the claim. For example, if a claim is brought against a physician, it is important to assess if that physician has any *specialized* knowledge in the field (as evidenced by advanced training, subspecialty board certification, etc.) in which the physician was practicing at the time of the negligent act. These considerations do not alter the basic premise that each person owes a duty to exercise reasonable care to others. However, what is "reasonable" may depend on the circumstances, and as shown above, an actor's status is key to understanding what the duty is in that specific case.

Relationship Between Actors

Another main factor in defining a person's duty is the relationship between the parties. In addition to the duty of reasonable care, some relationships trigger a specific duty or determine that a person owes no duty at all to the other party. It is necessary to identify the type of relationship between each actor involved in order to understand if the allegedly negligent actor owed a duty to the other and, if so, what that duty is.

A key example of a relevant relationship is when a negligence claim is brought against a landowner for an injury that occurred on that landowner's property. A property owner with hazardous conditions could be liable to persons lawfully on the land. However, in some jurisdictions, a landowner does not owe any duty at all to unknown trespassers on the property. In this scenario, understanding the relationship between the landowner and trespasser, as compared to the landowner and lawful occupant, is a critical distinction to determining the landowner's duty.

Certain special relationships are important, because an actor owes the other a duty of reasonable care regarding the risks that arise in the scope of that relationship. Examples of these relationships include, but are not limited to, common carriers with passengers, innkeepers with guests, employers with employees, and landlords with tenants (Restatement (Third) of Torts, 2012). In these types of relationships, there is an affirmative duty of reasonable care that usually is limited in scope and time to the relationship. In many jurisdictions, these relationships call for a heightened duty of care to be exercised. Specific relationships that dictate a duty, or when there is no duty at all, can vary across jurisdictions.

The relationship between actors is also critical when any type of professional negligence is alleged. In a professional setting, an actor's duty may be defined by the professional's relationship to the other actor. The most common example of this is in cases involving medical malpractice, in which the medical provider's relationship to the patient is what dictates the pertinent duty. In medical malpractice claims, a medical provider's duty is defined by the applicable standard of care in that field. (See Chapter 10 for a detailed discussion of the standard of care pertaining to healthcare providers.)

When pursuing a product liability claim, a cause of action for negligent failure to warn is common. Here, the manufacturer has a duty to warn of risks that it has reason to know of, when it also knows that those using the product will be unaware of such risks. This duty arises when a plaintiff can establish that the warning might have been effective in reducing the risk of harm. A manufacturer also has a duty to adopt necessary precautions to protect against these risks if it is foreseeable that a risk of harm remains even with the presence of warnings (Restatement (Third) of Torts, 2010). Additional product liability claims based on negligence are available in different jurisdictions, and the requirements of these claims can vary. (See Chapter 13 for more information on product liability.) This illustrates that the specific cause of action and actors involved help define the defendant's actual duty.

The party claiming negligence has the burden to first prove that a duty existed. In rare circumstances, a court may find that no duty existed based on moral or policy considerations. However, in the vast majority of cases, there is indeed a duty to use reasonable care. The duty to exercise "reasonable care" is a key, basic premise underlying all negligence claims. However, what is "reasonable" can only be assessed by determining if the accused had any pertinent status and identifying any relevant relationship between the parties. Only by considering all the facts can a person's duty truly be defined.

Example

While driving on the road, Driver Doe runs a stop sign and strikes Driver Smith's vehicle. Driver Smith files a lawsuit alleging that Driver Doe was negligent while operating the vehicle. Driver Doe had a duty to exercise reasonable care in the operation of the vehicle to prevent injury to others. Driver Smith will next have to prove (and likely can prove) that by running a stop sign, Driver Doe breached this duty.

Example

Landowner Doe owns two acres of private property that is used only for personal purposes. Trespasser Smith has never met Landowner Doe and has never been invited onto Landowner Doe's property. Trespasser Smith decides to walk on Landowner Doe's property, unbeknownst to Landowner Doe. While on the property, Trespasser Smith trips and falls, breaking a leg. Landowner Doe did not owe any duty to Trespasser Smith, because Trespasser Smith was trespassing on the land. Trespasser Smith is unable to proceed with a cause of action for negligence.

Example

Commuter Smith is riding on a commuter train operated by Common Carrier Company. The train was operated at a higher rate of speed than necessary, causing Commuter Smith to fall from the seat and become injured. Because of its special relationship, Common Carrier Company owed Commuter Smith a duty to exercise reasonable care to its passengers; therefore, Commuter Smith is able to proceed with a negligence claim.

Breach of Duty

Once the actor's duty is defined, the party claiming negligence has the burden of establishing that the actor breached that duty. The alleging party must present sufficient evidence to support a finding that the actor's conduct lacked reasonable care under the circumstances. Whether the actor's conduct lacked reasonable care is typically a question left for a jury to decide based on the facts and evidence presented in the case. When reasonable minds can differ, it is the jury's role to determine the pertinent facts and whether or not the conduct in question lacked reasonable care (Restatement (Third) of Torts, 2010). A jury is left to decide whether the duty was breached based on all facts in evidence, unless there are certain exceptional circumstances.

Certain facts can be used to assist a jury in determining whether conduct constitutes a breach of duty. For example, compliance with custom in a community or the conduct of others in similar circumstances may be used as supporting evidence that the actor's conduct is not negligent. Similarly, departure from custom might support a finding of negligent conduct. Examples include industry standards or guidelines that exist in the relevant field. These types of facts are not determinative but may be considered by a jury to reach its decision.

Negligence per se is a legal principle that exists only in certain jurisdictions. Under this principle, if (1) the actor violates a statute that is designed to protect against the type of occurrence at issue and (2) the victim is in the class of persons that the statute is designed to protect, then that actor is negligent (Restatement (Third) of Torts, 2010). If these factors are met, violation of the applicable statute, rule, or regulation is determinative of a finding of negligence. On the other hand, compliance with an applicable statute may be evidence of non-negligence but does not necessarily preclude a finding of negligence. For example, the fact that a driver of a vehicle was traveling the speed limit at the time of a collision does not preclude the possibility that the driver was still negligent in the operation of the vehicle.

Whether the actor breached the duty is typically a question of fact to be assessed in each case. Though different cases can be used to draw comparisons and distinctions, the decision from one case is rarely binding on another, because this determination is often very fact-specific. Factual inquiry should be pursued on a case-by-case basis.

Example

Driver Doe was driving on the roadway behind Driver Smith's vehicle. Driver Doe followed Driver Smith's vehicle too closely. When Driver Smith's vehicle slowed down at a red light, Driver Doe was not able to stop in time. Driver Doe rear-ended Driver Smith's vehicle, causing an injury. Driver Doe had a duty to exercise reasonable care when operating the vehicle. By following Driver Smith's vehicle too closely, Driver Doe breached this duty and operated the vehicle in an unreasonable manner. Driver Doe's conduct was negligent.

Example

Pharma Company manufactured Product X. Customer Smith purchased Product X and was injured when Product X malfunctioned. Customer Smith alleges that Pharma Company was negligent by failing to exercise reasonable care in the development of the product and that it negligently failed to warn about the risks associated with the product. Customer Smith presented evidence at trial that Pharma Company did not perform certain testing on its product prior to putting it on the market. Customer Smith also presented evidence that Pharma Company learned of the risk of the specific malfunction prior to putting Product X on the market but did not take precautions to fix it or add warnings about this risk to the public. This evidence will be weighed by the jury to determine whether Pharma Company's actions or inactions breached its duties.

Causation

Simply proving negligent conduct is not enough to succeed in a negligence claim. It is necessary that the party alleging negligence also prove that this conduct actually *caused* the resulting injury. Causation is a complicated concept that truly must be interpreted on a case-by-case basis. The specific facts of each case will need to be analyzed to determine if an actor is liable. There are two causation principles that must be assessed in each case: factual cause and proximate cause.

Factual Cause

For an actor to be held liable for negligent conduct, such conduct must be the factual cause of the injury. Factual cause is also sometimes referred to as "legal cause" or "cause-in-fact." Conduct is the factual cause of harm when, without the conduct, the harm would not have occurred. Commonly referred to as the "but-for" test, factual causation exists when the outcome would not have occurred *but for* the negligent conduct (Restatement (Third) of Torts, 2010).

This test requires a hypothetical analysis of what would have occurred absent the conduct in question. The first step in this analysis is to identify the actual injury or harm. The second step is to identify clearly the negligent act or conduct. Then it must be determined if the harm, or extent of harm, would have occurred without such conduct. Factual cause can be established even when there are multiple causes that contribute in some way to the harm. The conduct in question must be a cause of the injury, but not necessarily the sole cause.

There may be instances when there are multiple acts that occur, and each one of those acts alone could be the factual cause of the harm. In other words, each independent act on its own was sufficient to have caused the injury at issue. When this occurs, courts typically will still permit a determination that the negligent conduct is the factual cause of the injury, as if the other independent causes did not exist (Restatement (Third) of Torts, 2010).

The plaintiff has the burden to prove that the negligent conduct was the factual cause of the injury. When there are multiple potentially liable defendants, the plaintiff has the burden to prove that the defendants' conduct was negligent and caused the injury in some way. The plaintiff may prove that each specific defendant caused the harm, or that all defendants caused the harm. There are circumstances when a plaintiff cannot reasonably be expected to prove which specific act or actor caused the injury. Once the plaintiff presents sufficient evidence that it cannot reasonably do so, courts will commonly shift the burden to the defendants to prove they did not cause the harm (Restatement (Third) of Torts, 2010).

Multiple negligent actors and causal acts can certainly create complex legal questions. In some jurisdictions, the court may consider the scope of each actor's role. For example, the court may assess if one act minimally contributed to the injury, compared to another that overwhelmingly contributed to the same injury. Courts in various jurisdictions will handle these situations differently, and it is of utmost importance to understand how the law applies in the case at hand.

A defendant may argue that there is an alternative or competing cause, other than its own negligent conduct, that was the sole cause of the injuries. If this arises, it must be determined if both acts were sufficient to cause the injury or if it was, indeed, the alternative act or conduct that did so. If both acts are sufficient to have caused the injury, then as discussed above, the court will assess the relative contributions of each act, and it is likely that there is still factual causation. However, if an alternative act or conduct is the sole cause of the injury, no factual causation exists for the defendant's alleged negligent conduct.

It is well-established that negligent conduct cannot be the factual cause of an injury that already occurred (Restatement (Third) of Torts, 2010). For example, a plaintiff who already has been diagnosed with a disease cannot prove a later negligent act caused such disease. However, this is distinguishable from cases when a pre-existing condition exposes a person to greater injury or when negligent conduct causes a worsening of a prior condition. In those instances, the question becomes one of the scope of damages that can be claimed.

Factual causation seems simple: if the conduct did not occur, would there be the same outcome? In some cases, it is just that simple; in others, it is significantly more complex. The following examples illustrate the application of determining factual cause.

Example

Driver Doe ran a red light and collided with Driver Smith's vehicle. Driver Smith suffered a broken arm. A physician determined that Driver Smith's arm broke as a result of the impact of

Driver Doe's vehicle against Driver Smith's vehicle. After hearing all facts and evidence, the jury will likely determine that Driver Doe was negligent and that Driver Doe's negligence is the factual cause of Driver Smith's injury, because but for Driver Doe's negligence, Driver Smith would not have a broken arm.

Example

Driver Doe operated a vehicle negligently and collided with Driver Smith's vehicle. Prior to this accident, Driver Smith was being medically treated for a lumbar spine disc herniation. After the accident, Driver Smith's condition worsened significantly, and physicians provided the opinion that this worsening was due to the impact of the accident. Driver Doe's negligence is not the factual cause of the disc herniation, which occurred before the collision. However, after hearing all the evidence, the jury will likely determine that Driver Doe's negligence is the factual cause of Driver Smith's increase in pain and suffering from the aggravated condition.

Example

J. Smith was exposed to a toxic substance at three different locations and files a lawsuit claiming negligence against three actors responsible for manufacturing the substance. As a result of exposure to the toxic substance, J. Smith developed a disease. It is determined that J. Smith's exposure at each location was sufficient to cause the development of the disease. Under the factual cause rubric, the negligent conduct of all three actors is the factual cause of J. Smith's injury.

Proximate Cause

In addition to establishing factual cause, a party must also establish proximate cause. Proximate cause is one of the most complex but important concepts in the law of torts. Liability is not imposed on any and all harm factually caused by negligent conduct. If that were the case, a defendant could be exposed to significant and widespread liability. Instead, the law limits the scope of liability by imposing limitations on how far liability can extend. A person's scope of liability is limited to harm that results from the risk that made the actor's conduct negligent. In other words, negligence limits the reasonable care requirement to foreseeable risks (Restatement (Third) of Torts, 2010).

The proximate cause analysis requires a determination of what risks made the conduct negligent in the first place and whether the injury suffered is within the scope of those risks. This can also be categorized as a question of foreseeability, both of the probability of the harm and severity of the harm. Almost all jurisdictions will utilize such a foreseeability test to assess negligence. The question of proximate cause is a question of fact for the jury to decide.

What is pertinent to the proximate cause analysis is the *type* of injury suffered. This is distinguishable from the *extent* of the injury. If the type of injury was foreseeable, that is sufficient to determine causation, even if the extent of the injury could not be foreseen. This typically arises in situations when the injured party has a pre-existing condition making them susceptible to serious injury. In most jurisdictions, a defendant must take the victim as they are; the defendant is liable for the full scope of injuries caused by the negligent conduct, even if the injuries exceed those of the average person in such circumstances. This is also referred to in many jurisdictions as the rule of the "eggshell plaintiff." (See Chapter 3 for more information on the eggshell plaintiff doctrine.)

Another well-established principle which may be subject to slight change across jurisdictions is the "rescue doctrine." Under this doctrine, when a person acts negligently and injures another, liability will extend to injuries sustained by a third party who attempts to rescue or aid the originally injured person (Restatement (Third) of Torts, 2010). The underlying principle of this doctrine is that injury to a rescuer is within the foreseeable scope of harm of negligent conduct. Liability in this instance will be limited to the type of harm that could be anticipated by the rescue (Restatement (Third) of Torts, 2010).

Proximate cause is another principle that can present legal challenges in complex cases. The analysis is factually intensive and will vary in each case. Due to the fact-dependent nature of this inquiry, there is rarely direct precedent to be applied. The following examples illustrate how proximate cause can be assessed.

Example

Driver Doe was driving a vehicle at a high rate of speed. Passenger Smith was a passenger in Driver Doe's vehicle. Suddenly, a tree fell over, struck the vehicle, and injured Passenger Smith. Driver Doe's negligent conduct is the factual cause of Passenger Smith's injury, because but for Driver Doe driving at a high rate of speed, the vehicle would not have been struck by the falling tree. However, Driver Doe's negligent act of speeding did not cause the tree to fall; instead, it simply placed the car at the location to be struck. Therefore, Driver Doe's negligent act of speeding did not increase the risk of the type of harm that was suffered. Passenger Smith cannot prove proximate cause and therefore cannot establish liability for negligence. Injury from the falling tree was not within the scope of the risks that made Driver Doe's conduct negligent.

Example

J. Smith had right knee surgery and, three days later, slipped and fell on water on the floor at a local establishment. The fall alone was not sufficient to cause significant injury. However, because of the recent surgery, J. Smith required multiple corrective surgeries. Proximate cause is established, because a knee injury is within the scope of risks of the negligent failure to maintain the premises. The extent of harm, though not necessarily foreseeable, does not prohibit liability.

Example

Commuter Smith was standing on a train platform. An employee of the railroad was assisting a passenger who was attempting to board a train while carrying a package. The passenger dropped the package, which exploded. The explosion caused a scale on the train platform to strike Commuter Smith, who sustained an injury. Commuter Smith alleged negligence against the railroad employee for the employee's conduct in assisting the passenger carrying the package. Commuter Smith cannot establish proximate cause, because the injury from being struck by the scale was not within the scope of risk that made the conduct negligent. See *Palsgraf v. Long Island R. Co.*, 248 N.Y. 339, 162 N.E. 99 (N.Y. 1928).

Damages

Once a party fulfills its burden to establish the existence of a duty, breach of that duty, and causation, that party must also prove harm, a legally recognized injury. In the absence of such a legally recognized injury, there is no viable negligence claim. The term "damages" refers to the amount of money that is awarded to the injured party for harm caused by the negligent actor's conduct (Restatement (Second) of Torts, 1979). The party claiming negligence has the burden of proving it experienced harm as a result of the negligent conduct, that it is entitled to damages, and what specifically those damages are. There are several categories of damages.

Compensatory Damages

Compensatory damages are intended to compensate a person for the actual harm suffered (Restatement (Second) of Torts, 1979). Compensatory damages are categorized as either special damages or general damages.

Special damages are identifiable economic losses such as medical bills, out-of-pocket expenses, and lost wages. These types of losses are specific values supported by evidence. For example, the actual medical bills incurred for applicable medical treatment should be entered into evidence to support a claim for damages for those medical expenses. Similarly, employment records and tax records are commonly used to support a claim for lost wages caused by the negligent conduct.

A plaintiff can claim past, present, and future damages including, but not limited to, future medical bills and future lost wages. When making a claim for future damages, expert testimony is likely necessary to establish the injury is such that these expenses will continue past the point of case resolution or trial. To illustrate, a medical expert may be necessary to offer the opinion that the plaintiff will require medical treatment in the future and to outline that treatment. This opinion can then be used to determine what monetary value should be awarded to compensate a plaintiff for that future care. An expert witness may also be necessary to provide an opinion on whether a person's capacity to work and earn wages was diminished due to the injury and, if so, what monetary value is lost. Special damages must be supported by evidence, and the jury will decide if such damages were indeed caused by the negligent conduct in question.

The term "general damages" refers to non-economic damages, primarily the monetary value awarded for past, present, and future pain and suffering caused by the negligent conduct. This figure is less defined than a special damages calculation, as there is not necessarily a number on paper that can be used to generate the specific damages to be allocated in this category. Plaintiffs and defendants are often in dispute as to what amount of damages for pain and suffering is appropriate, and this is ultimately a jury determination. The monetary value determined for pain and suffering should be supported by the physical evidence, expert opinions, and any testimony available in the case.

Other examples of general damages include loss of function, loss of enjoyment of life (in some jurisdictions), inconvenience, fear resulting from the incident, embarrassment, and the emotional pain of disfigurement. These factors, among others, are commonly accounted for in the pain and suffering calculation.

Loss of consortium is a specific category of damages that is compensation for family members of the injured party. For example, a monetary value might be awarded to the spouse of an injured person for the losses incurred due to those injuries. Jurisdictions differ greatly on whether loss of consortium damages are available at all and, if so, which family members are entitled to recover such damages. Further, jurisdictions may limit the scope of what type of losses are subject to the payment of damages. See Chapter 3 for more information on loss of consortium.

Punitive Damages

Punitive damages are a monetary figure awarded to the plaintiff and are intended to punish the defendant for its egregious behavior and deter similar conduct by others in the future. There must be a viable underlying cause of action for punitive damages to be awarded. The defendant's actions, motives, relationship to the plaintiff, and wealth may be considered by the jury (Restatement (Second) of Torts, 1979). Punitive damages are only available to plaintiffs in certain jurisdictions. In some states, no such damages may be awarded regardless of the circumstances. Further, where punitive damages are permissible, it is at the discretion of the jury, who is not required to make such an award and will reach a determination based on the evidence presented. Punitive damages must be reviewed on a case-by-case basis due to the intricacies involved in each jurisdiction.

It is imperative that the laws of the applicable jurisdiction be evaluated to determine what damages are available in each case and what evidence is necessary to support each category of damages. Some states have statutes that dictate caps on damages in certain claims; it is common to see such caps in medical malpractice cases, for example. Similarly, who is entitled to recover damages can vary across jurisdictions when a wrongful death claim is made. Jurisdictional limitations as to the types of damages available and who is entitled to recover damages must be considered.

Apportionment of Damages

When two or more negligent actors are liable to a plaintiff for an indivisible injury, damages may be apportioned between those actors. There is no majority rule for how this is determined; it depends strictly on the rules of the jurisdiction and is often dictated by statute. In this scenario, an assessment of applicable laws is critical.

In states that apply the principle of "joint and several liability," an injured person may recover the full amount of damages from any one defendant, regardless of that defendant's percentage of fault (Restatement (Third) of Torts, 2000). Jurisdictional laws will determine which defendants are considered "jointly and severally liable" and, therefore, exposed to liability for the full amount of damages. For example, in some states, any defendant at least 1% at fault is considered so; in some states, a defendant must be 51% at fault. Under this principle, a plaintiff can bring a claim against one, several, or all of the negligent actors to recover the full amount of damages owed.

In states that apply the principle of "several liability," the injured party may only recover damages in proportion to that person's percentage of fault. If a defendant is found to be 30% at fault, then that specific defendant is only required to pay damages equal to 30% of the total damages award. A plaintiff must consider, then, which actor is best suited to be named as a defendant (Restatement (Third) of Torts, 2000).

When a plaintiff brings a negligence claim against a defendant, that defendant may also allege in its defense that the plaintiff's own negligence was a cause of the injury. The defendant then has the burden to prove each element of plaintiff's negligence as outlined within this chapter. States also differ as to how this comparative negligence impacts an award of damages. If a plaintiff is partially negligent, certain states require that a damages award is reduced by the percentage of fault of the plaintiff. Some states dictate that if a plaintiff's negligence exceeds a certain percentage, it is a complete bar to that plaintiff's recovery. This is a jurisdictional question. (See Chapter 3 for more information on contributory and comparative negligence.)

A plaintiff must establish as an element of negligence some harm (legally recognized injury) entitling it to a monetary award (damages). What damages are available to a plaintiff will depend on the type of claim at issue, the injuries sustained, the personal circumstance of the plaintiff, and the jurisdiction of the case.

Summary

Negligence can be alleged in many different legal contexts and in countless numbers of factual circumstances. Such a claim can be simple and straightforward or fact-intensive and complex. Regardless of complexity, any party alleging negligence must (1) show that the opposing party failed to use reasonable care and (2) satisfy each element of proof outlined in this chapter. It is important to remember that the application of fact to the general legal principles discussed in this chapter requires the study of the applicable law of the jurisdiction where the case is pending. The specific nuances in law and the differences in how courts interpret the law around the country must be considered when determining how to approach a case. When pursuing or defending against a negligence claim, an attorney and legal nurse consultant must be prepared to fully learn and understand all evidence and to present that evidence strategically and successfully to establish or refute these elements of proof.

References

Restatement (Second) of Torts, §§ 901–910 (1979).
Restatement (Third) of Torts: Apportionment of Liability §§ 1, 4, 5, 7, 10, 11, 16, 17 (2000).
Restatement (Third) of Torts: Physical and Emotional Harm §§ 3, 7–19, 26–36 (2010).
Restatement (Third) of Torts: Physical and Emotional Harm §§ 40, 42, 49–54 (2012).
Palsgraf v. Long Island R. Co., 248 N.Y. 339, 162 N.E. 99 (N.Y. 1928).

Test Questions

1. Which of the following are types of legal claims in which negligence can be alleged?
   A. Products liability
   B. Personal injury
   C. Medical malpractice
   D. All of the above
2. Which of the following is NOT an element of proof in a negligence claim?
   A. Duty
   B. Breach
   C. Knowledge
   D. Causation
3. In most jurisdictions, which factor should NOT be considered when determining a person's duty?
   A. Actor's status
   B. Below average skill of the actor
   C. Relationship to the injured party
   D. Facts of the event in question
4. When proving causation, a party must show that:
   A. The injured party had no prior similar injury
   B. The harm was within the scope of the risk of the negligent conduct
   C. The negligent conduct was the sole cause of the injury
   D. There was only one negligent actor
5. Which of the following is not a type of compensatory damage?
   A. Medical bills
   B. Lost wages
   C. Punitive funds
   D. Pain and suffering

Answers: 1. D, 2. C, 3. B, 4. B, 5. C

Chapter 5

Initiating Litigation, Discovery, and Disclosure

Peter I. Bergé, JD, MPA, PA-C Emeritus

Contents

Objectives

- Explain the considerations and steps involved in initiating litigation
- Describe the fundamental concepts of civil procedure
- Identify frequently encountered evidentiary requirements in relation to discovery in civil actions
- Discuss the steps in the discovery process and analyze the function of each
- Compare and contrast the role in the discovery process of the legal nurse consultant from the plaintiff and defense perspectives and from the role of the nurse expert witness

Introduction

The legal strategies and nuances of initiating litigation and, particularly, the discovery process far exceed the content of this chapter. While management of pre-trial discovery is the domain of the attorney, the legal nurse consultant (LNC) is a valuable asset in discovery in cases involving medical issues and may play a major role in case development using specialized knowledge.

Initiating Litigation

Before progressing to the core of the discovery process, a brief explanation of the steps leading up to the mandatory exchange of information is needed.

A critical consideration when first evaluating a potential medical malpractice or other personal injury claim is whether any potential defendant is entitled to a *notice of tort claim*, also known as a tort claim notice. Public/governmental entities are often entitled to a formal notice that a lawsuit against the entity or its employees or agents is being considered. The law usually requires that the notice be served on the agency within a specific period of time after the potential claim became known to the claimant, and that time may be very short, for instance, 90 days. The law may also give the public entity the right to require that its own form be used to file the tort claim notice. It is essential to be aware of the necessity of serving a tort claim notice in compliance with the statutory requirements, because failure to do so may preclude filing of the lawsuit. The LNC who performs intake interviews of clients must promptly determine who the potential defendants may be and discuss with the attorney whether any are entitled to a notice of tort claim.

Before considering the initiation of a lawsuit, plaintiff's counsel must assure that the claim meets the requirements of the jurisdiction, which may include obtaining a certificate (or affidavit) of merit (COM/AOM). A product of the tort reform movement, the COM/AOM requirement is intended to assure that professional malpractice claims are likely to have merit by involving a review by a professional with relevant expertise. The contents of the COM/AOM, what type of professional may execute one (or whether a professional must execute the document), the timing of when it must be obtained, and whether the document is served on the defendant vary among jurisdictions. It is incumbent on LNCs to familiarize themselves with the relevant details of COM/AOM requirements in the jurisdictions where they work. Other requirements arising from tort reform efforts may include review of medical malpractice claims by an expert panel early in the litigation process.

Once the attorney has met requirements for a COM/AOM, if any, pleadings are prepared. Pleading is the umbrella term used for the legal documents that initiate and respond to a lawsuit. These basic documents frame the issues for trial. Litigation is initiated when counsel for the plaintiff files a complaint. The required elements of the complaint are, typically, a) a statement regarding the grounds for jurisdiction (i.e., "personal jurisdiction" over the parties or "subject matter jurisdiction" over the type of case); b) short and plain statements of the claims (averments); and c) demand for judgment (also known as the "prayer for relief" or "wherefore" clause) (Fed.R.Civ.P. 8(a), 2014; Appendix A). The complaint identifies the causes of action, i.e., the specific legal claims for which the plaintiff is seeking compensation. Examples of causes of action include negligence, wrongful death, vicarious liability, loss of consortium, and lack of informed consent.

It is essential for the LNC to remember the plaintiff bears the burden of proving allegations regarding negligence and damages. In a civil action, this standard is "by the preponderance of the evidence." Similarly, the standard of proof for medical causation is "to a reasonable degree of medical (or nursing, engineering, etc.) probability/certainty." In practical terms, this is usually considered to be a likelihood of greater than 50%, or "more likely than not." Legal nurse consultants should familiarize themselves with the key wording required in the relevant jurisdiction regarding expert causation opinions.

The complaint will specify the factual and legal basis for the lawsuit and must be filed in the court of proper jurisdiction. Also called subject matter jurisdiction, the requirement refers to the court's authority to hear and rule on a specific legal matter. The defendant is the person being sued and is initially the recipient of the complaint. Together the plaintiff(s) and defendant(s) are referred to as the parties.

When the complaint is filed, the Court Clerk issues a summons (or a summons is prepared by plaintiff's counsel in the name of the Clerk of the Court), and it, along with the copy of the complaint, must be served on the defendant(s) or its designated agent (in the case of a corporation, business, or government entity). The summons identifies the parties named in the suit, the court in which the case is venued, the type of suit (e.g., medical malpractice, product liability, etc.), and (depending on the jurisdiction) a date that triggers certain deadlines for the defendants, such as by when they must file an appearance and a pleading responsive to the complaint (e.g., an answer). Together the summons and complaint are known as *the process*. When the summons and complaint have been delivered to the defendant or its registered agent by procedures required by the rules of court, this is known as service of process. The rules of the jurisdiction dictate who can serve and accept the process, the methods by which service of process can be accomplished, and the time frame by which it must be completed.

Once officially served the complaint and summons, the defendant will need to file a responsive pleading known as the *answer.* The time frame for filing an answer is subject to the rule outlined in Federal Rule of Civil Procedure (FRCP) 12 (Fed.R.Civ.P., 2014; Appendix A) or other applicable rules of court/rules of civil procedure. A civil case in federal court would require an answer to be filed within 20 days of service of the complaint and summons unless otherwise ordered by the court. Time to answer in state courts varies by state. Prior to filing an answer, the defendant's counsel in federal court may file a request to revise the complaint, a motion to strike certain counts in the complaint, or a motion to challenge the adequacy of the complaint. For example, the defendant may file a Motion to Dismiss, alleging the service of process was insufficient, the court does not have the legal authority to preside over the specific case, the complaint fails to state a cause of action, or the complaint is lacking a statutory requirement (such as an expert affidavit or good faith certificate). In state courts, there may be provisions for stipulations between parties to extend the time to file the answer. For example, a healthcare professional may receive process, then turn over the papers to the hospital-employer's risk management department. Risk management might evaluate the claim, initiate the hospital's internal review processes, and send the papers to the insurance carrier. Some time may pass before the carrier assigns an outside law firm to answer the complaint and defend the claim. By then, little time may remain for the defense attorney to review the papers and communicate with the defendant prior to the deadline for answering.

If the defendant does not file a Motion to Dismiss or the court denies the motion, the defendant must answer the complaint. In the answer, the defendant must admit, deny, or plead ignorance to each and every specified fact. The defendant's answer must also contain any affirmative defenses and objections (Fed.R.Civ.P., 2014; Appendix A).

Affirmative defenses are concise statements explaining legal theories of why the plaintiff's claims are unfounded. Defendants, through their counsel, may assert arguments or new facts that, if valid, would defeat the plaintiff's claim. Examples of affirmative defenses include contributory or comparative negligence, assumption of risk, and running of the statute of limitations. Affirmative defenses are unique, because they may shift the burden of proof, which otherwise rests with the plaintiff, to the defendant, i.e., what the defense alleges, *it* now must prove. While some jurisdictions may have rules discouraging the routine use of a list of affirmative defenses that are pled regardless of the details of a particular claim, such lists, or "boilerplate" defenses, are commonly included in responsive pleadings.

The complex issue of apportionment of liability may be raised in responsive pleadings or later in litigation. In general personal injury litigation, the defense may attempt to apportion liability to the plaintiff under theories of contributory or comparative negligence. An example is alleging that the plaintiff's failure to exercise due care was a contributing factor in the resulting injuries. In medical malpractice matters, defendants may seek apportionment of liability or damages to existing co-defendants or may attempt to join new parties as apportionment defendants. In either instance, the original defendant has the burden of proving the allegations against the new or existing apportionment defendants.

Overview of the Discovery Process

Terminology

For greater clarity in delineating the distinct roles of the nurse expert witness and the LNC in the discovery process, these roles will be defined as follows:

- ▪ "Expert" refers to testifying experts, who are consulted with the expectation they may testify in deposition and at trial, if the case progresses to that point.
- ▪ "Legal nurse consultant" refers to the behind-the-scenes legal nurse consultant who provides specialized medical-legal services to the attorney during the discovery phase. The LNC may be either in-house (an employee of the attorney or law firm) or an independent contractor.

The terms disclosure and discovery are not mutually exclusive. For conceptual purposes, this content will distinguish between the broad category of "pre-trial discovery" and the individual activities of disclosure and discovery engaged in by each party to the litigation. In general, the discussion here of "discovery" refers to pre-trial discovery. However, one may think of individual discovery practice as what a party does to obtain information another party has. In contrast, "disclosure" is considered the act of one party revealing information to the other party or parties.

Much like healthcare providers, attorneys have distinct styles and preferences. Even though adherence to the jurisdictional rules and guidelines offers a certain measure of flexibility in the pre-trial litigation process, the discovery steps outlined here follow the general, rule-of-thumb order. It is worth noting that, in the law, there are exceptions to the general rule, and each step may be influenced by the individual attorney or judge's preference.

The FRCP which govern pre-trial discovery in federal courts have not been adopted by all states. State rules of civil procedure may vary minimally or greatly from the FRCP, and the discovery process may also be governed by local rules and procedures specific to a given vicinage (e.g., particular county or regional courts).

It is important to keep in mind that medical malpractice litigation is a specialized subset of personal injury practice. All personal injury practice involves medical issues to some extent, and LNCs may have significant involvement in pre-trial discovery in some general personal injury cases, particularly if the damages rest on complex medical issues.

Legal nurse consultants possess extensive knowledge and may work in a broad spectrum of legal environments, making it a formidable task to present work samples in this chapter that address the full spectrum of legal settings. For demonstration purposes, the appendices contain samples of work product and provide the rules of procedure and evidence commonly encountered in medical negligence actions.

Purpose of Discovery

Discovery is defined as, "The act or process of finding or learning something that was previously unknown" (Garner, 2014, p. 564). The purpose of discovery is to provide the parties the opportunity to limit surprises at trial, narrow the issues to be decided, and establish support for their legal positions. The process of discovery in medical malpractice cases is accomplished through five core instruments:

1. interrogatories
2. request for production of documents or things (RFP)
3. depositions
4. physical and mental examination and
5. requests for admission (RFA) (Fed.R.Civ.P. 30, 33, 34, 35 and 36, 2014; Appendix A)

Key to the discovery of information sought is that it must be "relevant to the subject matter involved in the pending action" under the FRCP [Fed.R.Civ.P. 26(b)(1), 2014; Appendix A]. This relevancy requirement is the guiding rule for the request for information and restrains the tendency to serve the opponent party with requests for material unrelated to the core legal issue.

Another typical requirement under state rules of court is that "the information sought appears reasonably calculated to lead to the discovery of admissible evidence…" [N.J. Court Rules 4:10–2(a)]. In other words, evidence properly sought in discovery may not necessarily be admissible at trial. The central criterion is that the information be sought with the intention that it may lead to discovering evidence that would be admissible. Objections to the effect that the discovery requested will likely be inadmissible at trial are, therefore, inappropriate during discovery in jurisdictions which have such a rule. Such objections are not likely to be sustained by the court.

State versus Federal Laws

Because the U.S. Constitution Bill of Rights provides for the right of states to independently govern their citizens through their legislators, each state is free to choose its own rules of civil procedure and evidence as long as it does not violate the U.S. Constitution (U.S. Constitution Amendment X). If the individual state so chooses, the state judiciary is free to adopt the federal rules in whole, in part, or not at all.

Many states have chosen to adopt the Federal Rules of Civil Procedure and the Federal Rules of Evidence (FRE), in part or in their entirety. Choosing to follow the FRCP and the FRE provides a measure of continuity and uniformity in the court system. However, as mentioned above, states are free to modify the FRCP, emulate them while tailoring the rules to the preferences of the state courts, or develop their unique rules.

Additionally, local vicinages (typically county or regional courts) may develop "local rules," which are additional procedures or requirements only used in that county or region. That practice is widespread despite being frowned on by some state administrative court offices because they decrease uniformity of procedures across a state. Complicating the lives of attorneys further is the imposition of individual judges of their own preferences. While the attorney is responsible for complying with the rules of civil procedure (referred to in some jurisdictions as rules of court) and rules of evidence, it is useful for the LNC to be generally familiar with the most relevant jurisdictional rules and evidentiary guidelines that equate to the federal rules in the jurisdiction(s) where the LNC works.

Disclosure

Disclosure in pre-trial discovery is either voluntary or required depending on the information to be disclosed. Disclosure is defined as, "The act or process of making known something that was previously unknown; a revelation of facts" (Garner, 2014, p. 562). Attorneys are ethically bound to disclose to the client conflicts of interest of which they become aware. This responsibility is found in the American Bar Association's (ABA) Model Rules of Professional Conduct 1.7: Conflict of interest; current clients and 1.16 (a): Declining or terminating representation (2018). Conflicts of interest should generally be considered to extend to those working as the attorney's agent (paralegal, LNC, law clerk, etc.). Not all states have adopted the ABA Model Rules of Professional Conduct, but disclosing potential conflicts of interest to a client is typically required by state ethics rules. The LNC hired by an attorney is duty-bound to immediately inform the attorney if a potential conflict of interest exists.

Mandatory disclosure in personal injury litigation is inherent to formal discovery. One mechanism for accomplishing consistent mandatory disclosure is the use of *form interrogatories*. These are sets of questions developed by the jurisdiction's judiciary that parties are required to answer. For example, in a State of Delaware Superior Court civil action, Form 30 Interrogatories accompany the filing of the complaint and require information from the litigant regarding seven areas that address: (1) the identification of the names and addresses for any witnesses, (2) names and addresses of any persons with knowledge of facts to the events being litigated, (3) names and addresses of any persons who have been interviewed regarding the events being litigated, (4) identification of persons in possession of documents related to the matter being litigated, (5) name and address of any expert witness presently retained, (6) names and addresses of medical providers, and (7) name/address/policy limit amount of any applicable insurance coverage (Del.R.Ann., 2007a).

Claims of Privilege and the Attorney Work-Product Doctrine

Nurses are educated about the principles of confidentiality as related to health care. The nursing tradition is steeped in the ethics of preserving the confidences of patient communication, diagnosis, and treatment. Similarly, the attorney–client privilege is primarily addressed in the Model Rule of Professional Conduct 1.6: Confidentiality of information, which directs attorneys regarding their duty to keep client confidences (2018). The hallmark case-citing of the intended purpose of this communication privilege is in *Upjohn Co. v. U.S.* (1981). In part, it states privilege exists to protect "not only the giving of professional advice to those who can act on it but also the giving of information to the lawyer to allow him to give sound and informed advice" (*id.* at 390). The attorney–client privilege applies to the communication process between the attorney and the client.

The attorney work-product doctrine, on the other hand, is intended to protect the attorney's legal theory, litigation strategy, legal opinions, and other thoughts and processes in preparation for trial. The origins of the attorney work-product doctrine are found in the Supreme Court case *Hickman v. Taylor* (1947), but this protection is extended to include those materials generated by persons other than the attorney if "prepared in anticipation of litigation" (Fed.R.Civ.P. 26(b) (1–5), 2014; Appendix A).

This protection, however, is not absolute and may, under very limited circumstances, be subject to discovery if the opposing party establishes a substantial need for such information, which must meet certain requirements, such as that it cannot be obtained through other means without undue hardship and would otherwise generally be discoverable. Take, for example, an allegation of spoliation (intentional destruction of evidence) against a hospital where the only surviving document is the incident report. Normally, material prepared in anticipation of litigation compiled by risk management and the hospital's legal counsel is protected. Due to the destruction of crucial evidence and without the incident report, the plaintiff's counsel may be able to show a "substantial need" and "undue hardship" in trying to obtain legal redress for the injured plaintiff. If the judge determined the incident report was subject to disclosure, the *factual* evidence in the report might be discoverable, but the defendant attorney's own spoken and written thoughts (mental impressions) about the document would likely remain shielded by the doctrine (Fed.R.Civ.P. 26(b) (3), 2014; Appendix A). An in-depth discussion of exceptions to the work-product privilege is not practical here. It is advisable for the LNC and expert witness to develop an understanding of the attorney work-product privilege rules relevant to a given case on which they are working. It is essential, for example, for independent LNCs and experts to know to what extent their oral and written communications with the attorney are subject to discovery by the opposing party. They should discuss that issue with the attorney-client before beginning work on a new matter.

Discovery and the Legal Nurse Consultant

As a practical matter, work done by a consultant who is an employee of the attorney is generally protected under the work-product doctrine. An in-house LNC's work-product is shielded by this doctrine. However, the LNC in this role should discuss with the attorney whether it is advisable to mark correspondence, e-mails, chronologies/medical summaries, and the like with a disclaimer such as "attorney work-product, privileged and protected."

Once privileged materials are inadvertently disclosed, or if client confidentiality is breached, privilege and protection are at risk. For this reason, it is critically important for the consultant to keep a strict system of isolating potentially protected documents from those subject to discovery. Independent LNCs and experts should determine, in consultation with the attorney, if notes, memos, and even "sticky notes" should be destroyed, and if so, at what point in time.

The December 2015 amendment to FRCP 26(b)(5) (Appendix A), however, allows one to assert a protective claim in the case of inadvertent production of trial preparation material or privileged information. It provides that, once the party seeking protection of materials notifies the receiving parties of the claim and its grounds for asserting protection, the receiving party must return, sequester, or destroy the information. The rule is mute on the waiving of protection and privilege in these circumstances, but it bars the receiving party from its use (2015). Also, state rules of court generally address these eventualities. Should an inadvertent disclosure jeopardize the client's position, the attorney may be exposed to liability. The attorney must be informed immediately if possibly privileged material may have been provided to an opposing party. The most prudent practice, however, is to prevent accidental disclosures. A systematic approach to protection of privileged information circumvents unnecessary and costly litigation and prevents delays in an otherwise already lengthy process.

Discovery and the Expert Witness

Anyone retained as an expert witness for purposes of testimony should assume, at a minimum, that opinions, reports, fee schedule, cancellation schedule, literature, curriculum vitae (CV) or resume, and prior testimony will be subject to discovery by opposing counsel. Even the expert's draft report of opinions and personal notations regarding the case may be subject to discovery, depending on the rules and law of the jurisdiction. While it may be safest to assume all materials generated by the testifying expert witness are potentially discoverable, the expert should clarify this issue with the attorney before beginning work on the case and, when indicated, separate file materials accordingly.

Interrogatories and deposition questions to, or regarding, testifying experts may seem quite intrusive, even within the guidelines allowed by law. Expert witnesses should anticipate inquiry of having been the subject of litigation, school class ranking, having passed licensure boards in first attempt, the percentage of actual clinical time compared with the time devoted to academic positions or expert testimony, and the total dollar amount derived from expert testimony in the preceding year, along with numerous other inquiries. Opposing counsel may go through the expert's CV line by line in deposition and question every entry. Some attorneys routinely obtain third party reports on experts' work history, fees, publications, testimony and other background areas, and attempt to exploit that information to discredit the expert or undermine the expert's opinions. The "banking" and exchanging of deposition transcripts is a common practice and can provide invaluable material for impeachment of the adversary's expert. Opposing counsel may attempt to "nail down" the expert's testimony (e.g., "it is your opinion that symptoms *never* develop more than four weeks after an injury such as this one, right?") and then introduce past deposition testimony that contradicts the opinion just given, in an effort to impeach the expert's credibility.

Electronic Discovery

In April of 2006, new amendments to the FRCP addressed the need to further clarify the inclusion and scope of requests for information specific to electronic discovery. By December 1, 2006, amendments specific to the discovery of electronic information (Fed.R.Civ.P. 16, 26, 33, 34, 37, 45 and form 35, 2014; Appendix A) went into effect (Supreme Court of U.S., 2006).

Known less formally as e-discovery, the scope of electronically stored information (ESI) is both extensive and complex. In the broadest view, it may encompass a vast array of categories, including, but not limited to, active and deleted e-mails and voice mails, archived and back-up systems, cookies, cached pages, audio and graphic files, temporary files, website logs, data, and programs files. The entire history of electronic information from conception to delivery to demise is subject to potential discovery.

Playing a key role in the evolution of e-discovery is the hidden but traceable text of documents (metadata) that provides a historical footprint of changes, deletions, and alterations to a document. While certain areas of litigation are more likely to be the hotbeds of activity (such as toxic tort, class action suits, and patent law), matters of e-discovery are becoming more prevalent in personal injury and health law where issues of federal pre-emption, corporate compliance, and documents stored on a litigant's personal computer take on heightened importance. Questions of spoliation and intentional alteration of records may also prompt in-depth e-discovery.

There are a few specifics of electronic discovery warranting special attention by the LNC. First, this is an ever-evolving area of litigation, so universally accepted guidelines defining the scope of electronic discovery have yet to be established by the courts. At this writing, as in all areas of the law, the LNC should understand the parameters governing this area will continue to be shaped and changed as judicial rulings and case law progress.

Second, early timing of the "preservation (or spoliation) letter," possibly as early as the pre-trial investigative period, is a key component of ESI. In matters where potential sources of information may be stored electronically, a letter or notice to opposing counsel is sent via certified mail or served in conformance with the jurisdiction's rules of court to protect and preserve such information. A well-crafted preservation letter will go a long way toward assisting the attorney in obtaining potentially discoverable information and preserving the information for the discovery process (Ball, 2008). The preservation letter ultimately seeks to prevent the destruction of ESI.

The LNC may play a pivotal role in identifying potential electronic information. For example, the LNC may be aware of the existence of videos and monitor tracings made as a matter of protocol when performing invasive medical procedures such as cardiac catheterization. The LNC should alert the attorney to the possible existence of these electronic formats and should consult with the attorney regarding the need to send a preservation letter to safeguard against the destruction or deletion of such evidence.

Finally, optimizing the production of ESI may require the involvement of an information technology (IT) expert. This role may be filled by in-house IT staff or an independent expert retained by the attorney for litigation support. Similar to the liaison role of the LNC in medical matters, the IT expert will clarify and translate unfamiliar terminology and processes, be familiar with the specifics of maintenance and disclosure of ESI, identify the likely locations and storage protocols of ESI, help establish the trail to the originating system, and alert the attorney to possible manipulation or deletion of materials, whether knowingly or unwittingly, by the adversary. E-discovery of medical records requires even more specialized expertise. While controversial, the amendments also make allowances forgoing sanctions for ESI lost or destroyed in the process of routine maintenance (Fed.R.Civ.P. 37(f) safe harbor provision, 2014; Appendix A).

Ethical Considerations for Discovery

In the true spirit of discovery, exchange of information not otherwise privileged or protected should occur in accordance with the relevant rules of civil procedure. In practice however, attempts to obstruct or evade discovery are not unheard of, and because the court does not directly oversee the process, the attorney exercises discretion regarding the nature and timing of what information to disclose and what items to produce. The ABA provides ethical direction for attorneys in the Model Rule of Professional Conduct 3.4: Fairness to opposing party and counsel. In part, the rule states that, "A lawyer shall not unlawfully obstruct another party's access to evidence or unlawfully alter, destroy or conceal a document or other material having potential evidentiary value. A lawyer shall not counsel or assist another person to do such act" (2018). Nonetheless, attorneys are bound to provide vigorous advocacy for their clients, which they may interpret to include resisting requests for discovery of material that may be prejudicial to their clients. Filing of motions to compel production and opposition to those motions, collectively referred to as "motion practice," often occur.

The Discovery Process

Motion Practice

The filing of one or more motions is often an integral part of the litigation process and the main area of judicial intervention in the discovery process. The filing of motions may begin as early as the investigative phase of case development and continue through trial. Motions are requests to the court to rule on a matter or take some specific action. Motions in trial may be made orally, e.g., a Motion to Strike Testimony, or in writing. Generally, in the discovery period, motions are made in writing and are accompanied by documents supporting the attorney's legal and factual position. As a rule, motions will involve a Notice of Motion specifying the time and date the motion will be heard by the bench (subject to change by the Court), the specific motion itself (often consisting of or including an attorney certification), exhibits (supporting documents), and a proposed form of judicial order granting the requested relief in case the judge finds in the moving party's favor. If the judge finds for the party requesting the motion, the order will be signed and filed with the court (see Appendix C).

Motions can be either dispositive or non-dispositive. Granting a dispositive motion, such as a motion for summary judgment, will dismiss or end the case or will decide an element of the litigation, such as liability. A non-dispositive motion will not have this effect even if granted. An example of a non-dispositive motion is a motion to compel discovery, in which the moving party asks the court to order another party to comply with demands for discovery, typically by a specified date. Whenever a motion is filed, the opposing attorney is permitted to file a response. Motions are presented to the motion judge, who may request oral arguments by the attorneys, after the Court rules on the request.

Roles of the Legal Nurse Consultant in the Discovery Process

The roles of LNCs during pre-trial discovery in plaintiff and defense cases are similar. Both roles require the identification of sources of potential information, which will likely support and give credence to the attorney's legal position. (See Chapter 7 for more information on sources of medical information.) Both plaintiff and defense LNCs will identify, strategize, and investigate the necessity of production of documents.

The plaintiff has the burden of proving the claim, so the LNC working for plaintiff's counsel has the task of supporting the plaintiff's claim under the attorney's direction. Discovery efforts are aimed at eliciting information that validates the allegations asserted by the plaintiff and revealing potential weaknesses in the adversary's anticipated and actual defenses. The LNC may work with plaintiff's experts to identify and obtain records and documents they will need for reports and testimony and to fill in gaps in information noted in the pre-suit period. Other discovery requests might explore and acquire information based on the defendant's answer to the complaint.

Since the burden of proof rests with the plaintiff, the defendant's LNC does not have the same challenge. Under the attorney's direction, the LNC's efforts are geared toward uncovering information that refutes the plaintiff's claims while exposing potential flaws in the adversary's legal strategy. The LNC's focus should be on exploring and acquiring information on each allegation asserted in the plaintiff's complaint and on the anticipated elements of plaintiff's litigation strategy.

Interrogatories

As a rule, interrogatories (aside from form interrogatories, previously discussed) are the initial tool of the discovery process. Interrogatories consist of written questions submitted by a party (the proponent) to the opposing party, who answers them under oath. In fact, the responses are often drafted by the attorney, with some information provided by the client. In general, the federal rules are more restrictive, allowing only 25 interrogatories (questions), without leave of court (judicial permission) or written stipulation (Fed.R.Civ.P. 33(a), 2014; Appendix A). Subparts to a question (sometimes known as "branch questions") are counted as separate toward the total. This is an area where states may dramatically diverge on discovery rules from the federal courts. For example, Delaware Superior Court follows the federal rules but does not specify a limit on the number of interrogatories that can be served on the opposing party (Del.R.Ann., 2007b). Again, the LNC should confirm the rules applicable in that state (see Appendix D).

Interrogatories, prior to the actual questions, may begin with instructions, definitions, clarifications, and clearly worded specifications of requested information. These clarifications may serve to circumvent unfounded objections to the request, such as uncertainty about the intended meaning of "communication" or "document" among other terms, but there is no guarantee.

The plaintiff LNC may draft interrogatories that inquire into board certifications, practical experience, and history of sanctions and disciplinary actions of the defendant, as well as facts at issue and treatment rendered, assuming such information was not already covered by form interrogatories. However, some attorneys prefer to cover those issues in deposition. In contrast, the defense's LNC would formulate questions about the plaintiff's medical history; information regarding injuries, accidents, and prior litigation; and any background information relevant to the case.

Both plaintiff and defense LNCs will shape questions designed to garner as much information as possible about the medical expert's opinion on the opposing side. Specifically, the interrogatories should seek to identify the basis of the expert's opinion. The LNC is most effective in establishing the literature or treatises to which the expert will turn, as well as recognized standards or protocols. The LNC should research and obtain any medical literature or authoritative sources identified by the opposing expert. The plaintiff's LNC will need to review the cost of obtaining such information with the attorney-client, because the cost is usually advanced by the plaintiff attorney, with the cost eventually recoverable from the client only if the litigation is successful. (This depends on the rules of court of the jurisdiction and the nature of the retainer agreement.) Conversely, the defendant's LNC will need to estimate the cost of obtaining such information with the attorney-client as the cost is passed on to the defendant client (generally the insurance carrier), so the number of billable hours to be used in obtaining the information, and any limits set by the contract with the client, may be determining factors.

The interrogatories may also be used to determine the existence of prior testimony by the expert. Obtaining the expert's prior transcripts allows the LNC to review previous statements made under oath for issues of bias or credibility. There are both private and commercial services that provide access to an expert's prior testimony. These "deposition banks" are usually searchable by the expert's name and are accessible for a fee or through membership. Some services may have restricted access for either plaintiff or defense firms.

Once responses to interrogatories are received, the LNC will review the answers, note any objections, and decide with the attorney if supplemental requests should be served.

Request for Production of Documents and Things

The request for production (RFP) is submitted to the opposing party to obtain key documents and other tangible items (records, photos, statements of witnesses, etc.) that would assist in proving or refuting the facts asserted in the complaint. The RFP is often filed simultaneously with the interrogatories, although this is not mandatory practice. The RFP again takes the form of a request, although in a statement (see Appendix E).

The rules require the receiving party to produce all requested information, not otherwise protected, within the party's "possession, custody, and control" pursuant to FRCP 34(a) (Fed.R.Civ.P., 2014; Appendix A). The fact the information is not immediately contained in the plaintiff's or defendant's file does not necessarily excuse production if the information is within the legal control of the party. For example, a plaintiff's medical records that predate the injuries alleged in the lawsuit are not necessarily in the plaintiff's or plaintiff counsel's immediate possession; however, the plaintiff and counsel are assumed to have control by using an appropriate authorization to obtain them. If there is no objection to the production, the responding party must be given at least 30 days to gather and produce the requested documents or items. State rules of court may eliminate the necessity of such requests by requiring plaintiffs to provide defense counsel with executed authorizations that are compliant with the Health Insurance Portability and Accountability Act of 1996 (HIPAA) and permit the release of protected health information.

From the plaintiff's perspective, the LNC's knowledge of the healthcare setting is used to make the attorney aware of the possible existence of videos, monitor tracings, films, internal reports, and written guidelines and policies intrinsic to procedures and treatment. This specialized knowledge also guides the requests to specify the appropriate department if the information is not kept with the primary chart. The plaintiff's LNC may investigate the defendant's history with regard to sanctions, disciplinary actions, and prior litigation if that function is not routinely performed by other personnel. Again, there are commercial services that will provide this information for a fee. In the case of a medical negligence action, the plaintiff attorney may serve a RFP to allow the LNC to inspect the original medical file (to look for inconsistencies with copies of the chart produced earlier). In some cases, billing statements from the hospitalization or for ancillary services may be requested and audited by the LNC. Billing statements will usually indicate medications dispensed, monitor use, invasive procedures, and equipment usage. In addition, billing statements often contain additional diagnosis and procedural codes for comparison with the chart. To use the LNC's time and skills more effectively, the attorney should determine the extent such information will be relevant to the claims advanced in the case.

Incident reports may be filed but not be incorporated into the chart. Quality assurance (QA) and peer review investigations are sometimes conducted in the case of an adverse outcome. The extent to which incident reports and the products of QA/peer review proceedings are subject to discovery varies among jurisdictions. Legal nurse consultants should determine whether such materials exist in a given case and recommend that they be obtained if they are discoverable.

From the defense vantage point, the LNC should closely scrutinize the plaintiff's present and past medical records for clues to alternative causation from pre-existing health problems, prior injuries, medication side effects, and issues of non-compliance. In the case of allegations of substantial cognitive injuries, the LNC may, in coordination with the defense neuropsychology or neurology expert, obtain school records to determine a baseline academic performance. In addition, the defense's LNC will want to obtain all pharmacy transmittals and consider requesting additional medical records of the plaintiff based on the identification of not-previously-identified healthcare providers who are copied on test results or records. Investigation such as surveillance tapes where permitted, previous insurance claims, income tax information for wage claims, and employment records for claims of lost earning capacity may yield valuable information.

Both the plaintiff and defense LNCs should review the adversary expert's CV (as well as their own expert's) with an eye for identifying and obtaining any publications the expert has authored relevant to the case. Critically analyzing these articles or texts for strengths and weaknesses can often provide valuable insight into the expert's position. The LNC should also be able to identify any professional resources, associations, licensing boards, certification boards, and practice acts, because they impact the issues. It is prudent to verify an expert's credentials, as well as to consult any available sources that would reveal lawsuits, payments made on the expert's behalf, and disciplinary actions. (For more information on researching expert witnesses, see Chapter 36.)

The RFP as a discovery tool also permits passage to "inspect the premises or enter the land" (Fed.R.Civ.P. 34(a), 2014; Appendix A). Inspection of electronic medical records at the point of entry in the form they appeared on the screen may yield information not available in print-outs, particularly after metadata and audit trails have been produced and analyzed. (For more information on electronic medical records, see Chapter 9.)

Both interrogatories and the RFP are subject to a requirement for supplementary responses if the original response is incorrect or incomplete or if new and relevant material is made known to the attorney (Fed.R.Civ.P. 26(e), 2014; Appendix A). It is also expected that answers to discovery will be generated in a "responsive manner." The responses are to be produced either as kept in the usual course of business or in a labeled and organized fashion that correlates to the numbered sequencing of the original request served (Fed.R.Civ.P. 34(b), 2014; Appendix A).

Organization and Follow-Up

Reviewing answers to interrogatories and taking inventory of opposing counsel's response to the RFP are essential steps throughout discovery. Responses that contain answers such as "to be provided" or boilerplate objections may be overlooked unless a tracking system is in place and uniformly utilized. By developing a system of follow-through, the LNC lays the groundwork for support should a motion to compel production be necessary. The in-house LNC will further assist the attorney by alerting of the possible need for supplemental interrogatories and requests for production, as well as supplemental responses as related to medical issues. By paying close attention to and respecting the attorney's and, ultimately, the court's deadlines, the LNC supports and enhances the attorney-client's legal strategy.

Requests for Admission

Federal Rule of Civil Procedure 36 (Appendix A) addresses the RFA as a discovery tool. The intent of the RFA is to limit the issues that will ultimately be presented at trial. These requests take the form of written factual statements served upon the other side, who must admit, deny, or object. If the receiving party does not deny or object to the admission statement(s) within 20 days of receiving the request, the statements are deemed admitted. Likewise, the receiving attorney may voluntarily admit to the requests. Regardless of how the statement is admitted, the effect will be the same; that fact will not have to be proven at trial. For example, if the defendant admitted that all the expenses incurred were valid medical expenses related to the injury the plaintiff sustained, *without conceding liability for the plaintiff's injury,* the total amount of medical bills would not have to be debated in trial (see Appendix F).

Under some state rules of civil procedure, however, RFAs are not limited to the discovery period. For example, the New Jersey Rules of Court specifically exempt RFAs from the constraints of the discovery calendar, meaning that RFAs may be served after the discovery end date has passed [N.J. Court Rules 4:24–1(a)]. This exemption highlights the role of RFAs in enhancing the efficiency of trials by reducing the number of issues that must be proven.

Deposition

Deposition practice is governed by FRCP 30 and 31 (Fed.R.Civ.P., 2014; Appendix A). More than any other tool in the discovery process, depositions may serve to provide vital information, facilitate negotiations, and reveal the strength or weakness of the opposing counsel's legal and factual position.

Some depositions are fact-finding missions. In addition to finding out what the witness knows, the deposition serves to size up the witness and develop an impression of how the witness would appear to a jury. The witness's demeanor, appearance, and method of delivery can dramatically influence settlement negotiations. Offers of settlement are often increased or withdrawn following the depositions of key witnesses.

Other depositions, particularly those of parties and experts, are intended to elicit opinions and admissions, including admissions of culpability or ignorance, that are so compelling that, from the plaintiff's perspective, a satisfactory settlement is all but assured, or from the defense perspective, the case will almost surely go to trial and no settlement will be discussed.

In all cases, however, the counsel involved are establishing the deposition record for use at trial (and sometimes at appeal), if the litigation proceeds that far. Counsel may ask questions about particular documents for the sole purpose of attaching them as exhibits to the deposition transcript, which facilitates their use as exhibits at trial (but does not guarantee admissibility). The LNC involved in providing deposition support for attorneys should keep in mind which records could be used as compelling trial exhibits and list those for use as potential exhibits at deposition.

Video Depositions

Due to distance, availability, or other constraints, it is sometimes necessary to take depositions by video or from a remote location via satellite. The decision to videotape a deposition is generally made to preserve testimony for trial due to the witness's lack of availability at the time, or location, of the trial. It is common, however, to have deponents give a discovery deposition in a location other than the attorney's office. Many litigation support services will make arrangements for witnesses to be deposed from a specific location, arranging for the court reporter and any equipment needed. Video depositions (even of the best witness) are not the most engaging testimony for the jurors; however, they have the advantage of being reviewed repeatedly to reveal the witness's nervous mannerisms and conflicting body language. Also, video depositions can be used to prepare the witness for giving trial testimony.

Role of the Legal Nurse Consultant in Deposition

Independent or in-house LNCs are likely to be involved from the outset with identifying witnesses for deposition and trial. They may be recruited to help draft deposition questions based on their review of medical records and the medical research conducted.

As the deposition nears, the LNC may become involved in the preparation of the attorney's expert medical witness. Familiarizing the witness with the deposition process will serve to assist with the deposition proceeding smoothly. A standard instruction to deponents reminds them that the court reporter will attempt to take down every word spoken in the deposition in order to prepare a transcript. If the case goes to trial, the transcript may be used to refresh the memory of the witness as to prior testimony, as well as to confront the witness with inconsistencies between sworn testimony at deposition and that at trial. The LNC may play a role in informing experts that they will be sworn in and should remember to answer each question verbally (instead of a nod or "uh-huh"). The LNC should remind the witness that, prior to the start of the recorded testimony, the court reporter will record every spoken word. For example, the expert should avoid talking out loud when looking for something in the medical record, as this would be recorded and transcribed and, when reviewed, may read as though the expert is unprepared or disorganized. Witnesses should also be cautioned against the use of sarcasm or irony, as the tone they use to convey that sense will not appear in the deposition transcript.

It is helpful, if known, to inform the expert of the deposing attorney's style of questioning (i.e., friendly, aggressive, pressured, etc.). While there is no formula approach to expert testimony, the retaining attorney may wish to discuss how hypothetical questions and matters of the expert's fee should be addressed. Additionally, procedural matters such as waiving the reading of the deposition transcript and the purpose of the *errata sheet* should be reviewed with the expert (in jurisdictions that permit or require such a procedure).

When it is used, the errata sheet is sent to the deponent's counsel, so the witness will have the opportunity to correct any transcription errors with regard to their testimony. Factual changes should not be made to the testimony. Rather, only technical errors on the part of the stenographer who took down the testimony or the service that produced the transcription should be corrected. A disclaimer on the errata itself addresses the fact that any changes are also assumed to be under oath. Some LNCs may be involved in tracking through the discovery process whether the expert completed an errata sheet following their deposition.

It is important to review with the expert that objections in deposition are handled differently from those in trial. Objections in discovery depositions are made to preserve the issue for trial and, as such, are not ruled on until that time. The reasoning is simple; the judge is not there to rule on each and every objection. Stopping the deposition to call the judge for each objection is neither practical nor likely to be appreciated. Once the objection is made, witnesses should pause for instruction from their attorney and should anticipate the attorney may instruct them to go ahead with their answer. By placing the objection on record, the attorney has reserved the issue for the judge to rule on either prior to or during trial. (For more information on preparing expert witnesses for deposition, see Chapter 36.)

The LNC may be asked to accompany the attorney to the deposition of the opposing side's expert medical witness or medical fact witnesses (such as subsequent treating providers). The LNC in this role should be aware of the attorney-client's style and preference in questioning. While most of the LNC's questions will be drafted and reviewed with the attorney prior to the actual deposition, during the deposition the expert may reference something that triggers a follow-up question from the LNC's educated perspective. If the LNC has questions to suggest during the deposition, the attorney and LNC should determine *prior* to the deposition how this should be communicated without obvious interruption and the extent to which simple techniques such as passing notes are desirable or permissible. Some law firms may use technology, including instant messaging, to allow the LNC to provide specialized input to the deposing attorney.

The LNC may formulate a question or point that would be invaluable to the case, only to have the attorney ignore it and conclude questioning. The LNC should not pursue this issue at deposition. It is imperative to understand attorneys are constantly forming legal strategy and may reserve this question for trial because of its significance. Conversely, the attorney may choose not to use this question even in trial because, by doing so, it may open the door to issues the attorney does not want to introduce. The LNC's role, in part, is to appreciate that the lead attorney is the only one who can ultimately decide how to present the case.

Upon entering the deposition room, the LNC will follow the attorney's lead but should anticipate presenting a business card to the court reporter, who will record the LNC's name and title as among those present for the deposition. The court reporter may need to note the reason for the LNC's attendance (i.e., whether with plaintiff or defense counsel).

The court reporter is arranged for and paid by the counsel requesting the deposition. The attorney will generally not require the attendance of both the paralegal and the LNC. If the attorney specifically wants an electronic version of the transcript (in addition to a paper copy), the LNC can make this known to the court reporter at deposition. When received, the e-transcript should contain a hyperlink to the free software needed to view the transcript. The receiving party will need to click on (open) this link and download the program to their computer to view the transcript. Attorneys who are comfortable with the technology may find use of digital versions of the transcript very convenient for use at trial. Instead of paging through a paper transcript to find a specific item to, for example, challenge witness testimony (and impeach the credibility of the witness), counsel can perform a string search leading directly to the relevant page and line.

During the deposition, the LNC will assist the attorney by taking notes; identifying follow-up questions; noting observations about eye contact, cues, and body language of the expert witness; identifying potential non-verbal coaching of the deponent by the adversary; recording any inconsistencies in opinion; and noting any areas that need further review. It is helpful to the attorney if the LNC can provide feedback after the deposition regarding the expert's approach to teaching and explanation, as well as impression of the expert's credibility. It is good practice to have a copy of the outline of the questioning by the attorney. While rare, if any question were missed, the LNC would be able to subtly call it to the attorney's attention.

It is helpful for the LNC to track exhibits during deposition by noting which side produces what information. The original exhibits at deposition are returned to the party producing them; however, copies of the exhibits should be included when transcripts of the deposition are received. Be sure to collect any exhibits that belong to the attorney-client after providing a copy for the court reporter. The *original* deposition transcript will ultimately be presented at trial and should be kept separate. In the interim, the attorney will work off a duplicate copy of the deposition transcript or a copy saved directly to the attorney's computer as in the case of an e-transcript.

It is essential for the LNC to take detailed notes if expected to prepare a memorandum summarizing the deposition. An in-depth discussion of deposition memos is beyond the scope of this chapter, but they may take different forms. One may be a summary prepared shortly after the deposition, based on notes taken and additional information, such as lists of exhibits. Another may be a digest, discussed below, which is prepared after the transcript is available, using information from the transcript which may be supplemented by notes taken during the deposition regarding observations that would not appear in the transcript.

Role of the Expert Witness in Deposition

It is the court's expectation that expert witnesses will offer an honest, well-supported opinion within the scope of their expertise. Based on FRE 702 (2014; Appendix B), the expert brings an opinion to the table that is qualified by "knowledge, skill, experience, training, or education." The distinctions between those terms are rarely relevant, but readers will note there is a significant degree of overlap. The opposing medical experts will offer conflicting opinions as to duty, breach of duty, proximate cause, and extent and permanency of injury. Attorneys are, of course, familiar with their expert's opinion prior to the deposition and have received and reviewed the written opinion of each adversary's expert witness.

Therefore, the deposition process is the opportunity for the attorney to find out in detail what the opposing expert is expected to say at trial. In addition, it provides the attorney with the opportunity to size-up the expert witness and ideally eliminate any surprise testimony. It can safely be assumed the attorneys in medical malpractice matters will want to depose one another's medical expert witnesses and will send a notice of intent to do so.

Depending on the attorney and expert's experience, the preparation of the expert witness may precede the taking of the deposition by several days or be a brief office, telephone, or video consultation shortly before the deposition. Regardless of the time reserved for preparation, the attorney should have provided the expert with all the necessary medical documentation and pertinent information well in advance of the expert's deposition. In general, those materials would have been used in the preparation of the expert's report. The attorney should also have reviewed with the expert what materials used in the report preparation and which communications with the attorney's office (if any) are not discoverable. In some jurisdictions, drafts of expert reports are not normally subject to discovery.

In return, it is the expert's professional duty to be familiar with the information provided by the retaining attorney in order to deliver an effective deposition. Materials that should be forwarded to the expert include:

1. complete medical records relevant to the matter being litigated
2. deposition transcripts of all healthcare providers, the parties, and, if relevant, other witnesses
3. opinions and the deposition transcript (when available) of the adversary's expert
4. literature or treatises the attorney intends to reference
5. relevant policies and procedures of the institution, facility, or office practice and
6. any other information that has a bearing on the expert's ability to provide an informed opinion

Federal and state rules may differ on the mandatory requirement of current or active clinical practice for qualifying an expert witness; however, this question should be anticipated at deposition and in trial as a strategy to establish or impeach credibility of the witness (see Appendix G).

One common pitfall of expert testimony is when the attorney (or staff) fails to ensure the expert has received all the updated medical information and dispositive information concerning the plaintiff. More than one expert (and chagrined attorney) has been taken by surprise when the expert's testimony is discredited during deposition because of not having received updated medical records and recent depositions given by parties to the litigation. While including, in the expert's report, the reservation of the right to amend one's opinion (should additional information become available) may help to address such an occurrence, it may cost the expert a measure of credibility in the opinions offered, as the expert's attorney must now rehabilitate the expert's testimony through follow-up questioning. The LNC may be asked to review with the expert what materials will be presented or available for the deposition. This procedure serves various ends. One, it assures that the attorney may become aware of documents the expert should have or does not have. Another is to prevent the expert from making available documents that are not discoverable, whether due to privilege or any other reason. It is helpful for the LNC (and the expert) to discuss with the attorney whether the file should be "sanitized," which is to say, purged of handwritten notes, sticky notes, etc. In some jurisdictions, any of those materials may be discoverable and should be preserved; in others, they are not and should be destroyed. That determination is made by the attorney. Having a standardized system for documenting what materials are sent to the expert helps the LNC and the attorney to determine if any further items are required and may even be used to remind the expert of what has already been provided. In some jurisdictions, experts are expected to list the materials they have reviewed, and counsel may be required to disclose what materials were provided to the expert.

From a plaintiff's perspective, when the deposition occurs in the defendant's or expert's office, the LNC should note what textbooks, patient educational materials, and references are present on the shelves. It is hard for all but the most astute expert to deny the reliability of a text or reference kept on the shelf as a resource. For the defendant's or medical expert's deposition, the LNC for the defense attorney or for the retaining attorney may suggest the deposition occur in a conference room or area other than the defendant's or expert's private office.

Digesting the Deposition

Digesting a deposition may be done by the attorney's junior associate, paralegal, or law clerk. However, given the nature of complex information in a medical negligence case, the attorney may prefer the LNC to summarize the deposition. There are a variety of ways to do this, but it largely depends on the attorney's personal preference. One technique involves noting or highlighting every entry of a keyword or statement by page and line number. Another practice is to provide the attorney with a document listing these entries. For example, to provide the attorney with a document that shows every time the expert referred to "dehydration" in the deposition, the document would read "dehydration" 3:21, 4:24, 7:18, and so on (i.e., references in the deposition to "dehydration" can be found on page 3, line 21; page 4, line 24; etc.). Some deposition transcripts automatically have this word index included when received from the stenographer or transcription service.

Yet another technique involves contrasting and comparing the written records (expert report or medical record) with the deposition for inconsistencies in opinion or facts. Whether this is done by hand or via a software program depends on the attorney's practice. These key passages or inconsistencies in statements may later be enlarged, highlighted, and used as exhibits in trial. Case management software can save countless hours of manual production by electronically organizing and digesting depositions if the attorney-client's budget allows for this type of technology.

Physical and Mental Examinations

As an additional discovery methodology, the defense is permitted to request the plaintiff attend a defense medical examination or independent medical exam pursuant to FRCP 35 (Fed.R.Civ.P., 2014; Appendix A) or relevant state rules. In its purest form, the medical examination is meant to provide an objective opinion regarding the nature, extent, and permanency of the plaintiff's injuries.

The healthcare provider conducting the examination is retained and paid by the side requesting the examination (the defense). This invites the debate of whether the exam can be truly objective or unbiased. Given the inherent conflict, this practice is likely responsible for the variety of acronyms associated with the exam: independent medical exam (IME), defense medical exam (DME), plaintiff medical exam (PME), or expert medical exam (EME). Regardless of the label, the purpose remains to substantiate the extent and permanency of injuries as related to the plaintiff's allegations.

The plaintiff LNC may be asked to attend the exam with the plaintiff and provide a report of the findings to the attorney. If psychological issues of the plaintiff are at issue, some rules of court may require that "good cause" be established by the defense before obtaining a mental examination. As it pertains to the discovery process, whether a physical or psychological evaluation, the plaintiff is entitled to receive a copy of the provider's report detailing the examination findings and ultimate opinion. (For more information on defense medical examinations, see Chapter 6.)

Subpoenas

One of the advantages to initiating litigation is the power of a subpoena. Prior to filing a suit, requests for information such as medical records may go unanswered, be subject to significant delays, and result in the receipt of incomplete records. Federal Rule of Civil Procedure 45 (Appendix A) governs the production of documents and things (and testimony) of non-parties. The equivalent state laws and rules of civil procedure apply to proceedings in state courts.

A Notice of Deposition and a Notice of Records Deposition address the appearance and production of documents at deposition with regard to deponent *parties* to the litigation. A simple *subpoena* is used to compel the attendance of a *non-party* deponent or witness. A *subpoena duces tecum* is issued to require a non-party to produce documents. For example, a medical records custodian may be served with a *subpoena duces tecum* to produce the requested documents in person on or before a specified date and location. If the records custodian produces the requested information to the requesting party on or before the specified date, the custodian's physical appearance is not required (see Appendix H). This also applies under many state rules. Although the HIPAA Privacy Rule allows HIPAA-covered entities who are not party to the legal proceeding to release protected personal health information in response to a subpoena (with certain restrictions), it is advisable to accompany the subpoena with a HIPAA-compliant authorization executed by the patient or authorized representative to expedite the process (Health & Human Services, 2013). Some states have specific language that must be included in a medical records *subpoena duces tecum* to comply with HIPAA notice regulations, so the person preparing the *subpoena duces tecum* should check with the locality to ensure the required wording is included. Depending on the jurisdiction, mental health records may not be subject to subpoena. In that case, a court order may be required.

Scheduling, Status, and Final Pre-trial Conferencing

The scheduling conference in federal cases may be held prior to any discovery or may occur after some discovery has been obtained [Fed.R.Civ.P. 16(b), 2014; Appendix A]. In state courts, this is highly variable, and some chief judges or motion judges schedule case management conferences very early in litigation. Such an initial meeting provides a framework for important dates related to the litigation process. It is scheduled and conducted by the judge assigned to the case, and it requires the attendance of the attorneys representing the parties involved, although the parties themselves do not attend. During this conference, issues of undisputed facts are determined, matters of law may be discussed, and the potential for settlement is reviewed. If settlement is unlikely, a trial date may be set.

From the scheduling or case management conference, a proposed scheduling order of key dates is generated, either by the court or by one of the parties at the request of the court. The scheduling order specifies when the exchange of discovery documents will stop, when the plaintiff's expert report will be due, when the defendant's expert report will be due, the date by which depositions must be taken, and the date all pre-trial motions should be filed. The order also provides basic instructions of procedure.

Status conferences (interim meetings) between the judge and counsel may occur between the scheduling conference and the pre-trial conference. As the trial date nears, the final pre-trial conference is scheduled pursuant to FRCP 16(d) (2014; Appendix A) or per state rules of court. The purpose of the pre-trial conference is to dispose of duplicative matters, finalize legal positions, address any preliminary objections, exchange pre-trial briefs outlining the key elements of trial including potential exhibits, and encourage settlement if such is possible.

Seasoned LNCs may find that familiarity with the judge's particular style and "standing orders" further assists them in maximizing efficiency in the discovery period, e.g., knowing the judge's personal bias toward granting or denying pre-trial motions filed to extend time in the discovery process. Some judges are more likely to deny an extension of time past the original scheduling date in order to keep the docket of cases moving. Other judges will entertain such requests as long as all attorneys stipulate (voluntarily agree) to the extension, and the request for additional time is reasonable.

Spoliation and Fraudulent Concealment

"The intentional destruction, mutilation, alteration, or concealment of evidence" is termed spoliation (Garner, 2014, p. 1620). In response to proof of spoliation, the trial judge may allow an instruction to the jury that the missing evidence may be assumed unfavorable to the party responsible. The difficulty in establishing spoliation of evidence lies in the remedy itself. It may be impossible to counterbalance the damage done by the destruction if there is no evidence to view and quantify the degree of prejudice the affected party has sustained.

Fraudulent concealment refers to the intentional suppression of a material fact or circumstance with the intent to deceive or defraud despite a legal or moral duty to disclose (Garner, 2014, p. 349). For example, a physician fails to disclose that a physician partner committed malpractice on a patient now under the second physician's care. As it applies to healthcare provider negligence, fraudulent concealment may toll (suspend or stop) the statute of limitations until the plaintiff discovers or should have discovered the negligence.

Both the chain of custody form and evidence log may be helpful in tracking and locating discoverable evidence and instrumental in establishing or defeating the charge of willful obstruction in the discovery process.

Summary

The in-house and independent LNC and the expert witness who master a basic understanding of the ethical guidelines and rules that govern the process of discovery stand ready to assist the attorney in the presentation of a formidable case or in the vigorous defense of a defendant. By staying informed of evolving case law, rules of court, and advancing technology, the LNC promotes the intent of the law in the exchange of information. By displaying integrity and professionalism in the discovery process, the LNC demonstrates the essence of the profession. These attributes combined make the LNC an invaluable member of the attorney's litigation team.

References

American Bar Association Model Rules of Professional Conduct 1.16(a). (2018). Retrieved from www.americanbar.org/groups/professional_responsibility/publications/model_rules_of_professional_conduct/rule_1_16_declining_or_terminating_representation/.

American Bar Association Model Rules of Professional Conduct 1.6. (2018). Retrieved from www.americanbar.org/groups/professional_responsibility/publications/model_rules_of_professional_conduct/rule_1_6_confidentiality_of_information/.

American Bar Association Model Rules of Professional Conduct 1.7. (2018). Retrieved from www.americanbar.org/groups/professional_responsibility/publications/model_rules_of_professional_conduct/rule_1_7_conflict_of_interest_current_clients/.

American Bar Association Model Rules of Professional Conduct 3.4. (2018). Retrieved from www.americanbar.org/groups/professional_responsibility/publications/model_rules_of_professional_conduct/rule_3_4_fairness_to_opposing_party_counsel/.

Ball, C. (2008). Piecing together the e-discovery plan. *Trial*, June, 20–29.

Del.R.Ann. Vol. I. Del.Super.Ct.R.Civ.P., Appendix of Forms 30 (2007a).

Del.R.Ann. Vol. I. Del.Super.Ct.R.Civ.P., 33(a) (2007b).

Federal Rule of Civil Procedure 26. (2015). Retrieved from www.federalrulesofcivilprocedure.org/frcp/title-v-disclosures-and-discovery/rule-26-duty-to-disclose-general-provisions-governing-discovery/.

Federal Rules of Civil Procedure with forms. (2014). Committee Print No. 8, 113th Congress, 2nd Session. Retrieved from www.uscourts.gov/sites/default/files/Rules%20of%20Civil%20Procedure.

Federal Rules of Evidence. (2014). Committee Print No. 10, 113th Congress, 2nd Session. Retrieved from www.uscourts.gov/sites/default/files/Rules%20of%20Evidence.

Garner, B. A. (Ed.). (2014). *Black's law dictionary* (10th ed.). St Paul, MN: Thompson Reuters.

Health & Human Services. (2013). FAQ: May a covered entity that is not a party to a legal proceeding disclose protected health information in response to a subpoena, discovery request, or other lawful process that is not accompanied by a court order? U.S. Department of Health & Human Services. Retrieved from www.hhs.gov/hipaa/for-professionals/faq/711/may-a-covered-entity-not-party-to-legal-proceedings-disclose-information-by-court-order/index.html.

Hickman v. Taylor, 329 U.S., 495 (1947).

N.J. Court Rules 4:10 (Rules governing the courts of the State of New Jersey—Rule 4:10. Pretrial discovery).

N.J. Court Rules 4:24–1(a) (Rules governing the courts of the State of New Jersey—Rule 4:24. Time for completion of discovery and other pretrial proceedings).

Supreme Court of the United States. (2006). Federal rules of civil procedures amended. Retrieved from www.supremecourtus.gov/orders/courtorders/frcv06p.pdf.

Upjohn Co. v. U.S., 449 U.S., 389 (1981).

U.S. Constitution Amendment X.

Test Questions

1. In response to a valid deposition notice, FRCP 30(b)(6) imposes all of the following duties on the named corporation EXCEPT:
   A. The duty to designate
   B. The duty to negotiate
   C. The duty to prepare
   D. The duty to substitute
2. The purpose of an errata sheet following a deposition is to
   A. Make factual changes to the testimony
   B. Waive the reading of the deposition
   C. Provide the deponent with the opportunity to change opinions
   D. Correct mistakes in the deponent's testimony due to transcription error
3. The attorney work-product doctrine functions to
   A. Protect the attorney/client communications with regard to legal representation
   B. Protect the testifying expert's opinion from discovery
   C. Protect materials prepared by the attorney in anticipation of litigation
   D. Protect confidential information even if inadvertently disclosed
4. All of the following are true about subpoenas EXCEPT:
   A. They are subject to the rules of the court of proper jurisdiction
   B. They are served on non-parties to the litigation
   C. They may be the subject of a Motion to Compel Discovery
   D. The receiving party must pay the cost of serving the subpoena
5. All of the following are true about objections to Interrogatories EXCEPT:
   A. The objection(s) must be timely filed
   B. The objection(s) must specify the exact reason for the objection
   C. In a multipart question, the respondent does not need to answer the question at all if objecting to any part of the question
   D. May be avoided if definitions and clarifications of terms are provided at the beginning of the document

Answers: 1. B, 2. D, 3. C, 4. D, 5. C

Appendix A: Summary of Select Federal Rules of Civil Procedure in the Pre-trial Period

The following is a summary of select FRCP in the pre-trial period. It is not meant to be an exhaustive list. Due to the complexity of the FRCP, only *excerpts* of the discovery rules more commonly encountered by the LNC are listed. The specific examples given are for illustrative purposes only. The FRCP may be found online at www.law.cornell.edu/rules/frcp/.

Federal Rule of Civil Procedure	Description and Examples
FRCP 3: Commencement of an Action	Filing the complaint.
FRCP 4: Summons	A court's written order (writ) requiring the defendant to appear in Court. The sheriff is directed to summon the defendant via the writ.
FRCP 5: Service of process	When the complaint and summons have been served to the defendant.
FRCP 7: Pleadings and motions	Speaks to the form each document must take.
FRCP 8: General rules of pleadings	The necessary legal elements and inclusions to properly form a complaint and answer according to court rules.
FRCP 8(a): Claims for relief FRCP 8(b): Defenses FRCP 8(c): Affirmative defenses	
FRCP 12: Answer	The defendant must respond to the plaintiff's complaint or file a motion to dismiss based on the perceived inadequacy of the complaint.
FRCP 13: Counterclaims and cross-claims	A counterclaim is a claim asserted by the defendant against the plaintiff. For example, the plaintiff filed suit against the defendant for the defendant's responsibility in a motor vehicle accident. The defendant counter sues, alleging the plaintiff was at fault. A cross-claim occurs when two or more parties being sued (defendants) believe one or the other should bear the liability. For example, a plaintiff slips and falls on ice in a parking lot. The property owner and the snow removal company are sued. The property owner files a cross-claim against the snow removal company for liability (i.e., they did not remove the snow as contracted, and the fault is theirs).
FRCP 16: Pretrial conference	Close to the trial date, the Pre-trial Conference is conducted to resolve pending matters, simplify the issues, and view and address objections to the intended exhibits and other legal matters. The judge has been provided with a pre-trial brief from each individual counsel.
FRCP 26(a)(1–5) FRCP 26(b)(1–5) FRCP 26(c–g)	Rules regarding discovery including duty to supplement responses, objections, privilege of materials, disclosure, and relevancy.

Appendix A Continued

Federal Rule of Civil Procedure	Description and Examples
FRCP 26(b)(1): Expert Witness Written Report	Addresses the disclosure of the identity of the expert witness, the written opinion of the expert, the reasons for the expert's opinion, the expert's qualifications and list of publications for the past 10 years, the expert's compensation, and the identification of cases in which the expert has been deposed or testified in the last 4 years.
FRCP 26(b)(3): Trial preparation: Materials	Provides limited protection to otherwise discoverable trial preparation and work-product materials. The work-product protection applies only to documents prepared in anticipation of litigation.
FRCP 26(b)(4): Trial preparation: Experts	Parties may depose expert witnesses who may testify at trial.
FRCP 26(b)(5): Claims of privilege or protection of trial preparation materials	The party withholding the information as privilege must provide the opposing side with the nature of documents or information to enable the opposing party to assess the claim of privilege.
FRCP 26(b)(5)(c): Covers the right to file a Motion for a Protective Order	For example, a trademark secret (such as a secret recipe) might otherwise harm a company's competitive standing in business if the information was made public by revealing the ingredients to its competitors, or a motion may be filed by defense counsel in insurance litigation to protect the claims-handling policies and procedures of a company.
FRCP 26(b)(5)(e): Addresses the duty to supplement responses to discovery	Answers must be supplemented when information that was initially correct but now no longer true or new relevant information has been made known to the party.
FRCP 27: Depositions before an action or pending appeal	For example, the plaintiff is terminal and may not live to testify at trial. A video deposition may be taken in advance of filing the complaint. This deposition is known as *de bene esse* (Latin for "of well-being") and is taken in anticipation of a future need.
FRCP 30: Deposition upon oral exam	Governs the guidelines for taking depositions.
FRCP 30(b)(5): Provides that a *party* to the litigation can be compelled to bring documents or tangible things to a deposition for examination, copying, and inquiry	For example, the designated representative of a 30(b)(5) notice is instructed to bring a written list of storage protocols for the defendant's information technology department.
FRCP 30(b)(6): Permits a party to notice the deposition of an organization's key representative and specify "the matters on which examination is requested"	In response to the notice, the organization must designate one or more individuals to testify on its behalf. These individuals must have knowledge of the subjects described in the deposition notice.

continued

Appendix A Continued

Federal Rule of Civil Procedure	Description and Examples
FRCP 31: Depositions upon written questions	Counsel may request a written deposition because the deponent is incarcerated and unable to be released from custody to attend.
FRCP 33: Interrogatories to parties	Written questions served to the opposing party that requires responses and are asserted under oath by the means of a signed affidavit testifying to the truthfulness of the answers.
FRCP 34: Request for production	Requests generated for tangible items, such as documents, tapes, photos, equipment, reports, etc.
FRCP 34(a): Documents and things	Also, allows for site inspections.
FRCP 35: Request for physical and/or mental exam	Physical exam: The defendant's counsel has the right to have the plaintiff examined by a physician of the defense's choosing to evaluate the alleged injuries asserted in the complaint. Mental exam: For example, the plaintiff alleges depression as a result of the injuries sustained in a motor vehicle accident. Conversely, a showing of "good cause" to obtain a mental examination will be required of the moving party if the plaintiff has not put a mental condition at issue.
FRCP 36: Request for admissions: To limit the issues that will need to be presented at trial	For example, if the plaintiff requests that the defendant admit that the total amount of the medical bills in question is related to the injury, and the defendant admits the matter, there is no longer a question of fact regarding that issue for the jury to decide, making the trial more efficient. This is not an admission of liability; the trier(s) of fact will still need to determine if the defendant is liable for the injury.
FRCP 37: Motion to compel and sanctions for failure to make discovery	For example, the defendant fails to produce the requested information despite the time frame allowed and repeated requests by plaintiff's counsel. A Motion to Compel will be filed with the court, and all attempts at requesting the documents should be attached as exhibits to show the court the effort made to obtain them. In reality, actually imposing sanctions (monetary or otherwise) for failure to comply with discovery requests is largely determined by the individual practice of the judge.
FRCP 45: Subpoena	Compels a *non-party* to appear for deposition or testimony. For example, the attorney for the plaintiff may want to take the deposition of a security guard that saw the plaintiff fall in the parking lot.
FRCP 45: Subpoena *duces tecum*	The attorney may issue a subpoena *duces tecum* to the *non-party* custodian of medical records to bring the requested documents to a specified time and place. If the records are produced on or before the specified date, the custodian need not appear.

Appendix B: Summary of Select Federal Rules of Evidence

The following is a summary of select FREs that commonly impact the discovery process. It is not meant to be an exhaustive list or an exact citation of the rules. The specific examples given are for illustrative purposes only. To view the complete FRE online, go to www.law.cornell.edu/rules/fre.

Article IV	*Relevancy and its Limits*
FRE 401: Definition of "relevant evidence"	Evidence that supports or refutes the material facts at issue.
FRE 403: Exclusion of relevant evidence on grounds of prejudice, confusion, or waste of time	"The Balancing Test." Gives judge authority to rule whether the evidence's probative (tendency to prove) value outweighs its prejudicial effect. For example, the judge must decide if an enlarged photo exhibit of a ventilator-dependent infant is too inflammatory (plays on the emotions of the jury) or if it is necessary to show what the parents are dealing with each day to determine damages.
FRE 409: Payment of medical and similar expenses	Offers or promises to pay medical expenses related to the injury in question, cannot be admitted as proof of liability.

Article V	*Privileges*
FRE 502: Lawyer-client	The client has the privilege to refuse to disclose and to prevent any other person from disclosing confidential communications made for the purpose of facilitating the rendition of professional legal services to the client. This duty to preserve confidences extends to those acting as the attorney's agent as well.
FRE 503: Mental health providers, physicians, psychotherapist-patient	For example, neither a physician nor those in his employ are permitted to disclose the patient's terminal condition to the family in the absence of the patient's express permission.
FRCP 503(2) and (3): Exceptions to privilege	An example is a court-ordered medical examination, because the plaintiff's injury or condition is an element of the claim.
FREFRE 507: Trade secrets	For example, if the trade secret becomes public knowledge, the party will suffer financial harm due to marketplace competition.
FRE 510: Waiver of privilege by voluntary disclosure	For example, the plaintiff is interviewed by the attorney regarding the events. The plaintiff insists that a family member stay and gives permission for this family member to be present for the conversation. The plaintiff has waived privilege should the opposing counsel call the family member to testify.

Article VI	*Witnesses*
FRE 612: Writings used to refresh memory	For example, at deposition, the witness may be asked to recall who was on duty in the emergency department the night of the alleged negligence. The witness is permitted to view the emergency department record to refresh the witness's memory, if needed.

continued

Appendix B Continued

FRE 613: Prior statements of witnesses	For example, prior deposition testimony or written opinion that is contradictory to the position an expert now asserts in the current litigation.

Article VII	*Opinions and Expert Testimony*
FRE 702: Testimony by experts	In matters too complex or technical for average jurors to understand, an expert witness of specialized knowledge and education may testify to aid their understanding. For example, the expert may testify about how to interpret arterial blood gases and how recognizing the patient's respiratory deterioration may have prevented the anoxic event the plaintiff suffered.
FRE 703: Basis of opinion testimony by experts	The materials and information relied upon by experts in forming their opinions are not necessarily admitted as evidence. For example, the expert witness testifies the patient's symptoms were consistent with the presentation found in the *Principles of Neurology*, 8th edition. While the expert relies on this information, it would be too cumbersome for the jury to review the text in its deliberations, so it will not be admitted as evidence.
FRE 705: Disclosure of facts or data underlying expert opinion	The materials and information relied upon by experts in forming their opinion are not necessarily to be produced for the court; however, the court reserves the right to require production.
FRE 706: Court-appointed experts	The parties may agree upon an independent witness or the court on its own volition can appoint an independent expert witness. For example, in *Daubert v. Merrell Dow Pharmaceuticals*, due to conflicting opinions, the court appointed three impartial witnesses.

Article VIII	*Hearsay*
FRE 803: Hearsay exceptions; availability of declarant immaterial	As a general rule, hearsay is inadmissible. Below are a few exceptions to hearsay, thereby admissible.
FRE 803(4): Statements for purposes of medical diagnosis or treatment	For instance, a nurse practitioner tells the jury that the physician told her the child had a urinary tract infection.
FRE 803(6): Records of regular conducted activity	For example, medical records, billing statements, on-call schedules for staff physicians, etc.
FRE 803(8): Public records and reports	For example, public health statistics or information found at under the Freedom of Information Act (www.foia.gov).
FRE 803(18): Learned treatises	For example, a core textbook used for medical students might be considered a learned treatise. Because it would be unrealistic for the author to appear to testify to its authenticity, as long as the expert witness recognizes the text as reliable, the expert can testify to the information within.

Appendix B Continued

Article IX	Authentication and Identification
FRE 901(a): Requirement of authentication or identification	For example, the need to identify and authenticate voice recognition or handwriting.

Article X	Contents of writings, recordings, and photographs
FRE 1002: Requirement of original	For example, if a Polaroid photo of a ventilator-dependent plaintiff is enlarged to be used as a trial exhibit, the original Polaroid photo should be available for examination by the Court.
FRE 1003: Admissibility of duplicates	For example, a certified copy of the plaintiff's medical record will be accepted in lieu of the original record.
FRE 1006: Summaries	For example, if the contents of the plaintiff's medical records are too voluminous to be examined in court, then a summary or chart of the medical records may be presented. The original or copy of the medical records summarized should be available for the Court.

Appendix C: Samples of Motion Practice

The following are samples of Motion Practice as they pertain to the FRCP in the pre-trial period. It is not meant to be an exhaustive list regarding the FRCP in filing motions. Due to the complexity of the FRCP, only *excerpts* of the motions more commonly encountered by the LNC in the pre-trial period are listed. The specific examples given are for illustrative purposes only.

Motion Practice	Description and Examples
Motion to Enlarge Time: FRCP 6(b)	For example, the Sheriff was not able to serve the defendants at their last known address. As the 120 days to perfect service nears, the plaintiff's attorney may wish to file a motion to permit an extension of time in which to serve the defendants. Otherwise, plaintiff's attorney would risk dismissal of the complaint.
Motion to Amend: FRCP 7(b)	For example, as the plaintiff's attorney is made aware of additional defendants in a medical malpractice action, it may be necessary to amend the complaint to add parties.
Motion to Dismiss (may also be asserted as defenses to the complaint): FRCP 12(b)(1–7)	May be based on: ■ Lack of jurisdiction over the subject matter ■ Lack of jurisdiction over person ■ Improper venue ■ Insufficiency of process ■ Insufficiency of service of process ■ Failure to state a claim upon which relief can be granted ■ Failure to join a party (under FRCP 19)

continued

Appendix C Continued

Motion Practice	*Description and Examples*
Motion for Protective Order: FRCP 26(c)	For example, the plaintiff's attorney is requesting to schedule a third deposition of the defendant company's maintenance supervisor. Without a showing of "good cause," the court will likely grant the defendant's motion based on a finding of annoyance and undue burden.
Motion to Compel Discovery: FRCP 37(a)	For example, the plaintiff's attorney has repeatedly requested fetal monitor tracings from the hospital's labor and delivery unit for several months. The attorney has provided a HIPAA-compliant authorization each time and spoke with defense counsel several times regarding this request with no response. The subpoena *duces tecum* was served and has gone unanswered. The plaintiff's attorney will likely assemble documentation of the attempts to secure the information, as well as applicable case law, and attach them as exhibits in support of a motion to compel.
Motion for Summary Judgment (as a Matter of Law): FRCP 56	May be filed after an adequate period of discovery. The purpose of the motion is to request the court to enter judgment without a trial. For example, the defendant's counsel files the motion on the grounds there is insufficient evidence to support a verdict in the plaintiff's favor (i.e., there is no genuine issue of material fact to be decided by the jury).

Appendix D: Sample Interrogatories

Court of Jurisdiction

	:	
John Q. Smith,	:	C.A. No.: 04-123-ABC
	:	
Plaintiff,	:	
	:	Non-arbitration Case
v.	:	
	:	
Healthcare Hospital, a hospital corporation, and Max I. Millan, M.D.	:	Jury Trial by Twelve Persons Demanded
	:	
Defendants.	:	
	:	
	:	
	:	
	:	

Plaintiff's Second Set of Interrogatories Directed to Defendant Hospital

These interrogatories are of a continuing nature; therefore, the answers should be kept current.

Throughout these interrogatories, whenever you are requested to "identify" a communication of any type, and such communication was oral, the following information should be furnished:

a. By whom it was made and to whom it was directed
b. Its specific subject
c. The date upon which it was made
d. Who else was present when it was made
e. Whether it was recorded, described, or summarized in any writing of any type; and if so, identify each such writing in the manner indicated below

If you are requested to "identify" a communication, memorandum, or record of any type, and such communication was written, the following information should be furnished (in place of identification, production is acceptable):

a. Its nature, for example, letter, memorandum, telegram, note, drawing, and so on
b. Its specific subject
c. By whom and to whom it was directed
d. The date upon which it was made
e. Who has possession of the original and copies

"Written" communications also encompasses e-mail and computer communications.

Whenever a person is to be "identified," you should furnish, except as otherwise noted:

a. Name and present or last known address
b. If a corporation, the state of incorporation

Interrogatories

1. Did any person, agency, group, committee, board, or faculty in or outside the defendant/ institution review the medical records of (plaintiff name) at any time from February 7, 2004 to the present? If your answer is yes, please state:
   a. The name, address, title, and position of said persons, agencies, groups, committees, boards, or faculty conducting such review
   b. The reason such review is made
   c. The date of each such review
   d. The results of each review of (plaintiff's name) charts and records
   e. Whether or not any minutes were kept at such review meetings and if so, where the minutes are located and who has custody of them

Answer

2. Did the defendant hospital have in effect on February 7, 2004 any by-laws, rules, policies, regulations, or procedures which required:
   a. That the medical staff strives to maintain the optimal level of professional performance of its members
   b. That the medical staff provide periodic in-depth reappraisal of each staff member? If so, please attach a copy of all such instruments which set out the hospital's requirements in regard to those items listed above and written protocol for the achievement of such requirements.

Answer

3. Identify by name, address, title, position, and responsibility of all the following persons:
   a. The nursing administrator responsible for the nursing department on February 7, 2004
   b. The nursing supervisors responsible for and in charge of the nurses rendering care to patient (plaintiff name) on February 7, 2004
   c. The head nurse responsible for and in charge of the nurses rendering care to patient (plaintiff name) on February 7, 2004
   d. The charge nurse responsible for and in charge of the nurses rendering care to patient (plaintiff name) on February 7, 2004
   e. Each RN, LPN, and nursing assistant who attended and rendered nursing care to patient (plaintiff name) on February 7, 2004
   f. Each technician and/or other individual at healthcare hospital who rendered care to patient (plaintiff name) at any time on February 7, 2004

Answer

4. Please identify by name, address, title, position, and responsibility of the medical staff and/or emergency room providers who rendered care to (plaintiff name) at any time on February 7, 2004.

Answer

5. Please identify by name, address, title, position, and responsibility of the nurse practitioner that rendered care to (plaintiff name) at any time on February 7, 2004.

Answer

LAW OFFICES OF PLAINTIFF
By: _____
Plaintiff Attorney (ID No. 0000)
Address
City, State, Zip Code
Phone Number
Attorney for Plaintiff

DATED:

Appendix E: Sample Request for Production

Court of Jurisdiction

John Q. Smith,	:	C.A. No.: 04-123-ABC
	:	
Plaintiff,	:	
	:	**Non-arbitration Case**
v.	:	
	:	
Healthcare Hospital, a hospital	:	**Jury Trial by Twelve**
corporation, and Max I. Millan, M.D.	:	**Persons Demanded**
	:	
Defendants.	:	
	:	

Plaintiff's Second Request for Production Directed to Defendant Hospital

The plaintiff requests defendant to produce for examination and copying at the office of the attorney for the plaintiff on or before thirty (30) days of receipt of this request:

1. A copy of all policies and procedures that were in effect on February 7, 2004, which set out or specified the scope of conduct of patient care to be rendered by the medical staff of the healthcare hospital emergency department.

Response

2. A copy of all The Joint Commission [formerly Joint Commission of Accreditation of Hospital Organizations (JCAHO)] reports and recommendations regarding the emergency department staff for the years 1997 through the present.

Response

3. A copy of the hospital wide policy on patient's rights and responsibilities.

Response

4. A copy of all policies and procedures that were in effect on February 7, 2004 and February 8, 2004, which set out or specified the scope of conduct of patient care to be rendered by the medical staff/emergency room nurses.

Response

5. A copy of the table of contents for every policy and procedure manual located in the emergency department.

Response

6. A list of references and textbooks in the emergency department.

Response

7. A copy of all written materials regarding the definition of the scope of practice in the emergency department.

Response

8. A copy of all evaluation tools and performance appraisal tools for medical staff and nursing staff in the emergency department.

Response

9. A copy of all policies and procedures regarding staffing and staffing requirements for emergency department nursing service.

Response

10. A copy of all policies and procedures regarding patient assignments.

Response

11. A copy of the log record for all patients admitted to the emergency department at healthcare hospital for the 24-hour period on February 7, 2004.

Response

12. A copy of any incident report, variance report, accident report, unusual occurrence report, exception report, generic screens, quality indicators, or any other report that was completed with respect to (plaintiff name).

Response

LAW OFFICES OF PLAINTIFF
By: _____
Plaintiff Attorney (ID No. 0000)
Address
City, State, Zip Code
Phone Number
Attorney for Plaintiff

DATED:

Appendix F: Sample Request for Admissions

Court of Jurisdiction

	:	
	:	
John Q. Smith,	:	**C.A. No.: 04-123-ABC**
	:	
Plaintiff,	:	
	:	
v.	:	**Non-srbitration Case**
Healthcare Hospital, a hospital	:	
corporation, and Max I. Millan, M.D.	:	
	:	**Jury Trial by Twelve**
Defendants.	:	**Persons Demanded**

Plaintiff's Requests for Admissions Concerning Medical Bills Directed to Defendants

Pursuant to Rule 36 of the Federal Rules of Civil Procedure, Plaintiff, John Q. Smith, requests that Defendants admit that the following statements are true for the purposes of this action, and with respect to any statements to which your response is not an unqualified admission, plaintiff requests, pursuant to Rule 36 of the Federal Rules of Civil Procedure, that defendants respond to the Accompanying Interrogatories.

Each Request for Admission and Interrogatory incorporates the following instructions.

Instructions

1. If you object to any admission requested, fully state the basis of your objection
2. If you believe you must qualify or deny part of the requested admission, specify so much of the requested admission as you believe true and qualify or deny the remainder
3. If you are unable to admit or deny any of the admissions requested, state your reasons

Request for Admission #1

That each of the following documents, exhibited with this Request, is genuine and authentic.

A-1   Bills from healthcare hospital, February 7, 2004 to March 11, 2004, in the amount of $22,044.08, page 3

A-2   Bills from Heart Ambulance, February 7, 2004, in the amount of $440.45, pages 4–5

A-3   Bills from Memorial General Hospital, September 20, 2004, in the amount of $5,979.00, page 6

A-4   Bills from Max. I. Millan, M.D., February 7, 2004, through November 11, 2004, in the amount of $11,803.00, pages 7–9

A-5   Bills from Expert Rehabilitation Services, June 29, 2004, in the amount of $1,137.00, pages 10–11

Answer

Supplemental Interrogatory #1

If the answer to Request for Admission #1 is anything but an unqualified admission, state all facts upon which the denial or partial denial is based.

Answer

Request for Admission #2

That the amount of each bill set forth in request number 1 is reasonable.

Answer

Supplemental Interrogatory #2

If the answer to Request for Admission #2 is anything but an unqualified admission, state all facts upon which the denial or partial denial is based.

Answer

Request for Admission #3

That the treatment for which each bill pertains is related to the incident of February 7, 2004.

Answer

Supplemental Interrogatory #3

If the answer to Request for Admission #3 is anything but an unqualified admission, state all facts upon which the denial or partial denial is based.

Answer

LAW OFFICES OF PLAINTIFF
By:

_____
Plaintiff Attorney (ID No. 0000)
Address
City, State, Zip Code
Phone Number
Attorney for Plaintiff

DATED:

Appendix G: Example of Information Asked of Deponent Expert Witness

While not all-inclusive, the following requests for information may be anticipated in the deposition of the expert witness.

1. Name, address, credentials, education
2. Current and past licensure(s)
3. Any past sanctions or disciplinary actions
4. Any licensure revocations
5. Class ranking and success with passing boards
6. The extent of prior testimony
7. If the produced CV of the expert is current and accurate
8. Whether previously deposed as an expert witness or subject of litigation
9. Board certifications and specialties
10. Fee for deposition, report, and trial testimony
11. Amount of time in active clinical practice
12. Division of testimony for plaintiff versus defense
13. Listing of previous cases in which the expert testified
14. Association with attorney that retained the expert
15. Basis for the expert's opinion and what was specifically relied upon in forming that opinion (i.e., medical literature and research, textbooks, etc.)
16. What records the expert reviewed in forming the opinion
17. Whether the expert ever examined the plaintiff
18. If the expert has reviewed the report (opinion) or deposition of the opposing expert witness and on what points does the expert agree/differ

Appendix H: Sample Subpoena *Duces Tecum*

Sample Subpoena *Duces Tecum* [Court of Jurisdiction]

John Q. Smith v. Healthcare Hospital, a hospital corporation, and Max I. Millan, M.D.	Subpoena in a Civil Case Civil Action No.: 04-123-ABC

To:
Name, Records Custodian
Address of Facility
City, State Zip Code

☐ **You Are Commanded** to appear in the United States District Court for the District of Delaware at the place, date, and time specified below to testify in the above case.

Place of Testimony	Courtroom
	Date and Time

☐ **You Are Commanded** to appear at the place, date, and time specified below to testify at the taking of a deposition in the above case.

Place of Deposition	Date and Time

[X] **You Are Commanded** to produce and permit inspection and copying of the following documents or objects at the place, date, and time specified below (list documents or objects):

A dispatch log and any audiotape and/or transcript of the 911 call placed by (witness name) regarding an ambulance accident that occurred near the intersection of Driveway Road and Exit Road in City, Delaware on February 7, 2004 at approximately 1:00 p.m.

Place	Date and Time
Law Office, City, State, and Zip Code	April 30, 2006 at 3:00 p.m.

☐ **You Are Commanded** to permit inspection of the following premises at the date and time specified below.

Premises	Date and Time

Any organization not a party to this suit that is subpoenaed for the taking of a deposition shall designate one or more officers, directors, or managing agents, or other persons who consent to testify on its behalf, and may set forth, for each person designated, the matters on which the person will testify. Federal Rules of Civil Procedure, 30(b)(6).

Requesting Party's Name, Address, and Phone Number
Attorney for Plaintiff Name, Address, City, State and Zip Code, Phone Number

Issuing Party's Signature and Title (Indicate If Attorney for Plaintiff or Defendant)	Date
Attorney for Plaintiff, Plaintiff Name	March 11, 2006

Proof of Service		
Served	Date	Place
Served on (Print Name)	Name of Service	
Served by (Print Name)	Title	
Declaration of Server		

I declare under perjury under the laws of the United States of America that the foregoing information contained in the Proof of Service is true and correct.

Executed on _____   _____
                 Date   Signature of Server

                                       _____
                                       Address of Server

Rule 45, Federal Rules of Civil Procedure, Parts C & D

(c) Protection of Persons Subject to Subpoenas.

(1) A party or an attorney responsible for the issuance and service of a subpoena shall take reasonable steps to avoid imposing undue burden or expense on a person subject to that subpoena. The court on behalf of which the subpoena was issued shall enforce this duty and impose upon the party or attorney in breach of this duty an appropriate sanction which may include, but is not limited to, lost earnings and reasonable attorney's fee.

(2) (A) A person commanded to produce and permit inspection and copying of designated books, papers, documents or tangible things, or inspection of premises need not appear in person at the place of production or inspection unless commanded to appear for deposition, hearing or trial.

(B) Subject to paragraph (d) (2) of this rule, a person commanded to produce and permit inspection and copying may, within 14 days after service of subpoena or before the time specified for compliance if such time is less than 14 days after service, serve upon the party or attorney designated in the subpoena written objection to inspection or copying of any or all of the designated materials or of the premises. If objection is made, the party serving the subpoena shall not be entitled to inspect and copy materials or inspect the premises except pursuant to an order of the court by which the subpoena was issued. If objection has been made, the party serving the subpoena may, upon notice to the person commanded to produce, move at any time for an order to compel the production. Such an order to comply production shall protect any person who is not a party or an officer of a party from significant expense resulting from the inspection and copying commanded.

(3) (A) On timely motion, the court by which a subpoena was issued shall quash or modify the subpoena if it

(i) fails to allow reasonable time for compliance,

(ii) requires a person who is not a party or an officer of a party to travel to a place more than 100 miles from the place where that person resides, is employed or regularly transacts business in person, except that, subject to the provisions of clause (c) (3) (B) (iii) of this rule, such a person may in order to attend trial be commanded to travel from any such place within the state in which the trial is held, or

(iii) requires disclosure of privileged or other protected matter and no exception or waiver applies, or

(iv) subjects a person to undue burden.

(B) If a subpoena

(i) requires disclosure of a trade secret or other confidential research, development, or commercial information, or

(ii) requires disclosure of an unretained expert's opinion or information not describing specific events or occurrences in dispute and resulting from the expert's study made not at the request of any party, or

(iii) requires a person who is not a party or an officer of a party to incur substantial expense to travel more than 100 miles to attend trial, the court may, to protect a person subject to or affected by the subpoena, quash or modify the subpoena, or, if the party in whose behalf the subpoena is issued shows a substantial need for the testimony or material that cannot be otherwise met without undue hardship and assures that the person to whom the subpoena is addressed will be reasonably compensated, the court may order appearance or production only upon specified conditions.

(d) Duties in Responding to Subpoena.

(1) A person responding to a subpoena to produce documents shall produce them as they are kept in the usual course of business or shall organize and label them to correspond with the categories in the demand.

(2) When information subject to a subpoena is withheld on a claim that it is privileged or subject to protection as trial preparation materials, the claim shall be made expressly and shall be supported by a description of the nature of the documents, communications, or things not produced that is sufficient to enable the demanding party to contest the claim.

Chapter 6

Defense Medical Examinations

Nikki Chuml, MSN/Ed, RNC-OB, PRN

Contents

Objectives

- State the purpose of a Defense Medical Examination
- Describe the role of the LNC observer when attending a DME
- Describe the reasons why a legal nurse consultant would pause an examination to contact the plaintiff attorney
- Identify items the LNC should include in a DME report

Defense Medical Examinations (DMEs)

An Independent Medical Examination (IME) or Compulsory Medical Examination (CME), also known as a Defense Medical Examination (DME), is "a medical examination made by an impartial healthcare professional, usually a physician." (Black's Law Dictionary, 2014). In theory, it is an objective evaluation by an examiner of defense counsel's choice pertaining to the cause and nature of the plaintiff's injuries. The examiner takes a verbal history of the client's issues since the incident, performs an examination of the affected areas of the body and generates a report, which is sent to the defense attorney and must also be produced to the plaintiff attorney within a certain period of time. The examiner may be called to testify regarding his exam if the case goes to trial.

During discovery, both plaintiff and defense counsel gather information and evaluate the strengths and weaknesses of the case. This includes determination of the cause, nature, and extent of the plaintiff's injuries, as identified by an expert medical examiner, as well as the plaintiff's treating physicians. Historically, this exam has been called an IME, but plaintiff attorneys generally refer to it as a DME because the defense hires and pays the examiner. This chapter will discuss the role of the LNC regarding these examinations and some of the legal requirements, which vary by jurisdiction.

Goals of a DME

The goals of a DME are to obtain an opinion from the examiner on the cause and extent of the plaintiff's injuries, as well as the extent of disability arising from these injuries. A DME examiner does not have a provider–patient relationship with the plaintiff, so this examiner does not provide treatment to the plaintiff. If the DME examiner concludes that the plaintiff's injuries are not as severe as the plaintiff contends or are due to an underlying condition not related to the defendant's negligence, this is advantageous for the defense as it potentially lessens the monetary value of the case. Of course, this is assuming the DME examiner's opinions will withstand cross-examination by the plaintiff's counsel. However, if the DME examiner essentially supports the nature and extent of the injuries alleged by the plaintiff, this is beneficial to the plaintiff's case and may result in the defense initiating settlement discussions. Most cases settle prior to trial, based on the evidence obtained during discovery and each side's risk assessment of taking a case to trial. For example, in a case that goes to trial, the plaintiff risks obtaining no monetary award or an award that is substantially less than desired and the defense risks a very high jury award. Settlement is a means for both sides to avoid these risks.

DME Procedural Rules

Federal procedural rules and substantive law apply to cases venued in federal court, whereas state standards apply to cases venued in state court. Procedural rules cover notice to plaintiff, conducting the exam and report requirements, whereas any substantive law would include court decisions pursuant to motions made by either side about DME issues in dispute. In general, defense counsel sends a formal discovery notice to the plaintiff attorney requesting a defense medical exam. The notice, otherwise known as The Demand (see Appendix A), includes the name of the examiner, the date and time of the exam, and the location, usually the examiner's office. Occasionally, the exam may take place in another agreed-upon location. Prior to the exam, defense counsel sends the examiner the pertinent medical records and imaging films. Some state DME rules require that intake questionnaires or other medical forms be sent to the plaintiff attorney in advance of the DME, while others allow for the refusal of the plaintiff to fill out any questionnaires or medical history forms (Schreiber, 2014).

Federal cases are governed by Rule 35 of the Federal Rules of Civil Procedure. State Court cases are governed by state procedural rules. The LNC should be familiar with the basic DME procedural rules pertaining to the applicable jurisdiction in a given case. While it is not required for the LNC to have a vast legal background, knowing the basics is important.

Most state rules hold that only one examination per specialty can be performed (Schreiber, 2014). If an exam does not go forward due to an examiner's conduct, the defense may lose the ability to have that type of exam completed. Thus, it is important for the defense to hire examiners who will conduct the exam in accordance with the applicable rules. Likewise, plaintiff's failure to appear for the examination at the scheduled date and time could give rise to a defense motion for sanctions, such as a request to preclude plaintiff's counsel from offering any evidence regarding plaintiff's medical condition. Every effort is made to schedule a date and time convenient for both parties.

State rules vary as to whether someone is allowed to accompany the plaintiff to the exam. If allowed, the person may be a family member, plaintiff counsel or representative, or the plaintiff's physician. The LNC attends as a representative of plaintiff's counsel. The Federal Rules state that "The Court has discretion to determine who may be present at the examination. Some courts allow the person being examined by a doctor to bring his own physician, others do not. It is also unsettled as to whether attorneys have a right to be present" (Baicker-McKee, Janssen, & Corr, 2018, p. 889).

In some jurisdictions, a formal set of DME rules are negotiated among counsel. For example, defense counsel may submit a Demand related to DME rules, following which plaintiff counsel submits a Response (see Appendix B) with counter-demands. Prior to the DME, a final set of rules is determined either by agreement among counsel or, if they cannot agree, by the Court.

The rules related to whether the exam can be audio or video recorded and the details regarding the examiner's report also vary with jurisdiction. The attorney will inform the LNC if the exam is to be audio recorded or filmed. (Hodge, Thomas, & Lacy, 2015).

DME Case Law

As noted above, the rules pertaining to physical and mental examinations of plaintiffs are governed by the applicable state or federal statutes. These statutes, like other types of statutes, are interpreted by case law. For example, in a New York State case, the plaintiff moved to disqualify the examining doctor because the examining doctor had "a history of inflicting pain during his examinations by exerting excessive force and pressure upon the injured body parts" (*Miller v. Holtz House of Vehicles*, 1991). The judge ruled that upon a review of all the evidence, an evidentiary hearing was warranted on the issue of the doctor's potential disqualification as the examining physician. In a New York State Appellate Division case, the Court noted that "plaintiffs are entitled to have a representative present at their physical examinations as long as the representative does not interfere with the examinations conducted by defendants' designated physician or prevent defendants' physician from conducting a meaningful examination" (*Santana v. Johnson*, 2017). Likewise, the California Code of Civil Procedure states, "The observer under subdivision (a) may monitor the examination but shall not participate in or disrupt it" (California Code of Civil Procedure, 2018). A subsequent New York State Appellate Division case cited to the Santana case confirmed that the plaintiff was not required to show "special and unusual circumstances" to be permitted to have a non-legal representative present at a DME (*Martinez v. Pinard*, 2018).

Types of DMEs

Consistent with the types of physical injuries commonly alleged in personal injury claims, most DMEs are orthopedic or neurological exams. If the plaintiff alleges cognitive deficits or emotional harm a psychological, neuropsychological, or psychiatric DME may be requested. The rules vary with jurisdiction as to whether an observer may attend such an exam and, if so, what constitutes appropriate observer conduct. For example, in California an LNC may attend and ask the psychiatrist/psychologist to audio record the interview portion of the exam. The LNC usually is not permitted by the examiner to stay in the exam room, but sets up the recorder and then sits in the waiting area until told the interview is finished and the recorder may be retrieved. The LNC may also stay in the waiting area during the testing portion of the exam, if requested to do so by the plaintiff attorney. Neuropsychological examinations involve a battery of tests, typically administered over several hours, often on more than one day. Thus, even if the rules permit an observer, the attorney may not hire an LNC to attend this type of DME, since these sessions do not involve a physical exam that can be observed. Other attorneys may decide that if allowed, there is a benefit to having an LNC observer present to support the plaintiff, especially with some clients.

The examiner conducting a psychiatric or psychological exam solicits information from the plaintiff about psychiatric and medical history, the accident at issue, resulting injuries, and a summary of the treatment received thus far, along with the plaintiff's perceptions of whether the treatment has been effective. The client may also undergo psychological testing to determine their status and future needs. These tests may include:

- The Mini Mental State Examination (MMSE)
- The Minnesota Multiphasic Personality Inventory (MMPI)
- The Beck Anxiety Inventory (BAI) or Beck Depression Inventory (BDI)
- The Bender Visual Motor Gestalt test
- The Career Ability Placement Survey (CAPS)
- The Halstead Category test

In some states, observers are not permitted at defense psychiatric exams. If allowed, LNCs attending such exams should take notes regarding the examiner's questions and corresponding answers, the nature of any formal testing done, the interactions between the examiner and the plaintiff, and the demeanor of the examiner towards the plaintiff.

Role of the LNC

Both in-house and independent LNCs may attend DMEs on behalf of plaintiff attorneys. The primary role of the LNC is to observe the exam and provide an oral or written report to the plaintiff attorney detailing what took place during the exam. If a dispute subsequently arises about what occurred during the exam, the LNC may be called to testify about what they observed during the exam. The LNC attending a DME is largely an observer; the LNC does not interrupt the exam unless the examiner violates agreed-upon terms between opposing counsel about the nature of the examiner's questions or exam. In jurisdictions that use Demand and Response Letters, the agreed-upon terms will be noted in the Response of the plaintiff to the Demand for the DME. The LNC should bring a copy of the Demand and Response for the examiner, in case a dispute arises during the exam. Rarely, the LNC may need to stop the exam if the examiner engages in inappropriate conduct towards the plaintiff, such as range of motion testing that causes undue pain or asking questions deemed inappropriate such as medical history or mechanism of injury. The LNC should confirm that the attorney can be reached by phone during the exam should anything occur requiring attorney intervention.

The role of the in-house defense LNC is generally limited to preparing a package of records and imaging studies for the examiner and discussing the examiner's report with the defense attorney managing the case. The defense LNC usually does not attend a DME or interact with the plaintiff.

Preparation for the DME

In-house LNCs typically are involved in a case from the outset with ready access to case information and medical records, whereas independent LNCs may not. Independent LNCs may discuss the client's primary injuries with the attorney; however, this is not a requirement and will vary with attorney practice. Independent LNCs who prepare clients for DMEs usually ascertain the nature of the client's injuries while discussing exam details or attorney instructions with the plaintiff. Independent LNCs do not usually review the plaintiff's medical records unless they are already working with the attorney on the case behind-the-scenes, as this would incur additional expense the attorney may not consider necessary. However, some attorneys send pertinent medical records and even deposition transcripts to the independent LNC so the LNC will be familiar with the case.

It is important for both independent and in-house LNCs to discuss any instructions or requests the attorney has, including permissible observer conduct. For example, the LNC may be instructed not to interrupt the examination unless the client is being treated inappropriately, the examiner is causing the client undue pain, there is a request for invasive or radiological testing, or the examiner intends to do something the attorney instructed the LNC to disallow (Hodge et al., 2015). The LNC should also confirm whether the client is allowed to complete a questionnaire or symptom chart at the exam, and whether the DME is to be audio or video recorded. If the attorney is requesting video recording, the LNC should confirm if a videographer will be recording the DME or if the attorney wishes the LNC to do this.

The LNC should discuss with the attorney how best to handle impermissible examiner conduct or questions. For example, prior to the client responding to a disallowed question, the LNC will object to this line of questioning if instructed to do so by the attorney. If a dispute with the examiner ensues due to the LNC's objection, the LNC can pause the DME to call the attorney to discuss the examiner's objections. The attorney will either approve the question or inform the examiner the client will not answer the question (or similar questions). If the examiner refuses to continue the exam, the attorney may instruct the LNC to leave with the client. The LNC should always contact the attorney prior to leaving an exam with the client to give attorneys for both sides the opportunity to resolve the issue so the exam can be completed. If not, the incomplete exam may count for the one exam allowed for the specialty.

Both in-house and independent LNCs may be involved with preparing the client prior to the exam. They may meet with the client, along with the attorney, to convey any special instructions; advise the client what to expect during the exam; determine whether the client uses any assistive devices; set up a meeting point outside the exam location just prior to the exam; and discuss general rules of client conduct during the exam. For example, the attorney will often instruct the client to be truthful and thorough when describing symptoms and functional limitations, but to refrain from embellishment. It is important that the client convey to the examiner an accurate picture of the injuries and their impact on their life. The client should be instructed to give full effort to range of motion and strength testing but to refrain from any motion that causes significant discomfort. The client may also be instructed to refrain from answering certain questions about the event, the mechanism of injury, and prior medical history already explored at the plaintiff's deposition. They will also be instructed on how best to respond to such a question if asked. Clients should be reminded that the staff will likely be observing them not only in the exam room but at other times, such as in the parking lot and the waiting room.

Independent LNCs should contact the attorney prior to the exam to determine if the attorney wishes them to prepare the client. The preparation should be the same whether it is done by the attorney or the LNC. Plaintiff law firm personnel are responsible for confirming the date, time, and location of the DME with the client, confirming the client has transportation to the DME, and confirming the defense firm has arranged for an interpreter when needed. Often, the client may be contacted the day prior to the exam to confirm all the details again with the client. If any concerns arise, the LNC should contact the attorney. The LNC should also reinforce the date, time, and location of the DME with the client as well as any special instructions from the attorney.

Items the LNC observer needs include directions to the exam location and the physician's office phone number, pens, paper, a business card, a watch or other timing device, and cell phone or recorder fully charged and in good working order if the LNC is audio recording the DME. The LNC should also exchange cell phone numbers with the attorney and client, in case communication with the client prior to the exam is necessary. If the LNC is responsible for recording the exam, the LNC should be sufficiently familiar with the recording equipment to produce a good quality audio or video recording of the entire exam. The LNC should also be familiar with the types of physical exam testing done on the client's type of injury so they can speak to the attorney about the thoroughness of the exam. It is essential that the LNC appear at the appointed date and time for the DME. If the LNC is late or does not appear for the examination, the exam will either continue without representation or the exam will be cancelled, and a fee charged to the plaintiff.

The DME

The day of the appointment, the LNC should arrive at the exam location at the agreed-upon time to meet with the client just outside the location prior to accompanying the client to the waiting area. Both the client and the LNC should check in at the reception desk and the LNC should provide a business card to the receptionist.

When meeting with the client prior to the exam, the LNC should remind the client about any attorney instructions and answer any client questions. For example, remind the client to inform the examiner immediately if any parts of the physical exam cause pain. If the client is allowed to fill out forms or questionnaires in whole or part, the LNC may assist with this. Advise the client that staff in the front office may report observations about the client to the examiner. The LNC should make a note of the client's arrival time and when the client is taken into the exam room. Some state rules impose limits on the wait time between arrival and start of the exam. However, if an excessive wait time occurs the LNC should contact the attorney prior to leaving the office.

The LNC should

■ accompany the client into the exam room, start the recording, and make introductions
■ ask whether the client needs assistance with disrobing, putting on a gown, or removing footwear (if asked to disrobe those parts of the body being examined)
■ note the wait time in the exam room prior to commencement of the DME
■ remain with the client at all times except when the client disrobes if the client prefers this. If present when the client disrobes, the LNC should note whether the client had difficulty disrobing or getting onto the exam table.

DMEs generally occur in two parts: a history and a physical exam (PE). The LNC should

■ note the name of the staff member who took the history (if not the examiner) and what time the questioning started and ended. It is important to take notes about the questions and especially the corresponding client answers, even though the interview is being audio recorded, in case the audio fails.
■ not interrupt the history taking unless the examiner poses an impermissible question. If this occurs and cannot be resolved, the LNC should pause the DME to call the attorney.
■ note whether the examiner brought any records, films, or notes into the exam room. This should have been approved by the attorney prior to the exam.

During the physical exam portion of the DME, the LNC should take notes regarding the type of testing done. Audio recording (if allowed) should continue during the PE. One caveat: since the LNC is the attorney's "eyes and ears," the LNC must observe the client closely during the PE to note the client's physical reactions to the tests. Copious note-taking may impede this continuous observation. Using drawings of the front and back of the body or listing types of exams with room to write results may assist the LNC with making notes during the PE without having to look away from the client for long periods while writing. The LNC should attempt to record measurements if taken and noted out loud. The LNC should ask all staff who assist with the exam to state and spell their names for the report. Should the examiner verbalize unsolicited information about exam findings, the LNC should note these. Also, if the examiner asks the client any questions during the PE, the LNC should note the nature of the questions and corresponding answers. The LNC should also note the general demeanor of the examiner and the client, and whether the client exhibits any pain behavior during the PE. When attending a dental, ophthalmic, otic or other DME in which it may be difficult to identify the specific testing done, the LNC should take notes describing the general nature and length of each test as well as any substantive conversation between the examiner and the client. The LNC should note the start and end time of the PE.

After the examiner leaves the exam room, the LNC should assist the client to get dressed if needed and accompany the client out of the building. Once outside, the client may wish to discuss the LNC's impression of how the exam went and the next steps. The LNC should reassure the client and remind them to contact their attorney with any concerns about the examiner's report, which will be provided to the client's attorney within the time frame designated by the applicable DME rules. If the client is waiting for someone to provide transportation home, the LNC should wait with the client until the driver arrives.

DME Problems

The LNC should be prepared to deal with problems that may arise during the DME. Client conduct that can be problematic includes failure to show up for a DME appointment or arriving late; failure to answer the examiner's questions honestly; failure to give full effort during exam testing; or hostility towards the examiner. The most effective means of preventing these problems is client preparation prior to the DME during the prep sessions with the attorney or LNC. The LNC should reinforce positive client attitude and compliance when meeting with the client just prior to the exam. The LNC must remember that the role of observer is primarily a silent one; speaking to the client during the exam may be interpreted by the defense examiner as coaching or interfering with the exam.

Problematic examiner conduct includes hostility or other inappropriate demeanor directed towards the client or LNC, asking impermissible questions, or causing the client excessive pain during the physical examination. Most examiners are hired regularly and know better than to engage in this behavior. Even though the examiner is hired by the defense, most conduct the exam in a professional and courteous manner. The LNC should ask to pause the DME to call the attorney-client if poor examiner behavior is witnessed. Based on the attorney's instructions, this may need to be reported before the examination continues.

LNC DME Report

Following the DME, the attorney may wish to speak briefly with the LNC about the LNC's general impressions of how things went during the exam and whether anything problematic occurred that did not necessitate contacting the attorney during the exam. If the DME was audio or videotaped, a copy of this should be given to the attorney right away. This can be done based on how the attorney wishes to receive it. The most common way is via secure email or file sharing program, unless the attorney requests a physical copy on CD or DVD. In some cases, the attorney may ask a staff member or an outside service to transcribe the recording of the DME. Legal nurse consultants are not usually asked to transcribe these recordings, as this would incur unnecessary expense.

The attorney may request that the LNC prepare a written report detailing all aspects of the exam. (See Appendices C and D for sample reports.) The report is prepared from the LNC's notes and memory, preferably as soon as possible after the DME when the LNC's memory about the exam is fresh. If the exam was audio recorded, the LNC should listen to the recording when preparing the report to ensure the accuracy of their observations. The LNC's written report is especially important if the examiner's subsequent report is not consistent with the LNC's recollection of what was said or done during the DME. If the examiner's report differs significantly from the LNC's verbal report, the attorney may then ask the LNC to complete a written report, if not asked to do so previously.

The LNC's report is typically in narrative format, but some attorneys find a table format easier to read. Sample reports in both formats are in Appendices C and D. The report should include details about every part of the exam. For example:

- The start and end time of each part of the exam
- The information conveyed to the examiner during the history portion of the exam
- The testing conducted during the physical exam, including position of the client, the technique of the examiner, and any results that are gleaned from the test
- Whether the client was unable to perform any requested tests, or did so with some discomfort
- Whether the client exhibited any verbal or non-verbal pain behaviors
- The LNC's opinion regarding whether the examiner conducted a complete exam for the injury being assessed (providing a reference to an authoritative text excerpt to justify their opinion is recommended)
- The examiner's demeanor towards the client and the client's response
- Whether the client completed any forms at the DME (if allowed by the rules)
- The nature of any unsolicited comments the examiner made, including about the physical exam results, treatment options, or the client's prognosis
- If the LNC needed to consult with the attorney during the exam and the instructions given to the LNC based on the issue in question

It is important to include as much detail as possible, especially if the DME was not recorded. The LNC should clarify with the attorney whether the rules in the jurisdiction of the case state the LNC's report is potentially discoverable or is considered attorney work product. If the report is possibly discoverable by opposing counsel, the LNC should include only objective content in the report, with opinions conveyed orally to the attorney. If the report has no possibility of being discovered and will remain attorney-client work product, the LNC may include their opinions about the exam in their report. See Appendix E for a sample report by an in-house LNC.

Billing Considerations for Independent LNC Observers

Prior to agreeing to attend a DME, the independent LNC should obtain written confirmation from the attorney regarding the LNC's DME fee schedule, not only for attending the DME, but for any future court testimony or if the client fails to appear for the DME. The LNC may require a signed agreement and retainer check. Legal nurse consultants charge either a flat fee or hourly rate for time spent speaking with the client prior to the DME, traveling to and attending the appointment, speaking with the attorney after the exam, and preparing a report. The LNC may also bill for mileage at the current IRS business rate and any out of pocket expenses, such as tolls or parking fees. Following the DME, the LNC should send an itemized bill to the attorney. For more information on independent LNC fee schedules, see Chapter 30.

LNC Observer Testimony

It is rare that an LNC testifies regarding attending a DME except in cases where there is a discrepancy between the examiner's report and the LNC's report or recollection of the events. If no report was completed the LNC may be called to testify at trial regarding what was said or done during the DME. In this setting the LNC's role is not to provide expert opinions, but to serve as a fact witness and defend the content of the LNC's DME report. Questions directed to the LNC may include what the LNC observed during the physical exam and heard during the interview phase of the DME, especially if the recording is unclear. The LNC may be asked to read their report into the court record and justify any contradictions they have to the examiner's report. Prior to testifying, the plaintiff attorney should meet with the LNC to review the attorney's direct examination and likely cross-examination by opposing counsel. For more information on serving as an expert fact witness, see Chapter 32.

Summary

Under state and federal procedural rules, the defendant in a civil case with an injury claim is entitled to have the plaintiff undergo a physical or mental examination by a medical provider of the defendant's choice. Under most state rules, the plaintiff is entitled to be accompanied by an observer at the exam. The purpose of the observer is to take notes about what happens during the exam, audio or video record the exam if allowed by state rules, pause the exam if the examiner is not compliant with agreed-upon rules, report back to the attorney, and if necessary provide testimony about what occurred during the exam. Nurses possess medical knowledge pertinent to evaluation of injuries, which makes them ideal DME observers. Prior to attending a DME, the LNC observer should be aware of the applicable state or federal procedural rules for the jurisdiction of the case, any special attorney instructions, and the plaintiff's alleged injuries. DME attendance is a valuable service an LNC can offer an attorney-client.

References

Baicker-McKee, S., Janssen, W. M., & Corr, J. B. (2018). *Federal civil rules handbook.* Toronto: Thomson Reuters.

California Code of Civil Procedure [CCP]. (2018). Part 4—miscellaneous provisions. Title 4—Civil Discovery Act. Chapter 15—physical or mental examination. Article 5—conduct of examination. Section 2032.510.

Hodge, S., Thomas, M., & Lacy, C. (2015). A guide to the independent medical examination. Retrieved July 29, 2017, from www.albanylawjournal.org/Documents/Articles/25.2.339-Hodge.pdf.

Independent Medical Examination, *Black's Law Dictionary* (10th ed., 2014).

Martinez v. Pinard, 71 N.Y.S.3d 345 (1st Dept. 2018).

Miller v. Holtz House of Vehicles, Inc., 152 Misc. 2d 727 (Sup Ct, Monroe County 1991).

Santana v. Johnson, 154 AD3d 452 (1st Dept. 2017).

Schreiber, M. (2014). Guidelines for counsel regarding compulsory medical examinations. Retrieved July 28, 2017, from www.ninthcircuit.org/sites/default/files/GuidelinesforcompulsoryMedicalExaminations October2014.pdf.

Additional Reading

Hodge, S., Thomas, M., & Lacy, C. (2015). A guide to the independent medical examination. Retrieved from www.albanylawjournal.org/Documents/Articles/25.2.339-Hodge.pdf.

Oertle, H., & Boothe, S. (2014). How to correctly approach independent medical examinations. Retrieved from http://apps.americanbar.org/litigation/committees/products/articles/summer2014-0714-how-to-correctly-approach-independent-medical-exams.html.

Schreiber, M. (2014). Guidelines for counsel regarding compulsory medical examinations. Retrieved from www.ninthcircuit.org/sites/default/files/Weiss%20Guidelines%20for%20Compulsory%20Medical%20Examinations.pdf.

Swiercinsky, D., & Naugle, R. (n.d.). Clinical neuropsychology 101 (An introduction). In *Module V. Neuropsychological assessments* (pp. 2–22). Utah: Division of Services for People with Disabilities.

Test Questions

1. What is a Defense Medical Examination?
   A. An examination to determine plaintiff's diagnosis
   B. A second opinion to determine the plaintiff's treatment options
   C. An examination of a client by a physician or psychologist chosen by the Defense to determine the nature and extent of injuries resulting from a negligent act
   D. A deposition to determine what happened to the client
2. The role of the LNC observer in a DME is:
   A. To observe the examination and then give testimony as to what was done inappropriately
   B. To observe and take notes regarding each aspect of the DME
   C. To determine what the examiner is going to testify to at trial
   D. To prove the examiner did something wrong
3. What items does the LNC need to bring to the examination?
   A. Audio recorder, pens, reflex hammer, and otoscope
   B. Video camera, audio recorder, pens, and wheelchair
   C. Pen light, ruler, audio recorder, and timing device
   D. Pens, paper, audio recorder, and extra batteries
4. What should the LNC include in their report?
   A. Timing of each portion of the exam, the client's responses to the examiner's questions, and tests conducted during the physical exam
   B. Opinions of the examiner
   C. Examiner's testing results
   D. Independent LNC's fees to attend the exam
5. When should the LNC pause the exam and contact the attorney?
   A. If the plaintiff answers a question wrong
   B. If the examiner refuses to conduct the exam unless x-rays are taken
   C. If the recording device malfunctions
   D. If the examiner wants the client to change into a gown

Answers: 1. C, 2. B, 3. D, 4. A, 5. B

Appendix A: Sample Demand

Smith, Jones & Cooper
100 N. Center Street
Sunnydale, CA 19874
Telephone: (800) 123–5432
Facsimile: (800) 987–4533

Attorneys for Defendant
ALL PEOPLE MEDICAL GROUP and
MADE A MISTAKE HEALTHCARE, INC

SUPERIOR COURT OF THE STATE OF CALIFORNIA
FOR THE COUNTY OF LOS ANGELES

Patricia Evans	)	Case No. SC 5678–9
	)	Honorable Yes Sir
Plaintiff	)	**DEMAND FOR INDEPENDENT**
		MEDICAL EXAMINATION
	)	
v.	)	Date Action Filed:
	)	November 11, 2011
	)	
All People Medical Group	)	Discovery Cutoff: 02/19/2013
and DOES 1 to 50, inclusive	)	Motion Cutoff: 03/04/2013
	)	Trial Date: 03/18/2014
Defendants.		

TO PLAINTIFF AND TO HER ATTORNEYS OF RECORD:

PLEASE TAKE NOTICE that defendant, All People Medical Group, hereby demands that plaintiff, Patricia Evans appear for an independent medical examination pursuant to *California Code of Civil Procedure* 2032 as follows:

INDEPENDENT MEDICAL EXAMINATION

DATE: **January 21, 2012**
TIME: **9:00 a.m.**
PLACE: **Nice Job Medical Group**
         3335 Downtown Street, Suite 120
         Sunnytown, CA 93333

The examination will be conducted by board-certified physician, John Doe, MD. At the time and place stated above, said examination will consist of a physical examination of plaintiff by Dr. Doe in a manner which is not painful, protracted, or intrusive. Said examination will also include taking a pertinent medical history. The examination may be recorded, in accordance with *Code of Civil Procedure* Section 2032(g)(2), and counsel for all parties may be present in accordance with *Code of Civil Procedures* Section 2032(g)(1).

Plaintiff is requested to respond to this demand by a written statement that plaintiff will either comply with the demand as specifically modified by plaintiff, or will refuse, for reasons specified in a response, to submit to the demanded physical examination, within 20 days hereof. Failure to do so shall require defendant to move for an order competing compliance with this demand and a request for the imposition of monetary sanctions. Any sanctions requested shall include, but not be limited to, any fee charged by the physician for plaintiff's failure to appear at the examination as scheduled, or failure to advise the physician thereof 24 hours prior to the scheduled examination.

DATED: January 10, 2012

By: _____

Attorneys for Defendant
ALL PEOPLE MEDICAL GROUP and
MADE A MISTAKE HEALTHCARE, INC

Appendix B: Sample Response

Jeffrey Jones
122 Valley View Lane
Los Angeles, CA 12345
Telephone: (800) 543–9876
Facsimile: (800) 987–6543

Attorneys for Plaintiff

SUPERIOR COURT OF THE STATE OF CALIFORNIA
FOR THE COUNTY OF LOS ANGELES—EAST DISTRICT

Patricia Evans	)	CASE NO.: SC 5678–9
	)	Assigned to Judge. Yes Sir, Dept. "A"
Plaintiff	)	
	)	
v.	)	**PLAINTIFF'S RESPONSE TO DEMAND**
	)	**FOR INDEPENDENT MEDICAL**
All People Medical Group,	)	**EXAMINATION**
and DOES 1 to 50, inclusive	)	
	)	
Defendants.	)	DATE: January 21, 2012
	)	TIME: 9:00 a.m.
	)	
		Complaint Filed: 11/11/2011

TO DEFENDANTS HEREIN AND TO THEIR ATTORNEYS OF RECORD:
COMES NOW the Plaintiff, Patricia Evans, and, pursuant to the terms and provisions of *Code of Civil Procedure* 2032.230, responds to the Demand for Independent Medical Examination as follows:

RESPONSE TO DEMAND FOR EXAMINATION
Plaintiff will submit to the demanded defense medical examination (hereinafter the DME) on January 21, 2012 at 9:00a.m., to be performed by **John Doe, MD**, (general and vascular surgeon). The following conditions will apply:

1. History of the Underlying Accident

Plaintiff will not discuss the manner in which the underlying accident, which gives rise to this litigation, occurred, other than to describe it in general terms (e.g., automobile accident). Should further information as to the mechanics of the accident be necessary to the defense medical examiner, defendant's counsel may provide a copy of the plaintiff's deposition, or a summary thereof, to the doctor prior to the examination.

2. Identification and Personal Information

Plaintiff recognizes the medical examiner's need to identify the plaintiff at the time of the examination and will provide the following information:

1. Full name
2. Date of birth

Plaintiff will *not* provide the defense medical examiner with additional personal information including, but not limited to, the following:

1. Residence telephone number
2. Medical insurance information or other insurance information
3. Employment history

The basis of this limitation is that the request of the above-listed information would invade plaintiff's right of privacy, is impermissibly overbroad, and, therefore, oppressive, burdensome, and irrelevant to the subject matter of this action. (See, *Britt v. Superior Court* (1978) 20 cal.3d 844.)

Further, any persons assisting the examiner must be fully identified by name and title to plaintiff and on audio recording or court reporter's record. No persons other than plaintiff, his representative, court reporter, doctor, and usual staff are allowed to be present during the examination. No defense observers will be permitted to attend or observe the examination.

3. Medical History

Plaintiff may *not* be compelled to create any items of potential documentary evidence and will *not* fill out *any* charts, new patient records, forms, or histories that may be requested or provided by the defense medical examiner. The basis of this objection is that it is oppressive to require plaintiff to complete any written forms, as opposed to answering questions orally. To require plaintiff to complete written forms would violate plaintiff's right not to create items of demonstrative evidence for defendant's use, and since plaintiff is not a patient of the defense examiner, she/he is consenting to this examination pursuant to the requirements of *Code of Civil Procedure* 2032.230.

Plaintiff recognizes the examiner's need to obtain a *relevant* medical history and will answer any reasonable *relevant* medical history questions posed by the examiner. Plaintiff will not provide a written medical history. Should such a written medical history be required, defendant's counsel may provide either copies of the plaintiff's deposition and medical records or summaries thereof prior to the examination.

Other than questions seeking reasonable, relevant medical history, all other medical history questions will be objected to as invading plaintiff's right of privacy, being impermissibly overbroad, oppressive, burdensome, and irrelevant to the subject matter of the action in that such questions seek disclosure of plaintiff's medical history which, except as answered, does not reasonably relate to the injuries which are the subject of this action. (See, *Britt v. Superior Court* (1978) 20 cal.3d 844.)

4. Financial Responsibility

Plaintiff will *not* assume financial responsibility for any of the medical billings arising as a result of this DME, nor will plaintiff execute an assignment of benefits form.

5. Limitation of X-Rays and Diagnostic Tests

Plaintiff, by and through plaintiff's counsel, has already, or will authorize, access to prior X-rays of the area of the body injured in the accident which gives rise to this instant action. Absent a court order compelling same, plaintiff will *not* submit to any additional X-rays of that area of the body that may be requested by the defense medical examiner.

Pursuant to *Code of Civil Procedure* 2032.220(a)(1), plaintiff will *not* submit to any painful, protracted, or intrusive studies or tests and specifically refuses to submit to any additional X-rays, EEGs, EMGs, blood tests, or urinalyses.

The examination must be limited to plaintiff's conditions, which are in controversy in this action, as provided by *Code of Civil Procedure* 2032.220(a)(1).

6. Timing of the Examination

Plaintiff will *not* be unduly inconvenienced by the defendant's demanded DME.

Plaintiff will appear at the examiner's office on the agreed to date and the requested appointment time. If the DME has not commenced within 30 minutes of the agreed to time, plaintiff will consider this protracted delay to be a waiver of defendant's right to the DME and will leave the medical examiner's office, pursuant to *Code of Civil Procedure* 2032.220(a)(1).

The total time for examination and testing, if applicable, will not exceed two hours. If any period of time exceeding 30 minutes goes by when plaintiff is not being examined by the doctor or his staff, then plaintiff will be free to leave.

Please take further notice that should the defense doctor fail to start the examination promptly and conclude it within the agreed-upon time frame, the examining physician, defense counsel, and/or defendant shall be held responsible for any costs incurred by the waste of time, including, but not limited to the attorney, attorney's representative, paralegal or legal assistant, and/or court reporter.

7. Attendance of Attorney's Representative

The attorney for the examinee or for a party producing the examinee, or that attorney's representative, shall be permitted to attend and observe any physical examination conducted for discovery purposes, and to record stenographically or by audio recording any words spoken to or by the examinee during any phase of the examination. *Code of Civil Procedure* 2032.510(a). Plaintiff's observer will be a registered nurse.

The defense counsel and examiner agree to neither obstruct the plaintiff's observer's view or opportunity to witness all portions of the examination, nor impede observer from reminding the plaintiff to take regular rest and comfort breaks as needed during the examination.

Any cancellation of the examination less than forty-eight (48) business hours before it is scheduled, or refusal to proceed with the examination once plaintiff and plaintiff's observer have arrived, will require the minimal payment of $150.00 as a cancellation fee charged by our observer before the examination can be rescheduled.

8. Doctor to be Provided with this Response

The defense examiner is to be served with a copy of this response prior to the examination.

9. Demand for Production of Report

Pursuant to the provisions of *Code of Civil Procedure* 2032.610, plaintiff demands copies of all reports and writings generated by the doctor of the defense medical examination setting out the history, medical record review, examinations, findings, including the tests and results of all tests made, diagnoses, prognoses, and the conclusions of the defense medical examiner and all record review reports within 30 days following the examination. (See *Kennedy v. Superior Court* (1998) 64 Cal.App. 4th 674.).

DATED: January 12, 2012   LAW OFFICES OF Jeffrey Jones

Jeffrey Jones
Attorney for Plaintiff

Appendix C: Sample Report Paragraph Style

File Name:	Mr. John Doe
Date of Exam:	March 31, 2012
Time of Appointment:	8:30 a.m.
Date of Event:	July 28, 2011
Injury:	Right Ankle and Knee, Back and Neck Pain
Examining Physician:	Dr. Robert Right
Time Observer Arrived:	8:15 a.m.
Time Client Arrived:	8:20 a.m.
Time Exited Office:	11:25 a.m.

Observer Report

Mr. John Doe and I met outside Dr. Right's office at 8:20 a.m. We spoke about the procedures during the exam and all questions were answered. We entered the office and checked in at 8:25 a.m. The recorder was started. The office staff requested a history form be filled out, and I instructed the staff that history forms will not be filled out at the request of the attorney. We had a seat in the lobby and the recorder was stopped.

At 8:40 a.m., we were called into the office. The recorder was started again. A staff member asked questions such as height and weight, current medications, pain level, area of body being examined today, and date of accident. After questions were answered, the staff member left the room and the recorder was stopped.

At 8:55 a.m. the physician entered the room. The recording was restarted. The physician started with an oral interview. He asked several questions. The questions and client responses were:

What date did the accident occur? *July 28, 2011*

So, I see you were hit from behind, is that correct? *Yes*

What part of your body was injured? *Right ankle, right knee, back and neck pain*
(Continued, but shortened for example)

At 9:20 a.m. the physical portion of the exam began. Mr. Doe lay on the table, supine. The examiner lifted the client's right leg and bent it at the knee slowly to approximately 90 degrees with the hip flexed at 90 degrees. Mr. Doe grimaced at approximately 70 degrees, but was able to push through to 90 degrees. The examiner then extended the client's right knee and flexed the hip as far as Mr. Doe could tolerate without causing pain. His leg went to 90 degrees with the knee straight and could go further with the knee bent. … *(Cut short for sample)*

At 9:50 a.m., the examiner had the client sit on the table with his legs hanging off the side. He had Mr. Doe raise his right leg to straighten it out at the knee. He asked the client to raise and lower the right leg three times and asked if there was any pain involved. The client was then asked to do the same with the other leg. … *(Cut short for the sample)*

At 10:05 a.m. the client was asked to stand up and walk forward, then back, 20 feet. The client had a slight limp, appearing to favor the left side and not bear full weight on his right side. The client stated, "I cannot bear full weight on my right leg." He was then asked to go up on his toes and back down again. The examiner asked the client to squat and the client was able to go down approximately half way. The client stated, "That's as far as I can go." He stood back up again and complained of pain as he did. … *(Cut short for the sample)*

At 10:45 a.m. the examiner asked the client when the last x-rays were taken. The client was unable to remember the date. The examiner asked to take x-rays of his right ankle, knee, and neck. I respectfully informed the physician that per the Response Letter no x-rays or invasive testing is allowed. The physician stated that he could not complete his report without new x-rays. I informed the physician that if he felt strongly about it, I would contact the attorney to ask. At 10:50 a.m. the physician exited the room and I contacted the attorney regarding the request. The attorney stated, "Absolutely not, there will be no x-rays allowed." At 10:55 a.m. the physician re-entered the room and I informed him of what the attorney stated regarding x-rays. He stated, "Well, I tried." At 11:00 a.m. the physical examination continued. … *(Cut short for the sample)*

At 11:20 a.m., the physician stated the exam was finished and exited the room. The client donned his socks and shoes, we exited the exam room, and walked out of the office at 11:25 a.m.. The recorder was stopped after exiting the office. We spoke briefly outside the office as we exited the building. In the parking lot, the client asked if he did ok and I responded, "yes." He asked what the next step was and I instructed him to speak to his attorney.

Respectfully,
Nikki Chuml, MSN/Ed, RNC-OB, PRN

Appendix D: Sample Report Table Format

Defense Medical Examination
Jane Doe
November 20, 2014
Plastic Surgeon
Dr. Daryl Right

Table 6.1

Time	Observations
2:40 p.m.	Arrived at Dr. Right's office.
3:10 p.m.	Client arrived at Dr. Right's office.
3:30 p.m.	Appointment time.
4:07 p.m.	Called into examination room by nurse. No questions asked by staff member.
4:08 p.m.	Dr. Right entered examination room.
4:10 p.m.	Interviewed by Dr. Right on the incident. Dr. Right asked the following questions: What time did you have your surgery? 11 a.m. You were in the recovery room when the incident happened? Yes Do you remember the event? Yes, it hurt so bad. …(Shortened for sample) Dr. Right asked if he could examine client with a gown on. Client agreed.
4:25 p.m.	Dr. Right left room.
4:26 p.m.	Nurse Nice entered room and helped client remove pants and shirt. Client was helped onto examination table and placed supine in frog-leg position. A paper sheet was placed over client's abdomen and pelvic area.
4:29 p.m.	Nurse Nice left room.
4:30 p.m.	Dr. Right entered room with Nurse Nice and camera.
4:30–4:33 p.m.	Dr. Right took one picture of the inner aspect of the right thigh and one picture of the inner aspect of the left thigh from the distance of approximately 18 inches. Dr. Right stated, "The skin on inner left thigh appears smooth and intact, with no redness noted. Skin on inner right thigh appears discolored, with reddened, raised bumpy areas. Perineal area appeared slightly reddened, intact, with no raised or bumpy areas noted." Client was kept in supine position, back of buttocks was not visible.
4:33 p.m.	Dr. Right left room for additional equipment.
4:33 p.m.	Dr. Right returned to room in 5–10 seconds with device for camera.
4:34 p.m.	Dr. Right took one additional picture of the inner aspect of the right thigh with the device attached to front of camera. Dr. Right stated the device was a close-up attachment.
4:35 p.m.	Dr. Right left room, Nurse Nice instructed client to dress.
4:36 p.m.	I stopped recording and told client she may leave when finished dressing then I left the room.
4:45 p.m.	Client left examination room. We then left the office. Client left without discussing exam with me.

Respectfully,
Nikki Chuml, MSN/Ed, RNC-OB, PRN

Appendix E: Sample Report In-house LNC

Memo to:
From:
Date:
Re: Jane Doe

On _____ I attended Jane's DME with Dr. Gray, who flew up from Conn. to do the exam. We met Dr. Gray at the office of Bradley Jones, MD on Silver Ave. We arrived 15 minutes early. He was waiting for us and saw Jane immediately. Jane was not requested to fill out any paperwork prior to the exam.

We entered the small exam room at 10:46 a.m. Dr. Gray had a laptop and proceeded to type the history Jane gave him on a form in his laptop. He told us that he was using the same history form he uses with his patients. He asked for my business card and gave me his business card.

The history portion of the exam occurred from 10:46 a.m. to 11:27 a.m. Following are the initial questions/answers he asked and Jane answered:

Identifying Information

1. Age, address, and DOB.
2. Date of injury—she told him that the injury occurred on the date Dr. Sweet did surgery. She could not recall the exact date.
3. Allergies—no known drug allergies. She does have eczema.
4. Current meds—Dilaudid 2mg PRN. She takes this when the pain is really bad. She does not take it unless the pain is really bad because the Dilaudid "makes her sick"—she gets N/V and dizziness when she takes Dilaudid. All pain meds make her "sick." On average, she takes Dilaudid three times a week. She has been on Dilaudid "for years." Dr. Brown recently gave her a Rx for a new pain med to trial—Lyrica.

(Cut short for the sample)

Family History

Dad died at age 44 of MI. Mom is 65 and healthy. Has one child who is 26 yrs and healthy.

Do any family members have any unusual disorders or medical conditions? Mom and sister have high blood pressure; brother has "some type of heart problem."

Social History

She has smoked since about age 16. Dr. Gray commented that this is "bad." Doesn't drink at all except a glass of wine on special occasions—very rare. Has been married for 18 years. Finished 9th grade and then got her GED. Last worked Dec 2000. She formerly did factory work—some assembly line work. This involved a lot of standing and work with her hands.

Review of Systems

Except for the pain, she generally feels well, i.e. if she didn't have pain, she would feel good. No ENT problems except for allergies. Recently had pain in her chest for three days. Saw the doctor on call who ordered a nuclear stress test—this was normal.

Dr. Gray rattled off a litany of conditions/symptoms (such as seizure, stroke, etc.) affecting the various body systems—she replied "no" to all. She did say that she has had eczema since childhood that she believes is exacerbated by stress and heat.

She reported being 5′6″ tall and weighing 134 lbs.

Current Complaints/Symptoms

Dr. Gray spent at least 20 minutes discussing her various complaints in great detail. Following is a summary of what she said:

> She has low back pain, which radiates down the left lateral buttock to the posterior upper thigh (hamstring), to the lateral side of her left knee, lateral calf, ankle and then to foot (lateral >medical side of left foot). Sometimes her whole leg "locks down" in spasm. All her toes are numb, but also hypersensitive. She has numbness on both the tops of her feet and on the soles.

Leg Pain

This is her worst pain.

The pain shoots down her left leg and feels like a hot burning pain. She described it as "burning, stabbing, and throbbing."

The pain is constant, but the intensity varies. Superimposed on the constant pain is an intense pain that makes her "want to die." This pain will occur if she stands in one spot too long or walks too long. When she has this type of pain (usually from overdoing it) she must rest for a couple days to get back to her baseline.

Back Pain

She has pain in the middle of her low back all the time—a constant ache. Laying down makes it a little bit better—about 10% better. Standing or sitting for too long makes it worse. Periodically shifting her weight while sitting makes the pain a little better. Her average pain on a scale of 1–10 is a "6."

(Cut short for sample)

Sleep

She does not sleep well at all. She sleeps poorly due to the pain.

Current Physicians

Her PCP (Dr. Pine) and Dr. Brown at the Pain Clinic.

What Does She Do in a Typical Day?

6 a.m.—awakens and feeds the dog and cat. Sits in a chair, talks to her husband, and watches the news. Goes back to bed after her husband leaves.

8 a.m.—Gets up again and sits in a chair—watches TV, talks on the phone, and reads. Has toast for breakfast.

Doesn't eat lunch. Mid-afternoon, 2–3 times per week, visits mom who lives about 2 miles away. She drives to see her mom. She may also give her son a ride to work which is also about 2 miles away.

(*Cut short for sample*)

Activities

The longest car trip she can take without exacerbating her pain is 20 minutes to a half hour. If she is in the car longer than this, she requires a period of recovery to get back to her baseline.

Associated Symptoms

Jane said that she has "charlie horses" all day long along the lateral left calf. If she moves her foot a certain way, it "locks down." By this she means it flexes down. Dr. Gray called this a "legitimate pain." When this happens, it usually lasts for 5–10 minutes. About once per week, the spasms will keep coming back during the course of the day with certain movements.

History of Present Illness

She is 43 yrs old and in good general health except for the complications of Dr. Sweet's surgery. The nature of her pain has changed over time. Until recently, she never had the burning pain in her left buttock area. Dr. Brown did not say what is causing this new buttock pain.

After Dr. White's revision surgery she did not get better. Dr. White told her there is nothing more he can do for her.

(*Cut short for sample*)

Physical Examination

This lasted for just about a half hour.

With Jane still dressed and seated in the same chair, Dr. Gray tested her cranial nerves and told us everything was WNL. Her BP was low at 102/62 and her HR was only 60. He listened to her lungs and heart and told her that she had a mitral systolic murmur.

He next had her put on a patient gown so he could examine her back. First, he asked her to squat (which she could do, although she told him it was going to make her left leg spasm) and then to rise up on her toes and heels. She was able to do this on the right, but not the left.

His first observation about her back (and he had me get up and move behind him so I could observe what he was doing) is that her scapulae are uneven—he said her back is "winged" in that the left scapula is higher than the right. It did indeed look as though the left scapula was higher than the right.

He also said that she has a functional leg length discrepancy related to a pelvic shift or rotation and the resulting "posture" is responsible for some of her back pain. Also, when he placed a finger on each side of her pelvis at approximately the same anatomical position, one finger did look higher than the other.

(*Cut short for sample*)

General Observations

At the outset of the exam, Dr. Gray told Jane that he was going to type her responses right into his laptop as they went along. He often read aloud what he was typing. He said that he was using the same intake forms he uses with his patients and was trying to get everything down accurately. He was pleasant and engaging. He told Jane that she looked younger than her age and at the end of the exam, said she was "charming."

He told us that he was hired as an "objective" examiner to "sort" everything out. He had about an inch of medical records and a letter from the [defense law] office.

Memo to:
From:
Re: Jane Doe—comments re Gray IME report
Date:
In general, the information documented in the HPI is consistent with what Jane told him.

I do think that several issues he raises need to be discussed with Dr. Brown—

1. Does he agree that she has a "pelvic shift. Left hemipelvis up. Prominent right scapula"? This is not documented in any other physician records including [six different treating physician] records.
2. Does he agree that she has a "thoracic scoliosis on two planes: vertical and rotational"? This is not documented in any other physician records including his records.
3. Assuming Dr. Gray is correct that she does have a pelvic shift and/or thoracic scoliosis, in what way, if any, would this play a role in her left leg pain, middle back pain, and charlie horses along the left lateral calf?
4. Assuming she has evidence of more shoe wear on the left than right, what is likely causing this?
5. Does he agree there is no evidence of atrophy? Visually, her left calf appears smaller than her right, but his measurements above and below the knee were identical.

(Cut short for sample)

Section III

Medical Records

Chapter 7

Sources of Medical Information

Patricia J. Bartzak, DNP, RN, CMSRN
Deborah Enicke, RN, CEN, COS-C, HCS-D
Patricia Ann "Stormy" Green, RN, BSHS, RNFA

Contents

Objectives

- Identify the components of a hospital record
- Describe five types of outpatient records
- Identify other types of records that may contain pertinent medical information

Introduction

Medical documentation is critical to establishing or disproving the elements of proof in medical legal tort claims (for additional information see Chapter 4). The LNC plays a critical role in identifying and analyzing the pertinent sources of medical information, which varies with type of case and alleged injuries. In medical malpractice cases, for example, the behind-the-scenes LNC identifies information pertinent to standards of care, causation, and damages. In other types of cases such as motor vehicle accidents, slip and fall, or toxic tort cases, the LNC identifies medical evidence pertinent to causation and damages. Nurse experts identify evidence pertinent to nursing standards of care and nursing causation in malpractice cases.

It is important for the LNC to identify and analyze those records pertinent to plaintiff's baseline health and prior injuries to the same body system or part. In some states, aggravation of a pre-existing injury is compensable. The LNC identifies records that may document the nature and consequences of the alleged injury including functional limitations, pain and suffering, and employment ability.

This chapter outlines numerous sources of medical information that may be encountered by the LNC. Although most providers now use an electronic health records system, some providers still maintain paper records or a hybrid of the two.

Inpatient Hospital Records

Hospital records, including inpatient and emergency department records, are among the most common (and voluminous) sources of medical information. Each hospital has a customized electronic health records (EHR) system and corresponding forms (which vary with the type of patient care unit). There are multiple vendors offering EHR, with the ability to customize a program for each healthcare system. EHRs produced for litigation in a PDF file do not look the same as the data on computer screens utilized by healthcare providers (for more information on electronic health records, see Chapter 9). The following types of medical information may be contained in a hospital record:

Face Sheet

The face sheet contains identifying information such as:

- Patient name and date of birth
- Medical record number
- Gender, ethnicity, or religion
- Patient contact information
- Admission date and time
- Discharge date and time
- Contact information for next of kin or other emergency contact
- Names of attending and primary care physicians
- Admitting diagnosis and ICD code
- Insurance carrier/s and identification numbers/s
- DRG Codes (Diagnosis Related Group)

Consent Forms

A patient must give verbal and/or signed consent prior to medical treatment being provided. Physicians and other providers such as advanced practice nurses and physician assistants, have a legal duty to provide patients with information about the risks, benefits, and alternatives of procedures they perform. The procedure consent form is one source of evidence pertaining to the informed consent discussion that took place between the provider and the patient. It typically identifies the procedure being performed, who will be performing the procedure, and the risks associated with the procedure. The provider, patient, and sometimes a witness sign and date the consent form prior to the administration of pre-procedure medication. Consent forms may also be required for certain courses of treatment (such as radiation therapy) or patient participation in a research study. In some states informed consent requirements are statutory and in others, they are found in common (case) law. For cases venued in federal court due to diversity, state laws regarding informed consent applies. For more information regarding informed consent, see Chapter 19.

Other types of consents found in a hospital record, include consents for admission to the facility, treatment by various departments, and those pertaining to billing matters.

Discharge Summary

The discharge summary is an overview of a hospitalization. It includes:

- Dates of the hospitalization
- Reason for admission and history of present illness
- Medical history and physical exam (H&P) upon admission
- Course of treatment, including procedures
- Response to treatment
- Any complications of conditions or treatment
- Patient's discharge status
- Post-discharge care recommendations

Discharge Instructions

The Joint Commission encourages hospitals to clarify the responsibilities of patients and their families regarding the patient's ongoing healthcare needs, providing the knowledge and skills they need to carry out these responsibilities (The Joint Commission, Division of Health Care Improvement, 2015). Many healthcare facilities require nursing staff to document patient receipt and understanding of discharge instructions. The patient or responsible party signs the discharge instructions acknowledging receipt and understanding.

Consultations

An attending physician or other provider (such as a resident, advanced practice registered nurse, or physician assistant) often requests consultations from various medical subspecialties to assist with a diagnosis and make treatment recommendations. This may include, for example, cardiology, infectious disease, orthopedic surgery, or neurosurgery. Patients with complex or life threatening medical conditions are likely to need multiple medical consultations. Allied health professional consultations such as nutrition, physical and occupational therapy, social services, etc. may also make recommendations.

History and Physical Exam Note

This note has five primary components:

- History
  - Chief complaint
  - History of present illness
  - Past medical history
  - Surgical history
  - Social history
  - Family history
  - Home medications
- Review of Systems
- Physical examination
  - Patient's baseline health
  - Findings of the physical examination
  - Vital signs
  - Diagnostic study test results (i.e., imaging, laboratory)
- Assessments
- Plan of care

According to The Joint Commission, "more than one qualified practitioner can participate in performing, documenting, and authenticating an H&P for a single patient. When performance, documentation, and authentication are split among qualified practitioners, the practitioner who authenticates the H&P will be held responsible for its contents" (The Joint Commission, 2018a).

Physician, Advanced Practice Registered Nurse (APRN), or Physician Assistant (PA) Notes

Physicians, APRNs, and PAs write progress or other notes in conjunction with direct patient encounters, as well as to report diagnostic test findings or discussions with other healthcare providers or family members. Information in such notes may include:

- Subjective complaints
- Objective findings
- Changes in the patient's clinical status, including new problems or significant medical events
- Patient's response to treatment
- Diagnostic test results
- Acknowledgment of consultants' recommendations
- Acknowledgment of assessment and care provided by allied health professionals
- Plan for future treatment

Imaging Reports (Non-interventional)

The minimum information in an imaging report should include (American College of Radiology [ACR], 2014):

- Patient and facility demographics
- Name of ordering provider(s) or notation that patient is self-referred
- Name or type of examination
- Date of the examination
- Time of the examination, if relevant
- Relevant history or clinical information
- Findings, using appropriate anatomic, pathologic, and radiologic terminology to describe the findings
- Comparison with relevant prior studies and reports
- An impression, along with a differential diagnosis when appropriate
- Recommendation for additional diagnostic studies to clarify or confirm the diagnosis when appropriate
- Significant adverse patient reaction to the study or contrast material (ACR, 2014)

Imaging Films

Many facilities use digital imaging systems, or DICOM (Digital Imaging and Communications in Medicine), to save radiology images. Law firms requesting such images receive them on compact discs (CDs), digital virtual discs (DVDs), or via a secure file-sharing site. Firm personnel (and their medical experts) will need to download the appropriate imaging software to view the images.

Laboratory Records

Laboratory tests are important to identify a patient's baseline and to track trends in test results. Each laboratory report may include:

- Ordering provider
- Date and time of order
- Name of test(s) ordered
- Date and time of specimen collection
- Test result, including date and time of result
- Preliminary result, when applicable (e.g., blood cultures)
- Normal range values for that lab
- Flagging of results below or above the normal range

Transfusion Records

The blood product label includes:

- Patient unit number
- Blood product type
- Volume

- Expiration date
- Antigen typing
- Patient label

The nursing administration record includes documentation regarding:

- Signatures of two individuals (one of whom must be an RN) verifying information identifying the donor unit and recipient and the patient blood type and Rh factor (to ensure blood product compatibility)
- Route of administration (i.e., peripheral IV, central line)
- Use of blood warmer
- Date and time transfusion started and ended
- Provider who started and ended transfusion
- Amount infused
- Vital signs according to facility policy (typically pre, during, and post-infusion)

If a reaction to the blood product occurs, the provider documents the time the transfusion was stopped, the type of reaction, the patient's medical status, nursing interventions, and time the physician was notified regarding the reaction.

Patient Orders

Licensed independent providers (LIPs), including physicians, APRNs, and PAs, issue written and oral patient orders. Facility policies and procedures dictate guidelines pertaining to patient orders. For example, verbal orders may require documentation of order verification such as a second witness to the order or documentation that the nurse read back the order. Verbal orders are a potential source of medical error and thus, often discouraged unless necessary.

LIP orders should include date and time of the order, the name and title of the issuing provider and co-signer when required by hospital policy. LIPs issue standing orders when the plan of care for a designated group of patients (e.g., post-operative patients, insulin dependent diabetics) is the same. In some cases, the LIP will individualize standing orders for a particular patient. Facility policies and procedures dictate guidelines pertaining to standing orders.

Medication Administration Records (MAR)

The MAR contains detailed information about all prescribed and administered medications, including:

- Name of medication
- Date medication prescribed
- Medication form (i.e., tablet), strength, and dose
- Route, frequency, and specific time medication is to be administered, if applicable
- Date and time of actual administration, along with name or initials of provider who administered the medication
- Duration of prescription
- Date medication stopped

Information regarding medication side effects, why a medication was not administered (i.e., patient refused), and the patient's response to certain medications (i.e., analgesics) should be recorded on the MAR, the nursing flow sheets, or progress notes.

The LIP, pharmacist, or nursing staff must enter medication allergies into the electronic health record. The computer system alerts the pharmacist about drug allergies, cross-sensitivity among drugs, or drug–drug interactions.

Data Flow Sheets

Electronic data flow sheets contain sequential data, sometimes from more than one patient care area. For example, flow sheets may contain vital signs and other data from the emergency department, post-anesthesia care unit (PACU), and the patient care unit. Data flow sheets contain information about a wide range of patient data, including:

- Vital signs
- Oxygen saturation
- Pain levels (may also be on MAR)
- Vascular access (i.e., IVs, arterial lines)
- Monitoring devices (i.e., heart monitor, bed alarms)
- Supplemental oxygen use (how administered and flow rate)
- Neurologic assessments and interventions
- Respiratory assessments and interventions
- Nursing assessments (see nursing assessments for details)
- Intake and output
- Urinary catheters
- Patient position
- Weights

Nursing Progress Notes

The bedside nurse provides skilled care throughout each shift, closely assessing and monitoring the patient's condition. Nursing notes document changes in the patient's baseline condition and progress toward care goals, as documented in the Nursing Care Plan. The LNC should determine whether the documentation system is exception-based or narrative-based. An exception-based documentation system provides documentation that is outside the patient's norm, whereas a narrative note provides a more comprehensive accounting of the patient's condition for each shift. When reviewing a medical malpractice claim, nursing notes can substantiate or contradict documentation elsewhere in the patient's hospital record.

Nursing Assessments

The nursing admission assessment documents important considerations for nursing care during the patient's stay. This includes the patient's physical limitations, functional status, mental status, any feeding problems, allergies, and a current list of medications. Nursing assessments include:

- Fall risk
- Pressure injury risk

- Obstructive sleep apnea evaluation
- Speech and swallow evaluations
- Substance abuse including smoking, alcohol, and drugs
- Neurological assessments and checks, including Glasgow Coma Scale
- Emergency Severity Index (ESI) score (emergency department)
- Pain assessment
- Review of Systems (ROS)
- Suicide risk assessment
- Stroke risk and assessment
- Sepsis bundle data
- Malignant hypothermia
- Domestic violence, elder abuse, child abuse, spousal abuse
- Human trafficking

Nursing Care Plan

The nursing care plan is the basis for administering nursing care to a patient. It includes a nursing diagnosis, nursing interventions, care goals, and evaluation of the patient's progress toward the identified care goals. Some documentation systems auto-generate nursing care plans based on responses to assessment questions. The nurse may have the option to modify the nursing care plan to reflect new or resolved problems. In a nursing negligence claim, the nursing care plan can be utilized as evidence or lack thereof, for the appropriate standard of nursing care.

Allied Health Provider Records

Allied health provider consultations are another source of medical information. This includes patient assessment by:

- Physical Therapy
- Occupational Therapy
- Speech-Language Therapy
- Respiratory Therapy
- Infusion Services
- Audiology
- Chaplain Services
- Social Services
- Dietary and nutrition
- Neuropsychology
- Mental health providers
- Social work
- Case management

Surgical or Procedure Records

Records for patients undergoing a surgical or other invasive procedure contain a number of surgical records including:

Pre-operative Nursing Records

- ■ Vital signs
- ■ Pre-operative testing results
- ■ Allergies
- ■ Last food or drink
- ■ Nursing assessments
- ■ Surgical/procedural consents
- ■ IV infusions and medications administered
- ■ Time any provider visited patient
- ■ Time patient was transferred from the pre-operative area and name of the person that transferred the patient
- ■ Names and credentials of all pre-operative providers

Intraoperative Nursing Records

According to the Association of periOperative Registered Nurses (AORN), nursing documentation should comply with local, state, and national regulatory requirements (AORN, 2015). Minimum intraoperative documentation includes:

- ■ Patient demographics
- ■ Date of procedure
- ■ A brief patient assessment (includes presence of dentures, glasses, medical devices such as pacemaker or artificial hip, etc.)
- ■ Allergies
- ■ Times:
  - – Patient admitted to the operating room
  - – Anesthesia start and end times
  - – Procedure start and end times
  - – Patient transfer from the operating room to the PACU
- ■ Names, roles, and times all providers present in the surgical or procedure suite including physicians, nurses, technicians (i.e., scrub, perfusionist), and other care providers (i.e., physician assistants, nurse practitioners), as well as sales representatives for devices implanted or utilized during the procedure
- ■ Actions taken to prepare the patient for the surgery or procedure (i.e., insertion of urinary catheter, arterial line, or intravenous access line)
- ■ Information related to patient positioning including position description (i.e., lithotomy), use of positioning devices or padding, and how the patient was secured, including extremities, and names of those involved in positioning
- ■ Equipment identification number (EIN) of all equipment used during the procedure, such as electric cautery unit, laser unit. The EIN may be the actual serial number, or it may be a number previously assigned by the facility. Most often, EINs are assigned by either a biomedical department or engineering department
- ■ Location of grounding pad site and skin condition after its removal
- ■ The sponge, instrument, and sharp counts before and after the procedure
- ■ Pre-operative and post-operative diagnoses
- ■ Procedures performed

- Topical medications used on the operative field
- Wound classification
- Implant information, including manufacturer and lot number
- Information about the nature and disposition of pathological specimens, hardware, or other objects removed during surgery
- Estimated blood loss

Time Out and Side/Site Marking

Time out and side/site marking, also known as Universal Protocol (The Joint Commission, 2018c) is a critical component of every operation or procedure. It was adopted pursuant to the World Health Organization (WHO) Guidelines for Safe Surgery 2009 (WHO, 2009). Its purpose is promoting patient safety by preventing wrong site, wrong procedure, and wrong person surgery. The time out should occur just prior to initiation of the procedure or just prior to incision. Whenever possible, the patient should be involved in the process. The person performing the procedure marks the operative site. All team members participate in the process with concerns addressed at this time. At a minimum, all team members must agree on correct patient identity, the correct site, and the planned procedure (The Joint Commission, 2012). Facility policies and procedures, which must comply with any federal and state regulations, dictate what information should be documented.

Anesthesia Records

The pre-operative anesthesia assessment is completed prior to the administration of anesthesia and includes information about:

- Past anesthesia experience
- Type of anesthesia planned
- Airway assessment
- Informed consent discussion pertaining to anesthesia
- American Society of Anesthesiologists (ASA) score

The ASA score is an assessment of the degree of the patient's health and their risk for anesthetic complications. It is determined by utilizing the Physical Status Classification System of the ASA (ASA, 2014). This assessment process assigns a category based on the ASA scale of P1 (Class 1), which indicates "a normally healthy patient," through P6 (Class 6), "a declared brain-dead patient whose organs are being removed for donor purposes." Patients assigned a higher ASA score receive more intensive anesthesia monitoring.

After the pre-operative workup, the anesthesia provider drafts an anesthesia plan for the patient including the pre-operative medication, the type of induction, and the type of anesthesia.

Either an anesthesiologist or a certified registered nurse anesthetist (CRNA) provide anesthesia and patient monitoring during surgical procedures. Some states allow a certified anesthesiologist assistant (CAA) to provide anesthesia care for patients undergoing operative procedures. CAAs must meet certain educational criteria and pass a national exam (American Academy of Anesthesiologist Assistants, 2017). Sometimes the induction is performed by a CRNA or CAA with an anesthesiologist present, who subsequently leaves the OR suite to oversee another anesthesia provider.

The anesthesia record includes:

- Date of procedure
- Anesthesia start and end times
- Procedure start and end times
- Time of patient transfer to PACU
- Type of anesthesia administered
- Information regarding airway maintenance
- All medications and IV fluids administered
- Intake and output
- Estimated blood loss
- Vital signs
- Names and titles of all anesthesia providers

Operative and Procedure Reports

Surgical procedures are performed in an operating suite. Other invasive procedures may take place in the radiology department, endoscopy unit, intensive care unit, or the pre-operative area. The provider who performed the surgery or procedure completes a procedure report, which must be completed within the period mandated by the facility's policies and procedures. For surgical procedures, the surgeon completes an interim operative report to ensure skilled care in the post-operative period and transition to next level of care (The Joint Commission, 2018b).

Information included on the procedure or operative report includes:

- Name of surgeon and assistant(s)
- Name of anesthesia provider(s)
- Type of anesthesia
- A brief history stating reason for procedure
- Pre-operative diagnoses
- Procedure(s) performed
- Post-operative diagnoses
- Operative findings
- Detailed description of procedure including patient positioning, surgical technique, complications, and management of any complications
- Identity and disposition of removed tissue, hardware, or other objects
- Implant information
- Estimated blood loss
- Sponge, instrument, and sharp counts

Pathology Report

The pathology department generates a report pertaining to all tissue or other specimens removed during a surgical procedure. They are identified and placed in separate containers. The report includes:

- Identity of specimen(s)
- A gross, or visual, description of each specimen including measurements, color, and texture

- A microscopic description of tissue specimens
- A final tissue diagnosis

PACU or Recovery Room Record

The PACU or recovery room record includes:

- Arrival time
- Time patient arrived along with name of person who transferred the patient and provided handoff information
- ALDRETE score (scale for determining when a patient can be safely discharged from the PACU to post-surgical unit or Phase II recovery area)
- Patient assessment and nursing response to findings
  - Vital signs
  - Pain assessment
  - Neurologic status
  - Condition of dressings
  - Medications administered and the patient's response to the medication
  - Observations specific to the procedure(s) performed
  - Ability to ambulate and urinate
- Time of transfer and mode of transportation to receiving unit
- Report to receiving nurse

The anesthesia staff also assesses the patient post-operatively, including response to anesthesia and monitoring of pain relief interventions such as patient controlled epidural analgesia (PCEA) and intravenous patient controlled analgesia (PCA).

For same day surgery patients, the post-surgery record also includes discharge instructions and means by which the patient was discharged (i.e., wheelchair, ambulatory, taxi, car).

Emergency Department

Components of the Emergency Department (ED) record include:

- Times of arrival, initial assessment by triage nurse, medical assessment (MD, PA, or APRN), transfer, or discharge
- Triage level assignment
- Chief complaint
- History of present illness
- Vital signs
- Lab test results
- Procedures done (i.e., imaging, suturing)
- Consultations
- Assessment
- Differential diagnoses
- Diagnoses
- Treatment plan
- Discharge instructions
- Names and titles of all providers

The Emergency Medical Treatment and Labor Act (EMTALA) is a 1986 federal law requiring that anyone who presents to the emergency department must be stabilized and treated irrespective of whether the patient has health insurance or the ability to pay for services (Centers for Medicare & Medicaid Services, 2012).

Professional associations such as those listed below promulgate emergency services practice guidelines:

■ American College of Emergency Physicians (ACEP)—a professional physician organization that establishes clinical policies, policy statements, provides education opportunities and conferences, and publishes a peer reviewed journal to keep emergency department physicians current regarding current trends in the emergency department
■ Emergency Nurses Association (ENA)—a national professional organization for ED nurses which publishes professional practice guidelines and a peer reviewed journal

Sources of Medical Information not Part of the Hospital Record

Facility Management Records

In some hospital or professional negligence claims involving a hospital employee, certain facility records are pertinent and may be produced during discovery including:

■ Staffing schedules and patient care assignments
■ Policies and procedures
■ Interdepartmental communications
■ Staff education logs
■ Facility equipment maintenance records
■ Incident reports
■ Infection Control logs
■ State and federal survey reports
■ Audit trails

Electronic Communications

Electronic communications include emails, texts, text pages, or other provider-to-provider communications. This data often resides on a facility server. When relevant, plaintiff's counsel can request production of this data during discovery.

Patient Portals

Providers are increasingly using electronic patient portals to convey test results and other medical information, respond to patient questions, and prescribe medications. Patients use portals to schedule appointments, complete healthcare surveys, request medication refills, and submit non-urgent medical questions to a provider. Some portals allow a patient to upload photographs, such as of a rash or wound.

Hospital Logs

Various hospital departments maintain logs.

Emergency department logs may contain information about staffing, training records for residents (i.e., number of procedures performed), and resuscitation data. They may also contain data about the number of patients admitted, transferred, treated, refusing treatment, and discharged.

Surgical areas maintain numerous logs including those pertaining to surgical equipment, the surgical environment, operating times and schedules, patient factors, and surgical specimens including:

- Temperature and humidity for each surgical suite (may also be found in the Engineering Department)
- Refrigerator and freezer temperatures
- Tissue specimens (may also be found in Pathology records)
- Laser logs for each laser used in the department
- Tissue banking logs (for breast milk, bone, cadaveric tissue)
- Sterilizer logs (may be found in Sterile Processing Department or Central Supply)
- Implant logs (implant identification and lot number, date implanted, surgeon)
- Patient positioning
- Sponge counts
- Surgery schedules (including procedure, surgeon, anesthesia provider, OR suite, special requests for instrumentation or beds)
- Presence of sales representatives in the operating room

Post-operative anesthesia care units maintain patient logs that track the census and nurse–patient ratios. For each listed patient, the log identifies:

- Surgeon
- Anesthesia provider
- Procedure
- Time the patient arrived in department
- Time the patient was discharged from department
- Discharge status (i.e., home, ICU)
- RN assigned to care for the patient

Radiology logs include the procedure performed and type of contrast used (if any). Some facilities also log resident training data.

Pharmacy logs or records including:

- Computerized records for each patient, including name of medication and prescriber
- Pharmacist preparing medication order and co-signer
- Product or medication ordering information including supplier, minimum needed, current inventory
- Temperature logs for temperature-sensitive medications
- Parenteral and enteral product labels and dispensing data
- Data required by law pertaining to administration and wasting of controlled substances
- Floor stock delivered to patient care units

- Medications stored in crash carts
- Maintenance records for IV and chemotherapy hoods

Electronic Fetal Monitoring (EFM)

The hospital preserves all electronic fetal monitoring done prenatally or during labor and delivery as part of the mother's record. However, a specific request for the EFM strip when requesting the mother's record may be necessary. Some fetal monitoring systems can produce enhanced strips that are color coded and enlarged, for more accurate strip interpretation. When available, plaintiff counsel may request production of the enhanced strip during discovery.

Photographs

Medical providers may take and preserve digital photographs of various medical conditions, treatment, or test results including:

- Burns, wounds, pressure ulcers, bruises
- Dermatological diseases
- Findings during endoscopy procedures
- "Before and after" photographs documenting cosmetic surgery results
- Ophthalmology imaging or scans

Providers may require a specific request for photographs or they may be produced during discovery.

Videotapes

Surgeons may authorize video recording of surgical procedures, primarily for teaching purposes. Families may also record births. The surgeon or obstetrician may request termination of recording if complications are encountered during the procedure or birth.

Emergency Medical Services (EMS)

Several entities provide EMS and ground or air transportation to hospitals including volunteer services, for-profit agencies, and fire departments. The hospital face sheet usually identifies the name(s) of the entities providing EMS.

Documentation on the EMS record typically includes:

- Times (of initial call requesting services; arrival at and departure from scene; arrival at receiving facility)
- Presence of other first responders at the scene
- Initial assessment, including history and physical exam
- Treatment (CPR, stabilization) provided at scene
- Interventions during transport (medications, procedures, monitoring)
- Assessments during transport, including when applicable, specialized assessments such as the Glasgow Coma Scale (GCS), Revised Trauma Scale (RTS), or a stroke assessment
- Communications with receiving facility
- Healthcare provider(s) at receiving facility assuming care of patient

EMS also provide non-emergency facility-to-facility transportation for patient requiring medical monitoring or services during transport.

Death Certificate

Death certificate forms and policies for completing them vary by state. In general, information of the form includes:

- Name and address of the deceased
- Date and time of death
- Place of death
- Social Security number
- Demographics, such as age, race, marital status, birthplace
- Medical certification:
  - Date and time of death if known
  - Primary cause of death
  - Contributory cause(s) of death
  - Manner of death
- If an injury had occurred:
  - The type of injury (i.e., accident, suicide, homicide)
  - The setting of the incident (i.e., home, school, industrial setting)
- The name and title of the provider completing the death certificate

Autopsy Report

Hospital staff pathologists conduct an autopsy at the request of next-of-kin following an in-hospital death. In addition, state law mandates referral to the County Coroner or Medical Examiner for investigation for some types of death. This may include, for example, accidental deaths and deaths from falls, vehicular accidents, explosions, firearms, or drug overdose, among others. In some states, the death certificate indicates referral to the medical examiner.

The pathologist commonly issues a preliminary report followed by a final report once toxicological testing, consultations, and microscopic or other studies are complete. It can take several months for the pathologist to issue a final report, which includes:

- Facility where autopsy was performed
- Name and title of the pathologist
- Date and time of death
- Date and time of autopsy
- Examination type (i.e., partial autopsy, complete autopsy)
- Names and titles of all prosectors (additional individuals involved in the dissection of corpses for examination or anatomical demonstration)
- Historical summary (brief medical history, diagnoses, circumstances that may have led to death)
- External examination—a gross, visual examination of the body including:
  - Photographs of the body
  - Height and weight
  - Skin color and condition, tattoos, scars

- Evidence of medical intervention such as tubes, puncture sites, bandages, or condition of recent incisions
- Evidence of postmortem changes which can assist the pathologist in interpretation of other findings

■ Internal examination:
- Body cavities including condition, and position of organs
- Description of each body part examined (i.e., brain atrophy, fecal material, or purulent debris present in abdominal cavity)
- Weight of organs
- Specimens taken for microscopic examination
- Organs recovered for transplant (i.e., for research, transplant)

■ Results of all lab tests (including toxicology, microbiology, or other tests performed)
■ Final anatomic diagnosis (FAD)—the cause(s) of death

The Medical Examiner's complete file includes additional documents such as photographs, medical literature, and interviews with witnesses that may be pertinent in some cases.

Pathology Specimens

Microscopic slides prepared from surgical specimens are stored in the pathology department. Specimens pertinent to autopsies are stored at the location of the autopsy. When relevant to a legal claim, the plaintiff attorney sends notice to the pathology department, requesting preservation of the slides (and remaining tissue blocks). In some cases, new slides with recuts of the pertinent tissue block are sufficient for expert pathology review. In other cases, experts on both sides analyze the original slides. Transport of original slides requires adherence to chain of custody requirements and care to prevent slide damage.

Medical Equipment Records

Defective medical equipment causing injury to patients or others is the basis for some products liability claims against the manufacturer. A hospital's failure to keep a piece of medical equipment in good working order may give rise to a hospital negligence claim. Hospitals should maintain identifying information on all medical equipment, including model number, serial number, manufacturer's name, and equipment identification number (EIN). They also maintain service and repair records for all rented, borrowed, or purchased medical equipment.

Outpatient Records

Physician Office Records

Most (not all) physicians now utilize an electronic health records system. The printed version produced to law firms varies with type of system. Physician office records contain multiple types of documents including:

■ Progress notes associated with each patient visit
■ Documentation pertaining to phone messages

- Lab, imaging, and other diagnostic testing results
- Correspondence with the patient and other healthcare providers
- Disability, insurance, and billing records

In addition, primary care physician office records typically include:

- Consultant reports
- Portions of inpatient, ED, or Urgent Care records
- Flow sheets tracking data such as height, weight, prescriptions, blood pressures, blood glucoses, preventive health screening, etc.

Primary care records contain important information pertaining to plaintiff's baseline health, pre-existing medical conditions, psychosocial issues, compliance with recommended treatment, response to treatment of injuries alleged in lawsuit, whether alleged negligence caused aggravation of pre-existing injury, etc. Thus, it is prudent in all types of medical-legal tort claims to obtain all of plaintiff's primary care provider(s) records dating back to at least 10–15 years prior to the alleged injuries. This is important to glean information regarding plaintiff's baseline physical and mental health, pertinent pre-existing condition, prior injuries or major illnesses, and any documentation that may impact plaintiff's credibility such as a history of substance abuse or non-compliance with recommended treatments (Zorn, 2015).

Pharmacy Records

Most prescription records are now computerized. They contain the drug name, dose, frequency and route of administration, quantity dispensed, prescriber name, and billing information. Prescription records are important sources of medical information pertaining to plaintiff's underlying medical conditions, need for analgesic medication, polypharmacy and treatment for mental health conditions, as well as identity of medical providers. Pharmacies also provide detailed informational sheets for all dispensed medications.

As of 2011, 37 states participate in a prescription drug monitoring program (PDMP), an electronic database that tracks controlled substances to combat prescription drug abuse, addiction, and diversion (US Department of Justice, 2016).

Chiropractic Records

Chiropractors treat neuromusculoskeletal complaints, including back, neck and joint pain, and headaches (American Chiropractic Association, 2018). Chiropractic records contain abbreviations, symbols, and diagnostic criteria unique to the profession making interpretation of their records challenging at times. Chiropractors have been slower to adopt EHR systems than medical doctors and there is minimal medical literature related to chiropractic EHRs (Taylor, 2017).

Chiropractic malpractice claims commonly involve failure to refer the patient for a neurologic evaluation when indicated or vertebrobasilar stroke following chiropractic manipulation (Kosloff, Elton, Tao, & Bannister, 2015).

Alternative Medicine

Patients often utilize alternative or holistic medicine therapies to treat medical conditions or seek pain relief. This includes:

- Naturopathy
- Acupuncture
- Ayurveda
- Homeopathy
- Chinese (or oriental) medicine
- Homeopathic remedies
- Herbal medicine
- Electromagnetic therapy
- Dietary supplements
- Massage therapy
- Reiki
- Healing touch
- Tai Chi
- Qigong
- Hypnosis
- Meditation
- Yoga
- Guided imagery
- Art, music, energy or movement therapies

It is important to obtain any records maintained by providers offering alternative therapies as they may contain documentation about subjective complaints and response to treatment. It is also important to obtain a complete list of plaintiff's supplements or herbs as they may cause adverse effects including those due to interaction with plaintiff's prescription medications.

Home Care Records

Home care records include documentation regarding treatment plans, patient assessments, care provided (skilled nursing, aide care, PT, OT), care outcomes, diagnostic test results, home medical equipment or therapies, and phone or electronic communications. Home health agencies receiving payment for Medicare or Medicaid patients must adhere to Conditions of Participation (CoPs) guidelines. CoPs dictate timelines for initial assessment, comprehensive assessment, and reassessment.

Home care records include:

- Written documentation that:
  - Patient and caregiver informed of all rights
  - Patient and caregiver received information regarding advance directive
  - Patient and caregiver were given number for home health hotline to address any questions or grievances
  - Patient and caregiver advised in advance of disciplines to provide care and the frequency of proposed visits

- Patient and caregiver advised in advance of any change to plan of care (POC) before changes are made
- Before care is initiated, amount of payment expected from Medicare, Medicaid, or other federally funded entities; charges not covered by Medicare; charges the individual may have to pay

■ Written plan of care that includes all disciplines and planned visit frequency for each
■ Comprehensive assessment and any planned follow-up assessments to include Outcome Assessment and Information Set (OASIS)
■ Coordination of care between disciplines at start of care and any subsequent episodes (case conference)
■ Written summary to physician at a minimum of every 60 days with summary of interventions provided and patient's progress or lack thereof
■ Documentation of timely communication with physician for patient status changes
■ Drug regimen review conducted at all clinician visits
■ Home health aide care plan contains vital sign parameters
■ Home health aide visit notes document communication with RN for any changes to patient condition or vital signs that fall outside of established parameters
■ Clinician visit notes reflect interventions included on plan of care
■ Supervisory visits of Licensed Practical Nurses (LPNs) and Licensed Vocational Nurses (LVNs) and Home Health aides (frequency will be determined by state guidelines)

Rehabilitation Services

Outpatient facilities and specialized inpatient units provide rehabilitation care. Documentation includes interdisciplinary assessment of the patient's functional limitations, therapies implemented to improve function (physical, occupational, speech-language, cognitive therapies), goals of therapy, patient response to therapies, and readiness to return home.

Military Health Records

The location of outpatient, dental, and mental health treatment records generated during active duty varies with the branch of service (National Archives, 2018b). Records from inpatient care during activity duty service are sent to the National Personnel Records Center (NPRC) by the facility that created them (National Archives, 2018a). Veteran's Administration facilities provide inpatient and outpatient care for retired military personnel. The contents of these records are similar to non-VA records.

Employee Health Records

Institutions with large numbers of employees may offer employee health services, including for follow-up care pertaining to work related injuries, health screening, acute illness, and employee wellness initiatives. These records contain documentation pertaining to each visit, diagnostic testing results, correspondence, etc.

Hospice Records

Hospice care is "a comprehensive set of services identified and coordinated by an interdisciplinary group (IDG) to provide for the physical, psychosocial, spiritual, and emotional needs of a terminally ill patient and/or family members, as delineated in a specific patient plan of care" (Department of Health & Human Services, 2010). Records vary with the services provided and may include the following documentation:

- Hospice Item Set (HIS): a patient level data collection tool
- Certification of Terminal Illness (CIT)
- Notice of Election (NOE)
- Interdisciplinary Group (IDG): members may include the hospice physician, registered nurse, social worker, and pastoral or other counselor. IDG members conduct comprehensive patient assessment at required time points.
- The care plan includes the needs identified in all patient assessments and reflects patient and family goals. It includes the types of services the patient is receiving as well as visit frequency. It is updated as patient needs change.
- Visit notes from each provider

Alcohol/Drug Treatment, Mental Health, and HIV Related Records

Due to the sensitive nature of the content in these records, their release in a medical-legal tort claim requires the patient's permission granting release of these specific records. For example, the injured party (or representative) may have to initial check-off boxes for these types of records on the HIPAA authorization. Some facilities providing psychiatric services or treatment for substance abuse require the plaintiff to sign their institution specific release.

Plaintiff's counsel may object to releasing these types of records, unless defense counsel can establish they are relevant. In general, if plaintiff asserts a claim for psychological damages, all pre-existing and post-incident mental health records will be discoverable. At times, discovery of these types of records becomes the subject of motion practice in which the judge decides whether all or a portion of the records must be released to defense counsel. Sometimes the judge decides to do an "in-camera" review of the records to decide which, if any, of the records are relevant.

Long-Term Care Records

Types of long-term care facilities include Assisted Living Facilities (ALF), Skilled Nursing Facilities (SNF), and Long-Term Acute Care (LTAC) facilities. Components of long-term care records are similar to those found in inpatient rehabilitation records. There are, however, additional pertinent records applicable to long-term care residents, including those required by the Centers for Medicare & Medicaid Services (CMS). This includes the Minimum Data Set (MDS), a clinical assessment of a resident's functional capabilities. MDS assessments are required on admission to and discharge from long-term care facilities, as well at mandated intervals during admission. Long-term care facilities provide MDS data to a national MDS database at CMS. ALFs are unique in that the level of care or services provided to the resident is dependent on the contractual agreement between the resident and the facility. For more information about long-term care, see Chapter 12.

Corrections Records

Corrections cases involving medical issues allege either medical malpractice (departure from accepted standards of medical care) or a violation of civil rights (i.e., right to access to care, right to a professional medical opinion, right to care that is prescribed, and right to care for serious medical needs). These latter cases are also known as "1983 cases" pursuant to 42 U.S. Code § 1983, Civil action for deprivation of rights (Legal Information Institute, 1983).

Following are the types of medical documents maintained by corrections:

Intake Form

Medical personnel (usually RNs) screen all new inmates upon admission for acute or chronic medical conditions (physical, mental health, and dental) and suitability to reside in the facility (National Commission on Correctional Health Care, 2018). For example, an inmate with open wounds or other recent injuries, signs of alcohol withdrawal, or suicidal ideation is not suitable for jail housing. The purpose of this intake assessment is to:

■ Identify inmates that require immediate medical care
■ Identify ongoing medical care needs
■ To avoid placing inmates who pose a threat to themselves or others with the facility's general population

The screening form includes:

■ Current and past illnesses
■ Dietary needs
■ Prescribed medications (type, amount, and last dose)
■ History of or current suicidal ideation
■ Past or current mental illness, including hospitalizations
■ Allergies
■ Substance abuse (legal and illegal)
■ Drug or alcohol withdrawal symptoms
■ Dental problems
■ Current or recent pregnancy
■ Past serious infectious disease
■ Symptoms of recent communicable illness (i.e., chronic cough)
■ General appearance (tremors, anxious)
■ Level of consciousness (alert, lethargic)
■ Gait
■ Body deformities

Ambulatory Health Record

If an inmate requires any health intervention after the intake screening, an ambulatory health record (AHR) must be established for the inmate. Records in the AHR include:

■ Medication administration
■ Substance abuse treatment

- Suicide prevention
- Restraint use
- Use of solitary confinement (isolation, segregation, or restrictive housing)
- Therapeutic diet
- Hospice or palliative care
- Juvenile health care
- Immunizations
- Dental care
- Women's health

Incident Report

An inmate injury or adverse medical event may require that corrections personnel complete an incident report. Corrections policies and procedures dictate what events require completion of an incident report. These reports are generally discoverable and must be disclosed to the inmate's counsel during litigation proceedings.

Logs

Corrections facilities maintain various logs to document operational activities within the facility. The logs include the date and time of each entry, the names of officers and other staff assigned to an area, the names of relief personnel, and a record of personnel at each change of shift. Logs kept in corrections facilities include those pertaining to housing, cell checks, showers, meals, library, official visits, fire drills, and visitors:

Video and Audio Records

Video cameras capture activity in many areas of a correctional facility populated by inmates, including their housing cells. Facilities also record inmate phone calls. State regulations dictate the length of time the facility must preserve such recordings.

Transfer Forms

Facility personnel complete a transfer form whenever an inmate moves to a different corrections facility or to a different section within the same facility. This form typically includes a medical history, mental health status, dental status, current medications, and pending appointments.

Other Sources of Medical Information

Other pertinent records pertaining to a plaintiff in a corrections case may include:

- Homicide investigation report (generated when an inmate dies in custody)
- Arrest report
- Inmate disciplinary records

The inmate's medical record may also include partial records from outside medical consultants as well as care rendered during an emergency department visit or inpatient hospital stay. For additional information regarding correctional cases, see Chapter 17.

Other Records Containing Medical Information

911 Transcripts

Emergency communication centers maintain digital recordings of calls to the center, calls from the dispatch center to first responders and between first responders. State law dictates how long they are preserved. Release of the recordings (and transcripts) generally requires a judicial subpoena.

Medical Billing Records

Billing records serve multiple purposes. Hospital billing records associated with inpatient stays document services, consults, diagnostic testing, medications, equipment, fluids, etc. provided and associated costs. Outpatient billing records document provider identity, nature of services provided, and associated costs. These records are a source of provider identity, dates of treatment, and medical costs associated treatment for plaintiff's injuries. Medicare billing records list payments made for Medicare eligible expenses. When negotiating a Medicare lien in anticipation of settlement, it is important to distinguish between expenses resulting from an underlying condition and those resulting from the alleged injuries. Life care planners utilize plaintiff's billing records to document local costs associated with medications, treatments, and services.

Patient Incident Reports

Patient injuries, such as sustained during a fall, prompt completion of an incident report. In many states, incident reports fall under the umbrella of Quality Assurance and are thus not discoverable by plaintiff's counsel. The rationale behind this is to encourage reporting of adverse events to track their incidence and implement preventative measures.

Work Site Injury Reports

Someone in a supervisory role completes report pertaining to all work site injuries. The report typically includes the time and date of the incident, names of witnesses, and medical or other interventions implemented in response to the accident. The facility is also required to file a report with Occupational Safety and Health Administration (OSHA). Such reports are relevant in Workers Compensation claims or in labor law cases in which the injured worker sues a contractor or building owner for injuries related to unsafe working conditions. In general, Workers Compensation law bars employees from suing employers for on the job injuries (FindLaw, 2018).

Police Accident Reports

A police officer completes an accident report for all motor vehicle crashes, including crashes involving pedestrians, in-line skaters, trains, animals, etc. The report includes, when applicable:

- Driver(s) name, address, DOB, license number, etc.
- Number of occupants in each vehicle
- Vehicle information (state where registered, type, make, year, etc.)
- Driver violations and tickets issued, if any
- Vehicle damage

- Accident description
- A diagram of the accident
- Traffic control information (traffic signals, work area, school zone, etc.)
- Light, roadway, and weather conditions
- Safety equipment involved (seat belts, child restraints, air bag deployment)
- Type of physical complaints
- Apparent contributing factors (alcohol use, fatigue, distraction, cell phone use, etc.)
- Name, rank, and signature of officer completing the accident report

Police accident reports are often computer generated. Each section of the report is numbered. For each section of data, the officer selects the most appropriate option from a list of descriptive options. For example, options for roadway surface conditions might include dry, wet, snow/ice, or flooded. A key is required to interpret all police accident reports.

School Records

Professionals who document in student health or academic records include registered nurses, licensed practical nurses, nurses' aides, classroom staff, health/therapy aid (audiologist, speech therapist) or therapy aides, and the school psychologist, social worker, or guidance counselor. In addition, the student's record may include reports from outside healthcare providers or academic testing.

Federal laws regulate certain health and academic aspects pertaining to children with special needs including:

- The Individuals with Disabilities Education Act (IDEA) of 1990, 1997, and 2004
- Americans with Disabilities Act (ADA) of 1990, and Section 504
- Rehabilitation Act of 1973
- No Child Left Behind Act (NCLB)
- Family Educational Rights and Privacy Act of 1974 (FERPA or the Buckley Amendment)

Pre-K Through High School

For injuries sustained by a child or young adult, K-12 academic and health school records may provide evidence pertaining to baseline cognitive abilities or decline in academic performance resulting from an injury. These records are also pertinent to claims against a school district for failure to accommodate identified students, or student injuries at school (or school-sponsored activities) or failure to respond to complaints of student bullying, among others.

Most states mandate the health and academic records that schools must maintain for each student. The student's health record typically includes:

- Nurse's notes for students evaluated in the health office
- Medication orders and records of administration
- Requests for limited physical activity
- Physical examination reports
- Notes pertaining to the physical or mental health of a student
- Psychosocial information pertaining to family members negatively impacting a student
- Orders from a student's healthcare provider

- Documentation of referrals for confidential services or outside medical or social services
- Incident reports after a student injury
- Emergency health plan (such as for students with severe allergies)
- Transportation plan
- Student's health history
- Annual health screenings
- Parental notifications regarding health issues
- Immunization records, including medical or religious exemptions
- Hearing screenings
- Attendance records

As mandated by federal law, students needing significant academic or medical support must have either an Individualized Education Program (IEP) plan or a 504 Plan depending upon their specific needs (The Understood Team, n.d.).

College/University Health Records

Like K-12, post high school academic and health school records may provide evidence pertaining to baseline cognitive abilities or decline in academic performance resulting from an injury. They are also pertinent in claims against the institution such as those involving improper medical care, a communicable disease outbreak, or failure to properly assess and respond to a student's significant substance abuse problem or suicidal ideation. In cases involving the latter, the school must balance the student's right to privacy with parental desire to be informed if the student has not signed a release allowing information to be shared with them.

Student health centers provide a range of health services, including acute care needs (flu, respiratory illness), mental health services, and women's health care. Their records include provider notes made in connection with each visit, recommended referrals, consult notes, diagnostic testing results, immunization records, and paper or electronic communications with the student.

Social Media Records

The duty to preserve data on social media platforms is triggered "when a party reasonably foresees that evidence may be relevant to issues in litigation" (DiBianca, 2014). The consequences for a party deleting relevant social media data can result in attorney and client sanctions. Thus, plaintiff attorneys are increasingly including written notice to their clients to preserve prior social media posts, video clips, photographs, and other data until case resolution.

Defense counsel is increasingly making demands for access to the plaintiff's social media sites, looking for evidence that might be inconsistent with the plaintiff's claimed injuries or that might impact the plaintiff's credibility. Typically, the Courts are reluctant to grant the requesting party full access to a party's social media account given that such accounts usually contain both relevant and non-relevant data. However, there are now several decisions in which a court has ordered a party to produce to opposing counsel login and password information in response to a discovery request (DiBianca, 2014). In some cases, the Judge will conduct an in-camera of a party's social media sites to determine which data is relevant (DiBianca, 2014).

Disability Records

Medical documentation in files maintained by Social Security Disability, Worker Compensation, and private disability companies include applications, medical records from treating providers, independent medical exam reports, and disability determinations.

Summary

There are numerous types and sources of medical information relevant to the elements of proof in medical legal tort claims. Identification and review of information contained in and outside of the medical chart can be pertinent to a thorough review of the facts. Skilled LNCs can play an important role in identifying and analyzing the relevant medical data in each legal claim. For more information on analysis of specific types of claims, see chapters in this textbook on case analysis.

References

American Academy of Anesthesiologist Assistants. (2017). Frequently asked questions. Retrieved from www.anesthetist.org/faqs.

American Chiropractic Association. (2018). What is chiropractic? Retrieved from www.acatoday.org/Patients/Why-Choose-Chiropractic/What-is-Chiropractic.

American College of Radiology. (2014). ACR practice parameter for communication of diagnostic imaging findings. Retrieved from www.acr.org/media/ACR/Files/Practice-Parameters/CommunicationDiag.pdf.

American Society of Anesthesiologists. (2014). ASA physical status classification system. Retrieved from www.asahq.org/resources/clinical-information/asa-physical-status-classification-system.

Association of periOperative Registered Nurses. (2015). *Guidelines for perioperative practice.* Denver, CO: AORN.

Centers for Medicare & Medicaid Services. (2012). Emergency Medical Treatment & Labor Act (EMTALA). Retrieved from www.cms.gov/Regulations-and-Guidance/Legislation/EMTALA/.

Department of Health & Human Services. (2010). CMS manual system. Retrieved from www.cms.gov/Regulations-and Guidance/Guidance/Transmittals/downloads/R65SOMA.pdf.

DiBianca, M. (2014, January). Discovery and preservation of social media evidence. *Business Law Today.* Retrieved from www.americanbar.org/publications/blt/2014/01/02_dibianca.html.

FindLaw. (2018). Workers' compensation: Can I sue my employer instead? Retrieved from https://injury.findlaw.com/workers-compensation/workers-compensation-can-i-sue-my-employer-instead.html.

Kosloff, T. M., Elton, D., Tao, J., & Bannister, W. M. (2015). Chiropractic care and the risk of vertebrobasilar stroke: Results of a case-control study in U.S. commercial and Medicare Advantage populations. *Chiropractic Manipulative Therapy, 23*(19). doi: 10.1186/s12998-015-0063-x.

Legal Information Institute. (1983). 42 U.S. Code 1983—civil action for deprivation of right. Retrieved from www.law.cornell.edu/uscode/text/42/1983.

National Archives. (2018a). Clinical (hospital inpatient) records for former active duty personnel. Retrieved from www.archives.gov/personnel-records-center/active-duty-medical-records.

National Archives. (2018b). Veterans' medical and health records. Retrieved from www.archives.gov/veterans/military-service-records/medical-records.html.

National Commission on Correctional Health Care. (2018). Health records. Retrieved from www.ncchc.org/health-records.

Taylor, D. (2017). A literature review of electronic health records in chiropractic practice: Common challenges and solutions. *Journal of Chiropractic Humanity, 24*(1), 31–40. doi: 10.1016/j. echu.2016.12.001.

The Joint Commission. (2012). The universal protocol for preventing wrong site, wrong procedure, and wrong person surgery. Retrieved from www.jointcommission.org/assets/1/18/UP_Poster1.PDF.

The Joint Commission. (2018a). Provision of care, treatment, and services/critical access hospitals: History and physical. Retrieved from www.jointcommission.org/mobile/standards_information/jcfaqdetails.as px?StandardsFAQId=1851&StandardsFAQChapterId=29&ProgramId=0&ChapterId=0&IsFeatured =False&IsNew=False&Keyword=.

The Joint Commission. (2018b). Standards interpretation frequently asked questions. Retrieved from www. jointcommission.org/standards_information/jcfaq.aspx?ProgramId=5&ChapterId=79&IsFeatured=Fa lse&IsNew=False&Keyword=&print=y.

The Joint Commission. (2018c). Universal protocol. Retrieved from www.jointcommission.org/assets/1/18/ UP_Poster1.PDF.

The Joint Commission, Division of Health Care Improvement. (2015) Transitions of care: Engaging patients and families. *Quick Safety.* Issue 18. Retrieved from www.jointcommission.org/assets/1/23/ Quick_Safety_Issue_18_November_20151.PDF.

The Understood Team. (n.d.). The difference between IEPs and 504 plans. Retrieved from www.understood.org/en/school-learning/special-services/504-plan/the-difference-between-ieps-and-504-plans.

US Department of Justice (2016). State prescription drug monitoring program. Retrieved from www.deadiversion.usdoj.gov/faq/rx_monitor.htm#4.

World Health Organization. (2009). WHO guidelines for safe surgery 2009. Retrieved from http://apps. who.int/iris/bitstream/handle/10665/44185/9789241598552_eng.pdf;jsessionid=EEF9872B2AD902 F53F464DA24B7515A3?sequence=1.

Zorn, E. (2015). In-house law firm legal nurse role: 30 year perspective. *The Journal of Legal Nurse Consulting, 26*(1), 26–32.

Test Questions

1. Which of the following is NOT part of an inpatient hospital record?
   A. Operative reports
   B. EMS record
   C. Consultation notes
   D. Allied health provider notes
2. Which source of medical information must conform to pertinent "chain of custody" requirements?
   A. Videotape of surgical procedure
   B. Electronic fetal monitoring strip
   C. Photographs
   D. Pathology slides
3. The following source of medical information generally requires a judicial subpoena:
   A. Patient incident report
   B. Work site injury report
   C. 911 transcript
   D. Mental health treatment records
4. School records may provide evidence regarding:
   A. Pre-accident cognitive function
   B. Decline in academic function post-injury
   C. Accommodations provided to students with disabilities
   D. All of the above

Answers: 1. B, 2. D, 3. C, 4. D

Chapter 8

Access to Medical Records

Rachael Arruda, BA, RN, LNCC®, CCM

Contents

Objectives

- Identify the regulations and standards governing the content and preservation of medical records
- Explain the reasons for confidentiality of the medical record
- Describe the process for accessing medical and health records, agency records, and other pertinent records
- Identify the discovery processes for accessing medical records

Introduction

The role of a legal nurse consultant (LNC) can vary depending on the job setting, but all LNC roles center around the medical record. The LNC must know how and where to obtain medical and other records and must be knowledgeable about what is contained in a typical medical record to determine what is missing. The LNC must also be familiar with rules that govern confidentiality, disclosure, and discoverability of medical records in order to protect all parties involved in the potential or actual litigation of facts.

Medical Records

A medical record is a document created over time of a patient's ongoing medical information, such as medical history, complaints, examination findings, test results, diagnoses, care and treatment received, medications taken, etc. (Medical record, n.d.). The contents of a medical record must meet all state and federal legal, regulatory, and accreditation requirements. The American Health Information Management Association (AHIMA) and The Joint Commission (TJC) also play significant roles in determining minimum content requirements by publishing guidelines and standards.

The AHIMA "is the premier association of health information management (HIM) professionals worldwide ... [and] is recognized as the leading source of 'HIM knowledge,' a respected authority for rigorous professional education and training" (AHIMA, 2018, para. 2). The AHIMA works to advance the accuracy, reliability, and usefulness of health data by leading key industry initiatives and advocating for consistent standards (AHIMA, 2017a). It provides knowledge, resources, and tools to advance standards for the delivery of quality health care (AHIMA, 2017b).

The Joint Commission (TJC) is an independent, not-for-profit organization that accredits and certifies tens of thousands of healthcare organizations and programs to fulfill its mission to continuously improve health care for the public (TJC, 2018). The Joint Commission is also an approved national accreditation organization by the Centers for Medicare & Medicaid Services

(CMS), because it has "standards and a survey process that meets or exceeds Medicare's require-ments" (TJC, 2017). Thus, TJC can conduct "deemed status" surveys of healthcare organizations to determine if they meet or exceed Medicare and Medicaid's requirements for participation in the programs (TJC, 2017). The survey includes determining compliance with the health and safety requirements (including documentation regulations) called Conditions of Participation (CoPs), which are set forth in federal regulations (TJC, 2017). Compliance with CoP standards is necessary for healthcare organizations to participate in and receive federal payment from Medicare or Medicaid programs (TJC, 2017). Adherence to TJC's standards is mandatory to attain and maintain accreditation.

Regulations/Standards

Federal Regulations

Institutions that participate in federal reimbursement programs are subject to federal regulations regarding the content of the medical record. These regulations are found in the Code of Federal Regulations, Condition of participation: Medical record services (42 CFR 482.24). They require medical records to contain data supporting admission and continued hospitalization, including support of the diagnosis and description of the patient's progress and response to medications and services. Different types of healthcare settings have specific regulations for the content of their medical records, and the LNC must become knowledgeable about the relevant regulations for the cases on which the LNC works.

State Regulations

Each state has regulations that define the content of the medical record. The regulations vary from detailed to general requirements, with specific regulations for various healthcare facilities. Many states' regulations share the same requirements as federal regulations, in that they require the medical record to contain sufficient information to identify and justify the admission, the diagnosis, treatment, and responses to the treatment and services. The LNC must become familiar with state regulations regarding documentation for the state in which the care was provided.

Institutional Regulations

Most institutions follow TJC guidelines, but if the policies of the institution are more comprehensive or stricter than those of TJC, the institution (and its employees and contractors) can be held to the higher standard by TJC. Although physicians may not be institution employees, the institution has a duty to monitor a physician's compliance with federal, state, and institutional documentation regulations. A physician's privileges may be suspended or revoked for non-compliance.

Professional Standards

In the mid-1990s, the American Medical Association collaborated with CMS to develop evaluation and management documentation guidelines to assist physicians with documenting and correctly coding procedures and services, thereby facilitating payment approval (Maley & Henley,

2017). The Centers for Medicare & Medicaid Services recommend that physicians' records be accurate, complete, legible, and compliant with general practices of accurate medical record-keeping to avoid charges of fraud or abuse in billing practices (Office of Inspector General, n.d.). They further recommend that documentation of each encounter with a patient include the reason for the encounter, relevant history, physical examination findings, prior diagnostic test results, assessment and clinical impression or diagnosis, health risk factors, and plan of care (CMS, 2017). All entries must include a date of service and the identity of the physician (CMS, 2017). The patient's progress and response to treatment as well as changes in treatment plans or any revision in diagnosis should be included in this documentation (CMS, 2017).

The American Nurses Association (ANA) published *Nursing: Scope and Standards of Practice* which includes the documentation requirements for registered nurses (ANA, 2015). Documentation of the nursing process must include the pertinent data collected; relevant nursing diagnosis; expected outcomes; planning strategies; evidence of plan implementation; and systematic, ongoing evaluation (ANA, 2015). It also requires that the nursing process be documented in a retrievable form (ANA, 2015).

Retention of Records

Once a medical record is generated, the holder or custodian of the medical record has the responsibility to safeguard the information. The Joint Commission, federal and state regulations, institutional policies, and professional standards determine the length of time that the medical record should be preserved. The Joint Commission requirements regarding how long medical information should be retained are based on law, regulations, and what the patient information is being used for (e.g., patient care, legal research, education, etc.). Federal law requires that institutions receiving federal reimbursement, specifically Medicare, retain records for a minimum of five years (42 CFR 482.24). State requirements vary widely (Health information and the law, 2016, para. 1):

> State law governs the length of time that providers must maintain medical records … Some states have different time limits applicable to certain types of providers and … patients … Where laws vary by provider, requirements may be specific to hospitals, primary care physicians, specialty care physicians, long-term care facilities, or other facility and provider types … Where laws vary by patient condition, the most prevalent distinction in requirements is between living and deceased patients (as of discharge).

At the institutional level, storage space and cost may influence a healthcare facility's retention of records policy.

The AHIMA (2013, State Record Retention Requirements section, para. 2) recommends that in the absence of specific state requirements, providers should keep health information for at least the period specified by the state's statute of limitations or for a sufficient length of time for compliance with laws and regulations. If the patient is a minor, the provider should retain health information until the patient reaches the age of majority (as defined by state law) plus the period of the statute of limitations.

A longer retention period is generally prudent, though, since the statute of limitations may not begin to run until the potential plaintiff discovers (or should have discovered) the causal relationship between an injury and the care received (AHIMA, 2013). The age of majority is determined by state statute and is the age that a person is granted, by law, the rights and responsibility of an adult (Age of majority, n.d.). The age of majority is 18 years in most, but not all, states. Birth and death records are retained permanently (AHIMA, 2013). Organizations with special patient populations such as research, minor, or behavioral health patients may be governed by other regulations (AHIMA, 2013). For example, the Food and Drug Administration requires that research records pertaining to cancer patients be maintained for 30 years (AHIMA, 2013).

Student health records for grades kindergarten through 12th grade are considered part of the academic record. The Family Educational Rights and Privacy Act (FERPA) protects the privacy of student education records and applies to all schools that receive federal funds (i.e., not elementary- or secondary-level private or parochial schools) (U.S. Dept. of Education, 2011, 2018). The United States Department of Education's Privacy Technical Assistance Center's Best Practices for Data Destruction (Privacy Technical Assistance Center, 2016) explains that

> FERPA does not provide any specific requirements for educational agencies and institutions regarding disposition or destruction of the data they collect or maintain themselves, other than requiring them to safeguard FERPA-protected data from unauthorized disclosure, and not to destroy any education records if there is an outstanding request to inspect or review them ... FERPA does not require educational agencies and institutions to destroy education records maintained as a part of the regular school or agency operations, and in fact, many jurisdictions require lengthy retention periods for student attendance and graduation records. For other student records, in order to minimize information technology costs and reduce the likelihood of inadvertent disclosure of student information, schools and districts will often elect to establish their own record retention policies, including time frames for eventual destruction of the records.

The Occupational Safety and Health Administration (OSHA) require certain industries to retain records of employee exposure to toxic substances or harmful physical agents for 30 years (Access to employee exposure and medical records, 2011). Employee medical records must be kept by the employer for at least the duration of employment plus 30 years (Access to employee exposure and medical records, 2011).

In accordance with AHIMA recommendations, organizations that are destroying health records must permanently maintain documentation of the destruction that includes the date of destruction, method of destruction, description of the disposed records, inclusive dates, a statement that the records were destroyed in the normal course of business, and the signatures of the individuals supervising and witnessing the destruction (AHIMA, 2013).

Confidentiality, Privacy, and Privilege

Patients reveal many details of their personal and private lives to their physicians and other healthcare providers. This is encouraged and expected, as it enables the healthcare provider to deliver appropriate care to the patient. Therefore, it is the ethical duty of the physicians and other healthcare providers to keep this information in confidence. This ethical duty of confidentiality extends from verbal communications to information in the written record. Both federal and state constitutions have provisions that afford an implied right of privacy, and courts have recognized that health information is protected by this constitutional right of privacy (Nass, Levit, & Gostin, 2009).

Health Insurance Portability and Accountability Act of 1996

Health Insurance Portability and Accountability Act (HIPAA), also known as the Kennedy-Kassebaum Act, was enacted by Congress on August 21, 1996 (Office for Civil Rights [OCR], 2013a). Because Congress did not finalize the proposed regulations according to the scheduled time period, the finalization and implementation passed to the Department of Health and Human Services (DHHS) (OCR, 2013a). The final version of the HIPAA privacy regulations was issued in December 2000 and went into effect on April 14, 2001 (OCR, 2015). A two-year grace period was included, so enforcement of the HIPAA Privacy Rules began on April 14, 2003 (OCR, 2015). Penalties for non-compliance could be applied from that date (OCR, 2015). The Health Information Technology for Economic and Clinical Health Act (HITECH) was enacted and signed into law in 2009 (OCR, 2017a). This act "addresses the privacy and security concerns associated with the electronic transmission of health information" and strengthens the civil and criminal enforcement of the HIPAA rules (OCR, 2017a).

Among other things, HIPAA incorporated rules covering administrative simplification, including making healthcare delivery more efficient (OCR, 2015). Portability of medical coverage for pre-existing conditions was a key provision of the act as was defining the underwriting process for group medical coverage (U.S. Dept. of Labor, n.d.). Another key element was the provision standardizing the electronic transmission of billing and claims information (OCR, 2017b).

In standardizing the electronic means of paying and collecting claims data, the U.S. Congress recognized the increased potential for abuse of people's medical information (OCR, 2015). Consequently, a key part of the act also increased and standardized confidentiality and security of health data (OCR, 2013a, 2013b). The HIPAA privacy regulations require that access to patient information be limited to only those authorized and that only the information necessary for a task be available to them (OCR, 2013a, 2013b). They also require that personal health information be protected and kept confidential (OCR, 2013a, 2013b).

> The HIPAA Privacy Rule requires that covered entities apply appropriate administrative, technical, and physical safeguards to protect the privacy of protected health information (PHI), in any form. See 45 CFR 164.530(c) … Entities must implement reasonable safeguards to limit incidental, and avoid prohibited, uses and disclosures of PHI which, including in connection with the disposal of such information … Covered entities must ensure that their workforce members [employees, independent contractors, etc.] receive training on and follow the disposal policies and procedures … Any workforce member involved in disposing of PHI, or who supervises others who dispose of PHI, must receive training on disposal. This includes any volunteers.
> (OCR, 2009)

The primary areas covered under HIPAA focus on controlling health information, ensuring patients understand their privacy rights, ensuring patient access to their medical records, and providing recourse if privacy regulations are violated (OCR, 2013a). Providers and health plans are required to give patients a clear, written explanation of how the covered entity may use and disclose their health information (OCR, 2013a). Patients are generally able to see and obtain copies of their medical records and request amendments in response to information they perceive as inaccurate (OCR, 2013a). Additionally, a history of most non-routine disclosures must be made available (OCR, 2013a). Patients now have the right to file a formal complaint with a covered provider or health plan or with DHHS related to violations of HIPAA provisions (OCR, 2013a).

Failure to comply with HIPAA may result in civil and criminal penalties (OCR, 2013a). The latest HIPAA Enforcement Rule was published by DHHS in October 2009 (HITECH Act Enforcement Interim Final Rule) (OCR, 2017c). Under this rule, for violations occurring prior to February 18, 2009, DHHS may impose civil fines of up to $100 per violation and up to a maximum of $25,000 for violations of the same HIPAA requirement during one calendar year (OCR, 2013a). For violations occurring on or after February 18, 2009, DHHS may impose fines of $100 to $50,000 or more per violation with a calendar year cap of $1,500,000 for violations of the same HIPAA requirement (OCR, 2013a).

Federal criminal penalties include up to $50,000 and up to one year in prison for obtaining or disclosing individually identifiable health information, $100,000 and up to five years in prison if the wrongful conduct involves false pretenses, and $250,000 and up to 10 years in prison if the wrongful conduct involves the intent to sell, transfer, or use identifiable health information for commercial advantage, personal gain, or malicious harm (OCR, 2013a).

The HIPAA provides for uniformity of rules and regulations from state to state and even from one healthcare organization to another. Where existing state laws or the policies and procedures of a covered entity are stricter than (but not contrary to) the HIPAA requirements, the state law, policy, or procedure supersede the federally mandated HIPAA requirements (Health Information Privacy Division, 2016; OCR, 2015). If state laws are contrary to the access provisions of the Privacy Rule, they are pre-empted by HIPAA unless a HIPAA Rule exception exists (Health Information Privacy Division, 2016). As such, these state laws do not apply when a person seeks access to personal health information (PHI) under HIPAA (Health Information Privacy Division, 2016).

Providers are entitled to charge reasonable, cost-based fees that cover the cost of copying (including supplies and labor) to provide a printed copy of the health information (Health Information Privacy Division, 2016). A fee cannot be charged for searching or retrieving the records (Health Information Privacy Division, 2016). The healthcare provider must provide the requested information, in whole or in part, no later than 30 calendar days after receiving the request (Health Information Privacy Division, 2016).

There are certain types of information that are excluded from the right to access PHI. Two categories that are expressly excluded from the right of access are:

■ Psychotherapy notes that are documenting or analyzing the contents of a counseling session and
■ Information compiled in anticipation of a civil, criminal, or administrative action or proceeding (Health Information Privacy Division, 2016).

Access to Medical and Other Records

Patient Access

Ownership of the medical record, including electronic records, imaging studies, and all other reports in the medical record, belongs to the facility or healthcare practitioner who created the record (Butler, 2017). This also includes billing records that are held by health plans. Requests for specific, unique records may need to be sent to a department other than a medical record department. This may include financial records maintained in a patient billing office, radiology records maintained in the radiology department, and electronic fetal monitor strips maintained in the obstetrical/labor and delivery department. The HIPAA Privacy Rule gives individuals who are the subject of a medical record the right to access their medical record (OCR, 2013a). However, individuals do not own the record and cannot have it destroyed. The HIPAA also mandates restrictions on the use and disclosure of the information contained in a patient's medical record to third parties (OCR, 2013a).

The OSHA mandates that employees have access to their records of exposure to toxic substances and any relevant medical records held by the employer (Access to employee exposure and medical records, 2011). If the employer has no record that specifically documents the employee's exposure levels, the employee may access exposure records of other employees who engage in similar work and may have experienced similar exposure incidents (Access to employee exposure and medical records, 2011). The Social Security Administration (SSA), through its Privacy Act (20 CFR 401, Subpart B), states that patients have a right to access their medical records, including any psychological information maintained by the SSA (Access to medical records, 2007).

The right to request the records of a minor patient or a patient with a mental impairment whose guardianship has been established resides with the parent or legal guardian (OCR, 2017d). In the case of divorced parents, the custodial parent is the one with the right to access the minor child's records (OCR, 2017d). For a deceased patient, a person with legal authority to act on behalf of the decedent or the estate may request the decedent's medical records (OCR, 2017d). An example is an executor or administrator of the estate. If relevant law applies, next of kin or other family members may have authority to review the decedent's medical record (Butler, 2017). A healthcare facility must reproduce a record even if there are outstanding bills (OCR, 2017e). Most states allow healthcare providers and facilities to charge a minimum fee for copying the record (OCR, 2017e).

Medical records requested by a potential plaintiff do not have to be certified unless certification is requested. Certification does not guarantee the record is complete; it only guarantees that it is an exact duplicate of the original (AHIMA, n.d.). A certified copy of the record meets the criteria for admission as evidence in a court of law. State laws may differ in the requirements for certification, but generally the requirement is fulfilled by a statement and signature provided by the record custodian attesting that the copy of the record is a true and accurate copy, the record was made and kept in the usual course of business at the time the medical record was made, and the copy was made by the person/persons having knowledge of the information in the record (AHIMA, n.d.).

Third-Party Access

Information may be released to a third party when the actions of the patient have implied consent or waiver (OCR, 2013c). For example, it is generally assumed that, when a spouse, family member, or significant other is present during a discussion of the patient's medical condition, the healthcare practitioner may speak freely concerning private information. If there are questions concerning which family members can have access to additional information at a later date, the healthcare practitioner should consult with the patient.

The healthcare provider must be very careful in the release of information concerning mental health issues and substance abuse, even to close family members (OCR, n.d.). Psychotherapy notes (defined as notes by a mental health professional documenting or analyzing the contents of a conversation with a patient during a counseling session) are kept separate from the patient's medical and billing records (OCR, n.d.). The HIPAA does not allow the provider to disclose psychotherapy notes without the patient's authorization (OCR, n.d.).

Access to sensitive information such as human immunodeficiency virus results and information indicating a diagnosis of acquired immunodeficiency syndrome (AIDS) may be denied to non-authorized individuals (OCR, 2017f).

Other information that requires special consideration includes the release of information regarding genetic information and adoption records (Child Welfare Information Gateway, 2016a; Equal Employment Opportunity Commission [EEOC], n.d.). Over the years, accessing records that contain sensitive information has undergone many changes. These changes have been developed to allow for disclosure of relevant medical history to adoptive children or the child's representative. States generally require adoption reports to include information about the birth parents' medical and genetic histories, family and social histories, and ethnic and racial backgrounds among other information (Child Welfare Information Gateway, 2016b).

In some states, a request for all medical records does not always include the complete record. A specific request may be necessary to identify the exact information (including sensitive information) the patient is willing to release.

Mandatory Disclosure of Medical Records

There are certain circumstances in which some types of confidential medical record information must be disclosed. The specific non-voluntary reporting requirements may vary from state to state, but every state has mandated the reporting of suspected child abuse (Child Welfare Information Gateway, 2016c). Each state also has laws that require certain diseases to be reported at the state level, and the data may be voluntarily shared with the Centers for Disease Control and Prevention (CDC) (CDC, 2018). With regard to human immunodeficiency virus (HIV), all 50 states have enacted laws or regulations requiring laboratory reporting of HIV, but only 43 states and the District of Columbia require laboratory reporting of all detectable and undetectable viral loads of HIV-positive individuals (CDC, 2015). Other disclosures include deaths, births, fatalities due to blood transfusions (21 CFR 606.170(b)) and medical devices (21 CFR 803), some congenital diseases (varies by state), and induced termination of pregnancy (CDC, 2017).

Freedom of Information Act

"Since 1967, the Freedom of Information Act (FOIA) has provided the public the right to request access to records from any federal agency" (U.S. Dept. of Justice [DOJ], n.d.a, para. 1.). Federal agencies are required to disclose any information requested under the FOIA unless it falls under an exemption which protects interests such as personal privacy, national security, and law enforcement (U.S. DOJ, n.d.b). The disclosure of personal or medical records would be an unwarranted invasion of personal privacy and would be considered exempt under the FOIA.

Open Records Act

Many states have enacted similar freedom of information acts for state and local agencies. These Open Records Acts provide a means by which the public can gain access to state government documents. Requests for records from police, fire, public health, and motor vehicle departments are examples of requests that would fall under the Open Record Acts. Medical records remain exempt from public disclosure.

Non-discoverable Information

Under HIPAA, an individual does not have the right to access certain documents or communications generated by healthcare facilities or practices that are used to make general business decisions and not decisions about the individual (Health Information Privacy Division, 2016). These documents can include various administrative or monitoring records pertaining to patient care, credentialing surveys, infection control committee reports, departmental logs, risk management data, utilization review reports, peer review reports, and incident reports.

Peer Review

Peer review is a process in which healthcare providers evaluate the quality of their colleagues' work to ensure that standards of care are being met. Hospitals, ambulatory surgery centers, independent diagnostic centers, etc. rely on peer review to evaluate a provider's competency. The laws of all states and the District of Columbia provide that peer review is privileged and not discoverable (Dennen, 2014). The records of the meetings are non-discoverable to a patient who may be pursuing legal action against the subject of the peer review; however, in some cases, federal courts have allowed discovery concerning the peer review process. The Health Care Quality Improvement Act (HCQIA) extends immunity to participants in the peer review process, however it does not make peer review proceedings privileged. The extent of what is discoverable also varies by state and may be restricted to notes, minutes, and reports.

Incident Reports

An incident report memorializes an event that is not consistent with the routine operation of a hospital or with routine patient care. The event may be an accident or a situation that could have resulted in an accident. If an incident report is filed as part of the medical record, it may be discoverable and may be admissible in court under the business records exception to the hearsay rule (AHIMA, n.d.). If the incident report is directed to the legal or risk management department of the facility, the facility can argue that the report was made in anticipation of litigation and should be considered non-discoverable (DHHS, 2016).

Discoverable Information

Discoverable information refers to materials, documents, or witnesses that must be made available to the opposing parties in a lawsuit. Discoverable information is not always admissible in court, and the judge decides whether the information is relevant to the case and will be admitted as evidence. For example, photographs of victims in a fatal motor vehicle accident may be available and discoverable to all parties, but they may be extremely graphic. Unless the party requesting admission of the photographs into evidence can show that the photographs are relevant to prove an issue that is in dispute, the judge may rule that the photographs are inadmissible, as they do not support or defend an issue in the case and they are more prejudicial than probative.

Electronic Health Records

An electronic health record (EHR) is an electronic record of patient health information that is maintained over time by the healthcare provider (CMS, 2012). It can include patient demographics, progress notes, problems, medication, past medical history, immunizations, laboratory data, and radiology reports (CMS, 2012). Additional information may include nurses' notes; operative reports; physical therapy, occupational therapy, and speech therapy notes; intake and output data; vital signs; and other information related to the care and treatment of the patient. The contents may vary based on the healthcare delivery environment: the EHR will be different when generated by an acute care facility versus a skilled nursing facility or physician's office. An EHR is designed to reach out beyond the health organization that originally compiled the information and share the information with other healthcare providers (CMS, 2015).

An electronic medical record (EMR) is a digital version of a paper chart in a clinician's office and is not easily shared with healthcare providers outside that office (Garrett & Seidman, 2011).

The EHR provides automation to information access and has the potential to streamline clinician workflow (CMS, 2012). Other advantages for the EHR include direct or indirect interface with other care-related activities including outcomes reporting, quality management, and evidence-based decision support (CMS, 2012). The EHR can also strengthen relationships between patients and clinicians by assisting the clinician to make better decisions and provide better care (CMS, 2012). This can be accomplished by:

- Reducing medical error, duplication of tests, and delays in treatment by improving accuracy and clarity of medical records
- Making health information readily available to patients and
- Keeping patients well informed so they can make better healthcare decisions (CMS, 2012)

The EHR may allow automated access to a patient's health information through a patient portal—a direct link through the provider's website to their health information. A patient or legal representative can also request a printed copy of her; it is expected that the provider will be able to comply with the request and provide a paper copy (Health Information Privacy Division, 2016).

Legal Access to Medical Records

Discovery

When a lawsuit is filed, the parties begin to investigate the facts or issues of the case through formal discovery processes. The goals of discovery are to narrow the legal and factual issues in the case, ascertain the plaintiff's allegations and any affirmative or special defenses pled by the defendant(s), obtain relevant information, preserve witness testimony, and eliminate the element of surprise at trial (American Bar Association, n.d.). In medical legal tort cases, the medical record is a very significant element in discovery. There are several methods of obtaining medical records through discovery.

Request for Production

A request for production is propounded by one party on another party in a legal action. It is a request for specific documents to be produced. If the party upon whom the request is made fails to provide the documents, a motion to compel the production of those documents can be filed with the court.

Record Retrieval by Subpoena

Another method of obtaining medical records through discovery is issuing a subpoena *duces tecum*, which is Latin meaning "you shall bring with you" (Cornell Law School, n.d.a). This type of subpoena requires the witness to appear (in court or at a deposition) with documents under penalty of law (Cornell Law School, n.d.a). In many instances, the person with the most knowledge relating to the storage, maintenance, and retrieval of the medical record is the recipient of the subpoena. Whether medical records can be produced via subpoena without the patient's written authorization may be dependent on the case law in the state in question. Before responding to the subpoena, the provider should notify the patient whose records are being requested so the patient has adequate time to object to the request before the information is produced (OCR, 2017g).

For more information on discovery, see Chapter 5.

Fraudulent Concealment

If one of the parties involved in litigation possesses relevant documents but refuses to grant the other party access to those documents, the theory of fraudulent concealment may be initiated. Fraudulent concealment is the deliberate hiding, non-disclosure, or suppression of material facts, which one is legally obligated to reveal, with the intent to deceive or defraud (Fraudulent concealment, n.d.). If a healthcare practitioner or facility fails or refuses to produce records within the usual statutory time frame, it is not protecting itself from a lawsuit, because the statute of limitations (the period of time after which a lawsuit can no longer be pursued) may not be triggered until the plaintiff discovers that the defendant is purposefully concealing material information.

Spoliation of Medical Records

Spoliation of evidence refers to the destruction or alteration of records, which deprives the court or parties to evidence in a dispute (Sullivan, 2012). The United States legal process relies on the compliance of all parties to produce relevant documents and other evidence that are in the care and control of the parties. The failure to preserve or produce evidence is one of the worst forms of discovery misconduct and can result in severe consequences, including punitive damages that are not covered by liability insurance policies (Cornell Law School, n.d.b). If the loss or destruction of evidence is unintentional or not essential to the case, the court is less likely to impose punitive damages.

A significant legal consequence of the loss or destruction of a medical record or other pertinent evidence is an adverse-inference instruction to the jury, which permits them to infer that the destroyed evidence was unfavorable to the person responsible for its safekeeping (Cornell Law School, n.d.b). This can adversely affect the defendant's position at trial, whether the loss was intentional or inadvertent.

Other consequences of evidence spoliation include discovery sanctions against the party that destroyed, lost, or withheld evidence (Cornell Law School, n.d.b). An example of such a discovery sanction is the entry of a default judgment against the culpable party (Cornell Law School, n.d.b). The healthcare facility or practitioner may face professional disciplinary actions or criminal penalties.

In product liability cases, spoliation may be an issue when a person claims injury from a defective product. The product manufacturer may claim the product has become "lost" and then attempts to have the case dismissed. Severe penalties may be imposed if this is determined to be evidence spoliation.

Summary

A complete and comprehensive medical record can be a decisive piece of evidence in a case that involves medical issues. Having a familiarity with the standards and rules pertaining to the content, retention, confidentiality, accessibility, and discoverability of medical records will enable the LNC to assist an attorney with gathering, organizing, and reviewing the entire medical record. This knowledge will also give the LNC a better understanding of what information should be contained in medical records, why and when medical records are confidential, how to obtain them, and how long they should be available.

References

Access to employee exposure and medical records, 29 CFR § 1910.1020 (2011).

Access to medical records, 20 CFR § 401.55 (2007).

Age of majority. (n.d.). In *USLegal.com legal definitions*. Retrieved from https://definitions.uslegal.com/a/age-of-majority/.

American Bar Association. (n.d.). How courts work: Steps in a trial: Discovery. Retrieved from www.americanbar.org/groups/public_education/resources/law_related_education_network/how_courts_work/discovery.html.

American Health Information Management Association. (n.d.). Legal process and electronic health records. Retrieved from http://library.ahima.org/doc?oid=59559#.Wq1qfJdG3IV.

American Health Information Management Association. (2013). Retention and destruction of health information. Retrieved from http://library.ahima.org/doc?oid=107114#.Wpw4mudG3IU.

American Health Information Management Association. (2017a). Mission vision & values. Retrieved from www.ahima.org/about/aboutahima?tabid=story.

American Health Information Management Association. (2017b). How AHIMA moves you forward. Retrieved from www.ahima.org/.

American Health Information Management Association. (2018). Who we are: Our story. Retrieved from www.ahima.org/about/aboutahima.

American Nurses Association. (2015). *Nursing: Scope and standards of practice* (3rd ed., pp. 53–62, 66). Silver Springs, MD: NurseBooks.org.

Butler, M. (2017). How to request your medical records. *Journal of the American Health Information Management Association*. Retrieved from http://journal.ahima.org/2012/03/01/how-to-request-your-medical-records/.

Centers for Disease Control and Prevention. (2015). State laboratory reporting laws: Viral load and CD4 requirements. Retrieved from www.cdc.gov/hiv/policies/law/states/reporting.html.

Centers for Disease Control and Prevention. (2017). CDCs abortion surveillance system FAQs. Retrieved from www.cdc.gov/reproductivehealth/data_stats/abortion.htm.

Centers for Disease Control and Prevention. (2018). National notifiable diseases surveillance system: Data collection and reporting. Retrieved from wwwn.cdc.gov/nndss/data-collection.html.

Centers for Medicare & Medicaid Services. (2012). Electronic health records. Retrieved from www.cms.gov/Medicare/E-health/EHealthRecords/index.html.

Centers for Medicare & Medicaid Services. (2015). Electronic health records provider fact sheet. Retrieved from www.cms.gov/Medicare-Medicaid-Coordination/Fraud-Prevention/Medicaid-Integrity-Education/Downloads/docmatters-ehr-providerfactsheet.pdf.

Centers for Medicare & Medicaid Services. (2017). Evaluation and management services. Retrieved from www.cms.gov/Outreach-and-Education/Medicare-Learning-Network-MLN/MLNProducts/Downloads/eval-mgmt-serv-guide-ICN006764.pdf.

Child Welfare Information Gateway. (2016a). Access to adoption records. Retrieved from www.childwelfare.gov/pubPDFs/infoaccessap.pdf.

Child Welfare Information Gateway. (2016b). Providing adoptive parents with information about adoptees and their birth families. Retrieved from www.childwelfare.gov/pubPDFs/collection.pdf.

Child Welfare Information Gateway. (2016c). Mandatory reporters of child abuse and neglect. Retrieved from www.childwelfare.gov/pubPDFs/manda.pdf.

Cornell Law School. (n.d.a). Subpoena *duces tecum*. Retrieved from www.law.cornell.edu/wex/subpoena_duces_tecum.

Cornell Law School. (n.d.b). Rule 37: Failure to make disclosures or to cooperate in discovery; sanctions. Retrieved from www.law.cornell.edu/rules/frcp/rule_37.

Dennen, K. C. (2014, July 17). Peer review is not always privileged. *The National Law Review*. Retrieved from www.natlawreview.com/article/peer-review-not-always-privileged.

Department of Health and Human Services. (2016). Patient Safety and Quality Improvement Act of 2005: HHS guidance regarding patient safety work product and providers' external obligations. Retrieved from www.gpo.gov/fdsys/pkg/FR-2016-05-24/pdf/2016-12312.pdf.

Equal Employment Opportunity Commission. (n.d.). Genetic information discrimination. Retrieved from www.eeoc.gov/laws/types/genetic.cfm.

Fraudulent concealment. (n.d.). In *Black's law dictionary free online dictionary* (2nd ed.). Retrieved from https://thelawdictionary.org/fraudulent-concealment/.

Garrett, P., & Seidman, J. (2011, January 4). EMR vs EHR—What is the difference? [web log comment]. Retrieved from www.healthit.gov/buzz-blog/electronic-health-and-medical-records/emr-vs-ehr-difference/.

Health information and the law. (2016). Medical record retention required of health care providers: 50 state comparison. Retrieved from www.healthinfolaw.org/comparative-analysis/medical-record-retention-required-health-care-providers-50-state-comparison.

Health Information Privacy Division of the U.S. Department of Health and Human Services. (2016). Individuals' right under HIPAA to access their health information 45 CFR § 164.524. Retrieved from www.hhs.gov/hipaa/for-professionals/privacy/guidance/access/index.html.

Maley, M. M., & Hanley, M. B. (2017). Documentation guidelines for medical decision making. Retrieved from www.aaos.org/AAOSNow/2017/Aug/Managing/managing01/.

Medical record. (n.d.). In *Merriam-Webster online*. Retrieved from www.merriam-webster.com/medical/medical%20record.

Nass, S. J., Levit, L. A., & Gostin, L. O. (Eds.). (2009). *Beyond the HIPAA privacy rule: Enhancing privacy, improving health through research*. Washington, DC: The National Academies Press. Retrieved from www.ncbi.nlm.nih.gov/books/n/nap12458/pdf/.

Office for Civil Rights of the U.S. Department of Health and Human Services. (n.d.). HIPAA Privacy Rule and sharing information related to mental health. Retrieved from www.hhs.gov/sites/default/files/hipaa-privacy-rule-and-sharing-info-related-to-mental-health.pdf.

Office for Civil Rights of the U.S. Department of Health and Human Services. (2009). What do the HIPAA Privacy and Security Rules require of covered entities when they dispose of protected health information? Retrieved from www.hhs.gov/hipaa/for-professionals/faq/575/what-does-hipaa-require-of-covered-entities-when-they-dispose-information/index.html.

Office for Civil Rights of the U.S. Department of Health and Human Services. (2013a). Summary of the HIPAA privacy rule. Retrieved from www.hhs.gov/hipaa/for-professionals/privacy/laws-regulations/index.html.

Office for Civil Rights of the U.S. Department of Health and Human Services. (2013b). Summary of the HIPAA security rule. Retrieved from www.hhs.gov/hipaa/for-professionals/security/laws-regulations/index.html.

Office for Civil Rights of the U.S. Department of Health and Human Services. (2013c). Does the HIPAA Privacy Rule permit a doctor to discuss a patient's health status, treatment, or payment arrangements with the patient's family and friends? Retrieved from www.hhs.gov/hipaa/for-professionals/faq/488/does-hipaa-permit-a-doctor-to-discuss-a-patients-health-status-with-the-patients-family-and-friends/index.html.

Office for Civil Rights of the U.S. Department of Health and Human Services. (2015). Privacy rule general overview. Retrieved from www.hhs.gov/hipaa/for-professionals/privacy/guidance/general-overview/index.html.

Office for Civil Rights of the U.S. Department of Health and Human Services. (2017a). HITECH act enforcement interim final rule. Retrieved www.hhs.gov/hipaa/for-professionals/special-topics/hitech-act-enforcement-interim-final-rule/index.html.

Office for Civil Rights of the U.S. Department of Health and Human Services. (2017b). HIPAA for professionals. Retrieved from www.hhs.gov/hipaa/for-professionals/index.html.

Office for Civil Rights of the U.S. Department of Health and Human Services. (2017c). The HIPAA enforcement rule. Retrieved from www.hhs.gov/hipaa/for-professionals/special-topics/enforcement-rule/index.html.

Office for Civil Rights of the U.S. Department of Health and Human Services. (2017d). Personal representatives. Retrieved from www.hhs.gov/hipaa/for-individuals/personal-representatives/index.html.

Office for Civil Rights of the U.S. Department of Health and Human Services. (2017e). Your medical records. Retrieved from www.hhs.gov/hipaa/for-individuals/medical-records/index.html.

Office for Civil Rights of the U.S. Department of Health and Human Services. (2017f). Information is powerful medicine. Retrieved from www.hhs.gov/hipaa/for-professionals/special-topics/information-is-powerful-medicine/index.html.

Office for Civil Rights of the U.S. Department of Health and Human Services. (2017g). Court orders and subpoenas. Retrieved from www.hhs.gov/hipaa/for-individuals/court-orders-subpoenas/index.html.

Office of Inspector General. (n.d.). A roadmap for new physicians: Avoiding Medicare and Medicaid fraud and abuse. Retrieved from https://oig.hhs.gov/compliance/physician-education/roadmap_web_version.pdf.

Privacy Technical Assistance Center. (2016). Best practices for data destruction. Retrieved from https://studentprivacy.ed.gov/sites/default/files/resource_document/file/Best%20Practices%20for%20Data%20Destruction%20%282014-05-06%29%20%5BFinal%5D_0.pdf.

Sullivan, J. (2012). Intentional spoliation: No evidence, no tort, no problem? Retrieved from http://apps.americanbar.org/litigation/committees/businesstorts/articles/summer2012-0712-intentional-spoliation-evidence.html.

The Joint Commission. (2017). Facts about federal deemed status and state recognition. Retrieved from www.jointcommission.org/facts_about_federal_deemed_status_and_state_recognition/.

The Joint Commission. (2018). About The Joint Commission. Retrieved from www.jointcommission.org/about_us/about_the_joint_commission_main.aspx.

United States Department of Education. (2011). Family Educational Rights and Privacy Act: Guidance for parents. Retrieved from https://studentprivacy.ed.gov/sites/default/files/resource_document/file/for-parents.pdf.

United States Department of Education. (2018). Family Educational Rights and Privacy Act. Retrieved from https://www2.ed.gov/policy/gen/guid/fpco/ferpa/index.html.

United States Department of Justice. (n.d.a). What is FOIA? Retrieved from www.foia.gov/about.html.

United States Department of Justice. (n.d.b). What are FOIA exemptions? Retrieved from www.foia.gov/faq.html#exemptions.

United States Department of Labor. (n.d.). Health plans & benefits: Portability of health coverage. Retrieved from www.dol.gov/general/topic/health-plans/portability.

Test Questions

1. To obtain a plaintiff's medical record:
   A. A verbal request to the healthcare provider is all that is required
   B. A dated and signed request for the record must be made by the patient or patient representative
   C. The plaintiff must request the record in person
   D. Payment must accompany the request
2. Advantages of utilizing an electronic health record include:
   A. Reducing medical errors
   B. Making health information readily available to patients
   C. Keeping patients well informed so they can make better healthcare decisions
   D. Streamlining clinician workflow
   E. All of the above
3. Which of these statements is true?
   A. Ownership of the physical medical record, including x-rays and all other reports in the medical record, belongs to the patient
   B. OSHA can deny an employee access to their record relating to toxic substance exposure
   C. The right to request the records of a minor patient or a patient with a mental impairment where guardianship has been established resides with the parent or legal guardian
   D. A patient has the right to have their medical record destroyed
4. Spoliation of the records
   A. Results in a summary judgment for the plaintiff
   B. Includes the destruction of records from natural causes
   C. Can result in civil and criminal charges against the healthcare practitioner
   D. Includes late entries that are inconsistent with earlier entries

Answers: 1. B, 2. E, 3.C, 4. C

Chapter 9

Electronic Medical Records

An Overview

Todd A. Jennings, Esq.

Contents

Objectives

- Examine the history of and transition to electronic medical records
- Differentiate between electronic medical records and electronic health records
- Identify the benefits and drawbacks of electronic medical records
- Discuss the value of metadata and audit trails and
- Recognize privacy and security concerns associated with electronic medical records

Introduction

Here in the 21st century, in the wake of the digital revolution, reliance on electronic media is inescapable. The Digital Age has arrived, and no one should still be in transition. Today, knowledge, once the objective of a personal quest, is now a simple search query, whether through a computer, tablet, smart phone, or even a watch. If not connected to information through a wireless network, today's generation considers such information to be virtually inaccessible. The government and industries have geared up for the new order and are dragging a sometimes reluctant medical profession with them. Also, as the nation focuses on population health management and quick access to medical data, the United States has taken several steps to expand the use of technology in the delivery of health care. The combination of modernization and government edict has resulted in electronic medical records (EMRs), which, depending on one's point of view, is part advancement and part Frankenstein.

Medical records, with some exceptions, are now stored in computer servers instead of file cabinets and are created by the strokes of a keyboard rather than the strokes of a pen. For the most part, gone are the days of deciphering a healthcare provider's handwriting to identify a diagnosis or engaging in extensive sleuth work to determine the identity of an individual whose notes and signature appear on a chart. Such determinations are more easily had when everything is written in Times or Courier font. However, the problem of "illegible paper records" has simply been replaced with the problem of "legible information overload" (Iyer, Leone, & Zapatochny, 2015). For good or bad, the EMR is revolutionizing the delivery of health care and the role of medical records in administrative and legal proceedings. This chapter will explore the benefits and drawbacks of the EMR, the EMR's role in medical legal tort claims, and best practices for handling issues related to EMRs.

The Electronic Medical Record and its Components

Traditionally, a patient's chart, or medical record, was an individual healthcare provider's or healthcare facility's paper file documenting the treatment provided to the patient. The chart typically documented, among other things, office visits or admissions, medical histories, diagnoses, laboratory results, and referrals. Historically, entries in the medical record were written by the healthcare provider contemporaneously with the provider's encounter with the patient. An EMR is, in the simplest of terms, a patient's chart with a particular healthcare provider or facility, in electronic form. The Office of the National Coordinator for Health Information Technology (ONC) defines EMRs as "digital versions of the paper charts in clinician offices, clinics and hospitals ... [that] contain notes and information collected by and for the clinicians in that office, clinic or hospital ... for diagnosis and treatment" (ONC, 2015).

Electronic medical records consist of various functions that operate in tandem to provide a reliable record of a patient's care and treatment. The layout and functions of the EMR are largely dependent on the software provider as well as the niche for which the software is designed. For example, a hospital will clearly have different needs than an internist's practice. Nonetheless, an EMR is generally comprised of administrative, clinical, imaging, laboratory, and billing components. The administrative component typically includes registration forms, insurance information, admission and discharge information, and other information related to the administrative aspects of a patient's care. The clinical component is typically the core of the EMR where providers, nurses, and other staff input progress notes, orders, operative reports, and the results of physical examinations, family histories, patient activity, and other information related to the clinical aspects of patient care. The imaging and laboratory components are self-explanatory, providing functions for the ordering, tracking, and reporting of imaging and laboratory results. The billing component integrates the medical record with the billing department, often generating billing information for the care provided as it is provided. These five components may include several subcomponents, especially in the hospital setting. For instance, the hospital EMR may contain separate components for healthcare provider and nursing progress notes or for emergency department care and inpatient care after admission. Similarly, an EMR may contain separate components for chemistry and hematology and for patient registration and legal documents.

The EMR is often confused with the "electronic health record" (EHR), but, although regularly swapped in daily jargon, the two are not synonymous. The EMR is typically limited to a particular healthcare provider who uses the EMR for diagnosis and treatment, and like paper charts, it is not meant to be shared or used outside of that provider's office(s). Meanwhile, the EHR contains "information from *all the clinicians involved in a patient's care*, and all authorized clinicians involved in a patient's care can access the information to provide care to that patient" (ONC, 2015). The EHR also shares information with laboratories and specialists and follows the patient from provider to provider and potentially across the country (ONC, 2015). Thus, while the EMR is meant to be used in a particular practice, the EHR is meant to be used throughout the community of professionals providing treatment to an individual patient. The focus of this chapter is on the EMR and its role in medical legal tort cases.

The Transition to the Electronic Medical Record

The advent of the EMR stretches back to before the turn of the century; however, it has only been in the last decade that EMRs have begun to take hold of the medical industry. The transition to EMRs gained steam in 2009 when the federal government enacted the Health Information Technology for Economic and Clinical Health (HITECH) Act (U.S. Department of Health and Human Services [HHS], n.d.). The HITECH Act established a federal office to coordinate health information technology, provided incentives to healthcare providers who met certain EMR requirements, and set forth a penalty (reduction in the Medicare/Medicaid fees paid) to providers who failed to meet certain EMR requirements by 2015 and beyond (Centers for Disease Control and Prevention, 2017). In 2008, prior to the HITECH Act's passage, only 42% of office-based healthcare providers utilized EMRs (ONC, 2016a). In 2016, 8 in 10 healthcare providers (78%) utilized EMRs (DeSalvo & Washington, 2016). This increase is likely due to a combination of providers embracing the new technology and working to avoid the fee penalties imposed by the federal government. Today, the use of EMRs by hospitals is nearly universal (DeSalvo &

Washington, 2016). This is significant to the legal nurse consultant (LNC) since a significant number of medical malpractice litigation involves hospitals and hospital records.

Benefits of the Electronic Medical Record

In encouraging the widespread conversion to EMRs, the ONC identifies the EMR's benefits as allowing healthcare providers to:

1. Track a patient's data over time
2. Readily identify patients who are due for preventive visits and screenings
3. Quickly determine how a patient measures up to certain parameters and
4. Ultimately improve the overall quality of health care (ONC, 2016b)

The EMR offers many benefits that can be appreciated in the daily practice of medicine. For instance, a healthcare provider no longer needs to wait for the delivery of a paper file to begin a consultation, because the patient's records are easily accessible via a laptop or tablet in the examination room. Medical histories are more accessible and can be reviewed more quickly and contemporaneously with the examination, which minimizes errors, time, and money. This efficiency allows healthcare providers, who now work harder for less fees, to see more patients and generate more revenue. Also, depending on the software, EMRs may alert the healthcare provider to allergies or medication conflicts (Andrasz, 2012).

Drawbacks of the Electronic Medical Record

The aforementioned benefits notwithstanding, EMRs also present many drawbacks not associated with paper records. Perhaps most intuitively, an EMR is only as reliable as the individual interacting with it. As with any new technology, there are many healthcare providers who are still transitioning to EMR and not yet proficient. For instance, consider an aging sole-proprietor healthcare provider who has transitioned to EMRs to comply with the HITECH Act and avoid a reduction in Medicaid reimbursements. This provider does not quite understand all the ins and outs of the EMR software, especially how it integrates with medical billing. In the progress notes, this provider consistently lists a certain diagnosis under "Impression," accompanied by the corresponding billing code. During a medical malpractice lawsuit, the various parties and counsel believe the critical testimony will be that of this healthcare provider—the only clinician who diagnosed the plaintiff with that particular disorder. However, at deposition, the provider admits the plaintiff's true diagnosis was not the one listed in the note. Instead, it was a related, more general condition that had little effect on the issues in the case. The healthcare provider could not find the billing code for the true diagnosis on the EMR's pull-down menu and, in the provider's confusion, selected the next best thing to ensure that the record was populated and the patient was billed for the service. A lack of proficiency may also appear when a healthcare provider must use an unfamiliar EMR software program, e.g., when joining a new practice or when an office changes EMR software programs. There will likely always be errors stemming from users' unfamiliarity with new software, and these errors are compounded when the erroneous information is carried forward in the EMR.

The EMR software features that allow for data repetition come in many forms, such as copy and paste functionality (which allows users to copy and paste information from one portion of the EMR to another) and pre-population functionality (which allows users to designate certain information like demographics, allergies, and lab results to be automatically pulled forward from other parts of the EMR) (Blanchard & Manning, 2016). Like most aspects of EMRs, such features prove both a blessing and a curse. Copy and paste functionality can help reduce the time a healthcare provider spends typing information in the records and can help ensure the information relied upon from another part of the EMR is accurately recorded for that encounter. Pulling information forward can also help a healthcare provider prepare for a patient encounter by having the information pre-populate the note before the encounter.

However, these data replication features hinder a meaningful interpretation of the record. The ease with which errors can be repopulated throughout a record can lead to a degradation in the accuracy and relevancy of the record and associated billing (Blanchard & Manning, 2016). They often result in the medical record regurgitating the same information over and over again and can make each patient visit virtually indistinguishable. When information is carried forward, it unnecessarily lengthens the medical record and makes the changes between each visit's record nearly indiscernible. Such repetitive entries make it difficult to determine, for example, the changes in a patient's presentation from visit to visit or a provider's differential diagnosis over time. One LNC succinctly described such an EMR as "pages & pages of repetitive information making a change in the norm difficult to find, sort of like a needle in a haystack" (Gatti, 2015, p. 32). This repetition may also cause the reader to glance over, rather than read, large portions of the medical record, thereby potentially missing small but critical changes. The indiscriminate use of these features also opens up the healthcare provider to scrutiny at deposition and may undermine the clinician's testimony.

The EMR is also lengthened by the amount of clinical data placed into it, which appears to be significantly higher than what was typically recorded in paper charts. This is because many EMRs have data pre-filled and included in templates that do not require a provider to input data but rather remove only what is not applicable to the patient. Thus, the sheer size of an EMR, in and of itself, can present challenges. In clinical practice, the quantity of data may overwhelm clinicians who are searching for information before or during a patient encounter (Iyer et al., 2015). For legal professionals, it can be challenging to piece together the puzzle of a patient's care and treatment.

Given their immense volume, EMRs can be defeating and onerous to review. Browsing thousands of pages of medical records in portable document format (PDF) to discover whether a nurse complied with a healthcare provider's order or whether a patient was administered a medication at correct intervals can feel like a fool's errand. Accordingly, some practitioners have suggested that EMRs simply replace one problem with another: deciphering illegible handwritten notes with making sense of massive amounts of legible information (Iyer et al., 2015). To assist with reviewing voluminous EMRs, many legal professionals and expert witnesses prefer to use document viewing software programs that allow the user to search for or bookmark specific content.

The unwieldiness of EMRs is compounded by what some may describe as their disjointed organization. As previously described, EMRs are generally organized into administrative, clinical, imaging, laboratory, and billing components, and these components are typically comprised of multiple subcomponents. For a short hospital stay, each subcomponent (e.g., emergency department notes, healthcare provider progress notes, provider orders, nursing progress notes, medication records, clinical patient information, etc.) may be comprised of dozens, if not hundreds, of pages which may be organized in, typically, reverse chronological order. The EMR software program may keep the records for each subcomponent grouped together, or it may place the entire record in reverse chronological order, thereby intermixing each subcomponent's records.

Since the information critical to assessing a patient's care is usually sprinkled throughout several categories of records, establishing a timeline of events necessitates the often cumbersome process of scrolling between these categories to correlate dates and times to various actions (Gatti, 2015). Likewise, piecing together a written narrative of the events critical to a legal proceeding can be frustrating and time-consuming for the legal professional and costly for the client. Depositions sometimes become a page-jumping odyssey of confusion with attorneys constantly asking what page the deponent is on.

A most unfortunate drawback to the EMR, a problem that presents itself primarily in the context of civil litigation, is that healthcare professionals interact with the EMR entirely through the software program on a computer screen and may only encounter the EMR in hard copy or electronically as a PDF when involved in a civil proceeding. To the contrary, legal professionals interact with the EMR almost entirely in printed or PDF form and may only view it through the EMR software program (i.e., as the healthcare professionals saw it clinically) when the need arises to obtain some discovery or evidentiary advantage. The reality is the EMR in printed or PDF form seldom, if ever, imitates the EMR as viewed through the EMR software program. This often presents difficulty in litigation or administrative proceedings when a healthcare provider is testifying from the EMR and, as is normally the case, does not have any personal recollection of the patient encounter (ONC, 2016b). Whether it is a nurse identifying a healthcare provider's order and confirming it was carried out or emergency department staff confirming a culture was reported to the provider, healthcare professionals will often have difficulty navigating the EMR in printed or PDF form. During depositions, it is not unusual for healthcare professionals to testify repeatedly that the medical records are unfamiliar as presented (in printed or PDF form) and do not resemble the EMR they interact with clinically.

This disconnect can complicate a legal team's efforts to solicit coherent and easily digestible testimony from a key witness. Furthermore, the witness's credibility may be impinged by the clumsy trek through the EMR. This disconnect can frustrate all involved and unnecessarily complicate and prolong a witness's deposition. It is important for the LNC to anticipate this issue and be involved in the preparation of the witness or attorney taking the deposition. Getting the attorneys and healthcare professionals on the same page is critical to a successful navigation of the medical records during deposition or trial, thereby creating smooth, uninterrupted testimony for the trier of fact.

Like any electronic data, EMRs present new privacy issues for patients and new legal concerns for both medical and legal professionals. Privacy and security will be discussed later in this chapter.

Metadata and Audit Trails

What is Metadata?

An entire textbook chapter could be devoted to this singular subject. Despite the growing recognition of its value in civil litigation, particularly in the medical malpractice context, metadata is still treated by many legal professionals as an alien concept, perhaps because its use in legal proceedings has only recently grown in prevalence. The simplest definition of metadata, the one often used by legal and other professionals, is "data about data." In fact, the Merriam Webster's dictionary concisely defines it as "data that provides information about other data" (Merriam Webster, 2016). More specifically, metadata is the automated logbook of a particular document, such as an EMR, that records what activity has taken place with respect to that document. Such activity may include when the document was accessed, who accessed it, whether changes were made, who made those changes, and when such changes were made. In the context of EMRs, one healthcare provider said it best when describing an EMR's metadata as being "tantamount to an audit trail..." (McLean, 2009).

In the context of EMRs, metadata can serve as a virtual lie-detector test. This is important in any litigation involving the testimony of healthcare professionals and even more so in the medical malpractice arena. Healthcare professionals often encounter a large volume of patients in any given year, and their testimony, typically years following a patient encounter, is commonly based on what is in the EMR, not on personal recollection. Accordingly, discovering what the metadata says about a particular EMR can often undermine the information contained in it as well as the testimony derived therefrom. Metadata can expose alterations made to an EMR days, weeks, months, or years after the patient encounter.

The Audit Trail

As implied above, when it comes to EMRs, metadata typically takes the form of an audit trail. The audit trail is the EMR's record of information about each encounter with the EMR, including any instance an individual has accessed, viewed, printed, downloaded, supplemented, or modified a patient's chart. The purpose of an audit trail in practice is threefold: security, medical billing, and data gathering (Greene, 2015). An audit trail enhances the security of the medical records by providing a record of the identity and location of the person(s) accessing the record (Greene, 2015). Such information may prove useful in assessing the extent of a breach of confidential patient information and planning defenses against future breaches. In many cases, audit trails also enhance the accuracy of medical billing by integrating the EMR with the billing department (Greene, 2015). The data collected by audit trails is also valuable for tracking diseases and other medical research purposes (Greene, 2015).

Depending on the software used, an EMR audit trail will typically identify, among other things:

■ The date and time a patient's medical chart is opened
■ The name or username of the individual(s) who accessed it
■ Where such individuals accessed it
■ The medical records reviewed and
■ The documentation entered, edited, and deleted

The audit trail is typically produced as a spreadsheet, and oftentimes the individual producing the trail can control the contents of the report through various search parameters. As an example, an audit trail may be generated for a particular patient's chart or healthcare provider's EMR activities (Greene, 2015).

The primary consequence of audit trails is the ability to detect changes made to an EMR, whether those changes occurred as soon as a bad outcome was known or once litigation is initiated. Accordingly, it is important for healthcare professionals to be aware that changes to the EMR will be well-documented in the audit trail, and such alterations will be heavily emphasized. Although not guaranteed, it is expected that misconduct involving "after the fact" alterations of EMRs will decrease (Courtney, 2011).

Audit trails may also reveal some helpful information about the care rendered by the healthcare provider. For example, it may demonstrate that care was being provided remotely, such as when a healthcare provider reviews imaging or labs or otherwise participates in the patient's care far from the bedside (Greene, 2015).

It is important to note that audit trails themselves are not impervious to tampering, and many healthcare providers have reported the ability to disable, alter, or even delete them (Greene, 2015).

When reviewing an audit trail, it is best to do so in conjunction with the medical records, because the audit trail is often meaningless without being viewed in the context of the EMR. This is because the content of the audit trail is limited to what actions were being taken with regard to the EMR itself, not the patient. For instance, an EMR may indicate that, at a certain date and time, a nurse reviewed a certain result. This information, in and of itself, holds little value. However, reviewing the audit trail in tandem with the EMR may reveal the nurse reviewed blood culture results at a specific time, which may corroborate the nurse's personal recollection. It is also worthwhile, if possible, to communicate with the custodian of the EMR or any other individual that may generate the audit trail to gain an understanding of the software and the meanings of certain terms or phrases generated in a report. Understanding how an audit trail is generated and the terms used are critical in accurately integrating the EMR and audit trail into one's analysis.

Metadata in Litigation

Metadata, or audit trails, under the right circumstances and after well-thought-out discovery, can prove to be a very effective litigation device. At first glance, the value of such evidence may seem elusive, but the scenarios in which it can assist in developing the facts or narrative of a case are plenty. Suppose, for instance, an orthopedic surgeon does not have a recollection of having reviewed x-rays during a consultation with a patient's primary care physician, who misdiagnosed the patient's condition. The audit trail may show the surgeon did, in fact, have access to the x-rays during the discussion. This information may precipitate the surgeon being included as a party to a medical negligence action (*Sweeney v. Adams County Public Hospital District No. 2*, 2016). An audit trail could show that a patient's films were not reviewed by a healthcare provider prior to surgery (*Paugh v. Parrott*, 2015). Consider also the allegation that a patient was not seen or evaluated by a healthcare provider prior to discharge from the hospital. While an audit trail would not demonstrate the full extent of the healthcare provider's efforts, the audit trail may reveal whether the provider even accessed and reviewed the patient's medical records and plan of care prior to discharge (*Gilbert v. Highland Hospital*, 2016). Such evidence may, at a minimum, undermine the healthcare provider's credibility, or it could confirm the provider's testimony and upend an allegation of negligence altogether.

An often-seen use of the audit trail is corroborating the testimony of healthcare professionals who claim to have made certain entries in a patient's EMR at or around the time of critical events. The audit trail may reveal the entries were made after the fact or by other healthcare professionals. An audit trail of a healthcare provider's EMR activities on a certain day could show the individual was not at a patient's bedside as claimed but rather was entering information into another patient's chart in a different room (Keel, 2014).

Before requesting an audit trail, legal professionals should think carefully about the needs of the case and the scope of the request. As a threshold matter, metadata or audit trails may not be discoverable in every setting. As with any request for information, a request for metadata should be relevant to the claims or defenses or reasonably calculated to lead to information that may be admitted at trial (Legal Information Institute, 2016). Additionally, a request should be tailored to the specific circumstances of the case. Broad, sweeping requests for metadata will often be thwarted by the courts (*Dahl v. Bain Capital Partners, LLC*, 2009).

Tips for Using Electronic Medical Records in Civil Litigation

As mentioned earlier, the EMR is usually handled by legal professionals in PDF format and, given the wealth of data stored therein, can often drown them with information, particularly in proceedings involving multiple or lengthy hospital stays or multiple healthcare providers. For example, consider a medical malpractice lawsuit in which the plaintiff alleges that several healthcare providers and hospitals missed a certain diagnosis over several years, resulting in chronic and permanent cognitive deficiencies. The plaintiff had several multi-day admissions at various hospitals and inpatient facilities, resulting in volumes of medical records, all of which were important to assessing causation and damages. Similarly, consider a medical malpractice lawsuit involving a complex autoimmune condition resulting in a hospital stay of over three months that generated over 11,000 pages of records. In both instances, the task of reviewing the records and providing legal advice as to potential liability and defenses may prove overwhelming. Proper organization is critical to thoroughly analyzing and successfully navigating EMRs in administrative and civil proceedings.

Organizing the EMR pages and using electronic bookmarks for easy access and navigation is essential, particularly for voluminous EMRs. If the EMR is not already page-numbered, it may be worthwhile to coordinate the bates-stamping with other parties' offices for uniformity and ease of access to a specific page. Organizing the EMR as early as possible is critical to facilitating the drafting of pleadings, discovery, and discovery responses; interviewing clients and team members; identifying necessary witnesses; preparing for depositions; and developing a trial theme and strategy.

Using the features of a PDF viewer software program can also be helpful when reviewing EMRs. In addition to the aforementioned bookmarking feature, many programs have highlighting features to accentuate key information. The LNC may wish to color code such information by healthcare provider, laboratory data, liability, causation, damages, etc. Most programs also have features allowing the LNC to place comments using sticky notes, call-out boxes, text boxes, etc. When using such features, it is imperative to clearly label the document as a work-product and maintain a separate "clean" copy of the EMR (i.e., a copy with no highlighting, commentary, etc.) to send to experts, use for exhibits, etc.

It is still important that a legal professional, particularly one with the benefit of medical training and experience, like an LNC, summarize the EMR and highlight notes of special interest. Most PDF programs now contain a text recognition tool that allows the program to recognize the text within the EMR, thereby enabling the legal professional to copy the text from the EMR and paste it into a spreadsheet or word processing document. However, be cautious with this tool in practice. It is easy to become complacent when using this feature and mindlessly copy and paste the record into the summary. From an attorney's perspective, it is still vital to prepare a succinct summary of only the relevant information by removing repetitive information that has been copied and pasted or pre-populated by the medical professional and to bold or highlight the information most relevant to the theories and defenses in the case.

The text recognition tool also allows the LNC to search the PDF to easily find all records pertaining to a particular healthcare provider, for example. This is useful in depositions involving nurses, whose involvement in a patient's care is sprinkled through nearly every component of the record.

It may also be helpful to have, for each defendant or witness, a separate document containing only those portions of the EMR in which the witness's activities are recorded. This quick reference to the witness's involvement can help the attorney when deposing the witness, drafting dispositive motions, and preparing for trial. This reference document can be created by extracting the relevant pages from the EMR and saving them as a separate PDF.

Privacy and Security

First and foremost, patient privacy has become the albatross of EMRs. Personal information, whether financial or otherwise, is more vulnerable in electronic form to being improperly accessed and disclosed than the same information in paper form. Although EMRs have improved the delivery of health care in many ways, they can expose the confidential information of millions of patients to identity thieves and the public. Such information includes social security numbers, dates of birth, addresses, signatures, insurance and payment information, etc. This personally identifying information can be used to obtain credit cards, apply for loans, commit tax fraud, and submit counterfeit medical bills to insurers (Sankin, 2015). While identity theft is a major concern with EMRs, in some instances, the medical information itself can be used to blackmail, publicly humiliate, or affect employment, especially if the information is particularly sensitive, such as a human immunodeficiency virus (HIV) positive status or substance or alcohol abuse. Susceptibility in the EMR software allows identity thieves to obtain this information in bulk through computer hacks or by intercepting electronic communications without physically entering the healthcare facility or practice. The ramifications are enormous. While the hacks of retailers like Target and Sony in recent years may have received world-wide attention, hackers accessed nearly 100 million medical records from two health insurers in 2015 alone (Gosk, 2015).

Hacking aside, there are a number of everyday circumstances wherein EMRs pose a significant threat to patient confidentiality. Examples include: (1) an unauthorized employee accessing patient data and viewing a patient's entire medical record, perhaps the record of a public figure or estranged spouse, (2) a disgruntled employee electronically transferring patient records to a personal email just prior to resigning, (3) the theft of a facility's computer that stores hundreds of thousands of unencrypted patient files, or (4) the inadvertent and public disclosure of patient data at the hand of a careless employee (Hseih, 2014). Each scenario presents the threat of significant harm to patients' reputation, finances, and psyche. Moreover, such scenarios may affect patients' health, as the exposure of personal information may affect their decision to seek future care (Hseih, 2014).

Legal nurse consultants, who often work the most intimately with EMRs in regulatory and civil proceedings, should be ever-cognizant of the privacy and security of the records they are handling. Legal professionals are not immune from computer and other cyber hacks (Hong & Sidel, 2016). All legal professionals should have appropriate cybersecurity systems in place and avoid responding to or following links in suspicious emails. The 2016 Presidential Campaign, wherein an email phishing scam led to the exposure of a decade's worth of Hillary Clinton's campaign manager's emails, should offer all professionals a valuable lesson (Uchill, 2016).

The Privacy and Security Rules

The federal government recognizes the importance of patient privacy and has created a complex web of laws and regulations governing the privacy and security of medical records that imposes serious penalties for non-compliance. At the turn of the century, the U.S. Department of Health and Human Services, in response to a legislative mandate for the adoption of federal privacy protections, formulated the Privacy Rule, which established federal standards for the protection of health information by healthcare providers and entities (U.S. Department of HHS, 2013a). Simply, the Privacy Rule provides that certain entities, including healthcare providers, may not use or disclose an individual's protected health information except under specific circumstances. For example, if specific conditions are met, a patient's protected health information may be disclosed in judicial or administrative proceedings or used in healthcare oversight activities (Legal Information Institute, 2013g). The Privacy Rule applies to all medical records and patient-identifying information. However, importantly, the subsequently formulated Security Rule applies only to electronic protected health information. The Security Rule sets standards for the protection of electronic personal health information, requiring healthcare providers and entities to have the appropriate safeguards in place to ensure the security of electronic protected health information (Legal Information Institute, 2013g, 2013h).

These rules extend beyond healthcare professionals to business associates, including consultants and law firms. Accordingly, it is important for LNCs to be aware of these issues and always keep privacy and security a priority when working with patient information.

Business Associates and the Security Rule

As discussed earlier, the HITECH Act was an important component of the evolution of EMRs. It was an equally important component of the law governing business associates and their responsibilities. In the context of EMRs, a business associate is a person or entity that uses protected health information to advance the activities of a healthcare provider (U.S. Department of HHS, 2013b). Business associates typically perform functions such as claims processing, quality assurance, and billing, and they include attorneys, accountants, LNCs, and other professionals that are retained, but not employed, by healthcare providers to perform services requiring the disclosure of protected health information (ONC, 2016b).

Prior to the passage of the HITECH Act, a business associate was not directly liable for violating the Privacy and Security Rules. Only healthcare providers could be directly liable, and even then, they could escape liability for the actions of their business associates by correcting the violation and mitigating any harm to the patients (Bakich & Hustead, 2017). Thus, a business associate's liability for a violation of the Privacy and Security Rules was generally limited to breach of contract or other harm incurred by the healthcare provider for which the business associate was providing services. For example, if a law firm violated federal regulations while handling protected health information in the defense of a hospital, it was only responsible to the hospital to the extent the hospital was harmed by law firm's violation (Bakich & Hustead, 2017).

Now, however, the HITECH Act makes legal professionals and other business associates directly liable for non-compliance with the Health Insurance Portability and Accountability Act (HIPAA), and they face the same penalties as healthcare providers. Accordingly, business associates must now comply with the requirements of the Security Rule or be exposed to the same civil and criminal penalties to which healthcare providers are exposed (Bradshaw & Hoover, 2010).

Pursuant to the Security Rule, healthcare providers and their business associates must establish and maintain administrative, physical, and technical safeguards to ensure the integrity of electronic protected health information (ePHI). Administratively, the Security Rule generally directs providers and business associates to have policies and procedures in place to ensure compliance with the rule's requirements. More specifically, healthcare providers and business associates must implement policies and procedures to prevent, detect, and contain security violations; control workforce access to ePHI; train workforce members; address security incidents; plan for contingencies; and re-evaluate the same (Bakich & Hustead, 2017). Healthcare providers and business associates are also required to appoint a security officer to ensure compliance with the administrative requirements of the Security Rule.

The physical safeguards mandated by the Security Rule essentially require healthcare providers and business associates to implement facility access controls that limit physical access to ePHI while allowing authorized workforce members' access to perform their job functions. Specifically, they must implement policies and procedures to safeguard their facilities, control and validate an individual's access to their facilities, document any maintenance at their facilities related to security (e.g., doors, locks, etc.), control how computer workstations are used, and restrict unauthorized access to such workstations (Legal Information Institute, 2013e). While physical safeguards concern physical access to the facilities and workstations containing ePHI, the technical safeguards required by the Security Rule relate to the electronic access to the information systems on which the ePHI is managed (Legal Information Institute, 2013f). Such requirements include policies and procedures to track the identities of computer users, mechanisms to encrypt and decrypt ePHI, safeguards against unauthorized access, and protection of ePHI from improper alteration or destruction. Some of the technical safeguard requirements are arguably not applicable to business associates, and business associates are encouraged to consult with experienced information technology professionals to ensure they are complying with the law (Bradshaw & Hoover, 2010).

HIPAA Breaches and Breach Notification

An important aspect of HIPAA privacy and security that all ePHI users should be familiar with is the requirement that healthcare providers and business associates notify the Department of Health and Human Services of any breach of unsecured health information (U.S. Department of HHS, 2013c). Unsecured health information is defined as "protected health information that is not rendered unusable, unreadable, or indecipherable to unauthorized persons through the use of a technology or methodology specified by [HHS]" (Legal Information Institute, 2013a, para. 5). In other words, ePHI is unsecured if it is not encrypted or has not been electronically sanitized (U.S. Department of HHS, 2013d). The details of the necessary encryption and sanitization are quite technical, and the LNC is best served by consulting with an experienced information technology professional.

A breach of unsecured health information occurs whenever there is an acquisition, use, or disclosure of protected health information that compromises its security and privacy (Legal Information Institute, 2013a). Examples of breaches were given in the first few paragraphs of this section on privacy and security. The notification process is complicated for EMR breaches due to the volume of patients who can be affected by a single intrusion of a healthcare provider's network. An entire chapter could be devoted to this topic, but this section will focus on the applicability of the breach notification requirements to business associates. Nevertheless, LNCs should take the time to familiarize themselves with the requirements applicable to healthcare providers. The

Department of Health and Human Services is a great resource and provides a wealth of information on its website (U.S. Department of HHS, 2013d).

Although seemingly intuitive, determining whether a breach has actually occurred requires a complex analysis of certain risk factors such as the type of information acquired (e.g., social security numbers, HIV test results, etc.) and whether the information was actually used or viewed. For example, the inadvertent disclosure of a signed HIPAA release form may not, in and of itself, be a breach, given that it is merely a boilerplate form signed by a patient. However, if the form required the patient's social security number, the disclosure of that document likely meets the definition of a breach. If the LNC accidentally discloses ePHI, say through an inadvertent email, or if the LNC's network is hacked, there is likely no breach if the information was encrypted pursuant to U.S. Department of HHS' guidelines, because the information was likely not unsecured (U.S. Department of HHS, 2013c). In any event, the U.S. Department of HHS presumes a breach occurred in the absence of evidence to the contrary (Legal Information Institute, 2013a). Legal nurse consultants and healthcare providers should consult with an attorney regarding any suspected breach.

Business associates face lighter reporting requirements than healthcare providers. Business associates are only required to notify a healthcare provider of a breach of that provider's unsecured health information. The business associate must include in its notification to the healthcare provider the identification of the individuals affected by the breach, to the extent possible (Legal Information Institute, 2013b). Additionally, the notification must include the information necessary for the healthcare provider to meet its own notification requirements to the affected individuals (Legal Information Institute, 2013b). Such information includes the dates of the breach and its discovery, a brief description of what happened, what type of information was involved, what is being done to investigate the breach, what individuals can do to protect themselves from potential harm, and contact procedures (e.g., toll-free number, email address, or website) for individuals to ask questions and learn more information (Legal Information Institute, n.d.).

Generally, healthcare providers must notify affected individuals in writing by first class mail within 60 days of discovering a breach (Legal Information Institute, n.d.). This is an important deadline for the LNC to know since healthcare providers can delegate the responsibility of notifying individuals of a breach to the business associate (U.S. Department of HHS, 2013c). If the business associate does not have up-to-date contact information for 10 or more affected individuals, the business associate must also post notice of the breach on the business website or advertise the breach in major print or broadcast media for 90 days (Legal Information Institute, n.d.). If the breach involves 500 or more individuals, which is increasingly the case with EMRs, the healthcare provider must also notify prominent media outlets serving the state or jurisdiction of the breach, normally through the issuance of a press release, within 60 days (Legal Information Institute, 2013c). If the breach involves more than 500 patients, healthcare providers must also provide notice to the U.S. Department of HHS within 60 days of the date of a breach. If less than 500 individuals are affected, notice must be provided within 60 days following the end of the calendar year (Legal Information Institute, 2013d). Reports to the U.S. Department of HHS are prepared and submitted online at the U.S. Department of HHS' website (U.S. Department of HHS, 2013c). The topic of breach notification is complex and lengthy, but the foregoing serves as a broad overview so the LNC is alert to the need to timely react to a potential breach of ePHI should the LNC, legal professionals, or healthcare providers experience a breach.

Summary

For better or worse, EMRs are changing the way health care is documented and how medical records are used in civil litigation. Knowing how to maneuver the various components of the EMR is key to succeeding in depositions, motion practice, and other aspects of civil litigation. It is also helpful to understand the drawbacks of EMRs and how the information can be pre-populated or copied throughout the record. Appreciating the value of metadata and carefully crafting a discovery strategy around the needs of a case can sometimes produce an eye-opening moment. Importantly, working with EMRs requires a heightened vigilance to protect against unauthorized disclosure, especially with the ease in which such information can be disseminated by email or other electronic means. Knowing how to identify and react to a breach is essential to ensure compliance with the law.

References

Andrasz, L. (2012, November). HIPAA and electronic medical records: Benefits and security issues. *DCBA Brief, 25*(2), 26–31.

Bakich, K., & Hustead, J. (2017). Business associates. *Employer's Guide to HIPAA Privacy Requirements*.

Blanchard, T., & Manning, M. (2016, June). Electronic medical records documentation: Inherent risks and inordinate hazards. *Health Law Handbook Journal, 7*.

Bradshaw, M., & Hoover, B. (2010). Not so hip?: The expanded burdens on and consequences to law firms as business associated under HITECH modifications to HIPAA. *Richmond Journal of Law and Public Interest, 13*(3), 313–341.

Centers for Disease Control and Prevention. (2017). Meaningful use. Retrieved from www.cdc.gov/ehrmeaningfuluse/introduction.html.

Courtney, M. (2011). The impact of the use of electronic health records on health care providers' potential legal liability. *Health Law Handbook* § 10:9.

Dahl v. Bain Capital Partners, LLC, 655 F.Supp. 2d 146 (D.Mass. 2009).

DeSalvo, K., & Washington, V. (2016, September 29). By the numbers: Our progress in digitizing health care. *HealthITBuzz*. Retrieved from www.healthit.gov/buzz-blog/health-data/numbers-progress-digitizing-health-care/.

Gatti, C. (2015). Roundtable discussion on electronic health records. *The Journal of Legal Nurse Consulting, 26*(2), 31–36.

Gilbert v. Highland Hospital, 531 N.Y.S.3d 397 (N.Y. Sup. Ct. 2016).

Gosk, S. (2015, May 27). Electronic medical records are latest target for identity thieves. *NBC News*. Retrieved from http://nbcnews.com.

Greene, S. (2015). Audit logs. *The Journal of Legal Nurse Consulting, 26*(2), 21–24.

Hong, N., & Sidel, R. (2016, March 29). Hackers breach law firms, including Cravath and Weil Gotshal. *The Wall Street Journal*. Retrieved from http://wsj.com.

Hseih, R. (2014). Improving HIPAA enforcement and protecting patient privacy in the digital healthcare environment. *Loyola University Chicago Law Journal, 46*(1), 182–184.

Iyer, P., Leone, A., & Zapatochny, R. (2015). Electronic health records: The promise and the reality. *The Journal of Legal Nurse Consulting, 26*(2), 14–20.

Keel, J. (2014, May). Follow the audit trail. *Trial, 50*(5), 29–33.

Legal Information Institute. (n.d.). Notification to individuals, 45 C.F.R. § 164.404. Retrieved from www.law.cornell.edu/cfr/text/45/164.404.

Legal Information Institute. (2013a). Definitions, 45 C.F.R. § 164.402. Retrieved from www.law.cornell.edu/cfr/text/45/164.402.

Legal Information Institute. (2013b). Notification by a business associate, 45 C.F.R. § 164.410. Retrieved from www.law.cornell.edu/cfr/text/45/164.410.

Legal Information Institute. (2013c). Notification to the media, 45 C.F.R. § 164.406. Retrieved from www.law.cornell.edu/cfr/text/45/164.406.

Legal Information Institute. (2013d). Notification to the secretary, 45 C.F.R. § 164.408. Retrieved from www.law.cornell.edu/cfr/text/45/164.408.

Legal Information Institute. (2013e). Physical safeguards, 45 C.F.R. § 164.310 www.law.cornell.edu/cfr/text/45/164.310.

Legal Information Institute. (2013f). Technical safeguards, 45 C.F.R. § 164.312 Retrieved from www.law.cornell.edu/cfr/text/45/164.312.

Legal Information Institute. (2013g). Uses and disclosures of protected health information: General rules, 45 C.F.R. § 164.502. Retrieved from www.law.cornell.edu/cfr/text/45/164.502.

Legal Information Institute. (2013h). Uses and disclosures for which an authorization or opportunity to agree or object is not required, 45 C.F.R. § 164.512. Retrieved from www.law.cornell.edu/cfr/text/45/164.512.

Legal Information Institute. (2016, December 1). Federal Rules of Civil Procedure. Retrieved from www.law.cornell.edu/rules/frcp.

McLean, T. (2009). EMR metadata uses and e-discovery. *Annals of Health Law, 18*(1).

Merriam Webster. (2016). Metadata. Retrieved from www.merriam-webster.com/dictionary/metadata.

Office of the National Coordinator for Health Information Technology. (2015). What are the differences between electronic medical records, electronic health records, and personal health records? Retrieved from www.healthit.gov/providers-professionals/faqs/what-are-differences-between-electronic-medical-records-electronic.

Office of the National Coordinator for Health Information Technology. (2016a). Office-based physician electronic health record adoption. Retrieved from https://dashboard.healthit.gov/quickstats/pages/physician-ehr-adoption-trends.php.

Office of the National Coordinator for Health Information Technology. (ONC). (2016b). What is an electronic medical record? Retrieved from www.healthit.gov/providers-professionals/electronic-medical-records-emr.

Paugh v. Parrott, No. 03-C-14-005315, 2015 WL 10558743 (Md. Cir. Ct. Aug. 24, 2015). Plaintiff's Opposition to Summary Judgment.

Sankin, A. (2015, April 26). The real reason hackers want your medical records. *The Kernel*. Retrieved from http://kernelmag.dailydot.com.

Sweeney v. Adams County Public Hospital District No. 2, 196 Wash. App. 1040 (Wash. Ct. App. 2016).

Uchill, J. (2016, December 13). Typo led to Podesta email hack: Report. *The Hill*. Retrieved from http://thehill.com.

United States Department of Health and Human Services. (n.d.). HITECH Act Enforcement Interim Final Rule: The Health Information Technology for Economic and Clinical Health (HITECH) Act of 2009. Retrieved from www.hhs.gov/hipaa/for-professionals/special-topics/hitech-act-enforcement-interim-final-rule/index.html?language=es.

United States Department of Health and Human Services. (2013a). Privacy Rule general overview. Retrieved from www.hhs.gov/hipaa/for-professionals/privacy/guidance/general-overview/index.html.

United States Department of Health and Human Services. (2013b). Business associates. Retrieved from www.hhs.gov/hipaa/for-professionals/privacy/guidance/business-associates/index.html.

United States Department of Health and Human Services. (2013c). Breach notification rule. Retrieved from www.hhs.gov/hipaa/for-professionals/breach-notification/index.html.

United States Department of Health and Human Services. (2013d). Guidance to render unsecured protected health information unusable, unreadable, or indecipherable to unauthorized individuals. Retrieved from www.hhs.gov/hipaa/for-professionals/breach-notification/guidance/index.html.

Additional Reading

Wilbanks, B. (2015). A review of electronic health records for legal nurse consultants. *The Journal of Legal Nurse Consulting, 26*(2), 8–13.

Test Questions

1. The EMR and EHR are not synonymous since the EMR:
   A. Contains information from all the clinicians involved in a patient's care, and all authorized clinicians involved in a patient's care can access the information to provide care to that patient
   B. Shares information with laboratories and specialists and follows the patient from provider to provider, and potentially across the country
   C. Is meant to be used throughout the community of professionals providing treatment to an individual patient
   D. Is limited to a particular provider who uses the EMR for diagnosis and treatment and, like paper charts, is not designed to be shared or used outside of that provider's office(s)
2. Copy and paste functionality of an EMR:
   A. Allows users to copy and paste information from one portion of the EMR to another
   B. Can help reduce the time a provider spends typing information in the records
   C. Can help ensure information from another part of the EMR on which a provider relies during a specific encounter is accurately recorded for that encounter
   D. All of the above
3. Metadata:
   A. Is the automated logbook of a particular document, such as an EMR, that logs what activity has taken place with respect to that document
   B. Can serve as a virtual lie-detector test for the EMR itself
   C. Can expose alterations made to an EMR days, weeks, months, or years after the patient encounter
   D. All of the above
4. According to the HITECH Act, who is directly liable for non-compliance with Health Insurance Portability and Accountability Act (HIPAA) regulations and can face penalties?
   A. Healthcare providers, legal professionals, and other business associates
   B. Healthcare providers
   C. Legal professionals and healthcare providers
   D. None of the above
5. Audit trails:
   A. Document actions taken in the EMR and actions provided to a patient
   B. Can determine when changes in an EMR occurred and may allow testimony that deviates from the EMR to be challenged
   C. Cannot discern if an individual accessed the EMR only to view it or if they created or edited entries
   D. Cannot be generated for a particular medical provider

Answers: 1. D, 2. D, 3. D, 4. A, 5. B

Section IV

Case Analysis

Chapter 10

Elements of Case Analysis
Screening Medical Negligence Claims

Tonia Aiken, RN, JD
Phyllis ZaiKaner Miller, RN
Marguerite Barbacci, BSN, RN, MPH, LNCC®

Contents

Objectives

■ Define the process of investigation and analysis of potential medical negligence cases
■ Name five considerations when screening potential medical negligence cases
■ Define the three types of damages and give an example of each
■ Explain the difference between negligence and "known complication"

Introduction

The analysis and investigation of medical negligence claims are as much about the medicine as they are about the law. The legal nurse consultant (LNC) supports the legal team by analyzing cases through the eyes of a healthcare provider (HCP), providing appropriate insights and advice from the unique legal nursing perspective. Not all attorneys handling medical negligence cases consider it their specialty. Even attorneys who specialize in medical negligence litigation do not always understand the subtleties of the medicine and science pertinent to the case. The role of the LNC is to assist the legal team in evaluating the case fact pattern in the context of the medicine, science, and law to create the foundation for a successful claim investigation.

Each party to a medical negligence claim conducts its own independent analysis of the case, including screening for any conflicts of interest, evaluating the statute of limitations, and analyzing the four elements of proof (see Chapter 4 for more information). The plaintiff's legal team screens the case at the outset to determine whether it is meritorious; the defense team analyzes the case upon receipt, whether pre-suit or in-suit. The plaintiff's side has an additional consideration: the economic viability of the case. Therefore, this chapter discusses screening medical negligence cases from the pre-suit perspective of the plaintiff. The reader should understand, though, that the defense undertakes a nearly identical evaluation of the case upon receipt.

The decision to proceed with or defer investigation of a potential claim and the manner in which the investigation will be conducted ultimately rests with the attorney. The LNC works in concert with counsel, helping the attorney-client avoid potential pitfalls. Sometimes an attorney may be eager to pursue a case, believing it has the potential for a large settlement or verdict because the potential plaintiff is catastrophically injured or because the story has "great jury appeal." After reviewing the case and carefully considering all of the information, a knowledgeable LNC may realize that further pursuit of that claim would be difficult, at best, based on other considerations of the claim. Although the information may not be what the attorney wanted to hear, the opinion of the LNC will be appreciated as long as the basis for a "less than optimistic" outlook for the potential success of the claim is based on sound analysis and judgment. Although the LNC may be the team member to deliver this news, the LNC's role is fulfilled if the attorney learns of the case's poor prognosis from the LNC early in the case screening and not from opposing counsel during discovery or deposition, long after the case has been filed and money expended.

Professional Negligence

The term "malpractice" is often used incorrectly as a "catch-all" phrase to describe the negligence of any HCP. However, malpractice, or professional negligence, extends beyond the medical arena; it is a breach of duty by any professional, be it a real estate agent, accountant, attorney, etc. A breach of duty by a physician or other HCP while performing duties as a professional is medical negligence, or medical malpractice.

Elements of Case Analysis

Conflict of Interest

Attorneys must avoid representing clients when doing so would present a conflict of interest. Conflicts of interest can be legal, personal, or practical (Zorn & Dickinson, 2014). A legal conflict of interest would exist if a plaintiff attorney previously represented an individual who is a potential defendant in the case at hand (Zorn & Dickinson, 2014). Most attorneys would also decline to handle a claim against their personal physician or a healthcare professional who was a neighbor, acquaintance, or friend, because this is a personal conflict of interest. If a potential defendant in the case at hand has worked with the plaintiff attorney on behalf of another plaintiff (e.g., as an expert witness or as a subsequent treater), this would be a practical conflict of interest. While practical conflicts of interest are not legal conflicts of interest, they may impact the attorney's other cases (Zorn & Dickinson, 2014). It is important to identify any possible conflicts of interest as early in the investigation as possible. The LNC can assist in this effort by identifying all HCPs and facilities that played a role in the care at issue and supplying these names to the attorney for conflict checking.

Statute of Limitations

The statute of limitations (SOL) is the law that sets the maximum period of time one can wait before filing a lawsuit, depending on the type of case or claim. The SOL for medical negligence claims varies with each state and will be different for cases involving minors or mentally impaired individuals. Some states have a different SOL for death claims or may define the SOL from the date the injury or negligence was (or should have been) discovered. Claims against the Veterans Administration and other federal healthcare facilities are actually federal claims against the United States, and there is a one-year SOL.

The attorney determines the SOL from the medical records and facts of the case, not from what the client believes or remembers. Although the LNC is not responsible for determining this legal deadline, it needs to be factored into the analysis of all potential claims early in the process. If the SOL runs while the attorney or LNC is investigating the case, the attorney may be exposed to a legal malpractice claim. Consideration of the SOL begins with carefully identifying the act of negligence that allegedly caused the injury. If there are multiple points of care with multiple providers, or care that crosses state lines, the LNC should carefully present the relevant facts and dates for the attorney's consideration in determining the SOL. In cases of delayed diagnosis, the LNC can assist the attorney in determining the SOL by carefully outlining the chronology of symptoms and missed opportunities for the patient to have received an appropriate diagnosis. Alert the attorney as soon as possible if a rapidly approaching SOL is suspected.

Four Elements of Proof

To prevail in a professional negligence claim, the plaintiff must prove four elements: duty, breach of duty, damages, and causation (Narang & Paul, 2017; Robinson & Nouhan, 2018). (See Chapter 4 for more information.) While the plaintiff must prove **all four** elements to prevail, the defense needs only to cast enough doubt about **any one** element to prevail at trial or reach a favorable outcome (Robinson & Nouhan, 2018).

As the initiator of the lawsuit, the plaintiff has the burden of proving these four elements by a preponderance of the evidence. This standard is less strict than in criminal cases, in which the claims must be proven beyond a reasonable doubt. In civil cases, the standard of proof is "more likely than not," "greater than a 50% chance," or "to a reasonable degree of probability."

Duty

In medical negligence claims, duty is dependent upon the existence of a provider–patient relationship. When an HCP consents to treat a patient, it becomes the HCP's duty to use reasonable care and diligence in the exercise of skill and the application of learning to accomplish the purpose for which the HCP was employed (Jerrold, 2015).

Breach of Duty

Breach of duty is often referred to as liability or a deviation from the standard of care (SOC). The standard of care is the degree of skill, care, and judgment a reasonably prudent similar healthcare professional would have exercised in similar circumstances (Brenner, Brenner, Awerbuch, & Howitz, 2012; Narang & Paul, 2017; Robinson & Nouhan, 2018). Although states have worded the concept of the standard of care in various ways, the basic premise is that healthcare professionals are bound to adhere to the applicable standard practice for their profession. Healthcare professionals are not required to deliver the highest degree of care possible, but they are expected to deliver standard care. Within the definition of "standard care," the healthcare professional is entitled to exercise individual judgment. Because the applicable standard of care is beyond the knowledge of the lay juror, breach of duty must be proven through expert testimony that sets forth the applicable standards in effect *at the time of the incident* and the specifics of the deviation(s) from those standards.

In the case of *McCourt v. Abernathy* (S.C. 1995), the jury delivered a plaintiff's verdict, as it was determined that the care provided by the treating physicians was substandard (Moffett & Moore, 2011). However, the jury instructions provided by the trial judge provided a primer on breach of duty:

> The mere fact that the plaintiff's expert may use a different approach is not considered a deviation from the recognized standard of medical care. Nor is the standard violated

because the expert disagrees with a defendant as to what is the best or better approach in treating a patient. Medicine is an inexact science, and generally qualified physicians may differ as to what constitutes a preferable course of treatment. Such differences due to preference … do not amount to malpractice. … [T]he degree of skill and care that a physician must use in diagnosing a condition is that which would be exercised by competent practitioners in the defendant doctors' field of medicine. … Negligence may not be inferred from a bad result. [The] law says that a physician is not an insurer of health, and a physician is not required to guarantee results. [The physician] undertakes only to meet the standard of skill possessed generally by others practicing in [the] field under similar circumstances.

The judge re-enforced that the care provided by a physician be minimally competent, may differ from the care of other physicians, and that a bad outcome does not mean that the standard of care was not met (Moffett & Moore, 2011).

Legal nurse consultants should not use their own experience as a guide to standard of care, as this may differ from what is done at larger or smaller institutions and may be out of step with current thinking. Researching the applicable standards *in effect at the time of the event in question* is paramount to LNC practice. If the initial evaluation of the case makes determining the applicable standard of care difficult because some facts are missing or would require specialized expert review, immediately discuss this with the attorney-client. If an expert will be required to determine the applicable SOC, the attorney should have the option of continuing the LNC's review, asking for an initial expert opinion, or declining the case. If records are missing, this must be communicated to the attorney-client as soon as identified by the LNC. Records of past health care and compliance are critical. Often, further investigation will be necessary to analyze the records and evaluate causation and damages (discussed later in this chapter). It is not prudent to spend time and money summarizing medical records and retaining an expert on standard of care if there may be problems proving the other elements.

Legal nurse consultants working with plaintiff attorneys on screening cases should understand that many potential plaintiffs, being unfamiliar with the elements of proof in negligence claims, believe they are due compensation because their injury occurred during the course of their health care; because they developed an infection, allergic reaction, or unexpected side effect; because a HCP was rude, late, or did not return their calls; or because a subsequent HCP stated "we never do that here," "this never should have happened," or even "I'm so sorry that happened." Less-than-perfect outcomes, unprofessional behavior, different practice patterns, and expressions of empathy are not proof of liability (Moffett & Moore, 2011; Moreira, Magalhaes, Dinis-Oliveira, & Taveira-Gomes, 2014; Oyebode, 2013). Although the potential plaintiff's theory of what was done "wrong" is useful, it should not limit the liability investigation. (For more information on client interviews, see Chapter 33.)

ADDITIONAL CONSIDERATIONS

When evaluating liability in medical negligence cases, some additional considerations include complication versus liability, errors in judgment, and hindsight.

Complication Versus Liability

Known or commonly occurring complications or side effects do not typically constitute liability. However, be mindful that an unusual complication may well suggest a breach of duty. An example is the transection of a major nerve during hip surgery. Although injuries to structures near the surgical site are generally considered a complication of the surgery, an injury to a major nerve that a reasonable surgeon is trained to identify and protect might constitute liability.

Failure to recognize and appropriately treat complications in a timely manner may be considered liability. An example is an injury to the bowel occurring during complex abdominal surgery. The bowel injury may not be considered a deviation from the standard of care, but failure to recognize and treat the injury in a timely manner may be a breach of duty.

Errors in Judgment

In most situations, HCPs are allowed wide latitude in judgment when it comes to choosing the appropriate treatment for their patients. As long as the treatment chosen was within the bounds of accepted standards, any adverse outcome generally would not meet the definition of liability. Three factors must be present for an action to be called an error in judgment rather than a breach of duty:

1. the healthcare provider's care must have conformed to the current professional standards of care
2. the healthcare provider must possess knowledge and skills similar to those of an average member of the profession and
3. the healthcare provider must use professional judgment to choose between alternative available treatments, both of which are within the standard of care (Zwaan & Singh, 2015)

Another example is the administration of an antibiotic that results in a severe reaction. The patient had no known allergies to antibiotics, and although other antibiotics were available, there was no basis for prescribing an alternative. On the other hand, if the prescription was for a medication with known cross-reactivity in the setting of a known allergy, such a prescription may be considered a deviation from the standard of care.

Hindsight

Do not evaluate liability with the benefit of hindsight. In a case of "failure to diagnose," remember that the potential defendant did not know then what the LNC and legal team know now. A defendant HCP's liability must be determined based on the information available at the time the care was rendered and under the circumstances described.

An example of hindsight bias frequently encountered is the autopsy confirming the cause of death or presence of undiagnosed disease or condition. The defendant likely did not have the information revealed by the autopsy, and treatment decisions and actions were based only on the information available at the time care was rendered.

COMMON AREAS OF LIABILITY

Common areas of healthcare professional liability include diagnostic errors, treatment issues, communication issues, monitoring, supervision, medication, and falls.

Diagnostic Errors

In 1940, a professor at the University of Maryland School of Medicine coined the phrase "When you hear hoof beats, think horses, not zebras," cautioning HCPs to first consider a commonplace explanation of illness before an exotic medical diagnosis. It is more likely that a cough is due to a common condition compatible with the patient's general health and co-morbidities, e.g., a smoker's cough in the morning or a cold with a runny nose and fever. Far less likely would be tuberculosis or heart failure in a healthy young person.

Healthcare providers are also taught that atypical presentations of common diseases are more frequent than typical presentations of rare diseases. These old maxims suggest HCPs will default to the most likely diagnosis as the first working theory of what might be wrong and begin treatment. Even if, in hindsight, the diagnosis and treatment proved to be wrong, it would be hard to prove liability if reasonable HCPs seeing those same signs and symptoms could have reached the same diagnosis. Singh, Meyer, and Thomas (2014, p. 728) judged diagnostic error to have occurred "…when adequate data to suggest the final, correct diagnosis existed at an earlier [visit or time] or if documented abnormal findings at the visit should have prompted additional evaluation that would have revealed the correct diagnosis."

In its 2015 book titled *Improving Diagnosis in Health Care*, the National Academy of Sciences, in concert with the Institute of Medicine, examined the rate and cause of errors in diagnosis. One cited study (Tehrani et al., 2013) analyzed 25 years of closed liability claims data and found that errors in diagnosis were the most frequent cause of malpractice payouts (28.6%) and responsible for the highest proportion of total payments (35.2%). Diagnostic errors were also quite often associated with patient deaths (Balogh, Miller, & Ball, 2015).

Some of the causes of diagnostic errors include cognitive error; internal biases; lack of knowledge, expertise, and experience with the medical issues presented; failure to collect information; system failures such as missing information in electronic health records; and reliance on initial impression even when conflicting data arises. Diagnostic errors also result from inaccuracies in diagnostic studies or misinterpretations of the studies and from diseases that have atypical presentations that are not recognized and diagnosed. Legal nurse consultants should review the records to determine whether the healthcare providers properly assessed the patient by:

- Obtaining a thorough history with consideration for the patient's mental status, ability to hear, ability to understand the questions, and language barriers
- Conducting a timely and thorough physical exam
- Ordering appropriate, timely, and properly performed diagnostic studies and
- Considering all working differential diagnoses (such that relevant testing, consultations, and evaluations were ordered and performed)

Considering differential diagnoses is one of the more difficult skills for LNCs to master, as it requires LNCs to think more like physicians than nurses. During patient care, identifying differential diagnoses involves considering a patient's history, complaints, symptoms, presentation, medications, vital signs, labs, etc. and identifying those that are outside of normal parameters. Then consideration is given to what process, disease, or illness might fit that picture. Sometimes one disease or illness will match the presentation; other times, more than one will. Those possibilities are prioritized in order of severity, and consideration is given to what further inquiry or testing is needed to narrow the list to identify the correct diagnosis.

Case example: A 37-year-old mother of two minor children was seen by a physician 19 times over a three-year span for complaints of blood in her stools. The physician diagnosed her as having a small hemorrhoid. Subsequently, the patient reported having rectal pressure, abdominal pain, constipation, and hematochezia (blood in the stool). The physician again diagnosed her as having a hemorrhoid. When making the same complaints to a different physician, she was referred to a gastroenterologist who performed a colonoscopy, removed polyps, and informed her they were cancerous. The patient was diagnosed with metastatic colon cancer and died one month after the colonoscopy. The case settled for $1,800,000 (Laska, 2002a).

Treatment Issues

Treatment issues occur in medical centers, hospitals, long-term care facilities, home health settings, and HCP offices to name a few. They involve a wide variety of potential breaches, such as:

- Failure to treat in a timely fashion
- Failure to provide the correct treatment
- Failure to timely and properly perform the treatment
- Failure to use equipment properly and
- Failure to treat in a timely manner when signs and symptoms of a deteriorating condition are evident

Communication Issues

Communication is crucial because of the many layers of healthcare professionals involved in the care and treatment of patients. Communication lines must be open and direct between the healthcare provider and all other team members. Communication failures may result in patient injuries (and thus medical malpractice lawsuits). Common types of communication failures include, but are not limited to:

- Failure to communicate at all
- Failure to communicate to the appropriate individual
- Failure to communicate in a timely manner
- Failure to communicate in a proper manner
- Failure to document the communication
- Failure to communicate the appropriate information
- Failure to act based on the communication received
- Failure to timely and properly inform the patient of test results
- Failure to follow up on communication until resolution of the issue and
- Inappropriate communication of confidential information

Communication breaches involve both verbal and written communications. With social media, texts, emails, and phone messages, communication breaches are being taken to a whole new level.

Monitoring

Monitoring a patient involves all levels of healthcare professionals from physicians to nursing assistants. A facility's policies and procedures that set out monitoring responsibilities are important for the LNC to review in cases alleging a failure to monitor. Monitoring breaches include, but are not limited to:

- Failure to properly monitor the care, treatment, and condition of the patient
- Failure to monitor in a timely fashion
- Failure to report changes in the patient's status
- Failure to document monitoring
- Failure to use the proper equipment to monitor the patient

- Failure to properly instruct and teach the patient about self-monitoring (e.g., glucose monitoring)
- Failure to use equipment properly when monitoring a patient (e.g., silencing the alarms) and
- Failure to report and replace equipment not working properly

Supervision

Supervisory issues have always been an area of great interest, whether they involve an attending surgeon in an operating room or a clinical instructor with a student. The common areas of potential liability vary. For instance, with unlicensed assistant personnel, there is great concern over the issue of who is actually supervising the patient.

Supervisory liability focuses on the failure to supervise properly and delegate properly. For example, if a supervisor knows that the staff does not possess the knowledge, experience, and expertise to perform a delegated task but still delegates it, liability may result if the patient is injured.

Additionally, if the supervisor gives incorrect or inadequate instructions, liability may occur. For example, a nurse asks a supervisor to demonstrate how to z-track an injection. The supervisor uses the nurse's forearm for demonstration purposes rather than a larger muscle. The nurse z-tracks the medication into the patient's forearm, causing severe necrosis and disfigurement. Both the supervisor and nurse may be held liable.

Supervisory breaches include failure to:

- Supervise properly
- Delegate properly
- Properly evaluate care delegated to others and
- Document that the staff has been oriented, trained, and evaluated

Medication

Medication errors are high on the list of potential areas for legal exposure. Errors can be acts of omission or commission. Breaches involving medication may include failure to:

- Administer the drug per provider orders
- Administer the correct medication
- Administer the medication at the correct time
- Administer the medication by the correct route
- Administer the medication to the correct patient
- Administer the correct dosage of medication
- Monitor the sites of intravenous medication administration
- Confirm or clarify medication orders
- Monitor for signs of adverse reaction or toxicity of medication
- Document the administration of medications and
- Use aseptic technique

Falls

Medical negligent claims related to patient falls are common. Falls can occur in any patient. The following types of patients are more susceptible to falls than others:

- Sedated patients
- Patients with mobility impairments

- Patients with cognitive impairments
- Patients with visual impairments
- Patients with a history of falls
- Patients in unfamiliar surroundings
- Patients with predisposing diseases/conditions such as Parkinson's disease, etc.
- Patients on multiple medications and
- Noncompliant patients

Sometimes it is difficult to predict which patient will fall. Falls can result in injuries that range from minor bruising to subdural hematomas and death. The LNC must carefully examine all documentation surrounding the fall. The following should be considered by LNCs when working on a fall claim, irrespective of whether it is for a plaintiff or a defendant:

- Was a fall risk assessment done?
- Was the patient assessed to be at high risk of falling?
- What interventions were in place to address fall risk?
- Did the healthcare professionals follow the facility's policies and procedures?
- Was the patient properly evaluated and treated after the fall?
- What injuries did the patient sustain?
- Did the fall exacerbate a pre-existing condition or cause a new injury?
- Were the HCP and family notified?
- Was the fall documented?
- What was the patient's account of the fall?

Legal nurse consultants working for the defense should confer with the risk manager and interview those involved in the patient's care.

Case example: A wheelchair-bound patient was being transported to a free-standing dialysis center by a medical transport company. The plaintiff claimed to have fallen from his wheelchair while being transported, alleging that the driver made a sharp turn, causing him to fall from his wheelchair and strike his head. He stated the vehicle was not equipped with a seat belt; nor did it have the proper means by which to secure the wheelchair. The driver claimed the patient had refused to wear the seat belt. The plaintiff sustained a hematoma to the scalp, which resulted in gangrene, and removal of half of his scalp to halt the gangrene spread. The action settled for $825,000 (Laska, 2002b).

Damages

The third element of proof in medical negligence cases is damages. The plaintiff (or decedent in wrongful death cases) must have been harmed or injured, whether physically, mentally, or economically. If there are no damages, there is no case, irrespective of the egregiousness of the alleged negligence (Denton, 2010; Nelson, Morrisey, & Kilgore, 2007). Damages are divided into three categories:

1. Special, pecuniary, or economic damages
2. General or non-economic damages and
3. Punitive damages

Special damages are those with actual monetary value that can be calculated in dollars and cents. Special/pecuniary/economic damages include past and future lost wages, loss of earning capacity, out-of-pocket expenses incurred by the plaintiff as a result of the alleged negligence, past and future medical expenses related to the negligence (e.g., expenses paid by insurance), special equipment needs such as wheelchairs or catheters, and other items such as home and vehicle modifications.

General damages are injuries on which the law is unable to place a dollar amount. General damages, sometimes referred to as non-economic or non-pecuniary damages, may encompass past and future pain and suffering; embarrassment; disfigurement; loss of function; and loss of aid, comfort, society and companionship. Some states recognize the value of pain and suffering in the days, weeks, or months before death if due to an act of negligence. If such a claim is recognized, it can considerably impact the total damages and the work required to document that suffering.

Punitive damages, also known as exemplary damages, are monetary compensation that exceeds special and general damages and is intended to punish the defendant, set an example, and deter future behavior considered "outrageous." Most jurisdictions will not even consider a motion for punitive damages until all the facts have been set forth. Many states have capped the amount of punitive damages that can be awarded. Punitive damages are often very difficult to prove in medical malpractice cases.

The monetary value of any claim is based on the plaintiff's special and general damages. At the outset, discuss with the plaintiff all potential and actual damages resulting from the alleged negligence. Documentation substantiating these damages can be acquired at a later date, but forming a general idea of the total amount of special damages and the approximate value of the general damages at the outset is necessary in the case screening process.

The assessment of special damages is generally straightforward and simply requires identifying and summing all expenses related to the alleged negligence. When evaluating special damages, it is important to consider the plaintiff's pre-existing medical conditions, functional limitations, disability, etc. The plaintiff would have continued to require treatment, equipment, medication, etc. for these regardless of the alleged negligence; therefore, these expenses would not be included in determining economic damages. Damages are based on the injuries and expenses incurred as a result of the alleged negligence.

In assessing general damages, consider how the plaintiff's life has changed because of the injury. Permanency of an injury and impairment of the plaintiff's ability to work or engage in activities of daily living should be considered in determining general damages (Denton, 2010). The value of damages is plaintiff-specific. For example, an injury resulting in a crooked fifth finger in an arthritic elderly person is less valuable than the same injury in a concert pianist. When considering injuries to children, think about future disability, future opportunities lost, educational hurdles, social difficulties as a teen, etc. In cases of death, consider whether the decedent's life expectancy would have been reduced even if there was no negligence. Death, even from clear negligence, of an octogenarian with significant co-morbidities does not carry the same value as the death of a young, working spouse and parent.

Finding and applying the morbidity and mortality statistics for the particular disease or illness in question is often necessary when assessing damages. If a disease or injury is very likely to be fatal or to result in significant morbidity even when timely diagnosed and properly treated, the defense could easily argue that the decedent would have died regardless of the alleged negligence or that this disease kills most people within a year of diagnosis even with effective treatment. Thus, such cases are easily defended, because damages are difficult or impossible to prove. Because the value of a wrongful death claim is largely based on estimated, pre-injury life expectancy, unexpected autopsy findings (i.e., of an unrelated but ultimately fatal disease process in advanced stages) can greatly impact damages.

Another possible theory of damages, recognized in some jurisdictions, is the "loss of chance" doctrine. The loss of chance doctrine refers to a patient's loss of chance of survival or loss of chance for a better recovery. The court views a person's prospect for surviving a serious medical condition as something of value, even if the possibility of recovery was less than 50%. Under this theory, the compensable injury is the lost opportunity to achieve a better result, not the physical or psychological injury. This theory applies when (1) a pre-existing injury or illness is aggravated by the alleged negligence such that the patient dies, when without the negligence, there might have been a better or substantial chance of survival, or (2) the patient had a chance of surviving the illness or achieving a better result but for a delay in diagnosis. Because of the negligence, that chance has been lost. This is different from the claim that the patient had a more than likely expectation of cure that has now been lost due to negligence (Jones, 2013).

Some states do not recognize "loss of chance." In states that do not recognize this doctrine, consideration is given to life expectancy, disease outcome, and prognosis when determining outcome. Causation in medical malpractice cases (which is discussed later in this chapter) must be shown as a matter of probability, i.e., "more likely than not" or greater than a 50% chance that the plaintiff's injuries would not have occurred but for the negligent actions of the defendant(s) (*Kilpatrick v. Bryant*, 1993). In some jurisdictions, a reduction in the chance of survival or lesser injury from 51% to 49% could be actionable, because the likelihood crossed the 50% threshold, taking the patient's chance from more likely (51%) or less likely (49%) (*Fennell v. Southern Maryland Hospital*, 1990).

There are additional questions to consider while assessing damages. Can the damages be easily seen and understood on x-rays, in photographs, wage loss documents, or hospital bills? If the injury is difficult to understand, presenting it to a jury to assign a monetary value may be a challenge. Cases in which the primary injuries cannot be seen by the jurors (e.g., soft-tissue injuries, mild head injuries, or mental distress) pose special problems (Tong & Almquist, 2017). Would a jury sympathize with the injuries? If the jurors have some ache, pain, or malady they suffer with every day that makes the plaintiff's injuries seem trivial, they are not likely to award significant compensation.

When assessing the impact of the damages, the astute LNC needs to think beyond the monetary value of the claim. All aspects of damages must be considered:

■ Will the jury understand the complexity of the injuries and the associated costs?
■ Will the plaintiff's pre-existing injuries overshadow any possible recovery?
■ Will the jury consider the full impact of the claimed injuries and how this translates into the monetary value of the claim?

After assessing the special and general damages, the plaintiff LNC and legal team must consider the economics of whether the plaintiff's damages are large enough to warrant further investigation.

ECONOMICS

Medical malpractice suits are costly, prolonged, and difficult to prove. Theoretically, any person can attempt to seek compensation for an injury caused by negligence, regardless of its severity, but most plaintiff attorneys will only pursue cases in which damages are significant and permanent. Cases with significant and permanent damages are likely to secure a higher settlement or jury award, which allows the plaintiff firm to bring in a profit after client compensation and payment of costs associated with the investigation and litigation (Eisberg, 1990; Sloan, Githins, Clayton, Hickson, & Partlett, 1993).

Another economic consideration is whether the state in which a claim would be brought has enacted caps (limits) on non-economic damages. In these states, no matter how severe the injury, non-economic damages are compensable only to the limit of the cap. While the plaintiff can still recover special damages (which are not limited by caps), a cap on non-economic damages (such as for pain and suffering) can significantly limit the recovery, especially for a catastrophically injured plaintiff. Take, for example, a claim involving the loss of sight in a retiree. This is a significant injury impacting quality of life, but special damages are minimal as future related medical needs are limited and there are no lost wages. Even if liability and causation are clear, some attorneys in states with a cap on non-economic damages might not pursue this case, as the expense of adjudicating the case (including expert fees) could exceed the limited potential award.

The potential recovery must always be balanced against the costs of investigation and pursuit of a claim. For this reason, many plaintiff law firms have a damages threshold. If the potential recovery of a prospective case does not exceed this threshold, the firm will typically reject the case, as it would not make economic sense to pursue it.

Most malpractice cases take three to five years to resolve. Most plaintiff attorneys work on a contingency basis, meaning they do not make money unless the plaintiff receives a settlement or award. In a contingency practice, time is money. The firm may subsidize a case for a prolonged period before receiving any reimbursement of expenses, if ever. In the meantime, the cost of maintaining the practice continues. Furthermore, when a claim is not pursued, plaintiff attorneys working on a contingency basis make no money and absorb the costs incurred to investigate the claim. Therefore, timely and effective case analysis is economically imperative for plaintiff firms. For more information on the economics of plaintiff and defense firms, see Chapter 29.

Causation

Causation is the direct link between the breach of duty and the damages incurred. For a medical negligence case to be meritorious, the plaintiff must be able to prove harm as a direct result of the defendant's liability. That direct causal link between the breach of duty and the damages is the element of causation. To prove proximate cause, the plaintiff must show the defendant's act or omission was a substantial contributing factor in bringing about or failing to prevent the injuries sustained. In other words, the injuries would not have occurred "but for" (without) the breach of duty. Please refer to Chapter 4 for more information on causation.

To understand causation, the LNC must think carefully about the following questions: Did the breach of duty cause the injury or damage? Was it a proximate cause or a less substantial factor? Could the injury have been caused by something else? Did the breach of duty cause all or only part of the plaintiff's injury? If only part, which part? Could the plaintiff have had the same outcome absent the breach of duty? In death cases, would the decedent have died of the disease absent any breach of duty? If so, what are the statistics on morbidity and mortality for that specific condition?

During a case investigation, as new facts are identified, the LNC should rethink causation and how the additional information fits into the existing causation theory. The relationship between liability and damages can become ambiguous or extremely complicated and thus be difficult for the trier of fact to understand. The application and importance of the *latest* science, disease theory, and physiology in the analysis of causation cannot be overstated. Consider, for example, a case in which a plaintiff is claiming that a misfiled or ignored routine mammogram report from

14 months ago resulted in failure to diagnose breast cancer. At the time of the actual diagnosis, the patient was in Stage IV disease with many positive lymph nodes and multiple metastatic brain lesions. The instinctive reaction is that the failure to act on the report was negligent, and the earlier cancer is diagnosed and treated, the better. However, science and disease theory infer that breast cancer does not progress from curable to Stage IV with multiple positive lymph nodes and visible brain lesions in 14 months. Disease theory and statistics hold that the plaintiff likely already had brain lesions and positive lymph nodes and was already at an advanced stage of disease, if not Stage IV, 14 months earlier. Therefore, it is likely that, even 14 months earlier, the plaintiff would have needed much of the same treatment and had a very similar chance of survival regardless of whether the mammogram report was reviewed. Therefore, proving the ignored report and consequent delay caused injury may be very challenging.

When evaluating causation, beware of the autopsy and death certificate. They are very sharp double-edged swords, and sometimes they are wrong (Smith Sehdev & Hutchins, 2001). Do not assume that all autopsies are conducted with the expected level of precision. Even experienced medical examiners in large cities admit to rarely even glancing at the medical records of a patient who died in the hospital. Moreover, the doctor performing the autopsy may not be a particularly curious person or someone who thinks outside the box. The cause of death listed and filed with the county may be in direct opposition to what the LNC or attorney thinks caused that person's death. In this situation, the LNC would use critical-thinking skills and consider several questions. How do the facts in the medical record or patient history compare with the findings at autopsy? Was anything missed? What was not taken into consideration? Were appropriate samples and specimens taken? The LNC may suggest a meeting with the medical examiner to fill in any missing information or diplomatically discuss the discrepancy. When presented with an alternative fact scenario taken directly from the medical records, medical examiners may change or amend the autopsy findings and cause of death.

Because causation is often a more complex concept than liability, it is easier for juries to understand liability than causation. However, they must understand (and find) both to render a plaintiff's verdict (Eisberg,1990). Since all medical malpractice plaintiffs had an illness or injury that caused them to seek health care, the defense will remind the jury that the plaintiff's underlying illness or injury can and does sometimes have a bad outcome even in the best of hands. The plaintiff's legal team must explain why that was not the case for this plaintiff and why recovery without sequela would have been the expected outcome. Therefore, the LNC must thoroughly understand the science and pathophysiology of the disease, injury, and sequela and must educate the attorney, thereby preparing the attorney to effectively teach and explain causation to the jury. It is expensive and time-consuming for the attorney to depend on outside medical experts for this preliminary teaching and thoughtful, analytical discussion. An LNC with a good understanding of causation and excellent teaching skills can be valuable to the attorney.

CONTRIBUTORY AND COMPARATIVE NEGLIGENCE

Some states recognize the doctrine of contributory negligence as a complete bar to a plaintiff's recovery. For example, if the jury finds the plaintiff did something that contributed to the alleged injury, even if the blame is only 1%, recovery is precluded. In other states in which the doctrine of comparative negligence is recognized, the jury can assign a percentage of fault to the plaintiff and deduct that percentage from any award. In some jurisdictions, the award may be reduced to zero if the percentage of fault attributed to the plaintiff is 51% or more.

Because of the impact these doctrines can have on the final award, it is imperative that the actions and inactions of the plaintiff be taken into consideration in the causation analysis and valuation of the claim. Did the plaintiff do anything to cause or aggravate the illness or injury? Was the plaintiff compliant with the prescribed course of care? Did the plaintiff follow the HCP's instructions, keep scheduled appointments, and inform the provider of new symptoms or problems? Was the plaintiff harmed by medication taken after being instructed to discontinue it (Cartwright, 1987; Eisberg, 1990)?

The following is an example of contributory negligence. A potential plaintiff wishes to pursue legal action against a physician for failure to diagnose and treat heart disease, which was ultimately diagnosed upon suffering a heart attack. A review of the physician's records revealed the potential plaintiff did not take antihypertensive medication as prescribed, lost no weight as instructed, continued smoking despite admonishments to the contrary, and was only minimally compliant with diabetes management. These behaviors continued even after the heart attack. A jury could conclude that much of the fault lies with the plaintiff, thereby precluding recovery.

Other Considerations and Case Types

Witness Assessment

Another factor when analyzing a potential claim is assessing the potential plaintiff as a witness. The LNC should consider the plaintiff's presentation and demeanor. Is the plaintiff likable, articulate, and believable? Does the plaintiff evoke sympathy? What are the plaintiff's motives for bringing a lawsuit? Be alert for issues suggesting credibility problems. If the record reflects one thing but the plaintiff reports another, this can impact the credibility and believability of the plaintiff. Given that some jurors have a bias towards HCPs, assessing how the potential plaintiff will likely be perceived by the jury is an important consideration.

Informed Consent

Claims involving only informed consent issues are generally difficult for the plaintiff to win, but they are sometimes successful when brought with other claims, such as negligence. In most jurisdictions, the plaintiff must prove that no reasonable person would have agreed to the treatment, medication, or surgery if informed that the outcome suffered could, in fact, happen. Because HCPs are not required to disclose every possible complication that can occur or every potential or rare side effect of every drug prescribed, the plaintiff also must prove, through expert testimony, that the standard of care required the particular risk to be disclosed. See Chapter 19 for more information on informed consent cases.

An example of a successful informed consent case involves a young adult with a subclavian artery obstruction near the junction of the carotid. It arose from adhesions in the vessel from a childhood trauma. The obstruction was causing ischemic changes in the patient's arm, and a vascular surgeon explained the obstruction could be opened using angioplasty with minimal risk and minimal time away from work. Consent was given, and the procedure was performed. During the angioplasty, multiple pieces of clot broke off and, unable to flow downstream past the obstruction, the debris traveled via the nearby carotid to the brain. The patient suffered multiple strokes and permanent brain damage. A lawsuit was brought against the surgeon.

Wrongful Life and Wrongful Birth

Some states allow a legal cause of action for wrongful life and wrongful birth claims. In a wrongful life claim, a child seeks damages for being born with a birth defect rather than not being born, essentially alleging the child would have been better off if not born at all (Zorn & Dickinson, 2014). Few states allow a wrongful life cause of action because of the high value placed on the presence of human life (Zorn & Dickinson, 2014). In a wrongful birth claim, the parents of a child born with birth defects seek damages for alleged negligent treatment or advice that deprived them of the opportunity to avoid conception or terminate the pregnancy (Zorn & Dickinson, 2014). The claim for damages is based on the extraordinary cost to the parents of raising a defective child (Zorn & Dickinson, 2014).

An example of a wrongful birth claim is a case in which the parents alleged a failure to conduct genetic testing after a first child was born with significant mental retardation. The parents stated that if they had known the terrible life their first child suffered was due to a genetic defect they carried, a defect that could have and should have been tested for, they would have opted to never have another child. They were only told of the genetic issue after the birth of their second child.

Retained Foreign Objects

In the common law of torts, *res ipsa loquitur* (Latin for "the thing speaks for itself") is a doctrine that infers negligence from the very nature of an accident or injury, such as retained foreign objects, regardless of any direct or inferred behavior by the defendant. The plaintiff can create a presumption of negligence by the defendant by proving the harm would not ordinarily have occurred without negligence, the object that caused the harm was under the defendant's control, the plaintiff was not responsible for the injury, and there are no other plausible explanations for the plaintiff's injury (Zorn & Dickinson, 2014).

However, whether an attorney pursues a claim for a retained foreign object may depend on damages. A surgeon who leaves an unintended object, such as a clamp or sponge, in a patient may be found to be negligent. However, because these objects often do not cause any symptoms or harm, they are often discovered, incidentally, many years later and may simply be left in place. In this instance, there is no damage and generally no claim. On the other hand, a retained foreign object may cause significant pain or illness and require removal. In that instance, a claim may be brought. The statute of limitations in these cases may depend on when the object was discovered and whether the state has a discovery rule or a special statute regarding the discovery of foreign objects, which may suspend (or toll) the statute of limitations until the foreign object was, or reasonably should have been, discovered.

Cooperation of the Subsequent Treating Provider

Whether the subsequent treating provider will be cooperative is a factor considered by attorneys when deciding whether to litigate a potential case. For example, in a case involving negligent surgery, the observations of the subsequent surgeon are of crucial importance. The second surgeon is the only ostensibly "neutral" person who has seen the site of the original surgery. Jurors will therefore give more credence to the observations of the subsequent surgeon than to the opinions of hired experts for either side.

Sometimes, subsequent treating providers or surgeons have more expertise than the potential defendant. They often receive patients whose care was begun elsewhere and ultimately required a higher level of expertise or technology. Many subsequent treating providers and surgeons rely on these less experienced providers in surrounding communities for referrals. Testifying against these referring providers or facilities would damage a crucial source of the subsequent treaters' business. For example, if a small rural hospital delayed transporting a critically ill patient to a tertiary care center, the receiving provider is not likely to impugn the treatment at the rural hospital, because it might cause the referring HCPs to feel their care will be scrutinized every time they transfer a patient. If the receiving provider did criticize the care, the tertiary care center and its providers could see a drop in the number of transfers and referrals from that rural facility.

Often, the only testimony a subsequent treating provider may be willing to give to either side in a malpractice case is an objective discussion of what was found and what treatment was performed. They may be unwilling to offer any opinions regarding the prior care. Their input is still valuable, particularly when gathering information about damages or a permanent injury. The LNC can assist the attorney by identifying subsequent treating providers, gathering information about their specialty or expertise, and suggesting those the attorney may want to contact.

Other Concerns

Potential cases that involve long complicated courses of treatment with multiple providers or multiple facilities that end in a bad outcome are challenging. Determining exactly which healthcare professionals and facilities were negligent and how that negligence was causally connected to the injury is difficult, time-consuming, and expensive to investigate and prove to a jury.

Another area of concern is if the potential case has been previously rejected by other plaintiff attorneys. If the issues were investigated and the case turned down by another attorney, it is useful to inquire about the rationale for the rejection, such as an inability to find expert support on liability. However, just because a case was rejected by one attorney should not necessarily preclude further investigation, but it should raise the level of concern (Eisberg, 1990).

Case Studies

The following examples provide information obtained during case screening (from interviews with potential plaintiffs and reviews of their medical records) followed by an analysis of the potential claim.

The Hysterectomy

A 47-year-old stay-at-home mother had a long history of painful uterine fibroid tumors and very heavy menstrual periods. She was prescribed iron supplements but remained anemic, which interfered with her ability to run marathons. The potential plaintiff sought definitive treatment and consented to undergo a hysterectomy as recommended by her gynecologist. The surgeon determined that an abdominal hysterectomy was the best option due to the likelihood of encountering pelvic adhesions from prior cesarean sections and other abdominal surgeries. The surgery was completed "without complication," as documented by the surgeon in the operative report. On post-operative day three, the patient's abdomen was distended, and she complained of severe abdominal pain. An ileus was suspected due to decreased bowel sounds and inability to pass flatus. Laxatives were prescribed, and ambulation encouraged. On post-operative day four, the patient was febrile with no discernible bowel sounds. A CT scan of the abdomen was performed and revealed an urinoma. The patient was returned to the operating room for an exploratory laparotomy, which revealed a severed right ureter. Surgical repair of the ureter was completed and included the placement of a percutaneous nephrostomy tube to drain urine from the kidney while the ureter healed. The patient was discharged home three days after her repair surgery with instructions to return for the removal of the nephrostomy tube in six weeks. Subsequent testing revealed normal kidney function with a functional right ureter.

Analysis: This case fact pattern is an example of a patient experiencing a procedural complication; negligence is less likely. Injury to the ureter could have occurred as a complication in the setting of dense adhesions, not as a result of negligence. This injury could have been caused by even the most careful surgeon under these circumstances. In this case, the surgeon anticipated finding adhesions and chose a surgical approach appropriate for the predicted complication. The delay in diagnosis of the damaged ureter may also be within the standard of care, as a urinoma presents in a similar way to an ileus, which is a more common complication of abdominal surgery. Although the patient experienced a less than desirable post-operative course, an earlier diagnosis of a ligated ureter would have led to the identical course of treatment, albeit a few days sooner. Further, the element of damages is problematic, as expenses over and above the cost of the initial surgery were relatively small, and the patient had no long-term injury or lost wages. The economics do not support pursuing a claim based only on a few days or weeks of additional discomfort in a patient who would have been recovering from surgery anyway. The final summary: the patient incurred a known complication of surgery with no evidence of negligence, little economic impact, and no permanent injuries.

Failure to Timely Diagnose Myocardial Infarction

A 62-year-old man presented to the emergency department (ED) of a local hospital with a chief complaint of burning chest pain that had developed while at work but had since subsided. His medical history was significant for elevated serum cholesterol, but he claimed to be "eating better since he found out." He also reported being prescribed blood pressure pills but was not taking them secondary to erectile dysfunction. An electrocardiogram (ECG) was performed, which revealed only non-specific changes. No further testing was done. He was diagnosed with gastro-esophageal reflux disease, given a "GI cocktail," and discharged home with a prescription for an H2 blocker and instructions to follow up with his primary care physician. The patient was also instructed to return to the ED if his symptoms returned or worsened.

A few days later, the patient returned to the ED, accompanied by his wife, complaining that the pain returned the previous evening, "worse than ever," and continued unabated. An ECG revealed an evolving acute myocardial infarction with ST segment elevation, and he underwent an emergent percutaneous transluminal coronary angioplasty with stent placement. An echocardiogram revealed an ejection fraction of 55%, and he was discharged home three days later with appropriate medications.

Analysis: This case fact pattern depicts strong liability, but problems with damages and causation and the possibility of contributory negligence make the potential for success unlikely. A retrospective analysis of the ECG done during the first ED visit revealed evidence of ischemia. In addition to the misread ECG, it was a deviation from the standard of care to not obtain laboratory testing in response to the abnormal ECG finding. Damages are a bit problematic, as the patient's ejection fraction remained within normal limits. There also may be an issue of contributory negligence, as the patient's failure to take his antihypertensive medication as directed may have contributed to the advancement of his cardiac disease.

Delayed Diagnosis of Breast Cancer

A 35-year-old woman received a diagnosis of breast cancer. She was told by her oncologist that the diagnosis should have been made more than a year earlier, as the lesion was present on her mammogram taken 14 months prior to her diagnosis. The patient underwent a lumpectomy and subsequent chemotherapy and radiation. The patient provided the LNC and attorney with copies of her medical records, including the pathology report, which described the 2 cm lesion with clear margins located in the upper outer quadrant of the breast as an infiltrating ductal carcinoma. The sentinel lymph node biopsy was positive with positive estrogen receptors, designating Stage II cancer.

Analysis: At face value, this case fact pattern suggests liability on the part of the first radiologist for failing to properly interpret the mammogram. The elements of causation and damages, however, will be more difficult to prove. A successful outcome of this claim would require the plaintiff to prove to a reasonable degree of medical certainty that the delay of 14 months led to a progression of the cancer and that this delay caused her harm. In other words, but for the delay in diagnosis, her outcome (treatment and prognosis) would have been better.

In all cancer cases, the first thing the LNC should investigate is the statistical survivability and progression of the cancer at all stages. If the cancer is not likely to be cured and will progress no matter the stage at which the cancer is diagnosed, the delay in diagnosis is of little concern. If there is a reasonable expectation of significantly longer life or significantly easier course of treatment, economics will dictate whether the claim is worth pursuing.

Stage II breast cancer is very curable with a very favorable prognosis. In this example, it must be proven that the plaintiff was at Stage I breast cancer when her mammogram was misread 14 months prior to her diagnosis and that her progression from Stage I to Stage II changed the likelihood that she would survive the cancer. The delay may have minimally reduced the survival odds, but she was still curable. If the attorney wished to pursue the claim based on the difference in prognosis between Stage I and II, the LNC must be aware that not all states recognize the "loss of chance" doctrine. In this case, the loss of chance (the difference in prognosis between Stage I and II) would not be statistically significant. The difference in treatment would be assessed in the same manner. Both Stage I and Stage II breast cancer would have required surgery and possibly radiation and/or chemotherapy.

The Failed Back Surgery

Mr. Jones underwent a two-level lumbar fusion at L3–4 and L4–5 with placement of hardware, including two pedicle screws and autologous transplant of bone harvested from his iliac crest. Post-operatively, Mr. Jones was no better despite completing a full course of physical therapy. He reported that, in some ways, his condition was worse. Imaging studies documented a non-healing fusion. Mr. Jones underwent surgery to have the hardware removed and the fusion redone. He remained in daily pain and was unable to return to work for a period of several additional months.

Mr. Jones and his wife were unable to pay his medical bills and went bankrupt. They were concerned that his surgery had been done incorrectly, because his pain was not relieved and he required additional surgery. Before the surgery, Mr. Jones' doctor assured him that he would be able to return to work 6 weeks after surgery. Mr. Jones reported he now has a diagnosis of failed back surgery and believed that, if he had been told there was a chance that the surgery would not work, he never would have gone through with the spinal fusion and hardware placement.

Analysis: This case is a good example of significant general and special damages in pain and suffering, medical bills, and lost wages. Unfortunately, failed fusions are not uncommon and are considered a risk of the procedure. Unless the plaintiff could prove that the fusion failed not by chance, but due to an act of negligence, there is no liability. On the informed consent issue, it is not likely that an attorney could convince a jury that a reasonable person would have opted for continued severe, daily pain (like Mr. Jones had pre-operatively) if informed of a small chance the surgery would not work. This case fact pattern does not warrant a recommendation for further investigation.

Failure to Diagnose and Treat Heart Disease

A young 29-year-old mother found herself becoming short of breath during routine daily activities. She complained of severe fatigue "to her bones" after an ordinary day. Her doctor told her it was just the burden of working and caring for a young family and suggested she get more sleep and to have her husband "pitch in more." Her fatigue and shortness of breath worsened, and she developed a chronic cough, which her physician diagnosed as seasonal allergies. Antihistamines were prescribed.

When the symptoms persisted into the winter and became increasing worse, a dust allergy was diagnosed and more antihistamines prescribed. Two years after this patient was initially evaluated for fatigue and shortness of breath, she decompensated to the point that she could hardly climb a flight of stairs in her own home. She was referred to an allergist. The allergist determined the woman's symptoms were likely not from allergies and referred her to a pulmonologist.

The pulmonologist was alarmed at the woman's constellation of symptoms and their duration. His fears were validated when her chest x-ray revealed severe cardiomegaly. He referred her to a major medical center that same day. She was diagnosed with end-stage idiopathic dilated cardiomyopathy and scheduled for heart transplant evaluation. After six months on a left ventricular assist device, a suitable donor was found and this young mother underwent successful heart transplantation.

Analysis: This case fact pattern describes a claim that would garner consideration for further investigation. Symptoms that do not respond as expected or worsen under treatment always require further evaluation. Unusual fatigue or new onset shortness of breath, particularly in women, should raise the suspicion of heart disease. Regarding causation, idiopathic dilated cardiomyopathy can be reversed or stabilized with proper treatment in the majority of cases. Disease progression will occur in a small minority of patients, whose hope for long-term survival rests with heart transplantation. The epidemiology of idiopathic dilated cardiomyopathy suggests that, with earlier diagnosis and treatment, this young woman more likely than not could have avoided transplantation and possibly reversed her disease. The delay in diagnosis left her with heart transplantation as her only viable treatment option.

The damages in this case are significant. The cost of treatment pre- and post-transplantation exceeded $1,000,000. Her life expectancy was reduced to the life of the transplanted heart. Future medical expenses are expected to be extensive and warrant a life care plan assessment. Non-economic damages, pain and suffering, and claims of loss of consortium by her husband and children are vast.

Summary

Successful LNCs understand the importance of effective and efficient case screening and have developed their analytical skills to provide this valuable service to attorneys. They understand the various elements and considerations that factor into the attorney's decision whether to pursue a potential claim, and they investigate and critically analyze these to present them to the attorney. This analysis includes recognizing not only the strengths of the potential case but also the issues that may be difficult to surmount. This careful, thorough, and detailed case analysis is invaluable to attorneys and critical to the LNC's success.

References

Balogh, E., Miller, B. T., & Ball, J. R. (2015). *Improving diagnosis in health care*. Committee on Diagnostic Error in Health Care; Board on Health Care Services; Institute of Medicine; The National Academies of Sciences, Engineering and Medicine.

Brenner, L. H., Brenner, A. T., Awerbuch, E. J., & Howitz, D. (2012). Beyond the standard of care: A new model to judge medical negligence. *Clinical Orthopaedics and Related Research, 470*(5), 1357–1364.

Cartwright, R. E. (1987). Evaluating a case. *Trial*, 62–64 (September).

Denton, D. R. (2010). Elements of actual damages in negligence cases. Retrieved from www.avvo.com/legal-guides/ugc/elements-of-actual-damages-in-negligence-cases-1.

Eisberg, J. (1990). *Minnesota medical malpractice*. St. Paul, MN: Merrill/Magnus Publishing.

Fennell v. Southern Maryland Hospital, 580 A.2d 206 (1990).

Jerrold, L. (2015). Litigation and legislation: Deliberations on duty and deportment. *American Journal of Orthodontics and Dentofacial Orthopedics, 147*(4), S133–S134.

Jones, C. (2013). The loss of chance doctrine in medical malpractice cases. *News & Knowledge*. Retrieved from www.troutman.com/the-loss-of-chance-doctrine-in-medical-malpractice-cases/.

Kilpatrick v. Bryant, 868 S.W.2d 594, 602 (Tenn. 1993).

Laska, L. (Ed.). (2002a). Failure to diagnose bowel cancer leads to death. *Medical Malpractice Verdicts, Settlements and Experts*, January 13.

Laska, L. (Ed.). (2002b). Ambulance driver fails to seat belt wheelchair-bound patient. *Medical Malpractice Verdicts, Settlements and Experts*, January 22.

Moffett, P., & Moore, G. (2011). The standard of care: Legal history and definitions: The bad and the good. *Western Journal of Emergency Medicine, 12*(1), 109–112.

Moreira, H., Magalhaes, T., Dinis-Oliveira, R., & Taveira-Gomes, A. (2014) Forensic evaluation of medical liability cases in general surgery. *Medicine, Science and the Law, 54*(4), 193–202.

Narang, S. K., & Paul, S. R. (2017). AAP committee on medical liability and risk management: Expert witness participation in civil and criminal proceedings. *Pediatrics, 139*(3), e1.

Nelson, L. J., Morrisey, M. A., & Kilgore, M. L. (2007). Damages caps in medical malpractice cases. *The Milbank Quarterly, 85*(2), 259–286.

Oyebode, F. (2013). Clinical errors and medical negligence. *Medical Principles and Practice, 22*, 323–333.

Robinson, K. J., & Nouhan, P. P. (2018). *Expert witness*. STATPearls. Retrieved from www.ncbi.nlm.nih.gov/books/NBK436001/.

Singh, H., Meyer, A. N. D., & Thomas, E. J. (2014). The frequency of diagnostic errors in outpatient care: Estimations from three large observational studies involving US adult populations. *BMJ Quality and Safety, 23*(9), 727–731.

Sloan, F., Githins, P., Clayton, E., Hickson, G. B., & Partlett, D. (1993). *Suing for medical malpractice*. Chicago, IL: University of Chicago Press.

Smith Sehdev, A. E., & Hutchins, M. (2001). Problems with proper completion and accuracy of the cause of death statement. *Archives of Internal Medicine, 161*, 277–284.

Tehrani, A. S., Lee, H., Matthews, S. C., Shore, A., Mackary, M. A., Pronovost, P. J., & Newman-Toker, D. E. (2013). 25-year summary of US malpractice claims for diagnostic errors 1986–2010: An analysis from the National Practitioner Data Bank. *BMJ Quality and Safety, 22*(8), 672–680.

Tong, E., & Almquist, J. (2017). Concussion—The invisible injury. *The Journal of Legal Nurse Consulting, 28*(3), 18–21.

Zorn, E., & Dickinson, J. (2014). Case analysis: Medical malpractice. In *AALNC Legal nurse consulting professional course* (module 8). Retrieved from www.aalnc.org/page/course-content#modules.

Zwaan, L., & Singh, H. (2015). The challenges in defining and measuring diagnostic error. *Diagnosis, 2*(2), 97–103.

Test Questions

1. All of the following could be considered complications, not negligence, EXCEPT:
   A. An infection in a surgical wound
   B. A stroke during a carotid endarterectomy
   C. Severe bleeding after lytic therapy for a heart attack
   D. Nerve injury from patient positioning during surgery

2. A contingency fee is:
   A. A percentage of the settlement or verdict
   B. Conditions attached to a contract that must be met to finalize an agreement
   C. The cost of experts retained for trial
   D. A percentage of the calculated value of the time spent on the claim plus costs

3. In medical negligence cases, the standard of care is defined:
   A. By the U.S. government as published in the Code of Federal Regulations
   B. As care that is reasonable and acceptable to professionals in the same or similar community as the defendant
   C. The most current medical literature
   D. As the care a reasonably competent and skilled HCP would provide under circumstances similar to those in which the alleged malpractice occurred

4. Contributory negligence might include all of the following EXCEPT:
   A. Failure to stop smoking despite strong recommendations to do so from HCPs
   B. Failure to fill prescriptions for recommended medications
   C. Following the prescribed treatment for hypertension
   D. Failure to attend a consultation visit as recommended by the HCP

5. Which of the following is not to be considered when evaluating damages in a potential claim?
   A. The amount of medical bills incurred for treatment
   B. Grief of a spouse in a wrongful death claim
   C. Compliance of the patient in treatment for injuries
   D. A statutory cap on non-economic damages for pain and suffering

Answers: 1. D, 2. A, 3. D, 4. C, 5. C

Chapter 11

Case Analysis
Personal Injury

Linda Luedtke, MSN, RN
Elizabeth K. Zorn, BSN, RN, LNCC®

Contents

Objectives

- Define the elements of proof in a personal injury action
- Describe the common affirmative defenses
- Identify the common experts utilized to establish damages
- Describe the legal nurse consultant's role in personal injury litigation
- Identify the purpose of accident reconstruction in motor vehicle accident litigation

Introduction

Personal injury (PI) litigation involves tort law. A tort is a civil wrong committed against a person, property, entity, or relationship. Tort law serves two purposes in the United States legal system; it:

- Provides a mechanism for awarding compensation to those injured as a result of the wrongful conduct of others and
- Provides an incentive to act safely in conduct that affects others

There are multiple types of torts. The two broadest categories are intentional and unintentional torts. Examples of intentional torts are assault, battery, defamation, and false imprisonment. Examples of unintentional torts are negligence and product liability.

Personal injury claims are torts that involve negligent actions resulting in physical, psychological, or economic harm to the injured party. This includes injuries sustained in motor vehicle collisions and other transportation modes, such as bicycles, airplanes, trains, and ships. Premises liability claims may result from slip and fall injuries, elevator and escalator accidents, or injuries caused by other dangerous property conditions. Injuries resulting from domestic pets may also give rise to a claim against the pet owner.

Workplace injuries may result in litigation related to improper conduct by the property owner, general contractor, or subcontractor. However, in many states, Workers' Compensation laws generally bar employees from suing their employer or a co-employee due to the exclusive remedy doctrine (Randall, n.d.).

The Tort of Negligence

Personal injury litigation involves the tort of negligence, which has four elements: (1) duty, (2) breach of duty, (3) causation, and (4) damages. (These are discussed in more depth later in this chapter.) The plaintiff must establish all four of these elements to prevail in a negligence claim. Courts also use the term "negligence" to refer to the defendant's failure to exercise reasonable care under the circumstances. Thus, this term refers to both a type of tort claim as well as the second element of proof in such a claim (Glannon, 2015).

The plaintiff has the burden of proving each of these four elements. The typical burden of proof standard for torts is "preponderance of evidence," which means more probable than not, or greater than 50%. Thus, to meet the burden of proof, the plaintiff must introduce evidence supporting a finding on each element that the claim is more probable than not. The defendant may also present evidence of one or more affirmative defenses. The defendant has the burden of proof for the affirmative defenses.

Affirmative Defenses in Negligence Claims

Once a PI case is filed and served, the defense attorney may assert affirmative defenses to the claims. An affirmative defense either defeats a claim entirely or seeks to reduce the damages. The specific rules related to affirmative defenses vary by jurisdiction (state or federal court). This section will outline a few of the common affirmative defenses to negligence in PI claims, including statute of limitations, assumption of the risk, failure to assert a valid cause of action, contributory and comparative negligence, and the seat belt defense.

Affirmative Defenses that Defeat a Claim

In this type of affirmative defense, a defendant's assertion of facts and arguments, if true, will defeat the plaintiff's claim, even if all the allegations in the complaint are true (Garner, 2014). Examples of this type of affirmative defense include statute of limitations, assumption of the risk, and failure to assert a valid cause of action.

Statute of Limitations

The statute of limitations is a law applicable to all tort claims that bars a claim after a specified period of time. The applicable time frame varies by type of case and jurisdiction. Failure to commence formal action before the statute of limitations expires bars the plaintiff from ever bringing a claim.

Assumption of the Risk

Inherent risk cases involve activities in which it is understood that the activity carries certain risks of injury, even if the individual uses due care when engaging in the activity. In such cases, participants assume the risk of injuries due to known dangers of the activity (Glannon, 2015). This defense typically applies in cases involving recreational activities that cannot be made entirely safe without materially altering the activity. Examples include snow skiing, water-skiing, river rafting, rock climbing, horseback riding, and martial arts. The defense of primary assumption of risk is based on the theory that these activities, by their nature, have inherent risks. The defendant has no duty to protect the plaintiff from the inherent risks of the activity. However, the plaintiff would not be responsible for unreasonable safety hazards not remedied by the defendant.

For example, the owner of a ski resort has no duty to remove trail markers, because the markers are an inherent part of the sport of skiing. Thus, the ski resort owner would not be liable for a skier's injuries resulting from running into a trail marker. However, the ski resort owner does have a duty to adequately maintain equipment, such as the tow cables. Injury from a broken tow cable would not be inherent to the sport of skiing and could be subject to recoverable damages.

Failure to Assert a Valid Cause of Action

A cause of action is a "factual situation that entitles one person to obtain a remedy in court from another person" (Garner, 2014, p. 266). It is also known as a right of action. Failure to assert a valid cause of action is an affirmative defense stating that, even if all the factual allegations in a complaint are true, they are insufficient to establish a valid cause of action. For example, if someone who witnesses a motor vehicle accident is sued for failure to render aid to someone injured in the accident, the case would be dismissed, because no duty exists between the injured party and the bystander. Another example of when this affirmative defense would be asserted is in a case brought against a governmental or charitable entity that is immune from civil lawsuits under the applicable law.

Affirmative Defenses that Seek to Reduce the Damages

Contributory and Comparative Negligence

In this defense, the defendant alleges the plaintiff, in whole or in part, caused the injury. It may be a complete or a partial defense. The pure contributory defense rule disallows any recovery if the plaintiff is even 1% at fault. Due to concerns that this rule is too harsh on plaintiffs, only four states currently recognize it (Matthiesen, Wickert & Lehrer, S.C., 2018). All other states have adopted either pure or modified comparative negligence, in which any plaintiff award is decreased in proportion to the plaintiff's negligence, as determined by the trier of fact (Glannon, 2015).

EXAMPLE 11.1

A person slipped and fell in a grocery store in a puddle of water that had been present for several hours. In the subsequent lawsuit, the defendant claimed the plaintiff was partially responsible for the injuries, because the plaintiff was not using a cane, which the plaintiff had been using since having a stroke the prior year. The jury found that the grocery store was negligent and awarded the plaintiff $100,000. However, they also found that the plaintiff was 40% liable for the injuries. Thus, the plaintiff received only $60,000 (minus attorney fees).

The Seat Belt Defense

The seat belt defense is one form of comparative negligence defense allowed by law in some states. It pertains to accidents in which an injured person was not wearing a seat belt. Depending on the jurisdiction, the recovery of damages is limited to the injuries which would have been sustained had restraints been worn. In other states, there may be a partial reduction in the damage award. The seat belt defense applies even when the plaintiff had no part in causing the accident, and it is unrelated to mandatory seat belt laws. The defense relies on research pertaining to mechanisms of injury and opinions of medical and accident reconstruction experts to establish the basis for a reduction in a monetary award based upon plaintiff's failure to use a seat belt.

EXAMPLE 11.2

The plaintiff was an unrestrained back seat passenger in a vehicle involved in a high-speed head-on collision. At the time of impact, the plaintiff was catapulted forwarded. The plaintiff's head struck the front windshield, causing a subdural hematoma. The defense hired a biomechanics expert who testified that, if a seat belt had been worn, the plaintiff's head would not have hit the front windshield. The jury declined to award any monies for the consequences of plaintiff's subdural hematoma, as they determined this injury was solely caused by plaintiff's failure to use a restraint.

Elements of Proof in a Negligence Claim

The basic premise of negligence law is that people owe others a duty to exercise reasonable care in their conduct. The duty does not require people to avoid all injuries to others, only that people avoid injuries due to carelessness (Glannon, 2015). In addition to the content below, see Chapter 4 for more information on the elements of proof in negligence claims.

Reasonable Care

In a negligence claim, reasonable care is "the degree of care that a prudent and competent person engaged in the same line of business or endeavor would exercise under similar circumstances" (Garner, 2014, p. 255). For example, in a motor vehicle case, stopping at a stop sign or red light is considered reasonable care.

Breach of Reasonable Care

Negligence, also known as a breach of care, is the failure to exercise the standard of care that a reasonably prudent person would have exercised in a similar situation. The standard of care protects others against unreasonable risk of harm and involves both what a reasonable and prudent person should or should not have done under the circumstances (Garner, 2014). For example, in a slip and fall case, breach of reasonable care might include failure of a business owner to shovel and salt a sidewalk in front of the business entryway after a snowstorm.

Causation

The specific definition of causation applied in personal injury cases varies in different jurisdictions. However, the definitions typically are versions of either the "but for" or "substantial factor" analysis. The "but for" version provides that the conduct at issue caused the harm if the harm would not have occurred but for that conduct. The "substantial factor" version provides that the conduct at issue caused the harm if such conduct was a substantial factor in bringing about the harm (Glannon, 2015).

For example, The New York Pattern Jury Instructions—Civil states

> An act or omission is regarded as a cause of an injury if it was a substantial factor in bringing about the injury, that is, if it has such an effect in producing the injury that reasonable people would regard it as a cause of the injury. There may be more than one cause of an injury, but to be substantial, it cannot be slight or trivial. [Jurors] may, however, decide that a cause is substantial even if [they] assign a relatively small percentage to it.
>
> (Association of Justices, 2018)

Evidence pertaining to causation includes that derived from the medical records, medical literature, treating physicians, independent medical examiners, and other expert opinions.

EXAMPLE 11.3

The defense challenged plaintiff's argument that blunt head trauma sustained by an eight-week-old infant in an motor vehicle accident (MVA) caused a subdural hematoma diagnosed four weeks after the MVA. On the date of injury, a head CT scan revealed bilateral extra-axial fluid but no bleeding. Approximately one month later, the infant was diagnosed with an acute subdural hematoma. The legal nurse consultant's (LNC's) medical literature research revealed that bilateral extra-axial fluid in infants is an anatomical variant which increases the risk for subdural hematoma, thus supporting plaintiff's claim that the MVA was likely a substantial contributing cause of the subdural hematoma. This is also an example of the "eggshell skull rule" described below.

Damages

In simple terms, damages is defined as "money claimed by, or ordered to be paid to, a person as compensation for loss or injury" (Garner, 2014, p. 471). Damages generally fall into three broad categories: economic (special damages), non-economic, and loss of consortium. Damages analysis also includes consideration of the eggshell skull rule.

Economic Damages

Economic damages include out-of-pocket medically related expenses, liens, and lost wages.

MEDICALLY RELATED EXPENSES

Plaintiffs are entitled to recover medically related "out-of-pocket" costs necessitated by their injuries. These include expenses paid up to the time the case is settled or litigated and the costs of predictable future care. Components of these damages include costs, co-payments, or deductible payments for:

- Inpatient and outpatient treatment
- Therapies
- Medications
- Medical supplies
- Home care services
- Costs of travel to and from appointments
- Durable medical equipment
- Modifications to the environment (such as ramps and safety bars) and
- Costs of help with services to assist with necessary household functions (e.g., shopping, housecleaning, lawn cutting, and even snow removal when appropriate)

LIENS

A lien in the context of PI actions is a third-party right to reimbursement from the plaintiff's recovery for payments made related to the plaintiff's injuries. Such liens could exist on behalf of health insurance providers (such as Medicaid, Medicare, and self-funded Employee Retirement Income Security Act plans) and Workers' Compensation carriers, among others.

LOST WAGES

Economic damages also include past and future lost wages resulting from the injury. Documentation of lost wages is demonstrated through wages and benefits statements; income tax records; and business records, such as profit and loss statements for a self-employed person.

Non-economic Damages

Non-economic damages are those for which there is no mathematical basis for valuing (Glannon, 2015). Although they are not easily quantifiable, a monetary figure is determined based on the severity of the damages, the impact on the plaintiff's life, and the amount other plaintiffs have been awarded for similar injuries. Non-economic damages typically include:

- Pain and suffering (both physical and emotional)
- Loss of function
- Loss of enjoyment of life (not a valid claim in all states)
- Inconvenience
- Fear resulting from the incident (such as fear of driving)
- Embarrassment and
- Emotional pain of disfigurement

Loss of Consortium

Consortium are the benefits that one person, especially a spouse, is entitled to receive from another, including companionship, cooperation, affection, aid, financial support, and between spouses, sexual relations. These benefits can flow from child to parent, parent to child, and spouse to spouse.

Loss of consortium is a separate claim most commonly asserted by a spouse in a personal injury action and, in some states, a wrongful death action. In some states, the law permits a child or parent of the injured party or decedent to make a claim for loss of these services. However, while spousal loss of consortium claims are well established, many states have rejected such claims made by parents or children (Glannon, 2015).

Eggshell Skull Rule

This legal doctrine is based upon the long-held recognition in common law that some people are more susceptible to injury or complicated recovery from injury as a result of an underlying condition(s) but that this should not be held against them when seeking damages from a defendant. This "take the victim as found" rule holds that the defendant is liable for injuries caused by improper conduct notwithstanding the frailty of the injured person based on a pre-existing medical condition or some other characteristic (Niebel, 2017).

Motor Vehicle Collisions

Motorized vehicles involved in PI claims include cars, trucks, motorcycles, golf carts, boats, all-terrain vehicles, snowmobiles, jet skis, amusement park rides, buses, motorized wheelchairs, and airplanes. With regard to motor vehicles operated on roadways and highways, there are various categories of MVAs. For example, motor vehicles can be rear-ended, side-impacted, hit head-on, rolled over, involved in a chain reaction event, or involved in a combination of two or more of these events. Motor vehicles may collide with each other or with pedestrians or cyclists.

Relevant Documents in Motor Vehicle Cases

Police reports may contain information that is important in evaluating the PI case. In general, police reports provide the victims' personal information, aberrant conditions at the time of the accident, vehicle data, diagrams, and airbag and seat belt status.

Eyewitness statements provide information regarding events that occurred just prior to, during, or after an accident and, sometimes, regarding the general nature of plaintiff's injuries. These statements are generated by private investigators or law firm personnel who interview eyewitnesses at the request of the attorney managing the claim. Eyewitnesses are often subpoenaed to appear at deposition or trial to give testimony about their report and what they observed at the time of the accident.

First responder reports may contain information regarding the activity at the scene. They contain data regarding the position of the vehicle occupants, the position of those ejected from the vehicle, safety restraint usage, airbag deployment, complaints of those involved, estimated or stated weights, description of visible injuries, information regarding possible use of alcohol or drugs, vital signs, and medical interventions performed in the field.

Data regarding the position of the vehicle occupants (especially those who were ejected), estimates of the intrusion distance into the vehicle's compartments, the use of the Jaws of Life or other extrication equipment on the vehicle, and other vehicle damage information (such as steering wheel deformation) is extremely important to the engineer and reconstructionist in simulating the event (e.g., determining the motion of the vehicle and the response of the occupants).

Automobile Insurance Coverages

Understanding the available insurance coverage in an automobile claim is important for identifying coverage for the plaintiff's bodily injury, medical expenses, and lost wages. The main types of automobile insurance coverages include bodily injury, supplemental uninsured and underinsured motorist coverage, excess, no-fault, medical payments, collision, and comprehensive. The first five pertain to personal injuries, and the latter two pertain to property damage. The minimal required coverage, if any, varies with state law.

Bodily Injury Coverage

Bodily injury (BI) insurance is the most basic type of automobile insurance coverage. If the insured causes an accident that injures another person, the insured's BI insurance pays the damages the insured is legally liable to pay the injured person (up to the limit of the policy). If a person is injured in an automobile accident caused by someone else, the at-fault person's BI coverage will compensate the injured person for the injuries. Some states require a minimum amount of BI coverage. New York, for example, requires a minimum of $25,000.

The limits of BI coverage represent the maximum amount of money that can be recovered from a liability insurance policy in a personal injury claim. Should the value of a plaintiff's injuries exceed the amount of the defendant's insurance coverage, the plaintiff can seek recovery from the defendant's personal assets, although this is not a usual occurrence because many defendants do not have sufficient assets. Cases in which the value of the injuries far exceeds the limits of BI coverage generally settle fairly quickly for the policy limits.

Supplemental Uninsured and Underinsured Motorist Coverage

Supplemental uninsured and underinsured motorist coverage (SUM) is provided under an individual's own insurance policy. It is insurance someone purchases to protect oneself in the event that another driver causes an accident and does not have insurance coverage (uninsured) or enough insurance (underinsured) to compensate the injured person(s) for bodily injuries.

Supplemental uninsured and underinsured motorist coverage is available only if the injured driver's SUM coverage policy limit and bodily injury damages exceed the at-fault driver's BI coverage and is triggered only after the full limits of the at-fault driver's BI policy have been paid. The SUM coverage policy limit represents the total, combined amount the injured driver can recover from both the at-fault driver's BI coverage and the injured driver's own SUM coverage. In other words, the amount of SUM coverage available is the difference between the at-fault driver's full BI policy limit and the injured driver's SUM coverage policy limit.

For example, an injured driver, who carries SUM coverage of $100,000, sustains $125,000 in BI damages in a motor vehicle collision caused by a driver who carries $25,000 in BI coverage. After the at-fault driver's full BI coverage of $25,000 is paid to the injured driver, a claim can be asserted against the injured driver's own SUM insurance, since the damages exceed the amount recovered from the at-fault driver's full BI policy. Subject to its own assessment of the value of the damages, the most the SUM insurance will pay is $75,000 ($100,000 minus $25,000).

Excess Coverage

Excess coverage is liability insurance above (or in excess of) an individual's primary automobile BI insurance coverage that protects the insured against judgments in excess of the primary policy's (and typically other policies', such as a homeowner's policy) limits. For example, an individual could have a primary automobile insurance policy with a $250,000 BI limit and an excess policy that provides up to $1,000,000 of additional BI coverage. Umbrella coverage is a type of excess coverage that broadens coverage for liabilities the primary policy might not cover.

No-Fault (Personal Injury Protection) Coverage

No-fault is a type of automobile insurance created by state/commonwealth law. Currently, Puerto Rico and the following states have no-fault insurance laws: Florida, Hawaii, Kansas, Kentucky, Massachusetts, Michigan, Minnesota, New Jersey, New York, North Dakota, Pennsylvania, and Utah (Insurance Information Institute, 2014). No-fault laws require each vehicle's insurance carrier to pay certain expenses up to specified limits for the occupants of the vehicle it insures regardless of who was at fault for the accident. The specific aspects of the no-fault laws vary from jurisdiction to jurisdiction. In general, injured persons can still sue at-fault drivers for damages in excess of their no-fault benefits if their damages exceed specified thresholds.

For example, under New York's No-Fault law, an injured person can sue an at-fault driver for economic damages beyond those covered by the mandated basic no-fault coverage and for non-economic injuries (e.g., pain and physical limitations) if the injured person has a statutorily defined "serious injury," which includes death, dismemberment, and fracture, among others (New York Insurance Law, 2018).

Medical Payments Coverage

As its name suggests, this coverage is for medical expenses incurred (typically within a specified time frame after an accident) by the insured or passengers while in an automobile or by the inured if hit while a pedestrian or bicyclist (Department of Motor Vehicles, 2018). Typically, this coverage is optional. If it has been purchased, it is available up to the limit specified in the policy regardless of fault. When healthcare insurance is also available, medical payments coverage may be used to supplement it by covering co-pays or deductibles.

Collision Coverage

This physical damage coverage is applicable up to a specified amount when an insured's car upsets, rolls over, or collides with another car or object. Collision coverage is not required by state law. It is optional and usually subject to a deductible, which is available at various levels. By increasing the amount of the deductible, the insured can lower the cost of the coverage (premium).

Comprehensive Coverage

Comprehensive coverage is somewhat of a misnomer. It does not cover physical damage from collisions caused by the insured driving the insured vehicle. It does cover physical damage to the vehicle from other causes such as theft, vandalism, contact with an animal, a falling tree, natural disasters, or any other cause of damage to the insured's vehicle other than collision. Like collision coverage, comprehensive coverage is not required by state law and is usually subject to a deductible. By increasing the amount of the deductible, the cost of the coverage (premium) can be lowered.

Experts Utilized in Motor Vehicle and Other PI Cases

Causation Experts

Medical causation experts in personal injury claims typically are treating or expert physicians called upon to render opinions about the cause and nature of the plaintiff's alleged injuries, including permanency. In death cases, a forensic pathologist may render an opinion regarding the cause of death. For example, a pathologist may testify how a blunt head trauma caused intracranial bleeding, leading to increased intracranial pressure, tentorial herniation, and brain death. The pathologist may also be able to determine which of multiple injuries actually caused the death.

Damages Experts and Evaluations

Depending upon the nature and severity of the alleged injuries, one or more damages experts may be retained in a PI case to provide opinions regarding the nature and consequences of the plaintiff's injuries. Below are the types of damages experts and evaluations that may be obtained by either side in a PI claim.

Neuropsychologist

Neuropsychologists are retained primarily to assess cognitive deficits associated with serious brain injuries. They implement a battery of tests, typically over several hours on different days, designed to test intellectual functioning, attention, memory, motor speed, language, and executive functions, among others. The neuropsychologist compares pre-accident cognitive function with post-accident function to determine what deficits likely derive from the alleged injuries (Zorn & Zorn, 2017).

Vocational Rehabilitation Specialist

A vocational expert may be used when plaintiff claims lost or diminished earning capacity or inability to work resulting from the injuries. This expert can determine the degree of plaintiff's impairment and disability, whether the plaintiff can perform specific job functions, and possibly the need for and feasibility of vocational rehabilitation if the plaintiff is not able to return to prior employment (Zorn & Zorn, 2017).

Functional Capacity Evaluation

Attorneys for either side may request the plaintiff undergo a functional capacity evaluation (FCE) to assess the plaintiff's ability to work, ability to participate in activities of daily living, or cognitive abilities. A work FCE, often done by occupational therapists, involves a battery of standardized assessments designed to measure the plaintiff's ability to meet the physical or cognitive demands of a particular job (The American Occupational Therapy Association, Inc., n.d.).

Impairment Ratings

Some treating and Workers' Compensation physicians utilize the American Medical Association's *Guides to the Evaluation of Permanent Impairment* (2017) to determine impairment level after an injury. Each chapter focuses on a body system and provides a description of methods used for assessing impairments, which are then converted into whole-person impairment percentages (Holmes, 2016).

Life Expectancy Expert

Life expectancy experts are actuaries, PhDs, and occasionally, medical doctors who render opinions regarding the plaintiff's life expectancy. Predicted life expectancy is important when future damages are calculated for the rest of an injured person's life.

Life Care Planner

A life care planner evaluates the future needs of an injured plaintiff and determines the cost of those products and services over the plaintiff's expected lifetime. This information is then incorporated into a life care plan. The life care planner's analysis is based upon a review of medical records, assessment of the plaintiff's home or other living facility, interviews with the plaintiff or responsible relatives, consultations with healthcare providers, and review of medical care and equipment cost references. Life care planners typically are registered nurses or vocational rehabilitation specialists with credentialing in life care planning (Zorn & Zorn, 2017).

Economist

The economist provides three main types of projections: future health care and related costs, lost future earnings and benefits, and lost future household services. Future healthcare costs typically are based upon the life care planner's cost analysis and account for inflation and life expectancy (Zorn & Zorn, 2017).

Independent (Defense) Medical Examiner

In personal injury actions, the defense is entitled to a physical or psychological examination of the plaintiff by a healthcare provider of the defense's choice who has expertise in the type of injury sustained by the plaintiff. The applicable procedural rules related to defense medical exams (DME) vary with the jurisdiction. Plaintiff LNCs often attend DMEs to represent the interests of the plaintiff. For more information on DMEs and the LNC's role, see Chapter 6.

Medicare Set-Asides Expert

Effective January 1, 2012, Medicare began requiring insurers and self-insured companies to report settlements, awards, and judgments that involve a Medicare beneficiary to the Centers for Medicare & Medicaid Services (CMS). This resulted from amendments to the Medicare Secondary Payer Act of 1980, stipulating that Medicare is the secondary insurer on all claims involving other sources of insurance (Helland & Kipperman, 2011).

For Medicare-eligible plaintiffs, Medicare Set-Asides (MSAs) may need to be considered for future accident-related medical expenses. An MSA is an account funded by settlement proceeds for future medical care that would otherwise be covered by Medicare. An MSA specialist determines these expenses, sometimes based upon the future medical care needs identified in a life care plan. The MSA can be funded either by a lump sum payment or structured payments (Zorn &

Zorn, 2017). However, it is important to note that "under the present applicable statutory and regulatory scheme, whether MSAs are required for liability settlements involving Medicare beneficiaries (other than Workers Compensation cases) remains unclear and a source of disagreement among personal injury attorneys" (Zorn & Zorn, 2017, p. 16).

Accident Reconstruction Expert

Accident reconstruction experts utilize engineering principles and physics laws to conduct a scientific collision analysis, primarily to determine how and why an accident occurred. This includes analyzing the role of the driver(s), road conditions, topography, and environmental conditions at the time of the accident. Such experts also calculate the forces involved in an accident (see section below on kinematics). The expert gathers pertinent evidence from inspection of the damaged vehicle(s) and the accident site as well as from review of photographs, deposition testimony, witness reports, police reports, and meteorological data at the time of the accident, among others.

After all the pertinent information is collected and analyzed, the accident can be recreated on a vehicle test track or via three-dimensional computer simulation to assess the plaintiff's body position, movement, contact points at the time of impact, and likely injury mechanism. Vehicle test track simulation utilizes instrumented exemplar vehicles (recording vehicle accelerations and other parameters) and anthropomorphic test devices (ATDs), frequently referred to as "crash test dummies" (recording the loads acting upon the occupant). The crash test dummy acts as a mechanical surrogate of the human and is used to evaluate occupant motion and injury potential during collisions. 3D laser scanning of the accident scene is being used for highly accurate computerized presentations and simulations.

Biomechanical Engineer Expert

Biomechanical/biomedical engineers analyze the effects of forces on the human body. In a vehicle collision case, such an expert utilizes identified forces such as accelerations or torques (twisting effort applied to an object that makes the object turn about its axis of rotation) applied to the plaintiff's musculoskeletal or other body system to determine the likely mechanism of injury. Other pertinent evidence utilized in this analysis includes knowledge of the plaintiff's medical diagnoses as set forth in the medical records, radiological imaging studies, human injury tolerance data (including bone-fracturing strengths), joint movement and injury thresholds, and soft tissue characteristics. The expert will also examine the damaged vehicle for evidence of occupant contact with the vehicle matching plaintiff's known injuries. For example, in the case of an injured driver with lacerations on the right side of the forehead and scalp, the engineer will examine the windshield's rearview mirror to see if it is cracked and askew with hair embedded in the glass fragments. A surrogate analysis would involve a "crash test dummy" of the same height and weight as the plaintiff, seated in an exemplar vehicle. Purposes for conducting a surrogate study include determining distances from specific body points to internal vehicle components and visualizing how the seat belt fits around the surrogate's body.

EXAMPLE 11.4

The driver of a van claimed that a young child was inside the rear compartment of the van when the rear lift gate door opened and the child fell out onto the ground. The child died as a result of the injuries sustained in the accident. The child's injuries, as described in the autopsy report, were diffuse subarachnoid hemorrhage, bilateral parietal skull contusions, fracture of the right femur, contusions of the right shoulder and thigh, fractures of the left parietal and temporal bones, scalp detachment on the left side of the head, and fractures of the left ninth and tenth ribs. The bio-mechanical engineer was able to demonstrate, by the bilateral distribution, location, and severity of the injuries, that the injuries were not consistent with a child falling out of a van. Rather, they were caused by the driver backing the van into the child while the child was walking behind the van; the van knocked the child to the ground with substantial force. The contusions on the right parietal skull and the right shoulder were determined to be from contact with the closed rear lift gate door of the van, the right femur fracture and right thigh contusions were caused by contact with the rear bumper of the van, and the left-sided head injuries and fractured ribs were deter-mined to be caused by contact with the ground as the child fell.

Mechanism of Injury and Kinematics

Occupant kinematics (from the Greek word *kinein*, which means to move) are utilized to support or refute the claimed mechanism of injury in a given case (i.e., did the person move in such a way that this injury could be generated?). To evaluate the occupant kinematics of a specific event, one must be familiar with the principles of Newton's Laws of Motion (Lucas, 2017).

Newton's first law states that a body at rest will remain at rest, and a body in motion will remain in motion unless acted upon by an external force. In other words, a body that is standing or sitting still will stay immobile unless acted upon by a force, and likewise, a body that is moving will con-tinue to move at that rate unless acted upon by a force. An occupant in a motor vehicle travels at the same speed as the motor vehicle. Force is defined as the cause or instrument that alters the motion of an object. Forces have two characteristics: magnitude (intensity) and direction, and both of these properties influence the motion of a body and thus the mechanism of injury.

Newton's second law explains the association between the force applied to a body to initiate its change of motion, the length of time the force is applied, the extent of velocity change (commonly called delta V) that the body experiences, and the body's mass. For example, assume that two vehicles of the same mass are traveling at the same speed, and both decrease their forward velocity to zero, but by different methods. The first vehicle slows down when the brake is applied, generating a force at the tire/road boundary that acts on the vehicle and causes it to decelerate and come to a stop. The second vehicle collides with a stationary object (such as a wall), generating a force at the wall/vehicle interface that acts on the vehicle and causes it to rapidly decelerate. The first experiences a *small* force over a *long* period of time, and the second experiences a *large* force over a *short* period of time. The occupant of the braking vehicle will slow as the vehicle slows, resulting in minimal motion of the body relative to the vehicle interior. When the second vehicle hits the wall, the wall does not move, and thus the majority of the energy is dissipated through deformation (e.g., crush-ing) of the vehicle structures (e.g., bumper, hood, etc.). When the vehicle hits the wall and stops suddenly, the occupant continues moving at the initial speed (e.g., the speed of the vehicle before impact). If the second vehicle's occupant is restrained, the occupant moves forward at the initial speed within the compartment until slowed by interaction with the seat belt or airbag, whereas an unrestrained occupant continues forward motion within the compartment with little reduction in speed and strikes the interior surfaces (e.g., steering wheel, dashboard, wind shield) that have slowed due to impact. These interactions with the seat belt, airbag, or interior structures can cause injuries that provide insight into the occupant's state of restraint use (e.g., belted or unbelted).

Newton's third and final law states that, for every force, there is an equal and opposite force or response. This is demonstrated when two cars hit each other head-on. Each vehicle experiences the force from the other pushing against its front bumper. Barring pre-existing deformation in either vehicle, these forces are equal. Also, when an unrestrained occupant contacts the vehicle interior, the force causing the injury to the body is matched by an equal and opposite force on the vehicle structure. This may result in physical evidence of contact, which is revealed by inspection of the vehicle after the accident.

Other Types of Personal Injury Cases

Premise Liability

Premise liability claims involve injuries resulting from, among others:

- wet floors
- carpet defects
- uneven, defective, or icy walkways, steps, or parking lots
- defective deck rails
- poorly placed decorative features and
- poor lighting

In cases involving injury resulting from a hazardous condition, such as a hole in a walkway or a puddle of liquid on the floor in a store, the defendant must have had actual or constructive notice of the dangerous condition. Actual notice, as the name implies, means that notice was given directly to, or received by, the defendant (Garner, 2014). Constructive notice holds the defendant responsible if the plaintiff can prove that the defendant should have known about the dangerous condition under the circumstances. In most states, if the plaintiff cannot prove that the defendant had either actual or constructive notice, there typically is no liability (Minick, 2013). The specific notice requirements vary by state law.

Dog Bites

In general, dog owners are liable for bites or other injuries caused by their dog. Specific laws related to owner responsibility vary by state. In some states, the owner is responsible for injuries even if the dog does not have a history of aggression or previous bites. In other states, the plaintiff must establish the dog was prone to aggression or had a history of actually injuring someone. If the injuries occurred on the homeowner's property, the laws may vary depending on whether the injured party was an invited guest or a trespasser. Liability coverage for dog bites is included in the dog owner's homeowner's insurance policy.

Foodborne Illness

Researchers have identified more than 250 foodborne diseases which result from eating food contaminated by pathogens such as bacteria, viruses, or parasites. Common offenders are E. Coli and Salmonella. Foodborne illness can also be caused by chemical toxins, such as mercury in fish or natural toxins such as poisonous mushrooms. Common symptoms of foodborne diseases are nausea, vomiting, stomach cramps, and diarrhea (Centers for Disease Control and Prevention [CDC], n.d.).

According to the CDC, about 48 million people in the United States get sick each year from foodborne diseases, 128,000 are hospitalized, and 3,000 die. In 2011, Congress passed the Food Safety Modernization Act (FSMA) which shifted the focus from responding to foodborne illness to preventing it. The rules of FSMA recognize that "ensuring the safety of the food supply is a shared responsibility among many different points in the global supply chain for both human and animal food. The FSMA rules are designed to make clear specific actions that must be taken at each of these points to prevent contamination" (Food and Drug Administration, 2018).

In a given case of food poisoning, there are multiple potential defendants including manufacturers of food ingredients, shippers and distributers of food products, and restaurant personnel. Potential areas of liability include improper handling, storage, or preparation of food or failure to protect the consumer from known contamination. In many cases, identifying the source of the contamination and how it could and should have been prevented can be challenging. An outbreak of foodborne illness among many individuals may give rise to a class action.

Foreign Objects in Food

Ingestion of food or beverages containing hard or sharp objects (such as glass or metal) can cause trauma including laceration, puncture, or other injury to organs anywhere along the alimentary tract. This includes the teeth, tongue, jaw, mouth, pharynx, esophagus, stomach, small intestine, and colon. Foreign objects in food are also potential choking hazards, and foods containing an unidentified food allergen could cause a life-threatening allergic reaction. Finally, the presence of an insect or animal in a food substance may give rise to physical or psychological injuries.

As with foodborne illness, many different entities are typically involved in the packaging and delivery process, including manufacturers, distributors, restaurants, and stores. Thus, identifying the source of the contamination can be challenging. Any foreign objects should be saved for analysis. If surgery is required to remove a foreign object from the gastrointestinal tract, the pathology department should be put on notice to preserve the object until conclusion of any litigation.

Discovery Phase in Personal Injury Litigation

The discovery phase of a personal injury case involves the collection, production (to opposing counsel), and evaluation of all documents and information relevant to a claim. The most important of these documents are the pertinent medical records. In addition, in slip and fall cases, there may be an accident report. In motor vehicle collisions, this may include police reports, photographs, videos, private investigator reports, or eye-witness reports. If there is a claim for lost wages, the attorneys will collect tax and employment records.

The other major events that occur during discovery are:

■ party and non-party depositions
■ inspection of the damaged vehicle or other object giving rise to an injury (such as a defective ladder or walkway condition)
■ expert reviews
■ independent (defense) medical exam and
■ settlement negotiations, including mediation

For more information about the discovery phase of litigation, see Chapter 5.

Role of the Legal Nurse Consultant in Personal Injury Litigation

Identification, Review, and Summary of Medical Records

In PI cases, the LNC is primarily involved in evaluating causation and damages, e.g., what are the provable injuries caused by the defendant's alleged negligent conduct? The first steps involve identifying, reviewing, and analyzing the pertinent medical records and preparing a narrative summary or chronology which should include excerpts from the medical records regarding:

- The nature and extent of injuries resulting from the subject accident
- All treatment received for the alleged injuries
- Prognosis related to the alleged injuries
- Plaintiff's medical history, including any underlying chronic medical conditions or prior injuries requiring medical treatment
- Whether any of the alleged injuries resulted in aggravation of a pre-existing or latent condition
- Whether there are alternative explanations for post-accident complaints, such as intervening injuries or participation in rigorous recreational or occupational activities
- Plaintiff's medications prior to and since the accident and
- Any information that might impact the credibility of the plaintiff

The majority of medical providers have transitioned to electronic health records. Thus, the LNC must be familiar with bookmarking and navigating digital medical records and radiology images and using software or other means to electronically link the medical records to facts in the chronology.

In motor vehicle cases, emergency department records provide descriptions of the external injuries (e.g., ecchymosis, abrasions, lacerations, redness, swelling, deformity, open fractures, etc.). Bruises appearing laterally on the neck, diagonally across the chest, or horizontally across the iliac crest area may be "seatbelt signs" caused by occupant loading of the seatbelt restraint system during the event. Documentation regarding automobile restraint use in the police report or hospital record is important, because plaintiff's failure to be properly restrained could give rise to a defense argument that plaintiff failed to mitigate damages and was therefore partially responsible for the injuries suffered. Radiological imaging identifies fracture, dislocations, and internal injuries such as organ damage and internal bleeding.

Operative reports from exploratory surgery may contain detailed descriptions of the plaintiff's internal injuries, such as internal organ lacerations, ruptures, contusions, or hemorrhage. Operative reports from open repair of fractures may contain a detailed description of the fracture and any hardware used to stabilize the fracture. Pathology reports describe any injured body parts removed. A final autopsy report includes information regarding all body systems, all injuries, and the primary and secondary cause(s) of death. In some cases, the primary or secondary cause of death may be unrelated to the subject accident. The final autopsy report may also include toxicological screening for certain prescription medications or illegal substances which may be important to evaluate whether the decedent was impaired in any way at the time of the accident.

The LNC's chronology or narrative should include as much detail as possible regarding the nature, extent, prognosis, and treatment of the alleged injuries. This includes any physical pain and suffering, functional limitations resulting from the injuries (e.g., decreased range of motion of a joint or limb paralysis), and the impact of these limitations on plaintiff's activities of daily living, recreational activities, or ability to engage in usual employment. All complaints of acute or chronic pain should be included, along with the effectiveness of pain relief measures.

The chronology or narrative should also include the details of plaintiff's emotional pain and suffering. However, the plaintiff attorney must balance asserting a legal claim for psychological or emotional harm with the reality that this opens up discovery of plaintiff's past or current mental health treatment records by defense counsel. In some cases, the plaintiff attorney may choose to forgo a claim for emotional damages for this reason.

The chronology should include documentation about treatment the plaintiff has undergone, especially invasive treatments such as surgical procedures, as these typically are associated with physical discomfort and thus relevant to the claim for pain and suffering. The LNC should document any complications of the initial injuries or from the treatments themselves. It is also important to include excerpts pertaining to the plaintiff's compliance with recommended treatment, such as physical therapy or other rehabilitative services. The failure to follow a recommended course of treatment may give rise to an affirmative defense that the plaintiff is partially responsible for the extent of injuries suffered. Periodically, the LNC should request updated medical records and revise the medical summary accordingly.

Documentation regarding prognosis or life expectancy is important to determine the likely monetary value of future damages once the plaintiff has reached maximum medical improvement.

In all PI claims, the LNC should recommend obtaining complete primary care records dating back at least 10 years prior to the subject accident. These records typically contain a great deal of information about the plaintiff's pre- and post-accident health, including that contained in progress notes, correspondence to and from other providers, diagnostic study reports, and disability reports, among others.

Plaintiff's medical history is pertinent in all PI cases, including to evaluate whether there has been aggravation of a pre-existing or latent condition which, in many jurisdictions, is compensable. It is also important to know whether the same body part was previously injured and, if so, whether the plaintiff recovered from that injury. The injured party's medical history, including maintenance prescription medications, sets forth plaintiff's baseline health and provides clues as to whether the alleged complaints or limitations may be due to an underlying condition unrelated to the subject accident. For example, a claim of right-handed weakness from a cervical injury may, in fact, be the result of a prior right carpal tunnel syndrome. However, as already noted, if the plaintiff is more susceptible to an injury or complication from an injury or treatment by virtue of a pre-existing condition, this is compensable under the "eggshell skull" rule (Niebel, 2017). Information pertaining to the plaintiff's medical history is not only gleaned from the plaintiff's medical records from primary care and other healthcare providers but also from the plaintiff's deposition testimony.

Attorneys for both sides will want to know whether there is any documentation that could be used to impugn the plaintiff's character or credibility, such as a history of substance abuse, excessive gambling, domestic violence, or criminal activity.

Preparation of Legal Documents

The in-house plaintiff LNC is often asked to draft the medical portions of plaintiff's interrogatory answers or, in some states, the Bill of Particulars. This typically includes:

- a detailed list of plaintiff's injuries
- complications of the initial injuries
- invasive treatments the plaintiff was caused to undergo
- complications of treatments
- functional limitations resulting from the injuries
- a list of permanent injuries
- physical or psychological pain and suffering
- a list of treating providers and
- a list of hospital confinements

The defense LNC reviews plaintiff's discovery responses to prepare a list of plaintiff's medical records that the defense needs to obtain. Once these records are received, the defense LNC completes a chronology and identifies additional records that should be obtained. Once all the records are received, the defense LNC:

- analyzes whether there is support in the medical records for plaintiff's claimed injuries, including alleged exacerbation of a pre-existing condition
- analyzes whether the plaintiff's course of treatment and recovery are consistent with the natural history of the alleged injury
- analyzes whether there may be other causes for the alleged complaints
- identifies any evidence that casts doubt on the plaintiff's credibility or non-compliance with recommended treatment and
- evaluates special damages (medical expenses)

Collaboration with Expert Witnesses

Both in-house and independent LNCs work with the attorney to identify the types of experts needed for a particular case. The LNC then identifies and evaluates potential expert candidates, especially those experts rendering medical opinions about causation or damages as noted earlier in this chapter. The LNC should interview prospective experts to clear any conflicts with the parties to the lawsuit and obtain information about how often the experts have previously testified, the approximate percentage of their prior work for the plaintiff side versus the defense side, and their fee schedule. It is also important to inquire whether any portion of their prior testimony has been excluded by a court pursuant to a Daubert motion. The LNC should also conduct a general Internet search for each expert to determine whether there is any negative information present which could impact the expert's credibility.

For experts who are then retained by the attorney, the LNC (or attorney) prepares a package of material for the expert to review, including the pertinent medical records, other documents containing medical data (such as the accident report), imaging studies, and legal documents, such as those containing plaintiff's alleged injuries. The attorney may also decide to send the LNC's medical chronology (containing facts only; no opinions or commentary), even though doing so might make it discoverable by opposing counsel.

All LNCs who identify potential experts for attorneys should maintain an expert database, including a list of experts by specialty and, for each expert, an updated curriculum vitae, fee schedule, list of cases the expert has reviewed or testified, and feedback from the attorney about the expert's performance at the conclusion of a particular case. For more information on the LNC's role working with experts, see Chapter 36.

Expert Fact Witness

The LNC who serves as an expert fact witness in a PI case testifies at mediation or trial regarding the illness, injury, course of medical treatment, and its impact on the plaintiff as documented in the medical records. For example, the expert fact witness might explain an injury, medical procedure, or the purpose of a medication or course of physical therapy, sometimes with the aid of demonstrative evidence such as anatomical drawings. The attorney retains an expert fact witness to aid the jury or judge's understanding regarding "the extent of a plaintiff's injuries, treatment, pain, and suffering"; however, the expert fact witness does not render standard of care opinions (American Association of Legal Nurse Consultants, 2017). For more information, see Chapter 32.

Medical Literature Research

Legal nurse consultants generally are not involved in researching liability issues in PI cases, e.g., did the defendant run a red light or did a place of business fail to properly salt an icy walkway? Rather, the LNC may be asked to conduct medical literature searches pertaining to causation or damages. This might include, for example, research regarding physical injuries associated with low impact motor vehicle crashes, the prognosis associated with a particular injury, or the known side effects of treatments. The LNC should compile results of this research in a narrative summary or annotated bibliography for attorney use in case preparation. For more information, see Chapter 34.

Deposition Preparation

Legal nurse consultants on both sides can assist the attorney to prepare for depositions by ensuring plaintiff's medical records and the chronology are up-to-date prior to depositions. The attorneys will utilize the chronology as a guide to the plaintiff's injuries and treatments. All attorneys will want to know whether there are any entries in the medical records which might cast doubt on the plaintiff's credibility or compliance with recommended medical treatment. If there are such entries, the plaintiff attorney will review with the plaintiff during the deposition preparation session how best to answer questions from opposing counsel about these issues.

Jury Verdict and Settlement Research

Legal nurse consultants on both sides may utilize online databases to research verdicts and settlements for a particular injury or combination of injuries in the same jurisdiction or at least in the same state. Research criteria also include similar aged plaintiffs (or decedents) and similar damages elements such as economic loss, functional limitations, and extent of pain and suffering.

Day in the Life Video

In a catastrophic PI case, the plaintiff attorney may hire a videographer to produce a "Day in the Life" video which documents the plaintiff's daily routine, activities, and treatments during waking hours. It is an effective means of conveying the plaintiff's struggles with activities of daily living, functional limitations, and pain. It may also include testimony from the family or other care providers regarding their emotional distress or hardships related to caring for a catastrophically injured family member. The plaintiff LNC can attend the filming to capture the most relevant footage and then work with the videographer in consultation with the attorney to edit the final video to include the most compelling footage. Day in the life videos are used during settlement negotiations as an exhibit to a demand letter or mediation submission. To be used as demonstrative evidence at trial, the plaintiff attorney must lay a proper foundation for its admission as evidence from the testimony of the injured party's primary care provider or life care planner.

Settlement

Settlement of a PI case can occur anytime during the life of a case from pre-suit up through trial and appeal. Settlement prior to commencement of litigation generally occurs only in those cases in which liability is clear and the outcome of plaintiff's injuries is well established. In many cases, the ultimate outcome of plaintiff's injuries is not known for many months or years following an accident.

Settlement discussions begin following plaintiff's submission of a demand letter (or settlement package) to the insurance carrier or its outside counsel. The demand letter sets forth plaintiff's theories of negligence and resulting injuries, including pain and suffering and functional limitations. It also details the economic damages, including lost wages, unreimbursed medical expenses, or other out-of-pocket expenses related to the injuries.

The plaintiff LNC can assist the attorney to draft or edit the medical portions of the demand letter, ensuring that there is support in the medical records for the claimed injuries. The plaintiff LNC may also meet with the attorney and the plaintiff's treating providers to obtain their opinions about what conditions were likely caused by the accident at issue, including aggravation of a prior condition. The defense LNC reviews plaintiff's demand letter and assists the attorney to analyze whether there is evidence to support the nature and extent of plaintiff's claimed injuries. If not, the defense LNC assists the attorney to prepare a response rebutting the disputed claims.

Some cases are settled at an alternative dispute resolution proceeding, such as mediation or arbitration. Mediation, generally a non-binding procedure, occurs before a mediator approved by both sides. Prior to the mediation, attorneys for both sides send the mediator (and sometimes opposing counsel) a mediation submission setting forth their arguments about liability, causation, and damages. The plaintiff and defense LNCs can assist their attorneys to draft or edit the medical portions of the submission and to identify exhibits such as anatomical drawings that may assist the mediator to understand the medical issues. In some cases, one of the attorneys may hire an expert fact witness, such as Registered Nurse, to educate the mediator regarding medical facts, treatments, or injuries. For more information regarding settlement, see Chapter 38.

Trial

Cases that do not settle are scheduled for trial. Attorney and staff preparation for trial is a very timing-consuming process. It includes drafting subpoenas, preparing motions in limine (to exclude certain testimony or evidence), and preparing testifying witnesses. The attorneys must also prepare their opening statements, direct and cross-examination questions for all witnesses, and closing arguments. Some attorneys hire jury consultants to assist with key witness preparation or *voir dire* (the preliminary questioning of potential jurors).

The LNC can assist the attorney to prepare for trial by:

- Ensuring the medical records are up-to-date
- Updating the medical chronology
- Forwarding updated medical records to any witnesses giving medical testimony and

■ Suggesting or creating demonstrative evidence such as charts, anatomical drawings, timelines, etc.

Attorneys are increasingly using trial or other presentation software to project medical records, deposition testimony, video footage, radiological imaging, demonstrative evidence, etc. to the jury. The LNC can assist the attorney to identity the relevant medical exhibits for these presentations.

During trial, the LNC can assist the attorney as needed. This includes listening to key witness testimony and providing feedback regarding the credibility of the testimony and how the witness was likely perceived by the jury. The LNC may also be called upon to research unexpected testimony regarding medical issues that arise during trial. For more information, see Chapter 39.

Summary

A skilled LNC is of invaluable assistance to attorneys handling personal injury claims. Most PI claims are venued in state court, and thus a basic understanding of the applicable substantive law and procedural rules assists the LNC to extract the relevant information from the medical records, identify the appropriate experts, and assist in an analysis of the causation and damages issues.

References

American Association of Legal Nurse Consultants. (2017). *Legal nurse consulting: Scope and standards of practice.* Chicago, IL: AALNC.

American Medical Association. (2017). *Guides to the evaluation of permanent impairment* (6th ed.). Chicago, IL: AMA.

Association of Justices of the Supreme Court of the State of New York, Committee on Pattern Jury Instruction. (2018). *New York pattern jury instructions—civil* (Vol. 1A, 3rd ed.). New York, NY: Thomson Reuters.

Centers for Disease Control and Prevention. (n.d.). Foodborne illnesses and germs. Retrieved from www.cdc.gov/foodsafety/foodborne-germs.html.

Department of Motor Vehicles. (2018). Medical payments coverage. Retrieved from www.dmv.org/insurance/medical-payments-coverage.php.

Food and Drug Administration. (2018). Food Safety Modernization Act (FSMA). Retrieved from www.fda.gov/Food/GuidanceRegulation/FSMA/.

Garner, B. A. (Ed.). (2014). *Black's law dictionary* (10th ed.). St Paul, MN: Thompson Reuters.

Glannon, J. (2015). *The law of torts* (5th ed.). New York, NY: Wolters Kluwer.

Helland, E., & Kipperman, F. (2011). Recovery under the Medicare Secondary Payer Act. *Rand Health Quarterly*, Summer *1*(2), 4.

Holmes, E. (2016). Impairment rating and disability determination. Retrieved from https://emedicine.medscape.com/article/314195-overview#a4.

Insurance Information Institute. (2014). No-fault auto insurance. Retrieved from www.iii.org/article/background-on-no-fault-auto-insurance.

Lucas, J. (2017). Newton's laws of motion. Retrieved from www.livescience.com/46558-laws-of-motion.html.

Matthiesen, Wickert & Lehrer, S.C. (2018). Contributory negligence/comparative fault laws in all 50 states. Retrieved from www.mwl-law.com/wp-content/uploads/2013/03/contributory-negligence-comparative-fault-laws-in-all-50-states.pdf.

Minick, J. (2013). What is constructive notice for slip and fall claims? Retrieved from www.minicklaw.com/what-is-constructive-notice-for-slip-and-fall-cases/.

New York Insurance Law § 5102(d) (Consol. 2018).

Niebel, L. (2017). Understanding the eggshell skull rule: The interplay between liability, damages, and apportionment. *Journal of Legal Nurse Consulting, 28*(3), 30–33.

Randall, A. (n.d.). The exclusive remedy provision: State-by-state survey. Retrieved from https://apps.americanbar.org/labor/lel-annualcle/09/materials/data/papers/087.pdf.

The American Occupational Therapy Association, Inc. (n.d.). Functional capacity evaluation. Retrieved from www.aota.org/About-Occupational-Therapy/Professionals/WI/Capacity-Eval.aspx.

Zorn, E., & Zorn, B. (2017). Evaluating damages in catastrophic injury cases: A primer for the new LNC. *Journal of Legal Nurse Consulting, 28*(3), 12–17.

Additional Reading

Melvin, J. W., & Nahum, A. M. (Eds.). (2015). *Accidental injury biomechanics and prevention* (3rd ed.). New York, NY: Springer.

Test Questions

1. Which statement is NOT true regarding the purpose of PI litigation?
   A. It provides a mechanism for awarding compensation
   B. It provides an incentive to act safely in conduct that affects others
   C. It determines criminal charges against those found liable
   D. It allocates accountability to the party with the most control over the conditions that cause risk
2. The burden of proof in a tort case is the preponderance of evidence standard. This means
   A. It must be proven beyond a reasonable doubt
   B. When just over 50% of the evidence is in favor of the party
   C. When less than 50% of the evidence is in favor of the party
   D. None of the above
3. The LNC working for the plaintiff attorney may assist in preparing documents. They would include all of the following EXCEPT:
   A. The accident report
   B. Bill of Particulars
   C. Demand Letter
   D. Mediation submission
4. Which of the following documents does NOT provide important information for the accident reconstructionist?
   A. The traffic collision report
   B. Eye witness accounts
   C. An informed consent form
   D. An injury diagram
5. When the medical provider documents the patient had a "seatbelt sign," what three body areas may be included?
   A. Neck, chest, and back
   B. Chest, abdomen, and thigh
   C. Neck, chest, and iliac crests
   D. Chest, iliac crests, and back

Answers: 1. C, 2. B, 3. A, 4. C, 5. C

Chapter 12

Long-Term Care Litigation

Elizabeth Murray BSN, RN, LNCC®

Contents

Objectives

- Identify the range of services and support included in long-term care
- Recognize the difference between long-term care facilities and assisted living facilities

- Communicate the long-term care/skilled nursing facility standards and regulations and how they differ from acute care facilities
- Recognize the key components of a long-term care facility medical record
- Discuss the major categories of liability in long-term care litigation

Introduction

Long-term care litigation is one of the fastest growing areas of litigation in the United States. A 2017 long-term care actuarial analysis by the insurance industry reported the projected 2018 loss rate (cost for settling or defending long-term care/skilled nursing facility [LTC/SNF] claims), which is a combination of claim severity (total dollar amount of a claim) and frequency, is expected to increase to $2,450 per occupied bed (Coleianne et al., 2017). Many facets of long-term care litigation rely on legal nurse consultants to successfully pursue or defend allegations. Legal nurse consultants should educate themselves on the regulations governing long-term care litigation and familiarize themselves with the major categories of liability.

Overview of Long-Term Care/Skilled Nursing Facilities and Assisted Living Facilities

The United States Department of Health and Human Services Administration on Aging reports that the elderly population, or persons 65 years old or older, numbered 49.2 million in 2016 (Administration on Aging, US Department of Health & Human Services, 2017). This represented 15.2% of the US population or about one in every seven Americans. By 2030, all "baby boomers" will be older than age 65, and one in every five residents will be elderly (Administration on Aging, US Department of Health & Human Services, 2017; US Census Bureau, 2018). Most persons in need of long-term care are elderly. Among the population aged 65 years and older, experts estimate that 69% will develop disabilities and 35% will eventually enter a long-term care (LTC) or skilled nursing facility (SNF) (Johnson, Toohey, & Wiener, 2007).

"Long-term care" refers to a range of services and support a resident may need while living in a facility, and it refers to assistance needed with the basic personal tasks of everyday life called activities of daily living (ADLs). Activities of daily living include hygiene (bathing, dressing, grooming, and oral care), mobility (transfer and ambulation), elimination (toileting), dining (eating, including meals and snacks), and communication (speech, language, and other functional communication systems) (American Health Care Association [AHCA], 2018). A resident of a nursing home or long-term care facility may or may not require skilled nursing services. When reviewing a LTC case, the legal nurse consultant (LNC) may find the case involves an elderly individual living in an assisted living facility (ALF).

An ALF is a community-based living option for older adults who are having difficulty living independently but do not need 24-hour skilled nursing care. An ALF provides housing; meals; and assistance with health care, activities of daily living, and instrumental activities of daily living. Instrumental activities of daily living are tasks such as managing money or cooking that are not as basic to self-care as ADLs but add to quality of life. According to a 2014 survey from the National Center for Health Statistics (NCHS), approximately 835,000 residents live in more than 30,000 assisted living buildings (Caffrey, Harris-Kojetin, & Sengupta, 2015).

Licensing and regulation of the ALFs are at the state level. Most states have different licenses to differentiate levels of care, which correspond with how much assistance residents need. The states also have unique terms and definitions for the different levels of care, admission/retention policies, staffing requirements, services, documentation requirements, medication provisions, provisions for residents with dementia, and inspection and monitoring.

The LNC evaluating a case involving an ALF should research the regulations, licenses, and nurse practice acts for the particular state in which the care occurred. Then the LNC identifies the unique state criteria that will pertain to that case (Carder, 2015).

Statutes and Regulations Governing Practice in Long-Term Care/Skilled Nursing Facility Administration

Regulations and standards for LTC/SNF differ from those for acute care facilities such as hospitals. In 1965, Congress enacted Medicare coverage for hospitals and mandated that hospitals accredited by The Joint Commission were eligible to participate. The federal government then had to create a set of regulations for nursing homes using the fundamentals of the hospital regulations. These new regulations, known as the Code of Federal Regulations (CFR) title 42 (Public Health) part 483, were created and are managed by the Centers for Medicare & Medicaid Services, which are federal agencies within the US Department of Health and Human Services. These regulations govern LTC/SNF practices (The Centers for Medicare & Medicaid Services [CMS] US Department of Health & Human Services, 2015).

The two main concerns were: (1) the physical safety of the facilities to be fire safe and clean and (2) adequacy of treatment and services. Early enforcement focused on safety and sanitation. These regulations remained almost unchanged into the 1980s. In 1986, the Institute of Medicine published a report, titled "Improving Quality of Care in Nursing Homes," which reported the nursing home regulatory system was inadequate and facilities needed better regulation. The Campaign for Quality Care launched, and soon after, the Federal Nursing Home Reform Act was signed into law by President Ronald Reagan (Wiener, Freiman, & Brown, 2007). Two federal statutes prompted CMS to revise these regulations:

- **Omnibus Budget Reconciliation Act of 1987 (OBRA '87)** was the first major revision of the CFR since its 1965 creation. It set forth national minimum standards of care for residents of long-term care and skilled nursing facilities. It had a major impact on general nursing care in these facilities, including the creation of the Minimum Data Set (MDS), requirements for a medical director, and a reduction of physical and chemical restraints.
- **Balanced Budget Act of 1997 (BBA '97)** expanded the discretion used by states in administering their Medicaid programs and created a per-diem prospective payment system (PPS) for skilled nursing services. These rates are set on an average of skilled nursing costs and are updated annually.

The CFR title 42 part 483 regulations are treated by the courts as the equivalent of statutory laws. They are labeled and referred to by an "F-Tag" and number. "F-Tag" is a designation that CMS uses in its Guidance to Surveyors for Long-Term Care Facilities to identify a portion of each requirement of participation (AHCA, 2018). Interpretive guidelines are derived by CMS for use by state surveyors in enforcing the regulations, and they consist of an explanation of the intent of the law, definitions of terms, and instructions on determining compliance with the law. These guidelines are found in the CMS State Operations Manual (SOM) Appendix PP (Guidance to Surveyors for Long-Term Care Facilities) and are regularly updated (CMS, 2017b).

In September 2016, CMS released revised Requirements for Participation and Reform of Requirements for the Long-Term Care Facilities rule. The new regulations reflected advances in the theory and practice of long-term care service delivery and safety, and they implemented sections of the Affordable Care Act. The overarching themes of the final rule were person-centered care and quality, the use of a facility assessment competency-based approach, care planning from a person-centered perspective, alignment with Department of Health and Human Services initiatives, comprehensive review and modernization, and implementation of legislation. The rules were reorganized and updated, making them consistent with current health and safety knowledge.

The Centers for Medicare & Medicaid Services released new interpretive guidelines as a revised version of Appendix PP in November 2017. A revised list of the F-Tags under each regulatory group is now available for use on the CMS website (CMS, 2017a). Since the regulations were restructured, some tags were combined, and others split into multiple subparts. For example, F-Tags for Abuse and Neglect were merged into a single tag—F600, and the new interpretive guidelines offer information on abuse and neglect, consent, involuntary seclusion, physical and chemical restraints, policies to prohibit abuse and neglect, and reporting requirements.

When analyzing either plaintiff or defense LTC/SNF cases, it is critical that the LNC review the interpretive guidelines that are relevant to the allegations. See Box 12.1.

Box 12.1

EXAMPLE ALLEGATION: The Nursing Home Defendant negligently failed to deliver care, services, and supervision during the Plaintiff's residency, including the failure to provide Plaintiff with adequate amounts of fluid to prevent dehydration, which resulted in acute kidney failure.

The F-Tag number related to standards of care for resident hydration is F692 and refers to this CFR:

§ 483.25(g) Hydration. Based on a resident's comprehensive assessment, the facility must ensure that a resident is offered sufficient fluid intake to maintain proper hydration and health.

The guidance to surveyors states the intent of the regulation, and the interpretive guideline states which sections of the MDS assessment correspond to the regulation, defines any terms used, gives risk factors for dehydration, and states the general guideline for determining baseline daily fluid needs. If a resident met the criteria for risk, or "triggers," the interpretive guideline lays out "probes," which help the surveyor determine if the care met the standard. Probes include: "What care did the facility provide to reduce the risk factors and ensure adequate fluid intake?" and "If adequate fluid intake is difficult to maintain, have alternative treatment approaches been developed, such as attempts to increase fluid intake by the use of popsicles, gelatin, and other similar non-liquid food?" The surveyor uses an investigative protocol to determine if the care plan for the resident was evaluated and revised based on the response, outcomes, and needs of the resident (CMS, 2017b).

Arbitration Agreements

Arbitration is a well-established, widely used means to end disputes, and an arbitration agreement is a written agreement between parties stipulating that, if a dispute arises, they will arbitrate (have a matter between contending parties determined by one or more unofficial persons), rather than litigate (dispute or contend the matter in the form of law) (Black's Law Dictionary Free Online Legal Dictionary 2nd Ed., n.d.; The Gale Group, 2008). Arbitration agreements are historically common in long-term care; however, as the volume of long-term care litigation has increased, so have the challenges to the enforcement of such contracts. (For more information on arbitration, see Chapter 38.)

The Centers for Medicare & Medicaid Services' final rule in November 2016 stated Medicare- and Medicaid-certified long-term care facilities must not enter or agree to binding arbitration with residents or their representatives until after a dispute arises between the parties. An industry group challenged CMS's legal authority and won a preliminary injunction in federal court, and the Trump administration ultimately dropped the matter and chose not to appeal to the U.S. Supreme Court (CMS, 2016b). In June 2017, the CMS Administrator proposed a rule that would "remove the requirement ... precluding facilities from entering into pre-dispute agreements for binding arbit- ration with any resident or resident's representative" and also proposed "removing the prohibition ... banning facilities from requiring that residents sign arbitration agreements as a condition of admission to a facility" (Medicare & Medicaid Programs, 2017, p. 26650).

As part of the initial review procedure, the LNC working on a long-term care case must first determine if an arbitration agreement was signed, when it was signed, and who signed it. The LNC should review the facility's chart, along with the administrative and financial files to deter- mine if the resident had the capacity to sign such an agreement. If the arbitration agreement was signed by an individual other than the resident, typically a family member, the LNC must deter- mine the legal authority of the signatory, such as a power of attorney (POA) or court-ordered guardianship. Also, the LNC should be aware of the difference between the various POAs a family member may hold. A general power of attorney is a document that authorizes another person (the "agent") to act on the principal's behalf in the event the principal cannot perform the tasks as stated in the document. A special POA, such as a durable power of attorney (DPOA) or a medical power of attorney (MPOA), may be immediate or go into effect after a specific event occurs, such as the disability of the principal. It is less costly than appointing a guardian. A DPOA is distinctive from a regular POA and allows the agent to act on the principal's behalf beyond the incapacity of the principal. A DPOA may vary from state to state and can be revoked or revised at any time as long as the principal is competent to make such a decision (Black's Law Dictionary Free Online Legal Dictionary 2nd Ed., n.d.).

Components of a Long-Term Care/Skilled Nursing Facility Record

During an initial review of the LTC facility's chart, the LNC should analyze the contents to determine if the chart is complete and identify any missing records that should be requested. In general, the chart should include the following components:

- ■ **Face Sheet:** Contains demographic information, allergies, diagnoses, primary care provider information, last hospital admission, and family members and POA.

- **Discharge Summary:** Includes admission and discharge dates and diagnoses, reports of condition and progress in therapy during residency, nutritional summary, ADL summary, skin condition, and disposition.
- **Physician's Orders:** Include admission orders, monthly orders, and telephone/verbal orders.
- **History and Physical:** Includes those from the admitting provider and possibly from the last hospitalization.
- **Physician's Progress Notes:** Contain information regarding when a physician or mid-level provider saw a resident, review of systems, a physical exam, assessment, and plan. A pitfall to many current electronic medical records is that sections of a progress note can be copied and pasted. If sections such as the physical exam are copied and pasted, the LNC should document as such.
- **Consultations:** Contain visits to other providers such as cardiologists, surgeons, and wound care centers as well as in-house visits such as dental, podiatry, and optometry. The LNC should note the consultations that are relevant to the allegations.
- **Graphic Records:** Include vital signs, neurological checks, weight, intake/output, etc.
- **Nursing Admission Assessment:** Contains full physical assessment, including any additional assessments such as an admission skin assessment, Braden scale, fall/injury risk assessment, Abnormal Involuntary Movement Scale, elopement assessment, and side rail assessment.
- **Minimum Data Set:** Contains entry and discharge tracking records, admission and discharge assessments, quarterly review assessments, change in status and change in therapy assessments, and PPS schedule assessments for a Medicare stay.
- **Care Plans:** Should be created and implemented within seven days of completion of the initial assessment, according to federal regulations. Regulation changes by CMS in effect as of November 2017 require care plans to be completed and reviewed with the resident or family within 48 hours.
- **Interdisciplinary Care Plan Meetings and Care Conferences:** Contain documentation of meetings of the interdisciplinary team members. Meetings are held at regular intervals and upon a change in condition to ensure care plans are updated and the family representatives are informed.
- **Nurses' Notes:** Should show monitoring of condition and implementation of written care plans. They may contain information regarding change of condition. Nurses' notes in an LTC facility may occur every shift or less frequently, depending on the resident's condition and plan of care.
- **Nurses' Assessments:** Include regular skin assessments, wound grids, Braden scale, and fall/injury risk assessment.
- **Activities of Daily Living Flow Sheets:** Are usually completed by nursing assistants and give a broader picture of how frequently care occurred, the resident's state of personal hygiene and skin, and specific information on intake and output.
- **Medication Administration Record (MAR):** Includes all scheduled medications. It may include diabetic glucose monitoring and sliding scale insulin administration as well as pain level assessments and narcotic logs. As with any charting done while the resident is out of the facility, it is of significance when a medication is marked as given when all other charting indicates the resident was at the hospital or on a leave of absence from the facility. The LNC should include this in the report.
- **Treatment Administration Record (TAR):** May include skin care treatments, weights and measures, Foley catheter care, and turning and repositioning. As mentioned above, the

LNC should note when treatment is marked as given when all other charting indicates the resident was not at the facility at the time.

■ **Labs:** May include indicators of infection, nutrition, and hydration, and can be used to evaluate for changes in condition. The facility's copies of lab results include handwritten notes as to whom aberrant results were reported and may possibly contain planned new orders.

■ **Social Services:** Can contain resident preferences, non-compliance issues, mental status, competency assessments, and family complaints or issues.

■ **Therapy Notes:** Includes speech therapy, physical therapy, occupational therapy, and restorative nursing program.

■ **Respiratory Therapy:** May contain pulse oximetry monitoring and breathing treatments given or refused.

■ **Nutrition:** Contains assessments to determine nutritional status upon admission and regularly throughout a residency, as well as intake and output flowsheets, weight records, and interventions implemented.

■ **Consents:** Are contained in the medical record and business file.

■ **Transfer Forms:** Contain a more detailed view of a resident's condition when received or upon discharge than nurses' notes alone.

Resident Assessment Instrument (RAI)

Each person in an LTC/SNF facility is a "resident." There are inherently unique challenges in the assessment of residents, as they are not in the facility merely to treat an acute issue but to live the quality life each deserves, whether they are participating in activities and relationships or receiving treatment for ongoing chronic conditions. The RAI strengthens the interdisciplinary nature of the LTC/SNF facility, which involves disciplines including dietary, social work, physical therapy, occupational therapy, speech-language pathology, pharmacy, and activities. According to the CMS's RAI Version 3.0 manual, this interdisciplinary assessment model is to ensure the facility helps residents achieve the highest level of functioning possible (quality of care) and maintain their sense of individuality (quality of life) (CMS, 2014). The RAI has three components: the Minimum Data Set (MDS) Version 3.0, the Care Area Assessment process, and the RAI Utilization Guidelines (CMS, 2014).

■ **Minimum Data Set**—The MDS is a standardized assessment tool facilitating care management in nursing homes and non-critical access hospital swing beds. The MDS contains a core set of screening, clinical, and functional status elements which form the foundation of a comprehensive assessment for all residents of nursing homes certified to participate in Medicare or Medicaid. The required subsets of the assessment are (CMS, 2016c):

  – Section A—Identification Information
  – Section B—Hearing, Speech, and Vision
  – Section C—Cognitive Patterns
  – Section D—Mood
  – Section E—Behavior
  – Section F—Preferences for Customary Routine and Activities
  – Section G—Functional Status

- – Section GG—Functional Abilities and Goals
- – Section H—Bladder and Bowel
- – Section I—Active Diagnoses
- – Section J—Health Conditions
- – Section K—Swallowing/Nutritional Status
- – Section L—Oral/Dental Status
- – Section M—Skin Conditions
- – Section N—Medications
- – Section O—Special Treatments, Procedures, and Programs
- – Section P—Restraints
- – Section Q—Participation in Assessment and Goal Setting
- – Section S—(Reserved)
- – Section V—Care Area Assessment Summary
- – Section X—Correction Request
- – Section Z—Assessment Administration
- ■ **Care Area Assessment Process**—This process assists the facility to interpret the information captured in the MDS. When a care area is "triggered," the care team uses resources to assess the problem and decide whether to develop a care plan for it. The process includes (CMS, 2016c):
  - – **Care Area Triggers (CATs)**—Specific responses of the MDS assessment determine if the resident has or is at risk for developing specific functional problems.
  - – **Care Area Assessment (CAA)**—A further investigation of care area triggers is done to determine if the responses require the development of a care plan.
  - – **CAA Summary (Section V of the MDS 3.0)**—This contains documentation of the care areas that were triggered and the decisions that was made whether to develop a care plan.
- ■ **RAI Utilization Guidelines**—These are instructions for when and how to use the RAI.

Surveys

State surveyors enforce federal standards in long-term care. There are two types of standard surveys to certify a skilled nursing facility to comply with the 42 CFR Part 483, Subpart B requirements to receive payment under the Medicare or Medicaid programs: Traditional Survey and a Quality Indicator Survey (QIS) (CMS, 2016d). Using the federal regulations, the surveyor determines if there are any substandard care issues and documents the evidence. The surveyor then categorizes the deficiencies regarding the degree of harm (actual or potential) related to the non-compliance. The severity level consideration is then used to determine the immediacy of the correction required, such as whether the non-compliance requires immediate correction to prevent serious injury, harm, impairment, or death to one or more residents. A facility then has a period of time to rectify the situation, after which a post-survey revisit is conducted to determine if the deficiencies were corrected. The LNC can use surveys to determine if the facility was found to have a deficiency in the area and time period relevant to the claim (CMS, 2016d). Legal nurse consultants can find more information on surveys at the website for The Centers for Medicare & Medicaid Services (www.cms.gov).

Major Categories of Liability

Allegations in long-term care cases generally can be classified into one or more of the five major categories of liability: nutrition, falls, infection, skin, and change of condition.

Nutrition/Dehydration/Weight Loss

Review of the LTC record for nutritional issues is important even if the resident did not gain or lose a significant amount of weight. Pathophysiologically, a resident's nutritional status affects infection and skin issues, as well as overall quality of life. An initial review by an LNC should consider the resident's admission weight, height, body mass index, pre-existing diagnoses related to nutrition, dental condition, and admission assessments of nutrition and hydration by the nursing staff and dietician. Assessment should be ongoing, and re-assessment should be apparent after the implementation of changes in diet, medication orders, and supplements. Care plans should be resident-specific with individual interventions identified, and they should be updated periodically and when the resident has changes in condition related to nutrition.

The interpretive guideline used by surveyors for nutrition is called F-Tag F692, and it is an excellent resource for the LNC to determine if a resident's nutritional care met federal regulations and facility policy (CMS, 2017b). As with most long-term care allegations, the evidentiary support is rarely black and white. A resident of a nursing home may need assistance with ADLs and medical care, but they retain free will and can decide the degree of compliance with dietary recommendations, nutritional supplementation, participation in speech therapy and restorative nursing programs, and hydration. Every effort should be made and documented by the facility to encourage healthy habits and compliance and to offer and provide the ordered and recommended diet and hydration, but the facility staff cannot force a resident to consume. Resident-specific care plans should show consistent re-evaluation by staff to improve nutrition and hydration when there is an issue.

Analysis of care planning and implementation may include weight loss or gain, a change in intake or edema, caloric or protein needs related to infection or wound healing, and lab values. The suggested parameters listed in F692 for determination of a significant weight loss is 5% in one month, 7.5% in three months, and 10% or greater loss in six months. An LNC can assist the legal team in understanding how a resident's medical and surgical history, disease process, and other factors can impact nutritional status, even with the implementation of multiple nutritional interventions (CMS, 2017b).

Falls/Fractures/Injury

An "accident" refers to an unexpected or unintentional incident which may result in injury or illness to a resident (CMS, 2017b). Not all accidents are avoidable. However, the standard of care for an LTC facility requires a systemic approach to assessing risk, care planning, implementing interventions to reduce individual risks related to environmental hazards, and monitoring for effectiveness (CMS, 2017b). While falls are the most common source of alleged injury in LTC, other hazards the LNC may encounter in LTC records are smoking injuries, resident-to-resident altercations, unsafe wandering or elopement, exposure to chemicals and toxins, unsafe water temperatures, electrical safety, and insufficient or too much light.

The interpretive guideline for accidents is called F-Tag F689 and encompasses accidents in LTC, including falls. A "fall" refers to unintentionally coming to rest on the ground, floor, or other lower level but not as a result of an overwhelming external force (such as a push). A fall without injury is still a fall, and the interpretive guidelines are clear that "unless there is evidence suggesting otherwise when a resident is found on the floor, a fall is considered to have occurred" (CMS, 2017b). However, for damages in a medical malpractice lawsuit, an injury must occur. For instance, an allegation may claim the resident fell 23 times, but if the defense can show there were no injuries, a tort may not have occurred. Long-term care facilities have great responsibility for the systematic assessment of risk and adequate supervision to prevent accidents, especially now that there is virtually no use of restraints in LTC (CMS, 2016a). In addition to the interpretive guidelines, an excellent resource for the standard of care in falls is the American Geriatric Society (AGS) Guideline for the Prevention of Falls in Older Persons. Contained in this reference are the most common risk factors for falls, which include (AGS Panel on Falls in Older Persons, 2001):

- Muscle weakness
- History of falls
- Gait deficiency
- Balance deficit
- Use of an assistive device
- Visual deficit
- Arthritis
- Impaired ADLs
- Depression
- Cognition impairment and
- Age >80 years

This clinical practice guideline is an evidenced-based document with risk factors, screening and assessment, and recommendations on interventions to prevent falls (AGS Panel on Falls in Older Persons, 2001). Formal fall risk assessment tools, such as the Morse Fall Scale and the Hendrich II Fall Risk Model, identify a resident's fall risks such as history, diagnoses, ambulatory aids, gait, medications, and mental status, and use the total score to predict future falls. Most importantly, these risk assessments should be used to develop a comprehensive plan of care to prevent falls based on risk factors (Hendrich, 2007; Morse, 2008).

The LNC should determine if the facts in the facility and hospital records support the allegations and if the resident was given a formal and accurate assessment of fall risk upon admission to the facility and regularly throughout residency. Care plans should contain resident-specific interventions; nurses' notes and other facility documentation should show the implementation of interventions. Should a fall occur, documentation should be assessed to determine what interventions were in place at the time of the fall and what changes were made to the plan of care to avert further falls. Resident (depending on the resident's cognitive capability) or family refusals to adhere to interventions should be documented.

Infection/Sepsis

Infection issues are a common allegation in LTC litigation and can be a serious complication in the elderly. Many residents of LTC facilities have diabetes or take medications which can mask the symptoms of infection, which further complicates the prosecution or defense of infection allegations. The standard of care for LTC facilities is to show the facility "developed, implemented, and maintained an infection prevention and control program to prevent, recognize, and control, to the extent possible, the onset and spread of infection within the facility" (CMS, 2016a).

The interpretive guideline F-Tag F880 is the umbrella under which regulations on controlling infection, preventing the spread of infection, and handling of linens are found. Urinary tract infections, respiratory infections (such as bronchitis and pneumonia), and skin and soft tissue infections represent the most common infections in nursing homes. Also prevalent are conjunctivitis, gastroenteritis, and influenza (CMS, 2017b).

The LNC must determine if records show assessments (including pre-existing colonization and medical history), vital signs, noted lab reports, and a resident-specific care plan with the creation of appropriate updates. Nursing staff should report changes in condition promptly, and ordered treatments should be carried out as per the TARs and MARs. In addition to interpretive guidelines, the American Geriatric Society publishes guidelines for infection prevention and control in the LTC facility (Smith et al., 2008).

Wounds/Pressure Injury/Skin Impairment

The intent of federal regulations related to skin impairment is that the LTC resident does not develop a pressure injury unless clinically unavoidable and that the facility provides care and services to promote the prevention of pressure ulcer development, promote the healing of pressure ulcers that are present, and prevent development of additional pressure ulcers (CMS, 2016a). The nomenclature of skin impairment is ever-evolving, and the leading authoritative voice in the field is the National Pressure Ulcer Advisory Panel (NPUAP). The panel publishes the most recent guidelines for staging, treatment, and prevention, as well as new research and guidance on unavoidable pressure injury. The most recent NPUAP Pressure Injury staging definitions were presented in 2016 (NPUAP, 2016). The NPUAP website also features content from other leading agencies, such as the Agency for Healthcare Research and Quality (AHRQ) and the Journal of Wound, Ostomy, & Continence Nursing (NPUAP, 2017).

As with other common allegations in LTC, the LNC will review the record for a systematic approach to prevention and treatment of skin impairment. The elderly can have many risk factors for skin impairment from pressure such as impaired or decreased mobility; co-morbid conditions such as end-stage renal disease, thyroid disease, or diabetes; medications such as steroids which affect wound healing; impaired blood flow; refusal of care and treatment; cognitive impairment; incontinence; poor nutrition or hydration; and a previously healed pressure ulcer, which are more likely to have recurrent breakdown (CMS, 2016a).

The LNC reviewing a record with an allegation of skin impairment should look for an initial assessment including risk factors and breakdown, records of the measurements and descriptions of existing breakdown, care planning, implementation of prevention strategies or treatment and medications for existing breakdown, communication of changes in condition, and updates to care plans. The LNC should also review the implementation of nutritional interventions as well as physical and occupational therapy to increase strength and mobility, thereby decreasing risk for skin impairment from pressure.

The CMS interpretive guideline on pressure ulcers is F-Tag F686 (CMS, 2017b). The research on unavoidable pressure injury is evolving, with an emphasis on the complexities of non-modifiable intrinsic and extrinsic risk factors. The LNC reviewing LTC cases should review the most up-to-date expert opinions on unavoidable pressure injury (Edsberg, 2014).

Change in Condition

Monitoring a resident after care planning is an essential part of the standard of care in long-term care. Regardless of the specific allegation, the LNC should review the records to determine if the LTC staff communicated a change in condition to the medical staff and the family representative. Allegations may include a delay in communication of a change in condition, which prevented a resident from being promptly evaluated and treated. While this is an integral theme throughout the CMS interpretive guidelines (CMS, 2017b), AHRQ and the Society for Post-Acute and Long-Term Care Medicine also publish clinical guidelines for acute change in condition in the long-term care setting. In the prosecution or defense of LTC cases, the LNC should obtain the most up-to-date guidelines in change of condition monitoring.

Summary

Long-term care is a fast-growing area of litigation in which a legal nurse consultant can have a significant impact on the way the legal team argues or defends these cases. Focus and analysis on the nursing process can shed light on whether the facilities followed the standards of care in these cases. An LNC's ability to keep abreast of the current regulations is key in working on cases in the LTC/SNF arena.

References

Administration on Aging, US Department of Health & Human Services. (2017). A profile of older Americans: 2017. US Department of Health & Human Services. Retrieved from www.acl.gov/sites/default/files/Aging%20and%20Disability%20in%20America/2017OlderAmericansProfile.pdf.

American Geriatric Society Panel on Falls in Older Persons. (2001). Guideline for the prevention of falls in older persons. *Journal of American Geriatrics Society, 49*(5), 664–672.

American Health Care Association. (2018). *The long term care survey November 2018 Edition.* AHCA.

Balanced Budget Act of 1997, Public Law 105–33 (105th Congress, August 5, 1997). Retrieved from www.gpo.gov/fdsys/pkg/PLAW-105publ33/pdf/PLAW-105publ33.pdf.

Black's Law Dictionary Free Online Legal Dictionary 2nd Ed. (n.d.). *The law dictionary.* (S. Danilina, Ed.). Retrieved from thelawdictionary.org.

Caffrey, C., Harris-Kojetin, L., & Sengupta, M. (2015). *Variation in operating characteristics of residential care communities, by size of community: United States, 2014.* Hyattsville, MD: NCHS Data Brief, no. 222. National Center for Health Statistics.

Carder, P. O. (2015, June 15). *Compendium of residential care and assisted living regulations and policy.* Retrieved from U.S. Department of Health & Human Services: https://aspe.hhs.gov/basic-report/compendium-residential-care-and-assisted-living-regulations-and-policy-2015-edition.

Centers for Medicare & Medicaid Services. (2014). *CMS's RAI version 3.0 manual.* CMS. Retrieved from www.aanac.org/docs/mds-3.0-rai-users-manual/11113_mds_3-0_chapter_1_v1-12.pdf?sfvrsn=6.

Centers for Medicare & Medicaid Services. (2016a, June 10). Appendix PP guidance to surveyors for long term care facilities. *CMS State Operations Manual.* CMS.

Centers for Medicare & Medicaid Services. (2016b). Final rule—reform of requirements for long-term care facilities. CMS, HHS. Retrieved from https://s3.amazonaws.com/public-inspection.federalregister.gov/2016-23503.pdf.

Centers for Medicare & Medicaid Services. (2016c). *Long-term care facility resident assessment instrument 3.0 user's manual version 1.14.* Department of Health & Human Services, USA.

Centers for Medicare & Medicaid Services. (2016d). *State operations manual appendix PP—survey protocol for long term care facilities.* HHS.

Centers for Medicare & Medicaid Services. (2017a). Guidance for laws and regulations—list of revised FTags. Retrieved from www.cms.gov/Medicare/Provider-Enrollment-and-Certification/GuidanceforLawsAndRegulations/Downloads/List-of-Revised-FTags.pdf.

Centers for Medicare & Medicaid Services. (2017b). Interpretive guidelines, CMS revision to SOM appendix PP. Retrieved from www.cms.gov/Regulations-and-Guidance/Guidance/Manuals/downloads/som107ap_pp_guidelines_ltcf.pdf.

Centers for Medicare & Medicaid Services, US Department of Health & Human Services. (2015). *Code of federal regulations, title 42*.

Coleianne, C., Riggins, D., Sakherzon, K., Vats, K., Huskey, M., & and Park, S. (2017). Aon/AHCA 2017 long term care general liability and professional liability actuarial analysis. Retrieved from www.ahcancal.org/research_data/liability/Documents/2017%20Long%20Term%20Care%20Benchmarking%20Report.pdf.

Edsberg, L. E. (2014). Unavoidable pressure injury: State of the science and consensus outcomes. *Journal of Wound, Ostomy & Continence Nursing, 41*(4), 313–334.

Hendrich, A. (2007, November). Predicting patient falls. *The American Journal of Nursing, 107*(11), 50–58. doi:10.1097/01.NAJ.0000298062.27349.8e.

Johnson, R. W., Toohey, D., & Wiener, J. (2007, May 1). Meeting the long-term care needs of the baby boomers. *Urban Institute*. Retrieved from www.urban.org/research/publication/meeting-long-term-care-needs-baby-boomers.

Medicare & Medicaid Programs; Revision of Requirements for Long-Term Care Facilities: Arbitration Agreements, Proposed Rule 82 FR 26649 (CMS 06 08, 2017). Retrieved from www.gpo.gov/fdsys/pkg/FR-2017-06-08/pdf/2017-11883.pdf.

Morse, J. M. (2008). *Preventing patient falls*. New York, NY: Springer Publishing Company.

National Pressure Ulcer Advisory Panel. (2016). NPUAP pressure injury stages. National Pressure Ulcer Advisory Panel. Retrieved from www.npuap.org/resources/educational-and-clinical-resources/npuap-pressure-injury-stages/.

National Pressure Ulcer Advisory Panel. (2017). *National Pressure Ulcer Advisory Panel*. Retrieved from www.npuap.org.

Omnibus Budget Reconciliation Act of 1987, H.R. 3545 (100th Congress 12 21, 1987). Retrieved from www.congress.gov/bill/100th-congress/house-bill/3545.

Smith, P., Bennett, G., Bradley, S., Drinka, P., Lautenbach, E., Marx, J., Mody, L., Nicolle, L., & Stevenson, K. (2008). Infection prevention and control in the long-term care facility. *American Journal of Infection Control, 36*, 504–535. doi:10.1016/j.ajic.2008.06.001.

The Gale Group. (2008). *West's encyclopedia of American law, edition II*. Retrieved from http://legal-dictionary.thefreedictionary.com/arbitration.

US Census Bureau. (2018). Older people projected to outnumber children for first time in U.S. history. Retrieved from www.census.gov/newsroom/press-releases/2018/cb18-41-population-projections.html.

Wiener, J., Freiman, M., & Brown, D. (2007). Nursing home care quality. The Henry J. Kaiser Family Foundation. RTI International. Retrieved from https://kaiserfamilyfoundation.files.wordpress.com/2013/01/7717.pdf.

Test Questions

1. Which of the following are major categories of liability related to LTC/SNF litigation?
   A. Nutrition/hydration
   B. Falls
   C. Infection
   D. All of the above
2. What is the standardized assessment facilitating care management in nursing homes and non-critical access hospital swing beds?
   A. Elderly Assessment
   B. Minimum Data Set (MDS) Assessment
   C. Medication Administration Record
   D. Pre-admission Screening and Resident Review (PASRR)
3. What is the governing agency over federal long-term care regulation?
   A. Federal Drug Administration (FDA)
   B. Joint Commission on Accreditation of Healthcare Organizations (JCAHO)
   C. Centers for Medicare & Medicaid Services (CMS)
   D. Department of Justice (DOJ)
4. According to federal regulations, when should care plans in long-term care facilities be implemented?
   A. Within 5 days
   B. Within 7 days
   C. Within 14 days
   D. Within 3 days
5. Which of the following would be considered a "significant weight loss" in a long-term care facility?
   A. 3% in one month
   B. 4% in one month
   C. 5% in one month
   D. 5% in three months

Answers: 1. D, 2. B, 3. C, 4. B, 5. C

Chapter 13

Pharmaceutical and Medical Device Product Liability Litigation

Vicki W. Garnett, RN, CCRC, LNCC®
Stacy Newsome, MSN, RN, LNCC®

Contents

Objectives

- Define product liability
- Compare theories of product liability
- Define three alleged defects associated with product claims
- List two possible ways to obtain information related to adverse events with product liability
- Describe significant roles for the legal nurse consultant (LNC) working with product liability claims

Introduction

Product liability cases may very well be one of the most complex, but fascinating areas of law a legal nurse consultant (LNC) encounters. The roles of an LNC in a product liability claim involving drugs and devices, will no doubt be extremely valuable to the legal team. To be successful, the LNC must have a clear understanding of the legal theories surrounding this type of law. Not only will the LNC be required to stay current with the new laws but also will have a proficient understanding of the rules and regulations of the Food and Drug Administration (FDA). Being familiar with the process of approving new drugs and medical devices, understanding post-market surveillance, staying current with new drugs and approved medical devices, as well as potential side effects, will be instrumental for the LNC. This chapter will highlight and explore product liability law, understanding that as a rule, the law may be different from state to state. The LNC will be provided with tools, examples, and resources along with basic key concepts, all to help develop effective and successful skills to aid in the review of product liability claims.

Product Liability—Definition

Product liability claims truly are a fascinating area in the legal arena but can be somewhat challenging for the LNC as well as the legal team, both on the defense and plaintiff's side of the law. Tens of thousands of product injury lawsuits are filed each year in the United States and it is important to understand that each state may have laws and specific statutes that will affect the product liability action. In addition, there may be several theories under which a plaintiff may state a claim and several defense arguments that can defeat that claim. Product liability is a view of the law that holds a manufacturer, distributor, or merchant liable or responsible for products on the market, meaning they can be held liable for placing a defective product into the hands of consumer. Responsibility for product defect that causes injury lies with all sellers of the product who are in the distribution chains. The underlying legal theories of product liability stem from common law, which is based on old English laws handed down from generation to generation, comprising the principle of law generally recognized in the U.S.

The American Law Institute (ALI), founded in 1923, consists of a group of the United States' most prestigious judges, law professors, and attorneys who promote the clarification of the common law and adapt to changing social needs. In 1998, the ALI published The Restatement (Third) of Torts: Products Liability, which specifies the rules on a wide variety of issues for product liability law. This Restatement (Third) of Torts: Products Liability expanded the categories of product defects (manufacturing, design, and inadequate instructions or warnings) as compared to section 402A in the previous Restatement (Second) of Torts with strict liability in addition to the omission of the "consumer expectations test." Although the restatements do not have the force of law, these have been traditionally influential in the courts (The ALI, 1998).

The key provision in The Restatement (Third) of Torts: Products Liability, Section 2, is that "a product is defective when, at the time of sale or distribution, it contains a manufacturing defect that is defective in design or is defective because of inadequate instructions or warning" (The ALI 1998, p. 14). Instead of the standard categories of negligence, strict liability, and breach of warranty, it provides a functional definition of the product defect in terms of design, manufacturing, and warning. It further defines each category of strict liability as follows (The ALI, 1998, p. 14):

- A product "contains a manufacturing defect when the product departs from its intended design even though all possible care was exercised in the preparation and marketing of the product" (Section 2a)
- A product "contains a design defect when the foreseeable risk of harm posed by the product could have been reduced or avoided by the adoption of a reasonable alternative design by the seller or other distributor, or a predecessor in the commercial chain of distribution and the omission of the reasonable alternative design renders the product not reasonably safe" (Section 2b)
- A product "is defective because of inadequate instructions or warnings when the foreseeable risk of harm posed by the product could have been rendered or avoided by the provision of reasonable instructions or warnings by the seller or distributor, or a predecessor in the commercial chain of distribution and the omission of instructions or warning renders the product not reasonably safe" (Section 2c).

Because there is no federal product liability law, product liability claims are governed by state law; however, it is important to recognize that occasionally the federal government will move to pre-empt an entire area of product liability from state control. Pre-emption law will be discussed later in this chapter.

Theories of Product Liability

As noted, product liability claims are based on applicable state laws and in most jurisdictions, there may be several theories where a plaintiff's cause of action may be made: Negligence, Breach of Warranty, Misrepresentation, and Strict Tort Liability (FindLaw, n.d.-a). When reviewing a product liability claim, it is important for the LNC to understand the applicable law in the jurisdiction the claim is asserted.

Strict Liability

Strict liability will almost always be part of the plaintiff's cause of action in a product liability claim. The Third Restatement, Section 2d, supports *strict liability without fault* for a manufacturing defect. The liability is based on the fact a defect existed at the time the product left the manufacturers, wholesalers, or retailers and the defect caused an injury. There is no need to prove it was unreasonably dangerous or not reasonably safe. Responsibility for drug or device safety is placed on the pharmaceutical or medical device company. This means if the company produces a drug or device that harms a person, the manufacturer may be held strictly liable for the injury regardless of the fact the medication may have been taken improperly or for an indication other than for which the drug or device is approved. In contrast, under a negligence theory, the plaintiff must prove the defendant knew or should have known the danger. The plaintiff's burden is less taxing under strict liability theory than under negligence, where fault must be shown. This theory extends responsibility for manufacturing defect product to all individuals who might be injured by the product, even in the absence of fault. All manufacturers, distributors, and retailers can be sued for strict liabilities. The intent of strict liability for manufacturing defects is to encourage manufacturers to place greater emphasis on product safety and for retailers to deal with reputable manufacturers and distributors.

Manufacturing defects typically occur when the product does not work as intended or as designed due to a problem with the parts, materials, or construction occurring in the process of assembling the device. The main difficulty in these cases is usually proving the defect directly caused the injury involved. In a strict liability case, the plaintiff must show:

- The defendant sold the product
- The product was defective
- The defect was proximate cause of the plaintiff's injuries
- The plaintiff has damages

There may be occasions when a product is defective due to design flaw; some courts may use one of two tests to find that the defendant has no liability (Legal Information Institute., n.d.-a). This includes:

1. Risk-Utility Test: "a test used in product liability cases to determine whether a manufacturer is liable for injury to a consumer because the risk of danger created by the product's design outweighs the benefits of the design" (FindLaw, n.d.-b)
   a. "the defendant is not liable for a design defect if evidence shows that the product's utility outweighs its inherent risk of harm" (Legal Information Institute n.d.-a)
2. Consumer Expectation Test: "a reasonable consumer would find the product defective when using the product in a reasonable manner" (Legal Information Institute, n.d.-a)
   a. "if a reasonable consumer would not find the product to be defective even when using it in a reasonable manner, then the defendant is not liable, even if the product's design flaw resulted in injury" (Legal Information Institute, n.d.-a)

When trying to prove a product is defective or unreasonably dangerous, the LNC must remember that some drugs and medical devices are designed and created with the inherent nature of causing side effects. In every case, drugs and devices used for medical purposes must be examined and analyzed from a risk/benefit ratio to assess whether or not these drugs and devices are unreasonably dangerous in the first place. It is important to examine whether the desired and foreseeable actions of the drug or device are sufficiently beneficial to justify the risk of adverse reactions. Manufacturers and suppliers of unavoidably unsafe products must give proper warnings of the dangers and risk of their products, so consumers may make informed decisions whether or not to use them. In manufacturing defects, plaintiffs have gained a reduced burden of proof with the implementation of strict liability, while defendant manufacturers will face the burden of proof the alleged defects were not in existence when the product left their possession.

Example 13.1

One of the known risks of the artificial heart valve is thrombogenicity, or risk of clot formation. Because the artificial heart valve is a foreign object and does not have the hemodynamics of a natural heart valve, thrombosis formation will occur in a certain number of patients. Thrombosis, as a result of artificial heart valve replacement, is considered a reasonable risk and if thrombosis does occur (in most cases) the valve would not be considered unreasonably dangerous or defective.

Negligence

Negligence is the absence of or failure to exercise proper or ordinary care (Garner, 2014). Meaning, an individual who had a legal obligation either omitted to do what should have been done or did something that should not have been done. The doctrine of *res ipsa loquitur*, when translated, *the thing speaks for itself*, shifts the burden of proof in some product liability cases to the defendant because the defect would not exist unless someone was negligent. If the doctrine is used successfully, the plaintiff is no longer required to prove how the defendant was negligent, rather, the defendant is required to prove they were not negligent. A manufacturing company can be held liable for negligence if there was a lack of reasonable care in production, design, or assembly of the product that caused harm. Strict liability, on the other hand, is liability without negligence and there is no need to show fault.

To recover under a theory of negligence (for additional information see Chapter 4, Elements of Proof in Negligence Claims) a plaintiff must prove several basic elements, including the following:

- *Duty*: The manufacturer owed a duty to the plaintiff, meaning the manufacturer must exercise ordinary care, diligence, and prudence of a reasonable manufacturer under like and in similar circumstances when manufacturing and distributing the product
- *Breach of duty*: The manufacturer breached a duty to the plaintiff, meaning it must be proven that the manufacturer did not exercise ordinary care, diligence, and prudence of a reasonable manufacturer under like and in similar circumstances when manufacturing and distributing the product
- *Damages*: The breach of duty was the actual cause of the plaintiff's injury, meaning the plaintiff must have suffered actual physical harm. It should be noted, in some jurisdictions, this harm may encompass emotional injuries for perceived or future physical harm.
- *Proximate cause*: The breach of duty was also the proximate cause of the injury, meaning the harm must be proximately caused by or have been created directly from the breach of the manufacturer's duty

A drug company has a duty to act prudently, and a breach of this duty would include, for example not performing an investigation, after several unexplained deaths in the first three months after Federal Drug Administration (FDA) approval of a new drug. The FDA approval does not in and of itself provide an adequate defense for the manufacturer when negligence is alleged. Alternatively, a product manufacturer may have breached its duty to act prudently by employing someone who is not qualified to run the clinical trials. Both are examples of a pharmaceutical or medical device manufacturer's failure to exercise ordinary care, diligence, or prudence, breaching its duty to the consumer or user of their product.

Breach of Warranty

A warranty is a type of guarantee a seller gives regarding the quality of product. This theory, Breach of Warranty, refers to the failure of a seller to fulfill the terms of a promise, claim, or representation made concerning the quality or type of a product. For product liability cases, this warranty can be either expressed or implied (Legal Dictionary, n.d.-a).

An express warranty refers to something written or stated. This includes information written on the product label, the packaging inserts, written instructions or any other paperwork included with the product. This express warranty could also be in the form of any advertising for that product.

An implied warranty refers to a law that automatically applies to the product. The Uniform Commercial Code (UCC), which has been adopted in part by every state, provides the basis for warranties in the United States. The UCC recognizes express warranties and two types of implied warranties: (1) the implied warranty of a merchantability and (2) the implied warranty of fitness for particular purpose (Legal Information Institute, n.d.-b, n.d.-c).

An implied warranty is a law that automatically applies to a product and does not have to be guaranteed by the manufacturer or suppliers. An implied warranty of merchantability is a promise that a product sold is in good working order and will do what it is supposed to do. The implied warranties applicable to a case will depend on the product and the circumstances surrounding its sale, keeping in mind, however, these may differ from state to state. Also, this theory can be used in both strict liability and negligence claims and recalls of a device or drug could fall under this category.

Misrepresentation

Some states may allow strict liability for manufacturers for misrepresentation. This theory refers to the "process of giving consumers false security about the safety of a product" and may be done by drawing attention away from the hazard of its use. This may be an intentional "concealment of potential hazards or in negligent misrepresentation." (Legal Dictionary, n.d.-a, n.d.-b, n.d.-c). To be actionable, a misrepresentation must be made knowingly or with reckless disregard for the facts.

Misrepresentation may be represented through advertising or sales promotion. The key to recovery requires that the plaintiff attorney prove reliability on the product representations made. Misrepresentation can also be claimed under the theories of breached express warranty or strict tort liability (Legal Dictionary, n.d.-c).

Example 13.2 Misrepresentation

MIRENA INTRAUTERINE DEVICE (IUD) PRODUCTS LIABILITY LITIGATION

In July 2016, a manufacturing company's summary judgment was granted after a decision of U.S. District Judge decided to dismiss 1,200 suits "alleging harm from Bayer Healthcare's IUD Mirena due to the absence of expert testimony" (Field, 2016; Overley, 2016).

In this unusual but interesting case, the labeling of an IUD, the Mirena, which is a T-shaped hormone-releasing insert used to prevent pregnancy, was critically examined. The product underwent numerous labeling changes over a period of years, which focused on wording of the timing for potential perforation risks during insertion of the device. Hundreds of cases in the multidistrict litigation alleged that Bayer failed to warn women that Mirena could perforate the uterus after and unrelated to insertion, claiming misrepresentation. However, as was described in a summary of the case, Mirena's labeling warned about the risk of perforation of the uterus, "most often during insertion," but said nothing about post-insertion risks during the 2008–2014 period covered by approximately 1,200 lawsuits. Bayer claimed that perforation was impossible after and unrelated to insertion. Of note, to understand why "expert witnesses" played a role and why the judge dismissed the claims, review U.S. Chamber Litigation Center (n.d.).

Federal Pre-emption of State Product Liability Law

When an individual alleges harm by a defective drug, product, or device, a lawsuit can be filed under state products liability law or plaintiff can threaten to sue, attempting to recoup money through a settlement. While products liability lawsuits are generally governed by state law, under certain circumstances the federal government can and will move to pre-empt an entire area of products liability law from individual state jurisdiction. The Supremacy Clause, found within Article VI of the U.S. Constitution, gives the federal government precedence over individual state laws and provides that the "... Constitution, and the Laws of the United States ... shall be the supreme Law of the Land; and the Judges in every state shall be bound thereby, anything in the Constitution or Laws of any State to the Contrary notwithstanding..." (Legal Information Institute, n.d.-d). Federal pre-emption is defined as the invalidation of a U.S. state law that conflicts with federal law. When federal law contradicts state law, laws enacted by the federal government supersede or "pre-empt" state law; therefore, judges in state courts must adhere to the rule of the federal government and cannot make additions or requirements to existing federal laws (Legal Dictionary, n.d.-b; Legal Information Institute, n.d.-e).

Federal pre-emption is divided into two categories, explicit or express pre-emption and implied pre-emption. Explicit pre-emption applies when Congress acts to explicitly pre-empt state law and there is clear pre-emptive language contained within a statute. The Medical Device Amendment to the Food, Drug, and Cosmetic Act (FDCA) includes an explicit pre-emption provision, 21 U.S.C. § 360k(a), preventing states from establishing any ruling in addition to or in opposition of a federal requirement that relates to the "safety or effectiveness" of a medical device (Legal Information Institute, n.d.-f). An example of explicit pre-emption is found in the ruling of *Riegel v. Medtronic, Inc.* (2008), which found the state law tort claims involving Class III medical devices were explicitly pre-empted by federal law (Minerd, 2018). Implied pre-emption is when Congress does not explicitly state a purpose to pre-empt. The FDCA also includes a provision, 21 U.S.C. § 337(a), which gives federal authority to any action used to enforce the FDCA. The

Supreme Court ruling *Buckman Co. v. Plaintiffs' Legal Comm.*, 531 U.S. 341 (2001), is an example of implied pre-emption. (Justia US Supreme Court, n.d.; Minerd, 2018)

The Supreme Court has recognized two subcategories of implied pre-emption, field and conflict pre-emption. Field pre-emption applies when a state statute is superseded by a federal statute that occupies a particular field and takes away the state's power to supplement. Conflict pre-emption applies when compliance with both the federal and state statute is not possible; therefore, the state law is in opposition to the legislative objective of Congress. An example of conflict pre-emption is *Geier v. American Honda Motor, Inc.* (2000), in which the Court granted summary judgment for the defendant when state law conflicted with the federal Department of Transportation (DOT) standard under the National Traffic and Motor Vehicle Safety Act, requiring manufacturers to place driver's side airbags in some but not all 1987 automobiles (FindLaw, n.d.-c). Manufacturing defect and failure to warn claims in products liability cases are often brought by the plaintiff to challenge implied or explicit pre-emption.

Defective Product Claims

In product liability litigation, there are three theories of recovery used regardless of whether negligence or strict liability is alleged. These theories include manufacturing defects, design defects, and marketing or labeling defects leading to failure to warn.

Manufacturing Defect

In products liability law, a manufacturing defect is an unintended defect. This kind of defect occurs when a product departs from its intended design and becomes more dangerous than consumers expected. As a very simple example, imagine if a desk left the warehouse completed, but one of the bolts was not secured correctly, this could be considered a manufacturing defect. Defective manufacture of a drug or device can be alleged if the product is defective because of the way it is manufactured, and the defect existed when the product left the manufacturer's control.

Design Defect

A design defect is inherent, meaning the defect existed before the product was manufactured. The product itself was the result of the intended design (a bad design). Defective design exists when a drug or device is not reasonably safe for its intended use or a use that can be reasonably anticipated. If a product's design is found to be defective, all products manufactured using that same design are considered to be defective. Considering the example above, for a design defect, let's say the desk was designed with only three legs, this could be considered a defective design because it tips over too easily. Sometimes, the designer did not perform adequate and appropriate testing of the product and the defect may not be discovered until after the product has been sold. This may result in a manufacturing product recall.

Marketing and Labeling Defect—Failure to Warn

Unlike a manufacturing defect or a design defect, a marketing defect is not a problem with the product itself. Instead, product liability claims that focus on a marketing or labeling defect, or failure to warn, refer to inadequate warnings where the plaintiff alleges the product had an inherent danger and the manufacturer of the product had a legal duty to warn of this danger but failed to do so. Defects in labeling and warnings can include improper instructions, inadequate wording, or other circumstances surrounding the way the warning is communicated and results in failure to warn consumers of the product dangers. Defects in marketing are identified in the way a product is sold. A simple example, a consumer is injured when taking a liquid allergy medication in combination with aspirin, observing both drugs are manufactured correctly and generally safe for use. The labeling failed to warn of a possible risk of the combination with aspirin, which resulted in injury to the consumer. Warning and labeling defects can occur with any type of product and the duty of the manufacturer to warn of the dangers associated with the use of a product is crucial in any drug or device case, whether the case encompasses strict liability, negligence, or both.

The concept with failure to warn is associated with inadequate instructions or lack of appropriate warnings, even when there is no design flaw nor any manufacturing defects. Manufacturers, distributors, and sellers may be held liable when there is failure to give appropriate warnings and a consumer suffers an injury. Also, failure to warn can be considered a marketing defect in a product liability claim. Manufacturers of drugs and devices must warn of hidden dangers in a product and how to use the product in a safe manner (Justia, n.d.). When failure to warn is alleged, a key issue is the adequacy of the product label. It is expected when a warning is given, the manufacturer may reasonably expect it will be read and followed. While that presumption works to benefit the manufacturer, when an inadequate warning is found, the pre-emption operates to benefit the plaintiff as if there were no warning, and the product can be presumed to be defective.

Drug and device companies routinely warn of adverse reactions in the labeling and package inserts, for example, in the case of drugs, the *Physicians' Desk Reference* (PDR) and a *Patient Package Insert* (PPI) and with medical devices, *Instructions for Use* (IFU). There are general device labeling requirements set forth by the FDA for medical devices (Electronic Code of Federal Regulations [e-CFR], 2018a). The regulations for content and format of prescribing information for human drugs and biological products, the FDA refers to the Physician Labeling Rule (PLR) described at 21 CFR, § 201.56, 201.57 (USFDA, 2017a, 2017b, n.d.-d). The FDA rules and regulations will be discussed later in this chapter; however, it is essential for the LNC to understand that the FDA must approve all product labeling. In addition, the FDA requires a labeling revision, supplementation to the package insert, and in some cases direct notifications to the physicians prescribing the product as soon as there is reasonable evidence of an association between a newly recognized serious hazard and a drug or device.

Example 13.3 Alleged Design Defect with Failure to Warn and Negligence

DIANE ALBRIGHT VS. BOSTON SCIENTIFIC CORPORATION

In an Ohio court hearing in 2016, the manufacturing company, Boston Scientific Corporation (BSC), was found not negligent, not guilty of defective design, and not guilty of failure to adequately warn the plaintiff's doctor of the risks. The plaintiff however appealed, arguing that letters from the FDA to BSC had been excluded from the previous trial. The case was sent to the Supreme Court, pursuing damages for injuries after a surgery where a "Pinnacle Pelvic Floor Repair" kit was implanted to treat a pelvic organ prolapse (POP). BSC sold and marketed the device as a safe implant to treat POP and received FDA clearance through the 510(k) processes.

Numerous experts, clinicians, and engineers for both the plaintiff and defense testified as well as a company spokesperson for BSC. For details to this case and findings, as well as how the labeling and material safety data sheet (MSDS) affected this case and why the FDA letters to the Company with regards to post-marketing observation and reporting were significant, see Commonwealth of Massachusetts (2016).

Learned Intermediary

The term "learned intermediary" originated in a 1966 decision, *Sterling Drug, Inc. v. Cornish* (Justia US Law, n.d.), when the courts decided in situations involving prescription drugs, that "the purchaser's doctor is a learned intermediary between the purchaser and the manufacturer" (Smith, 2012). This doctrine has been a part of product liability laws for years. Basically, this idea implies the manufacturer's duty to warn goes to the physician rather than the patient. The physician, in turn, has the duty to warn the patient. The prescribing physician acts as a "learned intermediary" between manufacturer and consumer and has the primary responsibility of warning patients of the hazards of prescribed pharmaceutical products and medical devices. There are justifications that may support this ruling including: (1) the device or drug can only be provided to the patient by a qualified healthcare provider (HCP) via a prescription. The HCP is in the best position to give the warnings and provide medical decisions regarding the use of that drug or device and determine if the use is an appropriate treatment for an individual patient; (2) manufacturers are not in a position to provide an effective way to communicate directly with each patient; and (3) enforcing a duty to warn by the manufacturer would interfere with the physician–patient relationship (Smith, 2012). These justifications sound appropriate, however, there are other considerations for an LNC to think about with legal claims that involve the learned intermediary doctrine. For example, what constitutes an HCP and what about direct-to-consumer advertising? Is the role of providing the warnings limited to only a physician?

Healthcare Provider Role

According to federal regulations, an HCP is defined as a doctor of medicine or osteopathy, podiatrist, dentist, chiropractor, clinical psychologist, optometrist, nurse practitioner, nurse-midwife, or clinical social worker who is authorized to practice medicine or surgery (as appropriate) by the state in which the doctor practices, or any other person determined to be capable of providing healthcare services, and performing within the scope of their practice as defined by state law, or a Christian science practitioner (e-CFR, 2018b).

Direct-to-consumer pharmaceutical advertising (DTCPA) has grown quickly in the past few decades and, in some ways, may be changing the doctor–patient relationship (Ventola, 2011). Patients influenced by DTC can make those patients seem familiar with the drug and may be less likely to question their doctor or inquire about rare side effects. There are, however, federal regulations for DTC ads for pharmaceutical companies. These regulations already require that the pharmaceutical companies include proper warnings with fair and balanced information in ads summarizing the side effects, contraindications, and effectiveness of the drug (see USFDA, 2017b).

The manufacturer's duty to warn is limited to an obligation to advise the prescribing physician of any potential dangers that may result from the drug's or device's use. The plaintiff, as the patient and consumer, must rely on the HCP to read and be familiar of the warnings. When a manufacturer provides adequate warning to a surgeon, physician, or other HCP, a barrier to liability against the manufacturer is created. This barrier, however, is weakened if the labeling information is inadequate. An LNC must understand the importance of labeling and package inserts when reviewing product liability claims. In addition, the LNC will need to consider the date of the injury. This is critical when obtaining and reviewing the correct version of the package insert or product labeling; making sure the version of the labeling correlates with the date of injury.

Example 13.4 The Learned Intermediary Doctrine

APPEAL OF: THEODORE F. JOAS AND DARLENE A. JOAS

In March 2018, during an appeal case, for ZIMMER NEXGEN KNEE IMPLANT PRODUCTS LIABILITY LITIGATION, a judged disallowed a failure to warn citing the learned intermediary doctrine.

Theodore Joas had a total knee replacement in a Wisconsin hospital and received a Zimmer NexGen Flex knee implant. After a few years, Mr. Joas experienced pain and x-rays confirmed that the implant had loosened which required a surgical revision. Joas brought numerous claims against Zimmer, Inc., the implant manufacturer, however his case was transferred "to a multidistrict litigation in the Northern District of Illinois, where it was eventually treated as a bellwether case. Applying Wisconsin law, the presiding judge entered summary judgment for Zimmer." Joas however appealed, citing failure to warn, claiming that Zimmer (1) failed to provide proper warnings directly to him as the recipient of the knee replacement; and (2) failed to provide proper warnings to his surgeon, who performed the surgery implanting the device. Discussions surrounding the warnings in the labeling specifically to the recommended amount of cement to use was debated. The judge excluded the claim stating the learned intermediary doctrine, which "holds that the manufacturer of a medical device has no duty to warn the patient as long as the manufacturer provides adequate warnings to the physician" (p. 4). Second, the judge pointed out that even if Zimmer had a duty to warn the surgeon, Joas

> has no evidence of causation because Dr. Larson testified in deposition that he did not read the packaging material Zimmer sent with the NexGen Flex implant. Rather, he testified that he based his surgical technique entirely on his general medical training and his surgical fellowship. So, an improved warning, the judge held, would not have made any difference.

> (pp. 4–5)

For details of this ruling and the case, review reference U.S. Court of Appeals (2018).

Over-the-Counter Products

There are many healthcare products not dispensed by prescription. These may include FDA class II, over-the-counter (OTC) devices and drugs, that do not require a prescription and may be taken by a patient without ever seeing an HCP. The FDA does, however, have regulations for OTC labeling which require adequate warnings of potential hazards, written in language that consumers can understand, and have information listed in a simply eye-catching, consistent style. There is no learned intermediary when using these products. Refer to the FDA website regarding new regulations regarding OTC products (www.fda.gov).

Adequate Warning: Conduct of the Manufacturer and Failure to Warn Claims

Whether the cause of action is negligence or strict liability there are certain principles taken into consideration with regards to the conduct of the manufacturing company, keeping in mind the adequacy of the warning included in the labeling is not only what is written, but in the manner in which it is presented. These principles or considerations with failure to warn include:

- Knowledge of risk
- The nature and timing of the duty to warn
- Language used to convey the warning

Knowledge of Risk

A manufacturing company is not held liable for failure to warn of adverse effects unless the adverse effects were known or scientifically reasonably known at the time the product was distributed by the manufacturer. But take note, this knowledge not only comes from the expectation of high standards within the company's own research reporting the adverse effects, but also with the knowledge of adverse reactions or events from outside sources such as peer-reviewed scientific literature.

Nature and Timing of Duty to Warn

The determination whether a manufacturer acted reasonably regarding warnings depends on the company's knowledge of the risk associated with the product at the time the product was distributed to the plaintiff. Here it is important to recognize the duty to warn does not end when the product is placed on the market, rather this is a continuous process. To be discussed in the FDA section of this chapter, there is a regulatory obligation of the manufacturer to investigate information regarding products and monitor all reported adverse events. If information becomes available regarding a new risk, this needs to be communicated and creates a responsibility to warn the physician and other HCPs as soon as reasonably practical. The laws do not allow the drug or device manufacturers to wait until a significant number of patients have been injured or until a causal relationship is established. With this issue, the court's view agrees with the FDA regulations requiring a labeling revision as soon as there is reasonable evidence of an association of a serious hazard with a drug. A causal relationship need not have been proved.

Language Used to Convey the Warning

The FDA regulates all prescription drug and medical device promotional activities that fall within the definition of labeling and advertising (see USFDA, 2017a). Once a determination is made to include a warning in a drug or device label, how this warning is conveyed is an important consideration. Product labeling includes not only written materials accompanying the product, but also any type of marketing materials, exhibits, press releases, even presentations by company spokespersons. This can extend to doctors representing the manufacturing company's product, as well as any "Dear Doctor Letters," sent out by the manufacturers informing HCPs about problems or concerns related to medications or devices.

The format and content of drug and device labeling is rigidly controlled by federal regulations. The product label is approved by the FDA during the drug and device approval process and is not a document arbitrarily designed by the drug or device manufacturing company. The FDA approved labeling must include certain criteria including but not limited to, indications, precautions, warnings, contraindications, dosage, and adequate directions. All subsequent promotional materials must conform to the language in the approved labeling. The FDA labeling regulations impose a continuing obligation on the manufacturer, and new data must be incorporated in the label as soon as it becomes available. The failure to share new information could result in the drugs being improperly labeled or misbranded. This would constitute evidence for the plaintiff in a product liability suit.

The adequacy of the warning included in the labeling is measured not only by what is stated, but also by the manner in which it is stated. The question of adequacy depends upon the language used and the impression such language makes upon the HCP or consumer. The wording must be simple and straightforward. There are several important considerations in the review of warnings including:

- Consider warnings ineffective and insufficient if printed in a body of other information of the same size and color. This means it is incumbent upon the manufacturer to make the warnings conspicuous and prominent.
- A warning is found inadequate if facts are insufficient, the response unduly delayed, or the manner of words reluctant or lacking in intensity.
- The warning must be expressed in a tone congruent with the nature of the risk.
- If a warning with the reference to particular side effect is labeled **rare**, the HCP might be more inclined to recommend the product than if the side effect were labeled **common or occasional**.
- Also, warnings must not be ambiguous or lack clarity or narrowness. The risk and types of possible adverse reactions must be very clear and straightforward. Overpromotion and activities such as direct consumer advertising may dilute the warnings or even render them insufficient.

Example 13.5

In the United States District Court for the District of Massachusetts, January 23, 2017, in *Liu v. Boehringer Ingelheim Pharmaceuticals, Inc.* (Leagle, 2017) wrongful death allegations were made regarding Dr. Zhensheng Liu, due to the side effects from taking the prescription drug Pradaxa. Claims were made against the drug's manufacturers and distributors for the negligent failure to warn, negligent design defect, and negligent design and testing. The defendants moved for summary judgment, arguing: (1) the design claims were pre-empted, (2) the plaintiffs failed to establish proximate cause, and (3) Pradaxa's label was adequate.

In 2010, Pradaxa, a brand name anticoagulant, was approved by the FDA. Dr. Liu, over 80 years old, with atrial fibrillation was prescribed the medication Pradaxa. Approximately one and one-half years later, Dr. Liu fell and suffered a cerebral hemorrhage and subsequently died from cranial bleeding. The plaintiffs claimed they were unaware of the risk or dangers associated with Pradaxa and had they known, Dr. Liu would not have taken the drug. The plaintiffs also claimed the defendants knew or should have known the dangers and through negligence caused Dr. Liu's wrongful death. The plaintiffs argued that "Pradaxa was defective in design because there were safer alternative designs, and the product did not comply with the specifications or performance standards, and Pradaxa was not as safe as other drugs in the same class" (Government Publishing Office [GPO], n.d.). Because the plaintiffs were unable to produce supporting evidence and failed to establish cause, "the Court granted the Defendants' motion for summary judgment on the issues of defective design and negligent design and testing" (GPO, n.d.). The plaintiffs argued the labeling did not adequately warn of the risk associated with prescribing the drug to patients over 80 years of age, claiming the defendants knew of an increased risk of major bleeding for patients over the age of 80 taking the drug, but did not include the risk and the products warning label; noting Dr. Liu would not have taken or been prescribed the drug if the defendants had included the appropriate information in the warning. The Court granted in part and denied in part the defendant's motion for summary judgment. Summary judgment was granted to the claims of negligent design and testing and denied as to the adequacy of Pradaxa's label and proximate cause.

A manufacturer has a duty to keep abreast of the current state of knowledge regarding products gained through research, medical literature, and adverse reaction reports. The subsequent toll and acquired knowledge requires a further duty to notify both HCPs and potential customers of any new information. Manufacturers have a duty to warn of all potential dangers either known or that should have been known in the exercise of reasonable care.

Food and Drug Administration Rules and Regulations

The Food and Drug Administration (FDA) initially started as part of the Agricultural Division in the Patent Office in 1848. Over the next two decades, over 100 bills were passed to protect consumers from fraud and abuses in the marketplace. Thus, in 1906, President Theodore Roosevelt signed the Food and Drugs Act which passed due to strong advocacy by then Chief Chemist of the Bureau of Chemistry of the U.S. Department of Agriculture, Harvey Washington Wiley, in response to unhygienic conditions in the Chicago stockyards. In 1927, the Bureau of Chemistry reorganized under a new United States Department of Agriculture (USDA) entity, the Food, Drug, and Insecticide organization. Three years later the title was shortened to the Food and Drug Administration and the position of Chief Chemist eventually evolved into the Commissioner of Food and Drugs (USFDA, n.d.-l).

In 1938, President Franklin D. Roosevelt signed into law the Food, Drug and Cosmetic Act to protect consumers from untested and dangerous pharmaceutical products that killed many patients, including children, upon introduction into the market. The Food, Drug and Cosmetic Act (FD&C) enabled the government to rein in more control over food and drugs, including consumer protection against unlawful cosmetics and medical devices as well as to enforce the law (Wax, 1995).

In 1962, the Kefauver-Harris Amendment to the FD&C Act raised the requirements for all new drug applications to demonstrate "substantial evidence" of the drug's efficacy and safety; requiring the manufacturers to use the generic name along with the trade or brand name of the drug; restricted drug advertising to FDA approved indications; and gave the FDA more authority to inspect drug manufacturing facilities. These changes lengthened the time required to bring a drug to market (USFDA, n.d.-m).

In 1984, the Drug Price Competition and Patent Term Restoration Act, also known as the "Hatch-Waxman Act" was enacted to reduce the overall cost of bringing generic drugs to the market and allowing the original manufacturer to maintain the profitability of developing new drugs. The original manufacturer received the benefit of extension of the patent exclusivity terms of new drugs as extensions to the length of FDA approval process was tied into the term for each drug. Generic manufacturers benefitted from a new approval mechanism, the Abbreviated New Drug Application (ANDA), requiring generic drug manufacturers to demonstrate the generic formulation of a drug had the same active ingredient, route of administration, dosage form, strength, and pharmacokinetic properties (bioequivalence) as the branded drug (Mossinghoff, 1999).

The Food and Drug Administration Modernization Act of 1997 (FDAMA) amended the FD&C Act to reform the regulation of food, drugs, and cosmetics. Important components of this act included the reauthorization of the Prescription Drug User Fee Act of 1992 (PDUFA), which sought to reduce the average time required for a drug review from 30 to 15 months. The FDA's Center for Drug Evaluation and Research (CDER) was created to evaluate new drugs prior to sales and marketing by the pharmaceutical company. In 2005, an independent Drug Safety Oversight Board (DSOB) was created by the FDA to oversee management and communication of drug safety issues to physicians and patients (USFDA, n.d.-n).

The Food and Drug Administration Amendments Act (FDAAA), passed in 2007 by President George W. Bush, reviewed, expanded, and reaffirmed FDA legislation, including permission to perform more comprehensive reviews of potential new drugs and devices; more authority to assess fees for drug approval applications; expanded clinical trial guidelines for pediatric drugs; and creation of the priority review voucher program (USFDA, n.d.-o).

Device Approval

Medical devices range from very basic products to complex, life-saving devices. Obtaining FDA approval of a new medical device before marketing, demands the manufacturer provide a reasonable assurance that the device is safe and effective when used for the approval that is sought. Safety is evaluated by weighing the probable benefits to health against the probable risks of injury, noting the risk/benefit ratio must be acceptable, but proof that the product will never cause harm or will always be effective is not required.

The FDA has classified approximately 1,700 different generic types of devices and grouped them into 16 medical specialties referred to as panels. (USFDA, n.d.-b, n.d.-k). Each generic type of device is assigned to one of the three regulatory classes listed below based on the level of control necessary to assure the safety and effectiveness of the device. The classification of the device is also based on the risk the device poses to the intended patient. Classification of medical devices are as follows (USFDA, n.d.-k):

- Class I—General Controls
  - Devices considered low risk for human use
  - Occurs with and without exemptions
  - If not exempt, a 510k is required prior to marketing the device
- Class II—General Controls and Special Controls
  - Considered a moderate risk for human use
  - Occurs with and without exemptions
  - If not exempt, a 510k is required prior to marketing the device
- Class III—General Controls and Premarket Approval
  - Considered high risk for human use
  - Premarket Approval Application (PMA) is required unless the device was on the market prior to the passage of the medical device amendments in 1976 or is substantially equivalent to such a device
  - If not, a 510k is required prior to marketing the device

A product is exempt from 510(k) if the pre-amendment device is not significantly changed or modified or if a Class I/II device is specifically exempted by regulation. A "pre-amendment device" is defined as a device legally marketed in the U.S. prior to May 28, 1978, which has not been significantly changed or modified since then and for which a regulation requiring a PMA application has not been published by the FDA. These devices are considered "grandfathered" and do not require a 510(k) (USFDA, n.d.-k).

When Premarket Notification [510(k)] submissions are required, the manufacturer must produce the submission to FDA. Then the submission is reviewed by the FDA's Center for Devices and Radiological Health (CDRH), the Office of Device Evaluation (ODE), and the Office of In Vitro Diagnostics and Radiological Health (OIR). Depending on type of device, the 510(k) submissions are reviewed by ODE and OIR staff, including biomedical engineers, physicians, microbiologists, chemists, and other scientific professionals (USFDA, n.d.-c).

Also, device classification is based on intended use and indications for use which determine whether or not a drug, device, or product fall within the specifications of the FD&C and can be regulated by the FDA.

When evaluating a products liability claim, it is important to evaluate the intended use and indications for use to determine if the product or device failed due to utilization of the product outside the intended use or "off-label" use. Guidelines for drug and device regulations can be found in the Code of Federal Regulations Title 21, § 801.4 (USFDA, 2017c, 2017d), which states,

> …intended uses … refer to the objective intent of the persons legally responsible for the labeling of devices. The intent is determined by such persons' expressions or may be shown by the circumstances surrounding the distribution of the article. This objective intent may, for example, be shown by labeling claims, advertising matter or oral or written statements by such persons or their representatives. It may be shown by the circumstances that the article is, with the knowledge of such persons or their representatives, offered and used for a purpose for which it is neither labeled nor advertised…

The manufacturer is required to provide adequate supplemental labeling to the FDA when a drug or device is marketed for use outside of the originally intended use.

Clinical Trials

Prior to a drug entering the market, extensive testing must be performed to ensure drug safety and efficacy meet FDA standards. While this process does not eliminate the occurrence of adverse events, it is intended to reduce the incidence of drug reactions and identify potential side effects included in the drug label, so the consumer can make an informed risk versus benefit analysis with their healthcare provider prior to ingesting a drug.

The clinical trial process starts with pre-clinical or animal testing of a compound. After pre-clinical or animal testing is complete, a pharmaceutical company will submit an Investigational New Drug Application (IND) and must produce pre-clinical testing results to the FDA and an Institutional Review Board (IRB) for evaluation of safety in human trials. The IRBs must review and approve clinical trial protocols, ensure the study is acceptable and subjects are fully consented prior to participation. Phase I clinical trials typically involve a small number of healthy subjects to determine metabolization and excretion of the drug as well as to identify the most frequently reported side effects. If a Phase I study is deemed safe, a Phase II study is initiated to establish effectiveness to treat a certain disease or condition. Generally, Phase II studies have a larger subject group and controlled trials compare the drug to an inactive substance or placebo (USFDA, n.d.-f).

After successful completion of a Phase II study, the FDA and pharmaceutical company collaborate to establish a Phase III trial, which further evaluates the safety and effectiveness of a product with a larger population of subjects. Prior to the submission of a New Drug Application (NDA), the FDA and pharmaceutical company again collaborate on the results of the Phase III results. Once an NDA is submitted, the pharmaceutical company has officially asked the FDA to consider approving a new drug for use in the U.S. The NDA includes the results of all studies in addition to information about how the drug works and manufacturing processes. Once an NDA is submitted, the FDA has 60 days to determine if the NDA is complete and ready to be filed. Once filed, the FDAs CDER division attempts to review most NDAs within 6 to 10 months, based on priority. The CDER doctors, chemists, statisticians, pharmacologists, and other experts review the studies to determine if the benefit of the drug outweighs the risks. As all drugs have varying degrees of side effects, no drug can be deemed absolutely safe and without risk. If a particular drug is a first in class or the first drug proposed to treat a particular indication, an Advisory Committee may also review the results of the studies (USFDA, n.d.-f).

Prior to approval, the FDA also reviews the drug labeling and inspects the facilities where the drug is manufactured. Sometimes, additional studies are required to establish safety and efficacy of a drug. Manufacturing issues can also delay the drug approval process. Once all requirements are sufficiently met, the pharmaceutical company will receive an approval letter granting an NDA, and the drug can be manufactured in the U.S. (USFDA, n.d.-f).

Post-marketing Surveillance and Drug Safety Labeling Changes

Unfortunately, adverse events related to drugs and devices do occur, and the FDA established a reporting system to conduct post-marketing surveillance and risk assessment programs to track adverse effects. As previously discussed, pharmaceutical and biologic products undergo extensive evaluation through the clinical trial process, and consumers can assume a reasonable expectation the drug will be safe and effective if consumed for the approved indication and dosage and the consumer adheres to the instructions outlined in the drug label. However, when a new drug is released to a broader population, post-marketing side effects are identified, and additional testing is sometimes required. The FDA Adverse Event Reporting System (FAERS; USFDA, n.d.-a, n.d.-e) is a database used to track, store, and analyze post-marketing safety surveillance reports. Reports are evaluated by CDER scientists to monitor and enforce drug safety. Based on CDER's analysis, the FDA may enforce regulatory action such as requiring the pharmaceutical manufacturer to revise the drug label, include a black box warning, send out a "Dear Health Care Professional" letter, or withdraw the product from the market (USFDA, n.d.-g).

The Division of Drug Marketing, Advertising and Communications (DDMAC) also monitors drug advertising and surveillance information. The FDA must assure companies adhere to the terms and conditions of approval described in the application and that the drug is manufactured in a consistent and controlled manner by periodic, unannounced inspections of drug product and control facilities (USFDA, n.d.-g).

When pharmaceutical companies are required to revise drug labeling, the company must submit revised changes to the FDA, who in turn must approve supplemental label changes based on factors such as side effects, dosage changes, and additional indications for use. The National

Institutes of Health (NIH) and U.S. National Library of Medicine (NLM) website DailyMed is another resource that contains over 100,000 drug listings submitted to the FDA and allows consumers to search for drugs based on name, National Drug Code (NDC), drug class, or set ID. DailyMed is the official provider of FDA label information or package inserts and can be accessed at https://dailymed.nlm.nih.gov/dailymed.

The manufacturer is required to submit reports of adverse events to the FDA. The National Coordinating Council for Medication Error Reporting and Prevention (NCCMERP) defines a medication error as,

> any preventable event that may cause or lead to inappropriate medication use or patient harm while the medication is in the control of the health care professional, patient or consumer. Such events may be related to professional practice, health care products, procedures, and systems, including prescribing; order communication; product labeling, packaging, and nomenclature; compounding; dispensing; distribution; administration; education; monitoring; and use.
>
> (NCCMERP, n.d.)

The CDER staff review medication error reports sent to the USP-ISMP Medication Errors Reporting Program and MedWatch, evaluate causality, and analyze the data to provide feedback to the FDA (USFDA, n.d.-g).

The FDA's Drug Safety Labeling Changes (SLC) database provides the consumer with approved safety and labeling changes from January 2016 to the present. The SLC database allows the consumer to search by drug name or date and can be accessed through the FDA website. Data prior to January 2016 can be found on the MedWatch website, which contains safety alerts for drugs, biologics, medical devices, special nutritionals, and cosmetics from the years 2000 to 2015. The FDA maintains archival MedWatch information from 1996 to 2007, and this can be accessed through the FDA website (USFDA, n.d.-i).

Recall/Reporting Systems

The FDA Manufacturer and User Facility Device Experience (MAUDE) database tracks medical device reports (MDR) of suspected device associated injuries, malfunctions, and even death. The FDA utilizes MDRs to monitor the performance of devices and to detect potential device-related safety issues. The MDR is submitted by mandatory reporters, such as manufacturers, importers, and device user facilities as well as voluntary reporters such as healthcare professionals, patients, and consumers. The LNC should be aware of how to access the MAUDE database via the FDA website to research other potential device-related complications when a new products liability suit is filed. Some information contained in the MAUDE database can be subjective, inaccurate, or incomplete, so trends gleaned from this data should be used with caution (USFDA, n.d.-e, n.d.-h).

Role of the Legal Nurse Consultant Evaluating Product and Device Liability Claims

When evaluating products liability claims, the LNC should follow the same four elements of proof in negligence claims, which are duty, breach of duty, causation, and damages. The LNC should evaluate and analyze other key elements in the medical records for products liability claims, such as product identification, IFUs, NDC codes, drug labeling, and other factors outlined below.

Medical Records

The LNC will play a significant role with pharmaceutical or medical device litigation teams, both in defense and plaintiff cases. Once the plaintiff attorney has decided to proceed with accepting clients for a product liability case, the plaintiff LNC may design and draft documents to be used as intake forms; provide explanation and training to complete client intake calls; order or provide direction in ordering the necessary medical records; provide instruction to the support staff on where and how to locate product identification and damages in the records.

Upon receiving a new product liability case, the defense LNC should first evaluate the complaint filed by the plaintiff to determine what injuries and claims are alleged. The LNC should determine if the suit is being filed by the injured party or on behalf of a minor, incapacitated person, or decedent. Also, all named defendants will be identified in the complaint, including the companies and any HCPs or facilities. Often, amended complaints are filed, which may include or exclude parties in the suit and allegations; therefore, the LNC should revise the analysis accordingly.

A complete and comprehensible medical record can be a key piece of evidence in a drug or device litigation case. Requesting, organizing, evaluating, summarizing, and analyzing medical records, then comparing and correlating records with the allegations of the complaint, are critical in pursuit of defense of the legal case. Establishing clear causation is vital when reviewing a patient's medical record. The LNC should be intuitive while reviewing the records, understanding the importance of the details of the complaint first, then being alert to the relevant information in the medical record. Once the records have been reviewed, the LNC should identify any additional records needed to evaluate the case. The LNC should maintain collaboration with the attorneys and may be asked to assist in the review and analysis of relevant literature, identification, and coordination of expert review materials, collaboration with experts to prepare disclosures and draft reports and assist with depositions and trial preparation.

The plaintiff LNC will also conduct a thorough review of the medical records and develop chronologies, create timelines and narratives to convey the events that lead to the conclusion. The plaintiff LNC will work with the medical experts to assist in communications, expert reports and briefs by the attorneys. As the case proceeds through filing and if chosen for trial, the plaintiff LNC may become an integral part of the trial team, collaborating with the attorneys and expert witnesses, providing cuts of the medical records to use as trial exhibits, maintain a list of trial exhibits, format visual aids to enhance work product for explaining the medical issues and procedures or may collaborate with other companies to create demonstrative evidence for use at trial.

Because the LNC has a unique knowledge of the elements that make up medical records, it is critical to identify and request missing records. It is important to understand it is just not timeliness but accuracy with an attention to detail, that an attorney will require from the LNC. Creating a list of symptoms or injuries specific to the allegations and producing an index of where to find these in the medical records will be helpful for the legal team. The process of obtaining and analyzing medical records can be involved, but the LNC's role is instrumental to the legal team, not only by identifying the missing critical documentation for the claim but by reducing the massive volume of records down to the most valuable evidence.

The LNC should identify any potential medical negligence or other contributing factors, which means examining the standard of care and collaborating with the attorney and expert as to whether or not the drug or device was used in accordance with the IFU or product label. Findings of medical negligence may shift liability in part or completely to the HCP, and experts in the same field are often used to establish the standard of care. While the LNC is not able to opine on medical standard of care issues, the LNC can assist the attorney in identifying what types of experts can opine on the standard of care as well as contacting potential experts to evaluate their qualifications and interest in serving as an expert witness.

The following questions should be evaluated as the LNC reviews medical records for product liability claim:

- Did the plaintiff provide appropriate product identification for the time frame and product alleged to cause an injury?
- Did the HCP document discussion of the risks, benefits, possible side effects, and adverse events with the patient or guardian and obtain informed consent if applicable?
- Were there clear instructions to the patient from the learned intermediary?
- Was there adequate follow-up with the HCP or issues of non-compliance with appointments or product use?
- Was there a misdiagnosis?
- Did the expert identify any shared liability or even a transfer of liability to the HCP?
- Was the device or drug prescribed used in the manner approved or instructed by the manufacturer or was the product prescribed for "off label" indications?

Medical History

When reviewing medical records, the LNC uses nursing skills to discover any deviations or "red flags" uncovering valuable information for the claim. For example, focusing on the patient's past medical history is essential. The LNC should determine if the plaintiff had any symptoms prior to the alleged injury or if there were pre-existing medical conditions that predispose the patient to complications or adverse side effects. Examine referrals to other doctors and review those records as well. Medical records can provide evidence of non-compliance or identify behavior by the plaintiff that may have contributed to the injury. For example, does the patient smoke or drink alcohol? As a nurse, the LNC is aware smoking not only increases health risk but slows the healing process with regards to surgery and recognizes alcohol may potentiate the effects of drugs. Pre-existing chronic medical conditions such as diabetes or immune deficiency can complicate healing and predispose rejection of a foreign material, such as an implantable medical device. Consideration of repeated complications with implantation of other similar medical devices should also be evaluated to establish a pattern of device complications in some plaintiffs.

When evaluating a medication products liability case, it is also imperative to focus on the patient's pharmaceutical history and any potential drug to drug interactions looking for drug induced side effects. For example, if the plaintiff is alleging weight gain from a particular drug, it is important for the LNC to identify what other drugs the plaintiff may have taken during the same time frame that are also known to cause weight gain. When evaluating the patient's pharmaceutical history, research for evidence of prescriptions from multiple HCPs as well as any emergency department (ED) visits where the patient may have received prescriptions. In addition, if a pain management group was treating the patient, obtain the patient's narcotic agreements, search for any evidence where patient may have been fired from a previous practice, and look for documented narcotic violations (e.g., drug screen reports). In states that recognize doctrines of comparative or contributive negligence, this information will be critical to uncover.

Medical Devices

While there are similar roles for the LNC when reviewing both drugs and devices claims, there are some unique considerations for a medical device claim; including one must determine if the product is a medical device (USFDA, n.d.-j). There can be numerous sources and medical records related to a patient's surgically implanted medical device. The LNC must constantly be on the lookout for pertinent medical information and ensure access for review. For example, in a plaintiff claim, the LNC will be examining the medical records for evidence pertaining to the lack of warnings and injuries related to the claim. In a defense case, the LNC will be searching for contributing factors and suggestions of non-compliance. Inspecting the progress notes and reviewing both the pre-operative visits that discuss the surgery as well as the post-operative visits that describe the patient's post-operative instructions and progress may uncover valuable information for the case. For example, did the pre-operative visit discuss the surgery and associated risks? Were the risks detailed by the HCP and was there an opportunity for the patient to ask questions? Did the HCP provide clear post-operative instructions? Is there evidence the patient followed those instructions? Understanding the alleged injuries and looking for evidence of failure to warn as well as contributing factors will be valuable to the case.

Operative Reports and Informed Consent Process

For implantable medical devices, operative reports provide details to the surgery. Many operative reports will not only contain details to the surgical procedure but may provide relevant facts to the patient's past medical history as well as the informed consent process. An informed consent is a process that results from a dialogue between the HCP and the patient. The consent form is an actual document reflecting that process. Details to the consenting process will be quite significant in a device legal case discovering the description to the patient during the surgical discussion as well as the informed consent process. Because implantable devices can only be provided to the patient by a qualified HCP via a prescription, the HCP is in the best position to give warnings and provide medical decisions regarding the use of that device and determine if the use is an appropriate treatment for an individual patient. As previously discussed, manufacturers are not in a position to provide an effective way to communicate directly with each patient, hence the HCP becomes the learned intermediary when describing the risks, benefits, and alternatives to the surgical procedure. Please refer to Chapter 19 for more information regarding informed consent.

Labeling with Medical Devices

In legal claims involving a medical device, the labeling of a product should also be a key focus for the LNC to review. As mentioned, the FDA has specific requirements to include with medical devices found in the package insert, or IFU (information for use; see e-CFR, 2018a). The IFU will have different versions, so it will be important for the LNC to review the version that correlates with the date of the implant and injury. The IFU will contain specific information such as indications for use, contraindications, and post-operative instructions. When reviewing the complaint, the LNC will need to compare the labeling information with the patients' clinical history. For example, in a plaintiff claim, does the informed consent process appropriately reflect the warnings and adverse events listed by the manufacturer? In a defense case, is there anything in the patient's past medical history or medical records that show evidence of non-compliance or conflict with the contraindications? The IFU will provide valuable information about the use of the device and should be a routine part of the LNC review.

Implant Logs

An implant log contains information that will identify an implantable device or tissue used in a patient's surgery. This log is found in hospital records in the peri-operative sections and typically not kept in the physician's records. The implant log is not always included as part of the medical records request and the LNC may need to specifically request that information. The information on the implant log may vary from hospital to hospital, but typically the part, serial, or lot number along with the manufacturer's information will be listed. Many times, the lot numbers will be instrumental in identifying the device and manufacturing company as well as researching the device history. For more information on the FDA guidelines and regulations for tracking medical devices, see e-CFR (2018a).

Product Labeling, Package Inserts (IFU), and Drug Labeling

Similar to the IFU for medical devices, the drug label provides the HCP and patient with critical information about the drug, including but not limited to prescribing information, dosage, indications for use, potential side effects, and guidelines for the HCP to discuss risks and benefits of the product with the patient. When evaluating pharmacy records, the LNC should request product handout or labeling information supplied to the plaintiff at the time of the pharmacy dispensing. The LNC should be aware of labeling changes and assist the attorneys to identify the proper label in effect at the time of the alleged injury.

As noted above, an LNC will need to evaluate and examine the medical records in addition to all relevant information available surrounding the claim. Then, in conjunction with the attorney, analyze the evidence to determine if the case supports a liability or negligence claim. It may be beneficial for the LNC to create a checklist when analyzing claims, understanding, however, each case will be unique. Below is a sample checklist that may be beneficial for an LNC to use as a guideline when evaluating products liability claims.

1. Was the product at issue affirmatively identified? For example, in a medical device case, does the implant log confirm manufacturer and lot number? In a pharmaceutical case, identify the NDC code.
2. Based on the product identification or NDC number, determine when and where the product was manufactured.
3. Based on the implant or pharmacy records, determine when and where the product was consumed or implanted.
4. Based on implant/explant or pharmacy records, determine the span of time the plaintiff ingested or used the product at issue.
5. Does the plaintiff continue to use the product at issue?
6. Did the product reach the user or consumer without substantial change from the condition in which it was sold?
7. Was there a learned intermediary?
8. Was there a signed informed consent prior to the implant or ingestion of a drug? If not, did the physician document a discussion of the risks, benefits, and alternatives with the plaintiff?
9. Do the medical records document the indication for implantation of a device or purpose for pharmaceutical prescription?
10. What were the instructions, contraindications, and possible side effects listed in the IFU or package insert? Does the alleged injury fall within the potential side effects?

11. Did the manufacturer change the labeling or IFU when the information of additional side effects become known? If so, did this occur before, during, or after the plaintiff's span of use?
12. Did the physician discuss any change in labeling or IFU with the plaintiff?
13. Have the warnings been changed since the time of the events alleged in the case?
14. What is the statute of limitations and/or statute of repose laws relative to the alleged product use and injury?
15. Was the product used "off label" or were the indications for use followed appropriately?
16. Was there any evidence of non-compliance or behavior by the plaintiff that may have contributed to the alleged injury?
17. Was the product excessively promoted? Are sales representatives also named in the lawsuit?
18. Did the advertising falsely create high expectations on the part of the consumer such that the warnings were disregarded?
19. Have there been any FDA enforcement actions regarding the product? If so, did the manufacturer comply with the FDA enforcement rulings?
20. Do the medical records support evidence of the alleged injury?
21. Does the plaintiff have co-morbidities or other factors that may have caused or contributed to the alleged injury?
22. Did a healthcare provider opine on the cause(s) of the alleged injury within the medical records?
23. What is the plaintiff's current condition? Did they die from the alleged injury or are they fully recovered with no residual health issues?

Summary

When analyzing medical product liability claims for drugs and devices, the roles for an LNC may be challenging and at times quite complex. The LNC will need to utilize both legal knowledge and medical expertise while remaining current with research regarding various drugs and devices that fall under the product liability statutes. The LNC must take an analytic approach when reviewing allegations then comparing the allegation to the medical records and product information. In addition, a solid knowledge of government rules and regulations as well as the regulatory requirements for manufacturing companies will be essential for the LNC when working with product liability claims. Attention to detail, while producing professional work products will prove to be successful in both the defense and plaintiff's strategies, making the LNC a valuable asset to the litigation team.

References

Buckman Co. v. Plaintiffs' Legal Comm., 531 U.S. 341 (2001).

Commonwealth of Massachusetts. (2016). Diane Albright vs. Boston Scientific Corporation, 90 Mass. App. Ct. 213. Retrieved from http://masscases.com/cases/app/90/90massappct213.html#back20.

Electronic Code of Federal Regulations. (2018a). 21 CFR, § 1, Subchapter H: Food and drugs: Medical devices. Retrieved at www.ecfr.gov/cgi-bin/text-idx?SID=e6052869ab2c483927920716cb03e6dd&mc=true&tpl=/ecfrbrowse/Title21/21cfrv8_02.tpl#0.

Electronic Code of Federal Regulations. (2018b). 29 CFR 29 § 825 Labor: The Family and Medical Leave Act of 1993. Retrieved from www.ecfr.gov/cgi-bin/text-idx?SID=30c1f2d2c089b526142b4bf4b514cd9b&mc=true&node=se29.3.825_1125&rgn=div8.

Field, E. (2016). The top product liability cases of 2016: Year-end report. Retrieved from www.law360. com/articles/865187/the-top-product-liability-cases-of-2016-year-end-report (subscription required for full report).

FindLaw. (n.d.-a). Legal basis for liability product cases. Retrieved from https://injury.findlaw.com/product-liability/legal-basis-for-liability-in-product-cases.html.

FindLaw. (n.d.-b). Risk-utility test. Retrieved from https://dictionary.findlaw.com/definition/risk-utility-test.html.

FindLaw. (n.d.-c). *Geier v. American Honda Motor Co.* Retrieved from https://caselaw.findlaw.com/us-supreme-court/529/861.html.

Garner, B. A. (Ed.). (2014). Negligence. *Black's law dictionary*. St. Paul, MN: Thomas Reuters.

Geier v. American Honda Motor, Inc., 529 U.S. 861, 120 S. Ct. 1913, 146 L. Ed. 2d 914, (2000).

Government Publishing Office. (n.d.). *Liu et al. v. Boehringer Ingelheim Pharmaceuticals Inc. et al.* Retrieved from www.gpo.gov/fdsys/pkg/USCOURTS-mad-1_14-cv-13234/content-detail.html.

Justia. (n.d.). Failure to warn. Retrieved from www.justia.com/products-liability/failure-to-warn/.

Justia US Law. (n.d.). *Sterling Drug, Inc., a Corporation, Appellant, v. Maxine F. Cornish, Appellee*, 370 F.2d 82 (8th Cir. 1967). Retrieved from https://law.justia.com/cases/federal/appellate-courts/F2/370/82/234870/.

Justia US Supreme Court. (n.d.). *Buckman Co. v. Plaintiffs' Legal Comm.*, 531 U.S. 341 (2001). Retrieved from https://supreme.justia.com/cases/federal/us/531/341/case.html.

Leagle. (2017). *Liu v. Boehringer Ingelheim Pharmaceuticals, Inc.* Retrieved from www.leagle.com/decision/infdco20170124b07.

Legal Dictionary. (n.d.-a). Product liability: Theories of liability. Retrieved from https://legal-dictionary.thefreedictionary.com/Theories+of+Liability.

Legal Dictionary. (n.d.-b). Preemption. Retrieved from https://legal-dictionary.thefreedictionary.com/preemption.

Legal Dictionary. (n.d.-c). Misrepresentation. Retrieved from https://legal-dictionary.thefreedictionary.com/misrepresentation.

Legal Information Institute. (n.d.-a). Products liability. Retrieved from www.law.cornell.edu/wex/products_liability.

Legal Information Institute. (n.d.-b). Uniform Commercial Code: § 2A-212. Implied Warranty of Merchantability. Retrieved from www.law.cornell.edu/ucc/2A/2A-212.

Legal Information Institute. (n.d.-c). Uniform Commercial Code: § 2A-213. Implied Warranty of Fitness Retrieved from www.law.cornell.edu/ucc/2A/2A-213.

Legal Information Institute. (n.d.-d). U.S. Constitution, Article VI. Retrieved from www.law.cornell.edu/constitution/articlevi.

Legal Information Institute. (n.d.-e). Preemption. Retrieved from www.law.cornell.edu/wex/preemption.

Legal Information Institute. (n.d.-f). 21 U.S.C. § 360k(a). Retrieved from www.law.cornell.edu/uscode/text/21/360k.

Liu v. Boehringer Ingelheim Pharmaceuticals, Inc., 230 F. Supp.3d 3, 8 (D. Mass. 2017).

Minerd, E. (2018, April). Express and implied preemption for premarket-approved medical devices: A dual shield against tort claims. *MED DEVICE Online*. Retrieved from www.meddeviceonline.com/doc/express-and-implied-preemption-for-premarket-approved-medical-devices-a-dual-shield-against-tort-claims-0001.

Mossinghoff, G. J. (1999). Overview of the Hatch-Waxman Act and its impact on the drug development process. *Food and Drug Law Journal, 54*,187–195.

National Coordinating Council for Medication Error Reporting and Prevention. (n.d.). What is a medication error? Retrieved www.nccmerp.org/about-medication-errors.

Overley, J. (2016). Bayer beats 1,200 suits over Mirena IUD injuries. Law360/Portfolio Media, Inc. @ www.law360.com (subscription required for Law360).

Riegel v. Medtronic, Inc., 552 U.S. 312 (2008).

Smith, C. (2012). The learned intermediary doctrine: Product liability/legal briefs. Retrieved from www.frostbrowntodd.com/resources-learned-intermediary-doctrine.html.

Sterling Drug, Inc. v Cornish, 370 F. 2d 82, 85 (8th Cir., 1966).

The American Law Institute. (1998). *Restatement of the Law, Third, Torts: Products Liability* (p. 14). Philadelphia, PA: The American Law Institute.

U.S. Chamber Litigation Center. (n.d.). U.S. District Court Southern District of New York, In Re: *Mirena IUD products liability litigation*. Retrieved from http://www.chamberlitigation.com/sites/default/files/cases/files/17171717/Opinion%20%26%20Order%20--%20In%20re%20Mirena%20IUD%20Products%20Liability%20Litigation%20%28USDC%20-%20Southern%20District%20of%20New%20York%29.pdf.

U.S. Court of Appeals. (2018). Appeal of Theodore F. Joas and Darlene A. Joas, No. 16–3957.

U.S. Food & Drug Administration. (2017a). 21 Code of Federal Regulations Title 21 § 201.56, 201.57. Retrieved from www.accessdata.fda.gov/scripts/cdrh/cfdocs/cfcfr/CFRSearch.cfm?CFRPart=201.

U.S. Food & Drug Administration. (2017b). Code of Federal Regulations Title 21 § 202 Prescription-drug advertisements. Retrieved from www.accessdata.fda.gov/scripts/cdrh/cfdocs/cfCFR/CFRSearch.cfm?CFRPart=202.

U.S. Food & Drug Administration. (2017c). Code of Federal Regulations Title 21 § 801 Labeling. Retrieved from www.accessdata.fda.gov/scripts/cdrh/cfdocs/cfcfr/CFRSearch.cfm?CFRPart=801.

U.S. Food & Drug Administration. (2017d). Code of Federal Regulations Title 21 § 801.4 Labeling: Meaning of intended use. Retrieved from www.accessdata.fda.gov/scripts/cdrh/cfdocs/cfcfr/CFRSearch.cfm?fr=801.4.

U.S. Food & Drug Administration. (n.d.-a). FDA Adverse Event Reporting System (FAERS) electronic submissions. Retrieved at www.fda.gov/drugs/guidancecomplianceregulatoryinformation/surveillance/adversedrugeffects/ucm115894.htm.

U.S. Food & Drug Administration. (n.d.-b). Class I/II Exemptions. Retrieved from www.fda.gov/MedicalDevices/DeviceRegulationandGuidance/Overview/ClassifyYourDevice/ucm051549.htm.

U.S. Food & Drug Administration. (n.d.-c). 510(k) submission process. Retrieved from www.fda.gov/MedicalDevices/DeviceRegulationandGuidance/HowtoMarketYourDevice/PremarketSubmissions/PremarketNotification510k/ucm070201.htm.

U.S. Food & Drug Administration. (n.d.-d). PLR requirements for prescribing information [21 CFR Subpart.201.56 and 201.57]. Retrieved from www.fda.gov/drugs/guidancecomplianceregulatoryinformation/lawsactsandrules/ucm084159.htm.

U.S. Food & Drug Administration. (n.d.-e). Medical product safety information. Retrieved from http://wayback.archive-it.org/7993/20170110235327/http:/www.fda.gov/Safety/MedWatch/SafetyInformation/default.htm.

U.S. Food & Drug Administration. (n.d.-f). FDA's drug review process. Retrieved from www.fda.gov/Drugs/ResourcesForYou/Consumers/ucm143534.htm.

U.S. Food & Drug Administration. (n.d.-g). Postmarketing surveillance programs. Retrieved from www.fda.gov/Drugs/GuidanceComplianceRegulatoryInformation/Surveillance/ucm090385.htm.

U.S. Food & Drug Administration. (n.d.-h). MAUDE—Manufacturer and User Facility Device Experience. Retrieved from www.accessdata.fda.gov/scripts/cdrh/cfdocs/cfmaude/search.cfm.

U.S. Food & Drug Administration. (n.d.-i). Drug Safety Labeling Changes (SLC). Retrieved from www.fda.gov/Safety/MedWatch/SafetyInformation/Safety-RelatedDrugLabelingChanges/default.htm.

U.S. Food & Drug Administration. (n.d.-j). Is the product a medical device? Retrieved from www.fda.gov/MedicalDevices/DeviceRegulationandGuidance/Overview/ClassifyYourDevice/ucm051512.htm.

U.S. Food & Drug Administration. (n.d.-k). Device classification panels. Retrieved from www.fda.gov/MedicalDevices/DeviceRegulationandGuidance/Overview/ClassifyYourDevice/ucm051530.htm.

U.S. Food & Drug Administration. (n.d.-l). When and why was FDA formed? Retrieved from www.fda.gov/AboutFDA/Transparency/Basics/ucm214403.htm.

U.S. Food & Drug Administration. (n.d.-m). Kefauver-Harris amendments revolutionized drug developments. Retrieved from www.fda.gov/forconsumers/consumerupdates/ucm322856.htm.

U.S. Food & Drug Administration. (n.d.-n). Milestones in U.S. food and drug law history. Retrieved from www.fda.gov/aboutfda/history/forgshistory/evolvingpowers/ucm2007256.htm.

U.S. Food & Drug Administration. (n.d.-o). Food and Drug Administration Amendments Act (FDAAA) of 2007. Retrieved from www.fda.gov/regulatoryinformation/lawsenforcedbyfda/significantamendmentstot   hefdcact/foodanddrugadministrationamendmentsactof2007/default.htm.

Ventola, C. L. (2011). Direct-to-consumer pharmaceutical advertising: Therapeutic or toxic? *Pharmacy and Therapeutics, 36*(10), 669–674, 681–684. Retrieved from www.ncbi.nlm.nih.gov/pmc/articles/PMC3278148/.

Wax, P. M. (1995) Elixirs, diluents, and the passage of the 1938 Federal Food, Drug and Cosmetic Act. *Ann Intern Med, 122,* 456–461.

Zimmer, NexGen Knee Implant Products Liability Litigation. Retrieved from http://media.ca7.uscourts.gov/cgibin/rssExec.pl?Submit=Display&Path=Y2018%2FD03-08%2FC%3A163957%3AJ%3ASykes%3Aaut%3AT%3AfnOp%3AN%3A2119394%3AS%3A0.

Additional Reading

American Law Institute. (n.d.). Publications: Restatement of the Law, Employment Law. Retrieved from www.ali.org.

DailyMed. (2017). Drug listing certification. Retrieved from https://dailymed.nlm.nih.gov/dailymed.

Electronic Code of Federal Regulations. (2018). 21 C.F.R. § 801 Labeling. Retrieved from www.ecfr.gov/cgi-bin/text-idx?SID=c76cbd1dcb862135a24a704b3664f67f&mc=true&node=pt21.8.801&rgn=div5.

FindLaw.com. (n.d.). Market share liability in DES and lead pigment cases: Bridging the gap: A suggested proposal to apportion liability in lead pigment cases. Retrieved from https://corporate.findlaw.com/litigation-disputes/market-share-liability-in-des-and-lead-pigment-cases-bridging.html.

FindLaw. (n.d.). The supremacy clause and the doctrine of preemption. Retrieved from https://litigation.findlaw.com/legal-system/the-supremacy-clause-and-the-doctrine-of-preemption.html.

Garner, B. A. (Ed.). (2014). Risk-utility test. *Black's law dictionary.* St. Paul, MN: Thomas Reuters.

LegalMatch. (n.d.). Failure to warn lawsuit—product liability. Retrieved from www.legalmatch.com/law-library/article/failure-to-warn-lawsuit.html.

Medical Device & Diagnostic Industry (MD+DI). (2017). Understanding a medical device manufacturer's broad duty to warn. Retrieved from www.mddionline.com/understanding-medical-device-manufacturer's-broad-duty-warn.

Owen, David G. (2007). The five elements of negligence. *Hofstra Law Review, 35*(4). Retrieved from http://scholarlycommons.law.hofstra.edu/hlr/vol.35/iss4/1).

Silvergate, S. (2015). The restatement (third) of torts products liability: The tension between product design and product warnings. Retrieved from www.thelaw.agency/products-liability/.

U.S. Food & Drug Administration. (n.d.). The impact of direct-to-consumer advertising. Retrieved from www.fda.gov/Drugs/ResourcesForYou/Consumers/ucm143562.htm.

U.S. Food & Drug Administration. (n.d.). Food and Drug Administration Amendments Act (FDAAA) of 2007. Retrieved from www.fda.gov/regulatoryinformation/lawsenforcedbyfda/significantamendmentstothefdcact/foodanddrugadministrationamendmentsactof2007/default.htm.

Test Questions

1. Product liability is generally governed by federal law? True or false:
   A. False
   B. True

2. In most jurisdictions, a plaintiff's cause of action may be based on one or more of these four theories: Negligence, Breach of Warranty, Misrepresentation, and Strict Tort Liability. Match the correct theory with the best explanation supporting that theory:
   ____Negligence
   ____Breach of Warranty
   ____Misrepresentation
   ____Strict Tort Liability
   A. refers to process of giving consumers false security about the safety of a product and may be done by drawing attention away from the hazard of its use—here, the key to recovery is the plaintiff attorney to prove that he relied upon the representations that were made
   B. the plaintiff's burden is less taxing under this type of theory than other theories, where fault must be shown
   C. a lack in the reasonable care in production, design or assembly of the product that caused harm—a duty-breach of that duty resulting in damages and a proximate cause
   D. refers to the failure of a seller to fulfill the terms of a promise, claim, or representation made concerning the quality or type of product—this can be either expressed or implied

3. When a manufacturer's "duty to warn" goes to the physician rather than the patient then the responsibility is on the physician to act as a _____ and will be expected to convey the labeling information to the patient that was provided by the manufacturer.
   A. Learned interpreter
   B. Informed consenter
   C. Informed labeler
   D. Learned intermediary

4. Which of these examples best describe a failure to warn claim?
   A. A cough syrup that does not include on its label a warning that it may cause dangerous side effects if taken in combination with another commonly taken drug such as aspirin
   B. A device manufacturing company learns of an unanticipated adverse event and completes its regulatory obligations with reporting to the FDA. The company investigates the adverse event and monitors for additional reports of similar adverse events
   C. A patient takes a medication for nausea and claims the medication made him extremely sleepy causing him to sleep through his alarm and subsequently he was late for work on three occasions. He was fired from his job for his consistent tardiness. The medication labeling listed that the drug may cause drowsiness, dizziness, and also warned against driving motor operating vehicles while taking the drug but did not list specifically that the drug could cause a deep sleep hence preventing an alarm to awaken you. Medical records indicated the patient also took more than the prescribed dose.

5. All statements are correct regarding FDA regulations, EXCEPT:
   A. The FDA regulates all prescription drugs and medical device labeling, but is not responsible for regulation of advertising materials from the manufacturing co.
   B. New drugs approvals focus on the safety and effectiveness of the drug uniformly whereas new device approvals focus on the risk/benefit ratio

C. While there is a voluntary reporting system by physicians and others, any time any adverse event or complaint in any form is reported to a manufacturer, this reportable event must be summarized and sent to the FDA within a specified timely manner—the FDA reviews and evaluates these reports provided by the manufacturing companies

D. ANY death or hospitalization related to a vaccine requires the physician to directly report this to the FDA

Answers: 1. A; 2. C, D, A, B; 3. D; 4. A; 5. A

Chapter 14

Evaluating Toxic Tort Cases

William P. Gavin, Esq.
Mark A. Love, Esq.
Wendie A. Howland, MN, RN-BC, CRRN, CCM, CNLCP®, LNCC®

Contents

Objectives

- List the common causes of action (claims) in a toxic tort claim
- State the difference between specific and general causation in toxic tort claims
- List common substances at issue in toxic tort claims
- Describe the legal nurse consultant's role in toxic tort claims

Introduction

The term "toxic tort" refers to any civil personal injury claim alleging an injury suffered as the result of exposure to an agent. These agents can be dusts (such as silica or asbestos), volatile organic solvents (such as benzene), or gases (such as chlorine or ammonia). Claimed injuries run the gamut from often-fatal cancers, non-malignant debilitating conditions, and fetal or fertility injury, to the need for future medical monitoring when no injury yet exists.

Most exposures are occupational. For example, there have been thousands of cases in which the plaintiff worked many years with asbestos, benzene, or silica and later was diagnosed with a cancer or disease, allegedly caused by these agents. Though somewhat less common, there are also claims related to environmental, home, and pharmaceutical exposures.

Toxic tort suits are filed throughout the United States in state and federal courts, with particularly heavy filings in Illinois, Pennsylvania, California, and Missouri. Some involve exposure to a single product with one or two defendants, but most have numerous defendants with complex litigation involving several different causes of action, products, and types of defendants. Toxic tort litigation also evolves constantly as new studies reveal agent toxicity, carcinogenicity, or relative safety.

Statute of Limitations in Toxic Torts

A claim for a toxic tort injury is governed by a statute of limitations requiring the injured party to file suit within a set time. Failure to timely file suit usually results in a suit being forever barred.

The limitations period will vary from state to state. Some states have an injury limitations period as long as six years[1] while others can be as short as one year.[2] The limitations period under the Federal Employers Liability Act (see below) is three years (45 USC § 56). Some states provide a different limitations period if the wrongful act causes death.

In a toxic tort action, the illness sometimes occurs long after first exposure, so the question arises: When does the limitations period begin to run? Most states and the Federal Employers Liability Act provide that the clock begins to run when the right to sue (known as a "cause of action") accrues.[3] Typically, this is when the injured party knows, or should know through the use of reasonable diligence, of an injury and that the wrongful conduct of another caused the injury.[4]

Medical records are an important source of information on the topic of when a plaintiff knew or should have known of an injury caused by another. The legal nurse consultant (LNC) can review the records to identify instances of when a plaintiff has given a history to a healthcare provider that supports or undermines an argument about when an injury or illness was first discovered.

Elements and Causes of Action

The specifics of pleading, and the elements of, a given cause of action can vary by jurisdiction, but generally, toxic tort claims at their core come down to strict product liability and negligence. In some venues, there are also claims for medical monitoring and fear of future conditions, chiefly cancer, as well as specific federal claims under the Federal Employers Liability Act (FELA) for railroad workers and the Jones Act (part of the Merchant Marine Act of 1920, which allows merchant sailors to bring claims directly against their employers).

Medical Monitoring and Fear of Cancer

Plaintiffs sometimes are confronted with a scenario in which they have been exposed to a toxic chemical or pharmaceutical in which there is no present apparent injury, but there could be harm in the distant future. Many toxic agents have long latency periods between exposure and future harm. For example, asbestos can cause cancer 40 years or more after exposure.

In light of potential future harms which may or may not occur, courts have recognized the need for economic damages for the plaintiff's costs related to medical examinations for early detection of potential harm (medical monitoring) and non-economic damages related to the concern felt by the plaintiff over the potential cancer that could be coming (fear of cancer).

The threshold to collect damages for medical monitoring varies by state, but generally it is met by showing that there was exposure to an agent, that exposure increased the risk of future harm, and that there are medical tests which can detect the harm early, allowing treatment.

The *Ayers v. Jackson Township* case in 1985 (*Ayers v. Jackson Township*, 493 A 2d 1314) and the California *Potter* case in 1993 (*Potter v. Firestone and Rubber Company*) established medical monitoring costs as a form of damages. Per the California Supreme Court in *Potter*, medical monitoring damages are available without a showing of a present injury, if it can be demonstrated "through reliable medical expert testimony, that the need for future monitoring is a reasonably certain consequence of a plaintiff's toxic exposure and that the recommended monitoring is reasonable."

Fear of cancer describes the present anxiety over developing cancer in the future. As discussed in *Potter*, "...a person's likelihood of developing cancer as a result of toxic exposure is difficult to predict because many forms of cancer are characterized by long latency periods (anywhere from 20 to 30 years), and presentation is dependent upon the interrelation of myriad factors."

Some courts have held that fear of cancer damages may be available if those fears are genuine and reasonable. Others, including *Potter*, have determined that fear of cancer damages are only available if there is reliable medical or scientific opinion that it is more likely than not that the toxic exposure will cause the plaintiff to develop the cancer in the future.

The Federal Employers Liability Act

The Federal Employers Liability Act, 45 USC §§ 51 et. seq., is a federal law which provides that a railroad employee injured in the course of employment may file suit and seek the full amount of the employee's damages. Typically, a work-related injury or disease suffered by an employee would be covered by workers' compensation laws and separately any liable non-employer parties. (See Chapter 15 for more information on workers' compensation.) However, FELA pre-empts state workers' compensation law; an employee covered by FELA has no right to state workers' compensation benefits.

The U.S. Supreme Court held that an occupational disease is an injury for the purposes of the FELA (*Urie v. Thompson*, 1949). Although FELA claims for occupational exposures date back to the first half of the twentieth century, such litigation burgeoned in the early 1980s when physicians and attorneys recognized the consequences of asbestos exposure in railroad repair shops. Early suits were primarily for asbestosis, but in the last two decades, claims for malignancies have become more common.

Under FELA, a railroad has a continuous non-delegable duty to provide a reasonably safe place in which to work (*Bailey v. Cent. Vermont Ry.*, 1943). "This continuous duty ... while measured by foreseeability standards, is broader under the [FELA] than a general duty of due care" (*Ackley v. Chicago & N.W. Transp. Co.*, 1987; *Ragsdell v. Southern P. Transp. Co.*, 1982). The duty to provide a reasonably safe place to work becomes more imperative as the risk to the employee increases (*Bailey*, 1943). The railroad employer must know the nature of the substances used in its business (*Del Raso v. Elgin, J. & E. Ry. Co.*, 1967; *Evinger v. Thompson*, 1954).

To recover under FELA, the employee must show that the railroad negligently breached its duty to provide a reasonably safe place to work. The trial must include evidence that the railroad knew or should have known that the agent at issue (e.g., asbestos) presented a risk of harm. An LNC could expect to assist attorneys to prepare this evidence by identifying and locating pertinent articles published in medical and occupational health literature.

The railroad's negligence need not be the only cause, a major cause, or even a significant cause of the alleged illness to impose liability on the railroad (*CSX Transportation, Inc. v. McBride*, 2011; *Rogers v. Missouri*, 1957). This principle is critically important, because most FELA toxic tort claims also involve exposures to injurious agent(s) related to lifestyle choices (principally smoking) and others outside of the worker's employment that combined with the work exposures to cause the injury.

The railroad industry is classified as heavy industry. In the steam era, railroads completely refurbished and repaired their rolling stock in their own locomotive shops. Many still perform heavy diesel repairs in diesel shops. There are many different jobs and activities in railroad employment, and therefore, other toxic exposures also occur in different circumstances. Railroad employment may involve past and present exposure to the following agents that have allegedly caused disease in railroad workers:

- Asbestos
- Silica
- Diesel fuel and exhaust

- Welding fumes
- Solvents (including chlorinated solvents and mineral spirits)
- Environmental tobacco smoke
- Herbicides and
- Creosote

The Jones Act

In 1920, the United States Congress adopted the Merchant Marine Act (46 USC § 30104). Included in the Act is a section, commonly referred to as "the Jones Act," which, in part, provides the right to file a lawsuit for damages against the employer of a vessel's crew member who is injured or killed in the course of employment. This section of the Jones Act incorporates the law governing suits by injured railroad workers (FELA). Accordingly, to recover under the Jones Act, the plaintiff must prove that the employer, or one of its agents, was negligent and that this negligence was a cause, in whole or in part, of the injuries.[5]

The Jones Act extends the FELA to sailors, so FELA provisions and court decisions apply to Jones Act suits. Toxic tort lawsuits against railroads are valuable precedent in a toxic tort suit brought by a sailor against an employer under the Jones Act.

Although case law under the Jones Act is extensive for traumatic injuries and death, toxic tort litigation has not been as active. However, damages have been sought for cancer and death caused by exposures to asbestos, benzene, and polycyclic aromatic hydrocarbons (*Bartel v. American Export Isbrandtsen*, 2014; *Wills v. Amerada Hess Corp*, 2004).

Like railroad workers, sailors work under a diverse set of conditions and can be exposed to toxic substances in many ways: emitted from cargo, port facilities, or vessels' components and fuels, for example. The issues in a Jones Act toxic tort suit are, broadly speaking, the same as the issues in an FELA toxic tort suit: (1) whether the employer negligently failed to provide a safe workplace place; and (2) whether the exposure to the toxic substance caused, in whole or in part, the alleged injury or death.[6]

Fear of Future Cancer in Federal Employers Liability Act Cases

In 2003, the Supreme Court of the United States ruled that an FELA plaintiff suffering from asbestosis, but not cancer, can legally recover damages for the fear of contracting cancer in the future from the exposure to asbestos which caused the asbestosis (*Norfolk & Western R. Co.*, 2003). The Supreme Court also ruled, however, that "It is incumbent upon such a plaintiff to prove that [the] alleged fear is genuine and serious." Since the Supreme Court's ruling, the question has been, "What evidence is sufficient to demonstrate 'genuine and serious' fear?"

Shortly after the Supreme Court's ruling, a lower court ruled that an FELA asbestosis plaintiff is not required to introduce evidence of objective physical or medical manifestations of the fear of future cancer (*Jones v. CSX Transp., Inc.* 2003). Subsequent FELA court decisions have centered on whether the trial court should instruct the jury on what to look for in the evidence to determine whether the alleged fear is genuine and serious[7] or whether the evidence the plaintiff has submitted is sufficient to meet the threshold of genuine and serious.[8]

Reported cases provide some insight as to what evidence will be sufficient. Courts appear to be suspicious and less convinced by vague statements such as, "I worry about getting cancer," etc. Testimony such as "[I] have some concern" about future cancer, "You ... think about it," or "I worry about it" have been held to be insufficient to establish a genuine and serious concern.[9]

The introduction of medical opinion testimony establishing the increased risk of cancer because of the exposures and underlying injury initially provides a basis for the jury to understand the magnitude of the risk of future cancer. Evidence that a plaintiff has consulted a personal physician about the prospects of future cancer, has undergone medical monitoring for the cancer, has sought counseling, and/or has been prescribed medication for the anxiety will then be much more persuasive.[10]

Jurisdiction Issues

A court must have jurisdiction over the subject matter and parties of a lawsuit to enter a valid binding judgment. A court's authority to rule on a particular subject matter (*subject* matter jurisdiction) is rarely an issue in toxic tort litigation. The issue of *personal* jurisdiction is more common.

Generally, when the party is a corporation,[11] the court has personal jurisdiction over the corporation when (1) it was incorporated in the state where the court is located; (2) the suit complains that it engaged in activities that allegedly caused harm in the state;[12] or (3) its business activities in the state are so substantial that the corporation is essentially at home.[13]

Causation

The complex, most hotly contested issue in toxic torts is causation. To recover, the plaintiff must prove that the alleged exposures caused the plaintiff's illness. The toxic tort defendant will usually contend that either the substance at issue does not cause the illness at issue or the alleged exposures did not cause the plaintiff's illness.

To prove causation, the plaintiff must introduce evidence that the substance causes the claimed disease in a population of humans. This is *general causation*. The plaintiff must then prove that the alleged exposures caused the plaintiff's illness. This is *specific causation*.

The parties in a toxic tort litigation will almost always present the opinion testimony of a retained expert witness or a treating physician to opine on the subjects of general and specific causation. Before such opinion testimony is admitted into evidence, however, the trial court must determine if the evidence is sufficiently reliable. There are several tests that courts in the United States apply to determine sufficient reliability. In the federal courts and in a majority of state courts, the test applied has become known as the *Daubert* standard (*Daubert v. Merrell Dow Pharmaceuticals*, 1995); another is known as the *Frye* standard (*Frye v. United States*, 1923). For more information on expert testimony reliability, see Chapter 36.

General Causation: Epidemiology

Epidemiology is a scientific discipline which, among other things, describes disease over time in specific populations, searches for hazardous factors affecting and influencing health in populations, and quantitatively estimates risks of specific diseases of persons exposed to hazardous factors. "Epidemiological studies examine existing populations to attempt to determine if there is an association between a disease or condition and a factor suspected of causing that disease or condition" (*Merrell Dow Pharmaceuticals v. Havner*, 1997). A study may show a positive, negative, or no association of a disease with a specific substance. All parties use epidemiological evidence to establish or refute a claim of general causation (Federal Judicial Center & National Research Council, 2011, p. 551). Epidemiology focuses on general causation, not specific causation.

Epidemiologists use several types of studies to determine whether an association exists between a disease and a suspected substance: experimental trials, cohort studies, case-control studies, and meta-analyses (Federal Judicial Center & National Research Council, 2011, pp. 555–556). Toxic tort expert witnesses most frequently rely on cohort studies, case-control studies, and meta-analyses published by others.

A cohort study compares the rate of disease in two groups of people—one exposed to the suspected substance and one not exposed to the substance (Federal Judicial Center & National Research Council, 2011, p. 557).

A case-control study also looks at two groups, one with the disease and one without the disease, to determine if an association exists between the past exposures and incidences of disease (Federal Judicial Center & National Research Council, 2011, p. 559).

Meta-analysis combines and analyzes the data from all comparable past available and relevant epidemiological studies to arrive at a single figure to represent all of the studies reviewed[14] (Federal Judicial Center & National Research Council, 2011, p. 581). The more studies included in the pooled data, the more reliable the meta-analysis.

While epidemiology may demonstrate the existence and strength of association between a substance and a disease, it cannot prove that a substance causes a specific disease. The strength of the association allows an inference as to whether a substance causes a disease by correlating the epidemiological evidence with what scientific knowledge an expert has on the subject (Federal Judicial Center & National Research Council, 2011).

The strength of an association between a substance and a disease is often expressed by epidemiologists as the *relative risk*. Relative risk is defined as the ratio of the incidence rate of disease in the exposed group to the incidence rate in the unexposed group: i.e., the incidence rate in the exposed group divided by the incidence rate in the unexposed group (Federal Judicial Center & National Research Council, 2011).

$$\text{Relative Risk} = \frac{\text{Incidence rate in the exposed}}{\text{Incidence rate in the unexposed}}$$

A relative risk of 1.0 means that the incidence rate in the exposed group is the same as the incidence rate in the unexposed group. To support a causal association between a substance and disease, the relative risk must be greater than 1.0 (Federal Judicial Center & National Research Council, 2011, pp. 566–567). The higher the relative risk, the more likely a substance causes the disease in a human population (Federal Judicial Center & National Research Council, 2011). Thus, a relative risk of 2.0 reflects a stronger association than a relative risk of 1.5. Some courts have established minimum relative risks that must be established to proceed with a case (*Merrell Dow Pharmaceuticals v. Havner*, 1997).

Since many diseases can have more than one cause, an epidemiological study reviewing the association between a substance and a specific disease must consider the impact of exposures to other causative agents (Federal Judicial Center & National Research Council, 2011, pp. 561–595). If an epidemiological study fails to do this, its conclusions may be suspect. For example, a study on lung cancer in asbestos-exposed workers that does not consider the impact of smoking may be considered flawed. Epidemiology alone does not establish general causation between a substance and disease. Determination of causation is a subjective judgment made by experts using different criteria, although relative risk is of great practical importance in the analysis.

Some experts use a *weight-of-the-evidence* analysis in deciding general causation. This analyzes the data from different scientific fields, primarily animal tests and epidemiological studies, to assess carcinogenic risks (*Magistrini v. One Hour Martinizing Dry Cleaning*, 2002). Supreme Court Justice Stevens stated that it cannot be "intrinsically 'unscientific' for experienced professionals to arrive at a conclusion by weighing all available scientific evidence" when the Environmental Protection Agency uses this methodology to assess risks (*General Electric Co. v. Joiner*, 1997).

Finally, in 1965, Sir Bradford Hill published an article listing what have become known as the "Bradford Hill criteria" to be used to determine causation between a substance and disease (Hill, 1965). The Bradford Hill criteria are:

- The temporal relationship between exposure and the onset of disease
- Strength of the association between the substance and the disease
- Dose-response between the exposure to the substance and the disease
- Replication of similar findings
- Biological plausibility between exposure and disease
- Consideration of alternative explanations
- Cessation of exposure
- Specificity of the association and
- Consistency with other knowledge (Federal Judicial Center & National Research Council, 2011, p. 600)

In toxic tort litigation, the Bradford Hill criteria are frequently applied to prove or refute general causation.

Specific Causation

Once there is sufficient evidence of general causation, the plaintiff's expert must opine that the plaintiff's exposures caused the disease. The specific causation expert typically employs the differential etiology method in formulating an opinion, identifying all known causes of the diagnosis, and ruling them in or out in the plaintiff's case (Federal Judicial Center & National Research Council, 2011, p. 617). Specific causation experts are commonly occupational medicine specialists or oncologists, less commonly PhD epidemiologists.

Epidemiology and medicine are often essential to toxic tort litigation. The methodologies and principles employed are complex and within the scope of expert witnesses.

Chemicals and Injuries at Issue in Toxic Tort Litigation

There is no way to provide an exhaustive list of all potential exposures or diseases. This is an ever-changing area, often on the leading edge of science. However, the following are among the more frequently filed, rare, or emerging types of claims.

Asbestos

The most commonly filed toxic tort claims relate to asbestos exposure. Asbestos includes two families of minerals, serpentine and amphibole, in widespread use until the early 1970s. The mineral fibers are heat resistant and were woven into cloth or used as a non-organic binding agent in insulation, plaster, drywall products, fireproofing, brakes, and gaskets. There were reports of workers in asbestos factories suffering from lung disease starting in the 1890s, though it was not until the 1960s that epidemiological studies began to show that even lower exposure levels by end users resulted in an increase in risk of disease.

Inhaled asbestos fibers can cause pulmonary fibrosis. At a sufficient lifetime dose level, asbestosis irreversibly restricts alveolar gas exchange and can also cause pleural cancer, called mesothelioma (Fritz, 2018). Mesothelioma occurs at lower doses than asbestosis and is almost always fatal. Additionally, asbestos exposure can cause lung cancer and has been linked in some studies with potentially increasing the risk of other cancers, including colon cancer and laryngeal cancer.

Organic Solvents/Benzene

Benzene is a volatile organic compound (VOC), a six-carbon ring that forms the basic structure for numerous other organic compounds such as gasoline, kerosene, and various historical cleaning agents. There are several other compounds that have benzene as a foundation (such as toluene and xylene) with different characteristics, but for purposes of this chapter, they are included in this category. Benzene is also found in smoke and diesel exhaust. Several studies have associated benzene exposure with an increased risk of leukemias and lymphomas (Agency for Toxic Substances and Disease Registry [ATSDR], n.d.).

Diesel Exhaust/Polycyclic Aromatic Hydrocarbons

Diesel exhaust is a complex mixture of particulate matter (soot), inorganic chemicals (e.g., nitrogen dioxide), and organic chemicals. The organic chemicals include many different kinds of polycyclic aromatic hydrocarbons (PAHs). Many of the chemicals found in diesel exhaust, including benzo(a)pyrene, are also found in cigarette smoke and environmental tobacco smoke. Some PAHs are recognized carcinogens. Likewise, some of the inorganic chemicals in diesel exhaust are pulmonary irritants. The PAHs in diesel exhaust are absorbed onto the soot in the exhaust. When inhaled, the smallest soot particles carry the PAHs to the alveoli.

That components of diesel exhaust cause disease has been the subject of study since at least 1775, when Sir Percival Pott, an English surgeon and the first to link an occupational exposure to cancer, demonstrated that young chimney sweeps had an increased rate of scrotal cancer due to their exposure to soot (containing PAHs) as they sat on chimneys to do their work. The advent of the diesel engine and the diesel era in the American railroad industry fueled continued research on diesel exhaust and its constituents throughout the 1900s.

The first known actual notice to the American railroad industry that diesel exhaust could be a carcinogen among railroad workers dates back to 1955, when Mr. Robert Straub, a general claims attorney for the Chesapeake & Ohio Railway Company, presented a paper entitled "Potential Dangers From Exposure To Diesel Locomotive Exhaust" to various claims representatives at a meeting of the General Claims Division of the Association of American Railroads (AAR), later published in a medical journal (Straub, 1955).

To support his presentation, Mr. Straub cited numerous scientific and industry publications.[15] His presentation to the railroad claims representatives accurately explained the constituents of diesel exhaust, including carcinogenic chemicals, and how respirable particles in diesel exhaust carry carcinogenic chemicals to the alveoli.[16]

Physicians employed by U.S. railroads continued to discuss the hazards of diesel exhaust at AAR meetings held in the 1960s, 1970s, and 1980s. Minutes from a 1965 meeting of the physicians list lung cancer as a possible illness caused by diesel exhaust.[17] Minutes from other AAR meetings show that the physicians renewed their discussions of the hazards of diesel exhaust in the 1980s after the publication of several epidemiological studies demonstrating an increased risk of lung cancer among railroad workers exposed to diesel exhaust.

In 1988, National Institutes for Occupational Safety and Health (NIOSH) issued Current Intelligence Bulletin 50, "Carcinogenic Effects of Diesel Exhaust," which notes "NIOSH recommends that whole diesel exhaust be regarded as 'a potential occupational carcinogen'..." This warning was based, in part, on medical studies in the 1980s that showed an elevated incidence of lung cancer among railroad workers (Garshick et al., 1987).

In 2002, the United States Environmental Protection Agency issued a report, "Health Assessment Document For Diesel Engine Exhaust," which concluded that diesel exhaust is "likely to be carcinogenic to humans by inhalation" (U.S. Environmental Protection Agency, 2002). This comprehensive report notes its conclusion is based on the totality of evidence from human, animal, and other supporting studies.

In 2012, the International Agency for Research on Cancer (IARC) concluded that diesel exhaust is a confirmed human lung carcinogen, placing it in the same category as asbestos and cigarette smoke.

Diesel exhaust has also been linked to bladder cancer, typically a urothelial transitional cell carcinoma. There is also some medical literature associating the PAHs in diesel exhaust to pancreatic and prostate cancers. Diesel exhaust has been further associated with heart disease, emphysema, asthma, and reactive airway disease.

Environmental Tobacco Smoke

Environmental tobacco smoke (ETS) is accepted as a human carcinogen. Over the last two decades, smoking in public places and workplaces has been strictly curtailed in response to the increasing acceptance of the risks of exposure. One state's laws (Illinois, 2016) contain this statement in the Act limiting smoking in public:

> [T]obacco smoke is a harmful and dangerous carcinogen to human beings and a hazard to public health. Secondhand tobacco smoke causes at least 65,000 deaths each year from heart disease and lung cancer according to the National Cancer Institute. Secondhand tobacco smoke causes heart disease, stroke, cancer, sudden infant death syndrome, low-birth-weight in infants, asthma and exacerbation of asthma, bronchitis and pneumonia in children and adults. Secondhand tobacco smoke is the third leading cause of preventable death in the United States. Illinois workers exposed to secondhand tobacco smoke are at increased risk of premature death. An estimated 2,900 Illinois citizens die each year from exposure to secondhand tobacco smoke.
>
> The General Assembly also finds that the United States Surgeon General's 2006 report has determined that there is no risk-free level of exposure to secondhand smoke; the scientific evidence that secondhand smoke causes serious diseases, including lung cancer, heart disease, and respiratory illnesses such as bronchitis and asthma is massive and conclusive...

The IARC recognizes ETS as a human lung carcinogen. Also, scientific literature shows workplace exposures to ETS have been implicated in other cancers and non-malignant diseases. There is evidence that the pollutants may cause:

- Coronary heart disease (U.S. Dept. of Health and Human Services [DHHS], 2006)
- Breast cancer (U.S. DHHS, 2006)
- Nasal sinus cancer (U.S. DHHS, 2006)
- Oropharyngeal cancer (Lee et al., 2008; Lee et al., 2009)
- Laryngeal cancer (IARC, 1979) and
- Pancreatic cancer (Vrieling et al., 2010)

The 2006 Surgeon General's report on "involuntary smoking" also contains this powerful statement:

> Active smoking is firmly established as a causal factor of cancer for a large number of sites including lung, urinary tract, upper aerodigestive tract, liver, stomach, pancreas, and many others. ... The absence of a threshold for carcinogenesis in active smoking, the presence of the same carcinogens in mainstream smoke and side stream smoke, and the demonstrated uptake of tobacco smoke constituents by involuntary smokers are compelling arguments for the hypothesis that secondhand smoke would increase the risk of cancer in other smoking-related sites in non-smokers.

The constituents of cigarette smoke have been well known since the Surgeon General published a report on smoking in 1967 entitled "The Health Effects of Smoking." Cigarette smoke contains numerous carcinogenic chemicals including PAHs (e.g., benzo(a)pyrene), N-nitrosamines, polonium 210, selenium, and phenols) (United States Department of Health, Education and Welfare, 1967).

In 1979, the Centers for Disease Control/NIOSH issued Current Intelligence Bulletin 31, entitled "Adverse Health Effects of Smoking and the Occupational Environment." This bulletin concerns smoking tobacco products in the workplace but also addresses "any by-products from their burning and/or use." The bulletin states:

> Smoking can interact with worker exposure to toxic materials found in the workplace resulting in more severe health damage than that anticipated from adding the separate influences of the occupational exposure and smoking. Asbestos provides one of the most dramatic examples of severe health damage resulting from interaction between the smoking of tobacco products and workplace exposures.

In 1986, the United States Surgeon General issued the report "The Health Consequences of Involuntary Smoking." The report states in its summary, "Involuntary smoking is a cause of disease, including lung cancer in healthy nonsmokers. The simple separation of smokers and non-smokers may reduce, but does not eliminate, the exposure of nonsmokers to environmental tobacco smoke" (U.S. Department of Health and Human Services, 1986).

In 1991, NIOSH issued Current Intelligence Bulletin 54, "Environmental Tobacco Smoke in the Workplace: Lung Cancer & Other Health Effects." The bulletin states:

> NIOSH therefore recommends that ETS be regarded as a potential occupational carcinogen in conformance with the [Occupational Safety and Health Administration]

carcinogen policy, and that exposures to ETS be reduced to the lowest feasible concentration. Employers should minimize occupational exposure to ETS by using all available preventive measures.

Federal Employers Liability Act lawsuits against railroad employers asserting ETS injuries have become more common in recent years. Typically, a transportation employee, such as an engineer or conductor, will allege an ETS-related injury as a result of spending many years in a locomotive cab with smoking co-workers. Office workers were also among the classes of railroad employees exposed to ETS daily.

Welding Fumes

Welding is a common process by which metal is fused, most commonly by manual electric arc, which produces an arc of electricity between an electrode and the metal. Temperatures created by the arc range between 3,000 and 4,000 degrees centigrade, causing the electrode and the metal to melt and fuse.

The electrode, also known as a welding rod, is held in a device sometimes known as a "stinger," which is connected to an electric power source. The arc is created by touching the tip of the rod against the metal being welded and moving it along the joint.

Welding rod composition varies, because it must be compatible with the metal. Most modern rods are coated with a material known as *flux*, which also melts during the process to form a cone around the weld. The cone of molten flux excludes atmospheric gases that could contaminate and weaken the weld, and it also strengthens the weld. Flux composition varies greatly but often contains silicates, fluorides, borates, aluminum, cadmium, and chromium.

The welding process produces fumes; their composition and quantity depend on the rods and metal used. Generally, however, fumes often contain cadmium, iron, zinc, lead, chromium, nickel, manganese, copper, and silicates (Beaumont and Weiss, 1981). In a claim involving welding, the composition of both the rods used and the metals welded must be investigated (Sjögren et al., 1991).

Numerous studies have identified an increased risk of lung cancer among welders.[18] According to one, "it is clear that welders have relatively high lung cancer risk" (Beaumont and Weiss, 1981). However, studies have not gone so far as to identify a specific carcinogen. A study published in 2017 states, "An excess lung cancer risk among welders is well established, but whether this is attributable to welding fumes is unclear" (MacLeod, Harris, Tjepkema, Peters, & Demers, 2017). This may be due to the wide range of substances that may be in the fumes or confounding factors in subjects. Known lung carcinogens have been identified in these fumes.[19]

Welding fume exposure is also associated with the following non-malignant diseases or conditions.

Siderosis is an accumulation of iron particles in the lungs. The particles are inhaled in the form of iron oxide, produced from the melting metal core. Most of the particles are absorbed by macrophages and transported to the lymphatic system. Lung biopsies, however, have shown iron particles in the alveoli and bronchioles (Artfield and Ross, 1978). Siderosis can be seen in chest x-rays (Doing and McLauglin, 1936). The changes resemble silicosis and are usually seen as nodular densities throughout the entire lung field, with the heaviest concentrations seen in the middle third of the lungs.

Metal fume fever is a temporary condition characterized by cough, chest pain, a feeling of pressure in the chest, fever, malaise, and nausea. It has been associated with inhaling fluorides, cadmium, chromium, and zinc (Fuortes, Leo, Ellerbeck, & Friell, 1991).

Pulmonary edema is linked to exposure to welding fumes (Morely and Silk, 1970). In the 1920s and 1930s, a number of deaths from pulmonary edema were reported, particularly among welders who worked in closely confined spaces. This was caused by exposure to ozone and nitrogen peroxide gases created when the welding arc comes into contract with air (Doing and McLauglin, 1936).

Obstructive airway disease has also been associated with exposure to welding fumes. It has been postulated that toxic gases and particles stimulate change in pulmonary cells, narrowing or distorting the airways (Kilburne and Warshaw, 1989).

Talc

Talc is a soft mineral made up mainly of magnesium, silicon, and oxygen. Talcum powder is widely used in cosmetics and baby powder. Chemically, it is similar to asbestos, though it does not come in an asbestiform fiber shape. However, talc is often found near tremolite asbestos.

Individuals with long-term and heavy inhalation exposure to talc, such as talc miners, have been known to develop pulmonary talcosis, a form of pulmonary fibrosis caused by breathing in talc dust. Such individuals are also at an increased risk of lung cancer. This is also seen in heroin inhalation when talc is used as an adulterant.

Most cases focus on talc's asbestos content. Cosmetic-grade talc is asbestos-free, though this is a contentious issue in talc-asbestos cases, particularly in cases related to talc exposure from decades ago. Plaintiffs have contended that manufacturers of talc-containing products did not control for or remove asbestos from products such as aftershave powders and baby powders, which the manufacturers deny.

Johnson & Johnson lost several significant verdicts since 2016 in a series of cases in which women argued they contracted ovarian cancer as a result of using talcum powder products, contending that talc applied genitally migrated to the ovaries and caused chronic inflammation. Generally, animal and epidemiological studies have found no increase in risk of ovarian cancer, or a small increase in risk in a few studies. According to the American Cancer Society, "For an individual woman, if there is an increased risk, the overall increase is likely to be very small" (American Cancer Society, 2017). A jury in an October 2018 Johnson & Johnson case concluded that talcum powder was not responsible for a plaintiff's mesothelioma (Bronstad, 2018).

Scleroderma

Scleroderma[20] is not a single disease but a group of a chronic connective tissue disorders which cause the abnormal growth of connective tissue supporting skin and organs. Collagen deposition causes thickening of the skin and potentially musculoskeletal changes and changes to the viscera, especially the lungs, heart, kidneys, and gastrointestinal tract (Bovenzi, Barbone, Betta, Tommasini, & Versini, 1995).

In localized scleroderma, changes are limited to the skin and sometimes the muscle beneath and do not spread to internal organs. Localized scleroderma can be patchy on the chest, stomach, or back (morphea) or down an arm or leg (linear scleroderma). Localized scleroderma often improves over time, but its effects are permanent, including potential disability (U.S. Department of Health and Human Services, 2017).

Systemic sclerosis affects the skin, subcutaneous tissue, blood vessels, and potentially the heart, lungs, kidneys, and gastrointestinal tract (Diot et al., 2002). A less serious form of systemic sclerosis develops gradually and typically affects only the fingers, hands, face, lower arms and legs. This limited form of systemic sclerosis is characterized by calcium deposits in the connective tissues, Raynaud's syndrome, esophageal dysfunction, thickened and tightened skin on the fingers, and erythema on the face and hands (U.S. Department of Health and Human Services, 2017).

Diffuse scleroderma may make it difficult to bend fingers, hands, and other joints. There can be inflammation of the joints, tendons, and muscles. Facial skin involvement can cause microstomia. The skin can lose or gain pigment, making areas of light or dark skin. Some people lose hair on the limbs, sweat less, and develop dry skin because of damage to hair follicles and sweat glands (Johns Hopkins Sclerodoma Center, 2018). Diffuse systemic sclerosis typically occurs relatively suddenly. Thickening of the skin begins in the hands and spreads symmetrically over the body.

Scleroderma was first associated with the dusty trades in 1914 (Bramwell, 1914). Later studies have associated silica exposure, with and without silicosis, with scleroderma (Diot et al., 2002; NIOSH, 2002; Sluis-Cremer, Hessel, Nizdo, Churchill, & Zeiss, 1985). The Occupational Safety and Health Administration (OSHA), in its final rule on silica, stated, "OSHA finds, based on the best available evidence in the published, peer reviewed, scientific literature, that exposure to respirable crystalline silica increases the risk of … autoimmune effects."[21] In a relatively recent meta-analysis, silica was found to be one of the two most likely substances related to the pathogenesis of systemic sclerosis (Rubio-Rivas, Moreno, & Corbella, 2017).

Solvents have been associated with the risk of developing systemic sclerosis.[22] The solvents implicated include tri-chloroethylene (TCE), tetra-chloroethylene (perchloroethylene), other chlorinated solvents, and white spirits (mineral spirits). Other organic chemicals including vinyl chloride, toluene, ketones, and aromatic hydrocarbons have been associated with scleroderma (Marie et al., 2014). Studies have also considered welding fumes (Diot et al., 2002; Magnant et al., 2005), diesel exhaust nanoparticles (Mastrofrancesco et al., 2014), and air pollution as potential occupational exposures associated with scleroderma (Farhat et al., 2011).

Research Sources

Litigating causation necessarily involves identifying and reviewing the epidemiological evidence. There are many sources for this, including international agencies, agencies in the United States, textbooks, and medical journals.

International Agency for Research on Cancer

The IARC, part of the World Health Organization and located in Lyon, France, is one of the most respected sources on carcinogenicity because of its independence and carcinogen classification methodology. Periodically, IARC brings scientists together to study the world's literature on whether substances are associated with cancer, subsequently issuing a monograph categorizing them as follows:

- ■ Group I—Carcinogenic to humans
- ■ Group 2A—Probably carcinogenic to humans
- ■ Group 2B—Possibly carcinogenic to humans
- ■ Group 3—Not classifiable as to its carcinogenicity to humans or
- ■ Group 4—Not carcinogenic to humans

An IARC monograph is valuable, because it contains a comprehensive review of animal, biologic, and human data on the association of an agent with cancer. Their conclusions are often of great importance to expert witnesses opining on general and specific causation. To date, IARC has published more than 120 monographs which have evaluated the carcinogenic risk to humans of many different agents including asbestos, diesel exhaust, silica, organophosphate insecticides and herbicides, nanomaterials, chlorinated solvents, tobacco smoking, and involuntary smoking (World Health Organization, 2018).

Agency for Toxic Substances and Disease Registry

The Agency for Toxic Substances and Disease Registry (ATSDR), based in Atlanta, GA, is a federal public health agency of the U.S. Department of Health and Human Services. It is tasked with protecting communities from harmful health effects related to natural and man-made hazardous substances. The ATSDR is directed by Congress to perform specific functions concerning the effect of hazardous substances on public health, including health consultations concerning specific hazardous substances and the development and dissemination of information. The ATSDR contains an index of many potentially hazardous substances, toxicological profiles, and related studies (ATSDR, 2018).

National Institute for Occupational Safety and Health

The National Institute for Occupational Safety and Health, part of the U.S. Centers for Disease Control and Prevention (CDC), is a federal research agency established by the Occupational Safety and Health Act of 1970 to study worker safety and health and to empower employers and workers to create safe and healthy workplaces. The NIOSH is sometimes described as the research agency that supports the work of OSHA.

Like ATSDR, NIOSH lists many chemicals and provides information about them on its website and in its publications. This information includes toxicity, target organs, chemical properties, handling suggestions, and exposure limits and is supported with citations to published scientific data.

In 1975, NIOSH began issuing the "Current Intelligence Bulletin" to inform the public on matters of public health. For example, in 1979, NIOSH published Current Intelligence Bulletin 31, entitled "Adverse Health Effects of Smoking and the Occupational Environment," which recommended that employers curtail the use of tobacco in the workplace where employees may be exposed to other substances that would interact with the tobacco smoke. The Current Intelligence Bulletins are supported with detailed scientific literature citations and are often used in toxic tort litigation as evidence of what was known or could have been known about the hazards of a particular substance or activity. Most of the Current Intelligence Bulletins are available from the NIOSH website (NIOSH, 2017).

Occupational Safety and Health Administration

The OSHA regulates the safety and health of workplaces in America by promulgating administrative regulations. When OSHA adopts a regulation, it publishes it and its scientific basis in the Federal Register.[23] Typically, OSHA describes its findings on health risks posed by a regulated substance with supportive scientific references. For example, the Final Silica rule states, "OSHA finds that employees exposed to respirable crystalline silica at the preceding PELs (permissible exposure limits) are at an increased risk of lung cancer mortality…"[24] The OSHA publications are a valuable resource and are themselves often used to show the standard of care required by employers.

PubMed

The PubMed website states that

> PubMed comprises over 28 million citations for biomedical literature from MEDLINE, life science journals, and online books. PubMed citations and abstracts include the fields of biomedicine and health, covering portions of the life sciences, behavioral sciences, chemical sciences, and bioengineering. PubMed also provides access to additional relevant web sites and links to the other [National Center for Biotechnology Information] molecular biology resources.[25]

Most online search engines will usually lead to references on the substance being investigated. These references can often be followed to the supporting scientific literature.

Emerging Issues

Genetics and Genetic Testing

Humans have 23 pairs of chromosomes, with a set coming from each parent. Chromosomes carry the genetic data—the genes—that code for the various building blocks of the body, made up of deoxyribonucleic acid (DNA). Deoxyribonucleic acid is made up of adenine, cytosine, thymine, and guanine in dedicated pairs: adenine-thymine and cytosine-guanine. Since chromosomes are paired, there should be a gene copy (allele) from each parent on each chromosome.

The sequencing of DNA has gotten cheaper and more efficient. Individual genetic data can now be examined to assess for gene mutations, which could give rise (or susceptibility) to diseases known to be caused by toxic exposure. To date, it appears that humans have about 20,000 genes. However, sometimes a switch occurs that affects coding for a gene, changing or eliminating its function. The changes can cause inherited genetic disease (such as cystic fibrosis) or potentially increase disease risks.

This prompts an interesting question: If a plaintiff suffering from cancer has a rare genetic mutation associated with an increased risk for that cancer, does that provide a defense (i.e., was that the cause, not the claimed toxic exposure?), or does it just mean that plaintiff's threshold for exposure was much lower (i.e., an "eggshell skull" plaintiff)? In the matter of *Easter v. Aventis Pasteur, Inc.* (2005), plaintiff claimed that the mercury-containing agent in a vaccine caused plaintiff's autism. Genetic testing performed in that case failed to find a susceptible mutation.

Breast Cancer Associated Protein 1 in Asbestos Litigation

Mesothelioma is a rare cancer of the lining of the lung closely associated with asbestos. Breast Cancer (BRCA) Associated Protein 1 (BAP1) is a tumor and metastasis suppressor gene discovered in 2011 (Testa et al., 2011). The scientific evidence showed that mesothelioma (and several other cancers) were common in individuals carrying a germline mutation of this gene. Two scientists who co-published on this genetic mutation discovery signed competing declarations in the first asbestos case in which this issue was raised as a defense (*Ortwein v. CertainTeed Corporation*, 2016). The case settled during trial, but the main question that would have been put to the jury is,

Does the presence of the BAP1 mutation in the germline of a plaintiff with mesothelioma mean that the individual was just highly susceptible to getting mesothelioma from a much lower than expected level of asbestos exposure, or does the presence of the mutation cause the cancer in the absence of any asbestos exposure?

Ultimately, defendants may be able to use the presence of mutations to argue genetic susceptibility (or as a complete cause of plaintiff's harm), but plaintiffs may be able to argue that an exposure to a lower than expected dose of a toxic agent was the cause of their harm because of their susceptibility. Litigators will need to consider what mutations may lurk in a plaintiff's genes, and how—or whether—genetic testing will impact a case.

Glyphosate—An Emerging Toxic Tort

In August 2018, a jury in San Francisco returned a verdict of $289 million against Monsanto. Plaintiff DeWayne Johnson was diagnosed with lymphoma following years of working as a groundskeeper with Monsanto's Ranger Pro herbicide. The primary agent in Ranger Pro and Monsanto's Roundup is glyphosate, which plaintiff's counsel contended was associated with an increased risk of lymphoma, pointing to a 2015 study that found a link. Monsanto argued the numerous studies that found no link were evidence that glyphosate was not carcinogenic. Bayer, which purchased Monsanto in May 2018 and discontinued its name, reported that it was facing 8,700 such lawsuits over its glyphosate-based weed killers (Allen, 2018).

The Legal Nurse Consultant's Role

Serious injuries or occupational illnesses with prolonged treatment usually produce thousands of pages of hospital, provider, and other records. Identifying all of the providers and analyzing the records for important evidence and medical issues is a challenge. In addition to reviewing initial records at case outset, a legal nurse consultant may be asked to:

- Identify, obtain, and review additional materials needed, e.g., medical, occupational, and educational records
- Assist the attorney to determine whether an individual meets stated criteria for inclusion in a class action (when multiple claimants make the same or similar allegations against a single defendant). Inclusion requires all members of the class to have a common legal or factual (e.g., medical) issue that is central to case resolution (Larkin & McGuiness, 2014).
- Identify case strengths and weaknesses based upon medical information collected
- Explain indications, methods, and normal findings of various medical procedures
- Locate medical literature that pertains to the issue at hand or merit
- Evaluate evidence for alleged exposure to the substance based on:
  a. The patient's medical presentation
  b. Occupational site clinic visits
  c. Safety Data Sheets (formerly "Material Safety Data Sheets") and
  d. Employee training records
- Produce chronological summaries
- Evaluate possible causation and damages, including consideration of
  a. Permissible dosage/exposure limits

b. Mitigating factors and
c. Alternative causation/exposures
▪ Identify the types of experts indicated for a given type of case, and contact, screen, and engage experts in consultation with the attorney. These experts may include:
a. Medical specialists: Oncology/hematology, dermatology, neurology, pulmonology, hepatorenal, cardiology, and psychology/neuropsychology
b. Toxicology: physician with board certification in toxicology, reproductive toxicologist (PhD or MD/DO), and risk management/occupational toxicology and
c. Epidemiology: environmental/occupational

Other non-medical experts may be indicated and will likely be located by other members of the legal team. Such non-medical experts may include regulatory expert, hydrologist, materials scientist, health physicist (if radiation is involved), industrial hygienist, geologist, meteorologist, and others.

The following is a representative entry from an LNC's chronology in a hypothetical occupational cancer case:

R. Jones, age 58, DOB 3/6/1960
ABC Company
Mesothelioma, diagnosed 5/6/2016, metastases

Table 14.1

Date/Time	Bates #	Fact Text (verbatim)	LNC's Comments
11/11/2016 03:00 p.m.	000123–5	**Mercy VNA Hospice Nursing Visit – J. Doe, RN** Next Visit Date: 11/14/2016 Plan: Assess, observe, symptom management Narrative: Patient is sitting in recliner. Lungs are diminished. Appetite is very poor; took only a few spoons of soup at lunch. Spouse is very tired and frustrated. Assurance given—spouse is doing a very good job caring for patient. Their child is coming tonight and will help care for the patient tonight. Med pack in the home. Taking sublingual morphine 40mg every three to four hours for pain. PPS 40%.	PPS = Palliative Performance Scale, a measure of physical status used in palliative care and hospice Criteria for 40%: Mainly in bed. Unable to do any work, extensive disease. Care done mainly by others. Oral intake normal to reduced. Level of consciousness may be full, drowsy, or confused. Change from PPS 60% in mid-October (Bates # 000085–6) indicates rapid decline. Sublingual liquid morphine indicates patient is too ill to swallow pills.

This single line item, one of many in a comprehensive chronology, provides counsel with several important pieces of information: it identifies potential witnesses (Nurse Doe, the spouse, the child) who can testify about the damages the plaintiff experienced as a result of the illness, describes aspects of the plaintiff's pain and suffering, and defines and explains terms that may be unfamiliar to the attorney (PPS).

A plaintiff or defense firm may retain an independent legal nurse consultant to testify as an expert fact witness. Expert fact witness testimony is an effective way to present a complicated history of treatment to a jury chronologically, explaining the multiple healthcare provider roles, test results, and other actions simply and clearly. In this role, the LNC may only explain the contents of the medical records; an expert fact witness may not offer opinions.

For more information on the LNC's role and other concepts in this chapter, see the following:

- Sources of Medical Information, Chapter 7
- Access to Medical Records, Chapter 8
- The Expert Fact Witness, Chapter 32
- Researching Medical Literature and Other Information, Chapter 34
- Report Preparation, Chapter 35 and
- Locating, Screening, and Communicating with Expert Witnesses, Chapter 36

Summary

Toxic tort cases require many of the same skills LNCs use in other cases: performing record reviews and literature research, developing chronologies and demonstrative evidence, clarifying terminology, and identifying and working with testifying experts. However, the LNC without previous experience in toxicology, occupational health and hygiene, or class actions may discover that these challenging cases come with a steep learning curve. Asking the right questions and using specialized resources to research unfamiliar legal and medical elements, such as those outlined in this chapter, will be fundamental to the LNC's success.

Notes

1. Maine and North Dakota.
2. Tennessee, Kentucky, and Louisiana.
3. See e.g. *Nolan v. Johns-Manville Asbestos*, 85 Ill.2d 161, 171, 52 Ill. Dec. 1, 421 N.E.2d 864 (1981) and *Urie v. Thompson*, 337 U.S. 163, 69 S.Ct. 1018 (1949).
4. See e.g. 735 ILCS 13/213(d) (2014).
5. *Ribitzki v. Canmar Reading & Bates, Ltd. Partnership*, 111 F.3d 658 (9th Cir., 1997), amended on denial of rehearing, amended on rehearing 1997 WL 34580081.
6. For a more in-depth discussion of toxic tort litigation under the Jones Act and general maritime law see L. Keefe & M. Warren, Toxic Exposure Litigation Under the Jones Act and the Longshore Harborworkers' Compensation Act, *Tort & Insurance Law Journal*, Vol. 24, No. 3 (Spring 1989) pp. 691–701.
7. *Hedgecorth v. Union Pacific R.R. Co.* 210 S.W.3d. 220 (Mo. Ct. App., E. D. 2006) and *Hensley v. CSX Transp., Inc.*, 278 S.W.3d. 282 (Tn. Ct. App. 2008), appeal denied, (Tn. 2008), cert. granted, rev'd, 129 S. Ct. 2139 (2009), rev'd, and new trial on damages only ordered, 2009 WL 2615849 (Tenn. Ct. App. 2009).
8. In *Asbestos Products Liability Litigation v. CSX Transp., Inc.*, 2013 WL 1628165 (E. D. Pa. 2013); *Aldrich v. CSX Transp., Inc.*, 2007 WL 9709703 (S. D. Ga. 2007); *Seaford v. Norfolk Southern, Ry. Co.*, 150 Ohio App. 3d 374, 824 N.E.2d 94 (2004); and *Cohn v. Diamond Offshore Management Co.*, 2003 WL 21750661 (E. D. La. 2003) (a Jones Act decision).

9. In Asbestos Products Liability Litigation, 2013 WL 1628165 at *3 and Seaford, 824 N.E.2d at 111.
10. See e.g. *Blackburn v. Illinois C. R.R., Co.*, 882 N.E.2d 189 (5th. Dist. 2008), appeal denied, 889 N.E.2d 1114 (Ill. 2008), cert. denied, 129 S. Ct. 497 (2008).
11. Most issues of personal jurisdiction in toxic tort litigation concern the defendant, which is most often a corporation.
12. *Goodyear Dunlop Tires, S. A. v. Brown*, 564 U.S. 915, 919, 131 S. Ct. 2846, 2851 (2011) and *Helicopteros Nacionales de Colombia, S. A. v. Hall*, 466 U.S. 408, 414, 104 S. Ct. 1868, nn. 8, 9 (1984). See also e.g. 735 ILCS 5/2–209 (2016).
13. Goodyear, 564 U.S. at 919. See also *BNSF Ry. Co. v. Tyrrell*, 137 S. Ct. 1549 (2017).
14. See also In re Bextra and Celebrex Marketing Sales Practice, 524 F. Supp. 2d 1166 (N.D. Cal. 2007).
15. Bailey, C. L., Javes, A. R., & Lock, J. K. (1959, January). 13. Investigations into the composition of diesel engine exhausts. In *5th World Petroleum Congress.* World Petroleum Congress. Henderson, U, (1943). *Noxious gases and the principles of respiration influencing the action* (New York, NY: Reinhold Publishing Corp.). Kotin, P., Falk, H. L., & Thomas, M. (1955). Aromatic hydrocarbons. III. Presence in the particulate phase of diesel-engine exhausts and the carcinogenicity of exhaust extracts. *Arch. Indust. Health, 11*(2), 113–20. H. H. Schrenk (1941). Composition of diesel engine exhaust gas, *Am. J. Public Health and Nation's Health*, 669.
16. Mr. Straub's presentation can be found in the minutes of the General Claims Division's Sixty-Sixth Annual Meeting held on May 4–6, 1955, compiled and maintained by the Association of American Railroads, pp. 63–72.
17. Minutes from the 1965 Forty-Fifth Meeting of the Medical and Surgical Section of the Association of American Railroads March 3, 4 & 5, 1965, pp. 151–153.
18. See Stern (1987). See also Becker, Chang-Claude, and Frentzel-Beyme (1991).
19. See Hull et al. (1989) and Morgan and Seaton (1984).
20. From the Greek words, sclerosis and derma, which taken together mean "hard skin."
21. Fed. Reg. March 25, 2016: Vol. 81, No. 58, pg. 16285, 16300.
22. Bovenzi, Barbone, Betta, Tommasini, & Versini (1995); Diot et al. (2002); Cooper, Makris, Nietert, & Jinot (2009); Kettaneh et al. (2007); Nietert et al. (1998).
23. See, e.g., Occupational Exposure to Crystalline Silica; Final Rule, 81 Fed. Reg. 58: 16285–890, March 25, 2016.
24. Occupational Exposure to Crystalline Silica; Final Rule, 81 Fed. Reg. 58: 16285, 16287, March 25, 2016.
25. www.ncbi.nlm.nih.gov/books/NBK3827/#pubmedhelp.PubMed_Quick_Start.

References

Ackley v. Chicago & N.W. Transp. Co., 820 F.2d 263, 267 (8th Cir. 1987).

Agency for Toxic Substances and Disease Registry. (2018). Toxic substances. Retrieved from www.atsdr.cdc.gov/toxicsubstances.html.

Agency for Toxic Substances and Disease Registry. (n.d.). Benzene: Health effects. Retrieved from www.atsdr.cdc.gov/toxprofiles/tp3-c3.pdf.

Allen, N. (2018). Bayer's Monsanto: 8,700 lawsuits over glyphosate. Retrieved from www.marketwatch.com/story/bayers-monsanto-8700-lawsuits-over-glyphosate-2018-09-05.

American Cancer Society. (2017). Talcum powder and cancer. Retrieved from www.cancer.org/cancer/cancer-causes/talcum-powder-and-cancer.html.

Artfield, M. D., & Ross, D. S. (1978). Radiological abnormalities in electric-arc welders. *Occupational and Environmental Medicine, 35*(2), 117–122.

Ayers v. Jackson Township, 493 A 2d 1314 (N.J. Super. Ct. App. Div. 1985).

Bailey v. Cent. Vermont Ry., 319 U.S. 350, 352–53 (1943).

Bartel v. American Export Isbrandtsen, 64 F.Supp. 3d 856 (M. D. La. 2014).

Beaumont, L. I., & Weiss, N. S. (1981). Lung cancer among welders. *Journal of Occupational and Environmental Medicine, 23*(12), 839–844.

Becker, N., Chang-Claude, J., & Frentzel-Beyme, R. (1991). Risk of cancer for arc welders in the Federal Republic of Germany: Results of a second follow up (1983–8). *Occupational and Environmental Medicine, 48*(10), 675–683.

Bovenzi, M., Barbone, F., Betta, A., Tommasini, M., & Versini, W. (1995). Scleroderma and occupational exposure. *Scandinavian Journal of Work, Environment & Health, 21*(4), 289–292.

Bramwell, B. (1914). Diffuse sclerodermia: Its frequency; its occurrence in stone-masons; its treatment by fibrolysin—Elevations of temperature due to fibrolysin injections. *Edinburgh Medical Journal, 12*(5), 387.

Brondstad, A. (2018). Johnson & Johnson wins verdict in New Jersey talcum powder trial. Retrieved from www.law.com/njlawjournal/2018/10/11/johnson-johnson-wins-verdict-in-new-jersey-talcum-powder-trial/.

Cooper, G. S., Makris, S. L., Nietert, P. J., & Jinot, J. (2009). Evidence of autoimmune-related effects of trichloroethylene exposure from studies in mice and humans. *Environmental Health Perspectives, 117*(5), 696–702.

CSX Transportation, Inc. v. McBride, 131 S. Ct. 2630 (2011).

Daubert v. Merrell Dow Pharmaceuticals, 516 U.S. 869 (U.S. 1995).

Del Raso v. Elgin, J. & E. Ry. Co., 84 Ill. App. 2d. 344, 228 N.E.2d. 470, 479 (1967).

Diot, E., Lesire, V., Guilmot, J. L., Metzger, M. D., Pilore, R., Rogier, S., ... & Lasfargues, G. (2002). Systemic sclerosis and occupational risk factors: A case–control study. *Occupational and Environmental Medicine, 59*(8), 545–549.

Doing, A. T. & McLaughlin, A. I. G. (1936, April 4). X-ray appearance of the lungs of electric arc welders. *Lancet*, 771–775.

Easter v. Aventis Pasteur, Inc. (358 F. Supp 2d 576 (E.D. Tex. 2005).

Evinger v. Thompson, 265 S.W.2d. 726, 731 (Mo. 1954).

Farhat, S. C., Silva, C. A., Orione, M. A. M., Campos, L. M., Sallum, A. M., & Braga, A. L. (2011). Air pollution in autoimmune rheumatic diseases: A review. *Autoimmunity Reviews, 11*(1), 14–21.

Federal Employers Liability Act 45 USC §§ 51 et. seq.

Federal Judicial Center, & National Research Council (U.S.). (2011). *Reference manual on scientific evidence*. Washington, DC: National Academies Press.

Fritz, R. A. (2018). Pathological diagnosis of malignant mesothelioma. *The Journal of Legal Nurse Consulting, 29*(1), 36–41.

Frye v. United States, 293 F. 1013 (D.C. Cir. 1923).

Fuortes, L., Leo, A., Ellerbeck, P. G., & Friell, L. A. (1991). Acute respiratory fatality associated with exposure to sheet metal and cadmium fumes. *Journal of Toxicology: Clinical Toxicology, 29*(2), 279–283.

Garshick, E., Schenker, M. B., Muñoz, A., Segal, M., Smith, T. J., Woskie, S. R., ... & Speizer, F. E. (1987). A case-control study of lung cancer and diesel exhaust exposure in railroad workers. *American Review of Respiratory Disease, 135*(6), 1242–1248.

General Electric Co. v. Joiner, 522 U.S. 136, 153–54, 118 S. Ct. 512, 139 L. Ed. 2d 508 (1997) (Stevens, J., concurring).

Hill, A. B. (1965). The environment and disease: Association or causation? *Proc R Soc Med., 58*(5), 295–300.

Hull, C. J., Doyle, E., Peters, J. M., Garabrant, D. H., Bernstein, L., & Preston-Martin, S. (1989). Case-control study of lung cancer in Los Angeles County welders. *American Journal of Industrial Medicine, 16*(1), 103–112.

Illinois; 410 ILCS 82/5 (2016).

International Agency for Research on Cancer. (1979). Some halogenated hydrocarbons. IARC monographs on the evaluation of the carcinogenic risk of chemicals to humans, 20.

Johns Hopkins Scleroderma Center. (2018). Types of scleroderma. Retrieved from www.hopkinsscleroderma.org/scleroderma/types-scleroderma/.

Jones v. CSX Transp., Inc., 337 F.3d 1316, 1317 (11th Cir., 2003).

Kettaneh, A., Al Moufti, O., Tiev, K. P., Chayet, C., Tolédano, C., Fabre, B., ... & Cabane, J. (2007). Occupational exposure to solvents and gender-related risk of systemic sclerosis: A metaanalysis of case-control studies. *The Journal of Rheumatology, 34*(1), 97–103.

Kilburn, K. H., & Warshaw, R. H. (1989). Pulmonary functional impairment from years of arc welding. *The American Journal of Medicine, 87*(1), 62–69.

Larkin, J. D., & McGuiness, A. J. (2014). Class actions 101: What every solo practitioner needs to know. Retrieved from www.americanbar.org/groups/litigation/committees/class-actions/articles/2014/summer 2014-0814-class-action-basics-what-every-solo-practitioner-needs-to-know/.

Lee, Y. C. A., Boffetta, P., Sturgis, E. M., Wei, Q., Zhang, Z. F., Muscat, J., ... & Zaridze, D. (2008). Involuntary smoking and head and neck cancer risk: Pooled analysis in the International Head and Neck Cancer Epidemiology Consortium. *Cancer Epidemiology and Prevention Biomarkers, 17*(8), 1974–1981.

Lee, Y. C. A., Marron, M., Benhamou, S., Bouchardy, C., Ahrens, W., Pohlabeln, H., ... & Bencko, V. (2009). Active and involuntary tobacco smoking and upper aerodigestive tract cancer risks in a multicenter case-control study. *Cancer Epidemiology and Prevention Biomarkers, 18*(12), 3353–3361.

MacLeod, J. S., Harris, M. A., Tjepkema, M., Peters, P. A., & Demers, P. A. (2017). Cancer risks among welders and occasional welders in a national population-based cohort study: Canadian census health and environmental cohort. *Safety and Health at Work, 8*(3), 258–266.

Magistrini v. One Hour Martinizing Dry Cleaning, 180 F. Supp. 2d 584 (D.N.J., 2002).

Magnant, J., de Monte, M., Guilmot, J. L., Lasfargues, G., Diot, P., Asquier, E., ... & Diot, E. (2005). Relationship between occupational risk factors and severity markers of systemic sclerosis. *The Journal of Rheumatology, 32*(9), 1713–1718.

Marie, I., Gehanno, J. F., Bubenheim, M., Duval-Modeste, A. B., Joly, P., Dominique, S., ... & Lagoutte, P. (2014). Prospective study to evaluate the association between systemic sclerosis and occupational exposure and review of the literature. *Autoimmunity Reviews, 13*(2), 151–156.

Mastrofrancesco, A., Alfè, M., Rosato, E., Gargiulo, V., Beatrice, C., Di Blasio, G., ... & Fiorito, S. (2014). Proinflammatory effects of diesel exhaust nanoparticles on scleroderma skin cells. *Journal of Immunology Research*.

Merchant Marine Act 46 USC § 30104.

Merrell Dow Pharmaceuticals v. Havner, 953 S.W. 2d 706, 715 (Tex. 1997).

Morgan, W. K., & Seaton, A. (1984). *Occupational lung diseases* (2nd edn., pp. 346, 669–670). Philadelphia, PA: W.B. Saunders.

Morley, R., & Silk, S. J. (1970). The industrial hazard from nitrous fumes. *Annals of Occupational Hygiene, 13*(2), 101–107.

National Institute for Occupational Safety and Health. (1979). Current Intelligence Bulletin 31: Adverse health effects of smoking and the occupational environment. Retrieved from www.cdc.gov/niosh/docs/79-122/.

National Institute for Occupational Safety and Health. (1988). Current Intelligence Bulletin 50: Carcinogenic effects of diesel exhaust. Retrieved from www.cdc.gov/niosh/docs/88-116/.

National Institute for Occupational Safety and Health. (1991). Current Intelligence Bulletin 54: Environmental tobacco smoke in the workplace: lung cancer and other health effects. Retrieved from www.cdc.gov/niosh/docs/91-108/default.html.

National Institute for Occupational Safety and Health. (2002). Health effects of occupational exposure to respirable crystalline silica. Retrieved from www.oem.msu.edu/images/abrasive_blasting/Appendix%20IV%20-%20NIOSH%20Silica%20Health%20Effects%2002-129pd.pdf.

National Institute for Occupational Safety and Health. (2017). Current intelligence bulletins. Retrieved from www.cdc.gov/niosh/pubs/cib_date_desc_nopubnumbers.html.

Nietert, P. J., Sutherland, S. E., Silver, R. M., Pandey, J. P., Knapp, R. G., Hoel, D. G., & Dosemeci, M. (1998). Is occupational organic solvent exposure a risk factor for scleroderma? *Arthritis & Rheumatism: Official Journal of the American College of Rheumatology, 41*(6), 1111–1118.

Norfolk & Western R. Co. vs. Ayers, 123 S. Ct. 1210, 1223 (2003).

Ortwein v. CertainTeed Corporation, No. RG13701633 (Alameda County, CA, 2016).

Potter v. Firestone and Rubber Company, 6 Cal 4th 965 (1993).

Ragsdell v. Southern P. Transp. Co., 688 F.2d 1281, 1283 (9th Cir. 1982).

Rogers v. Missouri P. R.R. Co., 352 U.S. 500 (1957).

Rubio-Rivas, M., Moreno, R., & Corbella, X. (2017). Occupational and environmental scleroderma: Systematic review and meta-analysis. *Clinical Rheumatology, 36*(3), 569–582.

Sjögren, B., Bäckström, I., Fryk, G., Jakobsson, R., Milerad, E., Plato, N., & Tornling, G. (1991). Fever and respiratory symptoms after welding on painted steel. *Scandinavian Journal of Work, Environment & Health*, 441–443.

Sluis-Cremer, G. K., Hessel, P. A., Nizdo, E. H., Churchill, A. R., & Zeiss, E. A. (1985). Silica, silicosis, and progressive systemic sclerosis. *Occupational and Environmental Medicine, 42*(12), 838–843.

Stern, R. M. (1987). Cancer incidence among welders: Possible effects of exposure to extremely low frequency electromagnetic radiation (ELF) and to welding fumes. *Environmental Health Perspectives, 76*, 221–229.

Straub, R. (1955). Potential dangers from exposure to diesel locomotive exhaust. *Indust. Med. & Surgery, 24*(8), 353–358.

Testa, J. R., Cheung, M., Pei, J., Below, J. E., Tan, Y., Sementino, E., ... & Hesdorffer, M. (2011). Germline BAP1 mutations predispose to malignant mesothelioma. *Nature Genetics, 43*(10), 1022.

Urie v. Thompson, 337 U.S. 163, 188–95 (1949).

U.S. Department of Health, Education and Welfare. (1967). The health consequences of smoking; A public health service review. Retrieved from https://profiles.nlm.nih.gov/ps/access/NNBBKM.pdf.

U.S. Department of Health and Human Services. (1986). The health consequences of involuntary smoking: A report of the Surgeon General. Retrieved from https://profiles.nlm.nih.gov/ps/access/nnbcpm.pdf.

U.S. Department of Health and Human Services. (2006). The health consequences of involuntary exposure to tobacco smoke: A report of the Surgeon General. Retrieved from www.surgeongeneral.gov/library/reports/secondhandsmoke/fullreport.pdf.

U.S. Department of Health and Human Services. (2017). Limited systemic sclerosis. Retrieved from https://rarediseases.info.nih.gov/diseases/9749/limited-systemic-sclerosis.

U.S. Environmental Protection Agency. (2002). Health assessment document for diesel engine exhaust. Retrieved from https://cfpub.epa.gov/ncea/risk/recordisplay.cfm?deid=29060.

Vrieling, A., Bueno-de-Mesquita, H. B., Boshuizen, H. C., Michaud, D. S., Severinsen, M. T., Overvad, K., ... & Kaaks, R. (2010). Cigarette smoking, environmental tobacco smoke exposure and pancreatic cancer risk in the European Prospective Investigation into Cancer and Nutrition. *International Journal of Cancer, 126*(10), 2394–2403.

Wills v. Amerada Hess Corp., 379 F.3d 32 (2d. Cir., 2004).

World Health Organization. (2018). IARC monographs on the evaluation of carcinogenic risks to humans. Retrieved from https://monographs.iarc.fr/agents-classified-by-the-iarc.

Additional Reading

Beasley, C., & Oldham, R. (2017). Case analysis: Toxic tort. In *AALNC Legal nurse consulting professional course* (module 12). Retrieved from www.aalnc.org/page/course-content#packages.

Kaufman, C. (2011). Life care planning for the cancer patient. *JNLCP, XI*(4), 519–535.

Lopez, K. (2013). 10 key expert witnesses to consider in your next toxic tort case. Retrieved from www.a2lc.com/blog/bid/66199/10-key-expert-witness-areas-to-consider-in-your-next-toxic-tort-case.

MSDSonline, SDS/MSDS Search. (n.d.). Online search for safety data sheets. Retrieved from www.msdsonline.com/msds-search/.

Paget-Bailly, S., Cyr, D., & Luce, D. (2012). Occupational exposures to asbestos, polycyclic aromatic hydrocarbons and solvents, and cancers of the oral cavity and pharynx: A quantitative literature review. *International Archives of Occupational and Environmental Health, 85*(4), 341–351.

Palliative Care Network of Wisconsin. (2017). Fast facts and concepts #53, sublingual morphine. Retrieved from www.mypcnow.org/blank-vghoc.

Villeneuve, P. J., Johnson, K. C., Mao, Y., & Hanley, A. J. (2004). Environmental tobacco smoke and the risk of pancreatic cancer: Findings from a Canadian population-based case-control study. *Canadian Journal of Public Health/Revue Canadienne de Santé Publique*, 32–37.

Yuan, J. M., Wang, X. L., Xiang, Y. B., Gao, Y. T., Ross, R. K., & Yu, M. C. (2000). Non-dietary risk factors for nasopharyngeal carcinoma in Shanghai, China. *International Journal of Cancer, 85*(3), 364–369.

Test Questions

1. Toxic torts are:
   A. Civil claims of injury resulting from exposure to an agent
   B. Criminal actions brought against employers by OSHA
   C. Dependent on future medical monitoring for cancer
   D. Related to definite temporal relationship with exposure
2. Epidemiology:
   A. Appraises the effects of toxic hazards on the health of individuals
   B. Can address general causation of exposure-related disease
   C. Makes qualitative estimates of risk of disease after toxic exposure
   D. Relies on meta-analysis to prove causation related to a toxic exposure
3. Relative risk:
   A. Determines the Bradford Hill criteria for validation of similar findings
   B. If less than 1.0 supports a causal relationship between substance and disease
   C. Is the strength of association between a substance and a disease
   D. Uses a weight-of-the-evidence analysis to decide general causation
4. The Federal Employers Liability Act (FELA), related to railroads, and the Jones Act, related to sailors:
   A. Are subject to state worker's compensation statutes and regulations
   B. Must prove that employer negligence cannot be the sole cause of illness
   C. Permit employers to delegate the duty to provide a safe workplace
   D. Require an employer to know about all substances used in its business
5. The LNC's role in a toxic tort claim includes everything EXCEPT:
   A. Identify industrial hygiene expert
   B. Evaluate causation issues
   C. Evaluate all possible exposures
   D. Identify relevant medical literature

Answers: 1. A, 2. B, 3. C, 4. D, 5. A

Chapter 15

Workers' Compensation Case Evaluation

Victoria Powell, RN, CCM, LNCC®, CNLCP®, CLCP, CBIS, CEASII

Contents

Objectives

- Describe five underlying principles of the workers' compensation system
- List the workers' compensation benefits provided to the employee or injured worker
- Discuss the role of the legal nurse consultant (LNC) in assisting with causation in workers' compensation claims
- Compare the plaintiff and defense LNC roles in workers' compensation claims
- Describe the role of the LNC in catastrophic injury claims

History of Workers' Compensation

The Industrial Revolution began the transformation of the workforce from agrarian to industrial. The workers' compensation system developed in response to dangerous work environments using newly invented production machinery. At the time, common law held an employer responsible for worker injury or death only if caused by a negligent event, and injured employees or their survivors would have to bring suit to establish employer negligence. This was difficult and out of reach of most employees. Frequently, injured workers did not prevail and never received compensation for injuries sustained during employment. With no compensation, the burden for the expense of medical treatment, as well as wage loss, became the responsibility of the injured worker's family and friends.

The centralization of manufacturing in huge factories and mass product shipping by railroad and steamship increased the demand for workers. However, workers found themselves at greater risk for injury. Machinery, with its exposed fast-moving parts and the crowded conditions in factories, made for a more dangerous work environment. Catastrophic injuries and work-related deaths rapidly increased (Devenny & Morgan, 2008).

The increased risk of injury to workers could have affected the rapid progress of the Industrial Revolution. As injuries to workers increased, workforce reduction slowed production. For example, when railroad injuries increased, transportation of goods was delayed, straining the industrial supply chain.

Maryland passed the first workers' compensation legislation in 1902. In 1906, federal law covered all federal employees, and by 1949, all states had some form of workers' compensation plan in place (Mullahy, 2014). Today, all 50 states and several United States territories have workers' compensation laws. Congress has enacted legislation to cover federal workers in several different programs (Powell & Tahan, 2008). See Appendix A for more information on workers' compensation laws.

In 1908, as a result of increasing railroad injuries, President Theodore Roosevelt pushed Congress to pass the Federal Employer's Liability Act (FELA). This act, still in existence today, created legislation allowing injured workers to sue the employer without the traditional common law employer defenses regarding proof of negligence (Devenny & Morgan, 2008).

Finally, in 1911, after the Triangle Shirtwaist Factory fire in New York City killed more than 100 workers including women and children, states began passing legislation providing benefits for the injured worker without regard to employer fault (no-fault system). By 1948, each state had adopted workers' compensation legislation giving the injured worker medical and wage replacement benefits (Devenny & Morgan, 2008). All jurisdictions require either a state industrial board or an insurance commissioner to approve coverage contracts. Most states require insurance coverage, but there are some states that allow employer self-insurance coverage for their employees. Federal legislation was enacted to cover federal workers in several different programs with benefits similar to those found in workers' compensation.

In the 1970s, the Insurance Company of North America, which later merged with Connecticut General Corporation to become CIGNA, developed an in-house rehabilitation nurse program. The nurses' role then is familiar today: assisting the worker to reach maximum medical recovery and managing treatment, equipment, lost time, and the employee/employer relationship to save money.

In the 1980s, workers' compensation insurance carriers and employers realized they could save money and get their employees back to work quicker while reducing costs. As states began to write rehabilitation benefits into their statutes, the need for medical and later vocational services increased.

Case management expanded tremendously. However, the cost of medical care began to skyrocket as providers came to view an injured worker as a blank check. There were no cost or service controls. In the first efforts to control medical costs, states instituted mandatory fee schedules (approved fees for medical care).

Group health carriers began to develop programs incorporating billing review, second opinion requirements, and pharmacy management. Many states improved efforts to manage work-related medical costs; workers' compensation carriers began adopting some of the same strategies developed and implemented by group health carriers.

The industry continues to improve cost management by using LNCs in many roles for complex cases. The LNC works for insurance carriers, national or regional case management companies, or in independent practice. Some LNCs are employed directly by legal firms; however, this is uncommon unless a firm handles more than one line of business.

Basic Principles of the Workers' Compensation System

Workers' compensation insurance is designed to indemnify injured workers (compensate them for lost wages) and provide medical benefits to them for injuries sustained during employment. An effective workers' compensation program should also promote safety and accident prevention.

While each state has its own individual statutes, there are certain common basic principles. Administration of the workers' compensation program falls under state, not federal, jurisdiction. All injured workers are entitled to prompt payment of benefits, such as medical, indemnity for lost work time, vocational benefits, catastrophic injury care, and death benefits. Compensability is addressed by individual states outlining what constitutes an injury or a disease to be covered. Lastly, workers' compensation is meant to be the exclusive remedy; no other carrier is involved.

No-Fault System

Workers' compensation insurance is no-fault; that is, it eliminates fault as a basis of recovery. Under state workers' compensation systems, the injured worker gives up the right to bring a tort claim against the employer after a work injury, regardless of fault or negligence. In return for relinquishing the right to sue the employer for negligence, the injured employee is guaranteed insurance coverage for medical and wage benefits. This decreases legal costs, lessens the judicial load of personal injury cases, and relieves demand on public and private financial and medical services. The result avoids treatment delays, and the employer avoids damages from a lawsuit. In the event of death, benefits are paid to the worker's dependents (Devenny & Morgan, 2008).

Administration of Workers' Compensation Laws by the State

Generally, workers' compensation claims are settled through a quasi-judicial system, with the courts serving an appellate function. In a few states, courts conduct initial administration of claims. Where the state's administration is not under the court, it is usually under the control of an industrial accident commission or labor and industry board. For example, the state of Louisiana has an Office of Workers' Compensation Court within the Louisiana Department of Labor that is a "statewide court having jurisdiction of claims for workers' compensation benefits, the controversion of entitlement to benefits, and other relief under the workers' compensation act" (Louisiana Government, 2008). Texas, on the other hand, eliminated its administrative commission known as the Texas Workers' Compensation Commission and placed administrative function in a division under the Texas Department of Insurance. New rulings and administrative hearings were set up to provide easier access and administration of the Texas workers' compensation acts (Texas Department of Insurance, 2013).

The labor boards or commission usually resolve disputes, and their decisions are binding. Appeals may follow if there is a question of law.

General Information on Benefits and Limits

State-specific workers' compensation statutes define the statutory benefits for medical payments, indemnity, and disability if injured workers are unable to return to their former job because of injury. These statutes include time limits and access requirements for treatment and payment, reimbursement for out-of-pocket costs, amount and duration of wage replacement, and how a qualified professional determines temporary and permanent impairment or disability. As stated previously, these rules are all state-specific.

Medical Benefits

Each state decides how to choose a treating physician, use second opinions, and determine when to end benefits. For example, in Arkansas, the insurance carrier can direct medical care to the physician specialist of its choice. The carrier can request an independent medical examination (IME) or second opinion as a pre-condition for any questionable procedure or diagnostic test.

The state regulates who assigns impairment ratings and how, and the number of weeks the worker is to receive benefits.

Some states, such as Texas, provide lifetime medical benefits (Texas Department of Insurance, 2013). Of course, there is a trade-off: a worker cannot settle for future medical benefits. Therefore, the injured worker does not need to hire an attorney. Limiting or eliminating attorney representation becomes a significant factor for legal firms and may limit workers' compensation practice in these states.

Indemnity for Time Lost from Work

Benefits for wage loss are typically a percentage of a worker's average weekly or monthly wage, usually 66.67% or more (Popow, 2011). Waiting periods (e.g., a waiting period of 7 consecutive days or 14 cumulative days before indemnity begins) and retroactive payment of loss wages vary by state. It is also important to know whether the average weekly wage includes overtime benefits or not, and how long a retroactive period applies. Indemnity may also be capped by statute.

Injured workers often seek legal counsel when unable to obtain indemnity for lost wages or if they receive incorrect amounts. It is important to understand how to calculate the average weekly wage as well as communicate waiting periods, retroactive payment of lost wages, and so on.

Vocational Benefits

States may or may not provide a statutory vocational training benefit if the injured worker becomes disabled from the previous work activity. Vocational rehabilitation may be voluntary if a state has its own vocational rehabilitation program.

Catastrophic Injury, Impairment, and Death Benefits

Catastrophic injuries usually result in permanent impairment and disability. Usually, the injured worker does not return to former work activities, because functional capacity is limited. Common catastrophic injuries for workers include spinal cord injury with paralysis, brain injury with cognitive and functional losses, upper or lower extremity amputation, and toxic exposure resulting in chronic respiratory problems.

Workers' compensation also provides for inpatient and outpatient rehabilitation, occupational services, durable medical equipment, home and vehicle modifications, long-term residential placement, and caregiver services, if deemed necessary. Benefits for catastrophic injuries can be very complex and expensive.

Workers' compensation also pays a death benefit in the case of fatality. Burial insurance and benefits are available to minor dependents in most jurisdictions. The LNC should be familiar with the applicable statutory death benefits in order to provide families with knowledgeable counsel.

Compensability: Injuries and Diseases Covered

Compensability refers to whether an injury is eligible for coverage. Although workers' compensation is required by every state for workplace injuries, neither all injuries and diseases nor all workers are covered. Compensability must be determined and accepted by the employer and the insurance carrier in order for the employee to receive workers' compensation benefits. This may require analysis of the relationship between the mechanism and timing of injury. Both accidental injury and occupational disease are compensable.

The term "accident" refers to an unanticipated or unexpected and unforeseeable event that occurs as a result of employment work duties during time of employment. An accidental injury, usually termed an "incident," has a defined time, place, and description of the mechanism of injury. Most states' workers' compensation acts contain the phrase "injury by accident" or "accidental injury." Some states have omitted the requirement that the injury be accidental in order to be compensable (National Federation of Independent Business, 2017). The LNC should be familiar with the law and regulations in the applicable jurisdiction.

There are several ways to determine the cause of an injury besides interpretation of a strict accidental event. For instance, a worker who bends over repetitively in the course of job duties to pick up cases of soda may someday suffer a herniated disc. The herniation of a lumbar disc may be unforeseeable or accidental, but the activities of repetitive bending over to pick up a case of soda are not. One could argue the employee's activities were not an "accident"; therefore, the injury may not be compensable. This distinction illustrates why it is important to understand the statutes in the particular jurisdiction where the injury occurs.

Occupational diseases, on the other hand, cannot always be defined by a specific time of when the disease began nor a specific place where the disease occurred, but they still must meet certain criteria to be compensable. All states deem compensable a disease that occurs as the result of causes and conditions characteristic of and peculiar to a particular trade, occupation, or employment, e.g., black lung in miners. Diseases to which the general public are equally exposed without regard to employment are called "ordinary diseases of life" and are not compensable. In fact, compensability decisions of most occupational diseases are scrutinized on the basis of whether or not they are distinguished from ordinary diseases of life (Popow, 2011).

Compensability decisions may also rest on whether the job exposure to a disease or condition places the worker at greater risk than the general population. For example, a nurse who has never had chickenpox may be at higher risk by working in a pediatric clinic compared with nurses who do not care for pediatric patients. Thus, the occupational disease does not result exclusively from the job but does place the employee at a greater risk than the general population. However, the distinction between increased risk from occupational exposure and risk of ordinary diseases of life may be arguable if the relationship is questionable.

Some occupational diseases have clearly been established as related to higher exposure risk, e.g., asbestosis, silicosis, lead poisoning, mercury poisoning, and latex allergy. Other exposures will need to be thoroughly investigated for compensability.

Other occupational diseases may be attributed to repetitive motion or cumulative trauma, such as carpal tunnel syndrome caused by repetitive grasping, twisting, flexing of the wrist, and other movements. Obviously, these injuries must have a clearly established relationship to job activities.

Determining the onset of cumulative trauma can be difficult but is vital to determining whether a current or previous employment is responsible. Sometimes the *last injurious exposure rule*, defined as the last (most recent) employment where activities of the job could have caused the disease or condition, determines onset (Popow, 2011). For example, even if a new employee performed similar job activities in a previous job, a current employer may be responsible for providing workers' compensation benefits for a new claim of cumulative trauma. This is because the new employee's current job activities provided the most recent exposure to the cumulative trauma injury.

Other states define cumulative trauma as an occupational disease, determining onset by the date the symptoms first appeared or the date the physician made the employee aware of the diagnosis. Obviously, the current employer would not be responsible for providing benefits in a situation where the diagnosis was known before hire. The LNC should be aware of the applicable jurisdictional statute.

Mental injury, stress, and hernia claims may have distinct compensability rules. Mental injury claims vary widely; some states require proof of an associated physical injury with a mental injury, and some states do not address mental injury at all. Hernias generally have associated rules for compensability that limit the occurrence to specific incidents such as lifting. These injuries are usually given other specific requirements, such as pain at the time of lifting, no pre-existing protrusion or rupture, and exertion. Benefit time may be limited to six weeks in some states.

Exclusive Remedy

Workers' compensation coverage is intended as the injured worker's *exclusive remedy*. This eliminates money and punitive damages for pain and suffering related to a compensable injury. As workers' compensation is no-fault, this applies even if the injured worker is at fault.

Two exceptions to the no-fault exclusive remedy rule are intentional tort actions (e.g., assault and battery in the workplace) and third-party cause of injury (e.g., a plumber injured by another vehicle while driving to the work site). In the latter example, the plumber will have both a civil tort claim against the other vehicle's negligent driver and a workers' compensation claim. A worker injured by defective equipment at a worksite can also bring a liability claim against the equipment's manufacturer. Generally, the workers' compensation carrier will have a subrogation interest against the damage awards of the third-party tort claim. This prevents double recovery by the injured worker and properly places the cost of the accident on the third party.

Causation

The LNC in a worker's compensation case may assist with the determination of causation. As with medical malpractice and personal injury claims, causation is an essential element in determining if a case is going to be assessed for damages. Case managers in workers' compensation may or may not be able to address causation depending on their particular jurisdiction guidelines.

The Employment Relationship

Each state specifically outlines the employee–employer relationship. For an injury to be compensable, the injured worker must be an employee of the employer. This seems obvious but is sometimes difficult to prove.

Several criteria define the employment relationship, such as control, consent, and consideration or wage exchange for services. Workers' compensation will not cover a volunteer offering services without regard to compensation. An independent contractor, not controlled in terms of how, when, and where work is performed, is not a covered employee when working for another business. Domestic workers and farm workers are often exempt. In many states, company owners can exempt themselves from coverage though they must cover their employees.

Arising Out of and In the Course of Employment

The critical phrase used in workers' compensation statutes is that the injury must *arise out of and in the course of employment.* For benefits to be granted, an injury must occur during the course of the injured worker's employment and while the injured worker is engaged in employment work activities. Both requirements must be met in most workers' compensation statutes. Exceptions depend on the state's rules and statutes, which may have redefined the original principle of arising out of and in the course of employment.

The LNC's reliable source for explanation for any state statute is the insurance adjuster and attorney with whom the LNC works. There are also several Internet sites that give access to the complete statutes, rules, and regulations of each state (see Appendix B). These sites are invaluable when dealing with jurisdictional differences and understanding their application to a particular claim.

"Arising out of employment" concerns the cause of the injury, which is different from *proximate cause* used in tort claims for determining causation. In workers' compensation claims, cause is based on the association with employment and its level of risk.

For example, a cocktail waitress working at a hotel restaurant in a city with a high crime rate may be at higher risk for sexual assault. If a sexual assault should occur in the hotel's public restroom, the employee can claim a compensable work injury even though not performing work duties in the scope of employment at the time of the assault. The court will rule that the assault arose out of employment, because the employment exposed the employee to a higher risk of crime (Jones, 1998).

Another example is the case of a worker who dies of a sudden cerebral vascular accident (CVA) at work. The death of the worker did not arise out of employment because the individual's medical illness existed regardless of employment. The CVA was not a result of employment; it was coincidental and could have occurred anywhere at any time with any activity. When there are very difficult medical issues regarding the exact nature of an injury that appears to arise out of employment, the assistance of an LNC is valuable.

"But for the Employment"

The important concept of *but for* the employment can guide determination of causation. If the injury or condition is the same to which the general public is exposed, *but for* certain aspects of employment, the injury or condition is considered a result of employment. An employee, after running errands for an employer, was caught in a thunderstorm. The employee was electrocuted by a fallen electrical wire upon stepping out of the car. The employee was not engaged in employment activities at the time, and the storm that brought down the wire was an event caused by the laws of nature. However, *but for* the fact the employee was in the course of employment at the time, the injury would not have occurred. Therefore, the employee's death by electrocution would be compensable.

Benefit Periods

Workers' compensation benefits are available until the person achieves pre-injury functional level or maximum medical improvement, as long as this occurs within the time parameters set by the state's rules. For example, an injured worker can receive temporary, permanent, or partial income benefits for a defined number of weeks. After this period, the worker will not receive additional income benefits until and unless a qualified physician makes an impairment rating to support further disability status. In Texas, for example, if the impairment rating is deemed to be more than 15% of the whole body, further supplementary benefit for up to 401 weeks can be awarded (Texas Department of Insurance, 2013). In contrast, Pennsylvania's workers' compensation statutes set the maximum time an injured worker can receive temporary partial disability benefits at 500 weeks while total disability benefits can be received for 104 weeks (Pennsylvania Department of Labor and Industry, 2011).

The Role of the LNC in Workers' Compensation

Workers' compensation demands a knowledge and understanding of pertinent terms, practices, and parameters not usually taught in a healthcare setting. Anyone working in this area must be familiar with industry terms and how to apply them. (See Appendix C for additional glossary terms.) They must also have general knowledge of their state's applicable rules and regulations, which directly affect the rehabilitation plan and feasibility of any recommendations.

Since the single largest factor affecting the value of a claim is the strength of the medical evidence, some insurance companies recognize the value of having a medical professional available to work with their attorneys. Workers' compensation litigation is complex. It is more economically justifiable for large defense firms specializing in workers' compensation litigation to hire an LNC. Many adjusters will contract with a case manager or LNC to address medical issues that have legal bearing on the claim.

An insurance company's planning for personal injury, commercial injury, and workers' compensation claims litigation depends on the financial exposure. Major insurance companies retain law firms to add significant value by successfully disputing and reducing inappropriate settlement amounts related to causation and medical necessity for future expenses. The LNC makes a vital contribution in defining the medical issues.

The workers' compensation insurance carrier will often call upon nurse case managers (NCMs) to assist the injured worker with obtaining and retaining necessary medical benefits to optimize care and recovery. Whether working for the defense or the plaintiff, the LNC brings medical expertise, analytical skills, the nursing process, and communication ability to the table when working with the attorney and claims adjuster.

Defense law firms are more likely than plaintiff firms to hire legal nurse consultants for workers' compensation claims. Plaintiff litigation may be financially limited due to state laws that circumscribe financial settlements. Due to the no-fault principle, the employer is not liable for damages. This can sometimes limit the need for LNC services on the plaintiff side.

When the law allows for settlement of future medical and disability needs, plaintiff attorneys help the injured worker obtain all benefits due. Sometimes, tort law applies because of a third-party lawsuit; the plaintiff attorney will often handle both. In suits involving third parties, the LNC's contributions are the same as in personal injury practice, i.e., providing the medical expertise to help define the medical damages in addition to the worker's compensation claim.

An LNC may also help to determine occupational disease compensability based on diagnosis and state-defined criteria for compensability. The LNC's expertise in analyzing medical records is critical to confirming compensability in occupational disease cases. The LNC may act as case manager, researcher, expert, educator, and investigator and serve as a source of information for the adjuster, attorneys, employer, and injured worker. Multi-tasking skills, self-motivation, and attention to detail are critical. The best LNCs recognize the value of education and are consistent lifelong learners as directed under the American Association of Legal Nurse Consultants' Scope and Standards of Practice (AALNC, 2017). The LNC in this role should have a minimum of five years of nursing experience.

Legal nurse consultants in workers' compensation encounter a great variety of stakeholders. A workers' compensation claim can be complicated and is often a protracted process. It is helpful to have experience in occupational health, medical management, discharge planning, orthopedics, or home health care. The LNC role can include:

- Helping to decrease workers' compensation and related healthcare costs
- Investigating claims for compensability
- Determining causality of an incident
- Educating parties about anatomy, physiology, and anticipated treatment
- Educating parties on medical treatment, terminology, responsibilities, and expectations and
- Monitoring the individual's medical progress

As with many areas of specialty practice, there is a language unique to workers' compensation. A glossary of terms and abbreviations can be found in appendices C and D.

The LNC as Case Manager

Because of their clinical assessment skills, multidisciplinary communication background, and experience in anticipating and coordinating needed treatment, nurses are invaluable resources to the field of case management (Riddick-Grisham, 2010). Effective case management relies on principles of the nursing process to create an integrated continuum with measurable outcomes. Case management in its broadest sense reflects the phases of the nursing process; it is process in action (Riddick-Grisham, 2010).

Today, case management plays a pivotal role in the evolving healthcare system by providing patient and family education, decreasing fragmentation of care and duplication of services, increasing communication and collaboration among all members of the care team, and improving patient adherence to treatment. These actions improve achievement of measurable and durable outcomes while using healthcare dollars efficiently.

Crossover in LNC Roles

Nurse case management and legal nurse consulting have different certification requirements, but both require analytical and research skills. Thus, an NCM may be capable of working as an LNC and vice versa without obtaining certification assuming each has the required skills and experience. However, insurance companies are increasingly requiring certification for NCMs (White & Hall, 2006), and it is likely that the growth of the legal nurse consulting specialty practice will see similar demands. A study by White and Hall (2006) reported an evolving trend for the NCM working in the specialty area of workers' compensation to manage complex patient populations. At least one state now requires case manager certification (CCM, RN-BC, CDMS, etc.) for its healthcare network's utilization review positions (Texas Department of Insurance, 2013). The LNC may also see a trend toward obtaining sophisticated knowledge to successfully practice in workers' compensation.

Essential LNC/Case Manager Skills

Those best suited for employment within workers' compensation possess skills unique to many other specialty areas of nursing. All LNCs should be well-versed in medical records analysis, medical research, and the ability to locate appropriate experts. Other legal nurse consulting skills helpful in workers' compensation include practiced documentation of physician/client interview and assessment during medical exams and the creation of demonstrative evidence such as charts, photos, or graphs. Desirable traits for LNCs and nurse case managers in workers' compensation include:

- Knowledge of orthopedics, neurology, emergency or occupational medicine, or rehabilitation
- Verbal and analytical reasoning skills
- Ability to communicate with others from a variety of backgrounds, education levels, or cultures
- Problem-solving, negotiation, and conflict resolution skills
- Knowledge of community resources and how to access them
- Critical-thinking skills for data analysis
- Pharmacology knowledge, especially of pain medications, NSAIDs, and muscle relaxants
- Understanding of pathophysiology associated with different injuries, diseases, and disabilities
- Understanding of the effects of trauma on coping and psychological functioning and
- Ability to speak up and advocate for patient care when the referring party wishes to deny essential treatment

LNC/Case Manager Activities

After an initial interview with the injured worker, the LNC identifies barriers that might prevent the employee from returning to work. Like all clinical nurses, the LNC, in this context, is a patient advocate but works only on aspects directly related to the accident. For example, a diabetic may have a difficult time healing without proper diabetic supplies. A smoker may have delayed healing. Neither the diabetes nor the smoking caused the accident, but both affect healing. With the LNC's guidance on the medical effects of these conditions, the adjuster may decide it is more cost-effective to address the underlying issue for a limited period of time to improve potential outcome. It may then become the LNC's responsibility to identify resources for the injured worker (e.g., diabetes support groups, low- or no-cost diabetic supplies, a smoking cessation program, etc.).

The LNC may need to obtain additional information to supplement available medical records. With rushed appointments, text-to-type dictation, and electronic medical record systems with their myriad checkboxes, medical records can be perplexing. The LNC may need to facilitate attorney–physician communication to clarify a treatment plan. For example, if the initial records indicate the employee suffered a strain/sprain type injury but it has been several months and the disability continues, it might be warranted to find out why there is a delay.

Questions the LNC might ask the physician include:

- What is the diagnosis?
- What is the current treatment plan?

- When might the plan be modified?
- Are there any alternative treatments to try?
- Is a referral to a specialist indicated?

These questions show the physician the carrier is not sitting idly by while the patient returns every 30 days after numerous failed attempts at conservative treatment. It indicates the LNC and litigation team are proactive in planning appropriate care.

The LNC may have firsthand knowledge of the conservative or aggressive nature of a physician's practice. Perhaps the patient is poorly educated and requires a physician with extra patience and impeccable interpersonal skills. The LNC can assist an attorney or adjuster in locating an appropriate provider.

An employee with a fractured wrist may discover in the emergency department that diagnostic testing also shows signs of a degenerative tendon tear and advanced arthritic changes including several large bone spurs. While these are not related to the fall that caused the compensable fracture, it may be medically appropriate to address them simultaneously in a single surgical procedure. The LNC can be invaluable in helping to develop interrogatories to be answered by the provider or even in making direct contact with the provider to have the physician differentiate between what is work-related and what is not. The outcome varies depending on jurisdiction. Some questions might include:

- How long would the injured worker expect to treat solely for the fracture?
- What is the typical post-surgical rehabilitation for an individual with this type of fracture who does not have tendonitis and arthritis?

The LNC should be familiar with resources such as the Medical Disability Advisor and the Official Disability Guidelines. These resources outline the expected trajectory of care and expected time out of work with evidence-based medical management guidelines.

Role of the LNC in Evaluating Workers' Compensation Claims: Defense

A non-medical person may think a given medical injury or condition arises out of employment simply because a work supervisor or employer files a claim (without asking appropriate questions such as what the injured worker was doing at the time of the accident and where and when the accident occurred). A claims adjuster investigates the facts. If the facts do not match up or if concerns emerge about whether the injury or condition arises out of employment, the adjuster may request an LNC's review of the claim.

Legal nurse consultants in workers' compensation defense cases can be independent contractors or employees of either the insurance company or the retained defense law firm. Most insurance companies choose not to contract with the LNC directly for budgetary reasons and may use in-house nurse case managers as LNCs. The LNC hired by a large insurance company usually works with the legal department, rather than the claims division. The relationship of the defense law firm to the insurance company may be one of an employee or a completely separate business entity.

Defense LNCs examine the medical aspects of claims and assist with compensability. The LNC can expect to review medical records to determine if the original injury has expanded. A claim is limited to the original injury. Insurance companies pay generously for measures to obtain successful outcomes for compensable injuries, but, reasonably, they will not pay for anything outside the scope of the injury.

If there is a discrepancy between a claimed injury and its reported cause, the LNC's knowledge of anatomy and physiology, medical treatment guidelines, and time frames for resolution of medical conditions will help the claims examiner determine the cause of injury and whether the injury arises out of employment.

Case Example 15.1: Spider Bite

An employee reports to work on Monday morning and tells the supervisor of a spider bite that occurred while at work the previous Friday afternoon. Upon questioning, the employee reports the first notice of the "spider bite" was on Saturday morning, and today the area has become more painful and red. Although a spider was not actually seen, the employee assumes the lesion is a "spider bite" that occurred last Friday when removing debris from the worksite. The employer writes up an injury report, submits a worker's compensation claim, and sends the injured worker to the Emergency Department (ED), where the injured worker receives a prescription for antibiotics and an out-of-work note for five days. The ED discharge orders state the employee is to be re-evaluated by a primary care physician in five days. Two days later, the employee becomes very ill and is admitted to the hospital for incision and drainage of an infected wound.

The medical records describe the wound as being deep with necrotic tissue. The damage to the underlying tissue is extensive, and a skin graft is necessary. The employee undergoes two incision and drainage procedures while in the hospital and received intravenous (IV) antibiotics. While hospitalized, the employee is diagnosed with adult-onset diabetes mellitus.

In the meantime, the employee's worker's compensation claim is reviewed by the employer's insurance company. The questions related to this claim are "Did the injury occur in the course of employment or not?" The adjuster decides to deny the claim based on lack of evidence that the incident occurred at work and during job duties. The employee could have been at home when the spider bite occurred, as the incident was reported after a weekend. Furthermore, if the spider bite did occur at work, it could have occurred at a time when the employee was not engaged in work activities.

The adjuster must also consider the financial exposure of a spider bite claim. At this point, the claim poses significant financial exposure, because costs now include ED visits, several days of hospitalization, surgeries, IV antibiotic medications, possibly home health services for continued IV medications, and wage loss. The worker's age and co-morbidities may compromise healing, which increases expenses. Furthermore, the injured worker is a laborer who is not qualified for modified work duties.

Several weeks later, the injured worker, having received some wage replacement checks, receives a letter advising the claim was denied. The letter states the indemnity payments will stop, and medical coverage will not be available. The injured worker calls the employer who explains the insurance company did not accept the claim, because there was no evidence the "spider bite" occurred while working. Furthermore, if the spider bite did occur at work, this is considered an ordinary event of life, because the employee is at no higher risk of injury than any other ordinary person that receives a spider bite.

The injured worker retains an attorney who specializes in workers' compensation law. The attorney immediately files for a contested hearing in order to get the plaintiff's claim reviewed. The attorney informs the claims adjuster that a lawsuit will be filed for breach of contract or bad faith against the insurance company, which could result in damages for the plaintiff if it is found that the claims adjuster unreasonably denied the claim. This is because the adjuster has a duty to provide good faith and fair dealing in regard to the insurance policy contract. To do otherwise may also be a breach of fiduciary duty (Jones, 1998). The insurance company assigns the claim to an attorney and an LNC.

The LNC reviews the employee's medical records and researches information regarding brown recluse spider bites. The LNC then prepares a report explaining the plaintiff was at higher risk for a brown recluse spider bite than the general public, because on the alleged day of injury, the job duties involved removing old debris from a vacant room in an old worksite. The LNC reports the brown recluse spider is indigenous to this geographical area, and although the plaintiff could have received a spider bite anywhere, the employment duties placed the employee in an environment where a brown recluse spider is known to inhabit, so this job placed the employee at higher risk. This claim will more than likely be found compensable by the state's workers' compensation judge.

The LNC confirms the likelihood of the spider bite incident arising out of, and in the course of, employment and reviews the medical records for progression of the illness or disease, extent of injury, current treatment plan, future treatment expected, and disability time frame. The information provided by the LNC allows the plaintiff to obtain workers' compensation benefits owed and prevents potentially severe legal problems and expenses for the carrier and employer.

Case Example 15.2: Carpal Tunnel Syndrome

A 50-year-old is hired by a company that provides transcription services for several physicians' offices. The employee is a consistently hard worker who is fast and accurate. A month after hire, the employee reports pain in both wrists, with greater pain in the left compared to the right. The employee files a worker's compensation claim and sees a physician.

The physician obtains electrodiagnostic studies confirming bilateral median nerve compression, also known as carpal tunnel syndrome (CTS). The adjuster understands the relationship of repetitive injury and CTS, but the employee was only employed for four weeks. A CTS claim can be expensive including permanency and future disability.

The employee's prior employment consisted of working part-time in retail and being self-employed for 12 years as a medical transcriptionist. The claims adjuster denies the claim based on the statutory definition of CTS as an occupational disease, the length of time the claimant worked for the insured being insufficient to cause or aggravate the diagnosis of CTS, and the electromyelogram/nerve conduction velocity findings identifying chronic changes that take longer than four weeks to develop. Based on these facts, the adjuster concluded the CTS did not arise out of the current employment.

The employee and the claims department retain attorneys. The defense attorney asks for consultation from the LNC who hypothesizes whether the diagnosis of CTS could have a relationship to the employee's previous self-employment activities as a medical transcriptionist. The LNC obtains current and all prior medical records and finds notes from the primary care physician documenting the employee's complaints of bilateral hand and wrist pain with an assessment of "possible CTS" written three months before the employee began working for the retail store.

The employee only worked six weeks for the retail store, and the job duties did not involve repetitive movements of the hands or wrists. The LNC finds that this state defines CTS as an occupational disease, not a repetitive-trauma injury, and confirms this with the attorney. The LNC gives the information to the claims adjuster and explains the CTS did not arise out of the employee's current employment, and no aggravation of the condition has occurred. The claim is successfully denied.

Most states distinguish between injuries that have worsened by using different terms so the responsibility for compensability is clear; that is, compensation is sought from either the current employer or the employer who provided compensation for the original injury. The terms commonly used are aggravation and reoccurrence or exacerbation.

Aggravation is defined as a worsening of a prior condition caused by a new injury, and a new claim is opened (Ferrell, Williamson, & LaFollette, 2016). Aggravation of a pre-existing repetitive-trauma injury is generally addressed in workers' compensation statutes as related to the last place the injurious action occurred (Popow, 2011). Reoccurrence or exacerbation is defined as a deterioration of an injury or condition as part of the normal progression of the injury or disease, and the existing claim is reopened (Ferrell et al., 2016).

This case points out why it is important for the LNC to know how occupational disease and cumulative trauma (injury) are defined by individual state statute, and the LNC must investigate other claim details, e.g., if the disease or condition worsened naturally or through aggravation.

Role of the LNC in Evaluating Workers' Compensation Claims: Plaintiff

The key factor affecting case value is the strength of the medical evidence. Injured workers usually retain attorneys when there is an actual or potential dispute about causation or the extent of injury or if there is fear that benefits and rights will be lost.

In some states, an injured worker can settle a worker's compensation claim for any future medical treatment, disability, or future loss of wages. In these cases, the injured worker can obtain a large lump sum settlement or some other type of financial payment structure, e.g., as an annuity. In other states, there is no statutory provision for settlement of future wage loss and medical treatment. In others, medical claims remain open (payable) for the life of the worker.

Most plaintiff personal injury attorneys practice in several areas of law and do not limit their practice solely to workers' compensation. This obviously provides more opportunities for employment for the LNC.

To provide the attorney with information that will affect litigation regarding current and future disability claims and settlement, the LNC may perform or participate in the initial interview with the injured worker. Important questions for this meeting include:

1. Mechanism of injury: How did the injury occur? What is the worker's job? What was the worker doing? What is the name of the worker's company and the name and phone number of the worker's supervisor?
2. When did the injury occur (date and time)?
3. Did the worker report the injury? If so, when (date and time)?
4. To whom did the worker report the injury? Did the worker tell anyone else about the injury or symptoms?
5. Does the worker know if the supervisor filed the injury form with the state? If filed, when (date)?
6. Was there a co-worker or supervisor who witnessed the injury? If so, what are their name(s)?
7. How soon after the injury did symptoms begin (date and time)?
8. When did the worker seek medical care? Obtain the date and time, name of facility, name of provider, diagnosis, treatment, prescription, return date, etc.

9. Does the worker's employer have a list of providers from which the injured worker can choose for medical treatment?
10. Was the worker told where to go for treatment?
11. Has the worker been evaluated by the worker's own provider?
12. Has a provider removed the worker from work? If so, when and for how long? (Obtain a copy of any disability or off-work notes from the provider.)

Next, the LNC will focus on other medical and vocational-related questions. The LNC should assess for and document any current symptoms causing obvious discomfort or alterations in movement, speech, or cognition. Finally, the LNC can determine if there is third-party liability or any potential cause to suspect retaliatory discharge or discrimination. Before ending the interview, the LNC should obtain a signed authorization for the release of health information.

Plaintiff cases are accepted on a contingency basis, so there are no legal fees paid by the injured worker. In fact, unlike personal injury cases, the decision to accept a case is not based, in part, on expected settlement. The plaintiff attorney may be paid a percentage of the injured worker's weekly wage or some other amount such as a percentage of the total value of the settlement. There may be other legal reimbursement fees paid by the insurance company based on state statute. Therefore, the attorney may receive payments from each worker's compensation case until settlement or maximum medical improvement is reached. However, in some jurisdictions, there is no prospective payment; if a case does not result in a settlement or judgment, the attorney is not paid. This means that attorneys may not accept a case that has a low chance of success.

Unfortunately, sometimes the benefit of keeping the injured worker off-work and disabled can be a monetary incentive to all parties involved in the plaintiff's worker's compensation case. This is not in the best interest of the injured worker. If the employer can accommodate light duty within allowable work restrictions, the injured worker benefits psychologically, physically, and financially. The LNC will need to apply proper ethical principles as an advocate for the injured worker despite any pressure to do otherwise.

Independent Medical Examinations

An independent medical examination (IME) is a medical examination performed by a physician or healthcare provider not involved in the care of the examinee, for the purpose of clarifying issues associated with the case (Benzon, 2014). There is no provider–patient relationship, and none should develop. The examiner or evaluator should be impartial, unbiased, and objective. The evaluation includes the basics of a medical assessment, history, examination, and review of diagnostic studies.

The insurance carrier is most likely to request an IME. However, the employer, employee, plaintiff or defense attorney, workers' compensation board, administrative law judge, and treating healthcare provider can also request one. Issues addressed during an IME can include diagnosis, causal relationship, degree and duration of disability, prognosis, and work capabilities. Treatment recommendations can be discussed but are never performed or provided by an IME physician.

All lines of insurance and all states use independent medical evaluations, although other terms may be used, such as expert medical examination (EME) or defense medical examination (DME) (by request of the defense). An EME has the same basic goal and concept. Some states, such as Texas and New York, require specialized forms to be completed during the scheduling process. The LNC must be aware of state guidelines for scheduling and attending IMEs.

For the defense attorney, the LNC serves a key role in outlining all medical care performed to date, producing a written chronology or timeline, and developing questions for the IME provider to answer. The LNC may obtain the appointment, gather all medical records and diagnostic imaging, coordinate delivery of the records to the provider, correspond with the provider on questions to address, obtain any contracts or prepayment, and expedite the adjuster's responses.

For the plaintiff (claimant) attorney, the LNC's role is typically limited to attending and possibly recording the examination. An LNC attending an IME should become familiar with the American Board of Independent Medical Examiners guidelines of ethical conduct (ABIME, n.d.) and be able to identify anything that occurs during the exam that is contrary to these published standards. For more information on IMEs/DMEs, see Chapter 6.

The LNC may also vet IME healthcare providers. Does the healthcare provider have the necessary credentials and criteria to perform IMEs? Are all professional and Drug Enforcement Agency licenses valid and current? Does the healthcare provider maintain an active practice? Has this healthcare provider ever treated the injured worker in the past as a patient? Is this healthcare provider familiar with the rules and regulations for the insurance?

A second opinion can help clarify a complex medical picture or suggest alternatives to a current or proposed treatment. This is presented to the claimant as proactive, and a case manager or LNC will usually attend. This is usually called for when there is a conflict between potential treatment plans (e.g., surgery versus conservative care), when the claimant requests one, when multilayered medical scenarios or a questionable treatment is under way, or when the existing treatment plan has not achieved the expected outcome (Mullahy, 2014). In contrast to IME, the patient may choose the second opinion provider to become the treating provider.

The LNC should understand the purpose of the exam as well as the requestor's expectations and needs. The examining provider should be given all available information in advance of the examination to ensure adequate time to review the materials.

Role of the LNC in Catastrophic Injury

Financial settlements for future medical and disability are usually provided in a formal structure, such as annuities that pay out over the life of the injured worker and dependents. Each state has very specific rules guiding catastrophic injury lifetime benefits. The insurance company and plaintiff attorney must insist that the injured worker apply these lifetime benefits in the most effective way; this process is often provided by structured settlement companies with particular taxation and benefit expertise.

The LNC practicing as a life care planner (LCP) will advocate for medical evaluations, healthcare providers, facilities, caregivers, supplies, and necessary equipment that will promote comfort while allowing as much independence as possible. The LCP's life care plan should be realistic, provide expectations and expenses, and accommodate changes when necessary. A life care plan needs to be reviewed annually to make sure the components of the plan support all reasonably foreseeable needs. The nurse consultant may be the only case manager. Continued advocacy is critical even after the acute rehabilitation period has passed, because the insurer may decide to cut medical costs in ways that would be detrimental.

The nurse consultant who works for a defense attorney or insurance company is likely to perform many of the same evaluations and assessments as with any other case, with the exception that more time may be devoted to the catastrophic case. The LCP will continually review current medical reports for updates on extent of injury and disability. Limiting services to only those related to the compensable injury requires medical expertise and research abilities, so medical treatment and services continue to be medically reasonable and necessary.

For example, an injured worker sustains an L4–5 (lumbar) complete spinal cord injury, resulting in paraplegia, as a result of a fall while installing a new roof. Two years later, the claims adjuster learns the primary care physician is requesting a drug treatment program for the paraplegic worker, who apparently developed an addiction to opioids. The adjuster is uncertain if the payment for a drug treatment program is the responsibility of the insurer. The defense attorney asks the LNC to determine whether the current opioid use is prescribed for pain stemming from this worker's compensable injury. (Remembering the principle of *but for* may help: *But for* the injury, the injured worker would not be taking narcotic medication.)

In reviewing the medical records, the LNC finds the worker was taking several different narcotic medications prescribed by two different physicians for migraine headaches before the injury. After the injury, the injured worker continued with these medications and obtained additional opioid prescriptions from the workers' compensation provider for back pain. Although the drug treatment program may be medically necessary to treat the injured worker's addiction to narcotics, the question is whether the narcotic addiction resulted from the injury. The LNC's research on narcotic addiction and review of the injured worker's medical records show that the addiction process likely started before the compensable injury; therefore, the treatment for drug addiction is not related.

Summary

Workers' compensation litigation is a complex and challenging practice area. Statutes and administrative rules vary widely from state to state. Changes occur frequently, and the LNC practicing in this specialty must obtain training and new information regularly. Fortunately, basic principles provide the foundation for those working with workers' compensation litigation. Understanding these principles, the LNC can provide considerable valuable medical expertise.

References

American Association of Legal Nurse Consultants. (2017). *Legal nurse consulting: Scope and standards of practice.* [e-publication]. Retrieved from www.aalnc.org/page/aalnc-online-bookstore.

American Board of Independent Medical Examiners. (n.d.). Guidelines of conduct. Retrieved from www.abime.org/node/21.

Benzon, H. T. (2014). *Practical management of pain.* Philadelphia, PA: Elsevier/Saunders.

Devenny, L., & Morgan, J. (2008). *Workers' compensation practice for paralegals.* Durham, NC: Carolina Academic Press.

Ferrell, K., Williamson, K., & LaFollette, S. (2016). Other LNC practice areas. In *AALNC Legal nurse consulting professional course* (module 17). Retrieved from www.aalnc.org/page/course-content.

Jones, J. (Ed.). (1998). *Principles of worker's compensation claims* (2nd ed.). Malvern, PA: Insurance Institute of America.

Louisiana Government. (2008). Louisiana administrative code, Title 40: Workers' compensation administration. Department of Administration, Office of the State Registry. Retrieved from www.lwcc.com/LinkClick.aspx?fileticket=ss1CxT0dvBQ%3D&portalid=0   www.doa.la.gov/orm/pdf/LWCCWorkersCompensationPolicy86037-S.pdf.

Mullahy, C. M. (2014). *The case manager's handbook.* Burlington, MA: Jones & Bartlett Learning.

National Federation of Independent Business. (2017). Workers' compensation law: State by state comparison. Retrieved from www.nfib.com/content/legal-compliance/legal/workers-compensation-laws-state-by-state-comparison-57181/.

Pennsylvania Department of Labor and Industry. (2011). The Pennsylvania Workers' Compensation Act 338 of 1915. Bureau of Workers' Compensation Information. Retrieved from www.legis.state.pa.us/WU01/LI/LI/US/PDF/1915/0/0338.PDF.

Popow, D. (Ed.). (2011). *Principles of worker's compensation claims* (3rd ed.). Malvern, PA: Insurance Institute of America.

Powell, S. K., & Tahan, H. A. (2008). *CMSA core curriculum for case management* (2nd ed.). Philadelphia, PA: Lippincott Williams & Wilkins.

Riddick-Grisham, S. (2010). The role of the nurse case manager in life care planning. In R.O. Weed and D. E. Berens (Eds.), *Life care planning and case management handbook* (3rd ed., pp. 27–40). Boca Raton, FL: CRC Press.

Texas Department of Insurance. (2013). The Texas Workers' Compensation Act, 83rd Legislature, 2013. Retrieved from www.tdi.texas.gov/wc/act/#html.

White, P., & Hall, M. E. (2006). Mapping the literature of case management nursing. *Journal of the Medical Library Association, 94*(2 Suppl.). Retrieved from www.ncbi.nlm.nih.gov/pmc/articles/PMC1463029/pdf/i1536-5050-094-02S-0099.pdf.

Additional Reading

Anchor, K. N., Shmerling, J. E., & Anchor, J. M. (Eds.). (2002). *The catastrophic injury handbook: Understanding vocational, economic, legal, and clinical aspects of complex physical and mental trauma.* Dubuque, IA: Kendall/Hunt Publishing Co.

Anderson, B. J., & Cocchiarella, L. (Eds.). (2004). *Guides to the evaluation of permanent impairment* (5th ed.). USA: American Medical Association.

Markham, J. (Ed.). (1991). *Medical aspects of claims* (1st ed.). Malvern, PA: Insurance Institute of America.

Rondinelli, R. D., Genovese, E., Katz, R. T., Mayer, T. G., Mueller, K. L., Ranavaya, M. I., & Brigham, C. R. (2009). *Guides to the evaluation of permanent impairment.* Chicago, IL: American Medical Association.

Test Questions

1. Which one of the following is NOT an underlying principle of workers' compensation statutes?
   A. Prompt payment of benefits
   B. Administration by the state
   C. Employer's negligence
   D. No-fault system
2. What are three benefits injured workers receive from workers' compensation?
   A. Medical, death, and indemnity benefits
   B. Medical, indemnity, and job security benefits
   C. Medical, job security, and vocational benefits
   D. Medical, vocational, and legal benefits
3. Compensability is a term referring to:
   A. Payment for all injuries and conditions that occur while working
   B. Payment for all accidents and injuries regardless of fault
   C. Determining if the claim has been accepted for benefits
   D. Determining whether the injury or occupational disease is covered under statute
4. The LNC may assist with determining whether an injury is compensable by reviewing records to:
   A. Make sure treatment is related to the injury
   B. Determine if the injured worker has any pre-existing conditions
   C. Determine if the injury or condition results from the performance of work activities while working for the employer
   D. Make sure treatment was pre-authorized
5. The LNC working for the plaintiff attorney may ask the plaintiff all of the following EXCEPT:
   A. Did the plaintiff's supervisor cause the plaintiff to have the accident?
   B. Does the plaintiff know if the supervisor filed a claim with the state?
   C. Did anyone witness the accident?
   D. Did the plaintiff report the injury to a supervisor?

Answers: 1. C, 2. A, 3. D, 4. C, 5. A

Appendix A: Workers' Compensation Laws

National Federation of Independent Business: Workers' compensation law: State by State: www.nfib.com/content/legal-compliance/legal/workers-compensation-laws-state-by-state-comparison-57181/.

Workers' Compensation Laws by State: www.insureon.com/products/workers-compensation/state-laws.

Workers' Compensation Laws by State: http://injury.findlaw.com/workers-compensation/workers-compensation-laws-by-state.html.

Insurance Requirements & Regulations by State: www.cutcomp.com/depts.htm.

Workers' Compensation Law Compendium: www.alfainternational.com/workers-compensation-law-compendium.

Appendix B: Resources and Internet Resources

Resources

Jasper, M. (2008). *Workers' compensation law*. Oxford, UK: Oxford University Press.

Larson, A., & Larson, L. (2000). *Larson's workers' compensation, desk edition* (3rd ed.). Albany, NY: Matthew Bender and Company, Inc.

Reed, P. (Ed.). (2005). *The medical disability advisor: Workplace guidelines for disability duration* (5th ed.). Westminster, CO: Reed Group Publisher.

Work Loss Data Institute. (2008). *Official disability guidelines* (16th ed.). Encinitas, CA: Work Loss Data Institute (WLDI).

Internet Resources

U.S. Department of Labor Office of Workers' Compensation Programs. www.dol.gov/eas/regs/compliance/owcp/wc.htm.

The International Association of Industrial Accident Boards and Commissions. www.iaiabc.org/links.htm.

Workers' Compensation Administrators Directory. www.comp.state.nc.us/ncic/pages/wcadmdir.htm.

Appendix C: Common Workers' Compensation Terms

Apportionment—the determination of how much of a worker's permanent disability is due to the work injury and how much is related to other disabilities

Defendant—Defense side of the case (the employer's side)

Excess loss—the amount of the claim over and above the primary loss that is used to calculate the experience modification factor, capped in most states at $100,000

Experience Modification Factor—The experience modification factor is a value that compares the claim profile of the employer to the claim profile that would be expected of an employer of similar size (payroll) in the same industry (class codes). A value of 1.00 is average, meaning the frequency and severity of actual losses equaled the expected losses. A mod factor greater than 1.00 means the employer experienced worse than expected losses during the rating period, and a mod of less than 1.00 indicates the employer's losses were better than expected for the rating period.

First Report of Injury—this is a form that contains the demographic information of the injured worker as well as insurance carrier's information, date of injury, employer contact and so forth.

Functional Capacity Evaluation—exam to determine a person's capacity for work. Oftentimes this exam is used to determine an individual's efforts. If the individual does not give full and valid effort, this provides objective data to this effect for the file.

Incurred—the total anticipated cost of claims or loss. This includes amounts paid for medical, indemnity, and expenses in addition to the reserves for future medical, indemnity, and expenses.

Lien—a legal right to possess something which one person or entity has over another as security for a debt or obligation owed. For example, an injured worker's health insurance carrier may have a lien on an indemnity payment to the injured worker that would reimburse the carrier for medical expenses that resulted from the work-related injury.

Managed care organization (MCO)—a group of healthcare providers set up by an insurer and approved to treat workers injured on the job (i.e., "in-network" providers).

Medical Record Fee—statutorily defined limits on the fees healthcare providers can charge for providing copies of medical records

Minnesota Multiphasic Personality Inventory (MMPI)—This is the most widely used and researched clinical assessment instrument used by mental health professionals. The test is often used in legal cases, as a screening tool for certain professions, or to evaluate the effectiveness of treatment programs. The test contains 567 test items and takes 60–90 minutes to complete. It is administered, scored, and interpreted by a professional who has received specific training in its use. This test is used in collaboration with other assessment tools and is not intended as a stand-alone test. There are 10 scales used to indicate different psychological conditions such as hypochondriasis, depression, hysteria, paranoia, etc. The test also includes scales to detect lies, faking, defensiveness, and other validity measures.

Permanent Total Disability (PTD)—the inability (because of a compensable injury or occupational disease) to earn any meaningful wage in the same or other employment.

Pro se—an injured worker who is self-represented in front of a judge in a worker's compensation hearing.

Respondent—Plaintiff side of the case (worker's side).

Scheduled injury—a partial disabling injury to any of the body parts allowed under a state's workers' compensation statute for which a predetermined amount of compensation is specified. Body parts that may qualify as a scheduled injury include thumbs, fingers, hands, arms, toes, legs, eyes, hearing, and face or head disfigurement. Each body part has a maximum number of weeks of PPD benefits allowed.

Second injury fund—If an employee has a permanent disability to one major body part and sustains a permanent partial disability as a result of a job-related injury to a second major body part, the employee may be entitled to benefits from the "second injury fund."

Social Security Income—disability payments for those without enough reported earnings to qualify for Social Security disability benefits.

Statute of Limitations—the statutorily defined time frame after which an injured worker is barred from filing a worker's compensation claim for a compensable injury, death, or exposure. The time frame may vary depending on whether any compensation is paid to the worker.

Temporary Total Disability (TTD)—the monetary benefit awarded to the injured worker while they are not able to work in any capacity.

Unscheduled injury—a permanent disabling injury that is not to a "scheduled" body part. These typically include back, neck, shoulder, and hip injuries.

Appendix D: Common Workers' Compensation Abbreviations

ADA—Americans with Disabilities Act
ALJ—administrative law judge
AMA—American Medical Association
AWW—average weekly wage
CMS—Centers for Medicare & Medicaid Services

COBC—Coordination of Benefits Center
CT—cumulative trauma
Depo—deposition
DME—Durable Medical Equipment or defense medical examination
DOI—date of injury
DOL—Department of Labor
EE—employee
ER—employer
FCE—Functional Capacity Evaluation
FCM—field case management
FD—full duty
FMLA—Family Medical Leave Act
FROI—first report of injury
IME—independent medical evaluation
IR—impairment rating
IW—Injured worker
JA—job analysis
LD—light duty
LDP—last day paid
LDW—last day worked
LOV—last office visit
LTD—long-term disability
LT—lost time
MCO—managed care organization
MD—modified duty (also known as transitional duty)
MDA—Medical Disability Advisor
Med Only—medical only (i.e., no time lost from work)
MMI—Maximum Medical Improvement
MMPI—Minnesota Multiphasic Personality Inventory
MSA—Medicare set aside
MSP—Medicare Secondary Payer
MSPRC—Medical Secondary Payer Recovery Contractor
NCM—Nurse case manager
NOV—next office visit
ODG—Official Disability Guidelines
OOP—out of pocket
Ortho—orthopedic surgeon or orthopedic clinic
OT—occupational therapy
OTC—over the counter (medications)
OV—office visit
P&S—permanent & stationary (i.e., stabilized and at MMI)
P&T—permanent and total (disability)
PD—permanent disability
POA—plan of action
POC—plan of care
POD—post op day
PPD—Permanent Partial Disability

PPL—push, pull, lift
Psych—psychiatrist, psychologist, or their offices
PT—physical therapy
PTD—permanent total disability
PTP—primary treating physician
RM—risk management
ROM—range of motion
RRE—Responsible Reporting Entity
RTC—return to clinic
RTC—rotator cuff
RTW—return to work
SCHIP—State Children's Health Insurance Program
SIF—second injury fund
SOL—statute of limitations
SSA—Social Security Administration
SSD—Social Security Disability
SSDB—Social Security Disability Benefits
SSDI—Social Security Disability Insurance
SSI—Social Security Income
SS—Social Security
STD—short-term disability
Subro—subrogation
TCM—telephonic case management
TPA—third party administrator
TPD—Total Permanent Disability
TTD—Temporary Total Disability
U&C—usual and customary (job duties or charges)
WC—Workers' Compensation/Work Comp

Chapter 16

Evaluating Forensic Cases

Marjorie Berg Pugatch, MA, RN, EMT-B, LNCC®
Deborah A. Wipf, MS, APRN-GCNS-BC, LNCC®
Sandra Higelin, MSN, RN, CNS, CWCN, CLNC
Jennifer Oldham, BSN, RN, CEN, SANE-A
Anita Symonds, MS, BSN, RN, CFC, CFN, SANE-A, SANE-P

Contents

Objectives

- Provide an overview of specific areas of criminal law, procedure, and evidence
- Describe the role, responsibility, and process of the legal nurse consultant in reviewing criminal cases and in assisting attorneys in the prosecution or defense of a criminal case
- Identify the differences between criminal and civil case proceedings
- Explain the purpose and procedures for maintaining chain of custody
- Describe the role and responsibility of sexual assault forensic examiners
- Detail the identification and evaluation of child and adult abuse cases

Introduction

This chapter provides an overview of the LNC role in assisting the attorney handling criminal cases through discussion of various topics such as, basics of criminal justice, types of crimes, forensics, and specific types of forensic cases seen in the ED. Legal nurse consultants with a forensics background are well suited to assist the criminal attorney, but LNCs without such specialized training may supply valuable support to attorneys in a criminal practice or with a focus on personal injury. The LNC with knowledge of the criminal and forensic arena will be more valuable to the criminal attorney.

Since both criminal charges and civil claims may arise from the same event, the LNC involved in litigating personal injury claims should be familiar with the records and reports generated in criminal cases. For example, an event leading to both a criminal charge and a civil negligence case, is the motor vehicle accident where personal injury occurs, and where a driver is charged with driving under the influence. The evidence supporting the criminal charge is available to the attorney pursuing a personal injury claim and will need to be reviewed and evaluated.

Another example can occur in elder abuse cases where a healthcare facility failed to provide or follow safety protocols effectively resulting in a negligence claim. Civil litigation brought by the family against the healthcare facility may follow the criminal case. The LNC who has familiarity with the criminal procedures and forensics may be at an advantage assisting in this type of case.

Criminal Justice System

Criminal vs. Civil Law

As noted, the same criminal act may give rise to both a civil and criminal cause of action. One important difference between these two types of actions is the standard necessary for a person to be found culpable (guilty). In the criminal justice system, the standard is "guilty beyond a reasonable doubt" (The Law Dictionary, n.d.-c). In the civil justice system, it is a "preponderance of evidence" (The Law Dictionary, n.d.-d). Although the law applying to criminal and civil cases is different, the basic concept of deciding the truth based on evidence is common to both. In criminal cases a guilty verdict results in punishment by the state while in civil cases a guilty verdict often results in a penalty, fine, or restitution in an effort to make the plaintiff whole.

A crime, "is an act committed or omitted, in violation of a public law, either forbidding or commanding it; a breach or violation of some public right or duty due to a whole community" (The Law Dictionary, n.d.-a). Criminal law is statutory, meaning laws passed by legislatures either state or federal and applied by the courts to specific situations (Legal Dictionary, n.d.).

Crimes

Misdemeanor vs. Felony

Crimes are divided into misdemeanors and felonies. A misdemeanor "is an act committed or omitted in violation of a public law either forbidding or commanding it" (US Legal, n.d.-g) and "an offense for which a sentence to a term of imprisonment not in excess of one year may be imposed" (US Legal, n.d.-g). Misdemeanors are tried in lower court, and include petty theft, disturbing the peace, simple assault and battery, public drunkenness, and various traffic violations. A felony "is an offense for which a sentence to a term of imprisonment in excess of one year is authorized" (US Legal, n.d.-d). A felony conviction results in a sentence based on the crime, sentencing guidelines, and jurisdiction. Proving criminal intent at trial is a necessary element to obtaining a felony conviction. Criminal intent is also known as *mens rea*, meaning the alleged perpetrator knew the crime committed was wrong at the time it occurred. It is also referred to as one's state of mind (The Law Dictionary, n.d.-e). Examples of felonies are murder, rape, assault, and burglary.

Definitions of Crimes

MURDER, MANSLAUGHTER

First-degree murder "is defined by federal and state laws, which may vary by state, but generally define it as a killing which is deliberate and premeditated" (US Legal, n.d.-e). Second-degree murder "is a death which results from an assault which is likely to cause death" (US Legal, n.d.-f).

Voluntary manslaughter, sometimes called criminally negligent homicide, "includes killing in heat of passion, in self-defense, or while committing a felony" (US Legal, n.d.-h); involuntary manslaughter "occurs when a death is caused during the commission of a non-felony, such as reckless driving" (US Legal, n.d.-h). Manslaughter "lacks the element of malice necessary to be found guilty of murder" (US Legal, n.d.-h). The difference between voluntary and involuntary is usually whether or not the victim's death is accidental or intentional.

SEXUAL ASSAULT/RAPE

The definition of rape may vary from state to state (FindLaw, n.d.) but generally refers to the act of non-consensual sexual intercourse in which the perpetrator forces the victim by physical force, threat of harm, or other duress. The victim's inability to consent to sexual intercourse may be due to a physical or mental impediment rendering the victim unable to say "no." Impairment could be the result of drugs or alcohol, age, or developmental disability. An established relationship between a perpetrator and victim does not preclude the possibility of rape such as a husband and wife/partner. Most states have provisions in the law, to determine the criminality of consensual sexual intercourse between an adult and an underage person considered too young to be able to consent. This provision is "statutory rape."

ASSAULT

Assault is classified as first, second, or third degree and defined by and varies by state law. First-degree assault is an "intentional infliction of fear of serious bodily harm, or intentional fear of injury caused by a deadly weapon" (Legal Match, 2015, para. 1). Second-degree assault is intentionally inflicting fear and third degree is recklessly inflicting fear. The first and second degrees are more intentional and therefore upon conviction result in longer sentences.

BATTERY

"Battery is a crime and a basis for a lawsuit as a civil wrong if there is damage. A battery is any:

- willful and unlawful use of force or violence upon the person of another;
- actual, intentional and unlawful touching or striking of another person against the will of the other;
- unlawfully and intentionally causing bodily harm to an individual."

(US Legal, n.d.-b, para. 1)

Police Report

The police report is a detailed document that includes victim and witness information and statements. It contains statements from all law enforcement officers responding to the crime scene and from those that collected evidence from the crime scene. The police report will confirm if victims are taken to the hospital for treatment, what evidence was collected, where the evidence is being stored, and if any of the evidence has been sent for forensic testing. Depending on jurisdictional procedures, redactions may appear on information in a police report. In some jurisdictions, the police report is not given to the defense until trial, while in other states it may be provided at the time of the preliminary hearing. If provided early, it is sometimes possible for the defense attorney to find out redactions made by discussing the police report with the alleged perpetrator of the crime.

Criminal Procedure

Arrest, Probable Cause, Arraignment, Preliminary Hearing, Grand Jury

Criminal procedures vary from state to state and jurisdiction to jurisdiction within a state. The federal government has its own procedures for processing felonies. Therefore, the LNC will need to explore the applicable jurisdictional practices and procedures.

This section discusses only felony arrests and prosecutions. A felony arrest is made either as the result of criminal conduct observed by a police officer or as the result of a sworn complaint by the victim. Probable cause requires an arrest be legal. Probable cause (The Law Dictionary, n.d.-f) exists when a law enforcement officer decides an individual commits an offense in their presence or when a person has sworn to facts and circumstances giving the officer reasonable cause to believe an offense has been committed.

Once a felony suspect is arrested, advised of their Miranda warnings (Miranda Warning, n.d.) and brought to the police station for processing, the suspect is then transported to court for an arraignment before a judge. At the arraignment, the accused receives a brief statement of the charges. The sole issue for the judge now is whether to set bail or release the suspect (now called the defendant) on the defendant's own recognizance. The prosecution does not need to disclose to the defendant any evidence supporting the charges. The disclosure of evidence comes later in the process. As the case proceeds and prior to trial, the accused will be entitled to review all relevant evidence.

In some states, the prosecutor will present evidence to a grand jury (an impartial group of citizens) and ask the grand jury to vote on an indictment. The federal government, however, must use the grand jury system for all felony crimes. With grand jury proceedings sealed, neither the accused nor the accused's legal counsel is permitted in the grand jury room. However, if the defendant wishes to testify at the grand jury, the defendant may do so but without legal representation.

An indictment merely signifies a majority of grand jurors have been convinced a crime has been committed and there is reasonable probability the defendant has committed the crime. By voting in favor of an indictment, the grand jury gives permission to the prosecutor to continue the case. The defendant can ask the judge to review grand jury testimony and minutes to determine if proper procedures were followed; and that, as a matter of law, enough evidence was submitted to the grand jury to justify the vote of the grand jurors to indict.

If an indictment is delivered from the grand jury to the judge, a hearing is held where the defendant will be asked to enter a plea of guilty, not guilty, or no contest. On the federal level, after entering a plea, a preliminary hearing is when the prosecutor presents enough evidence to support the charge. If the judge feels there is good evidence to support the charge, a trial is scheduled or if the evidence does not persuade the judge, the charges will be dismissed (U.S. Department of Justice [U.S. DOJ], n.d.-c).

Criminal trials usually occur within a year of the indictment as opposed to civil cases in which several years may pass before a case reaches a trial calendar. This transpires because the defendant may be incarcerated during this period of time, depending on the seriousness of the crime, and has the constitutional right to a speedy trial.

Prosecution and Defense

Prosecution and Proof

The prosecutor must prove intent along with each element of the crime to support a conviction for felony and bears the entire burden of proof beyond a reasonable doubt. The criminal defense attorney does not have to prove anything. The Fifth Amendment to the U.S. Constitution protects against self-incrimination. A defendant cannot be forced to testify where testimony might implicate the defendant (Legal Information Institute, n.d.-a). After the prosecution has presented its case, the defense may present witnesses on behalf of the accused. However, the defense may rest (not present any witnesses) upon the presumption the prosecution did not meet its burden of proof. If the accused elects to present a defense in a criminal case, a common defense tactic is to seek to disprove the facts presented by the prosecution that support the elements of the crime or to create doubt in the mind of the judge or jury. For example, a person charged with a crime may present alibi witnesses who place the person in a different location at the time of the offense, attack the reliability of evidence used by the prosecution, or present other evidence not previously entered by the prosecution that exonerates the defendant.

If the prosecution does not secure a conviction, they may not subject the accused to another criminal trial using the same elements of the crime. (Legal Information Institute, n.d.-a). The Double Jeopardy Clause is in the Fifth Amendment to the U.S. Constitution (Legal Information Institute, n.d.-a). The Sixth Amendment to the Constitution "guarantees the rights of criminal defendants, including the right to a public trial without unnecessary delay, the right to a lawyer, the right to an impartial jury, and the right to know who your accusers are and the nature of the charges and evidence against you" (Legal Information Institute, n.d.-b).

Prosecution and Defense Strategy

The verdict must be unanimous and returned as guilty or not guilty. A crime is against the state, the prosecution has the state's resources (or federal government resources) at its disposal in investigating and developing cases. This includes law enforcement agencies; the office of the medical examiner/coroner; the state crime laboratory; and other state agencies, such as family and children's services, mental health, etc.

The criminal defense attorney is the advocate for the accused. As such, the attorney assures the client's civil rights are respected. The goal of any defense strategy would be to obtain an acquittal or to place doubt on the prosecution's evidence to pursue a plea bargain that would be in the best interest of the defendant.

The criminal defense attorney does not have access to state resources as the prosecution does, and at times must utilize private laboratories and forensic scientists in private practice for testing and consulting. The conclusions or test results provided by these entities might challenge or refute conclusions or test results (i.e., breathalyzer results) provided by the state and may also provide a sufficient basis to create a reasonable doubt for a jury concerning the state's case. An effective defense strategy can make the difference between incarceration and freedom. The development of a defense strategy depends on the facts of case and usually emerges once information about the case begins to surface. This includes discovery material provided by the prosecution and the defendant's account of the criminal act (Criminal Law Lawyer Source, n.d.).

The type and amount of information discoverable in a criminal case is dependent upon individual state laws. Therefore, the criminal defense attorney may or may not be privy to the state's case theory, depending upon the working relationship between the criminal defense attorney and the district attorney's office or the usual practices of the municipality. The criminal defense attorney will need to become an expert on any anticipated theory the state may utilize. The LNC can assist the defense attorney in developing case theories and strategies. The LNC can produce medical literature on case topics. The LNC can also locate, identify, retain, and work with experts in the field as part of case development.

Post-conviction Relief

Once a defendant has been convicted of a criminal offense either by a jury or the judge during a bench trial, there are several motions and appeals the defendant can file. An appeal is a right of convicted defendants to request a higher court to review their case. All defendants are guaranteed the right to a minimum of one appeal (King, 2014). The purpose of an appeal addresses "errors of law." The appellate court does not review any new evidence or re-evaluate evidence admitted in the original trial. A decision by the appellate court to grant a new trial is based solely on the court record made at the time of trial (King, 2014). However, defendants who have pled guilty have waived their right to appeal when they entered their plea into the court record. There are exceptions, including lack of effective counsel (U.S. DOJ, n.d.-a).

Mitigation

Mitigation is a term used to describe the process of gathering facts about a defendant during the criminal process. The aim of mitigation is to present evidence after conviction but prior to sentencing to lessen the penalty the judge may impose. Once the defendant is arraigned and a defense attorney is hired or appointed, the process for collecting information regarding the defendant's medical and mental health background can begin. Performing mitigation work for attorneys is an area that the LNC is well suited for. Possessing interviewing, critical thinking and analytic skills coupled with healthcare knowledge and experience is a valuable skills set for defense attorneys to tap into for mitigation support (Kopishke, 2004).

The LNC gathers information about any acute or chronic medical conditions, and medications the defendant might be taking. Using information gathered, the defense attorney argues for a lesser punishment or advocates for treatment rather than incarceration depending on information about the defendant's medical and mental health status. Mitigation also has a specific role in capital murder trials (US Legal, n.d.-i).

Forensic Science, Criminalistics, and Evidence

Forensic science is the application of sciences to matters of law (National Institute of Justice, 2017). Pathology, toxicology, biology, serology, chemistry, anthropology, odontology, psychiatry, computer technology and others are all forensic sciences. One branch of forensic science is criminalistics, dealing with the study of physical evidence related to a crime. It encompasses analysis of firearms, tool mark comparison, fingerprints, photography, evidence collection kits, and trace elements, among others (National Institute of Justice, 2015). Forensic experts provide written and oral testimony at trial. Such testimony may be a critical component of the case. The LNC assisting with cases where forensics science reports are available would need to be able to read and understand the results of these reports or can be expected to research the significance of the results and assist with locating and interfacing with expert witnesses.

Direct and Circumstantial Evidence

"Direct evidence is evidence of a fact based on a witness's personal knowledge or observation of that fact" (NYCourts, n.d., p. 1). For example, one can testify it was raining on a certain day because one was walking down the street and experienced the rain firsthand (direct evidence). Using the same example, one can infer it was raining outside because the witness saw people come into the building wearing wet raincoats and carrying open, dripping umbrellas. This is an example of circumstantial evidence or indirect evidence because inferences made or deduced from facts leads to a conclusion (NYCourts, n.d.). In order for a defendant to be found guilty of a crime by direct evidence alone, such evidence must satisfy a jury beyond a reasonable doubt that the defendant committed the criminal act. An example of direct evidence would be surveillance video of a person robbing a convenience store, or a witness who saw a person stealing a car. Evidence that comes from a person who saw or heard the criminal act is direct evidence. On the other hand, circumstantial evidence in a murder case may include "threats made, fingerprints at the crime scene or the presence of the accused in the vicinity of the crime" (US Legal, n.d.-a, para 1).

In terms of weight or importance, the law draws no distinction between circumstantial evidence and direct evidence. Direct evidence or circumstantial evidence may be enough to establish guilt beyond a reasonable doubt. Beyond a reasonable doubt means "there are no other logical explanations resulting from the case facts that anyone other than the defendant could have committed the crime" (Yeshion, n.d., para. 3).

Testimonial Evidence

Testimonial evidence includes sworn statements of witnesses made in court in both oral and written form. This may include statements made to the police. Testimonial evidence is about what the witnesses saw, heard, or know about the facts of the case. The most common example of testimonial evidence is the sworn statement of an eyewitness (The Law Dictionary, n.d.-g).

Hearsay evidence (see Chapter 39, Trial Preparation and the Trial Process) is an oral or written statement about an out-of-court declaration attributed to someone other than the testifying person. As an example, the witness on the stand states: "He told me he killed his neighbor." Such evidence is inadmissible because the person to whom the statement is attributed cannot be cross-examined to ascertain its factual basis, which is a violation of the defendant's Sixth Amendment rights (the right of the accused to confront witnesses). The purpose of disallowing hearsay is to make sure the evidence at trial is reliable and factual. However, the Federal Rules of Evidence (FRE) defines the many exceptions to this rule (Federal Evidence Review, 2015, Article VIII).

Physical Evidence

Physical evidence can be anything from massive objects to microscopic items, generated as part of a crime and recovered at the scene or at related locations. … Except for physical evidence, all other sources of information suffer from problems of limited reliability. Physical evidence, when it is recognized and properly handled, offers the best prospect for providing objective and reliable information about the incident under investigation.

(United Nations Office on Drugs and Crime, 2009, p. 4)

Scientific Evidence

Scientific evidence developed from a scientific procedure is meant to help the trier of fact. Examples include DNA analysis, fingerprint testing for purposes of identification, blood testing, breathalyzer testing to determine alcohol consumption, and ballistics testing of bullets and the area of impact. A witness qualified as an expert by knowledge, skill, experience, training, or education may testify in the form of an expert opinion (Federal Evidence Review, 2015).

DNA Analysis

The DNA analysis falls within scientific evidence and involves the extraction of genetic material from bloodstains, seminal stains, hair shaft, and epithelial-containing cells such as saliva and hair roots. Bite marks, fingernail scrapings, blankets, sheets, pillows, clothing, hat, bandanna, tissue, washcloth, cigarette butt, toothpick, rim of bottle or glass, dental floss, tape, or ligature can all provide potential DNA samples.

With the creation of the combined DNA indexing system known as CODIS, DNA evidence from separate criminal cases can now be linked together to identify perpetrators who have committed other criminal acts in unsolved cases (James, 2012; National Institute of Justice, 2010). The changes and advancements in DNA analysis enable its use in serious crimes such as murder and rape. Even hit-and-run, burglary, robbery, and assault cases can use DNA analysis. In response to challenges of DNA admissibility, guidelines for conducting quality assurance audits were developed. These guidelines were developed by the National Research Council, the FBI, and the technical working group on DNA analysis (James & Nordby, 2005). The DNA evidence was initially subjected to rigorous legal arguments and challenges. It is now generally accepted in most states and jurisdictions as admissible in a criminal proceeding and is rarely challenged. The Federal Bureau of Investigation (FBI) promulgated detailed quality assurance standards for forensic DNA testing in laboratories (FBI, 2011).

If the admissibility of DNA analysis is challenged, it is challenged for the following reasons: integrity of the evidence collection with questions regarding chain of custody; sample mix-up and sample contamination; integrity of the laboratory as to its accreditation, quality assurance procedures, or compliance with established guidelines and standards: integrity of interpretation of the results or the statistical inferences (Strutin, 2010; Thompson, n.d.; U.S. DOJ Archives, 2017).

Chain of Custody

Another important concept related to evidence collection and preservation is chain of custody. Chain of custody refers to the procedures used to document every person who has contact with the evidence. Chain of custody records establish the integrity of evidence, proving it has been preserved from the time of collection to the time it is produced in court. Documenting the procedures for accepting, storing, and retrieving the evidence is critical. There are strict accounting procedures for everyone involved in the collection, processing, and transportation of evidence (US Legal, n.d.-c). All types of containers use tamper-evident seals and containers are labeled with specific identification information. As the evidence travels from one individual or agency to another, record keeping includes date, time, and the name of the person who handled it.

A proper chain of custody at trial requires three types of testimony:

- that a piece of evidence is what it purports to be (e.g., a litigant's blood sample)
- continuous possession from one individual to the next individual (audit log) from the time seized until the time presented in court
- by each person who has had possession of the evidence indicating at trial that the particular piece of evidence remained in substantially the same condition from the moment one person took possession until the moment that person released the evidence into the custody of another

Chain of custody documentation must be maintained throughout the life of the evidence and documentation of contact with the evidence and the action performed on it. Maintaining an audit log is critical to the support of chain of custody (Coons, 2015).

Types of Criminal Cases and their Analysis

Driving Under the Influence

A critical issue in traffic accident investigation is determining if drugs or alcohol played a role (Centers for Disease Control and Prevention [CDC], 2017b). A blood alcohol level (BAC) of 0.08% is a standard value determining intoxication for legal or medical events. Most states recognize this level as equating with an inability to operate a motor vehicle in a safe and prudent way. The amount of alcohol necessary to reach a level of 0.08% varies from one individual to another (Alcohol Policy Information System, 2016). Law enforcement agencies across the country have routine procedures for analyzing blood, breath, and urine for drug and alcohol levels. This requires blood and urine samples collected in a medically approved manner and within chain of custody procedure parameters. Ordinary hospital lab collection and lab results are not used in a court of law. Technicians or officers, certified in breath intoxylizers, conduct the breath tests.

The LNC's analysis of a driving under the influence or driving while intoxicated (DUI/DWI) case includes determining if the driver has a previous history of driving under the influence and such questions as, has the driver's license ever been revoked or suspended and if so, the reason behind revocation and suspension.

The LNC reviews the police report to understand the driving/weather conditions, road conditions, speed of impact, presence or absence of skid marks, time of day, and appearance and behavior of the driver. The police report indicates if any drug paraphernalia or bottles containing alcohol were found in the vehicle or at the scene of the MVA. The LNC reviews field sobriety results, if done. The review includes the tester's training and the process followed, and the log of intoxylzer calibrations. Also, the LNC would determine, analyze, and make suggestions if treatment for intoxication is required.

The police report indicates if anyone in the vehicles was transported to the hospital. The LNC obtains emergency medical services (EMS) records and ED/hospital records to review the injuries sustained and if there were any references to "AOB" (alcohol on breath) or "ETOH (alcohol) present" or behaviors described consistent with the use of alcohol. The LNC pays attention to the description of the driver's condition at the scene and at arrival to the ED.

Additional reviews concern drug and alcohol test results. The LNC determines if blood or urine, or blood and urine tests were done and if proper chain of custody protocols were followed. The LNC ascertains how much time elapsed between drug/alcohol ingestion, the time of the accident, and time test samples were obtained. It is important to find out if the driver possesses a prescription for narcotics and the last time taken. The LNC determines if narcotics administered in the ED were given before or after toxicology samples were obtained. The LNC considers the following factors when evaluating a DUI case:

■ Physical makeup of the individual
■ Existing and pre-existing medical conditions including diabetes (hypoglycemic behavior may mimic excessive alcohol ingestion and breathalyzer results may be affected by the presence of acetone if ketoacidosis from hyperglycemia was evident)
■ Current medications (including over-the-counter medications) with specific reference to those medications known to affect driving ability (anti-anxiety, central nervous system depressants, stimulants)
■ Proper evidence collection and preservation of physical evidence
■ Quantity/amount of prescription medication found in laboratory samples

An expert witness, such as a toxicologist or accident reconstructionist, is often called to assist with the case. The LNC may provide the expert with the pertinent documents for review.

Challenges to DUI claims due to known prescribed medications or medical conditions such as diabetes are on the Internet. One such source is the National Traffic Law Center of the National District Attorneys Association (2013) website. The LNC should be aware of these challenges and other current research as DUI is an ever-evolving area, to include the legalization of marijuana and the implications of driving (National Institute on Drug Abuse, n.d.).

Electronics in motor vehicles and cell phones may play an increasing role in DUI cases including sensors and ignition locks in cars that may detect when a driver is under the influence or computer technology in the car that tracks speed and erratic driving maneuvers. As recently as the writing of this chapter, Washington State has enacted a new "E-DUI" law for driving under the influence of cell phones (distracted driving), (Fox News, 2017).

Sexual Assault/Rape

According to the National Sexual Violence Resource Center (2015), one in five women and one in 76 men has been sexually assaulted in their lifetime; more than half of sexual assaults are not reported to police. Forensic nurses such as Sexual Assault Nurse Examiners (SANEs) and others specially trained, such as Sexual Assault Forensic Examiners (SAFE), have demonstrated competency in performing sexual assault examinations. The role of the SANE/SAFE is to collect evidence, document evidence collected, testify in court (American Nurses Association (ANA) & International Association of Forensic Nurses (IAFN), 2015) and participate in chain of custody process.

> Example 16.1: Crystal and Rick were drinking at a party. Crystal passed out on a bed in the back of the house. When she woke up, Rick was on top of her. She told him to get off, but he had intercourse with her. She got up and grabbed her clothes and went into the bathroom and dressed. She was very upset and left shortly thereafter. She went home, showered, told a friend, and called the sheriff; consenting to an evidentiary examination was transported to a Sexual Assault Response Team (SART) center by law enforcement for an examination. Since Crystal suspected a drug was slipped into her drink, blood and urine toxicology tests were obtained. The examination took several hours. She was treated, given referrals and taken home. An investigation and an arrest ensued.

The LNC prepares for the defense or prosecution of the case. One fact the LNC should be aware of is similar genital injuries are found in both consensual sex and non-consensual sex in both adults and children (Henry, 2012). There are two common defenses to sexual assault, denial of involvement and intercourse was consensual.

The LNC assisting in this type of case reviews 911 calls, interviews all parties and witnesses, and reviews medical examinations and other investigative materials (Henry, 2012). Since alcohol was involved, the LNC should consider finding a fact witness or expert witness to present at trial.

The LNC finds answers to the following questions:

- Did the crime lab analyze the evidence collection kit?
- Was the chain of evidence fully followed and documented?
- Were the evidentiary examination findings of the victim positive or negative?
- Was a suspect examination completed? By whom?
- Were there positive or negative findings on the suspect examination?

A health history is obtained and reviewed to determine if any medications, illnesses, or other factors may have affected the physical examination findings (ANA & IAFN, 2015).

Child Sexual Abuse

> Broadly, child sexual abuse (CSA) is using children (under age 18) for sexual gratification. This can include sexual touching, penetration, and sexual acts such as flashing, masturbation, peeping, or exposure to pornography that may not involve touching. Child sexual abuse can be perpetrated by older youth as well as adults. The term child sexual assault may be used in reference to sexual violence perpetrated against a minor youth by a peer.
> (Washington Coalition of Sexual Assault Programs [WCSAP], 2016, para. 1)

The LNC working on this type of case either as a criminal case or civil matter should consider the concept of the differential diagnosis ensuring premature decisions about the event are avoided (Adams, 2011).

The best approach to child abuse cases is utilizing a multidisciplinary center that provides services in the local community such as a Children's Advocacy Center (CAC). The evaluation of the child is multifaceted. Components include the medical history both past and current, physical examination with diagnostic and forensic tests, forensic interview, and all the referrals that might be needed for the child and family (National Children's Alliance, 2014).

The perpetrators of this crime usually know and have access to the child. Most children who are subject to abuse do not report the incident in a timely fashion (72–120 hours or fewer). This is important to understand, as reporting delays result in little visible evidence. Children heal quickly and often do not report the abuse for many reasons. Many sexually abused children have normal anogenital exams, and sexual abuse may or may not leave permanent physical scars or marks (Jenny and Crawford-Jakubiak, 2013).

> Example 16.2: Patty, a 5-year-old, disclosed to her mother that "Uncle John" had touched her bottom. Her mother notified the sheriff, the child was interviewed. Patty was a poor historian and could only state this had happened 10–15 times when Uncle John was her babysitter. The medical examination revealed no findings.

The LNC assists the attorney by finding child abuse experts to analyze and opine about the case. For example, the medical expert will speak to the genital findings or lack of findings. The LNC gathers all the medical reports and helps with analysis for the prosecution or defense. The LNC evaluates the child's medical history both past and present; explores medical problems that mimic sexual abuse such as dermatological conditions or certain congenital findings; explores any descriptions of injuries that appear accidental such as bruises or bite marks.

The LNC obtains relevant information about the forensic interview including, was one completed, by whom, and whether it was videotaped. Securing the videotape and/or report is necessary as well as obtaining the protocol used for the forensic interview (Newlin et al., 2015). The LNC seeks information about family history including a prior history with child protective services (CPS) and whether the victim or other children in the family were removed from the home in the past. The LNC determines and investigates child care providers. A review of school records is necessary. The child's behavior, behavioral changes, and psychological problems are important aspects for the LNC to fully explore including how and to whom behavioral changes and problems are reported.

It can be frightening for a child to testify and confront the adult in court. Many children do not make good witnesses. There are court programs that will assist the child in learning about the courts. The advocates help during the testimony process for children (Court Appointed Special Advocates for Children [CASA], 2012).

Following the close of the criminal case, a civil case can commence. The LNC assists in civil suits by providing summaries of the information culled from the criminal case and again assists in locating experts for review and testimony.

Elder Abuse

"Elder abuse is an intentional act, or failure to act, by a caregiver or another person in a relationship involving an expectation of trust that causes or creates a risk of harm to an older adult (An older adult is defined as someone age 60 or older)" (CDC, 2017a, para 1). There are various types of elder abuse including the following: physical, financial, emotional, sexual, neglect, and self-neglect. Elder victimization can occur in any setting (home, hospital, nursing homes, and long-term care facilities).

Prevalence studies estimate 2–5 million Americans aged 60 and older have been injured, exploited, or otherwise mistreated by someone whom they depended on for care and protection. Based on statistical figures, the average number of reported abuse cases is approximately 2,150 each year. It is estimated for every case of elder abuse or neglect reported to authorities 14–23 go unreported. In 2014, the National Ombudsman Reporting System (NORS) documented 188,599 complaints involving abuse, gross neglect, or exploitation (National Center on Elder Abuse [NCEA], 2012). The National Council on Aging (NCOA) estimates 1 in 10 of those 60 years of age or older have been abused in one form or another (NCOA, n.d.).

"Abusers are both women and men. In almost 60% of elder abuse and neglect incidents, the perpetrator is a family member. Two thirds of perpetrators are adult children or spouses" (NCOA, n.d., para 3). Adults with dementia are at an even greater risk of elder abuse. Prevalence rates for abuse and neglect in people with dementia range from 27.5% to 55%. In one large study, "every point lower in global cognitive function was associated with an increased risk of physical abuse, emotional abuse, caregiver neglect and financial exploitation" (Dong, Simon, Rajan, & Evans, 2011, p. 212).

Adult protective services (APS) serves adults age 18 or older who are mentally or physically incapacitated to the extent they cannot provide self-care or manage their own affairs. The APS is utilized for those residing in the community setting. Adult Protective Servicers provide an 800 hotline in each state. In long-term care facilities, the Ombudsman advocates for residents. Complaints of abuse are also reportable to state regulatory agencies for health and safety. Mandated reporters include medical personnel, law enforcement, government agencies, and care custodians.

It is common for the elderly abused to not report abuse. Some victims are mentally incapable of communicating the abuse due to cognitive impairment. Elder and dependent victims often feel embarrassed and fearful. They may be reluctant to come forward for fear they are a nuisance, or fear reprisal. The elderly may be unwilling or unable to go to court. Elders typically want to protect family members.

Based on 2010 NORS Data provided to the National Center on Elder Abuse, abuse complaints in nursing homes were broken down and consist of physical abuse (29%), sexual abuse (7%), psychological abuse (21%), financial abuse (7%), gross neglect (14%), and resident to resident abuse of (22%) (NCEA, 2012).

The LNC plays a key role in elder abuse cases by interviewing clients, family, and witnesses. In addition, the LNC requests, reviews, analyzes, and reports on documents. These documents would include the following:

■ Medical records and reports from all healthcare providers/facilities in the past 10 years or number of years determined by retaining attorney
■ Policies and procedures of healthcare facilities involved in the case
■ Relevant photos
■ Depositions
■ Regulatory state surveys

The LNC locates and confers with expert witnesses to support or refute claims made by the plaintiff. This would include obtaining and reviewing expert curriculum vitae (CVs) and any resources the experts intend to use to formulate their opinions.

When evaluating or interviewing the abused (or presumed abused) elderly, the LNC should investigate these concerns (Hoover & Polson, 2014):

- Bruising in areas not usually subject to bruising, bleeding in the globe area, any unusual marks suggesting physical restraints were used
- Burns in unusual patterns that might be consistent with intentional or forceful immersion
- Nutritional deficits such as dehydration, malnourished or cachectic appearance, lack of food in the geriatric household, weight loss not explained by a medical condition
- Pressure injury, poorly healing wound(s), fractures, urine burns
- Fecal impaction
- Hygiene deficits, unkempt appearance
- Agitation, confusion, or fearfulness
- Dressed in inappropriate clothing for the weather
- Evidence of being over- or under-medicated
- Delay in medical attention
- Utilities not delivered (no electric service, for example)
- Specifics of in-home assistance organizations providing care (home health aide, housecleaning, visiting nurse) with contact information

If the elderly abused were cared for in a nursing home or other type of healthcare facility, the LNC prepares a potential list of witnesses and defendants elicited from interrogatories or deposition questions to include the following:

- Names of all licensed and unlicensed personnel involved in the care of the patient
- Names of all nursing supervisors
- Names of all involved physicians and
- Names of administrators, chief nursing officers, and directors of nursing

The LNC assists the attorney with elder abuse cases by thorough record review. The LNC must look beyond the documentation while performing these chart reviews to find out the precipitating events, the medical history, and factors related to patient outcomes. Also, the LNC identifies and may be asked to interview the people responsible for the plaintiff's care including: family members, caregivers, nurses, doctors, certified nursing assistants, rehabilitation therapists, dieticians, supervisors, administrators, chief nursing officers, and directors of nursing. It is imperative to review all facility policies and procedures. The LNC is in an excellent position to identify the breaches in standard of care in order to assist the attorney with the case.

The following example demonstrates why it is important to review all relevant medical records and utilize the appropriate expert witness who can opine precisely and accurately.

> Example 16.3. The patient underwent surgery for an excision of an abscess. The procedure left a deep narrow open wound. The treatment order was to pack the wound with Nu Gauze strips. The patient was sent home with home health aide to provide wound care treatment. The wound did not heal and became infected. Subsequently the patient was rehospitalized and underwent surgical debridement of this wound. During the debridement procedure, a 4×4 gauze packing was found in the wound cavity. It was alleged the home health nurses had not removed all of the packing material during dressing changes resulting in the wound infection requiring surgery, longer rehabilitation, emotional and physical pain and suffering.

The LNC reviewing this case identified and requested all medical records from hospitalizations as well as the home health records. Once the LNC reviewed the records, a certified wound expert also reviewed the records. The expert established that the 4×4 gauze pad found by the surgical team while debriding the infected wound was left there during the **first surgery**. The home health nurses had comprehensively documented their wound treatment and the use of Nu Gauze strips.

The issues of elder abuse are very complex. Aging of the baby boomers comprise the fastest growing group over the next 20 years with an increase from 12% to 31% (Hoover & Polson, 2014). Due to our aging population, more elder abuse cases are anticipated.

Domestic Violence

Domestic violence is a

> pattern of abusive behavior in any relationship that is used by one partner to gain or maintain power and control over another intimate partner. Domestic violence can be physical, sexual, emotional, economic, or psychological actions or threats of actions that influence another person. This includes any behaviors that intimidate, manipulate, humiliate, isolate, frighten, terrorize, coerce, threaten, blame, hurt, injure, or wound someone.
> (U.S. DOJ, n.d.-b, para 1)

In the U.S., the trend in some large urban areas is to have a domestic violence emergency response team (DVERT) to deal with domestic violence promptly. This team consists of law enforcement, advocates, social workers, and medical personnel. All team members generate documentation and reports. In communities that do not have such teams the victim of domestic violence can seek out a healthcare provider or go to the local emergency department for health care. To assist the attorney, the LNC reviews and analyzes the reports generated by all sources.

In a case of domestic violence, the LNC should find out whether this is the first incident. If not, all records from previous incidents (police reports, complaints, arrest records, court records, etc.) will need to be obtained, reviewed, analyzed, and evaluated. The LNC would want to find out what steps (if any) the victim has taken to separate or move away from the perpetrator; or what steps were taken to have the perpetrator removed? Were any prior protective orders or warrants served on the perpetrator? If so, what was the response of the perpetrator? Has the victim dropped previous charges against the perpetrator? If so, why? Has the victim ever sought refuge in a shelter? If so, what happened? Has the couple undergone any type of counseling or therapy? If so, what were the conclusions? What was the victim's account of the incidents?

Other questions the LNC should ask include the following:

■ What is the medical history of the victim?
■ Is there a history of pet abuse?
■ What is the medical history of the perpetrator?
■ Are there children involved? If so, what is the medical history of the children?
■ Have children been removed from the home? If so, how many times?
■ Was CPS (Child Protective Services) involved?
■ Were the children interviewed?
■ Are the children in foster care or in the care of other family members?

- Who is the caseworker?
- Was there any evidence or indication of emotional, physical, or sexual abuse of the children?

The LNC should consider the following questions when working with a DV client:

- Were physical injuries photographed?
- Was evidence obtained? If so, where is the evidence?
- Find out the diagnostic tests performed, and what were the results?
- Were statements made to medical professionals documented?
- What was the psychological/emotional state of the victim at the time of exam?
- How much time elapsed from the time of the physical abuse to the time treatment started?
- If rape occurred, was it reported?
- Was a sexual assault examination performed? If so, what were the findings?

Variables for the LNC to consider in the record review of the perpetrator of this crime include:

- Is there a previous criminal history?
- What does the police report say?
- Are the officers who took the report available to discuss the report?
- What is the medical history of the perpetrator? Drug and alcohol abuse? Psychological or mental problems?
- Has there been an evaluation by a mental health provider?

Strangulation

Strangulation is now recognized within the medical and legal community for its high risk of lethality. As of 2014, 44 states, the District of Columbia, the federal government, and two territories have passed felony strangulation laws (National District Attorneys Association [NDAA], 2014). Physicians, forensic nurses, medical professionals, and even law enforcement are utilized as experts and testify in court about strangulation. Strangulation can be especially challenging to medical and law enforcement personnel due to the lack of external signs of injury (Training Institute on Strangulation Prevention, n.d.). Even in fatal strangulation cases, there are often no external signs of injury to the neck (Hawley & Heisler, 2012). "Lack of visible evidence is common and should not be used to minimize either the forensic significance or the medical risk to life" (Strack & Gwinn, 2015, p. 77).

"The odds of becoming an attempted homicide increased by about seven-fold for women who had been strangled by their partner" (Glass et al., 2008, p. 329; New York State Office for the Prevention of Domestic Violence [NYSOPDV], n.d.). Although this is seen more frequently in domestic violence, it is also seen in sexual assault and child abuse.

When reviewing a case where strangulation is at issue, the LNC evaluates the police report, EMS records, and 911 recordings. An added benefit to obtaining the 911 recording, assuming the victim was the caller, is to assess for change in voice of the victim. In some jurisdictions, a special supplemental strangulation form becomes part of the police report. The questions on the form requests details specific to symptoms related to strangulation.

Where a healthcare forensic team is involved in the care of the strangulation victim, the LNC should be aware that some teams obtain neck swabs. This is useful for collecting potential epithelial cells for DNA if skin to skin contact was reported. Others are using alternative light sources to assist with the strangulation examination. Forensic records may not be included in the regular medical record of a healthcare facility, and may need to be requested separately.

Potential sources of DNA include (Magalhães, Dinis-Oliveira, Silva, Corte-Real, & Nuno Viera, 2015):

- Skin
- Blood and bodily fluids
- Feces
- Urine

It is important to have an expert review all medical records when dealing with a strangulation victim. The strangulation expert has the ability to recognize specific symptoms and indicators of the seriousness of strangulation. For example, petechiae on the face indicates the jugular veins were occluded, but the carotid arteries remained patent during at least part of the strangulation event. Loss of consciousness can occur within 10 seconds, and death within minutes (Faugno, Waszak, Strack, Brooks, & Gwinn, 2013).

Expert review is useful because it can provide an opinion as to whether a strangulation occurred and/or whether the event meets state specific criteria to substantiate a strangulation charge. Some of the issues the expert addresses and the LNC should be aware of include the following:

- Does the strangulation event description meet the requirements for strangulation charge?
- Is there a previous history where domestic violence has been associated with strangulation?
- Did the victim experience a change in voice during the strangulation and was the voice recorded on the 911 tape?

Death Investigations

The LNC assisting the criminal attorney must be familiar with the process of death investigation. This includes understanding the roles and responsibilities of the investigation team as well as being familiar with the forensic autopsy. A medical physician performs the forensic autopsy. In some areas of the country the responsible persons in charge of the forensic autopsy are medical examiners or forensic pathologists or even coroners. Some coroners are forensic pathologists while others are elected officials without medical training (CrimeSceneInvestigatorEDU, n.d.). Coroners without medical training would lead the investigation but would not perform autopsies; rather they contract out the autopsy.

The LNC working on these types of legal cases needs to have a practical understanding of the underlying cause of death, such as gunshot wound (WHO, n.d.), mechanism of death, the physiologic derangement resulting in death such as hemorrhage (Medical Dictionary, n.d.-a) and manner of death, how the death came about such as from natural causes, homicide, suicide, or accident (Medical Dictionary, n.d.-b). The LNC may need to review records involving the following list of causes of death:

- Gunshot and firearm wounds
- Cutting wounds

- Stabbing wounds
- Blunt force injuries
- Poisoning
- Asphyxia deaths (strangulation)
- Autoerotic deaths
- Arson and fire deaths
- Drowning
- Suicides

> Example 16.4: Law enforcement received a report that a female body was in a shallow riverbed. The victim's domestic partner told police investigators the victim fell off an overpass into the river. Attempts to rescue the victim by her partner were in vain. There were noticeable cuts and bruises on the body, which would corroborate the story. After the autopsy, it was determined many of the injuries did not match the description of the incident. Upon further investigation, it was determined the victim's domestic partner had recently taken out an insurance policy on the victim.

The LNC considers several questions when given this scenario. Was there a history of domestic violence? What interpersonal characteristics did this couple display prior to this event? What were the toxicology findings of the autopsy? Was anything found at the scene that would be consistent with the types of blunt injury wounds to the victim's head? Were there any findings at the time of autopsy to indicate the head trauma was the fatal injury? Were there any findings consistent with drowning? What was the affect and response of the domestic partner at the time police arrived on the scene? Who reported the incident? What was the financial situation of the couple? What was the work history of the boyfriend? Was anyone else with the couple? If so, what was their relationship to the victim?

Forensic Nurses: Education and Training; Scope and Standards of Practice

Forensic nursing education varies from a certificate program to advanced degree programs. Forensic nurses are certified in a practice area, such as sexual assault, examination of adult or pediatric patients (SANE-A or SANE-P). Conferring certifications is by examination verifying a specific knowledge base (IAFN, n.d.). Graduate degree programs in forensic nursing at both the Master's and Doctoral levels are available in several areas of the United States (Hammer, Moynihan, & Pagliaro, 2013). Emergency department nurses have a degree in nursing and may have either a certification or a certificate in specific forensic areas.

The American Nurses Association (ANA) and International Association of Forensic Nurses (IAFN) co-publish standards of practice for forensic nursing. The IAFN website has a resource section to include educational content on SANE training (IAFN, n.d.).

Hospitals not only have hospital wide policy and procedures but unit based policies and procedures. Also, nursing has clinical practice guidelines providing evidenced based standards of care. The LNC should be aware that sometimes the hospital's forensic team has specific policies and clinical practice guidelines (CPG). The forensic nurse may testify for the defense or prosecution. The forensic nurse's goal is to communicate and educate the court on evidentiary findings. The forensic nurse may testify as an expert fact witness (testify without offering an opinion) or an expert witness (may offer opinions) (see chapters 31 and 32), depending on experience. As an expert fact witness, the forensic nurse educates the trier of fact about what is in the chart, verifies chain of custody as to collection and preservation of evidence, and authenticates photographs taken by the forensic nurse. Depending on the forensic nurse's experience, testimony can include information about the consistency or inconsistency between injuries and history provided by the patient.

Forensics Within the Emergency Department

Hospital emergency departments may or may not have a designated forensic nurse (or team) on staff or available to the department on an on-call basis; and some hospitals have contracts with independent forensic nursing companies to provide "on call" availability as needed. The LNC reviews hospital forensic policies and procedures to determine how forensic cases are handled in the ED.

LNC Review of Emergency Department Records

When the LNC reviews forensic documentation of injuries in an ED record, there may appear to be conflicting documentation, or different types of documentation. A triage sheet includes only a minimal amount of information. This is a quick assessment to make decisions as to the level of care needed. Few, if any details are on the triage sheet, and sometimes the chief complaint changes when the victim is in the privacy of a room. For example, in triage, the chief complaint may be a trip and fall down a set of stairs, but once in the privacy of a treatment room, the patient may disclose being hit by a domestic partner. If the hospital is a teaching institution, the LNC may see one to two physician documentation sheets. The resident and attending physician might each fill out a history and injury description note.

Most hospitals have separate policies and protocols for the management of forensic cases (sexual assault) with a separate documentation tool as well as a special consent form that covers evidence collection. There are two services provided to the sexual assault victim: medical care and evidence collection. The victim of sexual assault has the right to consent or refuse treatment and consent or refuse evidence collection. The sexual assault victim may refuse to involve the police. A minor may give informed consent without parental consent for services in some states. Likewise, in some states, a minor can refuse to consent to services. In some states some adults are legally mandated to report abuse of a minor to the authorities. The LNC would need to be familiar with the laws in the state in which the incident occurred.

When a victim is a trauma patient, the trauma flow sheet may also contain injury documentation. Documenting trauma injuries is very important. Non-life-threatening injuries may be missed by the trauma team, but may be very important in the forensic nurse's assessment. Although the trauma team makes every effort to do a full assessment, in the presence of life-threatening injuries a forensic evaluation is deferred, which explains any gaps in the patient's time of arrival and the beginning of a forensic assessment. For example, if a victim presents as a trauma patient with a knife wound in the chest, causing massive amounts of blood loss and also has multiple abrasions on the knees; addressing the cause of the blood loss will stop the assessment until the bleeding is under control. The abrasions may not show up on the ED documentation at all. If a forensic nurse is documenting injuries in addition to the bedside nurse delivering immediate care, missed injury documentation decreases.

When reviewing medical records related to gunshot wounds (GSW), the LNC should be aware that medical record documentation has the potential to lead the reader down the wrong path. Some staff including nurses, emergency physicians, and surgeons may erroneously identify entrance and exit wounds. "Contrary to popular opinion, exit wounds are not always larger than entrance wounds" (Hanlon & Srivastava, 2012, para. 8). Determination of entrance and exits wounds is best determined by ballistics experts, specially trained forensic nurses, physicians, or forensic pathologists. These specialists have extensive training in GSW and can justify those findings based on science. For instance, a shooter might claim self-defense yet the victim states he was running away when shot in the back ("entrance wound") and the bullet "exited" through the chest per ED documentation, this assertion might later prove wrong and misleading by a forensic specialist.

The forensic nurse has received specialized training in injury recognition and documentation; trained to document only what they see using specific injury terminology. Conflicts in documentation between the regular emergency chart and the forensic chart can happen. Emergency department nurses, without forensic training, may describe the wound in less precision words. For example, the definition of what a laceration is in forensic terms versus an incised wound. ED staff commonly use laceration to describe any break in the skin. Forensically, a laceration is a blunt force injury (jagged wound, tear in skin) while an incised wound occurs from a sharp edge such as a knife (Rozzi, 2014; The Free Dictionary, n.d.).

Physical Evidence Collection in the ED

The LNC should be aware of various significant factors related to evidence collection obtained in the ED. Maintaining a chain of custody can be challenging in the ED setting. The following discussion of evidence collection in the ED serves to demonstrate the difficulties encountered in this setting.

Clothing Evidence

Clothing evidence may place a person at a crime scene or relate to the crime itself. The following examples are illustrative of the importance of physical evidence: (1) a pedestrian struck by a vehicle may have identifiable tire marks on the clothing, (2) a belt buckle on the pedestrian may have left a mark on the vehicle and (3) the clothing of a gunshot victim may have soot and powder that can assist with range determination.

Care and treatment of the victim in the ED can directly affect the clothing and potentially destroy important evidence. When a person has life threatening injuries, articles of clothing are removed as fast as possible with little movement of the victim to prevent further injury. The best way to remove clothing is to cut the clothing off the victim. Many first responders are taught not to cut through existing holes or tears but that does not mean it does not happen in the rush to save a life. Not all clothing arrives at the ED with the victim. It is possible articles of clothing may be left at the scene, in the transporting ambulance or at the first facility if the victim was transported from another medical facility.

There are several issues the LNC considers regarding clothing evidence collection. Removal technique can affect the quality of the evidence. Placing the clothing in paper bags or plastic can affect the clothing. If the clothing was not completely dry, plastic can facilitate mold growth. Clothing placed in individual bags versus in one bag can affect an evaluation of the clothing. The background of the person collecting the clothing also matters. Was clothing collected by a police officer, forensic nurse or the ED treating nurse? Other issues include finding out when clothing was collected and if photographed when it was photographed prior to bagging it. A forensic nurse may or may not photograph the clothing. If done it would be for the purposes of basic identification of the clothing. Photographing the clothing would depend on individual policies of the hospital forensic program. If there is a forensic nurse attending a crime victim within the ED there is an expectation that the clothing collected is evidence and therefore collection is done with preservation in mind. When clothing arrives to the police department from the ED or crime scene, it is removed from the bags or packaging, dried, if needed, and photographed with a focus on any marks, cuts or holes.

Sources of DNA

There are opportunities for someone trained in DNA collection to obtain samples from victims in the ED. For example, when a victim arrives at the ED and a bite mark is present, obtaining a DNA swab for testing is done. Likewise, broken or chipped fingernails may indicate a struggle took place between the victim and the attacker. Sampling the fingernail material may yield DNA of the attacker and lead to identification.

Weapons

During handling, knives are packaged to avoid injury to others and to preserve potential fingerprints and other evidence such as blood and tissue. Most hospitals have policies for handling weapons, especially firearms. Only properly trained hospital personnel handle firearms found on patients. In regard to evidence, it is rare to find an identifiable fingerprint on a firearm. This is partially due to the design of the firearm where irregular surfaces combined with recoil power tends to cause smudging of fingerprints (DiMaio, 2015). Handling firearms may necessitate the involvement of a third party in the chain of custody such as hospital security. The forensic nurse documents where the firearm is found and who removed it prior to transferring to police.

Bullets

Some bullets have identifiable marks matching a particular firearm. Therefore, the way a bullet is removed from a victim or a crime scene becomes a critical issue. Using a soft tipped hemostat would decrease the chances of adding a stray mark onto the bullet during removal. Unfortunately, most hemostats in the hospital are stainless steel and may create additional marks on the bullet. Additionally, there are times where a surgeon decides not to remove the bullet from a patient. An LNC would carefully review all the medical records including operative reports to find out what is removed, how it was removed, what was left in situ, and if the chain of custody was appropriately followed and documented.

Trace Evidence and Unidentified Substances

Trace evidence consists of small bits of material such as skin, hair, blood flecks, fibers, grass, soil, or glass easily lost at the scene, in the ambulance, or in the ED. When rolling a victim during injury assessment, at the scene, or in the ED, leaves or grass may drop from the victim and be left at the scene or on the ED floor. The sheet from the stretcher of the transporting ambulance contains potential trace evidence as well. On occasion, when a victim is moved from a bed at home or elsewhere, the EMTs sometime use bed linen to move the victim to the stretcher. The bed sheet may contain trace evidence. If the victim's clothing is dropped on the floor of the ED, the potential exists that trace evidence not related to the crime will be inadvertently picked up or evidence on the clothes may be lost on the floor. Chain of custody procedures are applied to unidentified substances such as pills, powders, leafy material, and liquids found on victims; once properly tagged, transfer to the police is done.

Photographic Evidence and Forensic Records

Photographic documentation of injuries can be a very powerful tool in explaining injuries to a jury. It is more effective for the jury to see photographs then describe an incised wound of the neck from one ear to the other ear caused by a sharp-edged object such as a knife or razor. When a jury views a photograph of a gunshot wound of the arm it may not show the real extent of the injury. However, the x-ray showing bullet fragments and a shattered humerus has greater impact.

It is imperative hospital procedures are followed in documenting and storing photos and obtaining photos before and after treatment is the optimal way. A ruler should be in each photo to show scale with date and time indicated. However, if the victim is in critical condition, the forensic nurse may only have seconds to take photos as physical assessment, rolling and moving the patient, and all manner of resuscitation efforts get underway. Invasive resuscitation measures may change the appearance of injuries. If the victim arrives with life threatening injuries, time in the ED may be for five minutes or less before going to the operating room. In this case, the forensic nurse may only have time to take one or two photos or none and those photos may not be ideal due to the circumstances.

When reviewing a chart, the LNC will look for detailed forensic documentation. The medical record should indicate whether a forensic nurse was in the ED, present during resuscitation efforts, and whether photos were taken. The LNC must be very specific when requesting records from a hospital. Sexual assault nursing examination (SANE) records, the forensic chart, and photographs taken in the ED will need to be specifically itemized in the request. In some hospitals, forensic records are stored separately from the usual medical records department to adhere to chain of custody principles. Some hospitals may print photos or copy photos while others use digital cameras and may make a compact disc for law enforcement. If others request forensic photos, they obtain them with a Health Insurance Portability and Accountability Act (HIPAA) compliant authorization.

Generally, the ED does not have a SANE nurse or forensic nurse in-house 24 hours a day. This lessens the chances of evidence being properly collected. However, some ED nurses with education on the principles of evidence collection and preservation can provide this service. These nurses maintain care of the patient as their first priority, and may not have the opportunity for forensic-related activities such as placing clothing in separate paper bags, documenting and photographing injuries and evidence. Items are collected but not according to the standards of an established forensic team. Emergency department nurses can testify to observations and procedures of care, injury assessment, and evidence collection, but the LNC should keep in mind they may not be comfortable testifying regarding forensic evidence and reluctant to do so.

The Role of the LNC

Criminal Case

The LNC's analysis of the facts of any case will be the same regardless of working plaintiff or defense. The scope of the LNC's duties may include obtaining, organizing, reviewing, and analyzing some or all of the following: (Note: The list is not intended to be all-inclusive, as the actions of the LNC will be determined by the type of criminal case.)

■ Medical or forensic reports to assess the extent of injuries and determine whether injuries are consistent with the time frame and history provided

■ Past medical records to assess old injuries (in the case of domestic violence, elder abuse, or child abuse) or whether an underlying medical condition or disease is present to explain the physical findings

■ Autopsy reports to:
   1. determine whether injuries match history (victim strangled, then house set on fire to make the death appear accidental)
   2. assess for previous old injuries
   3. ascertain if entrance/exit wound has been determined in gunshot cases in order to substantiate claims of self-defense or distance from firearm
   4. identify the type of weapon used (blunt instrument, tire iron, rock, knife, electrical cord) from wounds in, on, and through the body
   5. determine cause and manner of death
   6. determine postmortem mutilation, injury, and the possibility that the body was moved
   7. identify approximate time of death
   8. determine whether the death was an accident, suicide, or homicide
   9. identify how much time elapsed between the fatal injury and the time of death

■ Forensic science reports to:
   1. determine whether the accused can be linked to the scene by trace evidence, fingerprints, bite marks, blood, semen, DNA
   2. determine whether illicit or prescription drugs or alcohol were involved
   3. determine the sex and race of skeletal remains
   4. assess the evidence gathered during a sexual assault exam (semen in body orifice or on the body, pubic hair not belonging to the victim)
   5. determine whether the weapon (if located) is consistent with the type of weapon used in the commission of the crime

■ Police reports to:
   1. glean information about the initial crime scene (from measurements, photographs, drawings, and descriptions contained in the report)
   2. identify witnesses and other investigators
   3. determine if persons and objects were moved or removed from the scene
   4. identify the disposition of the injured or killed

■ Supplemental investigative reports (police, fire, EMS, 911 voice recordings if available and call logs)

■ Investigation reports from the prosecuting attorney's office or private investigators working for the criminal defense attorney to obtain information concerning witnesses and witness statements and the additional gathering of evidence by the investigators involved in the case

■ Psychological testing/reports to:
1. evaluate the competency of the accused to stand trial
2. assess the state of mind of both the perpetrator and the victim at the time of the crime
3. evaluate the effect of the crime on the victim
4. determine whether the accused had a history of mental illness (diagnosis, treatment, medications, compliance)
5. assess recommendations made by healthcare professionals
6. assess psychological profiles in the case of serial offenders

In addition, the LNC may be involved in:

■ Interviewing clients, witnesses, and potential experts to gather information about the crime and to determine whether the information supports or refutes physical evidence. If differences exist, the task is to determine how to reconcile the differences and to provide information to experts regarding the case
■ Locating experts and acting as liaison between expert and attorney
■ Assisting the expert by researching the literature and providing case materials to the expert
■ Performing research in scientific disciplines as indicated (medical, forensic science, law enforcement)
■ Preparing narrative reports, chronologies, and case progress reports
■ Educating the attorney on the medical issues involved in the case and
■ Preparing for and assisting with trial

Civil Litigation

After the conclusion of a criminal case, a civil lawsuit may ensue against the defendant or against an entity that should have prevented the crime; the entity may have been a named defendant in the criminal case. The particulars of the civil case will determine the LNC's role. As an example, a nursing home or assisted living facility may be named in a lawsuit in a case of an assault, sexual assault/rape, or elder abuse perpetrated by an employee. This type of claim may include (among others) failure of the nursing home or assisted living facility to provide a safe environment and wrongful hiring of the perpetrator/employee. In the above example, the LNC would obtain (or attempt to obtain) and analyze the following:

■ Criminal prosecution file (a list of witnesses and other valuable information)
■ Plaintiff's current and past medical records to determine injuries; assess for pain and suffering and diminution of abilities due to the injuries sustained
■ Nursing home policies and procedures including employee training logs
■ Investigation records performed by nursing home or the assisted living facility (if discoverable)
■ Employee time sheets (to determine potential witnesses and level of staffing)
■ Nursing home human resource file of perpetrator (employee)
■ State and/or federal surveys and/or inspection reports
■ Past complaints filed with survey agencies and/or state health department, federal government against nursing home facility
■ Past investigations by police as well as healthcare surveyors, past sanctions and or penalties against the nursing home/assisted living facility and
■ Past history of owners and operators of nursing home/assisted living facility

The LNC would assist the plaintiff attorney in developing the case including preparing reports, working with expert witnesses, and providing research as needed. The LNC on the defense side would function in a parallel role to the plaintiff LNC to refute the allegations.

Summary

The LNC possessing knowledge about the criminal justice system and the field of forensics is in an advantageous position to assist the criminal attorney with cases that involve medical findings (abuse, sexual abuse/rape, assault, driving under the influence, strangulation, murder). Understanding types of evidence and chain of custody procedures, issues involving chain of custody and processing of evidence will assist the LNC in both criminal cases and civil cases that may arise subsequent to a criminal case. Legal nurse consultants with a strong clinical background will be able to understand the victim's medical record and will be aware of how to procure the forensic information for use in case development. Additional exploration, training, and education in forensics will undoubtedly add to the LNC's knowledge base making the LNC a more valuable member of the legal team.

References

Adams, J. (2011). Medical evaluation of suspected child sexual abuse. *Journal of Child Sexual Abuse, 20*(5), 588–605. doi:10.1080/10538712.2011.606107.

Alcohol Policy Information System. (2016). Blood alcohol concentration (BAC) limits: Adult operators of noncommercial motor vehicles. Retrieved from https://alcoholpolicy.niaaa.nih.gov/Blood_Alcohol_Concentration_Limits_Adult_Operators_of_Noncommercial_Motor_Vehicles.html.

American Nurses Association, & International Association of Forensic Nurses. (2015). *Forensic nursing: Scope and standards of practice*. Silver Springs, MD: NurseBooks.org. Retrieved from www.nursebooks.org/Main-Menu/Standards/A-G/Forensic-Nursing-Scope-and-Standards-of-Practice.aspx.

Centers for Disease Control and Prevention. (2017a). Elder abuse. Retrieved from www.cdc.gov/violence prevention/elderabuse/definitions.html.

Centers for Disease Control and Prevention. (2017b). Motor vehicle safety: Impaired driving. Retrieved from www.cdc.gov/motorvehiclesafety/impaired_driving/impaired-drv_factsheet.html.

Coons, P. (2015, July 1). How to document your chain of custody and why it's important. [D4 Blog post]. Retrieved from http://d4discovery.com/discover-more/how-to-document-your-chain-of-custody-and-why-its-important#sthash.q0lL5zod.dpbs.

Court Appointed Special Advocates for Children. (2012). Rationale and methods for preparing children for success in the court room. *Judges' page newsletter archive*. Retrieved from www.casaforchildren.org/site/c.mtJSJ7MPIsE/b.8173513/k.1FB7/JP_10_NCAC.htm.

CrimeSceneInvestigatorEDU. (n.d.). Crime scene investigator resources. Retrieved from www.crimesceneinvestigatoredu.org.

Criminal Law Lawyer Source. (n.d.). How to develop a defense strategy. Retrieved from www.criminal-law-lawyer-source.com/tips/defense.html.

DiMaio, V. (2015). *Gunshot wounds: Practical aspects of firearms, ballistics and forensic techniques* (2nd ed.). Washington, DC: CRC Press.

Dong, X., Simon, M., Rajan K., & Evans, D. A. (2011). Association of cognitive function and risk for elder abuse in a community-dwelling population. *Dementia and Geriatric Cognitive Disorders, 32*(3), 209–215. doi.org/10.1159/000334047.

Faugno, D., Waszak, D., Strack, G., Brooks, M. A., & Gwinn, C. (2013). Strangulation forensic examination: Best practice for health care providers. *Advanced Emergency Nursing Journal, 35*(4), 314–327. doi: 10.1097/TME.0b013e3182aa05d3.

Federal Bureau of Investigation. (2011). FBI quality assurance standards for forensic DNA testing laboratories. Retrieved from www.fbi.gov/file-repository/quality-assurance-standards-for-forensic-dna-testing-laboratories.pdf/view.

Federal Evidence Review. (2015). Hearsay. Retrieved from http://federalevidence.com/rules-of evidence#802.

FindLaw. (n.d.). Definition of rape. Retrieved at http://criminal.findlaw.com/criminal-charges/rape.html.

Fox News. (2017). Police and law enforcement. Retrieved from www.foxnews.com/us/2017/07/18/washington-state-enacts-new-e-dui-law-for-driving-under-influence-phones.html.

Glass, N., Laughon, K., Campbell, J. C., Block, C. R., Hanson, G., Sharps, P. W., & Taliaferro, E. (2008). Non-fatal strangulation is an important risk factor for homicide of women. *Journal of Emergency Medicine, 35*(3), 329–335.

Hammer, R., Moynihan, B., & Pagliaro, E. (2013). *Forensic nursing: A handbook for practice* (2nd ed.). Burlington, MA: Jones and Bartlett.

Hanlon, D., & Srivastava, A. (2012). Gunshot wounds: Management and myths. *Trauma Reports.* Retrieved from www.ahcmedia.com/articles/76797-gunshot-wounds-management-and-myths.

Hawley, D., & Heisler, C. (2012). Strangulation and suffocation. National Adult Protective Services Association (NAPSA) Conference 2012. Retrieved from www.napsa-now.org/wp-content/uploads/2012/11/102.pdf.

Henry, T. (Ed.). (2012). *Atlas of sexual violence.* St. Louis, MO: C.V. Mosby.

Hoover, R. M., & Polson, M. (2014). Detecting elder abuse and neglect: Assessment and intervention. *American Family Physician, 89*(6), 453–460. Retrieved from www.aafp.org/afp/2014/0315/p453.html.

International Association of Forensic Nurses. (n.d.). Education offerings: Online pediatric and adult SANE training. Retrieved from www.forensicnurses.org/?page=EducationMainPage.

James, N. (2012). DNA testing in criminal justice: Background, current law, grants and issues. Prepared by Congressional Research Service. Retrieved from https://fas.org/sgp/crs/misc/R41800.pdf.

James, S. H., & Nordby, J. J. (2005). *Forensic science: An introduction to scientific and investigative techniques.* Boca Raton, FL: CRC Press.

Jenny, C., & Crawford-Jakubiak, J. E. (2013). The evaluation of children in the primary care setting when sexual abuse is suspected. *Pediatrics, 132*(2), e558–e567. doi:10.1542/peds.2013-1741.

King, N. J. (2014). The judicial system: Appeals and post conviction review. In A. Redlich, J. Acker, R. Norris, & C. Bonventre (Eds.), *Examining wrongful convictions: Stepping back, moving forward* (pp. 1–19). Durham, NC: Carolina Academic Press. Retrieved from https://law.vanderbilt.edu/files/publications/King-CH13.pdf.

Kopishke, L. (2004). Mitigation specialist: A natural role for the LNC. *Journal of Legal Nurse Consulting, 15*(3). Retrieved from www.aalnc.org/page/journal-v2.0.

Legal Dictionary. (n.d.). Statute. Retrieved from http://legal-dictionary.thefreedictionary.com/statute.

Legal Information Institute. (n.d.-a). Fifth amendment. Retrieved from www.law.cornell.edu/wex/fifth_amendment.

Legal Information Institute. (n.d.-b). Sixth amendment. Retrieved from www.law.cornell.edu/constitution/sixth_amendment.

Legal Match. (2015). What is 3rd degree assault? Retrieved from www.legalmatch.com/law-library/article/what-is-3rd-degree-assault.html.

Magalhães, T., Dinis-Oliveira R. J., Silva, B., Corte-Real, F., & Nuno Vieira, D. (2015). Biological evidence management for DNA analysis in cases of sexual assault. *The Scientific World Journal.* Retrieved from www.hindawi.com/journals/tswj/2015/365674/cta/doi:10.1155/2015/365674.

Medical Dictionary. (n.d.-a). Mechanism of death. Retrieved from http://medical-dictionary.thefreedictionary.com/mechanism+of+death.

Medical Dictionary. (n.d.-b). Manner of death. Retrieved from http://medical-dictionary.thefreedictionary.com/manner+of+death.

Miranda Warning. (n.d.). Miranda warning: Understanding your rights. Retrieved from www.miranda-warning.org.

National Center on Elder Abuse. (2012). Abuse of residents of long term care facilities. Retrieved from https://ncea.acl.gov/RESOURCES/docs/Abuse-LongTermCare-Facilities-2012.pdf.

National Children's Alliance. (2014). How the CAC model works. Retrieved from www.nationalchildren-salliance.org/cac-model.

National Council on Aging. (n.d.). Retrieved from www.ncoa.org/public-policy-action/elder-justice/elder-abuse-facts/.

National District Attorneys Association. (2014). Criminal strangulation/impeding breathing. Retrieved from www.ndaa.org/pdf/strangulation_statutory_compilation_11_7_2014.pdf.

National Institute on Drug Abuse. (n.d.). Does marijuana use affect driving? Retrieved from www.druga-buse.gov/publications/research-reports/marijuana/does-marijuana-use-affect-driving.

National Institute of Justice. (2010). What is codis? Retrieved from www.nij.gov/journals/266/pages/backlogs-codis.aspx.

National Institute of Justice. (2015). Forensic sciences: Types of evidence. Retrieved from www.nij.gov/topics/forensics/evidence/pages/welcome.aspx.

National Institute of Justice. (2017). Forensic sciences. Retrieved from www.nij.gov/topics/forensics/Pages/welcome.aspx.

National Sexual Violence Resource Center. (2015). Statistics about sexual violence. Retrieved from www.nsvrc.org/sites/default/files/publications_nsvrc_factsheet_media-packet_statistics-about-sexual-violence_0.pdf.

National Traffic Law Center of the National District Attorneys Association. (2013). Challenges and defenses II. Claims and responses to common challenges and defenses in driving while impaired cases. Retrieved from www.ndaa.org/pdf/Chalenges%20and%20Defenses%20II.pdf.

Newlin, C., Steele, L. C., Chamberlin, A., Anderson, J., Kenniston, J., Russell, A., Stewart, H., & Vaughan-Eden, V. (2015). Child forensic interviewing: Best practices. *Juvenile Justice Bulletin*. Retrieved from www.ojjdp.gov/pubs/248749.pdf.

New York State Office for the Prevention of Domestic Violence. (n.d.). Domestic violence and strangula-tion: A guide for victims and professionals. Retrieved from www.opdv.ny.gov/professionals/health/strangulation.pdf.

NYCourts. (n.d.). Circumstantial evidence. Retrieved from www.nycourts.gov/judges/cji/1-General/CJI2d.Circumstantial_Evidence.pdf.

Rozzi, H. (2014). Laceration or incised wound: Know the difference. *ACEP Now*. Retrieved from www.acepnow.com/article/laceration-incised-wound-know-difference/.

Strack, G., & Gwinn, C. (2015). Use of experts: Tips for prosecutors and expert witnesses. In *Responding to strangulation in Alaska: Guidelines for law enforcement, health care providers, advocates, and prosecutors* (Chapter 9). Retrieved from http://dhss.alaska.gov/ocs/Documents/childrensjustice/strangulation/strangulation.pdf.

Strutin, K. (2010). DNA identification evidence in criminal prosecutions. *Law and Technology Resources for Legal Professionals*. Retrieved from www.llrx.com/2010/03/dna-identification-evidence-in-criminal-prosecutions/.

The Free Dictionary. (n.d.). Laceration, incision. Retrieved from www.thefreedictionary.com/laceration.

The Law Dictionary. (n.d.-a). What is crime? *Black's law dictionary free online legal dictionary* (2nd ed.). Retrieved from www. thelawdictionary.org/crime.

The Law Dictionary. (n.d.-b). Misdemeanor. *Black's law dictionary free online legal dictionary* (2nd ed.). Retrieved from www.thelawdictionary.org/misdemeanor./.

The Law Dictionary. (n.d.-c). What is proof beyond a reasonable doubt? *Black's law dictionary free online legal dictionary* (2nd ed.). Retrieved from http://thelawdictionary.org/proof-beyond-a-reasonable-doubt/.

The Law Dictionary. (n.d.-d). What is preponderance of evidence? *Black's law dictionary free online legal dictionary* (2nd ed.). http://thelawdictionary.org/preponderance-of-evidence/.

The Law Dictionary. (n.d.-e). What is criminal intent? *Black's law dictionary free online legal dictionary* (2nd ed.). Retrieved from http://thelawdictionary.org/criminal-intent/.

The Law Dictionary. (n.d.-f). What is probable cause? *Black's law dictionary free online legal dictionary* (2nd ed.). Retrieved from http://thelawdictionary.org/probable-cause/.

The Law Dictionary. (n.d.-g). What is testimony? *Black's law dictionary free online legal dictionary* (2nd ed.). Retrieved from http://thelawdictionary.org/testimony/.

Thompson, W. C. (n.d.). The potential for error in forensic DNA testing. *Council for Responsible Genetics, Genewatch.* Retrieved from www.councilforresponsiblegenetics.org/genewatch/GeneWatchPage.aspx?pageId=57.

Training Institute on Strangulation Prevention. (n.d.). Impact of strangulation crimes: Important facts. www.strangulationtraininginstitute.com/impact-of-strangulation-crimes/important-facts/.

United Nations Office on Drugs and Crime. (2009). Crime scene and physical evidence awareness for non-forensic personnel. Retrieved from www.unodc.org/documents/scientific/Crime_scene_awareness__Ebook.pdf.

U.S. Department of Justice. (n.d.-a). U.S. attorney's criminal resource manual, section 626 plea agreements and sentencing appeal waivers: Discussion of the law. Retrieved from www.justice.gov/usam/criminal-resource-manual-626-plea-agreements-and-sentencing-appeal-waivers-discussion-law.

U.S. Department of Justice. (n.d.-b). Office on Violence Against Women. Retrieved from www.justice.gov/ovw/domestic-violence.

U.S. Department of Justice. (n.d.-c). Preliminary hearing. Offices of the United States Attorneys. Retrieved from www.justice.gov/usao/justice-101/preliminary-hearing.

U.S. Department of Justice Archives. (updated 2017). Using DNA to solve crimes. Office of the Attorney General. Retrieved from www.justice.gov/archives/ag/advancing-justice-through-dna-technology-using-dna-solve-crimes.

US Legal. (n.d.-a). Circumstantial evidence. Retrieved from https://definitions.uslegal.com/c/circumstantial-evidence/.

US Legal. (n.d.-b). Battery. Retrieved from www.definitions.uslegal.com/b/battery.

US Legal. (n.d.-c). Chain of custody law and legal definition. Retrieved from https://definitions.uslegal.com/c/chain-of-custody/.

US Legal. (n.d.-d). Felony. Retrieved from www.definitions.uslegal.com/f/felony.

US Legal. (n.d.-e). First degree murder. Retrieved from www.definitions.uslegal.com/f/first-degree-murder/.

US Legal. (n.d.-f). Second degree murder. Retrieved from www.definitions.uslegal.com/s/second-degree-murder.

US Legal. (n.d.-g). Misdemeanor. Retrieved from www.definitions.uslegal.com/m/misdemeanor./.

US Legal. (n.d.-h). Voluntary manslaughter. Retrieved from www.definitions.uslegal.com/v/voluntary-manslaughter.

US Legal. (n.d.-i). Mitigation law and legal definition. Retrieved from https://definitions.uslegal.com/m/mitigation/.

Washington Coalition of Sexual Assault Programs. (2016). Child sexual abuse. Retrieved from www.wcsap.org/child-sexual-abuse.

WHO. (n.d.). Mortality. Retrieved from www.who.int/topics/mortality/en/.

Yeshion, T. (n.d.). The myths of circumstantial evidence. *The Forensic Teacher Magazine.* Retrieved from www.theforensicteacher.com/Evidence.html.

Additional Reading

Barry, A. E., Chaney, B. H., & Stellefson, M. L. (2013). Breath alcohol concentrations of designated drivers. *Journal of Studies on Alcohol and Drugs, 74*(4), 509–13.

Bizzaro, A. (2010). Challenging the admission of forensic evidence. State Bar of Wisconsin. Retrieved from www.wisbar.org/newspublications/wisconsinlawyer/pages/article.aspx?Volume=83&Issue=9&ArticleID=1892.

Brady, J. E., & Li, G. (2012). Prevalence of alcohol and other drugs in fatally injured drivers. *Addiction, 108*(1), 104–114. doi: 10.1111/j.1360-0443.2012.03993.x. Retrieved from www.ncbi.nlm.nih.gov/pmc/articles/PMC3467360/.

Connolly, M.-T., Breckman, R., Callahan, J., Lachs, M., Ramsey-Klawsnik, H., & Solomon, J. (2012). The sexual revolution's last frontier: How silence about sex undermines health, well-being, and safety in old age. *Generations, 36*(3), 43–52.

DiMaio, V. J. M., & Dana, S. E. (2007). *Handbook of forensic pathology.* Boca Raton, FL: CRS, Taylor & Francis.

Forensic Blood Specimen Collection and Handling. (n.d.). Retrieved from http://lems4n6.com/downloads/online%20course-forensic%20blood%20specimen%20collection%20and%20handling.pdf.

Governors Highway Safety Association. (n.d.). Alcohol impaired driving (access to state laws). Retrieved from www.ghsa.org/state-laws/issues/Alcohol-Impaired-Driving.

James, N. (2012). DNA testing in criminal justice: Background, current law, grants and issues. Prepared by Congressional Research Service. https://fas.org/sgp/crs/misc/R41800.pdf.

Legal Information Institute. (n.d.). Trier of fact. Retrieved from www.law.cornell.edu/wex/trier_of_fact.

Mt. Sinai Medical Center Sexual Assault Files. Retrieved from http://icahn.mssm.edu/static_files/MSSM/Files/Departments/Emergency%20Medicine/Manual/SUB26_4.pdf.

National Institute of Justice. (2012). DNA evidence: Basics of identifying, gathering and transporting. Retrieved from https://nij.gov/topics/forensics/evidence/dna/basics/pages/identifying-to-transporting.aspx.

Spitz, W. U., Spitz, D. J., & Fisher, R. S. (2006). *Spitz and Fisher's medicolegal investigation of death: Guidelines for the application of pathology to crime investigation.* Springfield, IL: Charles C. Thomas.

Test Questions

1. What type of crime is the most serious?
   A. Misdemeanor
   B. Felony
   C. Petty
   D. First degree
2. Which of the following is NOT a post-conviction challenge?
   A. Lack of probable cause
   B. Constitutional violation
   C. Trial error
   D. Judicial error
3. In order to be found guilty of a crime, the defendant must be
   A. Proven guilty by a preponderance of the evidence
   B. Proven guilty by 51% of the evidence
   C. Required to testify
   D. Proven guilty beyond a reasonable doubt
4. Chain of custody is defined as:
   A. The process used by the police to arrest a suspect
   B. The transportation of evidence to the police laboratory
   C. The procedures used to maintain evidence integrity
   D. DNA evaluation of a physical piece of evidence
5. Which of the following is the LNC least likely to analyze in a criminal case?
   A. Emergency room record
   B. Psychological testing results
   C. Autopsy report
   D. Auto body shop repair bills
6. In which of the following scenarios would it be appropriate to consult a strangulation expert?
   A. A domestic violence victim that reported a strangulation event to police five days post assault
   B. A child abuse victim that was strangled and seen by an emergency room physician with 30 years of experience
   C. An elderly nursing home patient who had no memory of assault, however multiple bystanders stated an employee strangled the patient
   D. A sexual assault victim who was found naked with a ligature around their neck and who self-reported acute alcohol intoxication at the time of assault
   E. All of the above.

Answers: 1. B, 2. A, 3. D, 4. C, 5. D, 6. E

Chapter 17

Correctional Health Care and Civil Rights

J. Thaddeus Eckenrode, Esq.
Cynthia A. Maag, BA, RN, LNCC®
Mariann F. Cosby, DNP, MPA, RN, PHN, CEN, NE-BC, LNCC®,
CLCP, CCM, MSCC

Contents

Objectives

- Understand the types of claims brought by incarcerated individuals related to healthcare services
- Recognize the differences between state and federal court claims, the burden required in each, and challenges to pursue such actions
- Identify the most common correctional facility medical issues that give rise to litigation
- Understand the defenses available to correctional medicine claims
- Learn how the LNC can have an active, hands-on role in the prosecution or defense of correctional medicine litigation

Introduction

Undoubtedly, the legal nurse consultant (LNC) who works for a law firm, corporation, hospital, or governmental entity involved in medical negligence claims or litigation will have substantial exposure to and experience with the type of tort actions that can be brought.

The first exposure to a correctional medicine case involving healthcare services provided to an incarcerated individual in a jail or prison will likely be eye-opening in many ways.

While such cases are frequently investigated and litigated in a manner similar in process to the way most medical malpractice claims are pursued there are a number of significant differences. These include everything from simple or subtle nuances in the recordkeeping to the substantial distinctions involving the types of legal causes of action or theories of recovery that are most often in issue.

Medical malpractice cases are general tort claims, in which a duty of care by the defendant and alleged breach of that duty are the primary issues. (See Chapter 4, Elements of Proof in Negligence Claims for additional information.) Medical negligence can occur through failures to diagnose or misdiagnoses of conditions, improper medication choices or mistakes in dosing, improper treatment or lack of treatment, failure to refer to specialists or higher level caregivers, injuries caused by treatment modalities, etc. The healthcare provider's intent is generally irrelevant. A finding of a deviation from the standard of care causing an injury is generally the basis a defendant provider is adjudicated as legally liable for damages. In the prison system, an injured inmate certainly has the right to bring a medical malpractice claim against a correctional system healthcare provider (HCP). However, more frequently those types of actions are brought in cases using a constitutional analysis founded upon conduct that is deliberately indifferent to a serious medical need. As explained below, one can be medically negligent, yet not liable under this deliberate indifference standard.

Of note, in this chapter the term primary care provider (PCP) includes medical doctor (MD), doctor of osteopathy (DO), nurse practitioners (NP), and physician assistants (PA). Healthcare providers include PCPs and mental health providers such as psychiatrists, psychologists, and social workers; and other licensed staff such as licensed practical nurse (LPN), licensed vocational nurse (LVN), registered nurse (RN), and psychiatric technicians.

Overview of Correctional Medicine

It is often stated the only people in the United States who have a constitutional right to health care are prisoners/inmates. That is because there have been numerous cases litigated over the years related to prison conditions and inmate rights, and those have resulted in a number of court rulings which have addressed the rights of inmates in general and in particular, with regard to their right to have access to healthcare services. The seminal case on this issue was *Estelle v. Gamble* 429 U.S. 97 (1976), a United States Supreme Court case that ruled inmates have a basic right of access to medical care, and denial of adequate care constitutes cruel and unusual punishment under the Eighth Amendment of the United States Constitution. This paved the way for inmates to bring *1983 actions* under 42 U.S.C. § 1983 (Civil Action for Deprivation of Rights) alleging violations of their civil rights. In such cases, inmates are required to prove under the guidelines handed down by the *Estelle* court, that the HCP has been deliberately indifferent to a serious medical need.

Congress enacted the Prison Litigation Reform Act (PLRA) in 1996 (Yale Law School, n.d.) due in part to the substantial increase in litigation after *Estelle*. Inmates filed lawsuits related to prison living conditions, alleged assaults, cruel and unusual punishment issues and pertaining to the provision of services (including medical care). The PLRA sets out various requirements that prisoner litigants must meet when filing suit, as well as limitations upon the types of claims pursued. It also establishes that inmates may initiate litigation without having to pay the normal filing fees involved in most litigation, by seeking to proceed *in forma pauperis*; literally meaning in the form of a pauper, or someone without the financial resources to pursue litigation.

Prison vs. Jail

Many people use the terms prison and jail interchangeably. In general, prisons are the correctional facilities maintained and run by a state or federal government to house those offenders who have been convicted of a crime and sentenced to a period of incarceration that generally exceeds one year. In contrast, jails are usually maintained and run by a local municipality (city or town) or a county. These jails typically house offenders who have been sentenced to a shorter term of incarceration (often under one year) usually for misdemeanor offenses. Also, jails typically house offenders who have only recently been arrested and await a court date or have not yet been able to post a pre-trial bond for release pending trial. Additionally, there are significant differences that have relevance to the issues of health care, as regulation of health care in both prisons and jails vary widely from state to state.

Convict vs. Pre-trial Detainee

As noted above, an offender sentenced to prison has almost always been convicted of, or pled guilty to, a crime, and is therefore transferred to the custody of the state's Department of Corrections (DOC) to serve out their sentence. At that point, the individual is considered a convict. One sentenced, even to a period of time in jail, is also considered to be a convict. Many correctional institutions and agencies have been trending away from the use of that particular term. It should be noted jails also house individuals who have not yet been convicted of any crime, but who merely have been unable to secure a bond (or in some cases are held without bond depending on potential flight risk or the particular heinousness of the crime alleged) pending trial. Persons in that category are known as pre-trial detainees.

The distinction between convicts and pre-trial detainees is ultimately not that significant in the context of correctional healthcare issues. As will be discussed in more detail below, one place where that difference applies is over the issue of whether one is attempting to measure the conduct of any institutional defendant (correctional officer [CO], HCP, etc.) under an Eighth Amendment cruel and unusual punishment standard, since, by definition, a pre-trial detainee has not yet been convicted of anything, and hence is not subject to punishment. The United States Supreme Court ruled in a 1979 case, *Bell v. Wolfish* 441 U.S. 520 (1979), that the same requirement of adequate health care applies to detainees who have not yet been convicted of a crime. As such, the difference between a convict and pre-trial detainee is a nuance that ultimately has little relevance to the issue of whether the medical care available and provided to an offender was proper within the framework of Constitutional application, but is still one about which those who work on these types of cases should be aware. However, at least in the context of claims related to correctional medicine, the LNC working on these types of cases should understand the pre-trial detainee has essentially the same constitutional rights as does a convicted inmate.

There are other differences between prisons and jails worth noting, as these issues frequently arise in the correctional medicine litigation setting. Due to their size, prisons often have medical staffing 24/7, access to more advanced care, and provide a wider range of medical services. Many jails do not have full-time nursing care and may have extremely limited physician care, if at all.

Often the inmate's first contact about medical issues is with the correctional officer (CO). Intake questions about medical conditions and episodic health issues are compiled and screened for the need of a medical evaluation by COs. In some facilities, COs deliver daily medications for inmates to then self-administer.

Many jails charge an encounter or visit co-pay to offenders seeking care. State laws, which vary depending on the jurisdiction, may place financial obligations on jailed offenders not usually present in the prison setting. It is not unusual to see claims made by offenders against jails and jail medical staff related to improper staffing, inadequate services, and being charged for services. Frequently, such complaints are raised by offenders who re-enter through the jail system after having spent time in a state's prison system where the offenders develop expectations about the type of medical care they think should be provided in any correctional facility.

Correctional Medicine Lawsuits

Federal vs. State Court

Inmates who pursue litigation over the quality of, or access to, healthcare services in a correctional setting primarily file cases in federal court. That is because the majority of those claims allege a constitutional deprivation of an offender's civil rights, predominantly arising through years of legal precedent handed down in past federal cases. If a case is filed in state court, the defendants (correctional facility or agency, HCPs, etc.) often employ the legal tactic available to them to move the case to federal court, since the federal courts have primary jurisdiction over cases involving a federal statute or constitutional issue. There are times, of course, when strategic reasons (defense-friendly judges or a plaintiff-inmate who may be viewed more negatively by a local jury than one made up from the area of an entire federal district, etc.) in a particular case might lead a defense team to allow a case to remain pending in state court. Cases brought by inmates that only allege a state law tort claim (medical malpractice) can be brought in state court. Likewise, while an inmate can bring a state law tort claim in federal court as well, that usually requires it is raised as a part of an action that also includes a federal statutory or constitutional claim. If an inmate brings only a tort claim (medical malpractice), that is usually filed in state court, a federal court judge is likely to remand the matter to state court by finding no federal question at issue.

Pursuing Legal Relief in Forma Pauperis

Inmates may initiate litigation without paying the normal federal court filing fee by seeking *in forma pauperis* status. As one might expect, the vast majority of inmates in both prisons and jails will meet the criteria for filing *in forma pauperis*. It does not require an individual be completely destitute, but simply established they cannot pay the normal cost of litigation. The applicant for *in forma pauperis* status can establish the right to pursue the claim in that manner. The courts review these applications directly and often without additional input from the party or the need for any type of hearing, grant such applications.

Tort and Medical Malpractice

In the majority of states today some type of initial legal hurdle must be overcome before one can bring or maintain a claim of medical malpractice. In correctional cases involving medical malpractice, these hurdles may not be able to be overcome. Some examples include the requirement of an affidavit from an expert witness or submission of the claim to a pre-litigation review panel. Invariably an inmate, especially one bringing the action *pro se* or without counsel, simply cannot meet those requirements either because the inmate cannot afford the review by an expert witness or because the circumstances of their incarceration, i.e., restriction of free and unlimited movement, prevents the inmate from appearing to present their case to any reviewing entity.

Tort claims, of course, are usually just negligence claims, and one couched as a medical malpractice claim simply requires a plaintiff to convince a jury it is more likely than not that a defendant committed an act of negligence (deviated from accepted standards of care) and caused resulting harm to the plaintiff. This burden, as discussed herein, is significantly easier to meet than trying to prove a defendant HCP was deliberately indifferent to the needs of an inmate. However, since pursuit of a medical malpractice tort claim invariably requires the testimony of an inmate's medical expert witness, whom the aggrieved inmate neither can afford to pay nor has the ability to meet, it becomes virtually impossible in most cases for an inmate at least those without counsel to succeed on a medical malpractice claim.

Deliberate Indifference and Constitutional Claims

The vast majority of cases alleging some issue with the provision of healthcare services in a correctional facility are brought under the Federal Constitutional theory that the defendants were deliberately indifferent to an inmate's serious medical need. As noted above, the seminal U.S. Supreme Court case on this topic was *Estelle v. Gamble* (1976), in which the court established that "deliberate indifference to serious medical needs of prisoners constitutes the 'unnecessary and wanton infliction of pain' proscribed by the Eighth Amendment." The court held a conduct meeting as such criteria is actionable under 42 U.S.C. § 1983, which provides for causes of actions by citizens allegedly deprived of their civil rights or privileges by any person acting under color of law. The foundational element of a prisoner lawsuit raising a Constitutional claim related to medical care, therefore, is that the correctional facility or persons working therein were deliberately indifferent to a serious medical need of the offender.

If an inmate prevails on such a claim not only would damages be awarded, but attorney fees in those cases where the inmate has counsel (appointed or privately retained) would also be awarded. This factor alone has significance, because should the jury find in favor of the inmate and even render a verdict of nominal damages, inmate's attorneys are then entitled to an award of fees, which could easily exceed $200,000 or more, depending on the case complexity and the amount of work done in the case.

Serious Medical Need

Defining a serious medical need is, to most physicians or other HCPs, a challenge. The same problem that presents as a minor inconvenience to one inmate may be life-threatening to another. Yet, as various courts have wrestled with the elements of actionable deprivations of civil rights, criteria had to be established that allow the alleged conduct to be measured, and to serve as a basis for evaluating the elements of a constitutional claim of deliberate indifference. Ultimately, federal jury instructions, quoting directly from one or more appellate cases on point, define serious medical need as "one that has been diagnosed by a physician as requiring treatment or one that is so obvious that even a lay person would easily recognize the necessity of a doctor's attention" (Eighth Circuit Jury Instruction 4.22 [8th Cir. Civil Manual, 2017a, p. 48], quoting *Schaub v. VonWald* 638 F.3d 905 [8th Cir. 2015]). Needless to say, this definition creates controversy in many cases, as inmates will contend their condition was obvious, while HCPs will argue about whether any treatment was required.

Constitutionally Actionable Indifference

Likewise, defining what constitutes indifference is also vague and must be resolved on a case-by-case basis. Generally, it involves conduct where the HCP seems to ignore an inmate or the inmate's complaints. In that regard, if an HCP can establish that some level of care was provided, even if inadequate from a standard of care perspective, that likely will overcome most claims of indifference and would support summary judgment (a decision made by the court before trial) in favor of the allegedly indifferent defendant. Numerous cases have made it clear that negligence or inadvertence do not constitute deliberate indifference. Courts have held that deliberate indifference is equivalent to criminal-law recklessness, which is "more blameworthy than negligence" (*Farmer v. Brennan* 511 U.S. 825 1994).

Perhaps the most critical element in establishing deliberate indifference is knowledge of a substantial risk of harm to an inmate. As defined by case law, deliberate indifference is established only if a defendant had "actual knowledge of a substantial risk" to the inmate (harm or injury the inmate would suffer) and the defendant "disregards that risk by intentionally refusing or intentionally failing to take reasonable measures to deal with the problem." See Eighth Circuit Civil Jury Instruction 4.23 (8th Cir. Civil Manual, 2017b, p. 49), citing *Farmer v. Brennan*, supra, at 825 and *Wilson v. Seiter* 501 U.S. 294 (1991).

Finally, inmates are not entitled to the care they want, so a mere disagreement with the choices of care (medications, treatment modalities, tests to be performed, etc.) does not give rise to an actionable claim.

Technical Defenses

There are a number of legal hurdles an inmate bringing a claim for deliberate indifference must overcome. Many of these are technicalities that will not require much action by the defendant, as many federal courts do their own aggressive form of case screening, arising from the requirements of the Prison Litigation Reform Act (PLRA).

FAILURE TO EXHAUST ADMINISTRATIVE REMEDIES

Pursuant to PLRA, a litigant must first exhaust all administrative remedies with regard to the issues raised in the suit. For example, an inmate claiming some issue with regard to the medical care provided must first pursue the applicable grievance procedure at the institution, if one is in place. To that end, the inmate must pursue it in a timely fashion and completely before proceeding with a lawsuit. An inmate who fails to file a grievance, fails to raise the grievance within the time constraints set out in that particular policy, fails to pursue all available appellate levels of the grievance, or fails to otherwise pursue the process properly may be subject to having the lawsuit dismissed for those deficiencies. This tends to be one of the main legal reasons supporting an early order granting summary judgment in favor of the defendants. The LNC working on these matters should obtain a full copy of the relevant institutional grievance procedure and the prisoner litigant's complete grievance file, including the confidential file. A review of this material can be used to assess the possibility of a valid dispositive motion (a motion to ask the court to terminate litigation pre-trial) on this issue.

PLEADING DEFICIENCIES AND FRIVOLITY REVIEW

After a suit is filed, many courts conduct a frivolity review. The District Court judge assesses the allegations in the inmate's complaint to see if the allegation articulates a legitimate claim. If the court determines the allegation does not articulate such a claim either in general or even as to some of the named defendants, the court may dismiss the case as frivolous or release some of named defendants. Likewise, the court may evaluate whether the pleading itself, even in a case that may not be frivolous per se, properly articulates a cause of action against each of the named defendants for which the court may grant relief. The court may find that, as pleaded, one or more of the defendants is not the proper target of the inmate's claims and may dismiss the case or bring in certain parties on its own (referred to as *sua sponte*), or allow the case to proceed on only certain legal theories or as to only certain defendants.

THREE STRIKES PROVISION AND THE PHYSICAL INJURY REQUIREMENT
(IN MENTAL HEALTH CLAIMS)

Likewise, the PLRA precludes an inmate from being allowed to file suit *in forma pauperis* if that person has had three prior suits dismissed as frivolous. This does not preclude an inmate from filing subsequent suits, but the inmate will have to pay the normal filing fees (which may be several hundred dollars), so this technical requirement has the impact of effectively precluding many inmate suits (Federal Rules of Civil Procedure, n.d.).

An inmate cannot claim monetary damages for a mental or emotional injury unless a physical injury can also be demonstrated (*Royal v. Kautsky*, 375 F.3d 720, 2004).

VIOLATIONS OF FEDERAL RULES OR COURT ORDERS

Often upon the filing of a suit, the federal judge conducting a frivolity review may allow the case to proceed, but may enter an early order requiring the inmate to amend the pleading in some regard, setting deadlines by which changes or amendments must be made or to take some other action to articulate the claim, and if the inmate fails to do so, the court may simply dismiss the case. Since the Federal Rules of Civil Procedure (FRCP) require early designations of witnesses with knowledge and documentary evidence of which a party is aware, an inmate's failure to make those mandatory disclosures is often a reason for the court to grant an early dismissal (Federal Rules of Civil Procedure,§ Rule 37, 2019).

Monell *Claims*

Unlike tort claims, in which a corporation may face vicarious liability (be responsible) for the tortious conduct of its employees, conduct constituting deliberate indifference is personal, and cannot be imputed to an employer. However, corporations and governmental entities can still face Constitutional claims under *Monell v. Department of Social Services*, 436 U.S. 658 (1978) for implementing policies and procedures that deprive inmates of Constitutional rights or liberties, or for allowing deliberately indifferent conduct to occur. Originally, the *Monell* decision stood for the proposition municipalities could be classified as "persons" under Section 1983 and be held liable for the implementation of ordinances, regulations, or laws that allowed governmental officers to violate one's civil rights. Over time, the *Monell* holding extended to private contractors (including correctional system HCPs), who may face liability for implementing a policy that leads to a violation of an inmate's civil rights. For the LNC working on correctional medicine cases, obtaining all of the prison or healthcare contractor's policies, rules, regulations, and guidelines is of critical importance to establish compliance or deviation in both the prosecution and defense of these cases.

Additional Correctional Facility Claims Raised

Inmates may also bring a number of other types of claims as a result of incarceration, many of which are not likely to relate directly to the provision of medical care, but could implicate HCPs. Prison living conditions (too hot, too cold, too dirty, too unsanitary, etc.) are claims most often directed against the governmental entity operating the facility. Claims of assault by other inmates, excessive use of force by COs, denial of access to law libraries, documents, telephone use, canteen items, etc., are issues that rarely involve healthcare personnel. However, some of these items might give rise to a claim against HCPs: (1) failed to take action to stop an assault they may have had warning of, (2) failed to treat injuries inflicted during assaults, (3) use of force events and conspired to cover up such events, or (4) allowed constitutional violations to occur (in spite of HCP's inability or lack of authority to do anything to affirmatively prevent such events). When alleged to have had a role, whether from an administrative perspective or directly, the medical records should again be thoroughly reviewed for any documentation of statements made by the inmate at or following the events in issue.

Types of Plaintiffs

Pro Se *Prisoners and Detainees*

The vast majority of prison litigation is filed by inmates or detainees *pro se*. The LNC who becomes involved, through a retained law firm, in litigation that is filed *pro se* will immediately note the

Complaint or Petition filed by the inmate is likely to look vastly different than those seen in most medical malpractice cases. Instead of following a format typical of a pleading, with nicely spaced and neatly typed paragraphs, one is likely to see a handwritten document, in which the narrative text ranges from relatively articulate statements of allegations to rambling diatribes that address a myriad of gripes and issues that have little to do with medical care. Some inmates have neat, legible handwriting, while others not only struggle to spell common words, but appear to use virtually indecipherable hieroglyphics as their method of documentation. It is not uncommon to see handwritten complaints that start out on a pre-printed federal court form used for *pro se* litigants that then meanders over several more pages, complete with arrows, drawings, and ink blotches.

Notwithstanding the unusual nature of *pro se* pleadings that may be filed, the defense team must take the document as a genuine pleading that must be addressed. The defense LNC may have the painstaking and time-consuming task of going through the allegations of the pleadings to compare dates (which an inmate has often simply guessed at or recalled from memory) with medical records to try to confirm whether certain inmate or provider interactions actually took place, etc.

Pro se prisoner litigants often rely upon or seek the help of other jailhouse attorneys who have experience with other cases, and whose advice may be either helpful (some such inmates can be quite good at articulating a straightforward claim) or challenging (others follow a philosophy of throw it all in and encourage complaints to be broad, unlimited, and frequently quite exaggerated). Since many inmates are aware of the existence of self-help publications such as Meeropol and Head (2010) to bring these suits, it behooves the LNC to locate and read these texts.

Appointed Counsel Cases

In criminal matters, indigent defendants have a constitutional right to counsel, and as such, counsel is appointed (whether a public defender or others who take *pro bono* appointments) in all cases where a defendant cannot afford an attorney. In civil matters, including claims related to the provision of medical care in correctional facilities, there is **no** absolute right to counsel, and a court's decision about the appointment of counsel is therefore made on a case-by-case basis.

In virtually every *pro se* civil case filed, the most common early (and frequently ongoing) request made to the court by a *pro se* inmate is for the appointment of counsel. Courts consider a variety of factors in determining whether to appoint an attorney for a litigant, most often citing its belief (when they do choose to appoint counsel) the case is relatively complex, and the litigation can most reasonably be pursued by an attorney. The decision to appoint counsel is up to the particular discretion of each judge before whom an action is pending. In those cases where counsel is appointed to represent an inmate, the defense team can expect a more substantial discovery effort than will be seen in the typical *pro se* case. The defense team's LNC will likely have to more carefully evaluate medical records for the identities of potential witnesses and more carefully evaluate the nuances of the medical issues involved. Some attorneys are, quite frankly, less than enthused about receiving a federal court appointment for an inmate in a civil matter, and often will do very little to fight a defendant's dispositive motion (request of the trial court to decide a claim without trial), confidentially hoping summary judgment is granted to bring their involvement in the matter to a quick end. However, given there is no compensation paid to court-appointed attorneys in these cases, the only way for such counsel to "break even" on efforts or time (and on the expenses likely to incur for copies, travel, depositions, etc.) is with an award of attorney fees, for which they will likely be eligible only if the attorney prevails at trial. That alone raises the stakes for the defendants and makes an appointed counsel case one that justifies more serious consideration of settlement instead of taking the chance on a loss at trial. The defense team can expect a much more vigorous battle, therefore, in an appointed counsel case. Likewise, the LNC working with the plaintiff's law firm that finds itself appointed to represent a prisoner litigant will probably find that much of the work otherwise managed by an attorney will be redirected to paralegal or LNC staff, and should understand the importance of thoroughly working up a case the firm desperately wants to "prevail" at trial. Appointed counsel may, of course, opt to also articulate and pursue a tort (malpractice) claim on behalf of the litigant for whom they are appointed, but that likely requires an investment of law firm resources and funds (to hire experts, etc.) and winning such a tort claim will <u>not</u> result in an award of attorney fees. Some attorneys likewise convince inmates to enter into standard contingent fee contracts if they choose to pursue a tort claim as an alternative.

Retained Counsel

Ultimately, it is the rare case where an attorney is retained by an inmate litigant in a civil matter related to medical care. As noted, most inmates have no resources to pay an attorney, so those cases taken on by counsel are almost always on a contingent fee basis. Not surprisingly, given that inmates don't make the most sympathetic of litigants in general, cases taken on by attorneys on behalf of an inmate almost always involve catastrophic injuries or deaths. In the latter instance, of course, it is usually an inmate's family who has retained counsel on their own behalf over the death of the family member while incarcerated.

For cases not involving an inmate's death, an attorney who considers taking on an inmate as a client for an injury sustained while incarcerated will realize that overcoming the strong jury bias against an inmate requires substantial evidence of liability. The more egregious the care, the more egregious the defendant's conduct, coupled with a significant injury to the inmate with which the jury can empathize, the better the potential outcome. In that regard, inmate cases involving medical malpractice where the inmate has retained an attorney, will more likely be filed as a tort claim (medical malpractice) than a deliberate indifference claim, given the substantially easier evidentiary burden required—although most commonly both types of claims will be pursued.

The LNC working for either a plaintiff or defense firm in a prisoner case related to medical malpractice claims will perform tasks on these cases similar to those of any typical medical malpractice matter. As noted below, however, understanding the differences between medicine as provided in a hospital or private practice setting compared to how it is provided in a correctional setting is critical, since that impacts the materials one may seek to obtain from the providers (and other documents kept by the correctional facility), the types of different records kept or maintained, and the type of expert witness(es) each party may need. For those reasons, it is often important to locate an expert who understands or has experience in correctional medicine.

Medical Issues that Arise in Correctional Settings

Intake

Regardless of who initiates the inmate's healthcare intake process or system utilized to record the information, the goal is to be as accurate as possible. Most of the information comes from the inmate in the form of a medical history, and is only as reliable as what an inmate may report. Inmates may not always provide an accurate history for a variety of reasons. Some may intentionally offer erroneous medical history in an effort to obtain better treatment. Others may fail to provide accurate history for various self-serving reasons, or be unable to provide an accurate history due to language issues or cognitive deficits (Titus & Gibson, 2017).

Some responses on intake may be contradictory to other responses and such discrepancies should lead to follow-up questions for clarification. For example, questions about medications an inmate reports to be taking should lead to more detailed inquiry about ailments, duration and dosages of medications, prescribing HCPs and side-effects. A lack of attention to detail and thoroughness during the intake process may contribute to healthcare personnel missing vital information important at later stages of the patient's incarceration.

Medications

Some medications an inmate may have taken before incarceration may not be continued in the correctional setting. Medications that are non-formulary such as narcotics or other opioid pain medications, and some psychotropic medications are a few examples. If adequate and effective substitutes are not prescribed or given, correctional HCPs can be exposed to claims related to the failure to treat or address ongoing and known medical conditions. Medication errors related to dosing, timely delivery or administration of medications, or administration to the wrong patient, are common issues in correctional settings.

Additionally, in many correctional facilities, medications are given only at preselected times during med pass, which is often just twice a day. This medication delivery schedule can lead to issues for patients who prior to incarceration may have been prescribed medications to be taken more frequently. When medications are passed or administered by clinical staff, it is often necessary to assure the inmate has not *cheeked* the pills/tablets and instead has swallowed the medication (Keller, 2012).

The rationale for this somewhat time consuming oral cavity inspection, sometimes referred to as watch take or direct observation, includes the inmate practice of using medications as a form of currency to barter goods or services among inmates. The non-ingested medication can lead to inadequate treatment of the inmate's medical condition. Additionally, the accumulation of cheeked medication for bartering and other purposes can be a safety and security risk. Medications may be ordered to be administered open and float or crush and float in a cup of water to mitigate the possibility of the inmate cheeking the medication.

In many smaller facilities and jails, often due to the scheduling of on-duty medical personnel, one or more of the med pass events may be performed by non-medical individuals or corrections officers. While some non-medical personnel may have had some level of training in the facility or by medical providers in anticipation of the need to do med pass from time to time, it is also not uncommon to see medications distributed on occasion by untrained custody officers (Anno, 2001, pp. 148–149, Appendix E section II C5a). While handing a tablet or pill to an inmate is not on its own challenging, the need for medication documentation, careful observation of the swallowing of medications, awareness of side-effects and complications all have the potential to lead to problems or mistakes. When medications are given by COs they should have had medication administration training and should use the same diligence as licensed staff.

Depending upon the setting and other factors, an inmate may be provided a 30-day supply of oral medication or inhalers to self-administer. These keep on person (KOP) medications are typically medications that do not pose a safety and security risk and are distributed to the inmate in one month quantities. For these medications, the inmate is held responsible for the timely self-administration and is viewed as a partner in the timely initiation of the renewal process that may be applicable (American Nurses Association [ANA], 2013, p. 11).

Addiction-Related

A high percentage of incarcerated individuals are (or at least initially present) addicted to narcotics (National Institute on Drug Abuse, 2017). Accurately diagnosing symptoms of withdrawal, as opposed to other serious medical issues, can be difficult and is often a basis for claims of medical negligence or deliberate indifference when medical personnel presume an inmate's seriously ill presentation is due simply to a withdrawal from medications and fails to assess the inmate for other ailments (National Commission on Correctional Health Care [NCCHC], 2016b). Quantitative monitoring tools such as the clinical institute withdrawal assessment of alcohol scale or the clinical opioid withdrawal scale can be used by clinicians to monitor patients experiencing alcohol or opioid withdrawal.

Mental Health

Perhaps the most challenging issue facing HCPs in the correctional setting is evaluating the mental health status of prisoners (NCCHC, 2015b). Likewise, the availability of qualified mental health providers (psychiatrist, psychologists, or mental health counselors) is often limited. For that reason, basic mental health evaluations often fall to the nursing staff or primary care providers who may not have the background or training to be able to tease out an inmate's emotional state, or history of past self-harm or suicidal ideation.

Comments in the medical records that suggest possible mental health diagnoses or issues should be reviewed for evidence of referrals to a qualified mental health professional (QMHP), or possible requests for psychotropic medications. Potential liability issues arise when an inmate commits suicide or self-injures and early signs were not recognized or properly evaluated, or a timely referral was not made to a QMHP for assessment and intervention.

Chronic Disease and Chronic Care

Based on self-report information from 2011 to 2012, upon admission to correctional facilities "half of state and federal prisoners and local jail inmates reported ever having a chronic condition" (Maruschak, Berzofsky, & Unangst, 2016, p. 1). Some common chronic conditions include hypertension, hyperlipidemia, diabetes, hepatitis C (HCV), human immunodeficiency virus (HIV), acquired immune deficiency syndrome (AIDS), chronic pain, and asthma, to name just a few. These conditions are addressed in prison settings at a chronic care clinic or as part of a chronic care program.

The NCCHC has promulgated policies and procedures related to chronic disease services in correctional facilities (NCCHC, 2018a, 2018b; Titus & Gibson, 2017). However, evaluations of these long-standing problems may tend to be cursory due to the well-known and long-documented appearance. For that reason, subtle changes in a patient's condition (weight gain, vital sign fluctuation, lab abnormalities, etc.) may be overlooked by HCPs. The LNC reviewing chronic care records should be alert to these changes and plot out fluctuations and consider possible expert witness evaluations of these conditions.

Diabetes

Diabetes is a chronic condition frequently seen in the correctional setting. Diabetic treatment requires careful monitoring and daily medications (and dosing adjustments). In diabetes, blood sugar fluctuations can be significant. Low blood sugars can lead to hypoglycemia or diabetic coma, and high blood sugars can lead to diabetic ketoacidosis. Insulin therapy, when needed, must be carefully adjusted and may require frequent communication between nursing or correctional staff and other HCPs. Merely placing an inmate on common sliding scale therapy may be inadequate and warrants careful monitoring by HCPs (American Diabetes Association, 2011). The LNC reviewing such cases should carefully evaluate and list all blood sugar levels measured, the time of the tests, the medical response (if any), and whether self-testing equipment is an option at the institution (ANA, 2013, p. 11; Ball, 2011).

Hepatitis C

Chronic hepatitis C virus (HCV) is one of the infectious diseases that have a disproportionally higher prevalence rate among individuals entering jails and prisons (Beckman et al., 2016; Sterling et al., 2018). Morbidity and mortality risks associated with HCV are significant for the individual inmate. The inmate risks include progression to cirrhosis, end-stage liver disease, and hepatocellular cancer (Sterling et al., 2018). In addition, there are health risks associated with transmission of HCV within correctional facilities via blood exposure (Keller, 2014; Sterling et al., 2018).

Treatment for HCV has been controversial in correctional health care due in part to the costs of direct-acting antiviral medications that entered the market a few years ago (Beckman et al., 2016; Keller, 2014; Rich, Allen, & Williams, 2015). However, national standards provide guidance for the testing, treatment, and management of HCV and the application of the standards to those who are incarcerated (American Association for the Study of Liver Diseases and the Infectious Diseases Society of America, 2018; Federal Bureau of Prisons, 2018; Sterling et al., 2018).

Through review of the provider physical exam findings, inmate symptoms, and lab records, the LNC should be able to assess the status of the monitoring, evaluation, and treatment timelines of the patient. Review for evidence of the fibrosis 4 score, a liver biopsy, or the newer fibroscan can provide evidence of diagnostic monitoring for severity of the condition and cirrhosis. Due to the volume of patients in need of HCV treatment, the LNC should request institutional guidelines or information about any processes that may be in place for inmate treatment selection and monitoring criteria.

HIV and Infectious Diseases

In the correctional setting, HIV and AIDS affects a disproportionate number of people when compared to the U.S. population at large (Johnson, Kondo, Brems, & Eldridge, 2015). The rate of HIV diagnosis is five times greater in state and federal prisons than the rate among people not incarcerated (Centers for Disease Control and Prevention [CDC], 2018). Due to the high prevalence and CDC guidelines for testing, there can be a high incidence of inmates who are on medications for treatment of HIV/AIDS (CDC, 2009, 2018; Johnson et al., 2015).

Inmates presenting with HIV must have laboratory values monitored regularly. Changes in values including changes in viral load may reflect a deterioration of condition necessitating medication adjustments or changes (NCCHC, 2014). The medical records must adequately demonstrate healthcare attention to those issues to at least overcome a deliberate indifference claim, if not a negligence claim. For those cases that involve an inmate with HIV, the LNC should evaluate and analyze the frequency of scheduled blood work, the evidence of medical monitoring, and track the changes to confirm medication adjustments were made based on laboratory values and changes in the inmate's condition.

Other uncommon infectious diseases can present challenges to the correctional HCPs due to a tendency to put off appropriate lab tests until after a trial of some of the routine antibiotics. Sometimes the broad spectrum formulary antibiotics are not effective in the treatment of more discreet infections. A delay in diagnosis associated with this practice may result in serious consequences. The legal team and LNC should carefully evaluate all of the patient's presenting signs, symptoms, and objective data to evaluate the appropriateness of the treatment plan and the patient's response.

Gender Dysphoria

Gender dysphoria is a growing issue in correctional facilities (Glezer, McNeil, & Binder, 2013). Deviations by healthcare providers from the transgender specific standards of care can serve as a basis for a liability claim (NCCHC, 2015c; World Professional Association for Transgender Health, 2011). Many states now recognize gender dysphoria as a medical diagnosis that represents a serious medical need. However, some correctional facilities or governmental entities continue to challenge that conclusion and avoid treating this condition as one that requires intervention, medication, or other therapy (Glezer et al., 2013). As a result, litigation arising out of the treatment of gender dysphoria is a growing trend and may lead to sexual reassignment surgery (Crimesider Staff, 2017; NCCHC, 2015c).

From a review of the medical records, the LNC should be able to evaluate the extent to which the inmate is receiving mental health services and consideration of treatment modalities. Key elements of evidence include mental health assessment, counseling, psychotherapy services, hormone therapy with regular laboratory monitoring, access to transgender specialists and other gynecologic and urologic care, and considerations for sex reassignment surgery. Custody driven elements to consider include housing and consideration for provision of other sexual preference items (NCCHC, 2015c).

Terminal Illnesses: Compassionate Release and Medical Parole

Inmates with medical conditions often seek medical parole. Although defined somewhat differently from jurisdiction to jurisdiction, it generally relates to having a terminal medical condition from which the person is not expected to survive. Based on the medical condition, the inmate requests to be paroled in order to pass away in hospice or at home. Not surprisingly, many times the person's conditions are not terminal. The inmate seeks medical parole based upon either a misunderstanding about what might constitute as grounds for medical parole or simply as an attempt to potentially shorten one's sentence.

Claims may be brought against correctional HCPs based upon a belief the HCP should have approved the medical parole request and intentionally refused to do so. Ultimately, however, while medical personnel may feel an inmate qualifies for consideration of such parole because of a medical condition, they rarely have formal authority to approve a medical parole. The decision to grant such paroles usually still lies with high level corrections officials who likely utilize a specific protocol and criteria that are medical and custody based (U.S. Department of Justice, Federal Bureau of Prisons, 2015).

Facility-Related Use of Force, Restraint, Assaults

As noted earlier, while use of force actions or injuries from employment of restraints are most often directed against COs instead of medical personnel, there are times when there is a medical component to such activities. Some correctional facility guidelines may require COs to obtain verification that there is no medical contraindication to certain types of force that may be employed. It is not unusual for these verification attempts to be hurried—or even requested after-the-fact—when the inmate conduct allegedly warranting a use of force by COs arises suddenly. A HCP may feel compelled to approve the use of force without careful review of the medical chart, and may miss prior medical history that would suggest a potential medical complication from, for example, the use of pepper spray (pulmonary history) or restraints (vascular or clotting issues), etc. Likewise, following a use of force action or some type of restraint application by COs, the offender may need (and prison policies often require) a medical evaluation. It is not uncommon for such evaluations to be somewhat cursory, either because the offender remains agitated and is acting out, or because the COs want to move the offender promptly to a cell. It isn't hard to miss a medical issue that might have been noted with a more thorough evaluation. Legal teams working on these types of cases should carefully explore the extent of the post-restraint or use of force medical evaluation for this reason.

Referrals and Outside Care

Medical issues that arise in correctional facilities also differ significantly from those outside the correctional setting with regard to referrals, tests, or other care that cannot be provided in the institution (Thompson, 2010). It might not be unusual for the average individual's PCP to refer the patient for medical issues to a specialist for consultation in many situations. In the correctional setting, however, the unique issues involved in sending any inmate to an outside HCP tends to compound the dynamics.

Inmates who must go off-site to obtain medical tests, x-rays, diagnostics, specialty consults, or for emergency care, must be transported using safety and security precautions. Correctional facilities have custody protocols to follow. The process frequently requires a number of COs to accompany an offender on any outside trip. Logistics in scheduling transportation, concerns about the safety of officers and the general public, and protection against potential flight or escape attempts are all concerns of the correctional facility.

The medical trips to the hospital, testing facility, or HCPs can take several hours. Given the impact such trips may have on the staffing at the correctional facility (especially small jails) when the transporting COs are off-site, outside referrals for medical services may not be viewed favorably unless truly necessary (Young & Patel, 2015). In that regard, a common complaint that arises in prisoner litigation is a claim the offender needed a referral, test, or emergency care and the correctional facility HCPs failed to order it or make timely arrangements.

Telemedicine services can be utilized to mitigate the off-site challenges related to safety and security (Young & Patel, 2015). In some jurisdictions, this mode of inmate encounter is also used for HCP visits. The LNC should look for documentation in the medical records for both elements of these encounters: the specialist and the on-site staff who assisted with the encounter.

Another issue in the area of outside or specialty referrals may be related to delays in timely consults following custody transfers to another institution. Due to new HCP assigned at the new institution and logistics of where the new institution is located, the referral process may restart.

Instead of seamlessly continuing the referral, the process starts over with a referral to a different specialist closer to the new institution. The LNC should evaluate the registered nurses' (RN) role regarding the continuity of care and care coordination efforts and the impact on the medical plan of care (ANA, 2013, p. 14).

The ongoing balance for correctional HCPs is to assess how important an off-site referral may be, whether care of the issue can be provided in house, and how the request for an off-site trip for an inmate may impact the overall function of the facility. Private HCPs may even face pushback under their contract, in which the healthcare entity has potentially suggested it can reduce or minimize off-site trips.

Perhaps no issue is more critical and frequently raised in correctional litigation than those claims that an inmate was denied timely and necessary emergency care because of a refusal to send the inmate out, or a delay in the decision to do so, leading to significant or serious sequelae.

Unique Correctional Issues

Privatized Medicine and Contract Issues

Healthcare services in jails and prisons may be provided by nurses, physicians, or other practitioners employed directly by the facility or by the state or local government operating the facility. It is becoming more common, however, for healthcare services to be contracted out to private companies (Andrews, 2017). The reasons vary, but ultimately turn on the cost to provide healthcare services in an institution and to employ medical staff, the enormous administrative burden in managing those services and effectively utilizing contract services, including specialty providers and services, purchasing and maintaining inventory of medications, drugs, supplies and equipment, scheduling and staffing the institution properly, etc.

Whether healthcare services in a correctional facility are provided by a private company or direct facility employees has no impact on the Constitutional requirements or standard of care expected. However, it can substantially impact discovery and trial strategies. Governmental employees may be subject to relevant Sunshine Law disclosures (laws that govern public access to government records) while private individuals may not. On the other hand, interest in the profits, management, history, and corporate structure of a private HCP will likely lead to a substantially different discovery effort by inmates.

Ultimately, arguments about how privatized healthcare services are delivered by the contracting company may afford the inmate an opportunity to paint the defendant healthcare providers in a more negative light. Contending a private company puts profit over patients is a common theme, and one that may make sense to many jurors on a base level. Private companies must generate profits to survive, so the argument that they cut corners, provide the minimum amount of care necessary, etc., tend to play right into the deliberate indifference burden. The correctional facility or government defendants likewise face the argument of contracting such vital services out to the low bidder, and therefore also contribute to the lack of appropriate care provided.

The LNCs involved in correctional healthcare litigation should anticipate the need to obtain the private healthcare providers' corporate protocols for care (if any), job descriptions for institutional staff providers, personnel files for the relevant providers, any statistics (utilization, inventories, outside referrals, etc.) maintained by the corporation, training material, and promotional or advertising material, etc. In particular, care should be taken to determine if the relevant HCP, whose care is at issue, complete all of the training the corporation contends it provides. In addition, did this particular HCP possess the requisite qualifications for the position advertised initially? Did this individual utilize the record-keeping system appropriately? Likewise, if the corporation does utilize any written care protocols or procedures, careful evaluation of those that may be in issue in the litigation should be conducted, to assess whether there were any deviations from the policy, even if simply how to document events or care.

Staffing

As noted, one of the greatest challenges for the institution or private care provider related to medical care in jails and prisons is properly staffing a correctional facility (NCCHC, 2012; U.S. Department of Justice, Office of the Inspector General, 2016). Correctional medicine is not a glamour job, so finding professionals willing to undertake such work is often difficult. It is not unusual, therefore, to see claims raised regarding the inadequacy of healthcare staffing in correctional facilities, especially given the Constitutional requirement that inmates have "access" to medical care. Generally, the staffing will depend substantially on the size of the correctional facility. Prisons with a population that may number in the thousands will often have nurses present around the clock with daily physician coverage. Jails typically are consistently less staffed. Smaller county or municipal jails may only have a physician or nurse practitioner coverage once every couple of weeks, and nursing staff only a few hours per week.

For private companies providing medical care coverage, a common response to staffing sufficiency questions in litigation is that they would be happy to provide more coverage, but the contracting facility or governmental entity chooses the level of coverage for which it is willing to pay.

Physician vs. Nurse Practitioner vs. Physician's Assistant

Most physicians in the correctional setting will have graduated from an accredited medical school and often have some level of prior medical experience. However, it is not uncommon to find some correctional medical providers (MD and DO) who have previously retired from the active practice of medicine or who have had difficulties or challenges in past medical employment settings. Likewise, these MDs and DOs may find themselves practicing medicine somewhat outside of their specialty training (most physicians in a prison setting are essentially practicing general primary internal medicine, but may have had other specialty training or experience in the past). It is important to thoroughly evaluate the background, training, and experience of any HCP involved in a correctional medicine case.

Although prisons usually have physicians on site, at least during the day, smaller jails may only provide non-physician practitioner coverage. The extent to which the non-physician practitioner can provide services on a level similar to that of physicians may vary from state to state, depending on the statutes or regulations that articulate the limits of such a practitioner's legal rights and duties. For the LNC involved in correctional medicine cases, obtaining the governing law or regulations related to the non-physician practitioner involved in a correctional medicine case is important to assess compliance with such regulations or possible actions beyond the scope of their defined responsibilities.

Similarly, it is not uncommon to find that routine care is provided by a retired physician with a specialty background that is wholly unrelated to the types of claims seen in the facility. This practice may not disqualify the physician from providing care, but may subject the physician to scrutiny in the litigation process regarding that physician's qualifications to treat the injuries or ailments at issue in a given case. Therefore, obtaining background information about the pertinent physician is also a critical part of the case work-up for the litigation team.

Nursing

Nurses provide a substantial amount of the medical care in correctional facilities. However, due to the various factors that contribute to staffing ratios, a national prison or jail health staffing model to fit all institutions does not exist (Anno, 2001, p. 119). It is more common to find nursing coverage provided by licensed practical nurses (LPNs) than RNs in many facilities. Therefore, the legal team involved in any correctional medicine case should obtain any regulations, statutes, professional licensing standards, and resources related to the different types of nursing professionals involved in the case (ANA, 2013; Blair et al., 2014; Knox & Schoenly, 2014; Schoenly & Knox, 2013). It is likewise important to request and obtain information about each nurse's personal training, experience, licensure status, and other qualifications documents.

Dental

Dental care in correctional facilities is far less commonly available than routine medical care, but in most institutions the need to provide some level of dental care is still mandatory (Angelici, 2015a, 2015b). However, dental staffing is often scheduled no more than monthly in many facilities, frequently causing a backlog of patients with dental needs. It is common for an inmate to raise claims about their continued tooth pain being ignored because dental care is not provided in a timely manner. While nursing staff and general medical providers do not usually involve themselves in treatment of dental complaints, they do often evaluate dental complaints as a part of their role, sometimes using a pre-printed dental care form. Whether they properly document the particular complaints noted by an inmate or not, their qualifications to evaluate the dental needs of an inmate in any particular circumstance may be questioned and serve as the underlying basis of a negligence or deliberate indifference claim.

Since dental issues can evolve into more serious infections if left untreated, delays in getting an inmate to a dentist can be substantially problematic for the facility's healthcare providers. In these cases, the contention that the condition was obvious to a layperson, can establish the knowledge requirement of serious medical need. Other inmates can testify to the agony or pain the inmate experienced. Further, they may have noticed the inmate's facial redness or swelling or puffiness, inability to consume food, and the presence of pus or foul mouth odor (Adu-Tutu & Shields, 2014).

Mental Health

Mental health issues are among the more common problems among incarcerated individuals. However, claims related to the provision or lack of mental health services is not as predominant as one might expect. This is due in part to the aforementioned requirement of some physical injury to pursue claims for mental injury. The difficulty of identifying problems that constitute a serious medical need may be ignored. If some care or counseling is being provided, then the likelihood of articulating deliberate indifference is negated.

When claims are made by inmates over mental health issues, they are more frequently raised as malpractice claims when counsel is involved for the inmate, or as constitutional claims when no mental health services are available to inmates who commit self-harm or otherwise demonstrate substantial and obvious mental issues.

Specialists

Specialty services from surgeons, obstetricians, infectious disease physicians, neurologists, etc., are rarely available or provided in the institutional setting. Inmates who have a need for such specialty care often have to be sent off-site, as noted above in the section on outside referrals (Anno, 2001, p. 31, 167–168). Similarly, specialty scans (MRI, CT, Venous Doppler, etc.) are often done off-site at the nearest hospital or by a mobile unit that comes to the facility once a week or periodically. Radiology services in the correctional setting are often done by a contracted radiology service. Many of the plain and flat plate films may be done on site.

The LNC working on correctional medicine cases should carefully evaluate the entries in the medical records from the on-site HCP. The LNC would ascertain if there was a desire to refer the inmate to a specialist, or for signs, symptoms, lab work, or other findings that might warrant referral to a specialist. The refusal to send an inmate out when the records justify a visit to a specialist can easily serve as the basis of a claim that defendants were indifferent to, or ignored, a serious medical need, especially when the condition giving rise to that referral subsequently leads to the inmate's deterioration.

Attempts by the facility healthcare providers to justify an alternative treatment plan after a documented suggestion for a referral should be carefully evaluated to determine the justification for denial of the referral and the medical legitimacy of the alternative care plan. Assuming the alternative care plan is arguably appropriate, then that becomes a choice of care issue that will potentially support only a medical negligence case but not a deliberate indifference claim.

Record-Keeping and Medical Chart

Given the staffing challenges faced in most correctional institutions, there can be a tendency for medical personnel to be spread thinly. Even to the extent they are able to cover the medical needs of inmates and the lack of available time often translates to limited record-keeping. With strong documentation being the most powerful weapon in defending the average medical malpractice case, it proves challenging in defending medical cases in the correctional setting because of the paucity of records.

An institution's medical records systems include handwritten records and electronic medical records (EMR) of various types, etc. Common documentation issues can include a lack of detailed narrative notes, incomplete examination findings, missing vital signs, incomplete forms, and carryover or cut-and-paste from prior records. The lack of complete records can be used by inmate attorneys to develop a theme related to lack of care, inadequacy of evaluation, and in these civil rights cases, deliberate indifference to a serious medical need.

The LNC should identify portions of histories, physical exams, vital signs, and lab data that may be absent. The LNC can use this process to help identify staff to interview or depose to evaluate whether the appearance of absent information is the result of a documentation deficiency, a lack of medical care, or some other record-keeping deficiency.

Grievance Procedures

As noted above, a technical defense available in all Constitutional claims brought by inmates is their failure to exhaust their administrative remedies, to wit: the institutional grievance process (Brady, Powell, & Hill, 2016). Upon the filing of a prison lawsuit over medical care, the LNC should immediately obtain a copy of the institution's formal grievance process and a complete copy of the inmate's grievance file. The file should include the initial grievance forms, and all institutional documentation through the appeals process to final resolution. The law makes it clear that, assuming the inmate was not prevented by circumstances from pursuing all grievance rights, the inmate must take all the steps to pursue the grievance fully. Should the inmate fail to appeal an adverse ruling or fail to raise the specific issue regarding the suit filed, grounds exist for dismissal of that lawsuit.

The Legal Nurse Consultant's Role in the Prosecution or Defense of a Correctional Medicine Case

Collecting Records

Whether the LNC is reviewing a case for the plaintiff or defense, collection of all the records is vital. Given the significant differences between the correctional healthcare system and the average physician's office or hospital, there are several places where the records may be located. Likewise, each individual correctional facility may be run differently, use different forms, electronic medical record (EMR) systems, or store records inconsistently. As such, there is no uniform methodology to find and obtain records. The LNC will have to be creative and thorough to request all relevant records.

Identifying All Healthcare Providers

Healthcare providers within the correctional system may be full time within that institution, covering for another physician or nurse, or a consulting physician outside of the institution. When requesting the records on behalf of the defense, especially if the HCP is a contractor and not a state or prison employee, the LNC may have to take time to clarify the defense team's role with the facility's record department, and the need for the firm to gather the complete records available. The plaintiff's counsel will have obtained the records from the inmate directly or from defense counsel when suit is filed. Once an inmate is out of prison, the LNC may have to request the medical records directly from the State Department of Corrections, since records are often stored and maintained differently once an offender has left the facility.

The correctional facility may or may not use some type of EMR. Frequently, the records may be a combination of electronic charting and hand-written or form charting. The records the LNC or paralegal will want to make sure to request generally include:

- Intake checklists or forms
- Videos/audio
- Cell check logs/housing logs
- Incident reports
- Pre-incarceration medical records
- Disciplinary hearings
- Death investigation/homicide investigation
- Day-to-day nursing and physician visits
- Specialty clinic visits, i.e., endocrine clinic, cardiovascular clinic, etc.

- Medical Service Requests (MSRs)
- Health Service Requests (HSRs)
- Medication Administration Records (MARs)
- Treatment records
- Signature pages
- Suicide watch forms
- Temporary Care or Licensed Unit (or similar unit within the facility for close observation or specialized care)
- Detoxification orders and records
- Vision Clinic (if needed)
- Dental Clinic (if needed)
- Referrals or referral requests and approvals
- Consultations (both inside and outside providers)
- Mental Health Records (if needed)
- Medical equipment forms
- Emergency treatment area

Institutions and states may vary how records are labeled and how departments are referenced. From these records, the LNC should be able to identify most of the healthcare providers involved in the care of the inmate. There are times when handwritten records or signatures are illegible or are listed as initials only. The defense LNC can contact the Health Services Administrator or Director of Nursing at that facility for names or timesheets during the time frame in question. The LNC working with the plaintiff law firm will want to create a list of uncertain handwriting or signatures and highlight those portions of the records so counsel may explore those with other witnesses in depositions to obtain missing details or clarity.

MARs may be initialed by date with the corresponding signatures usually found on the front or back of the page. The reviewing LNC should attempt to confirm all of the initials (which are usually noted in a key on the MAR form but may be located elsewhere) to verify who administered or distributed each of the medications the inmate was prescribed.

Determining the level of the HCP is also essential in review of the records. A nurse can be a LPN, LVN, RN, or NP. A doctor or PCP can be a MD or DO, or might be a NP or PA. A mental health provider can be a technician, psychiatrist, psychologist, or licensed clinical social worker. Many correctional facility records do not clearly make these distinctions, but simply title the entry as a nurse visit, doctor visit, or MH (mental health) visit. Some jail records provide the level of the HCP in the signature; others may be electronic. In a jail setting, the person providing health care may be an unlicensed CO especially after hours or on weekends (Anno, 2001, pp. 148–149, Appendix E section II C5a).

Chronology

A detailed chronology is a necessity in a corrections case. The medical records, especially in the prison case, may not be easily placed in date order. The electronic medical records may be printed out of day and month order and on occasion, out of year order. Likewise, these records can be voluminous, depending on how long the inmate has been incarcerated.

Jail records are typically easier to manage and not as voluminous, since most inmates in a jail are incarcerated at those facilities for less than a year. Like any other chronology, not every entry in the medical record will be necessary. Focusing on the issues and dates raised in the inmate's complaint(s) will be the most useful. Inserting Bate-stamps to the records on the front end of the review process can be helpful for chronology preparation and especially useful in depositions and at trial.

Custody and Corrections Records

As mentioned in the healthcare providers section, the healthcare records in a jail setting may be quite different from a prison setting, depending on the state. Jail records should be easier to organize and follow chronologically. In the jail setting, a nurse may only cover the clinic for eight hours in a day or less, and may not be available on weekends or holidays. The COs then often become the source for medical care, having been trained by the company providing the medical service (Anno, 2001, pp. 148–149, Appendix E; Tompkins, 2016). Documentation provided by a CO may often be found on a protocol or procedure form provided by the healthcare contractor or other service that is complaint-specific (i.e., abdominal pain, shortness of breath, etc.) The COs may document the inmate's complaint, take vital signs, then call the HCP on call for the facility and report the findings to the covering doctor.

The LNC should assist the litigation team in determining the extent of medical care offered or available to inmates when medical personnel are not available. In some states COs who have been trained, may take telephone treatment directions or orders from an on-call HCP. These after-hours telephone decisions to treat in some manner, offer medication, provide no treatment, or send the inmate to an off-site emergency department if necessary, are the source of substantial inmate litigation.

Suicide watch is ordered when an inmate voices suicide ideation or plan to COs, healthcare staff, or mental health providers. The inmate will be evaluated, usually daily, to discuss feelings or mood to decide when the inmate may come off of watch. Nurses check on the inmate daily for any health needs and to administer medications. Forms used for suicide watch should reflect the inmate was observed in 15-minute intervals (or whatever the facility's policy may be) during the entire suicide watch (Hayes, 2017).

The inmate's arrest records may or may not be a part of the file. If not, the jail records will have to be requested directly from the jail. Arrest records will often provide the LNC with information about the need for subduing the inmate at the time of arrest, whether intoxicated, under the influence of illicit drugs, or whether they were already injured prior to incarceration.

Prison records may be extensive depending on how long the inmate has been incarcerated. Some of these records may go back several decades. The LNC may not need to request all of these records. The request may be limited to those years listed in the petition or complaint at least initially. If additional records are needed, then the request can be broadened. Orders and progress notes in a prison case may be found in the electronic medical record or in a hard chart depending on the facility. Some correctional facilities may have a temporary care unit (TCU) or similar short-term observational area for those inmates who have undergone surgery, are infectious, or otherwise in need of more intensive care than provided in the medical unit itself. If an inmate was moved for more intensive care during incarceration for any reason, the LNC will need to make sure those records are included during the initial review, if the records cover the time span noted in the complaint.

Consultations and outside referrals may be in separate sections of the records. Sometimes the referrals are entered into the electronic format, and other times are kept within another part of the chart. Medical Service Requests (MSRs) or Health Service Requests (HSRs) should be included in the initial records requests. An MSR or HSR should tell the LNC if the inmate had specifically asked to be seen by a nurse or doctor, and those records often reflect if such a visit took place or if the inmate was referred to an HCP at an upcoming visit. Likewise, an MSR may simply be a request for a renewal of medication, which may be signed by a nurse with referral to the HCP for renewal.

Grievances and Appeals

The inmate has a right to question or complain about the healthcare system and that right is protected by the grievance process (Brady et al., 2016). While the grievance process for most prisons will be consistent from prison to prison in the state's correctional system, a jail's grievance system may differ significantly from the state prison system and even other jails. The LNC needs to check into the specific site's grievance process and protocol for healthcare complaints. The inmate's complete grievance file along with the medical records should be requested when reviewing a case.

The grievance file is likely housed separately from the medical records. Depending upon the process, there could be a local or facility file and a headquarter file or DOC file. Additionally, it is important for the LNC to be cognizant of the fact that there is a healthcare and a custody grievance process. Contact with the correct entity within the DOC is essential to obtain the healthcare grievance records.

A grievance or appeal process addresses inmates' complaints or issues about health services. State regulations or local policies include the time frames for the process and responses which typically involves multiple reviews and levels of authority. The process delineates the formal steps the inmate must follow to have fully exhausted the administrative remedies (refer to section on Technical Defenses, Failure to Exhaust Administrative Remedies).

Since the grievance process may include issues regarding the quality of the healthcare delivery system, it is an important component of a facility's quality improvement program (Schoenly, 2016). Driven by state or local guidelines, one may find evidence of attempts by healthcare staff to informally resolve the inmates' complaints regarding a particular healthcare issue. If it can be resolved in this manner, the process may not go to the next level of review if the inmate withdraws the complaint or grievance or chooses to not pursue exhaustion of administrative remedies (Brady et al., 2016).

Outside Records

During a record review, the LNC may find reference that an inmate was referred to an outside healthcare provider, or was hospitalized or was seen in the emergency department. There may or may not be a copy of those records within the records received, but there should be some reference as to where to find them. If those records were not provided, the LNC will need to request those records from the separate entity.

Police Reports

Jail records frequently contain a copy of the original police or arrest report, but these are often kept separate from the medical records of the jail, depending on the facility. There are facilities that will retain the ownership of both the jail and medical records. Depending on the healthcare company supplying the medical personnel in that facility, the LNC may not be able to request records from the medical department of the jail. Therefore, if the jail is not a party to the suit, the LNC will need to obtain a release of information for the jail in order to obtain all records. The police report (booking report) will answer pertinent questions regarding reason for arrest, where the arrest took place, the name of arresting officer, and most importantly, often gives vital information about the inmate's medical condition upon arrival at the jail, which can serve as a baseline against which to compare the inmate's subsequent condition.

Medical Research

Medical research obtained for a correctional healthcare case will be somewhat different than a typical hospitalization or physician negligence case. Correctional health care is similar, but not the same. Research and literature about medical conditions or illnesses will certainly be the same no matter where the inmate is seen, but the type of care provided or what services are actually available to incarcerated patients may be quite different.

For example, some specialty medications are not allowed due to abuse among the inmates. So while the medication may be what the inmate was prescribed prior to incarceration, it may not be provided in prison or jail. The healthcare provider may have a list of approved or a correctional facility medication formulary to choose from. As in the community, some medications are prescribed and tried before the more expensive non-formulary options are considered. Research on the efficacy of substitute medications given in the correctional facility is a frequent task for the LNC (NCCHC, 2018c).

Some issues that may arise will revolve around timing of a procedure or diagnosis. Again, timing will be different in correctional care because of the referral, transportation process and security that must be considered.

Identifying Standards

There are a number of sources for global standards for correctional health care and include accreditation entities (Anno, 2001, p. 78; Rich et al., 2014). The NCCHC is one of the accreditation bodies that provide recommendations for the management of a correctional health services system.

The NCCHC provides separate volumes for prisons, jails, and juvenile confinement facilities, in addition to a manual for medical health services and opioid treatment programs (NCCHC, 2015a, 2015b, 2016a, 2018a, 2018b). The standards cover the areas of care and treatment, health records, administration, personnel, and medical-legal issues. The NCCHC website (www.ncchc.org) also provides position statements to augment the standards and offers expert advice in the *CorrectCare* publication.

The Federal Bureau of Prisons (n.d.) is another source for global standards. Access to clinical practice guidelines, national medication formulary, and other reports on population health and infectious disease management specific to correctional health care is available via the website. In addition to community health and disease specific management, the clinical practice guidelines include guidance on a variety of health related practices including prescribing antibiotics, durable medical equipment, and pain management.

Like all such standards, these standards constitute guidelines and are not meant to be mandatory. Nevertheless, a law firm representing any party in a correctional medicine case should carefully review the various standards for anything that may address the case at hand. Compliance with the published standards can serve as a solid basis for articulating a defense to claims brought by inmates.

To the contrary, if an HCP has done something different than what is set forth in the standards, it can be used as evidence to support a claim of medical negligence or deliberate indifference in conjunction with expert testimony. The LNC working on these types of cases should obtain copies of the relevant standards at the earliest possible time in the litigation and review for relevant statements on the case-related issues.

Nursing and HCP standards should also be obtained and considered (ANA, 2013).

Nurse practitioners and physician assistants are often involved as PCPs in jails and some prisons. Nurse practitioners and physician assistants are regulated by state statutes. Therefore the LNC should research the respective HCP's duties as it pertains to their role at that facility. Nursing assessment protocols are typically facility driven through policies and procedures and may utilize those from the NCCHC. The policies and procedures should cover everything from the intake process through emergency situations (Knox & Schoenly, 2014).

The LNC should also determine if the inmate was housed in a licensed healthcare area of the prison for the care in question, such as a Correctional Treatment Center or hospice (California Health Facilities, n.d.). If it is determined this was the case, then the pertinent state and federal statutes and regulations should also be obtained as part of the review process.

Mental health services may also be available in the institution, directly or through referral. Facilities may have someone available certain days of the week. Qualified mental health professionals includes psychiatrists, psychologists, psychiatric social workers, licensed professional counselors, psychiatric nurses or others who are permitted by law to evaluate and care for the mental health needs of patients. As a standard of care, inmates are expected to receive mental health access to meet their serious mental health needs. The facility should have a designated mental health authority responsible for mental healthcare services (NCCHC, 2015b).

Locating Expert Witnesses

When locating experts for cases involving correctional facilities, it is important to find out if the facility named in the lawsuit is a member of NCCHC and find experts well versed in NCCHC standards. Many of the experts in correctional cases work in facilities that are accredited by the NCCHC and are familiar with those standards of care. It should be clear that correctional healthcare physicians are the most knowledgeable about correctional health care. Likewise, nurse experts, mental health professionals, administrators, etc. should, at a minimum, have relevant correctional experience in the specialty as a consideration by the retaining side. Locating a specialist for case review for correctional cases is no different than finding one for any other case.

Assisting with Deposition and Trial

Selecting records for deposition or trial in correctional cases will be the same as preparing for any trial. The pertinent records will be used as an exhibit, along with any outside records, the grievance file, depositions, and any internal documents that were used in discovery by one side or the other. Expert witnesses will be utilized by each side. The LNC will often help coordinate the timing of the expert's arrival on the day of testimony, help orient them to the courthouse, and escort them out when their testimony is completed.

Protocols and polices of the institution and the healthcare provider will be needed for use at trial. In a jail case, the protocols and policies of the jail will be needed (if they are a co-defendant in the case) along with the healthcare company that provides services for that jail. In a prison case, the healthcare company will have their own protocols and policies, and the institution's protocols and policies will be that of the state DOC (if they are a co-defendant in the case).

Summary

Cases involving claims of improper medical care in correctional facilities are similar in many respects to the average medical malpractice case that may be brought against any HCP, healthcare facility, or system. However, there are significant differences. The LNC should be knowledgeable about both the legal claim differences and the differences related to providing health care within a system whose primary mission is not health care (Schoenly & Knox, 2013, p. 1). The correctional safety and security mission confounds and compounds the ability of healthcare providers to deliver healthcare services equivalent to community standards.

The LNC should understand the elements of the legal claim(s) being made and whether the inmate will be required to prove a deviation from the standard of care or deliberate indifference to a serious medical need, and the types of issues particular to the correctional institution. The issues can include limitations on the diagnostic tools and services available, the quality and education of the healthcare providers, and the reasons why otherwise seemingly necessary care might not be provided or may be delivered in an alternative manner (Schoenly & Knox, 2013, p. 1).

While most experts would agree that the same level of care should be provided in a correctional setting as in the community, the inherent nature of the differences in the setting is likely to be the foundation for a substantial trial battle. Given the limitations on equipment and supplies, the use of certain formularies and contract-specific services, the challenges and difficulties in effectuating referrals and specialty visits, it is likely not reasonable to expect that medical services provided to an incarcerated individual will be identical to a community setting. Yet that may be the most debated issue among the expert witnesses in the case, since the average expert without correctional medicine experience will likely assert that there is no legitimate reason why a national standard of care cannot be met. The LNC and legal team working on these cases should be aware that these nuances in correctional medical care will be a focus of the litigation as a case moves forward.

References

28 U.S.C. § 1915 (2010 ed). (Federal Rules of Civil Procedure).

42 U.S.C. § 1983 (2006) (Civil Action for Deprivation of Rights).

42 U.S. Code § 1997e (e) (Suits by prisoners, Limitation on recovery).

Adu-Tutu, M., & Shields, T. E. (2014). Guidelines for a correctional dental health care system. Retrieved from www.ncchc.org/filebin/Resources/DentalHealth-Care-2014.pdf.

American Association for the Study of Liver Diseases and the Infectious Diseases Society of America. (2018, May 24). HCV guidance: Recommendations for testing, managing, and treating hepatitis C. Retrieved from www.hcvguidelines.org.

American Diabetes Association. (2011). Diabetes management in correctional institutions [Position statement]. *Diabetes Care 34*(Supplement 1), S75–S81. https://doi:10.2337/dc11-S075.

American Nurses Association. (2013). *Corrections nursing: Scope and standards of practice* (2nd ed.). Silver Spring, MD: Author.

Andrews, J. (2017). The current state of public and private prison healthcare. Public Policy Initiative. [Blog]. Penn Wharton, University of Pennsylvania. Retrieved from https://publicpolicy.wharton.upenn.edu/live/news/1736-the-current-state-of-public-and-private-prison/for-students/blog/news.php.

Angelici, D. R. (2015a). Effective management of the prison dental program (Part 1 of 2). *CorrectCare, 29*(1), 10–12. Retrieved from www.ncchc.org/correctcare-archive.

Angelici, D. R. (2015b). Effective management of the prison dental program (Part 2 of 2). *CorrectCare, 29*(2), 14–15, 21. Retrieved from www.ncchc.org/correctcare-archive.

Anno, B. J. (2001). *Correctional health care: Guidelines for the management of an adequate delivery system.* Washington, DC: National Institute of Corrections, U.S. Department of Justice. Retrieved from www.ncchc.org/filebin/Publications/CHC-Guidelines.pdf.

Ball, K. (2011). KOP glucometers in prison? It's working great in California. *CorrectCare, 25*(4), 12–14. Retrieved from www.ncchc.org/correctcare-archive.

Beckman, A. L., Bilinski A., Boyko, R., Camp, G. M., Wall, A., Lim, J. K., ... Gonsalves, G. S. (2016). New hepatitis C drugs are very costly and unavailable to many state prisoners. *Health Affairs, 35*(10), 1893–1901. https://doi: 10.1377/hlthaff.2016.0296.

Bell v. Wolfish 441 U.S. 520 (1979).

Blair, P., Knox, C., Lee, J., Muse, M., Pinney, B., & Voermans, P. (2014). Nurse's scope of practice and delegation authority [white paper]. Retrieved from www.ncchc.org/filebin/Resources/Nurses-Scope-2014.pdf.

Brady, J., Powell, T., & Hill, K. (2016). Grievances: Turn lemons into lemonade and reduce legal risk. *CorrectCare, 30*(4), 8–10. Retrieved from www.ncchc.org/correctcare-archive www.ncchc.org/filebin/CorrectCare/30-4.pdf.

California Health Facilities. (n.d.). Licensed facility listing report. Retrieved from http://hfcis.cdph.ca.gov/Reports/GenerateReport.aspx?rpt=FacilityListing.

Centers for Disease Control and Prevention. (2009). HIV testing implementation guidance for correctional settings. Retrieved from www.cdc.gov/hiv/pdf/group/cdc-hiv-correctional-settings-guidelines.pdf.

Centers for Disease Control and Prevention. (2018). HIV among incarcerated populations. HIV/AIDS. Retrieved from www.cdc.gov/hiv/group/correctional.html.

Crimesider Staff. (2017). California funds 1st U.S. inmate sex reassignment surgery. *The Associated Press.* Retrieved from www.cbsnews.com/news/california-funds-1st-u-s-inmate-sex-reassignment-shiloh-heavenly-quine.

Eighth Circuit Civil Manual. (2017a). 4.22 Serious medical need. *Manual of model civil jury instructions for the district courts of the eighth circuit.* Retrieved from www.juryinstructions.ca8.uscourts.gov/8th%20Circuit%20Manual%20of%20Model%20Civil%20Jury%20Instructions.pdf.

Eighth Circuit Civil Manual (2017b). 4.23 Deliberate indifference. *Manual of model civil jury instructions.* Retrieved from www.juryinstructions.ca8.uscourts.gov/8th%20Circuit%20Manual%20of%20Model%20Civil%20Jury%20Instructions.pdf.

Estelle v. Gamble 429 U.S. 97 (1976).

Farmer v. Brennan 511 U.S. 825 (1994).

Federal Bureau of Prisons. (2018). Evaluation and management of chronic hepatitis C virus (HCV) infection. Clinical guidance. Retrieved from www.bop.gov/resources/pdfs/012018_hcv_infection.pdf; www.bop.gov/resources/health_care_mngmt.jsp.

Federal Bureau of Prisons. (n.d.). Health management resources. Retrieved from www.bop.gov/resources/health_care_mngmt.jsp.

Federal Rules of Civil Procedure Title V. Disclosures and Discovery Rule 26 Duty to disclose; General Provisions Governing Discovery. Retrieved from www.law.cornell.edu/rules/frcp/rule_26 Provisions Governing Discovery.

Federal Rules of Civil Procedure. (n.d.). 28 USC § 1915. Proceedings in forma pauperis, Retrieved from www.federalrulesofcivilprocedure.org/28-usc/section-1915-proceedings-in-forma-pauperis\.

Glezer, A., McNiel, D. E., & Binder, R. L. (2013). Transgendered and incarcerated: A review of the literature, current policies and laws and ethics. *Journal of the American Academy of Psychiatry and the Law, 41*(4), 551–559. Retrieved from http://jaapl.org/content/41/4/551.

Hayes, L. (2017). Controversial issues in suicide prevention. *CorrectCare, 31*(2), 12–14. Retrieved from www.ncchc.org/filebin/CorrectCare/31-2.pdf www.ncchc.org/correctcare-archive.

Johnson, M. E., Kondo, K. K., Brems, D., & Eldridge, G. D. (2015). HIV/AIDS research in correctional settings: A difficult task even even harder? *Journal of Correctional Health Care, 21*(2), 101–111. https://doi.org/10.1177/1078345815572347.

Keller, J. E. (2012). Inappropriate medications in jails and prisons. *CorrectCare, 26(2)*, 14, 24. Retrieved from www.ncchc.org/correctcare-archive.

Keller, J. E. (2014). Hepatitis C treatment between a rock and a hard place. *CorrectCare, 28(2)*, 8–9, 20. Retrieved from www.ncchc.org/correctcare-archive.

Knox, K. M., & Schoenly, L. (2014). Correctional nursing: A new scope and standards of practice. *Correct-Care, 28*(1), 12–14. Retrieved from www.ncchc.org/correctcare-archive.

Maruschak, L. M., Berzofsky, M., & Unangst, J. (2015, revised 2016). *Special report: medical problems of state and federal prisoners and jail inmates, 2011–12*. U.S. Department of Justice, Office of Justice Programs, Bureau of Justice Statistics. Retrieved from www.bjs.gov/content/pub/pdf/mpsfpji1112.pdf.

Meeropol, R., & Head, I. (Eds.). (2010). *The jailhouse lawyer's handbook* (5th ed.). New York, NY: Center for Constitutional Rights and National Lawyers Guild. Retrieved from https://ccrjustice.org/sites/default/files/assets/Report_JailHouseLawyersHandbook.pdf.

Monell v. Department of Social Services 436 U.S. 658 (1978).

National Commission on Correctional Health Care. (2012). Licensed health care providers in correctional institutions [Position statement]. Retrieved from www.ncchc.org/position-statements or www.ncchc.org/filebin/Positions/Licensed_Health_Care_Professionals.pdf.

National Commission on Correctional Health Care. (2014). Administrative management of HIV in correctional institutions [Position statement]. Retrieved from www.ncchc.org/filebin/Positions/Administrative_Management_of_HIV.pdf.

National Commission on Correctional Health Care. (2015a). *Standards for health services in juvenile detention and confinement facilities*. Chicago, IL: Author.

National Commission on Correctional Health Care. (2015b). *Standards for mental health services in correctional facilities*. Chicago, IL: Author.

National Commission on Correctional Health Care. (2015c). Transgender, transsexual and gender nonconforming health care [Position statement]. Retrieved from www.ncchc.org/filebin/Positions/Transgender-Transsexual-and-Gender-Nonconforming-Health-Care.pdf.

National Commission on Correctional Health Care. (2016a). *Standards for opioid treatment programs in correctional facilities*. Chicago, IL: Author.

National Commission on Correctional Health Care. (2016b). Substance use disorder treatment for adults and adolescents [Position statement]. Retrieved from www.ncchc.org/substance-use-disorder-treatment-for-adults-and-adolescents.

National Commission on Correctional Health Care. (2018a). *Standards for health services in jails*. Chicago, IL: Author.

National Commission on Correctional Health Care. (2018b). *Standards for health services in prisons*. Chicago, IL: Author.

National Commission on Correctional Health Care. (2018c). Management of noncancer chronic pain. [Position statement]. Retrieved from www.ncchc.org/position-statements.

National Institute on Drug Abuse. (2017). Treating opioid addiction in criminal justice settings. National Institutes of Health, U.S. Department of Health and Human Services. Retrieved from www.drugabuse.gov/publications/treating-opioid-addiction-in-criminal-justice-settings/treating-opioid-addiction-in-criminal-justice-settings.

Rich, J. D., Allen, S. A., & Williams, B. A. (2014). The need for higher standards in correctional healthcare to improved public health. *Journal of General Internal Medicine, 30*(4), 503–507. https://doi:10.1007/s11606-014-3142-0.

Royal v. Kautsky 375 F.3d 720 (2004).

Schaub v. VonWald 638 F.3d 905 (8th Cir. 2015).

Schoenly, L. (2016). Manage inmate grievances to improve quality and reduce risk. *CorrectCare, 30*(3), 16, 25. Retrieved from www.ncchc.org/correctcare-archive.

Schoenly, L., & Knox, K. M. (Eds.). (2013). *Essentials of correctional nursing*. New York, NY: Springer Publishing.

Sterling, K. R., Cherian, R., Lewis, S., Genther, K., Driscoll, C., Martin, K., … Sanyal, A. J. (2018). Treatment of HCV in the Department of Corrections in the era of oral medication. *Journal of Correctional Health Care, 24*(2), 127–136. https://doi: 10.1177/1078345818762591.

Thompson, J. H. (2010). Today's deliberate indifference: Providing attention without providing treatment to prisoners with serious medical needs. *Harvard Civil Rights-Civil Liberties Law Review, 45*, 635–654. Retrieved from http://harvardcrcl.org/wp-content/uploads/2009/06/635-6541.pdf.

Titus, T., & Gibson, B. (2017). Spotlight on the standards. *CorrectCare, 31*(3), 4. Retrieved from www.ncchc.org/correctcare-archive.

Tompkins, F. (2016). Delegation in correctional nursing practice. *Journal of Correctional Health Care, 22*(3), 218–224. https://doi:10:1177/1078345816654229.

U.S. Constitution: Eighth Amendment. Retrieved from www.law.cornell.edu/constitution/eighth_amendment.

U.S. Department of Justice, Federal Bureau of Prisons. (2015). Compassionate release/reduction in sentence: Procedures for implementation of 18 U.S.C §§ 3582©(1)(A) and 4205 (g). [Change notice]. Retrieved from www.bop.gov/policy/progstat/5050_049_CN-1.pdf.

U.S. Department of Justice, Office of the Inspector General. (2016). Review of the Federal Bureau of Prisons' medical staffing challenges. Retrieved from https://oig.justice.gov/reports/2016/e1602.pdf.

Wilson v. Seiter 501 U.S. 294 (1991).

World Professional Association for Transgender Health. (2011). *Standards of care for the health of transsexual, transgender, and gender conforming people* (7th version). Minneapolis, MN: Author. Retrieved from www.wpath.org/publications/soc.

Yale Law School. (n.d.). The Prison Litigation Reform Act (PLRA). Retrieved from https://library.law.yale.edu/prisoner-litigation-reform-act.

Young, D. J., & Patel, M. (2015). HIV subspecialty care in correctional facilities using telemedicine. *Journal of Correctional Health Care, 21*(2), 177–185. https://doi.org/10.1177/1078345815572863.

Additional Reading

ACLU (2011). Know your rights: The prison litigation reform act (PLRA). Retrieved from www.aclu.org/files/assets/kyr_plra_aug2011_1.pdf.

AELE.org. (2009). Civil liability for inadequate prisoner dental care. *AELE Monthly Law Journal, 9, AELE Mo. L.J. 301 Jail & Prisoner Law Section.* Retrieved www.aele.org/law/2009all09/2009-09MLJ301.pdf.

American Bar Association. (2017). Standards on treatment of prisoners. Retrieved from www.americanbar.org/publications/criminal_justice_section_archive/crimjust_standardstreatmentprisoners.html#23-2.5.

Andrews, J. (2017). The current state of public and private prison healthcare. *Inside Penn Wharton Public Policy Initiative, 6*(3). Retrieved from https://publicpolicy.wharton.upenn.edu/live/news/1736-the-current-state-of-public-and-private-prison/for-students/blog/news.php.

Colwell, J. (2017). Caring for prisoners. *ACP Hospitalist.* Retrieved from https://acphospitalist.org/archives/2017/10/caring-for-prisoners.htm.

Court Listener. (n.d.). *Shaub v. VonWald*, 638 F.3d 905 (8th Cir. 2011). Retrieved from www.courtlistener.com/opinion/215420/schaub-v-vonwald/.

Federal Bureau of Prisons. (n.d.). Health management resources, clinical practice guidelines. Retrieved from www.bop.gov/resources/health_care_mngmt.jsp.

Federal Bureau of Prisons. (2016). Dental services. Retrieved www.bop.gov/policy/progstat/6400_003.pdf.

Federal Bureau of Prisons. (2018. June). Durable medical equipment: Clinical guidance. Retrieved from www.bop.gov/resources/health_care_mngmt.jsp.

Macmadu, A., & Rich, J. D. (2015). Correctional health is community health. *Issues in Science and Technology, 32*(1). Retrieved http://issues.org/32-1/correctional-health-is-community-health/.

National Center on Addiction and Substance Abuse at Columbia University. (2010). Behind bars II: Substance abuse and America's prison population. Retrieved from www.centeronaddiction.org/addiction-research/reports/behind-bars-ii-substance-abuse-and-america%E2%80%99s-prison-population.

National Commission on Correctional Health Care. (Originally appeared in the Fall 2011 issue of *Correct-Care*.) Regulations, standards and policies. Retrieved from www.ncchc.org/cnp-regulations.

Pew Charitable Trusts. (2017). Prison health care: Costs and quality. Retrieved from www.pewtrusts.org/~/media/assets/2017/10/sfh_prison_health_care_costs_and_quality_final.pdf.

Schoenly, L. (n.d.). Correctional nursing. International Association of Forensic Nurses. Retrieved from www.forensicnurses.org/page/correctionalnursing?.

Sonntag, H. (2017). Medicine behind bars: Regulating and litigating prison healthcare under state law forty years after *Estelle v. Gamble. Case W. Res. L. Rev., 603*, 68 (2). Retrieved from https://scholarlycommons.law.case.edu/caselrev/vol. 68/iss2/9.

Thomas, D. L., Kelley, W., Thomas, J. A., Kennedy, T., & Edmonds, T. A. (2014). Who wins in a lawsuit? How to ensure constitutional medical care for inmates. *Corrections Today*. Retrieved from www.aca.org/aca_prod_imis/Docs/Corrections%20Today/2014%20Articles/May%20Articles/Thomas.pdf.

Thomas, J. R. (2018). Dwindling oversight heightens concern over medical, mental health care for inmates. *CT Mirror*. Retrieved https://ctmirror.org/2018/03/06/__trashed-2/.

U.S. Department of Justice, Federal Bureau of Prisons. (2014). Program statement. Retrieved from www.bop.gov/policy/progstat/6031_004.pdf.

Test Questions

1. What is the difference between a prison and a jail?
   A. The conviction of the inmate and the time sentenced to incarceration
   B. The difference is how many inmates the facility holds
   C. One is run by the state and the other by the federal government
   D. None of the above
2. Why do most lawsuits in a correctional setting end up in federal court?
   A. The majority of the inmates are represented by an attorney
   B. The majority of the claims do not allege a constitutional deprivation of the offender's civil rights
   C. The majority of the claims allege a constitutional deprivation of an offender's civil rights
   D. The majority of the inmates represent themselves
3. Which of the following claims might one see filed against the healthcare personnel in a correctional facility?
   A. Denial of access to the law library
   B. Failure to refer to an outside specialist
   C. Failure to monitor blood sugars
   D. Both B & C
4. Who else besides medical personnel may provide health care to the inmate if needed?
   A. Any inmate may treat another inmate
   B. Only licensed medical personnel may treat an inmate
   C. Custody Officers may provide care to an inmate if trained by the company providing health care to that facility
   D. Any non-medical personnel may provide treatment to an inmate
5. Which of the following is true regarding the grievance process?
   1. For cases alleging a claim of deliberate indifference, an inmate's lawsuit may be dismissed if the person fails to file a grievance and properly follow the process
   2. The healthcare grievance process arises from the Prison Litigation and Reform Act
   3. Grievance records are typically found in the medical record
   4. The grievance process is an important component of a facility's quality improvement plan
      A. 1, 2, 3
      B. 1, 2, 4
      C. 1, 2
      D. 2, 4

Answers: 1. A, 2. C, 3. D, 4. C, 5. B

Chapter 18

Employment Law and Occupational Health and Safety

Kathleen P. Buckheit, MPH, BSN, RN, CEN, COHN-S/CM, CCM, FAAOHN
Moniaree Parker Jones, EdD, MSN, RN, CCM, COI

Contents

Objectives

- Identify the major regulatory agency which addresses occupational health and safety issues
- Describe at least five major employment laws, standards, and regulations related to occupational health and safety
- Describe the role of the LNC in the area of occupational health and safety

Introduction

Understanding occupational health and safety is an important role for the legal nurse consultant (LNC). The LNC needs to be knowledgeable about the laws and regulations affecting this complex area of healthcare practice. Federal and state laws such as the Occupational Safety and Health Act (OSH Act) were enacted to protect the health and safety of workers. Employers not in compliance may receive fines and citations depending on the severity of the violation. The role of the LNC can be enhanced by having familiarity with the scope of practice of the Occupational and Environmental Health Nurse (OEHN). The knowledge of records that may exist to assist in the investigation and support of a case involving occupational safety and health issues is helpful to the discovery process.

Employment Laws

Employment laws, also referred to as labor laws, are designed to keep workers safe and ensure employees are fairly treated, although some laws protect employers' interests as well. Employment laws are based on federal and state legislation, administrative rules, and court opinions. Labor laws in the United States resulted from public outrage against the working conditions and practices of the Industrial Revolution. In the early 20th century, the first employment laws prohibited child labor, provided compensation for injured workers, implemented the minimum wage, and created a standard work week. In the 1960s and 1970s, federal laws prohibited discrimination and unsafe work conditions (HG.org Legal Resources, n.d.).

In order to clarify different legal applications of labor laws, definitions will be included to include doctrine, statute, and constitutional claims. According to USLegal.com,

- Doctrine is a legal principle that is widely adhered to. It is a rule or principle of the law established through the repeated application of legal precedents.
- Statute is the law passed by a legislative body. It is the written law passed by legislature, parliament or elected or appointed houses of assembly on the state or federal level. A statute may forbid a certain act, direct a certain act, make a declaration, or set forth governmental mechanisms to aid society. The term statute signifies the elevation of a bill from legislative proposal to law. A statute is also called legislation.
- Constitutional claim means a person's assertion of a right or interest established by the Constitution.

(USLegal.com, n.d.)

Discrimination in the workplace is another basis for many employment law cases. The Civil Rights Act of 1964 and subsequent legislation makes it illegal to treat workers differently because of ethnic, religion, gender, age, or disability issues. In most states, the law presumes that employment is considered "at will," which means employers and employees are free to terminate the relationship at any time and for any reason, unless a contract is in place; discriminatory conditions exist; or in retaliation for filing a worker's compensation claim or disclosing a violation of law (whistleblowing). A few states prohibit terminating employees in bad faith, such as to avoid paying a bonus or other benefits (HG.org Legal Resources, n.d.).

The United States Supreme Court held that a state may not condition public employment on an employee's exercise of First Amendment rights. The First Amendment prevents the government, except in the most compelling circumstances, from the power to interfere with an employee's freedom to believe and associate or to not believe and not associate. An employee improperly discharged depends on the situation and circumstances as not every discharge may result in a lawsuit. Wrongful termination lawsuits may arise from issues related to job performance, racial or national origin discrimination, sexual harassment, retaliation, reprimands, whistleblowing, military status or service, demotion or denial of promotion, Family Medical Leave Act matters,

Wage and Hour, and overtime disputes, and other personnel concerns. These cases can be heard in federal and state courts and in administrative agencies at all levels (Pollack, 2017).

Economic damages assessed in wrongful termination cases can be a challenge. The role of the LNC or legal expert may include assessment of damages and factors such as job finding success may differ by age, education, race, economic conditions, and tenure of last job. It is important for the LNC to understanding that forensic economists who assess economic damages in civil litigation usually assess damages based on economic theory, empirical studies, and prior legal cases. However, the LNC is aware that the role of the expert is to assist the trier of fact who adjudicates the claims and that not all claims made are recoverable (Macpherson & Stephenson, 2016).

Although wrongful discharge or retaliatory discharge is most frequent, there is also the theory of constructive discharge referring to the situation where the employer did not expressly terminate an employee for reasons such as the basis of race, color, sex, religion, or national origin but, creates working conditions such that no reasonable employee would be expected to endure in that environment. The infliction of emotional distress may include the employee who is subject to religious harassment or racial ridicule lending to a hostile work environment. Apart from the exception of federal legislation, each state determines its own stance on the employment-at-will doctrine (Tomlinson & Bockanic, 2009).

The analysis of the medical records by the LNC focuses on causation or damages (not liability) to determine the relationship of medical claims supported by the medical records. The LNC looks for potential pre-existing medical conditions pre-dating the incident in question. The employee history is key to determine past mental health issues, to include: emotional distress, substance abuse, unexplained human behaviors, being fired for not following medical orders if employed as a nurse or physician, or any discrepancies in the role of acting as a patient advocate. Regardless of the nature of the employee termination, it is important to interview all involved parties, investigate thoroughly to obtain a clear picture of the pertinent facts, document all evidence gathered, and look at the facility policies and procedures related to the termination. For additional information on employment laws, the Department of Labor (DOL) website is a great resource for the LNC to research (U.S. DOL, n.d.).

Occupational Safety and Health Act

The most comprehensive occupational safety and health federal legislation today is the Occupational Safety and Health Act (OSH) Act, signed into law by President Richard M. Nixon on December 29, 1970. The major goal of the OSH Act is:

> to assure safe and healthful working conditions for working men and women; by authorizing enforcement of the standards developed under the Act; by assisting and encouraging the States in their efforts to assure safe and healthful working conditions; by providing for research, information, education, and training in the field of occupational safety and health; and for other purposes.
>
> (U.S. Government Printing Office, 1990, p. 1)

The OSH Act created three separate bodies: the Occupational Safety and Health Administration (OSHA), the National Institute for Occupational Safety and Health (NIOSH), and the Occupational Safety and Health Review Commission (OSHRC) to administer the major requirement of the act. An advisory committee joins all three bodies.

Occupational Safety and Health Administration

In 1970, the United States Congress and President Richard Nixon created the Occupational Safety and Health Administration (OSHA), a national public health agency dedicated to the basic proposition no worker should have to choose between their life and their job. The creation of the agency has delivered remarkable progress in the prevention and reduction of illnesses and injuries in the nation by more than 65%. OSHA has tackled deadly safety hazards and health risks by establishing common sense standards and enforcement against those who put workers at risk. OSHA standards, enforcement actions, compliance assistance, and cooperative programs have saved thousands of lives and prevented countless injuries and illnesses (U.S. DOL, OSHA, 2016, pp. 3–4).

Occupational Safety and Health Administration covers most private sector employers and workers in all 50 states, the District of Columbia, and other U.S. jurisdictions either directly through the federal agency, itself, or through an OSHA-approved state plan. In 26 states or territories, state plans have been approved by OSHA providing job safety and health programs. The state plans are monitored by OSHA, providing as much as 50% of each program's funding. State OSHA programs must be at least as effective as the federal OSHA program. Additional information on federal and state OSHA guidelines are available on the website (U.S. DOL, OSHA, n.d.-a). OSHA does not cover: the self-employed; immediate family members of farm employers; or workers covered by other federal agencies, such as the military and state and local government employees. The OSHA-approved State Plans cover state and local government employees. Although OSHA does not fine federal agencies, OSHA's protection applies to all and monitors these agencies and conducts federal workplace inspections in response to reports of hazards (U.S. DOL, OSHA, 2016). A listing of OSHA-approved State Plans may be found on the OSHA website: www.osha.gov/dcsp/osp/index.html.

The National Institute for Occupational Safety and Health

The OSH Act established the National Institute for Occupational Safety and Health (NIOSH) as part of the U.S. Centers for Disease Control and Prevention (CDC) in the U.S. Department of Health and Human Services (DHHS). NIOSH is the federal agency charged with conducting research and promulgates recommendations and practical solutions to identified problems preventing worker injuries and illnesses. NIOSH is mandated to assure "every man and woman in the Nation safe and healthful working conditions and to preserve our human resources" (U.S. DHHS, CDC, & NIOSH, 2015).

The National Occupational Research Agenda (NORA) is a partnership program that encourages and funds innovative research and improved workplace practices. In its third decade (2016–2026) with an enhanced structure, NORA consists of 10 industry sectors based on major areas of the U.S. economy, and 7 health and safety cross-sectors addressing the major health and safety issues affecting the U.S. workforce (U.S. DHHS et al., 2016a).

NIOSH conducts research to finds ways to reduce worker injuries and illnesses by providing support for academic degree and non-degreed training programs and research, in disciplines such as industrial hygiene, occupational health nursing, occupational medicine, and occupational safety (U.S. DHHS et al., 2016b).

Occupational Safety and Health Review Commission

The Occupational Safety and Health Review Commission (OSHRC), an independent agency of the executive branch of the U.S. Government, was created to decide contests of citations or penalties resulting from OSHA inspections of workplaces. This agency provides administrative trial and appellate review with procedures for (1) conducting hearings, receiving evidence, and rendering decisions by its Administrative Law Judges (ALJs) and (2) discretionary review of ALJ decisions by a panel of Commissioners (U.S. OSHRC, n.d.).

National Advisory Committee on Occupational Safety and Health

The OSH Act established a 12-member National Advisory Committee on Occupational Safety and Health (NACOSH) that provides advice, counsel, and recommendations to the Secretaries of Labor and Health and Human Services about the administration of OSHA. Committee members are representatives from labor, management, occupational safety and health professionals, and the public (U.S. DOL, OSHA, n.d.-b).

Standards, Laws, and Regulations Applicable to Occupational Safety and Health

The OSHA mission is to assure safe and healthful workplaces by setting and enforcing standards, and by providing training, outreach, education, and assistance. Under the OSHA law, employers are responsible for providing a safe and healthful workplace for their workers (U.S. DOL, OSHA, 2016, p. 4).

The OSHA agency is responsible for promulgating, modifying, and revoking legally enforceable standards with which employers must comply. Generally, OSHA standards require employers to maintain conditions and adopt practices reasonably necessary and appropriate to protect workers on the job; be familiar with and comply with standards applicable to their establishments; and ensure employees have and use personal protective equipment as required for safety and health. Also, employers must comply with the General Duty Clause of the OSH Act. This clause requires employers to keep their workplaces free of serious recognized hazards and is generally cited when no specific OSHA standard applies to the hazard (U.S. DOL, OSHA, n.d.-a). The general duty clause, Section 5(a)(1) states that each employer must "furnish ... a place of employment ... free from, recognized hazards that are causing or are likely to cause death or serious physical harm to his employees" (U.S. DOL, OSHA, 2016, p. 10).

Standards are written for a wide variety of workplace hazards, including toxic substances, harmful physical agents, electrical hazards, fall hazards, trenching hazards, hazardous waste, infectious diseases, fire and explosion hazards, dangerous atmospheres, machine hazards, and confined spaces (U.S. DOL, OSHA, 2016, p. 5). A few of the standards that often involve the Occupational and Environmental Health Nurse include the Bloodborne Pathogens Standard, Hazard Communication Standard, Recording and Reporting of Occupational Injuries and Illnesses Standard, Access to Medical and Exposure Records Standard, Occupational Noise Exposure Standard, and Personal Protective Equipment Standard (Appendix A). All standards may be accessed via the OSHA website (U.S. DOL, OSHA, 2016, p. 4). For a more in-depth discussion of the role of the OEHN, see the section on Occupational and Environmental Health Nursing later in the chapter.

Bloodborne Pathogens Standard

Bloodborne pathogens are infectious microorganisms present in blood that can cause disease in humans. These pathogens include, but are not limited to, hepatitis B virus (HBV), hepatitis C virus (HCV), and human immunodeficiency virus (HIV), the virus that causes AIDS. Workers exposed to bloodborne pathogens are at risk for serious or life-threatening illnesses (U.S. DOL, OSHA, 2011).

The OSHA Bloodborne Pathogens Standard (29 CFR 1910.1030; see Appendix A) enumerates steps employers must take to protect workers who have the potential to be occupationally exposed to blood or other potentially infectious materials (OPIM) while performing the job, such as skin, eye, mucous membrane, or parenteral contact with blood or other potentially infectious materials (U.S. DOL, OSHA, 2011).

In general, the standard requires employers to:

- Establish a written exposure control plan to eliminate or minimize exposures
- Update the plan annually with changes in tasks, procedures, and positions that affect exposure, and technological changes, including documenting soliciting input from workers in identifying, evaluating, and selecting effective engineering and work practice controls
- Implement the use of universal precautions (treating all human blood and OPIM as if known to be infectious for bloodborne pathogens)
- Identify and use engineering controls that isolate or remove the bloodborne pathogens hazard from the workplace, such as sharps disposal containers, self-sheathing needles, and safer medical devices, such as needleless systems
- Ensure the use of safe work practice controls to reduce exposure by changing the way a task is performed, such as appropriate handling and disposing of contaminated sharps, specimens, laundry, and cleaning contaminated surfaces and items
- Provide personal protective equipment (PPE), such as gloves, gowns, eye protection, and masks with worker training on use and care at no cost to the employee
- Provide hepatitis B vaccinations and training to all workers with occupational exposure within 10 days of initial assignment to a job with occupational exposure
- Provide post-exposure evaluation and follow-up at no cost to any worker who experiences an exposure incident, such as in a specific eye, mouth, other mucous membrane, non-intact skin, or parenteral contact with blood or OPIM. The healthcare professional will provide a limited written opinion to the employer and all diagnoses must remain confidential
- Use labels, signs, red biohazard bags to communicate hazards affixed to any containers of contaminated equipment or waste
- Provide initial and annual training to workers that covers all elements of the standard
- Maintain worker medical and training records, including a sharps injury log

(U.S. DOL, OSHA, 2011)

The Needlestick Safety and Prevention Act was signed into law November 6, 2000. Congress identified occupational exposure to bloodborne pathogens from accidental sharps injuries in healthcare and other occupational settings continued to be a serious problem, and a modification to OSHA's Bloodborne Pathogens Standard was accomplished. This modification set forth greater detail and made OSHA's requirement for employers to identify, evaluate, and implement safety-engineered sharp devices more specific. Also, this Act mandated additional requirements for maintaining a sharps injury log and for the involvement of non-managerial healthcare workers in evaluating and choosing devices (U.S. DOL, OSHA, n.d.-c).

Hazard Communication Standard

The Hazard Communication Standard (HCS) (29 CFR 1910.120; see Appendix A) was first promulgated in 1983 covering manufacturing and later expanded to include all industries where workers were potentially exposed to hazardous chemicals. While chemicals have utility and benefits, they also potentially cause adverse effects. These include both health hazards (e.g., carcinogenicity and sensitization), and physical hazards (i.e., flammability and reactivity properties). To protect workers by reducing chemical source illnesses and injuries, employers need information about the chemical hazards and recommended protective measures. Workers have a right and a need to know this information, so they protect themselves as necessary (U.S. DOL, OSHA, 2014).

To ensure workplace safety, hazard information about how the chemical's employees are exposed must be available and understandable to workers. In 2012, the HCS aligned with the Globally Harmonized System of Classification and Labeling of Chemicals (GHS). This update to the HCS provides a common and coherent approach to classifying chemicals and communicating hazard information on labels and safety data sheets to include: (1) hazard classification, (2) labels, (3) safety data sheets, and (4) information and training (U.S. DOL, OSHA, n.d.-d).

Recording and Reporting of Occupational Injuries and Illnesses Standard

In 1971, the original Recording and Reporting of Occupational Injuries and Illnesses Standard (29 CFR 1904; see Appendix A) was enacted and amended in 2002. This standard allows the identification of high hazard industries and the notification to employees of their employer's safety record. The information helps employers, workers, and OSHA evaluate the safety of a workplace, understand the hazards, and implement worker protections to reduce and eliminate hazards, preventing future workplace injuries and illnesses (U.S. DOL, OSHA, n.d.-e).

Employers with more than 10 employees are required to keep a record of serious work-related injuries and illnesses that result in death, significant injuries or illnesses, loss of consciousness, lost work time, restricted work or job transfer, hospitalization, and receiving medical treatment. The standard provides an algorithm to assist in determining if an injury or illness is considered occupational in nature and includes a detailed list of first aid definitions, which does not meet the medical treatment definition. Records are maintained for at least five years. The OSHA Form 301 is for the employer to post workplace summaries in a prominent area for employees to see and copies may be requested by current and former employees, or their representatives (U.S. DOL, OSHA, n.d.-e).

Until now, employers only had to keep these OSHA Logs for five years after recording the incident and some industries and facilities were also required to "report" this information annually to the Bureau of Labor Statistics (BLS). Effective July 1, 2017, OSHA now requires certain employers to electronically submit this data they are already required to record on the OSHA Log. Data analysis will result in more efficient use, enforcement, and compliance assistance resources. Also, some data will be posted to the OSHA website to encourage employers to improve workplace safety and provide valuable information to workers, researchers, and the public (U.S. DOL, OSHA, n.d.-e). In addition, employers are required to report to OSHA within 8 hours any injuries or illnesses that result in death, and within 24 hours all work-related inpatient hospitalizations, all amputations, and all losses of an eye (U.S. DOL, OSHA, n.d.-e).

Access to Medical and Exposure Records Standard

The OSHA Access to Medical and Exposure Records Standard (29 CFR 1910.1020; see Appendix A) gives an employee, who had a possible exposure to or uses toxic substances or harmful physical agents in the workplace, the right to access relevant medical and exposure records. This knowledge may help the employee detect, prevent, and seek treatment for occupational disease (U.S. DOL, OSHA, 2001). The standard identifies who has the right to access the medical and exposure records; describes types of exposures that may be included; and defines access, employee exposure records, and employee medical records.

The records may be accessed by:

- A current or former employee who is or may have been exposed to toxic substances or harmful physical agents
- An employee assigned or transferred to work involving toxic substances or harmful physical agents and
- The legal representative of a deceased or legally incapacitated employee who was or may have been exposed to toxic substances or harmful physical agents

(U.S. DOL, OSHA, 2001)

The toxic substances and harmful physical agents may include the following:

- Metals and dusts, such as lead, cadmium, and silica
- Biological agents, such as bacteria, viruses, and fungi and
- Physical stress, such as noise, heat, cold, vibration, repetitive motion, and ionizing and non-ionizing radiation (U.S. DOL, OSHA, 2001)

Access is defined in the standard as the right to examine and copy medical and exposure records. Employee exposure records include monitoring results of workplace air or measurements of toxic substances or harmful physical agents in the workplace; biological monitoring results, such as blood and urine test results; and safety data sheets (SDS) containing information about a substance's hazards to human health. Employee medical records include medical and employment questionnaires or histories; results of medical examinations and laboratory tests; medical opinion; diagnoses; progress notes; recommendations; first-aid records; descriptions of treatments and prescriptions; and employee medical complaints. Medical records must be maintained for the duration of the employee's employment plus 30 years and exposure records for 30 years (U.S. DOL, OSHA, 2001).

Occupational Noise Exposure Standard

The purpose of the Occupational Noise Exposure Standard (29 CFR 1910.95; see Appendix A) is "to protect workers with significant occupational noise exposures from hearing impairment even if they are subject to such noise exposures over their entire working lifetimes" (U.S. DOL, OSHA, 2002, p. 1). The standard requires employees exposed to noise at or above 85 decibels (dB) averaged over eight working hours, or an eight-hour time-weighted average (TWA) are included in the company hearing conservation program.

Hearing conservation programs aim to prevent initial occupational hearing loss; preserve and protect remaining hearing; and equip workers with the knowledge and hearing protection devices necessary to safeguard themselves. Employers must measure noise levels; provide free annual hearing exams, hearing protection, and training; and evaluate the adequacy of the protectors being used (U.S. DOL, OSHA, n.d.-f). A hearing conservation program requires five components: (1) sound exposure monitoring, (2) noise controls, (3) education and motivation, (4) hearing protection, and (5) audiometric monitoring. Sound exposure monitoring must be conducted during a typical work situation and include all continuous, intermittent, and impulsive noise within an 80 dB to 130 dB range (U.S. DOL, OSHA, 2002).

Engineering and administrative noise controls are OSHA's preferred method of abatement. Examples of engineering controls are to eliminate the noise source or redesign the process to reduce sound levels; however, this is not always possible. Administrative controls include work practices such as rotating workers to areas of lower noise levels. Efforts to implement engineering and administrative controls should be documented.

Education, motivation, and compliance of workers are key to the success of the program. Employees who understand the need to protect their hearing and the reasons for the hearing conservation program will be more motivated to wear their hearing protection. Employees must be trained at least annually, and training documented (U.S. DOL, OSHA, 2015).

When engineering and administrative noise controls are not possible, employers must provide personal protective equipment (PPE); this includes ear plugs, ear muffs, and canal caps. All employees must wear hearing protection if exposed to eight-hour TWA noise levels of 85 dB or above for six months with no baseline hearing test; have incurred a standard threshold shift; or are working in an area where noise levels are 90 dB or above.

Audiometric testing is used to monitor an employee's hearing during employment. Baseline audiograms are performed at time of hire or when transferred from a low-noise to a high-noise level work area requiring monitoring. Annual tests are performed and compared to the baseline for changes in hearing levels (U.S. DOL, OSHA, 2002).

Personal Protective Equipment Standard

Controlling the source of a hazard using an engineering control is the best way to protect employees. Depending on the hazard or workplace conditions, OSHA recommends the use of engineering or work practice controls to manage or eliminate hazards to the greatest extent possible. When engineering, work practice, and administrative controls are not feasible or do not provide sufficient protection from any workplace hazard, employers must provide personal protective equipment (PPE) to their employees and ensure its use (U.S. DOL, OSHA, 2004, p. 4).

The Personal Protective Equipment (PPE) standard (29 CFR 1910.132; see Appendix A) was promulgated to provide information on the types of protection available for employees where engineering and administrative controls were not available or effective in controlling occupational hazards. The PPE is equipment worn to minimize exposure to hazards, such as contact with chemical, radiological, physical, electrical, mechanical, or other workplace hazards that can result in serious workplace injuries and illnesses. Besides hearing protection, the PPE may include items such as gloves, safety glasses, safety shoes, hard hats, respirators, coveralls, vests, and full body suits (U.S. DOL, OSHA, 2004, p. 4).

The PPE program must address the hazards present; the appropriate equipment selection based on the hazard; maintenance, care, and use of PPE; employee training and monitoring of use; and monitoring of the PPE program to ensure its effectiveness (U.S. DOL, OSHA, n.d.-g).

Employers' responsibilities for the PPE program include the following:

■ Perform a "hazard assessment" to identify and control safety and health hazards
■ Identify and provide appropriate PPE free of charge to the employee
■ Train and monitor employees in the use, care, and maintenance of PPE
■ Maintain PPE, including replacing worn or damaged PPE and
■ Review, update, and evaluate the effectiveness of the program

Employees' responsibilities of using PPE include the following:

■ Properly wear when required, care for, and store PPE as trained
■ Participate in training programs on PPE and
■ Inform management of PPE requiring repair or replacement

(U.S. DOL, OSHA. 2004, p. 4)

Workers' Compensation

Workers' compensation programs are promulgated by the individual states and as such vary state to state. Under the various workers' compensation systems, insurance is purchased or provided by employers through individual insurance companies, funds, or self-insurance plans to provide the worker with the indemnity and medical benefits required by the various state laws. The purpose of these laws is all the same: to provide oversight for workers' compensation benefits for the injured worker for loss of wages and medical benefits and providing guidance to the employer. All are meant to be self-executing, constantly changing and protecting not only the worker, but the employer as well (U.S. Workers Comp.com, n.d.).

In the United States, most employees who are injured on the job have suffered a compensable injury or illness while in the course of employment AND have a right to receive medical care for that injury or illness and, in many cases, monetary payments to compensate for any resulting disabilities from the initial injury or illness, whether permanent or temporary. These benefits may include lost wages, payment of medical treatment, provision of vocational rehabilitation or job placement, and in a resulting death, benefits to the employee's dependents (USLegal.com, 2016).

Equal Employment Opportunity Laws

The U.S. Equal Employment Opportunity Commission (EEOC) is responsible for enforcing federal laws that make it illegal to discriminate against a job applicant or an employee because of the person's race, color, religion, sex (including pregnancy, gender identity, and sexual orientation), national origin, age (40 or older), disability, or genetic information. It is also unlawful to discriminate against any employee or applicant for employment regarding hiring, termination, promotion, compensation, job training, or any other term, condition, or privilege of employment because of an association with anyone based on race or color, religion, sex, or national origin. In addition, an employer may not retaliate because of a complaint, filing charges, or participating in an employment discrimination investigation or lawsuit (U.S. EEOC, n.d.-a). The U.S. EEOC website provides information on:

- **Title VII of the Civil Rights Act of 1964 (Title VII)**
  Title VII makes it illegal to discriminate against employees or applicants based on race, color, religion, national origin, or sex. Employers must reasonably accommodate applicants' and employees sincerely held religious practices, unless doing so would impose an undue hardship on the operation of the employer's business (U.S. EEOC, n.d.-b).
- **The Pregnancy Discrimination Act**
  The Pregnancy Discrimination Act amended Title VII to prevent discrimination against a woman because of pregnancy, childbirth, or related medical condition (U.S. EEOC, n.d.-b).
- **The Equal Pay Act of 1963 (EPA)**
  The Equal Pay Act of 1963 (EPA) makes it illegal to pay to men and women different wages if they perform equal work in the same workplace (U.S. EEOC, n.d.-b).
- **The Age Discrimination in Employment Act of 1967 (ADEA)**
  The Age Discrimination in Employment Act of 1967 (ADEA) protects people who are 40 or older from discrimination because of age (U.S. EEOC, n.d.-b).
- **Title I of the Americans with Disabilities Act of 1990 (ADA)**
  Title I makes it illegal to discriminate against a qualified person with a disability. The law also requires that reasonable accommodations be provided for physical or mental limitations of an otherwise qualified applicant or employee with a disability, unless this would pose undue hardship for the employer's business (U.S. EEOC, n.d.-b).
- **Sections 102 and 103 of the Civil Rights Act of 1991**
  Among other things, this law amends Title VII and the ADA to permit jury trials and compensatory and punitive damage awards in intentional discrimination cases (U.S. EEOC, n.d.-b).
- **Sections 501 and 505 of the Rehabilitation Act of 1973**
  Sections 501 and 505 of the Rehabilitation Act of 1973 makes it illegal to discriminate against a qualified person with a disability in the federal government. The law also requires that reasonable accommodations be provided for physical or mental limitations of an otherwise qualified applicant or employee with a disability, unless this would pose undue hardship for the employer's business. Section 501 prohibits employment discrimination against individuals with disabilities in the federal sector. Section 505 contains provisions governing remedies and attorney's fees under Section 501 (U.S. EEOC, n.d.-b).
- **The Genetic Information Nondiscrimination Act of 2008 (GINA)**
  The Genetic Information Nondiscrimination Act of 2008 (GINA) prevents discrimination against employees or applicants because of genetic information. Genetic information includes an individual's genetic test information. It covers test results family members, as well as information about any disease or condition of a family members (i.e., an individual's family medical history) (U.S. EEOC, n.d.-b).

Rehabilitation Act of 1973

The purpose of Rehabilitation Act of 1973 is to provide a statutory basis for the Rehabilitation Services Administration, and to authorize programs to: (1) implement comprehensive state plans to provide vocational rehabilitation services to handicapped individuals, and (2) to prepare them for employment or at least to improve the quality of their lives through improved methods of rehabilitation and services. Also, it provides for research, special projects, and demonstrations to develop new methods of applying advanced medical technology, scientific achievement, and psychological and social information to solve rehabilitation problems, and develop new and innovative methods of providing rehabilitation services (U.S. EEOC, 2000).

The Rehabilitation Act of 1973, Section 504 protects qualified individuals from discrimination based on a disability. The non-discrimination requirements apply to employers and organizations receiving financial assistance from any federal department or agency, including DHHS, hospitals, nursing homes, mental health centers, and service programs. Under this law, individuals with disabilities are persons with a physical or mental impairment, substantially limiting one or more major life activities. For purposes of employment, qualified individuals with disabilities are persons who with reasonable accommodation can perform the essential functions of the job. Reasonable accommodation requires an employer take reasonable steps to accommodate the disability unless it causes the employer undue hardship (U.S. DHHS, Office for Civil Rights [OCR], 2013).

Americans with Disabilities Act

The Americans with Disabilities Act (ADA) of 1990 is one of the most comprehensive pieces of U.S. civil rights legislation, prohibiting discrimination and guaranteeing people with disabilities the same opportunities as everyone else to participate in American life. It provides opportunities to be employed, purchase goods and services, and participate in state and local government programs and services. The ADA is modeled after the Civil Rights Act of 1964 (prohibiting discrimination based on race, color, religion, sex, or national origin), and Section 504 of the Rehabilitation Act of 1973, making the ADA an "equal opportunity" law for people with disabilities. A person must have a disability, defined by the ADA, as a physical or mental impairment substantially limiting one or more major life activities. A person who has or is perceived by others to have such an impairment, or a person who is perceived by others as having such an impairment, is covered by the ADA (U.S. DOJ, Civil Rights Division [CRD], n.d.-a).

The ADA expands on the requirement of Section 504 of the Rehabilitation Act, by requiring state and local government programs that receive federal financial assistance to provide equal opportunity to individuals with disabilities to participate and benefit. Public services may not discriminate against individuals with disabilities. All government programs, services, facilities, and communications must be accessible, consistent with the requirements of Section 504 of the Rehabilitation Act.

Under ADA Title I: Employment, employers with 15 or more employees must provide individuals with qualified disabilities an equal opportunity to benefit from the full range of employment-related opportunities available to others. The Act prohibits discrimination in recruitment, hiring, promotions, training, pay, social activities, and other privileges of employment. Questions about an applicant's disability before a job offer is made is prohibited. Also, the Act requires employers make reasonable accommodations for otherwise qualified individuals unless it results in undue hardship (U.S. DOJ, CRD, n.d.-a).

Under ADA Title II: State and Local Government Activities, all state and local governments, regardless of size or receipt of federal funding, are required to give people with disabilities an equal opportunity to benefit from all programs, services, and activities (e.g., public education, employment, transportation, etc.). All governments must follow specific architectural standards in new construction and alteration of existing buildings, unless that would result in undue financial and administrative burdens. All governments are required to make reasonable modifications to policies, practices, and procedures where necessary to avoid discrimination, unless they can demonstrate that doing so would fundamentally alter the nature of the service, program, or activity. Also, Title II addresses modifications in public transportation and Title III addresses public accommodations. Title IV establishes the requirement for telephone and television access for people with hearing and speech disabilities and the telecommunications relay services (TRS) that operate 24 hours a day (U.S. DOJ, CRD, n.d.-a).

The Family and Medical Leave Act

The Family Medical Leave Act (FMLA) entitles eligible employees of covered employers to take unpaid, job-protected leave for specific family and medical reasons with continuation of group health insurance coverage with the same terms and conditions. Eligible employees are covered in one of two of the following situations:

1. 12 workweeks of leave in a 12-month period for:
   ■ birth of a child and care given for the newborn within one year of birth
   ■ placement of a child for adoption or foster care with the employee and to care for the newly placed child within one year of placement
   ■ care for the spouse, child, or parent who has a serious health condition
   ■ serious health condition causing inability to perform the essential job functions
   ■ any qualifying emergency arising from the employee's spouse or partner in legal same-sex marriage, son, daughter, or parent is a covered military member on "covered active duty" or
2. 26 workweeks of leave during a single 12-month period to:
   ■ care for an eligible employee's spouse or partner in legal same-sex marriage, son, daughter, parent, or next of kin who is a covered servicemember with serious injuries or illnesses (military caregiver leave)

(U.S. DOL, Wage and Hour Division [WHD], n.d.-a)

The U.S. Department of Labor's Wage and Hour Division is responsible for administering and enforcing the FMLA. In most instances, an employee also has the right to file a private lawsuit under the FMLA in any federal or state court (U.S. DOL, WHD, n.d.-b).

The FMLA applies only to "covered" employers who may be a private-sector employer, a public agency, or a school, which must provide FMLA benefits and protections to eligible employees and comply with other responsibilities required under the FMLA and its regulations at 29 CFR Part 825 (see Appendix A). A covered private-sector employer employs 50 or more employees in 20 or more workweeks in the current or previous calendar year. An employee is employed each working day of the calendar week if the employee works any part of the week. The workweeks do not have to be consecutive. Public agencies, including the federal government, are covered employers under the FMLA, regardless of number of employees (U.S. DOL, WHD, n.d.-b).

Health Insurance Portability and Accountability Act

The Health Insurance Portability and Accountability Act of 1996 (HIPAA) required the Secretary of the DHHS to develop regulations ensuring the privacy and security of health information by publishing the HIPAA Privacy Rule and the HIPAA Security Rule. The Privacy Rule, or Standards for Privacy of Individually Identifiable Health Information, establishes national standards for protecting of health information. The Security Rule or Security Standards for the Protection of Electronic Protected Health Information implemented a set of national security standards to protect health information held or transferred in electronic form. The Security Rule provides the protections contained in the Privacy Rule by addressing the technical and non-technical safeguards that organizations must use to secure individuals' "electronic protected health information" (e-PHI). Within HHS, the Office for Civil Rights (OCR) has responsibility for enforcing both rules with voluntary compliance activities and financial penalties. The Security Rule applies to health plans, healthcare clearinghouses, and any healthcare provider who transmits health information in electronic form (U.S. DHHS, HIPAA, n.d.). A major goal of the Privacy Rule is to assure that health information is protected yet allowing the exchange of health information required for high quality health care. The Rule balances important uses of information, while protecting the privacy of patients (U.S. DHHS, HIPAA, n.d.).

Department of Transportation

The Department of Transportation (DOT) agencies, i.e., Federal Railroad Administration (FRA), Federal Motor Carrier Safety Administration (FMCSA), Federal Transportation Administration (FTA), Federal Aviation Administration (FAA), and Pipeline and Hazardous Safety Materials Safety (PHMSA); U.S. Coast Guard (USCG); and Homeland Security have regulations requiring certain employers (see www.dot.gov/odapc/am-i-covered) to comply with specific drug and alcohol testing regulations that outline what employees are subject to their testing regulations. The DOT regulations include employees involved with safety-sensitive transportation and enforces regulations governing transit. This involves medical clearance to perform safety-sensitive jobs including alcohol and drug testing of employees in those positions. Use of illegal drugs and misuse of alcohol are not compatible with performing specific vital functions. Each DOT agency-specific regulation spells out who is subject to testing, when, and in what situations for a transportation industry (U.S. DOT, Office of Drug and Alcohol Policy and Compliance, 2015).

Drug-Free Workplace Act of 1988

The Drug-Free Workplace Act of 1988 requires some federal contractors and all federal grantees agree to provide drug-free workplaces as a pre-condition of receiving a contract or grant from a federal agency. Although all contractors must maintain a drug-free workplace, the specific components of the Drug-Free Workplace Act vary based on whether the contractor or grantee is an individual or an organization. The requirements for organizations are more extensive, because organizations must take comprehensive, programmatic steps to achieve a workplace free of drugs (U.S. DOL, elaws, n.d.-a; n.d.-b).

All organizations covered by the Drug-Free Workplace Act of 1988 are required to provide a drug-free workplace by taking the following steps:

1. <u>Publish and give a policy statement</u> to employees stating that it is unlawful to manufacture, distribute, dispense, possess, or use controlled substances, specifying actions against violators of the policy

2. Establish a drug-free awareness program of a) the dangers of drug abuse; b) the policy of a drug-free workplace; c) available drug counseling, rehabilitation, and employee assistance programs; and d) penalties for drug abuse violations

3. Notify employees that a condition of employment by a federal contract or grant is that employees must a) abide by drug-free policy; and b) notify the employer (5 calendar days), if convicted of a criminal drug violation in the workplace

4. Notify the contracting or granting agency (10 days after receiving notice) that an employee has been convicted of a criminal drug violation in the workplace

5. Impose a penalty or require satisfactory participation in a drug abuse assistance or rehabilitation program by any employee convicted of a reportable workplace drug conviction; and

6. Make a good faith effort to maintain a drug-free workplace by meeting the requirements of the Act

(U.S. DOL, elaws, n.d.-b)

State legislation legalizing medical marijuana is full of competing information and research. Although this drug poses several health risks, cannabinoids (chemicals found in the marijuana plant) are being prescribed as a possible treatment for a wide range of diseases. In 1996, California was the first to pass medical marijuana legislation and since then various states and interest groups have taken on this issue. It is important to consider the impact medical marijuana could have on employee functioning, health, and safety in the workplace and, ultimately on business (Working Partners.com, 2017).

Environmental Protection Agency Worker Protection Standard

Federal law and regulations require anyone who applies or supervises the use of restricted use pesticides (RUPs) be certified as a private or commercial applicator. The Environmental Protection Agency (EPA) has finalized stronger standards for workers who apply RUPs. These revisions to the Certification of Pesticide Applicators rule are intended to reduce harm from the misapplication of toxic pesticides. Pesticide use is expected to be safer with increased supervision and oversight and help to ensure RUPs are used safely (U.S. EPA, n.d.-c).

EPA's Agricultural Worker Protection Standard (WPS) focuses on reducing the risk to agricultural workers and pesticide handlers from pesticide poisoning and injury. The WPS offers occupational protections to agricultural workers involved in the production of agricultural plants and to pesticide handlers who mix, load, or apply crop pesticides. The EPA periodically revises the WPS to implement stronger protections for agricultural workers, handlers, and their families. These revisions aim to decrease exposure incidents among farmworkers and families. Each year, preventable pesticide exposure incidents occur at establishments covered by the WPS. Three requirements became effective on January 2, 2018 to include:

■ pesticide safety training that includes the expanded content of the WPS
■ pesticide safety information (posters) must reflect the revised standards and
■ handlers must suspend applications if people are in the application exclusion zone

(U.S. EPA, n.d.-d)

Youth Health and Safety

All states have child labor standards. When federal and state standards are different, the rules providing the most protection to young workers apply. There are specific wage rules for workers under 18 years old; the occupations and industries in which they can work; and the hours they may work. The Fair Labor Standards Act (FLSA), administered and enforced by the DOL's WHD, is the federal law addressing minimum wage, overtime pay, child labor, recordkeeping, and special minimum wage standards. The FLSA provides civil and criminal remedies and provisions for individual employees to file lawsuits. The 1989 Amendments to FLSA added a provision for civil money penalties (CMP) for repeated or willful minimum wage or overtime violations (U.S. DOL, WHD, n.d.-c). The child labor provisions of the FLSA are located on the WHD's "Youth Rules!" website (www.youthrules.dol.gov) and provide information and resources that help promote positive and safe work experiences for young workers. Also, OSHA offers assistance for young workers, their employers, and parents to help keep them safe at work. These resources include e-tools on the safe employment of youth in restaurants and in agriculture (U.S. DOL, WHD, n.d.-d).

Child labor rules under FLSA are designed to protect the educational opportunities of youth and prohibit the employment of youth in jobs that are detrimental to their health and safety. FLSA restricts work hours for those under 16 years of age and identifies hazardous occupations considered too dangerous for young workers. Federal law establishes certain safety standards and restrictions for workers under age 18, prohibiting employment in occupations the Secretary of Labor has declared as hazardous (U.S. DOL, WHD, n.d.-d).

Additionally, agricultural work has its own set of job restrictions to include:

- Under 12: May work with parental consent outside of school hours in non-hazardous jobs on a small farm exempt from federal minimum wage provisions
- If 12 or 13: May work with written parental consent outside of school hours in non-hazardous jobs on a farm
- If 14 or 15: May work outside of school hours in non-hazardous agricultural job
- 16 or older: You can work in any farm job at any time
- Youth of any age may work at any time in any job on a farm owned or operated by their parent or person standing in place of their parent

(U.S. DOL, WHD, n.d.-e)

Whistleblower Protection Act

The OSHA Whistleblower Protection Program enforces the provisions of over 20 whistleblower statutes that protect workers who report violations of various workplace safety and health laws and regulations to include: airline; commercial motor carrier; consumer product; environmental; financial reform; food safety; health insurance reform; motor vehicle safety; nuclear; pipeline; public transportation agency; railroad, maritime, and securities laws. Some of the rights provided by these protection laws include worker participation in safety and health activities; reporting a work-related injury, illness, or fatality; or reporting a violation of the statutes. Employers are prohibited under the OSH Act from discriminating against workers who exercise their rights under the OSH Act. These include filing an OSHA complaint; participating in an OSHA inspection or talking to an inspector; requesting exposure and injury records; reporting an injury; and reporting a safety or health complaint. Workers must file a complaint with OSHA within 30 days of the alleged retaliation (U.S. DOL, OSHA, n.d.-h).

Occupational and Environmental Health Nursing

The American Association of Occupational Health Nurses [AAOHN] (2017) defines occupational and environmental health nursing (OEHN) as follows:

> Occupational and environmental health nursing is the specialty practice that provides for and delivers health and safety programs and services to workers, worker populations, and community groups. The practice focuses on promotion and restoration of health, prevention of illness and injury, and protection from work-related and environmental hazards. Occupational and environmental health nurses (referred to as OHNs) have a combined knowledge of health and business that they blend with healthcare expertise to balance the requirement for a safe and healthful work environment with a "healthy" bottom line.

Modern roles of OEHNs are as diverse as clinicians to educators, case managers to corporate directors and consultants. Responsibilities have expanded immensely to encompass not only the responsibilities previously stated, but also a wide range of job duties such as care coordination of injured workers; counseling and crisis intervention; FMLA coordination; health promotion and risk reduction; legal and regulatory compliance; and worker and workplace hazard detection (AAOHN, 2017).

Scope of Practice/Standards of Practice in Occupational and Environmental Health Nursing

Standards of Practice developed by AAOHN for the OEHN define the practice and provides a framework for evaluation. These authoritative statements describe the accountability of the practitioner and reflect the values and priorities of the profession.

> AAOHN has identified 11 professional practice standards that describe a competent level of performance with regard to the nursing process and professional roles of the occupational and environmental health nurse. Criteria developed for each standard are key indicators of competent practice and permit occupational and environmental health nurses to evaluate their practice relative to the standards.
>
> (AAOHN, 2015)

Maintaining Professional License and Skills

Also, OEHNs must maintain and increase competency through continuing professional development. This may occur through self-study, reading and researching professional literature, networking with peers and other professionals, and participating in conferences, seminars, and

Box 18.1 The AAOHN Standards of Occupational and Environmental Health Practice

Standard I: Assessment

The Occupational and Environmental Health Nurse systematically assesses the health status of the client(s).

Standard II: Diagnosis

The Occupational and Environmental Health Nurse analyzes assessment data to formulate diagnoses.

Standard III: Outcome Identification

The Occupational and Environmental Health Nurse identifies outcomes specifically to the client(s).

Standard IV: Planning

The Occupational and Environmental Health Nurse develops a goal-directed plan that is comprehensive and formulates interventions to attain expected outcomes.

Standard V: Implementation

The Occupational and Environmental Health Nurse implements interventions to attain desired outcomes identified in the plan.

Standard VI: Evaluation

The Occupational and Environmental Health Nurse systematically and continuously evaluates responses to interventions and progress toward the achievement of desired outcomes.

Standard VII: Resource Management

The Occupational and Environmental Health Nurse secures and manages the resources that support occupational health and safety programs and services.

Standard VIII: Professional Development

The Occupational and Environmental Health Nurse assumes accountability for professional development to enhance professional growth and maintain competency.

Standard IX: Collaboration

The Occupational and Environmental Health Nurse collaborates with clients for the promotion, prevention, and restoration of health within the context of a safe and healthy environment.

Standard X: Research

The Occupational and Environmental Health Nurse uses research findings in practice and contributes to the scientific base in occupational and environmental health nursing to improve practice and advance the profession.

Standard XI: Ethics

The Occupational and Environmental Health Nurse uses an ethical framework as a guide for decision making in practice.

Source: From American Association of Occupational Health Nurses, Inc. Copyright 2012. With permission.

academic courses. Each state has its own continuing education requirements for nursing licensure renewal.

Certifications

The American Board for Occupational Health Nurses, Inc. (ABOHN) is the sole certifying body for OEHNs in the United States and awards three credentials: Certified Occupational Health Nurse (COHN); Certified Occupational Health Nurse-Specialist (COHN-S); and Case Management (CM). Accredited by The National Commission for Certifying Agencies (NCCA) and The American Board for Nursing Specialties (ABNS), ABOHN uses predetermined standards of nursing practice derived from AAOHN Core Curriculum, standards, and competencies to validate an individual registered nurse's qualifications, knowledge, and practice in specific areas of occupational health nursing in the U.S. (ABOHN, 2017).

Standing Orders

The professional OEHN is a licensed registered nurse working within the scope of practice set by the state's board of nursing and is also guided by the scope and practice of occupational and environmental health nursing established by the professional society. The OEHN uses nursing judgment and follows acceptable clinical practice protocols as a treatment plan based on a nursing assessment. These protocols should be reviewed by the nurse and physician. Standing orders or clinical guidelines, signed by a physician, provide a legal framework for the OEHN to use treatments outside the scope of practice, such as administering prescription medications. Standing orders should be reviewed regularly by healthcare providers, usually once a year. In the development and implementation of clinical protocols, individual state nurse practice acts must be followed (Rogers, 2003).

Documentation and Medical Records

As with any health record, the OEHN must maintain strict control over the health information to ensure confidentiality. However, most workplaces do not employ OEHNs and medical records are maintained by Human Resources, remaining separated from personnel records. The OEHN does not divulge personal health information to the employer, supervisor, or other workers. Rules for health record documentation apply to occupational health nursing as in any specialty's nursing notes.

Confidentiality

One of the reasons nurses have a special relationship with the employees is the understanding that nurses are to be trusted in keeping patient health information confidential. The employee is the patient who is in the care of the nurse. As with the HIPAA laws, responsible and ethical nurses are required by their scope of practice to maintain confidentiality of health information and, therefore, the trust of the employees in the nurse is maintained. "Unauthorized release of health records could result in personal liability, suspension of license to practice nursing by the state agency responsible for regulating the practice of nursing, or termination of employment by the employer" (Strasser & Knoblauch, 2014, p. 158).

Confidentiality of health information is integral to the practice of nursing, regardless of role or specialization. Adherence to laws and regulations as well as professional codes of ethics promotes public trust with the assurance of protected health information. The ethics providing confidentiality can also be found in the AAOHN Standards of Occupational and Environmental Health Nursing (2012). However, in occupational and environmental health settings, exceptions to the legal protection for health information may exist resulting in ethical conflicts for the nurse when asked to provide health-related records without workers' knowledge or consent (AAOHN, 2015).

Standards of Care

The Standards of Care provided by the American Nurses Association (ANA) and other nursing specialty associations describe a competent level of nursing care. AAOHN has developed the *Core Curriculum in Occupational and Environmental Health Nursing.* Rogers states that "the Core Curriculum delineates concepts and principles to support the knowledge base of the specialty practice" (Rogers, 2003, p. 692). "AAOHN has developed *Competencies and Performance Criteria in Occupational and Environmental Health Nursing,* which includes nine competency categories delineated by three levels (competent, proficient, and expert) and performance criteria for each stated competency" (Rogers, 2003, p. 692). The levels of care are demonstrated through the nursing process, which is the foundation of clinical decision-making and includes actions taken by nurses in providing care.

Within each category, three levels of practice are identified as: (1) competency, (2) proficient, and (3) expert. The competent level is considered the core for practice in this specialty. Proficient implies increased ability based on experience to evaluate client situations and act on them appropriately. The expert level has extensive experience and knowledge, enabling the OEHN to assess a situation quickly and initiate appropriate action. The code of ethics, standards of practice, core curriculum, and competencies provide the basis for scope of practice, knowledge, skill, and the legal and ethical framework in occupational and environmental health nursing. Standards of care are important if a legal dispute arises over whether a nurse practiced appropriately in a particular case (AAOHN, 2015).

> According to AAOHN Advisory, Managing Professional Risk (2007), plaintiffs usually allege the employer is liable for negligent actions of a nurse employee under the principle of respondeat superior so that the plaintiff can recover from the employer for the employee's negligence. This principle of law holds that when an employee or "agent" is found liable for the negligent actions, the employer or company must accept responsibility for their actions if the employee was acting within the scope of employment. The employer may use this as a defense if the employee was not acting within the scope of their employment. If OEHNs act outside the scope of their employment, job responsibilities or provide inappropriate or unsafe care, the nurses will be accountable for their actions.

The AAOHN advisory continues to state that malpractice, or liability in professional practice, occurs with professional misconduct, improper discharge of professional responsibilities, or the professional's failure to meet the standard of care that results in harm to others. This is also known as a "breach of care" or "breach of standard of care." The standard of care is defined by standards of practice or "what's reasonable under the same circumstances by a similarly qualified professional" (AAOHN, 2007).

The Role of the Legal Nurse Consultant in Occupational Health and Safety

Legal nurse consultants have diverse backgrounds, i.e., case management (CM), risk management, insurance, or critical care and some have experience in occupational and environmental health nursing leading to a better understanding of the role of the OEHN. Occupational and environmental health nursing is a specialty field of registered nurses who independently observe and assess the worker's health status with respect to job tasks and hazards. Also, OEHNs recognize and prevent health effects from hazardous exposures, coordinate patient care, educate patients, and treat workers' injuries/illnesses (U.S. DOL, Bureau of Labor Statistics, 2015).

The LNC may interface with the OEHN during case witness interviews, investigations, depositions, record discovery, and expert testimony. The LNC, depending on the nature of the case, may work with the OEHN to compare facts in a case, identify possible witnesses, and determine additional sources of records. For example, the OEHN interface with the LNC working on a chemical exposure case can provide valuable information, because the OEHN is likely familiar with the workplace chemical and able to give important details about the exposure source, as well as treatment protocols for the industry. This information is helpful in identifying questions for the attorney to present during depositions and mediations.

Occupational Health Records

OSHA Recordkeeping for First Aid Visits, Injury and Illness Reports

First aid is emergency care provided for injury or sudden illness before emergency medical treatment is available. A workplace first aid or injury program includes management and employee involvement, worksite analysis, hazard prevention and control, and safety and health training. The aim is to minimize the adverse outcome of accidents or exposures. The OSHA has certain requirements regarding first aid and injury reports in the workplace. As previously described, employers are required by OSHA standard (29 CFR Part 1904 and 1952; see Appendix A) to abide by certain recordkeeping obligations. It is essential data recorded by employers to be uniform and accurate for validity and for statistical use by OSHA. Some employers may be subject to additional recordkeeping and reporting requirements, such as record retention, exposure monitoring, inspections, or other activities relevant to occupational safety and health.

Workplace incidents that result in injuries and illnesses meeting the OSHA definitions of "recordable" are required by the employer to complete three OSHA forms (U.S. DOL, OSHA, n.d.-i).

- **Form 301: Injury and Illness Incident Report** for each recordable incident
- **Form 300:** Log of Work-Related Injuries and Illnesses to record each incident on a list) and

■ **Form 300A**: Summary of Work-Related Injuries and Illnesses to provide the year-long number of recordable injuries and illnesses and their impact on the employee's ability to perform the job

Criteria for classifying the effects of the incident includes:

1. Death
2. Days away from work (DART)
3. Restricted work days or job transfer (remains at work)
4. Other reason to record (medical treatment more than first aid as defined by OSHA and remains at work)

Recording an injury or illness on an OSHA log does not necessarily indicate qualification for workers' compensation or benefits and, at the same time, not all compensable cases are recordable by OSHA definition.

The OSHA recordable case must demonstrate three things: (1) an injury or illness has occurred; (2) the employer has determined OSHA's definition of work-relatedness applies to the incident; and (3) the result of the injury or illness met the definition of OSHA recordable. Many OSHA recordable cases are also compensable under the state workers' compensation system, while others are not. When an injury or illness occurs, the employer must take into consideration both OSHA recordability rules and the specific requirements of the individual state's workers' compensation system to decide if a case is recordable, compensable, or both. The aggravation of a pre-existing condition by a workplace event or exposure also can make a case work-related. Records are used by employers to implement safety and health programs with recognized importance in workplace tracking and problem solving (U.S. DOL, OSHA, n.d.-j). The LNC's job is to understand and relate the medical facts of a case in a format easily understandable to the attorney. A strong contribution to the litigation process can be made when the LNC is familiar with OSHA recordkeeping rules for cases involving work-related injuries and illnesses. Knowledge of the rules allows the LNC to describe any red flags in the medical chronology as well as present the standards of care related to OSHA guidelines. Basic knowledge of the recordkeeping process is an added benefit to refining the medical and regulatory issues in work-related cases.

Accident Investigation Reports

Accidents occur throughout the United States every day. The failure of people, supplies, equipment, or surroundings to behave or react as expected is the cause of most accidents. Incident investigations determine how and why the failures occur (U.S. DOL, OSHA, n.d.-k). Information gained through an investigation may help prevent similar or perhaps more disastrous accidents as well as help determine cause and harm important to case investigation and best practices. In reviewing accident investigation records, the LNC's primary role is to determine if reports were included in subpoena records and in the medical chronology report during the fact-finding process. For example, the LNC might uncover from the reports an unsafe act caused the accident, or that the employer failed to provide adequate safety equipment.

Workers' Compensation Claims

Workers' compensation is designed to be an alternative dispute resolution designed to provide benefits to the injured or disabled employees and limit monetary exposure to the employers thus replacing conventional litigation that may be expensive. State workers' compensation statutes establish the framework for most employment. Federal workers' compensation statutes are enacted to cover federal employees, or those workers employed in some significant type of inter-state commerce. The federal Employment Compensation Act provides compensation for non-military, federal employees. The federal Employment Liability Act, while not a workers' compensation statute, provides that railroads engaged in interstate commerce are liable for inju-ries to their employees if negligent. The Black Lung Benefits Act provides compensation to miners suffering from "black lung disease" (U.S. DOL, Division of Coal Mine Workers' Compensation [DCMWC], 2017). It is important for the LNC to be aware these federal laws exist to research and interpret work-related medical records appropriately for the attorney. Certain lung diseases, asbestosis for example, require B-Reader radiologists by federal law. The LNC using knowledge of these laws can determine if the standard of care has or has not been met.

In every state in the United States, workers' compensation is a benefit system designed to be "no fault," as it is irrelevant whether the cause or contribution to the occupational injury or illness was from the employer's negligence. It requires that a workplace injury or development of an occupational disease occurs in the course of employment (WorkersCompensationLawFirms.com, 2018).

Many states have established the uninsured employers fund to cover benefits for an employee who suffers a work-related injury or illness when the employer does not have workers' compensa-tion coverage. Except Texas, every state requires most employers with few exceptions to either carry workers' compensation insurance or be self-insured. However, there are also employers who illegally do not have workers' compensation coverage. In this event, a worker who sustains a work-related injury or illness can still file a workers' compensation claim and be compensated through the uninsured employers fund in their state (U.S. Workers Comp.com, 2018).

It is illegal in most states for an employer to terminate an employee for reporting a work-related injury or illness or for filing a workers' compensation claim. Since state laws differ, it is best to consult the regulating state agency or the DOL Employment Standards Administration for any veri-fication of wrongful termination laws. Most states also prohibit employment refusal to candidates previously having filed a workers' compensation claim. Employers can consult commercial databases of claims data, however, making it difficult to prove an employer discriminated against a job appli-cant. It is considered fraud under penalty of law for anyone, vendor, or organization to participate or engage in fraudulent workers' compensation claims. To identify fraud, employers sometimes hire private investigators to videotape claimants engaged in acts disproving claims. The LNC needs to be knowledgeable about all aspects of workers' compensation claims to determine if prompt and appro-priate care was received, panel physicians were offered when indicated (specialty physicians listed by employer from which the injured or ill employee may choose for their care), compliance with the American Disability Act was carried out, and any other red flags. The LNC handling workers' com-pensation claims must be familiar with the applicable statutes and laws specific to each case as well as become familiar with available resources to conduct a thorough investigation and complete the analysis for the legal team. The LNC may want to complete a Critical Facts Summary to assist the attorney with the chronology and various other information helpful in handling the claim and is not to be shared outside of the legal team. The value of the LNC's work in developing these summaries is often critical to the case and extremely valuable.

Exposure Monitoring Records

Toxic substances and harmful physical agents may include the following: metals and dusts, such as, lead, cadmium, and silica; biological agents, such as bacteria, viruses, and fungi; physical stress, such as noise, heat, cold, vibration, repetitive motion, and ionizing and non-ionizing radiation. Understanding the basics of exposure monitoring records is important to the LNC who may need to prepare medical summaries, exposure charts, or timelines related to a formal complaint. Lack of knowledge in how or where to research information could lead to inadequate reports. The Access to Exposure and Medical Records rule, found in 29 CFR1910.1020 (see Appendix A), and often seen as a companion standard to the hazard communication rule, allows for the examination of the results of monitoring and any measured level of exposure to chemicals as well as any medical records providing information about health status and the relationship of the exposure. The access rule also includes exposure to biological hazards such as bacteria, viruses, fungi, and physical hazards such as radiation and vibration (U.S. DOL, OSHA, 2001).

The Standard defines a record as "any item, collection or grouping of information regardless of the form or process by which it is maintained (e.g., paper, x-ray, microfilm, or automated data)" (U.S. DOL, OSHA, 2001). The Standard differentiates between medical records and exposure records. The medical record is defined as "a record concerning the health status of an employee which is made or maintained by a physician, nurse or other healthcare personnel or technician" (U.S. DOL, OSHA, n.d.-l). Medical records include: questionnaires, histories, medical examination results, physicals, laboratory tests, biological monitoring records, medical opinions, progress notes, recommendations, first aid records, treatment, prescriptions, and employee medical complaints. Exposure records are defined as "employee exposure records" containing any of the following information: environmental workplace monitoring or measuring of a toxic substance or harmful agent; biological monitoring that directly assesses the absorption of a toxic substance or harmful physical agent; and Safety Data Sheets (SDS) that reveal the identity of a chemical or substance. The Standard covers records documenting the amount of employee exposure to "toxic substances and harmful physical agents." Other examples include exposure to ultraviolet light emitted from welding operations or exposure to radiofrequency energy at a transmitting antenna tower or microwave dish (U.S. DOL, OSHA, n.d.-l).

Medical records must be preserved and maintained for at least the duration of employment plus 30 years (with some exceptions), unless a specific occupational safety and health standard provides a different period of time. Employee exposure records must be maintained for at least 30 years (with some exceptions). The access rule has provisions for trade secrets. An employer can withhold trade secret information in an otherwise disclosable record provided three conditions are met: (1) the claim information held is a trade secret can be supported, (2) the employer informs the requesting party the chemical is a trade secret, and (3) all other available information on the properties and effects is disclosed. There is also an emergency provision for trade secret release if a physician or nurse determines an emergency exists (U.S. DOL, OSHA, 2001).

Any LNC may be involved in toxic tort cases, which are civil actions for recovery of damages related to exposure to a chemical, an emission, or to a substance which may have allegedly caused physical or psychological harm. This type of complex litigation often involves multiple contacts, different jurisdictions, and numerous witnesses. The LNC may be involved in interviewing industrial hygienists, safety officers, physicians, OEHNs, and other healthcare and safety team members regarding these types of cases. The LNC must be cognizant of the existence of exposure monitoring records and which members of the workplace may have access to these records. It is essential for the LNC involved in toxic tort litigation to understand federal and state rules affecting this type of litigation and knowledge of where to do research concerning exposure records.

Safety Data Sheets

A Safety Data Sheet (SDS) is a document prepared by the manufacturer of a hazardous chemical which describes its physical and chemical properties, hazards for handling, storage, and proper disposal. These informational sheets are extremely important to workers and emergency personnel since they contain the procedures for handling or working with that substance in a safe manner. The SDS may be obtained by contacting the manufacturer. It is extremely important these sheets be kept updated according to the standard and that they are accessible to all employees (U.S. DOL, OSHA, 2012a). The LNC should be familiar with the definition of an SDS and where and how one would be obtained immediately should there be a need for this information in a case. The information found on the SDS can be important in this specialized area of litigation. The attorney may need to know the limits of exposure for example, and the SDS would identify this information. The SDS can be helpful in determining if adequate treatment was sought based on the manufacturer's written warnings for the product that would be of interest to the attorney in case fact-finding.

Medical Screening and Surveillance Documentation

Medical screening and surveillance are two basic strategies for optimizing employee health. The terms are used interchangeably; however, they are quite distinct concepts. Medical screening is one component of a comprehensive medical surveillance program. The purpose is early diagnosis and treatment of the individual and has a clinical focus. Surveillance is to detect and eliminate the underlying causes such as hazards or exposures of any discovered trends and thus has a prevention focus. Surveillance may also be part of obtaining a health baseline for comparison should a hazard or exposure occur. Both contribute significantly to the success of worksite health and safety programs. The OSHA requirements are generally focused on the medical, work histories, physical assessment, and biological testing with information obtained from the clinical processes used in the monitoring and analysis elements of medical surveillance (U.S. DOL, OSHA, n.d.-m).

The LNC needs to be familiar with where to find OSHA protocols governing surveillance examinations and proper monitoring. For example, when reviewing records related to an employee involved in a vinyl chloride chemical exposure, the LNC would need to look at the appropriate OSHA standard for the medical surveillance section to determine if the standards were met. OSHA standards may include mandatory tests in a specified time frame for employees working in certain areas.

The Vinyl Chloride Standard (29 CFR 1910.1017; see Appendix A) requires an employee have liver function tests yearly for fewer than 10 years of service in an exposed area, and every six months for employees who have worked in an exposed area for greater than 10 years. Exposure to vinyl chloride from any previous industry must be included in the calculation of exposure time. This means, if an employee worked previously at a vinyl plant for five years, and has now been employed at the current plant for five years, liver enzyme testing must be done every six months rather than yearly. Knowledge of these types of legal standards becomes important in the LNC's medical summaries, which may include assurance of proper record maintenance, company policies, employee performance tests and interpretation, maintenance of confidentiality of records, record retention, record storage, health education, and counseling or referral for conditions of exposure or possible exposure (Strasser & Knoblauch, 2014). Familiarity with the above helps determine confidentiality breach or lack of breach, as well as expected adherence or lack of adherence to protocols and standards.

Employee Training Records

Several OSHA standards require the employer to train employees in the safety and health aspects of their jobs. Other standards require the employer to limit certain job assignments to employees who have been trained or certified as qualified for the job with the goal of safety in mind. One such example is the OSHA requirements found in the Process Safety Management of Highly Hazardous Chemicals Standard (29 CFR 1910.119; see Appendix A), which contains several special requirements. The location of a written hazardous chemical training program must be communicated, readily accessible to all employees, and training records must be kept. There must be safe handling of hazardous chemicals with controls in place to protect workers. Labeling systems for hazardous chemicals must be in place, and training must be provided with emphasis on emergency procedures in the event of an exposure. Training must include contract workers and be maintained on a regular basis to include training for life-threatening emergencies (U.S. DOL, OSHA, 2012b).

Employee training records are of special interest to the LNC to determine company compliance and likelihood of injury. These records may hold answers to questions during investigation of harm such as: did the employee have the proper training, was the employee qualified to operate certain equipment, and who were the trainers and were they qualified?

Discovery

Legal and ethical issues frequently occur in the occupational setting. The LNC involved in occupational health cases will need to be familiar with state and federal regulations. Malpractice involves negligence and a professional misconduct or unreasonable lack of skill. Negligence can include failure to take action, failure to communicate danger, delay in assistance, medication errors, and failure to obtain consent. The interpretation of laws, rules, and regulations may change as new cases decide common law and precedents established (Strasser & Knoblauch, 2014). Knowing how to do an effective critical facts summary or medical chronology is important to the litigation process. The LNC who is familiar with the employment law and worker's compensation is valuable to case discovery. The LNC has the ethical obligation to inform the attorney of negative aspects in a case as well as any critical information that could impact the case either negatively or positively. The LNC must be knowledgeable in many areas and often act as a case manager, researcher, analyzer, risk assessor, and valuable member to the legal team (Jones, 2008).

Summary

The LNC must understand the dynamics of occupational health and safety issues and the care provided to employees and understand the many laws and regulations affecting the workplace enacted for the protection of the workforce. To appreciate health care provided, the roles and responsibilities of the Occupational and Environmental Health Nurse (OEHN) requires a legal platform that governs the scope of nursing practice in each state. Knowledge of occupational recordkeeping requirements can provide the LNC great time-saving assistance in investigations during the discovery process.

References

American Association of Occupational Health Nurses. (2007). Managing professional risk. Retrieved from www.aaohn.org/practices/advisories/.

American Association of Occupational Health Nurses. (2012). Standards of occupational health nursing. *American Association of Occupational Health Nurses, Inc., 60*(3), 97–103. https://doi.org/10.1177/216507991206000301.

American Association of Occupational Health Nurses. (2015). Confidentiality of worker health information. Retrieved from http://aaohn.org/page/position-statements.

American Association of Occupational Health Nurses. (2017). AAOHN: What is occupational & environmental health nursing. Retrieved from http://aaohn.org/page/what-is-occupational-and-environmental-health-nursing.

American Board for Occupational Health Nurses. (2017). Becoming certified. Retrieved from www.abohn.org/certification.

HG.org Legal Resources. (n.d.). Employment law—Guide to legal law. Retrieved from www.hg.org/employ.html.

Jones, M. P. (2008). Strategies for an effective medical chronology. *Journal of Legal Nurse Consulting, 19*(3), 7–11.

Macpherson, D., & Stephenson, S. (2016). Assessing economic damages in wrongful termination cases. *Journal of Legal Economics, 23*(1), 31–48.

Pollack, D. (2017). Wrongful termination of Public Human Service Employees. *Policy and Practice, 75*(2), 25–34.

Rogers, B. (2003). *Occupational and environmental health nursing—Concepts and practice* (2nd ed.). Philadelphia, PA: Saunders.

Strasser, P., & Knoblauch, D. (2014). Legal and ethical issues. In *AAOHN Core curriculum for occupational & environmental health nursing* (4th ed., pp. 128–131, 158). Pensacola, FL: AAOHN.

Tomlinson, E., & Bockanic, W. (2009). Avoiding liability for wrongful termination: "Ready, aim, … fire!" *Employee Responsibilities and Rights Journal, 21*, 77–87.

U.S. Department of Health and Human Services, Centers for Disease Control and Prevention, & National Institute for Occupational Safety and Health. (2015). NIOSH fact sheet (NIOSH Publication # 2013-140, October 2015). Retrieved from www.cdc.gov/niosh/docs/2013-140/pdfs/2013-140.pdf.

U.S. Department of Health and Human Services, Centers for Disease Control and Prevention, & National Institute for Occupational Safety and Health. (2016a). About NORA. Retrieved from www.cdc.gov/niosh/nora/about.html.

U.S. Department of Health and Human Services, Centers for Disease Control and Prevention, & National Institute for Occupational Safety and Health. (2016b). Training and workforce development. Retrieved from www.cdc.gov/niosh/training/default.html.

U.S. Department of Health and Human Services, Health Insurance Portability and Accountability Act. (n.d.). Health Information Privacy. Summary of the HIPAA Security Rule. Retrieved from www.hhs.gov/hipaa/for-professionals/security/laws-regulations/index.html.

U.S. Department of Health and Human Services, Office for Civil Rights. (2013). Know the rights that protect individuals with disabilities from discrimination. Retrieved from www.hhs.gov/sites/default/files/knowyourrights504adafactsheet.pdf.

U.S. Department of Justice, Civil Rights Division. (n.d.-a). Introduction to the ADA. Retrieved from www.ada.gov/ada_intro.htm.

U.S. Department of Justice, Civil Rights Division. (n.d.-b). Summary of HIPAA security rule. Retrieved from www.hhs.gov/hipaa/for-professionals/security/laws-regulations/index.html.

U.S. Department of Justice, Civil Rights Division. (2003). Summary of the HIPAA privacy rule. Retrieved from www.hhs.gov/sites/default/files/ocr/privacy/hipaa/understanding/summary/privacysummary.pdf.

U.S. Department of Labor (n.d.). Summary of the major laws of the Department of Labor. Retrieved from www.dol.gov/general/aboutdol/majorlaws.

U.S. Department of Labor, Bureau of Labor Statistics. (2015). Registered Nurses: *Occupational outlook handbook*. Retrieved from www.bls.gov/ooh/healthcare/registered-nurses.htm.

U.S. Department of Labor, Division of Coal Mine Workers' Compensation. (2017). About the Black Lung Program. Retrieved from www.dol.gov/owcp/dcmwc/.

U.S. Department of Labor, elaws. Drug-free workplace advisor. (n.d.-a). Drug-Free Workplace Act of 1988 requirements. Retrieved from http://webapps.dol.gov/elaws/asp/drugfree/screenr.htm.

U.S. Department of Labor, elaws. Drug-free workplace advisor. (n.d.-b). Drug-Free Workplace Act of 1988 requirements of organizations. Retrieved from http://webapps.dol.gov/elaws/asp/drugfree/require. htm.

U.S. Department of Labor, Occupational Safety and Health Administration. (n.d.-a). OSHA law and regulations. Retrieved from www.osha.gov/law-regs.html.

U.S. Department of Labor, Occupational Safety and Health Administration. (n.d.-b). National Advisory Commission on Occupational Health and Safety. Retrieved from www.osha.gov/dop/nacosh/nacosh. html.

U.S. Department of Labor, Occupational Safety and Health Administration. (n.d.-c). OSHA needlesticks—frequently asked questions. Retrieved from www.osha.gov/needlesticks/needlefaq.html.

U.S. Department of Labor, Occupational Safety and Health Administration. (n.d.-d). Hazard communication. Retrieved from www.osha.gov/dsg/hazcom/index.html.

U.S. Department of Labor, Occupational Safety & Health Administration. (n.d.-e). OSHA injury and illness recordkeeping and reporting requirements. Retrieved from www.osha.gov/recordkeeping/index.html.

U.S. Department of Labor, Occupational Safety and Health Administration. (n.d.-f). Occupational noise exposure—hearing conservation. Retrieved from www.osha.gov/SLTC/noisehearingconservation/ hearingprograms.html.

U.S. Department of Labor, Occupational Safety and Health Administration. (n.d.-g). OSHA personal protective equipment. Retrieved from www.osha.gov/SLTC/personalprotectiveequipment/.

U.S. Department of Labor, Occupational Safety and Health Administration. (n.d.-h). The whistleblower protection programs. Retrieved from www.osha.gov/dep/ola/whistleblower/index.html.

U.S. Department of Labor, Occupational Safety & Health Administration. (n.d.-i). Injury and illness recordkeeping and reporting forms. Retrieved from www.osha.gov/recordkeeping/RKforms.html.

U.S. Department of Labor, Occupational Safety and Health Administration. (n.d.-j). OSHA recordkeeping—final rule issued to improve tracking of workplace injuries and illnesses. Retrieved from www. osha.gov/recordkeeping/finalrule/index.html.

U.S. Department of Labor, Occupational Safety and Health Administration. (n.d.-k). The incident investigation. Retrieved from www.osha.gov/dcsp/products/topics/incidentinvestigation/index.html.

U.S. Department of Labor, Occupational Safety and Health Administration. (n.d.-l). Access to employee exposure and medical records, 1910.1020. Retrieved from www.osha.gov/pls/oshaweb/owadisp.show_ document?p_table=STANDARDS&p_id=10027.

U.S. Department of Labor, Occupational Safety and Health Administration (n.d.-m). Medical screening and surveillance. Retrieved from www.osha.gov/SLTC/medicalsurveillance/.

U.S. Department of Labor, Occupational Safety and Health Administration. (2001). Access to medical and exposure records (OSHA Publication No. 3110). Washington, DC: Author. Retrieved from www. osha.gov/Publications/osha3110.pdf.

U.S. Department of Labor, Occupational Safety and Health Administration. (2002). Hearing conservation (OSHA Publication No. 3074). Washington, DC: Author. Retrieved from www.osha.gov/Publications/OSHA3074/osha3074.html.

U.S. Department of Labor, Occupational Safety and Health Administration. (2004). Personal protective equipment (OSHA Publication No. 3151-12R). Washington, DC: Author. Retrieved from www. osha.gov/Publications/osha3151.pdf.

U.S. Department of Labor, Occupational Safety and Health Administration. (2011). OSHA fact sheet—bloodborne pathogens standard. Retrieved from www.osha.gov/OshDoc/data_BloodborneFacts/ bbfact01.pdf.

U.S. Department of Labor, Occupational Safety & Health Administration. (2012a). Safety data sheets. Retrieved from www.osha.gov/pls/oshaweb/owadisp.show_document?p_table=standards&p_id=10103.

U.S. Department of Labor, Occupational Safety & Health Administration. (2012b). Training requirements in OSHA standards and training guidelines. Retrieved from www.osha.gov/Publications/osha2254.pdf.

U.S. Department of Labor, Occupational Safety and Health Administration. (2014). Hazard communications for small business entities (OSHA Publication No. 3695-03). Retrieved from www.osha.gov/Publications/OSHA3695.pdf.

U.S. Department of Labor, Occupational Safety and Health Administration. (2015). Training requirements in OSHA standards (OSHA Publication No. 2254-09R). Retrieved from www.osha.gov/Publications/osha2254.pdf.

U.S. Department of Labor, Occupational Safety and Health Administration. (2016). All about OSHA (OSHA Publication No. 3302-11R). Washington, DC: Author.

U.S. Department of Labor, Wage and Hour Division. (n.d.-a). Family and Medical Leave Act. Retrieved from www.dol.gov/whd/fmla/.

U.S. Department of Labor, Wage and Hour Division. (n.d.-b). The employer's guide to the Family and Medical Leave Act. Retrieved from www.dol.gov/whd/fmla/employerguide.pdf.

U.S. Department of Labor, Wage and Hour Division. (n.d.-c). Major laws administered/enforced. Retrieved from www.dol.gov/whd/regs/statutes/summary.htm.

U.S. Department of Labor, Wage and Hour Division, YouthRules. (n.d.-d). Know the limits. Retrieved from www.youthrules.gov/know-the-limits/hazards/index.htm.

U.S. Department of Labor, Wage and Hour Division, YouthRules. (n.d.-e). Working in agriculture. Retrieved from www.youthrules.gov/know-the-limits/agriculture/index.htm.

U.S. Department of Transportation, Office of Drug and Alcohol Policy and Compliance. (2015). What employers need to know about DOT drug and alcohol testing. Retrieved from www.transportation.gov/sites/dot.gov/files/docs/ODAPC_Employer_Guidelines_%20June_1_2015_A.pdf.

U.S. Equal Employment Opportunity Commission. (n.d.-a). Overview. Retrieved from www.eeoc.gov/eeoc/.

U.S. Equal Employment Opportunity Commission. (n.d.-b). Laws enforced by EEOC. Retrieved from www.eeoc.gov/laws/statutes/index.cfm.

U.S. Environmental Protection Agency, Pesticide Worker Safety. (n.d.-c). Pesticide worker protection standard. Retrieved from www.epa.gov/pesticide-worker-safety/revised-certification-standards-pesticide-applicators.

U.S. Environmental Protection Agency, Pesticide Worker Safety. (n.d.-d). Agricultural worker protection standard. Retrieved from www.epa.gov/pesticide-worker-safety/agricultural-worker-protection-standard-wps.

U.S. Equal Employment Opportunity Commission. (2000). History—the Rehabilitation Act of 1973. Retrieved from www.eeoc.gov/eeoc/history/35th/thelaw/rehab_act-1973.html.

U.S. Government Printing Office. (1990). Public Law 91–596, 91st Congress, S. 2193, 29, 1970, As amended by Public Law 101–552, 3101, November 5, 1990.

U.S. Occupational Safety and Health Review Commission. (n.d.). About how OSHRC works. Retrieved from www.oshrc.gov/about/how-oshrc-works/www.oshrc.gov/about/how-oshrc.html.

U.S. Workers Comp.com. (n.d.). What is workers compensation. Retrieved from www.usworkerscomp.com/workers-compensation.

USLegal.com. (n.d.). Legal definitions and legal terms defined. Retrieved from ttps://definitions.uslegal.com/d/doctrine/.

USLegal.com. (2016). Workers' compensation. Retrieved from https://workerscompensation.uslegal.com/.

WorkersCompensationLawFirms.com. (2018). Workers compensation benefits. Retrieved from www.workerscompensationlawfirms.com.

Working Partners.com. (2017). Medical marijuana in the workplace. Retrieved from www.workingpartners.com/publications/medical_marijuana.asp.

Additional Reading

Legal Information Institute (n.d.). 29 CFR Part 1910 Occupational Safety and Health Standards. Retrieved from www.law.cornell.edu/cfr/text/29/part-1910\.

U.S. Department of Labor, Regulations (Standards-29CFR) Toxic and Hazardous Substances (2017). Retrieved from www.osha.gov/pls/oshaweb/owadisp.show_document?p_table=STANDARDS&p_id=10027.

Test Questions

1. What agency promulgates the workplace standards that employers are required to follow?
   A. National Institute for Occupational Safety and Health (NIOSH)
   B. Environmental Protection Agency (EPA)
   C. Occupational Safety and Health Administration (OSHA)
   D. Department of Transportation (DOT)
2. Mandatory <u>reporting</u> to OSHA is required of any workplace incident that results in:
   A. Hospitalization of one employee from an occupational exposure
   B. Employee who misses at least three work days
   C. Fatalities only
   D. Medical treatment within one week of a workplace injury
3. The LNC reviewing medical surveillance programs would find specific mandatory requirements in the:
   A. OSHA Standards
   B. DHHS policies
   C. WHO protocols for industry
   D. NIOSH Updates
4. The LNC handling workers' compensation claims must be familiar with the fact that:
   A. Employee exposure records must be maintained for three years
   B. Record retention is left up to the particular industry standards
   C. Records must be preserved and maintained for at least 10 years
   D. Employee medical records must be maintained for at least the duration of employment plus 30 years
5. The Occupation and Environmental Health Nurse (OEHN) who works with employees in several different states must be licensed by the state in which:
   A. The OEHN resides
   B. The OEHN provides care for the worker
   C. The employer has corporate headquarters
   D. The employee resides

Answers: 1. C, 2. A, 3. A, 4. D, 5. B

Appendix A: Code of Federal Regulations

29 CFR Part 825	The Family and Medical Leave Act of 1993	www.law.cornell.edu/cfr/text/29/part-825
29 CFR 1904	Recording and reporting occupational injuries and illnesses	www.law.cornell.edu/cfr/text/29/part-1904
29 CFR 1910, Subpart I	Personal Protective Equipment	www.law.cornell.edu/cfr/text/29/part-1910/subpart-I
29 CFR 1910.95	Occupational noise exposure	www.law.cornell.edu/cfr/text/29/1910.95
29 CFR 1910.119	Process safety management of highly hazardous chemicals	www.law.cornell.edu/cfr/text/29/1910.119
29 CFR 1910.120	Hazardous waste operations and emergency response	www.law.cornell.edu/cfr/text/29/1910.120
29 CFR 1910.1017	Vinyl Chloride	www.law.cornell.edu/cfr/text/29/1910.1017
29 CFR 1910.1020	Access to employee exposure and medical records	www.law.cornell.edu/cfr/text/29/1910.1020
29 CFR 1910.1030	Bloodborne Pathogens	www.law.cornell.edu/cfr/text/29/1910.1030
29 CFR 1910.1200	Hazard communication	www.law.cornell.edu/cfr/text/29/1910.1200
29 CFR 1952	Approved state plans for enforcement of state standards	www.law.cornell.edu/cfr/text/29/part-1952

Chapter 19

Informed Consent

Karen Wilkinson, MN, ARNP, LNCC®, CNLCP®
Deborah A. Wipf, MS, APRN-GCNS, LNCC®

Contributor:
Elena Capella, EdD, RN, CNL, CPHQ, LNCC®

Contents

Objectives

- Describe informed consent and the process of obtaining informed consent
- Identify major issues related to informed consent
- Describe the elements of proof in cases alleging a lack of informed consent

Introduction

Informed consent is the legal process that protects a patient's right to know the risks, benefits, and alternatives of a proposed treatment or procedure and the risks and benefits of the alternatives, including no treatment (American Medical Association, n.d.-a). Understanding the elements of informed consent is an essential part of the role of healthcare providers (HCPs), including nurses, regardless of practice setting. Patients' rights regarding their personal medical decision-making have become more important due to longer lifespans, which can lead to increasing chronic illnesses and co-morbidities. When implementing the informed consent process, HCPs and registered nurses (RNs) have an ethical duty to promote patient rights and self-determination issues (Congress.gov, n.d.). The American Medical Association (AMA) and the American Nurses Association (ANA) codes of ethics discuss specific information regarding patient rights and self-determination (AMA, n.d.-a, n.d.-b; ANA, 2015, 1.4 and 3.2 provisions). In addition, many professional organizations have established ethic white papers that address the informed consent rights of an individual. The legal nurse consultant (LNC) should reference the HCP's specific professional codes or white paper when reviewing informed consent cases.

This chapter will discuss the concept, process, and limitations of obtaining informed consent, and the elements of proof in cases alleging a lack of informed consent will also be discussed.

Informed Consent

A medical definition of informed consent is:

> The process by which a patient learns about and understands the purpose, benefits, and potential risks of a medical or surgical intervention, including clinical trials, and

then agrees to receive the treatment or participate in the trial. Informed consent generally requires the patient or responsible party to sign a statement confirming that they understand the risks and benefits of the procedure or treatment.

(MedicineNet, n.d., para 1)

Also, Black's Law Dictionary (Garner, 2014, p. 368) defines informed consent as:

A patient's knowing choice about a medical treatment or procedure, made after a physician or other healthcare provider discloses whatever information a reasonably prudent provider in the medical community would give to a patient regarding the risks involved in the proposed treatment or procedure.

Informed consent is grounded in principles of respect for individuals and individual autonomy. A properly executed informed consent reflects the HCP's respect for the patient's right to make medical care decisions as well as the HCP's desire to maintain the patient's trust. The elements required to elicit full informed consent from a patient are:

■ Discussion of the reason for and nature of the proposed procedure or therapy
■ Discussion of any reasonable alternatives to the proposed intervention
■ Disclosure of the relevant risks, benefits, and unknowns related to each option, including no treatment
■ Evaluation of the patient's understanding and
■ Decision by the patient about which option to pursue

(De Bord, 2014)

The legal standard for informed consent is set forth in a state's statutes or case law, and each state has laws and requirements for the essential elements. For federal institutions and certain procedures (e.g., clinical trials), federal rules and regulations regarding informed consent will apply.

The professional standards that guide healthcare providers are influenced by accreditation standards, medical specialty boards, professional organizations such as the AMA, and regulations. The Joint Commission has also been influential in stressing the importance of the communication process between the HCP and the patient (The Joint Commission, 2016). Obtaining a patient's signature is not as important as the thorough discussion of the risks, benefits, and alternatives to performing the procedure.

When Is Informed Consent Required?

There is no inclusive source that lists all procedures and treatments requiring informed consent. The most common approach is to consider that any invasive test or procedure should require informed consent to be obtained prior to the procedure or treatment. If there are side effects of the treatment or procedure that could result in a temporary or permanent loss of limb, function, or life, the informed consent process must be obtained after completely informing the patient of these potential side effects (FindLaw, n.d.-b). Federal and state statutes may require signed consent for some procedures (Legal Information Institute, n.d.-b, n.d.-c, n.d.-d). These mandates can be found in institutional and professional licensing requirements or in conditions of participation in payment programs, such as Medicare (Centers for Medicare & Medicaid Services [CMS], 2013). When consent is required, the method of documentation may be up to the HCP or restricted to a specific written consent form. The health code of a jurisdiction should be consulted to determine the applicable law in that state. In some jurisdictions, specific language is required by statute for certain forms.

When patients are to be transferred to another facility (or have refused a recommended transfer) for health treatment under emergency circumstances, federal law requires the HCP to inform them of the risks and benefits of transfer (Legal Information Institute, n.d.-a). This federal law also mandates the hospital, and not the physician, to take responsible steps to obtain a patient's informed consent or informed refusal for transfer under emergency conditions.

Medical Informed Consent Process

Informed consent is the process that involves dialogue between the patient and the HCP. It is not simply a signature at the bottom of a form. The elements that should be included in the medical informed consent process include: (1) diagnosis (when known), (2) the nature and purpose of recommended interventions, and (3) the burdens, risks, and expected benefits of all options, including forgoing treatment (AMA, n.d.-a). The dialogue culminates in an informed consent or an informed refusal. A written informed consent form should include the nature of the illness or injury, the procedure or treatment being consented to, the purpose of the proposed treatment, the risks and probable consequences of the proposed treatment, the date, and the signatures of the patient, HCP, and witness. There may be additional documentation required by regulatory bodies or organizational policies, such as a statement that the patient or authorized agent appeared to understand and agree to the procedure.

Guiding Principles of Informed Consent

The patient must provide consent for a specific procedure, and the HCP may not perform any other procedure outside the scope of the consented procedure. The patient has the right to refuse treatment or a procedure after receiving information on its risks, benefits, and alternatives. The HCP performing the procedure:

- is the person responsible for obtaining informed consent
- should have a complete understanding of the patient's medical condition and history
- should ensure the patient is legally and mentally competent to give consent for the procedure
- should provide the patient sufficient information at a level the patient can easily understand regarding the procedure and its risks, benefits, and alternatives
- should provide the patient an opportunity to ask questions concerning the procedure and its risks, benefits, and alternatives and
- should not coerce the patient into signing the consent form

(Findlaw, n.d.-a; Legal Information Institute, n.d.-d)

The clinical nurse's role in informed consent is to ensure the patient understands the information provided during the informed consent discussion, remembering the nurse is the patient's advocate and should recognize the patient's right and self-determination (ANA, 2015). If the nurse determines the patient does not comprehend the information, the nurse should inform the HCP obtaining the informed consent to ensure there is a complete understanding before the patient signs the consent form (Cook, 2014; Menendez, 2013).

Documentation of Informed Consent

A consent form is a document reflecting the consent process, but it does not replace the dialogue between the patient and the HCP. In all cases in which informed consent is required, there should be documentation that consent was, in fact, obtained by the person who had the duty to obtain it. Sometimes oral disclosure is sufficient, but the proof becomes problematic if the only witnesses to the conversation are the HCP and the patient. If a form is not signed by the patient, then the HCP should document what information was included in the informed consent discussion(s). Executed consent forms should be a part of the patient's permanent medical record.

Consent forms can be general, such as consent to medical care or to the release of certain information, or they can be specific to a treatment or procedure, such as consent to the administration of blood or blood products. The form must be signed by the patient or an authorized agent, and it must be witnessed. The witness is usually a nurse or other person who should ascertain the patient has, in fact, received from the HCP the information required to give informed consent, has no further questions prior to signing the form, and has given informed consent based on the discussion. The person witnessing the individual's signature should not be taking part in the treatment or procedure. The witness should sign and date the informed consent form while in the presence of the patient. If a patient does not speak English, a qualified interpreter should be involved in the informed consent process and should also sign the consent form.

If no form is required or used in a particular facility, the HCP should document narrative notes in the patient's medical record. The LNC and legal team also look to the deposition testimony of the plaintiff and defendant as additional evidence regarding the informed consent process.

Exceptions to Informed Consent

Emergency Situations

When a patient who is unconscious or otherwise unable to provide express consent needs immediate treatment necessary to save life, and harm from failure to treat is imminent and outweighs the potential harm of the proposed treatment, consent is implied (AMA, n.d.-a). In such cases in which it is "not medically feasible" to obtain informed consent, the courts will not hold the HCP liable for failing to obtain informed consent, even if complications occur that would be considered both inherent and material. In this context, the courts also suspend the rule requiring parental consent for a minor, if the minor needs emergency treatment and the parents are not available to give consent.

Therapeutic Privilege

In rare cases, an HCP may choose to withhold information that reasonably could hinder treatment or prove harmful to the patient. This concept may be employed by a defendant HCP to justify non-disclosure on the basis it was in the best interest of the patient not to do so. For example, in *Barclay v. Campbell*, a case involving a psychotherapeutic drug that resulted in the side effect of tardive dyskinesia, the doctor argued the patient's schizophrenia rendered the patient unable to have the reactions of a reasonable person, justifying non-disclosure of the risk. The court disagreed, holding the patient's right to disclosure was not negated just because the doctor did not believe the patient was reasonable (Justia US Law, n.d.).

Who May Sign the Informed Consent Form?

The person giving consent is usually the patient unless the patient is unable to do so for some reason. It is important for the HCP to evaluate each situation and follow the healthcare facility's policy. Most healthcare facilities establish their consent policies based on the state's laws and regulations, except federal facilities which follow federal laws.

Competent Patient 18 Years of Age or Older

There is a legal presumption that persons who have reached the age of majority (usually 18 years) are competent and may make their own decisions about medical care. For informed consent, competence refers to decision-making capacity, or the patient's ability to engage in rational decision-making. For example, in *Fosmire v. Nicoleau* (1990), the court found that competent individuals have the right to make their own medical choices regardless of their medical condition or religious belief.

Parent of a Child under 18 Years of Age

In the case of minors, parents must give consent by proxy (Pozgar, 2016). If the parents are divorced or in a custody battle, the parent with custody of the child at that time should be the one to consent for the child. If parents are unavailable in a given situation, certain others, usually next of kin in a hierarchical fashion, may be authorized under the jurisdiction's family code. The parent must consent for neonatal treatment before the delivery of the baby. Many times, the nurse in the labor and delivery area obtains consent for the newborn's treatment when consent for the mother's treatment is obtained.

Emancipated Minors

Each state determines when minors can consent for themselves. For example, some family codes stipulate that a minor does not need parental consent in order to obtain treatment for sexually transmitted diseases, drug addiction, or pregnancy. In addition, emancipated minors (e.g., minors who are married or legally emancipated) can consent to treatment without parental participation. What constitutes an emancipated minor differs from state to state, and the HCP should consult each state's family code for those laws. In *Parham v. J.R.* (1979), the United States Supreme Court issued a landmark ruling establishing a definite standard for juvenile admissions to mental health facilities. The parent may authorize the admission of the juvenile, but a neutral individual must determine if statutory requirements for admission have been satisfied (Justia US Supreme Court, n.d.; Pozgar, 2016).

Mentally Incompetent Persons

The family codes or the mental health codes of a particular state may contain provisions allowing procedures to be performed without the usual consent when the patient is mentally incompetent or committed to a mental institution and unable to give informed consent because of that mental condition. The law assumes an individual is competent until a statutory process has deemed the individual to be incompetent (Steiner, 2014).

Legal Guardian or Surrogate

A legal guardian may be appointed by the legal system to handle the affairs of another individual (Pozgar, 2016). This most often occurs when there is a physical or mental issue that prevents the individuals from making decisions and caring for themselves, when the individuals are in danger of substantial harm to themselves or others, or when the individuals have no person already legally authorized to take responsibility of them, such as when a child's parents are deceased and there are no other family members available.

The legal guardianship may be in place for a limited period of time or an undetermined period of time. Regardless, the legal guardian is responsible for the individual's residence, health care, food, and social activity. The guardian should consider the wishes of the individual in any decisions made regarding these items. The courts will monitor the decisions made by the legal guardian to ensure the individual is benefiting from the legal guardian's services. The courts may terminate a legal guardianship at any time (Legal Information Institute, n.d.-d).

Medical Power of Attorney

If a person lacks decision-making capacity, the HCP must determine if there is another individual who can provide the consent or whom the patient had previously identified to do so through a medical power of attorney. A medical power of attorney, or sometimes called the Power of Attorney for Healthcare, is established by a competent individual, known as the "principal," who identifies another person, known as the "agent," to make decisions regarding the prinicpal's health care should the principal become unable to do so for whatever reason. When that scenario arises, the medical power of attorney becomes effective immediately and remains in effect until it is revoked or replaced by a more recent version or until the principal becomes competent to make clinical decisions. The agent may begin to make healthcare decisions for the principal after an HCP has certified in writing that the principal is incompetent or unable to make such decisions. Some medical associations recommend that a copy of the medical power of attorney be included in the principal's permanent medical record (Pozgar, 2016).

The medical power of attorney may allow the agent to make all healthcare decisions, or it may limit the agent's decision-making authority. Each state may have specific laws regarding what the agent may consent to, regardless of the medical power of attorney. Also, states differ on whether an agent can consent for commitment to a mental institution, convulsive treatment, psychosurgery, abortion, or the discontinuance of comfort care.

Informed Consent Process for Research Subjects

In 1981, the U.S. Food and Drug Administration (FDA) enacted regulations regarding the Protection of Human Subjects. This regulation states "No investigator may involve a human being as a subject in research covered by these regulations unless the investigator has obtained the legally effective informed consent of the subject or the subject's legally authorized representative" (FDA, 2018). The regulations state the consent must be in a language understandable to the subject or representative, and the subject may not waive legal rights or relieve anyone involved from liability for negligence. There are exceptions to this rule as stated in Sections 50.23 and 50.24 of the regulation.

Consent to research is also grounded in ethical codes, statutes, and administrative regulations. The federal statutes spell out the basic elements of research informed consent (Government Printing

Office, n.d.). The consent process is outlined in the Code of Federal Regulations (Legal Information Institute, n.d.-e). The informed consent for research has been developed based on historical information and the need to protect the subjects of the research. However, patients often do not understand what they are signing and often do not read the information before they sign. If they were to read the document before signing it, research has shown participants frequently do not remember the information they read, and there is concern about participants' reading-level and comprehension of information on the informed consent (Cordasco, 2013; Foe & Larson, 2016).

There are individual state laws governing research and the informed consent process, and there are additional protections required by institutional review boards (IRB) or human research review committees for vulnerable populations, such as pregnant women, children, and prisoners. There are special rules for children and adolescents participating in research, but that discussion is beyond the scope of this chapter. The LNC should review the American Academy of Pediatrics' Section on Bioethics (www.aap.org) and the relevant Codes of Federal Regulations (Legal Information Institute, n.d.-e, n.d.-f) in cases involving pediatric research.

Issues with Informed Consent

Many articles and research studies identify issues and limits with the informed consent process. According to Ittenbach, Senft, Huang, Corsmo, and Sieber (2015), fewer than 50% of the study patients read the entire consent form, and 27% said they understood it "very little." The main issues with informed consent identified in the literature revolve around the concepts of mental competency, comprehension, and incomplete disclosure (Steiner, 2014).

Decision-Making Capacity and Competency

There are many reasons why a patient may not be able or competent to give informed consent. For example, patients who may not be able or competent to give consent are those under the age of 18 or those who are mentally impaired, demented, confused, unconscious, or drug-dependent, to name a few. Alzheimer's disease and other forms of dementia affect patients in varying degrees. It is often difficult to determine if a patient with these diagnoses is competent. Alzheimer's is a disease that takes many years to manifest itself to the furthest degree (Palmer et al., 2017). Palmer et al. (2017) conducted a study to accurately measure the decision-making capacity of patients with Alzheimer's and found it would be difficult to indicate whether a patient was capable or incapable of giving informed consent. The researchers concluded a structured assessment is needed to determine capacity to consent.

An HCP may have questions about a patient's decision-making capabilities when the patient refuses a course of treatment recommended by the HCP (Legal Information Institute, n.d.-d). The HCP should assess the patient's ability to participate in decision-making by assessing the patient's ability to: (1) understand the situation; (2) understand the risks associated with the decision; and (3) communicate a decision based on that understanding (De Bord, 2014).

According to 38 CFR 17.32(e), the persons authorized to consent for patients who lack decision-making capacity are, in order of priority: (1) healthcare agent; (2) legal guardian or special guardian; (3) next-of-kin: a close relative of the patient who is 18 years of age or older, in the following priority: spouse, child, parent, sibling, grandparent or grandchild; or (4) close friend (Legal Information Institute, n.d.-d). In such cases, the HCP must document the decision-making capacity of the patient. Simply because the patient can consent to a procedure or treatment does not mean the patient has the capacity to decide to either undergo or refuse treatment. The process of informed consent balances concern for the patient's wellbeing with respect for the patient's self-determination (Pozgar, 2013). De Bord (2014) discusses exceptions to full informed consent, which include:

■ If the patient does not have decision-making capacity, e.g., a patient with dementia for whom a proxy or surrogate decision-maker must be found
■ If the patient lacks decision-making capacity and there is inadequate time to find a proxy without harming the patient, e.g., a life-threatening emergency in which the patient is not conscious
■ If the patient has waived informed consent and
■ If a competent patient designates a trusted loved one to make treatment decisions

Comprehension and Understanding of Informed Consent Content

During the informed consent process, the HCP must assess several influencing factors, including: (1) the patient's understanding of the informed consent content, (2) the patient's proficiency in the English language, (3) whether any elements of informed consent are incomplete, and (4) whether the informed consent content is above the patient's reading and comprehension level (Cordasco, 2013). Language barriers can be a significant obstacle to informed consent. Many facilities only have informed consent forms in English, despite many patients having a low proficiency in the English language. The use of interpreters is haphazard at best, with many HCPs utilizing family and staff to provide the translation. The quality of their translation is unknown and suspect to being incomplete or incorrect. (Noori, 2017). When a language barrier is present, the HCP has liability if a qualified medical interpreter is not utilized to obtain informed consent. In addition, courts have held it is the ethical duty of the HCP to protect patients' privacy, and whenever an interpreter is used, the HCP should ensure the interpreter is competent and protects the patient's privacy rights. Using family members and hospital staff for interpretation presents more compromise in the consent process than utilizing professionally trained interpreters.

In the case of *Quintero v. Encarnacion* (Court Listener, n.d.), a physician used the English and Spanish languages to obtain consent from a Ramuri-speaking patient who was only able to communicate minimally utilizing a few Spanish words. The Court of Appeals held that "if the patient's capacity to understand is limited by a language barrier, and the physician proceeds without addressing this barrier ... the physician may be liable for failing to obtain informed consent from the patient" (Association of American Medical Colleges & Association of Schools of Public Health, 2012, p. 13).

Incomplete Disclosure

Incomplete disclosure is one of the most debated topics regarding informed consent. Clinicians and researchers have published many articles regarding what should be disclosed to a patient during the informed consent process for medical care and research. The landmark case regarding informed consent is *Schloendorff v. New York Hospital* (1914), in which the judge concluded, "Every human being of adult years and sound mind has a right to determine what should be done with his own body" (Steiner, 2014). In medical malpractice cases, the main issue of disclosure is regarding what was known and when it was known (Steiner, 2014).

Informed Refusal

Patients have the right to refuse treatment, and the decision to limit, withhold, discontinue, or forgo treatment must be carefully and very specifically documented by the HCP. Most court cases related to the right to refuse treatment have involved patients with a terminal illness, or their families, who want to discontinue life support. In those cases, the courts must consider quality end-of-life care as an ethical obligation, but since the decision of non-treatment or discontinuing support involves establishing what "end-of-life" means, these cases are difficult to resolve. Another area of increased liability for HCPs related to the right to refuse treatment is childhood vaccinations. It is important for the HCP to use the Vaccine Information Statement (VIS) tools to assist parents in gaining a good appreciation of the benefits, risks, and consequences of agreeing to or declining vaccination of a child (Rozovsky, 2014).

If an HCP has made all reasonable attempts to educate and inform the patient about a treatment or procedure and why it is being recommended, and the patient still refuses, the HCP must ensure every reasonable explanation was provided for the patient to make an informed decision and then document the patient's informed refusal. The informed refusal process, and documentation thereof, should include:

- An explanation of the risks involved in not having the treatment or procedure and
- A determination of the patient's capacity to refuse based on having all the facts necessary to make an informed decision

When care is refused, healthcare facilities typically have crafted forms for patients and families to sign and drafted policies for the HCP to follow based on state statutes. The patient's ability to refuse treatment can be challenged, and the HCP can attempt to prove the patient is not competent to make decisions.

Proof in Court

When asserting a lack of informed consent cause of action, plaintiffs must prove duty, breach of duty, causation, and damages (see Chapter 4). Specifically, plaintiffs must prove:

1. The HCP owed a duty to the patient to provide the necessary information for the patient to make an informed decision
2. The HCP breached that duty and failed to disclose the complication or condition in question, which was a material risk in the procedure performed
3. A reasonable person fully informed of this material risk would not have consented to the treatment in question (decisional causation) and
4. The patient/plaintiff was, in fact, injured by the occurrence of this complication or condition about which the patient was not informed (physical causation and damages)

Depending on the jurisdiction, decisional causation may be decided by an objective or subjective standard. The method most typically utilized in court is the objective standard—what a hypothetical "reasonable person" would have done if the risk in question had been disclosed during the informed consent process. The plaintiff must prove a reasonable person would not have consented to the procedure if advised of the risk in question. The reasonable person standard in the context of informed consent cases was established in the landmark 1972 case of *Canterbury v. Spence* (CaseBriefs, n.d.). In this case, the physician informed the patient that back surgery could result in weakness but did not disclose the possibility of partial paralysis. The court found causation based on the fact that, if the physician had disclosed the potential risk of the procedure, the patient would have never consented to have the procedure done, and others in a similar situation would make the same determination.

Expert testimony is offered regarding the inherency and materiality of the risk in question as well as the risks and benefits of the treatment alternatives (Pozgar, 2016). By comparing the risks and probable outcomes of all available options, the fact-finder (i.e., jury or judge) determines whether a reasonable person would have elected the procedure or treatment actually undertaken by the plaintiff or an alternative (including no treatment). They must not look at this from hindsight.

In some jurisdictions, the objective standard is one of the reasonable HCP, a variation of the reasonable person standard. Under this analysis, the plaintiff must prove the defendant did not disclose to the plaintiff information that a reasonable provider would have presented to another similar patient. In other words, the question is what a reasonable HCP would do when informing a patient, as opposed to what a reasonable person (the patient) would do had the risk been disclosed. Healthcare provider experts are utilized to support what a reasonable provider would have disclosed (Pozgar, 2016).

The second way decisional causation can be decided is the subjective standard. In this method, the fact-finder must decide whether the *plaintiff* would have undergone the procedure if additional information regarding the risks and alternatives had been disclosed. This is different from the objective approach in that it focuses on the plaintiff specifically, not just a hypothetical reasonable person. The subjective approach has been adopted by only a small number of states for the determination of decisional causation (Pozgar, 2013).

Informed consent is rarely the sole cause of action in a claim. It is more commonly brought in combination with a medical negligence claim. Informed consent and medical negligence claims are both considered unintentional torts. However, informed consent claims can also be brought in cases claiming battery; fraud, deceit, and misrepresentation; and breach of contract.

Battery

Battery is an intentional tort (meaning it resulted from an intentional act). The law protects the patient from unwanted physical touching of the patient's body by someone without permission. For a plaintiff to allege battery in an informed consent case, one of the following actions had to occur:

■ The HCP performs a procedure without the patient's consent
■ The HCP performs a procedure substantially different from the procedure to which the patient consented
■ The HCP exceeds the scope of the consent by expanding on the procedure performed or
■ A different HCP performs the procedure other than the HCP listed on the consent form

As a result of the battery and failure to obtain informed consent, the plaintiff may be compensated with a monetary award even if the procedure was properly performed and beneficial to the plaintiff (Steiner, 2014). In these cases, consideration may need to be given to the HCP's use of medical discretion. For example, if a surgeon performing a transurethral resection of a prostate for benign prostatic hypertrophy finds and removes bladder tumors during the surgery, the removal of these tumors is necessary but was not consented to pre-operatively.

Fraud, Deceit, and Misrepresentation

An informed consent may be found to be invalid if obtained by fraudulent misrepresentation, non-disclosure of important information, or concealment (Steiner, 2014). To prevail in a fraudulent concealment claim, the plaintiff must prove:

- The defendant HCP concealed or suppressed a material fact
- The defendant was under a duty to disclose the fact to the plaintiff
- The defendant intentionally concealed or suppressed the fact to defraud the plaintiff
- The plaintiff was unaware of the fact and would have acted differently if the concealed or suppressed fact had been disclosed and
- The plaintiff sustained damage as a result of the concealment or suppression of the fact

Breach of Contract

Breach of contract is another claim that may be brought in combination with a lack of informed consent claim. To prevail in a breach of contract claim, the plaintiff must prove:

- A contract existed between the defendant HCP and the plaintiff
- The plaintiff's duties under the contract were fulfilled
- The defendant failed to perform a term of the contract and
- The plaintiff sustained damages as a result of this breach of contract

For example, in *Belin v. Dingle* (1999), Ms. Belin, a surgical technician, consulted Dr. Dingle, a general surgeon, to perform a laparoscopic cholecystectomy. Knowing that the surgery would be performed at a teaching hospital, Ms. Belin insisted that Dr. Dingle perform the actual cutting and removal of the gall bladder and that a resident be used only if absolutely necessary. Dr. Dingle agreed, and Ms. Belin presented for surgery. Without Ms. Belin's knowledge or consent, the resident actually performed the surgery while Dr. Dingle retracted tissue. The resident dissected and clipped the common bile duct instead of the cystic duct, resulting in leakage of bile into the abdominal cavity and the need for additional surgery. Ms. Belin brought claims for negligence, lack of informed consent, and breach of contract. Regarding the latter, Ms. Belin claimed Dr. Dingle breached their oral contract when he failed to perform the surgery as agreed.

Viability of the Lack of Informed Consent Cause of Action

Practically speaking, it is often difficult to persuade a jury to find for the plaintiff in informed consent claims, especially if the procedure or treatment in question was lifesaving, curative, or necessary for a serious medical condition. When lack of informed consent becomes an issue in a medical malpractice case, it is often difficult to prove what occurred during the informed consent discussion. There are frequent discrepancies between the HCP's and plaintiff's versions of the information exchanged during this conversation. Such disputes typically center around whether a particular risk was discussed, even if the HCP documented it was. Many HCPs specifically document the informed consent conversation in their progress notes as well as on the informed consent form. This may occur more often when the HCP is getting consent for high-risk surgical procedures.

In cases in which the defendant HCP was compliant with the statutory or common law duty and completed a properly executed consent form, the plaintiff may resort to claiming the scope of the disclosure was inadequate and questioning the validity of the consent. In that regard, plaintiffs may claim they did not have the capacity to give consent or did not sign the form. In this type of situation, the plaintiff may make contractual claims such as fraud, mutual mistake, accident, and undue influence.

While it may be difficult to persuade a jury to find for the plaintiff, the reasonable person standard makes it difficult for an HCP to obtain summary judgment, because the defendant must counter the argument that knowledge of a particular risk would have influenced a reasonable person against the procedure or treatment in question. This is typically a question of fact for the jury rather than a question of law for the court.

Trends

There are some current trends that will affect how informed consent is determined in the future. In some cases, the HCP or the facility are videotaping the consent process. Some are utilizing recorded educational programs to explain the surgery, procedure, or treatment. Increasingly, interactive media and websites are being used as part of the informed consent process.

There is also a growing expectation of transparency, with patients asking HCPs what their complication rates are for a procedure, how many procedures the HCP has performed, and so forth. Research is currently being conducted to determine the severity of a procedure's risks to assist in the determination of what should be (or what does not need to be) disclosed to the patient.

Summary

Many healthcare providers do not fully understand the importance of the informed consent process and that it is not simply the patient's signature on a form. Furthermore, the nurse or other designee too often has the patient sign the informed consent form and witnesses the patient's signature without really knowing whether the patient has, in fact, received from the HCP the information required to give informed consent and whether the patient appeared to understand, had an opportunity to ask questions, and gave consent.

Failure to properly obtain informed consent prior to any treatment or procedure requiring it could result in litigation. There should be documentation in the medical record that informed consent was obtained appropriately, i.e., that the patient was presented with the appropriate information, understood what was presented, and consented to proceed. There should be documentation of the methods utilized to overcome any limitations to the consent process, such as language barriers and readability of the consent documents. It is only through proper documentation of what and how information was discussed with the patient that the medical record can substantiate a proper informed consent process in the event of a lawsuit.

The LNC reviewing an informed consent case should scrutinize the medical records and the healthcare facility's policies and procedures regarding informed consent. The LNC should also be mindful of the relevant federal or state statutes and case law that will assist the legal team in evaluating an informed consent case.

References

American Medical Association. (n.d.-a). Code of medical ethics 2.1.1: Informed consent. Retrieved from www.ama-assn.org/delivering-care/informed-consent.

American Medical Association. (n.d.-b). Code of medical ethics opinion 2.1.2: Decisions for adult patients who lack capacity. Retrieved from www.ama-assn.org/delivering-care/decisions-adult-patients-who-lack-capacity.

American Nurses Association. (2015). *Code of ethics for nurses with interpretive statements*. Silver Springs, MD: The Publishing Program of ANA. Retrieved from www.Nursesbooks.org.

Association of American Medical Colleges, & Association of Schools of Public Health. (2012). Cultural competence education for students in medicine and public health: Report of an expert panel. Retrieved from https://members.aamc.org/eweb/upload/Cultural%20Competence%20Education_revisedl.pdf.

Belin v. Dingle, 127 Md.App. 68, 732 A.2d 301 (1999).

CaseBriefs. (n.d.). *Spence v. Canterbury*, 1972 U.S. LEXIS 348, 409 U.S. 1064, 93 S. Ct. 560, 34 L. Ed. 2d 518. Retrieved from www.casebriefs.com/blog/law/torts/torts-keyed-to-epstein/the-negligence-issue/canterbury-v-spence-2/.

Centers for Medicare & Medicaid Services. (2013). Conditions for Coverage (CfCs) & Conditions of Participations (CoPs). Retrieved from www.cms.gov/Regulations-and-Guidance/Legislation/CFCsAndCoPs/index.html.

Congress.gov. (n.d.). H.R. 4449 Patient Self Determination Act of 1990. Retrieved from www.congress.gov/bill/101st-congress/house-bill/4449.

Cook, W. E. (2014). "Sign here": Nursing value and the process of informed consent. *Plastic Surgical Nursing, 34*(1), 29–33. DOI: 10.1097/PSN.0000000000000030.

Cordasco, K. M. (2013). Chapter 39: Obtaining informed consent from patients: Brief update review. In AHRQ, Evidence Report/Technology Assessment (No. 211), Making Health Care Safer II: An Updated Critical Analysis of the Evidence for Patient Safety Practices. (pp. 461–471; AHRQ Publication No. 13-E001-EF). Rockville, MD: AHRQ/DHHS. Retrieved from www.ahrq.gov/sites/default/files/wysiwyg/research/findings/evidence-based-reports/services/quality/patientsftyupdate/ptsafetyII-full.pdf.

Court Listener. (n.d.). *Quintero v. Encarnacion*, 98–3129 (10th Cir. 1999). Retrieved from www.courtlistener.com/opinion/157983/quintero-v-encarnacion/.

De Bord, J. (2014). Ethics in medicine: Informed consent. Retrieved from https://depts.washington.edu/bioethx/topics/consent.html.

FindLaw. (n.d.-a). Understanding informed consent and your rights as a patient. Retrieved from https://healthcare.findlaw.com/patient-rights/understanding-informed-consent-a-primer.html.

FindLaw. (n.d.-b). Informed consent and unauthorized treatment. Retrieved from https://injury.findlaw.com/medical-malpractice/unauthorized-treatment-and-lack-of-informed-consent.html.

Foe, G., & Larson, E. L. (2016). Reading level and comprehension of research consent forms: An integrative review. *Journal of Empirical Research on Human Research Ethics, 11*(1), 31–46. DOI: https://doi.org/10.1177/1556264616637483.

Food and Drug Administration. (2018). 21 CFR, 50.20, a guide to informed consent. Information sheet: General requirements for informed consent. Retrieved from www.fda.gov/RegulatoryInformation/Guidances/ucm126431.htm#general.

Fosmire v. Nicoleau, 75 N.Y.2d 218, 222, 551 N.E.2d 77, 78, 551 N.Y.S.2d 876, 877 (1990) Retrieved from www.questia.com/library/journal/1G1-10375630/fosmire-v-nicoleau.

Garner, B. A. (Ed.) (2014). *Black's law dictionary* (10th ed., p. 368). St Paul, MN: Thompson Reuters.

Government Printing Office. (n.d.). 21 CFR 50.25 elements of informed consent. Retrieved from www.gpo.gov/fdsys/granule/CFR-2012-title21-vol. 1/CFR-2012-title21-vol. 1-sec50-25/content-detail.html and www.gpo.gov/fdsys/pkg/CFR-2012-title21-vol. 1/pdf/CFR-2012-title21-vol. 1-sec50-25.pdf.

Ittenbach, R. F., Senft, E. C., & Huang, G., Corsmo, J. J., & Sieber, J. E. (2015). Readability and understanding of informed consent among participants with low incomes. *Journal of Empirical Research on Human Research Ethics, 10*(5), 444–448. DOI: https://doi.org/10.1177/1556264615615006.

Justia US Law. (n.d.). *Barclay v. Campbell*, 704 S.W.2d 8 (Tex. 1986). Retrieved from http://law.justia.com/cases/texas/supreme-court/1986/c-3854-0.html.

Justia US Supreme Court. (n.d.). *Parham v. J.R.*, 442 U.S. 584 (1979), No. 75–1690. Retrieved from https://supreme.justia.com/cases/federal/us/442/584/.

Legal Information Institute. (n.d.-a). 42 U.S. Code § 1395dd Examination and treatment of emergency medical conditions and women in labor. Retrieved from www.law.cornell.edu/uscode/text/42/1395dd.

Legal information Institute. (n.d.-b). 21 CFR 50.20 General requirements for informed consent. Retrieved from www.law.cornell.edu/cfr/text/21/50.20.

Legal Information Institute. (n.d.-c). 21 CFR 50.25 elements of informed consent. Retrieved from www.law.cornell.edu/cfr/text/21/50.25.

Legal Information Institute. (n.d.-d). 38 CFR 17.32 Informed consent and advance care planning. Retrieved from www.law.cornell.edu/cfr/text/38/17.32.

Legal Information Institute. (n.d.-e). 45 CFR Part 46—protection of human subjects. www.law.cornell.edu/cfr/text/45/part-46.

Legal Information Institute. (n.d.-f). 45 CFR 46.116 General requirements for informed consent. Retrieved from www.law.cornell.edu/cfr/text/45/46.116.

MedicineNet. (n.d.). Informed consent. Retrieved from www.medicinenet.com/script/main/art.asp?articlekey=22414.

Menendez, J. B. (2013). Informed consent: Essential legal and ethical principles for nurses. *JONA's Healthcare, Ethics, and Regulation, 15*(4), 140–144. DOI: 10.1097/NHL.0000000000000015.

Noori, M. (2017). Convenient access to professional interpreters in the hospital decreases readmission rates and estimated hospital expenditures for patients with limited English proficiency. *Journal of Emergency Medicine, 52*(5), 790. DOI:10.1016/j.jemermed.2017.03.043.

Palmer, B. W., Harmell, A. L., Pinto, L. L., Dunn, L. B., Kim, S. H., Golshan, S., & Jeste, D. V. (2017). Determinants of capacity to consent to research on Alzheimer's disease. *Clinical Gerontologist, 40*(1), 24–34. doi:10.1080/07317115.2016.1197352.

Pozgar G. D. (2013). *Patient care case law: Ethics, regulation, and compliance.* Burlington, MA: Jones & Bartlett Learning. Retrieved from www.jblearning.com/catalog/9781449604585/.

Pozgar, G. D. (2016). *Legal and ethical issues for health professionals* (4th ed.). Burlington, MA: Jones & Bartlett Learning. Retrieved from www.jblearning.com/catalog/9781284036794/.

Rozovsky, F. A. (2014). *Consent to treatment: A practical guide* (5th ed.). New York, NY: Aspen Publishers, Wolters Kluwer.

Schloendorff v. New York Hospital, 211 N.Y. 125, 129–130 (1914). Retrieved from http://biotech.law.lsu.edu/cases/consent/schoendorff.htm.

Steiner, J. E. (2014). Decision making concerning individuals. In *Problems in health care law: Challenges for the 21st century* (10th ed., pp. 209–250). Burlington, MA: Jones & Barlett Learning. Retrieved from www.jblearning.com/catalog/9781449685522/.

The Joint Commission. (2016). Quick Safety: *Informed consent: More than getting a signature* (Issue 21, February). Retrieved from www.jointcommission.org/assets/1/23/Quick_Safety_Issue_Twenty-One_February_2016.pdf.

Additional Reading

Legal Information Institute. (n.d.). 42 CFR 416.50—Condition for coverage—Patient rights. Retrieved from www.law.cornell.edu/cfr/text/42/416.50.

Legal Information Institute. (n.d.). 38 U.S. Code § 7331 Informed consent. Retrieved from www.law.cornell.edu/uscode/text/38/7331.

Martin, L. J., Zieve, D., & Conaway, B. (2017). Informed consent—adults. Retrieved from https://medlineplus.gov/ency/patientinstructions/000445.htm.

Nolo.com. (n.d.). Informed consent. Retrieved from www.nolo.com/dictionary/informed-consent-term.html or www.law.cornell.edu/wex/informed_consent.

Perrault, E. K., & Nazione, S. A. (2016). Informed consent: Uninformed participants: Shortcomings of online social science consent forms and recommendations for improvement. *Journal of Empirical Research on Human Research Ethics, 11*(3), 274–280. DOI: https://doi.org/10.1177/1556264616654610.

Wagner, R. A., Keany, J. E., Talavera, F., & Taylor III, J. P. (n.d.). Informed consent. Retrieved from www.emedicinehealth.com/informed_consent/article_em.htm#what_is_informed_consent.

Zur, O. (n.d.). Ethics codes on record keeping and informed consent in psychotherapy and counseling. *Zur Institute*. Retrieved from www.zurinstitute.com/ethicsofrecordkeeping.html.

Test Questions

1. The legal standard regarding informed consent is determined by:
   A. American Medical Association
   B. The healthcare facility's policies and procedures
   C. Federal or state statutes and case law
   D. American Nurses Association's Code of Ethics for Nurses
2. A neurosurgeon is planning on performing an aneurysm repair on a patient. Who is responsible for obtaining informed consent?
   A. The internist who performed the pre-operative history and physical
   B. The admitting nurse who prepared the patient for surgery
   C. The intern on duty when the patient is admitted
   D. The neurosurgeon performing the surgery
3. All of the following are elements of informed consent recommended by the American Medical Association EXCEPT:
   A. The decision a reasonable person would make
   B. Diagnosis (when known)
   C. Nature and purpose of the recommended interventions
   D. The burdens, risks, and expected benefits of all options, including forgoing treatment
4. A patient is admitted after a car accident unconscious and unable to give consent. The patient needs immediate, life-saving treatment, but there are no documents or information available regarding next of kin. Does the surgeon need to obtain informed consent?
   A. Yes
   B. No
5. According to Ittenbach et al., less than what percentage of patients read an entire consent form?
   A. 80%
   B. 50%
   C. 30%
   D. 15%

Answers: 1. C, 2. D, 3. A, 4. B, 5. B

Chapter 20

Medical Treatment Decisions

The Patient's Choice

Kelly Tanner, BSN, RN, CCRN-A, CNLCP®
Paula J. Yost, Esq., LPCA

Contents

Objectives

- Identify the differences in advance directives
- Differentiate between a Power of Attorney and an Executor
- Describe the medical professional's responsibilities when a patient makes a healthcare plan for treatment
- Summarize a minor's rights in healthcare decisions
- Articulate standards for substitute decision-making when patients do not have the capacity to make decisions for themselves

Introduction

Today, healthcare services and delivery are complex, and numerous participants are involved in the medical decision-making process when patients enter healthcare systems, including the federal government, state and local governments, public and private healthcare insurers, hospitals, healthcare facilities, social service agencies, healthcare providers (i.e., physicians, advanced practice registered nurses, and physician assistants), and therapists. Any healthcare decisions made must always respect the patient's wishes. The responsibility of the legal nurse consultant (LNC) is to be cognizant of the legal documents and federal and state statutes regarding patient medical decision-making rights and the multiple participants involved to fully understand and explain the rationale behind decisions reflected in the medical record. Also, the LNC's duty is to determine medical compliance with the patient's wishes and affirm or challenge the allegations presented.

Theory for Making Informed Medical Treatment Decisions

Patient Autonomy and Self-Determination

The concept of patient autonomy, which governs the act of making informed decisions, has further evolved through laws such as the Patient Self-Determination Act (PSDA) and the adoption of professional codes, such as The American Nurses Association's Code of Ethics. These documents emphasize the importance of autonomy in providing patient care. In respect to patient autonomy, a patient has the right to be informed of, and a provider has the duty to disclose, the medical treatment that will be given and the reason for it (DeWolf & Sue, 2007). Respect for patient autonomy and information disclosure is part of the informed consent process mandated by the PSDA. (See Chapter 19 for more information on informed consent.)

Healthcare Provider's Duties

The PSDA provides requirements that healthcare entities must meet if they participate in Medicare programs, including healthcare management organizations. These requirements include the stipulation that competent adult patients are provided with a written notice of their rights to consent to or refuse care. Written policies and procedures must be in place addressing the required elements of PSDA (Selde, 2015).

Liability issues may arise when allegations are made that the patient was not fully informed, not competent to make decisions, or given erroneous information. Families and surrogate decision-makers can complicate the situation if they disagree with a patient's medical decisions to refuse care. Failure to respect a patient's right to refuse medical treatment may give rise to a civil suit by the patient for damages and, in some cases, battery (unconsented physical contact). In addition, withholding or withdrawing treatment pursuant to a patient's alleged wishes can also lead to liability if the family disagrees or claims the patient did not want treatment withdrawn. If a healthcare provider is in doubt as to the proper course of action, a prudent step is to involve the court.

Patient Rights

In 1973, the American Hospital Association issued a Patient's Bill of Rights to be implemented throughout the United States for all hospitals and healthcare professionals to follow to ensure the patient was provided holistic, patient-centered care. In 2003, the Patient's Bill of Rights was replaced with *The Patient Care Partnership: Understanding Expectations, Rights and Responsibilities* (American Hospital Association, 2003). This document describes what patients should expect during their hospital stay as well as what is needed from them to allow the healthcare personnel to provide quality care. These expectations include:

- High-quality hospital care
- A clean and safe environment
- Involvement in one's care
- Protection of one's privacy
- Help when leaving the hospital
- Availability of interpreters when needed and
- Accommodations for people with disabilities

Patients exercise the rights listed above, within the framework of their identity. Individual culture and ethnicity influence the decision-making process. It is imperative to understand the medical profession is a culture within itself. That is, medical professionals have their own belief systems of what is right, wrong, valuable, indifferent, or optimal regarding medical treatment. In contrast, patients have their own deep-seeded values from which they launch all life-long decisions. The patient's medical treatment decisions are based upon that same decision-making process and from the same personal value system.

Patient values versus those of the medical profession are another important aspect of case analysis, especially when analyzing the patient's medical decision-making process. It is critical to note that treating providers typically do not scrutinize a patient's decision to accept and proceed with the recommended medical treatment. However, when a patient hesitates to agree to, or outright refuses, a medical recommendation, the reasons for that decision are more likely scrutinized.

The plan of care for each patient is individualized and specific to that patient. To ensure a patient's autonomous, informed decisions are respected, it is important to consider the impact of the patient's personal values and culture on the care plan and carefully review the medical records for evidence of how medical treatment decisions are made and recommended. Such analysis has the potential to reveal hidden aspects of the case that are crucial to, or may even change, the outcome.

The medical record should indicate evidence of the language used to discuss the patient's illness and disease, including the degree of openness in discussing the diagnosis, prognosis, and death. Documentation should reflect healthcare providers' discussions with the patient including education regarding the disease process, treatment recommendations, alternative treatments, risks, benefits and burdens, expectations and outcomes, and the patient's response to these discussions. Sometimes within the medical culture, it is uncomfortable to raise the issue of impending death or even the possibility of death. Although the culture is changing, it is something to consider during case analysis.

When reviewing the case records, determine whether decisions are made by the patient or a larger social unit such as the family. Look for documentation of who was present during provider-to-patient discussions and whether the patient voiced a choice in the presence of family members. Did the patient express, or did the provider inquire about, a preference for which individuals, if any, should be present for treatment discussions and decision-making?

Consider the relevance of religious beliefs, particularly about the meaning of death, the existence of an afterlife, or a belief in miracles. This may help to explain why a patient is making decisions contrary to medical recommendations. A patient, for example, may be choosing to suffer pain in this life so as not to have to endure eternal suffering in the next. Without careful exploration of such beliefs, the overt appearance of refusing pain medication may be falsely interpreted as non-compliance. Another example is the well-known religious belief held by Jehovah's Witnesses in refusal of blood and blood products. Social workers' and chaplains' documentation in the patient's medical records should reflect the healthcare team's respect for social and religious dimensions of holistic patient care. Lack of such involvement from either of these two disciplines should raise concern for the LNC reviewing the case.

Evidence of how the healthcare provider assessed and respected the patient's autonomy, personal values, religion, and culture may be relevant during case analysis. In conducting such an analysis, the LNC should consider:

- Evidence of how hope for recovery is negotiated within the family and with healthcare professionals. For example, in a case in which a patient was in a persistent vegetative state, look for documentation of discussions regarding the family's beliefs. Does the family hope the patient will awaken and be cured, or is their hope for comfort care or a peaceful death? Are these hopes and desires reflected in the orders and code status written by the treating providers? Is there documentation indicating negotiation between family and providers? Is there evidence of a degree of fatalism versus an active desire to control events into the future? Does the patient have an advance directive? Are there documented prior discussions between patient and provider of a medical plan of care? Are there documented information-sharing discussions among family members and healthcare providers at crucial crossroads during the patient's care?
- Issues of age, generation, gender, culture, and power both within the patient's family and

with the healthcare team. For example, in some cultures, the wife does not make any decisions. In others, the children depend on their parents to make decisions for them. In still other cultures, the healthcare provider makes all the medical decisions for the patient, and the patient would not think of asking questions or challenging the treating provider's medical treatment decisions. Also, some nurses may believe they are servants to the physician or provider and thus do not share assessments or insights into their patient's values, wishes, preferences, and beliefs. Therefore, the LNC should always consider the nurse-provider relationship.

■ The political and historical context, refugee status, past discrimination, poverty, and lack of access to care. If patients have never experienced optimal care due to lack of community, religious, familial, financial, or insurance resources, they may have few expectations and may not feel empowered or knowledgeable as to how or what to ask for on their own behalf.

To aid the complex effort of interpreting the relevance of cultural and religious dimensions of a case, LNCs should make use of available resources and experts, including community or religious leaders, family members, and language translators. The LNC should look for evidence that these issues were considered, because what appears to be patient non-compliance may not be if this information was overlooked or not addressed in the patient record.

The merit of a case may change if the patient does not have a clear understanding of the facts due to cultural or language barriers or if the patient has religious objections that were not considered. The patient's motivation for making treatment choices is important and should be confirmed. The LNC should look for evidence as to the steps the healthcare team took in deciding whether and how personal religious and cultural beliefs affected a patient's medical treatment choices. This is yet another key to determining whether a patient's autonomous, informed medical treatment decision is respected.

Evidence of the healthcare team's efforts to understand the context in which a patient made treatment decisions should be reflected in the documentation in the patient's medical record. How did the patient describe the reasons for seeking medical treatment? Where did these discussions take place? Who was present during the discussions? Who provided patient education regarding diagnosis and treatment recommendations? Was the education provided in a language and format the patient understood? Was there documentation of the patient's understanding? Were resources consulted to understand the patient's religion and culture? Was any effort made to understand the patient's community and its values, which may have influenced the patient's behavior?

If these factors are considered, then evidence of such discussions should begin the minute the patient seeks medical attention, throughout treatment, and until and beyond discharge from care. The LNC should look for a team approach to the holistic care received by the patient, no matter how extensive the team (i.e., whether a two-person provider and nurse team or a full team of social workers, therapists, chaplains, nurses, providers, and specialists). Is there documentation of multidisciplinary team meetings? What is the routine or policy for addressing these issues within the institution? And most importantly, how was the patient included in these discussions?

This is important since medical treatment decisions should reflect the patient's values, wishes, and desires. If a surrogate made the medical decision, the decision should reflect the patient's values and desires. Evidence of whether these issues were addressed appropriately may change the outcome or merit of the case.

Important Legal Documents

Advance Directives

Making medical treatment decisions known ahead of time provides patients with the assurance their wishes will be honored and offers their providers a clear guide to follow. Failure to make one's medical treatment wishes known beforehand is paramount to choosing to have others make those decisions on one's behalf. Unless patients share their end-of-life care preferences, their family and healthcare providers must substitute their judgment, making it possible the patients will receive medical care they would not necessarily want for themselves.

Patients have the right to make decisions about receiving health care that reflects their values, preferences, and wishes. To support this right, federal law requires patients be told of their right to complete an advance directive (AD). Advance directives are written statements prepared by patients that define their medical decisions if they are later unable to make them for themselves. If they choose not to complete an AD, it is important they understand they will still receive care. Many hospitals have personnel that assist patients in filling out these forms.

Advance directives are written instructions about a patient's future medical care. They go into effect when the patient is no longer able to make decisions. Advance directives allow patients to decide ahead of time what medical procedures they do or do not want to receive. This usually involves decisions about breathing machines, cardiopulmonary resuscitation (CPR), the receipt of nutrients and water if unable to take them by mouth, and the administration of certain medicines such as antibiotics. Also, the AD helps the family make decisions based upon the patient's wishes and ensures theses wishes are followed if different from the family's wishes. There are two types of advance directives: a living will (LW) and a Durable Power of Attorney for Health Care (DPAHC).

Living Will

A living will, also known as a healthcare treatment directive, is a legal document which states the patient's desires about withholding or withdrawing treatment in the event the patient has a condition that cannot be cured and is not expected to live for more than a few months. Living wills direct caregivers when the patient is not able to make healthcare decisions known. It is called a "living will" because it must be signed formally like a regular will, but its terms take effect before death.

A living will may:

■ Spell out the measures the patient does and does not wish to have taken to extend life when death is imminent
■ State whether the patient wants breathing machines, feeding tubes, oxygen, intravenous fluids, or other medicines to be used and
■ List specific conditions (e.g., coma, fatal illness with no hope of recovery or cure, end-stage dementia) under which the terms of the living will are to go into effect

For a living will to be legal, the patient must be competent, and the document must be witnessed. All adults are presumed competent unless a judge has declared them incompetent. Requirements vary from state to state, but usually the witnesses must not be the patient's relative, creditor, heir, or healthcare provider.

A person should prepare a living will when healthy and not wait until illness or hospitalization. It is important to note living wills only cover decisions about a patient's health care in cases of terminal illness and when death is imminent. Some illnesses, such as stroke, may not be covered by a living will. While most states have laws that recognize ADs, some do not recognize ADs as binding, and some do not recognize living wills drafted in other states. Consequently, it is necessary to check the laws of the state where the AD was completed and executed. Given the limitations inherent in a living will, patients should have another AD in place so their wishes are respected.

Durable Power of Attorney for Health Care

A Durable Power of Attorney for Health Care appoints a family member or friend to follow the patient's wishes only in the event the patient is unable to make medical treatment decisions. The DPAHC, also known as the healthcare proxy, is the agent or surrogate decision-maker who will make medical decisions for the patient who is unable to make them. The decisions should reflect the patient's own values, preferences, and wishes and not the treatments the agent wants for the patient.

The DPAHC is different from a LW in that a LW only goes into effect if the patient is dying. A DPAHC goes into effect any time the patient cannot make medical treatment decisions, whether temporarily or permanently. If the patient suffers from a temporary condition, the patient will resume decision-making when it is determined the patient has the capacity and competency to make decisions.

Some people prefer the DPAHC to a living will, because it is more adaptable. The patient must be competent at the time the DPAHC is signed for it to be legally valid. Sometimes, due to a medical or mental condition, a person can be confused about time and place but still able to understand choices if carefully explained. Healthcare providers and mental health specialists can assess the patient's ability to make decisions. If the patient demonstrates an ability to understand the questions asked; the medical decision to be made; the risks, benefits, and burdens of that decision; the available alternatives and their respective risks, benefits, and burdens; then the person is said to have decision-making capacity (DMC) and those autonomous, informed decisions should be respected. Decision-making capacity is different from legal competency, which is established in a court of law.

A court must decide if the person is legally competent. Legal competence is based on whether the person has a condition that affects mental capacity such as a mental illness or dementia, is able to make or communicate decisions, and is able to manage money or make healthcare decisions. The patient is legally competent if the patient is making an informed decision and understands the consequences of that decision. In addition to DMC and legal competency, it is required the patient be at least 18 years old (minors are discussed later in this chapter). If a person is legally incompetent, the court may appoint a legal guardian. Guardianship may cover all areas of someone's life, or it may cover only certain areas. For example, an older person may be able to make decisions about health care but not finances.

Consider the case in which a patient has a progressive medical condition (such as Parkinson's disease). The patient may wish to draw up the DPAHC papers early in the illness. The agent's duty is to follow the patient's wishes, so it is most helpful if the patient discusses treatment wishes while still able to do so. In states that recognize such documents, families and healthcare providers cannot override a patient's living will or the agent's decision. If it is unclear as to the patient's decision-making capacity at the time the LW or DPAHC was completed, the court should determine competency. If the patient is not competent to express wishes or make medical treatment decisions, the court should appoint a legal guardian with the authority to make medical decisions in the patient's best interest.

Once a patient has signed a LW or DPAHC, this document(s) should be kept in a safe, easily accessible place. It is a good idea for patients to discuss their wishes with their friends, family members, and especially their doctors and provide them with copies of their LW or DPAHC.

Sample forms for writing AD are available on-line and conform to the laws of each state. Also, the National Hospice and Palliative Care Organization provides copies of state-specific ADs free of charge. A patient's state health department, local hospitals, or state bar association may be able to provide state-specific ADs. Completing an AD does not require an attorney; however, a patient may wish to ask an attorney for assistance in drawing up an AD.

It is also important to note that being a Power of Attorney (POA) and an Executor of an Estate are not the same thing. The authority of a POA dies with the individual. An Executor named in a will may or may not be the same person as the POA. If an individual has a POA but did not name an Executor, the POA can employ an attorney's assistance to become the Executor (called an Administrator in many states).

Do Not Resuscitate

When in a clinic, hospital, or nursing home, a patient or resident may be asked to sign a code status sheet. This tells healthcare personnel what measures the patient wants taken if the patient stops breathing, has a lethal arrhythmia and needs defibrillation, or has asystole. The patient may change the code status at any time.

A full code means the patient wants every effort for revival attempted, including CPR, electrical shock, emergency medications, and ventilation. A limited code may exclude ventilation, dialysis, or other kinds of support. A no code or do not resuscitate (DNR) order may be written.

A DNR order excludes only CPR—an emergency procedure that may save the life of someone whose heart has stopped beating and who is not breathing. A DNR order does not limit other types of treatment; it does not mean do not treat. Patients should still receive other necessary medical and nursing care. If determined in advance the person has a terminal illness or multi-system failure and death is imminent, and if that condition is established and documented by two or more providers, then CPR is no longer an option and is not required or offered as a treatment option if the patient's heart stops. However, each state has different laws, and the LNC should be familiar with the relevant laws when analyzing a case involving such issues.

Failing to respect a patient's AD or DNR by taking actions prohibited by them or failing to take actions directed by them can result in a civil suit against the healthcare provider. Therefore, when reviewing a case involving end-of-life decisions, the LNC should search the medical record for documentation of discussions about the patient's end-of-life wishes and the existence of an AD and code status sheet.

Standards for Substitute Decision-Making—Health Care Surrogate Act

While competent persons make their own informed medical treatment decisions, most state statutes provide that a person who is incompetent or lacks DMC cannot consent to medical treatment. A person may be incompetent due to a variety of reasons and circumstances. For example, the person may be under the state's legal age of consent, unable to understand the treatment decision to be made, or unable to communicate a treatment decision. For whatever reason, if the patient is unable to make informed decisions, the individual cannot consent to medical treatment.

As of 2009, all 50 states enacted statutes (Health Care Surrogate Acts) which create a healthcare surrogate for patients who lack DMC and do not have an AD. The acts designate who can serve as a patient's surrogate, such as spouse, adult child, parent, legal guardian, sibling, close friend, healthcare provider, etc. The surrogate then speaks for the incompetent patient. Surrogate decision-makers look to the law for guidance regarding their authority, the standard on which they base their decisions, and the limits to their authority.

According to each state's Health Care Surrogate Act, without the expressed wishes of the patient, the surrogate must rely on other factors when making healthcare decisions presumptively believed to be what the patient would have made. Some factors a surrogate could consider are the patient's present level of functioning; quality of life; life expectancy; the prognosis for recovery with and without treatment; the various treatment options; the degree of humiliation, dependence, and loss of dignity resulting from the condition and treatment; and the opinions of family members, the reasons behind those opinions, and the motivations of family members.

During case analysis, if a patient's capacity to make healthcare decisions is in question, carefully review the patient's DMC. If DMC is lacking, then identify who is the patient surrogate according to the patient's AD. If the patient did not have an AD, identify who is the legal surrogate decision-maker according to the state's Health Care Surrogate Act. Finally, if the patient has a healthcare surrogate, is there evidence the surrogate made healthcare decisions as the patient would have made?

If, for example, a surrogate makes the decision to continue life support for a patient, is it because the surrogate cannot let go of the patient, or is the surrogate buying more time in anticipation of a miracle? If the latter, is this decision based on the surrogate's beliefs, wishes, preferences, desires, and personal grief, or is there evidence the patient would have made this same decision? The patient's medical record should reflect discussions with the surrogate, including inquiries regarding whose wishes they are considering. This will help to determine if the surrogate is making medical treatment decisions as the patient would have made.

Standards for Minor Patients

In 1976, the American Academy of Pediatrics (AAP) recognized that children should participate in decision-making commensurate with their age. According to the AAP, children should provide assent to care whenever reasonable (AAP Committee on Bioethics, 2016; Guttmacher Institute, 2018). Recognizing the "informed consent" process has limited direct application in pediatrics, i.e., it is limited to parents or guardians who have the legal right and capacity to made decisions on behalf of the child, the AAP provided an updated analysis of the following concepts:

1. Informed consent
2. The ethics of informed consent
3. The right to refuse treatment
4. "Proxy consent"
5. Parental permission and child assent and
6. Informed consent of adolescents

Parents' Rights

The AAP holds that treatment decisions involving the care of all minor children are the shared responsibility of the pediatrician and parents, and such decisions include all the elements of the informed consent process (see Chapter 19). Although the law provides parents with the authority to make informed decisions for their children, there are other laws that protect children from abuse and neglect, making it clear that sometimes parents can breach their obligations toward their children. Therefore, professionals who provide care to minors have the obligation to carefully assess parental decision-making as it relates to the best interests of the child. If, in the case of recommended life-saving treatment, the parents' motives and capability are questioned and all reasonable attempts have been made to educate them about the importance of the treatment, then the healthcare provider has a professional obligation to protect the child and should consider legal steps to override parental wishes or decisions.

Care Choices in the Neonatal Intensive Care Unit

The medical treatment of infants should be based on what is in their best interest. However, because the infant's "best interest" is not always clear, parents and healthcare givers face difficult treatment decisions when confronted with a severely ill, extremely premature, or terminally ill infant. Consequently, parent autonomy, clinical prognosis, the infant's rights, and the meaning of futility and inhumane treatment often stimulate legal battles around treating infants with debilitating birth defects and providing life-prolonging treatment deemed futile by the healthcare provider. Complex conversations between providers and parents are overshadowed by parental emotion and medical uncertainty. Treatment decisions under these conditions are overwhelming and devastating. When reviewing neonatal cases, LNCs need to identify the choices the parents faced, the medical implications of those options, the timing of their education regarding these implications, and whether the method of teaching matched their learning style. All circumstances discussed between healthcare providers (inter-professional team) and parents should be reflected in detail in the documentation (Carter & Rosendrantz, n.d.).

Pediatric Assent for Medical Care

Treatment decisions that involve the health care of older children and adolescents should include, to the greatest extent feasible, the assent of the patient as well as the participation of the parents and the provider. Assent should include at least the following (AAP Committee on Bioethics, 2016):

■ Helping the patient achieve a developmentally appropriate awareness of the nature of the condition
■ Telling the patient about the expectations of tests and treatments
■ Making a clinical assessment of the patient's understanding of the situation and the factors influencing the patient's reasoning (including whether there is inappropriate pressure to accept testing or therapy) and
■ Soliciting an expression of the patient's willingness to accept the proposed care. Of note, the AAP advises that no one should solicit a patient's views without intending to weigh them seriously. In situations in which the patient will have to receive medical care despite objections, the patient should be informed of the facts and should not be deceived.

Examples of situations in which the AAP encourages providers to seek the consent of the parent as well as the assent of the older school-age child include: venipuncture for a diagnostic blood test in a 9-year-old, diagnostic testing for abdominal pain in a 10-year-old, or application of an orthopedic device to manage scoliosis in an 11-year-old. While, in some cases, treatment may proceed over the objection of the patient, providers and parents should understand that overriding the child may undermine their relationship with the child.

If the minor patient refuses to assent or outright refuses treatment, there should be adequate evidence in the medical record of the healthcare provider's efforts to respect the patient's wishes, understand the situation, and address the child's fears or other concerns of the proposed care. Family meetings about these discussions should be recorded in detail. In addition, evidence of social service and chaplain involvement are avenues the healthcare team may explore in an effort to understand and discuss these concerns. Coercion should be a last resort.

Adolescents' Rights

While medical treatment decisions of minor patients should be meticulously explored during case review, other aspects of the care of minors should also be considered, including confidentiality and disclosure. With the exception of life-threatening situations, confidential care of adolescents is essential to overall health, and parental consent or notification should not necessarily be a barrier to receiving medical care or disclosing when minors have accessed treatment. Three specific situations in which minors' access to treatment may be disclosed without parental authorization include handling medical emergencies, reporting child abuse, and communicating among program staff (American College of Obstetricians & Gynecologists, 2018; English & Ford, 2004). Minors deemed "mature" may have decision-making power and control over the disclosure of their medical information.

Emancipated Minors

Emancipation is a legal procedure that frees children from the custody and control of their parents or guardians before the children reach the age of majority. If a minor becomes emancipated, the minor is able to do certain things without parental consent, including consent to medical treatment. There are three ways a minor can become emancipated:

- Get married (this requires parental consent and permission from the court)
- Join the armed forces (this requires parental consent and acceptance by the service) and
- Obtain a declaration of emancipation from a judge. If a minor wants to be declared emancipated by a judge, the minor must convince the judge that ALL of the following requirements are met:
  - The minor is at least 14 years old
  - The minor willingly wants to live separate and apart from the parents, who consent or acquiesce (i.e., the parents do not object to the minor living apart from them)
  - The minor is able to manage finances and
  - The minor has a source of income that does not come from any illegal activity

Sensitive Situations and Issues

Sensitive situations and issues (those in which adolescents may not seek medical attention because of reluctance to inform parents or guardians) include birth control, sexually transmitted diseases, and pregnancy. In addition, minors' access to abortion and contraception as well as substance abuse and mental health treatment without parental involvement is often regulated separately by widely variable state laws. Finally, the AAP believes that, in most cases, providers have an ethical and legal obligation to obtain parental permission for recommended medical interventions. In many circumstances, providers should also solicit patient assent when developmentally appropriate. In cases involving emancipated or mature minors with adequate decision-making capacity, or when otherwise permitted by law, providers should seek informed consent directly from adolescent patients (Duffy, 2016; Legal Information Institute, n.d.).

The Right to Refuse

Patients have the right to refuse recommended medical treatment. The aforementioned evolution of the Patient's Bill of Rights to *The Patient Care Partnership: Understanding Expectations, Rights and Responsibilities* reflects a major shift in the concept of who is the healthcare plan decision-maker. Whereas the provider was once the decision-maker, with little question of authority, the patient is now the primary healthcare decision-maker. In making one's own healthcare decisions, there are certain rights and responsibilities that pertain to the patient, healthcare provider, and institution. The patient has the right, and is encouraged, to obtain current and understandable information concerning diagnosis, treatment, and prognosis from the providers and other direct caregivers. Except in emergencies when the patient lacks decision-making capacity and the need for treatment is urgent, the patient is entitled to the opportunity to request and discuss information related to the recommended procedures and treatments, the risks involved, the length of recuperation, and the alternative medical options along with their accompanying risks and benefits (American Hospital Association, 1992; Selde, 2015).

Emergency Medical Treatment and Active Labor Act

The Emergency Medical Treatment and Active Labor Act (EMTALA) was signed into federal law by President Reagan in 1986 as part of a larger body of legislation, the Consolidated Omnibus Budget Reconciliation Act. The EMTALA incorporates regulations adopted by the Centers for Medicare & Medicaid Services (CMS), a division of the Department of Health and Human Services, to regulate the delivery of necessary emergency services (CMS, 2012).

The essential provisions of the law are as follows: Any patient who comes to the emergency department (ED) requesting examination or treatment for a medical condition must be provided with an appropriate medical screening examination to determine if the individual is suffering from an emergency medical condition. Once the patient presents to the emergency department, the facility is obligated to either provide the patient with treatment until stable or to transfer the patient to another hospital in conformance with the statute's directives (Zuabi, Weiss, & Langdorf, 2016).

The EMTALA applies only to hospitals that satisfy two criteria: (1) it receives Medicare funds, and (2) it provides emergency treatment services. It does not matter whether a hospital operates a formal ED or not. As long as the hospital provides services to treat emergency conditions, it will be subject to EMTALA and must comply with certain statutory and regulatory requirements. Furthermore, providers who practice within that hospital are also subject to specific obligations.

Since signed into law, there have been many updates to clarify portions of the original law. For example, CMS clarified the concept of "parking" to be when Emergency Medical Services

(EMS) personnel bring a patient to the ED, and EMS remain in attendance of the patient rather than the ED personnel assuming care. Parking is considered a violation under EMTALA (Assid, 2007).

Other issues, such as emergency preparedness and the need for clarifications of ambiguities and interpretation by the CMS, will compel EMTALA to evolve. For healthcare institutions that meet the criteria, education on these changes must be ongoing. What the facility does to comply and stay current with the evolution of EMTALA are areas to scrutinize during an investigation. A facility must show it provides updates on EMTALA and makes compliance efforts on a proactive and continuing basis.

The LNC should stay current on the law and, in cases that may involve an EMTALA violation, request the facility's EMTALA policies and procedures. Moreover, the facility's risk manager must update and revise these policies and procedures and review compliance in the healthcare facility to stay current with EMTALA. For more information on EMTALA, see www.emtala.com/faq.html.

Summary

It is a patient's right to make choices about accepting or refusing medical care. There are, however, life circumstances that could deprive the patient of that right unless the patient plans in advance for medical treatment under those circumstances. Without an advance directive in place, the providers and family must guess what kind of medical care the patient would have wanted. Patients can maintain their right to accept or refuse treatment if they have provided a written statement of their wishes in an AD.

Pediatric and adolescent patients also have the right to participate, as appropriate, in their care and the decision-making process. Providers should engage in age-appropriate discussions with these patients to attain assent and, when appropriate, consent.

Legal nurse consultants reviewing a case involving medical treatment decisions should look for evidence of when and how these decisions were made, the patient's role in the discussions, and the patient's understanding of the treatment recommendations. The ethical behavior of the medical professionals involved will help determine if the patient had the opportunity to make informed, individualized, and personal medical treatment decisions. Because of their clinical experience, LNCs are adept at identifying and understanding evidence of the ethical practices defining the patient's medical decision-making process, which can assist in supporting or challenging the validity of the case.

References

American Academy of Pediatrics Committee on Bioethics. (2016). Informed consent in decision-making in pediatric practice. *Pediatrics, 138*(2). Retrieved from http://pediatrics.aappublications.org/content/pediatrics/138/2/e20161484.full.pdf DOI: 10.1542/peds.2016-1484.

American College of Obstetricians & Gynecologists. (2018). Committee opinion: Adolescent confidentiality and electronic medical records. Retrieved from www.acog.org/Clinical-Guidance-and-Publications/Committee-Opinions/Committee-on-Adolescent-Health-Care/Adolescent-Confidentiality-and-Electronic-Health-Records.

American Hospital Association. (1992). A patient's bill of rights. Chicago, IL, catalog no. 157759. Retrieved from www.americanpatient.org/aha-patient-s-bill-of-rights.html.

American Hospital Association. (2003). The Patient Care Partnership: Understanding expectations, rights and responsibilities. Retrieved from www.aha.org/system/files/2018-01/aha-patient-care-partnership.pdf.

Assid, P. A. (2007). Emergency medical treatment and active labor act: What you need to know. *Journal of Emergency Nursing, 33*(4), 324–326.

Carter, B. S., & Rosendrantz, T. (n.d.). Ethical issues in neonatal care. Retrieved from https://emedicine.medscape.com/article/978997-overview#a1.

Centers for Medicare & Medicaid Services. (2012). Emergency Medical Treatment & Labor Act. Retrieved from www.cms.gov/Regulations-and-Guidance/Legislation/EMTALA/index.html.

DeWolf, B., & Sue, M. (2007). When respecting patient autonomy may not be in the patient's interest. *JONA's Health Care Law, Ethics, and Regulation, 9*(2), 46–49.

Duffy, S. (2016). Providing confidential care to adolescents in healthcare settings. *Rhode Island Medical Journal, 99*(8), 16–18.

English, A., & Ford, C. (2004). The HIPAA privacy rule and adolescents: Legal questions and clinical challenges. Retrieved from www.guttmacher.org/journals/psrh/2004/hipaa-privacy-rule-and-adolescents-legal-questions-and-clinical-challenges.

Guttmacher Institute. (2018). An overview of minors' consent law. Retrieved from www.guttmacher.org/print/state-policy/explore/overview-minors-consent-law.

Legal Information Institute. (n.d.). Condition of participation: Patient Rights, 42 CFR 482.13(b)(2).

Selde, W. (2015). Know when and how your patient can legally refuse care. *Journal of Emergency Medical Services, 40*(3). Retrieved from www.jems.com/articles/print/volume-40/issue-3/features/know-when-and-how-your-patient-can-legal.html.

Zuabi, N., Weiss, L. D., & Langdorf, M. I. (2016). Emergency Medical Treatment and Labor Act (EMTALA) 2002–15: Review of Office of Inspector General patient dumping settlements. *Western Journal of Emergency Medicine, 17*(3), 245–251. http://doi.org/10.5811/westjem.2016.3.29705.

Additional Reading

Hsuan, C., Horwitz, J. R., Ponce, N. A., Hsia, R. Y., & Needleman, J. (2018). Complying with the Emergency Medical Treatment and Labor Act (EMTALA): Challenges and solutions. *Journal of Healthcare Risk Management, 37*(3), 31–41. DOI 10.1002/jhrm.21288. Retrieved from www.ncbi.nlm.nih.gov/pubmed/29116661.

Test Questions

1. What constitutes informed consent to a recommended treatment?
   A. The patient allows the surgery
   B. The patient allows the surgery after being informed of its risks, burdens, and benefits as well as the alternative treatments and each of their risks, burdens, and benefits
   C. The patient nods yes when asked if consenting to the medical treatment
   D. The patient has a life-threatening emergency and immediate care must be given
2. If a patient makes a medical decision deemed to be a poor choice by the provider, should that decision be respected?
   A. Yes, it is the patient's choice
   B. No, the healthcare team is in a better position to make the medical choices
   C. Yes, if this is an informed decision with an understanding of it consequences, and it is confirmed the patient has decision-making capacity
   D. Yes, if the patient has a psychological diagnosis
3. A legal document that states the patient's desires about withholding or withdrawing treatment in the event the patient has a condition that cannot be cured and is not expected to live for more than a few months is a:
   A. Durable Power of Attorney for Health Care
   B. Living Will
   C. Do Not Resuscitate Order
   D. Substitute Decision-Making Will
4. One situation in which the healthcare provider should seek assent from an adolescent patient is:
   A. Organ donation
   B. Vaccination
   C. Blood transfusion
   D. All of the above
5. What is a hospital's obligation to patients when it is operating under the provisions of EMTALA?
   A. To immediately transfer a patient to a facility with the best medical care specific to treating the particular condition
   B. To stabilize a patient before considering patient transfer
   C. To treat all patients despite their ability to pay medical bills
   D. To give each patient a medical screening exam if the facility provides emergency care and stabilize the patient if necessary before transferring

Answers: 1. B, 2. C, 3. B, 4. D, 5. D

The Employee Retirement Income Security Act and Health Maintenance Organization Litigation

Diane Trace Warlick, RN, JD

Contents

Objectives

■ Discuss different types of managed care products
■ Define terms related to the Employee Retirement Income Security Act (ERISA), health maintenance organizations (HMOs), health insurance coverage, and litigation issues involving these topics
■ Identify how the ERISA has affected HMO litigation cases in the past and how legislative changes will impact future cases
■ Assist in the development of cases involving HMOs covered under the ERISA

Introduction

Evolution of Managed Care

Managed care is an approach to healthcare delivery that seeks to control medical costs through collaboration and coordination of services, ideally to provide the highest quality of medical care at the lowest possible price. It emerged in the early 1980s in response to escalating healthcare costs, fueled in part by the enactment of Medicare and Medicaid in 1965.[1]

Medicare and Medicaid are single-payer government-funded healthcare insurance programs for the elderly, disabled, and poor. They provide coverage for inpatient hospital charges [Part A] and specified medical costs [Part B], which include medically necessary physician services and outpatient medical and diagnostic fees.[2] These programs were not intended to [and do not] "manage care" per se; however, Medicare and Medicaid regulations have a considerable impact on our healthcare system, primarily by serving as the payment source for a large, previously uninsured segment of the population.

Beginning with enactment in 1965, the Medicare/Medicaid Program paid the "reasonable and customary" fees for hospital services and services performed by individual healthcare providers under Medicare Part B. Physicians were authorized to "balance bill"[3] patients for fees not otherwise covered under the Program. These financing mechanisms led to escalating healthcare costs as they fully subsidized rapidly increasing costs of physician and ancillary medical services. As a consequence, Congress enacted a series of limitations on the amount providers could be paid by the Government, for example, by setting restrictions on annual physician fee increases [1975], and statutorily limiting the annual percentage fees could lawfully increase [1984–1991].[4]

Congressional action and DHHS[5] regulations now govern many aspects of healthcare services from minimum standards of care, eligibility for services, allowable charges, and payment systems. They affect not only federal healthcare programs, but also private health systems through mandatory compliance with Medicare and Medicaid regulations.[6] Any physician or hospital system providing services to Medicare or Medicaid beneficiaries is required to implement and enforce federal standards called Conditions of Participation.[7]

In 1993 healthcare expenditures accounted for about 13.4% of the gross domestic product (GDP); this had risen to 15.3% by 2003 (Smith, Cowan, Sensenig, Catlin, & the Health Accounts Team, 2005), and reached 17.5% GDP in 2014.[8] By the end of the fiscal year 2016, total federal healthcare spending on all programs reached $3.4 trillion, 17.9% GDP. As cost continued to escalate, government authorities and insurance companies sought alternative ways to provide and pay for health care.[9] In part, the unrestrained costs led to the emergence of managed care.[10]

Managed care operates on three basic principles: (1) oversight of medical care given (utilization review); (2) contracts with care providers and organizations; and (3) benefits furnished in accordance with the employer's health plan terms, which can vary from employer to employer or even member to member. Millions of Americans are now covered by managed care health plans, primarily health maintenance organizations (HMOs), and preferred provider organizations (PPOs). Other forms of managed care include point of service providers (POSs), exclusive provider organizations (EPOs), and hybrid consumer-directed health plans (CDHPs). Recently, the focus has shifted in the industry to rewarding physicians for high levels of patient satisfaction and quality service, as health care has moved to the evidence-based practice (EBP) model.

Overview of HMOs

The Social Security amendments of 1972 (Public Law 92-603), the first major adjustment to Medicare, actively encouraged enrollment in HMOs and granted the Social Security Administration authority to conduct managed care demonstration programs.[11] In the early 1980s, federal healthcare programs and insurance companies adopted the HMO healthcare model, as a means of controlling rising healthcare costs.

HMOs provide employers with an affordable means of providing healthcare coverage to their employees. Some HMOs, known as the "staff model," directly employ physicians and ancillary healthcare providers for the sole purpose of providing care to their members. The "group model" HMO involves contracts with physicians in a group or professional association or a professional corporation. The health plan pays the group, and the group manages compensation of the individual provider group members (arranging contracts with hospitals and other healthcare providers, such as home health agencies and durable medical equipment [DME] companies) who provide these services to the patients assigned to the group.

As the managed care industry has developed, strategies for cost containment associated with this model of healthcare delivery continue to evolve. Although implemented as cost containment measures, criterion such as utilization review and management[12] came to be viewed by consumers as a method for denying care. Likewise, guidelines, "critical pathways," and mandatory conditions of participation for treatment of more common disease processes have come under suspicion as simply a mechanism for withholding treatment. Provisions creating financial incentives legitimized restrictions on "overuse" of common tests and diagnostic procedures under the banner of healthcare reform. Incentives also restricted referrals to specialists by primary healthcare providers; many patients viewed this as a denial of care.

Frustration with these aspects of managed care has gradually led to a transition away from the strict HMO form of healthcare delivery. The predominance of HMO coverage versus PPO plans versus POS plans has been shifting as a result of legislative, regulatory, and market changes. PPOs more than doubled the amount of subscribers versus HMO plans in the last 10 years (Kaiser Family Foundation & Health Research and Educational Trust, 2007). In 2004, 39% of Americans were enrolled in managed care organizations, 25% of them in managed care HMOs, and 55% in PPOs. As shown by the Kaiser Foundation Annual Employer Health Benefits Survey, by the end of 2015, HMO enrollments had dropped to 19% of the market versus 58% participation in PPOs (Distribution of Health Plan Enrollment for Covered Workers, by Plan Type, 1988–2006).

Overview of the Employee Retirement Income Security Act

Congress adopted the "Employee Retirement Income Security Act" (ERISA), in 1974. It began as a way to ensure that employees of companies providing retirement and pension plans receive their promised benefits. The U.S Department of Labor, Pension and Welfare Benefits Administration and the Internal Revenue Service jointly administer Title 1 of ERISA (U.S. Department of Labor, 2008).

Title 1 establishes minimum standards and creates a framework for administration of voluntary employee benefit plans. Employee benefit plans may be established and offered by an employer, an employee organization (such as some types of unions), or a combination of both. Different types of employee benefit plans include pension plans (defined benefit and defined contribution) and "welfare" plans such as health, disability, and life. ERISA governs most private-sector employee benefit plans but does not apply to plans created or maintained by government bodies, churches, and benefit plans, maintained for the sole purpose of complying with workers' compensation, disability, and unemployment laws. In addition, ERISA does not apply to benefit plans that are maintained outside the continental United States. Health Maintenance Organizations ("HMOs"), and Preferred Provider Organizations ("PPOs") are types of managed care programs that fall under the ERISA umbrella, and are required to meet statutory requirements.

ERISA was enacted to ensure that employee benefit plans are established and maintained in a financially sound manner. It created minimum standards for employee benefits in accordance with the ERISA fiduciary rules guidelines.

These guidelines include the following:

■ The plans are provided for the exclusive benefit of plan participants (employees) and their dependents/beneficiaries
■ The plan fiduciaries discharge their duties in "a prudent manner," while avoiding transactions that appear to be a conflict of interest
■ The plan fiduciaries comply with limitations in employer investments in securities and property
■ The plan funds benefits according to legal requirements and plan rules
■ The plan discloses information on benefits, management, and the financial condition of the plan to the appropriate government entities and plan participants (e.g., financial reports and summary plan descriptions [SPDs])
■ The plan provides documents required by government regulations to validate compliance with ERISA guidelines (Employee Retirement Income Security Act, 1974)[13]

ERISA guidelines also limit the legal remedies available to healthcare consumers. It restricts recoveries in litigation to (1) the amount equal to the denied benefit, (2) authorization to utilize the benefit, or (3) obtaining the requested medical care (when it was not originally a covered benefit).[14] Claimants cannot recover compensatory or punitive damages under the ERISA, but a plaintiff may recover attorneys' fees where the administrator of a plan is found to have made a denial in bad faith, or to have breached a duty to the plan participant. In 1985 the Supreme Court held that Congress crafted ERISA to be a self-contained legislative scheme, including an integrated system of procedures for enforcement, with which the "Court should not tamper."[15]

ERISA Pre-emption

The managed care industry became concerned very quickly that it would never be able to get a fair hearing in medical malpractice and negligence lawsuits as a result of a commonly held belief that HMOs provide substandard care (Blakely, 1998). The rapid growth of for-profit managed care plans, and their cost control efforts, generated a widely held perception that insurers and plan administrators were more interested in saving money than improving the availability and quality of health care. Consumers quickly realized that managed care decreased the time physicians spent with their patients and made it harder to see medical specialists, yet it did not produce significant healthcare savings.[16] However, in the 1980s the for-profit managed care industry did subdue, for a time, the medical cost inflation by reducing unnecessary hospitalizations, redirecting care to outpatient management wherever possible, and implementing other strategies to increase efficiency.

Although ERISA permits patients to sue for reimbursement of the costs associated with wrongfully denied benefits, ERISA does not permit the award of damages for any injuries resulting from alleged negligence or malpractice of an individual provider or the managed care company. These perceptions created a discernible "backlash" against the managed care industry.

ERISA expressly immunizes employer-sponsored HMOs from state law causes of action traditionally regulated by the states, for physical or mental harms. Section 514(a) of ERISA declares that ERISA "supersedes any and all state laws" insofar as they "relate to" any employee benefit plan. "State laws" includes "all laws, decisions, rules, regulations, or other state actions having the effect of law, of any state." Considerable litigation has since focused on the meaning of the words, "relate to," specifically with respect to allegations of malpractice and negligence.[17] The courts have consistently applied this doctrine to claims arising under HMOs, and other managed care providers. As a result, ERISA precludes state medical malpractice and negligence actions against managed care entities and their employees that involve care provided through an ERISA-governed plan. Claimants challenging care administered through an HMO are limited to recovery of benefits payable under the terms of the plan 29 U.S.C. § 1132(a)(1)(B)). The impact of ERISA on healthcare plans and insurers continues to evolve through statutory changes and the outcome of ongoing litigation, but clearly, ERISA is no longer a safe harbor for the managed care industry.

In the late 1990s, a number of states enacted laws that attempted to get around the ERISA preclusion of state tort actions for injuries suffered as a result of treatment decisions made by employees of managed health plans. Texas was the first state to enact such legislation in 1997. The Texas Health Care Liability Act (THCLA) authorized enrollees of HMOs and other insurers to sue for damages resulting from the failure of its agents or employees to exercise ordinary care in making healthcare treatment decisions in state courts.[18] In 1998, healthcare providers challenged the restrictions on recovery in the federal district court, which upheld the statute. The district court found that the Act allowed individual suits against HMOs and insurance carriers for negligence (*Corporate Health Ins. Inc. v. Texas Dept. of Ins.*).

Other states quickly followed Texas' lead, enacting similar laws reserving a claimant's right to sue for malpractice in state court actions. Georgia and California passed the "right to sue" legislation in 1999. Washington, Arizona, Maine, and Oklahoma did the same in 2000, followed by West Virginia, New Jersey, and Oklahoma in 2001 (Hellinger, 2005). These laws were intended to address the wrongful denial of patient care, and to create legal remedies in addition to mandating the treatment (which was often too little and too late). The insurance companies quickly challenged the legality of these state laws and in 2004, the Supreme Court struck them down. In *Aetna Health, Inc. v. Davila 542* U.S. 200 (2004) the Supreme Court held that these state causes of action fall within ERISA § 502(a)(1)(B) and are therefore completely pre-empted by ERISA § 502.

Despite the Supreme Court's decision, litigation continues to question "to what extent" ERISA pre-empts medical malpractice claims challenging care administered under an HMO or other managed care plan. Supreme Court Justice Ruth Bader Ginsburg has acknowledged that Congressional legislation "may be the only mechanism available to provide patients with adequate compensation for damages incurred as a result of coverage decisions made by employer-sponsored health plans" (Hellinger, 2005, p. 222). In Texas, as in all other states that challenged the ERISA pre-emption, aggrieved patients are entitled to recover only the benefits payable under terms of their plan or other appropriate equitable relief in the case of a breach of fiduciary duty (see 29 U.S.C. § 1132).

Material Misrepresentation	37%
Personal liability (trustee, director officer)	18%
Remedies	70%
Self Dealing	32%

New causes of action to hold HMOs and other managed care entities liable for errors, inappropriate care and financial mismanagement, actions for negligence and malpractice are not included.

HMO Liability

With the advent of patients' rights, patients' bill of rights, and the focus on results-oriented or evidence-based care, the courts have begun to recognize HMO corporate responsibility for the design and administration of employee benefit plans, and the appropriateness of utilization decisions. Courts have recognized viable causes of action against HMOs, primarily directed at management decisions, fiduciary obligations, and plan eligibility issues. In 2009 a study of the frequency of causes of action identified in cases brought against HMOs were:

ERISA LITIGATION STUDY
Pension Litigation Data, April 2009.[19]

Cause of Action	Percent of Cases Alleging
Adherence to plan documents	75%
Breach of fiduciary duty	100%
Duty to disclose	22%
Failure/duty to monitor	21%
Interference with benefits	65%
Loyalty	62%

Theories of liability, including calling malpractice by another name to get around the state law prohibition, have failed to qualify as/for equitable remedies.

As previously noted, an HMO is a healthcare plan or system, generally operated for profit, that seeks to control medical costs by contracting with a network of providers who also act as gatekeepers. The primary approach is an emphasis on preventive care and early intervention and treatment of illness processes to keep enrollees out of the hospital and reduce the need for specialist care. These preventive services offered, among others, vaccinations for infants and children, influenza and pneumonia vaccination programs for the elderly and at-risk populations, prenatal care and "well baby" visits, smoking cessation programs, and community health fairs. Over time, the HMOs observed that few members availed themselves of these "added-value" benefits. Unfortunately, what became evident was that on average, participants in HMOs experienced illness, injury, and chronic medical conditions as much as the participants in other types of managed care and those covered by traditional indemnity insurance.

Cost Control for the HMO

Monetary compensation for contracted providers may take the form of capitation, a per-member/per-month payment, or a flat fee for contracting with the plan. Other forms of remuneration have included bonuses based on the lack of referrals to specialists, reduced inpatient hospital stays, low pharmacy utilization, and other similar scenarios. Financial rewards were established for physicians with a low utilization of these services, but the physicians were penalized when usage was high. These financial motivators are referred to as "incentives."

In standard HMO models, the money paid to the plan from member premiums is "pooled" after payment of administrative expenses and costs. The pool may then be equally divided among the contracted providers or left in one unit. Any "extra" care that is provided to a member outside of routine office visits, such as an emergency room visit or a referral to and treatment by a specialist, diminishes the value of the pool.

Although the incentives appear to motivate providers to refuse referrals to specialists, deny emergency room treatment, and discharge patients prematurely from hospitals in order to retain their pools, the original impetus to providers was to eliminate any unnecessary or extraneous referrals and services. The intent was to avoid prolonged hospitalizations and unnecessary referrals. For example, a patient presenting to her primary care physician with a sore throat might have been referred to an otolaryngologist for treatment when the patient's physician (who may be a pediatrician or internal medicine physician) was quite capable of treating the condition.

For HMOs to remain competitive in the healthcare marketplace, other sources for the savings HMO models promised their administrators, members, and employers had to be identified. Utilization review and case management looked to be promising solutions to the dilemma. The primary purpose of utilization management is to monitor and control patient usage of unnecessary medical or hospital services.[20] Originally, utilization plans generally authorized or approved only the most necessary procedures, supplies, and days in the hospital. Decisions regarding benefit denial, or non-authorization of medical care, were typically initiated by a nurse employed by the plan to periodically review the patient's records and determine whether the procedure, service, hospital stay, or supply was medically necessary. The preliminary decisions were reviewed by a medical authority, usually a physician or the plan's medical director, and a final disposition would be made. Utilization review has expanded to apply beyond hospitalization and utilization of expensive equipment and supplies, to apply to referrals to specialists, home health care, and customized equipment and supplies. Utilization review continues today, but in a less restrictive manner than before, at least partly as a result of successful litigation regarding denials of benefits. Decisions by HMOs today do not appear to have had the significant adverse impacts on patients as previously anticipated. According to a journal article, "Health maintenance organizations (HMOs) and other managed care plans are a major and growing source of health insurance for the near-elderly" (those aged 55 to 64) in the United States (Xu & Jensen, 2006, p. 521). They generally operate on a "capitation" basis (reimbursement of physicians with a set fee per patient, regardless of services provided), saying it motivates providers to order fewer tests or perform fewer procedures or see the patient less frequently. This poses a question to some physicians whether the capitation method incentivizes HMOs to put the patient's needs last. Research has shown to the contrary, that HMOs do not appear to adversely affect the health of the elderly and near-elderly and may benefit those with chronic health conditions (Xu and Jensen, 2006).

Another cost-control measure, pay-for-performance incentives, are employed by approximately half of U.S. HMOs, but their use depends on health plan type and physician payment arrangements.[21] Recent studies supported by the Agency for Healthcare Research and Quality (HS13992), found that "physicians view some financial incentives as encouraging and others as discouraging services to patients," however "70% of physicians considered that their financial incentives had a neutral effect on the quantity of services provided."[22]

A newer incentive for physicians emerging in recent years is "the high-performance network." Quality indicators are collected from insurance companies, evaluating the past performance of physicians, based on cost per episode of care or measures such as preventive care testing. Insurers then encourage subscribers to choose those physicians who score higher on efficiency and quality. The belief here is that physicians may lose enough patients to colleagues who scored better than them, and they, in turn, would improve their efficiency and quality in order to compete (Ginsburg, 2006).

Example 22.1

The following is an illustration of a prolonged hospital stay scenario:

A patient enters the hospital for surgery. The physician and patient anticipate a hospitalization of six days. The intensity of service/severity of illness criteria utilized by the HMO indicates that the average hospital length of stay for this particular type of surgery, barring any severe complications, is three days, and that is what is "pre-authorized" by the plan. Unless there was a medical reason for the patient to remain in the hospital after the approved three-day stay, the patient would be financially responsible for charges for any additional days. Also, the physician would more than likely be responsible for the "overutilization" of inpatient days and be penalized by the plan.

A joint pool is shared by multiple providers. It creates an incentive for physicians to attempt to influence each other by recommending the authorization of fewer referrals and services, thereby creating a larger balance to share. This concept is known as "risk sharing." One of the benefits of a shared pool applies to doctors in the same group practicing together, or professional organizations or partnerships. This program structure facilitates referral of plan patients, to various specialists within the group practice, thereby controlling extraneous referrals and maintaining the pool money within the group. All these incentives and healthcare delivery models are a type of utilization management.

Case management is a type of utilization management, overseen by a "case manager" usually a nurse or social worker employed by the HMO (or other insurance provider). Case management differs from utilization management in that "utilization management examines how services are being utilized, whether or not the services are effective and how much money it costs to provide the services," while case management "coordinates care and assists the patient to navigate social service systems to attain the highest quality of care."[23]

The role of the case manager is to anticipate the patient's needs and treatment requirements and make cost-effective arrangements for delivery of these services by providers within the HMO network. The case manager should be familiar with clinical pathways, or usual and predictable courses for the treatment of a given condition. Based on the criteria set, medical necessity is determined, and care and services are authorized and delivered in a controlled, closely monitored environment. This model of utilization management falls short of delivering promised savings when the patient's medical condition does not follow the normal course of resolution. In addition, not all HMOs are capable of contracting every type of provider that a patient may potentially require, and in these situations, the case manager must consider out-of-network arrangements while still attempting to provide savings to the plan. To combat escalating costs to the HMO, case management has evolved into "care management."

"Care management" is a hybridized or refined case management system of coordinating the patient's care from a proactive viewpoint. This facilitates more of a partnership between the provider and the patient. The care manager is not only a liaison for the health plan but may also perform patient advocacy and physician/service coordination. This type of case management is usually restricted to specific and often common disease processes and has been found to reduce costs in some patient diagnoses that utilize the largest volume of healthcare services: diabetes, congestive heart failure, and asthma. Case managers have "care maps" they use to guide the care of patients with these chronic conditions. The successful results with these patient populations have encouraged this approach for the treatment of obesity, tobacco addiction, and depression (Mason, Leavitt, & Chaffee, 2007). Additionally, innovative ideas for encouraging wellness participation by subscribers are emerging. "They include, for example, small cash payments for the completion of a health risk assessment, gift cards, gym membership discounts, and reimbursement for weight management programs, such as Weight Watchers" (Draper, Tynan, & Christianson, 2008).[24]

Managed care has "come of age." Benefit denial decisions were initially seen as being arbitrary decisions determined by HMO accountants and financial officers as well as non-medical clerical staff based solely on cost. In reality, most ethical and prudent HMOs leave the medical decision-making authority to the medical staff, which usually includes nurses, social workers, physicians, and a committee of a variety of healthcare workers as a backup system. Medical decisions compare the patient's symptoms and physical condition to a national data set, or utilization guidelines, often referred to as intensity of service/severity of the illness criteria. Two of the more popular sources of this information are InterQual Criteria and Milliman Care Guidelines, which along with other such resources, provide general guidelines for lengths of stay and the appropriate times during the progression of an illness to perform diagnostic tests or decide which ones are needed. Criteria deemed necessary for a patient to be considered appropriate for discharge from care are likewise evaluated.

Decisions independent of these guidelines are required when a patient appears to progress at a rate faster than that outlined in the criteria and treatment ends sooner than expected. On rare occasions, a decision to accelerate treatment ahead of the guidelines standard turns out to be disastrous for both the patient and the plan. Early discharges can result in a relapse of the condition, or unseen complications that might have been evident had the patient remained hospitalized under a watchful clinical eye or undergone more diagnostic studies.

Data published in the *Journal of the American College of Cardiology* reported that compared with other types of health benefit plans, HMOs have historically authorized fewer procedures, but reported longer hospital stays for acute myocardial infarction admissions (Every, Fihn, Maynard, Martin, & Weaver, 1995). This may be due, in part, to the lack of access to the appropriate facilities, providers, or specialists, or diagnostic equipment and procedures within the HMOs network. The proper balance between the cost of purchasing and maintaining equipment versus referring patients to a diagnostic facility may be difficult to strike, given that the enrollee's needs and level of health care does not constitute a static number.

With the advent of the patients' rights movement in 1999, plans turned to compliance and quality programs. One of the more popular "watchdog groups" to review plan activity according to higher industry standards is the National Committee for Quality Assurance (NCQA). This is a not-for-profit organization independent of other insurance organizations and healthcare plans, whose main function is to monitor plans in order to ensure quality of services. "Quality health care can be defined as the extent to which patients get the care they need in a manner that most effectively protects or restores their health. This means having timely access to care, receiving treatment that medical evidence has found to be effective and appropriate preventive care" (NCQA, 2008).

Measuring quality is accomplished through member surveys, strict credentialing guidelines, and monitoring of Health Plan Employer Data and Information Set Data (HEDIS), a "report card" that indicates how a plan is performing compared with its peer group. Quality assurance organizations generally accredit or certify a plan only after a rigorous on-site review of administrative and clinical practice processes and verification of contracting practices. These organizations and others like it are holding the current standard of health plans to a more patient-friendly level. Although meticulous and painstaking to undertake, successful accreditation or certification reviews also serve the plan by increasing its marketability and credibility as a quality health plan.

HMO management has been scrutinized by many courts, state and federal. Each case provides legal guidance on the appropriate administrative policies for the operation of HMOs and other managed care organizations. Court opinions may also shed light on best practices for functioning within the managed care system and establishing profitable inter-relationships. It appears that HMOs may be evolving into more user-friendly, cost-effective answers to the coverage of healthcare benefits, as the courts attempt to balance competing legal and financial interests.

Role of the LNC in HMO Litigation

HMO and managed care litigation do not focus on errors and mistakes that may harm a patient and serve as the basis for malpractice actions. Thus, the LNC's focus, when requested to review records and provide a professional evaluation of the issues presented must shift the focus from patient care issues to more administrative tasks. The key issue is to determine whether or not the client is covered by an ERISA plan. The ERISA status is generally confirmed by the attorney prior to accepting a case or undertaking a medical record review, but the LNC should be familiar with how this is determined.

As a general rule, ERISA applies to any employer-provided health plan provided for employees. ERISA does provide a "safe harbor" for certain insurance coverage offered directly to employees. To fall within the "safe harbor," and be exempt from ERISA coverage, the coverage must satisfy four criteria: (1) premiums must be paid 100% by the employee; (2) coverage must be entirely voluntary; (3) employer can collect and remit premiums but cannot profit; and (4) employer cannot endorse the coverage or the insurance (26 C.F.R. 1.401(k)-3—Safe harbor requirements). Endorsement has a fairly low threshold; for example, simply putting the company name on a policy may be enough to constitute an endorsement.

All ERISA-governed plans must adopt reasonable procedures for the filing and processing of claims (29 C.F.R. § 2560.503-1, Claims Procedure). The plan documents (usually the insurance policy) and SPD (summary plan description) are required to clearly spell out the steps for filing the claim or requesting a review of a benefit denial in terms easily understood by the employees. The claimant must have prior notice of the process and the steps must be strictly followed by both the plan administrator and the claimant.

ERISA requires that a plan provide notice of a denial in writing and clearly delineate the steps to follow to obtain a review of the decision (26 C.F.R. 1.401(k)–3(d)).[25] The claimant must have sufficient time for the claim review process to take place. Time limits for deciding an initial claim and filing an appeal are prescribed by statute/regulations and vary based on the type of claim under review. For example, an urgent care claim must be decided within 72 hours; a pre-service claim must be decided within 15 days, and a post-service claim must be decided within 30 days (29 C.F.R. § 2560.503-1). In other words, the plan administrator may not delay a review for such an extended time that the claimant suffers ill effects simply because of the delay.

Persons involved in the claim process are subject to ERISA's fiduciary provisions. While employers are under the law to establish the benefits structure and administer their own plans, there is an inherent conflict-of-interest in the arrangement. However, the law clearly establishes the manner in which a fiduciary (responsible plan administrator) must conduct business for the exclusive purpose of providing benefits to the plan participants. A fiduciary has a very strict obligation to manage and protect the assets of the plan and act for another's benefit. The law provides that the fiduciary must act solely in the interest of plan participants and their beneficiaries and with the exclusive purpose of providing benefits to them; carrying out their duties prudently; following the plan documents (unless inconsistent with ERISA); diversifying plan investments; and paying only reasonable plan expenses (U.S. Department of Labor, n.d.-b).

The LNC Checklist

The primary objective of the LNC involved in assisting with HMO litigation is to determine whether the HMO delivered the promised healthcare benefits to the claimant. The attorney will most likely have ascertained the nature of the administrative issues associated with the case, such as scope of benefit coverage and the type of benefits selected by the claimant, but it is necessary for the LNC to at least be familiar with some of the legal nuances that distinguish this type of litigation from all others. The following is a checklist of matters the LNC and/or the attorney must investigate and undertake when relevant:

1. Request the certificate of insurance, plan documents, SPD, explanation of benefits, and the actual contract signed by the HMO member when the plan was elected. The LNC will also need to review any policies, procedures, or rules that were relied on in making the claim determination and obtain a copy of the complete claim file. The LNC must be aware of which benefits the plan member selected (known as election of benefits). The elected benefits will control whether a benefit(s) denied was a covered benefit to which the client was entitled. This information should be available either in the contract or as an addendum to the contract. Pharmacy benefit plans, formularies, and durable medical equipment (DME) coverage plans may also be relevant to the legitimacy of a claim.
2. When an exception to the contracted benefit plan has been requested by the HMO member and denied by the plan administrator, it will be necessary to evaluate whether or not the benefit meets industry standards. An industry standard is a benefit routinely provided by comparable HMOs and managed care organizations (MCOs). Information on standards may be gleaned from reviewing benefit plans established by professionally recognized HMOs. They may provide access to sample benefit plans on their website's home

page or make the pertinent parts of their plan available upon request. The Internet is a veritable gold mine of information on nationally accepted standards of care through the managed care association, medical association, and insurance association websites. The Department of Labor also provides very detailed information on ERISA plans.

3. Determine whether or not the SPD information is decisive and clearly understood by the reader. The SPD must clearly inform the plan beneficiaries of the following, among others:

   ■ Name of the plan, plan sponsor, plan administrator and plan coverage year
   ■ Employer tax identification number
   ■ The type of plan, and administration procedures
   ■ Summary of the benefits and detailed description of plan benefits for group health plans
   ■ Plan contributions—amount, when, and by whom
   ■ Claims procedures
   ■ Statement of ERISA rights

The plan must clearly enumerate the medical procedures/services/supplies that are and are not covered. Language that might be used to describe a lack of coverage could be similar to what "is considered experimental and therefore not a covered benefit," or "is not a covered benefit under this plan due to the lack of medical evidence that this is a required procedure." Consider for whom the information is written. For example, if the HMO member only speaks Spanish, the information must be available in Spanish. The plan should also contain language that specifically grants the plan administrator the discretionary right to interpret benefits.

4. When changes occur to the client's plan, the member must be notified in a timely manner, such that the impact of the change can be evaluated in time for the member to decide whether to choose another plan or make other arrangements for coverage. A stipulated timeline is usually established and documented in the plan with language and amendments describing the time limitation. As a general rule, these changes occur and are presented immediately prior to the annual enrollment period.

5. Inquire whether the member has exhausted all administrative remedies required under the terms of the plan. The plan's claim procedures must include at least an initial claim, and a right to appeal, with some plans also providing a second-level appeal.

6. If a member fails to exhaust the plan's claim procedures, the claimant may be foreclosed from filing suit in court. The courts have unanimously held that the claim procedures established under ERISA are mandatory. The LNC and attorney should be aware that the timelines associated with the steps necessary to comply with an appeal process or grievance hearing may be extremely rigid.

7. Determine whether the claim at issue is an "urgent care claim," or one involving emergency-type care. If the claim is an urgent care claim, the plan must render its initial coverage decision within 72 hours and any appeal must also be decided within 72 hours (29 C.F.R. § 2560.503-1(f)(2)(i)). If a participant decides to receive treatment before the plan renders a decision, he or she may be responsible for the charges, depending upon the nature of the emergency.

8. Obtain a copy of the document (notice) outlining a denial and all supporting information. A notice must include a statement of all the criteria (such as InterQual Criteria [InterQual Length of Stay Criteria©, 2008]) or plan provisions that are the basis for the denial. A denial letter must include the specific information cited under ERISA: the reason for

denial, notification to the client on the specific steps to take in order to have the request reviewed, and a list of any information that the member may be able to submit that supports the claim and any appeal.

9. Obtain authoritative sources for the standards of care related to the member's health condition(s) and the benefit requested. In these days of evidence-based practice (EBP), many physicians are following a kind of "care map" for patient care. These can include managed care, nursing and medical standards, and standards for specialty fields that some specialists (physicians and nurses) are held to above and beyond the more common standards of general medical and nursing practice. Ask for a copy of the standards to determine whether they are met in any particular situation. Supporting information can also be obtained from governmental or authoritative agencies such as the Food and Drug Administration (FDA), the National Institutes of Health (NIH), and the Centers for Disease Control.

10. In some cases, the HMO member may never receive a notice of denial or the letter may be vague or deficient in the information required by ERISA. The member must act immediately on learning about the denial and the grounds, whether or not it is in writing. While the absence of written notice usually delays the time limits for filing objections or appealing, the LNC must not take that possibility for granted. The employee or LNC acting on the beneficiary's behalf should take action to protect all rights under the plan.

11. Denial letters, to meet ERISA requirements, must refer to the specific language in the healthcare plan on which the plan administrator is relying for denial of benefits. If there are differences between the language in the SPD, the denial notices the client received, and the actual plan or contract language, the plan will carry the greater weight. It is the plan itself that constitutes the contract. Alternatively, if the SPD appears to be conferring benefits that are not included in the plan, the SPD usually prevails. Assessment skills and knowledge of medical terms and procedures equip the LNC with the ability to notice the subtle differences in the contract language. Attorneys will find the LNC's knowledge base helpful to clarify medical terminology and to review the SPD for appropriate scope of coverage.

12. Gather any and all documents, sources, and information possible to support or refute the member's claim. Information submitted to the plan for the reconsideration of the denial, must provide enough information for the plan administrator to make an informed, well-supported, and well-substantiated decision. This includes procedural errors, conflicting or questionable language in the documents, and "arbitrary or capricious" behavior in the administration of the plan benefits.

13. The opinions of the treating physician are generally allowed significant weight by the court; however, in the *Nord* decision, the U.S. Supreme Court held that the plans are not *required* to give deference to the treating MD's opinion. Still, the value of a face-to-face meeting with the treating physician cannot be overestimated. The LNC has the ability to communicate with the physician in "medical lingo" and can, therefore, bring the most value to the understanding and development of the case.

14. Gathering documentation to pursue a case involving ERISA and HMOs is not that different from the standard record requests as far as the medical record is concerned. The LNC will need to obtain a copy of the SPD, however, and that may require a particular release form. Many resources are available via the Internet with sample forms. Also, medical and legal libraries have books of examples of forms that can be adopted for requesting information from HMOs, physicians, and medical facilities. In addition,

networking with other LNCs and professionals is an extremely valuable source of information and may provide support necessary to fully understand this complex situation.

15. There is a fine line of distinction between the HMO representative suggesting a less expensive alternative versus making a medical decision by denying an intervention (test, procedure, medication). The LNC must determine on which side of the line a decision falls. Denial of a service without reference to alternative resources for intervention in the situation is a clear indication that the decision falls on the side of an unauthorized medical decision and is simply denying care. The distinction between making a medical decision and an administrative decision is a key factor in understanding the issues of the case. An example of medical decision-making by the HMO could be denying the necessary medical treatment or refusing to provide the needed medical devices without posing an alternative. In such a case, it must be determined whether or not the member suffered or will suffer any harm as a result.

Evaluating HMO Liability

In the analysis of a managed care case, preliminary questions must be assessed to determine the remedies potentially available to the client and how to pose them to the attorney. Three fundamental questions must be addressed by the legal team at the outset:

1. Does the case involve significant injuries?
2. Does the case involve an ERISA plan, or is the HMO coverage/insurance coverage provided by a non-ERISA entity or an ERISA-exempt entity? The answer to this question will control the causes of action the client may pursue as well as remedies that may be available.
3. Is the managed care entity an HMO, PPO, traditional indemnity insurance, or point of service contract?

Medical Malpractice

A medical malpractice claim will not be available unless the managed care plan is not subject to the ERISA prohibition. In a non-ERISA situation, the facts must be investigated to identify the existence of a duty, breach of duty, causation, and damages. The LNC should obtain a copy of or have access to authoritative sources or standards of care related to the member's condition and benefit request. These can include managed care standards, and applicable standards of care for nurses and physicians. Ascertain whether the applicable standards were followed. Supporting information can also be obtained from such entities as the FDA and NIH. (See Chapter 4 for more information about the evaluation of medical malpractice cases.)

Significant Injury

The first step in case analysis is to determine whether the client has suffered "significant injuries" because of the managed care plan's actions. Because of the costs and time associated with pursuing any medically related cases are extensive, it is not feasible to pursue every case. Only cases involving serious, long-term injuries or potentially significant long-term consequences resulting from the denial of care can justify the considerable financial expense and substantial time commitment required to pursue or defend the claim. While the LNC should fully explain the medical merits of the case to the attorney, ultimately it is the attorney who must decide whether or not to pursue a claim.

ERISA and HMO Coverage Summary

When ERISA does not apply, a client's claim may be governed by state law and pursued in the state courts. Potential causes of action to consider against an indemnity carrier or PPO company not involving an ERISA plan include breach of contract, medical malpractice, fraud in the inducement, intentional infliction of emotional distress, breach of fiduciary duty, common law negligence, and insurance bad faith. Insurers are held to a fiduciary standard in handling claims potentially covered by the insurance policy (U.S. Department of Labor, n.d.-a). If a claim is denied unjustifiably, the insurer may be liable for punitive damages for bad faith in state court proceedings.

HMOs, on the other hand, are generally not subject to state insurance bad faith laws because they are not considered health insurance carriers. The potential causes of action against an HMO not subject to ERISA include breach of contract, medical malpractice, breach of fiduciary duty, common law negligence, fraud in the inducement, intentional infliction of emotional distress, and state statutory causes of action. They may also include claims for vicarious liability as well as agency theories against the HMO for the actions of its physicians, nurses, and ancillary staff.

As discussed earlier, when a managed care claim *is* subject to ERISA, an enrollee has no right to pursue any cause of action seeking damages for personal injury in state court. The ERISA-plan client's only option would be to pursue the administrative remedies according to the policies and procedures required by the managed care plan. In some situations, the case may begin with an in-house review by the insurance carrier or the HMO for the wrongful denial claims. If the client disagrees with the findings of the in-house review, the client can allege in any subsequent federal court action that the in-house review was arbitrary, capricious, and in violation of the plan requirements. Otherwise, a participant or beneficiary may only bring a civil action for "the recovery benefits due to him under the terms of the plan, enforcement of his rights under the terms of the plan, or to clarify his rights to future benefits under the terms of the plan" (ERISA 502(a)(1)(B)).

In states where the laws hold insurance companies liable for the harm they cause, this should be reviewed on a case-by-case basis, since the area is very gray and is still being argued in court today.

When a client's claim arises from an ERISA-based plan, the potential causes of action against a managed care provider must be analyzed by the attorney and are beyond the scope of the LNC's analysis. It would be appropriate for the LNC to alert the attorney that the managed care plan may be employer provided, and thus invoke ERISA.

Type of Entity

The final question to be determined is whether the managed care entity is an HMO, PPO, traditional insurance, point of service contract, or other such insurance plan. If coverage is provided by an insurance carrier such as a PPO, point of service, or traditional health insurance contract, then the claim is a basic "denial of coverage" dispute. If the managed care plan is an HMO, then other standards will also apply.

Summary

HMOs are generally subject to statutory and regulatory duties. The LNC can assist the attorney by identifying the type of managed care provider at issue. If the managed care provider is an HMO, then the attorney will determine what statutes and regulations apply. The LNC can be an invaluable asset to the legal team when determining potential injuries, long-term effects of the denied benefit, and the ultimate effects on the client's life.

Notes

1. See www.ssa.gov/history/briefhistory3.html.
2. Part B provides insurance coverage for a range of preventive treatments, tests, services, and supplies, including: medically necessary physician services; screenings; ambulance transportation; outpatient hospital care, including some physical or occupational therapy; mental health services; home healthcare services; and durable medical equipment.
3. "Balance billing" permits a healthcare provider to directly bill patients for any difference between the charges covered by insurers, including Medicare, and the actual physician fee. Source: www.healthinsurance.org/glossary/balance-billing/.
4. For a year by year list of Congressional legislation affecting Medicare, see http://kff.org/medicare/timeline/medicare-timeline/.
5. Department of Health and Human Services at www.dhhs.gov.
6. 42 U.S. Code Chapter 7, Subchapter XVIII—Federal Old Age, Survivors and Disability Insurance Benefits, PARTS A–E.
7. Medicare standard of care regulations, called "Conditions of Participation" are set forth in the Code of Federal Regulations, 42 CFR Chapter IV, Subchapter G—Standards and Certifications.
8. See www.cms.gov/Research-Statistics-Data-and-Systems/Statistics-Trends-and-Reports/CMS-Fast-Facts/index.html.
9. See www.cms.gov/Research-Statistics-Data-and-Systems/Statistics-Trends-and-Reports/NationalHealthExpendData/Downloads/DSM-16.pdf. Centers for Medicare & Medicaid Services, Office of the Actuary, National Health Statistics Group.
10. See www.thebalance.com/causes-of-rising-healthcare-costs-4064878. "Between 1993 and 2010, prices rose by an average of 6.4 percent a year. In the early 1990s, health insurance companies tried to control costs by spreading the use of HMOs once again."
11. P.L. 92–603, approved Oct. 30, 1972 (86 Stat. 1329) http://kff.org/medicare/timeline/medicare-timeline/.
12. Process intended to evaluate both prospectively, and in hindsight, the necessity, quality, effectiveness, and efficiency of health care ordered and provided.
13. Title 29 U.S. Code, Chapter 18—Employee Retirement Income Security Program.
14. 29 U.S.C. § 1132.
15. See, *Massachusetts Mutual Life Ins. Co. v. Russell,* 473 U.S. 134, 147 (1985). The Court concluded that ERISA's breach of fiduciary duty provision, § 409(a), 29 U.S. C. 54 § 1109(a), provided no express authority for an award of punitive damages to a beneficiary and declined to find an implied cause of action for punitive damages, noting that "[W]here a statute expressly provides a particular remedy or remedies, a court must be chary of reading others into it."
16. See Blendon et al. (1998). See also The Kaiser Family Foundation and Health Research and Educational Trust (2007).
17. 29. U.S.C. §1144 ERISA § 514(c)(1).
18. Texas Health Care Liability Act, Tex Civ. Prac, & Rem. Code Anno. §§ 88.001-.001 (West Supp. 2000) (*as amended*).
19. www.mcguirewoods.com/news-resources/publications/taxation//taxation/Survey%20of%20ERISA%20Litigation%20Trends.pdff.
20. See Gray and Field (1989).
21. Agency for Health Care Research and Quality, Nov. 2006, https://archive.ahrq.gov/research/nov06/1106RA26.htm; See "Pay for performance in commercial HMOs," by Meredith B. Rosenthal, Ph.D., Bruce E. Landon, M.D., M.B.A., Sharon-Lise T. Normand, Ph.D., and others, in the November 2, 2006, *New England Journal of Medicine,* 355(18), 1895–1902.

22222222

22. Community Tracking Study Physician Survey, of over 12,000 physicians. https://archive.ahrq.gov/research/nov06/1106RA25.htm. More details are in "Effects of compensation methods and physician group structure on physicians' perceived incentives to alter services to patients," by James D. Reschovsky, Ph.D., Jack Hadley, Ph.D., and Bruce E. Landon, M.D., M.B.A., in the August 2006 *HSR: Health Services Research, 41*(4), 1200–1220.
23. Utilization Review, The Role of the Nurse, Brannon, Ann RN, retrieved from www.ehcca.com/presentations/racsummit5/brannan_pc1.pdf.
24. Volume 2, Chapter 7, "The Legal Nurse Consultant as a Case Manager," provides more information on case/care management.
25. See also, 29 U.S. Code § 1021—Duty of disclosure and reporting.

References

29 U.S.C. § 1132(a)(1)(B).
29 U.S.C. § 1132.
29 U.S.C. § 1144.
29 C.F.R. § 2560.503-1.
29 C.F.R. § 2560.503-1(f)(2)(i).
Black & Decker Disability Plan v. Nord, 538 U.S. 822 (2003).
Blakely, S. (1998). The backlash against managed care. *Nation's Business, 86*(7), 16–18, 20, 22–24.
Blendon, R. J., Brodie, M., Benson, J. M., Altman, D. E., Levitt, L. Hoff, T., & Hugick, L. (1998). Understanding the managed care backlash. *Health Affairs, 17*(4), 80–94.
Distribution of Health Plan Enrollment for Covered Workers, by Plan Type, 1988–2017. Exhibit 5.1. Retrieved from kff.org.
Draper, D. A., Tynan, A., & Christianson, J. B. (2008). *Health and wellness: The shift from managing illness to promoting health*. Washington, DC: Center for Studying Health System Change. Retrieved from www.issuelab.org/resources/9592/9592.pdf.
Employee Retirement Income Security Act of 1974. (2008). U.S. Department of Labor. www.dol.gov/dol/topic/health-plans/erisa.htm.
Every, N., Fihn, S. D., Maynard, C., Martin, J. S., & Weaver, W. D. (1995). Resource utilization in treatment of acute MI: Staff model HMO versus fee-for-service hospitals. *Journal of the American College of Cardiology, 26*, 401–406.
ERISA 502(a)(1)(B).
Ginsburg, P. B. (2006). *High-performance health plan networks: Early experiences*. Washington, DC: Center for Studying Health System Change.
Gray, B. H., & Field, M. J. (Eds.) (1989). *Controlling costs and changing patient care? The role of utilization management*. Institute of Medicine (US) Committee on Utilization Management by Third Parties. Washington, DC: National Academies Press. Retrieved from www.ncbi.nlm.nih.gov/books/NBK234995/.
Hellinger, F. J. (2005). Health plan liability and ERISA: The expanding scope of state legislation. *American Journal of Public Health, 95*, 217–223. www.ncbi.nlm.nih.gov/pmc/articles/PMC1449155/.
InterQual Length of Stay Criteria©. (2008). InterQual Products Group, McKesson Corp., San Francisco, CA. Retrieved from www.mckesson.com/en_us/McKesson.com/For%2BPayors/Private%2BSector/InterQual%2BDecision%2BSupport/InterQual%2BDecision%2BSupport%2Bfor%2BPrivate%2BPayors.html).
Kaiser Family Foundation, & Health Research and Educational Trust. (2007). Employer health benefits 2007 annual survey. Health care market place project. Retrieved from www.kff.org/insurance/.
Mason, D., Leavitt, J., & Chaffee, M. (Eds.). (2007). *Policy and politics in nursing and healthcare* (5th ed.). St. Louis, MO: Saunders.
National Committee for Quality Assurance. (2008). *Health plan report card*. Retrieved from www.ncqa.org/tabid/60/Default.aspx.

Smith, C., Cowan, C., Sensenig, A., Catlin, A., & the Health Accounts Team. (2005). Health spending growth slows in 2003. *Health Affairs, 24*, 185–194.

U.S. Department of Labor. (2008, March 9). Employee Benefits Security Administration. Meeting your fiduciary responsibilities. Retrieved from www.dol.gov/ebsa/publications/fiduciaryresponsibility.html.

U.S. Department of Labor. (n.d.-a). Fiduciary responsibilities. Retrieved from www.dol.gov/general/topic/retirement/fiduciaryresp.

U.S. Department of Labor. (n.d.-b). Health plans & benefits: Fiduciary responsibilities. Retrieved from www.dol.gov/general/topic/health-plans/fiduciaryresp.

Xu, X., & Jensen, G. (2006). Health effects of managed care among the near-elderly. *Journal of Aging and Health, 18*, 507–533.

Additional Reading and Resources

Baumberger, C. (1998). Vicarious liability claims against HMOs. *Trial, 34*(5), 30–35.

Bloche, M. G. (2008, August). *How do law & politics shape health systems change?* Washington, DC: Johns Hopkins University Press.

Connette, E. (1998). Challenging insurance coverage denials under ERISA. *Trial, 34*(5), 20–29.

Duffy, S. (2004). 3rd Circuit Boots Theory allowing bad faith ERISA legislation. Incisive Media US Properties. Retrieved from www.law.com/almID/900005540339/?slreturn=20190517233814.

Kongstvedt, P. (1996). *The managed care handbook* (3rd ed.). New York, NY: Aspen Publishers.

Milliman Care Guidelines©, Milliman, Seattle, WA. Retrieved from www.careguidelines.com/.

Websites: The following websites can offer more information on the subject of managed care:

www.hcfa.org.

www.ncqa.org.

www.managedcaremag.com.

www.mcareol.com.

Test Questions

1. ERISA is a law that:
   A. Describes how to perform utilization management
   B. Stipulates that lawsuits involving HMOs are to be argued in the state court
   C. Denies benefits when they are too costly
   D. Governs the administration of certain employee benefits plans
2. ERISA covers:
   A. Individual retirement account (IRA)
   B. State employee pension plan
   C. Corporate defined benefit plan
   D. Coverdell savings account
3. Utilization management is a form of:
   A. Healthcare cost containment
   B. Documenting the use of healthcare services
   C. Healthcare statistics
   D. Keeping a record of what physicians do
4. When a healthcare provider is paid by the health plan to administer healthcare services to a group of members, it is known as:
   A. Capitation
   B. Per member/per month
   C. IS/SI (intensity of service/severity of illness)
   D. Per capita
5. SPD is an acronym for:
   A. Standard pertussis/diphtheria
   B. Summary plan description
   C. Start percutaneous dialysis
   D. Superior portal ductus

Answers: 1. D, 2. C, 3. A, 4. A, 5. B

Other Legal Nurse Consultant Practice Areas

Chapter 22

Risk and Patient Safety for the Legal Nurse Consultant

Bruce Edens, MD
Andree Neddermeyer, RN, MBA, CPHRM, CSSGB

Contents

Objectives

- Articulate principles of patient safety, the relationship to case review, risk management, and LNC activities
- Explain ways healthcare organizations promote "safe culture" and comply with regulatory, and/or accreditation requirements governing patient safety
- Discuss methodologies for case investigation and development
- Identify resources for additional patient safety information and training

Introduction

Risk, its management, and the identification of risk elements, whether from the perspective of mitigation or investigation, is fundamental to the work and role of the legal nurse consultant (LNC). Reduced to its most basic least common denominator, **risk** is harm which creates an unproductive expense or cost to the individual or organization. In some cases, these costs have a real value in budget and operating revenue, in others, the dollar cost is less well defined and subsumed in the economic impact to the business, whether market share decline or loss of reputation or trust. In this chapter, the LNC is introduced to and will become familiar with the many facets of risk faced by an individual or organization in the provision of health care. This includes the management of risk from the prevention/mitigation through investigation of risk issues or events.

Role of the Legal Nurse Consultant

It is the role of the LNC to understand the risks inherent in delivery of healthcare services and provide non-clinical legal professionals or regulatory agencies with necessary knowledge to successfully investigate and litigate, when appropriate, incidents of patient harm or statutory non-compliance. Often a healthcare organization has a risk manager who may function in an advisory or managerial capacity for activities to help avoid, recognize, or mitigate organizational risk. The LNC needs to understand the risk manager role and to engage this individual effectively to glean information about the organization's approach to management of healthcare risk as well as to efficiently comply with requests for information or evidence.

Historical Perspectives on Risk, Error, and Patient Harm

The nature of the human condition includes life, injury, disease, and disability. There will always be undesirable, sometimes catastrophic personal events. Bad outcomes do not equal harm. Harm is an unanticipated bad outcome resulting in physical or mental injury to oneself or others which might not have occurred with a different action, decision process, system process, or failure of a protective process. In the arena of healthcare delivery, the opportunity for patient injury is occasioned when there is an actual failure or series of failures in a process or treatment, perhaps with additional failure of an intended prevention usually in combination with human error and results in patient harm.

The notion that care delivery can cause patient harm is not new. The first recorded literary reference suggesting the existence of preventable patient harm through delivery of medical care occurs in Hippocrates' (c. 460–377 BC) oath with the admonishment to abstain from doing harm (Hasday, 2013). Despite this counsel and the oath's status as part of the oldest and most widely recognized texts of medical ethics, the enormity of healthcare related preventable harm had to wait until its renaissance of interest in the late 20th century when the sheer magnitude of the patient harm and the need for preventive measures became evident to the medical establishment.

Regarding human error, its role in the cause of industrial accidents and disasters came to the forefront of attention after a variety of 20th century calamities affecting nuclear power, aviation, space exploration and the like. During the 1980s, a British psychology professor, James Reason, conducted research related to the causation of errors (Reason, 2000). Reason's studies and insight proved pivotal to understanding human error and how designing reliable processes can help humans make fewer errors. Reason proposed that accidents and harm could be analyzed from the perspective of personal factors such as inattention, negligence, or recklessness and from system considerations related to inadequacy of barriers to nullify effects related to inevitable human fallibility. Addressing the personal approach requires implementation of a just reporting culture. To address the errors attributed to the systems approach, Reason proposed the "Swiss cheese model" (Figure 22.1) with active and latent breakdowns in defensive barriers, the "holes" lining up momentarily to permit an unobstructed trajectory of accident opportunity.

The Concept of Patient Safety Culture

Patient safety is the risk management discipline addressing the prevention, recognition, and mitigation of these potential or actual patient injuries. Prior to 1999, there was little to no recognition of the enormity of medical error and its impact on patient harm. A body of literature and research

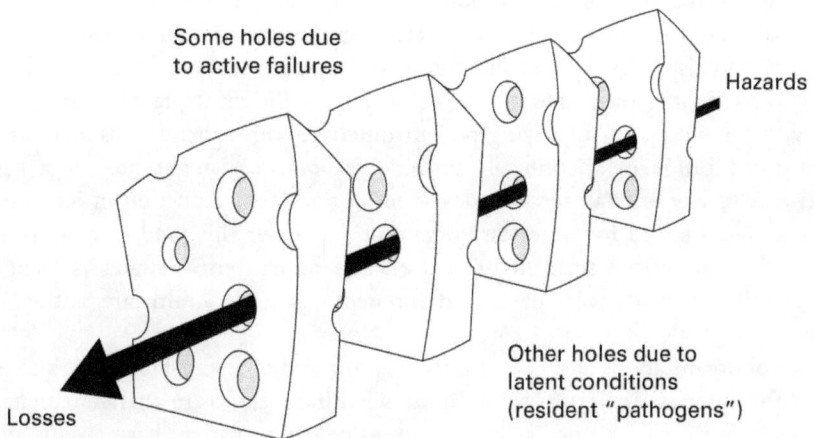

Figure 22.1 Swiss Cheese Model.

Source: Reproduced from BMJ Quality & Safety, Reason JT, Carthey J, de Leval MR, 10:ii21–ii25, © 2001 with permission from BMJ Publishing Group Ltd.

already existed; however, and nonetheless demonstrated the value of using the scientific methods to analyze patient care and improve patient outcomes. As early as 1850, Semmelweis reported that handwashing prevented postpartum infections in women. Around this same time Florence Nightingale published statistical analysis of mortality rates of Crimean War patients, showing that they were more likely to die from hospital infection than their war injuries. Nightingale also demonstrated that interventions to reduce infection caused a dramatic reduction in mortality from a staggering 42.7% to 2.7%, which proved to be lower than the contemporaneous rate at some of the best hospitals in London (Neuhauser, 2003).

In 1999, the Institute of Medicine (IOM) published its seminal article, "To Err Is Human." The information presented was of considerable interest to the public and the news media, who were astounded at the unwarranted cost of human lives and resources (98,000 deaths per year due to medical error). The cost of deaths from these medical errors was estimated to be between 17 billion and 29 billion dollars (Kohn, Corrigan, & Donaldson, 2000). In the same study, fatalities from medication errors (7,000 deaths per annum) were cited to exceed the number of worker deaths (6,000 per annum), so effectively taking your medicine was deadlier than working your job. The public demanded accountability and action presumably to weed out incompetent and dangerous healthcare providers. This public outcry prompted congressional hearings and piqued the interest and attention of government agencies, medical and professional organizations and insurers to validate and understand the situation and look for solutions.

What was originally missed in the article, however, was the assertion that this patient harm for the most part was not caused as much by human error as by the complicated sometimes poorly designed systems used in providing care (Donaldson, 2008). As more investigation and research demonstrated an unacceptably high incidence of patient harm in health care, the need to address and reduce this harm was recognized and ultimately gave rise to the discipline of patient safety. Understanding grew that in health care as in other industries, accidents and harm resulted from the interplay of system failures due to complex, ineffectively designed, and unreliable processes, triggered by poor understanding, judgments, or errors made by the humans involved. Healthcare delivery is complicated and often urgently administered resulting in frequent variances even within small functional areas of the same organization creating opportunities for system failures and consequently harm and risk. Despite best intentions, conscientiousness, dedication, and integrity of healthcare workers, poorly designed barriers to failure are insufficient to prevent harm.

Similarly, prior success in improving patient outcomes through rigorous analysis prompted the hope that institution of scientifically proven best practices might provide a pathway for improvement. A variety of strategies first developed for accident reduction in industrial settings were proposed and adapted for healthcare organizations. Over time and in concert with background research in industrial accident prevention and human error, strategies using the same industrial scientific methods were developed for deployment in healthcare settings to reduce patient harm.

A number of organizations and institutions for promoting patient safety were also established as a result of this interest. Their goal being to use scientific methods to analyze patient harm and to develop scientifically based action plans to prevent or reduce patient harm events and to share best practices widely so all patients in all healthcare settings could benefit. Over 20 years has passed since the publication and the data included in the IOM publication is still referenced in work to help move the needle towards a more reliable safety culture in health care.

The implementation of a robust comprehensive reporting system needed for data collection is a key component necessary to capture, assess, and rectify these system failures to reduce harm. Healthcare workers are still held accountable for their actions, but primary focus of remediation efforts was redirected to the cause(s) of broken systems. Regarding process and outcomes improvement, healthcare organizations again adapted industry inspired techniques like Lean Six Sigma, training many of their quality managers in the strategy using current healthcare issues as their training projects. Regulatory and accrediting organizations also were swept up in this movement as they implemented requirements and standards embracing the patient safety culture.

Risk Exposure in the Delivery of Medical Care

There needs to be awareness and acceptance that plans for management of healthcare specific risks and patient safety need to be part of the global enterprise business plan, not just an overlay. Typically, this is accomplished through integration of patient safety principles and practice into business strategic planning and results in a written, organizationally approved risk management plan which integrates with the business plan, mission, goals, and vision of an organization. Risk Management Plans are foundation documents that define how risks associated with the healthcare organization will be identified, analyzed, mitigated, and managed through the lifecycle of the plan. The plan provides templates or practices for capturing data and prioritizing risks by the Risk Manager or Risk Management Team. The Risk Management Plan is usually approved at the level of Board of Directors, or its designee.

Risk is inherent in the provision of health care in the usual ways that affect any business enterprise. Typical business enterprise risks are summarized in Table 22.1. These include risks

Table 22.1 Enterprise Risks

Risk	Example of Mitigation Strategy
Enterprise Liability	■ Insurance
Customer Service	■ Policy, Training, Satisfaction surveys
Enterprise Integrity and Regulatory Compliance	■ Compliance Training
Contract Management, Oversight, and Fulfillment	■ Errors and Omissions Liability
Regulatory and Licensing	■ Engagement ■ Transparency
Workplace Safety and Worker Safety	■ Safe Newsletter and Training
Security and Background Checks	■ Bonding ■ Identification Badges ■ Compliance Training
Technology	■ Environmental Monitoring ■ Data Encryption ■ Data Usage
Employment Practices	■ Sexual Harassment Training ■ Discrimination Training
Market Strategy and Financial	■ Advertising ■ Alignment Goals, strategy ■ Contract management

associated with general liability, customer service, regulatory compliance, contractual obligations, workplace safety and technological risks, and civil rights.

Risks Specific to Delivery of Health Care

Organizations delivering health care have the additional burden of risk associated with the provision of quality care and service in a setting and at the same time may expose workforce and patients/clients to new health risks. These health risks occur daily, at a granular level and may threaten economic viability, bodily function, disfigurement, or even death of the customer/patient or member of the workforce.

The Centers for Medicare & Medicaid Services (CMS) provides the funding for the health care of a significant proportion of US citizens and has been instrumental in establishing and codifying federal healthcare policy and practice. Specifically, the CMS has opined on the definitions of several healthcare risk terms including:

- Risk: a measure of the extent to which an entity is threatened by a potential circumstance or event, and typically a function of: (i) the adverse impacts that would arise if the circumstance or event occurs; and (ii) the likelihood of occurrence (CMS, 2012a).
- Risk Management: the program and supporting processes to manage information security risk to organizational operations (including mission, functions, image, reputation), organizational assets, individuals, other organizations, and the Nation, and includes: (i) establishing the context for risk-related activities; (ii) assessing risk; (iii) responding to risk once determined; and (iv) monitoring risk over time (CMS, 2012a). The Risk Management Plan for a healthcare delivery organization must take into account there are amplified risks related to professional liability and regulatory compliance as well as additional risks occasioned by the nature of the enterprise that are above and beyond risks in a typical business organization. Some of these unique healthcare delivery associated risks are summarized in Table 22.2.

Providing quality health care is not easy. The demands are round the clock and unpredictable with respect to volume and acuity. Often only a few staff are available to flawlessly execute simultaneous urgent salutary actions to restore health and save lives. There is always the specter of a bad outcome, patient/customer dissatisfaction, and an adverse outcome causing serious harm, disability, or death. The challenge is to deliver rapid, reliable, and reproducible quality care for the patients served and retain competent and engaged staff. Active interaction, training, education, and coaching of staff by senior leaders has tremendous power in developing situational awareness of risk. The value placed on risk mitigation by leaders is demonstrated by keen interest in the organization's safety environment through executive rounding and hiring of talented directors/managers of risk and safety programs who continuously promote safe actions throughout the enterprise.

Competent Qualified Staff

Fundamentally, quality and patient safety begin with the recruitment and retention of expert qualified staff capable of providing health care and services necessary with the referral resources when necessary care requires a higher-level of care, training, or equipment.

Table 22.2 Unique Risks Related to Healthcare Delivery

Risk Area	Specifics	Potential Consequences
Professional Liability & Competence	■ Inappropriate provider or employee actions, judgment, behavior ■ Credentials, competence, and training gaps ■ Inappropriate scope of practice and supervision ■ Lack of orientation/in-service	■ Harm to patients or staff ■ Civil/Legal Action ■ Licensing or Professional Board Action ■ Damage to reputation ■ Judgments, penalties, regulatory action
Personnel/Human Capital	■ Insufficient staff and retention efforts ■ Inappropriate acuity work assignments ■ Poor attitudes and engagement	■ Harm to patients or staff ■ Legal action and liability ■ Limited opportunities for process improvement or mitigation
Incident Management	■ Ineffective incident reporting system ■ Poor service recovery efforts ■ Ineffective policies and compliance ■ Communication gaps and misunderstood chain of command ■ Lack of effective investigation and due diligence ■ Lack of transparency	■ Harm to patients or staff ■ Patient and family dissatisfaction, legal claims ■ Regulatory or accreditation queries and inspection surveys
Work Environment	■ Unavailability of equipment and supplies ■ Distractions ■ Poor governance, policies, and communication ■ Defective workload management ■ Ineffective teamwork and poor handoffs ■ Low job satisfaction ■ Cumbersome documentation and system interfaces ■ Non-compliance with workforce statues	■ Harm to patients or staff ■ Low job satisfaction engagement ■ Costly inefficiencies ■ Care delays ■ Rework secondary to deterioration, relapse, readmission
Environmental Safety	■ Ineffective security precautions ■ Deficient planning for self-sufficiency, service interruption, and disasters ■ Poor infection control practices, disinfection, cleanliness ■ Failure to prevent and mitigate radiation, MRI, chemical and drug exposures ■ Unsafe maintenance of medical care equipment	■ Patient or staff harm ■ Workers compensation claims ■ Reportable events, inspections, penalties ■ Discredited reputation

continued

Table 22.2 Continued

Risk Area	Specifics	Potential Consequences
Materiel Management	■ Slow or absent monitoring and management of product safety and recalls ■ Non-compliance with manufacturer's product recommendations ■ Failure to manage off-label product usage ■ Flawed processes for product procurement and usage monitoring ■ Lack of oversight for contracted services	■ Patient or staff harm ■ Delay in treatment ■ Unnecessary waste expense
Regulatory Oversight & Compliance	■ Non-compliance with state and federal law ■ Confidentiality breaches ■ Inaccuracy of medical documentation supporting billing charges ■ Violations workplace ethics ■ Incomplete regulatory required employee training	■ Investigations, e.g. CMS, OIG, OCR, state agencies ■ Denial of payment and restitution of unsubstantiated claims ■ Corporate Integrity Agreement (CIA) ■ Penalties, incarceration
Reputation	■ Adverse public reports and news ■ Adverse public organizational and consumer rankings	■ Lost revenue

Organizations need to validate credentials and training of subject staff members as well as ensure proper levels of training and supervision when new equipment, procedures, or personnel are involved in care delivery. Through the credentialing process, the organization confirms their entire licensed workforce meets all of the requirements including current licensure for treating patients. The effectiveness of this process is a critical component of regulatory and accreditation scrutiny. Expectation of these bodies is the practice of "primary source verification" which means the organization confirms directly with the licensing agencies current active status of licensure.

Practice without appropriate current credentials poses a significant indefensible risk to the practitioner, is a breach in the standard of care, and represents significant financial and reputation risk to both the practitioner and the organization should a patient or individual sustain harm when care is being provided. The credentialing process is more robust and regulatorily stipulated in organizations who submit to an accreditation process from the variety of vendors providing such oversight for physicians and advanced care practitioners is more complex in healthcare facilities or organizations delivering substantial or inpatient medical care services. Such organizations typically have Credentials and Privileging committees reviewing the education, training, current licensure and certifications of applicant practitioners initially and at intervals, often based on the licensing interval. Based on this review, the governing body grants "privileges" which determines what types of care and procedures these healthcare providers may perform within the organization. There is usually a period of time during which a new healthcare provider's care is observed or proctored.

Although technically a Quality Improvement activity, evidence of Peer Review and ongoing practitioner quality of care review has become a requirement for Joint Commission accreditation and by default a requirement for CMS Medicare participation and in some states an institutional licensing requirement.

Peer review is an evaluation of current competency and medical decision making of a healthcare provider after an incident occurs during delivery of care services. The evaluation is conducted by similarly situated individuals with like practices and qualifications and based on meeting standards of care and duty. The Joint Commission (TJC) has further required evidence for ongoing professional practice evaluation (OPPE) for all healthcare providers at a frequency less than yearly and focused professional practice evaluation (FPPE) for healthcare providers who are new to an organization or whose care performance falls outside performance expectations. The expectation is that commensurate corrective actions will address deficiencies.

Credentials, privileging, and peer reviewed activities, as part of the spectrum of quality oversight, generally protected from discovery during legal case review. The final actions and status, e.g., whether discussed in committee, limitation of privileges, the imposition of action plan, may be discoverable.

Scope of Practice

It is critical to the delivery of licensed healthcare services, that healthcare providers deliver care within their scope of practice. Minimum scope of practice permissions may vary from state to state (Kaiser Family Foundation [KFF], 2015a, 2015b) and may be further curtailed at the discretion of an organization providing healthcare services. Scope of practice delineates activities a professional licensee may perform. In most cases, healthcare providers in training have the same scope of practice as do fully licensed counterparts so long as their care and services are appropriately supervised. It is up to the professional staff to meet and maintain their qualifications for current licensure.

The provision of medical care requires due diligence to ensure patients are receiving appropriately supervised care by any trainees in health care (medical, nursing, as well as a variety of technicians) involved in their care, supervisors typically have qualifications to independently function at the institution in the role for which the student is training. Evidence of this supervision is best formally documented as a part of the medical record with confirmation the supervising licensed professional guides and approves care provided. The requirements for supervision differ from state to state. New physicians and advanced care providers who have no experience practicing within the organization should be observed or proctored by senior independently functioning peer members of the healthcare organization who can evaluate their competence and judgment as well as familiarity and compliance with organizational policies and procedures.

Professional Liability

Licensed independent practitioners can be mandated by their malpractice carriers or organization where each practice, to carry appropriate, and, where specified, minimally statutory levels of professional liability coverage. Many states, for example: Colorado, Connecticut, Kansas, Massachusetts,

New Jersey, Rhode Island, and Wisconsin regulate physician malpractice limits of coverage (Weger, 2017). It is important that care delivery organizations in not only these states, but all states confirm that independent practitioners on their professional staffs are compliant with the law to protect themselves from claims of negligence and co-liability and are knowledgeable of any statutory changes specifically addressing this issue.

In states where malpractice insurance is not mandatory, physicians and independent practitioners may be required to register and contribute to a Patient Compensation Fund (PCF). The PCF is similar to standard professional liability insurance. The funds provide public benefit because they enable more practitioners to be willing to provide care services without fear of going out of business due to excessive malpractice insurance costs. Administered by the state, the PCF provides funds for awards to patients or their families when courts find that practitioners have caused harm through acts or omissions during medical treatment and there are otherwise no or insufficient funds to pay the awards. (American Medical Association [AMA], 2008). The PCFs work in conjunction with a physician's primary professional liability insurance policy, rather than replacing the physician's insurance policy. States with active PCFs include: Pennsylvania, Wisconsin, Kansas, Indiana, Louisiana, New Mexico, Nebraska, and South Carolina. In Florida and Virginia, PCFs only cover malpractice judgments for infants who have suffered a neurological injury. A medical care organization needs to maintain its own malpractice liability coverage to address claims of negligence or injury related to care provided by employed staff, e.g., nurses and medical technicians. This liability includes employee physicians and, in some instances, even licensed independent practitioners (LIPs) particularly when the hospital does not intervene when they have quality concerns or demonstrated patient endangerment regarding LIPs (Boeschen, 2015). Professional liability may also extend to an LIP when they may be "considered an employee" because the organization controls their work schedule, vacation, or professional charges (Boeschen, 2015).

In addition to professional malpractice liability of its employees, the healthcare business or organization must protect itself from liability related to:

■ use and maintenance of medical devices and monitoring systems
■ a healthy and secure environment
■ confidentiality breaches
■ effective up to date staff training and competence
■ adequacy of employee staffing to ethically and statutorily meet patient safety and employee work standards
■ appropriate policies and workflows
■ error free identification of patients and their test specimens
■ compliance with patient rights

Workforce Staffing and Communication

The nature of medical care delivery requires accommodation to a 24/7 schedule. It is steady work of varying, unpredictable intensity, acuity, and volume. Management must provide adequate resources to provide: (1) a safe level of staffing based on the complexity of the patient needs including off duty time for breaks and lunch, (2) appropriate and well maintained equipment and supplies to do their work well, (3) time for communication of both patient and organizational information, and (4) a work environment that supports staff emotional wellbeing and safety in order to keep workers feeling valued and wanting to continue working for the organization. In some states, staffing ratios and break time may be regulated (Lippincott Solutions, 2018), however, these standards should be considered minimums and all managers should be empowered to make necessary adjustments in staffing to maintain a safe environment for patients, staff, and visitors.

Effective management of healthcare risk, whether for an individual or enterprise, requires the recognition and engagement of senior leadership. The senior leader sets the expectation for performance, demonstrates commitment to the cause, and serves as a model for engaging in best practices to prevent risk. Effective communication is key to this endeavor. Operational policies must be clearly formulated and effectively disseminated with confirmation of understanding and clarity.

Policies are a method of communication. When well written, they help to standardize practice and ensure all pertinent and relevant actions are always considered and executed, if applicable. Policies can address infrequent occurrences and ensure that practice is always compliant with rules and statutory regulations. There may be several levels of policies. Administrative policies address organizational norms in a broad overarching fashion. Administrative policies may specify both business as well as clinical practice, such as specifying which two identifiers are used for fail safe patient identification. Service line and department policies may address the same topics but in a more granular way, service line and department policies may be customized to the work procedure of the service line or department but should always be consistent with the overarching administrative policy. As an example, service line department policies may specify how the two-identifier process is applied to the foot instead of the wrist of a newborn, but the practice would still need to use two identifiers per the administrative policy. Labeling of specimens provides another example which would be consistent across service lines (administrative) though the collection methods and equipment might vary based on department needs.

Regulatory Oversight

Professionals and organizations providing health care must comply with a variety of federal and state regulatory requirements aimed at protecting the health and safety of customer/patients and workforce while medical care issues are being addressed. Regulatory and accrediting organizations such as CMS, TJC, Det Norske Veritas Healthcare (DNV), Leapfrog Group, National Committee for Quality Assurance (NCQA), Occupational Safety and Health Administration (OSHA), and state departments of public health are among the entities assessing whether a healthcare organization meets contractual performance expectations and has implemented strategies to ensure delivery of quality of care and improved patient care outcomes. The Affordable Care Act (2010) specifically requires qualified health plans to only use hospitals with over 50 beds and healthcare providers who implement patient safety evaluation systems (PSESs), quality improvement processes, and comprehensive hospital discharge programs reducing possibility incomplete health recovery (Public Law, 2010). Collection and submission of performance data allows regulatory and private organizational comparisons and can affect the bottom line as reimbursement for care delivery is more frequently tied to results (CMS, 2018). In many states there are regulations which require reporting of significant adverse events and trigger audits for investigation of specific events or require monitoring of continuing quality and safety efforts through some of the agencies listed above (Hanlon, Sheedy, Kniffin, & Rosenthal, 2015). Corrective actions or even cease and desist orders can be imposed as appropriate.

There is a particularly unique aspect of medical care delivery services (and consequently risk) demanding that the environment of care—including air, food, living spaces, products, drugs, and equipment—be confirmed salutary and maintained in that condition for use in, on, or around patients and staff. This can be particularly challenging when medical care, by its very nature, involves situations in which patients or staff can be exposed to noxious agents or infectious diseases.

A large body of state and federal regulations govern the delivery of medical care and services. When assessing risk, it is important to understand which of these apply in the jurisdiction of interest. State licensing agencies have practices and activities based on existing state codes and regulations. The federal government, through Health & Human Services (HSS) and CMS, similarly has codes and regulations which not only address quality and safety aspects of care, particularly through the contractual Conditions of Participation for reimbursement, but also address fair business practices, preservation of civil rights, including Health Portability and Accountability Act (HIPAA) protections for protected health information and guarantees access to emergency care services regardless of ability to pay (CMS, 2012b).

Certain incidents of patient harm may require reporting to regulatory agencies who can investigate and levy fines for infractions like "never events" (PSNet, 2018b) which include wrong site surgery, infant abductions and the like. Reports may need to be submitted within specified time frames. Patient harm reports often result in a regulatory survey and sometimes a series of inter-agency surveys as reports of patient harm are widely shared. In some instances, particularly CMS surveys, state and federal inspectors are the same individuals wearing different hats but evaluating care against different agency standards.

Substantiated deficiencies in compliance with regulations can have serious consequences including organizational penalties, payor sanctions prohibiting participation in care delivery for beneficiaries, criminal prosecution with possibility of fines or incarceration and civil litigation. In most instances, the report of deficiencies is available to the public. Local media reporters often alert the public when there is a fine issued to a specific healthcare organization for a violation of a federal or state statute. A product of the new millennial digital age is the risk associated with online sharing of official regulatory investigative reports and actions, and perhaps more significantly, the assessments and rankings of service and work product quality by consumers on social media sites.

Enterprise Risk Management in Health Care

Historically, attempts at managing risk focused on the implications to a medical care organization's financial bottom line, with blaming individuals and getting rid of the perpetrators. Even after publication of the IOM's article, "To Err Is Human," there was very slow progress in decreasing the incidence of patient harm events. As the understanding of factors causing harm and the interface with human errors became clearer and more widespread, it became obvious that factors such as lack of reliability, variation and complexity of medical systems and processes, misalignment of outcomes and goals, poor communication, and failure to anticipate and plan for system breakdowns were the primary continuing drivers of patient harm. The classical steps of risk management apply then as now: (1) risk identification, (2) analysis, (3) planning, (4) response, (5) monitoring, and (6) evaluation and are useful in analysis and corrective action plans for incidents. The key, however, to improved patient safety is using these tools predictively through by gathering of pre-injury near-miss information, changing culture to avoid blame and encourage easy staff reporting, analyzing near misses, coaching team work and communication skills rewarding while also awakening in leaders the value of embedding clinical and enterprise risk management principles into the basic organizational operations, decision making, and strategic planning. Risk management and promotion of patient safety involve both the assessment and planning for risk before it occurs as well as the management of risk events after the fact.

Identification and management of risks in health care is perhaps the first step in developing a plan to address and mitigate healthcare enterprise risks. The American Society for Health Care Risk Management (ASHRM) (Carroll, 2014) has suggested eight domains or categories of risk which need consideration in management of these risks. These domains include operational, clinical/safety, strategic, financial, human capital, legal/regulatory, technology and hazard categories. Similar risk groupings with examples have been discussed earlier in this chapter where they were separated into common business enterprise risks (Table 22.1) and clinical risks (Table 22.2).

The approach to risk management in healthcare organization is well described in the referenced ASHRM white paper (Carroll, 2014) which speaks to creating a supporting organizational structure for managing risk which includes as its cornerstone, governance buy-in for creation of a transformative organizational culture which includes strategies that support workforce spirit, teamwork, reliability, critical thinking and engagement. In the rapidly changing healthcare environment, these plans and strategies must be nimble and adaptable. Objectives need to be doable, timely, and based on measurable outcomes using scientific methodologies. Optimally this commitment to prevent harm is demonstrated in creation of a written risk management strategy and initiative. Plans should be reviewed annually with consideration of major revision on a biennial basis at a minimum (Carroll, 2014). They need to address all elements of risk known or suspected within an organization as well as prescribe the process for analyzing incidents of harm including near misses.

The role of administrative leadership in supporting a robust risk management plan cannot be overemphasized. Leaders set the tone and create the culture for an organization with respect to how risk management fits in the overall strategic plan. Management of risk is not generally perceived as an obvious focal point of a healthcare organization whose mission is providing reasonably priced health care, achieving patient satisfaction, with good outcomes, and increasing business opportunities and market share. Failure to successfully integrate risk management into the fabric of a healthcare organization, however, puts all the organizational goals in jeopardy. Risk management cannot be the sole responsibility of a small elite group of managers or directors. Senior leaders set this expectation through their interest, words, and deeds. Interest, by leadership, is evidenced through activities like executive rounding which gives leadership the opportunity to see what is happening at a frontline level and to communicate face to face with employees about issues and concerns. Rounding also demonstrates leadership compassion and commitment. One of the primary needs of a successful risk management program is the unwavering support and commitment of the senior leaders and governance of the organization.

Factual and effective communication is another key component of the risk plan. Communication must be clear, in concert with organizational cultural values, and widely distributed with clear reinforcement of performance goals and expectations. Widespread sharing is particularly important in addressing issues of patient safety as there is a great tendency for repeat of same or similar events across functional areas when underlying common systems issues are not recognized or addressed (Wolf, 2008). Concise and clear organization-wide policies and procedures support and codify expected actions and behaviors and keep the staff compliant with best practices, regulations, and accreditation standards.

Expanding on the concept it takes a village to achieve the highest level of performance, leaders must employ knowledgeable and passionate risk and patient safety directors whose accountability is to develop, communicate, and facilitate the execution of a comprehensive risk and safety work-plan. The most effective workplans are developed in collaboration with the process leaders, address strategies for assessment and prevention of risk, as well as those for investigation, analysis, and mitigation of actual risk events and include trends in health care, or retrospective trends reported via the incident reporting systems. High level findings and recommendations are shared with the workforce. The risk management strategic initiative and work plan also involves deliberate opportunities for scheduling interactive coaching sessions. Through guidance and coaching, risk management and patient safety culture become an integral part of usual and customary daily activities of staff.

Information relative to healthcare trends, incident reports, regulatory mandates, and prioritized topics serve as measurable elements of the Risk Management plan and workplan. For additional guidance in developing or assessing the completeness of a healthcare risk management plan and areas of current national concern, review of focus areas highlighted in publications by private independent patient safety promoting organizations like TJC, the National Quality Forum, the ASHRM, the Institute for Healthcare Improvement, and the National Patient Safety Foundation as well as government entities such as the Agency for Healthcare Research and Quality and the CMS can be helpful.

The Joint Commission has been instrumental in promoting patient safety culture through its accreditation of US and international hospitals. Since 1995 it has recommended the reporting of sentinel events and issued its first sentinel event reporting policy in 2007. The initial policy largely called out what was termed "Never Events" (as in never supposed to happen) by Ken Kizer, MD of the National Quality Forum in 2002. These are now officially known as Serious Reportable Events (PSNet, 2018b). Many states and other organizations have incorporated variations of the list into their statutory requirements for patient harm reporting.

Most recently TJC has defined a sentinel event as one that reaches a patient and results in death, permanent harm, or severe temporary harm and intervention required to sustain life (TJC, 2017b). The Joint Commission has been promoting National Patient Safety Goals (NPSGs) since 2002. Compliance with these has become a condition of participation in TJC accreditation process and trended data collection for the NPSGs demonstrates the organization's compliance to the respective goal. The NPSGs highlight some of the more common and critical patient safety issues currently facing the healthcare delivery organizations. In sum, the NPSGs include expectations for maintaining processes which correctly identify patients to prevent errors particularly during administration of blood products, timely communication of critical test results, safer medication use through better labeling practices, monitoring of anticoagulant therapy and medication reconciliation across the spectrum of care, better use and response to clinical alarms, reduction in healthcare associated infections, identification of patient safety risks inherent in the population served, and continued adherence to universal protocol methodologies in order to prevent wrong side/site surgery.

Incident Management

A robust and easily useable method for capture of both incidents and near misses is a key component in reduction of healthcare risk and preventable harm. The system used for reporting should be simple and reporting of events seen as necessary for improved processes and improved care delivery. The organizational culture should demonstrate a safe culture, one that staff feel comfortable reporting adverse outcomes or near misses in. Implementation of a digital technologic methodology for capturing incident data is usually advantageous from the perspective of 24/7 availability, confidentiality, and analysis. Though confidentiality may encourage participation, confidentiality sometimes is limiting since additional information needed to fully understand or complete an investigation may not be available.

Tools for and methods of investigation of near misses and actual incidents are similar. In contradistinction to the usual adversarial legal investigation, a key feature of this incident investigation is transparency. Transparency encourages full, active participation and disclosure of all pertinent circumstances so causality can be accurately pinpointed. There is still personal accountability but recognition that most patient harm results from systems failures with varying contributions from human error, typically related to mistakes or inexperience. Mistakes can be reckless, risky, or inadvertent. Corrective actions for systems issues involve establishment of barriers to failure. Corrective actions for human error are based on a Just Culture model (Lightizer & Thurlo-Walsh, 2012) which takes into account systems failures and appropriately addresses the human component. The final goal of the process being reduction or elimination of harm through correction of responsible systems issues to prevent future occurrences.

Time is of the essence in investigating a reported incident. Healthcare delivery is typically often a 24/7 enterprise, so the reporting and initial interventions need to be started within the same time frame. It is important to capture details, initiate any mitigation processes, protect patients, staff, and facilities from related fallout, and to sequester and preserve any pertinent evidence including devices. Depending on jurisdiction, regulations may require timely notification of state and federal oversight agencies when serious or critical harm events occur. Organizational policies need to specify the "chain of command" for communication of incidents within the organization and the process for reporting, evidence preservation, process for causality evaluation, analysis and implementation of corrective actions. A Crisis Communication Committee/Plan is reserved for catastrophic events and is the initial mode of organization communication of incidences.

Once the initial response and data gathering after an event is complete, it is necessary to schedule a working meeting including an experienced facilitator together with those involved in the event in order to formally determine why it happened. The value of this analysis is that it provides objectives for process improvement and targets for creation of barriers to prevent system failures. The process of determining causality is referred to as a Root Cause Analysis (RCA) and sometimes as a Comprehensive Systematic Analysis (CSA) (World Health Organization [WHO], 2012). This process of analysis is applicable to untoward events in many industries including healthcare delivery. The Joint Commission was one of the first patient safety organizations to require evidence of CSA evaluations for sentinel events which they included in their sentinel event policy published in 1996 (TJC, n.d.). Several methodologies have been popularized for event analysis with the goal to determine the primary cause of harm in order that actions can be taken to prevent future occurrences. The steps in analysis include: (1) identification of all possible causes and contributing factors; (2) determining the root or primary cause; (3) developing an action plan to address the cause and prevent future events; (4) communicating the plan and expectations to the workforce; (5) use of scientific and statistical methodologies to check and maintain improvement (TJC, 2015; WHO, 2012). Techniques used commonly in identification of the root cause include asking the "5 'why's," flow charting, Ishikawa fishbone diagrams, pareto, run charts, and cause and effect analysis (WHO, 2012). Action plans are created to address the major and minor causal factors. When there is a high volume of similar types of incidents or a common area of barrier failure, Failure Mode Effects Analysis (FMEA; CMS, 2011) is a quality improvement technique that can be used to pre-emptively re-design a process to avoid or prevent situations which frequently lead to risk or harm (Tague, 2004).

Just Culture is an analysis algorithm to assist in attribution of culpability when risk and harm occurs (Boysen, 2013). Just Culture analysis looks at the likelihood a similarly situated worker would have made the same error. The analysis is useful for determining whether the human behavior or actions associated with an incident resulted from decisional impairment, maliciousness, recklessness, risky behavior, or was unintentional and potentially a system failure. Using this technique, appropriate corrective actions and discipline, if appropriate, can be instituted and risks managed.

Once an incident or series of incidents is analyzed and causality determined, corrective action plans need to be implemented to mitigate the current situation and prevent repeat occurrences. All corrective actions may not need to be initiated at the same time, but most important is addressing and mitigating any ongoing situations which place workforce, staff, patients, families, and friends at serious risk of loss of life, limb, function, or disfigurement. Such occurrences may include events characterized as "never events" and the ongoing threatening situation referred to as a condition of "Immediate Jeopardy" (IJ) (see below). Immediate action on the part of the care delivery organization is necessary to mitigate future additional harm and risk, avoid application of sanctions by regulatory agencies, and to create a favorable perception of organizational transparency, ethical behavior, accountability, and due diligence should litigation or regulatory scrutiny occur as a consequence. An official designation of IJ is particularly serious when issued by a regulatory agency because if not resolved quickly, such designation typically triggers additional scrutiny and sanctions can be imposed. The CMS has defined an IJ as "a situation in which the provider's noncompliance with one or more requirements of participation has caused, or is likely to cause serious injury, harm, impairment, or death to a resident" (CMS, 2014). An "IJ" status requires rapid correction as CMS further stipulates that if not resolved or abated within 23 days, to its satisfaction, actions will be taken to terminate the organization's authorization to participate in care for Medicare and Medicaid beneficiaries (CMS, 2014). The corrective actions for less dangerous situations should be implemented in a timely fashion but the timetable for this can accommodate the organization's ability to effectively institute necessary changes, educate staff, modify policies, and secure necessary products or devices for implementation. In the case of staff education regarding procedure and policy changes, demonstration that training has percolated throughout the organization is documented by review of plan, educational materials, attendance lists for information shared at staff meetings, plans and lists for makeup education, and evidence all staff and providers, including temporary employees and providers in training, have received the information.

Results of investigations and corrective action plans as well as composite summaries of organizational risk and harm performance should be shared with senior executives, Medical Executive Committees, and Boards of Directors, as appropriate, since these leaders have the ultimate authority and responsibility for management of risk and compliance with applicable regulations and organizational ethics. It is also important to share de-identified general incident and action plans with all department managers and employees, since the systemic nature of error and harm makes similar risk situations likely in other areas of the organization where healthcare services are delivered.

Various local, state, and federal jurisdictions may have statutes requiring reporting of certain serious events causing harm to patients, visitors, or employees to regulatory or accrediting agencies. Submission of quality outcomes data for comparative purposes may also be required in some settings. While these quality reports do not typically reveal specific details of harm and risk incidents, poor performance on such reports may create an economic risk to a healthcare organization if, as a result, private or governmental payors decide to terminate care delivery contracts with the caregiver or organization or to limit authorization or licensure of the same to offer care services. If publicly reported, economic consequences and risk can result from damage to the organization's professional reputation or rating in social or other media venues (TJC, 2016).

Some of the major incident voluntary and statutory reporting requirements are summarized in Table 22.3. Some agencies, e.g., TJC and some state agencies, may additionally require the provider or healthcare organization to post information advising patients/consumers of their right to lodge complaints against healthcare providers and contact information for communication of the complaint. Some specific comments regarding protected health information (PHI) are appropriate. The Health Portability and Accountability Act (HIPAA) was passed by Congress in 1996. HIPAA was necessary to support development and use of digital health records in which patients

Table 22.3 Statutory and Voluntary Incident and Quality Measures Reporting

Agency	Report	Notes and References
CDC	NHSN ■ Hospital Acquired Conditions ■ Epidemic Diseases Influenza Legionnaire's Ebola Zika ■ Food Borne	Coordinated with State infection control agencies CLABSI, CAUTI SSI, VRE, MRSA, C. difficile Influenza Immunization
CMS	■ NHSN ■ eCQM	www.cdc.gov/nhsn/cms/index.html www.cms.gov/Regulations-and-Guidance/Legislation/EHRIncentivePrograms/eCQM_Library.html
OSHA	Serious employee injury	www.osha.gov/report.htm
FDA	MAUDE MedWatch	www.fda.gov/MedicalDevices/DeviceRegulationand Guidance/PostmarketRequirement/ReportingAdverseEvents/ucm127891.htm www.fda.gov/Safety/MedWatch/default.htm
OIG	■ Serious Reportable Events	Serious Reportable Events in Medicare Beneficiaries analysis and report to Congress. State collected data.
State Agencies	■ Serious Reportable Events ■ Disruption of Services ■ Abuse ■ Food Borne Illness ■ Infectious Disease	
TJC	■ ORYX ■ Sentinel Events ■ Consumer Complaints	www.jointcommission.org/assets/1/18/2017_2018_ORYX_Reporting_Requirements_201801311.PDF www.jointcommission.org/.../Why_Organizations_Self_Report_Sentinel_Event.
OCR	HIPAA	www.hhs.gov/hipaa/for-professionals/breach-notification/index.html
OPA	Consumer Complaints	www.opa.ca.gov/Pages/ComplaintDataReports.aspx

potentially faced new electronic unauthorized or hacking risks through loss of privacy and identity (HHS, 2015). Among the provisions of HIPAA were the designation of certain data elements and terms as protected health information (PHI). Authorized review and use of PHI were limited by law to treatment, payment, and healthcare operations (TPO) in delivering health care.

The degree of access by members of the workforce to a patient's PHI is dependent on their functional TPO role in their healthcare delivery organization. Inappropriate access or release of PHI outside of TPO activities for the patient is considered a breach of the civil personal right to confidentiality and privacy. Breaches are subject to reporting, penalties per incident, and imprisonment of violators depending on the incident severity. Many states also have overlapping regulations similarly addressing inappropriate access, release, and use of PHI (O'Connor & Matthews, 2011). State fines and penalties may also apply, but ultimate oversight occurs through the federal Office of Civil Rights.

Managing Medico-Legal Risk of a Healthcare Adverse Event

Communication as well as engagement and accountability of the patient or their legal guardian begins with informed consent. Informed consent is a process wherein the patient or their legal guardian is helped to understand the diagnosis or problem, potential treatment options, and the risk of treatment as well non-treatment. In a situation of shared decision making, the patient and family can make decisions about care options they want to receive consistent with their acceptable quality of life and spiritual values. Untoward outcomes are easier to accept when the seriousness of the situation and the risks were understood up front (WHO, 2012).

When an unexpected or catastrophic event occurs during healthcare delivery, open lines of communication lines between the patient, family, providers, workforce, and organization create empathy. As part of the risk strategy, many organizations have included a Disclosure Plan for addressing adverse outcomes and how to communicate this information to patient, family, and staff. Conversations need to occur as soon as possible after the event and perhaps repeated if the treatment conditions have temporarily impacted the patient's ability to understand. Conversations should be concise, consistent with the facts, avoiding speculation. A discussion with those involved in the event should take place as soon as possible to provide the organization with steps to prevent further harm to patient and others in the future. The Risk Manager is often the individual who can establish the logistics, timing, and content to be shared in these discussions. A sincere apology is appropriate. In two-thirds of states, some parts or all information in an apology, without accepting liability, have been legally protected from use in a malpractice claim (Saitta & Hodge, 2012). Studies have shown that empathetic disclosure conversation often makes the difference between patient satisfaction or contentious lawsuit (Kachalia, 2013; Kachalia et al., 2010). Documentation of disclosure should be entered in the medical record and similarly should be limited to the facts without speculation.

Research shows effective disclosure discussions have resulted in significant reduction in malpractice claims and legal fees and more expeditious claim resolution (Kachalia et al., 2010). The Joint Commission has required disclosure of unanticipated outcomes of care since 2001 and 10 states have mandatory regulations for disclosure to patients of medical errors and unanticipated outcomes (PSNet, 2018a).

The physician and staff providing care are often "second victims" in this setting (Hall & Scott, 2012). They typically have little training or experience in handling these stressful situations. It is 'very easy during the initial shock, to have conversations with patients, families or even with staff or write clinical notes which acknowledge culpability or speculation as to cause or contributing factors. Such words, however well intended or cathartic, potentially put the healthcare providers and organization in a nearly indefensible position for mitigating risk associated with the event. Coaching and drills prior to need can be helpful in producing successful disclosure outcomes when healthcare providers and caregivers need to achieve this at times when they themselves may be emotionally distraught.

Following critical events and despite best attempts at communication, antagonism and distrust between parties can ensue. In such situations, some organizations have reduced risk using an ombudsman. The ombudsman is an employee of the healthcare organization who is impartial, i.e., neither an advocate for the provider, the organization, nor the patient. The participation of the ombudsman ensures a patient's or family's concerns are equitably acknowledged and evaluated with appropriate and sufficient time for effective communication.

Another tool that can be helpful for reducing risk following a serious adverse event is a process of "early resolution" (Ksiazek, 2015). Several states have statues which support this principle which is intended to avoid lengthy litigation of malpractice claims. There typically is an acknowledgment of injury, (perhaps not necessarily culpability) and a negotiation of restitution terms. Typical benefits include faster speed of resolution, significantly reduced legal costs, and justifiable and appropriate payouts.

Opportunities and Pitfalls in Healthcare Risk Management

Many of the risks associated with healthcare delivery, perhaps excepting malpractice or failure of duty, arise from patient safety considerations. Review of the annual Joint Commission NPSGs gives some insight to major patient safety concerns (TJC, 2018). The Joint Commission has identified a need to correctly identify the patient and effectively communicate for all settings, the planned treatment amongst all caregivers and patient/family including medications, procedures, and surgeries while preventing hospital acquired infections and surgical mistakes. Clear, understandable, and factual communication, whether oral or written, is perhaps the most fundamental aspect of both creation and mitigation of risk. The effectiveness of communication is an area of focus for both the LNC who is trying to reduce risk and the one who is trying to expose failure of duty to support a legal claim or action.

Inaccurate communication is perhaps the real cause of patient misidentification. As well, the role of inaccurate or incomplete communication undoubtedly contributes to surgical mistakes and is the reason why TJC expects participating accredited organizations to mark the surgery site and to pause prior to the start of surgery. Delivery of health care is by nature complex, fast paced, and unpredictable with the possibility of devastating outcomes. Whereas caregivers early on in training become familiar with the unique terms and syntax of medical language, they do not typically practice effective communication skills or receive instruction in appropriate content. The workload demands, staffing, and frequency of urgent/emergent situations created a need for brevity and directness in communication between healthcare providers when giving care. Even now, effective communication can be thwarted by the perceived subservient role of persons in training, nurses, or techs who are fearful to speak up or annoy staff physicians when they have observations, questions, or concerns about a patient's care.

Workload and urgency of intervention in the past also affected the brevity, quality, and legibility of written notes or orders and is possibly responsible for the notion that doctors have illegible handwriting (Borscherds, 2015). Recognizing the need for legible and shareable medical care communication, the federal guarantors for the medical benefits, the CMS, fundamentally changed the documentation environment for health care by incentivizing the adoption of computerized health records and "meaningful use" with the passage of the Health Information Technology for Economic and Clinical Health (HITECH) Act, enacted as part of the American Recovery and Reinvestment Act of 2009 (HHS, 2009).

The advantages of such computerized health documentation are many and include legibility, completeness, structured, searchable, and consistent data entries as well as opportunities for cross platform, cross agency, and cross country sharing of information (HealthIT, 2018). Computerized health records also allow greater scrutiny with respect to demonstrating the level and quality of care provided, including comparison of outcomes based on severity of disease thus assuring full compliance with contractual service agreements and fair charges and appropriate reimbursement for services provided. Of course, all of these "benefits" then become risks and liabilities when documentation fails to adequately support expectations for care delivery, even though it may have been provided.

With implementation of the electronic health record (EHR) with structured data entry and Computerized Physician Order Entry (CPOE), legibility is no longer the issue, but the ability to communicate clinical information electronically continues to be a significant problem because of the use of a myriad of unapproved non-standard abbreviations, numerous pre-existing often personal clinical acronyms, "textese," job specific chart views, pre-completed clinical flow records with documentation by exception, and voluminous, randomly organized daily clinical notes containing fragments of text are cut, copied, and pasted from the notes of others without proper attribution (Menachemi & Collum, 2011). The sheer volume of additional data input creates new risks as the accountability of caregivers shifts from giving patient care to completing the entry of medical record data. New workflows are developed which support the data entry rather than the patient care process. Flowsheets may be utilized as shortcuts for documentation by exception but have an inherent risk that healthcare providers can fail to proofread and correct pre-filled flowchart entries. Copy, cut, and paste functionality allows intentional or inadvertent insertion of documentation which may pertain to a different patient, different encounter, or different author. Notes can become excessively long and repetitive to the degree it is no longer possible to determine the current patient status. Often the same data can be recorded in several locations which are not linked and can become a source of contradiction or confusion.

Advantages and risks of the EHR are summarized in Table 22.4. Most of these risks are intrinsic properties of the EHR in attempting to make all healthcare providers and staff conform to the same documentation process using conventional operating system functionality. Most of these EHR shortcomings are secondary to human factors. The typical mitigation occurs through careful adoption of effective policies and procedures. This is not a fail safe process, but rather dependent on the engagement and commitment of the human user. Perhaps the greatest irony in all of this is that medical care, by nature, is fast paced, unpredictable, complex, and sometimes distracts with catastrophic outcomes, using a documentation system that relies on amped up healthcare providers to process and enter data in a careful, accurate, proscribed fashion that communicates effectively with other healthcare providers, analysts, and business operations specialists.

Lack of effective communication at the bedside can also affect care and lead to increased risk. Staffing shortages and handoffs when staff are on a break or transitions in care with changes in level of care, transportation for clinical testing and discharge, all present times of greater risk. Distractions during care delivery are another source of miscommunication. The Joint Commission identified care handoffs as an NPSG in 2006 and has underscored the continuing issue with a

Table 22.4 Advantages and Risks of EHR

EHR feature	Advantage	Risk
Structured data entry	■ Improved legibility ■ Data collection and reporting ■ Process improvement	■ Not provider's preferred terms, chooses closest match ■ Multiple entries with similar wording differ at end of string ■ Pointer imperceptibly moves during selection process ■ Provider fails to proofread
Customized screen views and workflows	■ Ease and completeness of workflow and data input	■ Team members don't see or recognize data ■ Staff focus on completing data entry, not "knowing" patient
Cut, copy, paste	■ Facilitates data entry	■ Obscures when and who made observation or intervention ■ Note bloat (excessively lengthy notes)
Auto alerts	■ Ensures complete data ■ Warns of risk	■ Frequency encourages bypass/ignore ■ More complex and longer time to enter data
Templates, charting by exception	■ Easy, complete data entry ■ Compliance with workflows and care bundles	■ Potential pre-charting ■ Inaccuracies (no proofreading) ■ Null flow chart entries may be omitted from official notes or reports
Bar coding	■ Fail safe identification and potential error warning	■ Equipment integrity and system integration failure ■ Time consuming, particularly independent double checks ■ Emergency care waiver ■ Staff workarounds
Chart availability, errors, and confidentiality breaches	■ 7/24 chart availability ■ Monitoring chart access ■ Simultaneous user access ■ Accurate date/time stamps ■ Improved chart completion ■ Timely billing and collections ■ Performance improvement activities	■ Easy chart access via designated monitors ■ Remote access ■ Clinical info and order input only limited by P&P ■ Limited appreciation of entry time stamps and sequencing ■ Users share passwords or access ■ "Need to know" access
Integration and interfaces	■ Ease of data entry	■ Access to legacy paper records and integration with digital records and data ■ Hardware malfunction ■ Systems calibration ■ Integration mapping errors ■ Information sharing with other EHR systems
Free text shortcuts		■ Reduced entry time but may be non-standard and of unclear meaning ■ Non-standard units of measure (lb vs kg)

sentinel alert 58 as well as developed resources to make healthcare organizations more aware and develop strategies for mitigation (TJC, 2012, 2017b).

As long as there is a need for human data collection, input and interpretation of data, highly intelligent skilled caregivers, due to the volume and fast pace of care, will develop shortcuts to streamline the process. The fail safe in this digital world is the cross check, the double signature, and team approach. The team approach to medical care delivery is not a new concept and lends itself easily to the development of highly reliable processes and team communication as popularized by TeamSTEPPS (Agency for Healthcare Research and Quality [AHRQ], 2017) and other programs. Key to the success of this effort is the ability to communicate orally in a clear and effective way, outside of the legacy hierarchical distinctions based on one's role on the team. In such a scenario, the ward clerk, housekeeper, medical assistant, nurse, physician, and surgeon have equal right and obligation to speak up when there are concerns around patient and staff safety. Unfortunately, there are still events in medical practice where some caregivers are intimidated by those who envision themselves as more superior or important than other members of the team.

Attention to environment of care is particularly important because work in healthcare delivery potentially involves exposure of patient/clients to infectious agents. Particular consideration needs to be focused on decontamination, sterilization, and practices that reduce the transmission of disease. Perhaps the most important principle in all of infection control, in addition to having a robust and responsive plan, is ensuring prevention and control practices and products utilized have published scientific evidence of efficacy (Chobin, 2017). Validating use of these proven effective measures should be one of the first orders of business for the LNC who is involved either in implementation and management of a Patient Safety/Risk organizational plan or in investigating an untoward patient outcome.

Simple and effective handwashing is one of the most effective ways of preventing disease transmission and, to this end, TJC has continuing annual NPSGs and standards which require an accredited organization employ "hand cleaning guidelines from the Centers for Disease Control and Prevention or the World Health Organization" (TJC, 2018). Additionally, TJC requires "use of proven guidelines for the prevention of post-surgical, central vascular access line, urinary catheter infections as well as difficult to treat infections, e.g., C. difficile and MRSA" (TJC, 2017a).

Healthcare organizations need to employ general cleaning, disinfection, and sterilization methodologies that conform with manufacturers' recommendations to ensure demonstrable effectiveness. Most products used in this way have already passed FDA scrutiny. Air flow, temperature, and humidity in patient care areas, operating rooms, and storage areas needs to be maintained within ranges which discourage presence and proliferation of organisms that cause or transmit disease.

Another highly regulated area of risk in organizations delivering health care involves all procurement, storage, and use of treatment products and medications. Most, if not all of these products require FDA evaluation and approval to be used for treatment. Often there are dates for expiration and specific storage requirements relating to light, temperature, and humidity, supported by scientific documentation of efficacy. Drugs and products may have black box warnings when there are particularly critical risks which the clinician should consider before using on a patient. Significant additional risks occur when the physician or surgeon uses medications and products "off label" meaning they don't have FDA approval for the indication for which they were used. Off label use may be rational and possibly lifesaving, but any resultant complications or injuries may be hard to defend. Human error has been cited as responsible for 80–90% of medical errors (TJC, 2015). Administration of the wrong drug is not an uncommon error (Keers,

Williams, Cooke, & Ashcroft, 2013). Management of anticoagulants is particularly of concern and is another TJC NPSG. Among the ways human error can be addressed include product engineering particularly in the realm of preventing drug errors. Drugs with similar appearance or names can be stored differently. Names can be printed with "tall man" lettering (Institute for Safe Medication Practices [ISMP], 2016) which better communicates subtle differences in naming which may prevent inappropriate and perhaps deadly administration. Tubing for different uses has been designed with incompatible connectors so that air can't be attached to an arterial line or vacuum attached to a chest tube (Food & Drug Administration [FDA], 2018).

Medical Risk Case Investigation for the Legal Nurse Consultant

The discussion of this chapter has been the identification of risk in healthcare delivery, the common risks of all organizations, and the specific unique risks associated with healthcare delivery. Discussion revolved around considerations in developing a management plan for preventing or mitigating risk. In this section, the role of the LNC as an investigative consultant will be addressed. The foundation of any case review is the documentation of care. It is essentially a third witness, written contemporaneously at the time the events occurred and suffers no memory loss. Physicians, perhaps because of the workload, the frequency of unpredictability and need for urgent action, and the emotional consequences of potentially poor outcomes and threat of lawsuit, often do a poor job of appropriate documentation. This is not just a medicolegal issue but may also impact reimbursement as well as ongoing quality assessment of care provided. Most healthcare providers and healthcare organizations have an EHR. The documentation of care in the EHR may be a totally digital system or a hybrid with both digital and legacy paper system. In many instances, test results and imaging studies may represent the bulk portion of legacy paper records. The reason for this is that much of the testing equipment, which also may have proprietary digital systems, does not electronically interface directly with the chosen EHR for automatic upload.

Clearly it is important to obtain and review all information records when performing a case investigation. It is important when requesting records to make it clear to the entity which of their care records are being sought. The timing and availability of some materials for review will likely depend on whether the investigation is for regulatory purposes or litigation. Some EHRs allow physical or digital printing of a record "report" on request. This "release" document may not include detailed flow chart records of vital signs or documentation of other routine nursing activities which may have value in review to understand what happened. In many care scenarios, nurses no longer write or compose detailed daily care notes, but rather capture activities and assessments in flow records and individualized plans of care.

Potentially helpful care information may be contained in other care documentation, perhaps not included in the official care report, e.g. timelines, which capture Admission, Discharge, and Transfer (ADT) information. Such reports may be very pertinent to the understanding of the case. These documents may be individually authorized or may be electronically extracted and aggregated from other information a nurse or staff member enters into the data collection modules of the EHR program.

Record review should include all healthcare provider notes, including history and physical, consultations, discharge summaries, interim and final operation and procedure reports, progress notes, informed consents, signed consent forms and authorizations, lab reports including pathology, imaging interpretations, and clinical photographs. Consent often provides the basis for litigation following patient harm events.

Some of the necessary information needed for researching a case may be outside the patient's medical record. Depending on the circumstances, review of operations policies in effect at the time of the event, equipment maintenance logs, evidence of device in-servicing and maintenance, awareness and compliance with manufacturers' recommendations, black box warnings, FDA Maude reports, and any photos taken of a failed explanted device may be beneficial.

Additionally, review of pertinent documents related to patient and family disclosure of untoward events may be in order. Analysis of situational factors in play prior to and during the event may have some bearing on legal causality and liability. Such information may be readily available if working for the healthcare organization but may be obscured for the LNC working on behalf of plaintiff's counsel. Workload, staffing, urgency and distractions, familiarity with the organization, its policies, and equipment, disruptive behavior, and substance abuse can impact patient safety at a variety of levels. Lastly it is important to be cognizant of the reputation of the organization and healthcare providers as well as their commitment to safety.

The LNC managing or consulting within an organization's risk department will likely have access to the specific organizational incident report and reporting system. These reports are typically considered "quality" related. Quality reports and peer review information is usually protected from legal discovery by federal and some state statutes, particularly when used for activities promoting patient safety. Pertinent federal regulations include the Patient Safety and Quality Improvement Act (2005) and the Patient Protection and Affordable Care Act (2010). The goals of this legislation are to encourage healthcare professionals and organizations to improve patient safety and quality of care through fearless reporting, discussion, analysis of patient harm with broadly shared learnings across state and national venues while preserving the patient's rights for redress of grievances and appropriate compensation for injury (Nash, 2011). These regulations protect the confidentiality of patient safety and quality information gathered under the auspices of Patient Safety Organizations (PSO). Though the intentions of the regulations may be clear and admirable, debate continues around the nuances of addressing both patient safety and personal injury. There is an expanding volume of case law resulting from litigation of unclear provisions of these regulations through the state courts (*Baptist Health Richmond v. Clouse*, 497 S.W.3d 759 [Ky. 2016]), and *Charles v. Southern Baptist Hospital of Florida*, 2017 WL 411333 (Supreme Court of Florida, Jan. 31, 2017). The LNC needs be alert to this continually changing body of law regarding discovery and admissibility of case information garnered during investigations of patient harm events.

Summary

This chapter presents a baseline foundation enabling the LNC to reflect upon and better understand the special risks faced by clinicians and organizations who provide medical care services. It is management and investigation of these healthcare related risks that provide the primary role and opportunity for the clinical expertise of the LNC. Over the last 20 years there has been a transformation in our understanding of the magnitude and complexity of healthcare delivery and the interplay of systems and human fallibility in causing unnecessary and unexpected patient harm. Our legislators, medical care communities, insurance payors, and most importantly our patients demand for reliable care in which they can trust. The discipline of Patient Safety has arisen consequently and continues to evolve to address the persistent menace of patient injury.

References

Agency for Healthcare Research and Quality. (2017). About TeamSTEPPS®. Retrieved from www.ahrq.gov/teamstepps/about-teamstepps/index.htm.

American Medical Association. (2008). State patient compensation funds. Retrieved from www.scribd.com/document/181171839/AMA-state-Patient-Compensation-Funds.

Boeschen, C. (2015). Medical malpractice: When can patients sue a hospital for negligence? Retrieved from www.nolo.com/legal-encyclopedia/medical-malpractice-patients-sue-hospital-negligence-30189.html.

Borscherds, M. (2015). Why is doctors' handwriting so bad? Retrieved from www.health24.com/News/Public-Health/Why-is-doctors-handwriting-so-bad-20141128.

Boysen, P. G. (2013). Just Culture: A foundation for balanced accountability and patient safety. *Ochsner Journal, 13*(3), 400–406. Retrieved from http://ochsnerjournal.org/doi/abs/10.1043/1524-5012-13.3.400.

Carroll, R. (2014). Enterprise risk management: A framework for success. *American Society for Healthcare Risk Management White Paper*. Retrieved from www.ashrm.org/pubs/files/white_papers/ERM-White-Paper-8-29-14-FINAL.pdf.

Centers for Medicare & Medicaid Services. (2011). Guidance for performing failure mode and effects analysis with performance improvement projects. Retrieved from www.cms.gov/Medicare/Provider-Enrollment-and-Certification/QAPI/downloads/GuidanceForFMEA.pdf.

Centers for Medicare & Medicare Services. (2012a). CMS risk management terms, definitions, and acronyms. *Enterprise Information Security Group, risk management handbook*, Volume 1, Chapter 10 [CMS-CSIO-2012-vI-ch10]. Retrieved from www.cms.gov/Research-Statistics-Data-and-Systems/CMS-Information-Technology/InformationSecurity/Downloads/RMH_VI_10_Terms_Defs_Acronyms.pdf.

Centers for Medicare & Medicaid Services. (2012b). Emergency Medical Treatment & Labor Act (EMTALA). Retrieved from www.cms.gov/Regulations-and-Guidance/Legislation/EMTALA/.

Centers for Medicare & Medicaid Services. (2014). State operations manual: Guidelines for determining immediate jeopardy (Appendix Q). Retrieved from www.cms.gov/Regulations-and-Guidance/Guidance/Manuals/downloads/som107ap_q_immedjeopardy.pdf.

Centers for Medicare & Medicaid Services. (2018). What are the value based programs? Retrieved from www.cms.gov/Medicare/Quality-Initiatives-Patient-Assessment-Instruments/Value-Based-Programs/Value-Based-Programs.html.

Chobin, N. (2017). Compliance with the manufacturer's instructions for use. Retrieved from www.infectioncontroltoday.com/sterile-processing/compliance-manufacturers-instructions-use.

Donaldson, M. S. (2008). An overview of "To err is human": Re-emphasizing the message of patient safety. In R. G. Hughes (Ed.), *Patient safety and quality: An evidence-based handbook for nurses* (Chapter 3). Rockville, MD: Agency for Healthcare Research and Quality (US). Retrieved from www.ncbi.nlm.nih.gov/books/NBK2673/.

Food & Drug Administration. (2018). Medical device connectors. Retrieved from www.fda.gov/MedicalDevices/ProductsandMedicalProcedures/GeneralHospitalDevicesandSupplies/TubingandLuerMisconnections/default.htm#misconnections.

Hall, L. W., & Scott, S. D. (2012). The second victim of adverse health care events. *Nursing Clinics of North America, 47*(3), 383–393. DOI: https://doi.org/10.1016/j.cnur.2012.05.008.

Hanlon, C., Sheedy, K., Kniffin, T., & Rosenthal, J. (2015). 2014 guide to state adverse reporting systems. Retrieved from https://nashp.org/2014-guide-state-adverse-event-reporting-systems/.

Hasday, L. R. (2013). The Hippocratic oath as literary text: A dialogue between law and medicine. *Yale Journal of Health Policy, Law, and Ethics, 2*(2 Art 4). Retrieved from http://digitalcommons.law.yale.edu/cgi/viewcontent.cgi?article=1045&context=yjhple.

Health & Human Services. (2009). HITECH Act enforcement interim final rule. Retrieved from www.hhs.gov/hipaa/for-professionals/special-topics/hitech-act-enforcement-interim-final-rule/index.html.

Health & Human Services. (2015). Summary of HIPAA privacy rule. Retrieved from www.hhs.gov/hipaa/for-professionals/privacy/index.html.

HealthIT. (2018). What are the advantages of electronic health records? Retrieved from www.healthit.gov/faq/what-are-advantages-electronic-health-records.

Institute for Safe Medication Practices. (2016). Special edition: Tall man lettering; ISMP updates its list of drug names with tall man letters. Retrieved from www.ismp.org/resources/special-edition-tall-man-lettering-ismp-updates-its-list-drug-names-with-tall-man-letters.

Kachalia, A. (2013). Improving patient safety through transparency. *New England Journal of Medicine, 369*, 1677–1679. DOI: 10.1056/NEJMp1303960.

Kachalia, A., Kaufman, S. R., Boothman, R., Anderson, S., Welch, K., Saint, S., & Rogers, M. A. (2010). Liability claims and costs before and after implementation of a medical error disclosure program. *Annals of Internal Medicine, 153*(4), 213–221. DOI: 10.7326/0003-4819-153-4-201008170-00002.

Kaiser Family Foundation. (2015a). Nurse practitioner scope of practice laws. Retrieved from www.kff.org/other/state-indicator/total-nurse-practitioners/?currentTimeframe=0&sortModel=%7B%22colId%22:%22Location%22,%22sort%22:%22asc%22%7D.

Kaiser Family Foundation. (2015b). Physician assistant scope of practice laws. Retrieved from www.kff.org/other/state-indicator/physician-assistant-scope-of-practice-laws/?currentTimeframe=0&sortModel=%7B%22colId%22:%22Location%22,%22sort%22:%22asc%22%7D.

Keers, R., Williams S., Cooke J., & Ashcroft, D. (2013). Causes of medication administration errors in hospitals: A systematic review of quantitative and qualitative evidence. *Drug Safety, 36*(11), 1045–1067. DOI: 10.1007/s40264-013-0090-2.

Kohn, L. T., Corrigan J. M., & Donaldson, M. S. (Eds.). (2000). *To err is human: Building a safer health system*. Washington, DC: National Academy Press.

Ksiazek, M. (2015). New Massachusetts law creates process for early resolution of medical malpractice claims. Retrieved from https://palawblog.stark-stark.com/2015/02/articles/medical-malpractice/new-massachusetts-law-creates-process-for-early-resolution-of-medical-malpractice-claims/.

Lightizer, B., & Thurlo-Walsh, B. (2012). Mitigate risk and drive organizational change with Just Culture. Retrieved from www.psqh.com/analysis/mitigate-risk-and-drive-organizational-change-with-just-culture/.

Lippincott Solutions. (2018). Update on nursing staff ratios. Retrieved from http://lippincottsolutions.lww.com/blog.entry.html/2018/03/08/update_on_nursingst-HJoe.html.

Menachemi, N., & Collum, T. (2011). Benefits and drawbacks of electronic health record systems. *Risk Management Healthcare Policy, 4*, 47–55. DOI: 10.2147/RMHP.S12985.

Nash, D. (2011). The Patient Safety Act. *Pharmaceutical & Therapeutics, 36*(3), 118. Retrieved from www.ncbi.nlm.nih.gov/pmc/articles/PMC3086102/.

Neuhauser, D. (2003). Florence Nightingale gets no respect: As a statistician that is. *British Medical Journal of Quality & Safety, 12*(4), 317. Retrieved from http://dx.doi.org/10.1136/qhc.12.4.317.

O'Connor, J., & Matthews, G. (2011). Informational privacy, public health, and state laws. *American Journal of Public Health, 101*(10), 1845–1850. http://doi.org/10.2105/AJPH.2011.300206.

PSNet. (2018a). Disclosure errors. Retrieved from https://psnet.ahrq.gov/primers/primer/2/disclosure-of-errors.

PSNet. (2018b). Never events. Retrieved from https://psnet.ahrq.gov/primers/primer/3/never-events.

Public Law 111–148 The Patient Protection and Affordable Care Act, 111th Congress (2010). Retrieved from www.gpo.gov/fdsys/pkg/PLAW-111publ148/pdf/PLAW-111publ148.pdf.

Reason, J. (2000, March 18). Human error: Models and management. *British Medical Journal, 320*(7237), 768–770. Retrieved from www.ncbi.nlm.nih.gov/pmc/articles/PMC1117770/.

Reason, J. T., Carthey, J., & de Leval, M. R. (2001). Diagnosing "vulnerable system syndrome": An essential prerequisite to effective risk management. *BMJ Quality & Safety, 10*, ii21–ii25.

Saitta, N., & Hodge, S. D. (2012) Efficacy of a physician's words of empathy: An overview of state apology laws. *The Journal of American Osteopathic Association, 112*(5), 302–306. Retrieved from http://dx.doi.org/10.7556/jaoa.2012.112.5.302.

Tague, N. (2004). *The quality toolbox* (2nd ed., pp. 236–240). ASQ Quality Press. Retrieved from https://asq.org/quality-press/display-item?item=H1224 and http://asq.org/learn-about-quality/process-analysis-tools/overview/fmea.html.

The Joint Commission. (2012). *Transitions of care: The need for a more effective approach to continuing patient care*. Retrieved from www.jointcommission.org/assets/1/18/Hot_Topics_Transitions_of_Care.pdf.

The Joint Commission. (2015). Human factors analysis in patient safety systems. Retrieved from www.jointcommission.org/assets/1/6/HumanFactorsThe_Source.pdf.

The Joint Commission. (2016). Public information policy. Retrieved from www.jointcommission.org/pip/.

The Joint Commission. (2017a). Infection control basics—key practices that are a must. Retrieved from www.jointcommission.org/assets/1/6/BPHC_IC_Workshop_6.16.17.pdf.

The Joint Commission. (2017b). Sentinel event alert 58: Inadequate hand-off communication. Retrieved from www.jointcommission.org/sentinel_event_alert_58_inadequate_handoff_communications/.

The Joint Commission. (2018). 2018 hospital national patient safety goals. Retrieved from www.jointcommission.org/assets/1/6/2018_HAP_NPSG_goals_final.pdf.

The Joint Commission. (n.d.). Public information policy. Retrieved from www.jointcommission.org/assets/1/18/Public_Information_Policy_final.pdf.

Weger, D. (2017). Going bare—are doctors required to have malpractice insurance? Retrieved from www.gallaghermalpractice.com/blog/post/going-bare-are-doctors-required-to-have-malpractice-insurance.

Wolf, Z. (2008). *Error reporting and disclosure in patient safety and quality: An evidence-based handbook for nurses* (Chapter 35). Agency for Healthcare Research and Quality. Retrieved from www.ncbi.nlm.nih.gov/books/NBK2652/.

World Health Organization. (2012). Root cause analysis. Retrieved from www.who.int/patientsafety/education/curriculum/course5a_handout.pdf.

Additional Reading

Aeroassurance. (2014). James Reason's 12 principles of error management. Retrieved from http://aerossurance.com/helicopters/james-reasons-12-principles-error-management.

American Association of Nurse Practitioners. (2015). Scope of practice for nurse practitioners. Retrieved from www.aanp.org/images/documents/publications/scopeofpractice.pdf.

Dimick, C. (2008). Documentation bad habits, shortcuts in electronic records pose risk. *Journal of the American Health Information Management Association, 79*(6), 40–43. Retrieved from http://library.ahima.org/xpedio/groups/public/documents/ahima/bok1_038463.hcsp?dDocName=bok1_038463.

Russ, A. L., Fairbanks, R. J., Karsh, B. T., Militello, L. G., Saleem, J. J., & Wears, R. L. (2012). The science of human factors: Separating fact from fiction. *MJ Quality & Safety, 22*(10), 802–808. Retrieved from http://dx.doi.org/10.1136/bmjqs2012-001450.

The Free Dictionary. (n.d.). Harm definition. Retrieved from https://medical-dictionary.thefreedictionary.com/harm.

Test Questions

1. Which of the following are risks unique to the healthcare business environment? Mark all that apply.
   A. Data security
   B. Inadequate work assignment for acuity
   C. Primary source credentials verification
   D. Legally protected identifiers
   E. Customer service and satisfaction

2. Which of the following are typically associated with Patient Safety? Mark all that apply.
   A. Just Culture
   B. Disciplinary action
   C. Transparency
   D. Patient disclosure
   E. Litigation

3. What are potential consequences of a significant adverse patient event? Mark all that apply.
   A. Malpractice litigation
   B. Patient harm
   C. Regulatory reporting
   D. Reputation damage
   E. All of the above

4. What are unexpected risks when using an Electronic Health Record (EHR)? Mark all that apply.
   A. Copy and paste attribution
   B. Chart entry errors
   C. Customized chart views
   D. Loss of patient engagement
   E. All the above

5. Which of the following is not necessarily part of the electronic medical record? Mark all that apply.
   A. History and physical
   B. Lab results
   C. Clinical notes
   D. Diagnostic Imaging results
   E. An incident report
   F. An audit trail

Answers: 1. B, C, & D; 2. A & C; 3. E; 4. E; 5. E & F

Chapter 23

The Life Care Planning Expert

Tracy Albee, BSN, RN, PHN, LNCC®, CLCP, FIALCP
Mariann F. Cosby, DNP, MPA, RN, PHN, CEN, NE-BC, LNCC®, CLCP, CCM, MSCC
Martha Heath Beach, MS, M.Ed., RN, CNS, ARNP, CNP, CRC, CCM, CDMS, CLCP, CNLCP®, CCRN, CNRN, CNOR, LNCC®, CCNS, ACNP-BC

Contents

Objectives

- Evaluate the utilization of a life care plan in assessment of damages in a case
- Understand the history of life care planning
- Identify facts involved in choosing a life care planner
- Discuss the steps required to complete a life care plan
- Analyze the steps of litigation as they apply to life care planners

Introduction

A life care plan (LCP) is a dynamic document based upon published standards of practice, comprehensive assessment, data analysis, and research, which provides an organized concise plan for current and future needs with associated costs for individuals who have experienced catastrophic injury or have chronic health care needs.

(Weed, 2018, p. 5)

Reviewed and vetted by 100 professionals experienced in preparing LCPs who took part in the first Life Care Planning Summit in 2000, the definition was adopted by the International Academy of Life Care Planning (IALCP) in 2003 and remains endorsed by the life care planning standards and summit proceedings (Albee, Gamez, & Johnson, 2017; Gamez & Johnson, 2017; International Association of Rehabilitation Professionals [IARP], 2015).

In addition to the definition of an LCP, the 2000 Life Care Planning Summit included discussions regarding the life care planning process (Preston & Johnson, 2012). Consensus and majority statements, or tenets, were established that denote that LCPs should be individualized to reflect specific needs and promote optimal health, function, and autonomy (Weed & Berens, 2012). The LCP should be comprehensive, based on multidisciplinary data, adaptive to change, and written in an objective and consistent manner (Weed & Berens, 2012).

> According to the International Academy of Life Care Planners (IALCP), life care planning is a transdisciplinary specialty practice. "Each profession brings to the process of life care planning practice standards which must be adhered to by the individual professional and these standards remain applicable while the practitioner engages in life care planning activities" (International Association of Rehabilitation Professionals [IARP], 2015, p. 5). Additionally, each practitioner is responsible for following the *Standards of Practice for Life Care Planners* (IARP, 2015). The standards of practice of two specialty life care plan (LCP) groups—nurses and physicians—are similar, with noted overlap amongst all three professional standards of practice documents.
>
> (Gamez, Johnson, & Stajduhar, 2017, p. 42)

Life care planners are often legal nurse consultants (LNCs) who have expanded their practice. Therefore, it is important for LNCs to understand all the practical aspects of life care planning and the varied parties who incorporate it into their businesses. The LNC should be knowledgeable of the damages side of the litigation process and understand the subtleties regarding the advocacy element of their scope of practice in this context (Schofield & Huntington-Frazier, 2015).

Today, life care planning is performed by a wide array of healthcare professionals, and several professional organizations have included life care planners among their membership as follows: the International Association of Rehabilitation Professionals—International Academy of Life Care Planners Section (IARP-IALCP); the American Association of Legal Nurse Consultants (AALNC); the Association of Rehabilitation Nurses (ARN); the American Association of Nurse Life Care Planners (AANLCP®); the Case Management Society of America (CMSA); and the American Academy of Physician Life Care Planners (AAPLCP™).

Many of these professional associations believe life care planners are multidisciplinary providers (Bond, 2017). However, two organizations were established with a specialty practice focus. In 1997, the AANLCP® was founded for registered nurses (RNs) practicing life care planning (Howland, 2015). The goal of establishing the organization was to recognize nurse life care planning as a professional specialty that implements the nursing process, to diagnose individuals and formulate LCPs (Howland, 2015). Over time the association evolved and currently offers a specialty certification based on the *Nurse Life Care Planning Scope and Standards of Practice* (Howland, 2015).

The AAPLCP™ was founded for Physical, Medicine, & Rehabilitation Physician Specialists, with the mission to champion the practice of life care planning by physicians (Gonzales, 2017). The AAPLCP™ reports commitment to elevate the discipline of life care planning through research and publication, the advancement of life care planning methodology, standards of practice, and education, training, and certification of qualified physicians (Gonzales, 2017).

Life care planners are utilized in litigation to present future medical damages in cases involving catastrophic injuries or illnesses. The LCP can serve multiple purposes, both in litigation and in the financing aspects of a non-litigated injury or illness. Also, it can be used as a financial planning document for individuals establishing trust accounts, or insurers setting reserves on catastrophic cases. Case managers often utilize an LCP to assist in determining costs and time frames for equipment and service needs for clients.

History of Life Care Planning

The basic principles, tenets, methodologies, and processes of life care planning began to emerge in the late 1970s in the United States. The utilization of an LCP as a tool in the case management process of catastrophic injury cases was first referenced and published by Deutsch and Raffa in 1981. The genesis of life care planning is the result of three spheres of influence: case management, clinical psychology, and developmental psychology.

These plans originally served as supporting tools to summarize, coordinate, and document the progress of complex rehabilitation after sustaining a catastrophic injury. As a result of these LCPs providing such consistency and organization to a complex process, the specialty attracted much interest. The insurance and legal community found enormous value in the use of the LCP. The plans served as a tool to mitigate costly complications as the result of inadvertently neglecting proactive treatment or failing to set accurate financial reserves for future care.

The field of rehabilitation counseling utilized the life care planning process to better manage the trajectory of recovery experienced with catastrophic disability. The injured individual, family, and medical professionals discovered immense value for its use and application to streamline care and ensure critical aspects of medical and rehabilitation were addressed in a timely manner. Today, life care planning has burgeoned into a sub-specialty highly sought after for its multiple applications; providing individualized, researched blueprints of current and future medical and rehabilitation needs for persons with disabilities (Weed & Berens, 2018).

Understanding the Value of a Life Care Plan in Litigation

The unspoken question foremost in civil litigation is "How much is this case worth?" In personal injury cases, including medical malpractice and product liability, damages are directly related to the injuries suffered by the plaintiff. These injuries may include bodily harm, psychological damage, loss of future earnings, and pain and suffering. A quantifiable estimate of future costs to the plaintiff resulting from the injuries is critical to the assessment of the case's value. In civil litigation, an LCP relates specifically to disability after the catastrophic illness or injury allegedly caused by the defendant. The pre-existing medical conditions are acknowledged in the plan, but other costs related to pre-existing conditions are not projected as a part of the plan unless those pre-existing costs are exacerbated by the injury or illness of the subject in the LCP.

The purpose of an LCP for an insurance carrier may be for other than a settlement, as they must be sure their cases are not underinsured for them to remain solvent. The carriers are often required by agreement with a reinsurance carrier to report and choose an appropriate and qualified life care planner.

Choosing an Appropriate and Qualified Life Care Planner

Selecting an LCP expert follows the standard process with regard to the Federal Rules of Evidence in Article VII, Opinions and Expert Testimony, Rules 701–706 that governs all testifying experts and how they form their opinions (Federal Rules of Evidence, 2018). In 2011, the wording was updated to reflect a more precise understanding of the intent of the rule. The most current writing of the rule is as follows (Legal Information Institute, n.d.):

A witness who is qualified as an expert by knowledge, skill, experience, training, and education may testify in the form of an opinion or otherwise if:

a. The expert's scientific, technical, or other specialized knowledge will help the trier-of-fact to understand the evidence or to determine a fact in issue
b. The testimony is based on sufficient facts or data
c. The testimony is the product of reliable principles and methods and
d. The expert has reliably applied the principles to the facts of the case

In June of 1993, the U.S. Supreme Court issued an opinion relating to how federal judges should decide when and whether to allow expert testimony in the courtroom. Prior to this, most federal and state judges considered two standards: relevance to a fact at issue, and whether it would be useful to the jury. The judges also looked to a 1923 ruling known as *Frye*, which held that conclusions must be generally accepted within the expert community.

In *Daubert v. Merrell Dow Pharmaceuticals, Inc.*, the U.S. Supreme Court sought to clarify these standards, by directing the judges to act as *gatekeepers* in the courtroom, to examine the scientific method underlying expert evidence, and to admit it only if determined to be both "relevant and reliable." Two later cases, *General Electric v. Joiner* and *Kumho Tire Co. v. Carmichael*, expanded upon this opinion.

When the U.S. Supreme Court issued its opinion in *Daubert*, it gave four primary criteria for determining admissibility (Tellus Institute, 2003):

1. Is the evidence based on testable theory or technique?
2. Has the theory or technique been peered reviewed?
3. In the case of a particular technique, does it have a known error rate and standards controlling the technique's operation?
4. Is the underlying science generally accepted?

An important factor for LNCs to understand, is while federal jurisdictions are relatively well settled, each state has its own case law and expert witness standards. A state may choose to follow Frye, Daubert, or some combination of the two. While the LNC may assist with expert selection the hiring attorney must ensure the expert hired for any given case can meet the expert requirements for that venue (Wilkinson, 2015). For example, when selecting an expert witness for a case in New York, the client must consider their expert witness's testimony will be subject to Frye standards, but in New Jersey, the testimony would be bound by the Daubert ruling. Staying abreast of recent court rulings can assist the LNC with this aspect of expert selection (Hanus, 2018).

During a jury trial, any challenge to an expert's testimony will typically be decided prior to or outside the jury hearing the person's opinions. Therefore, it is vital the life care planner be able to address these issues knowledgeably and confidently with the attorney in the initial interview. According to Rule 702, it is imperative the life care planner can articulate the principles and methods used in preparation of the LCP and the reliability of such standards and methods as they apply to the specific case for which the life care planner is retained.

One way for the LNC to assess the life care planner's knowledge is through review of the potential expert's education, experience, training, skills, and recognized credentials. Significant and current experience in the care of persons with chronic, lifelong disability, and catastrophic illness and injuries, or both would likely be a major advantage for any life care planner but is not required. Additionally, the life care planner with case management experience, a role that includes coordination of services to the catastrophically ill or injured, could also be determined as beneficial. Familiarity with vendors and healthcare providers, and the ability to find these sources in various locales, is essential. It is preferable for the expert to have a professional background and experience relevant to the diagnosis, age, and medical needs of the injured or ill individual.

Given that LCPs are completed by professionals from varied backgrounds, each professional possesses differing credentials, licensure, and certifications. As a result, the attorney or LNC needs to understand the various educational programs and certifications relevant to life care planning to determine the most appropriate person for the case. Advanced academic preparation demonstrates an enriched knowledge base with commitment to professionalism. Membership in professional associations, attendance at professional meetings, conferences, and continuing education courses all confirm ongoing acquisition of current skills and knowledge. These activities are an important component to the assessment process for the LNC (Bond, 2017; Kwass & Bailey, 2017).

Requesting a sample LCP may provide information such as writing style, past recommendations, and formatting (see Appendix A example). In general, this will provide information helpful to the LNC in understanding the plan's interventions and the underlying methodology utilized by the life care planner.

While all LCPs should contain certain components that demonstrate the report meets the standards (assessment, analysis, collaboration, and research), the format may differ. Some life care planners utilize standard formats and templates (Howland, 2015; Powell, 2015; Riddick-Grisham & Deming, 2011; Weed & Berens, 2018). Other life care planners use software planning programs or a self-developed format unique to their business practice or case.

Credentials

Many life care planners hold certifications in life care planning beyond those usually seen in the general healthcare field in which the professional practices. Valid certifications are offered by professional organizations, and awarded by a third-party, standard-setting organization, which should be independent of special interests. Knowing the difference between a certificate and a certification should be part of the LNC's knowledge base when interviewing experts (see Chapter 1, History, Entry into Practice, and Certification).

The following is a list of credentials specific to life care planning that are often held by life care planner professionals:

■ Certified Life Care Planner (CLCP) (ICHCC, n.d.-b): This is a multidisciplinary life care planning specialty practice certification program for qualified healthcare practitioners, administered by a corporation, the International Commission on Healthcare Certification (ICHCC). The ICHCC is currently in the application process for accreditation under the National Association for Certifying Agencies (NCCA), at the time of this 4th edition publication (ICHCC, n.d.-a).

■ Certified Nurse Life Care Planner (CNLCP®) (CNLCP®, n.d.): This is a certification program administered by the Certified Nurse Life Care Planners Certification Board, a non-profit entity that collaborates with the AANLCP® Executive Board. An application for accreditation by the American Board of Nursing Specialties Accreditation Council (now the

Accreditation Board for Specialty Nursing Certification) was submitted in August of 2007, and at the time of this publication the board continues to work towards approval. Standards of practice specific to the nurse life care planner are integral to the certification process (Howland, 2015).

■ Fellow in the International Academy of Life Care Planners (FIALCP): The Fellow designation was first established through the IARP-IALCP in 1996 with its goal to service the advanced practice needs of life care planners and to promote the application of standards of practice for life care planners in the field. To hold the credential of FIALCP, the applicant must submit work that demonstrates it meets specific criteria as evaluated by their peers (Shahnasarian, 2015).

■ Certified Physician Life Care Planner (CPLCP™) (n.d.): This is a new certification, as of 2017. The examination is administered by the CPLCP™ Certification Board by Professional Testing Corporation.

There are other healthcare provider credentials not included in the above list (e.g., occupational therapists and physical therapists), but would be important for the LNC to investigate when necessary (Gamez et al., 2017). Although holding a current accredited certification is an important indicator for the evaluating LNC, inclusion of the above certifications in this chapter does not imply validation by the AALNC. The retaining attorney or the firm's LNC must evaluate the validity of certifications presented by life care planners, and the appropriateness of their role in the case.

Steps Required for Developing a Life Care Plan

Data Collection and Analysis

Life care planners must obtain the data needed to analyze the injured or ill individual's past and present health status. Additionally, the life care planner must begin to form a basis for research into future care needs. In the initial stages of data collection, the life care planner may have medical records, employment records, school records, and other documents to review, which provide history and direction.

Assessment

The life care planner collects detailed data pertinent to the injured or ill individual's health status and need for ongoing medical, psychosocial, educational, and vocational needs. Often the life care planner begins this process with a comprehensive review of all available medical records. The life care planner completes an on-site assessment of the injured or ill person's status whenever possible. When an on-site visit is not possible, and after documentation of such a request by the life care planner, the damages evaluation may need to be performed based on a record review. A review of all available records relevant to damages is paramount.

The LNC can play a valuable role in collaborating with the life care planner to obtain a complete set of medical records and documents. It may be necessary to request ongoing treatment records and additional assessments to build an adequate foundation for the opinions of the LCP. A literature search may be needed to define the expected course and treatment of a diagnosis. The life care planner typically relies on evidence-based literature for opinions included within the LCP.

An on-site meeting with the injured person is always beneficial. It should be noted that when the life care planner is retained by a defense attorney, the opportunity to evaluate the plaintiff in-person is often denied. At times, the defense-retained life care planner may be allowed to observe the defense-retained physician's medical examination, if approved in advance by plaintiff's counsel. For the plaintiff-retained life care planner, the injured person's home is usually the most productive environment for the gathering of information, given the ability to view equipment, medications, and needs for modification in the individual's usual residential setting. The assessment life care planning interview should include the primary caregiver(s), whenever possible. When the injured person has sustained cognitive injuries, is unable to communicate, or is a minor child, the caregiver may be the primary source of information regarding daily care.

When hired by the plaintiff's counsel, the injured person's healthcare providers are often solicited for input into future care when appropriate. When future care is not discussed in the records, it is appropriate to seek additional information directly from the physician or other providers, after seeking applicable legal permission. In litigation, the life care planner would discuss this option with the referring attorney prior to any contact with current or past treatment providers. Due to the enactment of the Health Information Portability and Accountability Act (HIPAA) in 1996, it is necessary to obtain signed medical release authorization forms from the injured or ill person, or their responsible party, prior to contacting treating medical professionals. The referring attorney often handles this. There are also times when the plaintiff or defense attorney may choose to take depositions of the treating providers, to gain more information as to their future treatment plans.

Collaboration

Frequently, the life care planner will also collaborate with other healthcare providers to collect supplemental information and data for the LCP. A brief listing of these providers follows:

■ Physiatrist:

> Physical Medicine and Rehabilitation (PM&R) physicians, also known as physiatrists, treat a wide variety of medical conditions affecting the brain, spinal cord, nerves, bones, joints, ligaments, muscles, and tendons. Physiatrists evaluate and treat injuries, illnesses, and disability, and are experts in designing comprehensive, patient-centered treatment plans. They utilize cutting-edge as well as time-tested treatments to maximize function and quality of life.
> (American Academy of Physical Medicine and Rehabilitation Physicians, n.d.)

■ Medical Case Manager: When working for an insurance carrier, the medical case manager coordinates the medical and non-medical needs of the injured individual with the person's physician, insurance carrier, and attorneys. Case managers provide ongoing monitoring of the injured person's medical and psychological status, in addition to the person's medical needs. There are also independent medical case managers. In certain instances, the case manager can be a resource for the life care planner to be assured that all the individual's medical and psychological needs have been included in planning for the future.

■ Certified Rehabilitation Counselor (CRC): The CRC, who may also be a vocational counselor, provides an evaluation of the injured individual's ability to perform certain jobs within the physical, emotional, and cognitive abilities, as outlined by a treating physician's restrictions. The CRC also researches and provides job leads, recommends job modifications, and can assist with interviewing skills, obtaining employment, and job retraining. In conjunction with life care planning, the CRC can also be utilized to evaluate and project lost wages to include loss of long-term benefits.

There can also be other collaborative disciplines, depending on the specific injuries and needs unique to the injured person. A few examples might include treating physicians, occupational therapists, physical therapists, prosthetists, neuropsychologists, psychologists or psychiatrists, home modification experts, and special-education consultants. The list can be extensive and must be unique to the individual life care plan. The physician-specialists involved in the life care planning collaboration process will be diagnoses-driven and specific to each case. A *special needs trust* specialist might also be involved if the injured party is a minor or has other special circumstances requiring a special needs trust be implemented.

Creating the Plan

Each recommendation in the LCP must be supported by medical records, input from healthcare professionals, the assessment of the life care planner, and evidence-based literature, as appropriate. These elements contribute to the *foundation* of the LCP and will be necessary in all litigated cases. Services and products must be available in reasonable proximity to the injured party's residence. The LCP should provide the reader with a clear rationale for the relationship between recommended services and the injury or illness. It is critical to evaluate duration and frequency of recommended services and products, as well as to delineate changes in frequency, which could be due to growth, disease process, complications, aging or other factors.

Although life care planners use a variety of formats, basic writing principles for expert reports apply. The goal is a clear picture of the injured person's needs and the relationship of these needs to the sustained injuries. The LCP should reflect the desired outcomes being rehabilitative, restorative, and supportive of the injured or ill individual's ongoing needs. Clarity and brevity are essential. A well-prepared LCP projects future care in a defensible, organized, and transparent report (see Appendix A).

Each plan is unique and comprehensive in nature. In the preparation of an LCP, collaboration with other healthcare professionals, vendors, and specialists, for the exchange of knowledge and ideas about how to best deliver health care, maximizes the quality and credibility of the finished product. Recognition of the expertise of others outside one's profession is often necessary and appropriate. In the end, regardless of its collaborative nature, the LCP contains the opinions and conclusions of its author.

The LCP must portray a fair and comprehensive picture of the injured or ill individual's needs, relative to the catastrophic injury or chronic illness. Components of an LCP may include medical care, skilled nursing care, attendant care, household services, therapeutic assessments, therapeutic modalities, monitoring by physicians, orthotics/prosthetics, orthopedics, preventive health care, equipment, supplies, medications, diagnostic testing, hospital care, accessibility (housing), transportation, psychological support, case management, educational and vocational needs. The goal of the LCP is to allow the injured or ill individual to approximate as closely as possible the levels of independent function and quality of life that could have been expected if the injury or illness had not occurred.

Medical care projections incorporate costs of care by physicians, allied health professionals, therapeutic modalities, costs associated with diagnostic testing, anticipated hospitalizations, and medical procedures. Surveillance or preventive care is included to avoid or retard further complications. A comprehensive plan may include the services of a case manager to direct future care and implementation of the plan (Busch, 2018b). Costs of durable medical equipment (DME) include replacement costs, length of expected service, and annual maintenance charges. Both unit cost and frequency of use is described when summarizing the costs for medications and supplies. When housing modifications are needed to improve accessibility, the life care planner provides a detailed assessment of the current or future home and specific modifications recommended. When modifications are extensive and outside the scope of one's practice, these costs can be obtained in collaboration with an appropriate professional.

In many LCPs, the costs of medications, attendant care, and respite services are the most expensive items. It is important to be able to justify the medical necessity of the level of home-care personnel recommended (RN, licensed practical nurse [LPN]/licensed vocational nurse [LVN] certified nursing assistant [CNA], unskilled attendant, or other in-home supportive services). Also, the frequency of service should be clearly explained, and services should not be duplicated. If services are provided to prevent complications, then the cost of those complications typically should not be included unless there is a reasonable likelihood of the complications occurring despite the recommended interventions.

Home care services are often the biggest issue of debate within the LCP. New employment laws in most states now prohibit home health agencies from providing live-in attendant care at a flat rate and these agencies must charge increasing hourly rates to cover over-time in those circumstances (Kreimer, 2016). Therefore, when 24-hour per day care is medically necessary, it is very important for the life care planner to understand how the agencies charge for services and be capable of explaining to the attorney-client why these costs are much higher now than in previous years.

Some life care planners project for live-in care to be provided as a private hire by the injured party. This may be appropriate, as long as the additional costs are factored in, when a home health agency is not involved. This may include but is not limited to: (1) advertising fees, (2) costs associated with checking references, (3) performing criminal background checks, (4) accountant fees for handling payroll, (5) employer-required taxes, (6) extra costs associated with weekend and holiday coverage, and (7) liability and workers' compensation insurance.

Cost projections in the LCP should be categorized and organized in a logical manner and are often separated into the years that the service(s) will be required or that the needs will more likely than not, change over time. A summary table significantly facilitates the economist's work and also allows the jury to understand that the life care planner has taken into account any changes the injured person is likely to undergo over the course of a lifetime.

Determining Costs

Costs in the life care plan are presented in today's dollars. The completed LCP may be forwarded to an economist, by the hiring-attorney, to compute the present value of future costs set forth in the LCP. If the plan is not well structured, it can pose difficulties for the economist to analyze (Dillman, 2018). It is for this reason that the life care planner includes start and stop dates, as well as frequency and duration for all equipment, products, and services, within the LCP. The attorney usually retains an economist to interpret the numbers; and to incorporate inflation, interest rates, and other economic factors; since these calculations are beyond the scope of expertise of most life care planners. The economist must ensure that the final cost projection conforms to local jurisdiction rulings. The life care planner should include costs for usual and customary rates in the geographic area proximate to the injured person's home (Busch, 2017).

When a life care planner utilizes and cites billing codes in a plan to obtain costs, it is important for the life care planner to be knowledgeable of the various coding types which may include: Current Procedural Terminology (CPT), International Classification of Diseases (ICD), Diagnostic Related Groups (DRGs), and Healthcare Common Procedural Coding System (HCPCS) (Busch, 2017, 2018a; Holakiewicz & Pacheco, 2012). There are many reputable databases available to assist the life care planner in obtaining expected cost information based on the various systems of billing coding (Maniha & Watson, 2018). It is important when such databases are relied upon; the life care planner understands the basics of how the data was derived (Maniha, 2012).

Some life care planners call various providers in the plaintiff's community to obtain expected costs of care. This is appropriate if the data can be replicated over and over again. Unfortunately, not all healthcare providers will release an accurate cost estimate for future care not currently scheduled. Therefore, each life care planner must determine the methodology for estimating costs and then be comfortable defending it. Some life care planners use the middle range of costs as a reasonable estimate of the cost within a particular future item; others show the entire range of costs to cover a broader spectrum of future provider accessibility.

Currently, there is much debate between plaintiff and defense attorneys as to what is the definition of *the cost of future medical care*. While the plaintiff attorney will generally argue the cost of medical care is the cash rate a plaintiff would need to pay a healthcare provider for care, if there was no healthcare insurance involved; the defense attorney will want to consider the amount the healthcare provider actually accepts from any given third-party payor. Historically, life care planners have relied upon the cash rate, but due to many state's legal rulings, these third-party payor rates, known as *collateral sources*, are often presented and considered in determining the value of the future medical care (Busch, 2018a).

Life Care Plan Reviews

In litigation, the life care planner may be retained by either a plaintiff or a defense attorney to provide commentary on the LCP presented by the opposing counsel. When performing this type of review, each issue should be evaluated for appropriateness to the injury or illness, relevance to the litigated damage, reasonableness of costs, absence of duplication in services, and availability of goods and services geographically close to the individual with the illness or injury. The attorney may be particularly interested in potential sources of investigation to delineate any pre-existing medical issues impacting the current claim. For example, examination of school records or work history may show pre-morbid cognitive deficits mitigating some of the alleged damages.

The attorney may request an oral report before receiving any of the life care planner's written opinions. In some cases, the defense attorney may request a complete LCP, independent of the plaintiff's submission.

As mentioned above, a review of any collateral sources, such as government or private agencies which may provide services and equipment, is often a request of the defense attorney. The life care planner will educate the attorney regarding collateral sources. Life care planners may be judicious or refrain from guaranteeing funding from collateral sources, understanding that approval of equipment and services is often based on legislative and budgetary criteria and not guaranteed from year to year. The admissibility of such collateral sources also depends upon the local rules of evidence. Use of collateral funding sources as an offset for projected costs depends on the local jurisdiction of the case, and this should be clarified with the hiring attorney.

Life Expectancy

The most relied upon basis for normal life expectancy is found in the Center for Disease Control and Prevention (CDC) life tables. This is a source often used by life care planners to provide the informational data on *normal* life expectancy that is used in the LCP. Although non-physician life care planners do not project life expectancy, opinions on life expectancy or economic considerations related to the LCP may be considered.

At the attorney's request, the life care planner may be asked to participate in determining life expectancy. In some cases, the life care planner may work with a structured settlement company, insurance underwriter, or statistician to obtain a rated age for life expectancy. A rated age assumes that the insured is older than the person's actual *age*, which is a way of saying that the person will not live as long as a standard risk, and is then used to determine the life expectancy. In other cases, the treating or retained medical doctor may be the one to provide a life expectancy opinion.

Preparing the Life Care Planner for Deposition

The life care planner is considered an expert and may be called for deposition to testify as to their opinions and how they came to the conclusions represented in the LCP. The LCP as an expert will adhere to the same process as other nursing experts as defined in Chapter 31, The Legal Nurse Consultant as Expert Witness.

File Review

Careful file review precedes the deposition. The deposition request usually includes a call for the expert's entire file. The opposing attorney is entitled to review all notes, drafts, resources, and records in the file. File maintenance should be a priority throughout all stages of consulting. The expert should bring an updated curriculum vitae (CV) to the deposition. Before the deposition, the life care planner should review any current medical records generated between completion of the report and date of deposition. An addendum to the LCP is often considered appropriate and is provided to both sides prior to testimony. The plaintiff's expert may contact the plaintiff or caregiver for an update, if the deposition takes place several months (or more) after the completion of the report. The defense expert could request an update on the plaintiff's condition through the defense attorney's office. Depositions and reports of fact witnesses' and other expert witnesses should be made available for review by the life care planner.

Review of Opposing Life Care Planning Opinions if Available

Prior to deposition, the life care planner may be provided the LCP prepared by the opposing expert. Defendants' counsel typically retains a life care planner to review and critique the plaintiff's LCP. At other times, defendants' counsel may choose to have their own independent life care planner create a life care plan. If the opposing expert's life care planning report is available, it is important to review it carefully and be prepared to comment and discuss it in detail during deposition. The focus should include the similarities and differences between the two plans: the life care planner's and the opposing expert's plan. If the opposing life care planner used a different methodology, an attempt should be made to understand how the person came to their conclusions. If there are discrepancies or elements in methodology not transparent, be prepared to discuss the specific areas or items where it is unclear how the work was approached.

It is important to keep in mind that at times, the differences in opinion may be directly related to the other collaborating professionals, i.e., physicians working on the case, having differing opinions. However, regardless of how the collaborating professionals see the future care needs of the injured individual, life care planners must stay consistent with their methodology and remain unbiased in their approach to the process.

Assure the Life Care Planner Can Clearly Explain and Defend Their Cost Research

Too commonly, life care planners may rely on cost research without really understanding it. It is important to review all back up support for the cost research in the life care planner's file and assure the expert can explain it thoroughly. For example, if using a national database, the life care planner should know how data is collected and collated; the life care planner must understand the differences between means, medians, and the various percentages that may be relied upon. When using the Internet to research costs of services, medications, or durable medical equipment (DME), the expert needs to be able to clearly explain why certain vendors are used rather than others; or if they are using an average cost from multiple vendors.

Preparing the Life Care Planner for Trial

File Review

File review was the first step in preparing for deposition. File review is paramount in preparing for trial testimony. If significant time has passed between the deposition and the trial, often due to trial continuances, then the file needs to be updated. There can be many months or years between preparation of the report and the trial date.

In most cases, if more than six months have passed, it is advisable to contact the attorney for more recent medical information, followed by updating of the LCP, if appropriate. Updated medical records and new relevant depositions must be obtained and reviewed. When possible, it may be helpful to speak with physicians, therapists, home health nurses, and vendors. In addition, the plaintiff or the plaintiff's caregiver could be contacted, and a new assessment interview is often appropriate for evaluation and reassessment. The expert should have a well-organized file for easy reference if necessary.

The life care planner should also have a knowledgeable and comfortable grasp of case details during testimony. Demonstrating knowledge of the plaintiff's condition without constant referral to the files is most convincing. Careful review of deposition testimony of the plaintiff, caregivers, other damage experts, and defendants provides critical information about the opposing attorney's theories in the case as well as the attorney's style of cross-examination.

It is helpful to review one's own deposition testimony. The opposing attorney may seek to elicit contradictions in prior testimony, while in front of the jury, by reading sections of the deposition. Having knowledge of one's own deposition allows for clarification and augmentation of information deleted by the opposing attorney. Explanations for any changes in opinions between deposition and trial should be carefully considered and discussed with the hiring attorney prior to trial.

Review of the Depositions Taken of the Collaborating Professionals

Before trial, the life care planner should request an opportunity to review the deposition transcripts of the collaborating professionals referenced in the report. There are times when physicians involved may be provided additional information that could change their opinion at the time of their deposition. If the collaborating professionals' opinions change over time, this could result in the life care plan report no longer being as accurate as possible.

If the life care planner is reading a transcript and notes a change in opinion of a referenced professional in the report, this should be brought to the attention of the retaining attorney, so that adjustments in the LCP can be made if necessary. If a life care planning report is changed after the expert has testified, this could open the life care planner up to a second deposition. Therefore, the retaining attorney must provide any updated reports to the other side as soon as possible after a change is made.

Review of the Opposing Life Care Planner and Opposing Physician Expert Deposition Testimony

Just as the life care planner wants to assure their report is as accurate as possible prior to trial, the expert also must completely understand the opposing opinions before testifying. It is typical for the cross-examination to include questions about the opposing side's conclusions and why the two sides may differ. While reviewing the opposing side's LCP before deposition is helpful, it is just as, or more, helpful to read the deposition testimony before trial, which will provide even more insight into the methodology used by the opposing side.

Pre-trial Meeting with Hiring Attorney

A pre-trial meeting, or at least a conference call, should occur before trial. The retaining attorney should carefully review all aspects of trial testimony with the life care planner. Some attorneys prefer to rehearse direct examination, while others prefer more general discussions of the points to be covered. Preparation is most critical regarding cross-examination questions. The attorney and life care planner must anticipate the strategy of the opposing attorney and consider concise answers to expected areas of attack. Expert testimony involving damages is usually presented toward the end of trial, which provides the opportunity to discuss previous testimony. It is helpful for the life care planner to know what the jury has already heard.

In addition, the life care planner should ask their attorney-client about the testimony of the other experts that collaborated with re-trial work, assuming they testified at trial before the life care planner. This is done so physician experts can set the life care planning foundation. There are times when the physician, who testified first, was pressed on an issue and then changed their opinion about a prior recommendation. When this occurs, a change to the LCP numbers may need to be done "on the fly" and in front of the trier-of-fact. This is a lot less stressful when the life care planner knows they will have to make a change, rather than learning of it while sitting in the witness box.

Trial Testimony

Testimony focuses initially on the expert's qualifications. The witness must be able to present background information and credentials in a clear, confident, and impressive manner. The trier-of-fact must regard the witness's testimony as credible and important to the verdict. Recent legal decisions have affected the process of qualifying experts. Some jurisdictions demand more rigorous standards of proof of expertise.

The life care planner will be asked about remuneration, in the attempt to assign a *hired-gun* status to the expert's testimony. The opposing counsel may ask if the life care planner was paid prior to their testimony and the amount of those charges. It must be clear the expert is objective and that fees are not related to the outcome of the case. The life care planning is paid for their time and not the opinions. It is usually helpful if the expert has testified in prior cases on behalf of both plaintiffs and defendants. They will often be asked to provide information regarding those cases they previously provided testimony for, the percentage of plaintiff and defense cases, and dates and location of the testimony.

During direct examination, the opinions expressed are presented by the life care planner. The attorney usually leads up to specific recommendations with an introduction to the life care planning process itself. The opposing attorney attempts to prove that the life care planner's opinions are invalid. A well-written, defensible LCP is the best preparation for cross-examination.

It is also important that the life care planner's testimony stays within the confines of the LCP development. Unless previously discussed with the retaining attorney, veering off the topic into liability elements of the case, such as the standard of care or fact witness testimony, are not recommended. Being clear as to the role the life care planner's testimony bears in the case is essential (Barros-Bailey & Dominick, 2017).

Importance of Continuously Assessing and Updating the Life Care Planner's Standard of Practice

History of Summits

Life care planning is an advanced specialty practice performed by a diverse community of professionals in various healthcare fields. Due to the diversity of professional backgrounds in life care planning and because this specialized practice continues to grow and develop, it is vital to promote a coordinated effort with standardized approaches. Education of emerging and experienced practicing professionals is a key aspect of fostering the advancement of the field. While process and standards of practice for life care planning have been established and published, consensus and unity in this diverse field is an evolving process. Through life care planning summits, life care planners have the opportunity to examine relevant issues, contribute to the resolution of these issues, and be involved in the evolution of the specialty practice (Albee et al., 2017; Johnson, 2012; Gamez & Johnson, 2017).

Life care planning summits are historically biennial events attended by life care planning practitioners with the goal of exploring the current state and future direction of life care planning. Since 2000, over 600 life care planners have participated in summits, demonstrating a commitment to addressing cutting-edge issues affecting the life care planning community (Albee et al., 2017). The results of each summit are published and then relied upon by life care planners in their practice. Each summit and subsequent publication add to and update what is known as *The Best Practices and Consensus and Majority Statements* (Albee et al., 2017; Johnson, 2015). These reinforce the life care planning methodology and performed work.

Conferences and Continuing Education

Attending conferences and obtaining continuing education is very important for life care planners. One must stay on top of both the cutting-edge medical care now available to injured individuals and be cognizant of changing methodologies and standards of practice in the industry. In addition, having a well-established network of other experts in the field is helpful when trying to obtain information on an issue that may be less familiar to a life care planner while doing their work. To maintain the various certifications life care planners hold continuing education is a requirement. Keeping careful records of the conferences attended and continuing education units obtained will make recertification much easier to complete when the time comes.

Exposure of the Life Care Planner

It is recommended for the life care planner to have professional liability insurance in the event an error or omission occurs in the report or expert services, or both. Furthermore, the LCP may assist in determining if any claims have been previously made of the expert related to errors and omissions. Areas of exposure might include, but are not limited to, omitting costly attendant care, hospital admissions, or future surgeries from an LCP. Therefore, factoring in additional, periodic updates in the original LCP may mitigate some of this exposure.

Essentially, the life care planner is an expert witness. Therefore, similar liability exists that exposes the life care planner to claims such as errors, omissions, and factual inaccuracies that may damage the case. A life care planner may also place themselves at risk of prosecution for perjury for any false testimony occurring during a deposition or trial appearance. These issues would expose the life care planner to claims against their practice. For malpractice to exist, it must be determined that the expert, or in this case, the life care planner, failed to perform at the minimum standard for the profession and that the failure caused injury to the party, albeit plaintiff or defense. To approach an allegation of malpractice or negligence, the party alleging malpractice or negligence of the expert must prove the expert deviated from the industry standard and the party would have won the verdict, if not for the malpractice of the expert.

Therefore, there are some legal risks life care planners assume in their duties performed both to the hiring party and the opposing party or counsel. In particular, due to the nature of an LCP being an evolving *dynamic document*, the testimony of an expert witness may change prior to trial from previous testimony. Even though expert witnesses benefit from a protection to testify based on the premise that witnesses should not fear reprisal from their testimony, for LNCs that perform life care planning services, it would be prudent for retainer agreements to be drafted to protect against these types of claims and demand arbitration.

Using the Life Care Plan after Litigation

Since insurance carriers do use LCPs as a tool in discerning those cases which are advantageous for them to settle, then it goes to follow that the LCP can be a means of outlining the plan for future case management. The case manager is dedicated to the coordination of claims requiring medical monitoring to avoid the development of complications.

Summary

Every trial has two sides: plaintiff and defense, and damages are a key part of trials. Plaintiffs use damage experts to present monetary values before the jury or trier-of-fact, and defendants may use damage experts to refute the opinions of plaintiff's corresponding experts. The life care planner is in a unique role to opine on future care needs based on sound methodology and evidence-based practices.

References

Albee, T., Gamez, J., & Johnson, C. (2017). 2017 Life Care Planning Summit proceedings. *Journal of Life Care Planning, 15*(3), 19–29. Retrieved from https://connect.rehabpro.org/newwww/publications/jlcp-index.

American Academy of Physical Medicine and Rehabilitation Physicians. (n.d.). What is a physiatrist? Retrieved from www.aapmr.org/about-physiatry/about-physical-medicine-rehabilitation/what-is-physiatry.

Barros-Bailey, M., & Dominick, B. K. (2017). The expert witness team in employment law cases. *Journal of Nurse Life Care Planning, 17*(2), 29–31. Retrieved from www.aanlcp.org/?page=JournalCopies.

Berens, D. E. (2018). *Example life care plan.* Atlanta, GA.

Bond, N. (2017). Hiring a life care planner. *Trial, 53*(4), 49–50. Retrieved from www.justice.org/node/134220.

Busch, R. M. S. (2017). Managing the notion of UCR in a life care plan. *Journal of Life Care Planning, 15*(3), 3–14. Retrieved from https://connect.rehabpro.org/newwww/publications/jlcp-index.

Busch, R. M. S. (2018a). Critical elements of healthcare costing. *Journal of Life Care Planning, 16*(3), 37–42. Retrieved from https://connect.rehabpro.org/newwww/publications/jlcp-index.

Busch, R. M. S. (2018b). Implementation of a life care plan after the development by a nurse life care planner. *Journal of Nurse Life Care Planning, 18*(1), 48–56. Retrieved from www.aanlcp.org/page/JournalCopies?.

Certified Nurse Life Care Planner®. (n.d.). Certified Nurse Life Care Planner certification board. Retrieved from http://cnlcp.org/.

Certified Physician Life Care Planner™. (n.d.). Certified Physician Life Care Planner certification. Retrieved from www.cplcp.org/Certification.aspx#.

Deutsch, P. M., & Raffa, F. (1981). *Damages in tort actions* (Vols. 8 & 9). New York, NY: Mathew Bender.

Dillman, E. G. (2018). The role of the economist in life care planning. In R. O. Weed & D. E. Berens (Eds.), *Life care planning and case management handbook* (4th ed., pp. 317–332). New York, NY: Routledge.

Federal Rules of Evidence. (2018). Rule 702. Testimony by expert witnesses. Grand Rapids, MI: Michigan Legal Publishing. Retrieved from www.rulesofevidence.org/article-vii/rule-702/www.rulesofevidence.org/.

Gamez, J. N., & Johnson, C. B. (2017). Why should you attend the 2017 life care planning summit? *Journal of Life Care Planning, 15*(1), 41–43. Retrieved from https://connect.rehabpro.org/newwww/publications/jlcp-index.

Gamez, J. N., Johnson, C. B., & Stajduhar, L. (2017). A comparison of life care planning standards of practice. *Journal of Life Care Planning, 15*(3), 37–44. Retrieved from https://connect.rehabpro.org/newwww/publications/jlcp-index.

Gonzales, J. G. (2017). *A physician's guide to life care planning.* Austin, TX: American Academy of Physician Life Care Planners.

Hanus, J. (2018). When is a Daubert "expert" not a Daubert "expert"? *Journal of Legal Nurse Consulting, 29*(1), 22–23. Retrieved from www.aalnc.org/page/the-journal-of-legal-nurse-consulting.

Holakiewicz, L., & Pacheco, M. (2012). Coding and cost research for the life care plan. *Journal of Nurse Life Care Planning, 12*(1), 548–558. Retrieved from www.aanlcp.org/?page=JournalCopies.

Howland, W. (Ed.). (2015) *Nurse life care planning scope and standards of practice.* San Bernardino, CA: American Association of Nurse Life Care Planners.

International Association of Rehabilitation Professionals. (2015). *Standards of practice for life care planners* (3rd ed.). Glenview, IL: Author. Retrieved from https://connect.rehabpro.org/lcp/about/scopeand-standards.

International Commission on Health Care Certification. (n.d.-a). About ICHCC. Retrieved from www.ichcc.org/about-us.html.

International Commission on Health Care Certification. (n.d.-b). Certified life care planner (CLCP). Retrieved from www.ichcc.org/certified-life-care-planner-clcp.html.

Johnson, C. (2012). The 2012 life care planning summit: Third time is a charm. *Journal of Life Care Planning, 11*(2), 3–8. Retrieved from https://connect.rehabpro.org/newwww/publications/jlcp-index.

Johnson, C. B. (2015). Consensus and majority statements derived from life care planning summits held in 2000, 2002, 2004, 2006, 2008, 2010, 2012, and 2015. *Life Care Planning, 13*(4), 35–38. Retrieved from https://connect.rehabpro.org/newwww/publications/jlcp-index.

Kreimer, N. (2016). Home care services costs and the fair labor standards act. *Journal of Nurse Life Care Planning, 16*(4), 559–582. Retrieved from www.aanlcp.org/?page=JournalCopies.

Kwass, D. L., & Bailey, E. A. (2017). Protect your life care plan. *Trial, 53*(4), 52–54. Retrieved from www.justice.org/node/134220.

Legal Information Institute. (n.d.). Federal Rules of Evidence, Rule 702 Testimony by Expert Witness. Retrieved from www.law.cornell.edu/rules/fre/rule_702.

Maniha, A. (2012). FAQs in costing and pricing. *Journal of Nurse Life Care Planning, 12*(1), 559–582. Retrieved from www.aanlcp.org/?page=JournalCopies.

Maniha, A., & Watson, L. L. (2018). Life care planning resources. In R. O. Weed & D. E. Berens (Eds.), *Life care planning and case management handbook* (4th ed., pp. 729–757). New York, NY: Routledge.

Powell, V. (2015). *Samples for success: Life care plans from practicing life care planners.* Arkansas: Remington Publishing.

Preston, K., & Johnson, C. (2012). Consensus and majority statements derived from life care planning summits held in 2000, 2002, 2004, 2006, 2008, 2010 and 2012. *Journal of Life Care Planning, 11*(2), 9–14. Retrieved from https://connect.rehabpro.org/newwww/publications/jlcp-index.

Riddick-Grisham, R., & Deming, L. M. (Eds.) (2011). *Pediatric life care planning and case management* (2nd ed.). Boca Raton, FL: CRC Press.

Schofield, S., & Huntington-Frazier, M. (2015). Advocacy on trial: Are the nurse life care planner's roles of advocate and expert witness in conflict? *Journal of Nurse Life Care Planning, 15*(4), 928–932. Retrieved from www.aanlcp.org/?page=JournalCopies.

Shahnasarian, M. (2015). Insights into the International Association of Life Care Planning Fellow program: Questions and answers from program developers. *Journal of Life Care Planning, 13*(4), 21–25. Retrieved from https://connect.rehabpro.org/newwww/publications/jlcp-index.

Tellus Institute. (2003). *Daubert: The most influential Supreme Court ruling you've never heard of.* A publication of the Project on Scientific Knowledge and Public Policy (SKAPP). Boston, MA: Author. Retrieved from www.phil.vt.edu/dmayo/personal_website/PhilEvRelReg/Daubert-The-Most-Influential-Supreme-Court-Decision-You-ve-Never-Heard-Of-2003%201.pdf.

Weed, R. O. (2018). Life care planning: Past, present, and future. In R. O. Weed & D. E. Berens (Eds.), *Life care planning and case management handbook* (4th ed., pp. 3–20). New York, NY: Routledge.

Weed, R., & Berens, D. (2012). Life care planning summit 2000. *Journal of Life Care Planning, 11*(1), 5–24. Retrieved from https://connect.rehabpro.org/newwww/publications/jlcp-index.

Weed, R. O., & Berens, D. E. (2018). *Life care planning and case management handbook* (4th ed.). New York, NY: Routledge.

Wilkinson, T. (2015). Nurse expert witnesses and the Daubert standard. *The Journal of Legal Nurse Consulting, 26*(3), 34–39. Retrieved from www.aalnc.org/page/the-journal-of-legal-nurse-consulting.

Additional Reading

Apuna-Grummer, D., & Howland, W. A. (Eds.) (2013). *A core curriculum for nurse life care planning.* Bloomington, IN: American Association of Nurse Life Care Planners.

American Academy of Physician Life Care Planners (AAPLCP™). (n.d.). Retrieved from www.aaplcp.org.

American Association of Legal Nurse Consultants. *The Journal of Legal Nurse Consulting.* Retrievable from www.aalnc.org/page/the-journal-of-legal-nurse-consulting.

American Association of Nurse Life Care Planners. *Journal of Nurse Life Care Planning.* Retrievable from www.aanlcp.org/?page=JournalCopies.

American Association of Rehabilitation Nurses. (2015). *The specialty practice of rehabilitation nursing: A core curriculum* (7th ed.). Chicago, IL: Author.

Casuto, D., & McCollum, P. (2000). Life care planning. In M. O'Keefe (Ed.), *Nursing practice and the law.* Philadelphia: F. A. Davis.

Deutsch, P. (1990). *A guide to rehabilitation testimony: The expert's role as an educator.* Orlando, FL: PMD Press.

Deutsch, P., & Sawyer, H. (1999). *Guide to rehabilitation.* Purchase, NY: Ahab Press.

Federal Rules of Civil Procedure (FRCP). (n.d.). Rule 26—Duty to Disclose; General Provisions Governing Discovery: Duty to Disclose, Disclosure of Expert Testimony (A), (B), (C). Retrieved from www.federalrulesofcivilprocedure.org/frcp/title-v-disclosures-and-discovery/rule-26-duty-to-disclose-general-provisions-governing-discovery/.

Federal Rules of Civil Procedure 2018 Edition. (2017). Michigan Legal Publishing, Ltd. Retrieved from www.federalrulesofcivilprocedure.org/frcp/.

Federal Evidence Review. (2015). VII: Opinions and Expert Testimony (Rule 701–706), pp. 30–32. In Federal Evidence Review, 2015. Retrieved from http://federalevidence.com/downloads/rules.of.evidence.pdf.

Field, T. F., & Stein, D. B. (2002). *Scientific vs. non-scientific and related issues of admissibility of testimony by rehabilitation consultant.* Athens, GA: Elliott & Fitzpatrick, Inc.

Holakiewicz, L. (2008). Lessons from the stand. *Journal of Nurse Life Care Planning,* 8(3), 10–15. Retrieved from www.aanlcp.org/?page=JournalCopies.

International Association of Rehabilitation Professionals. *Journal of Life Care Planning.* Retrievable from https://connect.rehabpro.org/newwww/publications/jlcp-index.

Legal Information Institute. (n.d.). Federal Rules of Civil Procedure, Title V. Disclosures and Discovery, Rule 30 Dispositions by Oral Examination (e) Review by the witness; Changes. Retrieved from www.law.cornell.edu/rules/frcp/rule_30.

Lexology. (n.d.). To what extent can you use errata sheets to correct testimony under Rule 30(e)? Retrieved from www.lexology.com/library/detail.aspx?g=a46a6e9b-1196-48c7-be5d-d81b80ce63ef.

Powell, V. (2013). Qualifying as an expert. *Journal of Nurse Life Care Planning,* 13(3), 112–122. Retrieved from www.aanlcp.org/?page=JournalCopies.

Powers, A. S. (1994). Life care planning: The role of the legal nurse. *National Association Rehabilitation Professionals Private Sector Journal, 9,* 51.

Yudkoff, M., & Iyer, P. (2001). The life care plan expert. In P. Iyer (Ed.), *Nursing malpractice* (2nd ed., p. 652). Tucson, AZ: Lawyers and Judges Publishing.

Test Questions

1. A life care planner's role in damages includes which of the following? Choose all that apply.
   A. Reviewing extensive medical records and testifying to the standard of nursing care
   B. Reviewing pertinent medical documents, school or employment records
   C. Recommending resources that meet future care needs of an individual
   D. Educating attorneys, jurors, and judges regarding disability issues
2. The life care plan may be utilized for which of the following? Choose all that apply.
   A. Portrayal of damages at trial
   B. For insurance reserve setting
   C. Within a special needs trust for resource allocation
   D. As a case management tool in Workers' Compensation claims
3. Which of the following exemplifies the underlying premise of life care planning?
   A. A certified life care planner is the best qualified person to do all life care plans
   B. A life care plan is a dynamic document that will be updated periodically as appropriate
   C. Case Managers rely on the life care plan to manage care in Workers' Comp cases
   D. Life care plans are used to litigate liability in medical malpractice cases
4. Which of the following would a life care planner working for the defense weigh carefully for exclusion in the review process?
   A. General needs of the plaintiff related to pre-existing medical diagnoses
   B. Accuracy of the costs projected
   C. Relation of the recommendations to the injuries alleged in the action
   D. Appropriateness of the recommendations
5. Which of the following would the life care planner expect to testify to at trial? Choose all that apply.
   A. Information clearly within limits of their professional expertise
   B. Information regarding objective assessment of the needs related to the injuries in the action
   C. Information advantageous to the referral source (plaintiff or defense)
   D. Information well supported by appropriate professional foundation

Answers: 1. B, C, D; 2. A, B, C, D; 3. B; 4. A; 5. A, B, D

Appendix A: Example of a Life Care Plan

The authors would like to extend our thanks for Debra Berens, PhD, CRC, CCM, CLCP, for allowing us to use a sample of her Life Care Plan as an example for our text. Dr. Berens has over 30 years of experience working in the field of rehabilitation including life care planning for pediatric and adult clients with catastrophic disabilities, and also serves as a professional speaker/ trainer, author, editor, and Clinical Assistant Professor in the Clinical Rehabilitation Counseling program at Georgia State University, Atlanta, Georgia.

Appendix 23.1 Example Life Care Plan

A 58-year-old male injured in a motor vehicle crash on 10/30/16 resulting in C_{5-8} spinal cord injury, incomplete. Client participated in an inpatient rehabilitation program as a result of the spinal cord injury during which time he developed complications with his lower extremities that resulted in bilateral amputations to his legs above the knee on 11/13/16. The client demonstrates no functional capabilities with his lower extremities, although has some slight movement of his upper extremities, left greater than right. He presents with swelling/edema of his thighs status-post bilateral AKA, as well as chronic sacral decubitus ulcers, suprapubic catheter, colostomy bag, and pain in his upper back and upper extremities.

LIFE CARE PLAN

Note: The following initials are placed in parentheses throughout the plan according to their respective recommendations:

(IBH) = I.B. Healthy, MD, physiatrist/PM&R

(JS) = John Skin, MD, wound physician

(DB) = Debra E. Berens, PhD, certified life care planner

Routine Future Medical Care—Physician Only			
Recommendation (by whom)	Frequency and Duration	Purpose	Expected Cost
Physiatrist (IBH) Mileage to physician office for one-way trip > 50 miles	2 × year (avg.) to life expectancy	Assess and monitor medical status related to SCI and bilateral AK amputations. Identify current and future rehabilitation needs over lifetime.	$273/visit plus Mileage: $36.70 per evaluation
Wound physician/ Wound specialist (JS)	1 × month for 6 months (avg.) then every 3 months (avg.) to life expectancy (assumes wounds healed), or more frequent depending on wound status	Monitor and treat chronic skin breakdown/decubitus ulcers related to SCI	$200/visit
Internist/Primary Care Physician (IBH)	2018 to life expectancy	Monitor overall condition and insulin-dependent diabetes since the incident	$95.75 per visit every 4–6 weeks. Does not include cost of 1 × year physical exam recommended for general population.

Any diagnostic/radiology studies and labs that are related to the injury would be an additional cost.

| Urologist (IBH) Renal ultrasound CT scan of kidneys IVP/video urodynamics Cystography Urinalysis + Urine Culture and Sensitivity | Every 6 weeks (avg.) for 12 months then 4 × year (avg.) to life expectancy Every 2 years (avg.) to life expectancy Same as above Same as above 1 × year (avg.) to life expectancy Estimate 2–4 × year (avg.) to life expectancy and as needed | Monitor neurogenic bladder, bladder management program, supra-pubic catheter replacements, and reduce/prevent urology complications, including UTIs as related to the SCI Treat expected urinary tract infections (UTIs) . | $133–346 per visit for suprapubic catheter change Renal ultrasound: $786 each CT scan kidneys: $1,542 ea IVP/video urodynamics: $1,090 each Cystography: $380/year (avg.) to life expectancy UA + C/S: $460–920/year @ $230 each occurrence |

Note: In addition to the above physician services, the client also may need evaluation and follow-up by infectious disease physician, orthopedist, neurologist, dietician/nutritionist for weight management, and other specialists depending on his status and at the discretion of his treating physicians. See also Potential Complications, p. 582

Projected Therapeutic Evaluations and Modalities—Non-physician (Allied Health Evaluations)

Recommendation (by whom)	Year Initiated/Suspended	Frequency/Duration	Expected Cost
Physical Therapy Evaluation (IBH) Occupational Therapy Evaluation (IBH)	2018 to life expectancy Same as above	4 × year each for PT and OT to assess and monitor in-home program, equipment check and recommendations, functional abilities, etc.	PT: $600–692/year @ $150–173 each OT: $520–760/year @ $130–190 each
Wheelchair Seating and Positioning Evaluation for proper positioning & support (IBH, JS)	2018	1 × evaluation to assess wheelchair seating needs and make equipment recommendations	$0. See Note below. Cost typically included in cost of wheelchair. See also p. 582 for wheelchair needs.

Note: The physiatrist ordered pressure mapping as part of the client's wheelchair evaluation. Contact with the wheelchair vendor revealed no charge for the evaluation or pressure mapping, assuming purchase of recommended pressure relieving equipment.

Recommendation (by whom)	Year Initiated/Suspended	Frequency/Duration	Expected Cost
Home Accessibility Evaluation by Qualified Accessibility Specialist (DB)	2018 (current need)	1 × evaluation only	$1,800–2,400 for evaluation and recommendations. See also Architectural Considerations, pg. 10.
Psychological Screen/Evaluation to assess adjustment, coping strategies, family relations, etc. (IBH)	2018 (current need)	Minimum 1 × initial evaluation then frequency unknown pending outcome	$150–300 for evaluation
Note: It is common for individuals with catastrophic injury to require counseling to deal with the permanency of their disability, loss of independence and functional abilities, changed familial/social roles, and to promote healthy adjustment and coping. An initial evaluation by a psychologist experienced in working with individuals with traumatic onset disability is recommended to assess the client's coping and problem-solving skills as related to his functional limitations. Life Care Plan may be amended in the future, as appropriate, pending psychologist's evaluation and recommendations for future services.			
Case Manager to trouble shoot, problem solve, coordinate medical appointments, liaison with medical providers, equipment needs, medications, supplies, in-home caregiver, etc. (DB)	2018 to life expectancy	4 hours per month (avg.) to life expectancy	$4,800/year to life expectancy @ $100/hour (avg.)
Diagnostic Testing			
Recommendation (by whom)	*Year Initiated/Suspended*	*Frequency/Duration*	*Expected Cost*
Not applicable as related to the injury			

Educational Assessment/Educational Plan

Recommendation (by whom)	Year Initiated/Suspended	Frequency/Duration	Expected Cost
Not applicable as related to the injury			

Aids for Independent Functioning

Recommendation (by whom)	Year Purchased	Replacement Schedule	Expected Cost
Allowance for miscellaneous items such as hand-held shower head (assumes accessible bathroom), Thera-putty, therapy balls for left hand, Thera-bands, reacher/grabber, built-up utensils, etc. (DB)	2018	1 × purchase only	$50/year (avg.) to life expectancy

Wheelchair Needs

Recommendation (by whom)	Year Purchased	Replacement Schedule	Expected Cost
Power wheelchair with joy stick control and tilt in space recline (IBH, JS) Gel batteries for power chair (DB)	2018 (current need) 2019 (or 1 year after wheelchair purchase)	Every 5–7 years (avg) Every 1–2 years (avg.) depending on use	Wheelchair: $8,995 and every 5–7 years (avg.) to life expectancy Gel batteries: $446 beginning 1 year after wheelchair purchased and every 1–2 years thereafter to life expectancy (do not include on years wheelchair replaced & batteries included)
Manual wheelchair as back-up to power wheelchair (IBH)	2016 (already has)	Every 7–10 years (avg.) to life expectancy, assumes light use	2023–26: $400 and every 7–10 years (avg.) to life expectancy

Note 1: The client currently has a basic power wheelchair; however, his wound physician recommends a power wheelchair with tilt in space recline to offset pressure on his backside due to chronic, non-healing wounds.

Note 2: A 24 volt battery charger comes with purchase of power wheelchair and, if properly used and maintained, is not expected to need replacement sooner than the wheelchair. No cost included in plan for battery charger.

Recommendation (by whom)	Year Purchased	Replacement Schedule	Expected Cost
Active Aid padded Roll-in Shower Wheelchair (IBH). Assumes roll-in shower. See also Architectural Considerations, pg. 10	2018 (current need). Assumes accessible bathroom.	Every 5 years (avg.) to life expectancy	$1,275 and every 5 years (avg.) to life expectancy

Wheelchair Accessories and Maintenance

Recommendation (by whom)	Year Purchased	Replacement Schedule	Expected Cost
Gel wheelchair cushion (JS) Spare cushion cover (DB)	2016 (already has) 2018	Every 1½–2 years (avg.) to life expect. 1 × year to life expectancy	$375–395 and every 1½–2 years to life expectancy $46–53/year to life expectancy
Portable folding wheelchair ramps for community access (DB)	2018	Every 10 years (avg.) to life expectancy	$235–500 and every 10 years (avg.) to life expectancy (Range is for 3'–6' ramps)
Wheelchair maintenance for power, manual, and shower wheelchairs (DB)	2019	1 × year and as needed to life expectancy	$300/year for service contract for general repairs and maintenance. Do not include service contract on years wheelchairs are purchase and warranty is in effect.

Orthotics/Prosthetics

Recommendation (by whom)	Year Purchased	Replacement Schedule	Expected Cost

Note 1: The client has bilateral above-knee amputations that typically would be able to be fit for prosthetic legs. However, he is not a candidate for prostheses given his spinal cord injury and resulting paralysis.

Note 2: Resting hand orthotics/splints may be indicated for his future use; however, specific type cannot be determined based on current level of function and no cost for hand splints is included in the life care plan.

Home Furnishings

Recommendation (by whom)	Year Purchased	Replacement	Expected Cost
Power hospital bed with side rails (IBH) Low air loss mattress (JS) Mattress maintenance (DB)	2016 (already has) 2016 (already has) 2018	Frame: N/A, lifetime warranty Every 5 years (avg.) based on manufacturer's warranty 1 × year and as needed to ensure proper function	Frame: N/A, already has. 2021: Mattress: $3,500–4,000 and every 5 years (avg.) to life (Note: No offset made for standard mattress) Estimate 5% cost of mattress per year to life expectancy for parts and labor (filters 1 × month, specialty sheets, etc.).
Note 1: The wound physician reports the client will always require pressure relieving equipment as part of his daily skin care and to minimize the effects of skin breakdown. Note 2: See also Potential Complications, p. 582, for more sophisticated specialty bed mattresses if significant skin breakdown or pressure sores continue or increase.			
Adjustable height bedside table to provide flat surface for care (DB)	2018	Every 7–10 years (avg.)	$12–25 every 7–10 years (avg.) to life expectancy
Overhead ceiling track lift system for bedroom and bath (IBH, JS) Overhead lift maintenance (DB) Portable power patient lift for transfers other than bed/bathroom Add'l lift sling (DB) Maintenance Agreement for power patient lift (DB)	2018, assumes home is structurally capable of supporting an overhead track lift 2019, or one year after installation in accessible home 2018 (already has Hoyer manual lift) 2018 1 year after purchase of lift	1 × installation 1 × year (avg.) to life expectancy Every 5–10 years (avg.) to life expectancy 1 × year (avg.) to life expectancy depending on wear and tear 1 × year maintenance	$7,500–10,000 (avg.) for 1 × only installation of single overhead track system to transfer from bed to bathroom 5% (avg.) cost of lift per year to life expectancy Portable lift: $2,800 and every 5–10 years (avg.) to life expectancy Sling: $194–374/year to life expectancy Maintenance: $120/year to life expectancy

Health and Strength Maintenance (Leisure Time Activities)

Recommendation (by whom)	Year of Purchase	Replacement Sched.	Expected Cost
Daily home exercise program by caregiver to include range of motion, stretching, and positioning activities (IBH)	2018	Daily	$0. Done at home by caregiver, see p. 581.

Transportation

Recommendation (by whom)	Year Purchased	Replacement Sched.	Expected Cost
Wheelchair accessible mini-van with wheelchair lift and tiedowns (IBH) Maintenance for van accessibility features (DB)	2018 (current need). Family uses a 2008 van purchased used. Beginning 1 year after purchase of vehicle.	Every 10 years (avg.) to life expectancy 1 × year after 1 year standard warranty expires.	$18,000–25,000 and every 10 years (avg.) to life for wheelchair accessibility features only (does not include cost of van itself) Maintenance: $750/year (avg. est.) to life expectancy for maintenance of accessibility features only.

Vocational Plan

Recommendation	Initiated/Suspended	Purpose	Expected Cost
Deferred to Vocational Expert report.			

Architectural Considerations

(List considerations for home accessibility and/or modifications)
The client has resided in his current home for over 30 years and states a desire to remain in his home as long as possible. The home in its present structure is not accessible and a qualified home accessibility specialist is recommended to evaluate the home to determine its potential and make recommendations for home modifications. At a minimum, the client requires a one-level, barrier-free home that is fully wheelchair accessible and includes covered parking and entrances for inclement weather, ramps to entrances/exits, hardwood floors and/or low-knap carpet for easy wheelchair maneuverability, widened doorways/hallways, enlarged and accessible bedroom, closet, and bathroom with roll-in shower, lever faucets and door handles, roll-under counters and sinks in bathroom and kitchen, and other wheelchair accessibility features. Life care plan may be amended with the cost for home modifications to current home, if found feasible, once an accessibility evaluation is completed, see p. 573.

Drug Needs

Drug needs and costs are representative of the client's current need and may change from time to time.

Recommendation (by whom)	Purpose	Cost per Unit	Cost per Year
The below medications are based on the client's pharmacy medication profile for the period 10/1/16 to the present. In addition to the regular medications, a yearly allowance is included to account for antibiotics, topical ointments, and other pharmaceutical items that are required PRN as related to skin breakdown, UTIs, and other sequelae from the incident. The client's treating physiatrist has confirmed that he will require the below medications (or similar classes of medications) throughout his lifetime.			
Hydrocodone/APAP (IBH)	Pain relief	$8.73 for 100 per month	$105/year to life expectancy
Gabapentin (IBH)	Neuropathic pain	$12.89 for 60 tablets	$157/year to life expectancy
Lantus, 100 units injected (IBH)	Insulin-dependent diabetes	$196.62 for month supply	$2,359/year to life expect.
ProSed DS (IBH)	management for trauma-induced diabetes since SCI	$132.38 for 60 tablets	$1,611/year to life expect.
Allowance for antibiotics for UTIs (Cipro, etc.), non-healing wounds (Triamcinolone, Mupirocin), Imodium AD, Stool softener (Easy Lax), Tylenol ES for pain relief, multivitamin to promote wound healing, etc. (IBH, JS)	UTI pain/discomfort Miscellaneous infections, skin care, bowel program, pain relief, etc.	N/A	$100/year (avg. est.) to life expectancy

Supply Needs

Supply needs and costs are representative of the client's current need and may change from time to time.

Recommendation	Purpose	Cost per Unit	Cost per Year
Chux blue underpads for bed	Protect bed from incontinence	$35.95 per 100	Bed underpads: $431/year to life @ 1 box per month
Large Adult Briefs	Incontinence	$68.95 per 72 briefs	Adult briefs (large): $827/year to life @ 1 case per month
Misc. allowance to include non-sterile gloves, personal hygiene wipes, sterile water, syringes, etc.	Personal care and hygiene	N/A	Misc. allowance: $50/year (avg. est.) to life expectancy
Hollister colostomy bags and supplies	Bowel management	$30–58 for 10 bags @ 1–2 bags per day (avg.)	Colostomy bags: $1,095–4,234/year to life expectancy
Supra pubic catheter kit and supplies/ irrigation kit	Bladder management	Supra-pubic catheter kit: $178.89/ month	Supra-pubic catheter kit: $2,147/ year to life
Wound care supplies: 4×4 sterile gauze pads, Hypafix tape, skin protectant cream, saline solution, lotion, moisture barrier paste, etc.	Chronic, non-healing skin breakdown/wounds/pressure sores	Sterile irrigation kit: $15.23/day	Sterile irrigation kit: $5,559/year to life
Diabetes supplies: True Track Glucometer, Lancets for Glucometer, Test Strips for Glucometer	Insulin dependent diabetes management for trauma-induced diabetes since SCI	N/A True Track Glucometer: $26.11 Lancets = $7.59/100 Glucose Test Strips = $52.99/100 (Note: Assumes glucose testing 3 × day avg.)	$100/year (avg. est.) to life expectancy True Track Glucometer: $26 every 5 years (avg.) to life Supplies: $667.95/year to life expectancy

Note: The client receives his urology supplies, colostomy supplies, wound care supplies, and diabetes supplies from the local pharmacy.

Future Medical Care, Surgical Intervention, Aggressive Treatment

Recommendation (by whom)	Initiated/Suspended	Frequency	Expected Cost
With regard to future surgical interventions, the wound physician states he recommends conservative wound care for the client and does not anticipate future surgical intervention as related to his chronic wounds.			

With regard to future hospitalizations, given the client's history of hospitalizations (at least 2 hospitalizations in 2018 with previous multiple hospitalizations in 2016 and 2017), it can be expected that he will require future hospitalizations related to the SCI, bilateral AKA, UTIs, wound care, infections, and other sequelae from the MVC. Published research shows that expected annual hospitalizations for individuals with spinal cord injury at the C5–C8 level = $5,064 per year (1992 dollars). (Source: Stover, S., DeLisa, J., & Whiteneck, G. (1995), *Spinal cord injury: Clinical outcomes from the model systems.* Aspen Publishers, as cited in Blackwell, Krause, Winkler, & Steins (2001), *Spinal cord injury desk reference: Guidelines for life care planning and case management*, Demos Medical Publishing, p. 146). **Economist** to update cost to 2018 dollars.

	Home/Facility Care		
Recommendation (by whom)	Initiated/Suspended	▪ Hrs/Shifts/Days	Expected Cost
Option 1. In-home (preferred option) In-home care to provide total assistance with activities of daily living/ADLs, wound care, skin checks, positioning, transfers, bathing, dressing, meal preparation, clean-up, etc. (IBH, JS) Housecleaning, Interior/Exterior, and Yard Work (IBH)	Preferred In-home: 2018 to life expectancy 2018 to life expectancy	Preferred In-home: 24 hours/day to life expectancy. See Notes 1 & 2 below. N/A	Preferred In-home: CNA: $140,160–166,440 per year to life expectancy @ $16–19/hour LPN/RN: $4,368–6,708/year @ $28–43/hour for 1 hour visit 3 × week for wound care, vital signs, medication set up, and compliance. **Economist** to calculate value of loss of household and interior/exterior home maintenance services due to injury.
Note 1: The client's physiatrist recommends 24 hour/day, 7 day/week assistance for the client to perform his ADLs, transfers/positioning/wound/skin checks, homemaking tasks, laundry, meal preparation/clean-up, dressing, bathing, and for safety and emergencies in the home due to the multiplicity of his injuries including spinal cord injury, bilateral above-knee amputations, chronic non-healing wounds/skin breakdown, as well as advanced age and overall debilitation since the incident. He currently receives the equivalent of 24-hour care from his wife and adult children. Note 2: An alternative to shift care may be a live-in caregiver; however, live-in caregiver was unable to be identified in the local area. If live-in available, cost = approx. $300/day. Cost of in-home care may be reduced if live-in attendant is available, long-term contract is negotiated with home health agency, if family continues to provide care, or through private hire. Cost for aide above includes one agency's non-published reduced rate for 24-hour care. Note 3: The client requires supra-pubic catheter changes to be done by the urologist, with less frequent changes done by the home health nurse. It is possible his bladder management and frequency of UTIs may improve to the point where the home health nurse may be able to change the catheter on a consistent basis, thereby reducing cost of urologist to change catheter (see urologist, pg. 2). However, likelihood of this is not yet determined and no additional cost for in-home nurse to change catheter is included in the life care plan.			
Option 2 (least preferred option): Community residential nursing home facility (IBH)	Least preferred option and assumes the client is no longer able to stay in his home	24-hour care, 365 days per year to life expectancy	Option 2, least preferred: $280/day for room & board only (supplies, medications, MD visits, equipment, therapies, etc. are not included in R&B)

Note: If the client is no longer able to be cared for at home, a nursing home residential facility would be an alternate, least preferred option. Per diem includes room/board, medical monitoring, 24-hour on-site nursing, and does not include physician charges, labs, radiology, medications, specialized therapies or equipment, etc. that are described elsewhere in this plan. No deduction made for average yearly living expenses (room & board) incurred of general adult population if client resides in a residential facility.

Potential Complications

Potential complications are included for information only. No frequency or duration of complications is available.

- Chronic skin breakdown/pressure sores that are non-healing and can lead to osteomyelitis, and other complications, and may require more specialized equipment and cushions to offload the pressure and reduce breakdown, and/or surgery for skin flaps or other aggressive wound treatment. A sophisticated skin pressure relief bed system that includes a programmable patient turning schedule and does not require the assistance of a caregiver may be appropriate at a significantly increased cost.
- Urological problems related to neurogenic bladder and supra-pubic catheter use. The client already has a history of chronic UTIs for which antibiotics and aggressive catheter care are needed.
- Stump complications related to bilateral above-knee amputations including neuromas, skin breakdown at site of amputation, phantom pain or phantom sensations, change in stump size, swelling, etc. If indicated, stump revision surgery may be needed.
- Orthopedic/Musculoskeletal problems related to SCI and non-weight bearing status.
- Metabolic and/or gastrointestinal problems including neurogenic bowel, dilated colon, ileus, obstructions, GI bleeding, digestive problems, significant weight gain or weight loss, poor diet/nutrition, etc. Weight changes including significant gain, loss or atrophy may need to be monitored by a registered dietician or nutritionist for proper diet, nutrition, weight management and control.
- Medical and/or therapeutic care that is more frequent and expensive than expected, including comprehensive inpatient rehabilitation program, increased outpatient physical and occupational therapy, additional or more specialized equipment, increased case management services to coordinate care, increased need for in-home skilled nursing, etc.
- Psychological adjustment to injuries which may result in need for increased counseling intervention for the client and/or his family who are his current caregivers.
- Increased risk for secondary injury due to impaired physical and functional abilities.
- Vascular compromise or other vascular or circulatory issues related to bilateral above-knee amputations.
- Cellulitis, sepsis, and/or adverse reaction to long-term use of medications.

Source: Berens, 2018. © 2018 by Debra E. Berens, PhD, CRC, CCM, CLCP. All rights reserved.

Chapter 24

Medicare Set-Asides

Jennifer C. Jordan, Esq., MSCC, CMSP-F
Leslie Schumacher, RN, CRRN, CCM, LNCC®, CLCP, CNLCP®, MSCC, CMSP-F

Contents

Objectives

- Discuss the legalities that infer the need for a Medicare Set-Aside in an insurance settlement
- Distinguish between identifying a future medical allocation in accordance with state workers' compensation law and preparing a Workers' Compensation Medicare Set-Aside Arrangement (WCMSA) for Centers for Medicare & Medicaid Services (CMS) approval
- Identify the components of a Medicare Set-Aside, particularly CMS preferences
- Discuss the WCMSA submission process and post-settlement obligations
- Discuss how Medicare benefit determinations may ultimately determine the adequacy of Medicare Set-Asides

Introduction

A Medicare Set-Aside (MSA) arrangement protects the interests of Medicare by "setting aside" funds from an insurance settlement to pay for future injury-related care anticipated after settlement so that Medicare does not. Medicare is "secondary" to all other forms of reimbursement (to be outlined later) that are primarily responsible for payment for injury-related care. Certain criteria trigger the need for an MSA in workers' compensation and other forms of insurance that include a payment obligation for related medical expenses when a Medicare beneficiary is involved.

The phrase "Medicare Set-Aside" or "MSA" does not appear anywhere in the Medicare Secondary Payer Act (MSP). This may be the reason why the concept of MSAs has remained so elusive for so long. The obligation to fund an MSA does not come from the Medicare Act as much as it does from an underlying legal obligation to make payments for medical expenses. Whether a group health, workers' compensation, auto, or any number of other forms of insurance that convey an obligation to pay for medical expenses, the obligations to make payment is primary to Medicare. And, should any of these organizations commute a future medical benefit into a lump sum to settle a claim to terminate any potential liability, Medicare continues to be statutorily excluded from payment until the insurance payment is spent on related medical expenses. It is that portion of the settlement payment that effectively becomes an MSA, with or without the CMS opinion as to its adequacy.

Despite the fact, Medicare was always intended to be a secondary payer to workers' compensation since the passage of the Medicare Act in 1965; it was not until July 11, 2001 the phrase Medicare Set-Aside (MSA) was adopted into the legal lexicon. With the release of an interoffice memo from its central office to its regional offices, CMS officially put into motion a fear campaign unrivaled by other federal agencies, outlining steps payers must take to protect Medicare interest in a workers' compensation settlement. It is well known by the general public what will happen if income taxes are not paid, the problem with MSA is, we have no idea what risks lie ahead. We assume Medicare could deny related payments but there is debate over whether it could make post-settlement conditional payments and attempt to seek reimbursement from those who already made the settlement payment. Without statutory or regulatory guidance, there is no way to know for sure if or when CMS would take action on the basis of an inadequate MSA, and there is little to no enforcement to date to take example from. Because Congress or CMS could create an enforcement plan at any time, MSAs should be treated as a risk management device more than anything. Medicare is in fact a secondary payer in any insurance settlement situation that forecloses liability for medical expenses; something should be done at the time of settlement in consideration of Medicare interests. It is the how and what is done that will gauge what the future risk exposures may be.

Statutory and Regulatory Support for MSAs

By statute, Medicare is prohibited from making payment in situations where "payment has been made or can reasonably be expected to be made" as required by a group health plan or under a workmen's compensation law or plan of the United States or a state or under an automobile or liability insurance policy or plan (including a self-insured plan) or under no-fault insurance. However, should payment not be made, or reasonably be expected to be made promptly, by the primary payer, then the Secretary is permitted to make payment conditioned on reimbursement (Legal Information Institute, n.d.-a). Because there is no language in the MSP that limits application of this statute to only events that occurred prior to settlement, CMS has taken the position that Medicare continues to be statutorily excluded to the extent of the primary plan's compensation for future medical compensation.

For workers' compensation, this exclusion is further supported in Title 42 of the Code of Federal Regulations (CFR) (Legal Information Institute, n.d.-b). Section 411.46 in particular discusses the commutation of future medical expenses into a lump sum upon settlement and how the Medicare exclusion will continue until medical expenses equal the amount of that payment (Legal Information Institute, n.d.-c). Although there is no indication as to how to calculate the amount of payment, the section does note that "[i]f a settlement appears to represent an attempt to shift to Medicare the responsibility for payment of medical expenses for the treatment of a work-related condition, the settlement will not be recognized," noting specifically attempts to maximize other areas of the settlement to avoid providing for medical expenses even though facts clearly show the medical condition to be related (Legal Information Institute, n.d.-c). In comparison, liability and no-fault limitations found in Part D provide no similar guidance (Legal Information Institute, n.d.-d). While this does not alleviate the statutory exclusion, it does leave more to the imagination as to how CMS will determine the extent of the exclusion in those types of insurance situations.

Because we are trying to mitigate this unknown future risk, it is important to understand some of the basic MSP concepts to identify who is at risk of future enforcement and to what extent. Additionally, because the WCMSA review program is voluntary and has no official administrative remedy, it is also important to have a basic understanding of Medicare and its recovery program. If an action is taken in the future based upon the adequacy of an MSA, that will be a benefit determination entitled to an administrative appeal under the Medicare Act (Legal Information Institute, n.d.-e). The parties have rights, legal obligations beyond the MSA, and options other than CMS' recommendations, but it is difficult to make decisions if not aware of the bigger picture.

Considering Medicare Interests

In any situation in which a party has a legal obligation to pay for medical expenses and some event (i.e., settlement) will sever that obligation, Medicare may have an interest to consider. There are times when Medicare has no interest to protect, but its interests should always at least be evaluated. The MSP has past, present, and future considerations to be analyzed to determine whether or not action is needed. Action in any one aspect of MSP compliance is not indicative of responsibilities in another, nor upon whom the responsibility may fall. So, it is important to recognize the red flags and exposures and how all of the different MSP issues tie together.

Present Interest—Mandatory Insurer Reporting

Although beyond the scope of this chapter, it is important to be aware of the concept of Mandatory Insurer Reporting to fully understand how CMS will know to look for an MSA at some point in the future. In Section 111 of the Medicare, Medicaid, and State Children's Health Insurance Program (SCHIP) Extension Act of 2007 (MMSEA), Congress created a legal obligation for "applicable plans" to do two things in any given insurance situation: (1) determine if it involved a Medicare beneficiary; and (2) report that information to the government (Legal Information Institute, n.d.-a). The statute created a $1,000 per day per claim penalty for non-compliance and left the details of how to report the data to the Secretary of Health and Human Services to later determine. What resulted was an electronic quarterly reporting process with nearly 150 data fields that tells CMS who all of the parties are, all of the medical diagnoses involved and in the event of a settlement, the total amount of that insurance payment. What it does not ask for is if an MSA was funded and if so, how much was allocated (CMS, n.d.-e).

Regardless of whether one is involved in any aspect of Section 111 reporting or not, is important to understand the reporting acts as the on/off switch for related Medicare benefits. When a "total payment obligation" (TPOC) is reported, Medicare is on notice to deny related benefits until the Medicare beneficiary reports that they have spent the funds received for related medical expenses. In workers' compensation and no-fault situations, insurers also have an obligation to report the initiation of the claim, known as "ongoing responsibility for medical" (ORM). This too flips the switch off and Medicare will deny payments related to the codes reported until such a time ORM is terminated or a TPOC is reported upon settlement. The point is, be cognizant of how CMS discovers information that may cause a claimant to be denied Medicare benefits or a payer or party to a settlement to incur a post-settlement reimbursement exposure.

It is also important to understand that MMSEA Section 111 reporting is not CMS's only source for notice of other potential payers. Centers for Medicare & Medicaid Services stores beneficiary data in the "common working file" (CWF) and all information gained from various data sharing programs with Social Security, the IRS, and from individual states will be noted in this database. Also, CMS will annotate the CWF if a beneficiary or their attorney self-reports an insurance claim. Finally, WCMSAs reviewed by CMS in situations where the claimant is not yet a Medicare beneficiary at the time of settlement will also put CMS on notice of potential primary payers even when MMSEA Section 111 reporting is not required.

Past Interest—Conditional Payment Reimbursement

Again, beyond the scope of this chapter, it is important to understand how conditional payments work. One of the risks of not funding an MSA when appropriate is that CMS could potentially make a conditional payment post-settlement and seek reimbursement from almost anyone involved in the settlement at CMS's sole discretion, leaving everyone exposed. It is desirable to the settling parties for CMS simply to deny payments as it is statutorily obligated to do, however as with payments made prior to settlement, Medicare frequently does not make them intentionally. Either beneficiaries present Medicare cards or healthcare providers do not ask the right questions about other potential coverage. The inaccurate coding of bills can also lead to improper payments. Regardless of how it happens, case law supports the government's right to full reimbursement, so it is best to take measures to avoid post-settlement conditional payments from ever occurring.

Beyond the MSP, it is important to understand any payment the federal government makes and was not obligated to make, is an "overpayment" entitled to reimbursement under a number of federal debt recovery laws beyond the MSP. Additionally, any act which causes the federal government to make an overpayment could be subject to the False Claims Act which carries treble damages and a civil money penalty. As with many aspects of the MSP, it is important not to be myopic. While the MSP carries some serious ramifications for non-compliance that does not alleviate other legal exposures.

It is recommended healthcare providers familiarize themselves with the CMS website for conditional payments (CMS, n.d.-b.). Methods of requesting conditional payment information and responding are regimented and failure to handle them properly could result in not receiving a response or missing a deadline that forever forecloses your ability to take further action.

Also, be aware CMS only recovers for Medicare payments made under Parts A and B. Medicare Parts C and D are administered by private health insurance companies under contract to provide Medicare benefits on behalf of the federal government and responsible for their own recoveries. Because too extensive to address fully in this chapter, simply take away an awareness that conditional payment recoveries are not handled the same for Medicare Parts C and D.

Future Interest—Medicare Set-Asides

As stated above, there is no legal obligation to fund an MSA. No one will find such a requirement in any state or federal law or regulation. Nevertheless, technically, an MSA has been created any time consideration is provided in an insurance settlement in exchange for a release from the legal liability for future related medical expenses. Medicare is excluded to the extent another payer is primarily responsible, so the fact that the insurer provided payment for related medical treatment in advance of its occurrence does not change Medicare's secondary payer status until that money has been spent on related medical expenses. An MSA report is nice in that it identifies the specific amount allocated and the calculation methodology used, but Medicare's statutory exclusion will occur without an MSA report just the same.

MSA Considerations

There are a number of reasons to do an MSA and those reasons will differ among each party to an insurance settlement. While the insurer has the potential to be forced to make payment twice, the claimant could lose Medicare benefits as well as face reimbursement obligations from non-medical settlement proceeds. Additionally, the attorneys who handle or receive funds could be required to make reimbursement, similar to healthcare providers who were paid from settlement proceeds. There is no order in which CMS must proceed against any of these parties, and law supports the government's ability to collect until made whole, so there is no way of knowing who really may be at risk or when. There is little evidence of post-settlement enforcement on CMS's part, so this is truly unchartered water, making this mainly a risk management exercise. The goal of an MSA is to make it unlikely to be subject of a CMS post-settlement recovery effort.

Understand that there is no cause of action for failing to do an MSA or alleging that it is inadequate. Centers for Medicare & Medicaid Services can only recover that which it paid conditionally and may bring a private cause of action under the MSP. Medical Set-Aside litigation among the parties however will come in the form of contract claims regarding the settlement agreement or motions to reopen workers' compensation claims, none of which are ripe until the MSA runs out. The best way to manage such future unknown risks is to best anticipate the possible litigation.

Who Should Obtain the MSA

There is no rule as to whose responsibility it is to do the MSA. In the liability context, it is commonly believed that it is solely the plaintiff's responsibility. In workers' compensation, the duty is generally assumed by the insurance carrier along with the cost. In reality, an MSA should be calculated the same regardless of who obtains it. If completed properly, the MSA will protect all the same regardless of their participation. Anyone with a reimbursement exposure should ensure that the MSA is obtained.

The responsibility for payment arises out of some unrelated legal obligation, typically a state law or contractual obligation in an insurance policy. For example, workers' compensation law commonly provides for lifetime related medical expenses, whereas auto insurance frequently includes personal injury protection (PIP) and homeowners may provide med pay. These legal obligations are enforced in state court under state workers' compensation, contract, tort, and insurance laws and it should not be assumed that federal pre-emption would apply.

Responsibility for Reimbursement

A party can admit or accept liability, but often the MSP is triggered by a settlement, judgment, or award. In the context of MSAs, any of those events constitute an insurance payment for purposes of triggering an MSP reimbursement obligation. If damages for future medical expenses were alleged and released, a portion of that consideration provided for that release will essentially be the MSA.

Even parties to a nuisance settlement that claims to not include medical damages or attempt apportionment arguments, because only pennies on the dollar were obtained, need to be cognizant of MPS implications. Centers for Medicare & Medicaid Services' position, supported by the courts, has been that just because the beneficiary elected to compromise his claim for damages does not mean that the government has to (*Hadden v. U.S.*, 2011). A settlement may include for a number of economic and non-economic damages that are all beings simultaneously compromised but often are not broken down line by line. An MSA is meant to expressly earmark those funds that represent the portion of the settlement that is compensation for the release from liability for future related medical damages otherwise covered by Medicare. The problem will be deciding how much compensation will be deemed adequate for CMS and/or the courts.

Primary Plan

The MSP states, that a primary plan, and an entity that receives payment from a primary plan, shall reimburse the appropriate Trust Fund (Legal Information Institute (n.d.-a). The statute defines a primary plan to include

> a group health plan or large group health plan, to the extent that [Medicare beneficiaries may not be excluded from plan benefits due to Medicare eligibility], and a workmen's compensation law or plan, an automobile or liability insurance policy or

plan (including a self-insured plan) or no-fault insurance, to the extent that clause (ii) applies. An entity that engages in a business, trade, or profession shall be deemed to have a self-insured plan if it carries its own risk (whether by a failure to obtain insurance, or otherwise) in whole or in part.

(Legal Information Institute, n.d.-a)

Receipt of Insurance Payment

Those in receipt of funds from a primary plan, regardless of relationship to the insurance claim, are also exposed to MSP recoveries. The United States may recover from "any entity that has received payment from a primary plan or from the proceeds of a primary plan's payment to any entity" (Legal Information Institute, n.d.-f). This can include the Medicare beneficiary, his or her attorney, and even medical providers who were paid from settlement proceeds.

When an MSA Is Not Needed

Due to irrational fears of potential CMS recovery actions, MSAs are often obtained as a routine function of the claims process. Often, they are requested as soon as a claimant reaches maximum medical improvement (MMI). An MSA is not needed until a settlement is actually in negotiation as it will only be useful for about six months. The parties know what treatment is being obtained and reserves already reflect future medical considerations, so an MSA is not needed to start settlement discussions. Obtaining the MSA prematurely just results in potentially unnecessary costs associated with updates.

It is important to also recognize that an MSA is not always necessary. For example, if medicals are left open and only indemnity settled, there is no MSA needed because the insurer remains the primary payer. If the settlement is a compromise and only compensation for past medical expenses provided, there is no MSA needed unless the settlement also has a commutation aspect (CMS, 2018a). Centers for Medicare & Medicaid Services specifically outlines three conditions that must be met before it will recognize that no MSA is needed because Medicare's interests are already protected:

a. The facts of the case demonstrate that the claimant is only being compensated for past medical expenses
b. There is no evidence that the claimant is attempting to maximize the nonmedical portions of the settlement to Medicare's detriment and
c. The treating physician concluded (in writing) that to a reasonable degree of medical certainty that the claimant does not require any additional related medical treatment

(CMS, 2018a)

This certainly does not mean that there may not be other potential situations where no MSA is needed, only that this is a set of facts that CMS expressly recognizes. Other scenarios may need to be defended to CMS or endure the administrative appeal process.

State Law Limitations

Every state has its own workers' compensation law that outlines exactly what medical expenses an employer or insurer is required to pay when an employee is injured on the job. There is no federal law that governs any minimum coverage standards, meaning that the states have exclusive jurisdiction over workers' compensation. The MSP is a reimbursement statute, meaning that if there is no underlying legal requirement to pay, then the federal law is never triggered. If the state workers' compensation law does not require payment, then nothing in the MSP creates a reimbursement obligation that otherwise did not exist simply because a Medicare beneficiary is involved. And that will be the case no matter how many times CMS provides reminders that federal law supersedes state law.

Centers for Medicare & Medicaid Services states that it will "recognize or honor any state-legislated, non-compensable medical services and will separately evaluate any special situations regarding WC cases" (CMS, 2018a). This includes state-specific statutes that limit medical treatment regarding the length or nature of future treatment. However, whether CMS accepts such legal arguments in a WCMSA submission will depend upon the manner in which it was presented, which will be discussed further herein.

Available Medical Insurance or Alternative Payment Source

The point of the MSA exercise is to prevent Medicare from making post-settlement payments for related medical care. Therefore, it can be argued that if a Medicare beneficiary has other available health insurance or payment source, that an MSA is not necessary. Perhaps the spouse is working and has group health coverage, or a retirement package provides for lifetime health benefits.

However, it is CMS's position that those situations could change or end at any time and Medicare would still be there, possibly as the beneficiary's only option for medical treatment. Because one cannot waive their statutory Medicare entitlement once it attaches, CMS recommends an MSA regardless.

Keep in mind, that it is the underlying legal obligation to pay that determines claim value. At settlement, the consideration provided in exchange for the release from the legal liability to pay for medical expenses is typically determined by estimating the cost of reasonably anticipated related future treatment. The MSP does not, or at least should not, change the value of the claim.

Zero MSAs

In addition to the criteria noted about when CMS will acknowledge that no MSA is necessary, it is also possible to obtain a zero-set-aside letter from CMS in denied or controverted cases. Knowing which facts CMS is looking for in such requests is vital to making recommendations as to whether that letter is attainable or not. First and foremost, make sure nuisance value is in fact nuisance value. Centers for Medicare & Medicaid Services is very suspicious of high dollar settlements that allege no compensation for medical. Furthermore, cases in which no payments were made have the best chance of getting approved. If a payment was made in error, it is necessary to show that it was reimbursed. If the state law requires payment for a certain amount of emergency services before the determination of liability, then it is recommended to provide a copy of the state law. The record must clearly reflect the denied or contested nature of the claim or CMS will not believe it.

Provide any and all documentation that supports why there is no future medicals needed. If arguing not causally related, obtain and attach a statement from the treating physician supporting there is no future medicals needed. If a court order supports the position, make sure that it was based upon a hearing on the merits, and not a stipulation of the parties. If the settlement does not have the appearance of a true compromise, CMS will never issue a zero set-aside letter. To view a sample of the letter, see Appendix 5 of the WCMSA Reference Guide (CMS, 2018a).

MSA Obligations Both Contractual and Statutory

Medicare is statutorily excluded from payments when another party is also responsible for payment of the same medical treatment. Accordingly, a Medicare beneficiary is obligated to first use other available insurance, help obtain reimbursement when Medicare conditionally pays, and make reimbursement from any payment received from a primary payer. These responsibilities are clearly outlined in the Medicare Act and its corresponding regulations. Everything about the Medicare program is governed by law or regulation, that is everything but the creation and administration of MSAs.

MSAs are created not because the Medicare Act expressly requires them, but due to Medicare's exclusion and the Medicare beneficiary's obligations to first use other available payment sources. The beneficiary is obligated to use an insurance settlement to pay for future related treatment when funds are provided for that purpose. But it is the settlement agreement that can contractually obligate the beneficiary to administer the funds in a manner consistent with CMS recommendations found in the WCMSA Reference Guide and the Self-administration Tool Kit. Centers for Medicare & Medicaid Services recommends that MSA funds be kept in a bank account separate from personal finances, only used to pay for related treatment at the rate the MSA was calculated, maintain an accounting of expenditures and perform an annual attestation, but none of those acts are legal obligations found in the statute or regulations. By incorporating these recommendations into the settlement agreement, the claimant becomes legally bound under state workers' compensation and contract law to administer funds provided for future medical expenses as CMS prefers. If he fails to do so, the primary payer would have recourse under state law.

WCMSA Submission Issues

Although not required by any law or regulation, obtaining CMS's approval of the amount set aside for future medicals does provide the added assurance that the government agrees with the amount allocated. However, that assurance comes at a price because CMS has made decisions about how to calculate future medical expenses that are not entirely consistent with the underlying workers' compensation legal obligations. Centers for Medicare & Medicaid Services expressly states that:

> [t]here are no statutory or regulatory provisions requiring that you submit a WCMSA amount proposal to CMS for review. If you choose to use CMS' WCMSA review process, the Agency requires that you comply with CMS' established policies and procedures in order to obtain approval.
>
> (CMS, 2018a)

Although there may be another way to calculate the future medical exposure in accordance with state law, this section is addressing only CMS preferences and will be denoted with the acronym WCMSA, as CMS uses, in this context. Medical Set-Aside is used in more generic applications of future medical allocations.

Review Thresholds

In addition to CMS approval not being required, it is also not available in all cases. At present time, CMS will only review proposals in workers' compensation settlements that meet certain dollar thresholds. The CMS review is available in cases involving a Medicare beneficiary and a total settlement in excess of $25,000. Additionally, review is available in settlements over $250,000 for those with a reasonable anticipation of Medicare entitlement within 30 months. This reasonable anticipation of entitlement includes:

- The claimant is 62½ years old
- The claimant has applied for Social Security Disability Benefits
- The claimant has been denied Social Security Disability Benefits but anticipates appealing that decision
- The claimant is in the process of appealing or re-filing for Social Security Disability benefits
- The claimant has been diagnosed with End Stage Renal Disease (ESRD) but does not yet qualify for Medicare on that basis

(CMS, 2018a)

Calculating Total Settlement Amount

When determining the total settlement amount for CMS, it is asking for the gross total settlement, not net proceeds to the claimant after fees and expenses. And CMS is looking for the lifetime payout, not just the amount tendered at the time of settlement. For example, if the settlement is funded using a structured settlement annuity, the total settlement amount includes the lifetime anticipated payout, not the premium amount or only the guaranteed payments. See CMS Workers' Compensation Medicare Set-Aside Arrangement Reference Guide (CMS, 2018d) for a list of inclusions and exclusions. In second injury fund or "reopener" states (e.g., New Jersey and Oklahoma):

- Include any prior settlement amounts in the total settlement amount, as well as any second injury fund settlement (in New Jersey) or "3e" settlement (in Oklahoma) being made at the same time the main injury is settling
- Do not include any estimated amounts for settlements contemplated for the future but not being made at the time of the main injury settlement

(CMS, 2018a)

Verification Letter

Centers for Medicare & Medicaid Services will not issue letters indicating the review thresholds were not met or that a WCMSA is not necessary (CMS, 2018a). For those submitting proposals through the WCMSA Portal (WCMSAP), submitting three non-threshold cases can result in loss of portal access.

WCMSAP Submissions

Although CMS will still accept paper or CD submissions, the majority of WCMSAs are submitted through the web portal. The system was implemented in 2011 and eliminated a number of contractors involved in mail handling and imaging which has vastly improved turnaround times. What once took several months, even years during backlogs, now can be completed in less than a week.

Workers' Compensation Review Contractor

In 2005, CMS created the Workers' Compensation Review Contractor (WCRC) for purposes of reviewing WCMSA submissions. Prior to that, CMS regional offices performed the task, in addition to their regular responsibilities, which proved to be too burdensome. Reviews took place when time permitted, and approvals took nearly a year to receive. With the implementation of the WCRC, approvals took less time, but due to the number of other contractors involved with mail processing and imaging, three to four months was still a common response time. Today there is a web portal that further reduced turnaround time to as little as a week.

WCRC Review Process

While this publication is not intended as a "how to," it is vital to understand what CMS is looking for and evaluating in the WCMSA submissions, to best advise the various parties or prepare WCMSAs. This will help determine if submission may be problematic or result in an adverse decision due to the record contents. This assists with avoiding development requests that unnecessarily delay obtaining CMS's approval. And most importantly, these issues may identify and avoid a costly counter-higher.

The WCRC follows a succession of 10 steps when performing its initial proposal review (CMS, 2018a). These steps are significant because these are decision points the WCRC must assess to determine if it can move on to the actual medical review. If information for that step is incomplete or inaccurate, the WCRC will likely request additional information, resulting in an avoidable delay. If the WCRC is ultimately not satisfied, it will close the case.

Demographics and Contact Information

The first job of the WCRC is to verify that all the claimant's personal data is present. This includes Social Security number, Health Insurance Claim Numbers (HICN) and Medicare Beneficiary Identifiers (MBI), date of birth, gender, and contact information for not just the claimant, but also the claimant's attorney, employer/insurer, defense counsel, and submitter. If professional administration is proposed, then the contact information of the administrator will also be verified. But most importantly, inclusion of the consent to release will be verified and checked for validity and signature of the claimant. If a Power of Attorney (POA) or guardian situation, documents supporting that relationship must be included or the review will not be conducted.

Total Settlement Amount

The total settlement amount is important mainly because of the WCMSA review thresholds. Centers for Medicare & Medicaid Services will only review cases within the stated monetary amounts. This not because other settlements do not matter, but because CMS does not have the budget and resources to look at every insurance settlement. Thresholds, however, should not be considered safe harbors under which a WCMSA is not needed. The regulations are clear, it is the amount allocated for future medical that determines Medicare's exclusion, with no mention of CMS approval or total settlement amount (Legal Information Institute, n.d.-c). However, the settlement amount may also factor into CMS's evaluation in contested cases. Centers for Medicare & Medicaid Services looks at the amount when parties are claiming nuisance value settlements with no allocation towards medical costs. Although there are situations with high dollar nuisance value, it is difficult to convince CMS that none of it is attributed to medical. In cases not obvious, provide as much documentation as possible to justify the situation being presented to CMS.

Date of Injury and Diagnostic Codes

Injury codes are a significant part of a WCMSA submission because they are housed in the common working file alongside MMSEA Section 111 reporting data, which together will trigger post-settlement exclusions. The WCRC will verify dates of injury and confirm that affected body parts are clear. The ICD-10 codes should be used for all claims that occurred after October 1, 2015, while ICD-9 codes can still be used for earlier dates of loss. But be aware both cannot be used in the same proposal. For example, while multiple claims for the same claimant can be settled together using one WCMSA, if dates of loss span over the 2015 date, then only ICD-10 should be used. Also, be cognizant of the fact all aspects of the body part must be closed out. The medicals cannot be settled while leaving the pharmacy portion open. The WCRC will consider the case ineligible for review and close the case.

Proposed Set-Asides Amounts

The WCRC compares the WCMSA proposal to the settlement documents to make sure the amounts match. If there are discrepancies, the WCRC will request more documentation causing delays in approval time. To avoid such delays, make sure the specific breakdown for medical and prescription is clear and that they add up to the proposed total. Also note, failing to break down between the two will cause the WCRC to assume the whole amount is for medical items and services.

Jurisdiction and Calculation Method

The submitter must state the calculation method used in the WCMSA proposal. While it is permissible to use actual charges or usual and customary figures, most submitters use the state workers' compensation fee schedule and that makes jurisdiction also an important factor. Typically, when claimant lives in the same state where the claim was filed, pricing is based on the claimant's zip code. If the claimant lives in a state other than the one where the claim was filed, then pricing will be determined using the employer's zip code. If both the claimant and employer reside in a state other than where the claim was filed, then the address of the claimant's attorney will determine pricing method. If not represented, the pricing is based upon the carrier's zip code. Finally, if the carrier is in a different state too, then the zip code of its attorney will be used. Note that the most current version of the fee schedule will be used. Be aware, CRC will apply a new or updated fee schedule as soon as it learns of the change, therefore cases already in the pipeline may suffer a counter higher or lower if the change results in a difference that exceeds the 5% tolerance.

Payment Method

Submitter must state whether the WCMSA will be funded as a lump sum or using a structured settlement annuity. If no such statement is made, the default will be lump sum. While CMS is tolerant of the use of structure settlement annuities, it is clear its preference is lump sum funding. If submitted as a lump sum and later decided an annuity will be used, CMS rarely revises its approval to reflect the change. However, cases that wish to convert to lump sum are seldom met with the same resistance.

If CMS approval is sought, understand that the annuity must be broken down into an initial seed deposit and equal annual installments calculated in CMS's preferred manner. To calculate the initial seed, CMS first looks for the first surgery and significant durable medical equipment (DME) replacement, subtracts them from the total WCMSA and divides by life expectancy. That amount is multiplied by two and added to cost of the first surgery and DME replacement to get the initial seed. Then to calculate the annual deposits, the initial seed is subtracted from the total WCMSA and then divided by the life expectancy minus one year, with the first payment scheduled one year from the approval. To confirm, it is best to total the annual payments plus the initial seed to ensure they add back up to the proposed WCMSA amount.

In cases not approved by CMS, other creative financing can be utilized, that may make funds available when anticipated. If for example a total knee placement was performed 10 years prior to settlement and a spinal cord stimulator installed five years later, both surgeries will be due for revision within the next five years, but only funding for one will have been included in the initial seed. The other surgical cost would have been broken into the annualized payments and not enough time passed for the surplus to add up the amount needed to pay for the second surgery, meaning the WCMSA fund will most likely temporality exhaust, leaving Medicare to pay for the rest. Granted the remaining annuity installments will be overfunded because that surgery Medicare paid for is no longer a consideration, but the WCMSA is less likely to temporarily exhaust in the future. Regardless, it is Medicare that leaves itself exposed to this possibility and therefore not a compliance problem for parties involved. However, had CMS approval not been involved, the parties could have arranged for the annuity to make payments the size of the anticipated surgical costs in or closer to the years the revisions were anticipated, better protecting Medicare's interests without CMS's help.

Life Expectancy

For cases submitted to CMS for review, CMS uses the most recently published National Vital Statists Report published by the Centers for Disease Control (CDC), which reflects final mortality statistics from 2014 (Arias, Heron, & Xu, 2017). There are 21 tables in total providing specific estimates reflective of age, sex, and race. However, for purposes of WCMSA review, CMS uses only Table 1, which is the life table for the total U.S. population where the overall life expectancy from birth is 78.9 years. Now the overall life expectancy for a male, in general, is 76.5, but more specifically is 76.7 for a white male, 72.5 for a black male, and 79.4 for a Hispanic male. The range is plus or minus three to four years on either side of the CMS preference, meaning that MSAs for these ethnic groups are not being fairly evaluated. While understandable, for purposes of this voluntary program only, given the variances, CMS established a common baseline for submitters to utilize. But submitters need to recognize those projections may not properly represent claimant's actual lifetime exposure as a non-submitted MSA could.

Rated Age

For those claimants with a diminished life expectancy, not necessarily caused by their work injury, CMS will recognize a rated age when determining life expectancy. A rated age is a life insurance term used when the insurance company acknowledges that the claimant may not live to normal life expectancy due to certain medical factors and will price insurance based upon the reduction. Poor health typically makes the cost of life insurance higher because a policy will likely pay out sooner than normal, whereas annuities cost less because there will likely be less payments made than projected.

Unfortunately for CMS, there is no central source for impairment ratings to direct submitters. Each life insurance company conducts its own review of a small sampling of medical records and provides its own rated age for use in their insurance quotes. And this analysis is not based exclusively on the medical condition. There are financial considerations of the insurance company in play, risk tolerance for substandard business being the most significant. Conservative companies tend to shy away from such business and provide minimal rated ages, whereas companies that accept risks provide much more aggressive rated ages. And those more aggressive companies may have a limit on how much substandard business it wants in any one given period and may adjust its rated age criteria from time to time to influence demand for its product. While a person does not need a life insurance license to calculate MSAs, it is important to understand how this system works to understand how it affects the calculation of MSAs.

Because of this variance, CMS now requires the median of all rated ages obtained to be utilized. Although none of the rated ages purely represent claimant's diminished life expectancy based solely upon the medical condition, the spread does represent the spectrum of possibilities and CMS is willing to accept the middle. Of course, its attempt to avoid submitters only using the best rated age obtained is thwarted when only one is obtained. Knowing which life insurance company provides the best result is a way to game the system.

In recent years, other sources of rated ages have been recognized by CMS. Technically, rate ages obtained by insurance brokers for purposes other than quoting insurance products are a violation of their broker agreements with the insurance companies. Accordingly, independent underwriters began offering rated ages specifically for use in MSAs. These are typically the same underwriters that contract with the insurance companies, however this analysis is based only on the medical factors because the specific insurance company financial considerations do not apply. Submitters often obtain this rated age for purposes of completing the MSA, then the MSA and medical records can be sent to the broker for purposes of obtaining rated ages for pricing the structured settlement annuity.

When the decision is made to obtain a rated age or not, do not make assumptions about the significance of various medical conditions. Although one may view cancer as a death sentence, it is typically not reflected in a rated age to the extent that might be expected. While at the same time, one might not expect much of a rating from something like deep vein thrombosis and end up surprised at the results. Submit medical records of all possible medical conditions, related to the claim or not. Heart conditions and diabetes are probably more significant in this analysis than paralysis or traumatic brain injury. And unlike CMS, underwriters are only looking for a few pages, so independent medical exams (IMEs) and hospital discharge summaries are sufficient.

With regard to CMS submission, not only must the submitter send all rated ages obtained, it must also include a statement of the same. Failure to include that statement will result in the WCRC using the claimant's actual age in the evaluation. Rated ages must be submitted on the letterhead of the source and the source must be independent of the submitter or the rated age will be considered invalid. Be aware, the WCRC may add years to the rated age based upon the issue date compared to the proposed settlement date. If a year has passed between the issue date and the proposed settlement date, the WCRC will add a year to the rated age, two if two years have passed. If three years have passed, the rated age will not be used. If there are multiple rated ages submitted from the same source, only the most recent from the issuer will be used. And finally, when calculating the median, know that the WCRC will drop the decimal and use only the whole number rather than round up. With all that in mind, if a valid rated age remains, the WCRC will use the age instead of the actual age unless one requests otherwise in writing.

Treatment Records

Centers for Medicare & Medicaid Services requires the last two years of medical records be included in any submission, even if the records are not current. If claimant has not been treated in some time, CMS wants the last two years of records from when last treated. If there are records from the past two years but that only includes medical examinations like an IME, Qualified Medical Exam (QME), or Agreed Medical Exam (AME) that reference when the claimant stopped treating, then CMS will want the previous two years from that last treatment date referenced. If claimant is receiving treatment from healthcare providers other than those covered by workers' compensation, CMS may still want to see them for purposes of its review. Centers for Medicare & Medicaid Services really has little regard for the limitations of what records may legally be outside the reach of the workers' compensation carrier, so participation of all parties in the submission can be vital to the process. Remember, CMS is under no legal obligation to complete its review if submission requirements are not met to its satisfaction.

Pharmacy Records

Records, whether medical or payment, must reflect dose and frequency of each medication taken by claimant. Absent that, a signed letter by the treating physician stating the same will suffice. The WCRC will compare medical records to payment records to see if they match, however be aware items that appear on one but not the other will often still be included in the WCMSA. For example, we see this when a physician continues to prescribe a medication the carrier has repeatedly denied and that has never been filled. Also, CMS assumes all drugs referenced in the past two years remain in use and will continue in perpetuity, often even in cases where new medications were trialed and discontinued, or dosing adjusted. As with most everything in the WCMSA process, CMS assumes the worse-case scenario and will require funding for the same.

In cases where the carrier has not made payments for prescriptions, but the WCRC believes prescriptions to be in use, the WCRC will develop for unrelated pharmacy records. The WCRC commonly requests records from claimant's local pharmacy for all prescriptions filled. In cases where no prescriptions exist, the WCRC has also been known to request payment records from all nearby pharmacies, essentially looking to prove the negative. In the interest of time, in any situation where there has been no treatment, it is best to secure as much supporting evidence prior to submission, otherwise a development letter requesting more information can be expected. If developed and one cannot respond to the WCRC's satisfaction, it is possible that it will decline to complete the review.

WCRC Medical Review

Again, while this publication is not intended as a "how to," it is important to understand certain standards CMS has adopted so recommendations can be made that will result in a proposed WCMSA obtaining CMS approval as expediently as possible. When seeking CMS approval of a WCMSA, the calculation must be consistent with CMS adopted practices; knowing there may be other acceptable methods of projecting future medical expenses, consistent with state laws and evidence based medical theories.

CMS Assumes Current Treatment Will Be the Standard in Perpetuity

It is best to submit WCMSAs for review only after claimant has reached MMI because CMS assumes the current course of treatment will continue in its same form for the remaining life of the claimant. Centers for Medicare & Medicaid Services will not assume improvements will be attained from recommended treatments that have not already been implemented. Ideally, the best time to submit a case for review is when there are four to six months of stable supporting medical reports that reflect the desired improvements are underway.

CMS Assumes Recommendations Will Be Pursued

If any recommended, but unpursued treatments appear in the medical records submitted to CMS, these will likely be included in the WCMSA. Even if it is well documented that the claimant has no desire to undergo such treatment and that failing to pursue it is not life threatening, CMS still assumes that if the physician recommended it, it must be necessary. In these situations, it is prudent to perfect the medical record and seek clarification from the physician that such treatment will not be medically necessary. Occasionally, CMS will consider affidavits from the claimant stating they have refused such treatment. Whatever evidence to the contrary that can be obtained, this evidence should be presented to CMS to keep such treatment out of the WCMSA.

In the case of open spinal cord stimulator (SCS) recommendations, another course of action to avoid its inclusion by the WCRC is to send the claimant to the psychological evaluation needed prior to surgery. In cases where the SCS is not wanted or inappropriate for the claimant for other reasons, the psychological evaluation should achieve the desired result of removing surgery from consideration. Failure to do so most often results in the trial, surgery, regular revisions, and semi-annual adjustments being required by CMS, even if never pursued.

Deference to Treating Physician Opinion

Although evidence to the contrary may exist, CMS tends to rely primarily on the current course of treatment and the treating physician's opinion. Centers for Medicare & Medicaid Services states the WCRC relies on evidence based guidelines, however reiterates these are guidelines and not rules (CMS, 2018a). Even if other medical specialists examine the claimant and arrive at a different opinion, CMS rarely strays from the treating physician's recommendations. In Section 9.4.5 of the WCMSA Reference Guide, CMS defends its position by stating a licensed physician is not limited to a given specialty within the scope of practice. It will however limit consideration of chiropractors to that of chiropractic care (CMS, 2018a).

In the case of IMEs that may carry weight at the state level, CMS says these are persuasive but is not bound to use their contents in its review. However, CMS will adhere to reports legally binding upon the parties, such as an AME or a final Independent Medical Review (IMR) in California. Although CMS is finally recognizing these types of reports regularly, as with any issue where the WCMSA recommendation relies upon state law, it would be prudent to reference the state law in question and even send a copy of the relevant statute to be sure.

Physician Follow-Up Frequency

For the most part, CMS will adopt the existing frequency of physician visits. If claimant is seeing the physician monthly, submitter can expect monthly visits in the WCMSA. However, if claimant's record is not showing physician follow-up, expect at least an annual visit or in the case of pharmaceutical use, at least quarterly follow-ups. To protect Medicare's interest, CMS will frequently cost out what claimant should be doing rather than what is actually occurring.

Diagnostics

More in the vein of recommended medical standards rather than actual occurrence, CMS believes regular imaging should be obtained for orthopedic injuries, even for the most stable of conditions. Claimant may not have had an x-ray since the date of accident, yet CMS will include regular imaging and depending on life expectancy and jurisdiction, that could add several thousand dollars to an MSA. X-rays are included every three to five years and MRIs every five to seven years. In cases where MRIs are inappropriate, such as with a metallic hardware, CT scans will be substituted every five years. The CTs and MRIs will be priced with contrast unless the record is clear that these diagnostic tests have always been ordered without contrast.

Revision Surgery Frequency

To obtain the number of revision surgeries CMS will include in its review, the submitter must divide the life expectancy by the frequency, then drop the decimal. Therefore, when making MSA recommendations, it is important to know that intrathecal pumps are replaced every seven years, spinal cord stimulators every seven years, and rechargeable spinal cord stimulators every nine years. Artificial joint replacements are revised every 15 years.

The CMS methodology should not be viewed as a treatment schedule, only as the calculation preferences for purposes of WCMSA approval. And this is significant in the context of WCMSA submissions because the WCRC uses straight mathematics in its evaluation. The difference in one year of life expectancy can add the full cost of an additional revision surgery to the MSA. But CMS's stated position is the inclusion of that last revision is not automatic. While not the experience of most submitters, CMS says it will consider the claimant's co-morbidities and overall condition and type of revision before including a surgery projected in the last 1–3 years of life expectancy (CMS, 2018a). As its example, it says that a hip replacement is unlikely in the last years of life but that a spinal cord stimulator would be revised if needed. In cases in which it is incredibly unlikely that a revision surgery would take place near the end of life expectancy, it is recommended that those general heath and co-morbid conditions be highlighted in the submission as reasons why that surgery should not be included for the best outcome.

Surgery Pricing

Surgery pricing includes physician, facility, and anesthesia fees and each must be determined separately and added together. For physician fees, Current Procedural Terminology (CPT) codes are used to identify fee schedule pricing, unless claimant resides in an actual charges state and usual and customary pricing used. Anesthesia fees are also calculated per fee schedule based upon a reasonable time for the procedure in question. Facility fees however require use of diagnosis-related group (DRG) codes to estimate inpatient procedures. CMS uses the pricing for a major medical center in that state, regardless of where claimant lives, unless the state fee schedule provides pricing for that DRG. If an outpatient procedure, the Ambulatory Payment Classification calculator is used for a facility in that state, again unless fee schedule provides a cap. More specific surgery calculation instructions and CPT codes can be found in Section 9.4.5 of the WCMSA Reference Guide (CMS, 2018a).

Therapy Frequency

In cases in which some form of therapy (i.e., physical, occupational, speech, etc.) has been recommended in the past or the WCRC views it as indicated, it typically appears in the WCRC review in quantities of 12. Most common is 24 sessions, however up to 48 sessions have been included on occasion. Each session is typically assumed to be 45 minutes in duration.

Pharmacy Considerations

The Medicare Modernization Act of 2003 created Medicare Part D, providing pharmaceutical coverage to Medicare beneficiaries for the first time in the program's existence (U.S. Government Publishing Office, 2003). Prior to its implementation on January 1, 2006, drugs were not a consideration in MSAs. Now drugs often comprise more than half of the total set-aside amount.

In the first year drugs were included in WCMSA submissions, a submitter could add a bottle of ibuprofen, at the lowest cost available, to the allocation regardless of what the records indicated, and it would be sufficient for the WCRC reviewer to check the box indicating drugs were provided. Today, CMS will add every drug referenced in the past two years whether they were filled or not and price them at an amount no one actually pays.

There are many pharmaceutical issues in MSAs worthy of discussing, but only if non-submission is being contemplated. If CMS approval is sought, there is only one way to calculate the MSA. That does not mean those issues are not valid and reasonable and defensible ways to project future pharmaceutical needs. It only means that in the voluntary CMS review program, submitters must follow CMS's preferred methods.

Average Wholesale Price

The most significant cost driver when calculating pharmaceuticals in WCMSAs for CMS submission is the pricing methodology. In order to establish a common method for future medication pricing for both review contractors and submitters, CMS selected a source of drug prices that is published and available to the general public. Granted that access does come at a cost and the publication does not report actual prices that drugs are sold for, but it is nonetheless a publicly available source.

Average wholesale price (AWP) was originally a term referring to the average price for drugs purchased at the wholesale level. Today, reimbursement amounts are typically based on AWP minus some negotiated percentage, making the published AWP grossly in excess of real prescription drug prices.

There is no one way to calculate an MSA and no law or regulation supporting CMS's adoption of AWP for any reason other than access and convenience. When advising clients, it is simply important to recognize that there are pricing options that would be a legally defensible basis for calculating future medical exposures. However, if submitting the WCMSA for CMS approval, then AWP is the only option.

Drug Utilization Review

Often when a carrier questions a prescription, it will send it to some form of peer review, most often drug utilization review (DUR). In many states, the workers' compensation law allows the carrier to rely upon the results when determining its payment obligations. In California, a process called independent medical review (IMR) was created and its outcome is legally binding. But for purposes of an MSA, such peer review is not persuasive to CMS unless the recommendations have actually been implemented or the findings final and not subject to further appeal.

Off-Label Drug Utilization

Medicare Part D does not provide for payment of drugs prescribed off-label, meaning not prescribed for the FDA approval indication. However, Medicare will allow payment for off-label drugs where peer review in certain compendia supports the use. However, studies persuasive to CMS for purposes of WCMSA review frequently only indicate that a severely adverse outcome was not achieved. For purposes of WCMSA submission, it is most likely off-label drugs will be included if there are any peer review studies available in the accepted publications.

Generic versus Brand Name Drugs

Centers for Medicare & Medicaid Services tends to price drugs as prescribed. If a physician prescribed a brand name drug, the WCRC will project the lifetime quantities at that price even if the insurer filled and paid for the generic version. Ironically, Medicare Part B requires generics be used, as do most formularies under Part D, yet for purposes of recommending what others pay for drugs, brand name pricing is preferred. Regardless, it is well established that the WCMSA process is a financial exercise and projecting future costs using a pricing standard higher than most pay is simply the cost of doing business.

Centers for Medicare & Medicaid Services also does not consider the anticipation of patent expirations and generic availability. If a costly drug is about to go generic and CMS approval is desired, it may be worth waiting on submission until that happens to incur the savings. However, sometimes there are no savings to be had. Often the initial generic pricing is not significant and may prove not worth the wait, which also carries its own associated costs. While all factors are worthy of consideration, none of them matter if CMS approval is sought.

Opioids

Despite the declaration of a national health crisis, CMS continues to project a lifetime supply of opioid medications in WCMSAs with no consideration of addiction and abuse issues. Centers for Medicare & Medicaid Services continues to refuse to use evidence based guidelines in projecting opioids use in MSAs even though research shows the ineffectiveness and risks of opioids for most injured workers. Essentially this policy is institutionalizing opioid abuse by providing Medicare beneficiaries with the means to pay for such medications when even Medicare may not. Centers for Medicare & Medicaid Services currently recommends Part D plans monitor opioid use in excess of 120 mg morphine equivalent daily dose for more than 90 days and with prescriptions from more than three prescribers/pharmacies. Yet in the WMSA process, CMS recommends primary payers provide a large lump sum payment directly to the injured worker to self-pay for the same drugs with no oversight to prevent Medicare from doing so. It is clear CMS is only interested in protecting Medicare and not the interests of the injured worker in the WCMSA process.

However, as with all other aspects of the MSA process, CMS recommendations are only applicable in the WCMSA approval process. If the parties wish to provide funding for alternative treatments or rehabilitation that will provide for the claimant post-settlement, it should simply not be submitted to CMS for approval. If state law supports a settlement inclusive of funding for such alternative treatment, then Medicare's MSP exclusion is established without CMS approval. This comes down to the parties' desire to set a limit with CMS upfront or after MSA funds have been exhausted and the allocation method is potentially in need of defending.

Weaning and Rehabilitation

Centers for Medicare & Medicaid Services will not consider a reduction in the current pharmaceutical use without evidence of actual implementation. This is the case even with supporting evidence that it is the treating physician's recommendation. Parties who wish to reduce MSA costs for such drug issues need to pursue the rehabilitation or pain management programs. Simply providing the estimated costs associated with the same will not be accepted by CMS in a WCMSA proposal.

WCRC Resources

To keep submitters and reviews on the same page, CMS publishes resources used by the WCRC when conducting the review of WCMSAs. Theoretically, if submitters use the same references and pricing tools, they would ideally reach the same conclusions reached by the WCRC. While it does not alleviate the subjective issues in the evaluation, it does establish a baseline from which all involved can rely. Specific resources used by the WCRC contactor are noted in Appendix 4 of the WCMSA Reference Guide and noted herein in the reference (CMS, 2018a).

WCMSA Approval Process

A WCMSA proposal may be submitted to CMS through the regular mail in paper or electronic form (CMS, 2018a), or as most people today do, it can be uploaded through the WCMSA web portal (WCMSAP) (CMS, n.d.-c). A complete resource for information regarding the use of the portal can be found on the portal website (CMS, 2018b).

Files must be named in a particular way when submitted. Section 10.0 of the WCMSA Reference Guide outlines the numbering system necessary for the various required documents. Of the nine prefixes provided, some are required while others are considered supplemental. If any of the required documents are not submitted, then the submission will be developed. Failure to supply request information will result in the case being closed. To avoid these problems, CMS provides a sample submission in Appendix 4 of the WCMSA Reference Guide to aid submitters organize their submission (CMS, 2018a).

CMS Responses

Upon receipt of the WCMSA submission, CMS first sends an acknowledgment letter. If the submission fails to meet review thresholds, CMS will send notice of the same. If additional information is required, CMS will send a development letter. If the development letter is not answered,

CMS will send a case closure letter. Following review, CMS will send either an approval letter or a letter proposing a different amount. All correspondences will be sent via the same method the submission was made and always copy the Medicare beneficiary and his or her attorney.

Development Letters

During its review, the WCRC may decide it requires more information to render its opinion. Typically, it will find that the payment history and the medical records do not match and request the missing medical records. The five most common development requests are:

- Insufficient or out-of-date medical records
- Insufficient payment histories, usually because the records do not provide a breakdown for medical, indemnity, or expenses categories
- Failure to address draft or final settlement agreements and court rulings in the cover letter or elsewhere in the submission
- Documents referenced in the file are not provided—this usually occurs with court rulings or settlement documents
- References to state statutes or regulations without providing sufficient documentation (i.e., to which payments the statutes/regulations apply or a copy of the statute or regulation or notice of which statutes or regulations apply to which payments

(CMS, 2018a)

If a development request is not answered in 20 days (or 30 days for cases submitted to the Benefits Coordination & Recovery Contractor [BCRC]), the case will be closed. If an insufficient response is received, another development request may result. If the reason the response was considered insufficient was because the requested records do not exist, CMS may accept supporting documentation explaining why the request cannot be answered. But understand, ultimately CMS is under no legal obligation to conduct this review or provide a written opinion letter, so if an impasse is reached, CMS approval may not be obtained. As with any submission to CMS, settlement should not be unconditionally dependent on CMS approval without a contingency plan.

Response Time

Centers for Medicare & Medicaid Services' stated response time is 45 to 60 days from the time all required documents are submitted. In reality, complete submissions made through the portal may receive a response within a week. Responses in general are primarily affected by the WCRC's workload. The status of the review can be viewed in the WCMSAP. Any time a claimant wants to check the status of the review or view any documents submitted, they may do so at MyMedicare. gov.

Re-Review

Any time CMS renders an opinion upon which the parties disagree, there is no formal appeal under the Medicare program. If the parties disagree with the conclusions reached by CMS, there is no recourse other than disregarding the recommendation or seeking an order from a court of competent jurisdiction clarifying why CMS was wrong. However, in cases in which CMS made an error, submitters may request a re-review. This can fix a math error or situation in which CMS overlooked a record already included in the submission. Re-review can also be requested in cases in which the submitter has additional documents dated prior to the submission that warrant a change in CMS's position.

Amended Review

Effective July 31, 2017, CMS allows a one-time request for re-review in cases that previously did not settle and there has been a significant change in treatment or even change in state law. The case must have been approved at least 12 months prior, but no more than 48 months, and not yet settled as of the date of the request for re-review. And the change in treatment must result in a new proposed WCMSA amount that represents a 10% or $10,000 change, whichever is greater. To request re-review, the submitter must send a new cover letter, a new proposal for future care, all medical records since the previous submission, the last six months of pharmacy records, and a new signed consent to release form. Additionally, submitter must return the previous recommendation sheet highlighting and explaining line items affected by the new proposal and when appropriate, cross-referencing medical records for support or the proposal to demonstrate replacement treatment. Failure to provide any of the required items will result in denial of amended review, as CMS does not permit supplementing the request. This determination will supersede the previous one regardless of whether it increased or decreased.

Resubmission

In cases that were closed due to inactivity for more than one year, a new full submission will be required. While re-review may be requested, it will still be considered in the order of receipt as if it were a new submission. Sometimes, resubmission is simply the best strategy for overcoming issues that resulted in the inactivity. Because the submission is new, the timeline resets and the proposal start with a clean slate. In cases with problematic records, submitters also have the ability to withdraw the proposal rather than wait for it to go inactive.

Post-settlement Issues

Obtaining CMS approval is just the beginning of WCMSA responsibilities. The WCMSA represents a lifetime of medical expenses, which means a lifetime of record keeping and interacting with CMS. Unfortunately for the claimants, these responsibilities are often borne by them alone, as the remaining parties to the settlement typically move on and seldom look back. But the following needs to be understood to ensure access to related medical treatment, whether paid through the WCMSA or Medicare.

Rendering WCMSA Approval Effective

Once the settlement is final, CMS requires that the approved final documents be submitted to render its approval of the WCMSA effective. This essentially notifies CMS that the case did in fact settle and the terms of the WCMSA will apply to exhaustion. The settlement will also separately be reported through MMSEA Section 111 (CMS, n.d.-a) mandatory insurer reporting if the claimant is already a Medicare beneficiary, however the parties should not assume that this substitutes for sending final settlement documents. Centers for Medicare & Medicaid Services wants to see that the terms disclosed in the approved WCMSA proposal are in fact how the case was settled and funded.

Administration

Centers for Medicare & Medicaid Services requests the WCMSA be administered by a "competent administrator." Short of someone already designated incompetent by a court or in a guardian or conservator situation, this has been a fairly ineffective request. Over 85% of all WCMSAs funded from workers' compensation settlements since the program's inception in 2001 have been self-administered, many by individuals with less than good intentions for proper exhaustion.

Centers for Medicare & Medicaid Services publishes "requirements" for self-administration. Keep in mind there is no law or regulation that mandates any of these acts. Despite CMS's constant use of the word "must," and other affirmative language, the contents of Section 17.0 of the WCMSA Reference Guide (CMS, 2018a) and the Self-Administration Tool-Kit (CMS, 2018c) are merely recommendations.

Interest-Bearing Account

Claimant is asked to deposit the total WCMSA amount into an interest-bearing account, separate from other personal accounts. While previous CMS guidance referenced Federal Deposit Insurance Corporation (FDIC) requirements, that is no longer articulated, leaving other financial institutions open as investment options. Centers for Medicare & Medicaid Services is more interested in availability of funds rather than earning large sums of interest and keeping up with medical cost inflation. In fact, prior to 2005, WCMSAs funded with structured settlements used to include a cost of living adjustment, but CMS ended that with a memo stating interest need not be considered.

Use of WCMSA Funds

Centers for Medicare & Medicaid Services limits use of WCMSA funds to medical expenses related to the work injury that would normally be paid by Medicare and paid at the rate the WCMSA was calculated. For help with determining what Medicare covers, CMS refers beneficiaries to "Medicare & You" (CMS, n.d.-d).

Centers for Medicare & Medicaid Services permits expenses related to maintenance of the account to be paid from the WCMSA, such as banking fees, postage, copying charges, and income tax on any interest earned. What CMS does not allow is payment from the WCMSA for professional administration costs or attorneys' fees.

Record Keeping

The Medicare beneficiary will need to keep an accurate accounting of payments made from the WCMSA fund to demonstrate proper exhaustion. Centers for Medicare & Medicaid Services may request to see these records, particularly when requesting that it lift the MSP exclusion. Additionally, the administrator must submit an annual attestation no later than 30 days after the annual anniversary of the settlement, signed and stating the total amount of payments for that year and that all payments made from the funds were for related Medicare covered expenses. While there is no penalty or fine for failing to submit an annual attestation, it may be more difficult to resume Medicare benefits upon exhaustion when CMS has not been kept privy to the account balance as requested.

Professional Administration

There are companies that provide professional administration for MSAs. The administrator has access to physician networks and discounted pharmacy and DME programs to stretch MSAs further than projected. In the event of an exhaustion, permanent or temporary, the administrator will notify CMS and coordinate getting Medicare benefits to resume.

The biggest benefit of professional administration over self-administration is the protection afforded all parties in the fact the administrator is an unrelated third party contractually bound to pay only related medical expenses otherwise covered by Medicare. There are no mistaken payments or possibility of borrowing from the account for unrelated expenses. Unfortunately, these services do not come for free. Because CMS will not count the cost of administration against proper exhaustion, the cost must be borne outside the MSA. Accordingly, the cost must be negotiated as a term of settlement, otherwise claimant would be left to pay for such services after realizing that it is harder than contemplated.

Funds Remaining Upon Death

If funds are left in the MSA account upon death of the Medicare beneficiary, the funds belong to the estate of the Medicare beneficiary, unless contractually directed elsewhere in the settlement. Medical providers may have up to 12 months to submit billing, therefore, CMS requests that MSA accounts remain open for some period to ensure all related bills are settled. Once accomplished, the funds may be dispersed in accordance with state law.

Account Exhaustion

Once the WCMSA funds have been spent on related medical expenses otherwise covered by Medicare, Medicare coverage will resume. The Medicare beneficiary or administrator must notify CMS funds have exhausted and may need to provide records to CMS for its review to ensure only Medicare covered related items or services were paid for from the account. If CMS is satisfied, the common working file will be noted, and Medicare will become primary payer for all related treatment. In the event CMS is not satisfied with the accounting and finds that some payments were not proper, it will inform the beneficiary how much more must be spent on related treatment before it will lift the exclusion.

In cases funded with a structured settlement annuity, it is possible to temporarily exhaust annually. Although a new deposit is made every year and any funds remaining in the account at the end of any given year must carry forward, it is possible a situation such as a surgery may arise that costs more than is available. If at any time the account balance goes to zero, CMS must be notified, and it will become primary until the next annuity check arrives. Once the next deposit is made, CMS will resume secondary payer status and payments will resume from the MSA.

Medicare Benefit Determination and Appeal

If the Medicare beneficiary has no funds remaining in the MSA account and requires medical treatment, CMS will be forced to make a benefit determination. If CMS denies payment, whether because it feels the MSA was inadequate or improperly exhausted, the inevitable outcome is that Medicare may deny the payment, or potentially pay it conditionally and seek reimbursement, and the Medicare beneficiary will be statutorily entitled to bring an administrative appeal. Any legal arguments that could not be made at the time of the WCMSA approval because no similar access to appeal existed may be heard at this time to defend the exhaustion.

Summary

Parties to any insurance settlement involving a Medicare beneficiary must be cognizant of the fact that Medicare is, by statute, a secondary payer. As such, any legal obligation to pay for medical expenses, past, present, or future must be honored before Medicare is permitted to pay. Therefore, when settling claims involving a commutation of future medical benefits, Medicare's interests should always be considered and if necessary, protected. The settlement funds constitute an insurance payment that triggers the Medicare exclusion, and any allocation for future medical expenses must be spent on related medical treatment before Medicare will resume coverage. This allocation is commonly referred to today as a Medicare Set-Aside. While Medicare Set-Asides allocators are often from rehabilitation and case management backgrounds, it is also an area in which some legal nurse consultants (LNCs) find their niche.

Parties who wish to obtain assurances that the future medical allocation is sufficient in the eyes of the federal government may voluntarily seek its approval by submitting a WCMSA proposal to CMS for review. The review program is not required or governed by any law or regulation, federal or state, meaning that in addition to there being no requirement to seek it, there is also no recourse for challenging the outcome. However, CMS states that should the recommended amount be funded, the agency will not seek additional funds in the future.

Centers for Medicare & Medicaid Services approval is currently only available in workers' compensation settlements that meet certain monetary thresholds, and unavailability should not be viewed as a safe harbor for not needing an MSA. There is an inherent cost in obtaining CMS approval because many of the calculation methodologies it requires exceed the underlying state law obligations, resulting in higher allocations than might otherwise be reasonable and defensible. But while there is no recourse for disagreeing with CMS's recommendation at the time of approval, parties should remember that once CMS makes an official benefit determination based upon what it deems an inadequate allocation, the administrative remedy under the Medicare Act will be available at that time.

Although not required, CMS approval continues to be preferred by most insurers. Accordingly, it is important to understand CMS calculation methodologies and post-settlement administration expectations when settling insurance claims. More importantly, parties must be clear in establishing a meeting of the minds with regard to such Medicare issues, so settlement terms will be enforceable. Because the Medicare Act only governs the exclusion and reimbursements, requirements regarding MSAs are predominantly contractual. But setting aside all the details contained herein, the most important objective here is to prevent Medicare from making payments that are the responsibility of some other entity. Accomplish that and the how and what was allocated becomes irrelevant.

References

Arias, E., Heron, M., & Xu, J. (2017, Aug 14). United States life tables, 2014. *National Vital Statistics Report*, 66(4). Retrieved from www.cdc.gov/nchs/data/nvsr/nvsr66/nvsr66_04.pdf.

Centers for Medicare & Medicaid Services. (2018a, Mar 19). Workers' Compensation Medicare Set-Aside (WCMSA) reference guide [COBR-Q1-2018-v2.7]. Retrieved from www.cms.gov/Medicare/Coordination-of-Benefits-and-Recovery/Workers-Compensation-Medicare-Set-Aside-Arrangements/Downloads/WCMSA-Reference-Guide-Version-2_7.pdf.

Centers for Medicare & Medicaid Services. (2018b, Apr 2). Self-administration toolkit [Version 1.2]. Retrieved fromwww.cms.gov/Medicare/Coordination-of-Benefits-and-Recovery/Workers-Compensation-Medicare-Set-Aside-Arrangements/Downloads/Self-Administration-Toolkit-for-WCMSAs.pdf.

Centers for Medicare & Medicaid Services. (2018c, July 2). Workers' Compensation Medicare Set-Aside Web Portal (WCMSAP) user guide [COBR-Q3-2018-v5.5]. Retrieved from www.cob.cms.hhs.gov/WCMSA/assets/wcmsa/userManual/WCMSAUserManual.pdf.

Centers for Medicare & Medicaid Services. (2018d, Oct 1). Workers' Compensation Medicare Set-Aside Arrangement (WCMSA) reference guide [COBR-Q4-2018-v2.8]. Retrieved from www.cms.gov/Medicare/Coordination-of-Benefits-and-Recovery/Workers-Compensation-Medicare-Set-Aside-Arrangements/Downloads/WCMSA-Reference-Guide-Version-2_8.pdf.

Centers for Medicare & Medicaid Services. (n.d.-a). Non-group health plan recovery. Retrieved from www.cms.gov/Medicare/Coordination-of-Benefits-and-Recovery/Workers-Compensation-Medicare-Set-Aside-Arrangements/Downloads/WCMSA-Reference-Guide-Version-2_7.pdf.

Centers for Medicare & Medicaid Services. (n.d.-b). Medicare–Medicaid coordination. Retrieved from www.cms.gov/Medicare-Medicaid-Coordination/Medicare-MedicaidCoordination.html.

Centers for Medicare & Medicaid Services. (n.d.-c). Workers' Compensation Set-Aside Web Portal (WCMSAP). Retrieved from www.cob.cms.hhs.gov/WCMSA/.

Centers for Medicare & Medicaid Services. (n.d.-d). Medicare & you. Retrieved from www.medicare.gov/medicare-and-you/medicare-and-you.html.

Centers for Medicare & Medicaid Services. (n.d.-e). Mandatory insurer reporting for non-group health plans. Retrieved from www.cms.gov/medicare/coordination-of-benefits-and-recovery/mandatory-insurer-reporting-for-non-group-health-plans/overview.html.

Hadden v. U.S., 661 F.3d 298 (6th Cir. 2011).

Legal Information Institute. (n.d.-a). 42 U.S. Code § 1395y Exclusions from coverage and Medicare as secondary payer. Retrieved from www.law.cornell.edu/uscode/text/42/1395y.

Legal Information Institute. (n.d.-b). 42 CFR Part 411, Subpart B—Insurance coverage that limits Medicare payment: General provisions. Retrieved from www.law.cornell.edu/cfr/text/42/part-411/subpart-B.

Legal Information Institute. (n.d.-c). 42 CFR § 411.46 Lump-sum payments. Retrieved from www.law.cornell.edu/cfr/text/42/411.46.

Legal Information Institute. (n.d.-d). 42 CFR Part 411, Subpart D—Limitations on Medicare payment for services covered under liability or no-fault insurance. Retrieved from www.law.cornell.edu/cfr/text/42/part-411/subpart-D.

Legal Information Institute. (n.d.-e). 42 CFR Part 405, Subpart I—Determinations, redeterminations, reconsiderations, and appeals under original Medicare (Part A and Part B). Retrieved from www.law.cornell.edu/cfr/text/42/part-405/subpart-I.

Legal Information Institute. (n.d.-f). 42 U.S. Code § 1395w-22 benefits and beneficiary protections. Retrieved fromwww.law.cornell.edu/uscode/text/42/1395w-22.

U.S. Government Publishing Office. (2003). Public Law No.: 108–173, § 301, 117 Stat. 2221, Medicare Prescription Drug, Improvement, and Modernization Act. Retrieved from www.gpo.gov/fdsys/pkg/PLAW-108publ173/pdf/PLAW-108publ173.pdf.

Additional Reading

Centers for Medicare & Medicaid Services. (2001–2011). Memorandums. Retrieved from www.cms.gov/Medicare/Coordination-of-Benefits-and-Recovery/Workers-Compensation-Medicare-Set-Aside-Arrangements/WCMSA-Memorandums/Memorandums.html.

Centers for Medicare & Medicaid Services. (n.d.). Workers' Compensation Medicare set aside arrangements. Retrieved from www.cms.gov/Medicare/Coordination-of-Benefits-and-Recovery/Workers-Compensation-Medicare-Set-Aside-Arrangements/WCMSA-Overview.html.

Centers for Medicare & Medicaid Services. (n.d.). Mandatory insurer reporting (NGHP). Retrieved from www.cms.gov/Medicare/Coordination-of-Benefits-and-Recovery/Mandatory-Insurer-Reporting-For-Non-Group-Health-Plans/Overview.html.

IBM Watson Health, Micromedex. (2018). Retrieved from https://truvenhealth.com/Training/Product/IBM-Micromedex-Clinical-Knowledge/IBM-Micromedex.

IBM Watson Health, Red Book. (2018). Retrieved from https://truvenhealth.com/Training/Product/IBM-Micromedex-Clinical-Knowledge/IBM-Micromedex-RED-BOOK.

Legal Information Institute. (n.d.). 42 CFR Part 422, Subpart C—Medicare Secondary Payer (MSP) procedures. Retrieved from www.law.cornell.edu/cfr/text/42/422.108.

MCG Health, Milliman Care Guidelines. (2018). Retrieved from www.mcg.com/careguidelines/careguidelines/.

National Center for Biotechnology Information, PubMed. (2018). Retrieved from www.ncbi.nlm.nih.gov/pubmed/.

National Institute of Health. U.S. National Library of Medicine. (2018). DailyMed. Retrieved from https://dailymed.nlm.nih.gov/dailymed/about.cfm.

Parra v. PacifiCare, 715 F.3d 1146 (9th Cir. 2013).

Stat!Ref, STAT!Ref Core Resources Collections. (2018). Retrieved from www.statref.com/.

Thompson v. Goetzmann, 337 F.3d 489 (2003).

U.S. Food and Drug Administration. (2018a). Drugs@FDA: FDA approved drug products. Retrieved from www.accessdata.fda.gov/scripts/cder/drugsatfda/.

U.S. Food and Drug Administration. (2018b). National drug code directory. Retrieved from www.accessdata.fda.gov/scripts/cder/ndc/default.cfm.

U.S. Food and Drug Administration. (2018c). Orange book: Approved drug products with therapeutic equivalence evaluations. Retrieved from www.accessdata.fda.gov/scripts/cder/ob/default.cfm.

U.S. v. Baxter, 345 F.3d 866 (2003).

Wolters Kluwer. (n.d.), MediRegs healthcare compliance software. Retrieved from https://lrus.wolterskluwer.com/product-family/mediregs.

Test Questions

1. CMS approval of a WCMSA is required by statute.
   A. True
   B. False
2. Medicare set-aside funds may be:
   A. Self-administered by the claimant
   B. Paid directly to Medicare
   C. Co-mingled with personal finances
   D. Used to pay for unrelated medical expenses
3. If a physician writes a prescription for a brand name drug, CMS will allow for generic substitution in its WCMSA approval.
   A. True
   B. False
4. WCMSA submission does not require:
   A. Most recent two years of medical records
   B. Release signed by the Medicare beneficiary
   C. Copy of the first report of injury
   D. Proposed settlement agreement
5. If a Medicare beneficiary is offered a $20,000 settlement, then no MSA is necessary.
   A. True
   B. False

Answers: 1. B, 2. A, 3. B, 4. C, 5. B

Chapter 25

Healthcare Provider Licensure Investigations and Administrative Proceedings

Julie Dickinson, MBA, BSN, RN, LNCC®
Marian Ead, BSN, RN

Contents

Objectives

- Explain the purpose of practice acts in regulating health professionals
- Discuss the laws governing the investigative process and administrative proceedings
- Detail the composition and function of a professional licensing board
- List the penalties a professional licensing board can impose
- Recall the types of complaints that can initiate an administrative investigation
- Examine the legal nurse consultant's role in the prosecution and defense of healthcare provider licensure investigations and administrative proceedings

Introduction

Each state has one or more administrative bodies under the executive branch of government responsible for protecting and improving the health and safety of the state's residents. Depending on the state, these administrative bodies might be in the public health department, department of professional regulation, professional licensing board, or other state-specific agency. The administrative bodies are responsible for assuring access to high-quality healthcare services and ensuring the safe practice of regulated health professions. To do this, each state's administrative body is tasked with administering and enforcing the statutes, regulations, programs, and policies pertaining to all licensed healthcare professions and facilities. Depending on the organization of each state, one or more of these administrative bodies will be responsible for investigating complaints against licensed healthcare facilities, licensed professionals, and unlicensed individuals performing duties which are restricted to licensed professionals. The administrative body is "charged with maintaining the balance between the rights of the [healthcare providers] to practice [their profession] and the responsibility to protect the public health, safety, and welfare of its citizens" (Russell, 2012, p. 37). The administrative body takes disciplinary action against those who violate the law or pose a risk to public health and safety (Knag & Garg, 2015). The subject healthcare provider (HCP) is afforded "several layers of due process to address allegations" that may result in sanctions (Knag & Garg, 2015, para. 18).

Legal nurse consultants (LNCs), as members of the prosecution team (i.e., employees of the administrative body) or as members of the defense team, are key players in the prosecution of or defense against such complaints. In this chapter, the role of the LNC during licensure investigations and administrative proceedings against HCPs will be explored. While the specifics of the administrative process vary between states and sometimes even between licensing boards within the same state, the fundamentals of the overall process are consistent. For ease of understanding, the term "professional licensing board" will be used throughout this chapter to describe the administrative body that handles complaints against licensed HCPs, but the actual name of the administrative body will vary by state. Of note, licensure investigations are entirely separate legal processes from civil lawsuits. A healthcare provider can have a parallel but distinct medical malpractice action in the judicial system while being investigated by a professional licensing board for the same incident.

Administrative Law

Each state is responsible for determining what constitutes a professional, who should be licensed, and for enacting administrative law related to professional licensure. Administrative law is defined as the body of law that allows for the creation of public regulatory agencies and contains all of the statutes, judicial decisions, and regulations that govern them. It is created by administrative agencies to implement their powers and duties in the form of rules, regulations, orders, and decisions.

(Administrative law and procedure, n.d.)

Regulatory, or administrative, agencies are created to enforce standards and safety and serve to "protect a public interest rather than to vindicate private rights" (Administrative law, 2017).

Administrative state agencies that oversee healthcare professions include state boards of nursing, medicine, pharmacy, physical therapy, etc. The specific healthcare professions that a board governs will vary by state. For example, some medical boards govern just physicians; others govern physicians and acupuncturists; and some may govern physicians, physician assistants, and physical therapists. When suspecting non-compliance with the state's applicable administrative laws, such agencies can investigate and hold hearings to determine if a violation has, in fact, occurred. Administrative investigations focus on quality of care and standard of care (not on the other elements of proof in a civil negligence claim—damages and causation).

Administrative agencies have the authority to issue a variety of disciplinary actions against an HCP's license when a violation of the administrative law related to professional licensure is confirmed. There is no financial compensation for the individual or entity who filed the complaint that resulted in the disciplinary action. If the state-imposed discipline is a monetary fine, the funds collected may go into the coffers of the agency that investigates the complaint. In Massachusetts, for example, the Board of Registration in Medicine keeps monies received from fines it imposes on physicians, as the Board has its own budget and is not dependent on the state of Massachusetts to fund it.

Practice Acts

Practice acts are laws that govern the practice of a regulated healthcare profession in a given state. These laws define the scope of practice for that profession; explain the application, examination, and licensure process as well as the renewal process; limit the use of that profession's title (e.g., the use of the title "Registered Nurse"); discuss the composition and duties of the licensing board for that profession and give the board the authority to regulate that profession and enforce the law. Practice acts also discuss the investigative and disciplinary process and list the ongoing requirements for licensure, such as continuing education, professional liability insurance coverage, etc. Licensed healthcare providers are required to comply with their specific state's practice act.

Legal nurse consultants working on licensure investigations should be familiar with the applicable laws regulating the healthcare profession in question, e.g., nursing, medicine, dentistry, chiropractic, and optometry (Dickinson, 2017).

Laws Governing the Investigative Process and Administrative Proceedings

Each state has laws governing the investigation and adjudication of administrative complaints. Both the HCP and the professional licensing board must abide by these rules and regulations.

A state's laws governing administrative proceedings may not contain a statute of limitations for administrative actions. However, some states hold that "constitutional due process standards require that disciplinary hearing be commenced within 'a meaningful time'" (Lagnese, Anderson,

& Santoro, 2015, p. 270). Considerations to assess whether a hearing has commenced within a meaningful time include "the length of the delay, the reason for the delay, the defendant's assertion of his right, and prejudice to the defendant" (Lagnese et al., 2015, p. 271).

For example, in *Baer v. Connecticut Board of Examiners in Podiatry* (1998),

> The defendant/podiatrist was first notified of the patient's complaint nine years after the first alleged negligent surgery and seven years after the alleged negligent procedure. At or about the time of the surgeries, at least 11 x-rays had been taken of the patient's foot. However, as far as state regulations require that x-rays be maintained for only three years, they were all destroyed prior to notification of the plaintiff's complaint. In light of the extreme delay, the lack of any explanation for the delay, the defendant's objection to the timeliness of the charges, and the prejudice to the defendant (podiatrist's expert witness indicated he was unable to form an opinion because of the absence of the x-rays), the court held that the podiatrist's right to due process of law had been violated.
>
> (Lagnese et al., 2015, p. 271)

To obtain medical records from the subject HCP and other relevant providers who treated the patient, the professional licensing board does not need an authorization, subpoena, or patient's consent (except, typically, for psychiatric records). The Code of Federal Regulations authorizes the HCP to release information without the patient's consent as part of the professional licensing board's health oversight activities (Legal Information Institute, n.d.). At the state level, a state's administrative law may also require that the administrative body have unrestricted access to records, or it may prohibit HCPs from denying access to a medical record based on the grounds that privilege or confidentiality applies. Each state will have enforceable actions it can take against HCPs should they fail to comply or cooperate with an investigation.

Hearings may also be subject to the procedures set forth in the state's administrative procedure act. The Model State Administrative Procedure Act (MSAPA) was published by the National Conference of Commissioners on Uniform State Laws (NCCUSL), also known as the Uniform Law Commission, to provide "a uniform minimum set of procedures to be followed by agencies subject to the act" (NCCUSL, 2010). Each state may have adopted the MSAPA or incorporated significant portions of it into their individual state administrative procedures acts (NCCUSL, 2010).

Legal nurse consultants working on licensure investigations and administrative proceedings should be familiar with the administrative laws governing licensure investigations and proceedings in their state (Dickinson, 2017).

Healthcare Provider Board

Composition

Typically, each state has a board or commission for each licensed healthcare profession. This may include a board of nursing, board of medicine, dental commission, chiropractic board, podiatry board, etc. The size and composition of each board, the requisite qualifications of its members, and term limits are defined by state statutes. For example, the Connecticut Nursing Practice Act: State Board of Examiners for Nursing (2012) asserts that the nursing board shall be comprised of

12 members—two licensed practical nurses, five registered nurses (one who teaches nursing, two with master's degrees in nursing, and one with a doctorate in nursing), one advanced practice registered nurse, and four public members. Legal nurse consultants should be familiar with the relevant statutes in the state(s) in which they work.

Function

State statute defines the functions of the professional licensing board. Some boards, such as nursing boards, may have duties related to regulations and standards for courses in their state that offer training for the profession. All professional licensing boards are responsible for interpreting and enforcing the laws and statutes that govern their respective professions, hearing and deciding matters concerning suspension or revocation of licensure, adjudicating complaints against HCPs, and imposing sanctions where appropriate.

The reasons for which a board may impose disciplinary action may also be listed in the state's practice act for that profession. Such reasons may include being incompetent or unfit to practice, engaging in cruel or indecent conduct towards patients, receiving a criminal conviction, aiding or abetting the unlicensed practice of a licensed profession, engaging in fraud or material deception, abusing drugs, or failing to comply with continuing education (Brous, 2012).

Penalties the Board Can Impose

State statutes also define the sanctions a professional licensing board can impose. The following are examples of actions a board can take, singly or in combination, upon finding the existence of good cause (Brous, 2012):

- Revoke a license or permit
- Revoke the right to renew a license or permit
- Suspend a license or permit
- Censure a HCP or permittee
- Issue a formal reprimand against a license or permit
- Place a license or permit on probationary status, with or without practice restrictions such as
  - Limit a licensee's scope of practice to specific areas defined by the board
  - Engage in mandatory education and competency assessment until a satisfactory degree of skill has been attained in those areas which are the basis for the probation
  - Implement monitoring by requiring the licensee or permittee to be evaluated regularly by a similar HCP or by reporting regularly to the board and
- Assess a civil penalty (fine)

Administrative agencies do not have the authority to imprison healthcare providers for administrative law violations. If criminal behavior is uncovered or suspected, a referral may be made to the attorney general's office for criminal investigation. Healthcare providers may be criminally prosecuted for egregious actions, such as sexual misconduct, tax evasion, or criminally negligent homicide.

Administrative Process and LNC Role

Types of Complaints

A professional licensing board may initiate an investigation of a healthcare provider upon receipt of a "complaint." There are various types of complaints that can trigger an investigation. Consumer complaints are those received from patients or families. They may allege substandard care (e.g., misdiagnosis, wrong site surgery, or fetal demise), misconduct, or impairment. Statutory complaints are reports received from mandated reporters, healthcare facilities, or government agencies such as a department of public health. Examples include a hospital reporting it has suspended a physician's surgical privileges due to an increased complication rate, a report from the Department of Social Services that a dentist has been submitting a high number of claims to the state Medicaid program for x-rays which is concerning for excessive radiation exposure and fraud, and a pharmacist reporting a physician may be overprescribing narcotics and benzodiazepines. Also, mandated reporting, if required by state law, includes self-reported incidents by HCPs regarding their own practice. For example, an HCP may be required to self-report if terminated due to incompetency, if disqualified from participating in the federal Medicare or Medicaid programs, or if diagnosed with a mental or physical condition that prevents one from practicing with reasonable skill and safety.

In addition, the board's receipt of a malpractice or settlement notification from an HCP's liability insurance company may generate an investigation. Lastly, high-profile incidents involving HCPs may trigger the professional licensing board to open an investigation. For example, if a prominent news source announces that a physician removed a healthy kidney on the wrong patient, the board may begin an investigation without having received an official consumer complaint or statutory report.

The Prosecution Process

All licensing boards function differently in how complaints are processed. Some licensing boards have no medically trained persons involved in the complaint review process, while others have staff with medical or legal training, which may include LNCs. Because of their clinical experience and expertise, LNCs play a significant role in helping to determine which complaints should be investigated. Priority is given to complaints that allege current substandard care practices, misconduct, and fraud. Complaints that involve now deceased HCPs or "stale cases" (i.e., the date of incident was more than six years prior) are difficult or impossible to investigate. The LNC role in licensure investigations is key. The nuances of the investigative process will vary by state and licensing board, but generally, the process is as follows:

- If the complaint involves a specific clinical concern (e.g., infection control issues, several patient deaths in close succession, an unlicensed person performing duties which are restricted to licensed professionals, etc.), the LNC may make an unannounced visit to the HCP's office. This site visit typically occurs before the HCP is notified that a complaint has been received.
- The LNC determines which pertinent medical records or documents to obtain and the need for any subpoenas or written requests for information, once obtained, reviews them to establish the issues in the case. In addition to the HCP's records, the LNC may obtain records from the patient's prior or subsequent HCPs.

- The LNC prepares chronologies and summaries of the pertinent medical issues.
- The LNC notifies the HCP of the complaint, provides the specific allegations, and requests the HCP's written response to the allegations. In addition to the complaint received, the board may add its own allegations based on the LNC's review of the records and based on the findings at the unannounced site inspection.
- The LNC determines key persons, in addition to the subject HCP, to interview. This may include the patient, family, and healthcare staff and administrators. The licensing board relies on the LNC's knowledge of hospital workings, nuances, and protocols and the LNC's critical review of the medical record to ensure all key persons are interviewed. For example, in a case where a mother hemorrhages and nearly dies during an emergency caesarean section (C-section), it would be critical to interview the obstetrician, the anesthesiologist, the scrub person, and the circulating nurse to determine what actually occurred in the operating room. What is *not* documented in the medical record may be just as critical, if not more so, than what *is* documented. Thus, the LNC's analysis may lead to an exploration of what prompted the C-section to be emergent. Was it preventable? Were the fetal heart monitor strips not properly interpreted? In order to answer these questions, it may be prudent to interview the labor and delivery staff who cared for the laboring mother prior to the emergent C-section.
- The LNC obtains and reviews the healthcare provider's credentialing file and employment file to determine if there is a history of complaints, competency issues, or high complication rates. For example, a surgeon's high complication rate could raise a red flag that would require more in-depth investigation.
- The LNC reviews the HCP's most recent license renewal application to determine if there are any new malpractice suits.
- The LNC reviews a HCP's malpractice history to determine if there is a pattern of alleged negligence. While being sued for malpractice is not automatically synonymous with being negligent, it may bear insight into the HCP's practice.
- The LNC conducts medical literature research to understand the clinical issues in the case, develop lines of questioning for the interview(s) with the HCP (and others), educate the licensing board on the clinical issues and their significance in the case, and intelligently converse with an expert about the case. For example, in a case alleging an ophthalmologist's care of several patients resulted in complications following cataract surgery, the LNC needs to gain knowledge on normal eye anatomy and the details of cataract surgery including potential complications. Acquiring this knowledge is a quintessential responsibility of the LNC.
- The LNC locates and screens experts to review the case if there are allegations of substandard care. The expert's area of clinical practice and expertise needs to be the same as that of the healthcare provider whose care is in question. However, to avoid a potential conflict of interest for the prosecution if the case goes to hearing, the educational and professional path of the expert should not intersect that of the HCP. The only provider who is able to evaluate another's practice is one who has the same training. For example, in a case involving the actions of a critical care registered nurse (RN), only another critical care RN would be qualified to opine on whether the care provided by the subject RN was within the standard of care. In addition, the expert must have been clinically active at the time of the event giving rise to the complaint, because standards of care can change over time and the expert will need to opine on the standard of care in effect at the time of the incident. The vetting of potential experts includes a review of their medical malpractice history and

any prior board complaints and disciplinary actions. An LNC working directly for a licensing board will have access to the licensure applications, complaint history (including dismissed complaints that are not public record), etc. for in-state providers who are being screened as potential experts.

■ The LNC makes telephone inquiries to one or two potential experts—to discuss the issues in the case, ensure those issues are within the expert's scope of practice, disclose the name of the HCP to check for any conflicts of interest, and review the board's process for investigating complaints. Also, depending on the individual state's process, the expert may be required to enter into a written contract, accept the remuneration offered, provide a written opinion, and testify if the case goes to a hearing. The LNC may have the authority to select the expert and frequently consults with the expert throughout the course of the investigation. Locating an expert can be a time-intensive undertaking, especially if the HCP being investigated is well-known or highly regarded in the field or if the HCP's practice is highly specialized.

■ Once an expert has been contracted, the LNC forwards case documents to the expert for review. These include a copy of the complaint (or a summary if the complaint is statutory), a copy of the HCP's written response to the allegations, and the pertinent medical records.

■ Once the expert submits a written opinion, the LNC and licensing board counsel meet, discuss the case, and prepare a legal memorandum addressed to and reviewed by the licensing board's complaint committee (which is typically a subset of the full board, such as two board members). The memorandum summarizes the complaint, the medical records, the interviews conducted, and the expert's opinion. It concludes with a recommendation as to whether the case should be closed or whether some form of discipline should be imposed. The Complaint Committee then issues its decision. The committee has the discretion to agree or disagree with the recommendation of the LNC and board counsel. For example, if the recommendation is for the HCP to have a practice restriction, the complaint committee could reject the restriction and instead issue a harsher discipline of revocation or a less severe reprimand. If the HCP accepts the discipline, the investigation is over, and the LNC's role is complete. If the HCP does not accept the discipline, the matter goes to hearing.

■ In extreme cases, the licensing board may move to summarily suspend an HCP's license if it believes there is a clear and imminent danger to the public if the HCP continues to care for patients (Knag & Garg, 2015). In such circumstances, the licensing board and HCP may agree to an interim consent order pending a final determination by the Board (Knag & Garg, 2015).

The Defense Process

Ideally, the defense firm is retained by the HCP or the HCP's liability insurance company from the outset, as soon as the HCP receives notice of the investigation. Many liability insurance policies have limits on coverage for the defense of administrative actions. For example, the insurance company may pay up to $25,000 in costs to defend the claims. Any expenses over this threshold are the responsibility of the HCP. The HCP may also be responsible for defense costs if the claims are related to fraudulent or criminal activity, and the insurance company may deny coverage.

While the process varies by state, the notice of investigation alerts the HCP that a complaint has been received or that an investigation is being conducted because of a statutory report, malpractice or settlement notification, or high-profile incident. The letter identifies the patient's (or "petitioner's") name and date of birth and requests the HCP (or "respondent") to submit a complete copy of the patient's records by a certain date. The specific allegations are not disclosed to the HCP at this stage to reduce the chance of record alteration. Some states also use this process as an opportunity to audit compliance with the state's statutory requirements for that profession, such as mandatory continuing education and liability insurance coverage. The HCP may be requested to submit proof of such compliance. The defense attorney and LNC educate the HCP about the investigative process, what to expect (including the time frame), and the next steps. While the case is pending, the LNC maintains contact with both the HCP and the liability insurance company, providing periodic status updates.

The defense LNC works with the HCP to ensure the patient's complete record is assembled (along with any other requested documentation) and monitors the submission deadline to ensure compliance. The attorney advises the licensing board that the HCP is now represented by an attorney, requests all further communication be through the attorney, and submits the records and other requested documentation to the licensing board on behalf of the HCP. The defense LNC conducts background research on both the HCP (including prior discipline on license and malpractice history) and the patient (including litigation history and criminal activity).

Upon receipt of the HCP's records, the licensing board provides the attorney and HCP with the specific allegations and requests a written statement of care and response to the allegations by a certain date. The attorney and LNC analyze the records relative to the allegations, discuss the case and allegations with the HCP, and interview any pertinent staff at the HCP's office. As needed, the defense LNC conducts medical literature research and educates the attorney on the clinical issues in the case. The LNC then uses clinical knowledge and persuasive writing skills to prepare an initial draft response to the allegations. This response is "an opportunity to explain why actions were taken, bring extenuating circumstances to the [Board's] attention, demonstrate support from relevant professional literature, [and] letters from other personnel and colleagues..." (Knag & Garg, 2015, para. 5). The attorney finalizes the draft and, once approved by the HCP, submits the response to the licensing board by the identified deadline, which the LNC has been monitoring to ensure compliance.

If the licensing board expert has concerns about care rendered, the HCP may have an opportunity to submit a rebuttal response, depending on the state's process for handling administrative complaints. The licensing board provides the HCP, through the defense attorney, with a copy of the licensing board's expert's report (obscuring the identity of the expert) and requests a rebuttal response by a certain date. The LNC reviews the expert's report to identify any reference to the provision or review of other material gathered by the licensing board (e.g., records from subsequent healthcare providers) and works with the attorney to obtain a copy of this same material for their review and consideration in preparing the rebuttal response.

Depending on the specifics of the case, the defense may obtain an expert review at this stage. Typically, the expert is in the same field of practice as the HCP. However, sometimes a specialist is sought. For example, an endodontist may be asked to review a case in which a general dentist performed a root canal procedure, or an anesthesiologist may be asked to review a case in which a family practice physician provided sedation. The defense LNC locates and screens potential experts, obtains their curriculum vitae and fee schedule, and proposes several qualified experts to the defense attorney who selects one to recommend to the HCP's liability insurance company. Once the insurer grants permission to retain the expert, the LNC prepares an expert package, which contains the allegations, the HCP's records and response to the allegations, the licensing board's expert's report, and any other relevant material (such as subsequent treatment records). The defense attorney, LNC, and expert discuss the expert's review, and if favorable, the LNC may prepare an initial draft expert opinion letter detailing the expert's conclusions. The attorney will finalize the draft for review and approval by the expert. (For more information on locating, screening, and liaising with expert witnesses, see Chapter 36.)

Meanwhile, the defense attorney and LNC also meet with the HCP to discuss the licensing board's expert's criticisms, any other material received, the rebuttal response, and whether any other supporting documents (e.g., affidavit, phone records, etc.) should be procured. The defense LNC prepares a persuasive initial draft of the rebuttal response and monitors the submission deadline to ensure compliance. Once the rebuttal response is finalized by the attorney and HCP, the attorney submits it and the defense expert's report to the licensing board, who in turn provides the report to its expert for review and consideration.

If the matter is not dismissed after the rebuttal response, the defense is provided with the licensing board's investigative file (which may include summaries or notes of its witness interviews). The final opinion letter of the licensing board's expert should be included in the file, and the identity of the expert is now made known to the defense. The LNC reviews the investigative file carefully to ensure receipt of all exhibits and documents referenced therein.

The licensing board attorney provides defense counsel with the draft statement of charges and proposed consent order. The statement of charges is similar to a complaint in civil cases and lists the facts that constitute grounds for disciplinary action. The consent order outlines the specific penalties proposed against the HCP. The defense attorney discusses these documents with the HCP and explains the available options (settle via consent order or go to hearing) and their pros and cons.

Settlement can be accomplished by either accepting the proposed consent order as is or successfully negotiating its terms. Settlement may be desired if there are clear standard of care issues, the defense was unable to secure a favorable expert review, the HCP does not wish to testify at a hearing, or the HCP will make a poor witness. The HCP may also wish to settle if the insurance policy limits are likely to be exceeded by going to hearing, as the HCP would be responsible for paying any overage. While there is no guarantee, settlement may garner less media attention than a public hearing. Accepting any consent order results in a public record of this disciplinary action on the HCP's license. It is also reportable to the National Practitioner Data Bank (NPDB) and on future licensure, credentialing, and liability insurance renewals/applications (NPDB, n.d.). Other states in which the HCP is licensed may take disciplinary action because of a consent order (Knag & Garg, 2015). If the consent order imposes a civil penalty, this is an out-of-pocket expense for the HCP, as such payments are not covered under liability insurance policies. (Civil penalties are payable to the state, not the patient. The patient receives no monetary compensation or award from an administrative action.)

Factors that may impact settlement negotiations include: (1) there are prior disciplinary actions on the HCP's license (especially for issues similar to the matter at hand), (2) the HCP is willing to agree to permanent practice restrictions, e.g., refrain from performing certain procedures, refrain from prescribing controlled substances, etc., and (3) the HCP is planning to retire or not pursue licensure renewal. The HCP should also be aware of, and carefully consider the impact of, any boilerplate language contained in a consent order. For example, some consent orders may state that, "for purposes of this or any future proceedings" before the licensing board, the HCP "has chosen not to contest the … allegations" and agrees that "this consent order shall have the same effect as if proven and ordered after a full hearing" (Connecticut Medical Examining Board, 2017, para. 3). This may be significant should the HCP face another disciplinary action in the future.

A hearing is akin to a civil trial in which both sides present evidence through witness and expert testimony. At this stage (i.e., when the licensing board does not dismiss the complaint after the investigation), a hearing is typically the only remaining avenue to secure a complete dismissal of the matter, if the hearing decision is in favor of the HCP. However, the HCP must be aware that, if the hearing decision is not favorable, the penalties imposed may be less harsh, as harsh, or harsher than those initially proposed in the consent order. Disciplinary action imposed from a hearing also results in a public record on the HCP's license and is reportable to the NPDB and on future licensure, credentialing, and liability insurance renewals/applications. In addition, the cost of going to hearing may exceed the HCP's policy limit and result in out-of-pocket expenses for the HCP.

The HCP weighs these options, considers the guidance of the defense attorney, and decides which path to pursue.

Disposition of the Case

If an investigation is not dismissed, some states may schedule a meeting between the defense attorney and the licensing board attorney. In Connecticut, for example, this is termed a Compliance Conference. The HCP may or may not attend the meeting, depending on strategic and other factors. This meeting is an opportunity for counsel to further explore and clarify the allegations and the HCP's care of the patient, present additional evidence, and discuss resolution of the matter. The defense attorney will pursue whichever disposition the HCP chooses (settle via consent order or go to hearing). Most licensing board investigations are closed either without discipline or with consent orders.

If the HCP wishes to settle, the defense attorney discusses the proposed consent order with the licensing board attorney and tries to negotiate its terms to be as favorable for the HCP as possible. The terms of an executed consent order are overseen and managed according to the individual state's administrative law and may be internal to the state administrative agency or provided by a private contractor.

If the HCP chooses to proceed with a hearing, the licensing board's attorney files the Statement of Charges in accordance with the state's procedural rules. The defense attorney submits an Answer to the Statement of Charges, and a date is set for the hearing. In some states, interrogatories may be exchanged between sides to gather additional information for the hearing, and the LNC can draft these interrogatories or answers for the attorney.

Depending on the particular state's process, a professional hearing officer, administrative law or superior court judge (as an employee of the government), or a subpanel from the professional licensing board presides over hearings involving a licensed professional.

Both sides prepare for the hearing as they would for a trial. Exhibits and witness lists are prepared and exchanged, and witnesses and experts are prepared for their testimony. The role of the LNC throughout the hearing process is essentially identical to that throughout a trial. Legal nurse consultants on both sides assist with strategizing, ensure the medical records and other documents are well-organized for ease of locating critical documents during the hearing, identify and prepare exhibits (including demonstrative exhibits), research the opposing expert(s) and witnesses, assist with witness preparation as needed, ensure the expert has all necessary materials for review (including the investigative report and its exhibits), and coordinate with the expert to schedule hearing testimony.

The hearing proceeds in a similar fashion to a trial with opening statements, evidence presented by the prosecution followed by the defense, and closing arguments. Since the person(s) presiding over the hearing is not always a healthcare provider (i.e., an attorney or judge could preside, or the licensing board subpanel could include public members), the evidence "should be structured using witnesses, documents and language that may be understood by members outside of the licensee's area of practice" (Knag & Garg, 2015, para. 14). The licensing board has the burden to prove the allegations against the HCP. The hearing may be less formal than a trial with the licensing board or presiding individual asking questions throughout the presentation of evidence. If the persons presiding are not attorneys (e.g., if they are members of the licensing board), they may be provided legal guidance during the proceedings by an attorney (such as an Assistant Attorney General). This attorney may be referred to as a hearing officer or magistrate.

Administrative hearings may not be governed by the same evidentiary rules as court proceedings (Lagnese et al., 2015). For example, hearsay evidence, which is generally prohibited in court proceedings, may be admissible in administrative proceedings. In addition, while expert evidence is generally required to prove a deviation from the standard of care, if the hearing is presided over by professional members (i.e., not public members) of the licensing board, they may use their "own experience, technical competence, and specialized knowledge in evaluating the evidence" and the charges (Lagnese et al., 2015, p. 267). Depending on how the evidence is evolving, if both sides feel risk in letting the matter proceed to decision, they may negotiate a consent order and settle in the middle of a hearing.

The LNCs are integral members of their respective legal teams during the administrative hearing. Both LNCs:

- Prepare intensely for the hearing by becoming intimately familiar with the significant clinical issues pertinent to the case
- Support their attorneys by educating them on the clinical topics, identifying discrepancies between testimony and what is contained in the medical records, and notifying the attorney of any such inconsistencies
- Evaluate the witnesses, observe the decision-maker(s), participate in strategy discussions, and assist with an overall analysis of the proceedings
- Maintain a complete set of exhibits, manage and run the audiovisual equipment used to display the exhibits, take detailed notes, and support the attorney, HCP or patient, and fact and expert witnesses as needed
- Maintain professionalism and uphold respect for the opposing side and
- Assist in preparing for closing arguments, including for the presentation of any exhibits or visual aids

(Dickinson & Fontaine, 2016)

The defense LNC may prepare a report for the HCP's liability insurance company summarizing the day's proceedings. (For more information on trial preparation, the trial process, and the LNC's role, see Chapter 39.)

After hearing all the evidence, the presiding person or panel issues a recommendation to the professional licensing board. The recommendation could be to dismiss the matter (if the evidence showed the HCP did not violate the standard of care) or to issue certain penalties against the HCP's license (if the evidence supported liability by the HCP). A quorum of the professional licensing board reviews the recommendation and decides whether to accept it. If the professional licensing board issues discipline against the HCP, the HCP can appeal the decision through the processes set forth by the state. An appeal does not, however, act as a stay of the licensing board's decision and penalties (Knag & Garg, 2015). Defense counsel would have to seek a stay after the board issues its decision.

Summary

Whether working for the prosecution or the defense, LNCs play a significant role throughout healthcare provider licensure investigations and administrative actions. Legal nurse consultants should be familiar with the applicable laws regulating healthcare professions and governing licensure investigations and administrative actions. Understanding the investigative process and proceedings will assist the LNC in becoming an invaluable member of the legal team.

References

Administrative law. (2017). In Legal Information Institute. Retrieved from www.law.cornell.edu/wex/administrative_law.

Administrative law and procedure. (n.d.). In The Free Dictionary by Farlex. Retrieved from https://legal-dictionary.thefreedictionary.com/regulations.

Baer v. Connecticut Board of Examiners in Podiatry, 1998 WL 13945 (Conn. Super. 1998).

Brous, E. (2012). Professional licensure: Investigation and disciplinary action. *American Journal of Nursing, 112*(11), 53–59. Retrieved from www.nccwebsite.org/resources/docs/Professional_Licensure___Investigation_and.26.pdf.

Connecticut Medical Examining Board. (2017). Consent order in re: Brian McCarthy, M.D.: Petition No. 2016–990. Retrieved from www.elicense.ct.gov/Lookup/ViewPublicLookupDocument.aspx?DocumentIdnt=2167345&GUID=2777BF80-66FF-4C2B-8EB1-8693E17EDF7E.

Connecticut Nursing Practice Act: State Board of Examiners for Nursing, CT. Stat. § 20–88(a) (2012).

Dickinson, J. (2017). Non-traditional legal nurse consultant roles: The role of the defense LNC in licensure investigations. *Journal of Legal Nurse Consulting, 28*(1), 35–36.

Dickinson, J., & Fontaine, C. (2016, Feb 1). The verdict is in! The vital role of LNCs at medical malpractice trials. American Association of Legal Nurse Consultants webinar. Webinar retrieved from www.aalnc.org/page/on-demandwebinars.

Knag, P. E., & Garg, T. (2015, May 11). Navigating health department disciplinary proceedings. *The Connecticut Law Tribune.* Retrieved from www.murthalaw.com/files/navigating_health_department_disciplinary_proceedings___connecticut_law_trib.pdf.

Lagnese, J. A., Anderson, C. B., & Santoro, F. H. (2015). *Connecticut medical malpractice: A manual of practice and procedure.* Hartford, CT: Connecticut Law Tribune.

Legal Information Institute. (n.d.). Uses and disclosures for which an authorization or opportunity to agree or object is not required, 45 CFR § 164.512(d). Retrieved from www.law.cornell.edu/cfr/text/45/164.512.

National Conference of Commissioners on Uniform State Laws. (2010). *Revised Model State Administrative Procedure Act.* Retrieved from www.uniformlaws.org/shared/docs/state%20administrative%20procedure/msapa_final_10.pdf.

National Practitioner Data Bank. (n.d.). NPDB guide to reporting state licensure actions. Retrieved from www.npdb.hrsa.gov/hcorg/reportingStateLicensure.jsp.

Russell, K. A. (2012). Nurse practice acts guide and govern nursing profession. *Journal of Nursing Regulation, 3*(3), 36–40. https://doi.org/10.1016/S2155-8256(15)30197-6.

Test Questions

1. Administrative law is the body of law that empowers public regulatory agencies, such as professional licensing boards, to regulate healthcare professions.
   A. True
   B. False
2. In administrative law, which of the following are true?
   A. There is typically no statute of limitations
   B. The patient in an administrative action does not receive monies from any fines imposed upon the healthcare provider
   C. Administrative investigations focus on quality of care, not on all four elements of proof required in a civil negligence claim (duty, breach of duty, damages, and causation)
   D. All of the above
3. The function of a professional licensing board includes all of the following EXCEPT:
   A. Hear and decide matters concerning suspension or revocation of a license
   B. Order imprisonment for particularly egregious behavior
   C. Adjudicate complaints against providers
   D. Impose sanctions where appropriate
4. Licensure investigations can originate from which of the following sources?
   A. Consumer complaint
   B. Statutory report
   C. Malpractice notification
   D. High-profile incidents
   E. All of the above
5. The role of legal nurse consultants in healthcare provider licensure investigations includes all of the following EXCEPT:
   A. Review medical records and other documentation
   B. Prepare written work products (e.g., chronologies, summaries, persuasive responses)
   C. Advise the client (i.e., provider or licensing board) on legal strategy
   D. Conduct medical literature research
   E. Locate, screen, and liaise with expert witnesses

Answers: 1. A, 2. D, 3. B, 4. E, 5. C.

Chapter 26

Fraud
Government and Private Sponsored Health Plans and General Case Evaluations

---

Rebecca Mendoza Saltiel Busch, MBA, CCM, RN, CFE, CPC, CHS-IV, CRMA, CICA, FIALCP, FHFMA

Contents

Objectives

- Describe the mechanics of healthcare reimbursement
- Discuss the elements of fraud within the context of health care
- Develop a case evaluation infrastructure for government and privately sponsored health plans

Introduction

Fraud is defined as an intentional deception resulting in injury to another (Fraud, n.d.). Assessment of fraud within a health plan is complex. This chapter will focus on distinguishing normal behavior patterns from those potentially fraudulent and which should trigger a more thorough review. Materials and data appropriate for such a review are discussed and applied to various scenarios. Appropriate guidelines for drawing conclusions from the information and materials reviewed are presented. After a review of this chapter, the legal nurse consultant (LNC) will have a fundamental guide and standardized approach for the evaluation of cases involving potential fraud or abuse within a government or private sponsored healthcare benefit plan.

Definition of Fraud

The elements of fraud are the following (Association of Certified Fraud Examiners [ACFE], 2012):

- Misrepresentation of a material fact
- Knowledge of the falsity of the misrepresentation or ignorance of its truth

- Intent
- A victim acting on the misrepresentation and
- Damage to the victim

Another important aspect of fraud is commonly referred to as the "Fraud Triangle" (ACFE, n.d.). The elements of the triangle include opportunity, pressure, and rationalization. Simply put, an individual faced with financial pressures finds an opportunity to initiate a fraud scheme and then rationalizes the behavior.

The following **Fraud Review Checklist** is useful in reviewing a potential fraud case. Please note each question should follow with "If so, determine who, what, where, why, when, and how?"

- Did any misrepresentation of a material fact occur?
- Did the perpetrator(s) have knowledge of the falsity of the misrepresentation or ignorance of its truth?
- Did the perpetrator(s) demonstrate intent?
- Did a victim act on the misrepresentation?
- Was there damage to the victim?
- In evaluating the perpetrator(s), how was the opportunity created? What pressures were involved? Finally, how was the behavior rationalized?

This model applies to any industry or issue in which fraud is the theme of case review. Fraud cases in the healthcare environment typically take the following form:

- Manipulating reimbursement and submitting a false claim
- Manipulating health information for advantageous gain or avoidance of liability
- Generating false health information to support a medically unnecessary service or a fictitious healthcare claim
- Illicitly using identities (Busch, 2017a) such as individual, medical, professional, corporate/business, e-identity, digital, and synthetic identity theft (see Appendix A) or
- Selling a fabricated, counterfeit product or service

The following section provides applicable concepts that specifically impact the healthcare industry.

Overview of Legislation Impacting Healthcare Fraud

Many statutes address the issue of fraud. For example, a perpetrator could be prosecuted under the Mail Fraud Act for an offense that may be a healthcare fraud scheme. Based on the evidence, the prosecution may choose statutes not directly defined within the health domain. This chapter will focus on the statutes most closely related to the healthcare industry, including:

- Health Insurance Portability and Accountability Act of 1996 (HIPAA)
- Federal False Claims Act (FCA)
- Civil FCA
- State False Claims statutes
- Medicaid False Claims statute

- Physician Self-Referral Law/Stark Laws
- Anti-Kickback Statute
- Civil Monetary Penalties Law and
- Patient Protection and Affordable Care Act of 2010

Health Insurance Portability and Accountability Act of 1996

The amendments to the HIPAA of 1996 further define and establish the scope of healthcare fraud via government/private sector sponsored benefit programs. The act defines a federal healthcare offense as "a violation of, or criminal conspiracy to violate" specific provisions of the U.S. Code, "if the violation or conspiracy relates to a health care benefit program" (Cornell Law School, 2010). A healthcare benefit program is

> any public or private plan or contract, affecting commerce, under which any medical benefit, item or service is provided to any individual, and includes any individual or entity who is providing a medical benefit, item, or service for which payment may be made under the plan or contract.
>
> (Cornell Law School, 2010)

Finally, **healthcare fraud** is defined as knowingly and willfully executing a scheme to defraud a healthcare benefit program or obtaining, "by means of false or fraudulent pretenses, representations, or promises, any of the money or property owned by … any health care benefit program" (Health care fraud, 2017). The HIPAA establishes specific criminal sanctions for offenses against both private and public health plans (Busch, 2007).

The HIPAA federalizes the crime of healthcare fraud by making it illegal for anyone to knowingly and willfully do the following (Centers for Medicare & Medicaid Services [CMS], 2015, 2016):

- Defraud any healthcare benefit program or obtain by false representations any money or property of a healthcare benefit program
- Make "false statements" that criminalize any false or fictitious statements "in any matter involving a healthcare benefit program"
- Embezzle, convert, or steal any funds, property, or assets of a healthcare benefit program and
- Obstruct, delay, prevent, or mislead the investigation of federal healthcare offenses

Federal False Claims Act

The FCA was passed by Abraham Lincoln during the Civil War to counter widespread fraud by suppliers to the Union Army. Illegally presenting "false, fictitious or fraudulent" claims (Cornell Law School, 2017; Cornell Law School: Legal Information Institute, n.d.; Office of the Law Revision Counsel, 2017) upon or against the United States shall result in not more than five years' imprisonment and be subject to fines. In 1986, amendments to the FCA mandated both fine and imprisonment for all convictions and included the following changes (JDSUPRA, 2018):

- Increasing penalties
- Revising the procedures for civil actions for false claims and
- Providing new incentives for private citizens to report suspected frauds

Criminal violations can incur fines of $250,000 for individuals and $500,000 for corporations (Busch, 2010a, p. 255). In addition, imprisonment can be up to 10 years. This criminal statute applies to any federal government department or agency. Additional information about the FCA can be found at the Office of Inspector General: U.S. Department of Health and Human Services (OIG-HHS, n.d.-b), Cornell Law School references (Cornell Law School, 2010, 2017; Cornell Law School: Legal Information Institute, n.d.), and Centers for Medicare & Medicaid (CMS, n.d., 2017a, 2017b).

In addition to bringing a criminal action, the government may also bring a parallel civil action seeking relief (Busch, 2008b). The new law affords the government the opportunity to recover three times the amount of sustained damages. Civil penalties range from $10,957 to $22,363 as of 2018 and will continue to be adjusted each year to account for inflation (Federal Register, 2018). It is important to remember the burden of proof in a civil case is by preponderance of the evidence. In a criminal case, the burden is beyond a reasonable doubt.

The FCA affords the private citizen new incentives to report suspected fraud. It also gives whistleblowers (typically employees who sue their employers) extensive protection from harassment and retaliation from employers, including providing safety and preventing harassment, firing, demotion, suspension, or reprisals of any kind. The law provides "make whole" relief, including reinstatement with full security, back pay with interest, and compensation for any damages sustained because of discrimination.

Civil False Claims Act

The Civil FCA is governed by Title 31 of the U.S. Code. It states that any person who knowingly presents, or causes to be presented, to the U.S. government a false or fraudulent claim for payment or approval; or knowingly makes, uses, or causes to be made or used, a false record or statement to get a false or fraudulent claim paid or approved by the government; or conspires to defraud the government by getting a false or fraudulent claim allowed or paid has violated the Act. Those who violate the Act are liable to the government for a civil penalty of not less than $5,000 and not more than $10,000 for each false claim filed, plus treble (threefold) damages sustained by the government (Cornell Law School: Legal Information Institute, n.d.).

State False Claims Statutes

Several states have followed suit and initiated a similar legislation via State False Claims statutes that provide remedies for false claims and other fraud against state healthcare programs. The OIG-HHS also provides a centralized resource to review specific State False Claims Act information (OIG-HHS, 2013). California adopted the first State False Claims statute in 1987 (Cal. Gov't Code Ann. §§ 12650–12655). Other states include Illinois (720 ILL. Comp. Stat. 5/46–5; Illinois General Assembly, 2012), Florida (FLA.STAT.ANN. § 68.081 through 78.092), and Louisiana (LA.Rev. Stat.Ann. § 46.437.1 through 46.440.4). Contacting an individual state's insurance department is helpful to determine if statutes address both Medicaid programs and private insurers.

Medicaid False Claims Statutes

The Medicaid False Claims statutes address false statements, representations made regarding any applications for claim of benefits or payment, and the disposal of assets under a federal healthcare program (OIG-HHS, 2013). The government must prove four elements to sustain a conviction under this statute:

- The defendant made, or caused to be made, a statement of material fact in an application for payment or benefits under a federal healthcare program
- The statement or representation was false
- The defendant knowingly and willfully made the statement and
- The defendant knew the statement to be false

Many states have Medicaid Fraud Control Units, and others have specific agencies focused only on healthcare fraud (OIG-HHS, n.d.-c). The insurance fraud division of an individual state is an excellent resource for finding a state legislative activity regarding fraud.

Physician Self-Referral Law/Stark Laws

The physician self-referral law is commonly known as Stark Laws after the initial passage by Congressman P. Stark (42 USC § 1395nn). Stark I was enacted as part of the Omnibus Budget Reconciliation Act of 1989 (Stark Law, 2010, 2013). The focus of this statute is to prevent inappropriate financial influences over physicians' decisions about the best care for their patients. However, the prohibitions set forth in this statute have caused uncertainty among providers as they struggle to respond to various market forces on cost constraints. The self-referral law, as enacted in 1989, prohibits a physician from referring a patient to a clinical laboratory in which the physician (or an immediate family member) has a financial relationship.

Stark I initiated the rule that physicians or immediate family members may not have a financial interest with certain entities providing clinical laboratory services, and in cases in which they did, they may not bill Medicare or Medicaid. Stark II provided additional amendments and expanded the referral and billing prohibitions to additional "designated health services."

The Phase III (I & II) Stark Final Rule (CMS, 2007; Federal Health Care Fraud & Abuse Laws, n.d.; Federal Register, 2007) is officially titled Medicare Program: Physicians' Referrals to Health Care Entities with Which They Have Financial Relationships (Phase III). It is commonly called Stark III, as it is an extension of Stark I and Stark II and sets limits on self-dealing and kickbacks with respect to treatment of Medicare and Medicaid patients. The effective date of Stark III was December 4, 2007. Details and updates to Stark provisions are found online at the Office of Inspector General website.

Anti-Kickback Statute

The Anti-Kickback Statute (42 USC § 1320a–7b(b) is similar in intent to the Stark Laws in that it prohibits offering, paying, soliciting, or receiving anything of value to induce any gains from federal healthcare program dollars. The distinguishing factor between Stark and the Anti-Kickback Statute is that Stark focuses specifically on self-dealing referrals by and among physicians, whereas the Anti-Kickback Statute addresses inappropriate self-referrals from anyone, not just physicians. A detailed comparison can be found on the Office of Inspector General website (OIG-HHS, n.d.-a).

Civil Monetary Penalties Law

The U.S. Securities and Exchange Commission (SEC) defines Civil Monetary Penalties (CMPs) as "any penalty, fine, or other sanction that: (1) is for a specific amount, or has a maximum amount, as provided by federal law; and (2) is assessed or enforced by an agency in an administrative proceeding or by a federal court pursuant to federal law" (U.S. SEC, 2001).

The Civil Monetary Penalties Law, Section 1128A of the Social Security Act (SSA), authorizes the Secretary of HHS to seek CMPs, assessments (additional money in lieu of damages sustained), and exclusion (from participation in federal healthcare programs) for many types of conduct (U.S. SSA, 2016). These include, but are not limited to:

- Filing fraudulent claims
- Misrepresenting medical credentials
- Filing claims while excluded from federal healthcare programs
- Charging for services that are not medically necessary
- A person excluded from government programs retaining control of an organization that participates in title XVIII (Medicare) programs
- Providing inducements to beneficiaries that could alter their healthcare decisions
- Knowingly contracting with an entity that is excluded from relevant federal programs
- Receiving kickbacks (per SSA 1128B(b)(1), (2))
- Failing to give the Inspector General of HHS a reasonable amount of time to conduct its work and
- Not reporting on overpayments from relevant federal programs

The Social Security Act § 1128A codifies these rules, as well as 42 U.S.C. § 1320a–7a and 42 CFR § 1003.102 (OIG-HHS, n.d.-d). Any person or entity (excluding beneficiaries) that engages in this conduct against a state agency is liable for damages.

Recently, the laws governing the maximum amount of money that can be sought have been amended. In 2015, the Federal Civil Penalties Inflation Adjustment Act Improvements Act was signed, requiring all government agencies to increase CMPs yearly according to inflation (U.S. SSA, 2015). For example, in 2016 the maximum amount that could be sought for knowingly filing false claims was $15,024, and in 2017, it was raised to $15,270 (Federal Register, 2017). This law was enacted for the purpose of increasing the "deterrent effect" of the penalties (CMS, 2017c).

Patient Protection and Affordable Care Act of 2010

The Patient Protection and Affordable Care Act states (HeathCare.gov, 2014):

> The Patient Protection and Affordable Care Act (PPACA), commonly called the Affordable Care Act (ACA) and nicknamed Obamacare, is a United States federal statute enacted by President Barack Obama on March 23, 2010. Together with the Health Care and Education Reconciliation Act amendment, it represents the most significant regulatory overhaul of the U.S. healthcare system since the passage of Medicare and Medicaid in 1965. Under the act, hospitals and primary physicians would transform their practices financially, technologically, and clinically to drive better health outcomes, lower costs, and improve their methods of distribution and accessibility.

The LNC should make note of the historical context of this legislation. Ongoing legislative updates are expected, and the CMS website is a source for current and pending legislative changes. The LNC can remain current by monitoring the resources and updates at the following URLs: (1) www.hhs.gov, (2) www.healthit.gov, (3) www.cms.gov, and (4) www.oighhs.gov.

Overview of Healthcare Expenditures and Reimbursement Methodologies

One of the most complicated factors within the healthcare market is the complexity of reimbursement methodologies. This complexity coexists in both the private and public markets. Of note, other insurers generally follow Medicare rules. Medicare is a health insurance program for:

- People aged 65 or older
- People under age 65 with certain disabilities
- People of all ages with end-stage renal disease (ESRD; permanent kidney failure requiring dialysis or a kidney transplant)

It is important to note, within Medicare, patients are referred to as beneficiaries (funded by employee wage tax, employer wage tax, and other government tax sources), while in the Medicaid program, they are referred to as recipients (funded by a combination of federal and state tax dollars). The LNC may reference CMS and Medicare Payment Advisory Commission (MedPAC) websites, under payment basics, for case-specific programs relevant to the matter under review. For example, detailed updates on Medicare Part A (Hospital Insurance) helps cover inpatient care in hospitals, including critical access hospitals (CAHs) and skilled nursing facilities. Medicare Part B (Medical Insurance) helps cover doctors' services and outpatient care. Medicare Part C is known as Medicare Advantage (MA) Plans. These private companies have contracted to provide Medicare Benefits such as health maintenance organizations and preferred provider organizations. Part C is part of the Medicare policy that allows private companies to provide Medicare benefits (Medicare Interactive, n.d.). Finally, Medicare Part D is a voluntary outpatient drug benefit program with private companies providing the coverage. For the LNC reviewing cases involving this complex program, the terms of the plan administration will need to be reviewed. From a patient perspective, it is also important to look at the current year's offering by plan options. This information is available by searching the CMS website for Medicare Part A, B, C, or D. Also see Appendix B.

Overview of Payment Systems

This section will introduce methodologies currently utilized by Medicare to reimburse Medicare-approved services. Table 26.1 provides a list of payment systems utilized within government-sponsored programs and an overview of their key attributes. Detailed formulas and ongoing updates may be found at the CMS website under payment basics (MedPAC, 2017).

The CMS has a payment methodology for each of the services noted in Table 26.1. Many private payers have adopted these methodologies. In evaluating a case, it is important to identify which payment methodology is involved. Obtaining those details will then identify the information that needs to be collected from identifiable stakeholders. Please note any audit, review, or case analysis would focus on ensuring the rules of the reimbursement model were followed.

Table 26.1 Key Attributes of Payment Systems Utilized Within Government-Sponsored Programs

Payment System	Key Attributes
Accountable care organization payment system	Accountable care organizations (ACOs) refers to providers who agree to be held accountable for the cost and quality of care for a group of beneficiaries. There are now three different Medicare ACO programs.
Ambulance services payment system	Ambulance services are made up of both emergency and non-emergency transport from the patient's pick-up point to a medical facility.
Ambulatory surgical center services payment system	Medicare provides coverage for free-standing and hospital-based ambulatory surgical centers (ASCs). Reimbursement is driven by surgical procedures in an ambulatory payment classification (APC) group. Please note the payment groups are the same as the outpatient prospective payment system (OPPS) services.
Clinical laboratory services payment system	Coverage is provided under Medicare Part B for medically necessary diagnostic and monitoring laboratory services. Medicare sets rates for at least 1,100 Healthcare Common Procedure Coding System (HCPCS) codes.
Critical access hospitals payment system	Critical access hospitals (CAHs) are small facilities limited to 25 beds. In addition, CAHs may have up to 10 psychiatric beds, 10 rehabilitation unit beds, and home health agencies. It is estimated about 1,300 hospitals have CAH designation. These tend to be in rural areas and are not paid on the Medicare diagnosis-related group (DRG) prospective payment system and are paid at 101% of allowable hospital reported costs. The reimbursement is based on cost accounting data from Medicare cost reports.
Durable medical equipment payment system	Coverage is provided for equipment in the home environment (including home oxygen equipment and related supplies). Reimbursement rates are determined by fee schedules noted by the HCPCS code.
Home healthcare services payment system	These patients are generally restricted to their homes. Medicare will reimburse for services that fall into the categories of skilled nursing care; physical, occupational, and speech therapy; medical social work; and home health-aide services. The reimbursement is typically based on 60-day window episodes. The patient may be assigned to one of 153 home health resource groups (HHRGs) based on clinical and functional status and service use. These measurements are based on a system referred to as Outcome and Assessment Information Sets. This system consists of three categories: (1) clinical factors, (2) functional factors, and (3) service utilization. A score is computed within each category.
Hospice services payment system	Medicare will provide palliative treatment services for beneficiaries who forgo curative treatment regimens. The CMS provides a list of services (updated annually) and may include facility or home-based support. The reimbursement rate is a calculated daily rate. The categories of payments include routine home care (RHC), continuous home care (CHC), inpatient respite care (IRC), and general inpatient care (GIC).

Table 26.1 Continued

Payment System	Key Attributes
Hospital acute inpatient services payment system	Patient classification is based on Medicare's acute inpatient prospective payments system (IPPS) known as diagnosis-related groups (DRG). Once again, the calculation rate for a specific DRG will be impacted by geographic factors, hospital wage index, adjustments for case mix, and patient characteristics for a final payment determination.
Inpatient psychiatric facility services payment system	Medicare beneficiaries with serious mental illnesses or alcohol and drug-related problems may be treated in inpatient psychiatric facilities (IPFs).
Inpatient rehabilitation facilities payment system	Reimbursement is under a prospective payment system defined within 92 intensive rehabilitation categories referred to as case-mix groups (CMGs).
Long-term care hospitals payment system	Long-term care hospitals (LTCHs) service clinically complex patients with multiple acute and chronic conditions. Services rendered are part of a prospective payment system referred to as long-term care diagnosis related groups (LTC-DRGs).
Medicare Advantage program payment system	The MA program (Medicare Part C plan) allows beneficiaries the option of receiving benefits from private plans. Also, the beneficiary may pay additional premiums for expanded benefits. The reimbursement methodology needs to be evaluated by the specific plan chosen by the beneficiary.
Outpatient dialysis services payment system	This payment plan is focused on patients with ESRD.
Outpatient hospital services payment system	Reimbursement is driven by the OPPS. The services are classified using the HCPCS. The services are categorized into one of the APCs.
Outpatient therapy services payment system	This program pays for therapy services including physical therapy, occupational therapy, and speech-language pathology. Reimbursement is driven by the HCPCS, with each code weighted by Relative Value Units (RVUs).
Part B drugs payment system	Medicare Part B covers drugs that are administered by infusion or injection in physician offices and hospital outpatient departments. It also covers certain drugs furnished by pharmacies and suppliers.
Part D payment system	Part D payment system adopted by Medicare offers a combination of stand-alone prescription drug plans (PDPs) and Medicare Advantage Prescription Drug plans (MA-PDs) that deliver the benefit.
Physician and other health professional payment system	Physician and other health professional services include office visits, surgical procedures, and a broad range of other diagnostic and therapeutic services specified by Current Procedural Terminology (CPT) codes.
Skilled nursing facility (SNF) services payment system	Skilled nursing reimbursement is based on a prospective payment system referred to as Resource Utilization Groups (RUG). There are 66 RUGs based on patient characteristics and service use.

Source: MedPAC (2017).

The various payment systems noted in Table 26.1 impact traditional factors such as geographic index, hospital wage index, adjusted case mix, patient characteristics, and other adjustments for extraordinary outlier costs. Each payment system will have unique attributes. For example, each skilled nursing facility has a base rate and computes with factors such as an adjustment for geographic factors, hospital wage index, adjusted for case mix, multiplied by a Resource Utilization Group (RUG) weight which impact the intensity of patient characteristics. The implication for the LNC is to focus on validation of patient characteristics that place a patient into a particular RUG group. An anomaly would be a paraplegic patient who is receiving gait training exercises. The LNC is looking for clinical attributes that cannot be validated or are insufficient in their documentation. Each payment basic formula has a unique attribute. The LNC should review the relevant reimbursement methodology listed in Table 26.1 and isolate the unique formula characteristic that manipulated results in an improper payment.

The private sector has various reimbursement methodologies for health plan offerings. These vary by type of plan, plan members, contractual agreements among stakeholders, respective regulatory requirements, and defined reimbursement methodologies. The critical first step is to correctly identify relevant stakeholders and the context in which they operate. Identify the name of the health plan, and determine whether the plan is self-funded or a true insurance plan. For example:

■ A private or publicly traded employer provides a self-funded healthcare benefit plan subject to Employment Retirement Income Security Act and hires a Third-Party Administrator (TPA) to administer and process claims received on behalf of its members.
■ An employer provides a group healthcare covered insurance plan (subject to state law). A monthly premium is paid, and the payer assumes the risk to process claims.
■ A state employer is self-funded, provides healthcare benefit plans, is subject to state statute, and hires a TPA to administer the plan.

Key questions to ask include:

■ Who is sponsoring the plan?
■ Who is administering and adjudicating the claims?
■ To which statutory requirement or regulatory agency are they accountable?
■ Which stakeholder is taking on the risk (insurance versus self-funded)?

Pricing and Reimbursement

Trends in pricing and reimbursement of healthcare claims continue to evolve in methodologies and approach. Traditional fee-for-service continues to exist. Many private stakeholders will contract to utilize reimbursement methodologies used within the Medicare program. It is important to understand the payment terms defined between the stakeholders. The following is a list of key terms and trends:

■ Usual Customary Reasonable (UCR): The value of services in context and condition for a specific service regardless of whether it is included in a health benefit plan (Busch, 2017b)
■ Maximum Allowable Amount (MAA): The maximum dollar amount allocated by the individual health benefit plan by and for specified services

- Allowed Amount: The amount considered the benefit value for an included specified service within the individual benefit plan
- Approved Charge: The amount considered paid in full by the individual's benefit plan
- Allowable Costs: The dollars allocated by a health benefit plan by and for specified services

Case Evaluation Methodology

Methodology is "a set or system of methods, principles, and rules for regulating a given discipline, as in the arts or sciences" (Methodology, n.d.). Methodology is the cornerstone of the efficacy of LNC work, whether involved in a support role or as a potential testifying expert. The U.S. Supreme Court's decisions in *Daubert v. Merrell Dow Pharmaceuticals, Inc.* 509 U.S. 579 (1993) and *Kumho Tire et al. v. Carmichael, et al.* No. 97–1709 (1999) requires expert testimony meet the general tests of reliability and relevancy. It is important to "ensur[e] an expert's testimony both rests on a reliable foundation and is relevant to the task at hand" (509 U.S. 579 [1993, para. 2]). The Court provides flexible guidelines for determining the admissibility of expert evidence, noting scientific evidence must be grounded in the methods and procedure of science. The expert must employ the same level of intellectual rigor as within and outside the courtroom when working in the relevant discipline (Busch, 2006). As a result, the following global methodology for case evaluation is offered (Busch, 2012):

- Step 1: Define the scope of the audit and case review
- Step 2: Define the data necessary for evaluation
- Step 3: Define the stakeholders to be interviewed
- Step 4: Conduct audit review and data analysis
- Step 5: Complete market comparison, research, analysis, and final report

In applying this methodology, six additional concepts will be introduced to initiate the steps listed. These concepts include the Primary Healthcare Continuum, Secondary Healthcare Continuum, Information Continuum, Consequence Healthcare Continuum, Transparency Continuum, and Rules-Based Continuum.

Primary Healthcare Continuum (P-HCC)

Figure 26.1 represents the primary healthcare continuum (Busch, 2007, p. 59). Please note one episode of care will impact multiple persons and entities within this continuum. Initially in case review, it is important to identify the stakeholders involved. Next, it is important to list the reimbursement methodologies involved in transactions. For example, does the case involve a dialysis patient versus an outpatient surgical patient? This chart illustrates the dynamics with respect to patients and plan sponsors, e.g., the patient may have both Medicare and secondary private insurance. The healthcare record file may have both home-care records and hospital-based records. The key concept to understand is the P-HCC represents direct and indirect participants in the delivery of a healthcare episode (Figure 26.1).

The implications of the P-HCC include the following sample questions:

- What type of patient is involved in the alleged scheme? Is it a Medicare recipient or a Medicaid recipient? Does the recipient have private insurance? If yes, is it through an employer or is it individually purchased?

- What type of provider is involved? Is it a professional such as an advanced practice registered nurse, physician assistant, naturopathic doctor, physician, dentist, chiropractor, or optometrist? Are facilities such as an acute hospital or nursing home involved?
- Are any third parties involved (e.g., the durable medical equipment [DME] company, pharmaceutical company, case manager, or billing agent)?
- What type of plan administrator or insurance company is involved? For example, is it a TPA or one of the common commercial healthcare insurance companies?
- Who is the plan sponsor? Is it a self-insured employer, a government plan, or both?
- With respect to organized crime, are there any "store front" operations involved?

Organized crime is defined as "criminal activities that are planned and controlled by powerful groups and carried out on a large scale" (Oxford English Living Dictionaries, 2017; Table 26.2). Organized crime features can be categorized as "activity," "organization," and "system." Health care is vulnerable. Opportunities exist for illegal use of protected health information, which may generate significant revenue streams for criminal organizations that use and access both legal and illegal systems to perpetuate criminal activity. Simply put, health care is a high-volume, cash-rich environment. Opportunities are boundless throughout our globalized economy (Busch, 2008b). Table 26.2 illustrates characteristics of organized crime (Busch, 2008a).

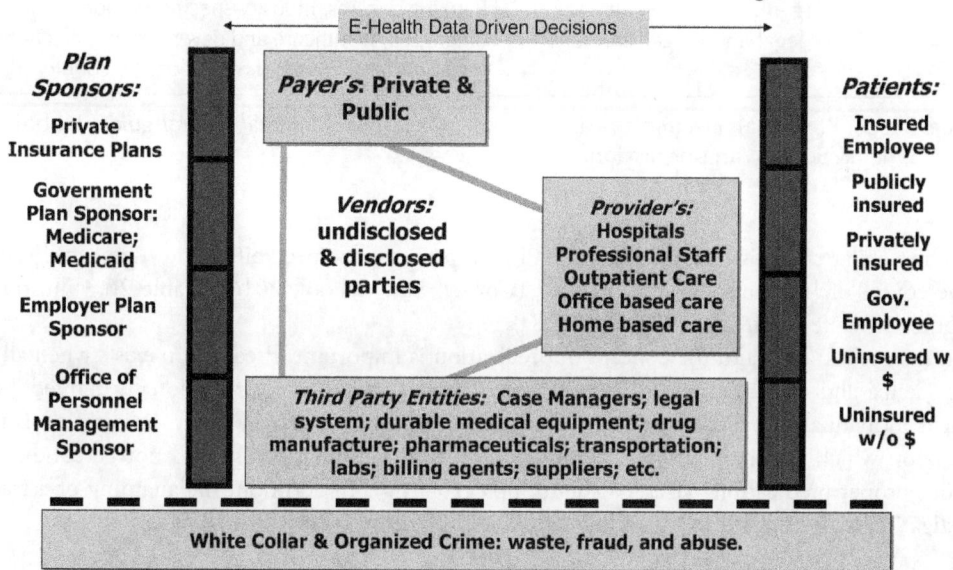

Copyright 2007 E-Heath Audit Guidebook, John Wiley & Sons, MBA Inc. 2007- 2008

Figure 26.1 Primary Health Care Continuum ("P-HCC"): Clinical, Service, Product, and Financial Integration.

Source: Busch, 2007. With permission from Wiley.

Table 26.2 Attributes of Organized Crime

Key Feature	Characterization of Organized Crime	Modern Technology
Activity	Organized crime = provision of illegal goods and services	Examples include: ■ Sale of new identities ■ Sale of medically unnecessary legitimate medications, health products, and procedures ■ Sale of counterfeit medications, health products, and procedures ■ Illegal and unethical marketing and recruitment schemes ■ Stealing resources and money from government programs, provider delivery systems, payer systems, and vendor systems ■ Intrastate or international theft of all the above activity Various schemes include: ■ Rent-a-patient ■ Pill mill ■ Drop box
Organization	Organized crime = complex	Organization: complex layered, multi-disciplined, multi-professional, and highly skilled
System	Organized crime = integration of legal and illegal structures	Banking systems, industry-specific vendors, employers, healthcare and payer systems, electronic mediums, and laws and regulations by country

Source: Busch, R. (2008a). *Electronic health records an audit and internal control guide.* Hoboken: Wiley & Sons. With permission.

White-collar crime is "a crime committed by a person of respectability and high social status in the course of [the person's] occupation" (Cornell Law School, 2016). Table 26.3 illustrates attributes of white-collar crime (Busch, 2008a).

In the context of fraud, the concept of predication is important. Predication exists when all of the evidence and circumstances of a case "would lead a reasonable, professionally trained, and prudent individual to believe a fraud has occurred, is occurring, or will occur. Predication is the basis upon which an examination is commenced. Fraud examinations should not be conducted without proper predication" (Busch, 2008b, pp. 178–180). In addition, the anatomy of a fraud investigation may be noted in the following (ACFE, 2012, p. I-7):

> Investigation of fraud consists of the multitude of steps necessary to resolve allegations of fraud, i.e., interviewing witnesses, assembling evidence, writing reports, and dealing with prosecutors and the courts. The investigation of fraud, because it deals with the individual rights of others, must be conducted only with adequate cause of predication.

In the context of data collection, it is important to appreciate the Secondary Healthcare Continuum (S-HCC), discussed further below, which represents the components of secondary users

Table 26.3 Characteristics of White-Collar Crime

Key Feature	Characterization of White-Collar Crime	Modern Technology
Activity	Crimes committed by the affluent or individuals in position of influence in the normal course of business. They tend to be self-dealing in nature.	■ Embezzlement ■ Misappropriation of resources ■ Collusion, price-fixing, and false advertising ■ Illegal pollution ■ False financials ■ Substandard products ■ Illegal tax avoidance ■ Illegal sale of unsafe products ■ Illegal unsafe working conditions ■ Misrepresentation of professionals, product, and service ■ False research ■ Sale of unnecessary medical services ■ Kickbacks ■ Undisclosed commissions ■ Other financial misrepresentations and/or falsifications
Organization	Individual or collective on behalf of the organization	Organization: complex layered, multi-disciplined, multi-professional, and highly skilled
System	Crime = intermingle with legitimate business activity—transparent	Banking systems, executive office, licensed professionals, industry-specific vendors, employers, healthcare and payer systems, electronic mediums, and laws and regulations by country

Source: Busch, R. (2008a). *Electronic health records an audit and internal control guide.* Hoboken: Wiley & Sons. With permission.

of health information in addition to market standards followed by stakeholders identified in the primary continuum. The primary purpose in this chapter is to understand that health information generated by the P-HCC can be found among the S-HCC users of information along with standards they must, or may be obligated to, follow. This channel of data may be important to appreciate during the discovery or investigation of an issue (Busch, 2008a).

Sample Case Study—Dr. Traveler (Busch, 2012)

Case History: Dr. Traveler is a licensed physician with a philanthropic edge in providing free healthcare examinations to the underinsured. The primary healthcare continuum market player in this case is defined as a licensed medical doctor, working in a free-standing clinic not affiliated with any other provider, taking care of privately insured patients, Medicare patients, and Medicaid patients. The LNC should show a general framework of the case; summarize the who, what, when, where, why, and how; and note the missing links:

■ Who: Dr. Traveler
■ What: Cardiologist specializing in home healthcare visits for the elderly population.

- When: Growing practice over last five years.
- Where: Home health visits.
- Why?
- How?

The following areas of concern were identified from a preliminary review of a recent data set:

- Insurance claims data indicate Dr. Traveler has a high percentage of home health visits to Chicago area residents.
- Dr. Traveler had a sudden increase in claim volume activity. The first year had a 30% increase; the following year had a 100% increase in patient volume activity. This occurred without adding any new staff, and all claims were submitted under the doctor's National Provider Identifier (NPI) number. The submitted claims appeared as if Dr. Traveler had rendered all of the services.
- The audit team referred the matter to the Special Investigations Unit (SIU), where further investigation of the claims data revealed trends not clearly plausible. For example, the SIU investigator mapped the addresses of the patients who received home visits from Dr. Traveler in a single day and questioned whether Dr. Traveler could have physically driven to these locations at the pace and volume he claimed. Further, Chicago is known for brutal winter weather, so the investigator profiled well-known adverse weather conditions and compared those to the claim file.
- Another example of implausible activity related to patients' dates of death. For instance, the claim file showed other providers had reported a patient passed away during a hospitalization. Since Dr. Traveler was not actually treating the patient, he was not aware that different providers had reported the patient as deceased.

Other claim data highlights include:

- During a blizzard in which 18 inches of snow shut down Chicago, Dr. Traveler billed for 31 home visits and 18 inpatient hospitals and nursing home visits.
- Dr. Traveler provided home health visits to 32 deceased patients.
- Dr. Traveler had 70-hour workdays.
- On one day of claims submission, Dr. Traveler generated 131 senior home visits.
- During one 24-hour period, the doctor conducted 187 visits in which the patients all had the same International Classification of Diseases (Diagnosis) code for congestive heart failure.
- On another day, Dr. Traveler treated 70 patients with one single home address (Dr. Traveler's own residence).
- Over a three-day period, a shortened holiday week, Dr. Traveler saw over 380 patients.
- Dr. Traveler's philanthropic contributions included being a frequent provider of free health screening exams at senior citizen complexes and private nursing homes around the Chicagoland area.

Table 26.4 shows the market players involved in the Dr. Traveler case study.

Secondary Healthcare Continuum (S-HCC)

The P-HCC could be used as a guideline to identify non-traditional stakeholders that may have relevant data to be collected. The S-HCC takes the process to a slightly different level. Based on the issues relevant of a case, this continuum may offer other opportunities to collect relevant data for analysis. For example, the P-HCC generates data as a result of indirect or direct patient care activity. The S-HCC members are often users of that information and, in turn, develop additional data or findings that could be utilized. For example, the S-HCC "public health" member may have studies based on a

Table 26.4 Primary Healthcare Continuum (P-HCC): Dr. Traveler's Case Study

Provider(s)	Doctor(s)	Dr. Traveler		
	Nurse(s)	–		
	Other	Dr. Traveler's office assistant Professional services provided by billing and collection agencies		
	Healthcare facility	Nursing homes, Hospitals, Home visits		
Payers	Public	Medicare, Medicaid		
	Private	All other insurance companies		
Vendors	Disclosed parties	N/A		
	Undisclosed parties	N/A		
Third party entities	N/A			
Patient Name	Patient's Condition	Treatment	Insurance Provider	Insurance Plan sponsor
Ms. Doe			Medicare	Government

Source: Busch, R. (2008a). *Electronic health records an audit and internal control guide.* Hoboken: Wiley & Sons. With permission.

particular toxin. Public policy may have studies on identified market issues. Reports on organized or white-collar crime activity may identify prior methodology utilized. When evaluating the S-HCC, ask the following questions: Of the list of entities or individuals previously identified within the P-HCC, do they interact with members of the S-HCC? How so? What type of data flow occurs between the two continuums? The identification of additional information or persons or entities involved should be added to a discovery list. Table 26.5 explores the S-HCC in the Dr. Traveler's case study.

Information Continuum (IC)

The third concept in gathering data is to appreciate the IC. As the market progresses into a true electronic environment, collecting information on the infrastructure in which evidence or documents are generated and held may impact an evaluation. The next figure names the components of the infrastructure that should be identified (Busch, 2012, Figure 26.2).

The components are important to understand in the context of discovery. For example, in one case, a copy of a specific medical record was required. The paper record was lost, but the intensive care unit (ICU) had an electronic record system. However, it was discovered during the retrieval of the electronic copy of the record that, for budgetary reasons, the ICU had only purchased enough memory for three months of patient records. Upon reaching the limit, the ICU would purge the records with no backup system.

The following checklist of items (people, process, and technology) is important with respect to the IC continuum:

- What electronic systems are utilized to generate data?
- How many and which type of computers are utilized?

- Who manages these systems?
- How are they networked?
- What are the current industry standards to maintain and manage systems?
- What software languages are used?
- What is the current storage capacity and technology utilized?

Another concept to understand is the use of metadata. Metadata is simply data about data (Rouse, 2014). It is the computer's record of any manipulations within a document. The implications for discovery will be the need for the right skill set to retrieve and analyze the information. The market's movement from paper records to electronic medical records (EMR) will impact the e-discovery process. The implication in litigation will be the process, using metadata, to authenticate the EMR production. Seeking metadata is an example of a data point noted when applying the attributes of the IC.

Table 26.6 explores the IC in the Dr. Traveler case study.

Table 26.5 Secondary Healthcare Continuum ("S-HCC"): Privacy, Security, Confidentiality, and Integrity Integration: Dr. Traveler's Case Study

Benchmarks for Perpetrator	Public Policy	Patients' right to receive healthcare screenings
	Certification Standards	License verification for Dr. Traveler and staff
	Market Standards	i. Did the healthcare facilities associating with Dr. Traveler perform credentialing appropriately?
		ii. Did Dr. Traveler's free health screening program at the healthcare facilities account for any privacy violations?
		iii. Did the senior center Dr. Traveler frequented receive any remuneration for allowing him to practice?
	Professional Services	i. Were all the healthcare claims submitted using the standardized claim form?
		ii. Were the appropriate or correct diagnosis and procedure codes selected in all claim forms?
	Public Health Data	Are procedures done by Dr. Traveler consistent with public health data? Refer to statistics on market occurrence of the disease group with respective procedures.
	Patient/Provider Autonomy Standards	Not relevant to this case
	Data Repositories	Information on weather events
	Data Intelligence Metrics	Volume of claims submitted by Dr. Traveler Rate at which claims were submitted by Dr. Traveler
	Data Analytics	i. Did Dr. Traveler submit false claims through phantom patients?
		ii. Did Dr. Traveler have staff who attended patients but submitted claims using Dr. Traveler's NPI?
		iii. Did Dr. Traveler submit claims for deceased patients?
		iv. Did the senior center Dr. Traveler frequented receive any remuneration for allowing him to practice?
	Information Network Standards	Dr. Traveler submitted hard copy claims forms through U.S. Mail. Is this a standard practice?

Source: Busch, 2012. With permission from Wiley.

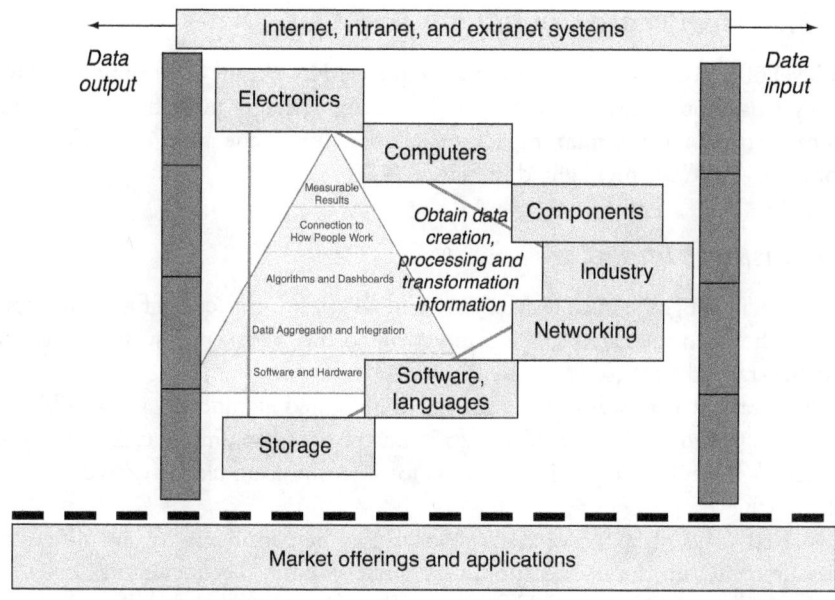

Figure 26.2 Information Continuum ("IC"): Change in Market and Industry Needs.

Source: Busch, 2007. With permission from Wiley.

Table 26.6 Information Continuum (IC): Dr. Traveler's Case Study (Busch, 2012)

Technology usage by perpetrator	Data input	Appointments scheduled in billing system Claim forms prepared by Dr. Traveler's office assistant for processing
	Data output Internal systems	Claim forms submitted to insurance companies 2 office telephone lines 1 fax landline 4 computers on a network Medical records filing that contains protected health information (PHI)
	External systems	Telephone and computer network at Dr. Traveler's residence
	Software used	Billing System
	Storage	Medical records filing that contains PHI Electronic and hard copies of claims filed Dr. Traveler's financial records
	Networking	Network connecting 4 computers at Dr. Traveler's office
	Other components	N/A

Source: Busch, 2012. With permission from Wiley.

Consequence Healthcare Continuum (C-HCC)

The fourth level of analysis is based on the Consequence Healthcare Continuum (C-HCC). The C-HCC analysis is about measuring damages. However, damages must first be fully identified. Often, this calculation and the total impact will change during the audit and investigation. Key attributes of the C-HCC are highlighted in Figure 26.3.

Economic Business Impact

In healthcare benefit programs such as Medicare and Medicaid, the loss of financial resources will affect patients who need the care. This is a direct hit to the taxpayers who fund these programs and the patients covered by these providers.

In the Dr. Traveler case study, the data sets highlighted significant, implausible anomalies projected with respect to claims data. Table 26.7 illustrates the volume of claims being generated by one physician. The billed and claim amounts for one physician clearly exceed what is physically possible to achieve.

Once a pattern is identified, several approaches may be considered in obtaining a monetary impact (measurement) on the claims submitted. First, assume the doctor did, in fact, provide home health visits but at a more plausible volume. The assumptions are as follows:

■ The doctor worked five days per week and, geographically, could provide home health visits in the morning and facility-based visits in the afternoon.
■ The physician devoted five hours per day for home health visits (five visits in one morning maximum, accounting for travel, movement, and documentation). Each visit is classified as a level three visit at $120.

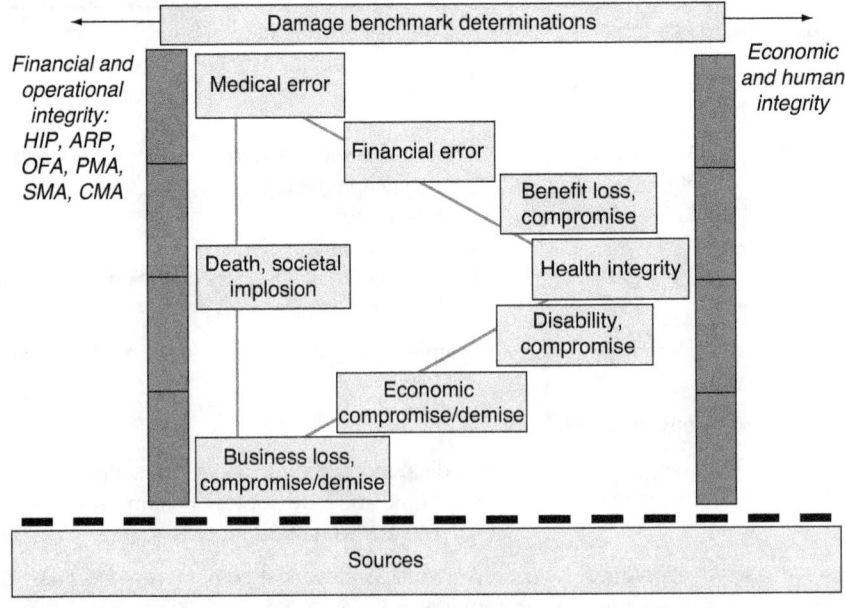

Figure 26.3 Consequence Healthcare Continuum ("C-HCC").

Source: Busch, 2007. With permission from Wiley.

Table 26.7 Claims Data

Claim Activity	7-Day Week Actual Volume	Volume Paid	Rate Level 3	Amount Billed per Week	Paid Amount per Week	Volume Submitted via Third Party	Paid per Week via Third Party	Annual Paid Loss	Annual Billed Amount
Home visits	420	225	$120	$50,400	$27,000	50	$6,000	$1,716,000	$2,620,800
Facility visits	40	12	$100	$4,000	$1,200	0	$0	$62,400	$208,000
Deceased	75	54	$120	$9,000	$6,480	0	$0	$336,960	$468,000
Total								**$2,115,360**	**$3,296,800**

Table 26.8 Adjusted Claims

Adjustment	5 adjusted Work Week Volume	Volume Paid	Rate Level 3/2	Amount Billed per Week	Paid Amount per Week	Volume Submitted via Third Party	Paid per Week via Third Party	Annual Paid Loss	Annual Billed Amount
Home visits	20	20	$120	$2,400	$2,400	0	$0	$124,800	$124,800
Facility visits	40	40	$75	$3,000	$3,000	0	$0	$156,000	$156,000
Deceased	0	0	$120	$0	$0	0	$0	$0	$0
Total								**$280,800**	**$280,800**

- The physician saw 10 facility-based patients (two patients per hour) at one facility in one afternoon. Each visit is classified as a level two visit at $75.

Although these assumptions provide the benefit of the doubt for no breaks during the day by the doctor, the volume is significantly more appropriate than the volume of claims actually submitted. Table 26.8 demonstrates an adjusted claims amount based on the assumptions noted above.

The damages assessment would begin by taking into consideration the two "annual paid loss" numbers. The difference between the paid amount of $2,115,360 and the adjusted amount of $280,800 yields the total illicit amount paid of $1,834,560. The doctor may be subject to fines based on the amount billed versus actually paid, plus treble damages.

Transparency Healthcare Continuum (T-HCC)

Known stakeholders may hold information that is unknown at the outset of an investigation that requires an intellectual connection and the application of certain assumptions to unveil. However, it is also necessary to understand and recognize there may be unknown stakeholders with critical information. The level of risk (loss, exposure, or other implications) is directly proportional to the amount of information known to be limited and to information not known at all (Busch, 2007).

Figure 26.4 illustrates the attributes of the T-HCC, and Table 26.10 explores the T-HCC in the Dr. Traveler case study.

Rules-Based Continuum (RBC)

Rules offer a framework for an audit or investigation. The rules both define the parameters for what is "normal" among a set of stakeholders and govern the relationship. When a perpetrator

Table 26.9 Consequence Healthcare Continuum (C-HCC): Dr. Traveler's Case Study (Busch, 2012. With permission)

Consequences	Economic business impact	$1,834,560
	Serviceability & Service Integrity	1. Risk of patients' PHI being compromised by Dr. Traveler by processing claims for phantom visits and treatments 2. Healthcare facilities associated with Dr. Traveler are exposed to risk of PHI theft
	Service, Medical, & Financial Errors	1. Since patients' medical records are compromised by Dr. Traveler, the patients are at risk of additional complications during any future treatments 2. Financial damages include cost of notifying patients of the error in their medical records and the cost of addressing that fabricated information
	Legal consequences	■ Criminal conviction ■ Civil lawsuits ■ Loss of license ■ Loss of escape out of the U.S.

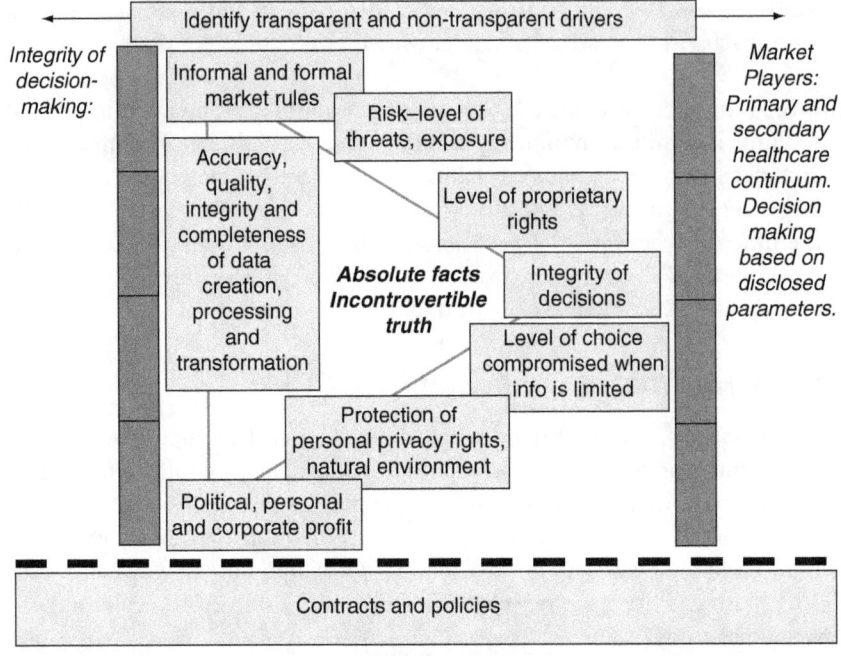

Figure 26.4 Transparency Healthcare Continuum ("T-HCC"):.

Source: Busch, 2007. With permission from Wiley.

Table 26.10 Transparency Healthcare Continuum (T-HCC): Dr. Traveler's Case Study

Transparency	Unidentified stakeholders	Billing company, collection agency
	Financial implication	Financial loss to patients because of Dr. Traveler's fraudulence is not clearly specified
	Health implication	Health implications to patients because of Dr. Traveler's fraudulence is not clearly specified

goes out to "play," they will become creative in adversely leveraging the rules. For example, if the provider is paid per diem, or a flat amount per day, the provider makes more money each day by keeping the patient in the facility; the provider increases profit by minimizing daily services. If an insurance company gets a flat rate per month in premiums, they make more money by denying claims. These are counterproductive, misaligned incentives. Regardless, the sophistication of circumventing rules has been impressive among the many devious schemes and forms of abuse (Busch, 2007).

Table 26.11 explores the RBC in the Dr. Traveler case study.

Applications

This section provides examples on how to apply the review model presented in this chapter, and it illustrates the scheme occurring may be relevant regardless of whether the patient is a Medicare

Table 26.11 Rules-Based Continuum (RBC): Dr. Traveler Case Study

Perpetrator's offenses and rules breached	Offenses	<ul><li>False claims</li><li>Phantom patients from free screenings</li><li>Medical believability</li><li>Tip seniors calling Medicare hot line</li></ul>
	Legislated and Contracted rules	<ul><li>False Claims Act</li><li>Use of stolen medical identities</li><li>Violation of privacy provisions of the patients in nursing homes and senior citizen complexes</li></ul>

beneficiary, Medicaid recipient, or private plan insured. For example, "patient dumping" is an issue regardless of the plan sponsor.

Illustrative Enforcement Actions

Patient Dumping

Brackenridge Hospital in Brackenridge, Texas, agreed to pay $25,000 to resolve allegations of failure to provide stabilizing treatment to an adult male presenting to its emergency department (ED) with complaints of having a severe headache for four days. A computed tomography scan revealed a subarachnoid hemorrhage. The Brackenridge ED physician determines the patient needs to be seen by a neurosurgeon and calls its on-call neurosurgeon. The on-call neurosurgeon refuses to go to the ED to examine or treat the patient; the neurosurgeon would only see pediatric patients. The patient was transferred to a hospital nearly 66 miles away and was hospitalized for three days (Busch, 2010a).

- Step 1: Define the scope of the audit and case review:
  - Review the allegation of patient dumping
- Step 2: Define the data necessary for evaluation:
  - P-HCC: medical records, hospital policy and procedure, relevant claims data, and reimbursement rules or inpatient prospective payment rules on diagnosis-related groups
  - S-HCC: any ED reporting data to the respective state, any relevant statistics from the Centers for Disease Control and Prevention regarding the diagnosis involved
  - IC: identify the sources and systems of the data, the manner in which they are contained and stored
  - C-HCC:
    - Serviceability: Since the patient was not treated properly at Brackenridge Hospital, the health of the patient could have been adversely affected
    - Medical errors: Brackenridge Hospital's ED did not have a clear process for requesting consultants, resulting in the wrong neurologist being summoned to treat the patient
    - Legal consequences: Criminal conviction, civil lawsuits, loss of license
  - T-HCC
    - Unidentified stakeholders: Hospital administration failed to prepare a clear process framework

- ■ Health Implication: Negligence from the hospital during an emergency would adversely affect the patient's health condition
- − RBC
- − Offense: Hospital's negligence, doctor's negligence
■ Step 3: Define the stakeholders to be interviewed:
- − The patient, the provider facility, and professional staff
■ Step 4: Conduct audit review and data analysis:
- − Organize the data for analysis and review
- − Utilize the nursing process of data, opinions, actions and procedures, evaluations, and follow-up data collection
■ Step 5: Complete market comparison, analysis, and final report

The submission of a false claim is often discussed from a provider perspective. The provider submits a claim for reimbursement that includes misrepresentation of service. The Brackenridge Hospital example involved a TPA altering the claim submitted by the provider. In the context of statutes discussed earlier, the negligent or criminal act is the submission of a false claim by a provider that is paid by a benefit plan sponsor. Likewise, the submission or processing of an altered claim by a TPA on behalf of the plan sponsor is also considered a negligent or criminal act.

False and Fraudulent Claims I

America's Health Choice, Inc. (AHC), Florida, agreed to pay $100,000 for allegedly violating the Civil Monetary Penalties Law (Busch, 2010b, p. 268). The OIG alleged AHC misrepresented or falsified information furnished to the Secretary of HHS. Specifically, AHC submitted documents to the Secretary misrepresenting the academic credentials of an AHC employee. The effectuation notices submitted to the Center for Health Dispute Resolution (CHDR) contained falsified dates of submission in an attempt to appear to be in compliance with CHDR's request for claims data (Busch, 2010b, p. 268).

- ■ Step 1: Define the scope of the audit and case review:
- − Review the allegation of false claims processing
- ■ Step 2: Define the data necessary for evaluation:
- − P-HCC: Credential documents, policy and procedures, claims data, adjudication procedures, management reports, TPA contracts, and performance incentives. Collect sample claims information from target patients and providers. All reimbursement schedules would apply since they are processing claims collectively for all types of facilities and providers.
- − S-HCC: Documents submitted to HHS, market data on claims processing standards to Department of Labor.
- − IC: Identify the sources and systems of the data, the manner they are contained and stored. Claims processing software, electronic data interchange processing, and clearing house information.
- − C-HCC
  - ■ Serviceability: An unqualified healthcare provider employee might provide substandard treatment to patients
  - ■ Service errors: Forging an employee's academic credentials will result in loss of credibility in America's Health Choice as a provider

- T-HCC
  - Unidentified stakeholders: Hospital administration employees involved who committed the forgery
  - Health Implication: Treatment provided by unqualified employee will expose the patients to risk of health complications due to wrong treatment
- RBC
  - Offense: False claims, forgery
  - Legislated and Contracted rules breached: Civil Monetary Penalties Law
■ Step 3: Define the stakeholders to be interviewed:
  - The operational staff, the payer management, and claims staff; selected patient and provider interviews
■ Step 4: Conduct audit review and data analysis:
  - Organize the data for analysis and review
  - Reconcile data from patient, provider, and claim file and
  - Utilize the nursing process of data, opinions, actions and procedures, evaluations, and follow-up data collection
■ Step 5: Complete market comparison, analysis, and final report

The AHC case is a great example illustrating the concept of a single episode of care impacted by multiple stakeholders and systems. In this case, information received by the patient can be reconciled with information maintained by the provider, the payer, and the plan sponsor. The multiple sources provide an opportunity to identify any anomalies.

The next example involves durable medical equipment (DME). This is a vulnerable area within the healthcare market. One of several rules includes coverage of DME payment and authorization by a licensed healthcare provider. Specifically, it is important to have the referring licensed healthcare provider meet the criteria for reimbursement. In addition, another pattern proves that many times the patient never actually receives the DME.

False and Fraudulent Claims II

Kay Medical Services Corporation in Florida agreed to pay $440,949 and be permanently excluded from participating in all federal healthcare programs for allegedly violating the Civil Monetary Penalties Law. The OIG alleged Kay Medical Services Corporation submitted claims that listed physicians as the referring licensed healthcare provider for certain DME services that were not provided as claimed and, thus, were false and fraudulent (Busch, 2010c, p. 269).

■ Step 1: Define the scope of the audit and case review:
  - Review the allegation of false and fraudulent DME claims
■ Step 2: Define the data necessary for evaluation:
  - P-HCC: The patient claim file, corresponding medical records, and physician listing for follow-up verification
  - S-HCC: Product information and market use, demographic information on diagnosis associated with the DME product provided
  - IC: Identify software utilized and retention policies for the retrieval of data for analysis
  - C-HCC:
    - Service errors: Fraudulent claims submission led to a heavy fine and exclusion from all federal healthcare programs

- T-HCC:
  - ■ Financial Implication: Exploitation and potential heavy loss to the payers (insurance companies) if they had provided reimbursements for the false claims
- RBC:
  - ■ Offense: Fraudulent claims
  - ■ Legislated and contracted rules breached: Civil Monetary Penalties Law, Stark Law
- ■ Step 3: Define the stakeholders to be interviewed:
  - The provider, the patient, and the DME representative
- ■ Step 4: Conduct audit review and data analysis:
  - Organize the data for analysis and review
  - Utilize the nursing process of data, opinions, actions and procedures, evaluations, and follow-up data collection
- ■ Step 5: Complete market comparison, analysis, and final report

Activity related to DME benefits from data mining tools. The data mining algorithms should reconcile the content of claims data (e.g., the NPI number for the physician, the diagnosis codes, and the actual equipment). Compare the data elements identifying NPI and product information with the recurring charges of quantity supplied and the duration of the product's life span.

The purpose of Stark is to avoid patient care decisions that have a financial basis among providers with a contractual relationship. In the following illustration, a clear direct financial arrangement was executed and in direct violation of the kickback and self-referral statutes.

Kickback and Physician Self-Referral

Advanced Neuromodulation Systems, Inc. (ANS), Texas, agreed to pay $2,950,000 and enter into a three-year corporate integrity agreement to resolve its liability for allegedly violating the Civil Monetary Penalties Law. The OIG alleged ANS offered and paid remuneration to potential and pre-existing referral sources in exchange for referrals to ANS for the purchasing, leasing, ordering, arranging for, or furnishing of medical devices manufactured by ANS and payable by a federal healthcare program. Other ANS practices raising kickback concerns included educational grants and fellowships, conferences held at resort locations, free dinners and gifts, and expenses paid to physicians under consulting agreements (Busch, 2010c, pp. 269–270).

- ■ Step 1: Define the scope of the audit and case review:
  - Review the allegation of kickback and physician self-referral
- ■ Step 2: Define the data necessary for evaluation:
  - P-HCC: Identify all contracted stakeholders; obtain claims data, medical records data, and all contracts signed between the stakeholders
  - S-HCC: Obtain market information of in-kind services or consulting arrangements
  - IC: Obtain marketing infrastructures
  - C-HCC:
    - ■ Service error: ANS opted for an illegal channel instead of adopting proper marketing techniques
  - T-HCC
    - ■ Unidentified stakeholders: Information on ANS employees involved in the scam, providers accepting kickbacks and providing referrals

- ■ Financial implication: Potential loss to the exchequer when the federal health program pays for ANS's product without validation
  - – RBC
    - ■ Offense: Corruption
    - ■ Rules breached: Civil Monetary Penalties Law, Corporate Integrity Agreement
- ■ Step 3: Define the stakeholders to be interviewed:
  - – The contracted stakeholders, representatives from educational grants and conference organizers
- ■ Step 4: Conduct audit review and data analysis:
  - – Organize the data for analysis and review
  - – Utilize the nursing process of data, opinions, actions and procedures, evaluations, and follow-up data collection
- ■ Step 5: Complete market comparison, analysis, and final report

In the ANS example, it is important to understand the marketing relationship in which the contracts were "sold." The next example addresses pricing issues. The physician agreed to the terms when accepting Medicare assignment. The physician circumvented this process by initiating an "association" program to collect additional compensation.

Overcharging Beneficiaries

Lee R. Rocamora, MD, North Carolina, agreed to pay $106,600 to resolve liability for allegedly violating the Civil Monetary Penalties Law. The OIG alleged the practitioner requests payments from Medicare beneficiaries in violation of agreed assignment. Specifically, the practitioner allegedly asked patients to enter into a membership agreement for the patient care program, in which patients paid an annual fee. In exchange for the fee, the membership agreement specifies the practitioner would provide members with (1) an annual comprehensive physical examination; (2) same day or next day appointments; (3) support personnel dedicated exclusively to members; (4) physician availability 24 hours a day, seven days a week; (5) prescription facilitation; (6) coordination of referrals and expedited referrals, if medically necessary; and (7) other service amenities as determined by the practitioner (Busch, 2010c, p. 270).

- ■ Step 1: Define the scope of the audit and case review:
  - – Review the allegation of overcharging beneficiaries
- ■ Step 2: Define the data necessary for evaluation:
  - – P-HCC: Collect patient contracts, marketing materials, and association materials; obtain claim file information from Medicare and the provider; and obtain any information on third-party support such as a billing agent
  - – S-HCC: Research data available on prior billing practices and offenses by the provider
  - – IC: Obtain systems for schedules, banking information, and invoicing process
  - – C-HCC:
    - ■ Financial error: Doctor was illegally overcharging the patients more (?) than that fixed by the government
  - – T-HCC:
    - ■ Financial Implication: Patients are cheated by paying extra money under the promise of better care

- RBC:
  - ■ Rules breached: Civil Monetary Penalties Law
- ■ Step 3: Define the stakeholders to be interviewed:
  - The patient, the provider, and any other third-party member
- ■ Step 4: Conduct audit review and data analysis:
  - Organize the data for analysis and review
  - Utilize the nursing process of data, opinions, actions and procedures, evaluations, and follow-up data collection
- ■ Step 5: Complete market comparison, analysis, and final report
  - This type of behavior is difficult to measure among the entire population. Patients must be educated to question and report such offerings from providers.

Summary

This chapter is an introduction to fraud assessment of private and public sponsored health plans. The critical components of fraud and its definition were reviewed. Key legislation highlighting potentially fraudulent behavior was presented. Historically, market behavior that initially materializes as abuse eventually is exposed and legislated as fraudulent activity. Monitoring the literature for behaviors studied as abuse can be an indicator of future legislation. The section on healthcare reimbursement highlighted 20 different models for reimbursement of healthcare services. If a case involves a specific type of model, the LNC should review the relevant information within the Medicare Manual available on the CMS website. The case evaluation methodology presented in this chapter meets the standard of Daubert and collectively targets the review to relevant data types addressing most types of cases encountered. Finally, the application section illustrated the methodology using actual fraud cases.

References

Association of Certified Fraud Examiners. (n.d.). *The fraud triangle.* Retrieved from www.acfe.com/fraud-triangle.aspx.

Association of Certified Fraud Examiners. (2012). *Fraud examiners manual.* Retrieved from www.acfe.com/uploadedFiles/Shared_Content/Products/Books_and_Manuals/INTRO%202012%20-%20final.pdf.

Busch, R. M. S. (2006). *MBA methodology healthcare expense analysis scientific methodology healthcare reimbursement: Usual & customary; Medicare set aside.* Westmont, IL: Medical Business Associates, Inc.

Busch, R. M. S. (2007). *Healthcare fraud auditing and detection guide.* Hoboken, NJ: Wiley.

Busch, R. M. S. (2008a). *Electronic health records: An audit and internal control guide.* Hoboken, NJ: John Wiley & Sons.

Busch, R. M. S. (2008b). *Healthcare fraud: Auditing and detection guide.* Westmont, IL: Medical Business Associates, Inc.

Busch, R. S. (2010a). Fraud: Government-sponsored health plans and general case evaluation. In L. Peterson & A. M. Kopishke (Eds.), *Legal nurse consulting: Practices* (3rd ed., pp. 251–272). Boca Raton, FL: CRC Press.

Busch, R. S. (2010b). Fraud: Government-sponsored health plans and general case evaluation. In L. Peterson & A. M. Kopishke (Eds.), *Legal nurse consulting: Practices* (3rd ed., pp. 267–268). Boca Raton, FL: CRC Press.

Busch, R. S. (2010c). Fraud: Government-sponsored health plans and general case evaluation. In L. Peterson & A. M. Kopishke (Eds.), *Legal nurse consulting: Practices* (3rd ed., pp. 269–270). Boca Raton, FL: CRC Press.

Busch, R. M. S. (2012). *Healthcare fraud auditing and detection guide* (2nd ed.). Hoboken, NJ: John Wiley & Sons.

Busch, R. M. S. (2017a, April). *Preparing for targeted third-party audits/investigations.* Williamsburg Fraud Conference conducted at Williamsburg, Virginia.

Busch, R. M. S. (2017b). Managing the notion of UCR in a life care plan. *Journal of Life Care Planning, 15*(3), 3–14.

Centers for Medicare & Medicaid Services. (n.d.). The False Claims Act ("FCA"). Retrieved from https://downloads.cms.gov/cmsgov/archived-downloads/SMDL/downloads/SMD032207Att2.pdf.

Centers for Medicare & Medicaid Services. (2007). Physicians' referrals to health care entities with which they have financial relationships (Phase III)—Final Rule (72 FR 51012). Retrieved from www.cms.gov/Medicare/Fraud-and-Abuse/PhysicianSelfReferral/Significant-Regulatory-History-Items/CMS1231349.html.

Centers for Medicare & Medicaid Services. (2015). Laws against health care fraud resource guide. Retrieved from www.cms.gov/Medicare-Medicaid-Coordination/Fraud-Prevention/Medicaid-Integrity-Education/Downloads/fwa-laws-resourceguide.pdf.

Centers for Medicare & Medicaid Services. (2016). Medicare fraud & abuse: Prevention, detection, and reporting (ICN 006827). Retrieved from www.cms.gov/Outreach-and-Education/Medicare-Learning-Network-MLN/MLNProducts/downloads/fraud_and_abuse.pdf.

Centers for Medicare & Medicaid Services. (2017a). Avoiding Medicare fraud & abuse: A roadmap for physicians. Retrieved from www.cms.gov/Outreach-and-Education/Medicare-Learning-Network-MLN/MLNProducts/Downloads/Avoiding_Medicare_FandA_Physicians_FactSheet_905645.pdf.

Centers for Medicare & Medicaid Services. (2017b). Medicare program: General information. Retrieved from www.cms.gov/Medicare/Medicare-General-Information/MedicareGenInfo/index.html.

Centers for Medicare & Medicaid Services. (2017c). Civil monetary penalties (annual adjustments). Retrieved from www.cms.gov/Medicare/Provider-Enrollment-and-Certification/SurveyCertificationGenInfo/Civil-Monetary-Penalties-Annual-Adjustments.html.

Cornell Law School. (2010). 18 U.S. Code 24—definitions relating to federal health care offenses. Retrieved from www.law.cornell.edu/uscode/text/18/24.

Cornell Law School. (2016). White-collar crime. Retrieved from www.law.cornell.edu/wex/white-collar_crime.

Cornell Law School. (2017). 18 U.S. Code 287—false, fictitious or fraudulent claims. Retrieved from www.law.cornell.edu/uscode/text/18/287.

Cornell Law School: Legal Information Institute. (n.d.). 31 U.S. Code § 3729—false claims. Retrieved from www.law.cornell.edu/uscode/text/31/3729.

Federal Health Care Fraud and Abuse Laws. (n.d.). Retrieved from www.oig.hhs.gov/compliance/provider-compliance-training/files/HandoutLegalCitations508.pdf.

Federal Register. (2007). Medicare program: Physicians' referrals to health care entities with which they have financial relationships (Phase III). Retrieved from www.federalregister.gov/documents/2007/09/05/07-4252/medicare-program-physicians-referrals-to-health-care-entities-with-which-they-have-financial.

Federal Register. (2017). Annual civil monetary penalties inflation adjustment (Document No. 2017–02300). Retrieved from www.federalregister.gov/documents/2017/02/03/2017-02300/annual-civil-monetary-penalties-inflation-adjustment.

Federal Register. (2018). Civil monetary penalty adjustments for inflation [Part 6]. Retrieved from www.federalregister.gov/documents/2018/01/08/2017-28230/civil-monetary-penalty-adjustments-for-inflation.

Fraud. (n.d.). In Lawserver.com legal dictionary. Retrieved from www.lawserver.com/law/legal-dictionary/fraud-definition.

HealthCare.gov. (2014). Patient Protection and Affordable Care Act (PPACA). Retrieved from www.healthcare.gov/where-can-i-read-the-affordable-care-act/.

Health care fraud, 18 USC § 1347. (2017). Retrieved from www.law.cornell.edu/uscode/text/18/1347.

Illinois General Assembly. (2012). Criminal offenses [720 ILCS 5/] criminal code 2012. Retrieved from www.ilga.gov/legislation/ilcs/ilcs4.asp?ActID=1876&ChapterID=53&SeqStart=36000000&SeqEnd=37300000.

JDSUPRA. (2018). Emerging trends in False Claims Act enforcement 2018 outlook. Retrieved from www.jdsupra.com/legalnews/emerging-trends-in-false-claims-act-88123/.

Medicare Interactive. (n.d.). Original Medicare: Medicare coverage overview. Retrieved from www.medicareinteractive.org/get-answers/medicare-basics/medicare-coverage-overview/original-medicare.

MedPAC. (2017). Payment basics. Retrieved from www.medpac.gov/-documents-/payment-basics.

Methodology. (n.d.). *Dictionary.com unabridged*. Retrieved from www.dictionary.com/browse/methodology.

Office of Inspector General: U.S. Department of Health and Human Services. (n.d.-a). Comparison of the anti-kickback statute and Stark Law. Retrieved from www.oig.hhs.gov/compliance/provider-compliance-training/files/StarkandAKSChartHandout508.pdf.

Office of Inspector General: U.S. Department of Health and Human Services. (n.d.-b). Fraud. Retrieved from www.oig.hhs.gov/fraud.

Office of Inspector General: U.S. Department of Health and Human Services. (n.d.-c). Medicaid fraud control units—MFCUs. Retrieved from www.oig.hhs.gov/fraud/medicaid-fraud-control-units-mfcu/index.aspc.

Office of Inspector General: U.S. Department of Health and Human Services. (n.d.-d). Civil monetary penalty authorities. Retrieved from https://oig.hhs.gov/fraud/enforcement/cmp/cmpa.asp.

Office of Inspector General: U.S. Department of Health and Human Services. (2013). State False Claims Act. Retrieved from www.oig.hhs.gov/fraud/state-false-claims-act-reviews/index.asp.

Office of the Law Revision Counsel. (2017). United States code. Retrieved from http://uscode.house.gov/browse/prelim@title31/subtitle3/chapter37/subchapter3&edition=prelim.

Oxford English Living Dictionaries. (2017). *Organized crime*. Oxford University Press. Retrieved from https://en.oxforddictionaries.com/definition/organized_crime.

Rouse, M. (2014). Metadata. Retrieved from http://whatis.techtarget.com/definition/metadata.

Stark Law. (2010). Stark Law: Information on penalties, legal practices, latest news and advice. Retrieved from www.hackensackumc.org/assets/1/7/STARK_LAW.pdf.

Stark Law. (2013). Stark Law. Retrieved from http://starklaw.org/stark_law.htm.

U.S. Securities and Exchange Commission. (2001). Final rule: Adjustments to civil monetary penalty amounts (17 CFR Part 201). Retrieved from www.sec.gov/rules/final/33-7946.htm.

U.S. Social Security Administration. (2015). Congress passes H.R. 1314, the Bipartisan Budget Act of 2015. Retrieved from www.ssa.gov/legislation/legis_bulletin_110315.html.

U.S. Social Security Administration. (2016). Compilation of the social security laws: Civil monetary penalties (SEC. 1128A.) Retrieved from www.ssa.gov/OP_Home/ssact/title11/1128A.htm.

Additional Reading

Burkhalter, C., & Crittenden, J. (2009). Professional identity theft: What is it? How are we contributing to it? What can we do to stop it? Retrieved from www.asha.org/uloadedFiles/asha/publications/cicsd/2009SProfessionalIdentityTheft.pdfwww.asha.org/uploadedFiles/asha/publications/cicsd/2009SProfessionalIdentity%09Theft.pdf.

Burton, L., Haller, C. C., McLean, P., & McLean, T. R. (2008). Electronic medical record metadata: Uses and liability. Retrieved from www.sciencedirect.com/science/article/pii/S1072751507016778.

Centers for Medicare & Medicaid Services: www.cms.gov/Medicare/Medicare.html.

U.S. Department of Health & Human Services (2017). Civil monetary penalties and affirmative exclusions. Retrieved from www.oig.hhs.gov/fraud/enforcement/cmp/index.asp.

U.S. Department of Health and Human Services. Office of Inspector General. (n.d.). Retrieved from https://oig.hhs.gov/fraud/enforcement/cmp/cmp-ae.asp.

U.S. Government Publishing Office. (n.d.). 31 U.S.C. 3729—false claims. Retrieved from www.gpo.gov/fdsys/granule/USCODE-2011-title31/USCODE-2011-title31-subtitleIII-chap37-subchapIII-sec3729.

U.S. Legal.com. (n.d.). *The US Legal dictionary*. Retrieved from https://uslegal.com.

Test Questions

1. Which of the following elements is required by the law for the allegation of fraud to exist?
   A. Overinflated billing cycles
   B. Victim acting on inaccurate information
   C. Lost or missing medical documents
   D. Gaps in service provided
2. Which of the following protections are available for "whistleblowers"?
   A. Protection from harassment and retaliation of employers
   B. Some protection for promotions and retirement
   C. Unpaid leave during suspension from work
   D. Protection from gossip in the workplace
3. Which of the following would an LNC expect to do in any fraud investigation? Choose all that apply.
   A. Interview witnesses
   B. Write reports
   C. Defend victims
   D. Negotiate settlements
4. Which of the following is most important for the LNC working in a fraud unit?
   A. Intimate knowledge of the local marketplace
   B. Experience in the courtroom setting
   C. Familiarity with literature describing behaviors that suggest abuse
   D. Previous experience in case management
5. Which of the following represent fraudulent activities? Choose all that apply.
   A. Deceased physicians billing for services
   B. Medically necessary services
   C. Billing for services post patient discharge
   D. Providing services under a contract agreement

Answers: 1. B; 2. A; 3. A, B; 4. C; 5. A, C

Appendix A: Identity Types and Potential Misuses and Illicit Use

- **Individual Identity Theft:** An intent to use another individual's identity (personally identifiable information) to commit, aid, or abet any unlawful activity (https://definitions.uslegal. com/i/identity-theft). **Illicit use:** A social worker at a hospital steals a baby's social security number, name, and date of birth then opens credit in this individual's name.
- **Medical Identity Theft:** An intent to use another individual's identity to commit, aid, or abet any unlawful activity within the healthcare arena (https://definitions.uslegal.com/m/medical-identity-theft/). **Illicit use:** An uninsured person used a sibling's identity to obtain open heart bypass surgery. The result is the co-mingling of protected health information under an assumed name in addition to depletion of benefit plan dollars.
- **Professional Identity Theft:** An intent to use another's professional identity to commit, aid, or abet any unlawful activity as a practicing professional. **Illicit use:** An individual assumed the RN licensure of a nurse, was hired, and worked within a healthcare facility taking care of patients under an assumed license. The result is the individual was criminally prosecuted. The healthcare facility had to refund Medicare and Medicaid for monies received for treating patients by the unlicensed individual (Burkhalter & Crittenden, 2009).
- **Corporate/Business Identity Theft:** An intent to use an organization's corporate identity to commit, aid, or abet an unlawful activity in the organization's name (https://definitions. uslegal.com/t/theft/). **Illicit use:** A criminal organization slightly modified the name of a well-known insurance company and pursued victims, sold a fake insurance policy, and collected premiums. The outcome was eventual criminal prosecution and numerous victims with very high healthcare bills for which they had expected insurance coverage.
- **E-Identity Theft:** An intent to use another individual's electronic or social media identity to commit, aid, or abet any unlawful activity, such as unauthorized electronic access. **Illicit use:** A individual obtains access to another person's online bank account and transfers financial assets. Other modes of theft are viruses attached to emails that will leave behind key logger software to collect an individual's interactions with electronic mediums. Note: this is a hybrid of identity theft known as electronic identity.
- **Digital Identity Theft:** An intent to use another's data identifiers to commit, aid, or abet any unlawful activity by misuse of data points associated with an individual's electronic identity. **Illicit use:** An employee left a computer on at work, and a co-worker accessed an Amazon account to obtain data identifiers that would support the retrieval of a lost password. The perpetrator could then make changes to the account, orders, deliveries, etc. Note: this is a hybrid of identity theft known as digital identity.
- **Synthetic Identity:** An intent to take real and fabricated information to create a new/hybrid identity to commit, aid, or abet any unlawful activity (https://definitions.uslegal. com/s/synthetic-identity-theft/). **Illicit use:** An individual with a newly created hybrid identity opened a series of credits cards and shopped until the bank froze the credit card. The victim is left sifting through what is real and what is not.

Appendix B: Medicare Coverage Sections: A, B, C, D

Medicare Part A (Hospital Insurance) helps cover inpatient care in hospitals, including critical access hospitals and skilled nursing facilities but not custodial or long-term care. It also helps cover hospice care and some home health care. Beneficiaries must meet certain conditions to get these benefits. Most people do not pay a premium for Part A, because they or a spouse already paid for it through their payroll taxes while working.

Medicare Part B (Medical Insurance) helps cover doctors' services and outpatient care. It also covers some other medical services that Part A does not cover, such as some of the services of physical and occupational therapists and some home health care. Part B helps pay for these covered services and supplies when they are medically necessary. Most people pay a monthly premium for Part B.

Medicare Part C is the Medicare Advantage Plan in which private companies contract with Medicare to provide Medicare benefits to beneficiaries. See: www.medicareinteractive.org/get-answers/medicare-basics/medicare-coverage-overview/original-medicare.

Medicare Part D was introduced in January 2006 as a voluntary outpatient drug benefit program, with private companies providing the coverage. Beneficiaries choose the drug plan and pay a monthly premium. Like any other insurance, if a beneficiary decides not to enroll in a drug plan when they are first eligible, they may pay a penalty if they choose to join later (www.cms.hhs.gov/MedicareGenInfo/). Medicare Part D includes stand-alone prescription drug programs and Medicare Advantage prescription drug plans. More information is available through www.cms.hhs.gov by searching Medicare Part D.

Chapter 27

The Role of the Legal Nurse Consultant in the Insurance Industry

Kari Williamson, BS, RN, LNCC®, CCM

Contents

Objectives

- Explain the difference between first-party and third-party claims
- Identify the defense environment participants
- Explain various factors to consider when evaluating the mechanism of injury and the clinical manifestations of an injury
- Identify effective arguments that will assist the defense team in mitigating damages

Introduction

Insurance companies, payer sources, and claims adjusters will use legal nurse consultants (LNCs) to assist with claims involving medical issues. Simply stated, these claims typically involve an injury and an allegation that the party responsible for that injury did not use reasonable care to prevent the damage/injury. The LNC is needed to help determine the medical damages and overall medical condition of the injured party, or claimant. This medical analysis is performed in the context of the inciting event and the case specifics, including the claimed injuries.

The LNC must also have a clear understanding of the type of insurance coverage involved in the claim, as this drives how the claim will be handled and processed. The coverage can also influence defense strategies should the claim go into litigation.

When reviewing medical records and case details, the LNC should be asking:

- Are the alleged injuries and subsequent treatment directly related to the event?
- Are there pre-existing conditions or injuries that may have been exacerbated by the event or that may impact the current conditions and recovery? What are the co-morbidities?

After analyzing the case, the LNC can then begin to work with the claims team to build a defense strategy and mitigate damages. The claims team (which may include the claims adjuster and defense counsel) will use this information to manage, negotiate, and settle the claim. Occasionally, the information is used to deny a claim.

Types of Insurance Coverage

An insurance policy is a contract between two parties: the insured (first party) and the insurer/insurance company (second party). The insured transfers the risk of loss to the insurer in exchange for paying a premium. Insurance coverage is then provided to the insured by the insurer in the event of a unforeseen or unwanted occurrence that is covered under the policy. The named perils, risks, or incidents for which coverage (protection) is provided are detailed in the insurance policy (Business-Dictionary.com; n.d.-a). Whether there is coverage for the claim under the policy is determined by the claims adjuster upon review of the claim, the policy, and the available information.

Non-Litigated versus Litigated

A non-litigated claim is an open claim for which no lawsuit has been filed by the claimant. In non-litigated claims, the LNC will work predominately with the claims adjuster to provide information regarding the medical aspects of the claim, including an analysis of the alleged injuries and the mechanism of injury. The LNC's medical analysis within the context of the allegations will be instrumental to help settle or deny the claim. The defense LNC may also be asked to provide assistance with mitigating damages (discussed later in this chapter). If a claim is not settled or is denied, the claimant may choose to file a lawsuit against the insured. Once a lawsuit has been filed, the claim is considered litigated. Internal steps and protocols within the specific payer/insurance company will be initiated.

In litigated claims, the LNC can expect to work with the claims adjuster and defense counsel. The defense counsel may be "in-house," external, or both. Litigated claims often involve complex medical issues and complicated injury information, requiring a deeper analysis, understanding, and formulation of defense strategies. The LNC must understand the assigned tasks and the goals of the individual claim. Often, the work product requires more than a simple chronology or timeline, because each member of the defense team may have different needs and goals. For example, the adjuster may simply want to understand the medical issue and how it relates to the injury; the defense attorney may want additional information to assist with a line of questioning or determining the genesis of the issues at hand.

First-Party Claims

A first-party claim is a claim made directly against the insurance company by an insured, policyholder, or beneficiary. A few examples of first-party claims include homeowners filing a claim under their homeowner's policy, business owners filing a claim under their commercial property insurance, and car owners filing a claim for physical damage to their own car under their automobile insurance policy.

Some policies, such as homeowners and personal auto, offer coverage for both first-party and third-party claims.

Third-Party Claims

A third party is a party who was injured by an insured. A third-party claim, also known as a liability claim, is a claim made against an insured who is covered by a liability policy.

Liability insurance is a "policy that covers civil liabilities to third parties, arising from bodily injury, property damage, or other wrongs due to the action or inaction of the insured. It covers only civil liabilities and not criminal liabilities" (BusinessDictionary.com, n.d.-b). *Liability* is responsibility, and *negligence* is a lack of responsibility (Prabhat, 2011). Negligence means the failure to exercise the reasonable care that an ordinary person would use under similar circumstances (TheLaw.com, n.d.). For example, driving under the influence of alcohol is negligence. The purpose of liability insurance is to protect the insured against potential exposure from a third-party claim alleging a breach of duties owed to others.

Any settlement for this type of claim will go to the third party, not the insured. A defendant (the insured) may draw other at-fault persons/entities into a claim to apportion liability and thus settlement. This is important, as it may affect the LNC's role within the claim since the goals of each defendant may be different. Examples of third-party claims include claims made by a pedestrian hit by the insured's automobile, by a patient injured by a surgeon, or by a visitor injured by a hazardous condition at a business or home.

For information on specific types of automobile insurance coverages, including bodily injury, supplemental uninsured and underinsured motorist coverage, umbrella, no-fault, medical payments, collision, and comprehensive, see Chapter 11.

Defense Environment Participants

Understanding the roles of the various members of the defense team is critical to being an effective defense LNC, as it allows the LNC to customize the work product to be helpful to the needs and goals of the defense team member using it. Strong collaboration is required.

Insurance Carrier

This is the company that offers and underwrites insurance. The insurance carrier will issue an insurance policy, thereby assuming the risk of that insured as provided by the policy. Insurance is a means of protection against loss. There are many types of insurance carriers as well as types of insurance coverage.

Third-Party Administrator

A third-party administrator (TPA) is a company or firm to whom an insurer outsources the handling of the insurer's administrative and claims duties. Many companies outsource to TPAs to avoid infrastructure costs. The TPA does not provide the specific insurance coverage; it simply handles claim-processing functions. The level of duties that are performed by the TPA can range from simply paying or processing a claim settlement to full investigation and adjudication of a claim. In many instances, the TPA claims adjuster will function as a traditional insurance-based claims adjuster. Third-party administrators handle all types of insureds and insurance lines and are paid a fee for the services rendered.

Self-Insured

A self-insured is a business that has set aside a large amount of money to self-fund its own risk of loss, instead of transferring that risk to an insurance carrier for a premium. In the case of a self-insured, there is no true "insurance"; there is just the monetary funds to cover the risk of loss. The benefit in this instance is the self-insured manages its own money and often will have strong influence over the management and payout of a claim. Self-insureds can also self-administer their claims, which means they have their own claims adjusters. In the self-insured environment, the adjuster functions in the traditional sense.

Excess Insurance Layer

This is a policy that adds an additional layer of insurance above the primary (or first) layer of coverage. In other words, it is a policy issued to provide limits in "excess" of the underlying liability policy (International Risk Management Institute, n.d.). Excess layers can be multiple layers held by multiple insurance carriers. The excess layer does not begin to pay for a loss until the primary layer has paid the limits of its policy. Companies that have potentially high exposure (such as manufacturers, contractors, trucking lines, hospitals, etc.) will have excess layers. When primary layer insurance companies do not want to carry the monetary risk over a certain dollar amount, say $1 million, an excess layer insurance policy is a cost-effective way of purchasing the higher limits of indemnity (Hiscox, 2012).

Adjusters from both the primary and excess carriers interact with each other. However, since the primary insurance policy money comes first, the primary insurance carrier/adjuster takes the lead on the claim and has the right to determine settlement and payouts of a claim within its layer. If the claim settles within the primary layer, the excess layer is not accessed. The settlement must exceed the primary layer before the excess layer can be accessed (Justia, n.d.).

Claims Adjuster

This individual manages the claim as it is submitted to the payer. The experience level of an adjuster, the specific line of insurance on which the adjuster works, and the level of authority vary. The "level of authority" usually refers to the maximum dollar authority (or amount) adjusters have been given by their management to settle claims on their own. As adjusters gain experience, they will be given bigger, more complex claims with higher dollar exposures, and their level of authority will increase. The complexity of the case and the potential dollar exposure often influence what the adjuster needs from the LNC. For example, a lower-value claim may not warrant an in-depth analysis that would be necessary for a higher-value claim.

The claims adjuster is also responsible for setting and adjusting the indemnity reserve for the claim. The indemnity reserve "is the money that is earmarked for the eventual claim payment. The claims reserve funds are set aside for future payment" (Kagen, 2018). The reserve can be adjusted up or down by the claims adjuster at any time based on claim information.

Claims adjusters have a responsibility to the insured, insurer/TPA, and claimant to timely, accurately, thoroughly, and fairly investigate and resolve claims; to follow the law; and to observe their fiduciary duty. On personal injury and medical malpractice claims, this necessarily means the claims adjuster must review and analyze the medical documentation within the context of the allegations and determine what injuries and economic damages are related to the incident that gave rise to the claim. The claims adjuster (and defense counsel) must be mindful of what is accepted versus what is denied, because any care, treatment, or diagnosis that is accepted can lead to subsequent additional associated or connected conditions or treatments. The insurer (acting through the claims adjuster) is obligated by law to accept and pay for what is related and deny the rest. In other words, any settlement should be fair—no less, no more. That is the principle of indemnity—the injured should only be restored to the approximate financial condition that existed prior to the loss.

In-house Defense Counsel

These are licensed attorneys who work for the payer source, whether the insurance carrier, a self-insured, or a TPA. The main goal of the in-house attorney is to monitor the legal issues of the company as well as the individual claims. Attorneys review contracts, identify specific claim issues, address coverage/policy questions, and interact with the payer source, claims adjuster, claimant's/plaintiff's counsel, and outside defense counsel. In-house attorneys for insurance carriers do not try cases, as their allegiance is with the insurer, not the insured. Attorneys for self-insureds can take cases to trial.

Outside Defense Counsel

These are licensed attorneys who work very closely with the payer source, but their allegiance (duty and ethical obligation) is to the insured. In broad terms, the payer source has the strongest influence over defense counsel selection, because the payer source (acting through the claims adjuster) retains the attorney, controls and pays for the legal defense, determines settlement issues, and pays any judgment or settlement. Sometimes the insurer's and insured's interests do not align, but typically, there is a system of checks and balances between the payer/insurer, in-house counsel, and outside defense counsel. Outside defense counsel can try cases on behalf of the insured.

Mechanism of Injury, Clinical Manifestation, and Treatment Evaluation

Mechanism of Injury

When evaluating the mechanism of injury (MOI), understanding the precipitating or inciting event is critical to building an effective defense. Throughout the medical records, the MOI as reported to various healthcare professionals should hold consistent. The details of the first reported version of the MOI/event are usually the most accurate. If the details change, the LNC should document and investigate this. Was a new diagnosis subsequently made that could account for the change? Could there have been an intervening event(s)/injury? If there are multiple versions of an MOI, this is a red flag and should be brought to the attention of the claims adjuster and defense attorney. Alternatively, the LNC should note if the details of the MOI are uncharacteristically vague.

While an LNC is not a biomechanical engineer, understanding the basics of the alleged MOI is essential to analyzing the alleged injuries and causation. For any type of injury, the LNC must always compare the injuries allegedly sustained with those expected from the alleged mechanism of injury. In other words, the LNC (1) reviews the injuries that reportedly occurred but are atypical for the type of accident and (2) considers the physical injuries that are generally expected from that type of accident but did not occur.

Falls

There are several types of falls, including slip, trip, stumble, tumble, etc. All have different inciting factors and occur for different reasons. Biomechanical basics such as center of gravity, base support, gravity line, and environmental factors are critical in fully understanding the MOI and the alleged injuries.

Motor Vehicle Accidents

In a motor vehicle accident (MVA), the MOI plays a critical piece in internal and external bodily injuries. When analyzing an MVA, the LNC should learn as much information as possible about the details of the incident, before reviewing the medical records, to obtain context for the alleged bodily injuries. The best document to provide the most accurate and unbiased report of the MVA is the police report and diagram. If the MVA was minor and police were not called to the scene, the claimant's initial description of the MVA will likely have to suffice.

The biomechanics of the occupant(s) are important and will help explain any sustained injuries. Where the occupant was sitting within a vehicle, whether the occupant was restrained, and how the occupant's body moved within the vehicle are important findings, as there will be different body impact points. Additionally, the size and speed of the vehicle(s) are important, as the energies and forces involved in the collision will vary. For more information, see Chapter 11.

Clinical Manifestation

If the biomechanics maxim "Does the injury fit the clinical findings?" holds true, then the medical records should reflect clinical findings (e.g., bruising, fractures, internal organ injury, etc.) that are consistent with the MOI and support the alleged injuries. The injured party's signs and symptoms are compared to the reported diagnoses and documented diagnostic findings in an effort to identify which injuries appear to be related to the accident.

While not all injuries result in visible trauma (e.g., lacerations, fractures, and contusions), the area of the body involved often exhibits associated symptoms that should be consistent with the MOI. Depending on the nature of the injury, its manifestation (and thus the claim) may occur several days, weeks, or months after the initial event. This is often the case with medical malpractice claims. Nonetheless, the LNC should carefully identify and evaluate any new injuries or conditions that are alleged well after the date of the accident. Understanding the medical or trauma timeline during any delay in clinical manifestation or injury reporting or during any lapse of care is a critical component of analyzing the medical record. It should be remembered that absent or negative examination findings can sometimes be more illuminating than positive findings.

The LNC will also look at pre-existing conditions and any documented soft tissue conditions or boney degeneration. Opposing counsel may focus on an abnormality or an allegedly related finding, but it should first be evaluated within the context of the claimant's age, clinical presentation, and overall clinical picture, as some findings maybe incidental or unrelated. The LNC should ask, "What is the best explanation for this clinical finding?" and "Is this finding consistent with the reported mechanism of injury?" If the finding correlates best with natural degeneration, the LNC can develop this possible argument to mitigate damages.

Treatment Evaluation

In addition to the clinical picture, the diagnostics utilized and the treatments prescribed are important considerations for the defense. If higher-level diagnostics or treatments were not implemented, the defense could argue the injuries were not that severe.

The LNC should also assess whether the medical treatment correlates with the alleged injuries. Was the treatment appropriate or excessive? Was it typical for the type of injury, i.e., did it follow the usual treatment protocols and time frames for this type of injury? Is there some other motivation behind protracted or extensive care? If there are indications of inappropriate treatment, including for asymptomatic findings, this can be a strong defense argument for over-treatment or unnecessary treatment. Was care provided that was unrelated to the alleged injuries? Was there a treatment gap? What was the response to treatment? Did the reported symptoms and injuries improve or resolve?

Mitigation of Damages

Damages

Damages refers to loss, injury, or harm to something or someone. In personal injury and medical malpractice claims, recoverable damages are generally medical costs, related expenses, wage loss, pain, and suffering. These compensatory damages are designed to help return injured persons to their pre-injury state (Naprawa, 2018).

Economic damages are easy to quantify. In an automobile claim, this might be the cost to repair vehicular damage. In personal injury and medical malpractice claims, it may be medical costs, out-of-pocket medically related expenses, and lost wages, which can be easily calculated from billing, tax, and employment records. Non-economic damages (such as pain and suffering) are subjective and difficult to quantify. See Chapters 4 and 11 for more information on damages.

Mitigation of Damages

On the plaintiff's side, it is the claimant's responsibility to seek reasonable care to address the injuries sustained. Claimants are expected to mitigate their own damages by appropriately and fairly taking protective action to avoid deliberately increasing, aggravating, or doing additional harm to the injury in question. If the claimant does not follow prescribed medical treatment and additional harm is done, the carrier may deny the portion of the claim related to this additional, preventable harm.

Example:

A person sustains a severe finger laceration in a car accident but does not follow the treating provider's orders regarding antibiotic use, wound care, and follow-up care. The person subsequently develops a severe infection resulting in the amputation of that finger. Under such circumstances, the claimant may be held liable for the additional care and treatment, because the claimant had a responsibility to comply with prescribed medical care to minimize foreseeable complications.

On the defense side, the carrier will review the alleged damages, compare them to the medical records, and determine what injuries, medical care, and treatment is directly related to the claim. The carrier cannot be arbitrary or unfair, but it will deny (not accept) care that is unrelated to the injury, that was due to the claimant's non-compliance/failure to mitigate damages, and that is deemed unreasonable, unnecessary, or outside the standard of care for the expected diagnosis or condition. The carrier can also help to reduce the value of the claim by reviewing the claimant's social media and obtaining surveillance of the claimant to gather evidence contrary to the claimant's alleged injuries. For example, if a claimant alleges limited shoulder function due to an injury, the defense team may use social media and surveillance to obtain photographs or video footage of the claimant lifting a grandchild overhead, participating in a vigorous exercise class, or retrieving an item from the top shelf at a store. These efforts by the defense help to minimize the claim's dollar value. See Chapter 11 for more information on damages evaluation, damages experts, and affirmative defenses that seek to minimize damages.

Role of the Legal Nurse Consultant within the Defense Environment

The LNC (whether an employee of the insurance company or an independent consultant) can be retained at any point during the life of a claim. The specific assignment(s) will vary depending upon the type of claim, allegations, and nuances of the case. Clear direction as to the scope and goal of the project and specific requests should be understood at the outset. The LNC may be requested to:

- Develop a medical record summary, analysis, and chronology
- Review billing records
- Provide information and illustrations of anatomy, injuries, etc.
- Interpret medical terminology and abbreviations in the medical record
- Identify missing records
- Recommend types of experts (e.g., causation, damages, independent medical examination, independent medical record review)
- Locate specific experts (see Chapter 36 for more information)
- Conduct a thorough and objective analysis of current medical literature
- Develop deposition questions
- Review deposition transcripts to compare the testimony to the medical records
- Participate in roundtable claims discussions
- Provide negotiation points for settlement
- Assist with trial preparation and prepare exhibits (see Chapters 37 and 39 for more information)
- Clarify medical issues at arbitration, mediation, and trial
- Assist with defense team strategies and
- Develop and deliver medical training sessions for claims adjusters

The goals of these projects assigned to the LNC may be to help the claims adjuster with:

- Determining the relatedness (causal connection) of the alleged injuries to the accident in question
- Determining whether a prior condition or injury was exacerbated or aggravated by the accident in question
- Identifying the severity and permanency of the sustained injuries
- Investigating the reasonableness and necessity of prescribed medical treatment, including medications
- Determining the potential medical outcomes and long-term prognosis of the claimant
- Evaluating whether the submitted medical bills are directly related to the claim
- Determining whether the related medical treatment charges are usual and customary for the provider and geographic location and whether they were billed (and bundled) appropriately (see Chapter 28 for more information)
- Identifying the implications of the sustained injuries and the potential need for future treatment and
- Determining the standard of care and deviations therefrom in medical malpractice cases

It is imperative that the LNC remain objective and support any opinions, conclusions, and recommendations with documentation from the medical records and from research of reliable medical literature. This will enhance the adjuster's credibility and effectiveness when using those findings in the settlement negotiations.

When evaluating a claim, the LNC should first attempt to establish the claimant's baseline health and medical conditions. The establishment of a baseline allows the LNC to logically evaluate the alleged injuries and course of treatment.

Some of the documents the LNC can expect to review include:

- Demand letter/documents from claimant's/plaintiff's counsel
- Prior medical records

- Police, accident, and incident reports
- Ambulance records
- Emergency department records
- Provider follow-up notes (e.g., primary care provider, chiropractor, orthopedist, surgeon, etc.)
- Claimant's statements and
- Adjuster's notes

The LNC will also use these documents to identify an accurate date of loss for the alleged injury and to determine the initial complaints and symptoms present from the outset or within a few days of an accident. Subsequent claims of injuries that are inconsistent with those initially documented may be questionable in terms of relatedness to the accident. The LNC's work product will note these inconsistencies as well as any evidence of possible fraudulent claim activity by the claimant. The LNC also analyzes whether the objective findings noted on physical examination are consistent with the claimant's subjective complaints.

The LNC's knowledge of the healthcare system and processes common to most hospitals and providers is of great value. The LNC knows what medical records to expect amongst the documentation provided in support of a claim. The astute LNC will identify any missing records or billing statements. For example, the emergency department (ED) record might have the forms completed in longhand, but not the provider's dictated note. In another scenario, an adjuster may question the necessity of taking two sets of wrist x-rays in the ED for a distal radius fracture. The LNC can explain that a second set of x-rays is routinely taken after a closed reduction of a fracture.

Pre-existing medical conditions are pertinent to injury claims but do not preclude an injury to the same area of the body. For example, it is possible for an individual with failed back syndrome and chronic low back pain to sustain an acute lumbar strain. Obtaining prior medical records may prove essential in determining the claimant's previous history of pain medications and dosages, pattern of medical treatment, and employment history immediately before the accident as compared with post-accident. In the absence of disclosure of such a pre-existing medical condition, a thorough review of medical records may suggest a relevant prior condition. For example, the presence of pain or anti-inflammatory medications being taken at the time of the accident, imaging studies being compared with previous studies done at the same facility, and billing records that reveal the claimant as an established patient with a spine surgeon may indicate a pre-existing condition.

The LNC also analyzes how the claimant's pre-existing conditions and co-morbidities impact the medical care for the injury in question and whether there are any intervening events that have influenced care, rehabilitation, outcomes, etc. In looking at the care provided and the treatment recommended, the LNC should also look for any business connection between healthcare providers, as sometimes, if there is a joint ownership, higher-level diagnostics and longer treatment patterns are seen. (See Chapters 26 and 28 for more information on fraud.)

To support or explain the medical issues and to determine whether a plausible causal connection exists between the accident and the alleged injury, the LNC may research the medical literature. (See Chapter 34 for more information on medical literature research.) Examples of questions that may require literature support include:

- Can new-onset diabetes occur as a result of abdominal trauma?
- Can trauma aggravate pre-existing degenerative changes of the spine?

- Can a pre-existing cardiac dysrhythmia worsen from steering wheel or airbag impact?
- Can first trimester pregnancy loss occur as a result of a slip and fall?
- Can post-traumatic stress disorder result from a car accident in which no party sustained serious physical injuries? and
- Can a closed head injury with or without cognitive deficits occur as a result from a minor/low impact rear end MVA with minimal vehicle damage?

On occasion, the LNC may identify the need to have the matter peer-reviewed by a similar healthcare provider (peer) to the claimant's primary treating provider. This independent record review can help clarify certain medical issues. The pertinent records (e.g., vehicle photos, accident reports, and medical records) are provided to the peer reviewer to obtain the peer's professional opinion on the claim. Some states have laws governing how such peer reviews are conducted. For example, in some states, reviewers may need to be certified insurance consultants. The LNC may coordinate the peer review, gather and provide the necessary records, generate questions for the reviewer, and communicate verbally on specific issues. Unlike independent medical examinations in which the healthcare provider interviews and examines the claimant, peer reviewers do not meet with or examine the claimant. Thus, these peer reviews are often referred to as "paper" or "desk" reviews. Similar to vetting experts, though, it is preferable to seek out healthcare providers who are board-certified in their specialties, in active practice, and in good standing with state boards.

The LNC's involvement tends to escalate as the claim moves forward. The LNC must work with new information as it becomes available, evaluating how these new details may impact the claim. The LNC may also be involved in discussions about whether the claim should be settled or defended.

The LNC working in the insurance industry is well advised to become familiar with the basic procedures and functions involved in the processing and adjusting of claims. This allows the LNC to better meet the needs of the claims adjuster. The LNC must understand the constraints and considerations under which adjusters operate, such as the available coverage, policy limits, critical time frames, statute of limitations, and the duty of good faith. The timely and fair resolution of a claim is the goal, and numerous factors are considered when arriving at a settlement offer, including:

- Severity and permanency of the injury
- Pre-existing conditions
- The extent of medical treatment (e.g., surgery versus medical management)
- Medical bills
- Wage loss
- Functional impairment
- Future treatment and
- Settlement and verdict values in similar cases in the same or nearby jurisdictions

Summary

By providing a thorough, objective analysis of the medical records and medical issues, LNCs can help insurance companies reach fair and equitable settlements of claims. This may involve the denial or defense of claims with questionable or unsubstantiated injuries or treatment. The detection of questionable or fraudulent injury claims not only helps the insurance company but also the insureds by constraining premium increases. The LNC can be a highly valued member of the claims team, working closely on the medical issues with the claims adjuster, who has the overall responsibility for investigating and managing claims, determining the liability, and negotiating and settling claims.

References

BusinessDictionary.com. (n.d.-a). Coverage. Retrieved from www.businessdictionary.com/definition/coverage.html.

BusinessDictionary.com. (n.d.-b). Liability insurance. Retrieved from www.businessdictionary.com/definition/liability-insurance.html.

Hiscox. (2012.). What is primary insurance? Retrieved from www.hiscox.com/blog/what-primary-insurance.

International Risk Management Institute. (n.d.). Excess liability policy. Retrieved from www.irmi.com/term/insurance-definitions/excess-liability-policy.

Justia. (n.d.). Types of personal injury damages. Retrieved from www.justia.com/trials-litigation/docs/personal-injury-damages/.

Kagen, J. (2018). Claims reserve. Retrieved from www.investopedia.com/terms/c/claims-reserve.asp.

Naprawa, A. (2018). How to determine pain and suffering in a car accident case. Retrieved from www.alllaw.com/articles/nolo/auto-accident/pain-and-suffering-from-car-accident.html.

Prabhat, S. (2011). Difference between liability and negligence. Retrieved from www.differencebetween.net/language/words-language/difference-between-liability-and-negligence/.

TheLaw.com. (n.d.) Negligence. Retrieved from https://dictionary.thelaw.com/negligence/.

Test Questions

1. The LNC in the role of a claims consultant is expected to do all of the following EXCEPT:
   A. Oversee the management of the claim
   B. Determine causal relationships
   C. Identify the mechanism of injury
   D. Determine pre-existing conditions
2. Which of the following will help the defense to mitigate damages?
   A. The initial version of the MOI has remained consistent
   B. The claimant declines immediate care
   C. The claimant is unable to return to work
   D. The claimant has no pre-existing conditions
3. Which of the following is an example of a first-party claim?
   A. A business invitee trips and falls over a store display and files a claim for a fractured wrist
   B. A car parked at home is damaged by a tree branch during a storm, and the car owner files a claim for the damage
   C. A patient's wrong leg is amputated, and the patient files a liability claim
   D. A pedestrian is hit by an automobile and files a claim with the car owner's insurance company
4. The goals of the projects assigned to the LNC may include which of the following?
   A. Identifying the severity and permanency of the sustained injuries
   B. Investigating the reasonableness and necessity of prescribed medical treatment
   C. Evaluating whether the submitted medical bills are directly related to the claim
   D. All of the above
5. The defense environment participants include:
   A. The police officer at the scene
   B. The emergency room nurse
   C. The in-house attorney
   D. The plaintiff

Answers: 1. A, 2. B, 3. B, 4. D, 5. C

Chapter 28

Bill Review
The Analysis of Claims for Healthcare Services

Rebecca A. Reier, BS, RN, CRNA (Ret.), CCS-P

Contents

Objectives

- Define "claims for healthcare services"
- Identify the three typical objectives of conducting bill reviews
- Describe areas with potential for fraud and abuse

Introduction

Claims for healthcare services are produced for virtually all aspects of medical care. Legal nurse consultants (LNCs) may be asked by insurers (government, commercial healthcare, liability), attorneys (both plaintiff and defense), practice groups, and facilities to analyze billing charges and procedure codes in the context of the related medical documentation. This chapter discusses the process of analyzing claims for healthcare services and introduces methodology and practical considerations.

Healthcare Claims Analysis

The term "fiduciary responsibility" has been introduced in the court systems to represent the fiscal duty of a healthcare provider (HCP) whose medical care decisions affect not only the health but the economics of the patient (International Risk Management Institute, n.d.; *Witherell v. Weimer*, 1981). This concept dates back to the "Hippocratic Oath" developed and evolved from the 3rd century BC to modern times in which the physician promises to consider the effect on the "person's family and economic stability" (MedicineNet, 2018).

Claims for healthcare services represent a defined economic value placed on care provided by a HCP or healthcare facility and submitted to a person or entity responsible for payment, such as the health insurer, motor vehicle insurer, or the patient. Healthcare claims analysis is the process of reviewing a claim for healthcare services, determining its accuracy and relevancy, and offering an opinion and recommendations. This involves reviewing applicable medical records and billing statements, conducting research, educating the retaining attorney or insurance company, opining on the merits of the claim for healthcare services, noting discrepancies, and identifying missing pieces of information needed for a full review.

The adjustor for the patient's/plaintiff's health insurance company is often the first to receive the actual claim. Claims for services provided by a healthcare provider or healthcare facility are most often received electronically by the health insurance company. The LNC may encounter these claims forms and the associated healthcare documentation at any point in the analysis process. In addition to the claim form, the file may include:

■ Documentation of the reserves, or monies, set aside by the insurance company to finance the claims
■ Communications among all parties involved in the case
■ Medical records and associated bills or invoices
■ Litigation materials such as interrogatories, answers, and depositions
■ Health or automobile insurance policies and
■ Expert reports that provide valuable information

In analyzing healthcare claims, the LNC should:

■ Interact with attorney-clients, insurance clients, or others in a timely and professional manner
■ Have a clear understanding of the assignment, including case type, type of report or opinion requested, and due date for case analysis completion

- Have knowledge of Current Procedural Terminology (CPT) codes, ICD-10 (International Classification of Diseases) codes, Healthcare Common Procedure Coding System (HCPCS) codes, insurance claim forms, and private and federal billing regulations and
- Analyze all pertinent records

Communication

During the healthcare claim analysis process, the LNC interacts with a host of clinical and non-clinical individuals. The LNC must be compliant with the Health Insurance Portability and Accountability Act (HIPAA) and HIPAA Business Associate Agreements when communicating with others. The LNC should be familiar with any limitations from the Federal Privacy Act as well as individual state Privacy Acts. The federal Privacy Act of 1974 (5 U.S.C. § 552a) "establishes a code of fair information practices that governs the collection, maintenance, use, and dissemination of information about individuals that is maintained in systems of records by federal agencies" (U.S. Department of Justice, 2015, para. 1). In addition, proprietary information should be protected.

As in all activities by the LNC, discoverability issues and written documentation requires care and clarification of expectations of the client.

Bill Review

Methodology

Billing information can appear as line-item invoices, official claim forms (e.g., CMS-1500 for services rendered by healthcare professionals and the uniform billing form UB-04 for hospital services), or simply a summary statement to the patient. Whatever the format, line-items containing the appropriate codes for services and diagnoses must be present to adequately evaluate the charges. Although ICD-10 codes were official in September 2015, the earlier version, ICD-9 codes, are encountered on claims prior to that date. The CPT and HCPCS codes are updated annually.

The UB-04 claim form for hospital services contains three-digit codes known as revenue codes. These allow the facility to break out charges and bill for some ancillary services, such as medical and surgical supplies, on a separate line. The CPT and HCPCS codes may not be listed on every charge on the UB-04 claim form, but every item is included in a revenue code. The line item descriptions (such as "surgical implant" or "unit of packed red blood cells") use terminology generally familiar to the LNC, who then can ascertain if such charges match the care and services documented in the medical record. Thus, the LNC is able to validate whether all charges on the UB-04 are reasonable and medically necessary.

When conducting a bill review, both the medical records and related charges must be available for side-by-side comparison. Obtaining the relevant medical records must be done promptly upon assignment of a bill review, since procurement of records can take significant time. Once secured, the LNC should review each item on the billing statement carefully, making comparisons and cross-references to the medical record.

Typically, bill reviews focus on assessing the charges, evaluating the procedural codes, and identifying any evidence of abusive or fraudulent billing practice.

Identifying Usual, Customary, and Reasonable Charges

The LNC may be confronted with the daunting task of identifying usual, customary, and reasonable (UCR) medical charges. This ubiquitous terminology requires careful differentiation (Health-Care.gov, n.d.; USLegal, 2016a). The term can be applied to the actual charges for healthcare services by an HCP as seen on the bill or invoice. It can also be applied to the allowed or covered amounts by a payer.

The American Medical Association (AMA, 2013) defines UCR as:

a. "usual" fee means that fee usually charged, for a given service, by an individual physician to [a] private patient (i.e., [the physician's] own usual fee)

b. a fee is "customary" when it is within the range of usual fees currently charged by physicians of similar training and experience, for the same service within the same specific and limited geographical area and

c. a fee is "reasonable" when it meets the above two criteria and is justifiable, considering the special circumstances of the particular case in question, without regard to payments that have been discounted under governmental or private plans

Alternatively, the payers in the health insurance industry (such as government or commercial payers) use the term UCR to define the specific allowance for a particular healthcare service (as opposed to the HCP's charge for that service). Generally, this allowance is a much lower figure than the HCP's charge. Some states have a personal injury protection (PIP) fee schedule. If the LNC is comparing the charges to such fee schedules, it is important to check the year in effect in relationship to date of service on the claim.

There are legal considerations pertaining to UCR as well. Some states have a collateral source rule, which states the plaintiff's economic damages will not be diminished by benefits received from an independent, collateral source. In other words, payments made by a health insurance company for medical treatment related to the alleged injury are irrelevant, and such evidence is inadmissible (USLegal, 2016b). However, in some states, the collateral source rule has been challenged in higher courts, because while the law typically allows a plaintiff to recover reasonable expenses incurred, an HCP's charges are not the amounts actually incurred by the plaintiff because of these collateral source payments (Wickert, 2018). The defense further argues that the charges are not reasonable, because they were adjusted (reduced or written off) by the insurer to the allowed amount (Wickert, 2018). Certain states permit the payer's allowance as evidence of UCR. The LNC should be familiar with the rules and laws applicable to the matter at hand.

The AMA definition of UCR introduces the concept that the reasonableness of fees may relate to what is customary in specific geographic areas, such as a zip code. A comparative review of customary charges can reveal abusive billing practices. It is imperative that the reference material used for analysis be the most demonstrable and broadest database available. The Centers for Medicare & Medicaid Services (CMS) and the American Hospital Association (AHA) list databases as resources. Another resource is Fair Health.

Evaluating Appropriateness of Procedural Codes

In 1996, the National Correct Coding Initiative (NCCI) was developed by CMS (CMS, 2018b, 2018c). The NCCI is the basic coding methodology utilized by virtually all coders, billers, and insurers to assess the validity and appropriateness of the charges. The NCCI is the authority when evaluating whether the healthcare provider or facility has assigned a CPT code appropriately to describe the services rendered. The Centers for Medicare & Medicaid Services state,

> The CMS developed the National Correct Coding Initiative (NCCI) to promote national correct coding methodologies and to control improper coding leading to inappropriate payment in Part B claims. The CMS developed its coding policies based on coding conventions defined in the American Medical Association's CPT Manual, national and local policies and edits, coding guidelines developed by national societies, analysis of standard medical and surgical practices, and a review of current coding practices. CMS updates the National Correct Coding Initiative Coding Policy Manual annually. The Coding Policy Manual should be utilized by carriers and [Form Locators] as a general reference tool that explains the rationale for NCCI edits. Carriers implemented NCCI Procedure-to-Procedure (PTP) edits within their claim processing systems for dates of service on or after January 1, 1996 and began implementing Medically Unlikely Edits (MUEs) on January 1, 2007.
>
> (CMS, 2018b)

The MUE is the maximum number of units one provider may charge for one procedure/service on one patient in one day. For example, there would be no circumstances in which a physical therapist would need to bill for more than one evaluation of the same patient on a single day. Another example is that most payers will not pay for more than six 15-minute time units of physical therapy. Billing for additional units of service in excess of an MUE requires documentation of medical necessity. In addition to practitioner MUEs, there are also MUEs for facility and durable medical equipment charges.

The LNC also utilizes clinical knowledge to identify items billed inappropriately (such as a pregnancy test for a male or a CT scan when an MRI was performed).

Identifying Abusive or Fraudulent Billing Practices

Healthcare fraud schemes are diverse and vary in complexity, with unscrupulous HCP and healthcare systems targeting both public and private health insurance plans. Identifying and addressing billing errors, abuse, and fraud is critical to the outcome of a claim for healthcare services. Healthcare fraud is actively pursued by the U.S. government and commercial insurers. Many cases of fraud and abuse are uncovered during legal proceedings.

The statistical evidence of the problem and the effectiveness of identifying and reporting the offenses continue to mount. In 2018, the U.S. Department of Health and Human Services (HHS) and the U.S. Department of Justice (DOJ) published the latest "Health Care Fraud and Abuse Control Program Annual Report," which details the dollar amounts recovered from law enforcement efforts to combat healthcare fraud and abuse (U.S. HHS & U.S. DOJ, 2018). According to the report, "during Fiscal Year 2017, the Federal Government won or negotiated over $2.4 billion in health care fraud judgments and settlements" (U.S. HHS & U.S. DOJ, 2018). In 2015, the Departments of Justice and Health and Human Services announced a recovery of $7.70 for every dollar spent on health-care related fraud and abuse (U.S. DOJ & U.S. HHS, 2015).

The CMS has issued an open invitation to the public to report medical billing fraud by providing information on the CMS website, on Explanation of Benefits provided to patients, and via an annual publication entitled "Medicare Fraud and Abuse: Prevention, Detection and Reporting" (CMS, 2017). This CMS report also lists Medicare fraud and abuse laws that the LNC should be aware of in reviewing billing fraud cases (CMS, 2017, p. 5). See Chapter 26 for more information on these laws.

According to CMS, Medicare fraud typically includes any of the following (CMS, 2017, p. 3):

- Knowingly submitting, or causing to be submitted, false claims or making misrepresentations of fact to obtain a federal healthcare payment for which no entitlement would otherwise exist
- Knowingly soliciting, receiving, offering, and/or paying remuneration to induce or reward referrals for items or services reimbursed by federal healthcare programs and
- Making prohibited referrals for certain designated health services

Further, federal Stark Laws prohibit self-referral and kickback activity unless a specific exception has been established (Stark Law, 42 U.S.C. 1395nn). See Chapter 26 for more information on the Stark Laws.

According to CMS, Medicare abuse "describes practices that, either directly or indirectly, result in unnecessary costs to the Medicare Program. Abuse includes any practice inconsistent with providing patients with medically necessary services meeting professionally recognized standards" and being fairly priced (CMS, 2017, p. 4).

The National Health Care Anti-Fraud Association (NHCAA) states the most common types of fraud committed by dishonest providers include (NHCAA, n.d.):

- Billing for services never rendered—either by using genuine patient information, sometimes obtained through identity theft, to fabricate entire claims or by padding claims with charges for procedures or services that did not take place.
- Billing for more expensive services or procedures than were provided or performed, commonly known as "upcoding," i.e., falsely billing for a higher-priced treatment than was actually provided (which often requires the accompanying "inflation" of the patient's diagnosis code to a more serious condition consistent with the false procedure code). Each service/procedure requires specific documentation to be valid. This has become a prime target area for auditors.
- Performing medically unnecessary services solely for generating insurance payments. This is seen very often in nerve-conduction studies, sleep studies, and other diagnostic-testing schemes.
- Misrepresenting non-covered treatments as medically necessary covered treatments for purposes of obtaining insurance payments. This is widely seen in cosmetic-surgery schemes, in which non-covered cosmetic procedures such as "nose jobs" are billed to patients' insurers as deviated-septum repairs.
- Falsifying a patient's diagnosis to justify tests, surgeries, or other procedures that are not medically necessary.
- Unbundling related charges (e.g., billing each step of a procedure as if it were a separate procedure).
- Billing a patient more than the co-pay amount for services that were prepaid or paid in full by the benefit plan under the terms of a managed care contract.
- Accepting kickbacks for patient referrals.

- Waiving patient co-pays or deductibles for medical or dental care and over-billing the insurance carrier or benefit plan. (Insurers often set the policy regarding the waiver of co-pays through their provider-contracting process; while, under Medicare, routinely waiving co-pays is prohibited and may only be waived due to "financial hardship.")

In addition, other classic examples of potentially abusive or fraudulent billing practices and suspicious activity include:

- Fraudulent cost reporting by institutional HCPs
- Excessive diagnostic procedures ordered by an HCP
- Suspicious HCP activity, such as frequently moving office locations, listing a post office address instead of a street address, frequently changing phone numbers, having high provider turnover in a practice, and repetitively referring patients to the same HCP
- Suspicious claimant (patient) activity, i.e., late reporting of an accident or injury; directly reporting to a chiropractor with a moderate or severe injury as opposed to seeking emergency treatment; and non-compliance with the prescribed treatment regimen, including gaps in treatment, failure to present for treatment, and lack of cooperation with a case manager
- An abusive pattern evidenced by the repeated use of "cut and paste" in the electronic medical record when it is obvious the information was neither reaffirmed nor new, i.e., there were no changes at all in constitutional measurements
- Excessive mark-ups from the actual cost of an item (e.g., a hospital or surgery center charges higher prices for implants and surgical devices as compared to on-line sellers, industry averages, or actual invoices paid; or a hospital charges the payer 500–1,000% more than the actual cost of an MRI)
- The performance of spinal fusions and implants at a surgery center, because there is a potential for a physician-owned distributor to supply the parts and implants—creating kickback issues, and
- The ownership by HCPs or their immediate family of an ambulatory surgery center (in such instances, the patient must be informed of this in writing)

Legal nurse consultants should be aware that errors in these areas could be as simple as insufficient knowledge and training by a new coder. Fraud is an *intentional* act to secure higher payment for services rendered. The LNC who suspects fraud must share the concerns with the appropriate authority for a comprehensive investigation.

In personal injury cases, the healthcare provider does not always submit the claim form through a clearinghouse before presenting it to the payer. This creates opportunities for fraudulent and abusive billing practices, because the HCP does not anticipate the claim form will be scrutinized by editing software, an auditor, or an LNC. The LNC analyzing these claims should validate the healthcare provider's signature and place of service for authenticity.

Verifying the place of service is important, because payment for healthcare services is affected by the "site of service," such as an ambulatory surgery center, hospital outpatient department, or an office setting. Payment to the healthcare provider for services provided in the hospital or ambulatory surgery center will be 20–60% lower than if the service had been provided in an office setting. This is referred to as "non-facility" versus "facility," because there is a transfer of overhead costs (and thus allowance and reimbursement) to the place of service (CMS, 2018a).

For more information on fraud, see Chapter 26.

Resources

What most laypersons do not understand is that clinical nurses, especially those in the hospital setting, have limited, if any, exposure to the intricacies of patient billing, insurance reimbursement, Medicare and Medicaid payments, self-pay discounts, and other billing specifics. However, bill review is an area in which the LNC can become educated by shadowing hospital coders, taking courses at a local community college, or learning through self-study programs. The use of coding reference materials and mentors (such as Certified Coders and Life Care Planners) may also provide excellent support for the LNC. The LNC should be aware of differences in billing statements among HCPs and healthcare systems and their specific billing software systems.

There are a multitude of resources available for the LNC who is conducting bill reviews. The websites of federal, state, and commercial payers are useful for both fee schedules and coverage options. The major professional organizations for specific medical specialties (e.g., American Academy of Pain Medicine) offer access to pertinent reimbursement data. The following are examples of professional health information management associations that can offer a wealth of resource material and valuable newsletters:

- Medical Group Management Association (MGMA)
- American Health Information Management Association (AHIMA)
- American Academy of Professional Coders (AAPC)
- Ambulatory Surgery Centers Association
- American Association of Nurse Life Care Planners
- Healthcare Business Management Association (HBMA)
- American Academy of Professional Coders
- American Institute of Healthcare Compliance and
- American Medical Association

While bill reviews may be done manually, the LNC may choose to take advantage of specific software programs. The ability to generate standardized reports may make auditing software an advantageous and economical tool.

Summary

The LNC's clinical knowledge and experience is critical to conducting bill reviews. This, coupled with knowledge of procedure and diagnosis codes and the ability to identify patterns and trends, prepares the LNC to recognize billing errors, such as billing for services which were not reasonable or medically necessary when compared with documentation in the medical record.

References

American Medical Association. (2013). Definition of usual, customary, and reasonable (UCR) [H-385.923]. *Policy Finder*. Retrieved from https://policysearch.ama-assn.org/policyfinder/detail/H-385.923?uri=%2FAMADoc%2FHOD.xml-0-3242.xml.

Centers for Medicare & Medicaid Service. (2017). Medicare fraud & abuse: Prevention, detection, and reporting [ICN 006827]. Retrieved from www.cms.gov/Outreach-and-Education/Medicare-Learning-Network-MLN/MLNProducts/MLN-Publications-Items/CMS1243333.html.

Centers for Medicare & Medicaid Services. (2018a). Medicare Claims Process Manual: Chapter 12: 20.4.2. Site of service payment differential. Retrieved from www.cms.gov/Regulations-and-Guidance/Regulations-and-Guidance.html.

Centers for Medicare & Medicaid Services. (2018b). National correct coding initiative edits. Retrieved from www.cms.gov/Medicare/Coding/NationalCorrectCodInitEd/index.html.

Centers for Medicare & Medicaid Services. (2018c). How to use the Medicare national correct coding initiative (NCCI) tools. Retrieved from www.cms.gov/Outreach-and-Education/Medicare-Learning-Network-MLN/MLNProducts/WebBasedTraining.html.

HealthCare.gov. (n.d.). UCR (usual, customary, and reasonable). Retrieved from www.healthcare.gov/glossary/UCR-usual-customary-and-reasonable/.

International Risk Management Institute. (n.d.). Fiduciary liability definition. Retrieved from www.irmi.com/term/insurance-definitions/fiduciary-liability.

MedicineNet. (2018). Medical definition of Hippocratic oath. Retrieved from www.medicinenet.com/script/main/art.asp?articlekey=20909.

National Health Care Anti-Fraud Association. (n.d.). The challenge of health care fraud. Retrieved from www.nhcaa.org/resources/health-care-anti-fraud-resources/the-challenge-of-health-care-fraud.aspx.

Privacy Act of 1974, 5 U.S.C. § 552a.

Stark Law, 42 U.S.C. 1395nn.

U.S. Department of Health and Human Services, & U.S. Department of Justice. (2018). Health care fraud and abuse control program annual report for fiscal year 2017. Retrieved from https://oig.hhs.gov/publications/docs/hcfac/FY2017-hcfac.pdf.

U.S. Department of Justice. (2015). Privacy Act of 1974. Retrieved from www.justice.gov/opcl/privacy-act-1974.

U.S. Department of Justice, & U.S. Department of Health and Human Services. (2015). Departments of Justice and Health and Human Services announce over $27.8 billion in returns from joint efforts to combat health care fraud. Retrieved from www.justice.gov/opa/pr/departments-justice-and-health-and-human-services-announce-over-278-billion-returns-joint.

USLegal. (2016a). Usual customary and reasonable charges (UCR charges) law and legal definition. Retrieved from https://definitions.uslegal.com/u/usual-customary-and-reasonable-charges-ucr-charges/.

USLegal. (2016b). Collateral source rule law and legal definition. Retrieved from https://definitions.uslegal.com/c/collateral-source-rule/.

Wickert, G. L. (2018, January 8). Medical billing, insurance write-offs, and the collateral source rule. Retrieved from www.mwl-law.com/medical-billing-insurance-write-offs-and-the-collateral-source-rule/.

Witherell v. Weimer, 421 NE2d 869 (1981).

Additional Reading

American Hospital Association. (n.d.). AHA resource center. Retrieved from www.aha.org/data-insights/resource-center.

Centers for Medicare & Medicaid Services. (n.d.-a). Details for title: CMS 1500. Retrieved from www.cms.gov/Medicare/CMS-Forms/CMS-Forms/CMS-Forms-.

Centers for Medicare & Medicaid Services. (n.d.-b). Details for title: CNMS 1450 (UB-04). Retrieved from www.cms.gov/Medicare/CMS-Forms/CMS-Forms/CMS-Forms-Items/CMS1196256.html.

Piper, C. (2013). 10 popular health care provider fraud schemes. Association of Certified Fraud Examiners. Retrieved from www.acfe.com/article.aspx?id=4294976280.

U.S. Department of Justice. (2018). National health care fraud takedown results in charges against 601 individuals responsible for over $2 billion in fraud losses. Retrieved from www.justice.gov/opa/pr/national-health-care-fraud-takedown-results-charges-against-601-individuals-responsible-over.

U.S. Department of Justice. (n.d.). Justice news: Health care fraud. Retrieved from www.justice.gov/news?keys=health+care+fraud&items_per_page=25.

Test Questions

1. The analysis of claims for healthcare services is best described as:
   A. A focused review of billing to discover fraud or abuse
   B. A global review of claims within the organization for common trends
   C. A systematic review of all components of a claim to determine its validity
   D. A data review to gather statistics for reporting purposes
2. A UB-04 is:
   A. A form the LNC utilizes during claim analysis to report the findings
   B. A form provided by the healthcare provider to the patient to obtain information
   C. A form mandated by the third-party insurer prior to reimbursement for services rendered by healthcare professionals
   D. A form utilized in the billing of hospital services
3. The primary reasons for conducting bill reviews include all of the following except:
   A. Identifying usual, customary, and reasonable charges
   B. Ensuring the correct use of CMS-1500 and UB-04 forms
   C. Evaluating the appropriateness of procedural codes
   D. Identifying abusive or fraudulent billing practices
4. According to CMS, Medicare fraud typically includes which of the following?
   A. Knowingly submitting false claims or making misrepresentations of fact to obtain a federal healthcare payment for which no entitlement would otherwise exist
   B. Knowingly soliciting, receiving, offering, and/or paying remuneration to induce or reward referrals for items or services reimbursed by federal healthcare programs
   C. Making prohibited referrals for certain designated health services
   D. All of the above
5. To constitute fraud, the perpetrator must be acting intentionally.
   A. True
   B. False

Answers: 1. C, 2. D, 3. B, 4. D, 5. A

Section VI

Legal Nurse Consultant Roles

Chapter 29

Legal Nurse Consultant Practice within a Law Firm

Elizabeth K. Zorn, BSN, RN, LNCC®
Julie Dickinson, MBA, BSN, RN, LNCC®

Contents

Objectives

- Identify the pros and cons of working in-house
- Describe the economics of a law firm
- Summarize the role of an in-house legal nurse consultant
- Identify the skills and attributes of successful in-house legal nurse consultants
- Summarize the professional responsibilities of in-house legal nurse consultants
- Identify the ethical and scope of practice considerations for in-house legal nurse consultants

Introduction

The role and title of a legal nurse consultant (LNC) in a law firm may vary considerably, depending upon the location and size of the firm, the nature of the work done, whether the firm does primarily defense or plaintiff work, whether the firm has worked with an LNC before, and the extent to which a particular legal community uses and values LNCs. In most areas of the country that utilize LNCs, the responsibilities of the LNC in a law firm have evolved significantly over the past 30 years. Now, most LNCs not only participate in the organization, review, and summary of medical records but also play an integral role in more complex and sophisticated activities, such as the analysis of liability in medical malpractice cases, determination of proximate cause, assessment of damages, case strategy, identification and vetting of medical and nursing experts, and trial preparation (Zorn, 2015). This chapter provides a general orientation to work in a law firm environment, including the roles of various law firm personnel. It also summarizes professional LNC responsibilities and practice issues as well as the skills and attributes necessary to function as a skilled in-house LNC.

Mission and Work of the Law Firm

The fundamental mission of any law firm is to act in the best interest of its clients in the provision of high-quality, ethical legal services. The types of claims handled by a law firm depends on whether the firm has limited its practice to a specific area of law and the particular work generated by that firm's clients. The practice of law is as diversified as the practice of nursing. Medium and large-sized firms, which may have satellite offices in different parts of the state, country, or world, offer a wide range of legal services with separate practice groups for different areas of the law. These may include litigation (trial), intellectual-property matters, real-estate transactions, environmental law, estate law, commercial law, bankruptcy law, family law, and employment-discrimination matters among others. Smaller firms and solo practitioners typically have a more narrowly focused legal practice, sometimes concentrating on a single area of law. Most firms that hire in-house legal nurse consultants either are engaged solely in medical legal litigation or have a medical legal litigation practice group.

Typically, litigation firms specialize in either plaintiff or defense work. Plaintiff medical legal litigation firms or practice groups represent injured individuals who wish to commence medical malpractice, personal injury, toxic tort, product liability, or workers' compensation claims, or who wish to file Social Security disability claims. Defense firms represent the individuals or entities being sued. For example, in medical malpractice cases, defense firms represent the defendant physician, healthcare facility, nurse, or other healthcare provider (e.g., chiropractor, dentist, podiatrist, physician assistant, nurse practitioner, etc.). Defense firms may also represent healthcare providers or facilities that are involved in one or more of the following: credentialing disputes or investigations by a state health department, social services department (for Medicaid fraud), consumer protection department, or human rights commission. In motor vehicle accident cases, the defense represents the individual allegedly at fault for the accident. In toxic tort cases, the defense represents those entities allegedly responsible for environmental contamination, illness, or property damage resulting from exposure to toxic substances. In product liability cases, defense firms represent the manufacturer, distributor, or designer of a particular product, drug, or medical device.

Most defendants in medical malpractice and personal injury actions carry liability insurance, and thus working for the defense usually means being retained by an insurance company (or group of self-insured entities) to represent the interests of the healthcare provider or other insured. Claims agents at the insurance company assign cases to one of several defense firms in the state in which the alleged incident occurred. They also monitor the work and billing of the assigned defense firm and give authority for settlement of claims. Some defense firms are retained by individuals directly and represent these parties in civil cases, criminal matters, or both.

Law Firm Personnel

Attorneys

There are distinctions in rank among attorneys depending on the size, structure, and economics of the firm. Generally, the attorneys are partners or associates. Partners are more experienced in the practice of law, typically having practiced for at least 8 to 10 years. Partners may have voting rights in the running of the firm depending on how the partnership is structured and have a monetary compensation formula different from associates. Attorneys are invited into the partnership of a firm once they have proven their worth to the firm. This generally requires demonstrating legal skill by managing cases effectively and bringing in new business. In large firms, there may be different levels of partnership, such as senior and junior partners or voting and non-voting partners. Some partners are recruited from outside the firm, known as a "lateral move," if the firm is looking for someone with a particular area of expertise. Another type of experienced attorney is "of counsel" to a firm. This typically means the attorney is associated with the firm but is not a partner. Examples are an attorney too experienced to be an associate but does not wish to become a partner, a retired attorney who still consults with the firm, and an attorney with a mutual referral relationship with a firm.

Associates are non-partner attorneys. They range in experience from recent law school graduates to attorneys with six or more years of experience on the verge of becoming partners. First-year associates generally have no prior legal experience (other than possibly summer internships at a law firm during law school, a clerkship for a judge, or prior work as a paralegal before or while attending law school). Associates are rarely in a position to bring in new business. Most new associates spend a large proportion of their time doing legal research. They also work on specific case projects under the close supervision of a more senior associate or partner. Although they may be gradually permitted to take depositions, associates generally cannot handle trials by themselves until they have gained considerable experience taking depositions, arguing motions before the Court, and assisting the senior attorneys at trial. In larger firms, there may be different levels of associates, such as senior and junior associates. New associates in larger, full-service firms (i.e., firms that handle work in many areas of the law) may rotate through the different practice groups to help determine which area of law they wish to pursue. Once they have completed their rotation, they typically become part of one particular practice group, working under the supervision of the partners and senior associates in that practice group.

With time and experience, associates on a "partner track" move up the ladder toward partnership. As the associates advance, they have more responsibility for the overall management and outcome of the cases assigned to them. They also have increasing responsibility to engage in direct client contact and to bring in new clients to the firm. The structure of some firms is such that associates may have the option to pursue a "non-partner track." Examples of this are an associate in a litigation firm who is involved in the preparation of cases for trial but does not actually try cases in the courtroom or an associate hired to primarily do legal research.

Paralegals

Paralegals, also known as legal assistants in some firms, work under the supervision of an attorney or non-attorney professional. They typically have a two- or four-year college degree and multiple job responsibilities that vary greatly depending on their level of experience and the firm and practice group in which they work. Often their responsibilities relate to the organization and review of large numbers of non-medical and medical documents, entry of case information into a computer database, preparation of draft legal pleadings for the attorney, investigative research, summarization of depositions, interview of clients or prospective clients with the attorney, preparation of exhibits and computerized presentations for trial, correspondence, and organization of files. Some firms even utilize paralegals to do legal research. Depending on the size of the firm, some paralegals may take on a supervisory role as a paralegal manager or coordinator.

Legal Nurse Consultants

The "titles" given to in-house LNCs vary greatly depending on the firm, the attorney's familiarity and experience with LNCs, the payer's (e.g., the liability insurance company's) familiarity with LNCs (in defense firms), the geographic area, and other factors. Titles may include "legal nurse consultant," "nurse paralegal," "nurse investigator," and simply "nurse consultant." Regardless of the title, LNCs are generally considered non-attorney professionals and receive commensurate respect, pay, and benefits. While some larger firms may be more hierarchical than smaller firms in their formal structure and the distinctions they make between the status of attorneys and non-attorneys, the contributions of the skilled LNC as a valued member of the legal team are increasingly recognized. Most attorneys who become accustomed to working with experienced LNCs are cognizant of the important role LNCs play in assisting the attorney to provide high-quality legal services in a cost-effective manner. The LNC has a large body of knowledge about anatomy, physiology, and medical and nursing practice that the attorney may not have. This allows the LNC to function as an educator, especially for less-experienced attorneys.

Other Firm Personnel

The additional categories of personnel in a law firm depend upon the size of the firm. Small medical legal litigation firms (fewer than 25 attorneys) typically have partners, associate attorneys, LNCs, paralegals, legal secretaries, a receptionist, and a bookkeeper/office manager. Many firms, especially small and medium-sized firms, contract with outside vendors for support services such as marketing and technology, though some firms may hire employees dedicated to those functions. Some firms also opt to have a Chief Operating Officer or Chief Financial Officer to oversee the business side of the law firm. Generally, the larger the firm, the more support persons and services are in-house. The purpose of employing ancillary staff is to support the attorneys, paralegals, and non-attorney professionals in the delivery of legal services and in the underlying business operation of the firm. Large firms (75 attorneys or more) typically have an array of additional support staff and services, such as librarians; private investigators; messengers; process servers; large-volume copying departments; audiovisual personnel; computer technicians; document coders and data entry persons; human resource, payroll, and benefits departments; continuing legal education and special-events coordinators; a business manager; marketing and public-relations staff; and office-supply and kitchen staff. In addition to LNCs, large firms may also have other non-attorney professionals, such as certified public accountants and environmental engineers to support their varied practice groups.

Firm Structure

Hierarchy

As in all businesses, rank distinctions among the employees and partners of a firm exist and are generally related to title, tenure, compensation and benefits package, productivity, and responsibilities within the firm. In a well-functioning and well-managed law firm, all personnel understand the importance of teamwork and have a common goal of providing quality legal services to their clients. This is most likely to occur in firms that value the role that each person plays in the delivery of client services.

Task Delegation

While task delegation in a law firm varies with the size and structure of the firm, most firms have a hierarchical order of task delegation. Generally, partners delegate tasks to any (non-partner) employee of the firm. Partners who are the chairperson of a practice group may even delegate responsibilities to another partner in that practice group. Large firms are also likely to have committees that delegate tasks to all categories of personnel in the firm.

Typically, partners or senior associates delegate tasks to those people with whom they directly work. For a given case, this would likely include a junior associate, paralegal, LNC, and legal secretary. Associates delegate work to paralegals, legal secretaries, and LNCs. Legal nurse consultants delegate work to paralegals and legal secretaries. Paralegals delegate tasks to legal secretaries. Paralegals and legal secretaries typically delegate tasks to in-house or outside ancillary support personnel, although anyone else higher in the hierarchy could also do this if appropriate. An effective partner or senior associate responsible for a given case will periodically confer with the team working on the case to make sure that assigned tasks are getting done in a proper and timely manner.

Although task delegation usually follows a predictable order, the nature of work in most law firms is such that during intensely busy times or when an important deadline is looming, roles overlap, the usual hierarchy is temporarily suspended, and everyone on the team does whatever they can to complete the job.

It is not uncommon to see overlap of tasks between the LNC and a paralegal. For example, in some firms, the paralegals organize, review, and summarize the medical records in simple personal injury cases, while the LNCs focus on the medical malpractice and other complex personal injury cases (Zorn, 2015). Given that the roles of the paralegal and the LNC vary considerably among firms, it very important that members of the litigation team understand the tasks for which they are individually responsible. The importance of this cannot be overstated. Failure to define each person's role on the litigation team can lead to tasks being done twice, which wastes valuable time as the case moves through the legal system. The alternative (an important task not being completed in a timely manner or not being done at all) can lead to unfavorable court rulings (including case dismissal) or sanctions. Thus, some firms develop "protocols" which set forth who is responsible for the many tasks that must be done throughout the life of a case.

Law Firm Management

The management of a law firm is a function of the partnership, which votes on all significant personnel and operational decisions at regular partnership meetings. Most firms appoint a managing partner to handle the many administrative tasks that must be dealt with day-to-day. Typically, the managing partner will set the agenda for the partner meetings and make administrative decisions that require no formal vote by the partnership. In smaller firms, the managing partner may also tend to personnel and financial matters. Larger firms may hire a business manager to coordinate the financial operation of the firm. Typically, this person's compensation package is tied to the financial success of the firm during a given year. In addition, larger firms typically have a Human Resources Department that handles benefits and personnel issues. It is very common for firms of all sizes to outsource their payroll activities.

Law Firm Culture

Like most business cultures, law firm culture can vary tremendously from firm to firm. Generally, large established firms are more formal, structured, and hierarchical. In these firms, decisions may take a long time due to the need to pass through several layers of approval. The larger the firm, the more likely it is that politics plays a role in the decision-making process. Within a large firm, different practice groups may have their own distinct cultures. In smaller firms, the relationships among partners and employees may be more informal. For example, it is not unusual for all employees in a small firm to have direct access to the managing partner. Medium-sized firms may fit anywhere along this continuum. As in other sectors of the business world, there has been a trend toward less-formal attire in most law firms.

The best way for prospective LNCs to glean the culture of a particular firm or practice group is to speak with past or current employees of that firm and practice group. Information about the culture and politics of a firm can also be obtained through the interview process directly (by inquiry) and indirectly (by observation). Typically, a prospective LNC interviews with one or more partners, associates, and LNCs already employed at the firm. Of particular interest to the prospective LNC is the extent to which the LNC role and work are valued by the partners, associates, and clients. This is evident in the responsibilities and tasks assigned to the firm's LNCs and whether the LNCs have adequate secretarial support, especially in firms in which LNCs have fairly heavy caseloads. Another indication is whether the firm profiles its LNCs on the firm's website and letterhead. Legal nurse consultants employed at the firm are the best source for information about the firm's regard for the LNC role.

Legal nurse consultants hired by firms with other LNCs derive great benefit from the orientation and ongoing mentoring from other LNCs familiar with the expectations at that firm. For LNCs applying for the first LNC position at a firm, developing a new role in the firm can be exciting and very rewarding. It can also be challenging, especially if the LNC has no experience in the legal field and if the attorneys have not worked with an LNC before. Networking with other nurses who work at law firms is especially important in this situation.

Pros and Cons of Working In-House

In-house legal nurse consulting practice is associated with both advantages and challenges. The in-house LNC benefits from frequent contact with the attorneys in the firm. Regular discussions between the LNC and the attorneys regarding the procedural status of cases, strategy, and the applicable legal standards allow the LNC to gradually develop the skills and knowledge necessary to analyze medical issues in the context of legal standards. If the firm has more than one LNC on staff, cases can be distributed more flexibly to prevent a single LNC from being overburdened.

The in-house LNC benefits from a steady income, with job security dependent upon the LNC's performance and the firm's ability to maintain an adequate medical-legal caseload. Other advantages of working in-house include health and disability insurance, retirement savings (typically with employer contributions), paid time off, and a regular work schedule with weekends and holidays off. The office setting also allows interaction and camaraderie with colleagues. Successful in-house LNCs may also receive bonuses based on performance or productivity measures.

Working in-house also means less flexibility with the LNC's work hours and schedule, as most firm employees work during standard business hours Monday through Friday. While some firms may allow LNCs to work remotely, most require their employees to work from the office. Relative to working as an independent consultant, in-house LNCs have less variety in the types of cases on which they work and in the attorneys with whom they work. In-house LNCs are also typically salaried employees (not hourly), and working beyond the standard 40-hour workweek can be expected, depending on the workload and trial schedule.

Trends in Law Firm Practice

Digital Practice

Technology has affected almost every aspect of practice in a law firm and is changing the way firms conduct business. From pleadings and discovery to depositions and trial, technology has transformed the way cases are handled. The use of technology is becoming necessary as clients, experts, the court, and other law firms trend towards paperless practice. Many courts are now only accepting electronic filing ("e-filing") of documents such as pleadings and motions and are using electronic means to provide court notices and rulings to attorneys. They are also encouraging law firms to accept electronic discovery, meaning the law firm agrees to receive case documents via email or other electronic means rather than by paper copy.

Most law firms have large-capacity computer servers on which electronic case data is stored. For example, a defense firm may have a drive on the server for active cases. That drive houses folders for every insurance company and other client for whom the firm does business. The insurance company's folder stores template documents and other information specific for that company, such as template letters, templates for case status reports, reporting guidelines, contact information, contracts, billing guidelines, etc. Within a particular insurance company's folder are subfolders for each individual case, such as *Smith v. Baker* and *Jones v. Rogers*. Each case folder has subfolders for varying types of documents, such as correspondence, pleadings, discovery, depositions, medical records, trial, etc. In some firms, these servers or drives can be "shared," allowing authorized, external users (such as the defendant's insurance company) to access the contents contained therein. This is especially helpful in cases with a large volume of medical records, staffing records, facility licensing/administrative records, etc.

Many law firms scan all hard copy documents received and save the electronic copy to the appropriate case folder. Any hard copy letters or documents sent by the firm will also be scanned and saved electronically. Firms that are paperless also save relevant emails to the electronic file.

Alternatively, there are numerous case management software programs available to firms. These programs integrate various aspects of a case (such as client communication, workflow, documents, reports, costs, billing, etc.) to streamline and coordinate processes, thereby increasing efficiency and productivity.

The digital age is also changing the way medical records are handled by law firms. Rather than managing hundreds, sometimes thousands, of pages of paper medical records, law firms are increasingly using technology to store, organize, review, analyze, and send medical records. Medical records not received electronically are scanned, converted to searchable text (called optical character recognition, or "OCR"), and saved to the case file. Most radiographs are now digital, and any older film x-rays can be converted to digital format by x-ray companies. Using software programs for documents in portable document format (PDF), records can be organized, paginated, highlighted, notated, bookmarked, searched, hyperlinked to internal pages and external documents or websites, added to as more records are received, etc. There are software programs that can be used to prepare medical chronologies. To maintain confidentiality and comply with the Health Insurance Portability and Accountability Act (HIPAA), digital medical records can be sent for discovery compliance, expert review, the client's review, etc. through technology such as secure email, encryption (password-protection), secure file sharing using software, or a proprietary secure file transfer program.

Deposition transcripts are now commonly received in electronic format, allowing the reader to easily search the transcript, add excerpts to the case management software program, bookmark testimony of interest, and hyperlink to referenced exhibits.

Technology is also impacting trials. Nearly gone are the days of large poster board exhibits and overhead projectors. Attorneys are now using projectors or large monitors to display digital exhibits. Modern day courtrooms have jury boxes in which each juror has an individual monitor to view these digital exhibits. Software programs can be used to aid the legal team in organizing and presenting their case. Using slideshows to highlight key closing arguments is another example of how technology has impacted the practice of law.

Economic Considerations

Law firm practice has also been affected by economic factors, which vary by state and region and by the laws in that jurisdiction. For example, some states have placed limits (or "caps") on the amount recoverable for non-economic damages (i.e., for pain and suffering), which has led some plaintiff firms to move away from handling medical malpractice cases. Some liability insurance companies are requiring defense firms to accept "flat fees" for certain legal services, instead of the traditional "per hour" fees. For example, a defense attorney who traditionally was compensated by an insurance company for each hour spent trying a case may now be required to accept a flat fee for the entire trial. This flat fee is often less than what the attorney would have made if the compensation was by the hour. The trade-off for accepting a flat fee payment structure is often the guarantee that the insurance company will use this attorney for many cases in that jurisdiction (so long as they remain satisfied with the quality of legal services). The economy is also impacting reimbursement for the defense of cases as more and more insurance companies are cutting back on and becoming stricter about expenses and charges for which they will compensate or reimburse a firm.

Economics of the Law Firm

A reasonable understanding of the economics of a firm is vital to any understanding of firm productivity measures. A law firm is a for-profit enterprise that brings in gross annual revenue, out of which overhead expenses, capital improvement expenses, marketing expenses, and salaries and benefits are paid. The remaining profits are distributed among the partners according to the partnership agreement. The salaries, bonuses, benefits, and hourly rates of employees are determined by the partnership based upon position in the firm, longevity, and performance. Partners evaluate associate attorneys. Partners and associate attorneys evaluate LNCs with whom they work. All attorneys and non-attorney professionals (e.g., LNCs) evaluate their staff, including legal secretaries and paralegals.

The economics of a law firm vary with its size and whether it is primarily a defense firm or plaintiff firm. Large firms have more complicated economic structures than small firms. Defense firms are usually paid on an hourly basis or sometimes have a flat-fee arrangement for certain legal work. Plaintiff firms usually generate income on a contingency-fee basis, which means they receive a percentage of a plaintiff's award when they settle a case or obtain a favorable jury verdict. The percentage of the award to which the firm is entitled varies by state and type of case. However, cases lost or dismissed generate no revenue for a plaintiff firm.

The economic success of all firms depends upon satisfying and retaining existing clients, as well as bringing in new clients through various practice development activities and advertising. Many insurance carriers and self-insured entities utilize several defense firms to handle their litigation claims. Thus, defense firms may compete for a proportion of business from a particular client. Many firms engage in practice development, such as networking and advertising activities, to bring in new business. For most firms, a certain percentage of their business comes from referral-based sources, such as other attorneys and existing clients. The ability to bring new clients into the firm is an important factor for an associate to be considered for partnership. Networking activities that may bring in new firm business include speaking engagements at continuing legal education seminars, participation in state and local Bar Association committees, and serving on not-for-profit boards of directors. Attorneys with the ability to bring in new profitable business consistently, often called "rainmakers," are very valuable to a firm.

The LNC can contribute to the economic success of a firm by providing the attorneys with high-quality work products and educating them about the medical issues in their cases. The LNC can enhance client satisfaction by maintaining regular contact with them to provide updates about the status and progress of their cases. This is especially true in plaintiff firms, where LNCs typically have a great deal of contact with clients. The LNC can also assist the attorney to nurture and satisfy relationships with referring attorneys by keeping them updated on the status of cases they refer to the firm. The LNC can also engage in marketing activities with the attorneys, such as attending or co-presenting at attorney or liability insurance seminars. Finally, the LNC can bring new business into the firm directly by networking with other LNCs and attorneys and joining professional groups and committees in the legal community.

Fees and Costs in Litigation

Legal fees cover the time and expertise of the attorneys and non-attorney professionals, the support staff's time, and the overhead of the firm. They do not cover costs or disbursements, which are out-of-pocket expenses that the firm incurs in the prosecution or defense of a case. Examples of disbursements are expert fees, copying charges, court-reporter and transcript charges related to depositions, and travel expenses. Ultimately, payment of disbursements is the responsibility of the client, whether a case is won or lost, although many plaintiff firms write off disbursements as a business expense if the case is lost. Most plaintiff firms advance payment of disbursements until the conclusion of a case. On the defense side, disbursements are typically either forwarded upon receipt to the client for payment or, if the expense is below a certain dollar amount, the firm may pay the bill and obtain reimbursement from the client. Disbursements in personal injury matters, especially medical malpractice claims, can be sizable. Thus, plaintiff attorneys and their LNCs must consider whether the potential economic recovery substantially outweighs the likely cost of prosecuting the claim.

Fees and Productivity Measurements in Defense Firms

Defense firms are paid regardless of case outcome. Most defense firms bill their clients by the hour for all timekeepers' time spent on a case. Timekeepers are the attorneys, LNCs, and paralegals, with few exceptions, who maintain a daily log of the amount of time they spend working on each case. Timekeepers generate billable hours that translate into firm revenue. Secretaries, copy clerks, and other support personnel do not generate billable-hour revenue for the firm and thus are not considered timekeepers. The billing rate of a timekeeper may vary from client to client or among different types of cases or different geographical locations for the same client. For example, large established firms in metropolitan areas generally command higher attorney billing rates than their counterparts in smaller cities or outlying areas. Some clients negotiate flat-fee arrangements for a portion of their legal services. For example, an insurance carrier might pay a set fee in malpractice cases for time spent from inception of the case through the conclusion of depositions.

Timekeeping by all billable personnel is documented on a daily time sheet, customarily in blocks of a tenth of an hour (0.1 or 6-minute increments) or sometimes a quarter of an hour (0.25 or 15-minute increments). Each time entry also includes the date, matter number, task, and explanation for each task. The particular requirements for timekeeping records, including how much time must be accounted for each day, vary from firm to firm. In addition, each client may have specific requirements regarding the descriptive nature of time sheet entries. Whereas historically time sheets were handwritten, the time entries and resulting client bills are now most often computer-generated using software programs which incorporate standardized task-based codes such as those promulgated by the American Bar Association (ABA). Some firms are moving towards using automated activity entry software to capture a timekeeper's computer and phone activity and to assist the timekeeper with capturing all billable work. Time sheets provide a basis for measuring the productivity of the timekeeper. Typically, there are certain minimum monthly or annual billable-hour expectations for each timekeeper. If the firm has an annual bonus program, the bonus may, in part, reflect billable hours over the minimum requirement. Non-billable hours are also accounted for each day. Non-billable time might include time spent attending educational seminars, participating in department meetings, or organizing medical-research or expert files.

Defense firm clients often scrutinize bills for legal services carefully and may dispute certain entries or refuse payment for others. For example, the client may feel that a billed task was administrative and should have been performed by ancillary personnel. Or the client may dispute the time billed for a particular project or task. Some clients impose billing guidelines on firms that may restrict the types of LNC projects for which they are willing to pay. It is critical that all timekeepers, including LNCs, generate accurate time sheets that reflect the exact nature of the work done and the actual time spent. If allowed, being more descriptive in time entries may help explain why a particular task took as long as it did or why it required professional, not administrative, staff. Typically, a firm has an assigned billing attorney for each client who reviews the bills for content and accuracy before they are sent to the client. The billing attorney knows the specific billing requirements of a particular client and should relay this information to all timekeepers. The billing attorney also has the authority to "write off" time before the bill is sent to the client or to reduce billable time if a dispute ensues after the client receives the bill. Unfortunately, time written off translates into lost revenue for the firm. A firm that utilizes time efficiently to generate high-quality services will ensure profits and future business from clients.

Most defense firm clients are insurance companies, self-insured hospitals, or other self-insured entities. Instead of working with one firm exclusively, each client typically has an approved list of several defense firms with which it works. This allows the client to utilize the expertise of a particular attorney for a case, manage conflicts that may arise (e.g., between co-defendants), and reap the financial benefits of competition among defense firms. Like any consumers, defense clients want high-quality service at reasonable rates.

Most clients recognize the value of having LNCs as an integral part of the legal team. Legal nurse consultants possess a body of medical knowledge based upon their education and clinical experience. They also have the ability to research medical issues and communicate effectively with medical experts. In many firms, LNCs perform work formerly done by attorneys at higher rates. This is cost-effective for the client and allows the attorney more time to engage in activities that only attorneys can conduct. Timelines, medical literature research, and other work product generated by the LNC enhance the attorney's knowledge and organization of the medical issues in a case. This assists the attorney in providing high-quality legal work for the client, increasing the chances for a favorable outcome for the client.

Fees and Productivity Measurements in Plaintiff Firms

Most plaintiff personal injury firms take cases on a contingency-fee basis (i.e., the firm is entitled to a percentage of any verdict or settlement). The percentage varies from state to state and sometimes with type of case. Cases against the federal government have a predetermined percentage that the plaintiff attorney can charge. In New York, state statute requires a sliding-scale contingency fee in medical malpractice cases that reduces the percentage of the attorney fee initially (from the typical 40% to 30%) and again in incremental amounts for all awards in excess of $250,000 (Contingent fees for attorneys in claims or actions for medical, dental or podiatric malpractice, 2017). For example, if a New York medical malpractice case settles for $1 million, the attorney gets 30% of the first $250,000 ($75,000), 25% of the next $250,000 ($65,500), 20% of the next $500,000 ($100,000), 15% of the next $250,000 ($0), and 10% of everything above $1,250,000 ($0) for a total fee of $240,500. In addition, plaintiff firms are also entitled to recover any disbursements not already paid by the client.

Many firms deduct these costs from the total award and then calculate their percentage on the remaining amount. Other firms deduct their fee from the total award and then deduct their costs. For example, in an auto case that settled for $100,000, the plaintiff attorney has a contingency agreement with the client for 40% and has spent $15,000 in out-of-pocket costs. $100,000 minus $40,000 (the attorney fee) minus $15,000 leaves the client with $45,000. If costs are first deducted, $100,000 minus $15,000 leaves $85,000, minus 40% equals $34,000 for the attorney's fee, leaving the client with $51,000. Some cases involve a split-fee arrangement with the referring attorney. While this reduces the fee of the attorney handling the case, it does not affect the amount of money that the client collects. The client collects the remaining amount of the award, assuming there are no liens on the recovery, such as Medicare, Medicaid, Workers Compensation, or from self-funded Employee Retirement Income Security Act plans. If a lien is involved, the attorney must consider this in any settlement negotiations. The attorney may be able to negotiate a reduction in the lien, especially if settlement of a case is economically beneficial to the lienholder.

Unlike defense firms that are paid for their time whether they win or lose a case, plaintiff firms doing contingency work generate revenue only when they settle a case or obtain a favorable jury verdict. The revenue generated from these cases depends upon the amount of the award and the costs associated with prosecuting the case. Keys to profitability in a plaintiff firm include maintaining continual sources of new clients, effectively screening cases, properly managing costs, and moving cases toward resolution in an effective and timely manner. A more detailed discussion of effective plaintiff LNC performance in the context of these four factors follows this section.

While many plaintiff firms do not utilize timekeeping records to track productivity of attorneys, LNCs, and paralegals, plaintiff firms that now use computerized case management software are increasingly doing so. Plaintiff firms also measure productivity in several other ways. Assessment of partner productivity and related compensation is complex and varies greatly among firms. Typically, partner compensation is based upon preset percentages or agreed-upon criteria (including cases resolved and administrative responsibilities) for allocation of profits as defined in the partnership agreement. Productivity of associate attorneys is based upon criteria set by the partners and is reflected in the associate's annual performance evaluation. Criteria may include number of resolved cases that year, new cases brought into the firm, quality of written work, and perceived effort. Associate salaries and bonuses are determined by the partners and are typically based upon seniority and performance. Likewise, LNC productivity is usually measured by the extent to which the associates and partners value the contribution of the LNC, as reflected in annual performance evaluations. In some firms, LNCs may also be asked to maintain an assignment or task list in which the LNC records assignments, deadlines for completing the assignment, and time spent on each project. In addition to tracking individual LNC productivity, such an assignment list can be utilized by the managing partner to determine whether LNC time is being appropriately and fairly shared among attorneys and for those cases that most merit the assistance of an LNC. In addition, timekeeping records kept in a plaintiff practice may be used to justify the contingency fees to the court when a settlement or verdict is awarded to a minor or incapacitated individual, who cannot act on their own behalf. The court is responsible for protecting the interests of these vulnerable persons and thus may review the timekeeping records for reasonableness.

As mentioned above, profitability in plaintiff firms is determined by four factors: client base, case screening, cost containment, and timely resolution of cases.

Client Base

Plaintiff firms depend upon the continual referral of new cases. Legal nurse consultants who engage in firm practice development (discussed later in this chapter) and who nurture relationships with referral sources (e.g., existing clients and referring attorneys) may generate case referrals to their firms.

Case Screening

Effective screening of potential cases is critical to the profitability of a plaintiff firm and is discussed later in this chapter. Many plaintiff attorneys rely on the knowledge, research, and advice of their LNCs when screening cases involving medical issues, especially medical malpractice cases. While ultimately it is the attorney's decision whether to accept or reject a case for further investigation, the in-house LNC may be in the best position to help identify claims that are non-meritorious or economically non-viable. An effective LNC assists the attorney to reject non-viable cases expeditiously. Discovering a major obstacle or a series of small ones at the outset results in less time spent on unprofitable cases. The productive LNC in the contingency fee setting recognizes how much information must be obtained to make an initial assessment of the likely merits of a case.

Cost Containment

Disbursements are associated with virtually all personal injury claims. Typical costs include those for copies of medical records, deposition transcripts, private investigator fees, and expert fees. These costs are especially high in medical malpractice cases, which may require the services of several experts and multiple depositions. A profitable plaintiff firm must contain costs in proportion to the anticipated economic recovery; otherwise, expenses will consume a disproportionate share of the client's recovery and the attorney's fee. The LNC can assist the attorney to achieve this balance by first providing a thorough assessment of the client's damages, including physical or emotional pain and suffering, functional limitations, lost income, and loss of services related to derivative claims. This allows the attorney to determine the likely settlement and verdict range in the venue for each case, assuming liability can be established. Second, the LNC can assist the attorney in deciding whether a particular expense is necessary to litigate the case properly, whether it is reasonable, given the expenses already incurred, and whether the timing of a particular expense is appropriate. For example, if a particular case moves toward settlement negotiations at the conclusion of depositions, it may be prudent to cease incurring additional costs unless settlement talks fail. Ultimately, case management decisions rest with the attorney. However, a knowledgeable LNC can assist the attorney to make prudent economic decisions that benefit both the firm and its clients.

Timely Resolution of Cases

Firms that accept cases on a contingency-fee basis do not generate revenue from those cases unless and until they negotiate a settlement or achieve a favorable jury verdict. Gross annual firm revenue is directly related to the number and value of cases successfully resolved that year. Productive LNCs accept responsibility for assisting the attorneys to move their cases toward resolution at each phase of litigation. This means providing the attorneys with timely work products at key points of the litigation process and trying to stay one step ahead of the attorneys, so they always have the information they need to move the case to the next phase of litigation. This may involve maintaining a chart that tracks the progress of an attorney's cases and setting up regular conference times with the attorney to review the status of all the attorney's cases and discuss cases that need attention in more detail, including the tasks to be done, who will be responsible for completing each task, and an agreed-upon time frame for completing each task.

Market Expectations for LNC Salaries and Benefits

Legal nurse consultant salary and benefits packages differ greatly with the size and location of the firm, whether it is a defense or plaintiff firm, and the extent to which the partnership values the LNC role. Prior to considering or interviewing for an in-house position, the prospective LNC should network with in-house LNCs in the area to get a feel for local benefits and salary packages (though they may vary significantly from firm to firm, even in the same region). Most in-house LNCs are salaried employees, and firms that have worked with skilled LNCs typically offer salaries higher than firms hiring an LNC for the first time. Full-time LNCs often work more than

40 hours per week but usually have the flexibility to work evenings, weekends, or at home and to take time off during the week when necessary. Many successful plaintiff and defense firms realize that a skilled LNC can perform analytical work previously done by associates and thus are willing to offer a salary in the range of an associate attorney.

The American Association of Legal Nurse Consultants (AALNC) conducted a compensation survey in 2011 (AALNC, 2011). A total of 505 LNCs completed the survey, of which 23.5% indicated they worked in a law firm. Of the 94 participants who indicated working full-time as an LNC for a law firm, 4.3% reported an annual salary between $40,001 and $50,000, 37.2% between $50,001 and $70,000, 38.3% between $70,001 and $90,000, and 20.2% over $90,000.

Some firms have bonus programs. A bonus is a portion of the firm's profits awarded to some or all employees, typically on a quarterly or annual basis. Calculation of bonus awards varies greatly from firm to firm. Typically, bonuses are utilized to reward superior performance or productivity and may be, for example, a percentage of profit generated from one's billed hours (defense). However, they may also be awarded solely based on seniority, be a percentage of salary, or be equal across all categories of employees.

Most salaried LNCs receive paid vacation and sick time. Additional benefits may include health and dental insurance, life insurance, short and long-term disability insurance, retirement plans, profit sharing, and flexible compensation plans. Some firms also pay the LNC's costs for state RN licensure renewals, AALNC national and local chapter dues, continuing legal or nursing education seminars, and membership in nursing organizations and bar associations.

Prior to accepting an offer for an in-house position, the prospective LNC should obtain detailed information about the firm's LNC salary, billing requirements, benefits, and bonus program. It is also important to request a job description and an overview of the process for evaluating performance and productivity, especially if this impacts compensation. See Appendices A and B for examples of in-house plaintiff and defense LNC job descriptions. Note that actual responsibilities may differ by firm. Some tasks may be delegated, as appropriate, to paralegals and other support staff.

The Role of an In-House LNC

The role of the in-house LNC has evolved over the years to encompass more complex responsibilities, such as analyzing liability, causation, and damages in medical malpractice cases and participating in case strategy discussions (Zorn, 2015). The exact role and responsibilities of an in-house LNC depend on many factors, including the firm's prior experience with LNCs; the locality, culture, and size of the firm; and the nature of the firm's work. While there are a few differences, the roles of LNCs do not vary greatly between plaintiff and defense firms. The biggest difference is the involvement of in-house plaintiff LNCs in the initial screening of medical malpractice cases. This is a very important undertaking that, as discussed above, directly affects the economic success of a plaintiff firm. This section discusses the plaintiff LNC's role in the screening and investigation of potential cases, followed by an examination of the role performed by both plaintiff and defense in-house LNCs once a case is in suit.

Initial Screening and Investigation

Legal nurse consultants at plaintiff firms are usually very involved in the initial screening and investigation of potential medical malpractice cases. The screening process begins when a client or the client's representative (e.g., family member, referring attorney, or friend) contacts the firm about a potential case. Typically, a paralegal or LNC obtains the initial intake information on the phone and records it on an intake sheet. The LNC then consults with an attorney about the disposition of the potential claim. The goal at this phase of the screening process is to obtain enough information to either accept the case for preliminary investigation or reject it right away due to lack of merit, conflicts of interest, expired or impending statute of limitations, insufficient damages, or facts that make prevailing on liability unlikely. It is common for plaintiff firms to reject many more cases than they accept. For cases that are rejected, the LNC may draft a "reject" letter for the attorney's signature.

If the attorney pursues an investigation of a potential claim, the LNC and the attorney typically meet with the client or representative in-person to gather more in-depth information about the facts of the case and the nature of the alleged injuries, including current medical status and prognosis. It is also important to obtain a complete medical history, a list of all prior and current healthcare providers and hospitalizations, and information about potential liens (e.g., Medicare). In death cases, it is important to inquire whether an autopsy was done. It is also helpful to request the client and family members to prepare a written narrative of their recollection of key events, because, over time, memories become less clear. Occasionally, clients or their family members may already have prepared a journal of events as they unfolded or a diary related to the client's injuries and functional limitations.

The next step in the investigation of a potential medical malpractice claim is to request the relevant medical records. The LNC identifies all records needed for the managing attorney and medical/nursing expert(s) to render an opinion about the merits of the case. Typically, the LNC's legal secretary, a medical records coordinator, or a paralegal sends out correspondence requesting the medical records that have been identified by the LNC. It is important to have a tickler system (a computerized reminder system) in place to ensure records are received in a timely manner.

Once all the medical records are received, the LNC bookmarks the electronic medical records (or organizes any hard copies) and reviews them to form an initial impression about the merits of the case. Due to the LNC's nursing background, the LNC is in a unique position to readily extract the relevant information contained in the medical records to analyze liability, proximate cause, and damages. Based on this analysis, the LNC may recommend not proceeding further with the case if the claim likely lacks merit or if the potential economic recovery does not justify the great time and expense involved in pursuing a medical malpractice claim. In this situation, the LNC may prepare a brief summary of the rationale for rejecting the case to use when conferring with the attorney. The attorney decides whether to accept the LNC's recommendation to reject the case or to move forward with an expert review.

If the case appears to have merit, the LNC may prepare a summary of the relevant documentation in the medical records. The format of the summary depends upon the nature of the case. It may be a narrative in paragraph form, a medical chronology of the sequence of events, or a multicolumn chart with very detailed information from a hospitalization. In addition to preparing a summary of the medical documentation, the LNC conducts a preliminary medical literature review, focusing on the medical conditions, signs and symptoms, and treatment options as they relate to the applicable standard-of-care issues relevant to the case. The goal of this research, in addition to learning about the medical issues, is to develop an informed opinion regarding the likelihood that a standard of care expert review would be favorable. The LNC also prepares a list of the potential defendants for review with the attorney.

Once these analyses are complete, the LNC may present the findings verbally or in writing to the assigned attorney. This includes an analysis of the strengths and weaknesses of the case;

an evaluation of the plaintiff's credibility, contributory negligence, and failure to mitigate damages; and an assessment of how a jury would likely perceive the plaintiff. It also includes an evaluation of whether the potential award for the plaintiff's injuries meets the firm's damage threshold, which is the firm's minimum requirement for potential economic recovery. Based on an assessment of pain and suffering, functional limitations, economic loss, and research of verdicts in the same or nearby venues for cases with the same or similar issues, a plaintiff firm identifies the verdict potential for the case being screened. If it is below the firm's damage threshold, the attorney will likely reject the case, as the legal fees would not adequately cover the considerable expense of adjudicating the case. Armed with a thorough workup by the LNC, the attorney either rejects the case at this point or sends it out for review by the appropriate medical/nursing expert(s).

The expert review is the last phase in screening potential medical malpractice cases. If the attorney proceeds with one or more expert reviews, the LNC plays an important role in this phase of the investigation by identifying the appropriate specialty and individual healthcare provider (e.g., physician, nurse, oral surgeon, etc.) to review the case. This includes vetting potential experts regarding any conflicts of interest and their clinical credentials, certifications, and practice. The LNC also consults with the attorney about whether more than one expert is necessary to address the liability and causation issues.

Once the LNC identifies a qualified expert who will review the case, the LNC prepares a package of materials for the expert's review. This includes an organized hard copy or bookmarked, "clean" digital copy of the medical records (i.e., it is devoid of any notes or highlighting from the LNC's or attorney's review of the electronic records); a summary of the facts as claimed by the plaintiff; photographs, radiology images, or other items if applicable; and generally a retainer check. A list of questions or issues for the expert to consider may be included in the letter. Sometimes, the attorney may send the LNC's medical chronology or timeline to the expert. The medical chronology or timeline sent to the expert should contain only excerpts from the medical records (and no commentary or opinions by the LNC), as any material sent to the expert is likely discoverable by the opposing side. Any such chronology should only be used as a reference guide for the expert, who must always review the relevant medical records in their entirety prior to forming opinions. The LNC's analysis memo is never sent to a potential expert, as it would be discoverable and contains topics to be explored with an expert, not all of which are issues in the case after it is filed. Attention to a detailed, organized package for the expert cannot be overemphasized. This facilitates a thorough review by the expert, whose primary job is to provide the attorney and LNC with an objective opinion about the merits of the case regarding one or more of the following: liability, causation, or damages. The expert's time is very costly and should not be spent organizing medical records. For more detailed information about identifying, vetting, and working with experts, see Chapter 36.

Once the expert's review is completed, the attorney and LNC confer with the expert about the merits of the case, including a detailed discussion about all aspects of the case and the basis for the expert's opinions. If the expert feels the case is meritorious, it is essential that the expert has a sound basis for conclusions that will hold up under intense cross-examination. Thus, the attorney and LNC should effectively "cross-examine" the expert about the basis for the expert's opinions. Using the analysis memo, the effective LNC discusses the medical issues in detail with the expert, serves as a liaison between the expert and the attorney, and ensures the expert has addressed all areas of concern. Based on the expert review, the case will either be rejected or pursued. Sometimes, the expert may recommend a review by an additional expert if some issues are not within the expert's area of expertise.

When filing a medical malpractice claim, most states require an affidavit of merit or expert opinion letter be affixed to the Complaint as proof that an expert has deemed the case is meritorious. The required content of the opinion letter is defined by the state's statutes, but generally, it states that, based on a review of the relevant medical records, a healthcare provider with similar education, training, and experience to the defendant has a good faith belief that the defendant violated the standard of care. The plaintiff LNC may draft this letter based on the discussion with the expert. While the attorney is ultimately responsible for ensuring all required content is covered in the opinion letter, the effective LNC is familiar with the statutory requirements and includes this content in the draft.

Before putting a meritorious case into suit, the attorney may approach the defendant's liability insurance carrier to solicit interest in discussing settlement prior to suit. If so, the LNC may draft a demand letter for the attorney, summarizing the facts and the liability, causation, and damages issues. Alternatively, the attorney may prepare the letter using the LNC's work.

The LNC at a plaintiff firm plays a prominent role in the overall management of medical malpractice cases under investigation. The goal in such cases is to conduct a thorough investigation in a timely manner well before the statute of limitations expires. This means the LNC must have a system for tracking cases under investigation to ensure that progress is made towards the timely disposition of each case, including regular conferences with the assigned attorney. The LNC may also have frequent contact with the client to provide updates about the progress of the case investigation.

Pleadings and Discovery

Once a plaintiff attorney commences a medical malpractice claim by the filing and serving of a summons and complaint, the defendant's liability insurance carrier assigns a defense firm to represent the interests of their insured. Depending upon the number of defendants, more than one defense firm may be involved in a case. The in-house defense LNC usually becomes involved as soon as the case is assigned to the firm. Following the exchange of legal pleadings and initial discovery demands in medical malpractice cases, the role of the LNC in both plaintiff and defense firms is much the same.

Both plaintiff and defense LNCs may assist attorneys with portions of the initial legal pleadings and discovery demands that are exchanged. For example, defense LNCs may draft the Answer and prepare interrogatories (or, in some states, a demand for a bill of particulars) and requests for production. The plaintiff LNC may draft answers to the interrogatories (or bill of particulars) that inquire about specific claims of negligence and injuries resulting from the alleged malpractice. For more information about the discovery process, see Chapter 5.

The plaintiff's interrogatory responses should contain a list of pertinent prior and current healthcare providers, and the plaintiff's responses to the defendant's requests for production should contain medical records or executed HIPAA-compliant authorizations. Upon receipt of these, the defense LNC goes through the same process conducted by a plaintiff LNC investigating a potential claim. The defense LNC requests, organizes or bookmarks, and summarizes the medical records; performs preliminary research about the pertinent medical conditions and applicable standard of care; and confers with the attorney about the relevant medical issues. The defense LNC also researches, vets, and proposes potential experts to the attorney. Because the defendant's liability insurance company pays the expenses to defend a claim, the company typically must approve the expert and the expert's fees before retention by defense counsel. Once approved, the defense LNC prepares an organized package of materials for the expert's review and then with the attorney, confers with the expert about the review and findings. The defendant's liability insurance company receives periodic updates on the case as it develops, so the defense LNC may prepare a summary of the expert's opinions for inclusion in the case status report to the insurance company. Both plaintiff and defense LNCs may draft their party's expert witness disclosure that summarizes the expert's qualifications and opinions.

If the defense has requested a defense medical examination (DME), it is helpful for the plaintiff attorney and LNC to meet with the client to discuss what to expect during the DME. The plaintiff LNC will often accompany the plaintiff to the examination, which is arranged by the defendant. The plaintiff LNC's role is to provide emotional support to the client and prepare a summary of the doctor's history-taking and examination for the attorney. This summary can be very useful if the examining doctor's report is inconsistent with what actually occurred. The plaintiff LNC should be aware of the state's procedural rules related to DMEs and should contact the attorney for guidance if any problems are encountered during the examination. For more information on DMEs, see Chapter 6.

Plaintiff and defense LNCs may confer with their attorney about which non-party witnesses should be deposed, and they often help their attorneys prepare for party, non-party, and expert depositions. Following are examples of how an LNC may help the attorney prepare for a deposition.

- For plaintiff's deposition, the defense LNC may:
  - Review and prepare a summary of all past and current medical records and inform the defense attorney about any factors that might affect the plaintiff's credibility or the liability, causation, damages, or contributory negligence issues
  - Notify the defense attorney regarding any inconsistencies between the plaintiff's statements (e.g., interrogatory answers, letters, etc.) and the documentation in the medical records, employment records, or insurance claim files
- For the defendant healthcare provider's deposition, the plaintiff LNC may:
  - Educate the attorney about the medical issues in the case, which may include the relevant anatomy and physiology, a detailed explanation of the surgical procedure, and medical literature research about the applicable standard of care
  - Conduct a background check and search for any relevant articles authored by the defendant
  - Attend the deposition to assist the attorney with understanding and responding to unanticipated testimony regarding medical issues
- For the opposing expert's deposition, the LNC may:
  - Conduct background research (e.g., any disciplinary actions on the expert's state license(s), any malpractice suits against the expert, etc.) to determine the validity of the expert's credentials and general standing within the medical community
  - Review the expert's prior depositions and publications for any opinions expressed by that expert that are contradictory to the opinions in the expert disclosure in the current case
  - Conduct an author search to determine whether the expert is published on the topic at issue in the case

Once the depositions are completed, the LNC provides the deposition transcripts to the expert(s), after which the LNC and attorney consult with the expert(s) to discuss any significant new information obtained during the depositions and whether this information changes the expert's opinions.

In addition to conferring with the attorney about the liability issues, the LNC may also provide a detailed assessment of the proximate cause and damages issues based upon information in the medical records, medical literature, deposition testimony, and the expert's review. This may include an assessment of:

- The nature of the injuries (both physical and emotional)
- Which injuries are likely to be permanent
- Whether there has been aggravation of a pre-existing injury
- The nature of any functional impairment
- Whether the plaintiff is partly responsible for the injuries
- Whether the plaintiff has failed to mitigate the damages
- Contributing causes for the plaintiff's alleged injuries and
- Apportionment of liability when there is more than one defendant

Throughout the discovery phase of a medical malpractice claim, LNCs at both plaintiff and defense firms regularly update the plaintiff's medical records; conduct more in-depth research about the standard of care, causation, and damages issues; communicate with experts; confer with the attorney about the strengths and weaknesses of the case; and often participate in case strategy sessions.

Adjudication

Settlement negotiations may ensue at any time during a lawsuit (including pre-suit and after a trial verdict). To prepare for negotiations, the attorney may ask the LNC and other law firm staff for their opinions about a good settlement range for the case. Many factors are considered when valuing a case, including physical and emotional pain and suffering, functional limitations, the age of the injured party, lost wages, cost of medical treatment related to the alleged damages, plaintiff's comparative negligence and failure to mitigate damages, previous awards for similar injuries in the same or nearby venues, and how the plaintiff and defendant are likely to be perceived by a jury. If both parties agree to try to resolve the case through an alternative dispute resolution procedure (such as mediation or arbitration), LNCs for both sides assist their attorneys to prepare by writing summaries and securing anatomical drawings to include in a persuasive document that sets forth their party's arguments and is submitted to the fact-finder (mediator/arbiter).

Plaintiff LNCs may be asked to coordinate the creation of a "day in the life" video that can be used for settlement purposes or at trial. These films are powerful visual tools that show a typical day in the life of a catastrophically injured client who may be unable to sit through a trial due to the injuries. The LNC may be asked to screen and choose a film company to make the video, give direction to the film company on the video's content and length, and be present during the filming and editing of the video.

Many LNCs also play a key role in setting up and participating in focus group case evaluations. A focus group usually consists of 8–12 people from a community similar to the community in which the case will be tried. Law firms can hire companies to find a location, advertise for the participants, and videotape the process. Normally, the participants are not told which side (plaintiff or defense) has convened the focus group. The participants are paid a nominal fee to hear brief versions of both sides of the case, deliberate based on what they have heard, and render a verdict. These groups offer insight into how a jury may perceive the attorney's arguments and the anticipated arguments of the opposing party. The LNC may assist the attorney by preparing demonstrative evidence, evaluating how the focus group reacts to various arguments, and reviewing the videotape of the deliberations with the attorney. A focus group can help both the attorney and the client understand how a jury may react to different issues and how they may value the case if a plaintiff verdict is reached. Often, focus groups bring unexpected issues to light, helping the attorney to better prepare for trial.

For cases that go to trial, the LNC plays an important role in assisting the attorney to prepare for trial. This may include identifying potential medical record exhibits, preparing or securing demonstrative evidence, preparing additional medical charts or summaries, conducting further medical literature research (including researching and analyzing the opposing expert's opinions), and obtaining and reviewing updated medical records. During trial, the LNC may assist the attorney with jury selection, help evaluate the testimony of key witnesses (which includes identifying any inconsistencies between trial testimony, deposition testimony, discovery responses, medical records, and other records), evaluate the jury's reaction to certain witnesses and evidence, and assist the attorney with issues that arise unexpectedly during trial. For more information on trial preparation and the trial process, see Chapter 39.

Skills of the Successful In-House LNC

At the most basic level, job security for the in-house LNC depends upon the firm maintaining an adequate volume of cases with medical issues. Beyond this, job security is directly related to performance. The LNC who develops the knowledge and skills to become a valuable and indispensable asset to attorneys in the delivery of high-quality legal services is most likely to enjoy long-lasting employment and a favorable compensation package. Although the skills required of the successful in-house LNC may vary from firm to firm (depending on the type of work done and the nature of the LNC's role at the firm), following are basic skills of all highly effective LNCs.

Writing

LNCs spend a significant portion of their time writing. The LNC's ability to prepare documents that are well-written, on-point with their purpose, written with the reader/audience in mind, and produced in a timely fashion is a key component of successful performance. Having the skill to draft succinct medical record chronologies or summaries, informative research summaries, properly constructed correspondence, comprehensive interrogatories or bills of particulars, and persuasive position statements or summaries regarding the merits of a case is a tremendous asset to the attorney in the delivery of high-quality legal services. For example, a detailed, accurate, and updated medical summary or timeline that contains the relevant documentation from the medical records can be used by the attorney at key points throughout the life of the case, such as during the preparation of pleadings, deposition outlines, and demand letters and during trial or alternative dispute resolution proceedings.

The quality of written documents submitted to clients, judges, experts, and opposing counsel is a reflection of the depth of analysis and competence of its author and of the firm. Written documents should be well-reasoned, concise, factually accurate, and carefully proofread for spelling and grammatical errors. These include documents drafted by the LNC for the attorney to send out as the attorney's own work product. The fewer the revisions required of the attorney, the more valuable the work of the LNC. Learning and adopting the writing style of the attorney who will sign the ultimate product is also very helpful. Legal nurse consultants who feel they need to improve their writing skills should engage the help of a mentor, enrolling in a writing course, or reading books designed to improve writing skills. See Chapter 35 for more information about report preparation.

Medical Literature Research

Personal injury attorneys rely heavily on the medical literature research done by LNCs to prepare their cases. Medical malpractice matters in particular often require the attorney to have an in-depth understanding of the anatomy, physiology, clinical presentation, treatment options, and prognosis for a given medical condition. In addition, research is also conducted on standard of care, causation, and damages issues. The LNC must develop the means to gather authoritative information from sources such as peer-reviewed medical journals, medical textbooks, and clinical practice guidelines promulgated by professional organizations. The Internet is an invaluable means for readily obtaining much of this information. The LNC must learn to conduct effective medical literature searches online and navigate the wealth of other professional medical information available on the Internet. Helpful websites relating to different medical topics should be categorized and saved for future use. See Chapter 34 for more information about researching medical information and literature.

Teaching

Once the relevant information is gathered, the LNC must decide how best to convey it to the attorney. The LNC may prepare a notebook with the pertinent medical literature highlighted and organized by topic or date or prepare a written summary of the research results, such as an annotated bibliography. The LNC must be prepared to teach any aspect of medicine to the attorney. Teaching aids such as anatomical drawings, charts, and models are very helpful. The degree of instruction that is necessary will vary greatly with the experience of the attorney and the particular medical issues involved. A young associate may need a lesson in basic anatomy and physiology to even understand the medical literature, whereas a senior partner may need explanations regarding only very obscure or complicated medical issues. The LNC's role in educating the attorney about all of the relevant medicine is critical. Medical malpractice attorneys must be able to interact effectively with their own medical experts, depose and cross-examine the opposing party's medical experts, and make persuasive oral arguments to a judge or jury about the medical issues. Medical experts also play a role in educating the attorney, but generally their availability to the attorney is somewhat limited (and expensive), whereas the attorney typically has frequent contact with the LNC in the firm.

Analytical Skill

Evaluating medical issues in the context of the applicable legal standards is the essence of the work done at both plaintiff and defense personal injury firms. Effectively analyzing the liability (in medical malpractice cases), proximate cause, and damages issues in personal injury cases is a very high-level skill that can be acquired only over time. It is imperative that the LNC understand the relationship between liability, proximate cause, and damages. All of these elements must be present for a case to have merit. To learn and understand the legal standards, the LNC can engage in discussions with the attorney about the applicable legal standards throughout the life of a case.

This allows the LNC to differentiate more effectively between the relevant and irrelevant information in the medical records or literature and to understand the legal issues that can impact a potential or actual claim, such as the statute of limitations. Understanding the applicable legal standards also allows a plaintiff LNC to prepare a persuasive draft demand letter to an insurance carrier or a defense LNC to draft a case status report for the client.

Organization

The LNC in a personal injury firm must keep track of tremendous amounts of information and large volumes of medical records. Most firms have a system (electronic, hard copy, or a combination) for maintaining case files, recording new information, and organizing documents. The LNC must adhere to the organizational system in place at the firm so information and documents are readily available to all members of the legal team when needed.

Personal injury firms request large volumes of medical records. Thus, it is essential that the firm have a tickler system in place so requested medical records are received in a timely manner. See Chapter 8 for more information about obtaining medical records.

It is very helpful to organize medical records chronologically into notebooks, with tabs and dividers for each care provider and hospitalization, or into an electronic format (PDF) with bookmarks to designate the various sections of a record. Some firms now utilize chronology software to organize digital records and electronically link chronology facts to the page in the medical record where that fact appears. Organized medical records are essential to an effective analysis of their content by both the LNC and the medical and nursing experts.

Prioritizing

An effective LNC must have the ability to balance multiple tasks on a daily basis. The LNC at a thriving personal injury firm typically has responsibility for a large volume of cases and, in plaintiff's firms, for potential new claims. This results in dozens of tasks and attorney-requests competing for the LNC's time on a daily and weekly basis. Balancing these tasks requires that the LNC develop a system for keeping track of and prioritizing the projects to be done.

First, the LNC must maintain a current "to do" list of all pending tasks and projects. For example, the LNC might maintain a database with all cases and their status and use it to generate weekly reports with tasks to be completed and their deadlines. It is also helpful to categorize projects such as by type of task (medical summary, literature research, organization of records, etc.) or amount of time required to complete the task (small v. large projects). Whatever the form of the "to do" list, it must be updated whenever the LNC identifies or is assigned new cases or projects. It should also be updated to reflect completed projects.

Second, the LNC should have a system for prioritizing the numerous pending projects and tasks. All cases being evaluated or managed in a litigation firm have statutory, procedural, or court-ordered deadlines. Failure to meet some of these deadlines may result in dismissal of a claim, sanctions, or even a legal malpractice action. All litigation firms have a system for tracking deadlines, and ultimately it is the responsibility of the managing attorney to meet them. However, the LNC must be aware of these deadlines and procedural dates (e.g., depositions, expert disclosure, and trials) so any projects needed by the attorney can be completed well before the deadline. Also, an LNC working in a plaintiff firm must consult with the attorney about the applicable statute of limitations in cases under investigation. Some medical malpractice cases require review of certain medical records or even legal research before the statute of limitations can be determined. Projects with these types of deadlines have priority over all other projects. Projects without specific or impending dead-lines should be completed in as timely a manner as possible and roughly in the order in which the projects were received. This promotes a sense of fairness when the LNC works with multiple attorneys. The LNC's "to do" list may be utilized by the LNC and managing partner to communicate with multiple attorneys about prioritization of the LNC's projects.

Computer Skills

Typically, every member of the legal team in a law firm has a computer and can access email, the firm's calendar, and electronic case files. Word-processing programs are the primary means for creating written documents in a law firm. In addition to mastering the word-processing program, LNCs must be able to create multicolumn charts and chronologies, which are typically done using spreadsheet programs or the table format in the word-processing program. Some LNCs utilize chronology software products that link facts to specific pages of a digital medical record or voice recognition software to create their timelines and chronologies. Depending on the specifics of a case, LNCs may create graphs to supplement the chronology or to maintain and tally economic damages.

The Internet is the primary means of doing various types of research in medical-legal cases, including performing medical literature searches; obtaining peer-reviewed journal articles; conducting background checks of witnesses, parties, and experts; and doing legal research. Legal nurse consultants must learn to effectively navigate the vast amount of information on the Internet, bookmark and organize the Internet sites that are most useful, and determine the reliability of the sites (i.e., peer-reviewed or professional association websites versus non-authoritative sites or personal postings/blogs).

Law firms are increasingly obtaining medical records and radiology studies in electronic format. Legal nurse consultants should learn to create chronologies while reading medical records in electronic format, which is typically accomplished using side-by-side computer monitors with the records on one screen and the chronology on the other. Legal nurse consultants frequently need to review, catalogue, and navigate digital x-rays, MRIs, CT scans, and other imaging studies on CDs and DVDs. The cost of obtaining and mailing radiology studies in this format is significantly less than that of studies obtained on radiology film. In addition, this allows radiology studies to be sent to experts electronically. There are various software programs used to view and manipulate electronic imaging studies, and the LNC must become familiar with navigating them.

As technology permeates all aspects of practice in a law firm, it is imperative that LNCs be computer-savvy and able to learn and navigate the computer programs used by the firm.

Other Attributes of the Successful In-House LNC

Personality Traits

Highly successful LNCs possess the personality traits that one would expect in attorneys, physicians, and other professionals. These include a strong work ethic, dedication to the mission and work of the firm, and a willingness to accept responsibility for seeing projects through to their conclusion. Litigation practice may involve the need to do research or produce a work product unexpectedly within a short time period, particularly when a case is at trial. This requires flexibility, including the willingness to work additional hours and reprioritize work projects during a crisis. Attorneys value the LNC who is independent, takes initiative to be aware of the procedural status of a case, anticipates work to be done to move the case forward, and suggests ways to improve the management of cases. They also value LNCs who take the initiative to learn applicable legal standards and strategy.

Legal nurse consultants spend a good deal of time communicating with many different people, including clients, medical experts, attorneys, other LNCs, and many personnel within the firm. Good interpersonal, conflict-resolution, and communication skills are essential. Legal nurse consultants who support and engage auxiliary staff are likely to enhance their productivity. Both plaintiff and defense LNCs must communicate empathetically with their respective party and be cognizant of the emotional toll that litigation can take on them.

Legal nurse consultants serve in a consulting capacity and thus must have the ability to express ideas and thoughts logically and coherently. Legal nurse consultants must also possess enough self-confidence and assertiveness to express their views and debate issues with highly educated attorneys and medical experts. Sometimes, the LNC is most valuable when playing devil's advocate or analyzing the case from the opposing side's viewpoint. Attorneys need as much information about the weaknesses of their cases as they do about the strengths. This is a high-level skill that can be acquired only over time through frequent discussions with the attorney about all aspects of a case.

Prior Clinical Practice

Most registered nurses with at least five years of prior clinical practice can learn to function effectively as LNCs. Because case analysis in personal injury firms requires evaluation of a wide range of medical conditions, in-depth knowledge of anatomy and physiology is essential. It is also helpful to have a clinical background in specialties requiring knowledge of many body systems and processes, such as critical care, trauma, and emergency room nursing. Firms with several LNCs may employ nurses with different areas of clinical expertise, including obstetrics and orthopedics.

Professional LNC Responsibilities

Mentoring

In-house LNC positions are commonly held by long-term, experienced LNCs who are often integrally involved in every aspect of a firm's medical-legal cases. This includes not only medical record analyses and medical literature searches but also regular conversations with attorneys related to the legal standards, case strategy, and case management. Thus, in-house LNCs are in a unique position to mentor other LNCs, especially those new to legal nurse consulting practice. This includes not only orienting and teaching LNCs new to the firm but also contacting new LNCs in the community through speaking engagements and local AALNC chapters and being available to field questions from local LNCs about legal nurse consulting practice and employment opportunities. In-house LNCs should also consider approaching the firm partnership about offering internships to LNCs seeking a mentoring experience. Ultimately, the success of the legal nurse consulting specialty practice rests with providing high-quality work products and advice, something which is learned through extensive experience working on actual medical-legal cases. Experienced LNCs have a responsibility to share their knowledge with less-experienced LNCs, advise legal professionals and those within the liability insurance industry about the benefits of LNC services, and facilitate the advancement of the legal nurse consulting specialty practice within the legal community.

Firm Practice Development

In-house LNCs are increasingly being profiled on firm websites, listed on firm letterheads, and included in firm advertising campaigns as attorneys realize the client and public appeal of having in-house LNCs. In-house LNCs who network within the medical legal community by joining their local bar or LNC associations, serving on committees, publishing articles, and procuring speaking engagements to groups of attorneys or prospective clients (e.g., healthcare providers or liability insurance companies for defense firms) assist their firm to become recognized as having special expertise in handling medical-legal cases, thereby generating case referrals and new clients.

Education

In-house LNCs have a professional responsibility to maintain competence in current legal nurse consulting practice (AALNC, 2017). Through reading the *Journal of Legal Nurse Consulting* and legal association journals, attending educational programs for LNCs, and networking with others in the specialty practice, in-house LNCs can continually develop, maintain, and expand their professional skills and knowledge.

In-house LNCs also benefit from learning about trends and issues in the clinical and legal arenas. This allows the LNC to keep abreast of the medicine, science, and clinical practice issues that may present in medical-legal claims and to understand the legal standards affecting case analysis.

Professional Practice Evaluation

In-house LNCs should continually strive to improve their practice and their contributions to the firm by regularly evaluating their own practice relative to professional practice standards (AALNC, 2017). This practice evaluation can originate from soliciting feedback from the firm's attorneys regarding the LNC's work products, engaging in self-evaluation to identify areas of strength and areas for growth, and interacting with other LNCs and medical-legal professionals to identify opportunities to enhance one's own practice or role performance (AALNC, 2017). Upon conducting such evaluations and identifying areas for improvement, in-house LNCs should set and achieve goals for professional growth.

Leadership

Leadership in both the practice setting and the specialty practice is another responsibility for in-house LNCs (AALNC, 2017). Most in-house LNCs have a paralegal, legal assistant, or legal secretary with whom they work closely. In-house LNCs delegate to and oversee the work of these team members. As leaders, in-house LNCs must develop a positive working relationship with these co-workers, building a foundation of respect, trust, and effective communication to achieve the firm's mission of providing high-quality legal services. In-house LNCs who demonstrate leadership and conflict resolution skills will be valued by the partnership.

In-house LNCs also have the responsibility to share their knowledge, experience, and leadership skills by participating in professional associations, such as the AALNC. Such participation advances the specialty practice and benefits other LNCs.

Ethical and Scope of Practice Considerations

Legal nurse consultants should be familiar with and follow the AALNC's Code of Ethics and Conduct (AALNC, 2015) and Legal Nurse Consulting: Scope and Standards of Practice (AALNC, 2017), which are voluntary ethical and practice guidelines developed to assist LNCs in their practice and to advance the legal nurse consulting specialty practice within the legal and liability insurance communities.

The firm is vicariously liable for the conduct of all its employees, including its in-house LNCs, who practice under the supervision of the firm's attorneys. This is also known as the doctrine of respondeat superior (Restatement of Torts, 2000). Thus, although experienced in-house LNCs may engage in higher-level skills, the attorney is ultimately responsible for any work product and for the management of cases.

In addition, all LNCs should be familiar with the relevant portions of the legal profession's ethical standards to align their legal nurse consulting practice with the professional obligations of the attorney. Each state has detailed ethical canons for attorneys, which hold the force of law and are modeled after the American Bar Association's Model Rules of Professional Conduct (ABA, 2016). Following are the general rules pertinent to a firm's use of LNCs.

Rule 1.6c [Confidentiality of Information]: "A lawyer shall make reasonable efforts to prevent the advertent or unauthorized disclosure of, or unauthorized access to, information relating to the representation of a client." This includes maintaining client confidentiality and abiding by HIPAA laws related to protected health information.

Rule 5.3b [Responsibilities Regarding Non-lawyer Assistance]: "A lawyer having direct supervisory responsibility over the non-lawyer shall make reasonable efforts to ensure that the person's conduct is compatible with the professional obligations of the lawyer."

Rule 5.7b [Responsibilities Regarding Law-Related Services]: The term "law related services denotes services that might reasonably be performed in conjunction with and in substance are related to the provision of legal services, and that are not prohibited as unauthorized practice of law when provided by a non-lawyer." This rule essentially requires that law-related services performed by a non-lawyer in a firm must not constitute the unauthorized practice of law. In essence, all non-lawyers are prohibited from performing services that call for the judgment of a lawyer. For example, LNCs are prohibited from giving legal advice to clients and engaging in procedural activities (such as arguing motions before the court and questioning witnesses at deposition and trial).

Summary

Over time and with a desire to learn, in-house LNCs can become invaluable members of the legal team and make significant contributions to a firm's mission to provide high-quality, ethical legal services. While the exact role of the LNC is determined by many factors, typically in-house LNCs are responsible for numerous projects from case inception through adjudication. Understanding the economics of a firm allows the LNC to contribute to the firm's success, and the LNC who observes the practice's ethical and scope boundaries and develops the requisite knowledge and skills to analyze medical issues in the context of legal standards is indispensable to attorneys.

References

American Association of Legal Nurse Consultants. (2011). Salary survey report. Retrieved from www.aalnc. org/p/cm/ld/fid=153.

American Association of Legal Nurse Consultants. (2015). Code of ethics and conduct with interpretive discussion. Retrieved from www.aalnc.org/page/what-is-an-lnc#Q10.

American Association of Legal Nurse Consultants. (2017). Legal nurse consulting scope and standards of practice. Retrieved from www.aalnc.org/p/pr/qu.

American Bar Association. (2016). Model rules of professional conduct. Retrieved from www.americanbar. org/groups/professional_responsibility/publications/model_rules_of_professional_conduct/model_ rules_of_professional_conduct_table_of_contents.html.

Contingent fees for attorneys in claims or actions for medical, dental or podiatric malpractice, N.Y. Jud. Law § 474-a(2) (Consol. 2017).

Restatement (Third) of Torts: Apportionment Liab. § 13 (2000).

Zorn, E., (2015). In-house law firm legal nurse role: 30 year perspective. *The Journal of Legal Nurse Consulting, 26*(1), 26–32.

Test Questions

1. Which of the following are skills of highly effective in-house LNCs?
   A. Writing
   B. Research
   C. Analysis
   D. Prioritizing
   E. All of the above

2. In a defense firm, all the following personnel generate billable-hour income for the firm EXCEPT:
   A. Paralegals
   B. Secretaries
   C. Legal nurse consultants
   D. Associate attorneys

3. In a plaintiff firm, clients are usually retained on what basis?
   A. Hourly
   B. Contingency fee
   C. Cost
   D. Tentative

4. When prioritizing work projects, the LNC should give the least priority to
   A. Procedural deadlines
   B. Statutory deadlines
   C. Date the request was made
   D. Court-ordered deadlines

5. The exact role and responsibilities of an in-house LNC are shaped by all of the following EXCEPT:
   A. The state's statutes
   B. Firm's experience with LNCs
   C. Nature of the firm's work
   D. Locality, culture, and size of the firm

Answers: 1. E, 2. B, 3. B, 4. C, 5. A

Appendix A: Plaintiff LNC Job Description

Plaintiff Law Firm
In-house Legal Nurse Consultant Position Description
Position: Legal Nurse Consultant (LNC)
Reports to: Supervising attorneys and managing partner

Position Purpose

The essential role of the LNC is to analyze medical issues in the context of the applicable legal standards, thereby assisting the attorneys to provide high-quality legal services consistent with the firm's Mission Statement and Core Values.

LNC Responsibilities

LNC duties are performed under the supervision of firm attorneys and are carried out based upon the discretion and preference of the attorney and established firm protocols for the management of the firm's cases.

LNC responsibilities include but are not limited to:

Medical Malpractice Cases—Screen Potential Cases for Merit

- Participate in initial client interview, obtaining prior medical history, client's version of the facts, and a list of all relevant hospitalizations and healthcare providers
- Identify medical records needed for initial case review
- Conduct preliminary medical literature search related to liability and causation issues
- Review and digitally bookmark the relevant medical records
- Prepare case screening memo for attorney
- Identify and screen potential medical and nursing experts
- Prepare package of materials for the expert, including an organized digital or hard copy of the relevant medical records and a letter to the expert setting forth the facts and a list of questions for the expert to consider
- Participate in the discussion with the expert about the merits of the case

Assist in the Ongoing Management and Evaluation of the Following Types of Cases

MEDICAL MALPRACTICE

- Identify defendants to name
- Review and edit Complaint
- Draft medical portions of discovery responses to defendants' demands (bills of particulars/ interrogatory answers)
- Prepare medical portions of discovery demands directed to defendant(s)
- Review relevant portions of defendants' production of records, policies & procedures, and other information
- Identify and review complete/updated medical records and prepare work products as appropriate (e.g., chronology, timeline, charts/graphs, other data analysis, etc.)

- Provide attorney with relevant anatomical drawings and procedure descriptions relevant to case
- Assist attorney to prepare for depositions, and attend depositions as requested
- Periodically communicate directly with clients regarding their medical status
- Periodically obtain updated medical records from client's current treating healthcare providers
- Conduct more in-depth medical literature searches as case issues become more focused
- Draft/edit demand letters, summarizing facts, liability, and damages issues
- Perform background research on defendants
- Attend selected defense medical exams and prepare memo summarizing exam
- Review and analyze opposing side's Expert Witness Disclosure(s)
- Assist with focus groups (mock trials)
- Assist attorney to prepare for trial, including selection of demonstrative evidence and preparation of additional charts, timelines, and exhibits for use at trial. Attend trial as requested

Other Personal Injury Matters (Auto, Slip & Fall, Labor Law, Dog Bite, Pedestrian, Etc.)

- Identify relevant medical records
- Review and bookmark digital medical records
- Prepare chronology to include relevant documentation in the medical records pertaining to causation and damages
- Periodically obtain updated medical records from plaintiff's current treating healthcare providers
- Attend selected defense medical exams and prepare memo summarizing exam

Assist attorney to prepare for trial, including selection of demonstrative evidence and preparation of additional charts, timelines, and exhibits for use at trial.

Product Liability and Toxic Tort

- Identify relevant medical records
- Prepare chronology to include relevant documentation in the medical records pertaining to causation and damages
- Conduct medical literature searches related to the drug, device, or toxic substance

Mass Tort

- Identify relevant medical records
- Bookmark and review digital medical records
- Draft medical portions of Plaintiff Profile Forms or other court-mandated documents

Long-Term Care (LTC)

- Identify relevant medical records and additional sources of documentation commonly used in LTC facilities

- Analyze medical records to determine if the care and services provided met the applicable standard of care and complied with federal and state regulations
- Obtain facility survey results and complaint investigation reports and identify cited deficiencies or complaints relevant to case
- Remain current with updates and changes to relevant federal and state regulations

Other Responsibilities

- Maintain database of potential/actual healthcare provider experts
- Work as a team player with other support staff and the attorneys
- Serve as a resource to the paralegals on medically related issues
- Maintain list of prioritized case projects
- Participate in regular meetings with attorneys to review the status of cases

Required Skills

- Strong work ethic and dedication to the firm's mission
- Excellent analytical and research skills
- Excellent reading and writing skills
- Excellent oral and written communication skills, including the ability to express opinions logically, coherently, and succinctly
- Excellent teaching and interpersonal skills
- Strong problem-solving skills
- Excellent organizational skills, ability to multitask, and ability to prioritize pending work projects
- Willingness to accept responsibility for seeing projects through to their conclusion
- Ability to work independently with minimal supervision and direction
- General working knowledge of the laws and rules & regulations applicable to medical malpractice, long-term care, and other personal injury cases
- Proficiency in various computer programs and software

Educational and Experience Requirements

- Registered Nurse
- Four-year BA or BS degree preferred
- At least five years of prior clinical nursing experience
- Prior experience working on medical malpractice or personal injury cases preferred
- LNCC® board certification preferred

Appendix B: Defense LNC Job Description

Defense Law Firm
In-house Legal Nurse Consultant Position Description
Position: Legal Nurse Consultant (LNC)
Reports to: Supervising attorneys and managing partner

Position Purpose

Within potential or actual legal cases, claims, or investigations, the essential role of the legal nurse consultant is to analyze medical issues in the context of the applicable legal standards and to contribute towards and support the firm's mission of delivering the highest quality legal representation.

LNC Responsibilities

LNC responsibilities are performed under the supervision of the attorneys and are carried out based upon the discretion and preference of the attorney and established firm protocols for the management of the firm's cases.

LNC responsibilities include but are not limited to:

Assist the Attorneys in the Evaluation and Management of Medical Malpractice, Other Personal Injury (Vehicle, Slip & Fall, Etc.), Toxic Tort, Product Liability, and Long-Term Care Claims or Cases

- Review Complaint (and in malpractice cases, the affixed expert opinion letter)
- Review relevant portions of plaintiff's discovery responses and production of records and other information
- Identify medical records to obtain
- Organize/digitally bookmark and review relevant medical records and prepare work products as appropriate (e.g., chronology, summary, timeline, charts/graphs, other data analysis, etc.)
- Provide attorney with relevant anatomical drawings and procedure descriptions relevant to case
- Conduct medical literature search (related to liability, causation, and damages issues in malpractice cases and related to causation and damages in other personal injury cases)
- Identify and vet potential experts
- Prepare package of materials for the expert
- Participate in the discussion with the expert to review the expert's analysis and prepare a summary of the expert's opinions
- Draft expert witness disclosure
- Assist attorney to prepare for depositions, and attend depositions as requested
- Periodically obtain updated medical records from plaintiff's current treating healthcare providers
- Conduct more in-depth medical literature searches as case issues become more focused
- Review and analyze opposing side's Expert Witness Disclosure(s) and transcript of expert depositions
- Perform background research on opposing experts
- Draft medical portion of case status reports to insurance company, mediation position statements, and other documents as requested
- Assist attorney to prepare for trial, including selection of demonstrative evidence and preparation of additional charts, timelines, and exhibits for use at trial. Attend trial
- Participate in regular meetings with attorneys to review the status of cases
- *For medical malpractice cases:*
  - Obtain defendant's complete records of the plaintiff and other relevant documents that may have been generated by the defendant (e.g., incident reports, survey data, etc.)

- – Perform background research on defendant and plaintiff
- – Participate in initial client meeting and obtain client's version of the facts
- – Prepare production of defendant's complete chart of plaintiff to comply with plaintiff's discovery request
- ■ *For product liability and toxic tort cases:*
  - – Conduct medical literature searches related to the drug, device, or toxic substance
- ■ *For mass tort claims:*
  - – Review plaintiff's Profile Form or other court-mandated documents
- ■ *For long-term care (LTC) cases:*
  - – Review facility's records of plaintiff/decedent to determine if Arbitration Agreement exists, and obtain related legal documents as needed (e.g., Power of Attorney agreement). Advise attorney of status
  - – Review Death Certificate to assist attorney with causation analysis
  - – Obtain and analyze LTC survey results and Complaint investigations for defendant facility, and compare to allegations in the case

Assist the Attorneys in the Evaluation and Management of Healthcare Provider Licensure Investigations

- ■ Obtain client's complete records of the petitioner
- ■ Perform background research on client and petitioner
- ■ Review and analyze allegations made against client
- ■ Participate in initial client meeting, and obtain client's version of the facts
- ■ Conduct medical literature search related to liability and causation issues, as needed
- ■ Draft response to the allegations
- ■ Review Department of Public Health's (DPH's) consultant's report
- ■ Identify medical and other records that need to be obtained
- ■ Identify and vet potential experts, as requested
- ■ Prepare package of materials for the expert, as requested
- ■ Participate in the discussion with the expert to review the expert's analysis, as requested
- ■ Draft rebuttal response, and draft expert opinion letter
- ■ Review DPH's investigative report and its exhibits, including their consultant's final report
- ■ Perform background research on DPH's consultant
- ■ Assist attorney to prepare for hearing, including selection of demonstrative evidence and preparation of additional charts, timelines, and exhibits for use at hearing. Attend hearing as requested
- ■ Provide periodic status updates to insurance company and client
- ■ Participate in regular meetings with attorneys to review the status of licensure investigation cases

Other

- ■ Maintain database of potential/actual healthcare provider experts
- ■ Maintain spreadsheet of the firm's statistical rate of dismissal for licensure investigation matters
- ■ Work as a team player with other support staff and the attorneys
- ■ Supervise paralegals in their work on the medical aspects of medical malpractice and other personal injury cases

Required Skills

- Strong work ethic and dedication to the firm's mission
- Excellent analytical and research skills and attention to detail
- Excellent reading and writing skills
- Excellent oral and written communication skills, including the ability to express opinions logically, coherently, and succinctly
- Excellent teaching and interpersonal skills
- Excellent organizational skills, ability to multitask, and ability to prioritize pending work projects
- Willingness to accept responsibility for seeing projects through to their conclusion
- Ability to work independently with minimal supervision and direction
- General working knowledge of the laws and rules & regulations applicable to medical malpractice, long-term care, and other personal injury cases and to licensure investigations
- Proficiency in various computer programs and software
- Strong problem-solving skills

Educational and Experience Requirements

- Registered Nurse with active license and no prior disciplinary actions
- Four-year BA or BS degree preferred
- At least five years of prior clinical nursing experience
- Prior experience working on medical malpractice or personal injury cases preferred
- LNCC® board certification preferred (or willingness to obtain within two years)

Chapter 30

The Independent Legal Nurse Consultant

Anne Meyer, BSN, RN, LNCC®
Cathy Weitzel, MSN, APRN

Contents

Objectives

■ Identify the advantages and challenges of being an independent legal nurse consultant
■ Describe services that independent legal nurse consultants provide for attorney-clients
■ Determine business relationships that are essential for the independent legal nurse consultant entrepreneur

The Role of the Independent Legal Nurse Consultant

Job opportunities for nurses are diverse and continue to develop. The nursing subspecialty of legal nurse consulting also offers much variety including, but not limited to, working as an independent legal nurse consultant (LNC), in-house LNC (at a law firm or legal nurse consulting firm), case manager, life care planner, and Medicare set-aside allocator.

In addition to providing behind-the-scenes consultation, some independent LNCs also offer services as an expert fact witness or, if they remain clinically active, as a nurse expert witness. This chapter focuses on the behind-the-scenes independent LNC. See Chapters 31 and 32 for more information on the nurse expert witness and expert fact witness roles.

Working as an independent LNC often allows a nurse to have exposure to many different types of cases and areas of litigation to determine if there is a particular niche that may be a better fit than another. The nature of an independent LNC's practice is directly related to the type of legal work done by attorneys who engage the independent LNC, as well as the services requested in a particular case. An LNC can provide a variety of services to attorney-clients and other professionals within the legal and insurance industries, including:

■ Identification of pertinent medical records
■ Medical record review and analysis for a variety of medical-legal tort claims including medical malpractice, personal injury, product liability, and toxic tort, among others
■ Preparation of a medical record summary (e.g., narrative, chronology, or timeline)
■ Medical literature research regarding standard of care, causation, and/or damages issues
■ Identification of the necessary expert specialties, and location and screening of potential experts
■ Provision of anatomical drawings, medical definitions, or other aids to assist in the attorney's understanding of the medical issues
■ Preparation (plaintiff LNC) or review (defense LNC) of the medical portions of discovery documents, such as interrogatory answers or Bill of Particulars
■ Identification, recommendation to obtain, review, and analysis of documents during discovery, such as healthcare facility policies and procedures
■ Review and analysis of expert reports
■ Review and analysis of deposition transcripts of witnesses and medical experts
■ Formulation or assistance with preparation of deposition questions
■ Attendance at defense medical exams (DMEs) and independent medical exams (IMEs) (plaintiff LNCs)
■ Analysis of liability, causation, and/or damages
■ Identification, securement, and/or preparation of demonstrative evidence for deposition, mediation, arbitration, or trial
■ Assistance in preparation of expert affidavits and

- Social media and background research on defendants (plaintiff LNCs) or plaintiffs (defense LNCs) as well as on experts and other witnesses

Becoming a Business Entrepreneur

The decision to become a business entrepreneur and launch an independent legal nurse consulting business is not to be taken lightly. Simply the idea of being an entrepreneur and "one's own boss" can sound very exciting and liberating, but there are many things to consider before taking that step. While being a legal nurse consultant requires a particular set of skills and qualities (see Chapter 1 for additional information), being a successful business owner requires additional attributes, including being a self-starter and having astute critical-thinking skills, self-confidence and discipline, positive mental attitude, problem-solving abilities, time management skills, the ability to work alone for long periods of time, and perseverance.

Self-reflection and a "pro versus con" approach may be helpful in the decision-making process of starting a business. Initially, the LNC must focus on the benefits and challenges and how a decision to move into an entrepreneurial role may affect professional and family life. The following are some benefits and challenges to consider (Carleo, 2017).

Benefits include:

- Flexible schedule
- Work from home
- Being one's own boss
- Set own hourly rate
- Bill by the hour (as opposed to a flat salary/no overtime pay)
- Take as much or as little work as desired
- Variety in types of cases
- Variety in attorney-clients and
- Self-accomplishment

Challenges include:

- Marketing and acquisition of work
- Competition from other independent LNCs
- Limited camaraderie with colleagues
- Variable income
- No paid time off
- Responsible for own health and liability insurance and retirement savings
- Responsible for one's own business taxes
- Responsible for following appropriate accounting procedures and
- Overhead expenses (e.g., office space, equipment, supplies, insurance, marketing, employees)

There are many professional and business resources available to assist in the decision-making process and to provide education regarding what is involved in the start-up of a legal nurse consulting business. These resources include:

- A small business course at a local community college
- Local Chamber of Commerce
- U.S. Small Business Administration (www.sba.org)
- SCORE (Service Corps of Retired Executives) (www.score.org) and
- Other seasoned independent LNCs

Contractor versus Subcontractor

A subcontractor is a person who, or business that, contracts to provide some service or material necessary for the performance of another's contract. Subcontracting is an option for independent LNCs to gain experience in this area of practice, to supplement their income, or perhaps work in this area of nursing without the responsibility of being a business owner. A subcontracting work agreement is a document which specifies the terms of the subcontractor's engagement, including issues pertaining to expectations, terms of payment for work done, and whether the subcontractor is expected to have liability insurance. Some, but not all, contractors include non-compete clauses in subcontractor agreements to protect their relationships with attorney-clients. It can be common for an attorney working with a subcontractor to try to contact that subcontractor directly for additional work. In these situations when there is a non-compete clause, it is expected that the subcontractor refer the attorney to the hiring LNC (contractor) to avoid any "under-cutting" of the relationship between the contractor and attorney-client.

The hiring LNC and subcontractor sign the agreement before work assignments commence, and if fees or other terms change by mutual agreement, a new contract is signed. It is important to read all subcontractor agreements very carefully; once signed, the terms are binding. Subcontracting agreements should *not* contain a clause stating the subcontractor will not be paid until the contractor is paid; such clauses are not permitted in some states. For example, in California, the Supreme Court found "Paid-If" and "Paid-When" provisions to be unenforceable and invalid (FindLaw, n.d.). Subcontractor pay rates vary and may be reflective of the subcontractor's level of experience or type of task being completed. Subcontractors may be paid a percentage of the contractor's billing rate, which takes into consideration the contractor's overhead costs, client management, project oversight, etc. The subcontractor is usually not informed of the contractor's fees; nor is this disclosed or discussed in subcontractor agreements.

Independent LNCs may find it necessary to hire subcontractors as their business grows, ideally matching the clinical expertise of the subcontractor with the issues in a particular case. Subcontractors offer the business owner the flexibility of addressing a waxing and waning caseload without some of the legal and financial responsibilities that comes with hiring employees. The LNC contractor is essentially responsible for the quality of the subcontractor's work product and, thus, should carefully screen and consider prior clinical, legal, and writing experience of prospective subcontractors. In addition, the LNC contractor should review any work done by a subcontractor before submitting the work product to the attorney-client.

The LNC who hires a subcontractor should utilize a subcontractor agreement. Contract law varies by state, so it is prudent for the LNC contractor to consult with an attorney when drafting a subcontractor agreement template. A business accountant can also educate the business owner regarding the differences between a subcontractor and an employee to avoid any legal or tax issues. If an attorney hires a legal nurse consulting firm, it is understood the work may be done by an LNC other than the firm owner. However, if a solo LNC contracts with a subcontractor, it may be prudent to advise the hiring attorney of this to avoid any credibility issues.

Business Development

Business Plan

The success of a business can be influenced by many things. The core elements of any successful entrepreneurship include:

1. Developing a strategic business plan
2. Determining individual business goals and philosophy (core values/mission statement) and
3. Seeking professional consultation in legal, financial, accounting, and liability issues

It is essential to develop a solid plan as the foundation of a business. A business plan in the business world is similar to a care plan in the nursing world. It drives the business decision-making process and orchestrates a systematic, goal-oriented approach. It is a roadmap to structure, run, and grow a new business. The main components of a business plan include the Executive Summary, Description of Business, Market Analysis, Marketing Strategy and Implementation, Human Resources, and an Appendix which contains personal resumes, financial statements, letters of intent, copies of key documents, etc.

Business goals are set by the LNC after market research or evaluation of potential work opportunities within a particular legal community. The goals should realistically reflect how much time the LNC can devote to setting up and building a legal nurse consulting business, as well as the LNC's economic needs. Many independent LNCs continue to work clinically while starting a business, until the business generates sufficient revenue. A business philosophy stated in marketing materials identifies the core values or mission statement of the business.

Choosing a business name is an important step in the business planning process. A business name may be a simple reflection of the LNC's name or the services being provided, or it can be something more creative. Simple Internet and domain name searches can determine if the proposed business name is unique or already claimed by someone else. Registering a business name will be necessary if not utilizing solely the LNC's name. This is an easy process that can be discussed with an attorney or accountant or found on state government websites for businesses or the Small Business Administration website.

Other Professional Business Relationships

Aside from the legal nurse consulting work, the LNC business owner will at least initially be required to do many jobs within the business, including business management, marketing, human resources, billing, and accounts payable. It is important to align with other business professionals to seek advice and direction related to the legal and financial implications of starting and maintaining a business. Such business professionals include a business attorney, accountant, banking institution, and an insurance broker.

A business attorney can assist the LNC with creating contracts to be used with attorney-clients and subcontractors and can advise regarding permits and licenses, business name registration, collections, and disputes. An accountant can offer guidance regarding business structure, tax filing and credits, and financial record-keeping. Internet resources (e.g., legalzoom.com or rocketlawyer.com) can also be useful for the LNC who does not have a business attorney or accountant to consult and may not have the funds budgeted for this expense. Opening a separate business bank account will be helpful to separate business and personal finances and stay legally compliant and protected (U.S. Small Business Administration, n.d.).

The LNC will want to consult an insurance broker and consider both professional liability and Errors and Omissions (E&O) insurance. Although it is very rare for a behind-the-scenes consultant or nurse expert to be sued for professional services, it is prudent to maintain liability coverage (Dickinson & Zorn, 2013). The American Association of Legal Nurse Consultants website also has information regarding professional liability insurance (www.aalnc.org).

Fees

Setting a fee schedule is part of the business plan. Fees for behind-the-scenes consulting are based upon the LNC's prior clinical nursing experience, legal nursing experience, and what the market will bear in a particular geographical area. The LNC should determine the fees for services offered. These fees can be an hourly charge for specific services or a project fee to encompass an entire project, and they may also include ancillary costs as incurred, e.g., fees to obtain research articles, mileage, etc. A fee schedule should include whether a late fee will be assessed for late payments. It is important for the new LNC not to try to build a business by offering budget services. It can be very difficult to make large increases in hourly fees later, and it diminishes the value of the services being provided.

It is common practice to request a retainer upon initiation of a new case. A retainer helps the LNC to offset costs while working on a case. The LNC may have a set retainer amount (e.g., the equivalent of two or three hours of the LNC's hourly rate) for all cases or determine an amount on a case-by-case basis related to the estimated hours to be worked. Replenishment of retainer funds may be requested upon depletion of the retainer.

The LNC should determine a method to diligently track time spent working on a case and invoice the attorney-client accordingly. The LNC should decide on a billing frequency (e.g., upon completion of X number of hours worked, when the bill reaches X dollars, monthly, or upon completion of the case). The LNC should be aware that not all law firms pay invoices within 15 or 30 days (often termed "net 15" or "net 30"). Some insurance companies only distribute payments every 60 days or quarterly. It is important to define the conditions of billing prior to commencing work. There are many inexpensive billing programs available online to manage clients, track time, and create professional-looking invoices to assist the LNC in organization and ease of fee collections.

The LNC should confirm what work the attorney-client wants completed, the LNC's fee for that service, and when invoicing will occur. It is imperative to maintain ongoing communication with the attorney-client regarding unexpected issues that arise during a review (such as illegible documents, receipt of additional records, and the attorney's request for additional services that can add further expense). It is better to have transparency than surprise the attorney when the invoice arrives. Lack of communication regarding billing can lead to delayed payment, not receiving new casework, and tarnished credibility. A contract between the LNC and the attorney-client identifying expectations can also be helpful to avoid issues.

A learning curve is expected for the new LNC or even for seasoned LNCs providing a new service or addressing an unfamiliar area of medicine. It is good business practice to take this into consideration when billing for services.

Networking

Business development relies on the LNC's ability to network with other professionals who work in the legal community, including attorneys and other LNCs. Networking, a form of marketing that involves developing and nurturing professional relationships, is important to gain leads about potential work. However, acquiring the skills to provide high-quality services (e.g., work product and advice) is crucial to ultimately achieve a successful business.

The independent LNC should seek networking opportunities with attorneys who handle medically related cases, including medical or nursing malpractice, personal injury, product liability, premises liability, and even post-conviction medical reviews for debilitated prisoners.

In general, the most productive networking results from personal contacts. The LNC should seek introductions by colleagues or friends to attorneys who may have a current or future need for legal nurse consulting services. The approach when meeting with a prospective hiring attorney about consulting work varies with whether the attorney has previously used and values legal nurse consulting services. The LNC should solicit the attorney's thoughts about legal nurse consulting services and convey knowledge about the ways a skilled LNC can assist the attorney to provide high-quality legal services. It is also helpful to attend or exhibit at educational seminars held by state or local bar associations or other professional associations for attorneys, such as the Defense Research Institute (defense counsel) or The American Association for Justice (plaintiff counsel). The fees for attending or exhibiting such events can be costly, so the LNC should be strategic, focusing on events frequented by attorneys who do medical legal work. The LNC can join the local bar association as an associate member, participate in a bar association sub-committee, or offer to speak at a seminar on a clinical topic within the LNC's area of expertise. Membership in a state or local bar association may allow the LNC to place classified ads in association publications.

Building relationships with other LNCs is important, especially in-house LNCs who typically have knowledge about a particular legal community including the attorneys who utilize legal nurse consulting services. When contract LNC work is necessary for a particular case, attorneys will seek recommendations from the in-house LNC. Although networking with other independent LNCs is important, some LNCs may be reluctant if the LNC seeking advice is viewed as a source of competition. Networking with other independent LNCs is also a valuable way to meet potential subcontractors for the LNC's business or to meet LNC contractors with whom the LNC may subcontract.

The independent LNC should identify which professional organizations would be most beneficial to continuing business development. Referral organizations, such as Business Network International (www.bni.com), provide opportunities for the LNC to develop business relationships in the local community. The U.S. Chamber of Commerce (www.uschamber.com) has a wealth of information regarding local events and opportunities for small business owners.

Marketing

The purpose of marketing is to gain the attention of attorneys who would benefit from legal nurse consulting services and to educate potential attorney-clients about ways in which these services could assist them to provide high-quality legal services. Marketing materials may include business cards, brochures, letterhead, a business logo, and a resume or curriculum vitae (CV). These materials do not need to be the most expensive, but they should be professionally designed, printed, and proofread to create a positive, professional impression. The LNC should dedicate a separate email address for all business communication, and the email address itself should sound professional.

Legal nurse consultants interested in remote consulting (behind-the-scenes) work may wish to set up a website to promote their services. Legal nurse consulting work can be done offsite, and there is no reason LNCs cannot conduct work across the country from their home office unless required by the attorney-client to attend face-to-face meetings. A website is always accessible and can drive business to the LNC even when the office is closed or the LNC is unavailable by phone.

The more technologically savvy LNC may be able to set up a website without assistance, but some may decide to hire a website developer. The website may be interactive or two dimensional and include a set of core values or a mission statement, an explanation of services, an active blog, and articles of interest to the attorney-client. Regardless of the website's functionality and proffered information, it is essential the graphics and text are professional and free from spelling and grammatical errors.

Publishing in legal nurse consulting or legal journals or writing newsletters read by attorneys or other LNCs lends credibility to the LNC and can be a marketing tool. Topics of interest to potential attorney-clients may include a description of legal nurse consulting services and clinical topics that may arise in the types of cases prosecuted or defended by attorneys that work on medically related cases.

Social media is used by a vast amount of the population and can be a useful tool to network and gain new business. There are many options available including Twitter, LinkedIn, and Facebook. A well done and complete profile on LinkedIn can also serve in place of a website for a new LNC. Legal nurse consultants can include a link in their email signature line to their LinkedIn profile to drive traffic to the profile. Consistent social media use and posting will allow for the most visibility. It is important for the LNC to remember these are social sites; postings should always be professional. It is prudent to have separate personal and business social media accounts.

Home Office Essentials

Organizational skills are essential for the successful operation of any small business. A dedicated workspace (separate from living quarters) allows the LNC to focus on work without interruption. The workspace should be of sufficient size to accommodate the LNC's files, office equipment, and reference resources. If home office space is not available, many areas offer shared work space or co-working office space for lease. Dependable, high-speed Internet service is imperative for electronic communications, medical literature research, and electronic transmission of medical records and work products. Wireless access allows the flexibility to work in other locations within a home when desired. A laptop computer allows the LNC to work in locations outside of the home.

Other Business Equipment and Software

While not necessary for business start-up, other helpful office equipment includes a copier/printer, fax machine, scanner, shredder, file cabinet, and dual monitors. There are many different software programs available to assist the small business entrepreneur to stay organized, maintain a professional presentation, and save time. These include programs for tracking cases, maintaining client and vendor contacts, time-keeping and invoicing, book-keeping, and creating chronologies and reports. The business information stored on a computer can be invaluable and cause a business to halt if the system is down or damaged. A computer back-up process should be utilized on a regular basis to ensure minimal loss if there is an issue. There are a number of cloud storage and file transfer companies available, but not all ensure compliance with the Health Insurance Portability and Accountability Act (HIPAA). Networking with other business and legal nurse consulting professionals regarding the equipment, software, and services they find useful can be very helpful to identify cost-effective options.

The LNC may spend considerable time on the phone with attorney-clients. Thus, phone service that is clear and reliable is essential. While a cell phone lends to the ability to be accessible at all times, a dedicated landline may be the most dependable option. Many business professionals utilize the same cell phone for both personal and business purposes; however, it is essential that a professional voicemail message be used.

Confidentiality and Security

Confidentiality is a common concept to nurses, and it is no different when practicing in the nursing subspecialty of legal nurse consulting. The LNC must ensure client confidentiality by utilizing password-protected computers and locked filing cabinets for storage of paper records and case documents. Any paper documents from closed cases should be shredded. Consideration may be given to utilizing a commercial document-shredding company that ensures secure destruction. Case and client details should never be discussed with anyone other than members of the legal team. The LNC must be familiar with and abide by HIPAA regulations when storing and transmitting medical records (Health and Human Services, n.d.). This includes the use of encrypted email or a secure file-sharing program. A dedicated work computer is advised to maintain confidentiality and minimize the risk for virus issues. Anti-virus software should be installed and updated regularly.

Summary

Independent LNC work can be very interesting, challenging, and rewarding. The role offers many options for the LNC attracted to diversity or a niche area of practice. The independent LNC also has the option to work as a business owner, contractor, and/or subcontractor. Legal nurse consultants interested in becoming entrepreneurs must consider if they have the skill sets to both provide quality legal nurse consulting work and operate a business. Although the LNC may be an excellent nurse, that does not necessarily translate into business acumen. The creation and implementation of a strong business plan is crucial to a good outcome, but the LNC must also consider one's ability to market, network with other business professionals, and afford the time and money to follow this plan. While starting and maintaining a business can be very intimidating, there are many other business professionals and resources available for the LNC entrepreneur to gain knowledge which can lead to a thriving business.

References

Carleo, S. (2017). Business principles & practices. In *AALNC Legal nurse consulting professional course* (module 13). Retrieved from www.aalnc.org/page/course-content#packages.

Dickinson, J. & Zorn, E. (2013). Liability lessons for legal nurse consultants part one: An analysis of claims involving legal nurse consultants. *Journal of Legal Nursing Consulting, 24*(2), 4–9.

FindLaw. (n.d.). *Capitol Steel Fabricators, Inc. v. Mega Construction Co.* Court of Appeal, Second District, Division 5, California. (2010). Retrieved from https://caselaw.findlaw.com/ca-court-of-appeal/1217658.html.

Health and Human Services. (n.d.). Summary of the HIPAA Privacy Rule. Retrieved from www.hhs.gov/hipaa/for-professionals/privacy/laws-regulations/index.html.

U.S. Small Business Administration. (n.d.). Open a business bank account. Retrieved from www.sba.gov/business-guide/launch-your-business/open-business-bank-account.

Additional Reading

Carpern, C. (n.d.). 3 easy ways to liven up your LinkedIn. Retrieved from http://ct-social.com/linkedin-connections/.

Carpern, C. (n.d.). How often should I be sharing posts on LinkedIn? Retrieved from http://ct-social.com/sharing-posts-on-linkedin/.

FindLaw. (n.d.). Compliance information and resources: State by state. Retrieved from https://smallbusiness.findlaw.com/business-laws-and-regulations/compliance-information-and-resources-state-by-state.html.

Nations, D. (2017). What is LinkedIn and why should you be on it? Retrieved from www.lifewire.com/what-is-linkedin-3486382.

Test Questions

1. An LNC subcontracting agreement may contain clauses related to all of the following EXCEPT:
   A. Pay rate per hour or per project
   B. Payment will not be made until the contractor receives payment
   C. Subcontractor must provide proof of liability insurance
   D. Subcontractor cannot market to attorneys within 100 miles of the contractor's location

2. Independent LNCs may subcontract to other LNCs when:
   A. They have a case that falls outside of their expertise
   B. They cannot complete the requested work in a reasonable time frame
   C. They want to grow their business without the responsibility of employees
   D. All of the above

3. The main components of a business plan include all of the following EXCEPT:
   A. Market Analysis
   B. Description of the Business
   C. Mission Statement
   D. Financial Statements

4. A legal nurse consultant's marketing material can include:
   A. Company website
   B. Brochures
   C. Blogging
   D. All of the above

5. Steps to ensuring security and HIPAA compliance for an LNC's home office include all of the following EXCEPT:
   A. Shredding of closed case documents
   B. Sending case emails from a shared family computer with virus protection
   C. Storage of case documents in a locked cabinet
   D. Discussion of case details with legal team members only

Answers: 1. B, 2. D, 3. C, 4. D, 5. B

Chapter 31

The Legal Nurse Consultant as Expert Witness

Mariann F. Cosby, DNP, MPA, MSN, RN, PHN, CEN, NE-BC, LNCC®, CLCP, CCM, MSCC
Tricia West, MBA/HCM, BSN, RN, CHN, PHN

Contents

Objectives

- Discuss the foundation for nurses serving as expert witnesses
- Describe routes by which nurses may assume the role of expert witness
- List steps for record review and analysis by expert witnesses
- Delineate expectations for communications by nurse experts
- Relate the legal definition of "standard of care" to the clinical definition
- Explain the testifying nurse expert's role in deposition and trial

Introduction

History of the Nurse as an Expert Witness

Legal proceedings employing expert witnesses date back seven centuries. Even then, courts called upon persons with special knowledge or experience to assist them. Just as it is today, the principal purpose of expert witness testimony was to provide the court with opinions based upon the expert's scientific, technical, or specialized knowledge, experience, skill, or training (Barros-Bailey & Dominick, 2017).

Black's Law Dictionary (Garner, 2014) defines an expert as: "someone who, through education or experience, has developed skill or knowledge in a particular subject, so that he or she may form an opinion that will assist the fact-finder" (p. 699). Experts provide expert evidence, defined as "Evidence about a scientific, technical, professional, or other specialized issue given by a person qualified to testify because of familiarity with the subject or special training in the field" (Garner, 2014, p. 675). The experts give their opinion to aid the court in a decision or judgment. They are questioned before being allowed to testify to ensure they are qualified to offer expert testimony on the topic. Today nurses are called upon to function as experts in a variety of legal proceedings.

A key distinction between an expert fact witness and an expert witness is that an expert witness may provide opinions on the standard of care whereas a fact witness does not. The specialized knowledge or skill that permits a person to form and offer opinions is what distinguishes the expert witness from a fact witness (Barros-Bailey & Dominick, 2017). For more information on expert fact witnesses, see Chapter 32.

In addition to approving the expert's qualifications, the court must determine the opinion evidence is relevant to the issues in the case, that it is reliable, and that it will assist the trier of fact. The trier of fact is usually a jury. However, in a bench trial, it could be a single judge or a panel of three judges.

Expert testimony is necessary when the judge's or jury's understanding of the science or technical facts are beyond the scope of a layperson. The landmark case that established the rule of *general acceptance* for scientific evidence is *Frye v. United States*, a federal case decided by the District of Columbia Circuit in 1923. The court in this case held that if an expert's conclusions are *generally accepted* in the scientific community, the expert's testimony is admissible evidence. "When the question involved requires special experience or special knowledge, then the opinion of the expert skilled in the particular science, art or trade to which the question relates is admissible in evidence" (*Frye v. United States*, 1923).

The general acceptance standard remained in place until the Federal Rules of Evidence (FRE) were adopted in 1975. The Federal Rules of Evidence adopted by the U.S. Supreme Court govern the introduction of evidence in civil and criminal proceedings in federal courts. While the Federal Rules do not apply to state court proceedings, many states model their evidence rules on the federal specifications (Paul & Narang, 2017).

Article VII of the Federal Rules of Evidence governs opinions and expert testimony. Rule 702, which applies to testimony that may be offered by an expert witness was amended in 2000 in response to the 1993 U.S. Supreme Court decision, *Daubert v. Merrell Dow Pharmaceuticals, Inc.* and its application in many other cases [Jan. 2, 1975, P.L. 93–595, § 1, 88 Stat. 1937; Apr. 17, 2000, eff. Dec. 1, 2000] (Federal Evidence Review, n.d.-a). The current rule, amended in 2011 as part the Federal Evidence style amendments, reads as follows (Federal Evidence Review, n.d.-b):

A witness who is qualified as an expert by knowledge, skill, experience, training, or education may testify in the form of an opinion or otherwise if:

a. the expert's scientific, technical, or other specialized knowledge will help the trier of fact to understand the evidence or determine a fact in issue;
b. the testimony is based upon sufficient facts or data;
c. the testimony is the product of reliable principles and methods; and
d. the expert has reliably applied the principles and methods to the facts of the case.

(FRE, 2018)

In Daubert, the Supreme Court charged trial judges with the additional responsibility of *gatekeeper*. In this role, the trial judge evaluates the methodology, reliability, and relevance of opinions presented by scientific experts. If the trial judge opines that scientific testimony is not supported by accepted scientific methodology, the judge can exclude the unreliable scientific expert testimony (Wilkinson, 2015). (See Chapter 36 for more information on Daubert, Frye, and FRE 702.)

Nursing has evolved into a profession with a distinct body of knowledge, university-based education, specialized practice, standards of practice, a societal contract, and an ethical code (American Nurses Association [ANA], 2015a, 2015b). The practice of nursing requires decision-making and skill based upon the principles of the biological, physical, and behavioral and social sciences, and evidence-based research for identifying risk factors and providing specific interventions. In the United States of America, every state has a Board of Nursing that is the state entity authorized to regulate nursing practice. Every state legislature has promulgated licensing standards and regulations for the nursing profession in their respective Nurse Practice Acts and Advanced Practice Nursing Acts. Under the nursing act, only a registered nurse would meet the qualifications for sitting for a registered nurse (RN) licensure examination, and as such be eligible for licensure as a registered nurse. The specifics of each state's Nurse Practice Act can be found online (Find Your Nurse Practice Act, n.d.).

Nursing is not practiced under the supervision of a physician. Although a physician writes medical orders for patients, which are carried out by nurses, physicians do not supervise, evaluate, or direct nursing care. Expert opinion is typically required to establish the applicable standard of care and the actual departure from standard practice. The expert witness must possess the necessary skill, knowledge, training, and experience to ensure that the opinion rendered is reliable.

Since the only expert qualified to render expert opinion testimony is a member of the same profession who practices in a substantially similar manner, only a nurse can testify to nursing standard of care and performance. However, for many years, physicians routinely testified to establish the standard of care for the nursing profession. Today courts acknowledge that nurses possess specialized knowledge that physicians do not have unless they have been trained and have practiced as nurses (Kaminski, 2015; Wilkinson, 2015). An exception to this is a physician who teaches nursing students in a formal university nursing program, and would be limited to the content of the course taught by the physician, which most likely would not include all components of the nursing process upon which nursing standard of care is based.

In a landmark case in 2004, *Sullivan v. Edward Hospital*, the Supreme Court of Illinois held that a board-certified internal medicine physician was not competent to testify as to the standard of care of a nurse. Citing the Amicus Brief submitted by The American Association of Nurse Attorneys, the court noted:

> A physician, who is not a nurse, is no more qualified to offer expert, opinion testimony as to the standard of care for nurses than a nurse would be to offer an opinion as to the physician standard of care. Certainly, nurses are not permitted to offer expert testimony against a physician based on their observances of physicians or their familiarity with the procedures involved ... Such testimony would be, essentially, expert testimony as to the standard of medical care.
>
> (*Sullivan v. Edward Hospital*, 806 N.E. 2d 645 Ill., 2004)

The common theme running through court decisions on this issue is that physicians have little firsthand knowledge of nursing practices and training. Physicians rarely teach nursing programs or write nursing texts. Therefore, a physician in most cases would not be familiar with the standard of care or with the nursing policies and procedures (P&P) governing the standard of care for nurses.

Guidelines for an Expert Witness

Expert witnesses are represented in many venues. Because they contribute to the process of determining whether the standards set forth in their profession are being upheld and as such are a valuable tool to the trier of fact in a court proceeding, their qualifications and credibility are of paramount importance. The following set of guidelines (Zorn, 2015) is instructive to any expert making oneself available to the triers of fact, and may enhance the expert's credibility:

- Do not work with unethical attorneys.
- Be wary of attorneys who are reluctant to provide all case materials. The expert will be questioned as to how one can make valid opinions without all information being provided.
- Avoid attorneys who are unwilling to pay for the expert to review all relevant case material.
- Always tell the truth. Do not accept cases as an expert that cannot be honestly supported.
- Be certain the retaining attorney has made the expert role in the case clear. Ask to see the designation as an expert document.
- Read all documents before rendering a final opinion.
- Know that everything the expert does inside and outside of a courtroom can affect the person's credibility as an expert.
- Always maintain a competent, professional and confident decorum.
- Use appropriate foundation and research when forming opinions.
- Carefully review all case documents.
- Request missing documents.
- Do not use the attorney's chronology as the basis of one's opinions. Review the actual medical records.

According to Babitsky (2005, p. 1), the "dangerous expert witness is an expert witness who puts fear into opposing counsel." As Babitsky further described, this is elicited by the expert's ability to communicate, their command of factual knowledge, teaching and communication skills, and skills in persuading a jury. Being a dangerous expert witness means mastering opposing counsel's tactics and turning the tables back on them. This makes cross-examining the witness very difficult for opposing counsel.

Attorneys frequently evaluate and consider credentials or qualifications that will be critically scrutinized when an expert witness is called to testify. Areas that the retaining attorney consider include:

- the expert's license and certifications
- formal education
- continuing education
- professional experience
- specialty training
- membership in professional organizations
- publications including peer-reviewed journals and textbooks
- consulting experience
- teaching and lecturing positions
- presentations

Therefore, the successful expert should consider these qualification guidelines:

- Avoid gaps in the curriculum vitae (CV) by providing assurance all of the credentials are correct and certifications are current
- Never include certifications or licenses that the expert does not have
- State only experience that has occurred and to which can be attested
- Carefully market expertise and services
- Provide or offer expert services to both plaintiff and defense attorneys as the expert's opinions should be based upon facts, and not biased
- Carefully review what to include on one's website. Be mindful of content, using sales language, case names, and stretching the truth
- Use professional discretion for social media posts. Be mindful of comments, pictures, and personal information that could taint the expert's reputation or credibility or be viewed as professional bias.

For additional information regarding the qualifications attorneys consider when screening potential expert witnesses, see Chapter 36.

The nurse expert witness is an integral part of the legal team. In professional negligence actions, through expert testimony, plaintiffs' attorneys provide the court with testimony to support the case allegations, and experts for the defendant healthcare providers offer opinions that rebut the allegations. In this context, experts testify to assist triers of fact (judge or jury) in reaching a decision by offering scientific and technical information that is more than common knowledge.

As a member of the nursing profession, the nurse expert witness identifies standard of care for nursing aspects of the case and objectively describes whether or not the standard of care was met or how the standard of care was breached. This role is an opportunity for nurses to integrate their professional education and knowledge with experience from clinical, administrative, educational, and research settings and apply them to situations in the legal arena.

The nurse who assumes the role as an expert witness must understand that it includes commitment to testimony at deposition and trial. Nurses should discuss their qualifications very carefully with retaining attorneys since legal qualifications for testimony as an expert witness vary from state to state. In some states, the expert must identically match the defendant in areas of specialty. The major responsibilities of nurse experts include the following:

- Offer opinions based on the standard of care and current practice guidelines, not on morals, motivations, political positions, or scruples of either side
- Render opinions based on their knowledge, experience, training, education, and facts in evidence
- Base an opinion on *a reasonable degree of nursing certainty* for each alleged act of negligence that constitutes a deviation from the acceptable standard of care
- For those jurisdictions that allow nurses to opine on causation, offer nursing opinions on causation
- Acknowledge that nurse experts *do not* advocate for either plaintiff or defendant—nurse experts are advocates for the standard of care

(Schofield & Huntington-Frazier, 2015)

Legal Culture versus Healthcare Culture

The legal arena is a forum that differs from healthcare culture in many ways. Nurses who propose to work as expert witnesses may find it helpful to visit the law library to review the textbooks and journals that attorneys use as they prepare cases. Practice-oriented journals for attorneys such as *Trial* and *For the Defense* describe specific communication techniques and strategies.

As members of a highly regarded profession, nurses may be shocked at the communication rules and adversarial style of the legal world. Experienced nurses are familiar and comfortable with indirect communication with physicians, such as querying potentially deleterious orders in a way that preserves the physician's ego and role in the healthcare hierarchy. Direct, powerful communication from attorneys may cause nursing professionals to feel uncomfortable. The nurse expert witness should not be intimidated by unfamiliar communication rules. Educational and professional preparations in critical thinking, and experience in clinical crises, provide a firm foundation for nurses to adapt to the foreign territory of the legal arena.

Obtaining Cases for Review

Professional reputation, clinical expertise, and communication skills are the most significant factors sought in nurse expert witnesses. Additionally, attorneys seek experts with whom they can communicate easily and candidly discuss strategies. Attorneys look for professionals with characteristics that will assist them in telling their story to the triers of fact. To win their cases, they need experts with strong teaching skills that can be adapted to the courtroom's unique environment, as well as an open, pleasant personality with a relaxed manner, and a sense of humor.

Such an expert must also possess the ability to explain rather than advocate, despite nursing's self-defined commitment to patient advocacy, as legal advocacy in the courtroom belongs to the attorneys (Schofield & Huntington-Frazier, 2015). Experts should possess the ability to offer and defend concise, clear, and objective opinions with honesty; and impeccable integrity, professional responsibility, and ethical conviction. They must exude professional authenticity and confidence (Powell, 2013; Zorn, 2015).

In some situations, novice nurse experts may have more credibility with juries than experts with extensive testifying experience. The ability to meet the requirements of the nurse expert role is more important than experience in the testifying role. It is not uncommon to find nurse experts who have worked on many dozens of cases yet have never testified at trial. This is due to the overwhelming number of cases that settle before trial.

Multiple sources exist for obtaining cases for review. Nursing colleagues may provide an expert's name to an attorney. Nurse expert witnesses experienced in case review may be asked to refer other nursing experts. Some legal nurse consulting firms either refer or subcontract RNs to requesting attorneys or claims adjusters who seek assistance for case review. The RN interested in expert witness review may refer colleagues to legal nurse consulting firms or may interview with a law firm directly. Legal nurse consultants (LNCs) who prefer to function in a non-testifying role, may provide referrals or do background work on cases.

Membership in the American Association of Legal Nurse Consultants (AALNC) is a valuable resource for obtaining cases to review. A listing on the LNC locator®, a service provided on the AALNC website (www.aalnc.org), may result in a case being referred to the expert. Attending local and national AALNC meetings, networking with colleagues and speakers, and distributing business cards are marketing options. Demonstrating professional expertise and strong communication skills by speaking at local and national meetings or publishing in journals and books is a reliable method for increasing the nurse's visibility to other professionals who seek such expertise.

Possible sources for case review referrals include:

- Nursing, legal, and medical colleagues
- Legal nurse consulting firms
- Expert witness referral services
- AALNC LNC Locator (www.aalnc.org)
- Networking with attendees, vendors, and speakers at AALNC National and Chapter events
- Legal Nurse Listserv
- Speaking at AALNC or Bar events, webinars, seminars, or meetings
- Publishing in peer-reviewed journals and books

Case solicitation must be done with care and consideration. The nurse expert witness is an expert clinician serving as case reviewer and analyst. Those nurse experts who choose to market their services as a business should target both plaintiff and defense firms to avoid the appearance of bias or lack of objectivity and the perception of being a *hired gun* whose opinions are for sale. This allows the LNC opportunity to describe in testimony how to practice ethically: addressing the facts of any case, without allegiance to either side (Kaminsky, 2015).

Unfortunately, there are those experts who can be hired to say whatever an attorney wants to hear. The ethical nurse expert witness bases case review, analysis, and opinions strictly on the standard of care and facts in the case. This speaks for itself in answering why and how an expert can testify for either side. Ethical experts simply address what happened and how and testify accordingly. They have no allegiance to either side; rather, their opinions are grounded solely in standards and ethics (Kaminski, 2015).

The ethical nurse expert's fees are based on time expended on the matter. Although time-based bills are created, opinions cannot be bought. It is unethical to contract with attorneys based on the outcome of the case. In other words, experts should not work on cases on a lien. For this very reason, it is highly recommended that all outstanding fees be paid prior to the nurse expert providing any testimony. Experts are paid for their education, training, experience, and time— not for their opinion. By waiting to be paid after an opinion is rendered, experts can be accused by opposing counsel of having been paid for their opinion.

As the length of testimony is unknown upfront, it is recommended that one get a retainer to cover the longest time likely for testimony. For trial testimony, some experts charge, for example, a one day minimum and keep the entire retainer even if the testimony does not last that long; others return any unused balance. This is a business decision for each expert to decide.

Accepting a Case

As outlined below, prior to accepting a case the nurse expert should query the retaining party for various case elements. This includes determining whether the retaining party is plaintiff or defense, if any conflicts exist, and the role that is being sought: consultant or expert witness. The attorney's expectations should also be clear about notes, written reports, and timelines. Additionally, services and associated fees should be clearly stated in writing. The nurse should be cognizant of the standard of care under consideration during this preliminary phase.

Check for Conflicts

The first order of business is to check for conflicts of interest. The nurse expert must confirm that no bias or impropriety exists. Depending upon the situation, personal or professional relationships with the opposing side may require the expert to refer the case to another expert. Examples of conflicts include the expert working clinically for a facility being sued or a personal or professional relationship with the plaintiff or defendant. The expert should discuss whether a prior or current relationship poses an actual or potential conflict with the retaining attorney. If a conflict does exist, the expert can suggest possible replacements to the attorney. If the expert identified a potential conflict, again the facts should be shared with counsel at the outset.

Once conflict checks are concluded, the attorney typically provides case details about the plaintiff, events, and specific expectations for the nurse expert. Acceptance by the nurse expert is based on the appropriateness of the nurse's education, research, publications, and experience in a clinical setting like the case. If doubt exists, the issue should be discussed in detail with the retaining attorney and may include a referral to a more qualified colleague. Maintaining a network of other qualified nursing and medical experts is a sign of professional involvement. Such referrals define the expert's integrity and invite future contact from the same attorney. Follow-up correspondence to thank the attorney for consideration in a specific case is always appropriate, even if the nurse expert does not accept the assignment.

Establishing One's Role

When an attorney or member of the attorney's firm first contacts the expert, it is important to ascertain whether the attorney represents the plaintiff or defense. Having this piece of information should assist the nurse expert in framing the initial conversation. The nurse expert must realize that there are differences specific to working with plaintiff versus defense counsel.

Although the nurse expert must always be impartial in developing and testifying opinions, knowing plaintiff and defense perspectives will help the expert communicate more effectively with each, as there are differences in their obligations and procedures.

Once a case is filed, an insurance company's defense attorney has no options, and must accept the case. Based on the facts of the case, the defense strategy may be to defend vigorously with a demurrer or motion for summary judgment (MSJ), or to negotiate a settlement. Plaintiff counsel, in contrast, is never obligated to accept a case, and may choose to decline it on its merits, ethics, financial basis, or due to client presentation.

Expert Witness or Consultant

The nurse needs to know what type of services the attorney is seeking. Is the requested role to provide services as an expert witness or consultant? Bear in mind that only an expert witness's materials are discoverable. A nurse consultant can create notes, comments, summaries, and opinions that will be considered privileged as attorney work product. However, if the attorney initially engages the nurse as a consultant and later wants the nurse to testify as an expert witness on the case, the privileged status becomes void and all documents and notes become discoverable. Therefore, when contacted by an attorney who may initially be uncertain about whether the nurse will be needed to testify, the nurse should err on the side of caution and approach the case as if retained as an expert witness.

Since written materials created by expert witnesses are subject to discovery, the expert should discuss the creation of written materials with the retaining attorney at the time the case is accepted, before any notes or reports are generated. It is important for the nurse expert to know what the attorney needs and expects before creating any potentially discoverable material. Determine whether verbal, written, or both types of work product meet the requirements of the case. Some experts will create a brief chronology that includes *just the facts*. This technique may be part of the expert's review and analysis.

Timelines/Deadlines

Case acceptance should be accompanied by a clear understanding of the case time frame as deadlines are critical in the legal arena. The nurse should not accept a case without adequate time to receive, review, and analyze all relevant materials sufficiently. It is accepted practice for an expert to charge a rush fee for a short turnaround. When this is likely, it is professional courtesy to apprise the retaining attorney in advance, preferably as part of the expert's retention agreement. Any potential changes to an agreed time frame should be discussed immediately with the retaining attorney as they arise.

Standard of Care Considerations

It is essential for the nurse expert to ensure the attorney's intent is evaluation of nursing care. While nurses may be knowledgeable about standards of practice for other healthcare providers, it is not appropriate for nurses to testify to the standards of care for other professions. If the retaining attorney is seeking opinions outside the nurse's scope of practice, the nurse should decline to offer such testimony and advise the attorney to obtain an expert with experience in that non-nursing area. Please see Chapter 2 for more information.

The nurse expert witness must base testimony on the legal standard of care, i.e., the ordinary degree of skill and care exercised by a like professional in the same condition and the same circumstances. Inexperienced expert witnesses often set and refer to their own personal standards of care, and these may exceed those of the legal definition. This may be appropriate for clinical practice, but it is not appropriate for legal work. Standard of care in litigation is written based on how a reasonable, average practitioner would act in comparable circumstances.

Standards of care were historically linked to the geographical community in which the event occurred. However, with advanced communications, standardized educational curricula, widely distributed professional publications, and standards promulgated by professional organizations, lower local standards of care are no longer acceptable justification for a lower level of current practice. This means, for example, that a patient with an acute myocardial infarction is entitled to the same standard of care in a rural area as in a major university medical center. The difference is that the rural provider must assess the patient enough to know when to transfer the patient elsewhere for the standard of care to be provided when status and needs exceed the rural facility's capability.

Rapid advances in technology may change the standard of care from year to year. However, in litigation, the testifying expert must realize that opinions based on standard of care must conform to those in force at the date or time of the event. This concept also applies to the expert's educational and clinical practice. Other considerations include changes in institutional and facility policies and procedures, state statutes and regulations, national professional standards, certification criteria, and academic curricula. Long statutes of limitations associated with obstetric and pediatric cases require attention in locating experts who were educated and practicing during the time of the instant case.

Establishing Nurse/Attorney-Client Relationship

Although a case may be accepted for initial review by telephone, the nurse expert should immediately write to the attorney to confirm details of the arrangement, fee structure, deadlines, and whether a report is being requested. This is typically accomplished with a professional service acknowledgment or engagement agreement confirming the terms of the attorney/expert relationship. This acknowledgment should be signed by the attorney and returned with the retainer check prior to beginning work on the case. Fee schedules should also be sent now, specifying what the expert is charging for time spent and any other charges that may be incurred during the case such as travel time, mileage, copying, Bates-stamping, courier services, postage, etc.

The expert's commitment to objective evaluation should be apparent in conversation and correspondence. Although initial screening thoughts may be shared based upon facts presented during this first conversation, it must be clear that any responses to counsel's queries are based solely on the information provided and may be subject to significant revision when all materials are available. Retaining counsel may omit facts or provide biased information, unintentionally or otherwise.

Careful review of the records may allow the seasoned expert to identify *a smoking gun*, a fact not previously noticed by counsel that serves as conclusive evidence; this may or may not be in the client's favor. In any case, the ethical expert should never proffer opinions before reviewing and analyzing all records available, before and after retention and as discovery proceeds.

As a legal strategy, to preclude one from being retained by the other side, attorneys may contact a well-known expert for a *curbside* opinion about a case. Having the non-retained expert provide even a verbal opinion could, therefore, prevent the person from being designated as an expert for the other side. This strategy serves to *block* the use of a strong potential expert for the opposing attorney. Additionally, the expert should be cautious in providing opinions prior to being retained, since one would not have all pertinent information on which to base an opinion. The ethical expert should be careful to always have solid facts prior to formulating an opinion.

After Accepting a Case: The Case Review

Elements of a Case Review

The attorney may not realize the value of some of the records; never rely solely on an attorney's summary or chronology. The careful expert will let the attorney know what records will give the most complete information, and look at them with a critical eye and an open mind. Depending on the particulars of the case, materials needed might include:

- Medical records from many providers
- Billing records
- Emergency medical records, paramedic run sheets, depositions of the plaintiff and others involved in the case, healthcare providers, and opposing expert
- Depositions of all relevant parties, experts, and witnesses
- Policies and procedures

- Payroll, schedules, and time sheets
- Inservice training records
- Employment files
- Material safety data sheets
- Accident reconstruction reports
- IT metadata reports, commonly known as audit trail reports

The expert should acknowledge receipt of any materials, listing them in order in communications. Document review may raise questions at any time and prompt the expert to request other materials as specifics indicate. Questions that the expert should keep in mind include: Can liability or causation be defended? Can any of the four required elements of malpractice (for additional information, see Chapter 4) be explained and therefore eliminated? As the expert begins the case review process, the expert must determine if additional records are needed, as all applicable records must be present to allow the nurse expert to develop coherent and complete opinions. Clinicians are aware of the variety of records that are created in any patient care situation, including notes and documents from a variety of physicians, nurses, and allied health personnel. Although the attorney may describe the allegations and central issues of the matter, the nurse expert and attorney should discuss which records are essential, because the expert's opinion cannot and should not be based on the attorney's or attorney assistants' summary.

The nurse expert should also be aware that case development can go on for several years. The nurse expert must create an organized filing system to maintain records safely and completely. Filing systems need not be elaborate but should provide for rapid retrieval and safe keeping of information. It is common for a cloud service to be utilized by counsel to provide medical records and exchange other case related materials.

Security

Case development can go on for several years, with more materials coming to light over time. Personal health information (PHI) included in records obtained from care facilities, providers, and health insurance carriers is covered by HIPAA law when it is provided to business associates, such as attorneys. Expert witnesses are covered under this provision, as the attorney firm is required to assure that their retained experts keep PHI secure. Therefore, an expert witness should have an HIPAA-compliant filing system. If records are transmitted via file transfer protocol (FTP) or other cloud-based means, both sender and receiver must be sure they will be handled securely (for additional information, see Chapters 8 and 9).

Organizing the Medical Records

Establishing a process for reviewing the medical records assures the best rate of success for being able to identify breaches in the standard of care and decreasing the chance of omitting salient information. The nurse expert's first perusal of the documents provided should focus on identification of potential missing records. Developing a list of case specific forms and documents that one should expect to see in the medical record can assist the nurse in this process. Additionally, other health related documents such as billing records or logs can be added to the list of records to request from the retaining attorney (for additional information, see Chapter 7).

Ideally, a complete set of all medical records associated with the event will be provided. These records should be organized by the expert in a logical manner that:

1. Corresponds to the way in which a nursing/medical expert would expect to find records in a medical chart
2. Will allow opinions to be developed
3. Provides easily retrievable data for discussion with the attorney and for testimony

It is common for legal office staff to create a master set of records which are Bates-stamped, to minimize confusion when pages are identified. If only abstracts or selected pages from a record are provided for the expert's initial overview, the opinion rendered should clearly express that it is based on limited information and thus subject to change if more information is provided. The nurse expert should ask whether all pages of the record have been sent, or it may be apparent from review of the Bates-stamping that some pages are missing, either accidentally or by design. In some situations, the nurse expert may decline to provide an opinion until appropriate documents are received and analyzed. Not always understanding the nurse expert's process, some attorneys will try to save money and provide select portions of the medical records that they think are important rather than all the records. An expert should be mindful of this cost saving tactic and request additional documents as needed.

Identifying the Critical Medical Record Information

Once the records are organized, reading and identifying the important facts serve to assist the nurse expert in developing opinions in the case. It will help in preparing for depositions, when for summary judgment and pre-trial motions, in and during trial. It is critical for assisting counsel in putting together facts as they relate to the standard of care. Familiarity with records provides a firm foundation for the nurse expert's review. Applicable sections of the medical record are examined in detail, with the framework of the nursing process and standard of care kept in mind to ensure objective evaluation. Time frames, nursing care (including all the elements of the nursing process), patient responses, and continuity of care are significant elements for meeting the standard of care. Validation of data from other healthcare providers (such as physicians, pharmacists, and other ancillary departments) is essential. Documentation from other providers that may support, diminish, or refute the nurse's initial opinion must be considered as case analysis progresses. To be as unbiased as possible, opinion formulation should be based on findings in the medical record and supported by information from published standard of care sources.

Some experts prefer to make notes on temporary stickers such as sticky notes or bookmarks in electronic records; some may create detailed notes, outlines, and chronologies. Others may prefer to read the material and formulate opinions without creating written materials of any kind. Since all written materials created by expert witnesses are subject to discovery, the expert should discuss the creation of written materials with the attorney at the time the case is accepted before any notes or reports are generated. Many attorneys prefer that no documents be created.

Chronologies

Most experts find developing a comprehensive chronology very beneficial and part of a critical thinking tool and case analysis framework. This process helps the nurse expert analyze all information, clarify the sequence of events, and identify key points, issues, and challenges. From the first documents received, assembling case facts in an accessible format can put the expert on track to assist the attorney with a courtroom victory.

An expert's fact chronology can also be a tremendous asset for both the expert's deposition and trial preparation without the need to create a separate set of notes. A good expert chronology makes it easy for everyone on the trial team to share case knowledge and brainstorm strategies. Chronologies can also help ensure complete discovery. What facts are disputed? Which facts will still need sources that will be acceptable in court?

Experts can construct a chronology with a proprietary data management tool (many are available for purchase/subscription) or using a simple spreadsheet program with appropriate headers, such as date, record source, Bates number, relevant points, and notes. Most such tools can accept links to PDFs or other content for ease in retrieval and can be searched and sorted by one or more columns. There are several methods by which an expert can create a chronology. It is important to include disputed facts that opposing counsel may present. Recording these in a chronology or database, may make it easy to identify those facts which support or refute opposing counsel's position. A chronology can also be an aid as one is reviewing the facts and information of the case, without spending time redoing notes. Further, it helps tremendously in conveying the essence of the case, supporting the opined conclusions when the time comes. For more information on chronologies and reports, see Chapter 35.

Formulating the Expert Opinion

Determining Nursing Standards

The nursing process defines each patient as unique, requiring individual assessment, nursing diagnosis, planning, interventions, and ongoing evaluation and re-evaluation. Although many professional commonalities are involved in meeting the standard of care, the expert must identify standards for the patients and clinical scenarios presented for review assuring that the time frame that pertains to the case is utilized.

Written standards may be found in:

■ State and federal statutes and regulations, including Nursing Practice Acts and Rules
■ Position statements by the state's Board of Registered Nurses and by the nursing specialty's professional organizations
■ State and proprietary accreditation agencies such as The Joint Commission
■ National specialty nursing associations, including specialties and sub-specialties
■ Academic curricula
■ Professional literature, particularly peer-reviewed publications
■ Institutional policies and procedures

Using published standards reduces subjectivity of opinions on standard of care. However, many documents accepted as standards contain disclaimers that suggest they are guidelines that are neither comprehensive nor limiting. Such disclaimers may weaken the strength of the information as published. Disclaimers also refer to the importance of tailoring care to individual patient circumstances. As the American Heart Association (2000) described in its discussion of application of algorithms to clinical care: If patient care could be reduced to a set of objective *cookbook* requirements, there would be no need for analysis by nurse expert witnesses—but professional responsibility requires a *thinking cook*. This means that the nurse expert must use informed critical thinking when analyzing records to form an opinion regarding standard of care.

When performing the medical record review, the nurse expert should also consider the following as part of the analytical process to determine whether the standard of care was met or breached:

- Published standards of practice
- Facility policies, procedures, and protocols
- Medications and treatments
- Equipment used
- Pathophysiology as applied to the case being reviewed

The expert should expect to opine on the following three issues: What demonstrates care below the standard? Where does the reasonable and prudent nurse test apply? What are considered known potential complications?

Deciphering the Medical Record

Knowing what is reasonable and expected in a medical record is only the beginning. A nurse expert must be able to decipher what is actually charted in the medical record. (See Chapters 7, 8, and 9 for more information on medical records.) Unreadable or undecipherable records should be revisited. Sometimes what is difficult to decipher or read becomes clearer as the context of the case and other portions of the medical record are read and analyzed. Remember that ignoring charting because it cannot be read, or for any reason, may be tempting but unwise. The expert may identify a *smoking gun* that had not previously been noted by counsel, an oversight that could be germane to the case.

There frequently are inaccuracies or conflicting information in the medical record. A healthcare provider may read and carry forward another's mistake in a history and physical, for example. These errors may have little bearing on the case, or they may carry major impact. The expert may discern inconsistencies in documentation regarding prior treatment or lack of treatment due to these cut-and-paste actions. The implications of these errors can be critical and the expert needs to validate or invalidate what the chart reports.

Documentation Scrutiny

As medical records are read and analyzed, the nurse expert should remember the mantra from nursing school: *If it wasn't charted, it wasn't done.* However, there are some caveats. The nurse expert should analyze documentation deficiencies very carefully. The nurse should look for trends in the documentation that reflect the expected standard of care as it relates to the case issues. Conversely, inadequate or absent documentation may reflect a pattern of inadequate care, case specific or otherwise. This is an essential part of the expert's medical record review.

Often, what is not said or is omitted in a medical record is just as important as or more so than what is documented. Here is an example of one of the caveats: Although not documented, it was done.

A patient was to receive intravenous (IV) fluid to replace a low sodium level. Documentation noted fluid type and rate given, and appeared consistent with the orders and the nursing standard of care. However, upon further review of other evidence and additional careful analysis of the IV fluid documentation, it was apparent that the records were missing documentation of several liters of fluid that had to have been administered to account for a rapid increase in serum sodium. This provided the causal link to damages.

In this case, although the additional IV fluids were not charted, case analysis concluded that they were given and ultimately led to the patient's demise. Even though it was not charted, it *was* done.

The reader is referred to Chapter 9 for identifying deficiencies associated with electronic medical records drop-down menus and issues with charting by exception.

State and federal regulations mandate adequate charting. For example, the California Code of Regulations Title 22 Division 5 Licensing and Certification contain regulations regarding health records in skilled nursing facilities. State specific and federal information is searchable and available online. For example, the California regulations for skilled nursing facility records include:

§ 72547 Content of Health Records.
  (a) A facility shall maintain for each patient a health record which shall include
  (b) Nurses' notes which shall be signed and dated. Nurses' notes shall include
  (c) Meaningful and informative nurses' progress notes written by licensed nurses as often as the patient's condition warrants. However, weekly nurses' progress notes shall be written by licensed nurses on each patient and shall be specific to the patient's needs, the patient care plan, and the patient's response to care and treatments.

The careful nurse expert will also look for behaviors such as assessments, treatments, and medication administration that may have been done although they are not evident in the chart documentation. For example, although urinary catheter insertion may not be documented, the output and monitoring of such is documented. Therefore, although not documented as inserted, it was done. However, who placed the catheter and under what circumstances may be important; standard for documentation will likely note that this should be included.

Not everything that is done for a patient and every conversation can be documented in the patient's record, as the nurse would be left with no time to actually provide care. However, documenting key care, instructions, and patient teaching is essential. For example, a nursing expert will be likely to know that for a patient at risk for pressure injury, it is critical that nurses document the patient's nutritional status, position changes, communication to the physician about any wound development, consultation by a wound care specialist, care planning to address pressure injury prevention, and the patient's response to all the above. The expert will recognize potential deficiencies in care if these do not appear in the record.

Reviewing Depositions

Depositions may not be available to the nurse expert early in case development, but the nurse expert should review and consider them as soon as they are available, checking for discrepancies with records for all disciplines.

Nurse Expert Deposition

Nurse expert witness deposition testimony often begins with an exploration of the expert's background (education and clinical experience), prior case review, and testimony experience. Whether both sides proffer expert reports depends upon the state in which the suit was filed or whether the case is in federal or state court. If a report is prepared, it is required to be provided to opposing counsel prior to deposition. The deposing counsel will explore the testifying expert's opinions as contained in the expert's report. If a report is not provided, opposing counsel will ask the expert about the person's opinions. Counsel will ask about the expert's familiarity with the care delivered and standards in the case. The expert will be expected to opine on both the care and basis for their opinion.

The nurse expert will be asked to review the opposing nurse expert's opinion, if there is one. An analysis of the opposing nurse expert's report or deposition should be done carefully, looking for discrepancies both within the deposition and from other case evidence. Did the opposing expert alter and misstate the facts in any way? Are the opinions supported based upon facts in the medical records or other depositions? Has the opposing expert addressed only the facts that match their case theory and ignored others? If the opposing counsel's nurse expert has critiqued one's own opinion, the retaining attorney may ask the nurse expert to prepare a written rebuttal, using the same criteria.

Witness Statements and Other Documents

At times, attorneys obtain written statements from the plaintiff or witnesses to an incident. These statements do not constitute sworn testimony and do not carry the same weight. The expert witness may be asked to review these as part of the case file.

Communication with the Attorney

Once the initial records are organized and reviewed, additional questions will often arise. The timing of the communications with the attorney will vary from case to case. The nurse expert may want to initiate a call to the attorney early on, before completing the entire review, to get some questions answered. At other times, a follow-up interview with the attorney may be in order once the bulk of the review is completed.

The nurse expert may suggest that counsel serve a request for the production of additional documents. Almost without exception, this will include the facility's policies and procedures (P&P). Rather than request entire volumes of P&P, which is time consuming and expensive to provide and review, it is more cost-effective for counsel to provide the expert with the facility table of contents of their policy and procedure manuals and then request which specific P&Ps are necessary. Again, what is requested is case specific.

Often, a response to a request for medical records omits certain types of documents. The nurse expert should suggest to the attorney what additional records to request. For a comprehensive list of documents to request for production, please refer to Chapter 7.

Initial Report to the Attorney

After initial case review, a conversation with the attorney provides the expert with an opportunity to ask questions, discuss opinions, and review case strategy. The nurse expert's clinical experience and education should be apparent in this conversation, as elements of nursing care are reviewed with the attorney to support opinions about the standard of care being met or breached. The expert's initial verbal report also provides more details of record analysis to assist the attorney, including suggestions for additional document requests, advice about other areas to investigate in the patient's care, and provision of literature pertinent to the case.

If the expert hired by a plaintiff attorney believes that no breach occurred, those opinions should be conveyed to the attorney as soon as possible to allow the attorney to decide about continuing with the case. This is especially true for plaintiff cases as the attorney pays all costs up front, recouping them only when and if a verdict or settlement for the plaintiff is found. On the defense side, if defensibility is questionable, a conversation with defense counsel about settlement should ensue.

Other times, the nurse expert may identify challenges in the case's fact pattern, which require reformulating the case strategy or taking an alternative approach. No matter which side retains the nurse expert, opinions should reflect a knowledge and understanding of the standard of care and how the medical record substantiates or refutes whether the nursing actions met the standard of care.

The nurse expert must always show personal and professional integrity. Most attorneys appreciate a frank discussion of case merits. If the expert's opinion is not strong, grounded in experience, education, literature, and clinical practice, it is inappropriate to continue as an expert in the case. Weak opinions are a disservice to all involved. If the expert's opinion is not strong or well-supported, the expert should offer to withdraw from the case. It would be unethical to proffer any specific opinion because of counsel's request to retain the business. Nurse experts' integrity is their stock in trade. Compromising it is unethical; opinions must always be based on the evidence. If the attorney's theory of the case does not align with the expert's opinions, the attorney may withdraw the expert and terminate the relationship for this case.

Written Reports

A report should not be written unless it is specifically requested by the attorney. If a report is requested, the expert should ask the attorney if a specific format or style is preferred. Whatever the format or style, the professional content must be defined by the expert's own opinion. Jurisdictions may have specific rules for expert reports that the attorney should clearly explain. It may be helpful to look at similar reports from other cases supplied by the attorney for writing and format techniques. The content must be the expert's own work and not be tainted by the attorney's input. Individual states may promulgate specific rules for expert reports that the attorney should clearly explain to the nurse expert. If not explained, and the nurse expert is not familiar, the expert should inquire regarding state specific rules.

Most expert reports include a list of documents reviewed, a description of the events that led up to the incident, a definition of standard of care, and the actual opinions of the expert about how standard of care was met or breached. Support such opinions with the basis of the expert's opinions. This would be from facts and examples from the medical record of specific nursing actions, or lack thereof and an explanation of the standard of care's relationship to them. The basis can also come from statements in sworn testimony such as depositions.

Reports should be concise, carefully organized, and clear, with flawless spelling and grammar. Rambling writing dilutes and muddles opinions. The elements of the nursing process: assessment, nursing diagnosis, planning, interventions, and evaluation; provide a simple framework to describe events and outcomes cogently. If the expert identifies more than one breach of standard, describing each should follow the same format for clarity.

Consider references to professional literature carefully before footnoting them in written reports to assure that the elements of the literature apply to the case specifics. Although the nurse expert may examine such documents as part of opinion formulation, the expert's background, education, and experience in similar clinical situations constitute the strongest foundation for opinions (The Academy of Experts, 2015).

Deposition Process and Trial Testimony for the Nurse Expert Witness

Pre-deposition Process

Pre-deposition planning includes a careful review of the documents and meeting with the retaining attorney. Although the nurse is not expected to have all records memorized, the expert is expected to know what is in them and be able to locate relevant records without much difficulty. This underscores the importance of having organized and numbered/Bates-stamped records and a chronology that allows the expert to quickly find the relevant records germane to the opinions. The preparation and ability to meet this goal is enhanced by strong professional background, personal confidence, calm demeanor, and careful attention to every word heard and spoken during the deposition. The expert needs to keep in mind that the court reporter's transcription of the deposition creates a permanent record that may be used at trial.

All depositions should be approached from the perspective that the expert is at trial. In preparing for the deposition, the nurse expert should consider the deposition testimony equivalent to trial testimony. The expert should spend the time needed to thoroughly review the case materials and formulate all opinions based on those materials.

Prior to the deposition, the retaining attorney should meet with the nurse expert to prepare. The meeting may occur days in advance or an hour or so just prior to the deposition testimony. The nurse expert should discuss the timing of this meeting in advance so that it best meets the needs of both parties. The attorney may discuss the formality and strict rules of deposition. This can create an environment that may be intimidating to the new nurse expert who is comfortable with clinical expertise, patient care, and healthcare culture and communication, yet a stranger to the legal world. Rules of discovery require that attorneys should not coach witnesses or obstruct information. The nurse expert must be able to explain opinions clearly, defending them in the face of a variety of questioning strategies from the opposing attorney. Above all, the expert must focus on the goal of this event—to clearly articulate opinions about the standard of care for the case.

Retaining counsel should be consulted about personal and professional items to be brought to deposition, since everything in the expert's file is discoverable. It is common to bring two copies of an updated CV, one for each attorney. The court reporter appreciates receiving a nurse expert's business card to verify identifying information that is part of the deposition, and a list of any technical words one might expect to be used during the deposition.

On the day of the deposition, the nurse expert should exhibit professional demeanor from the moment of arrival at the deposition, because attorneys from both sides will evaluate the expert's potential for strong courtroom appearance and testimony. The nurse expert should mentally rehearse good posture, pleasant facial expressions, and positive body language. Conservative business attire and accessories should be selected. A good night's rest, a healthy breakfast, and allowing extra travel time will help in decreasing stress. Electronic devices such as cell phones and pagers should be turned off.

Since most cases will settle prior to going to trial (greater than 90% generally speaking in medical malpractice cases), the nurse expert should remember that the deposition is an important factor in the outcome of the case. A strong and credible nurse expert is likely to have a positive impact.

Deposition Questioning

Opposing counsel conducts the deposition to discover information about the case and to develop the case for trial. Nurse experts should not minimize the importance of discovery and case development. Opposing attorneys craft specific strategies to discredit testimony or individuals. Experts take an oath to be truthful when testifying. Nurse experts can expect to have any element of their professional practice queried, often in a negative style, which is designed to intimidate and reduce the expert's credibility. Education, clinical experience, research, publications, and fees are often discussed. Part of the opposing counsel's job is to minimize the impact the expert's testimony provides in the case. Careful consideration of the exact question asked and formulation of an answer that is responsive to the question are essential. A responsive answer provides only the information requested by the single question. Rambling explanations should be avoided because this may provide points for reducing credibility. Familiarity with attorney questioning strategies described in legal practice literature can be very helpful for nurses entering the legal arena (Combs, 2015).

The nurse expert should be careful to keep testimony focused on nursing practice without venturing into practice areas of other healthcare providers. If opposing counsel asks hypothetical questions, the expert should provide hypothetical answers. Hypothetical questions sometimes lead to complicated lines of questioning and potential for confusion. It is always appropriate to request that the question be repeated or clarified. This is especially true when the question is hypothetical rather than about the specific circumstances of the case.

Questions about authoritative literature must also be carefully considered, in light of the multiple factors that create the standard of care and the fact that no author's every word is completely authoritative. All answers should be visualized in their future black-and-white transcript format. Playful quips or humorous remarks are likely to diminish the expert's credibility when the opposing attorney reads them aloud later in the courtroom. Fine distinctions of language and meaning that are minimized in daily life become paramount in the legal system.

Other attorneys who are present at the deposition may object to certain questions or answers. The nurse expert should be prepared for this eventuality with instructions from the retaining attorney in the pre-deposition meeting. Objections constitute a legal procedure for the record. If the expert finds the objections to be distracting the expert can request to have the question reread by the court reporter. An objection does not negate the need to answer the question; however, it may impact the wording and timing of the answer.

The retaining attorney may choose to withhold questions or may ask questions that further clarify the expert's opinions. The nurse expert or any of the attorneys may request a break at any time. The deposition ends when all the attorneys, including the retaining attorney, are finished with their questions.

Regardless of whether the expert's opinions are expressed verbally or in writing, the expert should always remember to reserve the right to modify opinions or add additional opinions based on new material reviewed. Acquisition of other information from depositions or opposing experts' reports may support the expert's opinion or may serve as a foundation for reanalysis of the records. The receipt of more medical records may also affect the expert's initial opinion. Thus, it should always be clear that the nurse expert's opinion is based on currently reviewed information and is potentially subject to change. If this possibility arises after the deposition, it is the expert's responsibility to contact the attorney immediately to discuss the matter and, if appropriate, consider a revision of the opinion.

The deposition may be videotaped, especially if the expert is not available for trial. While the presence of the camera may be intimidating at first, the nurse expert should consider that the film will preserve a verbal and visual record of the testimony. Maintaining a calm demeanor and a professional presentation of information is essential. Refrain from using papers or one's hands to cover one's face. Look at the attorney who is doing the questioning. Videotaped testimony can create a positive record of the nurse's opinions and communication skills, which is especially noteworthy when faced with negative or badgering behavior by opposing counsel.

- Be certain to explain medical and nursing concepts and terminology in layperson's terms for better understanding by the attorney, jury, or judge
- Reserve the right to review and make non-substantive edits to one's deposition transcript
- Do not exaggerate
- Do not guess
- Say, "I do not know" if that is the case
- Say, "I do not remember" if that is the case
- Stay within the expert's scope of practice and area of expertise
- Remain calm and do not get frustrated or flustered
- Speak only in response to questions
- Listen carefully before answering the question
- Be well prepared to explain one's qualifications and why the methodology used to formulate one's opinions is reliable
- Watch for, and do not agree with, mischaracterizations of one's testimony or opinion

(Mangraviti, Babitsky, & Donovan, 2016)

Reviewing the Transcript

Following the deposition, the nurse expert should plan to review the deposition transcript. It should be closely checked for accuracy. Any changes should be noted on the corrections form (errata sheet), including the rationale for each change (such as spelling error, typographical error, or obvious omission of a word). Such errors may be corrected, but the substantive nature of the content must not be changed by this process. If the nurse expert believes that a change in the substance of the testimony must be made, the retaining attorney should be contacted immediately before notating any change on the errata sheet provided with the expert's deposition.

Trial Testimony Preparation

Most cases settle prior to trial. If the case proceeds to trial, the nurse expert's court testimony is required. Since a lapse between deposition and trial is common, the expert must prepare with another review of all the case material, with attention being given to one's own deposition. Well-organized files and a strong chronology, and consultation with the retaining attorney, will simplify this process. The retaining attorney will appreciate the organized expert in that this secondary review will be far less time consuming and therefore less expensive.

Personal and professional preparation for trial follows the same rules as for deposition, with even more emphasis on appearance, demeanor, communication, and unequivocal testimony. The nurse expert must be prepared for the content of testimony, trial-scheduling uncertainties, anxiety that may be associated with the unfamiliar environment of the courthouse, and development of techniques to enhance communication with the jury.

The Witness Stand

The witness's testimony starts by swearing or affirming to tell the truth. The retaining attorney does the initial questioning, starting with credentials and CV to establish credibility as an expert.

This supporting data is then offered to the court to accept the nurse as an expert who is qualified to testify for the trial. Opposing counsel may question credentials now or wait until cross-examination.

After the judge accepts the nurse as a qualified expert, the retaining attorney asks specific questions about the circumstances relevant to the case. The nurse expert's testimony then addresses the standard of care and the specific issues that are in question for the jury. At this point, the nurse expert may feel quite comfortable in the teaching role, which is an inherent part of nursing care, as explanations are made to help the jury of laymen understand the intricacies of healthcare and patient outcomes.

The opposing attorney then questions the nurse in cross-examination, which is often focused on eliciting information that discredits the nurse expert. The nurse expert must display an extremely calm demeanor, focus on the elements of the case, and communicate clearly in the face of hostility. Although cross-examination is not comfortable to endure, it gives the well-prepared expert an opportunity to show true professionalism to the jury. The retaining attorney then has the chance to redirect, questioning answers or ideas that need to be emphasized to the jury. Finally, the opposing attorney has the opportunity for re-cross-examination. The appendix provides information about common cross-examination strategies.

In *Tips for Preparing the Expert Witness* (2016), Tedder-King and Czyz discuss how witnesses can look and sound good for the jury. Confident eye contact with the jury, word delivery, and body language make witnesses look good. Talking into space or down to the floor or shirtfronts reduces communication. Vocal support with full, relaxed breathing techniques, and clear and strong speech articulation and volume, enhances communication. Speech volume should not fade at the end of sentences. It is recommended that experts practice these techniques with a warning that *practice* does not mean *memorize*. The expert should become comfortable with expressing the substance of testimony utilizing a variety of wording.

Demonstrative evidence and visual aids may be helpful to the judge and jury because they provide emphasis and concreteness and memorialize evidence. The nurse expert may play an important role in developing this evidence which may be as simple as an enlargement of a medical record page or as complicated as computer-generated graphics that demonstrate physiology or mechanism of injury. Pieces of medical equipment may also be shown in action. Part of the nurse expert's testimony may include teaching the jury about the role of these pieces of evidence in the case. Visual aids should follow rules of simplicity, readability, and easy comprehension.

Summary

Although professionals set their own personal standards of care, these are not necessarily the same as the legal definition for standard of care. Courts use expert testimony to describe and interpret these standards as they relate to specific clinical events. Nurses are well-prepared to assume the role of expert witness, making appropriate consideration of the demands and challenges of the role. Educating the judge and jury about standard of care and how it was met or breached allows the plaintiff's counsel to build a case and the defense counsel to rebut allegations. It is a natural extension of nursing's professional responsibility to uphold the standards of care.

References

American Heart Association. (2000, August 22). Guidelines 2000 for cardiopulmonary resuscitation and emergency cardiovascular care. Part 6: advanced cardiovascular life support: section 7: algorithm approach to ACLS emergencies: section 7A: principles and practice of ACLS. *Circulation, 102*(8 Suppl.): 1136–1139.

American Nurses Association. (2015a). *Code of ethics for nurses with interpretive statements.* Silver Springs, MD: Nursebooks.org.

American Nurses Association. (2015b). *Nursing scope and standards of practice* (3rd ed.). Silver Springs, MD: Nursebooks.org.

Babitsky, S. (2005). *How to become a dangerous expert witness: Advanced techniques and strategies.* Falmouth, MA: SEAK.

Barros-Bailey, M., & Dominick, B. K. (2017). The expert witness team in employment law cases. *Journal of Nurse Life Care Planning, 17*(2), 29–31. Retrieved from www.aanlcp.org/?page=JournalCopies.

Combs, L. (2015). Nurse experts: Are you prepared for cross-examination? *The Journal of Legal Nurse Consulting, 26*(3), 31–33. Retrieved from www.aalnc.org/page/journal-v2.0.

Federal Evidence Review. (n.d.-a). Federal rules of evidence. FRE 702, Opinion testimony by lay witnesses and advisory committee on rules. Retrieved from http://federalevidence.com/changing-rules.

Federal Evidence Review. (n.d.-b). Federal rules of evidence 2011 (Before Dec. 1 2011 restyled amendments). Retrieved from http://federalevidence.com/old-rule.

Federal Rules of Evidence. (2018). *Rule 702. Testimony by expert witnesses.* Grand Rapids, MI: Michigan Legal Publishing. Retrieved from www.rulesofevidence.org/article-vii/rule-702/.

Find Your Nurse Practice Act. (n.d.). Retrieved from www.ncsbn.org/npa.htm.

Frye v. United States, 293 F.1013 (D.C. Cir. 1923).

Garner, B. (Ed.). (2014). *Black's law dictionary* (10th ed.). St. Paul, MN: Thomson Reuters.

Kaminski, S. M. (2015). Tips for LNC expert witness location. *The Journal of Legal Nurse Consulting, 26*(3), 26–33. Retrieved from www.aalnc.org/page/journal-v2.0.

Mangraviti Jr., J., Babitsky, S., & Donovan, N. (2016). Chapter 7: Understanding & defeating counsel's depositions tactics (pp. 201–207). *How to be an effective witness at deposition and trial: The SEAK guide to testifying as an expert witness.* Falmouth, MA: SEAK Inc.

Paul, S. R., & Narang, S. K. (2017). Expert witness preparation in civil and criminal proceedings. *American Academy of Pediatrics, 139*(3). doi:10.1542/peds.2016-4122.

Powell, V. (2013). Qualifying as an expert. *Journal of Nurse Life Care Planning, 13*(3), 112–122. Retrieved from www.aanlcp.org/?page=JournalCopies.

Schofield, S., & Huntington-Frazier, M. (2015). Advocacy on trial: Are the nurse life care planner's roles of advocate and expert in conflict? *Journal of Nurse Life Care Planning, 15*(4), 928–933. Retrieved from www.aanlcp.org/?page=JournalCopies.

Sullivan v. Edward Hospital, 806 N.E. 2d 645 (Ill. 2004).

Tedder-King, A., & Czyz, K. (2016).) *Tips for preparing the expert witness.* Retrieved from www.thejuryexpert.com/2016/04/tips-for-preparing-the-expert-witness/.

The Academy of Experts. (2015). What is an expert? Retrieved from www.academyofexperts.org/guidance/users-experts/what-an-expert-report.

Wilkinson, T. (2015). Nurse expert witnesses and the Daubert standard. *The Journal of Legal Nurse Consulting, 26*(3), 34–39. Retrieved from www.aalnc.org/page/journal-v2.0.

Zorn, E. (2015). Serving as an expert witness: A virtual roundtable discussion. *The Journal of Nurse Consulting, 26*(3), 40–44. Retrieved from www.aalnc.org/page/journal-v2.0.

Additional Reading

Iyer, P. (2016). *How to be a successful expert witness.* Fort Myers, FL: The Pat Iyer Group.

Matson, J. V. (2013). *Effective expert witnessing: Practices for the 21st century* (5th ed.). Boca Raton, FL: Taylor & Francis Group.

National Expert Witnesses LLC: Books for experts listed here: http://national-ew.com/?page_id=102.

Test Questions

1. Marketing nurse expert witness services is best achieved by:
   A. Commercial advertising in legal journals
   B. Networking with LNC colleagues
   C. Paying attorneys for referrals to their colleagues
   D. Purchasing listings in commercial expert witness directories
2. Fees for expert witness work should:
   A. Depend on the outcome of the case
   B. Include a bonus for the nurse expert if the retaining attorney wins the case
   C. Be negotiable depending on the potential award amount
   D. Be completely time-based
3. Which is true about deposition testimony?
   A. It is an opportunity for opposing counsel to discover the nurse expert's opinions
   B. It is considered unimportant except as a partial rehearsal for trial
   C. It may not be admitted into the evidence at trial
   D. The retaining attorney conducts the deposition to allow the nurse expert witness to clarify opinions
4. Record review and analysis by the nurse expert witness should include:
   A. Detailed note-taking and outlining of all case elements in a timeline
   B. Colored highlighting of critical elements of the original medical record
   C. Ensuring that all appropriate pages of the record are present
   D. Advising the attorney that a detailed written report is essential
5. The nurse expert witness's case analysis should hold nursing actions to which standard?
   A. Actions expected of a reasonably prudent nurse in similar circumstances
   B. Actions expected of advanced-practice clinicians in the same specialty
   C. The universal standards for all healthcare providers
   D. The highest possible standards in order to improve patient care

Answers: 1. B, 2. D, 3. A, 4. C, 5. A

Appendix A: Cross-Examination Techniques

The expert witness will encounter several strategies used by attorneys in cross-examination. This appendix provides an overview of some of the more common techniques. The expert can become more skilled at identifying and reacting to these techniques by anticipating them and knowing effective ways of responding. Each strategy is briefly explained, followed by sample dialogue. "A" stands for "Attorney" and "E" stands for "Expert." Comments in parentheses are provided by the authors.

1. Expect detailed probing into the expert's background, fee structure, and experience as an expert. The expert should calmly, and without being defensive, provide the answers to these questions.

A: Nurse __, where did you go to nursing school?

E: University of Louisiana.

A: Do you have any advanced degrees in nursing?

E: Yes, I have a Master of Science in Nursing.

A: You don't have a doctorate in nursing?

E: No.

A: And yet you feel qualified to be an expert in this case?

E: Yes, I do, based on my experience as a nurse and my education. [A doctorate in nursing is not the entry-level degree for expert witness review.]

A: Where have you worked as a staff nurse?

E: Baton Rouge Medical Center and University of Alabama Hospital.

A: You realize that the nurses who were sued in this case worked in Denver?

E: Yes.

A: And yet you have never worked in Denver, have you?

E: I have not.

A: Why do you feel qualified to comment on the standard of care for nurses who work in Denver?

E: The standard of care is a national standard. The nurses in Denver are expected to adhere to the same standards as the nurses in the state in which I work.

A: How much do you charge per hour to review a case?

E: $250 per hour.

A: How much? [The attorney acts shocked.]

E: $250 per hour. [The expert repeats answer calmly.]

A: Do you know how much nurses earn who work in hospitals in Denver?

E: No.

A: Why are your fees so much higher?

E: They reflect my education, training, and expertise. Our work process is not the same.

A: How much are you being paid for your opinions today?

E: I am not being paid anything for my opinions. I am being paid for my education, training and experience and time at $400 per hour. [The expert should be clear that his/her time is being paid for, not his/her opinion.]

A: How many cases have you reviewed as an expert?

E: Twenty.

A: So, you are really a novice at this work, aren't you? [This question is an effort to intimidate the expert.]

E: No. I have twenty plus years of experience, my education and training.

A: How much money did you earn last year doing expert witness work? [The courts generally permit the expert to provide a percentage of income rather than reveal the expert's income.]

E: My expert witness earnings represented about 15 percent of my income.

A: Are you going to be paid a percentage of the recovery that plaintiff hopes to get in this case?

E: No. [It is unethical for experts to work on contingency.]

2. Asking questions in no obvious order—this is designed to prevent the expert from seeing a pattern in the questions. The expert should answer each question as clearly as possible.

A: Let's talk about your opinions in this case, all right?

E: All right.

A: What is your understanding about the responsibilities of the nurse for keeping the doctor informed of changes in the patient's condition?

E: The nurse should report significant changes in the patient's condition.

A: What is the purpose of giving insulin to diabetics?

E: It is a medication that manages blood sugar.

A: What is a patient acuity system?

E: It is a system which assists administration to determine how to staff a nursing unit and adhere to nurse patient staffing ratio.

3. Deliberate mispronunciation of words—the attorney is trying to present an uneducated air so that the expert's guard will be let down. The expert should ignore the mispronunciations.

A: Nurse____, this case is about a patient who had hypertrophy of the ventricles. [Mispronounces words.] Is that right?

E: Yes. The patient's echocardiogram showed that the patient had hypertrophy of the left ventricle. [Pronounces it correctly.]

A: What is that?

E: [The expert explains this term.]

4. Flattery—the opposing attorney acts impressed with the expert's credentials to lower the expert's guard. The expert should politely acknowledge the flattery and wait for the next question.

A: You went to nursing school, right?

E: Yes, I did.

A: You went to one of the finest nursing schools in the country to get your degrees, didn't you?

E: Yes.

A: You have written several articles that have been published in prestigious journals, correct?

E: Yes.

A: Why, I bet you know more than about 99 percent of the nurses in this country, don't you?

E: I have no way to know what all nurses know so I cannot answer that. I do know the standard of care and how it applies to this case.

5. Goading the expert—the attorney is hoping the expert will lose his or her temper or respond in a flippant way. The expert should remain calm.

A: Did you speak to any of the nurses who were sued in this case? [This is a misleading question to ask in front of a jury, because it implies that the nursing expert was not being fair to the defendants by not allowing them to tell the expert their side of the story.]

E: I did not, as it is my understanding that I am not permitted to contact the defendants.

A: Did you think it was important to know what they had to say about how this incident occurred?

E: I did, and that is why I read their deposition transcripts.

A: Have you heard the expression that hindsight is 20/20?

E: Yes.

A: Wouldn't you agree that the nurses taking care of the patient did not have the benefit of hindsight?

E: It is my position that the nurses should have followed the standard of care. [Whenever opposing counsel starts a question with "wouldn't you agree…" the expert needs to listen carefully as they are most likely being asked to agree to something that is not correct.]

A: You have testified that it is your opinion that the nurses did not follow the standard of care, isn't that right?

E: Yes, I have.

A: You are telling this jury that these dedicated nurses, who work day in and day out, made a mistake, aren't you?

E: Yes, they deviated from the standard of care.

A: You want the jury to believe that these nurses were negligent, don't you? [This is a blatant effort to attack the nursing expert. The expert must remain firm in his or her convictions.]

E: Yes they were negligent. They failed to follow the standard of care.

6. Using body language to intimidate—pointing fingers, shouting, and leaning into the expert's space are often tactics that the attorney who retained the expert can bring to a halt by objecting.

7. Asking questions in a rapid manner—the attorney may be hoping that the expert will mimic the pace of questioning and give a careless answer in haste. The expert should think through the answer to each question and establish a pace that is comfortable for the expert, remembering that a pause does not show up on a transcript.

8. Asking repetitive questions—the expert should provide consistent answers to the same question asked several times.

A: Now, let me be sure I have this right. You are saying that you don't think the nurses did anything wrong with respect to the care that was provided to my client, right?

E: Yes, I am.

A: And you believe, in your professional opinion, that the standard of care was met?

E: Yes, I do.

A: There was nothing that should have been done differently, is that right?

E: That is true.

A: You are very sure about that?

E: Yes.

9. Asking vague or complex, convoluted questions—whether on purpose or because of difficulty framing questions—the attorney should be asked to rephrase the question so that it is clear.

A: What is nursing all about?
E: I don't understand your question.
A: What do you do as a nurse?
E: In what context?

10. Questioning the expert about details in the medical record to test the expert's memory—the expert can refer to the materials that were reviewed and does not have to answer questions based on memory alone.

11. Use of silence—the attorney may pause after the expert's answer, hoping the expert will elaborate on the answer. The expert should answer the question and wait for the next one.

12. Asking about nursing literature to identify "authoritative texts"—the attorney should prepare the expert to answer these questions based on the jurisdiction's case law.

A: What texts do you believe are authoritative in the field of medical surgical nursing?
E: I find several to be generally reliable.
A: Do you rely on those texts for information?
E: Yes, but no text is completely up to date because of the lag time from sending it to the publishers and getting it into print.

13. Hypothetical questions—the expert needs to be sure that the details included in the hypothetical question match the case issues.

A: Now, Nurse ___, I'd like you to assume that the following is true. The patient has been admitted to the hospital for a breast reduction. She tells the nurses that she has numbness and tingling in her legs after surgery. She complains each shift to each nurse. What is the standard of care regarding notifying the physician of these changes?
E: I am having difficulty with your hypothetical because it is not based on the facts of this case. My review of the medical record and the depositions of the nurses show that the patient complained on only two shifts.
A: You are aware of my client's testimony that she complained to each nurse who took care of her?
E: I read her testimony to that effect, but it is contradicted by the nurse's testimony.
A: Can you answer my question?
E: If I accept the facts of your hypothetical, I would want to know how often her physicians were visiting her and what they were documenting about her legs.
A: Nurse ___, I am not asking you about what the doctors were doing. I am asking you about the nursing standard of care. Do you understand that?
E: Yes.
A: Now can you answer my question?

E: I would have to say, if I accepted your hypothetical, that I would expect the nurses to report this finding to the doctor if it was a new symptom, but I understand from the testimony of the nurse that the patient said this was not new.

14. Failing to bring materials to the deposition will make it more difficult for the expert to answer questions. This dialogue illustrates the difficulties in not bringing the materials.

A: Do you have with you the copies of materials that were provided to you for review in this case?

E: I do not have a copy with me, but Ms. Wilson does have the materials that I reviewed to supply this expert report.

A: When you say Ms. Wilson has copies of those materials, did you bring your copies with you today?

E: Ms. Wilson has a copy of my nurse expert report and she has copies of all the material that was sent to me from her office that I reviewed in compiling the report.

A: I realize that she has copies of those materials, but does she have your copies of the materials?

E: No, my copies are at home.

15. Making derogatory remarks on the material that was reviewed is not advisable. The attorney has the right to look at anything in the expert's file.

A: Did you make any notations or marks of any kind on the materials you reviewed?

E: Yes, I did.

A: May I see your file? [Looks at materials.] Why did you highlight this sentence in Nurse Perry's deposition?

E: I thought it was significant.

A: What was significant about it?

E: It conflicted with what the doctor said happened.

A: I see a comment in the margin of the report that was prepared by Nurse Watson, who is the expert for the plaintiff. What does this mean: "She should stick to obstetrics where she belongs and not review this case?"

E: I thought the expert was not qualified to review this case.

A: What does this comment mean: "What a jerk?"

E: I thought his conclusion was not correct.

16. Failing to read and consider all information—the expert should ask for pertinent documents, depositions, and other records needed to formulate an opinion.

A: When you undertook this assignment, did you want to render a fair opinion? The following dialogue illustrates the problems that can occur.

E: Yes, I did.

A: And to render a fair opinion, did you think it was important to know as much as you could about the facts of this case?

E: Yes.

A: Did you read the depositions of the nurses?

E: No, I did not.

A: Why did you not read them?

E: They were not sent to me.

A: Did you ask the attorney for them?

E: No. [This question is designed to make the expert look unfair. The expert is placed in an awkward position if the attorney does not provide the expert with the depositions. The expert can prevent this type of trap by asking the attorney for all relevant material. If the attorney does not provide the depositions, respond that they were requested them but have not yet been received.]

17. Failing to listen to the question and failing to stay focused are shown below.

A: Could you explain to the jury why Mrs. Queen was admitted to the hospital?

E: She stayed in the hospital after her fractured hip because they were trying to find a nursing home bed.

A: I asked you why she was admitted. What caused her to be hospitalized?

E: She was unsteady on her feet and falling frequently.

A: Can we agree that there does not appear to be an order for taking these compression stockings off this patient?

E: No.

A: No, we can't agree or —

E: We can agree.

18. Failing to be responsive, especially giving more explanation or more information than is asked for, is not recommended.

A: Did the job as an instructor involve teaching emergency nursing to students?

E: Yes, I took the students into the emergency room for one semester. They were assigned to observe the triage nurse and to perform simple treatments. At times, they would observe cardiac arrests, of course always standing in the back of the room where they would not be in the way. Many of them found this to be the most traumatic experience they had as students, although I did have one student one time who fainted when the doctor started suturing a head laceration on a child. [This was a yes-or-no question.]

19. Failing to stand behind **your** expert report is ill-advised.

A: It says in your report that Nurse Williams did not deviate from the standard of care when she administered morphine to my client.

E: Yes, that is what it says.

A: Do you hold that opinion today?

E: I have changed that opinion.

A: What have you changed about your opinion?

E: I now believe that she should not have given 35 mg of morphine at one time, when the doctor ordered 10 mg. [This expert should have come to this realization long before the deposition.]

20. Going too far out on a limb—not being flexible—creates problems for the expert.

A: How often does the tube-feeding bag need to be changed?

E: It should be changed every 24 hours.

A: What is the purpose of changing the tube-feeding bag?

E: It is to keep the bag sanitary.

A: You have heard testimony that Mrs. Viglione's family saw fungus growing on the inside of the tube-feeding bag, correct?

E: Yes, but that does not really matter.

A: Why is that?

E: The stomach is not sterile, so fungus will not hurt it.

A: Would you eat bread that has mold growing on it?

E: No.

A: Why is that?

E: [long pause] I would not want to get sick.

A: If a fly flew into the tube-feeding solution, would you feed the fly to the patient?

E: Yes, I would, because the stomach is not sterile. [This is actual testimony by a nursing expert.]

    21. Testifying to issues outside his or her expertise is inappropriate.

A: Do you have an opinion as to whether Dr. White should have prescribed Keflex® to this patient?

E: Yes, I do.

A: And your opinion is?

E: Even though I am not an orthopedic surgeon he should not have prescribed the Keflex, since the patient herself had requested that she not be given this drug.

    Defense attorney #1: Can we just take a two-minute break? I want to talk to her outside.

    Defense attorney #2: I object to any break.

A: Are you through with your response?

E: I still believe that Dr. White should have, based on his medical judgment, not given Keflex to the patient.

    [Attorney #1 puts his hand on expert's arm, whispers in her ear, and forces her to stand up.]

    Defense attorney #2: Let the record reflect that the attorney is coaching the expert during this deposition. His witness did not ask to speak to counsel. Counsel has asked to speak to his expert. The expert and her attorney are leaving the room.

    Defense attorney #1: I object to the use of the word "coach" in terms of characterizing because I want to speak to my expert witness. I just want to talk to my expert in private about the scope of her testimony that we will hope to use at the time of trial. I would like to clarify with her, and I don't consider that coaching at all about anything. We will be back in a few minutes after I have had that opportunity to speak with her.

    Defense attorney #2: "Coaching" is a good word, and I stand by my description of what you are doing here, Counsel.

A: Before you leave, are you able to put on the record the scope of this witness's intended testimony?

    Defense attorney #1: I intend to do that when I come back.

A: You can't do that beforehand?

    Defense attorney #1: I will come back and do it.

    Defense attorney #2: That's after he coaches her.

    [Expert and defense attorney #1 leave room for a minute, then return.]

    Defense attorney #1: Before we begin, I would like to put a statement on the record about my conversation with the witness.

A: Which the record should reflect was three minutes.

Defense attorney #1: I have had the opportunity to discuss with the expert the scope of her review. I was concerned that she might have some questions about her role. She is being offered as a nursing expert who will address the standard of care for the nurse. At the end of her report, she has a paragraph that seems to conclude that Dr. White prescribing Keflex may have been a cause of the problems.

A: Let me ask you this.

Defense attorney #1: Go for it.

A: Will this witness be testifying about causation? In other words, what damages, if any, were caused by administering Keflex?

Defense attorney #1: We are offering her as an expert witness as to the standard of care of the nurse. We are going to limit her testimony to the duty of the nurse.

Defense attorney #2: Exactly! [The nursing expert may not testify about the physician standard of care and vice versa.]

22. Failing to know the topic is problematic.

A: What is the nursing process?

E: It is the process by which we give nursing care.

A: Can you be more specific?

E: No, I can't.

A: Can you list any of the steps of the nursing process?

E: No.

23. Using terms such as "always" and "never" can be too sweeping and trap the nurse.

A: Does a nurse read the entire medical record before she takes care of a patient?

E: Yes, nurses always read the chart.

A: So, without exception, nurses always read about the patient before they take care of him, is that correct?

E: Yes.

A: The standard of care requires the nurse to always read the medical record, is that what you are saying?

E: Yes, it is.

A: Can you give me a reference to an article or textbook that says that the nurse should always read the medical record before taking care of the patient?

E: No, I can't.

A: So, this is your opinion on what the nurse should do?

E: Yes, it is.

A: In your practice as a nurse, have you seen nurses sit down before taking care of the patient and read the entire medical record?

E: No, I have not. But they should do it. [It is difficult to maintain that this is the standard of care if the expert cannot support her opinion with a text or common practice.]

24. Trying to be an attorney is not advisable. The nursing expert should avoid adopting legal language.

A: Do you believe that the patient did anything wrong?
E: Yes, I believe she was contributorily negligent.

25. Being biased or an advocate is to be avoided. The expert's role is to be objective and an educator about the standard of care.

A: Nurse __, you have been retained to be an expert in this case, isn't that correct?
E: Yes, I was hired to defend the nurses.
A: I'm confused; isn't Ms. Corner the defense attorney?
E: Yes, she is.
A: What do you see as your role?
E: My role is to make sure that these nurses don't have to pay for something that was not their fault. It was not their fault that the patient did not follow instructions. There would be far fewer lawsuits if patients just did what they were told!

26. Being argumentative, evasive, aggressive, or too clever is not recommended. The expert often comes out on the losing end of this type of tactic.

A: It is your opinion that the nurses at Major Hospital did nothing wrong, is that right?
E: Yes, it is. I think the nursing care was perfectly fine.
A: Do you have an opinion about whether this order sheet existed?
E: [Smiling] I have an opinion that will remain private.
A: Why?
E: I find it interesting that this order sheet was supposed to be in the chart, and it is the most crucial document in this case and it is missing. I find it unusual that it is missing because it should be there. I mean, I have never seen this type of patient being cared for in the hospital without that type of order sheet in place.
A: I don't think you have answered my question as to what your belief is as to whether that order sheet ever existed.
E: I cannot testify with any certainty that the document existed because I was not there to see it. Based on my review of the deposition of the nurse and her answers to interrogatories, I feel that a possibility does exist that this order sheet was there, and then destroyed.
A: When I asked you the question originally, and I know that the reporter can't take this down, but you gave a little smile as to indicate that perhaps you did have an opinion as to whether this existed. What is your opinion about whether it really existed?
E: I think anything is possible at this point since we have so many pieces of paper involved in this case.
A: Yes or no? In your opinion do you believe is it more likely than not that the paper existed?
E: I would say no, that it probably did not exist. It is a possibility either way, 50/50. [This response is completely ambiguous and not helpful.]

27. Answering two-part questions with one answer—each part of the question should be answered separately, or the attorney should be asked to rephrase the question.

A: Do they read the whole chart or just portions of the chart?
E: Yes.

28. Speculating about the actions of others is dangerous.

A: What is the purpose of the medical record?
E: It is to document the assessment of the patient, significant aspects of patient care, track responses to care—medical and nursing, as well as allow for continuity of care from one healthcare provider to another.
A: Would you expect the physician to document significant observations about the patient?
E: Yes, I would.
A: You are aware that the house doctor recorded that there was a strong pulse in the patient's right leg at 10:00 a.m.?
E: Yes, I read that.
A: You are also aware that the vascular surgeon came in at 10:45 a.m. and recorded that the patient had compartment syndrome in the right leg?
E: Yes.
A: Is it possible that the patient had a strong pulse in the right leg at 10:00 a.m.?
E: Anything is possible. [The expert may find it more useful to say that it is highly unlikely.]
A: Do you believe that it was likely that the patient had a strong pulse at 10:00 a.m.?
E: No, I do not.
A: Why do you believe the house physician documented the presence of a strong pulse?
E: Sometimes when there is a bad outcome there is a cover-up. [This may be viewed as an inflammatory statement.]

29. The attorney may ask the expert to speculate. The expert must analyze information provided to him/her and should not speculate.

A: Do you know how long the nurse was with this patient?
E: I don't know for a fact, no.
A: Do you have an opinion as to when the nurse saw this patient?
E: I have an opinion that she saw her at the end of the evening shift rather than at the beginning of the evening shift, based on her testimony at the deposition.
A: Is there anything in the medical record to indicate that valuables had been taken from the patient?
E: I did not find anything to that effect.
A: If valuables are taken from a patient, does that usually include jewelry?
E: Not necessarily.
A: What does that usually include?
E: It depends on what the patient has.
A: Could that include rings, necklaces, and money?
E: It depends on what the patient comes into the hospital with.
A: In a situation when a patient comes in with a drug overdose, when a hospital will take valuables from a patient, what does that generally include? [The expert is being asked to speculate.]

E: I can't answer that question.

A: Why not?

E: Because I don't know what the patient had. Patients come into the hospital with all kinds of things.

A: You have no understanding what general hospital procedure would be in terms of removing a patient's valuables under those circumstances?

E: No. The definition of "valuables" is highly variable.

30. Do not charge fees that are difficult to justify to the jury.

A: What do you charge to come to court for the day?

E: My trial fee is $5,000 per day.

31. Explain medical terms in the language of laypersons to avoid talking over the heads of the jury. Avoid doing what this expert did:

A: Could you explain to the jury what type of surgery Mrs. Wilson had?

E: She had a bilateral salpingo-oophorectomy and a vaginal hysterectomy with fulguration of areas of endometriosis. [The jury will have no idea what she just said.]

32. Avoid talking down to the jury.

A: Could you explain to the jury what type of surgery Mrs. Wilson had?

E: Women have a uterus, two ovaries, and two fallopian tubes. The eggs are stored in the ovaries. The male seeds are called sperm. The male seeds meet the egg in the tube and the egg travels down the tube to the uterus or womb. The fertilized egg becomes a fetus where they grow in the uterus until the baby is ready to be born. The baby comes out the birth canal or vagina. The patient had removal of her ovaries and tubes. Her uterus was removed through her vagina. She had areas of endometriosis, which are made up of cells from the uterus that travel outside of the uterus. Each month when a woman has her menses, these cells swell and this causes pain. The doctor used cautery to burn these cells.

33. Avoid making statements that defy the common sense of jurors.

A: Do you accept as true everything that the nurse said happened?

E: Yes, I do. I believe in her honesty.

A: So if I told you that she testified yesterday that she took care of the patient on February 30, would you believe her testimony was true?

E: Yes, I would.

34. Referring to the insurance company is to be avoided.

A: Have your bills been paid by my firm?

E: No, I have gotten my checks directly from the insurance company. [The jury is not supposed to know that an insurance company is involved in the case.]

35. Being able to cite sources of information makes the expert's testimony stronger.

A: What do you base your opinion on that restraints may not have been mandated on the evening shift?

E: I based my opinion on the testimony of the plaintiff and on the medical record. Both stated that the patient was cooperative, awake, alert, and oriented.

36. The attorney may ask questions of the expert to trap the expert into admitting that she has committed malpractice.

A: Have you ever been a staff nurse assigned to a patient who was in restraints of any nature where the patient sustained an injury?

E: No.

A: Have you ever been a staff nurse assigned to a patient who sustained an injury because of not being restrained?

E: No.

A: Have you ever been a staff nurse assigned to a patient who sustained an injury in a hospital?

E: Yes.

A: Tell me about those circumstances. First, on how many occasions?

E: Do you mean when I was caring for the patient?

A: Yes.

E: I can recall taking care of an elderly person with frail skin. I inadvertently applied pressure to the skin and the skin tore. I recall that situation. Other than that, I don't recall other situations.

A: Okay. Have you ever cared for a patient where a patient fell out of bed?

E: No.

A: Have you ever committed malpractice?

E: Not that I know of.

A: Have you ever been sued for malpractice?

E: No.

37. The expert should avoid being backed into a corner.

A: Is it your opinion that any time the patient sustains an injury while in four-point restraints, malpractice has occurred?

E: I would be hard pressed to agree to a blanket statement like that. I would have to know the circumstances.

A: Have you cared for patients who were in four-point restraints because they were being abusive, combative, and at risk to themselves or others if they were not restrained?

E: Yes.

A: And in those situations, is it possible that the patient could sustain an injury while in four-point restraints, in the absence of nursing malpractice?

E: I personally have not seen it happen. I've seen many efforts to try to avoid friction, irritation, tightness, and problems with circulation. It's my opinion that if the standard of care is followed, the probabilities of the patient sustaining injury are greatly reduced.

A: So, would that allow for the possibility that even if the appropriate standard of care was followed for monitoring a patient in four-point restraints, an injury may happen in any event?

E: It would be a very remote possibility.

A: Is it possible that a combative patient in restraints can create a friction burn?

E: Yes, it is possible, if the patient was continuously pulling.

A: Okay. So even if they are being monitored to make sure that the restraints are not too tight, and they are being released from them periodically as the protocol requires, that could occur?

E: The answer to that question is not simple because when a nurse observes that type of continuous friction and pulling against the restraint, the nurse is obligated to consider alternatives to avoid the friction. These could include putting padding under the restraint to prevent the abrasion, to considering the fact that the very act of restraining the patient can cause combativeness. The combativeness can be independent of the underlying medical reason that the combative behavior might have existed. There must be some efforts at problem-solving with respect to how to avoid damage to the skin. So, your question was can it cause abrasion? Yes, it can, but there are multiple interventions to avoid that outcome, and I do not see that those were taken in this situation.

38. The attorney may question the knowledge of the expert or realize that he has just laid a trap for himself.

A: Your criticism that Ms. Winters failed to release the restraints is based on the patient's testimony, correct?

E: Well, Ms. Winters also testified that she did not release the restraints.

A: That's your recollection? Let's strike that.

E: Would you like me to show her testimony to you?

A: No.

Chapter 32

The Expert Fact Witness

Medical Summary Preparation and Testimony

Patricia W. Iyer, MSN, RN, LNCC®

Contents

Objectives

- Describe the role and purpose of an expert fact witness
- Discuss marketing the role to attorneys
- Describe the approach to organization and presentation of medical records to a jury
- Identify steps in preparing to testify as an expert fact witness

Introduction

The individuals who make decisions (render a verdict) about the facts of a court case are the "triers of fact"—judges, mediators, arbitrators, and jurors. Yet, they are laypersons and have little understanding of what occurs within the healthcare system. The triers of fact and the attorneys presenting the case need to understand the clinical facts. Medical records used as evidence during a trial are often incomprehensible to the average juror, and the medical abbreviations and symbols used therein are usually meaningless to laypeople.

Cases involving plaintiffs or decedents who have undergone complex or lengthy treatment or allege significant injuries often involve thousands of pages of medical records that a jury would be forced to read and comprehend on its own (Heron & Lewallen, 2014). Clearly, this is impossible.

To overcome the barriers created by incomprehensible medical records, attorneys educate the triers of fact by using healthcare professionals to explain medical information. Attorneys rely on a variety of professionals. Some use treating physicians to explain medical treatment to the jury. Although a treating doctor understands care provided to the plaintiff, it is rare that this doctor will read all the medical records from beginning to end (not just the doctor's own records). Even if requested to do so, few practicing physicians have time to read a medical record thoroughly and prepare a detailed report.

Some attorneys ask physician expert witnesses to prepare reports summarizing medical records. In the author's experience, few physicians understand how to prepare a detailed report or can clearly explain complex medical terms so that non-medical people can easily understand them. Moreover, the cost of having a physician do so would be beyond the resources of many attorneys.

At trial, family members may describe what they observed during the plaintiff's treatment. These persons typically have no medical training and cannot provide accurate medical explanations for the triers of fact.

Thus, the nursing expert fact witness is the ideal person to explain medical information to the triers of fact. This chapter discusses the role of the nurse as an expert fact witness—a role that teaches attorneys, claims adjusters, judges, mediators, arbitrators, and jurors.

Definition of the Role

Legal nurse consultants can testify as expert fact witnesses. This role is also variously named Rule 1006 witness (based on the Federal Rule of Evidence 1006 explained below), summary witness, summary provider, or, depending on the focus of the testimony, a kind of damages expert. None of these terms are universally used or understood by attorneys and legal nurse consultants (LNCs). There are many individuals who have not heard of the role, including judges, attorneys, experts, and LNCs.

This chapter uses the term "expert fact witness" although it does not yet appear in standard legal dictionaries. This term combines two types of witnesses: expert witness and fact witness. An *expert witness* provides opinion testimony (typically addressing liability, causation, or damages issues) to aid the trier of fact in matters that exceed the common knowledge of ordinary people. A *fact witness* (sometimes called a *non-party witness*) may be a treating physician, nurse, family member, or anyone who is not a defendant but has first-hand knowledge of the events that occurred, thereby acting as a witness to the events.

The expert fact witness is one who by special knowledge, skill, training, or experience is qualified to provide *non-opinion* testimony to aid the trier of fact in understanding matters that exceed the common knowledge of laypeople. This witness does *not* offer opinions about the quality of care and treatment rendered but summarizes and explains the facts contained in the medical records to educate the judge or jury about that care and the plaintiff's response to it.

In this role, an expert fact witness evaluates, summarizes, and explains the contents of medical records in an *objective, unbiased* way. The expert fact witness would avoid, for example, making statements such as "In my opinion, this person suffered tremendously" or "I believe this person was malingering." The expert fact witness does not just address care and response to it but provides a summary of the medical records to aid the fact-finders' understanding.

Most often, the expert fact witness's summary is a written report. The expert fact witness submits the report to the attorney client, who then provides the report to opposing counsel. The expert fact witness may offer testimony at deposition, mediation, or arbitration. If the case proceeds to trial, the expert fact witness's testimony aids the jury in understanding the facts contained in the medical records. Depending on the case and the attorney's goal for the testimony, the expert fact witness may focus on the plaintiff's treatment, injuries, or pain and suffering (Iyer, 2017a).

The expert fact witness's expertise is helpful in preparing a detailed explanation, from the records, of the events surrounding the injuries through the end of care (if the person survives). In the types of cases that involve expert fact witnesses, injuries, care, and related pain and suffering frequently represent substantial damages.

An expert fact witness's concise and simple explanation of the plaintiff's medical care from the medical records assists with the judge and jury's understanding of the medical information. Also, these explanations can increase the fact-finders' comprehension of the information presented by other experts in the case. On the defense side, this testimony is particularly useful in cases involving lengthy hospitalizations in which calling each individual healthcare professional who cared for the plaintiff to explain their documentation, care and treatment, and the plaintiff's response would be nearly impossible, fragmented, and not in an easily understandable, chronological order. On the plaintiff side, this testimony is beneficial in cases in which the plaintiff is unable to testify due to cognitive impairment, language barrier, or young age, or in cases in which the patient died.

At trial, the plaintiff's expert fact witness's presentation of the details contained in the medical record bridges the gap in testimony between liability for the injury and the life care plan (if one has been prepared for the case). The jury needs a clear, concise, and understandable accounting of events and the plaintiff's injuries based on medical records to understand the necessity of the recommendations made in the life care plan. Frequently, the plaintiff's expert fact witness's testimony concentrates on presenting facts in the medical records that support the allegation of the plaintiff's pain and suffering, which is a key component of damages for the judge or jury to understand.

By virtue of the plaintiff's burden to prove that damages occurred, it is much more common for plaintiffs' attorneys to hire expert fact witnesses. However, the expert fact witness may be retained by the defense to summarize and educate the fact-finders about the care and treatment rendered or to refute claims by summarizing parts of the medical records that can be used to mitigate damages.

Federal Rule of Evidence 1006

The Federal Rules of Evidence (FRE) govern the introduction and use of evidence in cases tried in federal courts. The important regulation that supports the role of expert fact witness is FRE 1006 Summaries to Prove Content. It states:

> The proponent may use a summary, chart, or calculations to prove the content of voluminous writings, recordings, or photographs that cannot be conveniently examined in court. The proponent must make the originals or duplicates available for examination or copying, or both, by other parties at a reasonable time and place. And the court may order the proponent to produce them in court.
>
> (FRE, 2017, para. 1)

Cases venued in state courts follow the state's rules of evidence, and a state-by-state Internet search found 42 states currently modeling their corresponding rule of evidence after FRE 1006 using the language verbatim or modifying it.

The report prepared by the expert fact witness constitutes a summary of medical records. Although no precise definition of "voluminous records" exists, the records generated when a plaintiff has sustained significant injuries can usually be described as voluminous. However, in the author's experience, a plaintiff attorney might hire an expert fact witness to explain the medical records of a person who had a brief period of consciousness before death, and a defense attorney might hire a nurse expert fact witness to teach the jury about a specific nursing procedure or treatment documented in the record.

Medical records form the basis of expert fact witness reports and testimony. Medical records are considered business records, recorded contemporaneously with events, and as such are admissible as evidence. Although not a witness to the actual events, the expert fact witness can act as a conduit of medical record information to the judge or jury. An expert fact witness typically focuses on medical records and *not* deposition testimony. However, this author has included plaintiff and family diaries in some expert fact witness reports.

Qualifications for the Role

Several attributes strengthen the role of the expert fact witness. Above all, the expert fact witness must be an analytical thinker. The ability to interpret and analyze medical records is essential for the role. Analysis of medical records requires the ability to be extremely detail-oriented. The expert fact witness must be able to identify missing records, extract essential data from the records, and prepare a clear report that articulates the events and injuries. The ability to prepare clear, logically organized, and accurate reports is essential. In addition, the nurse should have strong speaking skills and the ability to clearly explain complex medical concepts to laypeople.

The expert fact witness should be familiar with the clinical specialty relative to the plaintiff's alleged injuries. It is not necessary for the expert fact witness to have experience in the exact nursing specialty, but an expert who has never worked in acute care, for example, may have difficulty explaining medical and nursing topics without some firsthand knowledge. The expert fact witness does not have to have been clinically active at the time of the incident in question. This may contrast with some state requirements for liability expert witnesses.

The expert fact witness must possess expertise to explain healthcare and medical records without providing opinions about the facts and must have a thorough understanding of several types of medical records.

The expert fact witness must possess technology competence. This includes the ability to work with various computer software and programs including spreadsheets, portable document formats, word processing, and custom software. It is also important to be able to work with the latest electronic hardware like universal serial bus drives, external hard drives, and a projector attached to a laptop. The expert fact witness, like all LNCs, should be aware of the requirements under the Health Insurance Portability and Accountability Act and use secure methods of handling medical records and reports.

Applicable Cases

The expert fact witness may be retained by either the plaintiff or defense attorneys to review records, prepare a report, and testify about the facts contained in the medical records.

Plaintiff

Plaintiff attorneys may retain an expert fact witness to focus on the plaintiff's injuries and treatment associated with bodily injury, medical or nursing malpractice, product liability, toxic tort, domestic violence, and criminal cases—in short, any case in which the plaintiff sustained injuries. Whenever there is documentation of significant injuries in the medical records, the expert fact witness has a role. Examples of the types of cases for which expert fact witnesses may be retained include:

- Surgical errors
- Chemical and thermal burns
- Paralysis
- Cancer or other damages that develop from exposure to pollutants
- Closed head injury
- Major trauma from motor vehicle accidents, pedestrians hit by cars, or those with work injuries
- Worsened prognosis caused by delay in the diagnosis of cancer
- Death or injuries from surgical or treatment errors
- Battering during domestic violence
- Death or permanent injuries caused by medication errors

- Perinatal death or permanent injury and
- Anesthesia errors

A plaintiff expert fact witness would not have a role in cases in which the injuries are insignificant or non-existent. As a practical matter, many plaintiff attorneys who try cases involving people with significant injuries but have great difficulty in proving liability may not wish to incur the expense of retaining an expert fact witness. Typically, the plaintiff attorney hires the expert fact witness after the liability is established through standard of care experts.

In summary, the plaintiff expert fact witness may be an effective part of presenting damages when:

- There are voluminous medical records covering long admissions or treatment lasting months or years
- The injured person is unable to describe pain and suffering due to death, disability, or lack of communication skills or memory
- The plaintiff experienced marked pain; required extensive pain treatment; underwent multiple medical, surgical and nursing interventions; or experienced noxious sensations or emotional suffering
- The attorney wants the expert fact witness to educate the jury about the plaintiff's experiences or
- The attorney wants to build maximum impact by having an expert fact witness testify to the plaintiff's pain and suffering rather than putting the plaintiff on the stand. The jury may perceive the plaintiff as whining or may not be able to express pain and suffering adequately (Iyer, 2011)

Defense

Defense attorneys may hire expert fact witnesses:

- To summarize and educate the fact-finders about the care and treatment rendered
- To summarize the treatment provided to a plaintiff during a lengthy hospitalization
- To teach the jury about a specific nursing procedure or treatment documented in the record
- To review and compare the plaintiff's expert fact witness's report to the medical records and identify discrepancies and
- To summarize and educate the fact-finders about parts of the medical records that can be used to mitigate damages, such as:
  - Facts supporting plaintiff's exaggeration of injuries
  - Facts supporting plaintiff's non-compliance with the plan of care
  - Facts that weaken plaintiff's pain and suffering claims due to underlying, pre-existing injuries
  - Facts that negate plaintiff's pain and suffering claims due to underlying, pre-existing opioid dependence issues and
  - Facts that support an absence of pain and suffering during the time between an injury and death

Marketing the Expert Fact Witness Role to Attorneys

In order for an expert fact witness to provide this service to clients in a particular state, the first consideration is whether the state has patterned a comparable evidentiary rule after the Federal Rule of Evidence 1006. In other words, does the state allow expert fact witness testimony at trial? If not, the LNC pursuing this area would need to focus marketing efforts to those attorneys involved in federal cases or work with attorneys in nearby states with a state rule similar or identical to FRE 1006.

Once the above issue has been resolved, the LNC's success as an expert fact witness depends on the ability to market, educate, and sell the role to the attorney. Initially, attorneys may have little or no understanding of the advantages of using an expert fact witness. Some common responses from attorneys when presented with information about the role are "I'll have the treating doctor testify" or "I'll find the treating nurses and bring them to court." The expert fact witness should point out the expense of having a doctor prepare a detailed report of the voluminous records and the impracticality of locating and coordinating dozens of nurses or other healthcare professionals as testifiers. It is often impractical to use treating professionals to testify about the facts in the medical records. Treating healthcare professionals may be difficult to locate, and they may be unable to remember the plaintiff. They may not be analytical thinkers, have the ability to communicate easily, or be able to establish a rapport with a jury. They often speak using complex medical terms making it difficult for laypeople to follow. They may be intimidated by the legal system or unable to remain unbiased and objective. Often, they may have no prior experience in testifying or presenting clear, logically organized, and accurate reports. Having multiple healthcare professionals testify would result in a piecemeal, disjointed presentation of the plaintiff's treatment, because healthcare professionals have a limited focus on only the care they rendered. On the other hand, a nurse expert fact witness can provide a clear, unbiased report explaining complex medical terms, abbreviations, and procedures so that a jury can better understand the extensive medical record.

If the attorney has previously used a doctor to explain treatment, the expert fact witness should show the attorney a sample written report (with identifying information redacted) to explain the differences in scope and content. A sample work product is an excellent visual method to help attorneys understand the value of the role of the expert fact witness. Additionally, the expert fact witness can address other advantages of employing nurses for these types of reports. Nurse expert fact witness reports are often broader in scope than those prepared by other healthcare professionals, because nurses have greater knowledge of the healthcare system, hospital functioning, medical records, and elements of pain and suffering—all of which are often a large part of medical malpractice or personal injury cases. Nurses are the healthcare professionals who perform the treatments, measure the pain, teach the patient, and record responses to interventions. In addition, they interact with all healthcare professionals in all types of medical settings.

Once attorneys thoroughly understand the role and evaluate a sample written report, it is common for them to realize the value of using a nurse expert fact witness in the applicable cases discussed earlier.

Marketing Specifics

The LNC providing expert fact witness testimony should market to current clients and potential new clients. Discussing the role with current clients who are handling cases with significant injuries has a much higher chance of success for the LNC than cold calling or cold visits to other attorney offices. Attorneys who know, like, and trust the LNC are more likely to hire the expert fact witness (Iyer, 2017b). Inquire about cases in their practice which would benefit from an expert fact witness summary report and court testimony of that report. Certainly, requesting referrals from existing attorney clients is another excellent way of opening a new door.

Expert fact witness services can be packaged as part of the LNC's services or may be used as the main focus. While performing one type of LNC service on a case such as a screening for merit, the LNC may find the same case to be particularly amenable to an expert fact witness summary and testimony. Legal nurse consultants with businesses focused on supplying expert witnesses should also discuss the services of an expert fact witness. These are excellent opportunities to present the role to the client.

The LNC as an expert fact witness needs to focus marketing to attorneys handling medically related cases with lengthy hospitalizations or substantial injuries as those cases would benefit the most from expert fact witness review. The Internet provides details of law firms that focus on particular cases. For example, a search for "medical malpractice catastrophic injury cases" provides a list from which to start marketing.

Being prepared with an "elevator talk" on the benefits of using a nurse expert fact witness over other healthcare professionals and the difference between an expert fact witness and a liability expert witness will enable the LNC to take advantage of every opportunity that presents itself. Develop simple, brief explanations of the role to discuss on the telephone and in emails. Sharing information about the expert fact witness role while exhibiting at attorney conferences or lecturing to attorney groups are other ways to educate attorneys. Marketing materials such as brochures and presentations brought to these types of events or sent to potential clients should be professional, consistent, and organized.

Discuss the role on the LNC's website or on other forms of social media. Write blogs about the benefits of expert fact witness reports, the types of cases in which the role is applicable, and the process of analyzing and summarizing medical records. Write a blog about a case worked on and the result the expert fact witness helped the client achieve (if the result is not subject to a confidentiality agreement). After a large settlement is publicized, write a blog about how an expert fact witness would add value to that case. Maintaining an updated CV on the LNC's website including client names (with permission) and types of cases reviewed as an expert fact witness will reinforce the LNC's depth of experience.

Although cold calling or cold visits to attorney offices is a challenging way to solicit business, it often results in talking to the gatekeeper: the receptionist or paralegal. They can be instrumental in allowing access to the attorney. Being brief in explaining the role to the gatekeeper and being friendly and courteous may be enough for them to pass on the information (verbal and written) to the attorney. Consider asking the gatekeeper for an appointment with the attorney to discuss the expert fact witness role or follow up with the gatekeeper at a later date to request a meeting with the attorney. Cold calling at non-lunch times and the beginning and end of the workday increases the chance of talking with a person instead of leaving a message (Iyer, 2016). Consider time zones when placing these calls.

Follow up and repetition are vital parts of a marketing plan. Demonstrate reliability by returning calls, as promised. Periodically contact clients to remind them of the LNC's availability to assist with cases that warrant the use of an expert fact witness report. If requested to mail or email information to the attorney, follow up with a call to confirm receipt of the information and answer any questions.

Remember clients and potential attorney clients at the holidays and send a professional-looking card. This is another way of increasing name recognition, so the attorney will contact the expert fact witness when a case requires this kind of help.

Marketing to gain new clients takes time, and since the role of the expert fact witness is very specialized, it can take longer to find new clients than general legal nurse consulting services. When the LNC is contacted by potential clients for expert fact witness services, it is useful to ask potential clients how they found the LNC. This identifies the LNC's more effective marketing strategies.

See Chapter 30 for additional information on marketing.

Networking

In addition to marketing efforts, networking is another way to disseminate information about the expert fact witness role (Iyer, 2017c). Network with other LNCs by joining the American Association of Legal Nurse Consultants (AALNC; www.aalnc.org). There are numerous opportunities to become involved in this national professional organization (joining a committee, writing for the *Journal of Legal Nurse Consulting*, volunteering for a leadership role) and interact with like-minded LNCs. The AALNC's LNC Locator® is a publicly accessible, searchable database of AALNC members. It is a well-known way for litigators to find LNCs and nurse experts. In addition, there are local AALNC chapters where networking and marketing opportunities are presented. Another avenue for marketing and networking is through LNC listservs where discussions are held, experts are requested, and informal learning occurs. Becoming known in the LNC community through networking efforts can result in more referrals for expert fact witness opportunities.

Related Business Aspects

The expert fact witness will need to address costs of this service up-front with the attorney. A thorough and ongoing discussion of costs is in everyone's interest so there are no surprises. Given the amount of information to be analyzed, extracted, and compiled, these reports are time-consuming; they represent a substantial investment. Ongoing communication with the attorney about the time preparing reports and an estimate of the amount of time needed to testify will avert surprises. In some circumstances, tailoring the report down to the bare bones may be needed when the attorney is unable to fund a more extensive report and presentation.

Keeping track of billing time and other material costs and providing a detailed billing report are necessary and expected business practices. The nurse expert fact witness should consider using a replenishing retainer to avoid waiting for fees to be paid.

Lastly, the nurse expert fact witness will need to set aside sufficient time to read, assimilate, and summarize the medical records. For these reasons, it is advisable to avoid last minute rush assignments. After all, the intent is to provide an excellent, thorough report and secure additional assignments; it therefore behooves the nurse expert fact witness to set aside the proper amount of time.

Record Organization

The expert fact witness should request the client supply the medical records in the format the witness prefers—electronic or printed. It is ideal if the attorney's office organizes and paginates the medical records so all people working on the file have an identical set. If the records the expert fact witness receives are not organized, it is necessary to organize them for maximum efficiency. The expert fact witness organizes the records using indexes, medical record tabs, bookmarks, etc.;

these allow the expert fact witness to locate information quickly. The expert fact witness then evaluates the records for completeness and provides a list of the incomplete or missing records to the retaining attorney so the records can be obtained or located.

Report Preparation

The focus of the report will depend on the case, retaining attorney, and specific assignment or goal of the expert fact witness summary. The volume of records relevant to the report will vary. For example, in a case in which a decedent succumbed within hours of a trauma, the record review may focus on the period of time between injury and death. Other cases involve more extensive records generated over months or years. Understanding the allegations in the case will allow the expert fact witness to focus on the most important medical records.

It is easy to get overloaded with details. Use a system that will enable easy location of key documents. Do not notate on or highlight the records. Flagging pages with electronic or paper sticky notes is one way to facilitate writing the report. It is also expedient to prepare the report while reviewing the records rather than reading through all the records first.

The goal is to summarize the records in an objective way. Do not speculate. For example, the report should not contain statements such as, "Plaintiff must have been scared to wake up in the emergency room with no recollection of the accident." Instead, the report might contain the statement: "The nurse described the plaintiff as anxious and asking, 'Where am I?'" Another example would be to avoid writing "Plaintiff was clearly exaggerating the reports of shoulder pain" and instead write "The physician documented 'no grimacing was observed during shoulder range of motion'."

When evaluating plaintiff's claimed injuries, be aware of the difference between pre-existing conditions and those caused by the accident. At the same time, note pre-existing conditions that were exacerbated by the new injuries. Provide explanations.

In analyzing the medical records objectively, the expert fact witness has an ethical obligation to tell the retaining attorney about potentially damaging information found in the medical records, such as data that contradict the attorney's theories of liability or causation. The attorney is responsible for determining how to use this information in the process of litigating the case.

The expert fact witness should not lose sight of the fact that laypeople will read the report. This requires the ability to view the healthcare experience from the layperson's perspective. Since nurses have a foundation in patient education, the expert fact witness is able to prepare the report for the layperson using lay terminology. Furthermore, the expert fact witness breaks down complex medical terms into simple language, avoiding slang, abbreviations, and incomplete sentences.

Expert fact witness reports focus on the most relevant information in the medical records. The report should not contain:

- Opinions on damages (such as "Plaintiff suffered extraordinary pain and suffering")
- Opinions about liability (such as "Plaintiff suffered due to the deviations from the standard of care")
- Assumptions and speculations
- Typographical or grammatical errors or
- Long and complex sentences

The report should include:

- Information from the medical records
- Definitions of medical terms and
- Organized and easy to read information with bullet points, tables, graphs, or other formats as appropriate

The aim of the report is to educate, and the best way to do that is to hold the interest of the lay readers by using color, headers, short segments of information, and simple non-technical words.

Do not use a spreadsheet format for a table consisting of words. The software has a limited number of characters in each cell and data that exceeds the limits will not be displayed or printed. A spreadsheet is excellent for numbers and calculations, but a word processing program is best for information that is predominantly words. Copying and pasting or inserting a table or graph into a word processing document is an effective way of showing information. For example, a spreadsheet is useful for graphing pain scores or a total number of milligrams of an opioid.

Report Formats

There are several ways expert fact witnesses may organize the material in the narrative report. Typically, every report begins the same way: it is set up as a letter to the attorney and starts with a listing of medical records the expert fact witness reviewed. The list identifies each set of documents reviewed, such as the name of the facility with the beginning and end date of care, the outpatient treatment with beginning and end date, and so on.

The report may contain a brief description of the plaintiff's medical and social status immediately preceding the injury. For example, "Plaintiff was a 42-year-old, self-employed accountant who worked full time, was physically active, went to the gym five times per week, and took no medications. Plaintiff was married with two teenage children." Plaintiff attorneys may use this information on the plaintiff's prior level of function to highlight the impact of the injuries. Defense attorneys may use this information to illustrate plaintiff's return to the prior level of functioning.

Depending on the case and the goal of the expert fact witness report, a brief summary of the plaintiff's health status at the time of the incident may be relevant.

Next, the remainder of the report can be organized in two ways: by problems or by time frame. A problem-based approach works for briefer medical records. The expert fact witness can read the records, extract the relevant data, and then begin the narrative section. The content is organized according to nursing needs or problems (e.g., discomfort, dependence on others, behavioral alterations, skin breakdown, etc.) or according to topic (e.g., exaggeration of injuries, non-compliance with plan of care, etc.).

The report that is organized by time frame presents a summary of the plaintiff's condition and treatment within a specific period of time. This type of approach allows the expert fact witness to summarize while reviewing the records. A brief acute care admission is best summarized on a daily or, if needed, hourly basis. It may be more meaningful to summarize a longer hospital admission on a weekly basis. Weekly summaries are often the best format for a longer rehabilitation or nursing home stay, where daily charting is not common.

See Chapter 35 for more information on report preparation.

Formatting Tips

Use tables in the report to provide quick summaries of key components, such as comments the plaintiff made about symptoms, the number of doses of pain medication, the dates plaintiff failed to show for medical appointments, and so on.

The following are tips for creating a table:

- Repeat the column titles at the top of each page of the table to make it easier to remember what information is in each column. Use the word processor's ability to repeat the header row so that manual insertion of headers is not needed.
- Choose an easy-to-read font style. A serif font, like Times New Roman, is more legible than a sans serif font, like Arial.
- Use a font size of at least 12 in a table and in the body of the report and a significantly larger font size for exhibits, graphs, and displays when they are enlarged for trial.
- When preparing a table, add a blank line above and below each row entry. This additional white space makes it easier to read the table.
- Include bulleted information or a numbered list when possible. Place a blank line above and below the list.
- Use full sentences.
- Define and explain medical terms using parentheses around the definitions and explanations to show they are not part of the medical records.

Opposition to the Expert Fact Witness Role

It is common for opposing counsel to want to limit the use of expert fact witnesses. Once the attorney serves the expert fact witness report to opposing counsel, there are usually objections even before the mediation or trial begins. Often, opposing counsel realizes the potential negative impact of the expert fact witness's testimony as the jury will gain a better understanding of the medical records. This realization turns to concern and leads to efforts to block testimony. The report may and often does stimulate efforts to settle the case.

After receiving the report, opposing counsel may file a motion in limine asking the judge to prevent the witness from testifying. The retaining attorney often appreciates the expert fact witness's help in rebutting opposing counsel's objections. These strategies are often helpful:

- With permission, supplying the names of clients who have successfully used the expert fact witness in court
- With permission, supplying briefs written by attorneys who have defended the use of an expert fact witness (with the names of the parties redacted) and
- Supplying the text of the Federal Rule of Evidence 1006 and the state's law that mirrors Rule 1006 (if available)

As is required for the acceptance of other expert witnesses, the attorney must offer proof to the court that the expert fact witness is qualified to testify in this role. Opposing counsel and judges may not understand that nurses are qualified to present medical record evidence by virtue of their specialized education; certification; clinical experience; and familiarity with medical procedures and processes, medical records, and medical terminology. As key members of the healthcare team, nurses spend more time with patients and medical records in the clinical setting than any other care provider. Nurses teach patients about health and diseases, medical terminology, diagnostic tests, procedures, and a wide variety of treatment modalities. Nurses are qualified to provide this same information to educate jurors. Ultimately, acceptance of the qualifications of the expert fact witness is at the judge's discretion after review of the motion in limine and objection thereto or after hearing oral arguments on the motion at the time of trial.

See Appendix A for examples of the kinds of objections raised by opposing counsel. This material is from an actual case which settled before trial.

Deposition of the Expert Fact Witness

Typically, depositions of expert fact witnesses are taken less often than depositions of liability expert witnesses. However, preparing for deposition is the same as preparation for trial since the information provided at deposition can be used at trial. The expert fact witness may request preparation time with the retaining counsel, particularly if the witness is new to the role of being a deponent. By thoroughly reviewing the expert report with counsel along with the pertinent parts of the medical records, the expert fact witness prepares for deposition. See Chapter 36 for more information on deposition preparation.

If opposing counsel is not familiar with the expert fact witness role, the attorney may be initially puzzled by the report and the role. The opposing attorney may ask about the expert fact witness's prior experience in preparing such reports or what the expert fact witness plans to say at trial. Opposing counsel commonly needs assurance that the expert fact witness will not offer liability opinions. The opposing counsel may ask the expert fact witness questions to discredit the expert or the report. As attorneys gain familiarity with this role, they may become more aggressive in an attempt to challenge the expert fact witness.

It is imperative that expert fact witnesses confine their testimony to the facts contained in the medical records. Do not guess, speculate, or overreach when providing answers. For example, the expert fact witness may be asked if a decedent realized death was imminent. If a healthcare professional did not document this observation, the best answer is, "I would have no way of knowing that. It was not documented in the medical records available for review." This is an appropriate response for any question aimed at trying to have the expert fact witness give an opinion or state a fact not in the records. Refocus back to the facts and do not provide any answers to "what if" type questions.

A measure of success of the expert fact witness's deposition is if opposing counsel files a motion in limine after the deposition to preclude the expert fact witness from testifying at trial. The opposing attorney knows the testimony of the expert fact witness will likely accomplish the retaining attorney's objectives, which will be damaging to opposing counsel's case.

Trial Preparation

Any expert witness, whether a liability expert or an expert fact witness, should assume that any case may go to trial, despite reassurance from the attorney client to the contrary. The retaining counsel may request further assistance beyond report preparation as trial looms.

Drafts of Trial Exhibits and Demonstrative Aids

The jury remembers visual images long after witnesses have left the stand. Collaborate with the attorney to creatively plan and develop effective exhibits. Trial exhibits may include lists, charts, graphs, photographs, diagrams, or illustrations.

Discuss exhibits the client has used in past trials or suggest exhibits from the prepared report or medical records that would be effective in educating the trier of fact. For example, timelines made from the narrative chronology are effective as a visual aid for the jury. Demonstrative evidence can incorporate images of normal anatomy, medical procedures, schematic drawings of pain medications, graphs, changes in laboratory values, or even enlarged pages of the medical records. Demonstrative evidence is simple, visually pleasing, and free of complex terminology and concepts. The expert fact witness reviews the exhibits for correctness, simplicity, and readability at every stage of production. Exhibits that are part of the expert fact witness's testimony may be supplied to opposing counsel in advance of the trial, as required by court rules.

The use of presentation software on a laptop computer is now common at trial, because it is an effective way to present information. The attorney may ask the expert fact witness for ideas for slides, while having a staff member create the slides. Many of the slides will be exhibits found in the expert fact witness's report.

For more information on demonstrative evidence and trial preparation, see Chapters 37 and 39, respectively.

Presentation Practice

Often the expert fact witness and the attorney client will meet or converse on the phone prior to the court date. The purpose of the discussion is to:

■ Plan how to present the expert fact witness's qualifications so the jury and judge will understand why the expert is suited to present testimony (see Appendix B)
■ Prepare an outline of the expert fact witness's testimony. In some cases, the attorney will ask how to condense the summary to avoid overwhelming the jury with too many details
■ Determine how and when to use the demonstrative evidence
■ Learn about any developments in the case which would affect the expert fact witness's testimony
■ Ask the attorney for help in anticipating cross-examination tactics
■ Ask the attorney about the style of the opposing counsel and
■ Inquire about the style of the judge

It is important to be very familiar with the report and medical records. However, memorizing word-for-word text is risky, because the courtroom's climate may differ greatly from the privacy of rehearsal. It can be helpful to practice responses to potential questions that try to lead the expert fact witness to provide an opinion or testify beyond the confines of the medical records.

Trial Testimony

If the judge deems the expert fact witness to be qualified, the judge may still restrict testimony to strict and narrow boundaries or extend liberal boundaries for testimony. It is important to understand and abide by any limits imposed by the court.

Expert fact witnesses must understand their role in presenting medical testimony relative to the other experts called by the retaining attorney. For example, is the retaining attorney also calling a treating surgeon to the stand to explain the surgical aspect of the case and thus the nurse expert fact witness's testimony will focus on the medical and nursing management of the plaintiff? Will the expert fact witness summarize and explain one hospital admission or the plaintiff's entire treatment, including rehabilitation, subsequent admissions, etc.? The retaining attorney may also limit how much testimony the expert fact witness gives in relation to how much information the jury can absorb.

Setting up in Court and Practical Considerations

When the expert fact witness is the first witness of the day, it is advisable to arrive early. This allows the witness to sit in the jury box in advance in order to arrange any material, adjust the microphone, and make sure that a glass of water is available. Keep in mind that the expert fact witness educates the court about the technical facts, issues, and events of the medical record. The first few minutes on the stand are critical to establishing rapport with the jury. The expert fact witness attentively listens to the questions asked by the attorney. Eye contact with each juror is vital. Testimony under oath requires accurate reporting without embellishment. It is difficult for the opposing side to discredit meticulous, accurate, and complete testimony.

The expert fact witness should listen carefully to each question, answering only the question asked. Use everyday analogies and lay terminology to explain the main points of the case but be careful not to bore the jury with too much detail.

Presentation skills are critical. Because the audience is laypeople, the presentation is geared to non-medical people. In complex cases with a large volume of information to present, the attorney may want to begin with an overview of the areas to be presented, proceed to details, and finish with a summary. The expert fact witness need not memorize the report but should be very familiar with it.

The attorney may decide to make the testimony more conversational or may ask the expert fact witness questions to avoid the appearance that the witness is presenting a one-sided lecture to the jury. The attorney's questions may follow the expert fact witness's report. Regardless of the format of the testimony, the information should flow logically from one topic to the next.

The use of demonstrative evidence should be interspersed throughout the presentation. For extra effect, the expert fact witness might leave the witness box to point to a particular part of an exhibit. Changing the method of presentation throughout testimony assists in holding the interest of the jurors and increases the likelihood of them remembering the information.

Cross-Examination

The opposing attorney may cross-examine the expert fact witness. In contrast to the extensive cross-examination the liability expert has come to expect, this cross-examination may be brief. Opposing counsel may want to get the expert fact witness off the stand and out of sight as soon as possible to diminish the impact of the testimony. The accurate introduction of the medical record evidence and clear explanations of treatment and medical terminology leave little room for questions.

Opposing counsel may question the expert fact witness about facts in the medical record which are related to the liability issues. It is a safe practice to ask to see any page to which the attorney is referring.

At some point in cross-examination, the opposing attorney may try to discredit or diminish the effectiveness of the testimony by asking detailed questions regarding the expert fact witness's professional background. The expert fact witness should rebut this effort to discredit the expert by answering matter of factly and not apologetically.

Summary

Legal nurse consultants who undertake to summarize medical record evidence should have a detail-oriented perspective, the ability to clearly summarize medical records, and the willingness to testify if needed. While physicians tend to concentrate on explanations of specific medical treatments and procedures, nurses are more likely to present a broader, more comprehensive view of the events described in the medical records to improve the court's understanding of the case.

Unlike the adversarial, confrontational nature of liability testimony, testifying as an expert fact witness is usually less so and can be more rewarding for the LNC. The testifying expert fact witness takes on the role of educator and provides the jury with an understanding of the pertinent issues in an organized, systematic, and memorable format. As more attorneys and judges understand the role of an expert fact witness, additional opportunities may arise to educate juries, judges, attorneys, mediators, and arbitrators.

References

Federal Rules of Evidence. (2017). Rule 1006—summaries to prove content. Retrieved from www.rule-sofevidence.org/article-x/rule-1006/.

Heron, J., & Lewallen, M. (2014). 1006 Summary Witness: The nurse as a summary provider. *Cleveland Academy of Trial Attorneys News*, 12–14. Retrieved from http://clevelandtrialattorneys.org/wp-content/uploads/2014/06/CATA-News-Spring-2014.pdf.

Iyer, P. (2011). Pain and suffering. In P. Iyer, B. Levin, K. Ashton, & V. Powell (Eds.), *Nursing malpractice* (4th ed., pp. 265–299). Tucson, AZ: Lawyers and Judges Publishing.

Iyer, P. (2016). *How to start a legal nurse consulting business.* Fort Myers, FL: The Pat Iyer Group.

Iyer, P. (2017a). The LNC role in describing damages. *Journal of Legal Nurse Consulting, 28*(1), 28–29. Retrieved from https://view.flipdocs.com/?ID=10004296_650486.

Iyer, P. (2017b). *How to get more clients: Marketing secrets for LNCs.* Fort Myers, FL: The Pat Iyer Group.

Iyer, P. (2017c). *How to get more cases: Sales secrets for LNCs.* Fort Myers, FL: The Pat Iyer Group.

Additional Reading

Carleo, S. (2017). Business principles & practices. In *AALNC Legal nurse consulting professional course* (module 13). Retrieved from www.aalnc.org/page/course-content#packages.

Federal Rules of Evidence. (2017). Rule 702—testimony by expert witnesses. Retrieved from www.rule-sofevidence.org/article-vii/rule-702/.

Thorson, B. (2010). In summary of summaries. *Federal Lawyer Magazine.* Retrieved from www.fedbar.org/Resources_1/Federal-Lawyer-Magazine/2010/The%20Federal%20Lawyer%20-%20May%202010/Features/In-Summary-of-Summaries.aspx?FT=.pdf.

Test Questions

1. Which of the following statements is NOT true?
   A. A judge may prevent a nurse from testifying as an expert fact witness
   B. The expert fact witness presents opinions about the standard of care
   C. A nurse who is not named as a defendant in a case may be a fact witness
   D. Opposing counsel may attempt to block the use of a nurse expert fact witness to explain medical records

2. Which of the following statements is true?
   A. Defense attorneys commonly hire an expert fact witness to explain the plaintiff's pain and suffering
   B. The term "expert fact witness" is widely understood by attorneys
   C. Opposing counsel may challenge the use of expert fact witnesses with any level of academic training
   D. The use of treating professionals to testify provides the same benefits as using an expert fact witness

3. Which of the following statements is NOT true?
   A. The expert fact witness may write notes on medical records
   B. The physician is the appropriate expert to testify about permanency of injuries
   C. The expert fact witness's report may contain trial-appropriate exhibits
   D. Depositions are an opportunity for opposing counsel to evaluate the credibility of the expert fact witness

4. Which of the following statements is true?
   A. Few trials require demonstrative aids
   B. Memorizing testimony is an effective way to prepare for testimony
   C. Knowledge of patient education principles is useful when testifying as an expert fact witness
   D. The expert fact witness should proofread demonstrative evidence thoroughly when arriving at the witness box

5. Which is the most essential way to prepare for the role of the expert fact witness?
   A. Develop strong written and oral communication skills
   B. Prepare a concise marketing package
   C. Locate attorneys who handle personal injury cases
   D. Visit local hospitals to view medical equipment

Answers: 1. B, 2. C, 3. A, 4. C, 5. A

Appendix A: Motion in Limine to Exclude Expert Fact Witness (Motion Denied)

JUDGE: Mr. Plaintiff Attorney, before you call your first witness, I understand that there is a motion to be heard. Jury, you may be excused ... Mrs. Defense Attorney, I understand that you have filed a motion in limine to preclude the testimony of Nurse Expert Fact Witness. You may present your position.

DEFENSE ATTY.: Your Honor, the defense objects to the use of Nurse Expert Fact Witness as an expert in this trial. She was not involved in the plaintiff's treatment in any way. There are no nursing issues involved in this case. There are no claims of medical malpractice in the care of this plaintiff. Since plaintiff intends to call her treating physicians as witnesses, Nurse Expert Fact Witness's testimony is cumulative of the testimony of her doctors and the plaintiff herself. Nurse Expert Fact Witness's report, exhibits, and slide show are highly prejudicial and inflammatory, and given the cumulative nature of the report, that prejudice far outweighs any marginal probative value.

Nurse Expert Fact Witness's background and expertise are strictly in nursing. She lacks any specialized medical education or experience. The practice of professional nursing is defined as "diagnosing and treating human responses to actual or potential health problems through such services as case finding, health teaching, health counseling, and provision of care supportive to or restorative of life and well-being, and executing medical regimens as prescribed by a licensed physician or dentist." Nurse Expert Fact Witness lacks the skill, training, knowledge, or experience to summarize plaintiff's medical records. The medical records consist of medical diagnoses, treatments, and prognoses. A medical doctor, and not a nurse, is competent to provide analysis and summary of medical records. Nurse Expert Fact Witness cannot provide such a summary. She is merely a nurse. Plaintiff's treating physicians are the appropriate personnel to explain the surgical procedures, diagnoses, and other purely medical details, as distinguished from nursing events. Nurse Expert Fact Witness's mere familiarity with these matters does not qualify her to provide an appropriate, accurate, and reliable medical summary.

The primary purpose of expert testimony is to assist the trier of fact in understanding complicated matters, not simply to assist one party in winning their case. An examination of Nurse Expert Fact Witness's report, exhibits, and slide show clearly demonstrates that she anticipates doing nothing more than selectively repeating the medical record without bringing any nursing expertise to bear upon issues pertinent to the fact-finder. Nowhere in the report does Nurse Expert Fact Witness comment upon plaintiff's nursing regimen or any nursing-care-related issues. Plaintiff is perfectly capable of testifying about her course of treatment and symptoms.

Finally, Nurse Expert Fact Witness's report and slide show contain photographs of the plaintiff's injuries. These photographs are highly prejudicial. Her report contains a diagram of plaintiff's fractured hip. This drawing is so rudimentary that it cannot properly be qualified or explained except by its author. Without the exhibit's caption, it is questionable whether anyone would know what it is.

JUDGE: Counsel, are you finished?

DEFENSE ATTY.: Yes, Your Honor.

JUDGE: Mr. Plaintiff Attorney, you may respond.

PLAINTIFF ATTY.: My esteemed adversary argued earlier that Nurse Expert Fact Witness was not qualified to summarize medical records. As Mrs. Defense Attorney herself noted, the practice of nursing includes health teaching and the provision of care supportive to or restorative of life and well-being, and executing medical regimens as prescribed by a licensed physician. For Nurse Expert Fact Witness to function as a nurse, she must be able to interpret and analyze medical records. Part of the role of the registered nurse is to be able to use and explain equipment such as Foley catheters, Hoyer lifts, Rotorest beds, nasogastric tubes, and the other equipment that is explained in her report. Patient education is a basic function of all nurses. Nurse Expert Fact Witness will be applying her expertise in patient education to help the jury understand the medical and nursing details of plaintiff's care.

As a registered nurse with 30 years of experience, Nurse Expert Fact Witness has specialized knowledge beyond that possessed by the jury. She has expertise in understanding and interpreting medical records.

Your Honor, my adversary has argued that nowhere in Nurse Expert Fact Witness's report does she comment on nursing-care-related issues. As you will note from reviewing her report, she comments on several nursing-care-related issues, including the symptoms my client experienced after she was run down by the bus driven by the defendant.

JUDGE: Now, Mr. Plaintiff Attorney, let's stick to the arguments. Save the dramatics for the jury.

PLAINTIFF ATTY.: I'm sorry, Your Honor. Nurse Expert Fact Witness's report describes the many sources of discomfort my client experienced, her difficulty eating, her emotional distress, her dependence on others, just to name a few. These are all issues that nurses are educated to treat as part of their role in providing care to patients such as my client. Further, my adversary has argued that my client can testify about her medical treatment and symptoms. My client was sedated for part of her admission, although capable of feeling and reacting to her medical treatment. She lacks the specialized knowledge and training that Nurse Expert Fact Witness has and is unable to explain to the jury why certain treatments were performed on her. Nurse Expert Fact Witness has the educational background to be able to explain the drawing of plaintiff's fractured hip, one that my adversary objected to as rudimentary. Clearly Nurse Expert Fact Witness was able to understand it, when my adversary could not! This is exactly why the jury needs Nurse Expert Fact Witness to help them understand what happened to my client. It is unclear how the defense can assert that Ms. Expert Fact Witness serves no useful purpose, whatsoever when in fact she has just assisted the defense counsel to understand the nature of plaintiff's pelvic fractures.

Further, the defense has had five months to obtain a counter expert, and they have no one. There is not a single defense expert who in any way questions the accuracy, appropriateness, or reliability of the medical information in Ms. Expert Fact Witness's report. The defense's orthopedic surgeon reviewed Ms. Expert Fact Witness's report as part of his medical opinion. He does not, in any manner, criticize her report. I'd like to stress that the defense argues that the plaintiff can testify to her course of medical treatment. My client, who had just been struck by a 30,000-pound bus going 55 miles per hour, was in no condition to even think! In a case such as this, where the plaintiff was in the hospital for three weeks, there would be testimony from at least 25–30 different healthcare professionals, including doctors, nurses, and therapists, to accurately convey that which Ms. Expert Fact Witness is conveying during approximately one hour's worth of testimony. To request that photographs of the plaintiff's injuries not be utilized at the time of the trial under the guise that they are prejudicial is simply wrong. In fact, it would be prejudicial to the plaintiff to not be able to accurately display the full extent of her injuries to the jury. These are simply photographs of bruises. Simply because the bruises may be a foot in circumference does not make them more prejudicial to the defense.

I would also cite Rule of Evidence 1006, which states that the "contents of voluminous writings, recordings, or photographs which cannot conveniently be examined in court may be presented in the form of a chart, summary, or calculation." Nurse Expert Fact Witness's report and testimony will assist the jury in understanding my client's voluminous medical records.

JUDGE: Are you finished?

PLAINTIFF ATTY.: Yes, Your Honor.

JUDGE: Mrs. Defense Attorney, do you have anything further?

DEFENSE ATTY.: Yes, if the court please. I want to add that Nurse Expert Fact Witness continually states her personal interpretation of plaintiff's medical treatments. She frequently comments on plaintiff's injuries, using such terms as "large amounts of bruising," "extensive bruising," "fortunately did not disrupt her elbow joint," "maximum assistance," "moderate assistance," and "minimal assistance." The subjective nature of Nurse Expert Fact Witness's characterization of plaintiff's injuries demonstrates that the sole purpose of this testimony is to excite the passions of the jury rather than to provide an accurate, brief, and objective summary of the medical record, which is too voluminous for the jury to otherwise comprehend.

JUDGE: Are you now finished?

DEFENSE ATTY.: Yes, Your Honor.

JUDGE: Counsel, any response?

PLAINTIFF ATTY.: Yes, Your Honor. The comments that my esteemed colleague has just cited are taken directly from the medical records of my client. The terms are not Nurse Expert Fact Witness's but those of the doctors, nurses, and therapists who attended my client. Why, if Mrs. Defense Attorney would like to see, I can point out each term and where it is in the medical record.

JUDGE: That will not be necessary, Mr. Plaintiff Attorney. I am satisfied that Nurse Expert Fact Witness has performed a thorough review of the medical record. I agree that she possesses specialized skill, knowledge, experience, and training well beyond that of the average layperson. She is familiar with medical terminology and has worked with medical records during her duties as a nurse. She has taken direction from medical professionals and implemented instructions and orders. I do not wish to spend excessive court time bringing in a parade of doctors and nurses to testify about the treatment they rendered to the plaintiff. Furthermore, I agree that the medical records are voluminous in this case and filled with symbols, abbreviations, and terms not understood by the average layperson. I find that the medical records are difficult to interpret without Nurse Expert Fact Witness's testimony. I do not believe that plaintiff's doctors are prepared to render such detailed and extensive testimony as Nurse Expert Fact Witness will in this case. I find that our state's Rules of Evidence permit this type of witness to testify. Further, I do not find the photographs of the plaintiff to be prejudicial. The images of normal anatomy are also acceptable, as they are intended to provide the jury with an understanding of the issues in this case. Her testimony is permitted, and I will allow the jury to hear her. Further, I will allow the jury to see the photographs of the plaintiff that are part of the slide presentation. Anything further, Mrs. Defense Attorney?

DEFENSE ATTY.: Judge, Nurse Expert Fact Witness's report does not constitute evidence in this case. We respectfully ask the court to prohibit Nurse Expert Fact Witness's report from being entered into evidence or being placed with the jury while they deliberate.

JUDGE: I disagree. Nurse Expert Fact Witness may testify, and her report will be placed into evidence. Mr. Plaintiff Attorney, you may call Nurse Expert Fact Witness to the stand.

Appendix B: Questions for Qualifying the Expert Fact Witness

Please tell us the extent of your education and schooling.

Do you take continuing education courses regularly? What types and how often?

Do you currently hold any professional licenses?

Where do you currently work?

What is your title?

Can you tell us about your clinical nursing background, please?

Have you ever treated patients who suffered _____(injuries similar to the plaintiff)?

Where?

Have you ever held an instructor or teaching position in the field of nursing?

Aside from that position, have you ever been responsible for teaching or educating professionals in the nursing field? If yes, please explain.

How many medical charts have you analyzed over the course of your career?

Have you reviewed the medical chart in this case from (names of facilities)?

Do these records contain medical terms and abbreviations?

How do you define voluminous?

Were these charts voluminous?

Have you performed the tasks the nursing staff at (name of facility) had to perform in their care of (plaintiff's name)?

How often have you been called upon to provide a summary of medical records of the nature you prepared in this case?

Your honor, at this time I offer registered nurse _____ to the court and ladies and gentlemen of the jury as an expert in the field of nursing and explaining medical records.

Legal Nurse Consultant Skills

Chapter 33

Communication with Attorneys' Clients in the Medical Malpractice Arena

Sharon K. McQuown, MSN, RN, LNCC®
Cheryl E. White, MSHL, BS, AS, RN, LHRM, LNCC®, MSCC, DFSHRMPS

Contents

Objectives

- Describe three components of interviewing skills that nurses acquire through their education and practice
- Explain two purposes for interviewing attorneys' clients in the legal setting
- List three potential barriers to communication with attorneys' clients
- Identify two legal issues the LNC may need to communicate to the attorney's client

Introduction

Strong written and oral communication skills are important when working with attorneys and communicating with their clients. It is essential that the LNC be able to communicate complex and confusing information in a way that can be understood by those without medical training. The LNC must also be a good listener, as that is one of the best ways to be a good communicator. This chapter addresses the role of the in-house or independent LNC during communication with an attorney's client (i.e., the plaintiff or the defendant), beginning with the initial client interview and continuing through the completion of the civil tort litigation. The LNC possesses a broad healthcare education as well as experience in communicating and establishing rapport with healthcare team members. The LNC uses these skills to communicate with the attorney's client, thereby helping the plaintiff or defense attorney manage a case effectively and efficiently.

Communication Defined

Dictionary.com defines communication as "the imparting or interchange of thoughts, opinions or information by speech, writing or signs" (Communication, 2018). The LNC will find that communication is an essential function of the job. Whether verbal or written, the LNC will be required to communicate complex medical issues and processes in simple and concise terms that can be understood by those with little or no medical knowledge. The LNC must not only communicate clearly to others but be an active listener and observer who is skilled at understanding communication from others, including reading their non-verbal cues.

Barriers to Communication

The LNC must be aware of potential barriers to communication that can thwart the successful exchange of information. Some may be more obvious than others. Barriers to communication include:

- Age
- Medical conditions resulting in speech, hearing, or cognitive impairments
- Distractions
- Language
- Emotional status

- Educational background
- Socioeconomic status
- Culture
- Religion
- Prior experiences and
- Personal bias

Much of today's written communication is performed electronically. Misinterpretation of information communicated by email often stems from the inability to hear the communicator's voice inflections or tone or see the communicator's facial expressions. In addition, miscommunication can occur by phone. Background noises, poor connections, use of conference mode, and distractions during the call can make communication by phone difficult.

The LNC who is a good communicator is mindful of these barriers to communication and guards against creating such barriers when communicating with the attorney's client by:

- Avoiding the use of medical and legal terminology
- Using a language interpreter or assistive communication devices
- Accounting for the attorney's client's age, education, culture, emotional status, religion, etc. and adjusting communications accordingly
- Being mindful of any personal bias or influence from past experiences
- Reading the attorney's client's non-verbal cues and modifying communications accordingly and
- Eliminating distractions and avoiding the performance of other tasks such as answering emails or reading documents while communicating by phone. Failure to pay attention during communication increases the risks for misinterpretation and errors by the LNC.

Multiple books have been written and courses developed to teach effective communication. One author stated, "[T]he biggest problem with communication is we don't listen to understand. We listen to reply" (Covey, 2011, p. 251). When the LNC listens to understand, there are fewer risks for misinterpretation and a greater chance of strengthening the overall communication, building trust with the client, and leaving the client feeling satisfied with the interaction.

Communication in the Legal Arena

Whether working with a plaintiff or defense attorney, the LNC will have the responsibility of communicating with multiple members of the legal team including the paralegal, legal secretary, the attorney's client and family, medical experts, and others. The defense team may also include adjusters from the defendant's insurance company, co-defendants, and risk managers from hospitals or other healthcare facilities. Each member of the legal team has different perspectives, needs, and expectations. The common goal for all team members is successful resolution of the case.

The LNC plays a key role in the communication process as the one person on the legal team with both healthcare and legal experience. Thus one role of the LNC is that of a liaison between the legal team members, the attorney's client, and medical experts. The LNC brings clinical knowledge, advanced communication skills, and empathy to the legal team.

Appropriate communication of information by the LNC helps the attorney's client to understand the risks and benefits of all case resolution options, decision points along the way, and the legal processes. The desires of the plaintiff or defendant in the matter must be carefully elicited, and they must make informed decisions based on the information provided to them.

Often the plaintiff's decisions in litigation are based more on emotional factors (love, grief, fear, and anger). Plaintiff clients who have been injured or lost a loved one often seek financial retribution and may also seek a public admission of fault from the defendant. Plaintiffs may be unable to see the facts of the case beyond the injuries sustained. It may be inconceivable to them that the defendant may not have been negligent or that negligence may not have caused the injuries. Furthermore, they may be shocked to discover that even if the defendant is found negligent, the defendant's professional license may not be at risk. The plaintiff's goals must be accurately identified. Education and emotional support from the attorney and LNC can then assist the client with the agreed goals.

The experience of being a defendant in a lawsuit can be very upsetting, time-consuming, stressful, and expensive for the healthcare practitioner. One of the most valuable resources defense counsel can utilize is the LNC. Defendants often recognize the LNC as a clinical colleague and may feel a certain comfort level communicating with the LNC from the outset. The legal nurse consultant can provide a needed perspective on the interrelationship between the medicine and the law and can bridge the gap between the facts in the case and the medical issues of the care and treatment in question.

The LNC's first communication with the attorney's client may be by phone. It is during this initial call that rapport is first built between the client and the LNC. This initial communication is an opportunity for the LNC to gather key information and to education the client (or potential client) on the next steps. For example, plaintiff firms often use a prepared intake form to collect initial information when screening calls from potential plaintiffs.

The Initial Interview

The initial interview serves many purposes including introducing the attorney's client to the litigation team, obtaining case facts, and evaluating the effectiveness of the plaintiff or defendant as a witness. The initial interview may take place over the telephone or in-person.

If the attorney conducts the interview, the LNC may act as the scribe. In this role, the LNC must demonstrate active listening. Active listening involves paying close attention to what is being said to not just hear it and take notes but to analyze the information and consider follow-up questions. Eye contact is important to demonstrate focus on the person and the conversation. The LNC should also observe the person's non-verbal signals which might convey confusion, anger, grief, or embarrassment.

Likewise, legal nurse consultants should be aware of their own body language and non-verbal cues that might impact the plaintiff's or defendant's willingness to speak openly and honestly. Avoid body language such as frowning, scowling, or eye-rolling which can negatively impact the effectiveness of an interviewer and may demonstrate a lack of empathy and respect for the attorney's client.

Interviewing is an acquired skill set that most LNCs developed as registered nurses when performing patient assessments. If the LNC is conducting the initial interview, the LNC should begin with introductions and an explanation of the LNC's role on the litigation team.

Early in the interview, it is important for the LNC to identify any actual or potential conflicts of interest that would prohibit involvement in the case. The names of all potential parties should be solicited. The LNC should also inquire about any previous involvement with the legal system and obtain the names of the attorneys and parties involved. If it is determined that an actual or potential conflict exists, the interview may need to be terminated until the conflict is resolved, if possible. (Defense firms typically screen for conflicts prior to accepting a case from the defendant's liability insurance company.)

If no conflict is evident, the interview should proceed to solicit more detailed information. The LNC should organize questions in a clear, logical, and easy format for the plaintiff or defendant to understand, because communication is successful only when the speaker and listener understand each other (McQuown & Cooper, 2014). Through a friendly tone, the LNC will encourage the plaintiff or defendant to engage in open and honest communication.

It is also important for the LNC to account for the attorney client's feelings and instill trust through the effective use of interviewing skills (McQuown & Cooper, 2014). The LNC should keep an open mind and demonstrate a respectful attitude throughout the interview. It is important that the LNC ask questions and restate key information during the interview for clarity. A well-trained LNC will always consider the opposite side's perspective—to look for strengths and weaknesses of the case.

Plaintiff

The LNC may begin the interview with the open-ended statement "Tell me what happened." Legal nurse consultants should allow plaintiffs to tell the story in their own words. Most plaintiffs are eager to tell their story to a nurse who understands the medical issues of their case. The LNC must direct the interview efficiently to sort relevant information from irrelevant information by guiding the story with specific questions or requests for additional details.

The LNC should ask what prompted the individual to contact the attorney and what the plaintiff wishes to accomplish by filing a lawsuit. Some plaintiffs may want financial compensation for their injury. Others may want to understand what caused their injury, and some want to prevent the same thing from happening to someone else.

The LNC will collect information regarding the date of the injury, extent of the injury, names of all healthcare providers and facilities involved, and possible witnesses. The plaintiff's complete health history is elicited and reviewed to determine past medical history, current medical problems caused by the injury, pre-existing conditions, and the effect of the injury on those pre-existing problems. It is important for the LNC to communicate to the attorney any negative behaviors of the attorney's client, such as drug or alcohol abuse, driving under the influence, and other offenses to the attorney.

The LNC and plaintiff should discuss how the plaintiff's life has been altered following the injury, including the impact of the injury on the plaintiff's health, lifestyle, and employment—that is, identify the damages.

The plaintiff LNC also serves as a resource to the plaintiff to answer questions about injuries, ongoing medical problems, and care. The LNC plays a vital role in communicating to the plaintiff the reasons for continuing prescribed therapies and compliance with the medical plan of care.

The plaintiff LNC understands that assessment through interviewing and questioning is an ongoing process lasting the life of the case, and this process should clearly identify the strengths and weaknesses in the plaintiff's case.

Defendant

The LNC conducting the initial interview with the defendant should remember the defendant may feel unjustly blamed. An LNC with strong communication skills can increase the defendant's confidence and perceived value of the legal team. Many defendants feel encouraged by the presence of a nurse on the legal team who understands the clinical issues and treatment.

The LNC will inquire about the defendant's education, work experience, certifications, publications, and any prior litigation or licensure actions. The LNC will also collect information about the healthcare professional's role and involvement in the plaintiff's care, including specifics about relevant examinations, testing, diagnoses, treatment, and follow-up.

The healthcare defendant will be requested to review the medical record concerning the event(s) in question to help refresh the defendant's memory and to interpret handwritten and electronic medical record entries and idiosyncratic abbreviations. The LNC will use this opportunity to question the defendant about routine care that may have been provided but not documented. The LNC assists the defendant in identifying pertinent documents which will be important to the case, such as policies and procedures, telephone logs, message books, incident reports, quality improvement reports, continuous education records, etc. The defendant will be given a preservation notice to retain any diaries, personal notes, calendars, etc. related to the case.

Both the plaintiff and defendant should be educated on the four elements of negligence that the plaintiff must prove to prevail in a medical negligence case, the legal definition of the standard of care, and the burden of proof. (Additional information concerning the four elements of proof in a medical negligence case can be found in Chapter 4.)

The LNC should also communicate the steps in the litigation process and offer a brief explanation of the next step in that process. (Plaintiff LNCs may prepare educational materials such as a booklet that can be provided to all plaintiffs.)

The interview should conclude with a discussion of the attorney-client privilege with instructions not to discuss the case with anyone other than the litigation team (and on the defense side, with the defendant's liability insurance company). Upon conclusion of the interview, the LNC prepares a written summary of the interview for the attorney containing the findings, facts, and key points gathered during the interview.

Legal Issues

Because of the rapport established between the attorney's client and LNC during the initial interview and because of the education provided by the LNC during that meeting, plaintiffs and defendants often reach out to the LNC directly with questions throughout the litigation process. Legal nurse consultants must be careful to avoid the unauthorized practice of law. See Chapter 2 for more information on this and other LNC liability issues.

The education provided by the LNC and legal team to plaintiffs often includes helping to adjust plaintiffs' perception of the legal issues and their expectation of the outcome. For example, the plaintiff should understand that the defendant healthcare professional's license may not be suspended or revoked in the event of a successful outcome. (Licensure actions are entirely separate from civil lawsuits, but any settlement or award against a licensed healthcare professional is reportable to the National Practitioner Data Bank and often to the state's licensing body for that profession, e.g., Board of Nursing or Board of Medicine. See Chapter 25 for more information.) Payout by the defendant's liability insurance carrier may be the only effect suffered by the defendant healthcare professional.

Plaintiffs and defendants should be instructed that their role in the litigation process is an active one and that they must respond to requests for subsequent information promptly and fully.

Plaintiffs and defendants need to understand the possible length of legal proceedings and the importance of avoiding discouragement by seemingly endless postponements and continuances.

Discovery

Once the suit is filed and the legal process begins, education continues for the plaintiff and defendant. Interrogatories and requests for production may be perceived by the attorney's client as a series of redundant, irrelevant questions. As the discovery process continues, the day of their deposition may be one of the most stressful events for the plaintiff and defendant.

It is important for the LNC to educate the attorney's client on how depositions differ from prior interviews. The tendency for both the plaintiff and defendant is to tell their story in an uninterrupted fashion. In depositions, the opposing attorney will ask the plaintiff or defendant a series of questions. Most of the questions will require a concise yes or no answer. The LNC or attorney should instruct the plaintiff or defendant to pause before answering so the attorney has an opportunity to object to the question. Once the objection is on the record, the attorney will often instruct the client to go ahead and answer the question. If there is no objection, the plaintiff or defendant should answer the question clearly, so it can be recorded by the court reporter and be preserved for later use by either legal team. The plaintiff or defendant must remember that non-verbal communication such as a head nod or shoulder shrug cannot be recorded, and thus a clear verbal answer must be provided to the opposing attorney. Additional information regarding discovery can be found in Chapter 5.

Mediation

The goal of all cases is resolution, and one opportunity for resolution is mediation. Mediation may be voluntary or court-mandated, and the LNC can be the communication liaison to the plaintiff or defendant regarding the mediation process.

Attorneys may utilize various presentation formats at mediation, including a hard-bound brochure book, a video brochure, demonstrative evidence, or simply a verbal presentation during the opening session. The personal connection the LNC has built with the plaintiff or defendant allows the LNC to assist the attorney in preparing a meaningful and effective presentation. For example, LNCs can work with plaintiffs to obtain photographs that reflect their life prior to the event in question or with defendants to obtain information about professional awards and accomplishments.

During the mediation, LNCs can answer questions posed by the plaintiff or defendant to assist them in understanding the nuances of the negotiations. As the discussion turns toward actual monetary offers, the LNC can clarify questions to or answers from the attorney so there are no miscommunications. Additional information regarding mediation can be found in Chapter 38.

Trial

When mediation fails, the parties proceed to trial. The attorney's client needs to be educated on how the jury pool is selected. The individuals selected to serve want to hear a clear and concise story. It is essential to keep jurors engaged throughout the process, which can be difficult in complex cases. As the witnesses and experts are presented, it is important to promptly address any questions or concerns from the plaintiff or defendant. Plaintiffs and defendants know this is their day in court. They may not understand the broad-brush strokes utilized with a certain witness.

During trial, the attorney's client may feel the LNC is more approachable than the attorney. In this case, it is the LNC's responsibility to communicate to the attorney any concerns verbalized by the client. For more information on trials, see Chapter 39.

Summary

Legal nurse consultants, as educators and skillful communicators, are critical to the litigation process. During their nursing training and clinical experiences, LNCs developed skills as active listeners and keen observers. In the legal arena, these skills enable the LNC to build trust with the attorney's client, collect and analyze data, and educate and communicate in a correct, clear, and concise manner, making the LNC a valuable asset to the attorney.

References

Communication. (2018). *Dictionary.com*. Retrieved from www.dictionary.com/browse/communication.

Covey, S. R. (2011). *The 7 habits of highly effective people: Powerful lessons in personal change*. New York, NY: Simon & Schuster.

McQuown, S., & Cooper, J. (2014). Interacting with plaintiff and defense clients. In *AALNC Legal nurse consulting professional course* (module 3). Retrieved from www.aalnc.org/page/legal-nurse-consulting-professional-course.

Additional Reading

Balzer-Riley, J. W. (2017). *Communication in nursing* (8th ed.). St. Louis, MO: Elsevier.

Browne, M. K., & Keeley, S. (2011). *Asking the right questions: A guide to critical thinking* (8th ed.). Englewood Cliffs, NJ: Prentice Hall.

Chay, A., & Smith, J. (1996). *Legal interviewing in practice*. Sydney, Australia: Law Book Company.

Filetti, D. M. (2012). The utilization of legal nurse consultants in the defense of medical malpractice cases. *DRI, 11*(31).

Harney, D. M. (2016). *Medical malpractice* (5th ed.). Charlottesville, VA: Michie Law Publishers.

Iyer, P., Taptich, B., & Bernocchi-Losey, D. (1995). *Nursing process and nursing diagnosis* (3rd ed.). Philadelphia, PA: W.B. Saunders.

Katzenbach, J. R., & Smith, D. K. (2015). *The wisdom of teams*. New York, NY: HarperCollins.

Louisell, D. W., & Williams, H. (2013). *Medical malpractice* (Vol. 7). New York, NY: Matthew Bender.

Nelken, M. L., & Schoenfield, M. K. (1992). *Problems and cases in interviewing, counseling and negotiation*. St. Paul, MN: National Institute for Trial Advocacy.

Silverman J., Kurtz, S., & Draper, J. (2013). *Skills for communicating with patients* (3rd ed.). Boca Raton, FL: CRC Press, Taylor Francis Group.

Smith, L. (1998). Medical paradigms for counseling: Giving clients bad news. *Clinical Law Review, 4*, 391.

Test Questions

1. Which of the following statements is NOT true?
   A. An LNC plays a key role in the communication process as the one person on the legal team with healthcare and legal experience
   B. A defendant's attitude depends, in part, on how the defendant feels about the attorney and legal team
   C. The plaintiff can often see the facts of the case beyond the injuries sustained
   D. The plaintiff's goals must be accurately identified
2. Which of the following is NOT true? An LNC with strong interviewing skills can increase the attorney client's:
   A. Confidence
   B. Perceived value of the litigation team
   C. Openness
   D. Monetary compensation
3. Which of the following is NOT a purpose of the initial client interview?
   A. Collect data from the attorney's client
   B. Determine the financial status of the attorney's client
   C. Educate the attorney's client
   D. Assess the effectiveness of the attorney's client as a possible witness
4. Which of the following is NOT a possible barrier to communication?
   A. Poor computer skills
   B. Emotional status
   C. Culture
   D. Educational background
5. Which information is NOT communicated to the attorney's client?
   A. The four elements of proving a medical negligence case
   B. The steps in the legal process
   C. Instructions to destroy all personal notes concerning the incident
   D. That all discussions between the attorney and client are protected

Answers: 1. C, 2. D, 3. B, 4. A, 5. C

Chapter 34

Researching Medical Literature and Other Information

Katy Jones, MSN, RN

Contents

Objectives

- Identify the steps in a database search
- List five National Library of Medicine databases other than MEDLINE® that can be helpful in accessing information on specific topics
- List two sources legal nurse consultants can use to research an author's credentials
- State two ways to determine the validity of published information
- List two sources for locating standards of care or clinical practice guidelines

Introduction

The American Association of Legal Nurse Consultants' Standards of Professional Performance state, "The legal nurse consultant integrates evidence and research into practice" (American Association of Legal Nurse Consultants, 2017).

As the specialty practice of legal nurse consulting becomes more familiar to the legal profession, the roles of legal nurse consultants (LNCs) will continue to expand. Attorneys are realizing and appreciating that LNCs have a vast knowledge base and many skills beyond the review and interpretation of medical records. Attorneys are thinking creatively and recognizing that LNCs can be helpful in multiple areas such as domestic, criminal, employment, and environmental cases as well as cases in which negligence involves critical medical errors. For example, a labor law attorney represents a client with a diagnosis of bipolar disorder. The plaintiff's employers fired the plaintiff, and the plaintiff alleges the behavior which led to the dismissal was due to the plaintiff's bipolar disease. The plaintiff is pursuing a legal claim of discrimination under the Americans with Disabilities Act. An LNC should be able to research medical and pharmaceutical information as well as interpret psychiatric and pharmacy records in this case.

Depending on the type and stage of a case when an LNC's involvement begins, an attorney may ask an LNC to:

- provide confirmation or rebuttal of the case allegations
- perform all or a portion of the medical research
- determine standards of care and standards of practice
- identify medical literature and other information relevant to the case or authored by an expert or fact witness
- identify potential expert witnesses
- provide background information on the plaintiff's or decedent's medical treatment and
- determine the necessity of future medical damages and treatment

Access to computers and the World Wide Web has become commonplace both at home and in the workplace. Information is just a click away on the Web, which has become a significant resource on which LNCs rely constantly. One of the many valuable services an LNC offers clients is the ability to identify and locate medical information specific to issues in a case. Some nurses are relatively comfortable doing research in health sciences libraries and often have had considerable experience in retrieving information from medical and scientific textbooks and journals. However, depending on their educational preparation and level of computer proficiency, some LNCs may be somewhat less confident performing in-depth medical research using the Web.

The Internet provides access to the most current information via online sources and has revolutionized the way LNCs perform their research projects. To establish the necessary elements of a case, the LNC can search the Internet and locate information about medical conditions, medications, procedures, and standards and practice guidelines that were relevant at the time of the subject incident or accident. Appendix A contains a complete list of all website references and multiple other websites.

The goals of this chapter are to help the LNC develop the skills of identifying and locating medical information, increase the LNC's personal knowledge base and awareness of available resources, and perhaps more importantly, help the LNC analyze the medical and scientific information relied upon for its validity and credibility.

Today's is a high-speed information society. Due to the mechanics of the publication process, much of the state-of-the-art knowledge may not be found in the traditional textbook. Considerable time (possibly years) may pass between the manuscript's acceptance and the textbook's availability. Therefore, textbooks often do not reflect the most up-to-date information. However, textbooks contain a wealth of in-depth material that is pertinent to the time frame in question and thus invaluable for many research projects.

The Nursing Process in Literature and Online Searches

The nursing process serves the LNC well when conducting research. Each element of the process is critical to the development of a research strategy that delivers the best results.

Analysis and Issue Identification

It is essential to know the type of case to properly direct the research. After determining the case issue(s), the LNC should work with the attorney to ascertain what additional information needs to be accessed and analyzed to meet the attorney's needs.

Failure to collect important data at the outset of the research may result in delays and produce incomplete or irrelevant results. In addition to knowing the topic to be researched, the LNC should also understand the issues involved in the case, the date of loss (i.e., the date when the incident or injury occurred), the plaintiff's demographics (i.e., age, gender, ethnicity, etc.), any past or concurrent medical conditions of the plaintiff, the plaintiff's medications, whether the attorney has a preference for specific literature, and any date restrictions to be applied to the information retrieved in the search due to the date of the subject incident.

The LNC must use analytical and critical thinking skills to sort out the primary issues to be addressed. The attorney may have identified one issue thought to be the key issue, whereas the LNC may have a different opinion after initial data retrieval and analysis. A discussion of the differences with the attorney will usually put the LNC's valuable teaching skills into practice once again.

Example 34.1

An attorney reports to the LNC the client is a woman who has asked the attorney to file a wrongful death suit against a hospital, arising from the death of her husband. After undergoing coronary bypass surgery, the husband became increasingly depressed and agitated. He presented to the emergency department (ED), accompanied by his wife, who informed the triage nurse that her husband needed medication to treat worsening depression and agitation as he no longer had any interest in normal activities and refused to eat. The ED physician medically screened the patient and asked the staff to page the patient's primary physician; however, the primary physician was on vacation. The staff paged the house physician, but the house physician was not one of the patient's Health Maintenance Organization (HMO) providers. The staff paged a third physician who was an HMO provider, but the physician failed to respond to the page. The patient waited in the ED for four hours and then left. That afternoon, he committed suicide.

The attorney asks the LNC about the standard of care for a triage nurse in the ED when a patient offers complaints of depression and agitation. The LNC agrees there may have been a breach in the standard of care by the triage nurse. However, the LNC explains that since the nurse attempted to reach three physicians but was unable to obtain authorization for treatment, perhaps the larger issue was the lack of protocol between the hospital and HMO to obtain authorization for treatment.

Outcome Identification

After collecting the initial data from the attorney, analyzing it, and identifying the primary issues, the LNC must then identify the desired outcome of the research effort. The LNC should consider these questions:

- What does the attorney need to establish?
- Is the subject matter controversial?

- Does the attorney want to view the full articles, or are article abstracts or synopses sufficient for the *preliminary* research?
- Are medical teaching materials needed to educate others on the legal team?
- What is the time frame for obtaining the materials?
- Are there time or budgetary constraints?

Planning

For the purposes of this chapter, planning involves determining which databases, core textbooks (if textbooks are required), and other materials outlined in Appendix A are required to research the primary issues. In the case of a computerized search for journal articles, planning involves selecting the most relevant search term for the MEDLINE database or browser, along with choosing appropriate filters in order to retrieve the most relevant articles. This step of the process may also extend to an LNC's investigation of a defendant healthcare provider's or expert's credentials. Planning expedites and focuses computerized literature searches.

Example 34.2

An attorney asks the LNC to research *abdominal rhabdomyosarcoma*, because a potential client claims that a delay in the diagnosis of her 14-year-old daughter's condition resulted in her death. The LNC may decide to look for pertinent information in pediatric oncology textbooks and perform a computerized literature search for medical journal articles relating to this issue via subscription databases as well as online Internet searches.

A search for relevant and authoritative literature about this condition may start at the National Comprehensive Cancer Network, which provides current national cancer guidelines for diagnosis, staging, and treatment of abdominal rhabdomyosarcoma. Another website to visit, no matter what the condition or diagnosis, is the National Library of Medicine's (NLM) website, which contains both current and historical literature. The NLM is the library of the National Institutes of Health (NIH). PubMed® is the NLM's main search engine for MEDLINE.

The LNC can use a combination of keywords in the search box and filters to obtain pertinent medical literature results. For example, if the LNC types *rhabdomyosarcoma* in the PubMed search box, the search result yields 13,076 citations (articles). To narrow the search further and retrieve only those articles most relevant to the specific case, the LNC may choose to limit the search further by clicking on the *Show additional filters* tab to the left of the search results. The LNC can then reduce the search parameters to adolescents (13–18 years) by selecting the *Ages* filter. To narrow the search even further, the LNC can select filters for English language, human studies, and publication within the last five years. In this way, the LNC can reduce the number of citations from 13,076 to 327.

Noting that many of the articles retrieved pertain to *rhabdomyosarcoma* at various sites of the body, the LNC may further limit the results by adding the keyword *retroperitoneal* to the word *rhabdomyosarcoma*. PubMed will automatically add the Boolean operator AND between *rhabdomyosarcoma* and *retroperitoneal* unless directed otherwise. This addition again decreases the number of resultant citations to only seven, but they are more pertinent to the primary issue than the 327 citations previously retrieved. The LNC may now decide to expand the date restriction to 10 years rather than just five, by changing the date limitations, and now this revised search retrieves 19 total citations.

It is also possible to limit the search to *abstracts only* by selecting the abstract box, although this narrows the results to only those articles containing abstracts. Choosing this option may result in the loss or omission of some relevant citations. However, the LNC may always obtain the articles that do not have abstracts, especially if the titles indicate the articles may be relevant to the topic.

Implementation

Implementation is the act of following through with the established plan. In Example 34.2, the LNC chose the appropriate search term and used filters to restrict the search parameters to match the specifics of the potential case. This decreased the number of citations retrieved from 13,076 to 7 from the last five years, a reasonable number to review.

Each case is different, and the LNC must use critical thinking skills to determine whether the resulting number of citations, once filters have been selected, is too small. The LNC may deselect filters, which results in a larger number of citations, but many of the articles may not be pertinent to the primary issue(s). Also, if the LNC filters the search to *review articles* (by checking the review box), it is likely the LNC will retrieve fewer citations, but review articles will provide an overview of the medical literature on a specific issue or topic. It is worth noting the LNC researcher should not rely *solely* on either abstract (due to brevity) or review articles (due to interpretation by someone other than the original author) when formulating final medical case strategy with the attorney.

To implement the plan, the LNC reviews the citations and abstracts and selects those appropriate for the case. The next implementation step is to prepare a list of selected citations and abstracts. The LNC researcher may then retrieve the journal articles from the library shelves, from an online source, or through a document delivery service. A discussion of the specifics of article retrieval occurs later in this chapter.

Evaluation

Before providing textbook information, articles, and other materials to the attorney, the LNC should review them to evaluate whether the information is relevant to the attorney's case and needs. The attorney may initially need only broad information on a medical topic to become familiar with a condition or disease before deciding whether to accept a case. In contrast, the attorney may need the information before deposing a medical professional or need reliable and authoritative information to support the case strategy. As previously mentioned, the LNC should have determined the attorney's specific needs early in the research process. Once the LNC retrieves the literature or other information, the LNC should then re-evaluate it in the context of its intended purpose to ensure it will meet the needs of the attorney.

The LNC must ask the attorney for guidance on whether the information meets the appropriate court rules and prior precedents concerning the rules of evidence. If not, then the LNC should formulate and implement another plan.

If the first three steps of the process (analysis/issue identification, outcome identification, and planning) are completed thoughtfully, successful implementation and evaluation should follow.

Research Evaluation

It is necessary for LNCs to evaluate the validity and reliability of research articles. Statistical validity corresponds to accuracy, while reliability refers to similar results under similar conditions. The least reliable research studies are those that are performed by the public. For example, a poll posted on social media that invites everyone to participate is neither valid nor reliable.

Peer-reviewed journals publish the results of the most reliable research studies. Peer-reviewed journals are publications that use experts in the field to evaluate submitted journal articles and research. The peer-reviewers evaluate the research methodology and suggest changes or reject the article if it lacks validity. Because peer-reviewed journals will not publish articles that fail to meet the standards of the profession, published peer-reviewed articles represent the best research practices in a specific field.

In addition to seeking peer-reviewed journals, LNCs should identify the following characteristics of reliable medical research:

- An abstract, which is a summary at the beginning of peer-reviewed journal articles
- Author's credentials
- Footnotes or citations to reference the sources of the author's discussion and findings. The references should be current except for the inclusion of any prior research on the topic that is accepted as the "classic" resource. An example of a classic resource is the original 1962 article by Kempe, Silverman, Steele, Droegemuellar, and Silver that defined battered child syndrome for the first time.
- Tone of the article. A formal, serious, thoughtful tone is common in peer-reviewed research articles.
- Originality. The LNC should assess if the research is original or a summary of others' research, not an opinion. The research should have a narrow focus that is explored in depth.
- Audience knowledge base. The target audience for the article should be individuals with a professional knowledge base as opposed to those with a layperson's knowledge base.
- Sample size. Generally, the larger the sample size, the more generalizable the results. Generalizability refers to applying the research conclusion to a larger population.

Legal nurse consultants should keep in mind, though, that research is not always generalizable and that all research has limitations. Research may not be generalizable, because the methodology involves a specific location, a specific population, and a specific time. For example, research done in rural Kansas would not necessarily apply to inner-city Detroit. Most reliable research articles will have a section that describes the limitations of the study. Limitations could include the lack of a control group or a very small control group, poor compliance, drop-out rates, and incomplete data.

Legal nurse consultants should also familiarize themselves with the distinct types of statistical analysis. The type of statistical analysis used will lend itself to the weight of any statistically significant findings.

Research Sources

The LNC should consult a variety of sources to identify the best available evidence-based medical information, to research information related to a healthcare professional's credentials, and to conduct social media queries. Primary, secondary, and tertiary sources are available for analysis (University of Minnesota Bio-Medical Library, 2017).

In the context of medical research, primary sources comprise journals or periodicals in which the authors directly participated in the research. It also includes documented individual experiences.

Two resources for primary research are the NLM's Health Services Research Projects in Progress and the database found at ClinicalTrials.gov, which allows access to current research and information pertaining to ongoing, suspended, or terminated clinical trials.

Secondary sources are resources not originating with the primary author or original research. Secondary sources of information include:

- consultation with a professional in the appropriate specialty or field
- textbook research either accessed online or in the library
- nonprofit organizations (e.g., American Cancer Society, National Kidney Foundation). Some non-profit organizations can also be primary sources of research. For example, the American Heart Association funds research and identifies treatment recommendations based on the research findings.
- the World Wide Web
- literature reviews using a bibliographic database such as MEDLINE
- directories such as The Official American Board of Medical Specialties (ABMS) Directory of Board Certified Medical Specialists and the International Medical Education Directory
- professional specialty organizations such as the American Association of Critical Care Nurses and American College of Obstetrics and Gynecology and
- governmental agencies such as the Food and Drug Administration (FDA), the Centers for Disease Control and Prevention (CDC), and the NIH. Some governmental agencies can also be primary sources of research. For example, the CDC and FDA publish their own investigative findings.

Tertiary sources summarize secondary sources which have been collected and distilled. Examples of tertiary sources include scientific textbooks, lay textbooks, encyclopedias, and almanacs.

Online Searches

Numerous sources of information are available on the Web. Awareness of that information and quick access to it can significantly enhance the LNC's value to the attorney and the case. The World Wide Web (abbreviated as www) is a huge library of online information from around the world. Legal nurse consultants can access online information on the websites of individuals, groups, and organizations through the Web. The Web is part of the Internet, which includes not only websites but also file transfers (uploads and downloads) and electronic mail (email) communication.

The Web is one of many interfaces of the Internet, making it easy to retrieve text, pictures, and multimedia files from computers without having to know complicated commands. Online information retrieval is the process of identifying desired information by direct, interactive communication with a computer.

A search engine is an enormous database of websites navigated by a software robot that seeks out and indexes websites and sometimes other Internet resources as well. A search engine "looks" for databases of documents and information to access based on the researcher's search terms. A database is a program that organizes specific information and "virtual" documents enabling a researcher to rapidly access subsets of information from the entire body of information for retrieval (analogous to finding the desired document in a filing cabinet). Medscape, PubMed, and TOXLINE are examples of document and image databases.

There are thousands of search engines (e.g., Google, Yahoo, Bing, Microsoft Edge, etc.), and they vary in speed, skill, depth of indexing, size of database, advanced search features, and presentation of results. Each search engine's method of searching is proprietary, the depth and breadth of its database are unique, and each possesses its strengths and idiosyncrasies.

Conducting a MEDLINE Search

The LNC can perform a MEDLINE search by accessing PubMed. The following steps should expedite and focus the search to achieve the best results. The LNC should:

1. collect adequate information from the attorney to formulate a focused search strategy
2. formulate the overall search strategy
3. input common keywords or the Medical Subject Headings (MeSH) term(s), author, or journal that addresses the focus of the search in the *Search Box* (see the sections below on MeSH Term Searches, Author Searches, and Journal Searches)
4. choose *Filters* for searching, if desired
5. click *Search* to retrieve the results of the search
6. view the citations and click on relevant citations to view the abstracts (if available)
7. prepare a list of search results (specifically the list of citations and relevant abstracts) and
8. locate or order articles

MeSH Term (Keyword) Searches

A MeSH term search is the most common type of search used in the MEDLINE database and entails entering one or more MeSH terms in the search box. The LNC can enter either a single term or multiple terms. Multiple terms can ensure a more focused search. If the LNC enters additional terms or further focuses the search, the LNC should insert Boolean operators (e.g., OR, NOT) in capital letters between the terms. PubMed now automatically adds the Boolean operator AND between multiple terms when retrieving citations; this narrows the search by increasing the terms that must be found.

Example 34.3

An attorney asks the LNC to research *malignant melanoma* for a case in which the primary issue involves the failure of the defendant physician to diagnose melanoma or refer the patient to a dermatologist in a timely manner. If the LNC performed a search using the single term *melanoma* in the search box, thousands of citations would appear, and most would be irrelevant to this case. To focus the search and keep the primary issue in mind, the LNC searches using *melanoma AND diagnosis*, because the most important articles are those that relate to early diagnosis of melanoma.

Filtering the Search

MEDLINE allows the researcher to filter searches to decrease the number of citations retrieved and, more importantly, to retrieve only the most relevant articles. In PubMed, after entering the search terms in the search box, the LNC should click on the word *Filters*. See the previous discussion on how to further filter the search.

Author Searches

Legal nurse consultants often use author searches when an attorney wants to review published works of opposing experts or their own experts. The search is usually simple and straightforward, and no search strategy or analysis is required. The researcher enters the author's last name, a space, and one or two initials (first and middle names and *no punctuation*) and then clicks *Search*. If the author's middle initial is not known, it is sufficient to enter the last name, a space, and the first initial. This calls up all authors with the same name and initial.

To narrow the search, the LNC should enter the middle initial, especially if the last name is common. If the author's last name might be mistaken for a search term (e.g., hand), the searcher can clarify an author search by entering the author's last name and two initials followed by the field tag for author in brackets: [au]. The author search would then read: hand js [au]. The total number of citations retrieved will appear at the top of the first page (in this case, 37). It is important to prepare the full list of citations. PubMed shows 20 citations per page by default. The LNC may change this parameter to as few as five or as many as 500 per page. When the LNC searches for a common name, narrowing the search by date parameters may once again reduce the amount of irrelevant citations.

The attorney may ask the LNC to analyze and prepare a synopsis of the author's articles once retrieved. The attorney may then request the LNC to review the expert's publications and deposition transcript (if the deposition has been taken) for any discrepancies that might provide a basis for impeachment.

Journal Searches

Limiting a search to one journal is time-efficient in certain situations. For instance, an attorney may learn from an opposing expert's deposition that an article relating to an issue in the case was recently published in the *Journal of the American Medical Association*. However, the attorney is unsure of the issue's publication date or the article's title. The attorney may relay this to the LNC for retrieval of the article.

To perform this type of search, the LNC should enter the name of the desired journal or the abbreviated title in the search box instead of, or in combination with, a keyword or author's name. A health sciences reference librarian can provide a list of accepted journal abbreviations if needed. The list is also available online through ftp://ftp.ncbi.nih.gov/pubmed/J_Medline.txt.

See Appendix B for checklists for conducting medical research via the Internet or the library.

Government Resources

Overview of the National Network of Libraries of Medicine

The NLM, a part of the NIH, is the largest and most prestigious medical library in the world and is based in Bethesda, Maryland. Its progeny, the National Network of Libraries of Medicine (NNLM), is a nationwide network of regional health sciences and biomedical libraries. The NLM serves as the overall coordinator and as a backup resource for all other regional libraries in the network. The NNLM provides the nation with access to the most comprehensive collection of biomedical information in the world. The subdivisions of the specific retrieval systems are under the umbrella of the NLM.

PubMed is a Web-based retrieval system developed by the National Center for Biotechnology Information at the NLM. It is the NLM's premier search system for health information available online without charge. Assistance for searching PubMed is easily accessible and offered with links to an online tutorial, overview of PubMed, Help, and frequently asked questions.

PubMed offers links to full-text articles, some without charge, at participating publishers' websites. Additionally, PubMed offers links to related articles as well as free access to other third-party sites such as libraries and sequencing centers.

MEDLARS/MEDLINE

The *Medical Literature Analysis and Retrieval System (MEDLARS)* is the computerized system of databases and databanks offered by the NLM. The NLM enters into agreements with public institutions in foreign countries to serve as International MEDLARS Centers. These centers assist health professionals in accessing MEDLARS databases, offer training in searching, provide document delivery, and perform other functions as biomedical information resource centers (NLM, 2017a).

MEDLINE (abbreviated from MEDlars onLINE) is the NLM's electronic directory to bibliographic references for over 5,600 biomedical journals selected for indexing with MeSH terms. The MEDLINE database contains more than 23 million references and abstracts of articles (NLM, 2017b). Each entry is assigned a PubMed ID (PMID) number.

> The subject scope of MEDLINE is biomedicine and health and is broadly defined to encompass those areas of the life sciences, behavioral sciences, chemical sciences, and bioengineering needed by health professionals and those others engaged in basic research, clinical care, public health, health policy development, and/or related educational activities.
>
> (NLM, 2017b)

NLM Gateway

The *NLM Gateway* is a Web-based system that allows users of the NLM services to initiate searches in multiple retrieval systems from one interface, providing "one-stop searching" for many of NLM's information resources. The NLM Gateway covers a wider range of information than PubMed. In addition to journal citations, the NLM Gateway collection contains multiple databases, some of which include audiovisual materials, serials, and monographs available for searching and retrieval. The NLM's network allows for concurrent searches of multiple databases.

LocatorPlus is one of the NLM free online catalogs. It is a guide to finding records for journals, books, reports, and audiovisuals in the NLM collection; records for serials and books not in the NLM collection but owned by regional libraries; and records for journals, books, reports, and audiovisuals on order, on loan, or in process at the NLM.

Clinical trials are research studies of specific health questions in human volunteers performed in a controlled environment. The purpose of clinical trials is to conduct research for determining new ways to use known treatments or to determine efficacy of experimental treatments or therapies. *Clinicaltrials.gov* is the address to access information about clinical trials.

The NLM is the gateway for many online directories and databases. Examples include *Directory of Information Resources Online (DIRLINE)*, *Development and Reproductive Toxicology/Environmental Teratology Information Center*, *Health Services Research Projects in Progress*, *the*

Hazardous Substances Data Bank, Toxline, ChemIDplus, Toxics Release Inventory, Genetics Home Reference, and *Online Mendelian Inheritance in Man.* To access any of these directories or databases, the LNC should go to *www.nlm.nih.gov* and search by keyword.

Nongovernment Resources

Embase is a pharmacological and biomedical database with access to over 11 million documents from 1974 to the present, including over 5,000 biomedical and pharmacological journals from 70 countries. The LNC can access Embase through major database vendors (e.g., Ovid Online, LexisNexis, and ProQuest Dialog).

EMedicine offers free information on numerous common diseases, conditions, tests, and procedures as well as first aid. EMedicine features health-related slideshows and medication information, including generic and brand names, dosing, interactions, drug classifications, prescription, or over-the-counter availability. This site contains a multitude of calculators for body mass index, temperature conversions, weight conversions, blood alcohol concentration estimation, diagrams of dermatomes, and burn surface area.

Google Scholar provides a way to search for scholarly literature across disciplines and sources including "theses, books, abstracts, and court opinions, from academic publishers, professional societies, online repositories, universities and other websites" (Google, 2017). *Google Scholar* is an invaluable resource to the LNC. To access Google Scholar, the LNC can search for it by the keywords Google and Scholar from any browser. One advantage to using Google Scholar is that the LNC can often find a version of an article that is accessible for free. At the bottom of the reference for the article, Google Scholar will have a link to "all versions." By following this link, the LNC may find the article from a vendor that has open (free) access, rather than retrieving the article from a journal that requires membership or a single-use fee.

ClinicalKey is a reliable online service enabling healthcare providers to perform expedient literature searches regarding clinical and treatment-based information. The site's content includes well-respected medical textbooks as well as more than 600 journals and Clinics of North America, numerous practice guidelines, thousands of patient education aids, online continuing medical education (CME) opportunities, medication information, and links to millions of PubMed abstracts. It also allows the user to search full text journals. Many North American medical schools subscribe to ClinicalKey. A subscription fee is required, which can be paid either annually or monthly (ClinicalKey, 2017).

UpToDate (www.uptodate.com) is another well-known subscription service that offers evidence-based standards and guidelines.

Many medical, nursing, and other healthcare journals are available online. Several well-known, peer-reviewed journals allow access to their full articles without a fee. Even those journals that charge a fee for current issues often have archives of the journals available at no cost, although the individual publisher's policies on this may vary.

Medscape offers medical journal articles, access to MEDLINE, free CME credits, important conference releases, medical news, and medication information. A free registration is required to access this database.

Ovid "provides access to online bibliographic databases, academic journals, and other products, concentrated on health sciences" (Ovid, 2017). Ovid is used across the world by librarians, researchers, clinicians, and students from foremost colleges and universities; medical schools; academic research libraries and library consortia; hospitals and healthcare systems; pharmaceutical, engineering, and biotechnology companies; HMOs; and clinical practices. Ovid is not accessible to an individual without password-granted access through one of the above.

The Virtual Library (through the University of Sheffield in the United Kingdom) offers links to complete text documents for evidence-based practice.

Accessing Standards and Guidelines

Legal nurse consultants who are new to the field often expect to find standards of care conveniently listed in books and readily accessible when needed for comparison to a healthcare worker's performance. Unfortunately, it is usually not that simple. The LNC may consult the following resources, many of which are available online, for clinical practice guidelines:

- ClinicalKey and UpToDate: subscription fees are required, which can be paid annually or monthly
- Professional Organizations: Most professional medical, nursing, and other healthcare organizations, such as the American Medical Association, American College of Surgeons, American Academy of Family Physicians, and American Nurses Association, promulgate Clinical Practice Statements and Practice Guidelines that can be invaluable to the LNC
- Medical journals: such as *CHEST® Journal* from the American College of Chest Physicians
- Core curricula medical, nursing, and other healthcare textbooks
- The archive of older standards of care and practice guidelines offered by the Agency for Healthcare Research and Quality (AHRQ)
- Nursing care plans and critical or clinical pathways
- Facility policies and protocols (these should be consulted first)
- Professional association scopes, standards of practice, guidelines, and consensus/position statements
- Comparative effectiveness research
- Certification course material
- United States Preventive Services Task Force
- State and federal statutes, rules, and regulations
- Department of Health inspection/survey reports
- National and state patient safety authorities and
- Emergency Medical Services state protocols

Retrieving Copies of Medical Literature

Legal nurse consultants who are employed by a hospital or medical center may ask the medical librarian to retrieve and copy articles, a service which is often free of charge. An independent literature retrieval service (or LNCs with easy access to a large medical library) offer document-retrieval services to other LNCs and will retrieve, scan and email, fax, or send full-text articles for a fee with an appropriate copyright and a facility permission.

Using a Retrieval Service

Loansome Doc® is the document retrieval system offered by the NLM. Through Loansome Doc®, users order full-text copies of articles located on MEDLINE from a medical library. The user must register with the NLM to use the service. The NLM website facilitates the user through the registration and ordering processes. Loansome Doc® requires an agreement with a local library that uses DOCLINE (the NLM's automated interlibrary loan request routing and referral system). If unsure about which library to contact, the user can identify appropriate NLM Regional Medical Libraries on the NNLM website. Loansome Doc® service charges a retrieval fee for the article(s).

Independent Retrieval Services

When emailing requests to an independent medical literature retrieval service, the LNC should include as much information as possible to accelerate access to the materials. Complete citations including authors, title, journal, volume, pages, and date of publication will ensure a timely and accurate delivery of the requested documents.

Libraries

If access to a local medical library is available, the LNC can obtain the articles and copy them (with appropriate copyright permission) at the library for a nominal fee. If the LNC is employed at a medical center or large law firm, it may be possible to order the articles from the medical-legal librarians or to set up an account with the publishers directly.

Online Sources Without the Use of a Retrieval Service

Healthcare journal articles are occasionally free of charge through PubMed. Links directly to the article archived in PubMed Central or in the actual journal are clearly displayed when an article is available for free. Searching the individual journal's website archives may also allow access without charge. Individual journals determine the amount of time before articles may be accessed without a subscription fee. ClinicalKey and UpToDate have access to full text articles from many journals available without an additional charge to the basic subscription fee.

Library Searches

Textbook Research

Well-recognized, core curriculum textbooks offer prevailing standards of care, wide-ranging protocols and procedures, and case descriptions. Many recognized healthcare textbooks are available online, although some publishers' Web-based databases require an annual subscription fee. Some pointers will help to safeguard the LNC who relies on printed information to support a position relating to a healthcare issue or topic. The LNC should:

- use grandfather texts, i.e., core-curriculum textbooks that are widely accepted in the general medical and scientific community. Grandfather texts are generally those used as textbooks in medical, nursing, and other healthcare professional schools, such as *Nelson Textbook of Pediatrics*, *Hematology*, and *Ferri's Clinical Advisor*;

■ ensure the book is time-appropriate to the case, especially when attempting to locate standards of care or clinical practice guidelines. If the LNC is researching a standard of care issue related to an incident in 2010 that is the subject of a medical malpractice lawsuit, the books consulted should have been published in or prior to 2010. Any information relating to standards or guidelines must have been available to the treating healthcare providers at the time of the subject incident. If the LNC is researching a causation topic, the most current, relevant medical literature can be used; and

■ refer to a minimum of three authoritative sources to confirm there is general agreement or controversy among experts in the field regarding the issues in question.

Prior to submitting printed materials (from textbooks and journals) to the attorney, highlight the pertinent information to expedite review of the materials. In some cases, the attorney may want the LNC to prepare a synopsis of each article submitted.

References and bibliographies at the end of textbook chapters may direct the reader to additional information on the subject. Also, editors and authors of authoritative texts may be potential expert witnesses, as they are considered experts in their specialties or subspecialties.

Reference Materials

The *American Board of Medical Specialties* is considered the "gold standard" of physician certification for medical doctors. The ABMS has 24 medical specialty member boards supervising the criteria for physician certification. Verification of certification is available online, by phone, and in hard copy. The hard copy includes dates of certification and recertification as well as profile information for each board-certified physician. The LNC can also refer to a website provided by the ABMS called Certification Matters (www.certificationmatters.org). However, Certification Matters only identifies current certification, not any certification lapses. In addition to the ABMS, the LNC may find board certification information for medical doctors from the website of the certifying board. For example, the American Board of Pediatrics offers verification of certification at www.abp.org/content/verification-certification. Only organizations can order verifications of certification for doctors of osteopathy at https://aoaprofiles.org/.

Advantages to Researching on the Internet or in the Library

The vast amount of information available on the Internet within seconds of the click of a mouse is equally the major benefit and the major drawback of researching on the Internet. The primary benefits of using the Internet to access information of any type are speed and availability 24 hours a day. Current technology enables rapid transmission of large files, including those with color images, sound, and motion pictures. Vast numbers of computer users can simultaneously send mail and take part in electronic bulletin board discussions.

A primary advantage of making a trip to a comprehensive medical library is having more than the current edition of multiple textbooks and the Physician Desk Reference on the shelves (which is often all that is available when researching online). Copies of older medical, nursing, and other scientific journals are also available for reviewing and copying relevant articles.

Disadvantages to Researching on the Internet

The major drawback of accessing information online is the volume of information the LNC must sort through. Because of the availability of so much information, evaluation of the search results can be time-consuming. When researching on the Internet, it is critical for the LNC to scrutinize, carefully evaluate, and appraise any information to make certain it is accurate, reliable, and authentic to the time under research.

As most of the information on the Internet is relatively current, information needed for cases involving incidents that occurred several years earlier may not be available online. The Wayback Machine, which has archived nearly 300 billion webpages, is a potential source for the LNC to locate Internet archives (Wayback Machine, 2017).

Verifying an Author's Credibility

The importance of verifying the author's or potential expert's qualifications to address the subject matter at issue cannot be overemphasized. This critical step may be achieved in one of several ways.

- A PubMed search will verify if the author has published articles on a particular topic in the author's field and specialty of practice.
- The author's curriculum vitae may or may not be available for the LNC's review and verification of credentials, employment, responsibilities, etc.
- Hospital and medical school faculty biographies may be available on the facilities' websites.
- Most states have a State Licensing Board website with a link to verify a license. Depending on the individual website, it may be possible to locate comprehensive information related to education, training, board certification(s), dates, and current address.
- The LNC can search the ABMS online or contact the certifying organization to verify board certification status.
- The LNC can search the membership data of the author's professional organization to identify office location, board certification(s), education, residencies and fellowships, locations of hospital admitting privileges, major professional activity, and group practice participation.
- Another way for the LNC to obtain data is to search Castle Connolly's *America's Top Doctors*. The organization conducts annual surveys to gather peer nominations to determine the top 1% of physicians in medical specialties and subspecialties. This publication contains in-depth data concerning each physician's education, training, and special expertise.
- Traditional Internet searches via various search engines may help to locate authors and their practice, publications, and presentations given to professional groups.

Westlaw and LEXIS-NEXIS databases contain very comprehensive information on many healthcare professionals/authors, including deposition and trial testimony, *Daubert* challenges, and media coverage. Westlaw and LEXIS-NEXIS require a subscription to access their databases.

Assessing the Validity of Medical Literature

There is a saying that people can prove anything they really want to prove. Not all published information is valid. The LNC should be mindful of this fact when selecting journal articles, and the nurse expert should consider this when using information to support a position.

Legal nurse consultants learn to develop critical-thinking skills to analyze the facts of their cases. This skill should extend into the area of analyzing medical literature.

For textbook research, LNCs should confine their research primarily to core curriculum texts. Healthcare education has used a major portion of these texts for many years. These textbooks have been reproduced in several editions since the original publication and have been published by reputable publishing houses (including but not limited to Mosby, W.B. Saunders, Lippincott, Williams & Wilkens, Appleton & Lange, and Elsevier). Additionally, the authors or contributors are healthcare professionals with extensive experience and expertise in the subject area. It is always good practice for the LNC to use at least three reputable texts to ensure there is general agreement or controversy regarding the issues being researched.

In addition to textbooks there are a host of other sources, such as scientific journals and continuing education resources, available to analyze medical information.

The medical community considers peer-reviewed journals to be more credible than non-peer-reviewed publications. Peer review prior to publication attempts to ensure that the methodology, results, and conclusions of the experiment, observation, study, or research are unbiased and meet the criteria for scientific research. Depending on the journal's readership and interest, the article inclusions may provide input and observations from highly regarded scientists and researchers that have passed peer review.

Professional association journals cover emerging trends, standards of care, legal issues, ethical issues, and reports on disciplinary actions, association news, and practice and business articles. Medical periodicals contain information related to emerging trends and techniques, prevailing philosophies on medical issues, practice and business articles, and profiles of practitioners. Continuing education information contains emerging practices and protocols, updates on medical issues, and state of the science at the time of the conference, seminar, or workshop.

There are seven levels of scientific research and medical literature. The hierarchy of evidence ensures that the LNC evaluates the highest quality of evidence (Melnyk & Fineout-Overhold, 2014). The first level is the best quality of evidence, followed by the second, and so on. The hierarchy includes evidence from

1. systematic reviews or meta-analysis of all relevant clinical trials
2. at least one randomized controlled trial
3. quasi-experimental, well-designed trials without randomization
4. cohort or case-controlled studies
5. a review of more than one descriptive and qualitative study
6. a review of a single descriptive or qualitative study and
7. the opinion of authorities or reports from committees of experts

Junk Science—How it Applies to Medical Literature

It is important to keep in mind that any literature referenced may be subject to *Frye* or *Daubert* standards for admissibility in litigation. Junk science is "faulty scientific information or research, especially when used to advance special interests" (Junk science, n.d.).

The landmark case of *Daubert v. Merrell Dow Pharmaceuticals, Inc.* (1993) defined the elements needed to authenticate scientific testimony and admissibility in trial. Under *Daubert*, all expert opinions, theories, and the literature on which they rely must meet the following criteria: (a) scientific methodology, (b) subject to peer review or publication, (c) a known rate of error, and (d) generally accepted within the medical/scientific community. While some states chose to follow the *Frye* (1923) rule (general acceptance by the scientific community), the federal courts apply the *Daubert* standard.

Literature Citation Tips

The *American Psychological Association (APA)* style is the accepted format to use when referencing sources of information from the healthcare professions. Due to the nuances of the APA format for various sources of information, the LNC should try to become acquainted with it. The APA website offers citation examples, and there are online tutorials available through many educational institutions' websites. In a Daubert Motion, medical literature must be cited using Blue Book format, not APA format.

Ethics

The procedural guidelines of information retrieval are universal for effective, competent, and ethical research. Below are several guidelines that are applicable to any researcher who acts as an intermediary between an attorney and the information, regardless of whether the information is obtained from printed or electronic sources. The following guidelines directly apply to LNCs. The LNC should

- use interview techniques to clarify the attorney's needs before doing research on any case and consider any budgetary restrictions or time constraints
- maintain awareness of the range of information resources to advise the attorney fairly and impartially
- maintain a reasonable and current skill level in the database systems available for performing online searches
- avoid bias in the selection of appropriate databases and systems when performing online searches and confirm the reliability, authority, and credibility of the retrieved literature
- maintain alertness regarding information that might be detrimental to the attorney's case and keep the attorney informed
- respect the attorney's schedule and deadline for the production of literature
- maintain strict adherence to copyright and reprint permission and
- maintain confidentiality of all case-specific data

Social Media

Social media searches are an important way for the LNC to obtain personal information about the parties involved in a lawsuit. For example, a social media search might show a plaintiff dancing at a party while the plaintiff alleges permanent leg damage due to a botched surgery. The

LNC may search several types of social media and should be aware that social media changes constantly. Therefore, the LNC should use websites that are current and popular.

One part of social media is a social network, which allows individuals to share personal information, photographs, and videos with family and friends. There are hundreds of social network sites, but Facebook is one of the best known with 1.2 billion users per month (Chaykowski, 2017). Because of its popularity, there is a good possibility that a party in a lawsuit will have a Facebook page with personal information on it. LinkedIn, with nearly 500 million users, is a popular social network site, particularly with business persons (Darrow, 2017). By accessing LinkedIn, the LNC can obtain a party's work history, which can aid the discovery process.

The LNC can also search the individual's blog and website. Websites are groups of interconnected webpages maintained by individuals, groups, or businesses. Blogs are websites that offer information and opinions and are usually updated regularly. The LNC can type the individual's name into a search engine to locate a blog or website.

Another type of social media is a microblog. With microblogs, users post short updates of text, videos, and photos. The content of each microblog post must contain 140 characters or less. Twitter and Tumblr are the best-known microblogs. Microblogs tend to contain the subjective opinions of individuals and, because of this, have been used to question the individual's credibility.

Photo and video sharing websites are another kind of social media for the LNC to search. Individuals can post photos using common photo sharing websites such as Instagram, Pinterest, and Photobucket. The LNC can enter the individual's name into the website's search box or type the keywords of "image" or "video" and the individual's name into a search engine. The LNC can also use a search engine to search for an individual photo by dragging the photo into the search box. The search results will then list all websites that display the photo.

The LNC can also search video-sharing websites, such as Vimeo and YouTube, for content posted by the parties involved in a lawsuit or for lectures, interviews, presentations, and procedures posted by the medical professionals or experts involved in the case.

An additional way for the LNC to search social media is through the deep web. The deep web includes content on the Web that is not indexed by standard search engines. Deep web search engines use a different kind of indexing that narrows topics. The content of the deep web mainly includes search engines for government, social sciences, business, and others. However, some deep web search engines locate information about people. Examples include Pipl and PeekYou, which search only for individuals and provide more depth to the search than a regular search engine.

Summary

Researching various aspects of medical information is challenging, demanding, labor intensive, and trying at times. It also enhances the LNC's knowledge base and is a valuable service to attorneys when the information retrieved is a major factor in the successful outcome of a case.

References

American Association of Legal Nurse Consultants. (2017). *Legal nurse consulting: Scope and standards of practice*. Retrieved from www.aalnc.org.

Chaykowski, K. (2017). Facebook messenger passes 1.2 billion users. Retrieved from www.forbes.com/sites/kathleenchaykowski/2017/04/12/facebook-messenger-passes-1-2-billion-users/#50afa91a1330.

ClinicalKey. (2017). Welcome to the ClinicalKey store. Retrieved from https://store.clinicalkey.com/.

Darrow, B. (2017). LinkedIn claims half a billion users. Retrieved from http://fortune.com/2017/04/24/linkedin-users/.

Daubert v. Merrell Dow Pharmaceuticals, 509 U.S. 579 (1993).

Frye v. United States, 293 F. 1013 (1923).

Google. (2017). About Google Scholar. Retrieved from http://scholar.google.com/intl/en/scholar/about.html.

Junk science. (n.d.). *Dictionary.com unabridged*. Retrieved from www.dictionary.com/browse/junk-science.

Melnyk, B. M., & Fineout-Overholt, E. (2014). *Evidence-based practice in nursing & healthcare: A guide to best practice* (2nd ed.). Philadelphia, PA: Wolters Kluwer; Lippincott Williams & Wilkins.

National Library of Medicine. (2017a). *International MEDLARS Centers* [Fact sheet]. Retrieved from www.nlm.nih.gov/pubs/factsheets/intlmedlars.html.

National Library of Medicine. (2017b). *MEDLINE* [Fact sheet]. Retrieved from www.nlm.nih.gov/pubs/factsheets/medline.html.

Ovid. (2017). The OvidVID experience. (n.d.). Retrieved from www.ovid.com/site/index.jsp?top=1.

University of Minnesota Bio-Medical Library. (2017). Primary, secondary, and tertiary sources in the health sciences. Retrieved from https://hsl.lib.umn.edu/biomed/help/primary-secondary-and-tertiary-sources-health-sciences.

Wayback Machine. (2017). About the Internet archive. Retrieved from https://archive.org/about/.

Test Questions

1. The LNC may use which of the following sources to locate standards of care?
   A. Well-respected medical and nursing textbooks
   B. Clinical practice guidelines
   C. The Agency for Healthcare Research and Quality
   D. Professional organizations
   E. All of the above
2. Which is a primary source of medical information?
   A. Encyclopedias
   B. Food and Drug Administration
   C. Observations conducted for research or scientific purposes
   D. Textbook research
   E. Consultation with a professional in the appropriate specialty
3. The LNC may retrieve medical literature by which of the following?
   A. PubMed
   B. The Internet
   C. Loansome Doc®
   D. Retrieval service
   E. All of the above
   F. None of the above
4. What site may be useful in retrieving archived webpages?
   A. The deep web
   B. Twitter
   C. The Wayback Machine
   D. The Virtual Library
5. Which website may an LNC use to identify personal information about parties in a lawsuit?
   A. Facebook
   B. Google Scholar
   C. The National Library of Medicine
   D. The American Psychological Association (APA)
6. Which of the following websites may an LNC use to research a physician's credentials?
   A. American Board of Medical Specialties
   B. Ovid
   C. Medscape
   D. AHRQ

Answers: 1. E, 2. C, 3. E, 4. C, 5. A, 6. A

Appendix A: Websites

Function or Specialty	List or Site	URL/Address
Accreditation	Joint Commission (formerly Joint Commission on Accreditation of Healthcare Organizations)	https://jointcommission.org/ (formerly www.jcaho.org)
Archive, digital library of Internet sites and other cultural artifacts in digital form	The Wayback Machine	https://archive.org
Author verification	Castle Connolly Top Doctors	www.castleconnolly.com/doctors/index.cfm
Cancer	American Cancer Society	www.cancer.org/
Cancer	National Comprehensive Cancer Network	www.nccn.org/
Certification and credentials for advance practice nursing	Nursing Credentialing Acronyms	www.medscape.com/viewarticle/575791 https://nurse.org/articles/nursing-certifications-credentials-list/
Certification and credentials, physicians	American Board of Medical Specialties	www.abms.org/board-certification/
Certifications and credentials, nursing	American Nurses Credentialing Center	www.nursingworld.org/ancc/
Citation database	MEDLINE® Fact Sheets	www.nlm.nih.gov/bsd/medline.html.
Clinical trials database	ClinicalTrials.gov	https://clinicaltrials.gov
Critical care	American Association of Critical Care Nurses; Standards	www.aacn.org www.aacn.org/nursing-excellence/aacn-standards
Data network for toxicology	TOXNET®	https://toxnet.nlm.nih.gov
Deep web people search	Pipl	https://pipl.com/
Deep web people search	PeekYou	www.peekyou.com/

Function or Specialty	List or Site	URL/Address
Direct access to MEDLINE searches	PubMed®	www.ncbi.nlm.nih.gov/pubmed/
Directory of the SIS at the NLM	Special Information Services	https://sis.nlm.nih.gov/
Document retrieval and delivery system of the NLM	LoansomeDoc® DOCLINE®	https://docline.gov/lonesome/login.cfm
Evaluation	Health on the Net Foundation; Web publisher	www.hon.ch/en/ www.hon.ch/web.html
Evidence-based medicine	The WWW Virtual Library	www.vlib.org/medicine
Evidence-based medicine and disease prevention	U.S Preventive Services Task Force	www.uspreventiveservicestaskforce.org/
Expert witness and deposition databanks	LexisNexis Expert Research on Demand	www.lexisnexis.com/experts-on-demand
Expert witness and deposition databanks for plaintiffs	Trialsmith	www.trialsmith.com/TS/
Expert witness background information	WestLaw	https://store.legal.thomsonreuters.com/law-products/ westlaw-legal-research/profiler
Expert witnesses	Expert.com Expert Pages	www.experts.com https://expertpages.com/
Family medicine	Family Practice Notebook.com	www.fpnotebook.com/about.htm
Fitness and exercise	Shape Up America!	www.shapeup.org
Forensic nursing	International Association of Forensic Nurses	www.forensicnurses.org/
Gastroenterology	American College of Gastroenterology	https://gi.org/
General medical resources	ClinicalKey (formerly MDConsult) Martindale's Virtual Medical Center	www.clinicalkey.com/info/ www.martindalecenter.com/Medical.html
General medicine	American Academy of Family Physicians	www.aafp.org/home.html

Function or Specialty	List or Site	URL/Address
Geriatrics	Alzheimer's Association The Gerontological Society of America	www.alz.org www.geron.org/
Glossary	Cochrane Handbook for Systematic Reviews of Interventions (formerly The Cochrane Collaboration)	https://training.cochrane.org/handbook
Governmental agency	DHS/Center for Medicare and Medicaid Services	www.hhs.gov/ www.cms.gov/
Government licensing, regulation, and recalls	U.S. Food & Drug Administration	www.fda.gov
Government statistics	CDC/National Center for Health Statistics	www.cdc.gov/nchs/index.htm
Guidelines	American College of Radiology Evidence-Based Guidelines	www.acr.org/Clinical-Resources/ACR-Appropriateness-Criteria
Guidelines	National Guideline Clearinghouse	www.guideline.gov
Guidelines for endocrinology	American Association of Clinical Endocrinologists	www.aace.com/publications/guidelines
Guidelines for chest physicians	American College of Chest Physicians	www.chestnet.org/Publications/CHEST-Publications/Guidelines-Consensus-Statements
Health insurance plans	America's Health Insurance Plans	www.ahip.org/ (formerly www.aahp.org)
Home health interpretive guidelines	Home Health Agency – CMS	www.cms.gov/Medicare/Provider-Enrollment-and-Certification/SurveyCertificationGenInfo/Downloads/QSO18-25-HHA.pdf
Infectious disease	Morbidity and Mortality Weekly Report	www.cdc.gov/mmwr/index2018.html
Internal medicine	American Medical Association	https://ama-assn.org/
Journal article retrieval	LoansomeDoc	www.nlm.nih.gov/loansomedoc/loansome_home.html
Kidney disease	The National Kidney Foundation	www.kidney.org/
Medical database	OVID	www.ovid.com/
Medical library	The National Library of Medicine	www.nlm.nih.gov/

Function or Specialty	List or Site	URL/Address
Medical resource	Hardin—MD University of Iowa	www.lib.uiowa.edu/hardin/
Medical subject headings	MeSH®	www.nlm.nih.gov/mesh/
Microblog	Twitter	https://twitter.com/microdotblog?lang=en
NLM Help	NLM Gateway	https://gateway.nlm.nih.gov/help.jsp
Nursing journals	Nursing Index – CINAHL	https://health.ebsco.com/products/the-cinahl-database
Nursing resources	Medscape for Nurses	www.medscape.com/index/nurses/journals
Obstetrics guidelines	American College of Obstetricians and Gynecology	www.acog.org www.acog.org/Clinical-Guidance-and-Publications/Practice-Guidelines-and-Reports-Search
Online catalog of the NLM	LocatorPlus®	https://locatorplus.gov/
Patient safety	AHRQ	www.ahrq.gov/professionals/quality-patient-safety/index.html
Patient safety	Institute for Healthcare Improvement	www.ihi.org/
Pharmacology	Drugs.com EMBASE	www.drugs.com/ www.elsevier.com/solutions/embase-biomedical-research
Pharmacy and medical database	ProQuest Dialog	http://proquest.libguides.com/proquestdialog
Physician certification	American Board of Medical Specialties	www.abms.org/
Physician licensing	Federation of State Medical Boards	www.fsmb.org/contact-a-state-medical-board/
Physician locator	e-physician.info	www.e-physician.info
Primary site of funding and research for disease	U.S. Department of Health and Human Services (HHS) National Institutes of Health (NIH)	www.hhs.gov/ www.nih.gov/
Public health statistics	National Center for Health Statistics	www.cdc.gov/nchs/index.htm
Scholarly literature	Google Scholar	https://scholar.google.com
Search engines	Bing Google Microsoft Edge Yahoo	www.bing.com/ www.google.com/ www.microsoft.com/en-us/windows/microsoft-edge www.yahoo.com/
Social media websites	Facebook Tumblr Twitter	www.facebook.com/ www.tumblr.com/ https://twitter.com/?lang=en

Function or Specialty	List or Site	URL/Address
Surgery	American College of Surgeons	www.facs.org/
Video sharing websites	Vimeo	https://vimeo.com/
	YouTube	www.youtube.com/

Note: All websites were current at the time of submission. However, it is possible some sites may be inactive at the time of publication.

Appendix B: Checklist for Medical Research

For Internet research, the LNC should

- gather and analyze relevant facts and define the medical issue
- determine whether field searches can be used (e.g., author, journal)
- identify and enter keywords if field searches are not appropriate
- utilize Boolean connectors (e.g., AND, OR, NOT) to expand or limit the results
- open Filters tab if needed to define very specific criteria to be included in the scope of the search
- review citations and abstracts
- mark the relevant citations
- verify the research is time-specific to the needs of the case
- save the search results and
- retrieve the article(s)

For library research, the LNC should

- gather and analyze relevant facts and define the medical issue
- determine the area of medicine to be researched
- use the online card catalog to locate learned treatises or books published on this issue and area of medicine
- review the area of medicine by using textbooks and medical dictionaries
- locate scientific and medical journals and peer-reviewed publications that deal with this area of medicine by referencing medical indexes
- verify that research is date-specific
- summarize or photocopy relevant research and
- create a paper trail of research findings using appropriate citation techniques

Chapter 35

Report Preparation
Principles and Process

Joahnna Evans Budge, BSN, RN, CCRN, CLNC

Contents

Objectives

■ Discuss the importance of attorney-client communication related to report writing
■ Describe the legal nurse consultant (LNC) report process
■ Define the different types of LNC reports, with examples provided

Introduction

Legal nurse consultants add value to the legal team through their knowledge, understanding, and experience as healthcare "insiders." A large part of nursing involves communication and the explanation of complex medical issues and terminology. This is a skill nurses have used throughout their careers, communicating with patients, physicians, and ancillary departments. Legal nurse consultants also use this skill when working with the legal team. Report preparation and presentation is an essential LNC tool. Through well-researched and well-prepared reports, the LNC communicates thoughts, ideas, and recommendations regarding case issues, case analysis, and case development. A concise, effective report will educate the attorney-client and legal team. Excellent verbal and written communication skills will enhance case development and improve case outcomes.

The LNC-Client Communication Process

Communication between the LNC and the attorney client is a critical element as the development of the case progresses. It is important for the LNC to have a clear understanding of the audience receiving the LNC's report and the intent of its use.

The LNC's verbal communication with an attorney is helpful to learn about the attorney's familiarity with medical issues and terminology and to discover the attorney's understanding of the case issues as well as theories that have been developed relative to the case. The astute LNC will also determine the attorney's willingness to receive new information about the case. Understanding these ideas can guide the communication style and report format needed to present the information effectively.

The goal of all communication should be that the intended target audience understands the information provided. Effective communication is a three-part process: the message is translated into words, verbal or written; the message is delivered to the target audience (verbal report, letter, memo, report style of preference), and the goal is achieved—the intended report audience understands the communicated message. Multiple factors can distort the way the intended message is communicated.

In communication, "noise" refers to anything that interferes with the communication process. According to Craig E. Carroll, "noise is like second-hand smoke, having negative impacts on people without anyone's consent" Carroll, 2015, p. 305). Noise includes such things as poor grammar selection, misspellings, poor organization, and sloppy thinking, all of which will hinder communication. Such "noise" is in the control of the author and speaker. The LNC author/speaker must guide the legal team audience toward the intended message. Medical issues are often complex and multi-faceted; the LNC takes into consideration the target audience, and prepares reports with attention to detail and professional standards.

Report Topic

Prior to beginning the case review and report process, the LNC should discuss the purpose of the report with the attorney-client. What is the attorney's theory of the case? The case issues revealed during the research and review process will drive the report topics. It may enhance or change the case focus and case theory.

Purpose of the Report

Depending on attorney-client preference and case process, either a written or verbal report is expected following the LNC's completion of the medical record review, research, case analysis, and conclusion. Throughout the report process, the LNC arranges the information with awareness of the purpose of the report, the case issues, the intended message, and target audience. The LNC must not produce generic or templated case reports. Every new case brings its own unique issues, circumstances, and attorney-client audience.

The LNC has been consulted by the client-legal team for the LNC's experience, education, training, and knowledge of health care, medical issues, and standards of care and practice. A thorough review of the medical records and other documents often reveals additional information, additional case issues, and alternative case theories that the LNC must communicate to the attorney-client in a timely manner. A thorough review with supported opinions is essential to case integrity and ultimate case outcomes. The LNC's report must include all relevant case issues accompanied by supporting research and documentation.

Prior to composing a case report, the LNC must verify the intended report audience with the retaining attorney-client. Is the report intended for the attorney alone, or for additional members of the legal team such as co-counsel and paralegals? Will other retained experts or expert witnesses be reviewing the report as part of their own case research process? These factors affect the discoverability of case reports. Will the report be produced to opposing counsel? A safe LNC "rule of thumb": Be prepared to support and defend anything you choose to put into writing at some future date.

Planning and Development of the Report Document

While some initial thought may be given to the report outline prior to completion of the LNC review and as case issues are identified, upon completion of the record analysis and research a report outline should be finalized to aid with the direction of the report.

Report Outline

The report outline should be focused on the case issues. The LNC should consider the type of report:

- Plaintiff or defense
  - Defense reports tend to be shorter and more targeted than plaintiff case reports because the burden of proof is on the plaintiff's legal team
- Case screening for merit
- In-depth review outlining deviations in standards of care and practice
- Chronology/timeline
- Expert witness review and summary
- Independent Medical Exam (IME)/Defense Medical Exam (DME) [Please see Chapter 6 for detailed information on the IME/DME process for LNCs]

The report outline is organized (and often reorganized) to present the case issues in the most compelling format. For example, a case involving a Code Blue is often best presented as a detailed timeline. A case involving allegations of negligence and malpractice may require a narrative format. See Appendices A and B for sample case reports.

Whether the report is verbal or written, a well-organized outline format ensures the most effective information delivery to the attorney-client audience. A common practice when preparing a report follows American writer Dale Carnegie's maxim: "Tell them what you're going to say; say it; then tell them what you've said" (Dale Carnegie Quotes, n.d.).

The outline should contain

a. Introduction
b. Body
c. Conclusion/summary
d. List of research resources used to prepare the report

The LNC should review the report outline for clarity of information and precise communication of the issues. The goal is a logical and sequential presentation of the information building to the conclusion.

Report Format

The method in which ideas, facts, issues, and information are organized and presented has the ability to influence the audience's comprehension. The LNC will develop a theme and support it with documentation, facts, and research while identifying and leaving out irrelevant information that would create "noise." The LNC presents facts in a format that is clear, sequential, thorough, and concise. It is essential that the LNC use authoritative literature and published standards of practice. Conclusions are based on the documented case issues, scientific evidence, and professional standards of care and practice.

When "writer's block" occurs, the LNC should take time to refocus. By briefly stepping away from a project, a reorganization of thoughts and ideas may allow the LNC to gain clarity.

Once satisfied with the report format and content, the LNC will finalize the report, using a recognized publication manual as a guide for the final report specifications. The *Manual of the*

American Psychological Association (APA) (2010), sixth edition, provides guidelines for documenting text citations within authored documents. Sources should be acknowledged in the text of the report itself and in an alphabetical list at the end of the report. A parenthetical citation should contain the author's last name, the date of the publication, and the page number from which the material is excerpted. APA format resources are available online, as well as in local libraries and bookstores.

The final LNC report product needs to be neat and professional in appearance. Final reports are submitted in a font and type size that are easy to read. A double-spaced document allows the attorney-client to make notations directly on the report and in the margins if desired. Spelling and grammatical errors will detract from the efficacy of the report. Requesting a colleague peer review of the report may affect the report's discoverability if the LNC is named as an expert in the case. It's possible that at deposition or trial, opposing counsel may ask if the case, case issues, or the report were discussed with anyone else.

Report Revision

Even the most carefully prepared report may require revision. Discovery of additional medical records and documents, research findings, and other information may render a revision necessary. Sometimes this occurs even after the report has been delivered to the attorney. Throughout the report process, it is imperative that the LNC maintain a list of the medical records and documents reviewed to date. All reports should contain the LNC's designation that the report is based on review of the "medical records and documents received to date," with the LNC reserving the right to amend the report should additional documents or information become available. This designation protects the report's integrity because additional documents may alter the LNC's opinions presented in the original report. Throughout the review and report process, the LNC is mindful of the initial case theories while remaining alert for new information that might require the prevailing case theories be updated or revised.

Discoverable vs. Non-discoverable Reports

Reports authored by an LNC retained as a *testifying expert*, are considered discoverable reports. These reports are reviewed by the retaining attorney-client and legal team, other experts involved with the case, as well as opposing counsel, and opposing counsel's experts. Designated expert reports may also be referenced in other experts' work product, or as a source of case research. Reports written by LNCs working "behind the scenes," retained as *consultants* are generally considered non-discoverable. Reports authored by LNCs are considered part of the attorney's education, research, and case development process. The LNC should always obtain the retaining attorney's permission prior to putting anything in writing. Find out if the LNC work product will be discoverable. The non-discoverable internal case report of an LNC consulting expert may contain opinions that an expert witness would not put into writing, such as the negligence of other healthcare providers, or suggestions for additional discovery, case experts, demonstrative evidence, and case development strategy. The LNC may consider marking each report page with "Confidential Attorney Work Product" to prevent the report from accidentally being included as a discoverable document. A testifying expert using a consulting expert's or consulting LNC's report as part of their case research could render the report discoverable. It bears repeating: be prepared to support and defend anything you put into writing at a later date.

Report Types

Memo

The word "memo" is short for "memorandum"; it is perhaps the most frequently used form of communication in any situation, and particularly in email communication. Memos are usually used to communicate to people within an agency or institution and follow the basic format given here:

> *Date:*
> To:
> From:
> Subject:

The memo is a brief, basic method of communication. A memo is shorter than a letter and summarizes the message in an introduction, body (discussion), and conclusion. To be effective, it should be concise, clear, and "user-friendly" (The Writing Center, Writing Business Memos, 2019). As a reminder, all written communication, including emails, between an LNC and the retaining attorney-client may become discoverable.

Informal Report

The informal report may be either a written or a verbal report. Some attorneys prefer a verbal report prior to receiving a written report from the LNC or the expert witness. A written informal report is shorter than a formal report. It does not require a title page, a table of contents, or reference page and does not need to follow a particular structure.

Formal Reports

Medical Research

It is common for a retaining attorney to request the LNC to summarize a piece of medical literature. It is the responsibility of the LNC to review and present the content of an article into language that is understandable for the attorney and other non-medical members of the legal team. The LNC's literature summary may be necessary for the legal team, the client, and the court's understanding of the medical terminology and complex medical issues. Summarizing detailed and complicated medical issues into an understandable, "user-friendly" format is a valuable LNC skill.

Chronology or Timeline

A chronology and a timeline are terms that an LNC may utilize interchangeably. A chronology is the sequential listing of pertinent case events related to the alleged injury or incident. A chronology may be broken down into segments that best portray the case events. The LNC determines the time frame most appropriate for each individual case chronology of events, and then documents the medical incidents and issues in chronological order. There are several excellent computer programs available to the LNC that assist with case chronology and timeline development and format. A case chronology must be objective, listing only the relevant facts. The LNC may choose to add a column for clinical commentary if the explanation would benefit understanding of the case events. When completed, both the chronology and the timeline read like road maps, leading sequentially from one medical fact to another. (See Appendices A and B for a sample case chronology and timeline.)

Medical Record Analysis and Report

The first page of the report should include the following:

■ Date of report
■ Patient-client name or case name
■ Name of the attorney requesting the report
■ File number given to the case by the attorney-client (if available/applicable)
■ Treatment dates
■ List of all medical records, documents, expert reports, depositions, and interrogatories that were reviewed for the analysis and report process

A medical record analysis provides the attorney with a complete account of the events, potential malpractice, potential witnesses and involved parties, and an evaluation of the significance of events in relation to the alleged injury or incident. The case issues and analysis are then presented in an organized, logical manner by the LNC in the written report, as formerly discussed. The case analysis report should "tell the story" in chronological order, allowing the attorney to use the information to construct a fact pattern relative to the alleged occurrence or injury. Legal nurse consultants often use sub-headings in case reports, such as "Medical History," "Sequence of Relevant Events," or "Recommended Experts."

The report should review and address the central issues of the case, clearly presented to the LNC's report audience. The LNC includes direct quotes or citations from the medical record for accuracy and case issue support. Abnormal patient findings and deviation from the standard of care are important to include, with clinical commentary explanation. The case analysis is followed by LNC clinical commentary and case recommendations, identifying additional involved parties, potential witnesses and experts, relevant missing records, and any additional discovery items. The LNC avoids introducing distracters or irrelevant case information that could cloud the case issues.

Expert Witness Report

The expert witness report differs from the LNC case consultant report. The expert witness report provides a review and analysis of the alleged malpractice, occurrence(s), and/or injury(s). The expert identifies the applicable standards of care and practice, and any deviations in acceptable standards of care and practice. The expert report addresses only case issues relating to the expert's area of clinical practice. The nurse expert witness comments on issues within the scope and practice of nursing. Medical issues are addressed by physician experts. The expert witness report should contain a summary of the expert's qualifications, a brief summary or chronology of the event, a discussion regarding the standards of care, and a professional opinion on whether or not the deviation from acceptable standards of care occurred and caused or contributed to the alleged malpractice, occurrence(s), and/or injury(s). Expert witness reports are discoverable. For additional information on expert witnesses, see Chapter 31.

Summary of Independent Medical Examination

(See Chapter 6 for IME/DME report writing information.)

Client Intake Interview

The LNC may be asked to conduct an initial client interview to gather preliminary information from the client about the alleged malpractice, occurrence(s), and/or injuries. The LNC should do the following:

- Note the date and time of the interview, the interviewee's name, address, and contact information
- Obtain and document the interviewee's recollection of the event(s):
  - Ask the interviewee to recall any significant dates and times of incidents, and contributing factors, recollection of physician orders, procedures, treatments, physical therapy, etc. Does the interviewee have a recollection of the medical team's behavior or comments surrounding the time of the alleged occurrence?
  - After the interview, the LNC prepares a written report objectively documenting the reported facts and alleged issues. The report should document whether the interview was conducted in person or on the phone. The intake interview report notes whether the interviewee "recalled," "confirmed," or "speculated" about different issues when relating to the alleged incident.

Summary

Case review, report preparation and presentation is a key LNC function. The LNC may author numerous reports, chronologies, summaries, memos, and other types of correspondence in this role. Effective communication to the attorney-client and legal team requires that the LNC consider the scope of case issues, the purpose or objective of the communication, as well as the audience's knowledge and familiarity level with the subject matter. The LNC's final report product presentation is clear, concise, and professional.

References

Carroll, C. E. (2015). *The handbook of communication and corporate reputation.* Oxford: Wiley-Blackwell.

Dale Carnegie Quotes. (n.d.). BrainyQuote.com. Retrieved August 14, 2018, from BrainyQuote.com Web site: www.brainyquote.com/quotes/dale_carnegie_156635.

Publication manual of the American Psychological Association. (2010). (6th ed.).

The Writing Center, Writing Business Memos. (2019) Retrieved from https://writingcenter.gmu.edu/guides/writing-business-memos.

Additional Reading

Legal Nurse Consultants. (2018). Nurse.org. Retrieved from https://nurse.org/resources/legal-nurse-consultant/.

Test Questions

1. An example of "noise" that can interfere with effective written communication is:
   A. An explanation of medical terms
   B. Spelling errors
   C. Text citations
   D. Current newspaper articles
2. A common style guide that provides ways of documenting text citations is:
   A. PAR
   B. SKR
   C. APA
   D. KFC
3. In the client intake interview, the LNC should NOT include
   A. Interviewee's recollection of the event
   B. Interviewee's recollection of contributing factors
   C. Interviewee's recollection of physician's orders
   D. What the plaintiff had for lunch before arriving at the IME
4. At the conclusion of a legal nurse consultant's case report, affidavit, or declaration, it is prudent for the LNC to add a paragraph regarding the author LNC reserving the option to amend the above report should additional case information come to the LNC's knowledge.
   A. True
   B. False

Answers: 1. B, 2. C, 3. D, 4. A

Appendix A: Sample Case Chronology

_____ P _____ v. _____, et al. (Case No. _____)

Summary of Medical Records and Deposition for Non-economic Damages

Date	Event/Care Provider	Source	Event/Description	Legal Nurse Consultant Clinical Notations (Article ref. #'s)
5/23/2003	Motor vehicle accident (MVA) EMS	Accident Report	South-bound on 101, turned wheels to R. Struck from behind by trash truck, vehicle pushed to R shoulder across a lane of traffic. Treated and released by paramedics on scene	Air bag would not have normally deployed with rear-end collision. Front of vehicle did not suffer any impact
5/28/2003	Initial treatment for back/neck symptoms after MVA	Chiropractic Office; Initial Visit	PT C/O [Complaints of]: Constant/mod/sha** low back pain (LBP), stiffness radiating down L hip; Neck pain radiating to both shoulders; HA [head ache] w/light sensitivity	C-Spine x-ray [cervical spine] Negative for fracture, Break in Georges line [indicates a sprain, possible fracture of neural ring] @ C4–5, C5–6
	Chiropractic Dr. H	Patient Data Form **0373–0376	**: "Neck pain, head aches, back spasms" and dizziness, "whiplash" symptoms began 5/23/2003 Dr.'s Notes: (**0375) (1) Neck pain and tension, had headache every day "6" [0–10 pain scale], shoulder pain, arms ache (2) R sided LBP and spasms "4" (3) Headache, sensitive to light "8" "Before accident felt fine" Chiropractic Treatment: 3 x/week	Article 2A Anatomy of a Normal Spine Article 2B Cervical Lines of Menstruation Article 2C Numerical Pain Rating Scale Denies taking any medications, so was not taking any pain meds after her lumpectomy (3/03, **0088) than would have affected her driving or judgment

Date	Treatment	Notes	References
5/30/2003	Follow-up chiropractic treatments Dr. H___	Treatment Notes (Hole was punched through **# ...)	** (S = subjective, patient's own words recorded by care practitioner): LBP and tension, very sore; L and R neck pain, having headaches	Article 4A Cervical Pain: Description and Diagnosis; Article 4B Evaluation of Patient With Cervical Spine Disorders, p. 5; Article 5A Low Back Pain
6/2/2003	Follow-up chiropractic treatments Dr. H___	Treatment Notes	** (S) "LBP improved" Notes upper back pain and tension	Improvements in pain were temporary. Her pain fluctuates according to her need for movement and daily activities as a mother, wife, and working adult
6/5/2003	Follow-up chiropractic treatments Dr. H___	Treatment Notes	(S) LBP and tension, L arm pain and tension, muscles tight R lower back	First noticed/mentioned L arm tingling and pain, approx two weeks after accident Article 4C Cervical Sprain and Strain
6/9/2003	Follow-up chiropractic treatments Dr. H___	Treatment Notes (Hole was punched through **#)	(S) Upper back pain and tension, Lower back pain Dr.'s notes: "Patient stopped treatment seeing MD."	Almost three weeks after the accident, a simple muscle strain should have been improving, and sought further treatment Article 4B, p. 3; Article 6A, p. 2

Appendix B: Sample Case Timeline

18:35	Patient received from the operating room to PACU s/p (R) carotid endarterectomy
18:40	Left arm weakness noted; paged surgeon
18:50	Surgeon returned call; informed of patient's left arm weakness
19:05	Surgeon and anesthesiologist at bedside; discussed plan of care with patient's wife—patient remains partially sedated
19:30	Patient returned to operating room

Chapter 36

Locating, Screening, and Communicating with Expert Witnesses

Julie Dickinson, MBA, BSN, RN, LNCC®

Contents

Objectives

- Describe the legal nurse consultant's role in identifying, screening, and communicating with expert witnesses
- Discuss the statutes, rules, and case law governing expert witness qualifications and testimony
- Differentiate the types of expert witnesses
- List five desired qualifications and personal attributes of a potential expert witness
- Summarize the key factors to evaluate when assessing an expert as a witness
- Describe how to prepare an expert for deposition and trial

Introduction

Medical-legal tort cases rise and fall on expert witness testimony. Because these cases typically involve specialized knowledge and medical terminology that are not familiar to a lay jury, an expert witness is often required to teach the judge and jury about the medical aspects of a case (Lagnese, Anderson, & Santoro, 2015). An expert witness is an individual qualified by knowledge, skill, experience, training, or education to opine concerning scientific, technical, or other specialized knowledge, such as standards of practice, anatomy and physiology, or a particular medical condition or treatment (Federal Rules of Evidence [FRE], 2018). Legal nurse consultants (LNCs) are instrumental in locating, screening, and communicating with expert witnesses and, as such, play a vital role in one of the most critical factors impacting the outcome of a medical-legal tort case.

Role of the Legal Nurse Consultant

Legal nurse consultants must understand the medical issues in the case, their party's case theory and strategy, the opposing party's case theory, and the jurisdiction's laws regarding expert witnesses. In-house LNCs (those who are employed at law firms) typically locate, screen, and communicate with expert witnesses throughout the life of a case. Independent LNCs are often hired to provide certain components of this process. Throughout this chapter, the specifics of the LNC's role will be discussed.

Historical Cases Regarding Nurse Expert Witness Qualifications and Testimony

Legal nurse consultants and nurse experts should be familiar with several historical cases pertaining to nurse expert witnesses and their qualifications and testimony.

> It appears straightforward that, generally, the most qualified expert to render expert opinion testimony regarding standards of care would be a member of the same profession who practices in a substantially similar clinical specialty as the potential defendant in the case. The courts are now generally acknowledging that nurses possess specialized knowledge that physicians do not have unless they have been trained and practice as a nurse.
> (American Association of Legal Nurse Consultants [AALNC], 2014, para. 3)

However, before 1980, courts allowed physicians to testify to nursing standards of care. Two landmark court cases, *Avret v. McCormick* (1980) and *Maloney v. Wake Hospital Systems* (1980), set the stage for courts to accept nurse experts, allow them to define the standards of care for nursing practice, and testify to causation when appropriate.

In *Avret v. McCormick* (1980), a trial court excluded a nurse expert from rendering a standard of care opinion on maintaining sterility of a phlebotomy needle. At trial, the defendant physician testified that phlebotomy is not exclusively limited to the professional skills of physicians. The Georgia Supreme Court held that the nurse was qualified as an expert witness, because a "nurse who had duly graduated from schools of nursing and was licensed in the state and who had drawn blood and given intravenous injections in numbers exceeding 2,000 was qualified to testify as an expert witness."

In *Maloney v. Wake Hospital Systems* (1980), the plaintiff sued the hospital for malpractice alleging that a nurse in its employ improperly administered undiluted potassium solution intravenously causing disfigurement of the skin on her hand. The trial court excluded certain testimony of a nurse who was an expert in the field of intravenous therapy and testified as to the cause of plaintiff's physical injury. The North Carolina Court of Appeals found that the trial court erred in excluding this testimony and held that a nurse expert is not disqualified from giving an expert opinion as to the cause of a physical injury simply because the nurse is not a medical doctor. This position has continued, as "in more recent years, nurses with specialized knowledge have been permitted in some venues to testify on causation, for example in cases involving wound care and infusion therapy" (AALNC, 2017, p. 5).

Sullivan v. Edward Hospital (2004) was another landmark case involving a patient fall during a hospital admission. The Supreme Court of Illinois held that a board-certified internal medicine physician was not qualified to render opinion testimony on the standards of care for nursing practice.

Statutes, Rules, and Case Law Governing Expert Witness Qualifications and Testimony

To be effective and proactive in their role, LNCs should be familiar with the applicable statutes, rules, and case law governing expert witness qualifications and testimony for their cases. For federal cases, these can be found in federal statutes: the Federal Rules of Civil Procedure (FRCP) and the Federal Rules of Evidence. For cases venued in state court, these are the state's statutes, rules of civil procedure, and rules of evidence. Many states have adopted or adapted the FRCP and FRE for their state rules.

In many states, expert opinion is generally required twice in medical-legal tort claims: first, to initiate the lawsuit and second, to prove or refute the claims at trial. First, to minimize non-meritorious suits, many states require an expert opinion letter or affidavit to commence a lawsuit. The state's statutes define expert qualifications. For example, for all civil actions alleging injury or death resulting from the negligence of a healthcare provider, Connecticut statute requires that the Complaint or initial pleading include a written and signed report of a similar healthcare provider opining that there appears to be evidence of negligence and detailing the basis for that opinion (Prior reasonable inquiry and certificate of good faith required in negligence action against a health care provider, 2011). A "similar health care provider" is defined in Connecticut statute as (Standard of care in negligence action against health care provider. Qualifications of expert witness, 2011):

(b) If the defendant health care provider is not certified by the appropriate American board as being a specialist, is not trained and experienced in a medical specialty, or does not hold himself out as a specialist, a "similar health care provider" is one who: (1) is licensed by the appropriate regulatory agency of this state or another state requiring the same or greater qualifications; and (2) is trained and experienced in the same discipline or school of practice and such training and experience shall be as a result of the active involvement in the practice or teaching of medicine within the five-year period before the incident giving rise to the claim.

(c) If the defendant health care provider is certified by the appropriate American board as a specialist, is trained and experienced in a medical specialty, or holds himself out as a specialist, a "similar health care provider" is one who: (1) is trained and experienced in the same specialty; and (2) is certified by the appropriate American board in the same specialty; provided if the defendant health care provider is providing treatment or diagnosis for a condition which is not within his specialty, a specialist trained in the treatment or diagnosis for that condition shall be considered a "similar health care provider."

(d) Any health care provider may testify as an expert in any action if he: (1) is a "similar health care provider" pursuant to subsection (b) or (c) of this section; or (2) is not a similar health care provider pursuant to subsection (b) or (c) of this section but, to the satisfaction of the court, possesses sufficient training, experience and knowledge as a result of practice or teaching in a related field of medicine, so as to be able to provide such expert testimony as to the prevailing professional standard of care in a given field of medicine. Such training, experience or knowledge shall be as a result of the active involvement in the practice or teaching of medicine within the five-year period before the incident giving rise to the claim.

In New York law, the Complaint for any action alleging medical or nursing malpractice shall be accompanied by a certificate stating the plaintiff attorney has consulted with at least one licensed physician who is knowledgeable in the relevant issues and, from this consultation, the attorney has concluded there is a reasonable basis to initiate an action (Certificate of merit in medical, dental and podiatric malpractice actions, 2015). If the attorney intends to rely solely on the doctrine of *res ipsa loquitur* (Latin for *the thing speaks for itself*), this certificate is not required, because negligence may be inferred from the very nature of the accident or injury (Lagnese et al., 2015).

Depending on the state's rules and case law, the expert opinion letter may not include the expert's name and other identifying information, but it may need to offer enough information for defense counsel to ascertain whether the expert's qualifications meet the statutory requirements (e.g., that the author/expert is a "similar health care provider" as defined by the state).

Knowing the pertinent rules and statutes, plaintiff LNCs are better positioned to recognize whether an expert opinion letter is required, identify a qualified expert, and assist in assuring the expert affidavit contains all of the information required by statute. Defense LNCs can identify whether a Complaint is lacking a statutorily required expert opinion letter or affidavit or whether the letter or affidavit is devoid of the information necessary to evaluate the author.

Second, expert opinions are typically required to prove or refute the medical-legal tort claims at trial. Medical malpractice cases generally involve details that are outside the average juror's knowledge, so expert testimony is typically necessary to prove or defend both liability and causation. Expert testimony may not be required "when the negligence is gross, when the medical condition is obvious, and when the plaintiff's evidence of injury creates a probability so strong that a lay juror can form a reasonable belief" (Lagnese et al., 2015, p. 113). Expert testimony on liability is also not required in cases applying the legal doctrine of *res ipsa loquitur*. This allows a jury to "infer negligence based on the circumstances of the incident even though no direct evidence of negligence has been introduced" (Lagnese et al., 2015, p. 116). For example, a case involving a retained surgical sponge could apply this doctrine.

The admissibility of all evidence, including expert opinion testimony, is governed by a jurisdiction's case law and evidentiary rules. Two cases, along with Federal Rule of Evidence 702, have established the guidelines for evaluating the reliability and relevance of expert witness testimony and thus for determining its admissibility (Morgenstern, 2017). Some states follow *Frye v. United States* (1923), most follow *Daubert v. Merrell Dow Pharmaceuticals, Inc.* (1993), and some follow a combination of the two (Morgenstern, 2017). Legal nurse consultants and expert witnesses should be familiar with applicable case law and evidentiary rules.

Frye v. United States (1923) established the "general acceptance" standard for opinion testimony. In *Frye*, the defendant was accused of murder, and at trial, defense counsel offered as an expert witness a scientist who had conducted a systolic blood pressure deception test on the defendant. This test was based on the theory that the utterance of a falsehood requires a conscious effort, which would be reflected in the blood pressure. The court disallowed this testimony, holding that the systolic blood pressure deception test had not yet gained standing, scientific recognition, and general acceptance among physiological and psychological authorities. The District of Columbia Court of Appeals affirmed this judgment.

Federal Rule of Evidence 702 applied a more liberal approach to the admission of expert opinion testimony in federal cases (FRE, 2018). Subsequently modified, FRE 702 states (FRE, 2018):

> A witness who is qualified as an expert by knowledge, skill, experience, training, or education may testify in the form of an opinion or otherwise if:
>
> **(a)** the expert's scientific, technical, or other specialized knowledge will help the trier of fact to understand the evidence or to determine a fact in issue;
> **(b)** the testimony is based on sufficient facts or data;
> **(c)** the testimony is the product of reliable principles and methods; and
> **(d)** the expert has reliably applied the principles and methods to the facts of the case.

In *Daubert v. Merrell Dow Pharmaceuticals, Inc.* (1993), two children and their parents as petitioners alleged that the children's birth defects were caused by the mother's prenatal ingestion of a prescription anti-nausea drug (Bendectin), which was marketed by Merrell Dow Pharmaceuticals. The trial court determined, and appeals court held, that the evidence presented by the petitioners' experts did not meet the "general acceptance" test. The Supreme Court reversed the decision, holding that "general acceptance" is not a necessary precondition to the admissibility of scientific evidence under the FRE, which assigns to the trial judge the task of ensuring that an expert's testimony both rests on a reliable foundation and is relevant to the task at hand. Thus, the trial judge, as the "gatekeeper," is responsible for deciding the admissibility of expert scientific testimony based on reliability (scientific validity) and relevance (application to the facts at issue). *Daubert* set forth a non-exclusive checklist for trial courts to use in assessing the reliability of scientific expert testimony. Such considerations include whether the theory or technique in question can be (and has been) tested, whether it has been subjected to peer review and publication, its known or potential error rate and the existence and maintenance of standards controlling its operation, and whether it has attracted widespread acceptance within the relevant scientific community. This inquiry focuses on principles and methodology, not conclusions.

Two subsequent cases, *General Electric Co. v. Joiner* (1997) and *Kumho Tire Co. v. Carmichael* (1999), extended the reach of trial judges under *Daubert* by allowing them to consider methodology and expanding their gatekeeper role to include non-scientific evidence (Morgenstern, 2017).

Knowing the nuances of the jurisdiction's statutes, rules, and case law regarding expert witness qualifications and testimony is essential for LNCs to help the attorney determine which type(s) of expert(s) will be needed for a particular case.

Types of Expert Witnesses

The types of experts needed for a case depends on the nuances of that case. Some cases may only need one expert; more complex cases may require multiple experts.

Standard of Care

Standard of care expert witnesses testify on the duty owed by the defendant to the plaintiff, based on the expert's education, training, and experience and on the standard of care in effect *at the time of the incident in question*. In medical malpractice cases, standard of care is the level of care, skill, and treatment that reasonably prudent, similar healthcare providers would recognize as acceptable and appropriate in light of all relevant surrounding circumstances (Lagnese et al., 2015). Therefore, the standard of care, or liability, expert is typically a similar healthcare provider to the defendant who, upon review of the relevant records and information, offers an informed opinion on whether the defendant complied with or deviated from the standard of care. State statutes often require experts to be actively engaged in the practice or teaching of their specialty within a specified period of time before the incident in question (Standard of care in negligence action against health care provider. Qualifications of expert witness, 2011).

Causation

Causation expert witnesses opine on the causal relationship (or lack thereof) between the alleged negligence and the claimed damages. In other words, was the alleged breach in the standard of care a proximate cause of the injuries alleged by the plaintiff (Lagnese et al., 2015)? Depending on the case, one expert may opine on both standard of care and causation, or different experts may be needed. For example, in a case alleging that an oral and maxillofacial surgeon's negligence in extracting a third molar resulted in a traumatic jaw fracture, an oral surgeon could opine on standard of care and causation, because both third molar extractions and jaw fractures fall within the expertise of an oral surgeon. In a case alleging that an oral surgeon's negligence in prescribing antibiotics for a surgical procedure resulted in sepsis, an oral surgeon could opine on the standard of care, but an infectious diseases physician would be required to testify on causation. Causation opinions are based on the expert's education, training, and experience and on the *most current medical literature available*.

Damages

In some, usually catastrophic or wrongful death, cases, experts are necessary to opine on the nature and extent of the plaintiff's or decedent's injuries, or damages.

Economic damages are the tangible expenses and quantifiable monetary losses incurred as a result of the defendant's negligence (Lagnese et al., 2015). These may include medical expenses such as doctors' appointments, durable medical equipment, surgery, and other care and treatment; past and future lost wages; and lost earning capacity. Life care planners, vocational experts, economists, and life expectancy experts may address economic damages (Zorn & Dickinson, 2014). Life care planners opine on types and costs of future care, equipment, supplies, home modifications, and support services that the plaintiff and family will require as a result of injuries. Vocational experts offer opinions on vocational rehabilitation, earning capacity, lost earnings, and cost of replacement labor (including lost ability to perform household services). Economists project the value of future expenses and lost wages over time. Life expectancy experts may be used in wrongful death cases to calculate and opine on future lost wages based upon how long the decedent likely would have lived and worked. They may also be used in cases involving brain-damaged children to opine on the child's likely life expectancy and to calculate medical expenses based on a life care plan.

Non-economic damages relate to the injuries suffered by a plaintiff that cannot be readily valued, such as past and future pain and suffering, mental or emotional distress, loss of chance, and loss of enjoyment of life (Lagnese et al., 2015). Pain and suffering experts are typically retained by the plaintiff to offer testimony establishing pain and suffering. These experts opine regarding the likely nature of the pain and suffering which, in death cases, would include whether the decedent likely knew that serious injury or death was imminent (Zorn & Dickinson, 2014). (For more information on pain and suffering experts, see Chapter 32.) Loss of chance experts, typically used in cases alleging delayed diagnosis or failure to diagnose, offer testimony regarding whether the defendant's alleged negligence reduced the plaintiff's chance for a better outcome (Zorn & Dickinson, 2014).

Expert Fact

An expert fact witness is a subject matter expert qualified by education, training, and experience to educate the judge and jury about case facts (Zorn & Dickinson, 2014). Expert fact witnesses offer unbiased, impartial testimony and do not opine regarding standard of care or causation. They may, for example, explain medically related evidence that is outside the common knowledge of laypersons, such as medical terminology, how a piece of medical equipment is used, or the nature of a medical procedure. An expert fact witness could also be a subsequent medical provider testifying about the observations and findings during an examination but not opining on the treatment rendered by the defendant. For more information on expert fact witnesses, see Chapter 32.

Locating Expert Witnesses

The information the LNC needs to begin locating expert witnesses varies by type of case and type of expert needed, but for malpractice cases, it may include the defendant's clinical specialty, the practice setting in which the care in question occurred, the date of the alleged incident, and the allegations of negligence and damages. When locating standard of care experts, LNCs should understand the specifics of the practice setting in question: type of facility (e.g., acute hospital, skilled nursing facility, physician office, outpatient surgery center, etc.), department, location, and specialty. For example, does an outpatient surgery center specialize in one type of surgery, or does it offer all kinds of outpatient procedures? Is the hospital a teaching facility or not? Does the emergency department handle complex pediatric patients, or is there a children's hospital nearby to serve them?

Once the LNC understands the relevant nuances of the case, the next step is to consider the appropriate specialty for the expert. For example, does the case require a general orthopedic surgeon or a specialized hand surgeon? Does the case need a triage nurse from a Level III rural community hospital or one from an urban Level I trauma center? Would a pharmacist or a toxicologist be better for a case of fatal drug interaction?

Before beginning to locate specific experts in the identified specialty, the LNC must be aware of any restrictions posed by the statutes of the jurisdiction. For example, the Tennessee Health Care Liability Act (1980) requires that healthcare professionals testifying as experts must be licensed to practice in Tennessee or a contiguous bordering state. Outside of any such statute, the LNC should also inquire if the attorney has any preferences related to expert witnesses. For example, some attorneys may wish to have their experts be located in, or as close as possible to, the jurisdiction. This helps minimize costs and shows that the attorney did not have to look far to find a favorable expert review. Knowing the attorney's preferences ensures the search for experts is efficient and cost-effective.

Potential experts can be (Zorn & Dickinson, 2014):

■ Faculty at academic medical centers
■ Authors and editors of peer-reviewed journals
■ Leaders of county, state, and national professional specialty practice associations and
■ Members of a state's licensing board for the profession in question

Other sources to locate potential experts include (Zorn & Dickinson, 2014):

■ Professional contacts made through listservs and networking
■ AALNC's LNC Locator®
■ State bar association's expert database
■ Expert witness directories and
■ Expert witness services

The LNC should check with the attorney before using expert witness directories and services. While these may be helpful, some attorneys prefer not to use them to avoid the appearance that the expert is a "hired gun" (experts who testify extensively, primarily for only plaintiffs or only defendants, and who derive a bulk of their income from expert witness work) (Zorn & Dickinson, 2014).

Screening Expert Witnesses

Qualifications and personal attributes establish an expert's credibility. Because fact-finders (i.e., jury, judge, mediator, arbitrator, etc.) decide cases based largely on the credibility of the expert witnesses, expert vetting is critical. The party with the more credible expert will likely prevail. See Table 36.1 for a sample expert screening form.

Preliminary Screening and Qualifications

After identifying potential experts, the LNC screens the prospects to narrow the selection down to one or two potential candidates to propose to the attorney. The initial screening can often be accomplished using the Internet. For example, physician biographies or curriculum vitae (CV) are typically available on practice or academic websites. Background information can also be found in state public health department physician profile or license verification sites and the American Board of Medical Specialties website. The LNC reviews the information to identify whether the potential expert's qualifications meet the specific needs of the case and the attorney.

The LNC should be familiar with the statutes regarding expert qualifications in the jurisdiction. This will allow the LNC to screen for experts who meet the most basic necessary qualifications. For example, the state's statutes may require active practice or teaching in the field during the five years prior to the incident in question.

For prospective standard of care experts, the LNC will evaluate their education, training, and experience relative to the defendant's. The more alike their paths without actually crossing, to avoid a potential conflict of interest, the more the prospective standard of care expert is a similar healthcare provider to the defendant.

Other qualifications to consider when screening potential experts include:

- Graduate of an accredited school. (Some attorneys may wish to only use experts who were educated and trained in the United States. The LNC should know the attorney's preferences.) Graduates of prestigious schools may have more inherent credibility; for-profit "degree mills" do not.
- Advanced training (e.g., fellowship).
- Additional advanced degrees (e.g., Ph.D.).
- Board-certification "based on independent, noncommercial, psychometrically-validated testing and … periodic proof of continued learning for re-certification" (Diehl & Howland, 2016). The LNC must recognize the difference between certification and certificates of course or program completion, particularly in nursing experts. Avoid "experts" who inflate their CV by listing such coursework as "certification" or a credential instead of clearly and accurately listing it as education. Opposing counsel can easily discredit an "expert" on cross-examination by pointing out these misrepresentations, resulting in disqualification. The LNC should always check to see whether any credential is appropriate for the expert's practice. For example, coursework intended for unlicensed caregivers would be inappropriate

for an RN to offer as evidence of special expertise; though it could be listed under education, it may not be to the expert's credit.

- Active practice in the field for at least five to 10 years.
- Current, active, unrestricted professional license with no disciplinary actions on any professional license (current or expired).
- Teaching/faculty appointments.
- Presentations and speaking engagements on relevant topics.
- Publications in peer-reviewed journals or textbooks on relevant topics, particularly if pertinent to the issues in the case. The LNC should carefully review these publications to discern any opinions that would be detrimental to the case. If the expert's review is favorable, but the expert's prior publications are not, opposing counsel will certainly point this out during cross-examination to impeach the witness.
- Participation on a journal editorial board/review panel.
- Research experience.
- History of achievement (e.g., awards and other recognition).
- Active in professional association(s) which indicates a "willingness to keep abreast of current trends and to advance the profession" (Diehl & Howland, 2016).
- Good standing with professional association(s) and certification board(s).
- Ideally no malpractice history or payouts in any state.

The LNC should carefully and meticulously research and verify the information on a potential expert's CV or biography. Does the expert hold the board certification listed? Is the expert's faculty appointment corroborated by the university's website? Is the journal truly peer-reviewed and not a publication in which authors pay to be published? Is the expert's participation on an editorial review board verified on the journal's website or publication? Is the membership organization legitimate? Does the professional association list the expert as a member? Researching potential experts and confirming their background, credentials, and experience is imperative to avoid issues later. Once an expert is disclosed, the opposing party will conduct this exact same research to identify any misrepresentations. These can cause irreparable damage to the case for the retaining party. Carefully researching and vetting a potential expert will also help to ensure the judge will qualify the expert and allow the expert's opinions into evidence at trial.

The LNC should also investigate whether the potential expert's professional association has guidelines for its members who serve as expert witnesses. These might include the association's proposed qualifications for member expert witnesses. Opposing counsel may use them to discredit an expert who does not meet them. For example, Section V.G.1.08 of the American Association of Oral and Maxillofacial Surgeons' (AAOMS) Code of Professional Conduct (2016) discusses expert witness testimony. It states "The oral and maxillofacial surgeon expert witness should be a diplomate of the American Board of Oral and Maxillofacial Surgery" (AAOMS, 2016, p. 13). It also advises against oral and maxillofacial surgeons serving as expert witnesses in cases "for which they also served as one of the patient's treating doctors" (AAOMS, 2016, p. 14).

The LNC should also conduct a general Internet and social media search of the expert's name and business name and review the expert's business website for "information that may support or oppose the liability and/or causation theories of the case at hand" (Zorn & Dickinson, 2014).

Further Screening and Personal Attributes

After the preliminary screening has narrowed the candidate field, the LNC further screens the remaining viable prospects by speaking with them about the case. Before contacting potential experts, the LNC should know any budgetary or time constraints for the case that would affect the expert review (Zorn & Dickinson, 2014).

The LNC typically calls the experts, identifies that the LNC is working with an attorney who represents a party in a lawsuit, and explains the need for an expert witness with this area of expertise. If the candidate is interested, the LNC provides a brief, factual summary of the case to determine if the potential expert's background and experience are a fit for the issues in the case. In medical malpractice cases, standard of care and causation experts must have knowledge and experience with the illness, injury, procedure, or equipment at issue. It is possible to work in the operating room, for example, but have no experience with open-heart surgery or to work in general medicine but not have encountered the illness from which the plaintiff suffered.

The LNC should clearly state whether the attorney is seeking an expert to testify, provide the trial date (if scheduled), and ensure the potential expert is willing to testify at deposition and trial (if the expert's opinions are favorable). Some candidates will not wish to get involved or testify or will not have the time or availability.

The LNC advises the potential expert of any time constraints or the expected turnaround time for the review. If the expert can meet the time frame, the LNC can then disclose the names of all parties and counsel to screen for conflicts of interest. Defense LNCs, particularly in small states, try to minimize any embarrassment for an individual defendant by not disclosing the name of the defendant until the final stage of the call with the potential expert. If the candidate has no conflict of interest, the LNC:

- Requests the expert's CV, fee schedule, and contact information (including mailing address, email address, cell phone, fax number, etc.). The LNC will review the expert's CV to confirm the accuracy of the information researched prior to the call.
- Determines the expert's preference for paper or electronic records.
- Discusses any budgetary constraints to ensure the expert can meet that need.
- Inquires about any disciplinary actions taken against the potential expert by a state's licensing board, any professional liability lawsuits against the expert, and any professional liability claims settled on the expert's behalf. For each, the allegations and outcome should be discussed. The expert's credibility could easily be tarnished by opposing counsel if the expert had a disciplinary action, lawsuit, or claim involving similar issues to the case at hand.
- Asks the potential expert about prior expert witness work. The attorney may or may not want the testifying expert to have experience as an expert witness. The LNC should be aware of the attorney's preference. Some prior experience as an expert witness may increase the likelihood that the expert will be an effective witness, having had exposure to and being more comfortable with cross-examination and understanding what to expect at deposition, mediation, arbitration, or trial. However, some attorneys prefer the novice witness to prevent any characterization of the expert as a "hired gun." Most of the expert's income should be derived from clinical practice and not from expert work.

Since expert witnesses are to be impartial and unbiased in their opinions, if the prospective expert has experience as an expert witness, it is ideal for the expert to have worked on both plaintiff and defense cases. The more closely the expert's work is evenly divided between plaintiff and defense cases, the more objective and balanced the expert will appear to be.

In addition, the LNC should inquire about the potential expert's testimony history and whether the candidate has ever been disqualified from testifying. The LNC should also ask whether the expert has opined in a case with similar issues and, if so, for which side. If the expert were to offer opinions in the current case that contradict those expressed in a prior, similar case, these inconsistencies will be used by opposing counsel to discredit the expert, causing irreparable damage to the case at hand.

Depending on the attorney's preferences and the expert's legal experience, the LNC should remind or educate the expert that, if the expert is ultimately disclosed, anything written by the expert about the case may be discoverable to the opposing side. Therefore, any notes the expert makes should be factual only and not contain opinions, impressions, or commentary. The expert should communicate with the attorney and LNC verbally unless otherwise instructed.

During this call, the LNC is also assessing the expert for certain personal attributes that can bolster an expert's credibility and jury appeal. While many such attributes cannot be assessed until after the expert has reviewed the case (see the "Assessing an Expert as a Witness" section later in this chapter), those that can be evaluated during a phone interview with a potential expert include:

■ Articulate with strong verbal communication skills
■ Likeable, approachable demeanor
■ Confident but humble
■ Poised and
■ Truthful and forthcoming in answering questions about one's background and experience

The expert should also respond to outreach efforts, returning calls and emails within a reasonable time frame and being available during the day to speak with the LNC. These characteristics, including being easy to work with and courteous, will help to ensure the expert is compatible with the legal team with whom the expert will be working closely.

Selecting an Expert Witness

Compensation and Fees

Expert witnesses are compensated for their time, not their opinions. Experts are paid even if their review yields an unfavorable opinion. In addition, it is unethical for expert witness compensation to be contingent upon case outcome.

Experts' fee schedules outline their expectations for compensation, and some experts require the attorney to contractually sign it. A fee schedule typically contains the expert's rates for record review, report writing, consultation, deposition testimony, and trial testimony. The LNC should ensure the expert will honor the agreed-upon rates throughout the life of the case. An expert may require:

■ A retainer before commencing work
■ Prepayment for deposition or testimony
■ Travel fees, related expenses, and cancellation fees and
■ Interest on late/unpaid invoicing

Table 36.1

EXPERT SCREENING FORM   Date: _____

Preliminary Research:
Demographic information:
Name:
Company/practice name:
Business address:
Mailing address (If different than business address):
Office phone number:
Facsimile number:
Cell phone number:
Email address:

Education and training:
Education:
Post-graduate training:
Other academic degrees:
Board certification:
Practice specialty:
Length of time in specialty:
Licensure: (List states, status, and any disciplinary history of each license held.)

Experience:
Past practice/positions:
Current practice/position:
Clinically active in specialty at time of incident or as statutorily required for an expert?
Academic appointments:
Lectures on topic in question:
Publications on topic in question:
Relevant editorial experience:
Relevant research:
Relevant awards or honors:
Relevant professional memberships:

Other:
Judicial history in states in which the expert has held professional licenses:
Expert witness guidelines promulgated by professional association? If so, does the expert meet the criteria?
Results of general Internet search:
Results of social media search:
Relevant information on expert's website:

continued

Table 36.1 Continued

Phone interview:
Case-specific:
Does expert's background/experience meet the needs of the case?
Willing to testify at deposition/trial if review is favorable?
If trial is scheduled, is the expert available?
Able to meet any time-constraints?
Any conflict of interest with parties or attorneys in the case?
Paper or electronic records?
Able to meet any budget-constraints?

Credibility:
Any disciplinary action by a licensing board? If yes, explain the allegations and outcome.
Ever named as a defendant in a professional liability lawsuit? If yes, explain allegations and disposition.
Any professional liability claims settled on behalf of the expert? If yes, explain allegations and settlement.

Experience as expert witness:
Prior expert work? If yes, # of years and # of cases reviewed.
% of income from expert work:
Breakdown of expert work plaintiff v. defense:
Prior testimony? If yes, # of depositions and # of trial testimony.
Ever disqualified from testifying?
Any prior cases with similar issues? If yes, explain nature of case and details of opinions.

Requests:
Expert's curriculum vitae (CV) or résumé
Expert's fee schedule
Email (if needed)
Cell phone number (if needed)
Prefer paper or electronic records?

If these are not specified in the agreement, the LNC should contact the expert and inquire about them to avoid misunderstanding later.

Generally, experts charge hourly rates equivalent to what they would make in an hour in their daily practice. This depends on the expert's profession, specialization, and geography. For example, a physician's fees will be higher than a nurse's. An advanced practice nurse will typically charge more per hour than a registered nurse, and a pediatric neurosurgeon will likely have hourly rates higher than a pediatrician or internal medicine physician. A rural family physician may charge less than a city counterpart.

Other factors that influence an expert's fees are the expert's experience with medical-legal work and the task to be performed. An expert new to medical-legal case reviews may have a lower hourly rate than an expert who has performed multiple reviews. "Newer experts need to be aware of the steep learning curve involved with performing expert reviews and should not charge the attorney for that" (Zorn & Dickinson, 2014). Experts typically charge one hourly rate for record review, report writing, and attorney conferencing; a higher hourly rate for deposition testimony; and a higher or flat half- or full-day rate for trial testimony. Finally, an expert's agreement may state that services are contracted to the firm and not to the firm's client and that prompt payment from the firm is expected.

The payer (plaintiff's counsel or defendant's liability insurance company) must review and approve an expert's fee schedule before an expert is retained. Strategic consideration must be given to the impact of the expert's compensation on a jury (Zorn & Dickinson, 2014). For example, is the expert's fee for trial testimony likely more than the average juror makes in three months? Does the opposing expert donate all expert income to a charity? These can be problematic and can affect the jury's perception. Therefore, it is important to use experts with reasonable fees that compensate for income normally derived from their daily practice.

Final Selection

Once the screening of potential experts has yielded several solid, qualified candidates, the LNC presents these prospects to the attorney. The LNC needs to make the attorney aware of any potential credibility issues identified during the screening process so the attorney "can make a judgment regarding whether the risks outweigh the benefits of using the expert" (Zorn & Dickinson, 2014).

On the plaintiff side, the attorney selects the final expert for the case. On the defense side, the attorney reviews the prospects and selects one, typically, to present to the defendant's liability insurance company with the expert's CV, fee schedule, and a brief biography. Some insurance companies also require an expert retention form. Unless it requires the expert's signature, the LNC can complete it with the expert via phone to avoid any risk of it becoming discoverable to opposing counsel should the expert ultimately be disclosed.

Communicating with Expert Witnesses

Expert Packages

Initial

Once the expert is retained, the LNC identifies the relevant materials to send to the expert for review. While it is essential to provide the expert with all materials that would be helpful in formulating complete opinions about the case, expert time is expensive, so the LNC should send only records germane to the issues on which the expert is opining (Zorn & Dickinson, 2014). The content of the expert package is determined by the type of expert (i.e., standard of care, causation, etc.) and the materials available (which depends on the stage of the case, i.e., pre-suit, early in suit, or later in suit). For example, if a standard of care expert is reviewing a pre-suit matter for a potential plaintiff, the only available and relevant records may be those of the potential defendant. If a causation expert is reviewing a case that has been in suit for some time, the available and relevant materials may include the Complaint, defendant's records, subsequent treaters' records, prior treaters' records, opposing expert disclosures, and deposition transcripts. Some attorneys may want the opposing party's interrogatory responses or bill of particulars sent to the expert.

Once the LNC has identified the records to send to the expert, the package should be prepared in whatever format the expert prefers (i.e., hard copy, electronic, or both). Hard copy records should be organized in chronological order with a tab for each provider/office/facility and sub-dividers to further organize the provider's records into sections such as progress notes, orders, lab work, radiology reports, medication, nurses' notes, etc. Records being sent electronically should be organized in the same way with electronic bookmarks to indicate the providers and subsections. The LNC should also include any relevant, non-traditional records such as digital x-rays, photographs, CDs with pertinent imaging studies, film x-rays, fetal heart monitor strips, etc. A well-organized expert package avoids wasting the expert's time and the payer's money and allows the expert's review to be more efficient and thorough.

The LNC prepares a cover letter to send with the expert package. The cover letter should contain a detailed description of the contents of the package, indicating, for example, that the second amended Complaint dated xx/xx/xx and Dr. Smith's paginated records (pages 1 through 57) are enclosed. This level of detail is helpful if questions arise later about whether the expert received certain materials. (For this purpose, some LNCs maintain a paper or electronic copy of all materials sent to an expert.) The cover letter should also reiterate whether the attorney desires a written or verbal report. If the expert is ultimately disclosed, work products and written communication between the expert and the attorney's office will likely be discoverable (depending on the jurisdiction's rules).

To streamline the expert's review, some attorneys may also wish to include a summary of the case facts or a chronology in the expert package. Because these would potentially be discoverable if the expert were later disclosed, the summary or chronology should contain only facts and excerpts from the medical records. They should be devoid of any editorial comments, analysis, case strategy, or opinions (Zorn & Dickinson, 2014). The cover letter, summary, and chronology should also avoid using inflammatory language, such as calling the case "tragic" (on the plaintiff side) or describing the allegations as "ludicrous" (on the defense side).

Depending on the attorney's preference, the cover letter may also include a list of questions for the expert's consideration during the case review. These questions should not be "leading" (Zorn & Dickinson, 2014). For example, instead of asking "Do you agree that Dr. Jones deviated from the standard of care in failing to prescribe antibiotics?," which is leading (i.e., it implies the answer), the LNC should ask "What is the standard of care for the prescription of antibiotics in this situation?"

The attorney should review and approve all letters and materials before they are sent to the expert. If an expert requests additional information to formulate complete opinions, the LNC should obtain and provide it.

Subsequent

As the case develops, additional depositions may be taken, updated medical records obtained, and further experts disclosed. It is imperative for LNCs to ensure their experts periodically receive all pertinent ongoing case materials. For example, if a plaintiff's expert who screened the case for merit pre-suit will continue as the expert in the case, the LNC provides the Complaint, additional medical records, defense expert disclosures, and deposition transcripts when available. If an expert's opinion is based on partial information, the expert's credibility could be undermined (Zorn & Dickinson, 2014). For example, a plaintiff's causation theory could be jeopardized if the plaintiff's expert is unaware of a pre-existing medical condition that might be responsible for the plaintiff's alleged injuries.

Invoices and Payment

In-house LNCs are typically more involved with handling expert invoices than independent LNCs. Ideally, expert invoices should be detailed enough to identify what the expert did and when. For example, an invoice should note that on xx/xx/xx, the expert spent two hours reviewing the deposition transcript of the plaintiff, and on xx/xx/xx, the expert had an hour-long phone conference with the attorney and LNC.

Generally, the party who requested the expert's time pays the expert's fees (Zorn & Dickinson, 2014). For example, if plaintiff's counsel retains an expert to review a case, the plaintiff pays for the expert's time to review the records, conduct any necessary medical literature research, confer with the attorney, and write a report. Since defense counsel would want to depose this expert to explore the expert's opinions and their basis, the defendant's liability insurance company pays for the expert's time at deposition and any related travel expenses or cancellation charges. Opposing counsel is typically notified beforehand of the expert's deposition, travel, and cancellation fees. Since plaintiff's counsel will want to prepare the expert for the deposition, the plaintiff is responsible for paying for the expert's preparation time. Plaintiff's counsel will also enlist the expert to testify at trial to aid in proving the case, so the plaintiff will incur the expense of the expert's time and travel for trial. Typically, payment is made for services already rendered, but occasionally, prepayment to the expert may be agreed upon. For instance, some experts may require prepayment from opposing counsel to set aside four hours during a workday for the expert's deposition, but this must be agreed upon by both parties beforehand.

Upon receipt of an expert's invoice, the LNC should review it to ensure the hourly rate billed is as agreed, that billed time appears reasonable for the task, and that calculations are correct. If a retainer was provided to the expert, the LNC should ensure this was reflected in the invoice properly. In providing the invoice to the attorney for approval, the LNC should point out any discrepancies or any unusual or unexpected charges. The LNC should obtain the expert's W-9 form and advise the expert of the expected payment time frame, particularly if the expert is unfamiliar with the differences between the plaintiff and defense sides. Plaintiff expert invoices are paid directly by the plaintiff's firm, and the payment turnaround time is generally quick. Defense payments can take longer to receive. Most defense firms have agreements with the liability insurance companies on how to handle such expenses. The insurance company may pay all invoices directly or may have a threshold over which they will pay invoices directly. If an invoice is under that threshold, the defense firm advances payment to the expert and is then reimbursed by the insurance company. If a defendant is private pay (i.e., the client retained the defense firm directly without going through an insurance company), the firm typically sends invoices directly to the defendant for payment.

As the expert's point of contact, the LNC may receive inquiries from experts about outstanding invoices. The LNC can contact the appropriate person (e.g., the firm's billing coordinator or the claim's handler from the insurance company) to ascertain the status of the expert's payment and report back to the expert. If payment is expected, for example, within two weeks of the inquiry, the LNC can follow up with the expert in two weeks to ensure payment was received.

Conferencing

Ideally, conferences with expert witnesses are held in-person, but if the expert is not local or if the expert is already known to the attorney, the initial conference may be telephonic. The conference should be scheduled for a time when the expert, attorney, and LNC can devote their full attention to the discussion without distractions or time constraints.

Prior to the conference, the LNC should confirm the expert has received all relevant and requested materials to complete the case review. If the expert needs additional information, the LNC should provide it as far before the conference as possible. In preparation for the conference, the attorney and LNC should be well-prepared to discuss the case issues with the expert. Such preparation may include reviewing the medical records and thoroughly understanding the medical issues in the case (which may require conducting medical literature research). The attorney and LNC may prepare a list of questions to ask or issues to discuss with the expert.

At the time of the conference, the attorney, LNC, and expert should have all case material (including the medical records) available. Paginated medical records can be very helpful for phone conferences, so all participants can know they are looking at the exact same record.

Depending on the expert and the expert's experience with legal cases, the attorney may begin the conference by educating the expert on the four elements of proof in negligence cases, the legal definition of the standard of care, and the burden of proof. The attorney may then ask the expert to summarize opinions and thoughts on the case. From there, the attorney and LNC ask questions, and the conference morphs into an in-depth discussion to identify and explore the expert's findings and opinions and their bases. The attorney and LNC consider the expert's opinions from the perspective of opposing counsel, and the attorney will essentially cross-examine the expert to determine whether the opinions are firmly rooted in science and able to withstand intense cross-examination. The attorney and LNC should inquire if there is any other information or material the expert needs to complete the review, and, if so, the LNC should ensure the expert receives these records promptly after the conference.

If the expert's opinions are favorable, the attorney may educate the expert on the litigation process (if needed) and ask the expert to confirm willingness to testify to those opinions under oath at deposition and trial. The expert should be reminded that the expert's entire file may be discoverable, so any communication with the attorney and LNC should be verbal unless otherwise instructed.

After the conference, the attorney and LNC should discuss the validity of the expert's opinions. Did the expert have a solid command of the medical records? Were the expert's opinions based in science and reinforced by peer-reviewed literature? This should also include an evaluation of the expert's credibility and how a jury would likely perceive the expert. (This evaluation is discussed in more detail in the next section.)

If the conference was audio-taped (if permitted by state law and preferred by the attorney), the LNC should proofread the transcript prepared by a staff member after the conference, and the audiotape or digital recording should be preserved for the life of the case (Zorn & Dickinson, 2014). Otherwise, the LNC should prepare a summary of the expert's opinions based on the detailed notes taken by the attorney and LNC during the conference. This memorandum should also include a brief evaluation of the expert's credibility and appeal as a witness.

On the defense side, this summary may be sent to the liability insurance company to update the claims representative on the expert's review. On the plaintiff side, if the expert review was the final step in screening a case for merit, the LNC and attorney should discuss the disposition of the potential claim and the next steps.

Assessing an Expert as a Witness

Meeting with an expert (ideally in person) to discuss the case is invaluable to further assess the expert's credibility and appeal as a witness. Characteristics and skills that bolster credibility and jury appeal include:

- Being articulate
- Having strong teaching and verbal communication skills
- Being able to explain complex or specialized concepts or procedures in simple, everyday language that a lay jury could easily understand
- Having a wholesome demeanor; warm, humble personality; and sincere, believable affect
- Being confident but not arrogant
- Being poised, non-reactive, and able to maintain composure, particularly when faced with aggressive, hostile cross-examination and
- Having a neat physical appearance, including being well-groomed, dressing conservatively, and avoiding strong perfume, aftershave, or other scented products

The expert witness must have an excellent command of the issues and intimate familiarity with the details in the records. This will enable the expert to identify and immediately correct misquotations or misrepresentations during cross-examination.

The expert should be able to identify and discuss both case strengths and weaknesses. It is valuable for the attorney to know these to prepare for issues that may arise. This also indicates the expert's assessment is honest and forthright.

It is essential that an expert remain truthful and avoid misrepresentation or exaggeration. The expert should be intellectually honest in the opinions proffered and typically should avoid "absolutes" (i.e., "always" or "never").

The expert must also understand the retaining party's legal strategy and the opposing party's case theory to understand the big picture, appreciate how the expert's opinions fit into it, and ensure the testimony supports this while remaining truthful.

Disclosure

Most states require some variation of expert disclosure prior to trial. The dates of disclosure are determined by the case's scheduling order, with plaintiff's experts being disclosed first, followed by a set time frame for the defense to depose plaintiff's experts (in states that take expert depositions). Then the defense has a deadline to disclose their experts, following which plaintiff's counsel is allotted time to depose the defense experts (in states that take expert depositions).

The exact information to be provided in an expert disclosure varies by state. In some states, the identity of the expert is not revealed, but the disclosure summarizes the opinions to which the expert is expected to testify. In other states, the expert's name, credentials, and practice location are disclosed along with a summary of the expert's opinions and a list of materials the expert reviewed to formulate those opinions.

The expert disclosure provides the boundaries for the expert's testimony. If the expert offers opinions that are not disclosed, opposing counsel can object to the testimony, because it is outside the scope of the expert's disclosure.

The LNC may draft the initial expert disclosure based on the opinions expressed by the expert during the expert conference(s). The attorney then prepares the final disclosure in conjunction with the expert and files it by the court-ordered deadline.

Deposition Preparation

Not all states engage in expert discovery. For those that do, expert depositions are an opportunity for the opposing party to explore the expert's opinions before mediation, arbitration, or trial. On rare occasions, an attorney may choose not to depose an expert to minimize expenses.

Before the deposition preparation meeting with the expert, the LNC should ensure the expert has received all relevant case material, including updated medical records and deposition transcripts. Since the plaintiff's expert is disclosed and deposed first, the defense expert should receive plaintiff's expert disclosure and deposition transcript before deposition. (The plaintiff's expert will receive the defense expert's disclosure and deposition transcript before trial.) The LNC should also ensure the expert has a copy of the expert's own disclosure, which summarizes all the opinions to which the expert is expected to testify and provides the confines of the testimony. The LNC should also confirm the expert has a copy of the deposition notice, which may have come with a list of materials the expert is requested to produce at the deposition. If the attorney objected to any of these requests, the LNC should notify the expert and ensure the expert understands what materials should be brought to the deposition.

How much deposition preparation is necessary depends on multiple factors, including the expert's testimonial experience and case complexity. Regardless, because expert testimony plays a crucial role in medical-legal tort claims, the importance of deposition preparation for an expert cannot be overemphasized. A strong expert deposition may trigger a favorable case outcome for the retaining party.

At the preparation meeting, which is ideally held in-person, the attorney, LNC, and expert will discuss the medical records, case facts, the expert's opinions (as detailed in the expert's disclosure), pertinent deposition testimony by parties and fact witnesses, opinions and deposition testimony of opposing experts (if available), and the case strengths and weaknesses and how to address them (Zorn & Dickinson, 2014). The expert should solidly understand the theories and strategies of the retaining party and how the expert's testimony fits into this big picture.

The attorney will review the questions planned for direct examination as well as anticipated lines of questioning from opposing counsel during cross-examination. Preparing for cross-examination is critical and should include reviewing any issues that may be raised by opposing counsel about opinions expressed in the expert's publications or prior testimony in other cases. It is not only helpful for the expert to practice responding to questions, but this is an opportunity for the attorney and LNC to critique the expert's answers, refine the expert's demeanor and presentation, evaluate the expert's ability to teach a jury, and assess how the expert may present to a jury (Zorn & Dickinson, 2014).

The attorney should explain the deposition process, including who may be there, the order of questioning by counsel, and that the expert is under oath. The usual ground rules of depositions should be reviewed. Such rules may include that the expert can ask to have any question clarified, rephrased, or broken down into smaller questions, but if the expert answers, it is assumed the expert understood the question. The expert can request a break at any point, but any pending question must be answered prior to the break. All answers must be verbal, as the stenographer cannot record nods or shakes of the head. Last, to help ensure the deposition transcript is easy to read, the expert and the questioning attorney should not interrupt each other or talk over each other so the full question and full answer can be transcribed.

The expert should pause before answering any question from opposing counsel to allow the retaining attorney to object, if necessary. The attorney should emphasize that, unlike trial, this is not an environment in which the expert is a teacher. Instead, the expert should answer each question concisely and should not volunteer any additional information. The expert should be alert to any misrepresentations of the case facts or the expert's opinions and should promptly correct any such errors. The expert should also be mindful of the confines of the expert's expertise and should not offer opinions outside of those limits. The expert should know, if different opinions are offered at trial, the opposing party can use the expert's deposition to impeach the expert.

Other deposition tips include:

- Maintain a professional, polite, sincere demeanor. Be cooperative and do not argue. Do not lose composure despite attempts by opposing counsel to incite anger or defensiveness.
- Be mindful of body language, and keep arms uncrossed.
- Answer honestly.
- Be aware of compound and hypothetical questions.
- Be careful about assumptions and absolute words such as "never" and "always."
- Dress appropriately.

At the deposition, the expert should request a copy of the deposition transcript once available. Within a specified time frame, often 30 days, the expert can review and correct the transcript and sign the errata sheet. Corrections to the transcription should be for spelling or other types of transcription mistakes. The corrections should not be substantive or change the opinions to which the expert testified. Such substantive changes will damage the expert's credibility. Substantive changes may also lead to further deposition, cause the retaining attorney to seek another expert to replace the existing expert (if disclosure deadlines allow), and can negatively affect the outcome of the case, such as forcing settlement.

Trial Preparation

Preparing an expert for trial is very similar to preparing an expert for deposition. The trial process should be explained to the expert, and if the expert is new to testifying, it may be helpful to have the expert view a real trial proceeding, a mock trial, or a video of a trial.

The attorney and LNC should review the pertinent medical records, case facts, opposing expert opinions, and relevant deposition testimony. Discussion should include case strengths and weaknesses, the retaining party's case theory, and the expert's role in that strategy/theory.

As with depositions, preparing for testimony and cross-examination is critical, and thorough preparation cannot be overemphasized. This should include reviewing the questions planned for the expert's direct examination as well as anticipated lines of questioning from opposing counsel. The expert should seek clarification of any confusing question and ask that compound questions be reduced to smaller questions. The expert should pause briefly before answering opposing counsel's questions to allow the retaining attorney an opportunity to object. The expert should answer only the question at hand and should answer all questions honestly, which helps maintain consistency when a question is asked several ways. The expert should know tactics that may be used by opposing counsel, including attacking the expert's qualifications; feigning amazement, sarcasm, or disbelief to undermine the credibility of the expert's testimony; and using the "best friend" approach to get the expert's guard down.

In addition, there are two key points specific to trial preparation. First, if the expert was deposed, the expert should carefully review the opinions offered at deposition to ensure consistent, unwavering testimony at trial. This will help to avoid impeachment from giving differing opinions under oath and will also allow the expert to quickly correct any misstatement or misrepresentation during trial of the expert's deposition testimony. If the expert was not deposed, the expert should be thoroughly familiar with the opinions in the expert's disclosure. Second, the expert's role at trial is to educate the jury or fact-finder. To connect with the jury, the expert should look at the jurors when answering questions and teaching them about the issues. Since the jury will be presented with differing opinions from opposing experts, both the content of the expert's testimony and its delivery are important (Zorn & Dickinson, 2014). "A prepared expert is more apt to be calm and confident and therefore present more favorably. The party whose expert is deemed more credible by the jury or trier of fact will prevail" (Zorn & Dickinson, 2014).

The expert should review, approve, and practice using any visual aids, diagrams, drawings, exhibits, etc. that will be used during testimony. The attorney and LNC should offer constructive feedback about the expert's responses, demeanor, and body language (including eye contact). They should also work with the expert to eliminate any distracting mannerisms, such as finger-tapping, knee-bouncing, eyebrow movement, "talking" with one's hands, etc. It can be very beneficial to videotape the expert's practice testimony, which allows the expert to critique responses and visualize body language and mannerisms. The expert's "performance" is crucial, as jurors may pay more attention to form over substance and to actions over words (Kuslansky, 2013). Juries perceive strong "performers" as more competent, even if a weaker performer is more credentialed and qualified (Kuslansky, 2013).

In the weeks and days leading to the expert's testimony, the LNC should maintain regular communication with the expert. Trials are fluid processes, and the exact date of the expert's testimony may not be known until after evidence begins. Once the date is known, the LNC should ensure the expert has the address of the courthouse, the location of nearby parking, and the time the expert should arrive. The LNC should remind the expert of the documents or exhibits the expert is expected to bring to the courthouse. Likewise, the expert should know what not to bring to the courthouse, including whether food and beverages are prohibited. During breaks in the trial, the attorney and LNC provide feedback to the expert on the expert's testimony and its delivery and may suggest adjustments based on how the jury appears to be responding to the expert.

Summary

Legal nurse consultants play a crucial role in one of the most important determinants of medical-legal tort cases—expert witnesses. These cases rise and fall on the testimony and credibility of expert witnesses. Legal nurse consultants fill a vital role in locating, screening, and communicating with expert witnesses from pre-suit through adjudication. It begins with understanding the types of expert witnesses and the rules governing their qualifications and testimony. Locating and carefully screening individuals who are experts in their field are critical steps the LNC takes to ensure the retention of compelling experts. Analyzing the expert's opinions, assessing the expert as a witness, and preparing the expert for testimony are instrumental skills the LNC employs to directly affect case outcome.

References

American Association of Legal Nurse Consultants. (2014). Providing expert nursing testimony regarding nursing negligence. Retrieved from www.aalnc.org/page/position-statements.

American Association of Legal Nurse Consultants. (2017). *Legal nurse consulting: Scope and standards of practice* [e-publication]. Retrieved from www.aalnc.org.

American Association of Oral and Maxillofacial Surgeons. (2016). Code of professional conduct. Retrieved from www.aaoms.org/images/uploads/pdfs/code_of_professional_conduct.pdf.

Avret v. McCormick, 271 S.E.2d 832 (Ga. 1980).

Certificate of merit in medical, dental and podiatric malpractice actions, NY CPLR § 3012-A (2015).

Daubert v. Merrell Dow Pharmaceuticals, Inc., 509 U.S.579 (1993).

Diehl, B., & Howland, W. (2016). Role of the nurse expert. In *AALNC Legal nurse consulting professional course* (module 16). Retrieved from www.aalnc.org/page/course-content#packages.

Federal Rules of Evidence. (2018). *Rule 702. Testimony by expert witnesses.* Grand Rapids, MI: Michigan Legal Publishing. Retrieved from www.rulesofevidence.org/article-vii/rule-702/.

Frye v. United States, 293 F. 1013 (D.C. Cir. 1923).

General Electric Company v. Joiner, 522 U.S. 136 (1997).

Kuslansky, L. (2013, May 8). The Jodi Arias trial—a case study in experts, witness ... or witless? [Web blog]. Retrieved from www.a2lc.com/blog/bid/64719/the-jodi-arias-trial-a-case-study-in-experts-witness-or-witless.

Kumho Tire Company, Ltd. v. Carmichael, 526 U.S. 137 (1999).

Lagnese, J. A., Anderson, C. B, & Santoro, F. H. (2015). *Connecticut medical malpractice: A manual of practice and procedure.* Hartford, CT: Connecticut Law Tribune.

Maloney v. Wake Hospital Systems, 262 S.E.2d 680 (N.C. Ct. App. 1980).

Morgenstern, M. (2017, April 3). *Daubert v. Frye*—A state-by-state comparison. [Web blog]. Retrieved from www.theexpertinstitute.com/daubert-v-frye-a-state-by-state-comparison/.

Prior reasonable inquiry and certificate of good faith required in negligence action against a health care provider, CT Gen. Stat. § 52–190a (2011).

Standard of care in negligence action against health care provider. Qualifications of expert witness, CT Gen. Stat. § 52-184c(b-d) (2011).

Sullivan v. Edward Hospital., 806 N.E. 2d 645 (Ill. 2004).

Tennessee Health Care Liability Act, Tenn. Code Ann. § 29-26-115(b) (1980).

Zorn, E., & Dickinson, J. (2014). Identification, evaluation, and collaboration with expert witnesses. In *AALNC Legal nurse consulting professional course* (module 7). Retrieved from www.aalnc.org/page/course-content#packages.

Test Questions

1. The Federal Rule of Evidence 702 states that a witness who is qualified as an expert by knowledge, skill, experience, training, or education may testify in the form of an opinion or otherwise if:
   A. The expert's scientific, technical, or other specialized knowledge will help the trier of fact to understand the evidence or to determine a fact in issue
   B. The testimony is based on sufficient facts or data
   C. The testimony is the product of reliable principles and methods
   D. The expert has reliably applied the principles and methods to the facts of the case
   E. All of the above

2. Criteria for admission of evidence according to *Daubert* do NOT include:
   A. Whether the theory or technique has been subjected to peer review and publication
   B. The potential error rate
   C. Whether the theory is tested
   D. Whether the theory meets the "general acceptance" test

3. Expert fact witnesses are NOT:
   A. Presented as subject matter experts
   B. Called to educate the jury about the case facts
   C. Able to offer opinion testimony
   D. Qualified by their education, training, and experience

4. Sources for locating potential expert witnesses include which of the following?
   A. Journals in which authors pay to be published
   B. Directories in which experts pay to be listed
   C. Board of directors of local businesses
   D. AALNC's LNC Locator®

5. Desired qualifications and personal attributes of expert witnesses do NOT include:
   A. Board-eligibility
   B. Advanced training
   C. Publications in peer-reviewed journals
   D. Strong verbal communication skills

6. Desirable expert witness characteristics do NOT include:
   A. Ability to explain complex or specialized concepts or procedures in simple, everyday language that a lay jury can easily understand
   B. Tendency to exaggerate the truth to support the retaining party
   C. Attention to detail with an excellent grasp of the case issues and familiarity with the content of the medical records
   D. Ability to identify and discuss both the strengths and weaknesses of a case

7. Preparing an expert for deposition or trial testimony should NOT include:
   A. A discussion of the case facts, medical records, and opposing expert's opinions
   B. A review of the questions planned for direct examination as well as the anticipated lines of questioning for cross-examination
   C. A reminder to respond to opposing counsel's questions with the same level of aggression used to ask the question
   D. A pointer to be alert to any misrepresentations by opposing counsel of the case facts or the expert's opinions

Answers: 1. E, 2. D, 3. C, 4. D, 5. A, 6. B, 7. C

Section VIII

Case Adjudication

Chapter 37

The Role of the Legal Nurse Consultant in the Preparation of Demonstrative Evidence

Kelly K. Campbell, RN, BSN, CP, CLNC, CLCP
Sean Dennin
Patricia W. Iyer, MSN, RN, LNCC®

Contents

Objectives

- Describe the purpose of demonstrative evidence
- Distinguish between demonstrative evidence, substantive evidence, and visual aids
- List different types of demonstrative evidence
- Describe the role of legal nurse consultant (LNC) in the preparation and presentation of demonstrative evidence

Introduction

Experts and attorneys in medical cases use terms that are unfamiliar to most jurors. There is a bewildering amount of complexity and detail to absorb. Trials may take weeks or months to litigate. A jury's attention to the facts of the case must be maintained during this slow process.

Substantive evidence, demonstrative evidence, and visual aids break up the tedium while helping jurors grasp the important concepts. Evidence, whether presented in physical or digital form, allows jurors to analyze and synthesize the mass of information presented during the trial. Legal nurse consultants play a vital role in creating the tools that help the jurors or judge decide a case.

Although most cases are resolved before trial and may involve the use of evidence and visual aids during a settlement conference or mediation, the focus of this chapter is the use of demonstrative evidence at trial.

Types of Trial Exhibits

There are three types of trial exhibits: substantive evidence, demonstrative evidence, and visual aids.

Substantive or real evidence may include objects actually involved in the plaintiff's case, for example: the blood-stained knife, medical record, incident report, halo brace, 911 recording, or videotape of a nurse's aide striking the patient. This evidence is part of the facts of the case, and the judge usually allows it to be admitted into evidence for the jury to view and consider during deliberations. Substantive evidence is that "offered to help establish a fact in issue" (Black's Law Dictionary, n.d.).

Some substantive evidence may be withheld from the jury or offered for viewing with the warning that it is gruesome. For example, death scene, autopsy, or pressure sore photographs may be considered too graphic for the jury, and defense counsel will likely object to their use, asserting they are prejudicial to the case. The judge will determine if the possible prejudicial effect of the substantive evidence outweighs its probative value (in proving something). For example, defense counsel objected to photographs that showed a plaintiff's bruised hips after being thrown from a bike as a result of being hit by a bus. In that case, the judge allowed the photographs to be included in the report, and they would have been shown to the jury had the case not settled. In another case, a juror expressed the likelihood of fainting if forced to see photographs of the plaintiff's foot scarred by multiple surgeries. The judge ruled that none of the jurors had to see the photos.

Demonstrative evidence is "physical evidence that one can see and inspect (i.e., an explanatory aid) and that while of probative value and usually offered to clarify testimony, did not play a direct part in the incident in question" (Black's Law Dictionary, n.d.). This type of evidence is usually created after the fact by the legal nurse consultant, expert fact witness, expert witness, medical illustrator, or attorney to illustrate key aspects of the case. Examples could include charts, graphs, medical illustrations, and more. Demonstrative evidence is shown to the jurors during a trial to help them understand the substantive evidence in conjunction with verbal testimony. Attorneys ask that demonstrative evidence be admitted into evidence so that the items can be used to assist a witness in testifying or to help the judge or jury better understand the case. However, depending on the judge's ruling, it may not be available to the jurors during deliberations (unlike substantive evidence).

Visual aids are not admitted into evidence and include items such as flip charts, whiteboards, and parts of a verdict form. Attorneys may use them to list key expenses in a life care plan or to summarize the witness's testimony, for example.

Evidentiary Foundations

A 1993 case called *Daubert v. Merrell Dow Pharmaceuticals, Inc.* set the standard for judges to assess whether an expert witness's scientific testimony is based on scientifically valid reasoning and applies to the facts of the case. This Supreme Court case defined five factors that the judge may consider in determining whether the methodology is valid:

1. Whether the theory or technique in question can be and has been tested
2. Whether it has been subjected to peer review and publication
3. Its known or potential error rate
4. The existence and maintenance of standards controlling its operation and
5. Whether it has attracted widespread acceptance within a relevant scientific community

A subsequent Supreme Court decision in 1999 called *Kumho Tire Company, Ltd. v. Carmichael* held that *Daubert* factors may apply to non-scientific testimony, meaning the testimony of engineers and other experts who are not scientists. These decisions affect the creation of demonstrative evidence. The sources used for demonstrative evidence must reflect scientific knowledge and accuracy.

Several of the Federal Rules of Evidence (FRE) were amended on the basis of the *Daubert* case. The LNC should be aware of the FRE, which are applicable to federal cases. Cases venued in state court follow the state's rules of evidence, which are often verbatim adoptions or adaptions of the FRE. Ultimately, the attorney and judge are responsible to ensure the evidence is admissible. See Table 37.1 and Chapters 3 and 5 for more information on the FRE.

Table 37.1 Selected Federal Rules of Evidence

Concept	Fed. R. Evid. Number	Wording
Relevance	401	To be relevant, evidence must tend to "make a fact more or less probable than it would be without the evidence and that fact is of consequence in determining the action."
Admissibility of relevant evidence	402	Relevant evidence is admissible, except as otherwise provided by the Constitution of the United States, a federal statute, by these rules, or by other rules prescribed by the Supreme Court pursuant to statutory authority. Irrelevant evidence is not admissible.
Exclusion of relevant evidence	403	Although relevant, evidence may be excluded if its probative value is substantially outweighed by the danger of unfair prejudice, confusion of the issues, or misleading the jury, or by considerations of undue delay, waste of time, or needless presentation of cumulative evidence.
Sponsorship by a competent witness	602	A witness may testify to a matter only if evidence is introduced sufficient to support a finding that the witness has personal knowledge of the matter. Evidence to prove personal knowledge may consist of the witness's own testimony. This rule does not apply to a witness's expert testimony under Rule 703.
Authentication	901	To satisfy the requirement of authenticating or identifying an item of evidence, the proponent must produce evidence sufficient to support a finding that the item is what the proponent claims it is.

Source: Federal Rules of Evidence. (2015). Cornell Law School. Retrieved from www.law.cornell.edu/rules/fre.

Preservation of Substantive Evidence

Because of their knowledge of how the healthcare system works, LNCs who are involved in a case (particularly pre-suit) may see opportunities to suggest how substantive evidence can be preserved. For example, if a piece of medical equipment such as a patient-controlled analgesia pump is implicated in an injury to a patient, the LNC would suggest securing the equipment and downloading its data before it can be used on another patient. The LNC would anticipate that a potentially defective piece of equipment might be sent to the Biomedical Department and then returned to use, thus losing the data specific to the injured patient.

Surveillance videos, 911 recordings, and other types of electronic data may only be available for a short period.

The Legal Nurse Consultant's Role

One of the most challenging aspects of medical case work is understanding and conveying complex medical issues in simple terms to a lay judge and jury. The LNC's value is the ability to glean relevant information from the medical record, depositions, discovery documents, or expert opinions and then consult with the attorney about how best to utilize demonstrative evidence at trial to establish the claims or defenses to the claims.

The LNC, using medical knowledge developed from nursing education and experience, identifies significant medical facts, educates the legal team about the pertinent medical issues, and plans and organizes the demonstrative evidence to convey these facts and issues to the judge and jury.

Clear communication between the LNC and the legal team is paramount to identifying, preparing, or outsourcing effective demonstrative evidence creation. The LNC must ensure research is from authoritative resources and all information provided for demonstrative evidence is accurate, reliable, and relevant. The expert witness who will present the demonstrative evidence is involved in its preparation and confirms the materials are accurate. The LNC often talks with the expert to ensure the expert is satisfied with the demonstrative evidence. As part of the litigation team, the LNC must understand the key claims and defenses in the case and determine how the attorney can effectively present them to the jury.

The LNC may work with the attorneys, paralegals, expert witnesses, photographers, accident reconstruction engineers, and medical illustrators (among others) to create a successful strategy for identifying and developing demonstrative evidence. Brainstorming sessions are integral to the development of cost-effective courtroom graphics, timelines, anatomical models, animations, and illustrations.

When identifying or developing demonstrative evidence, the LNC must focus on the judge and jury's (i.e., the triers of fact's) ability to comprehend sometimes complex medical information. The LNC's recommendations on the use of timelines, graphs, illustrations, anatomical models, and video testimony simplify this data and assist the attorney to ensure the triers of fact will understand and retain the information presented.

Preparation of Demonstrative Evidence

The LNC's involvement in preparing demonstrative evidence may start months before a settlement discussion or trial, or it may begin later in the process.

Ideally, the LNC will have three to five months before trial to plan and create the demonstrative evidence. The initial meetings with pertinent members of the litigation team focus on what the managing attorney wishes to convey when utilizing demonstrative evidence. This is followed by a discussion of which type of demonstrative evidence best satisfies the attorney's goals and the cost constraints. If the work is being outsourced to a medical illustrator or graphic artist, the LNC will have enough information at the conclusion of these initial litigation team meetings to interface with the person preparing the demonstrative evidence.

Legal nurse consultants may find people qualified to prepare demonstrative evidence by exploring the companies who exhibit at attorney conferences, advertise in attorney journals, or are available through outsourcing platforms such as Fiverr.com or Upwork.com. These platforms provide a forum for examining the work of illustrators or artists and handle the financial arrangements. The law firm does not pay for the finished work until the attorney is satisfied with the work product.

Practical Considerations

Several factors influence the type of demonstrative evidence the LNC prepares in conjunction with the legal team. These include practical considerations like complexity, cost, the attorney's comfort level, and the trial setting.

Complex demonstrative evidence takes longer to prepare, with greater risk of inaccuracies, typographical errors, and high costs. Simple exhibits with pictures or symbols are often effective. The recommendation to keep wording at an eighth grade reading level guides the LNC in exhibit creation.

Cost drives the preparation of demonstrative evidence. An exhibit may be designed to be reused, borrowed, or rented, rather than custom-designed for one specific case. Creation of a costly computer animation or digital display of information may not be warranted in a lower damages case. The law firm's financial resources, the value of the case, and the strength of the liability claim affect budgets for demonstrative evidence.

The attorney's comfort level also guides the type of demonstrative evidence an LNC may prepare. Some attorneys are satisfied with low-cost exhibits mounted on foam core board, flip charts, or whiteboards. They argue that managing a trial involves juggling constantly competing priorities and pressures, and that little can go wrong with these methods of presenting evidence. There are no bulbs to burn out, no hardware failures, and no chance of not having an accessible electrical outlet in the courtroom. The jury can look at the exhibits in the jury room; they don't disappear when the projector is turned off.

Other attorneys are comfortable with technology or have the funds to hire a person to run the digital show and consider foam core boards or transparency projectors as archaic presentation methods.

The courtroom setting is the final consideration when planning demonstrative evidence. Many courthouses were built decades before anyone even thought of using computers or transparency projectors. Lighting, space, wall surfaces, projection screens, wall outlets, and tables are all critical to the effective display of images. It is essential for the attorney to be familiar with the courtroom likely to be used before planning exhibits with the LNC.

The attorney gives final authorization for demonstrative exhibits based on consideration of these factors. It is imperative after completion of the project to have a last review of the demonstrative evidence with the litigation team and others important to its final presentation. It is wise to always *overestimate* the amount of time it will take to prepare demonstrative evidence.

Types of Demonstrative Evidence

A variety of software can be used to create exhibits, from simple word processing programs to more complex presentation or graphic art programs. The LNC may be the person to envision and create the exhibit or to supply the data to the person who creates the exhibit. Because graphic artists usually do not have a medical background, it is always important for the LNC to oversee the accuracy of their work.

Simple mistakes like confusing the left and right sides of the body can invalidate an exhibit. For example, in a case alleging a healthcare provider perforated the plaintiff's lung with a nasogastric tube, the demonstrative evidence included an animation of the tube being advanced correctly into the stomach. A second presentation for this case included an animation of the tube placement through the lung. The animation would need to depict the correct lung.

Charts, Graphs, and Tables

Charts, graphs, and tables are inexpensive to prepare and display and are effective for depicting data visually in easy-to-understand forms. Legal nurse consultants may create many styles of data charts and graphs, such as column charts, line graphs, pie charts, bar charts, area graphs, scatter graphs, stock charts, surface charts, doughnut charts, bubble graphs, and radar graphs.

Graphs are effectively used to portray changes in numbers such as weight loss over time (Figure 37.1), number of milligrams of pain medication required, pain scores (Figure 37.2), or changes in vital signs (Figure 37.3) right before a patient complaining of chest pain went into cardiac arrest.

A jumble of numbers or words that blur together can become much more meaningful when they are displayed in a table. It can be as simple as a table showing pain scores with gray boxes and numbers (Figure 37.4) in a case involving a young patient who developed toxic epidermal necrolysis after a fatal overdose of chemotherapy. Figure 37.5 shows how an LNC changed material written by an attorney to make it easier to understand. The attorney wrote it in narrative form; the LNC organized it into a table.

Design considerations affect the creation of tables. Such considerations include the amount of data, shading, repeat headers, and footnoting.

Amount of data: The LNC should design tables to be enlarged and will determine how much data to include by knowing if the table will be part of a slide presentation or enlarged on a board. It is often better to display less information on a page and allow sufficient white space, so the jury can easily read the content.

Some attorneys use transparency projectors in court. The size of the viewing plate will dictate how much information the LNC will place on the page. An overhead projector that uses transparencies may have a plate that measures 9 × 9 inches. These projectors do not have zoom lenses for close-ups.

Electronic projectors, also known as visual presenters or optical projectors, can zoom in on small objects or hard copies of documents, x-rays, MRI or CT scans, or other radiological images. They do not require transparencies. However, they also have a limited viewing area.

The LNC needs to be aware of the size of the plate when creating tables. In one case, an expert fact witness's table included 22 columns, which was too much data to be displayed all at

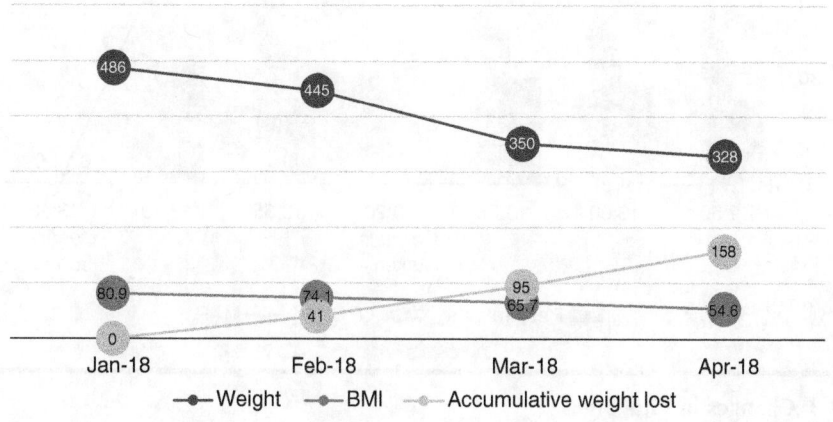

Figure 37.1 Weight Loss Graph.

Source: Created by Kelly Campbell.

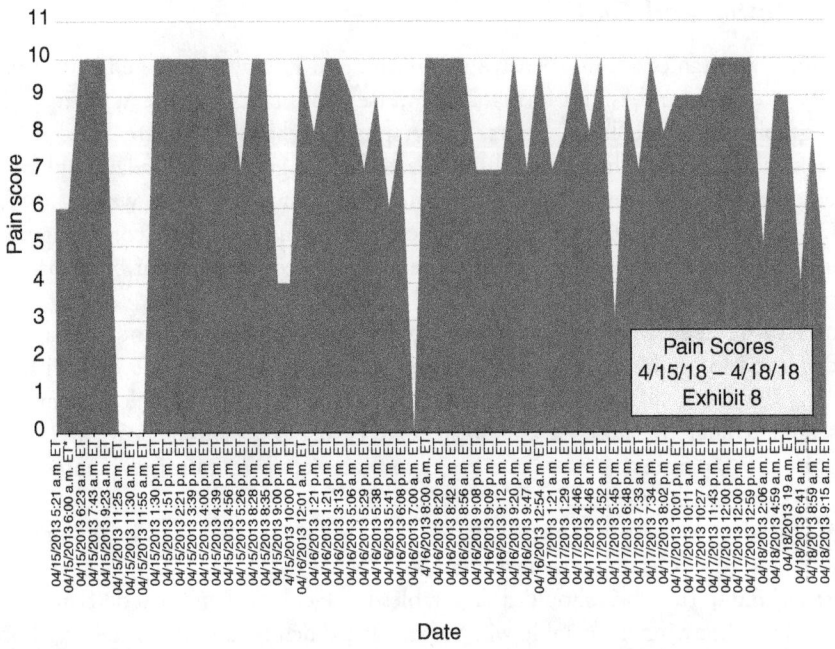

Figure 37.2 Pain Scores.

Source: Created by Pat Iyer.

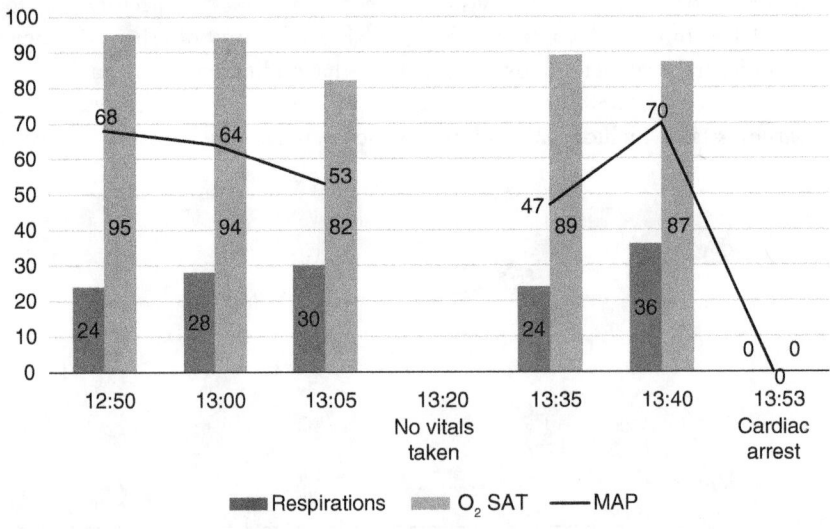

Figure 37.3 Changes in Vital Signs.

Source: Created by Kelly Campbell.

Date	Time	Pain Level									
		1	2	3	4	5	6	7	8	9	10
08/31	10:25 PM									9	
	10:50 PM								8.5		
09/01	2:30 AM								8.5		
	5:30 AM								8		
	7:00 AM								8		
	9:00 AM								8		
	10:40 AM							7.5			
	10:30 PM							7			
	11:00 PM						6.5				
09/02	6:00 AM							7			
	8:30 AM							7			
	6:15 PM						6	7			
09/03	8:00 PM								8		
09/04	12:00 AM							7	8		
	4:00 AM				4	5					
	4:30 PM							7	8		
	8:00 PM							7			
09/05	12:00 AM						6	7			
	5:00 AM							7			

Figure 37.4 Pain Levels in a Table.

Source: Created by Pat Iyer.

once. As soon as the attorney slid the paper over so the expert fact witness could testify about the columns on the far right of the page, the left side of the page was no longer visible.

Figure 37.6 was created (as an example of a large table) after a 31-year-old diabetic patient developed necrotizing fasciitis from a rectal boil. The patient required multiple debridements and finally high leg amputation. Each of the surgeries that took place in March are indicated by a shaded column. This figure would be easier to view on an optical projector if it was broken into two or three time periods, although separating it would lose some of the impact of the multiple surgeries.

Figure 37.6 also includes a key at the bottom to explain to the attorney and fact-finders that the shading in the columns indicates days the patient had surgery. The terms "fever" and "rapid heart rate" are also defined.

Shading: Apply shading to visually separate rows but be careful to avoid obscuring words.

Repeat headers: Repeating the header row and column helps the jurors when data is continued from one page to the next.

Footnoting: Occasionally, an attorney may request the facts in a table be footnoted to include the page of the medical record where this fact is noted. This is very time-consuming and should not be routinely done. In one case, the attorney requested a footnoted, revised report after the expert's deposition in which opposing counsel questioned where the expert found several facts. Figure 37.7 shows a revised table in a report that contained 1,514 footnotes. The case resulted in a multi-million-dollar award to the parents of a child who went into liver failure after receiving acne medication.

The Statement of Charges alleges:

o Dr. provided incomplete and/or inappropriate restorative care for
   tooth #13.
   • Only evidence was subsequent recommended treatment on
      a surface examined by Dr. but found to not need treatment.
o Dr. failed to properly treat areas of dental defect in one or more
   teeth numbered 4, 5, 13, 20, and/or 29.
   • No specific evidence of failure to treat an area that
      warranted treatment on April 14, 2015.
   • No specific allegations regarding alleged negligent treatment
      of any specific tooth.
o Dr. failed to diagnose and/or treat decay in tooth #30 from ~April
   13, 2015 through ~May 2, 2015.
   • No credible evidence that tooth #30 warranted treatment
      during the time Dr. treated her.

Statement of Charges alleges:	The evidence shows:
Dr. provided incomplete and/or incomplete and/or inappropriate restorative care for tooth #13.	Only evidence was subsequent recommended treatment on a surface examined by Dr. but found not to need treatment.
Dr. failed to properly treat areas of dental defect in one or more teeth numbered 4, 5, 13, 20 and/or 29.	No specific evidence of failure to treat an area that warranted treatment on April 14, 2015. No specific allegations regarding alleged negligent treatment of any specific tooth.
Dr. failed to diagnose and/or treat decay in tooth #30 from ~April 13, 2015 through ~May 2, 2015.	No credible evidence that tooth #30 warranted treatment during the time Dr. treated her.

Figure 37.5 Comparison of Same Information Presented Two Ways.

Source: Created by Julie Dickinson.

Major Problems	April																													
	1	2	3	4	5	6	7	8	9	10	11	12	13	14	15	16	17	18	19	20	21	22	23	24	25	26	27	28	29	30
													Discomfort																	
Pain	✓	✓	✓	✓	✓	✓	✓	✓	✓	✓	✓	✓	✓	✓	✓	✓	✓	✓	✓	✓	✓	✓	✓	✓	✓	✓				
Right leg weakness & stiffness							✓	✓				✓	✓								✓	✓		✓	✓		✓			
Right leg swelling								✓																						
Dizziness																														✓
Weakness	✓																											✓	✓	
Sore throat/dry mouth	✓	✓																												
Nausea		✓			✓	✓	✓		✓	✓				✓				✓	✓											✓
Vomiting		✓				✓		✓	✓	✓			✓																	
Diarrhea													✓			✓						✓							✓	
Decreased appetite			✓																				✓							
Severe weight loss																					✓									
Rapid heart rate	✓	✓	✓	✓	✓	✓	✓	✓	✓	✓			✓		✓	✓	✓	✓	✓		✓		✓	✓	✓	✓	✓	✓		✓
Fever	✓	✓	✓	✓	✓	✓	✓	✓	✓	✓		✓	✓	✓										✓	✓	✓	✓	✓	✓	✓
Chills															✓															
Skin breakdown left lumbar area																											✓	✓	✓	
Skin breakdown right thigh & buttock							✓	✓																						
Large amount of drainage	✓																													
Unable to urinate on own	✓	✓	✓	✓	✓	✓	✓	✓	✓	✓	✓	✓	✓	✓	✓	✓	✓	✓	✓	✓	✓	✓	✓	✓	✓	✓	✓	✓	✓	✓
													Emotional																	
Anxiety																	✓													✓

⬚ = Surgery Fever = 100° or higher Rapid heart rate = 100 beats per minute or higher

Figure 37.6 Major Problems Chart.

Source: Created by Pat Iyer.

Symptoms	March						
	22	23	24	25	26	27	28
Abdominal pain	✓i	✓ii					
Fever			✓iii		✓iv	✓v	✓vi
Rapid heart rate	✓vii	✓viii	✓ix	✓x	✓xi	✓xii	✓xiii
Abdominal distention	✓xiv	✓xv	✓xvi		✓xvii	✓xviii	✓xix
Swelling in extremities	✓xx				✓xxi	✓xxii	
Jaundiced	✓xxiii				✓xxiv	✓xxv	✓xxvi
Dark brown skin color		✓xxvii	✓xxviii	✓xxix		✓xxx	✓xxxi
Fecal impaction					✓xxxii		✓xxxiii
Stage II sacral pressure sore	✓xxxiv	✓xxxv	✓xxxvi	✓xxxvii	✓xxxviii	✓xxxix	✓xl
Unable to breathe on own	✓xli	✓xlii	✓xliii	✓xliv	✓xlv	✓xlvi	✓xlvii
Unable to eat solid food	✓xlviii	✓xlix	✓l	✓li	✓lii	✓liii	✓liv
Lung congestion	✓lv	✓lvi	✓lvii	✓lviii	✓lix	✓lx	✓lxi
Abdominal infection	✓lxii	✓lxiii					
Worsening renal function			✓lxiv				
Acute drop in blood pressure	✓lxv						
Septic shock		✓lxvi					

3/23/04	= Exploratory laparotomy and washout
3/26/04	= Exploratory laparotomy, abdominal washout, replace JP drain, fecal disimpaction
3/28/04	= Exploratory laparotomy, fecal disimpaction, abdominal washout

Footnote	Book	Tab
i HOSPITAL 00200	2	Progress Note
ii HOSPITAL 00204	2	Progress Note
iii HOSPITAL 00207	2	Progress Note
iv HOSPITAL 02317	3	Critical Care Flow Sheet
v HOSPITAL 00214	2	Progress Note
vi HOSPITAL 02329	3	Critical Care Flow Sheet
vii HOSPITAL 00200	2	Progress Note
viii HOSPITAL 02299	3	Critical Care Flow Sheet
ix HOSPITAL 00207	2	Progress Note
x HOSPITAL 02311	3	Critical Care Flow Sheet
xi HOSPITAL 02311	3	Critical Care Flow Sheet
xii HOSPITAL 02323	2	Critical Care Flow Sheet
xiii HOSPITAL 00219	2	Progress Note
xiv HOSPITAL 00200	2	Progress Note
xv HOSPITAL 00204	2	Progress Note
xvi HOSPITAL 00207	2	Progress Note
xvii HOSPITAL 02318	3	Critical Care Flow Sheet
xviii HOSPITAL 00217	2	Progress Note
xix HOSPITAL 00219	2	Progress Note
xx HOSPITAL 00202	2	Progress Note
xxi HOSPITAL 02318	3	Critical Care Flow Sheet
xxii HOSPITAL 00214	2	Progress Note

Figure 37.7 Footnoted Table.

Source: Created by Pat Iyer.

xxiii	HOSPITAL	00202	2	Progress Note
xxiv	HOSPITAL	02318	3	Critical Care Flow Sheet
xxv	HOSPITAL	02320	3	Critical Care Flow Sheet
xxvi	HOSPITAL	02330	3	Critical Care Flow Sheet
xxvii	HOSPITAL	02300	3	Critical Care Flow Sheet
xxviii	HOSPITAL	02302	3	Critical Care Flow Sheet
xxix	HOSPITAL	02312	3	Critical Care Flow Sheet
xxx	HOSPITAL	02324	3	Critical Care Flow Sheet
xxxi	HOSPITAL	02330	3	Critical Care Flow Sheet
xxxii	HOSPITAL	00211	2	Progress Note
xxxiii	HOSPITAL	00912	4	Report of operation
xxxiv	HOSPITAL	02295	3	Critical Care Flow Sheet
xxxv	HOSPITAL	02295	3	Critical Care Flow Sheet
xxxvi	HOSPITAL	00208	2	Progress Note
xxxvii	HOSPITAL	02312	3	Critical Care Flow Sheet
xxxviii	HOSPITAL	00212	2	Progress Note
xxxix	HOSPITAL	02324	3	Critical Care Flow Sheet
xl	HOSPITAL	02330	3	Critical Care Flow Sheet
xli	HOSPITAL	00200	2	Progress Note
xlii	HOSPITAL	00204	2	Progress Note
xliii	HOSPITAL	00207	2	Progress Note
xliv	HOSPITAL	02313	3	Critical Care Flow Sheet
xlv	HOSPITAL	00211	2	Progress Note
xlvi	HOSPITAL	00217	2	Progress Note
xlvii	HOSPITAL	00219	2	Progress Note
xlviii	HOSPITAL	00201	2	Progress Note
xlix	HOSPITAL	02302	3	Critical Care Flow Sheet
l	HOSPITAL	00208	2	Progress Note
li	HOSPITAL	02314	3	Critical Care Flow Sheet
lii	HOSPITAL	00212	2	Progress Note
liii	HOSPITAL	02326	2	Critical Care Flow Sheet
liv	HOSPITAL	02332	2	Critical Care Flow Sheet
lv	HOSPITAL	00200	2	Progress Note
lvi	HOSPITAL	00204	2	Progress Note
lvii	HOSPITAL	00207	2	Progress Note
lviii	HOSPITAL	02312	2	Critical Care Flow Sheet
lix	HOSPITAL	02318	2	Critical Care Flow Sheet
lx	HOSPITAL	02324	2	Critical Care Flow Sheet
lxi	HOSPITAL	00219	2	Progress Note
lxii	HOSPITAL	00202	2	Progress Note
lxiii	HOSPITAL	00212	2	Progress Note
lxiv	HOSPITAL	00209	2	Progress Note
lxv	HOSPITAL	02297	2	Critical Care Flow Sheet
lxvi	HOSPITAL	00205	2	Progress Note

Figure 37.7 Continued.

Calendars

Legal nurse consultants may create calendars to show, for example, the extensive treatment a plaintiff needed, the number of times in a given time period the plaintiff received care from various healthcare professionals, the number of medication doses required to control a plaintiff's symptoms, or the amount of time that passed before the plaintiff first reported an issue related to the care in question. Figure 37.8 was created after the expert fact witness provided the data to a

L. T.
Medications for
Symptoms 2/28/18 to
3/31/18 - Exhibit 13

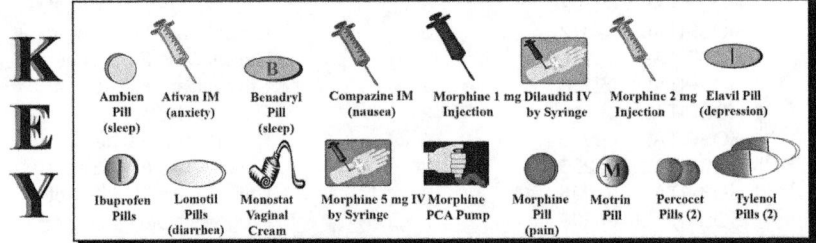

February and March 2018

Figure 37.8 Medication Calendar.

Source: Created by Pat Iyer.

graphic artist, who used a software program to create the calendar. Figure 37.9 was created by a defense LNC in a case in which the plaintiff alleged immediate, debilitating dental sensitivity after a teeth-whitening procedure. These types of exhibits work best when the colors are sharp and distinct. They lose meaning when printed in black and white.

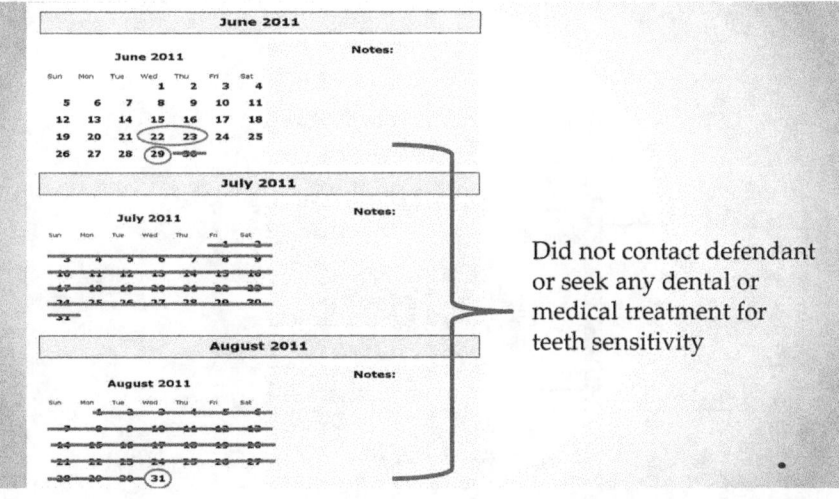

Figure 37.9 Calendar.

Source: Created by Julie Dickinson.

Timelines

Timelines are invaluable in illustrating the most important concept: the relationship between events. The timeline tells the story of what occurred, based on meticulous dissection of the sequence of events. The jury sees the time span at a glance. A timeline is useful for many types of cases. They can show the actions of a healthcare provider, such as the staff caring for a woman with low blood sugar (Figure 37.10), or the extensive treatment needed after a woman fell into an

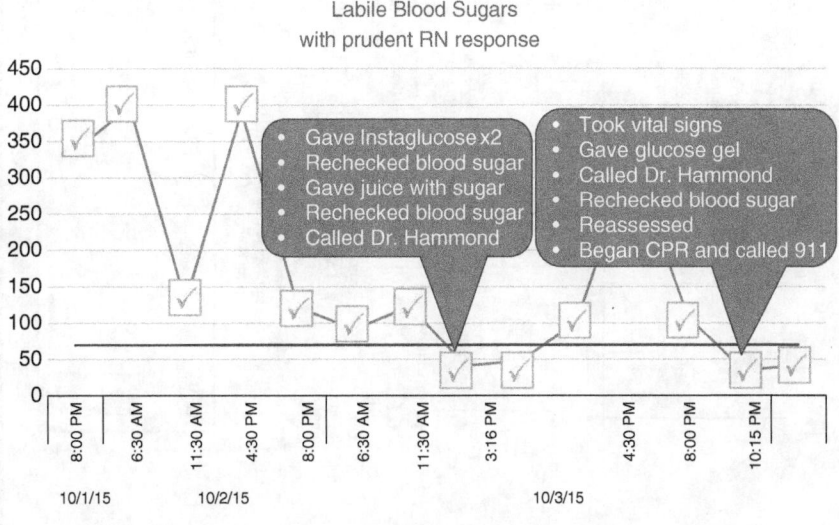

Figure 37.10 Timeline of Labile Blood Sugars with Prudent RN Response.

Source: Created by Julie Dickinson.

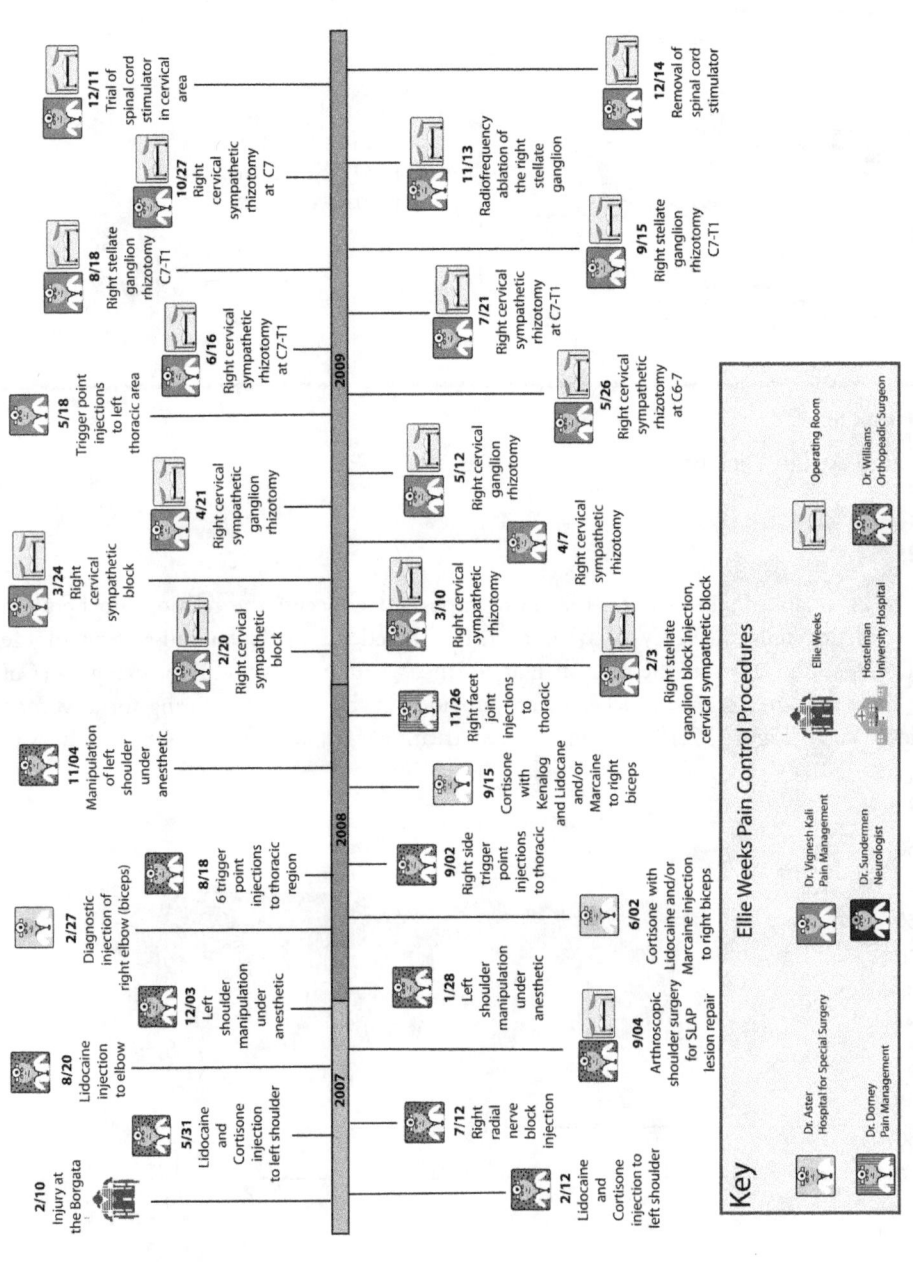

Figure 37.11 Timeline of Pain Control Treatment.

Source: Created by Pat Iyer.

elevator shaft (Figure 37.11). A timeline can highlight discrepancies in testimony or documents or guide the testimony of an expert witness.

Timelines are typically prepared with a horizontal line depicting time and events above or below the line. The LNC uses color to enhance the facts. Red is often associated with important information. The combination of yellow and black draws the viewer's attention to key facts also. Timelines should be prepared to scale so that each time period is of a similar size. Every detail on timelines should be checked and double-checked for accuracy.

Medical Records

Pages from medical records or police reports may make effective exhibits. The LNC's detailed examination of medical records may reveal pages that would convey significant details to the jury. These might include diagrams showing burns or abrasions, consent forms with shaky or firm signatures, Glasgow Coma Scores, and drawings made by healthcare providers. The pages should be scanned at as high a resolution as possible, so they will be clear when enlarged.

Figure 37.12 is the police diagram created after a person riding a motorcycle with defective brakes hit an oncoming car. The person was thrown several feet to the grass and died later that day.

Photographs

Medical records may contain or refer to actual photographs of the plaintiff. The LNC's careful reading of the records may lead to discovery requests and uncover important pieces of substantive evidence. The LNC may be involved in suggesting which images may have the biggest impact on proving or disputing liability or damages.

It is also important for the LNC to consider and suggest that photographs be taken of injuries (e.g., the evolution and final cosmetic outcome of a patient who survived Fournier's gangrene), the location at which an injury occurred (e.g., a pothole in the sidewalk), evidence related to an injury (e.g., the contents and bottles of antidepressant medication left behind by a non-compliant patient who committed suicide), or equipment associated with an injury. For example, an LNC

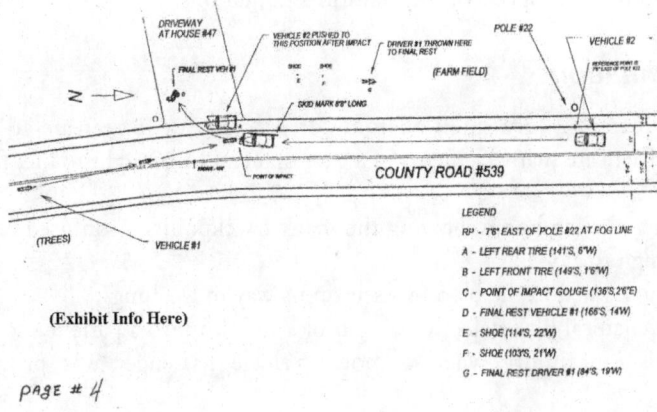

Figure 37.12 Police Diagram.

Source: Supplied by Pat Iyer.

worked with a photographer to take pictures of a syringe, insulin vial, and Lasix vial in a case of a patient who opened an unlocked medication cart. The plaintiff self-injected the contents of both vials and suffered brain damage from the hypoglycemic event. This substantive evidence was shown to the jury at trial.

Visitors and patients often capture images within and outside of healthcare settings with a smart phone. The quality of the camera in cell phones has improved dramatically, but a professional photographer's use of lighting and equipment will produce superior trial exhibits.

In one case, the LNC created an exhibit of photographs of a plaintiff who lost 80 pounds after a medical malpractice event. The LNC arranged them so the oldest photograph showing the plaintiff at a healthy weight was in the upper left corner of the display. The photo taken days before the plaintiff died was in the lower right corner. The pictures were laid out on a diagonal to show the change in the plaintiff (now decedent) who became unrecognizable by the time of death.

Video

A video taken by a patient, visitor, or other observer may be useful at trial. Freezing the video and taking a screenshot yields useful photographs, as well. The LNC may also be involved in observing surveillance video, such as that taken of a person who claimed to be incapacitated yet is observed running a marathon. With so many hidden cameras present in buildings and streets, the LNC may be involved in observing video taken during an incident. For example, a group of four prison guards removed a prisoner from the cell and pressed the prisoner facedown into a pillow. Video in the facility captured the incident, as well as the leisurely response of the infirmary nurses. The prisoner suffered anoxic brain damage. Had the case not settled, the attorney would have showed the video to the jury at trial.

The goal of a "day in the life" video, from a plaintiff's perspective, is to depict the involved and often uncomfortable care a plaintiff requires. Scenes may be video recorded at a hospital or rehab facility or at home. "Day in the life" videos do not need to capture an entire day and are usually edited to no more than 30 minutes of viewing time in order to maintain their impact on the jury. The LNC working with the plaintiff attorney may offer to plan the filming with the videographer to capture key aspects of the plaintiff's limitations.

Computer Animations

Animations used to teach a jury about anatomy or processes or to recreate an event can have a powerful impact. There are many elements of a case that can be brought to life, for example:

- the inside of a nursing home showing the many checkpoints a confused person would have to walk through to elope
- how a clot moves within the blood vessels on its way to the lungs
- the way a mechanical lift's defective sling broke and dropped a patient and
- the mechanism of injury when a motor vehicle passenger was propelled through a windshield

There are many computer animations available for purchase that are not case-specific, for example those that show normal anatomy or physiology. Case-specific animations are time-consuming and very expensive to produce. Attorneys and LNCs need to know the factors that will ensure the animations are admissible at trial including that the animation is supported by the testimony of an expert witness and the evidence and that it follows scientific principles.

Anatomical Images

Medical textbooks, peer-reviewed journal articles, guidelines promulgated by professional associations, drug labels, and authoritative Internet resources including online anatomical and other images can be used as resource materials when preparing anatomical images for use as demonstrative evidence. These resources aid the LNC's understanding of the medical issues in the preparation of effective demonstrative evidence or when consulting with an outside demonstrative evidence vendor. Medical experts testifying at trial will often recommend anatomical drawings or models that will assist them in teaching the jury.

Anatomical photographs or illustrations found on the Internet are either available at no charge or can be purchased and downloaded for use as demonstrative exhibits. Many sites require subscription activation to access information and photos or illustrations, but government-owned sites such as the National Institutes of Health (NIH) may have free resources for use as exhibits. Graphics may also be purchased and downloaded from online stock art vendors such as www.presentermedia.com, and stock anatomical exhibits can be purchased from medical exhibit companies such as www.adamimages.com, www.medicalexhibits.com, or www.precise-law.com.

When purchasing demonstrative evidence from exhibit companies, the LNC may encounter explicit instructions and limitations as to how images can be used. Copyright restrictions will apply, and the fee paid is not a purchase price but a usage license fee, typically licensed for use at only one trial. Images scanned from authoritative medical textbooks are sometimes used as exhibits but should only be used with adherence to the copyright regulations assigned by the medical publisher.

In many cases, stock demonstratives will not satisfy the needs and specifics of a particular medical subject. An expert witness is unable to explain improper technique during a surgery by utilizing stock depictions of the procedure, because usually it is illustrated as being performed properly. A custom illustration, anatomical model, or animation can convey important aspects of a surgery or procedure in which mistakes were allegedly made. (See Figure 37.13 for an example.) These custom, case-specific demonstratives should be the result of careful collaboration between the expert, attorney, LNC, and creative consultant (medical illustrator or animator). Custom-made demonstrative evidence requires time to create and revise the final exhibit until it is completely satisfactory to the expert intending to use it at trial.

Custom-made exhibits are more expensive than purchasing stock exhibits. Thus, on the plaintiff's side, the LNC should discuss the projected cost of the exhibit with the managing attorney to make sure the potential economic recovery is sufficient to justify the cost of the exhibit. On the defense side, the costs associated with any exhibits may need to be approved by the defendant's liability insurance carrier. Typically, the creative consultant provides a written cost estimate and schedule for completing the work. Copyright, number of draft revisions, and final format (e.g., printed exhibit, digital presentation, compact disc) can also be included in this proposal.

When outsourcing the preparation of demonstrative evidence, the LNC will assemble information, medical documents, or imaging needed by the creative consultant and work with the consultant on custom demonstratives such as medical illustrations, custom 3D models, or animations as approved by the attorney. See Figure 37.14, which depicts a severe injury to the cervical spine. Here, the LNC's careful attention to detail is needed to ensure the illustrator has created an accurate image.

Inflammation During Multiple Attempts at Intubation

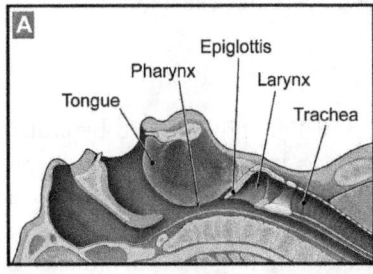
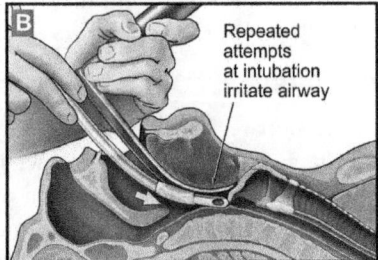
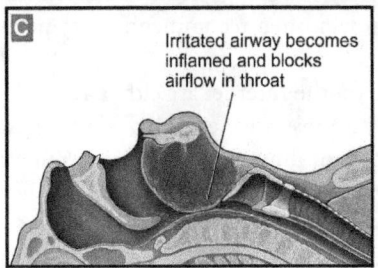
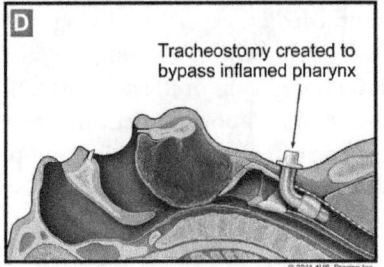

Figure 37.13 Inflammation During Multiple Attempts at Intubation.

Source: Created by Sean Dennin, AVS-Precise, Inc.

Cervical Spinal Cord Injury

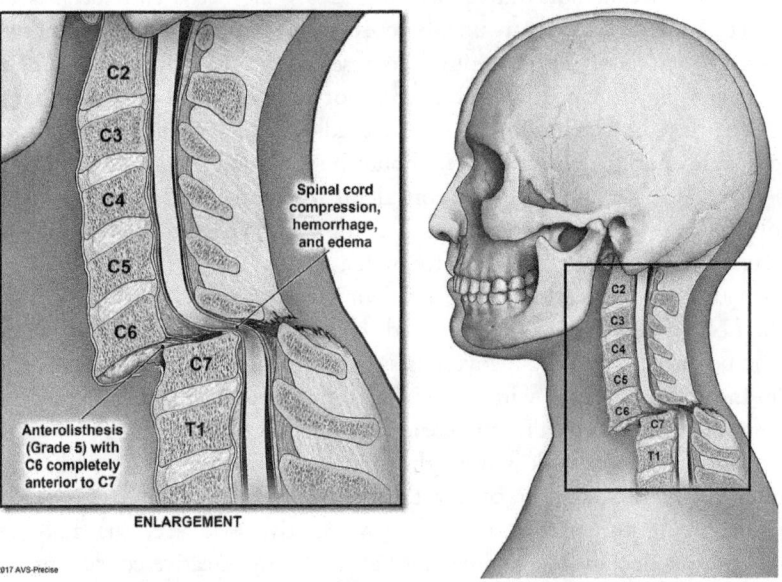

Figure 37.14 Cervical Spinal Cord Injury.

Source: Created by Sean Dennin, AVS-Precise, Inc.

Slide Presentations

Slide presentations help the jury comprehend key points and add variety to the presentation of testimony. An LNC serving as an expert fact witness, expert witness, or in a consulting role may be involved in preparing or supervising slide preparations. The tips in Box 37.1 provide design principles. The help function in the slide presentation software is a great resource for learning how to carry out these principles.

Box 37.1 Slide Design Principles

1. Learn how to use the slide master to create a uniform format for the slides. This feature allows the user to pick a font, center titles on a slide, select fonts for headers, and set up a footer with page numbers.
2. Use readable fonts such as Arial, Tahoma or Verdana. They should be readable at a distance of about 20 feet. Avoid script fonts or other non-standard fonts.
3. Color combinations are crucial for visibility. Use one of these combinations: black or dark letters on white background, black letters on yellow background, or white letters on black or dark blue background.
4. Warm colors draw attention to an important point. Red, orange, green, and yellow are effective. Cool colors, such as violet, blue, or green, are useful for backgrounds.
5. Avoid slides filled with bullet points. Instead, use images, diagrams, charts, or graphs to convey concepts.
6. Avoid clip art, which looks dated. Use modern icons.
7. Crop images to allow the viewer to focus on the important part of the image.
8. Keep the layout simple. Avoid busy designs with too many images on the slide.
9. Align words and images. Avoid centering an image, with a title over it. (This is visually uninteresting.)
10. Observe the direction of the image when placing words next to it. For example, if the image has a photograph of a person turned to one side, the direction of the image should lead to the text instead of to a blank area.
11. Use a variety of slide layouts.
    a. Place the title at the top of the slide and fill the rest with an image.
    b. Use a full slide image and superimpose words onto the image.
    c. Fill one side of the slide, top to bottom, with an image, and use the other part for words.
    d. Place text in the upper left and an image in the lower right of the slide.
12. Avoid using anything but conservative animations. Words that appear or fade in with a click are appropriate. Words that bounce on the screen, drop from the top, twirl around, or explode into pixels may not be acceptable to the judge who reviews the slide presentation in advance.
13. Add polish to the slides with semitransparent boxes to draw attention to words or hold the content of a slide together.
14. Format photographs to add subtle shadows.
15. Create a slide library so slides can be reused in future presentations.
16. Proofread the presentation. Ask another person to proofread it also.

Created by Pat Iyer

Summary

Effective demonstrative evidence is critical for ensuring the judge and jury understand the complex medical issues in a case. The LNC brings essential skills to the litigation process: the ability to teach, analyze, synthesize, and organize information. The litigation team benefits from the medical knowledge and detail-oriented eye of the LNC in the preparation of exhibits for demonstrative evidence. Medical illustrations, video snapshots, photographs, charts, etc. are valuable assets to support the attorney-client's case. Demonstrative evidence based on medical record and other facts will not only educate the attorney and triers of fact but also elevate the LNC's value as a key member of the legal team (Carlson & Walker, 2018).

References

Black's Law Dictionary Free Online Legal Dictionary 2nd ed. (n.d.). *The law dictionary*. (S. Danilina, Ed.). Retrieved from thelawdictionary.org.

Carlson, M., & Walker, J. (2018). Medical record fact witness and the use of medical illustration in LNC reports: When a picture IS worth a thousand words. *The Journal of Legal Nurse Consulting, 29*(3), 16–19.

Daubert v. Merrell Dow Pharmaceuticals, Inc. 509 U.S. 579 (1993).

Kumho Tire et al. v. Carmichael, et al. No. 97–1709 (1999).

Additional Reading

Federal Rule of Evidence 401. Test for relevant evidence, www.law.cornell.edu/rules/fre/rule_401.

Federal Rule of Evidence Rule 402. General admissibility of relevant evidence, www.law.cornell.edu/rules/fre/rule_402.

Federal Rule of Evidence Rule 403. Excluding relevant evidence for prejudice, confusion, waste of time, other reasons, www.law.cornell.edu/rules/fre/rule_403.

Federal Rule of Evidence Rule 602. Need for personal knowledge, www.law.cornell.edu/rules/fre/rule_602.

Federal Rule of Evidence Rule 901. Authenticating or identifying evidence, www.law.cornell.edu/rules/fre/rule_901.

Gonzalez, Ervin A. (2014). Demonstrative evidence, 14 *The Florida Bar Journal* 1.

Gonzalez, Ervin A., & Teal, Kyle B. (2015). No ideas but in things: A practitioner's look at demonstrative evidence, 89 *The Florida Bar Journal* 17.

Test Questions

1. What court decision was instrumental in changing the way evidence was reviewed?
   A. *Smith v. Jones*
   B. *Daubert v. Merrell Dow Pharmaceuticals, Inc.*
   C. *Webster v. Merriam*
   D. *Darrell v. Clarke Enterprises*
2. The main point to remember regarding the admissibility of evidence for legal proceedings is:
   A. Length
   B. Content
   C. Reliability
   D. Color
3. Which of the following is NOT an important aspect of the presentation style and use of graphics?
   A. Color
   B. Contrast
   C. Scale
   D. Age
4. Which of the following is likely to be the costliest type of exhibit to prepare?
   A. Page from medical record mounted on foam core board
   B. Table displayed on an optical projector
   C. Custom-made computer animation
   D. Slide presentation
5. Which of the following Federal Rules of Evidence refers to the definition of "relevant evidence"?
   A. FRE 104
   B. FRE 611
   C. FRE 401
   D. FRE 1008

Answers: 1. B, 2. C, 3. D, 4. C, 5. C

Chapter 38

Alternative Dispute Resolution

Arbitration, Mediation, and Other Settlement Modalities

Margaret M. Gallagher, RN, MSN, LNCC®, CLNC
Annalese H. Reese, Esq.
Paul K. Reese, Esq.

Contents

Objectives

- Define "alternative dispute resolution (ADR)"
- Define "arbitration" and compare and contrast the processes of binding arbitration and non-binding arbitration
- Discuss the role of the legal nurse consultant (LNC) in the arbitration process
- Define "mediation"
- Identify the steps in the mediation process
- Discuss the role of the LNC in the mediation process
- Identify the steps in preparing a settlement brochure for mediation
- Discuss other settlement methods

Introduction

Court dockets are more congested; the costs of lawsuits are on a dramatic rise; and judges are formally ordering parties to attempt to resolve their disputes through "alternative dispute resolution." Alternative dispute resolution has become an increasingly popular process within the United States justice system and is a method used to aid in resolving lawsuits outside of the courtroom. In its "Findings and Declaration of Policy" for the Alternative Dispute Resolution Act, 28 U.S.C. §§ 651–658, Congress noted that ADR may have the potential to provide a variety of benefits including reduction of the large backlogs of cases.

The United States Department of Justice (DOJ) Use and Benefits of Alternative Dispute Resolution Fiscal Year 2017 Report notes that success rates for voluntary ADR proceedings during the 2013–2017 time frame ranged from 69% to 82%. Success rates for court-ordered proceedings during the same time frame ranged from 52% to 77%. Monetary and time saving benefits were achieved in 57% to 77% of unresolved cases during the same reporting period. This DOJ report also shows ADR saved litigants millions of dollars and years of man-hours during the 2013–2017 reporting period (United States DOJ, 2018).

The Alternative Dispute Resolution Act defines "ADR" as "any process or procedure, other than an adjudication by a presiding judge, in which a neutral third party participates to assist in the resolution of issues in controversy, through processes such as early neutral evaluation, mediation, minitrial, and arbitration ..." (28 U.S.C. § 651(a)). Alternative dispute resolution also includes conciliation, cooperative problem solving, dispute panels, facilitation, fact-finding, interest-based problem solving and bargaining, settlement conferences, ombudsing, peer review, settlement negotiations, or any combination thereof. While ADR may be used in cases involving many types of issues, it is perhaps most useful in those cases involving personal injuries, medical malpractice, employment issues, financial institutions, and contract disputes. As healthcare and malpractice costs continue to rise, there is growing interest in tactics such as early apology, mediation, and arbitration in the medical arena (Sohn & Bal, 2012, p. 1370). In some states, litigation filed in court is automatically assigned before trial to ADR resolution.

There has been a general increase in all forms of ADR in recent years because of the numerous advantages ADR offers. The benefits of ADR are well-recognized and far reaching:

- Both sides typically avoid the cost of expensive litigation
- ADR allows a claim or dispute to be resolved in a timely fashion
- ADR methods tend to value and preserve the parties' relationship
- ADR is a future-looking means of resolving disputes without forcing a winning/losing mentality, fostering a sense of mutual benefit and
- ADR methods conserve judicial resources

(Goldberg, 2014, pp. 4–6)

This chapter focuses on the LNC's role in the two most common methods of ADR: arbitration and mediation. Other settlement modalities are also discussed.

Arbitration

Arbitration is historical and legally recognized as a process for the resolution of disputes outside the court system. The parties agree (or may be ordered by a court) to submit their controversy to an independent third party—an impartial person or panel of impartial persons often known as "arbitrators" or an "arbitral tribunal." The arbitrator's or panel's decision is referred to as the "award." Arbitration is an option for a lawsuit ready to go to trial in order to avoid a court trial or clogged court calendars (Garner, 2014). As noted in the Revised Uniform Arbitration Act, currently adopted by approximately one-third of the states:

(1) Arbitration, as a form of alternative dispute resolution, offers in many instances a more efficient and cost-effective alternative to court litigation

(2) The United States has a well-established federal policy in favor of arbitral dispute resolution, as identified both by the Federal Arbitration Act, 9 U.S.C. §1, *et seq.*, and the decisions of the Supreme Court of the United States

(3) Arbitration already provides participants with many of the same procedural rights and safeguards as traditional litigation, and ensuring that those rights and safeguards are guaranteed to participants will ensure that arbitration remains a fair and viable alternative to court litigation and guarantee that no party to an arbitration agreement is unfairly prejudiced by agreeing to an arbitration agreement or provision

(as noted in Myerson, 2015)

Arbitration may be voluntary, required by a dispute settlement provision in a contract between the parties, or mandated by statute or court order. Mandatory arbitration typically involves cases in which established contractual relations are present, such as labor–management disputes, insurance claims (personal injury), securities industry disputes, and auto accident injury cases in no-fault states[1] (Uniform Law Commission [ULC], 2018). Trade associations and professional insurance liability carriers utilize arbitration to resolve conflict as a matter of course. Often, parties select a retired judge or a respected attorney to serve as the arbitrator or panel member. Parties may also agree to rely on an established and experienced professional organization, such as the American Arbitration Association (AAA), to provide this alternative dispute resolution service. Many contracts include an arbitration clause specifically naming the AAA as the agreed-upon organization to oversee an arbitration.

The AAA is a not-for-profit organization with offices throughout the United States and is one of several arbitration organizations that administers arbitration proceedings. The AAA's services include assisting in the appointment of mediators and arbitrators, setting hearings, and providing users with information on dispute resolution options, including settlement through mediation (AAA, 2018). Arbitrators are often chosen in accordance with the parties' agreement. The AAA offers dispute resolution services abroad through its International Centre for Dispute Resolution (ICDR). Established in 1996, the ICDR provides conflict-management services in more than 80 countries (AAA, 2018).

There are two categories of arbitration—binding arbitration and non-binding arbitration. Each can be either mandatory or voluntary.

Binding Arbitration

Binding arbitration involves the agreed-upon submission of a dispute to a neutral party who hears the case and makes a decision in lieu of a traditional trial presided over by a judge or heard by a jury. The arbitrator's decision is final, binding, and enforceable in a court of law. The grounds for appealing or setting aside a binding arbitration decision are very limited and, sometimes, not available at all. If a person signs a contract that has a mandatory, binding arbitration agreement, that individual gives up the right to go to court, except to enforce the arbitration award (Alabama Center for Dispute Resolution, 2018).

Arbitrators typically have experience in the commercial or social area of dispute and have expertise and knowledge of the specific case, as provided by the arbitrating parties in written briefing statements and argument. The goal of the parties' submissions is to provide the arbitrator with a substantive factual and legal basis for rendering informed decisions and awards.

The trend toward arbitration in the past three decades has enabled corporations to insert arbitration clauses (requiring the submission of disputes to binding arbitration) into contracts with employees and customers (Stone & Colvin, 2015).

Non-binding Arbitration

Non-binding arbitration is one step above mediation in the spectrum of ADR processes. A non-binding process is more formal and involves more mandatory procedures than mediation, which is discussed in greater detail later in the chapter. Indeed, non-binding arbitration resembles conventional arbitration in that some discovery and briefing usually take place, and there are often formal hearings at which evidence is presented and witnesses are examined and cross-examined. A non-binding arbitration award differs from a traditional arbitration award only in that it is not binding. However, in some circumstances, it could become binding. Many states, such as Florida, sponsor ADR programs that offer non-binding arbitration, sometimes for cases valued under a certain amount.[2] These programs usually provide that the award *will* become final unless one of the parties files a request for a new trial *de novo* within the time provided in the statute or rules (Bennett, 2006).

Judicial Enforcement of Arbitration and Arbitration Agreements

Although arbitration was originally intended to be used for disputes between commercial entities of similar sophistication and bargaining power, it has increasingly been extended to disputes between parties of significantly unequal negotiating position such as consumer disputes, civil rights, and other employment disputes (Szalai, 2016).

It is now well accepted that the Federal Arbitration Act (FAA) pre-empts state law. In fact, the FAA (2012) specifies that arbitration agreements are "valid, irrevocable, and enforceable save upon such grounds as exist at law or in equity for the revocation of any contract" (9 U.S.C. §§ 1–16, § 2). Arbitration agreements are binding except in very specific circumstances.[3]

When buying a new car, health insurance, or any other product that requires a written purchase agreement, an arbitration clause is typically included. They are in hundreds of millions of consumer contracts, according to the National Association of Consumer Advocates. Amazon, Groupon, Netflix, and Verizon are among the companies to name a few whose contracts have the clauses. These agreements are in the fine print of terms for car loans and leases, credit cards, checking accounts, insurance, investing accounts, student loans, and even certain employment and nursing home agreements (Walker, 2015). Courts currently enforce binding, pre-dispute arbitration agreements routinely, and as one should expect, medical malpractice arbitration agreements are not an exception (Larson, 2016).[4]

There is a widespread belief that alternative dispute resolution methods, particularly mandatory binding arbitration agreements, have become the rule in healthcare delivery (Rolph, Moller, & Rolph, 1997). Because binding arbitration decisions are final and subject to judicial enforcement, the arbitration process may be covered by state statutes that outline specific protections, guidelines, and warnings to the participants about the consequences of entering into arbitration, as well as the validity of medical malpractice arbitration agreements (Shieh, 2014, pp. 1808–1809).

In Texas, for example, Vernon's Annotated Statutes, Article 4590i, § 15.01(a) (2018) states as follows:

> SUBCHAPTER J. ARBITRATION AGREEMENTS
> Sec. 74.451. ARBITRATION AGREEMENTS.
> (a) No physician, professional association of physicians, or other health care provider shall request or require a patient or prospective patient to execute an agreement to arbitrate a health care liability claim unless the form of agreement delivered to the patient contains a written notice in 10-point boldface type clearly and conspicuously stating:

> UNDER TEXAS LAW, THIS AGREEMENT IS INVALID AND OF NO LEGAL EFFECT UNLESS IT IS ALSO SIGNED BY AN ATTORNEY OF YOUR OWN CHOOSING. THIS AGREEMENT CONTAINS A WAIVER OF IMPORTANT LEGAL RIGHTS, INCLUDING YOUR RIGHT TO A JURY. YOU SHOULD NOT SIGN THIS AGREEMENT WITHOUT FIRST CONSULTING WITH AN ATTORNEY.

The Texas statute also states that violations of the above section by a physician or professional association of physicians constitute violations of the Medical Malpractice Act. This action would be subject to enforcement provisions and sanctions.

Arbitration agreements mandating arbitration of medical malpractice cases have been upheld in other states as well (Larson, 2016, p. 74). As of 2018, 20 states (with Massachusetts pending) have adopted the Uniform Arbitration Act (2000), which may apply to healthcare arbitration agreements (ULC, 2018).

The Arbitration Process—Generally

Binding arbitration involves submitting a contested matter to a designated arbitrator, a process generally governed by three mechanisms: the terms of the arbitration agreement, the laws related to that arbitration agreement, and applicable rules of arbitration procedure.

Terms of the Parties' Contract and Agreement to Arbitrate

Arbitration is a "creature of contract." As a result, under the FAA and equivalent state laws, the specific terms under which arbitration will occur are typically determined by the agreement of the parties. In many instances, parties choose to adopt the rules of an arbitration-sponsoring organization such as the AAA. But parties are also free to adopt their own ad hoc procedures (sometimes based on elements of the rules of an arbitration-sponsoring organization) or to use the rules of an arbitration-sponsoring organization as a base and modify those rules to suit their needs (Bennett, 2013, p. 221).

Laws Related to the Arbitration Agreement

The FAA applies to the parties' agreement to arbitrate disputes whether or not it is expressly mentioned in that agreement. Although the FAA applies generally and broadly, the U.S. Supreme Court has recognized that the FAA permits the contracting parties to change the arbitration process to suit their needs if the parties' intent to do so is expressly reflected or incorporated into their agreement. The Court has held that the parties may add portions of a state's arbitration law to the FAA's provisions or opt out of the FAA's provisions entirely (Trantina, 2015).

An example of a state statute which may address the arbitration process is noted in the earlier discussion of Texas's arbitration agreements statute. Some states have adopted the Revised Uniform Arbitration Act, which also addresses the arbitration process (National Conference of Commissioners on Uniform State Laws, 2000).

Applicable Rules of Arbitration Procedure

Private arbitrators or arbitration-sponsoring organizations, such as JAMS[5] (formerly known as Judicial Arbitration and Mediation Services, Inc.), often establish formal written rules and procedures for arbitrations they conduct. For example, JAMS's "Comprehensive Arbitration Rules and Procedures" address various issues including commencing the arbitration, service, notice, withdrawal, preliminary matters, pre-hearing submissions, the hearing, awards, enforcement of awards, and confidentiality (JAMS, 2014).

Arbitration agreements are involved in numerous legal actions related to nursing home disputes and are the subject of ever-evolving federal regulations related to the use of arbitration agreements in nursing homes (Center for Medicare Advocacy, n.d.).

The Arbitration Process in Nursing Home Litigation

In a lawsuit involving an alleged injury in a nursing home, the first and primary task for the LNC is to review the admissions paperwork, or administrative file, to locate and secure a copy of any relevant arbitration agreement.

Is there a Valid Arbitration Agreement?

An arbitration agreement in the long-term care (LTC) setting is typically in writing. Some nursing home admission contracts may include language addressing arbitration, but more often, a separate, stand-alone arbitration agreement exists. In either case, depending on the administrative procedures of the respective LTC facility, arbitration provisions most often are located in the "administrative" file with other admissions documents—not as part of the resident's "medical chart." If an executed arbitration agreement is located, it should be brought to the attention of counsel. Other documents related to the execution of the arbitration agreement may be very important.

Did the Signatory of the Arbitration Agreement have Capacity or Authority to Sign?

On some occasions, the resident who is admitted to a nursing home may be *non compos mentis*, a Latin phrase meaning legally insane or not competent to manage one's own affairs (Legal Information Institute, n.d.). In that case, the resident's signature on an arbitration agreement may not be legally binding. It is relevant, then, whether the resident had legal capacity or mental competence to execute the arbitration agreement. This is discussed in more detail below.

In some cases, a family member or legally designated representative, typically with a power of attorney, will execute an arbitration agreement during the admission process to a nursing home. A power of attorney is a writing or other record that grants authority to an agent to act in the place of the principal (Uniform Power of Attorney Act, 2006).

What Documents are Relevant to the Determination of a Resident's Capacity or Representative's Legal Authority to Execute an Arbitration Agreement?

a. **Pre-Admission Screening:** is a standardized document created at the hospital or other institution that is prepared and verified BEFORE coming to the nursing home and typically contains (i) demographics such as the existence of a guardianship, power of attorney, medical power of attorney, living will; (ii) medical assessment; (iii) mental illness/mental retardation assessment (explicitly/implicitly contains data regarding a resident's decision-making capacity); and (iv) physician recommendations.

b. **Admission Record:** identifies: (i) emergency contacts and perhaps a power of attorney (discussed further below); and (ii) diagnosis information (e.g., Alzheimer's, dementia).

c. **Physician Determination of Capacity:** certifies whether a patient has sufficient mental or physical capacity to appreciate the nature and implication of healthcare decisions and, if incapacitated, identifies the relevant diagnosis.

d. **Medical records from discharging provider:** are records from the resident's last care before LTC residency (often a hospital) and may contain information related to capacity issues such as medications or diagnoses which raise a question of capacity. Aside from medical conditions, which provide more apparent clues about mental infirmity, the LNC should note medications, quantities, and interactions.

e. **Power of Attorney (POA):** is a legal document giving one person (called an "agent" or "attorney-in-fact") the power to act for another person (the "principal"). The agent can have broad legal authority or limited authority to make legal decisions on behalf of the principal, including the principal's property and finances. A POA may grant express or implied authority to sign the arbitration agreement.

f. **Court-ordered Guardianship:** is a formal appointment by a local court of an individual as guardian or conservator of the resident or resident's estate. Typically a formal court order will be entered; some or all of the proceedings may be sealed.

In addition to securing the arbitration agreement and gathering necessary information for a preliminary assessment of the resident's legal capacity or POA's legal authority, the LNC should request and inspect admission and administrative forms, patient information forms, and contractual service forms from all of the resident's relevant medical care facilities to determine whether they contain arbitration clauses or other alternative dispute resolution clauses. Medical care facilities should encompass a broad spectrum of providers or related enterprise entities and include, among others, hospitals, nursing homes, medical device facilities, pharmacies, ambulance/medical transport, diagnostic study suites, physical therapy, laboratories, cyber health care practice such as telemedicine, managed healthcare organizations, health plans, healthcare insurance, and doctor's offices—in short, any care provider whose care may be connected to a culpable injury (Mal & Brenner, 2010; Sacopulos & Segal, 2009, pp. 427–433).

Initiating and Conducting an Arbitration

Often the role of the LNC employed at a law firm is to initiate the process of preparing the submission to the arbitrator(s). For example, in a case in which the AAA is the arbitrator, the initial process is accomplished by following established AAA procedures:

1. Log onto the AAA's website (www.adr.org) to determine where a local state office can be found.
2. Submit names, addresses, and phone numbers of the LTC facility's liability insurer, claimant, and their attorneys or representatives.
3. Complete the case, claim, or docket numbers.
4. Provide a brief synopsis of the claim along with the dollar amount involved in the case.
5. Add any additional information that may assist the AAA to position the case for arbitration or mediation. At this point, the parties will stipulate whether the arbitrator's decision will be binding or non-binding.

Once an agreement to arbitrate is established, the AAA appoints an experienced arbitrator from its panel of neutral attorneys. A biographical sketch of the arbitrator is sent to all parties to review and, if a conflict of interest is identified, to object. Following the appointment of an arbitrator, a hearing is scheduled at a convenient location.

Although the arbitration hearing is less formal than a court trial, the process is as important to the parties as a trial. Hearings are conducted in a manner that affords a fair presentation of the case by both parties. Opening statements are made to describe the case and detail what each party is seeking. This aids the arbitrator in understanding the relevance of the testimony that will be presented and of the decision being sought. The arbitrator decides what evidence or testimony is relevant in understanding the issues and can reject evidence deemed unnecessary or even prejudicial. The claiming party customarily presents first; each party states its position, trying to convince the arbitrator of the correctness of that position. This is not the strict "burden of proof" that would have to be met in a civil court trial. Witnesses are utilized to clarify issues and identify documents and exhibits. Cross-examination is permitted. Closing statements include a summary of the facts and arguments as well as refutation of points made by the opposing party.

The arbitrator closes the hearing and usually has approximately 30 days to review all the evidence and testimony in order to determine an appropriate decision and award. The award is a brief statement detailing which party will be providing a specific relief. This decision must be adhered to in a binding arbitration.

Similar to litigation, the LNC assists in gathering and preparing demonstrative and medical evidence relevant to the case. The LNC may also be tasked with identifying, locating, and interacting with medical experts, as well as searching for relevant medical literature. If attorneys choose to have witnesses and experts interviewed prior to the arbitration hearing, the LNC may assist to educate these individuals and verify they understand the format of arbitration and the importance of their testimony. For more information on the role of the LNC at trial, see Chapter 39.

The Mediation Process

Mediation is, by far, the preferred process for most litigants considering ADR (Feinberg, 1989, p. 5).[6]

> During the last thirty years the use of mediation has expanded beyond its century-long home in collective bargaining to become an integral and growing part of the processes of dispute resolution in the courts, public agencies, community dispute resolution programs, and the commercial and business communities, as well as among private parties engaged in conflict. Public policy strongly supports this development. Mediation fosters the early resolution of disputes. The mediator assists the parties in negotiating a settlement that is specifically tailored to their needs and interests. The parties' participation in the process and control over the result contributes to greater satisfaction on their part. ... Increased use of mediation also diminishes the unnecessary expenditure of personal and institutional resources for conflict resolution, and promotes a more civil society. For this reason, hundreds of state statutes establish mediation programs in a wide variety of contexts and encourage their use.
> (National Conference of Commissioners on Uniform State Laws, 2003, para. 1–2)

Mediation is a voluntary and, typically, confidential[7] means of dispute resolution without handing over the decision-making power to someone else (such as a judge, jury, or arbitrator). It is an attempt to settle a legal dispute through active participation of a third party (mediator) who works to find mutually agreeable points between the participants in order to facilitate an agreed resolution. The mediator does not make findings, nor does the mediator tell the opposing parties what to do. The mediator does not formally draw legal conclusions or make a formal decision and award; the mediator does not formally judge which party is right or wrong.[8] Control over the outcome of the case remains with the involved parties who agree to try and resolve their differences through a negotiated settlement agreement (Studdert, Mello, & Brennan, 2004). Mediation has become very common in the resolution of domestic relations disputes, such as divorce, child custody, and visitation.

Mediation has also become more frequent in contract and tort cases related to healthcare claims.[9] In this forum, the plaintiff and defendant agree to conduct a settlement conference before an impartial third party known as a mediator. The case needs to have reached a mature status—exhibits having been collected and discovery nearing completion—to be ready for mediation.

The financial cost of mediation is far less than litigating the matter in court. Mediation may achieve early settlement and an end to the anxiety of litigation and its often unpredictable results. Mediation also saves judicial resources and is often ordered by the judge.

Retired judges and attorneys with the appropriate legal experience, special expertise, and training offer services as mediators. In some states, non-attorneys with training in mediation proceedings and expertise in a specific field of practice (e.g., physicians, nurses, psychologists, educators) make excellent mediators. The mediator's fee is agreed upon in advance by all parties.

Mediators use appropriate techniques and skills to open and improve dialogue between disputants. Although the mediator is an impartial third party, it is important to educate and inform the mediator about the issues of the case prior to the settlement conference. One tool frequently used by the parties is a settlement brochure, which is discussed in depth later in this chapter. Such brochures are confidential submissions of the separate parties (*ex parte*—from one party only) to the mediator and are typically not exchanged between the parties. They ideally will emphasize the submitting party's strengths and the opponents' weaknesses that are likely to reflect the potential outcome in the courtroom. The mediator can study the brochure to analyze, identify, and learn about the factual and legal issues in the dispute. The ideal result of mediation is for the mediator to facilitate negotiation and persuade both sides to meet somewhere on middle ground, thus resolving the claim absent a jury trial.

Agreements to mediate, mediation rules, and court-based referral orders may require disclosure of information by all parties. Mediators may also have express or implied powers to direct the parties to produce certain case-related documents or reports. In court-referred mediations, the parties are usually required to exchange all material normally available through discovery or disclosure rules were the matter to proceed to a court hearing (Omer, 2009).

During mediation, the settlement conference itself often has a friendly atmosphere. At the beginning of the settlement conference, all parties typically meet together with the mediator, and counsel for each side presents a brief oral synopsis of the case. The parties then proceed to separate conference rooms for confidential caucuses between the mediator and the respective parties. Meeting privately with each party, the mediator strives to influence the opposing parties to adjust their respective expectations, focusing on the strengths and weaknesses of each party's claim. The ultimate goal is to resolve the differences between the parties and reach a settlement that is satisfactory to both sides. For successful mediation to occur, the presence of party representatives who possess authority to finalize settlement agreements is a prerequisite.

The following activities and discussions can assist in preparing for the mediation process; however, not all will apply to every mediation:

- Is mediation the right dispute resolution process at this time? Are the parties ready to settle? Has the court established a time frame to conduct mediation?
- Readiness has great importance. Overwhelming emotions may render objective decision-making extremely difficult. In some cases, an injury may not have had sufficient time to heal, making any residual loss difficult to quantify. Precise diagnosis, enlightened prognostications, and ample expert support enable the parties to more accurately determine the "value" of the matter.
- Although entering into a mediation to settle the entire dispute may seem inappropriate, it may be appropriate to mediate particular issues.
- Identify who should participate in the mediation. Laws give decision-making power to certain individuals, typically parties to the dispute or their designated agents. These individuals are essential to the mediation, and their attendance at the proceedings is crucial.

Other important participants may include attorneys, accountants, experts, interpreters, or spouses.

■ Convening a mediation session requires as much care as convening any other important meeting. Consider a location that best fosters settlement. Do any participants have special needs? What date and time works best? How much time might mediation require?

■ The task of selecting the right mediator occurs more readily when participants allow time to analyze the dispute. What is the dispute about? By identifying disagreements, parties clarify the issues in dispute. Is it possible there is missing information which, if shared by all parties, would settle the matter quickly? The law and facts surrounding the dispute provide a natural parameter for selection of a mediator experienced in issues related to that controversy.

■ What information do participants require in order to make good decisions?

■ Do pictures, documents, corporate records, receipts, medical records, bank statements, expert reports, and so on exist that parties need to gather, copy, and bring to the mediation?

With all of the information at hand at the mediation, one may avoid the need to adjourn the meeting to a later date while the parties gather other information.

The LNC's Role in Mediation

The LNC often plays a very visible role in mediation, both before and during the settlement conference. In a medical malpractice case, for example, an LNC could be employed by either the plaintiff or defense to audit the opposing party's presentation during mediation to detect discrepancies or inaccuracies. The LNC would, of course, privately relay such information to the employing attorney. The LNC can also serve as an informed educator at the mediation forum. When complex medical issues are introduced, the mediator sometimes needs more information on the standard of care, the medical issues in dispute, or explanations of medical terminology. The LNC can be a resource liaison to the mediator.

An LNC can offer valuable assistance in mediations as an educator regarding the medical issues of a malpractice or personal injury case. The following outlines the medical aspects of a mediation presentation:

1. Overview of the case
2. Health history of the plaintiff
3. Injuries sustained and definitions and
4. Questions and clarifications

Production of a Settlement Brochure

Prior to the settlement conference, the LNC is a major contributor to the production of a settlement brochure, which is also frequently referenced as "Confidential Submission of Plaintiff [Defendant] to the Mediator." The term "brochure" is somewhat of a misnomer. Brochures, as the term is typically used, are often simple trifold documents. Here, a brochure used as a settlement tool may be several inches thick and bound with dividers. The settlement brochure can vary in size depending on the issues and evidence to be presented and any length restrictions posed by the mediator. Both plaintiff and defense counsels prepare brochures, although the plaintiff's brochure is usually more extensive. A settlement brochure serves three purposes:

1. It aids the legal team in focusing on specific medical issues that may later be raised at trial
2. It educates the mediator as to the strengths and weaknesses of the medical aspects of the case and
3. It demonstrates that the parties are prepared for trial

The Plaintiff's Brochure

A number of formats are used in preparing an effective brochure from the plaintiff's perspective. The LNC may choose to divide the document into six sections titled Table of Contents, Brief Statement of the Case, Detailed Discussion of Medical Management Issues, Negligence, Damages and Injuries, and Exhibits.

1. The Table of Contents refers the reader to the pages where specified information is located.
2. The Brief Statement of the Case is a precise statement of position. An example is: "Plaintiff collapsed and died from cardiac arrest while waiting to be evaluated at ABC Hospital." Avoid conveying a description of the case in the statement. The theme of the case can sometimes be used in the brief statement.
3. The Detailed Statement of Medical Management Issues should be prepared by the LNC in consultation with the attorney. An in-depth study of medical records and medical references enables the LNC to prepare a detailed synopsis of the medical issues.
4. Negligence or gross negligence can also be addressed by the LNC. Breaches in the standard of care or deviations from policies and procedures fall within the area of the LNC's expertise. Expert reports and experts' curricula vitae are also presented in this section. Authoritative papers, guidelines, and standards written by specialty or other organizations should also be included.
5. The LNC may also have input into the section on damages and injuries. The one purpose of this section is to humanize the plaintiff, showing the impact of the injuries on the individual and the family—what they can and cannot do anymore. An example is a plaintiff whose left leg was amputated. An avid skier, the plaintiff used to take yearly vacations with family during the holidays to ski, snowboard, and cross-country ski. The settlement brochure would include photographs of last year's ski vacation. Poetic license is often used to dramatize the plaintiff's injuries and damages. The damages section should include an itemized accounting of the economic losses (e.g., medical expenses, lost earnings, property damage, etc.). An offer of settlement is also noted.
6. The section for exhibits consists of pertinent medical records (appropriately highlighted), medical expense invoices, funeral and burial expense invoices, photographs, greeting cards, letters, school records, employment records, certificates, graphs, charts, and so on. This section contains references to supporting data for the brochure. These exhibits are numbered and may be referred to in the narrative of the brochure by number.

The Defendant's Brochure

A defense brochure can be divided into six similar sections:

1. The Table of Contents refers the reader by page number to the desired section.
2. The Brief Statement of the Case is offered from the defendant's viewpoint.

3. The Detailed Statement of Medical Management Issues may or may not be addressed by the defense. In its place, the defense may wish to insert the defendant healthcare professional's qualifications, experience, and a listing of professional and community services.
4. The negligence or gross negligence issue may be addressed by the defense by discussing the defense expert's opinions about the standard of care. Any contributory or comparative negligence of the plaintiff could be discussed in this section as well.
5. The section for damages and injuries could be used by the defense to address any mitigating factors.
6. The exhibits section may or may not be applicable for defense brochures. In general, a settlement brochure may present any factor or aspect of a case on which either side wishes to focus. There are no rules or requirements. This is a place where the evidence can be presented creatively for effect. Mediators are generally experienced in trial tactics and strategies, and while creativity may be helpful and appreciated, one should avoid hyperbole and over-reaching, as mediation is a process of narrowing rather than expanding differences.

Other Settlement Modalities

Minitrials

A minitrial is not a trial but, rather, a settlement process that goes beyond the ADR. The parties present highly summarized versions of their respective cases to a panel of officials (i.e., representatives of each party—usually high-level business executives) who have authority to settle the dispute. The presentation generally takes place outside of the courtroom in a private forum. After the parties have presented their best case, the panel convenes and tries to settle the matter. The process is particularly suitable for larger, more complex disputes in which there are points of law or substantial issues of fact. Typically, a case that might last several weeks or months in a courtroom would be dealt with in a minitrial within two or more days.

A minitrial represents a pre-trial alternative attempt to settle the matter before lengthy trial begins. It is usually conducted after formal litigation has been undertaken and involves the presentation of each side's case, usually without live testimony, with opening and closing statements and an outline of evidence intended to be produced at trial. Parties of a lawsuit generally stipulate to "stay" pending litigation (to put a hold on further advancement of the litigation) until the minitrial is concluded. The outcome of the minitrial is generally confidential and advisory only. The parties may proceed to trial if settlement negotiations fail (Bennett, 2001).[10]

Focus Groups and Mock Juries

Focus groups and mock juries can be used to develop the themes of a case before entering into settlement discussions or going to trial. They can give the trial team valuable information about what a disinterested third party feels about the facts of a case, the plaintiffs, the defendants, and the experts. This information can be crucial to strategic planning and development of the case. Such sources of information can help to determine the overall chances of obtaining a satisfactory verdict or judgment. This impartial information can assist the LNC and attorney in evaluating complex medical issues in the case to see whether additional explanations or evidence are necessary. The legal team may use a variety of consultants to aid them in these processes, including trial consultants.[11]

Typically, focus groups are more helpful early in the discovery process and allow attorneys to present different themes of the case and strategies to a panel. After presenting their theories, the attorneys receive feedback from the panel about which ideas were appropriately conveyed and which could be improved or further developed.

A mock trial, on the other hand, is performed toward the end of the litigation process and allows the litigation team to present a full trial or parts of a trial to a pool of potential jurors. A mock trial begins where the actual trial begins—with a conflict or dispute that the parties have been unable to resolve on their own. Most mock trials use some general rules of evidence and procedure, an explanation of the basic facts, and brief statements for each witness.

Mock jury trials are usually used in cases that involve either a large dollar demand or multiple parties, such as class action suits. The LNC or legal team works with marketing firms that gather a sample of 50–80 persons representative of the demographic area where the trial is to be held. These individuals, who may be randomly selected, receive payment for spending one or two days listening to and observing the mock trial. Simplified steps in a mock trial are as follows:

- Opening statement: First, the prosecutor (in a criminal case) or the plaintiff attorney (in a civil case) presents what the evidence will be and what the evidence will show. The defendant's attorney follows with an explanation of what the defense evidence will be and what the evidence will show.
- Plaintiff's case: Witnesses are called to testify, and physical evidence is introduced. Each witness called is cross-examined by the defense.
- Defendant's case: Witnesses are called to testify, and physical evidence is introduced. Each witness called is cross-examined by the plaintiff.
- Closing statements: An attorney for each party reviews the evidence presented and asks for a favorable decision.
- Jury instructions: The Judge explains to the jury the appropriate rules of law that they are to consider in weighing the evidence. The prosecution or plaintiff attorney must meet the burden of proof in order to prevail.

The jurors may record their responses on a computerized handheld device, and the information is entered into a database for future statistical analysis by the trial team. The LNC may be involved with the statistical analysis of the material or may role-play the expert witness to the jury.

After the closing arguments, the mock jury breaks into smaller groups for deliberation. Often, members of the trial team sit behind one-way mirrors to observe how the "jurors" discuss the testimony. Each group renders a decision (verdict). The verdicts are important, because they provide a representation of what an actual jury may render at trial. If all deliberating groups render a higher dollar amount than expected by the defense, then the insurance company will likely be compelled to settle the case.

The Medical Review Panel

The Medical Review Panel process is a review of the claim by a panel of healthcare providers. The process is intended to reduce the number of medical malpractice lawsuits by allowing the patient to receive an early opinion about whether or not the healthcare provider met the standard of care (Louisiana Medical Mutual Insurance Company, 2018). According to a 2014 report of the National Conference of State Legislatures (NCSL), 17 jurisdictions have requirements that medical liability or malpractice cases be heard by a screening panel before trial (NCSL, 2014a).

The goals of such panels are as follows:

- Reduction of the court's caseload
- Reduction of the costs of medical malpractice litigation
- Prevention, when possible, of the filing of court actions against healthcare providers and their employees for professional liability situations where the facts do not permit at least a reasonable inference of malpractice and
- Provision of an objective expert view for both plaintiff and defense counsel. The panel's decision may induce a settlement or convince a plaintiff to reconsider filing a lawsuit. Expensive litigation in court is thus avoided.

The LNC helps prepare the case for the panel presentation in the same way the LNC prepares it for mediated settlement conferences or trial. The LNC may attend the panel presentation and play a vital support role helping to detect errors in the opposition's case presentation and analyzing the strengths and weaknesses of the case.

Apology Laws

Saying "I'm sorry" are two words people have come to expect from other individuals. Physicians and nurses use these words often in practice. For example, a physician may say "I'm sorry" when relaying that the pathology report confirms a malignancy, and a nurse often says "I'm sorry" if an intravenous medication causes burning. These examples reflect healthcare professionals' empathetic way of communicating. The complex issues surrounding medical malpractice liability often prohibit a healthcare professional from expressing empathy for a patient. Further, directives from insurers and employers in the healthcare industry often disallow physicians and nurses from apologizing when a mistake is made. However, Apology Laws were enacted to allow healthcare professionals to issue an apology and not automatically be found liable, because the laws make the apology inadmissible in subsequent malpractice trials.

Massachusetts was the first state to enact an apology law in 1986 (Cohen, 2004, pp. 21–22). The premise was that patients and their family would value the open human communication and not pursue litigation. This premise was supported by studies at the University of Michigan Health System, which instituted a disclosure and apology program that resulted in fewer medical malpractice claims and lower legal costs. As of 2014, 36 states, the District of Columbia, and Guam have provisions regarding medical professionals making apologies or sympathetic gestures (NCSL, 2014b).

An LNC should be aware these laws vary from state to state similar to state nurse practice acts. It is important that an LNC understand that state statutes have different terminology such as "apology with the admission of fault" (otherwise known as apology) and "apology without admission of fault" (otherwise known as sympathy) (Klauer, 2015).

In 2018, a study conducted at Vanderbilt University put forth that:

> The underlying assumption regarding the potential efficacy of these laws is that, after receiving an apology, patients will be less likely to pursue a malpractice claim and will be more likely to settle those claims that are filed. However, once a patient has been made aware that the physician has committed a medical error, the patient's incentive to pursue a claim may increase even though the apology itself cannot be introduced as

evidence. The net effect on medical malpractice liability costs could be in either direction. Despite apology laws' status as the most popular, recently enacted tort reform and one of the most widespread tort reforms in the country, there is little evidence that they achieve their goal of litigation reduction.

(McMichael, Van Horn, & Viscusi, 2018, p. 1)

Strengths and Weaknesses of ADR

Advantages of ADR include:

- Far less time to reach a final resolution than if the matter were to go to trial
- Usually (but not always) costs significantly less money
- More flexibility (with arbitration) in choosing what rules will be applied to the dispute. (The parties can choose to apply relevant industry standards, domestic law, the law of a foreign country, a unique set of rules used by the arbitration service, or even religious law, in some cases) and
- The choice by parties to have their dispute arbitrated or mediated by a person who is an expert in the relevant field, saving a great deal of time and money typically spent educating the judge and jury, just so they can make an informed decision

(Lorman, 2018)

The disadvantages of ADR are that it:

- Typically resolves disputes that only involve money
- (Arbitration) Cannot require one party to perform or refrain from a specific act
- May not include some of the procedural safeguards available in court, such as liberal discovery
- Offers very limited opportunity for appeal or other judicial review of an arbitrator's decision
  - Some arbitration services provide a process for internal appeals, which generally occur when the arbitration agreement is invalid such as when the consent to arbitrate is obtained by fraud or force
  - Though a difficult standard to meet, if the decision of the arbitrator is patently unfair, it will not be enforced and
  - The fact that the arbitrator made a decision that the court would not have made is not, by itself, a basis to overturn the decision

(Lorman, 2018)

Research continues to test the efficacy of ADR. According to David Sellinger, a Washington, DC attorney and mediation proponent, "[l]itigators in today's economic environment have to think about ADR in most every case they handle" (Hoffman, 1999, p. 30). Choosing to utilize one of the various methods of ADR can be a matter of economically achieving the right results for all parties. Attorneys must decide with their clients how best to proceed with a case, while at the same time evaluating their clients' satisfaction and desire to create solutions and participate in the ADR process.

Arbitration has been widely accepted as an enforceable alternative to the civil justice system for decades. The FAA was signed into law by President Calvin Coolidge back in 1925. Now, over

90 years later, issues surrounding arbitration are being hotly debated in many courts around the country. Probably the most hotly debated issue regarding arbitration is the waiver of the parties' right to trial by jury (Lowe, 2008).

The most recent federal arbitration legislation efforts continue to establish that a pre-dispute arbitration agreement is not valid or enforceable if it requires arbitration of an employment, consumer, antitrust, or civil rights dispute (9 U.S.C. § 1, *et seq.*, 2018). Further, the validity and enforceability of an agreement to arbitrate shall be determined by a court, under federal law, rather than an arbitrator, irrespective of whether the party resisting arbitration challenges the arbitration agreement specifically or in conjunction with other terms of the contract containing such agreement (H.R. 1374, 2017–2018).

With regard to nursing home litigation, two recent decisions by the U.S. Supreme Court have specifically enforced mandatory arbitration agreements in nursing homes in West Virginia and Kentucky. Both decisions emphasize the lynchpin application of the Federal Arbitration Act (9 U.S.C. § 2). Legal nurse consultants working on nursing home cases involving an executed arbitration agreement may find the following cases to be applicable: *Kindred Nursing Centers L.P. v. Clark*, 137 S. Ct. 1421, 1424 (2017), and *Marmet Health Care Center, Inc. v. Brown*, 565 U.S. 530 (2012).

Summary

An LNC, together with an attorney, can provide the best representation for the client. Working to achieve a win–win outcome can be a rewarding experience for a nurse preparing a case to be presented before an alternative forum of adjudication.

Notes

1. Twelve states have true no-fault auto insurance, including: Florida, Hawaii, Kansas, Kentucky, Massachusetts, Michigan, Minnesota, New Jersey, New York, North Dakota, Pennsylvania, Utah, and Puerto Rico (Insurance Information Institute, 2014).
2. For example, please see Fla. Stat § 44.103(2): "A court, pursuant to rules adopted by the Supreme Court, may refer any contested civil action filed in a circuit or county court to nonbinding arbitration."
3.
    A court may invalidate an arbitration agreement based on "generally applicable contract defenses," but not on legal rules that "apply only to arbitration or that derive their meaning from the fact that an agreement to arbitrate is at issue[.]" The [FAA] thus preempts any state rule that discriminates on its face against arbitration or that covertly accomplishes the same objective by disfavoring contracts that have the defining features of arbitration agreements.
    Kindred Nursing Centers L.P. v. Clark, 137 S. Ct. 1421, 1424 (2017) (citing *AT&T Mobility LLC v. Concepcion*, 563 U.S. 333, 339 (2011))

4. See *Marmet Health Care v. Brown*, 132 S. Ct. 1201, 1203 (2012) ("The [FAA] statute's text contains no exception for personal-injury or wrongful-death claims").
5. JAMS represents itself as the largest private alternative dispute resolution provider in the world.
6. Among the various alternative dispute resolution methods, mediation stands out as particularly advantageous. Mediation has several special features, including being informal, flexible, and completely voluntary and nonbinding. These make it preferable not only to litigation but often to other alternative means of dispute resolution as well (Feinberg, 1989).
7. The Prefatory Note in the 2003 Uniform Mediation Act, Section 8 establishes that mediation communications are confidential to the extent agreed by the parties or provided by other law or rule. § 2.2 includes mediation "briefs" and other reports that are prepared by the parties for the mediator under the umbrella of

confidentiality. Communications outside the context of the mediation proceedings may be controlled by local statute or agreement of the parties (National Conference of Commissioners on Uniform State Laws, 2003).

8. For further discussion of a mediator's obligations for impartiality and confidentiality, see Prefatory Note §§ 9(d) and 9(g) (National Conference of Commissioners on Uniform State Laws, 2003).

9. A growing sense that the tort system was broken prompted the formulation of a number of alternatives for achieving compensation and deterrence, including proposals to route medical malpractice claims through structured mediation.

10. The American Bar Association (ABA) defines "mini-trial" as

> a private, consensual process where the attorneys for each party make a brief presentation of the case as if at a trial. The presentations are observed by a neutral advisor and by representatives (usually high-level business executives) from each side who have authority to settle the dispute. At the end of the presentations, the representatives attempt to settle the dispute. If the representatives fail to settle the dispute, the neutral advisor, at the request of the parties, may serve as a mediator or may issue a non-binding opinion as to the likely outcome in court.

(ABA, 2018)

11. Trial consulting typically employs social scientists, particularly psychologists, communication experts, and economists, to aid attorneys in the presentation of a trial. Modern trial consultants help the legal team to prepare witnesses, improve arguments and rhetoric, and select juries. The traditional mainstays of trial consulting include witness preparation, shadow juries, jury selection, mock trials, focus groups, community attitude surveys, and expert assistance with trial presentation (Wiener & Bornstein, 2011).

References

9 U.S.C. § 1, *et seq.* (2018).

9 U.S.C. §§ 1–16, § 2.

9 U.S.C. §2.

28 U.S.C. §§ 651–658.

28 U.S.C. § 651(a).

Alabama Center for Dispute Resolution. (2018). What is binding arbitration? Retrieved from http://alabamaadr.org/web/publicinfo/Arbitration/index.php.

American Arbitration Association. (2018). Retrieved from www.adr.org/about.

American Bar Association. (2018). Mini-trial. Retrieved from www.americanbar.org/groups/dispute_resolution/resources/DisputeResolutionProcesses/mini-trial.html.

AT&T Mobility LLC v. Concepcion, 563 U.S. 333, 339 (2011).

Bennett, N. (2001). Mini-trials and summary jury trials. Retrieved from http://gov.news/press/2001pres/01fsprivacy.html.

Bennett, S. (2006). Non-binding arbitration: An introduction. *Dispute Resolution Journal, 61*(2).

Bennett, S. (2013). Conflicts between arbitration agreements and arbitration rules. Retrieved from http://cardozojcr.com/wp-content/uploads/2013/11/Bennett.pdf.

Center for Medicare Advocacy. (n.d.). Reversing Obama rules, Trump administration proposes allowing nursing homes to require pre-dispute arbitration clauses as a condition of admission. Retrieved from www.medicareadvocacy.org/reversing-obama-rules-trump-administration-proposes-allowing-nursing-homes-to-require-pre-dispute-arbitration-clauses-as-a-condition-of-admission/.

Cohen, J. (2004). Toward candor after medical error: The first apology law. *Harvard Health Policy Review, 5,* 21–22.

Feinberg, K. (1989). Mediation—a preferred method of dispute resolution. *Pepperdine Law Review, 16*(5).

Fla. Stat § 44.103(2).

Garner, B. A. (Ed.). (2014). *Black's law dictionary* (10th ed.). St Paul, MN: Thompson Reuters.

Goldberg, J. (2014). Online alternative dispute resolution and why law schools should prepare future lawyers for the online forum. *Pepperdine Dispute Resolution Law Journal, 14*(1).

Hoffman, E. (1999, June). The impact of the ADR Act of 1998. *Trial.*

H.R. 1374, introduced in the 115th Congress (2017–2018).

Insurance Information Institute. (2014, Feb. 3). Background on: No-fault auto insurance. Retrieved from www.iii.org/article/background-on-no-fault-auto-insurance.

JAMS. (2014). JAMS comprehensive arbitration rules & procedures. Retrieved from www.jamsadr.com/rules-comprehensive-arbitration/#Rule 1.

Kindred Nursing Centers L.P. v. Clark, 137 S. Ct. 1421, 1424 (2017).

Klauer, K. (2015, Oct. 1). Apology laws: Better read the fine print. Retrieved from www.ahcmedia.com/articles/136295-apology-laws-the-complexities-of-apologies-and-error-disclosure.

Larson, D. (2016). Medical malpractice arbitration: Not business as usual. *Yearbook on Arbitration and Mediation, 8*(69).

Legal Information Institute, Cornell Law School. (n.d.). Retrieved from www.law.cornell.edu/wex/non_compos_mentis.

Lorman. (2018, Apr. 16). Advantages and disadvantages of alternative dispute resolution. Retrieved from www.lorman.com/resources/advantages-and-disadvantages-of-alternative-dispute-resolution-16190.

Louisiana Medical Mutual Insurance Company. (2018, Jan. 3). Louisiana Medical Review panel process: The basics. Retrieved from www.lammico.com/article/MRPbasics.

Lowe, C. (2008). Mandatory binding arbitration: Is anyone really getting their day in court? *Medical Malpractice Law and Strategy, 25*(9).

Mal, B., & Brenner, L. (2010, Mar.). Physician-patient arbitration agreements: Make sure they are understood by all. *Orthopedics Today.*

Marmet Health Care v. Brown, 132 S. Ct. 1201, 1203 (2012).

McMichael, B., Van Horn, R., & Viscusi, W. (2018). Sorry is never enough: How state apology laws fail to reduce medical malpractice liability risk. *Stanford Law Review, 71*(1).

Myerson, B. (2015). The Revised Uniform Arbitration Act: 15 years later. *Dispute Resolution Journal, 71*(1).

National Conference of Commissioners on Uniform State Laws. (2000). Uniform Arbitration Act: Prefatory note. Retrieved from www.uniformlaws.org/shared/docs/arbitration/arbitration_final_00.pdf.

National Conference of Commissioners on Uniform State Laws. (2003). Uniform Arbitration Act: Prefatory note. Retrieved from www.uniformlaws.org/shared/docs/mediation/uma_final_03.pdf.

National Conference of State Legislatures. (2014a, May 20). Medical liability/malpractice ADR and screening panels statutes. Retrieved from www.ncsl.org/research/financial-services-and-commerce/medical-liability-malpractice-adr-and-screening-panels-statutes.aspx.

National Conference of State Legislatures. (2014b, Jan. 21). Medical professional apologies statutes. Retrieved from www.ncsl.org/research/financial-services-and-commerce/medical-professional-apologies-statutes.aspx.

Omer, S. (2009). Exploring the concept of power in mediation: Mediators' sources of power and influence tactics. *Ohio State Journal on Dispute Resolution, 24*(3).

Rolph, E., Moller, E., & Rolph, J. (1997). Arbitration agreements in health care: Myths and reality. *Law and Contemporary Problems, 60*(153).

Sacopulos, M., & Segal, J. (2009, Feb.) Limiting exposure to medical malpractice claims and defamatory cyber postings via patient contracts. *Clinical Orthopedics and Related Research, 467*, 427–433.

Shieh, D. (2014). Unintended side effects: Arbitration and the deterrence of medical error. *New York University Law Review, 89*, 1806, 1808–1809.

Sohn, D. H., & Bal, B. (2012). Medical malpractice reform: The role of alternative dispute resolution. *Clin Orthop Relat Res., 470*(5), 1370–1378.

Stone, K., & Colvin, A. (2015, Dec. 7). The arbitration epidemic. Retrieved from www.epi.org/publication/the-arbitration-epidemic.

Studdert, D., Mello, M., & Brennan, T. (2004, Jan. 15). Medical malpractice. *New England Journal of Medicine, 350*(3).

Szalai, I. S. (2016). Exploring the Federal Arbitration Act through the Lens of History Symposium. *Journal of Dispute Resolution.* Retrieved from http://scholarship.law.missouri.edu/jdr/vol. 2016/iss1/9.

Trantina, Terry L. (2015). What law applies to an agreement to arbitrate? *Dispute Resolution Magazine*, Fall. Retrieved from www.americanbar.org/content/dam/aba/publications/dispute_resolution_magazine/fall-2015/7_trantina_what_law_applies.authcheckdam.pdf.

Uniform Law Commission. (2018). Arbitration Act (2002). Retrieved from www.uniformlaws.org/Act.aspx?title=Arbitration%20Act%20(2000).

Uniform Power of Attorney Act. Final Act § 102(7), (2006). Uniform Law Commission, enacted in 26 jurisdictions with 2018 introductions in DC, Mississippi and South Dakota. Retrieved from www.uniformlaws.org/Act.aspx?title=Power%20Act%20Attorney.

United States Department of Justice. (2018). Use and benefits of alternative dispute resolution by the Department of Justice. Retrieved from www.justice.gov/olp/alternative-dispute-resolution-department-justice.

Vernon's Annotated Statutes, Article 4590i, § 15.01(a) (2018).

Walker, M. (2015, Sept. 29). The arbitration clause hidden in many consumer contracts. *Consumer Reports*.

Wiener, R. L., & Bornstein, B. H. (2011). Introduction: Trial consulting from a psycholegal perspective. *Handbook of trial consulting*. Boston, MA: Springer.

Additional Reading

Craver, C. (1999, June). Mediation: A trial lawyer's guide. 35 *Trial* 37.

Emery, J., Edwards, L., & Edwards, J. (2000). *Civil procedure and litigation*. New York, NY: West Legal Studies.

Hechler, D. (2001, June 25). ADR finds true believers companies make the leap—and save tens of millions of dollars. *The National Law Journal*.

Meek, S. (1996). *Alternative dispute resolution*. Tucson, AZ: Lawyers and Judges Publishers Inc.

State statutes by topic: Alternative dispute resolution. (2001). Retrieved from http://gov.news/press/2001pres/01fsprivacy.html.

Tex. Rev. Civ. Stat. Ann. art. 4590i, § 15.01.

List of litigation research firms found at http://wwwdomoz.org/Society/Law/Services/litigiation_Support/.

Test Questions

1. What is the most widely used format of ADR that may issue a binding decision?
   A. Mediation
   B. Arbitration
   C. Negotiations
   D. Minitrials

2. An LNC's role in arbitration may include all of the following EXCEPT:
   A. Preparing evidentiary material
   B. Interviewing experts
   C. Educating the litigation team and arbitrator about medical issues
   D. Discussing the facts of the case with the arbitrator after the hearing ends and before the award is rendered

3. Components of a settlement brochure include:
   A. Brief statement of the case
   B. Medical management issues
   C. Damages
   D. Exhibits
   E. All of the above

4. During mediation, what role does the LNC carry out?
   A. Negotiates the mediator's fee
   B. Serves as a resource to the attorney and mediator
   C. Prepares written negotiated agreement
   D. Cross-examines witnesses

5. A decision rendered by an arbitrator or a tribunal of arbitrators is referred to as
   A. Award
   B. Decision
   C. Verdict
   D. Memorandum of understanding

Answers: 1. B, 2. D, 3. E, 4. B, 5. A

Chapter 39

Trial Preparation and the Trial Process

Diane L. Reboy, MS, BSN, RN, LNCC®, CNLCP®, CCDS

Contents

Objectives

- Describe the purpose of well-organized trial and witness notebooks
- Explain the difference between admissible and inadmissible medical records
- State issues of concern regarding the use of deposition testimony, documents, and physical and demonstrative evidence at trial
- Discuss the role of the LNC in witness preparation, jury selection, and testimony presentation
- Discuss important issues affecting verdict determination and jury awards, including comparative and contributory negligence and punitive damages

Introduction

Trial preparation and trial are the culmination of all efforts put forth in developing a case. Depending on the nature of the case and its jurisdiction, the LNC and the trial team may have spent years working on the lawsuit. Thorough preparation is the key to a successful outcome, and the attorney relies on the LNC to assist in organizing, preparing, and presenting the case in a logical fashion.

The LNC may work with just the trial attorney to prepare for trial or may be part of a larger trial team (LNC, paralegal, legal assistant, associate attorney, lead attorney, and informational technology specialist). When working as part of a larger legal team, all the members need to be aware of what tasks each is to perform to eliminate duplication of efforts and prevent an important task from being missed. The successful trial team displays the true meaning of the word "team" in that a cooperative effort is necessary for things to run as smoothly as possible. The jury can easily detect a lack of preparedness in the trial team, which can impact the jury's perception of the team's competence.

The LNC's involvement in trial preparation and trial will include some, if not all, aspects of the process from preparing and organizing trial materials to anticipating the needs of the trial attorney in the courtroom, and preparing for the next trial day. In addition, the LNC's contributions continue post-trial. Trials can be rewarding and exciting but, at the same time, stressful. The LNC's organizational skills and ability to anticipate the next steps are invaluable attributes to the trial attorney.

One of the major changes in trial preparation and trials over the past 10 to 15 years is the development of and reliance upon technology by attorneys, law firms, and even courts. Many traditional courtrooms now allow electronic and other technological equipment to be utilized during trial, including large monitors, laptops, projectors, etc. It is not unusual for courts to have wi-fi access. Some trial teams may use software programs specifically designed for organizing and presenting information and evidence at trial. The use of technology in the courtroom allows for enhanced organization of and access to information, and it also enables the attorney to present the case in new, dynamic ways that are more interesting and convincing. The LNC may be responsible for bringing in permissible equipment or utilizing the court's existing equipment (Arkfeld, n.d.).

Trial Notebooks

Trial notebooks, whether paper or electronic, compile all pertinent information in a convenient, easily accessible format. There are two schools of thought regarding when to create the trial notebook (Ducote & Holmes, n.d.). The first is to wait until a trial date is known. In many states and law firms, trials are double- and triple-booked with the court to start on the same day, because it is anticipated most cases will settle before that date arrives. Therefore, to start a trial notebook for every case would be a waste of human, electronic, and paper resources.

The other school of thought is to start creating the trial notebook from the very beginning of litigation to avoid a last minute pre-trial rush. This can be especially critical when the LNC is responsible for several trials at the same time. The LNC needs to be aware of the trial attorney's practice preferences and the general percentage of cases the attorney litigates that settle or go to trial (Drummond, 2009).The exact content of trial notebooks depends on the attorney's preferences, but they typically contain relevant pleading and discovery documents from all parties, such as the Complaint, interrogatory answers or bill of particulars, expert disclosures, and deposition transcripts. The LNC may also wish to incorporate some, or all, of the following materials into the trial notebook (whether traditional or electronic) or have these items available in the courtroom in some other form:

■ Motions in limine
■ Proposed jury instructions
■ Notes on *voir dire* examinations

- Notes on opposing counsel's opening statement
- Notes on opposing counsel's closing argument
- Pre-trial orders
- Court's docket/case number assigned to this specific case
- List of plaintiff and defense witnesses
- Order of proof (the order witnesses will be called)
- Plaintiff's list of exhibits admitted at trial
- Defendant's list of exhibits admitted at trial
- Co-defendant's list of exhibits admitted at trial
- Relevant portions of medical records at issue
- Medical timeline or chronology along with summaries and definitions of pertinent medical terminology
- Pertinent medical literature
- Relevant portions of other significant records (education, employment, etc.)
- Expert reports
- Opposing experts' curriculum vitae, prior testimony, impeachment documentation
- Opening statement and
- Final argument

Traditional Trial Notebooks

Traditional trial notebooks may take on many different forms, ranging from simple manila file folders organized by subject to three-ring binders with tabbed subject dividers, all the way to a large, legal size, pre-divided, five-hole punched binders, specifically prepared for trials. The best format to use is the one the attorney prefers.

When organizing a trial notebook, color coding various sections may be helpful. The LNC should prepare a concise table of contents with enough detail to allow the attorney or anyone working with the attorney instant access to pertinent documents. If there are several trial notebooks, a table of contents and index should be in each notebook, and the notebooks should be clearly labeled on the front cover and spine.

Medical records are typically organized in a separate notebook and divided by healthcare provider. The notebook should also contain the medical chronology or timeline and any pertinent medical literature (supportive and non-supportive).

Electronic Trial Notebooks

Electronic trial notebooks are simply computer folders and subfolders organized as a hard copy notebook would be. For example, there may be a folder for pleadings, a folder for interrogatory responses or bills of particulars, a folder for deposition transcripts, and a folder entitled "Medical Records" with bookmarked portable document formats (PDFs) of each provider's records (or subfolders for each provider).

"Computer-driven technologies have had a substantial impact on the effectiveness and ease of trial preparation" (Miller, 2017). Advantages to the use of electronic trial notebooks include the convenience of having the entire file in one place on a flash drive, CD, or loaded onto a laptop. Electronic documents stored as PDFs are easily organized, bookmarked, and searched. Paper documents can be quickly scanned as PDFs, and electronic documents can be printed (Masters, 2013). Pages within PDFs can be reorganized, added, and deleted with just a key stroke. Contrast that with the traditional notebook, in which additions and deletions require changes to the table of contents or index each time a change is made (Arkfeld, n.d.).

As federal and state trial courts are continually renovated with updates in electronic capabilities, the LNC needs to be aware of the type of electronic technology the specific court uses or what equipment the trial team has available to bring into the courtroom (e.g., screen, projector, laptops, etc.). The trial team must ascertain whether the trial judge will allow the use of such technology. Some judges still rely on paper formats in courtrooms, making it necessary for the trial team to prepare traditional hard copies of exhibits as well as having an electronic copy to project for the jury.

Witness Notebooks

In addition to a trial notebook, the attorney may require a separate notebook (paper or electronic) for each witness. The witness notebook may include:

- The witness's contact information
- Copies of correspondence sent to, or pertaining to, the witness
- Notes taken during meetings with the witness
- Any written item or statement prepared by witness
- Compressed transcript (mini script) of deposition with concordance (a word index or alphabetical list of the words present in the transcript)
- Signed errata sheet with revisions to the deposition testimony
- Summary of deposition or line and page outline
- Outline of direct or cross-examination for trial
- Copy of report (for expert witnesses)
- Copy of curriculum vitae and bibliography (for expert witnesses)
- Other pertinent documents (e.g., medical literature authored by the expert witness, notes made by the expert witness regarding significant entries in medical records) and
- Pertinent investigative reports

Burden of Proof

To prevail at trial, the plaintiff has the burden of proving the four elements of negligence that are discussed in Chapter 4: duty, breach of duty, damages, and causation. The defense must only raise enough doubt about any one of these four elements to defeat the plaintiff's efforts.

In civil cases, the plaintiff must prove the "preponderance of the evidence," whereas in a criminal case threshold for proof is "beyond a reasonable doubt" (Findlaw, 2017a; Legal Information Institute, n.d.-a). Some states now use "clear and convincing evidence" as the standard for civil trials. That is, the scales must tip only slightly toward one party for the jury to find in favor of that party. For more information on the differences in the burden of proof between civil and criminal cases, see Chapter 16.

Comparative and Contributory Negligence

In addition to understanding the applicable burden of proof for a case, LNCs should also appreciate if the case is being tried in a jurisdiction that recognizes the doctrines of comparative or contributory negligence. In those jurisdictions, the jury may find the defendant negligent but may also find the plaintiff responsible for the injury as well.

Most states (46) use some form (pure or modified versions) of the comparative negligence standard, in which recovery is based on proportional fault (Wickert, 2013). In pure comparative negligence, plaintiff's total damages are reduced by the percentage to which the plaintiff was responsible for the injury. If a plaintiff was awarded $100,000 and found to be 25% responsible, the final award would be $75,000. If this plaintiff was found to be 75% responsible, the final award would be $25,000. In modified comparative negligence, the plaintiff does not recover any award if found to be equally or more responsible for the injury than the defendant. If a plaintiff was found to be 75% responsible, there would be no recovery. If the plaintiff was found to be 25% responsible, an award would be recovered.

An example of comparative negligence is a worker who is taking a personal cell phone call while carrying lumber through a construction site. The worker slips in a hole and fractures a leg. The employer was at fault, because the hole should have been covered to avoid an employee from falling and sustaining a serious physical injury. However, the worker was at fault too, having been distracted by the personal phone call and not paying attention. In a jurisdiction that recognizes the doctrine of comparative negligence, the jury, upon finding negligence, will be asked to assign a percentage of fault to all parties. In this example, the jury may find the employer (defendant) to be 80% negligent and the worker (plaintiff), 20% responsible. If the jury awarded $100,000, the plaintiff would receive $80,000, because the plaintiff carried 20% of the responsibility.

In jurisdictions that recognize the doctrine of contributory negligence, recovery is barred if the actions or inactions of the injured party have contributed in any way (even as little as 1%) to the injury. There are four states that use a contributory negligence standard (American Bar Association [ABA], 2016; The-Injury-Lawyer-Directory.com, n.d.-a, n.d.-b).

While the plaintiff has the burden of proving the claims asserted in the Complaint, the defendant has the burden of proving the comparative or contributory negligence, because it is an affirmative defense asserted by the defendant. Thus, these cases can be difficult for both sides to prove, and settlement may occur more often.

Evidence

Evidence is information presented to a jury for their consideration in deciding a case. Evidence encompasses testimony (from both trial and deposition) and exhibits, including medical records, physical evidence, and demonstrative evidence. What evidence can be presented to the trier of fact, how it can be presented, and how its admissibility can be challenged are governed by the applicable rules of evidence. In federal court, these are the Federal Rules of Evidence (FRE, 2019). Most states have adopted or adapted the Federal Rules of Evidence for their state's rules. The rules of evidence aim to standardize admissibility to allow fair, timely, and economic case presentation.

Evidence can be challenged for a myriad of reasons, including:

- The evidence is prejudicial
- The evidence lacks relevance
- The evidence proffered as scientific is not generally accepted, valid, or reliable (Daubert or Frye challenge)
- The expert witness lacks expertise and is not qualified to testify and

- There were lapses in the chain of custody that disqualifies physical evidence (See Chapter 16 for more discussion on the chain of custody)

Understanding the rules of evidence and evidentiary issues is a complex area of the law, and whole textbooks are devoted to the subject. The LNC should strive to become familiar with common rules of evidence associated with medical malpractice and personal injury cases.

Deposition Testimony

Trial testimony will be discussed later in this chapter, but deposition testimony can play an important role at trial, too.

A deposition is testimony given under oath outside of court and is part of the discovery process. It is a formal interview conducted by attorneys for all parties in the lawsuit and recorded by a court reporter using stenography and increasingly by videotape. After the deposition, the court reporter prepares a transcript of the testimony (questions and answers), and the deponent can make corrections in a signed statement listing the changes and the reasons the changes were made. (See Chapter 5 for more information on depositions.)

Deposition testimony is not only used for discovery but is also used to impeach or question the veracity of the witness testifying in court by comparing the witness's deposition testimony to statements made on the stand at trial (Federal Rules of Civil Procedure, 2017). In addition, deposition testimony can be used to preserve a witness's statements and present them at trial when the witness will not be testifying live due to unavailability, illness, or death. In this circumstance, the attorneys identify the portion(s) of the deposition testimony they wish to offer into evidence. The opposing attorneys identify the portions within the proposed testimony to which they object. These offers and objections are exchanged between counsel prior to trial, and if disagreements persist, the court will rule on them to finalize the specific excerpts to be read to the jury at trial, typically by a neutral, non-involved person. If the witness's deposition was videotaped, various procedures also apply to introducing videotaped deposition at trial. This includes hearings to review the edited videotape without the jury present to ensure only the agreed-upon or ruled-upon excerpts will be played.

Exhibits

Trial exhibits assist the party in telling the story to the jury. An exhibit is a document (such as a medical record), physical evidence (such as a pathology slide), or demonstrative evidence (such as an anatomic model or computer simulation) shown to the court during the trial. Exhibits are used to present proof of the case facts, aid the jury's understanding of an expert's technical testimony, help the jury to "see" the event, and enhance the jury's retention of key elements of the testimony. Visual evidence keeps the jurors engaged, as technical testimony presented without visual exhibits can become monotonous and tiring.

Exhibits marked for identification (typically demonstrative evidence) may be viewed by the witness, discussed with the jury, and perhaps shown to the jury, but they are not available to the jury during deliberations. Full exhibits can be provided to and viewed by the jury during deliberations. For example, a medical record may be admitted as a full exhibit, but an enlargement of a specific portion of the record may be used as demonstrative evidence. A police officer's accident report may be admitted as a full exhibit, but a computer simulation that reconstructs the accident would be demonstrative evidence.

Prior to trial, the attorney decides which documents to present as exhibits at trial and in what order. Depending on the practices of the law office, the LNC may be involved in organizing the exhibits either in hard copy or electronically and submitting them to the court. If the LNC is involved in preparing exhibits, the following may be helpful:

- Create a separate folder for each exhibit
- Groom the document to ensure it has no highlights, underlines, or attorney-made marks on it apart from those found on the original document
- Carefully review the document to ensure compliance with any granted motions in limine (discussed below)
- Mark the document as "Plaintiff Exhibit ___" or "Defense Exhibit _____" according to local procedural rules
- Prepare a corresponding exhibit list
- Whenever possible, use the original document and have copies available in the exhibit folder. There should be enough copies of each exhibit to provide one to the lead attorney for each party, the judge, and the court (to mark as the official exhibit for use during trial and jury deliberations) and
- If the original document is not available, insert a note in the folder indicating the location of the original document and how it can be obtained

If the LNC is coordinating exhibits with a co-defendant, the LNC determines, ahead of time, which defendant will be responsible for a particular exhibit. This prevents the submission of duplicate exhibits and helps to minimize trial preparation costs.

Each party submits an exhibit list to the court in accordance with the jurisdiction's submission requirements. In some jurisdictions, exhibits are exchanged between the parties before the trial begins. The LNC must maintain an accurate and current list of all exhibits from all parties. This will be discussed further later in the chapter.

The LNC must also be aware of whether the attorney intends to introduce specific documents, records, or other exhibits into evidence through a particular witness by having that person authenticate them under oath. The LNC assures those documents are assembled and organized before that witness takes the stand.

Medical Records

Medical records are vital evidence in trials of medical-legal tort cases. To introduce medical records at trial, they must be accepted as admissible by the court. Admissibility procedures are determined by jurisdiction with much variability from state to state. Not adhering to the relevant admissibility requirements can result in crucial medical records being disallowed as evidence in court, which could have dire consequences on the outcome of the case. Therefore, the LNC needs to know and adhere to the jurisdictional requirements. For example, in Texas, medical records are admissible if obtained in response to a subpoena *duces tecum* or a medical authorization (that is compliant with the Health Insurance Portability and Accountability Act) and accompanied by an affidavit from the records custodian. In New Jersey, hospital records are admissible only if they are certified by the hospital as being a complete copy of the medical records. In some states, the party that orders the records by subpoena receives the original, or court, copy, while in other states, the records are sent directly from the healthcare facility to the court.

BUSINESS RECORDS EXCEPTION TO THE HEARSAY RULE

Typically, hearsay evidence is inadmissible at trial. Hearsay evidence is witness statements made about what someone said to them or overheard by the person testifying. It includes statements made to the witness about certain documents or records, and it may include video, audiovisual, and computer-generated evidence (Joseph, 2016). The concern regarding hearsay evidence is the person who originally made the statement to the witness is not available for cross-examination. There are, however, many types of hearsay evidence and many exclusions and exceptions to the hearsay rule (FRE, 2018). Examples of exceptions include statements for purposes of medical diagnosis or treatment, public records, and reports and statements made under belief of impending death. As business records, medical records and medical bills are exempt from the hearsay rule (The LSU Medical and Public Health Law Site, 2009).

Physical Evidence

Physical evidence is any tangible item used or displayed as an exhibit during trial. An example of physical evidence is a medical device (e.g., intravenous infusion pump or fetal monitor) affirmatively identified as the one used (or representative of the one used) during the medical procedure or care at issue. The item must be authenticated and deemed admissible by the court and is then appropriately marked by the court reporter and identified on the exhibit list. Any physical evidence used at trial may be held by the court for years after the trial is over. Therefore, the attorney, client, and LNC must carefully weigh whether a specific item or, alternatively, a duplicate can be placed into evidence.

Demonstrative Evidence

Demonstrative evidence allows an attorney to present certain issues to the jury in a way that facilitates understanding of complex concepts. Demonstrative evidence can be in the form of a chart, table, diagram, illustration, video, or animation. The LNC, as the person on the litigation team most familiar with the medical records, can be particularly helpful in identifying issues best presented through demonstrative evidence. The LNC can enlarge a document contained in the medical record to focus the jury's attention on a specific point. Medical models and illustrations are helpful in explaining anatomical matters, and computer-generated animation is especially helpful for accident reconstruction, allowing the jury to see the dynamics of how an accident occurred. The LNC should consider what the case theories are and what the trial attorney is trying to prove (plaintiff) or cast doubt on (defense) to determine the best presentation of information.

Depending on which members of the litigation team will be at trial, the LNC or paralegal is responsible for making sure the proper equipment is in the courtroom for demonstrative evidence presentation. Prior to trial, the LNC or paralegal should contact the court clerk to determine the availability of any audiovisual equipment in the courtroom and, if none is available, arrange to bring the necessary equipment. In many jurisdictions, the judge must grant a request to bring audiovisual equipment into the courthouse. Also, it is important to check with the judge regarding the type of demonstrative evidence planned to ensure it will be permitted (Arkfeld, n.d.).

Many companies create demonstrative exhibits for courtroom use. Some companies provide the necessary equipment to present the demonstrative evidence and can assist with the actual court presentation. The person on the legal team (LNC or paralegal) responsible for demonstrative evidence should factor in additional trial preparation time for an outside vendor to create exhibits. The LNC or paralegal should discuss with the trial attorney the cost of an elaborate demonstrative exhibit relative to its desired benefit of conveying the party's theory to the jury. Testifying experts should be consulted on any demonstrative evidence planned for use during the expert's testimony and should review it prior to trial to ensure the exhibit is accurate and error-free.

Demonstrative evidence can also be an effective way to present closing arguments of a case through a slide show presentation. Closing argument is the last chance a party has to convince the jury of the party's case theory. The slide show presentation is used to visually summarize the facts of the case as well as "undercut the opposing party's case" (Dickinson, 2017, slide 7).

For more information on demonstrative evidence, see Chapter 37.

Medical Literature

In preparation for trial, the LNC organizes the relevant medical literature collected during discovery and throughout case development that supports the trial attorney's theory of the case. When identifying medical literature to be used at trial, the LNC must be aware that literature addressing standard of care issues must pre-date the alleged incident (to show the standard was in effect at the time of the incident). However, the most current articles that speak to causation issues can be used. Also, the LNC should be aware of major court decisions that impact what may be admissible, such as *Daubert v. Merrell Dow Pharmaceuticals, Inc.* (1993) which limits "junk science." (See Chapter 34 for more information on researching medical literature and Chapter 36 for more information on the Daubert case.)

A medical literature notebook may be organized electronically or in a three-ring binder. Articles can be organized by topic, alphabetically by author or title, or by the expert who will be testifying about the topic addressed in the article. To locate articles quickly and easily, a tabbed index is prepared. Depending on the attorney's preference, an abstract of each article may be prepared containing the supportive information as well as any information that negatively impacts the case theory.

Witnesses

Types of Witnesses

Witnesses take center stage at trial and, through their testimony, the story is told to the jury. Three types of witnesses may testify in a civil trial: expert witnesses, fact witnesses, and expert fact witnesses. An expert witness is one who has education, training, specialized experience, and superior knowledge about a specific subject that is beyond the common knowledge of lay jurors. Without the testimony of the expert witness, jurors would be incapable of forming an accurate opinion or deducing correct conclusions. Expert witnesses must be qualified by the court before they are permitted to testify (i.e., the judge must consider the expert's education, training, and experience and the basis for the expert's opinions to determine whether the opinions are scientifically sound and generally accepted and whether the expert is, in fact, qualified to provide such opinions to the jury). For more information on expert witnesses, see Chapters 31 and 36. To learn more about expert witnesses and scientific testimony, review: *Daubert v. Merrell Dow Pharmaceuticals, Inc.* (1993) (and its derivative cases) and *Frye v. United States* (1923).

In a healthcare provider professional negligence trial, the role of expert witnesses is to explain the medical issues of the case to the jury. These issues include standard of care, causation, and damages. Plaintiff's standard of care expert will describe the care that should have been provided and how the defendant deviated from the accepted standards of care. An expert witness will offer testimony on causation and teach the jury how the deviation was a direct cause of the alleged injuries. The plaintiff may present damages experts to describe the physical and emotional injuries and the financial damages and to project their impact on the plaintiff's future. The defense will also call expert witnesses to testify on standard of care, causation, and damages and to rebut the testimony of the plaintiff's experts.

In other types of medical legal tort cases not involving professional negligence (e.g., motor vehicle crashes, slip and falls, product liability, etc.), medical expert witnesses do not testify about standard of care issues but may testify on causation and damages to explain the injuries, treatment, and projected impact of the injuries in the future. Defense expert witnesses present rebuttal testimony concerning causation and the impact of the plaintiff's injuries. They may highlight other probable causes of the injuries; including pre-existing conditions that could have caused or exacerbated the claimed injury.

Fact witnesses are individuals with firsthand knowledge of issues pertaining to the case. Fact witnesses may include a healthcare provider who is not the focus of the negligence claim but who was present during the incident in question and can testify to the facts surrounding what actually occurred. For example, in a case in which the defendant is an obstetrician, the labor and delivery nurse may be called as a fact witness. Family members or close friends of a plaintiff or decedent may be called as fact witnesses to testify about their observations of the care provided or about the impact the injuries have had on the plaintiff and how it has changed the plaintiff's lifestyle. Fact witnesses may also include employers or co-workers, ministers, etc.

Expert fact witnesses are individuals with specialized education, training, knowledge, and experience who teach the jury by offering unbiased testimony about the facts of the case (which are beyond a lay juror's understanding), but they do not offer any opinion testimony about standard of care, causation, or damages. Their testimony is impartial and fact-based and thus would be the same regardless of whether they were hired by the plaintiff or defense side. An expert fact witness could be a nurse teaching the jury about a nursing procedure or how a piece of equipment is used or summarizing and explaining voluminous medical records to the jury. An expert fact witness could also be a subsequent medical provider testifying about the observations and findings during an examination but not opining on the treatment rendered by the defendant. For more information on expert fact witnesses, see Chapter 32.

Witness Preparation

The role of the LNC in assisting with witness preparation is determined by the trial attorney's preference and the law firm's standard practice. The LNC, as a member of the trial team, may assist in any or all of the witness preparation tasks discussed in this section.

The goal of witness preparation is to present the best possible trial testimony to the trier of fact. This not only includes what a witness will testify to but how the witness sounds and looks on the stand. All witnesses need some preparation before trial. This may take several hours or even several days; thus, witness preparation requires time and patience. When a witness is unavailable for in-person preparation, videoconferencing can be employed. In many cases, the witness has never been inside a courtroom, and therefore, a review of courtroom procedures helps to familiarize the witness with the process and allay any fear, anxiety, and concerns. Witness preparation is also an opportunity for the trial team to establish a rapport with the witness and assess how the witness will appear to the jury. This assessment includes physical appearance, non-verbal communication, and demeanor. If needed, a trial consultant may be brought into the case to help with witness preparation.

Part of the process involves preparing the witness for answering questions on the stand. The witness is instructed on the following:

- Listen carefully to the question asked, and answer only that question. Do not volunteer information beyond what was asked. Answer succinctly and concisely.
- Do not answer the question if it is not understood. Ask the attorney to repeat or rephrase the question.
- Tell the attorney if the information sought is not known. Never guess or speculate.
- If the attorney rephrases a previously asked question, give the same answer.
- If the witness was deposed, thoroughly review the deposition transcript and give consistent answers at trial.
- Be certain the attorney is finished asking the question before beginning to answer.
- Reflect on an answer before responding. This allows the opposing attorney time to object to the question, if needed.
- If an objection to a question is made, do not answer the question. Rather, wait for the judge to rule on the objection. If the objection is overruled, proceed with answering. If the objection is sustained, await the next question.
- Speak clearly, slowly, and loud enough to be heard without straining.
- When answering a question, use one's own words and do not adopt the attorney's phrasing or language.
- If necessary, rephrase the attorney's question before answering to ensure understanding.
- If the attorney references a specific document in a question (e.g., a medical record or journal article), request a copy of the document and read it carefully before responding.
- If the attorney asks for a "yes" or "no" answer only and this would yield an incomplete answer, inform the attorney the answer will be inaccurate.
- Always tell the truth.
- Do not sound rehearsed.

Witness preparation also involves giving the witness guidance on appearance and demeanor. Such instructions include:

- Maintain a polite and sincere demeanor, especially when answering questions on cross-examination.
- Be aware of body language and avoid arm-crossing, knee-bouncing, fidgeting, excessive hand movements, eye-rolling, etc.
- Maintain eye contact with the attorney while the question is being asked, and then look at the jury while answering the question.
- Dress appropriately for court (business casual for fact witnesses and suits for expert witnesses). Instruct anyone accompanying the witness, such as family or friends, to dress appropriately for the courtroom.
- Do not discuss the case anywhere inside or outside of the courthouse except on the stand or with the trial team. More than one case has been lost by an overheard discussion in the courthouse bathroom during a break.

The trial team reviews with the witness any materials that could be used to impeach (challenge) the witness's credibility by the opposing counsel. These include deposition testimony, answers to interrogatories, answers to requests for admission, and any oral or written statements made previously (including social media posts). For expert witnesses, these may also include published medical literature, information on the expert's website, prior deposition or trial testimony, prior expert reports, etc. All such material may be reviewed by the LNC to identify any content that is contrary to or otherwise harmful to the case at hand.

During witness preparation, the trial team also discusses the expected trial testimony of other witnesses for that party (such as family or friends for the plaintiff or a co-worker of the defendant who witnessed the care in question). This aids in identifying any potential inconsistencies in trial testimony between the various witnesses for that party. The trial attorney, if not involved in this part of trial preparation, should be advised of any inconsistencies as soon as possible. The trial team reviews and discusses any exhibits the trial attorney will use while the witness is on the stand and ensures the witness understands the purpose of the exhibits.

Even if all parties agree on which witnesses will appear at trial, the attorney may prefer or be compelled by jurisdictional rules to serve a subpoena or notice on all witnesses who will be called, even friendly ones (those who willingly agree to testify and are supportive of the theory of the case). In that circumstance, the trial team informs the witnesses ahead of time to expect to be served by the process server and explains the rationale for such service with the witnesses.

Trial Documents, Equipment, and Supplies

A member of the trial team (i.e., legal assistant, paralegal, LNC) will organize case materials (medical records, legal documents, exhibits, trial notebooks, witness notebooks, medical literature notebooks, etc.), technology/audiovisual equipment (laptop, flash drives, projector, screen, power cords, etc.), and office supplies in preparation for trial. All materials and equipment are securely packaged and arrangements made for delivery to the courthouse (Whalen, 2016). Numbering each trial box (i.e., 1 of 25, 2 of 25, etc.) and listing each box's content is beneficial for the trial team, as it provides easy identification and access to the contents during a trial.

Key Elements of Trials

Trial is conducted in the following order:

- Motions in limine
- *Voir dire*
- Opening statements
- Trial examination of witnesses
- Directed verdict (if applicable)
- Closing arguments
- Jury instructions and deliberations
- Verdict and
- Post-trial activities

Initial Trial Proceedings

Motions in Limine

A motion in limine is a written request usually made before the beginning of a jury trial for a protective order against evidence that is immaterial, inadmissible, or prejudicial. The purpose of such a motion is to avoid injection into the trial of matters irrelevant (immaterial), inadmissible (evidence that, according to law, cannot be entered; evidence that was illegally seized; and certain types of hearsay), or prejudicial (a preconceived opinion). For example, if a plaintiff has a remote history of illicit drug use that played no role in the underlying issues of the case, plaintiff's counsel may file a motion in limine seeking to preclude this information from coming into evidence, as it is more prejudicial than probative. If a motion in limine is granted, then medical records, exhibits, and any other evidence are carefully reviewed and redacted or altered to remove the information. Failure to adhere to a motion in limine may result in attorney sanctions (punitive measures) or a mistrial.

Voir Dire *(Jury Selection)*

Cases are either tried before the court (known as a bench trial in which the judge is the finder of fact *and* law) or before a jury (in which the jury decides the facts and the judge rules of matters of law). Most malpractice cases are tried before a jury, because plaintiffs' attorneys believe a jury will be more sympathetic to the injured party (the plaintiff) and provide a substantial verdict award (Washington, 2016).

> The trial jury in either a civil or criminal case is chosen from a list called a **venire** or jury pool that has been compiled by the court. The method of selecting names for the venire varies. In many states, the list is compiled from voter registration lists or drivers license lists. (In some jurisdictions, the federal and state courts use the same lists for a given area.) The jury pool is sometimes compiled with the help of jury commissioners appointed by the presiding judge. Most states require that a court official screen the list of potential jurors to eliminate people unqualified or ineligible under state law. Traditionally many people were exempted from jury duty because their jobs were considered so important to society they couldn't be released from them for jury duty. These automatic exemptions and excuses are becoming less and less common. In many states, exemptions have been sharply cut back or completely eliminated.
>
> (ABA, 2017a, para 1–2)

Voir dire comes from the Latin phrase, *verum dicere*, meaning to give a true verdict. It is a process in which the judge and attorneys for all parties question prospective jurors from the jury pool. Sometimes, written questions are answered by perspective jurors and analyzed prior to oral examination; this is called "silent *voir dire*." Such questions may include demographic information, such as education, occupation, any arrests or convictions, marital status, significant other's name and occupation, children's names and occupation, and the name and occupation of any other persons living at the juror's residence. The *voir dire* process varies widely depending on where the case is venued.

DISQUALIFICATION FOR CAUSE

To begin *voir dire*, the judge shares general information about the case (including the names of the parties, attorneys, experts, and witnesses) and asks the jurors if they are unable to render a fair and impartial verdict. Jurors responding in the affirmative are often excused. The judge may also inquire if any of the prospective jurors have language, visual, hearing, or reading difficulties that may prevent the person from being an effective juror. Following this, the judge and the attorneys may ask specific questions of individual jurors. The questions posed vary widely depending on the case but may include the prospective juror's connection to any one of the parties or legal counsel, any financial interest in the case or outcome, or any prejudicial or biased belief on the prospective juror's part. The potential juror may also be asked about any prior jury experience, whether it was favorable or unfavorable, and whether that experience will impact the juror's ability to be fair and impartial. Other questions may include whether the juror or a close family member has been a party to a lawsuit, the nature of the lawsuit, and whether the process will affect the juror's perspective. Any of these may result in the prospective juror being disqualified for cause, also known as a causal strike. There is no limit on the number of causal strikes allowed.

PEREMPTORY CHALLENGES

The initial *voir dire* results in elimination of prospective jurors for cause. Following this, each party's attorney is entitled to strike additional jurors to secure a jury more harmonious to that party. During this *voir dire*, the focus is on assessing the jurors' attitudes toward the issues in the case. The attorneys evaluate the perspective jurors with the goal of choosing jurors most sympathetic to their side. They accept or strike perspective jurors, aiming to equalize potential bias.

In federal court, each party is limited to three peremptory challenges, and attorneys are not obligated to offer any reason for striking a juror. In state courts, the number of challenges can vary. In some criminal cases, peremptory challenges are complicated by the Batson challenge, which is an objection to the peremptory challenge on the grounds that it was used to strike a potential juror based on race, ethnicity or sex (*Batson v. Kentucky*, 476 U.S. 79 1986).

ROLE OF THE LNC

The LNC plays a crucial role during jury selection, because nurses are trained to observe details. The LNC may draft questions for the attorney to use during *voir dire*, and during the questioning, the LNC observes the jurors' reactions to the questions posed. The LNC should also take accurate and detailed notes that identify whether the responses fit the profile of the ideal juror for that party. Notes taken during the *voir dire* process should be kept in a separate notebook (paper or electronic) and should be easily accessible, as the attorney may need to refer to these notes during trial.

JURY CONSULTANTS

A jury consultant is a skilled observer trained in behavioral science, psychology, and possibly law or criminal justice. While human behavior is not always predictable, jury consultants help the trial team, particularly in high profile civil and criminal cases, to pick a jury most advantageous for the party. The jury consultant can assist the trial team in developing questions to ask during the *voir dire* process. During the *voir dire* process itself, the consultant assesses verbal and non-verbal communication (e.g., body language, facial expressions, dress, and mannerisms) for clues to the prospective juror's ability to listen, visually respond, and more (Latiolasis-Hargrove, 2009). The consultant analyzes the responses of perspective jurors to identify who may influence the jury for either side and assesses socioeconomic status, life experience, attitudes, educational levels, marital status, and more to identify jurors favorable (and unfavorable) to the case. Jury consultants may also assist attorneys in running jury focus groups and trial simulations to identify the types of jurors that would be beneficial to the case.

During trial, the jury consultant observes the jurors for their reactions to how the attorney presents the case and observes witnesses and how the jury reacts during each witness's testimony. The consultant notes any emotional reactions or discomfort by the jury, as this may influence deliberations on the verdict, possibly leading to a hung jury and causing a mistrial. Based on these observations, jury consultants can make recommendations to the attorney about adjusting various aspects of the witness examination, such as length, forcefulness of questioning, etc.

Opening Statements

The plaintiff and defense attorneys introduce their respective sides of the case in opening statements (National Paralegal College, n.d.). The opening statement tells the jury of the issues involved in the case, giving the jury a general picture or overview so they will be able to understand the evidence. The attorneys may tell the jury about the witnesses they expect to call to present their case. Trial begins with the plaintiff attorney's opening statements. The defense attorney can then present an opening statement or can choose to wait until the beginning of the defense portion of the case.

It is the responsibility of the LNC to take notes during opening remarks and analyze the opposing counsel's statements to identify any new theories requiring a change in trial strategy, emphasis, or additional follow-up. The LNC should be prepared to discuss these and strategize with the retaining attorney.

Trial Examination of Witnesses

Following opening statements, the judge instructs the plaintiff attorney to begin presenting the case. The evidence is presented to the jury through the examination of witnesses and the introduction of exhibits. After the plaintiff's evidence is presented to the jury, the defense presents its case in rebuttal to that of the plaintiff.

Regardless of whether a witness is presented in the plaintiff's or defendant's case, all parties can examine each witness. Examination of witnesses occurs in the following order: direct examination, cross-examination, redirect examination, re-cross-examination, and rebuttal.

Direct Examination

The attorney that initially calls a witness to the stand directs the examination of that witness. Questions may be open-ended to allow the witness to elaborate (e.g., "Please describe the appearance of the plaintiff during the initial visit?") or may be close-ended requiring a brief response, such as yes or no (e.g., "Did the plaintiff ask any questions prior to signing the informed consent form?"). Close-ended questions may be used for adverse or hostile witnesses from whom a simple answer without elaboration or explanation is desired.

During direct examination, leading questions are generally not allowed. A leading question implies the answer. Examples are "When you approached the intersection, you saw the red light, correct?" and "Isn't it true the fetal heart monitor showed decelerations during the two hours prior to the delivery?"

After a witness's initial testimony, an attorney reserves the right to recall any witness.

Cross-examination

After direct examination, the other party or parties conduct cross-examination. The scope of questioning during cross-examination is limited to the subject matter elicited during direct examination. When the witness being cross-examined is adverse to the party performing the questioning, cross-examination attempts to undermine or discredit the witness, and the tone of the questioning is often intentionally adversarial. Questions may be leading, such as "You did not step on the brake, correct?" Through counsel's aggressive questioning, witnesses may experience intimidation, anger, and confusion, impacting the jury's perception of the witness and the witness's credibility. Thus, an effective cross-examination can make or break a case, especially in medical malpractice trials, which hinge on the credibility of the expert witnesses.

Redirect and Re-Cross-examination

Cross-examination is followed by redirect examination, which is further direct examination of a witness by the party who conducted the initial direct examination. The attorney uses this examination to clarify or reinforce previous testimony, but its scope is limited to the topics covered during cross-examination. Redirect examination is usually followed by re-cross-examination (further cross-examination of a witness by the party who conducted the initial cross-examination). Like redirect, re-cross-examination is used to clarify or emphasize specific testimony. Its scope is limited to the content of redirect examination.

Rebuttal

After the defense rests, the plaintiff may choose to call rebuttal witnesses to contradict or dispute specific testimony given by a defense expert witness. Rebuttal testimony provides an opportunity to respond to the testimony of the defendant's witnesses by means other than cross-examination. Examination of rebuttal witnesses follow the same order: direct, cross, redirect, and re-cross.

The LNC's Role during Trial Testimony

The LNC may be responsible to ensure all experts are available when called for testimony. This may mean meeting an expert at the airport and transporting the expert to a hotel or courtroom. This transportation time is an opportunity to discuss testimony and consult with the expert about issues that have arisen during the trial. The LNC may also continue to serve as the liaison to the experts throughout the course of the trial, including notifying them if the case settles before the expert testifies or advising them of the outcome of the trial.

Many courtrooms today have real-time court reporting, allowing all parties to immediately access testimony transcripts during trial. When real-time transcripts are not available in court, the LNC takes detailed notes of the witness's responses. The LNC then uses the real-time transcript or notes to suggest specific questions or further areas of questioning for the attorney. The LNC is also invaluable when identifying inconsistencies in the witness's testimony. For example, the LNC may utilize a digital copy of the witness's deposition transcript to perform key word searches to quickly retrieve relevant deposition testimony to identify any discrepancies between the witness's deposition and trial testimony. If the expert quotes from an article or textbook, the LNC advises the attorney if the testimony given is incorrect, inaccurate, or incomplete. The LNC, who should be very familiar with the relevant medical records, can point out inaccuracies between the testimony and the medical records. Inconsistencies in testimony require immediate attention for effective impeachment, so it is imperative that the LNC bring these to the attorney's attention while the witness is still on the stand. The attorney often consults with the LNC in the courtroom before concluding the examination of the witness. The LNC uses this opportunity to report any inconsistencies as well as any suggestions for additional questions or areas of questioning. The LNC may need to provide this information in written form if the court discourages verbal conferences in the courtroom.

The trial transcript or the LNC's notes are also invaluable later when the attorney is strategizing, preparing for upcoming witnesses, arguing motions, and developing closing arguments. Where real-time transcripts are not available, electronic or traditional hardcopy court transcripts can be purchased daily if available.

Throughout the trial, the LNC should listen to each witness's testimony to analyze its impact on the case. Trial strategy is dynamic and may change during the trial. The LNC, as a member of the trial team, must always be cognizant that the trial is a onetime opportunity for the plaintiff or the defendant to tell the story. Critique and discussion of the testimony and exhibits after the trial will not help win the case. The LNC should feel comfortable providing honest, constructive feedback to the attorney to allow for real-time modifications to trial strategy. For example, if jurors do not appear to be listening to specific testimony or do not appear to understand testimony, alterations in questions or demeanor of the attorney or witness must be corrected at once. As an observer and a nurse with training in reading body language and other non-verbal cues, LNCs are in a unique position to positively affect trial strategy and make suggestions based on observations in the courtroom.

Trial testimony can be frustrating for the LNC, a primary observer to the process. Witnesses may not respond as planned, and the opposing party may undermine well thought out theories. The LNC may need to conduct additional literature searches on specific topics to develop new theories or expand on earlier ones. The attorney will communicate new theories to witnesses in preparation for their testimony.

It is important for the LNC, paralegal, or legal assistant to keep an accurate record of all trial exhibits, including the dates they were introduced, offered, and accepted into evidence as full exhibits or marked for identification. Not only does this allow the exhibits to be easily identified, referenced, and accessed, but it is crucial if the court allows each party to confirm the full exhibits being sent with the jury for deliberation. See Table 39.1.

Table 39.1 Sample List of Exhibits

Exhibit #	Exhibit	Date	Introduced	Offered	Accepted	Full or ID
1	ER report	1/1/19	11/4/19	11/4/19	11/4/19	Full
5	Consent	1/2/19	11/4/19	11/4/19	11/5/19	Full
8	Consent	1/10/19	11/5/19	11/5/19	11/5/19	Full
14	Autopsy report	2/1/19	11/6/19	11/6/19	11/6/19	Full
15	Death certificate	2/1/19	11/4/19	—	—	
22	Anatomic model		11/6/19			ID

Depending on which members of the trial team are assisting at trial, the LNC may have numerous other ancillary responsibilities during trial. These may include transporting material (such as audiovisual equipment, medical record notebooks, the party's copies of exhibits, etc.) to and from the courthouse and securing them, setting up and handling the audiovisual equipment (such as overhead projectors, slide projectors, computer projection equipment and easels for charts or enlargements), and bringing office and other supplies for use during trial.

Trials can be exhausting and invigorating at the same time. Long hours may be necessary to ensure the client's case is presented clearly and convincingly. It can be rewarding to see years of work by the trial team and client come together to tell the complete story to the jury.

Directed Verdict

After the plaintiff's evidence has been presented, the attorney will state the plaintiff rests. The defense may then choose to make a motion for a directed verdict, also known as a motion for judgment as a matter of law. The basis of the motion is to argue that the plaintiff has failed to meet the burden of proof and that no reasonable jury could, based on the evidence presented, reach a conclusion to the contrary (Legal Information Institute, n.d.-b). After hearing arguments, the judge will either grant, deny, or defer ruling on the motion until after the jury reaches its verdict. If granted, the case ends in favor of the defendant. If denied, the defense presents its side and the case goes to the jury to decide. Deferring the ruling allows the judge to reduce the likelihood that a decision to grant the motion for directed verdict will be appealed and overturned, because the motion is moot if the jury renders a defense verdict.

Summation/Closing Arguments

Closing arguments are the summation of evidence presented during trial. The attorneys present conclusions in the best possible light for their party and point to where the opposing party failed to establish the promised evidence made during opening statements. A slide show presentation can be used to assist the attorney during summation by visually emphasizing important points of the case. Closing arguments are the final words from the attorneys and may be given before or after the judge's charge to the jury (discussed below). The arguments by the attorneys do not constitute evidence, cannot introduce any new information, and may be time-limited by the judge. The plaintiff usually presents first followed by the defense. Depending on the rules for the jurisdiction, each party may be given a brief time to rebut the opposing party's closing arguments. During summation, the LNC's role is to take notes of all party's closing arguments to assist the attorney to prepare for any rebuttal.

Jury Instructions, Deliberations, and Verdict

Jury instructions, also called the jury charge, are the explanations of the laws jury members must follow to determine the outcome of the case. Before the start of trial, each party submits its proposed jury instructions to the judge. Either before or during the trial, the attorneys and the judge discuss the proposed jury instructions, but ultimately the judge decides which instructions to present to the jury. Then either before or after closing arguments, the judge charges the jury (reads the instructions to the jury) and provides any necessary explanations or clarifications (ABA, 2017b). (See Appendix A: Samples of Medical Negligence Jury Instructions).

The jury then retires to the jury room and deliberates privately (i.e., outside the presence of the judge and counsel) during the hours set by the judge. During deliberations, the jury may request clarification of jury instructions by the judge or request portions of the trial transcript be read to them (or the recording of that testimony be played back to them). Sometimes the jury will ask to see exhibits to assist with the deliberation process. In most civil trials, the jurors are not sequestered; that is, they may go home each evening during the presentation of evidence and during deliberations.

In most, but not all, jurisdictions, jurors must reach a unanimous verdict. This may depend on whether the case is civil or criminal, whether the court is federal or state, and the length of time the jury has been deliberating. Some state courts permit a majority vote after six hours of deliberations. The time a jury takes to reach a verdict usually depends on the complexity of a case. In civil cases, the verdict is either for the plaintiff or for the defendant. In criminal cases, it is guilty or not guilty.

Once the jury reaches a verdict, they must complete the forms required by the jurisdiction. These forms will vary and may be called the jury ballot, verdict form, and jury interrogatories. The forms may be standard templates or may be customized by plaintiff's counsel or by input and agreement of all counsel. Typically, in civil cases, the forms require the jury to answer whether the plaintiff has proven, by a preponderance of the evidence, that the defendant deviated from the standard of care and, if so, whether that deviation caused the plaintiff's injuries. In jurisdictions with comparative or contributory negligence, the jury must decide what percentage, if any, the plaintiff's actions or inactions contributed to the injuries. If the verdict is in favor of the plaintiff, the jury must also award damages (discussed below).

In most cases, once all the forms are completed, the bailiff or court clerk is informed, and jurors are brought back to the courtroom where the jury foreperson reads the verdict. In some instances, the verdict is given to the parties by the judge by telephone (ABA, 2017c). Any party may request a polling of each juror's verdict (i.e., asking the jurors individually whether they agreed with, and still agree to, the verdict). If the verdict is not unanimous or not upheld by the number of jurors required to reach a verdict, the judge may direct the jury to deliberate further or may order a new trial.

If the verdict is accepted by the court, the judge signs the verdict form, and it is entered into the public record. If it is a plaintiff's verdict in a civil case, the judgment will usually state the monetary award (see Damages subsection below). Unless sealed by a judge, this information is public record.

Damages

Damages are any loss, detriment, or injury that directly results from a breach in the standard of care (Zorn & Dickinson, 2014). The term "damages" also refers to the monetary compensation awarded to the plaintiff for proven or established injuries. Financial reparation (compensatory damages) may be awarded to indemnify (compensate) the plaintiff for the injuries and related expenses. Compensatory damages are comprised of special damages and general damages. Special (or economic) damages are the quantifiable expenses incurred by the plaintiff, such as medical expenses (e.g., hospitalization, medical appointments, therapy, assistive devices, medication, etc.), lost wages, household help, funeral expenses (in a wrongful death case), etc. General (or non-economic) damages are intangible injuries suffered by the plaintiff, such as pain and suffering, mental anguish, loss of function, disfigurement, embarrassment, loss of enjoyment of life, loss of chance, etc. Non-economic damages may also include loss of consortium, which is usually a derivative claim brought by the plaintiff's or decedent's significant other for deprivation of the benefits of a family relationship, including intimacy, affection, companionship, and sexual relations (Zorn & Dickinson, 2014). Some jurisdictions have statutory limits (or caps) on the amount of money that can be awarded for non-economic damages.

Punitive or exemplary damages are awarded over and above compensatory damages when the defendant's actions are found to be egregious or grossly negligent, i.e., blatantly careless, indifferent, and without regard for the safety or lives of others (Zorn & Dickinson, 2014). Punitive damages are granted to punish the defendant, set an example, and deter future gross negligence (Zorn & Dickinson, 2014). When punitive damages are demanded, the trial may be bifurcated, that is, divided into two separate phases: liability and damages. The jury first hears testimony on liability and causation and then deliberates on these issues. If the jury finds the defendant was negligent and the negligence caused plaintiff's injuries, then the second phase of trial begins in which the jury is presented with evidence on damages. For more information on damages, see Chapter 4. For more information on damages experts, see Chapters 32 and 36.

If the jury found in favor of the plaintiff, they must consider the evidence presented regarding economic and non-economic damages and decide upon a monetary amount to award the plaintiff.

Sometimes, particularly in cases in which a judgment may be excessive and the economic damages are large, the parties may choose to enter into a high–low agreement before the jury renders its verdict. The jury, and oftentimes the judge, is not aware of the parties' agreement. A high–low agreement is a settlement agreement in which the parties essentially insure the other against an excessive verdict or no monetary award. Regardless of what the jury's verdict will be, the parties agree to the maximum and minimum monetary award to be given to the plaintiff. At a minimum, the plaintiff will receive X dollars (the low); at a maximum, the plaintiff will receive Y dollars (the high). For example, the parties may agree to a high–low of $1,000,000 and $100,000. If the verdict is in favor of the plaintiff and the jury awards $2,000,000, the plaintiff will receive $1,000,000 from the defendant. If the verdict is in favor of the plaintiff and the award is between $100,000 and $1,000,000, the plaintiff will receive the dollar amount specified by the jury. If the verdict is in favor of the plaintiff and is less than $100,000 or if the jury finds for the defendant, the plaintiff still receives $100,000 (Findlaw, 2017b).

Post-trial Activities

Jury Interviews

The LNC may be tasked with interviewing jurors after the trial concludes. The LNC is the perfect individual to conduct post-trial juror interviews, as LNCs are usually approachable and less intimating to jurors than an attorney. The jurors are under no obligation to talk to any party but are free to do so if there is no violation of applicable laws. Juror interviews can provide valuable information to the legal team for future trials. Questions about the attorney's presentation, including demeanor, the exhibits, or the witnesses, may identify areas for change or improvement in the attorney's next trial. When encouraged to do so, jurors are often willing to provide constructive feedback on the attorney's courtroom performance. In addition to the LNC, jury consultants also provide this service to attorneys.

Bill of Costs

A bill of costs is an itemized list of expenses incurred in an action by a party. Some jurisdictions allow certain expenses to be reimbursed to the prevailing party by the non-prevailing party. The costs subject to relief vary by jurisdiction and may include filing fees, fees for service of process, printing and copying expenses, and costs associated with subpoenaed witnesses. In federal court, an affidavit attesting to the accuracy and necessity of the costs is required. The deadline for filing the Bill of Costs is usually 10 to 30 days from judgment, and a copy of the bill should be provided to all other parties.

Post-trial Motions or Appeal

The non-prevailing party may file post-trial motions or an appeal to seek relief from the judgment. Post-trial motions are filed with the trial court and are typically ruled upon by the judge who presided over the trial. They may include motions for a new trial and for judgment notwithstanding the verdict (JNOV). A motion for a new trial is based on the principle of prejudicial error occurring during trial that ultimately affected the outcome. These motions are not granted lightly and would result in a new trial with a different jury. A motion for JNOV, which may also be referred to as a *renewed* judgment as a matter of law (emphasizing its relationship to the motion for directed verdict), asks the judge to overrule and reverse the jury's verdict because no reasonable jury could have reached the given verdict based on the evidence presented. When a motion for JNOV is granted, the original verdict is overturned with a new judgment in favor of the other party.

In civil cases in which the plaintiff prevails, the defendant can also file a motion for remittitur (reduction in the amount of money awarded to the plaintiff). Likewise, the prevailing plaintiff can file a motion for additur (increase in the jury's award) if it is believed the verdict is inadequate in light of the evidence presented.

Another way to obtain relief is through post-trial appeal of the verdict. The non-prevailing party, believing errors occurred during trial, appeals a higher court to review the lower court's decision. "An appeal is not a retrial or a new trial of the case" (ABA, 2017d, para. 4). An appeal may result in a new trial or some other modifications if the higher court finds that errors were made. There are attorneys who specialize in the appeals process, as it has its own set of procedures.

Summary

Trial preparation and the trial are the culmination of years of effort by the legal team to develop and present a case. They are increasingly becoming more technology-dependent and electronically based events.

As a critical contributor to the preparation and presentation of a case, the LNC assists the trial team in bringing the client's thoroughly prepared and well-organized story to the jury. The LNC's contributions begin pre-trial with strategizing with the trial team, preparing reports and exhibits, organizing binders and notebooks, working with witnesses, conducting research, being versed on the experts' opinions, and overseeing the preparation of the trial box. During the trial, the LNC assists with *voir dire*, identifies testimonial discrepancies, evaluates witnesses, maintains exhibits, manages the audiovisual equipment, orders and reviews transcripts, takes detailed trial notes, participates in ongoing trial analysis and strategy, anticipates the attorney's needs, and assists with any number of other tasks. After the trial, the LNC may be involved with post-trial tasks such as conducting jury interviews and assisting with post-trial motions and appeals (Dickinson & Fontaine, 2016).

The LNC brings many attributes and skills to the trial team and the case, including nursing expertise, an ability to educate and communicate, organizational skills, an ability to analyze and strategize, meticulous attention to detail, and critical thinking skills. In addition, anticipation is an all-important trial skill. The most successful LNC at trial anticipates the attorney's next steps, courtroom procedures, and witness needs.

References

American Bar Association. (2016). 50 state survey comparative fault. Retrieved from www.americanbar.org/content/dam/aba/events/lawyers_professional_liability/ls_lpl_2016_fall_conf_50_state_survey_comparative_fault.authcheckdam.pdf.

American Bar Association. (2017a). How courts work: Jury pool. Retrieved from www.americanbar.org/groups/public_education/resources/law_related_education_network/how_courts_work/jurypool.html.

American Bar Association. (2017b). How courts work: Jury instructions. Retrieved from www.americanbar.org/groups/public_education/resources/law_related_education_network/how_courts_work/jury instruct.html.

American Bar Association. (2017c). How courts work: Verdict. Retrieved from www.americanbar.org/groups/public_education/resources/law_related_education_network/how_courts_work/verdict.html.

American Bar Association. (2017d). How courts work: Appeals. Retrieved from www.americanbar.org/groups/public_education/resources/law_related_education_network/how_courts_work/appeals.html.

Arkfeld, M. R. (n.d.). Using multimedia in legal proceedings. *The digital practice of law*. Retrieved from www.elawexchange.com/.

Batson v. Kentucky, 476 U.S. 79 (1986).

Daubert v. Merrell Dow Pharmaceuticals, 509 U.S. 579 (1993).

Dickinson, J. (2017). Visual rhetoric: The effective use of PowerPoint during closing arguments. 2017 AALNC Forum. Obtained from author.

Dickinson, J., & Fontaine, C. (2016). The verdict is in! The vital role of LNCs at medical malpractice trials. Retrieved from www.aalnc.org/page/on-demandwebinars.

Drummond, M. A. (2009). The trial notebook. Retrieved from www.americanbar.org/publications/tyl/topics/professional-development/the_trial_notebook.html.

Ducote, D., & Holmes, M. (n.d.). A paralegal's guide to preparing a trial notebook. [PowerPoint presentation]. Retrieved from www.NALS/resources/collection/100414.Lit_Civil_Holmes_Ducote.

Federal Rules of Civil Procedure. (2017). Rule 32: Using depositions in court proceedings. Retrieved from www.federalrulesofcivilprocedure.org/frcp/title-v-disclosures-and-discovery/rule-32-using-depositions-in-court-proceedings/.

Federal Rules of Evidence. (2018). Article VIII: Hearsay. Retrieved from www.rulesofevidence.org/article-viii/.

Federal Rules of Evidence. (2019). Retrieved from www.rulesofevidence.org/.

Findlaw. (2017a). Criminal defense strategies. Retrieved from http://files.findlaw.com/pdf/criminal/criminal.findlaw.com_criminal-legal-help_criminal-defense-strategies.pdf.

Findlaw. (2017b). High–low agreements: A viable settlement alternative. Retrieved from http://corporate.findlaw.com/law-library/high-low-agreements-a-viable-settlement-alternative.html.

Frye v. United States, 293 F. 1013 (D.C. Cir. 1923).

Joseph, G. P. (2016). *Modern visual evidence*. Newark, NJ: Law Journal Press.

Judicial Council of California Civil Jury Instructions. (2018a). Standard of care for health care professionals. CACI No. 501. Retrieved from www.courts.ca.gov/partners/documents/caci_2018_edition.pdf.

Judicial Council of California Civil Jury Instructions. (2018b). Success not required. CACI No. 505. Retrieved from www.courts.ca.gov/partners/documents/caci_2018_edition.pdf.

Judicial Council of California Civil Jury Instructions. (2018c). Alternative methods of care. CACI No. 506. Retrieved from www.courts.ca.gov/partners/documents/caci_2018_edition.pdf.

Judicial Council of California Civil Jury Instructions. (2018d). Duty of hospital. CACI No. 514. Retrieved from www.courts.ca.gov/partners/documents/caci_2018_edition.pdf.

Judicial Council of California Civil Jury Instructions. (2018e). Duty of hospital to screen medical staff. CACI No. 516. Retrieved from www.courts.ca.gov/partners/documents/caci_2018_edition.pdf.

Judicial Council of California Civil Jury Instructions. (2018f). Standard of care for nurses. CACI No. 504. Retrieved from www.courts.ca.gov/partners/documents/caci_2018_edition.pdf.

Latiolasis-Hargrave, J. (2009). *Strictly business: body language: Using nonverbal communication for power and success* (2nd ed.). Dubuque, IA: Kendall-Hunt Publishing Company.

Legal Information Institute. (n.d.-a). Preponderance of the evidence. Retrieved from www.law.cornell.edu/wex/preponderance_of_the_evidence.

Legal Information Institute. (n.d.-b). Motion for directed verdict. Retrieved from www.law.cornell.edu/wex/motion_for_directed_verdict.

Masters, D. L. (2013). How to conduct a paperless trial. Retrieved from https://apps.americanbar.org/litigation/litigationnews/trial_skills/073013-tips-paperless-trial.html.

Miller, D. (2017). Best practice tips for electronic trial preparation. Retrieved from http://www2.law.columbia.edu/johnson/syllabus/TrialPresentationTips.pdf.

National Paralegal College. (n.d.). Opening statements, burdens of proof. Retrieved from https://national-paralegal.edu/public_documents/courseware_asp_files/researchLitigation/TrialPractice/Opening Statements.asp.

The-Injury-Lawyer-Directory.com. (n.d.-a). Contributory negligence vs. comparative negligence. Retrieved from https://the-injury-lawyer-directory.com/contributory-negligence-vs-comparative-negligence/.

The-Injury-Lawyer-Directory.com. (n.d.-b). Comparative fault by state. Retrieved from https://the-injury-lawyer-directory.com/comparative-fault-state/.

The LSU Medical and Public Health Law Site. (2009). The hearsay rule. Retrieved from https://biotech.law.lsu.edu/map/TheHearsayRule.html#Topic248.

Washington, S. M. (2016). Jury vs. bench trial—which one is better? *DUI Trial*. Retrieved from www.smwashingtonlaw.com/blog/2016/08/jury-vs-bench-trial-which-one-is-better.shtml.

Whalen, D. (2016). Technology tips for your civil litigation practice. Northeastern College of Professional Studies Colloquium 2012, October 25–26, 2016. Boston, MA. Retrieved from https://ofaolain.com/wp-content/uploads/2012/10/technology-tips-for-litigation.pdf.

Wickert, G. (2013). Understanding comparative fault, contributory negligence and joint & several liability. *Claims Journal*. Retrieved from www.claimsjournal.com/news/national/2013/09/05/235755.htm.

Zorn, E., & Dickinson, J. (2014). Case analysis: Medical malpractice. In *AALNC Legal nurse consulting online course* (module 8). Retrieved from www.aalnc.org/page/course-content#packages.

Additional Reading

Bennon, J. (2015). How to replace all the binders in your law office—a pictorial walk through. *Above the Law*. Retrieved from http://abovethelaw.com/2015/06/how-to-replace-all-the-binders-in-your-law-office-a-pictorial-walk-through/.

Black, N. (2016). Today's tech: A medical malpractice lawyer: A paperless office and an app. *Above the Law*. Retrieved from http://abovethelaw.com/2016/08/todays-tech-a-medical-malpractice-lawyer-a-paperless-office-and-an-app/.

Hendrickson, T. (2013). Trial notebook for iPad review. Retrieved from https://lawyerist.com/62253/trial-notebook-for-ipad-review/.

Hendrickson, T. (2016). Today's tech: A medical malpractice lawyer: A paperless office. *Above the Law*. Retrieved from http://abovethelaw.com/2016/08/todays-tech-a-medical-malpractice-lawyer-a-paperless-office-and-an-app/.

Hinderaker, A., & McFarland, I. (2015). Demonstrative evidence under the rules: The admissable and inadmissable. Retrieved from www.merchantgould.com/News-Room/Articles/85803/Demonstrative-Evidence-Under-the-Rules-The-Admissable-and-Inadmissable?find=85803&printver=true.

Legal Information Institute. (n.d.). Rule 30: Depositions of oral examination. Retrieved from www.law.cornell.edu/rules/frcp/rule_30.

Lexis Nexis' Concordance and Summation. www.summation.com.

Mauet, T. A., & Maeroweitz, M. P. (2016). *Fundamentals of litigation for paralegals* (9th ed.). New York, NY: Wolters Kluwer.

Microsoft Office Tutorials. (2016). Create a new trial notebook in Microsoft OneNote for lawyers [video file]. Retrieved from www.officetutes.com/create-a-new-trial-notebook-in-microsoft-onenote-for-lawyers/.

Miller, D. (2017). Best practice tips for electronic trial preparation. Retrieved from http://www2.law.columbia.edu/johnson/syllabus/TrialPresentationTips.pdf.

Monteleone, L. V. (2016). OneNote in OneMinute—screen clipping. [video blog]. https://paperlessprosecutor.wordpress.com/2016/03/24/onenote-in-oneminute-screen-clipping/.

New York State Bar Association. www.nysba.org/WorkArea/.

Polchinski, P. D. (2010). *The cross-examination edge: A guide to effective questioning*. Tucson, AZ: Lawyers & Judges Publishing Company.

Sanbar, A. A., Firestone, M. H., Fiscina, S., et al. (2007). *Legal medicine* (7th ed.). Philadelphia, PA: Mosby Elsevier.

Shandell, R. E., & Schulman, F. A. (2017). *The preparation and trial of medical malpractice cases*. Newark, NJ: Law Journal Press.

Singer, A. (1996). Trial consulting: A much-in-demand, highly effective and nicely profitable professional subspecialty for legal nurse consultants. *Journal of Legal Nurse Consulting, 7*(2), 2.

Statsky, W. P. (2016). *Introduction to paralegalism* (8th ed.). Independence, KY: Cengage Learning.

Tanford, J. A. (2009). *The trial process: Law, tactics and ethics* [Kindle Cloud Reader]. Retrieved from www.amazon.com/reader/1422472213/ref=rdr_sb_li_hist_1&state=01111.

The Personal Injury Law Directory. (n.d.). Retrieved from www.the-injury-lawyer-directory.com/negligence.html.

Trimm, H. H. (2005). *Forensics: The easy way*. Hauppauge, NY: Barrons Educational Services, Inc.

Wellman, F. I. (2016). *The art of cross-examination legal interrogation techniques*. Colorado Springs, CO: CreateSpace Independent Publishing Platform.

Test Questions

1. Motions in limine are used to:
   A. Highlight the key points of the trial strategy
   B. Prohibit introduction of certain evidence into trial
   C. Determine the order of witnesses
   D. Object to the other party's witnesses
2. An attorney may use a peremptory challenge to:
   A. Dismiss a potential juror without specific cause
   B. Object to a question by the opposing attorney
   C. Question the qualifications of an expert witness
   D. Attempt to remove a judge from the case
3. Demonstrative evidence is:
   A. Evidence used by the jury to show how they reached a verdict
   B. Evidence used to assist the jury in understanding complex concepts
   C. Sent to the jury room with the jurors for deliberation
   D. Evidence used only in opening statements or closing arguments
4. Cross-examination:
   A. Reinforces the credibility of the witness
   B. Is a process by which leading questions are not permitted
   C. May appear to be theatrical
   D. Is of little consequence to the outcome of the trial process
5. When comparative negligence is found by the jury, the plaintiff's:
   A. Award is compared with other awards for similar injuries
   B. Contributions to the injury are compared with the defendant's and the plaintiff's award is reduced proportionately
   C. Injuries are compared to those of individuals in similar cases
   D. Contributions to the injury are compared to the defendant's but the plaintiff's award is not changed

Answers: 1. B, 2. A, 3. B, 4. C, 5. B

Appendix A: Samples of Medical Negligence Jury Instructions from the Judicial Council of California Civil Jury Instructions (Judicial Council of California Civil Jury Instructions. 2018 ed.)

Standard of Care for Health Care Professionals (CACI No. 501)

[A/An] [insert type of medical practitioner] is negligent if [he/she] fails to use the level of skill, knowledge, and care in diagnosis and treatment that other reasonably careful [insert type of medical practitioners] would use in the same or similar circumstances. This level of skill, knowledge, and care is sometimes referred to as "the standard of care." [You must determine the level of skill, knowledge, and care that other reasonably careful [insert type of medical practitioners] would use in the same or similar circumstances, based only on the testimony of the expert witnesses [including [name of defendant]] who have testified in this case.]

> (Judicial Council of California Civil Jury Instructions, 2018a. CACI No. 501, p. 412, para. 1)

Success Not Required (CACI No. 505)

[A/An] [insert type of medical practitioner] is not necessarily negligent just because [his/her] efforts are unsuccessful or [he/she] makes an error that was reasonable under the circumstances. [A/An] [insert type of medical practitioner] is negligent only if [he/she] was not as skillful, knowledgeable, or careful as other reasonable [insert type of medical practitioners] would have been in similar circumstances.

> (Judicial Council of California Civil Jury Instructions, 2018b. CACI No. 505, p. 423, para. 1)

Alternative Methods of Care (CACI No. 506)

[A/An] [insert type of medical practitioner] is not necessarily negligent just because [he/she] chooses one medically accepted method of treatment or diagnosis and it turns out that another medically accepted method would have been a better choice.

> (Judicial Council of California Civil Jury Instructions, 2018c. CACI No. 506, p. 425, para. 1)

Duty of Hospital (CACI No. 514)

A hospital is negligent if it does not use reasonable care toward its patients. A hospital must provide procedures, policies, facilities, supplies, and qualified personnel reasonably necessary for the treatment of its patients. [When you are deciding whether [name of defendant] was negligent, you must base your decision only on the testimony of the expert witnesses who have testified in this case.]

> (Judicial Council of California Civil Jury Instructions, 2018d. CACI No. 514, p. 438, para. 1)

Duty of Hospital to Screen Medical Staff (CACI No. 516)

A hospital is negligent if it does not use reasonable care to select and periodically evaluate its medical staff so that its patients are provided adequate medical care.

(Judicial Council of California Civil Jury Instructions, 2018e. CACI No. 516, p. 442, para. 1)

Standard of Care for Nurses (CACI No. 504)

[A/An] [insert type of nurse] is negligent if [he/she] fails to use the level of skill, knowledge, and care in diagnosis and treatment that other reasonably careful [insert type of nurses] would use in similar circumstances. This level of skill, knowledge, and care is sometimes referred to as "the standard of care." [You must determine the level of skill, knowledge, and care that other reasonably careful [insert type of nurses] would use in similar circumstances based only on the testimony of the expert witnesses [including [name of defendant]] who have testified in this case.]

(Judicial Council of California Civil Jury Instructions, 2018f. CACI No. 504, p. 421, para. 1)

Glossary

Noreen Sisko, PhD, RN

Abbreviated New Drug Application (ANDA): Contains data that, when submitted to the Food and Drug Administration's Center for Drug Evaluation and Research's Office of Generic Drugs, provides for the review and, ultimately, the approval of a *generic* drug product.

Abbreviated New Drug Application Number: A six-digit number assigned by the Food and Drug Administration staff to each application for approval to market a *generic* drug in the United States.

Access to Medical and Exposure Records Standard: An Occupational Safety and Health Administration standard allowing those exposed to toxic substances access to their medical records and any analyses of employee medical and exposure records provided that all employee identifiers have been removed.

Accident Reconstructionist: An engineering expert who utilizes scientific analysis to determine how and why an accident occurred.

Accreditation: In health care, a process that allows organizations to demonstrate their ability to meet regulatory requirements and standards established by a recognized accreditation organization.

Accreditation Board for Specialty Nursing Certification (ABSNC): Formerly the American Board of Nursing Specialties (ABNS) Accreditation Council. An organization that offers a peer-review mechanism that allows nursing certification organizations to obtain accreditation by demonstrating compliance with the highest quality standards available in the industry.

Action Level: An Occupational Safety and Health Administration and National Institute for Occupational Safety and Health expression of a health or physical hazard indicating the level of a harmful or toxic substance/activity which requires medical surveillance, increased industrial hygiene monitoring, or biological monitoring.

Adjuster: See Claims Examiner.

Administrative Action: A legal proceeding by a state's administrative agency.

Administrative Law: The body of law that allows for the creation of public regulatory agencies and contains all the statutes, judicial decisions, and regulations that govern them. It is created by administrative agencies to implement their powers and duties in the form of rules, regulations, orders, and decisions.

Administrator/Administratrix of an Estate: A person appointed by a court to administer the estate of a deceased person who left no will.

Admissible Evidence: Any testimony, document, or tangible evidence that may be introduced to a fact-finder to establish or to bolster a point put forth by a party to the proceeding. For evidence to be admissible, it must be relevant, without being unfairly prejudicial, and it must have some indication of reliability.

Adverse Drug Reaction Reports: Summaries of adverse experiences with a specific product reported to the Food and Drug Administration.

Affidavit: A written or printed declaration or statement of facts, made voluntarily and confirmed by the oath or affirmation of the person making it. The oath is taken before an officer having authority to administer such an oath.

Affidavit of Merit: A written, formal, sworn statement of fact, signed by a qualified expert, stating that, in the expert's opinion, the named malpractice case is meritorious (i.e., the defendant was more likely than not negligent in the care of the plaintiff). Also referred to as Certificate of Merit.

Affirmative Defense: A defense to a cause of action (claim) for which the defendant has the burden of proof. Comparative negligence is an example of an affirmative defense.

Age of Majority: The threshold of adulthood as recognized or declared in law. It is the moment when minors cease to be under the control and legal responsibilities of their parents or guardians.

Agency for Healthcare Research and Quality (AHRQ): Formerly known as The Agency for Healthcare Policy and Research (AHCPR). Establishes standards of practice for a variety of patient care issues.

Agency for Toxic Substances and Disease Registry (ATSDR): An agency in the U.S. Department of Health and Human Services responsible for evaluating the impact on public health of the release of hazardous substances into the environment.

Alleged Injury: An injury represented as existing or as being described but not so proved.

Allowable Costs: Dollars allocated by health benefit plans by and for specified services.

Alternative Dispute Resolution (ADR): A method used to aid in resolving lawsuits outside of the courtroom.

American Board of Nursing Specialties (ABNS): A membership organization focused on improving patient outcome and consumer protection by promoting specialty nursing certification. Members are nursing credentialing organizations, such as the American Legal Nurse Consultant Certification Board.

American Legal Nurse Consultant Certification Board (ALNCCB®): The certification board associated with AALNC that determines the eligibility criteria for the LNCC® examination, audits applications for compliance with the criteria, sets fees, and sets maintenance criteria for renewal of certification. The ALNCCB® is charged with the responsibility of maintaining the LNCC® examination so that it is valid, reliable, and legally defensible. It confers the LNCC® credential upon passing the certification test.

Answer: A pleading filed by the defendant that is responsive to each allegation set forth in the plaintiff's Complaint.

Appeal: A request to a higher court to review a decision of a lower court.

Arbitration: Informal hearing held before a neutral third party who renders a decision and issues an award. A process for the resolution of disputes outside the court system.

Arbitration Agreement: A contract providing for compulsory arbitration or determination of a matter or matters between contending parties by one or more unofficial persons, in case of dispute as to rights or liabilities under it.

Arbitrator: A disinterested third party chosen by the parties or appointed by the court to render a decision in an arbitration.

Arraignment: The stage of the criminal process in which the defendant is formally advised of the charges and can enter a plea.

Assault: The unlawful intentional, or attempted, inflicting of injury upon another. Classified as first, second, and third degrees; first degree assault is intentional infliction of fear of serious bodily harm; second degree is knowingly inflicting fear; and third degree is recklessly inflicting fear.

Assessment: As a legal nurse consultant standard, the collection of data to support the assessment of medical-legal issues related to a case or a claim.

Associates: Non-partner attorneys employed by a law firm.

Assumption of the Risk: A defense based on the theory that some activities, such as snow skiing, by their nature, have inherent risks, and the defendant has no duty to protect the plaintiff from such risks. By choosing to engage in the activity, the participant (plaintiff) assumes the risk of injuries due to known dangers of the activity.

Audit Trail: Paper or electronic trail that gives a step by step documented history of a transaction or record entry. It enables an examiner to trace the financial data from general ledger to the source (invoice, receipt, voucher, etc.). In electronic medical records (EMR), it is a record of information about each encounter with the EMR, including any instance an individual has accessed, viewed, printed, downloaded, supplemented, or modified a patient's chart.

Authorization: In insurance, the process by which permission is granted by the insurance plan for a member to receive a treatment or service by a healthcare provider.

Auto-generate: A computer feature that auto-populates parts of the medical record with certain content, such as the patient's history of present illness or providers' orders, being carried over from one day to the next.

Average Weekly Wage: The sum used by the Workers' Compensation Commission to calculate compensation rates for injured workers. Can include overtime wages.

Bad Faith: In insurance, an insurance company's unreasonable and unfounded refusal to provide coverage in violation of the duties of good faith and fair dealing owed to an insured.

Bates Stamping: Organizational labeling system which places a number on each page of a medical record or legal document.

Batson Challenge: Refers to an objection to the validity of a peremptory challenge, on grounds that the other party used it to exclude a potential juror based on race, ethnicity, or sex. See *Batson v. Kentucky*, 476 U.S. 79, 89 (U.S. 1986) in civil cases and *Snyder v. Louisiana* 552 U.S. 472 (2008) in criminal cases.

Battery: The unlawful use of violence against another, without the person's consent.

Behind-the-Scenes Consultants: Legal nurse consultants who are either employees of firms or independent contractors who do not testify or sign affidavits.

Bench Trial: A trial heard and decided by a judge, as opposed to a jury. A bench trial can be requested in place of a jury trial.

Beneficiary: An individual who is entitled to benefits under a defined health plan.

Bill of Costs: An itemized list of expenses a prevailing party in a lawsuit or action paid for services procured from an attorney. Some jurisdictions allow these costs to be recovered from the defeated party. Recoverable costs vary by jurisdiction but often include copying fees, filing fees, travel expenses, court reporter fees, and electronic legal research costs.

Bill of Particulars: A legal document in which the plaintiff sets forth the specific negligence and damage claims. It is used by only a few states and is similar to interrogatories. When referred to as Verified Bill of Particulars, it has been signed by the plaintiff and notarized.

Billable Hours: Hours worked on cases or projects billed to a client.

Binding Arbitration: An arbitration in which the arbitrator's decision is final, binding, and enforceable in a court of law.

Blood Borne Pathogens Standard: One of the standards developed by the Occupational Safety and Health Administration in order to limit workers' occupational exposure to blood, bodily fluids, and other potentially infectious materials.

Bodily Injury (BI) Insurance: The most basic type of automobile insurance coverage. It covers the insured for third-party claims up to the amount purchased, if the insured causes an accident that injures another person. If a person is injured in an automobile accident caused by someone else, the at-fault person's BI coverage will compensate the injured person for the injuries.

Boolean Operators: Words (AND, OR, and NOT) used to produce focused searches in some search engines by combining or excluding keywords. Modern search engines do not need Boolean operators.

Bradford Hill Criteria: Criteria published by Sir Bradford Hill to determine epidemiologic causation between a substance and disease. Used to prove or refute general causation.

Breach of Duty: Failure of an actor to exercise reasonable care under the circumstances.

B-Reader: A licensed radiologist who received special training and experience in x-rays for the purpose of identifying lung disease, such as asbestosis and silicosis.

Burden of Proof: The amount of proof required to prove an element of a cause of action or an affirmative defense. In civil cases, the amount of proof required is a preponderance of the evidence. In criminal cases, the amount of proof required is beyond a reasonable doubt.

Business Associate Agreement (BAA): A contract, generally required under the Health Insurance Portability and Accountability Act, between a covered entity and a business associate to ensure the business associate will appropriately safeguard protected health information.

Capitation: A specific, fixed dollar amount paid to healthcare providers per patient for the cost of providing health care.

Care Area Assessment: A process used by long-term care/skilled nursing facilities to interpret the information captured in the minimum data set and determine if a care plan is needed based on the data.

Carrier: A company that provides insurance.

Case-Control Study: A study that looks at two groups, one with the disease and one without the disease, to determine if an association exists between the past exposures and incidences of disease.

Case Management Software: Computerized database used by law firms to integrate various aspects of a case (such as client communication, workflow, documents, reports, costs, billing, etc.) to streamline and coordinate processes and increase efficiency and productivity.

Case Outcome Identification: As a legal nurse consultant standard, the participation in the identification of the optimal outcome for a case or claim.

Case Planning: As a legal nurse consultant standard, the development of a work plan that contributes to optimal case outcome.

Catastrophic Injury: A physical injury that creates permanent and life-long disability, such as a brain or spinal cord injury.

Catastrophic Loss: A loss of an extraordinary large value.

Causal Strike: A method of eliminating potential members from the jury panel. Also referred to as challenge for cause or removal for cause. The basis for a causal strike is typically a prospective juror's partiality.

Causation: The causal relationship between the alleged breach of duty and the claimed injuries. There are two types of causation: factual cause and proximate cause, and both must be proven.

Causation Expert: An expert witness who opines on the casual relationship (or lack thereof) between the alleged breach of duty and the claimed injuries.

Cause of Action: A factual situation that entitles one person to obtain a remedy in court from another person (*Black's Law Dictionary*, 10th ed., 2014). A claim made in a Complaint along with alleged supporting facts that, if proven, would constitute all the elements of proof required to prevail on that claim. Examples of causes of action include negligence, breach of contract, loss of consortium, and fraud.

Centers for Medicare & Medicaid Services (CMS): A federal agency within the U.S. Department of Health and Human Services that administers the Medicare program and, in conjunction with state governments, the Medicaid program.

Certificate of Completion: Confirmation of completing an activity or course of study. Not a professional credential.

Certificate of Merit: See Affidavit of Merit.

Certification: The formal recognition of the higher level of knowledge, skill, and expertise within a specialty practice than is expected from nurses with the minimal qualifications required for entry into the practice setting. It is demonstrated by the achievement of standards identified by the nursing specialty.

Certified Medical Records: A copy of a patient's medical records that is authenticated by the records custodian or healthcare facility as being an accurate version of the documents requested.

Certify: To issue a court order allowing a class of litigants to maintain a class action; to create (a class) for purposes of a class action.

Chain of Custody: The movement and location of physical or electronic evidence from the time it is obtained until the time it is presented in court. It is evidenced by a paper trail/chronological documentation that records the sequence of custody, control, transfer, analysis, and disposition of physical or electronic evidence in a criminal case.

Circumstantial Evidence: Evidence made by inference or deduction.

Civil Action for Deprivation of Rights: A law that essentially allows a person who is deprived of constitutional rights by a state actor to bring a cause of action against the person/entities (i.e., police officers, correctional officers, state and municipal officials, and private parties acting the color of law). Also called "Monroe" for the 1961 Supreme Court case *Monroe v. Pape*.

Claim: In the judicial system, a demand for money, property, or a legal remedy to which one asserts a right. In insurance, a demand by an individual or corporation to recover, under a policy of insurance, for losses that may come within that policy.

Claimant: The person making an injury claim; the individual petitioning for or receiving benefits.

Claim Reserves: The money that has been earmarked and set aside for claim-related payments, including the indemnity/loss payment or payments of expenses related to defending the claim.

Claims Examiner: A person designated to represent an insurance company in the investigation and negotiation of a claim in order to reach an agreement on the amount of a loss or the insurer's liability. Also known as a Claims Adjuster or, in some areas, a Resolution Manager.

Client: For independent legal nurse consultants (LNCs), the individual requesting or hiring the services of the LNC. The client is typically an attorney/law firm, insurance company, governmental agency, etc. Independent LNCs do not work directly for the plaintiff or defendant; rather, they work on the party's behalf through the client as an intermediary.

Closing Argument: A summation of evidence presented during trial.

Code of Ethics: A set of guidelines designed to define acceptable behaviors for members of a group, association, or profession.

Code of Federal Regulations (CFR): Codification of the general and permanent rules published in the Federal Register by the executive departments and agencies of the federal government.

Cohort Study: A study that compares the rate of disease in two groups of people, one exposed to the suspected substance and one not exposed to the substance.

Collision Coverage: Automobile insurance for repair or replacement of an insured vehicle up to a specified amount when an insured's car collides with another car or object.

Common Law: In general, a body of law that develops and derives through judicial decisions.

Comparative Negligence: A proportional division of the damages between the plaintiff and the defendant in a tort action according to their respective share of fault contributing to the injury or damage. It is measured in percentages according to the degree of contribution to the injury.

Compensation: Money awarded in court or through alternative dispute resolution to the plaintiff for loss, injury, or suffering.

Competent: Duly qualified; answering all requirements; having enough capacity, ability, or authority; possessing the requisite physical, mental, natural, or legal qualifications.

Complaint: The original or initial pleading by which an action is commenced. It sets forth a claim for relief.

Comprehensive Coverage: Optional automobile insurance that covers damages to the insured vehicle from causes such as theft, a falling tree, and natural disasters. It does not cover damages from collision.

Conditional Payment: A Medicare payment for services rendered to a beneficiary that another payer may be responsible for and, thus, is conditioned upon reimbursement by the other insurer (the primary payer).

Conditions of Participation (CoPs): Standards developed by the Centers for Medicare & Medicaid Services that healthcare organizations must meet in order to begin, and continue, participating in the Medicare and Medicaid programs.

Conflict of Interest: A situation in which one person has information that may potentially be used to influence a case and cause harm, injury, or prejudice to a party.

Consent Order: A written agreement between a healthcare professional or facility and a professional licensing board that identifies the facts found during investigation and details the specific penalties imposed upon the professional or facility.

Consent Proxy: A document that delegates the authority to make healthcare decisions to another adult when one has become incapacitated or unable to make decisions.

Conservatee: A person deemed by a judge to be unable to care for oneself or to manage one's financial affairs and for whom a conservator is appointed.

Consortium: The alliance between two people, such as between spouses, and their respective right to each other's cooperation, affection, aid, and companionship. Loss of consortium is often claimed in personal injury lawsuits.

Constitutional Deprivation: A crime, pursuant to Section 242 of Title 18, in which a person acting under the color of law willfully deprives a person of a right or privilege protected by the Constitution or laws of the United States.

Constitutional Law: The body of law deriving from the U.S. Constitution and dealing primarily with governmental powers, civil rights, and civil liberties.

Consumer-Directed Health Plans (CDHP): A type of medical insurance or plan that typically has a higher deductible and lower monthly premiums.

Consumer Expectation Test: A test used to determine whether a product was negligently manufactured or whether its warning is defective. A product is considered defective if it fails to meet the reasonable, widely accepted minimum expectations of consumers about the circumstances under which the product should perform safely.

Contingency Fee: A fee arrangement in which the plaintiff attorney receives a percentage of the plaintiff's settlement or verdict.

Contractor: One who contracts to work for another party; the person who retains the control of the means, method, and manner of the project result.

Contributory Negligence: Negligent conduct by the plaintiff that contributed to the injury. In states that recognize this doctrine, a finding of any fault by the plaintiff is a total bar to recovery by the plaintiff.

Control Group: In experimental research, a group that does not receive treatment.

Correctional Medicine: The medical specialty in which healthcare providers care for people in prisons and jails.

Corrections Record: Documents maintained by corrections facilities (prisons or jails) that contain medical information.

Cost-Benefit Analysis: Economic analysis that assigns a numerical value to the cost-effectiveness of an operation, procedure, or program.

Coverage: The assurance against losses provided under the terms of an insurance policy.

Covered Entity: An entity that is covered by (i.e., that must comply with) the Health Insurance Portability and Accountability Act. Covered entities include health plans, healthcare clearinghouses, and certain healthcare providers.

Credentialing: A review process to approve a healthcare provider applying for a contract with a health plan or healthcare facility.

Credentials: Evidence of one's qualifications, achievements, etc. Degree credentials (e.g., BSN, MS, JD) are awarded based on the completion of an educational program. Licensure credentials (e.g., RN, LPN) are awarded based on completion of a specified educational program and the successful passing of a national licensure exam. National certifications (e.g., LNCC®) are awarded upon meeting criteria set by a nationally recognized, usually accredited, certifying body.

Credibility: Worthy of belief; must be preceded by establishment of competency (i.e., that an expert is legally fit to testify).

Criminal Intent (*mens rea*): One's state of mind during a crime. There is criminal intent when an alleged perpetrator knew the crime committed was wrong at the time it occurred.

Cross-examination: The process in which a witness or party is questioned by the opposing party during a trial, hearing, or deposition.

Cruel and Unusual Punishment: Punishment prohibited by the Eighth Constitutional Amendment; includes torture, deliberately degrading punishment, or punishment that is too severe for the crime committed.

Cumulative Trauma: An injury or illness that occurs over a period of time (e.g., carpal tunnel syndrome).

Curbside Opinion: A verbal opinion from a non-retained expert.

Current Procedural Terminology (CPT): A uniform language that accurately describes medical, surgical, and diagnostic services.

Custodial Parent: The parent who is given physical or legal custody of a child by a court order.

Damages: A sum of money awarded to a person injured by the tort of another.

Damages Cap: A maximum amount of non-economic damages that can be awarded in a case. Caps are imposed by state-specific laws.

Damages Expert: An expert witness who opines on the nature and extent of the plaintiff's or decedent's injuries (damages).

Daubert Hearing: A hearing conducted by federal district courts and most state courts to determine whether proposed expert testimony regarding scientific knowledge meets the applicable evidentiary requirements for relevance and reliability, as clarified by the Supreme Court in *Daubert v. Merrell Dow Pharms., Inc.*

Daubert Standard: The standard to which federal district courts and most state courts hold expert testimony regarding scientific knowledge to determine whether it is admissible under the applicable evidentiary rules.

Decedent: A person who has died.

Decision-Making Capacity (DMC): A person's ability to understand information provided and make decisions congruent with one's own values and preferences.

Deductible: A predetermined amount of money that an insured must pay before an insurance company will pay a claim.

Defective Design: A flaw in the way a drug or device was designed, rendering it not reasonably safe for its intended use or a use that can be reasonably anticipated.

Defendant: The person or entity against whom a lawsuit is brought.

Deliberate Indifference: The conscious disregard of the consequences of one's actions or inactions. In law, the courts apply the deliberate indifference standard to determine if a professional has violated an inmate's civil rights by disregarding an excessive risk to an inmate's health or safety.

Delta V: Change in velocity; the difference between the speed just prior to an impact and the speed immediately after the impact, as determined by an accident reconstructionist.

Demand Letter: A letter from the plaintiff attorney to the defendant's attorney or insurance company that details the claims, their bases, and the injuries and sets forth a dollar amount the plaintiff would accept for settlement of the case.

Demonstrative Evidence: Evidence in the form of objects (e.g., maps, diagrams, or models) that, in itself, has no probative value but is used to illustrate and clarify the factual matter at issue.

Dependent Adult: An adult 18 years of age or older who is not capable of meeting one's own needs and relies on others to supply care and support.

Deposition: Pre-trial sworn testimony of parties or others, such as witnesses, to elicit information about the claims and defenses. Depositions are conducted outside of the courtroom and are also known as examinations before trial (EBT).

Digital Imaging and Communications in Medicine (DICOM): The standard for the communication and management of medical imaging information.

Direct Evidence: Evidence of a fact based on a witness's personal knowledge or observation of that fact.

Direct Examination: The process in which a witness or party is questioned during a trial, hearing, or deposition by the party who called that witness to give evidence.

Directed Verdict: A ruling entered by a judge after granting one party's trial motion which argued the opposing party has insufficient evidence to reasonably support its case. In granting the motion, the judge determined there is no legally sufficient evidentiary basis for a reasonable jury to reach a different conclusion. It takes the case decision out of the jury's hands. Also known as a Judgment as a Matter of Law.

Disbursements: The out-of-pocket expenses a law firm incurs in the prosecution or defense of a case, such as fees for copies of medical records, deposition transcripts, private investigators, and experts.

Discoverable: Able to be discovered; subject to legal discovery by the opposing party.

Discovery: Pre-trial devices that can be used by one party to obtain facts and information about the case from another party in order to assist the requesting party's preparation for trial.

Dispositive Motion: A motion asking for a court order that entirely disposes or ends one or more claims in favor of the moving party (usually the defendant). The most common are the motion to dismiss and the motion for summary judgment.

Double Jeopardy: Legal protection in the U.S. Constitution for a criminal defendant from facing prosecution more than once for the same crime.

Durable Medical Equipment (DME): Any equipment that provides therapeutic benefits to a patient in need because of certain medical conditions or illnesses.

Durable Power of Attorney (DPOA): A power of attorney that remains in effect during the grantor's incompetency.

Durable Power of Attorney for Healthcare (DPOAHC): An agent allowed to make healthcare decisions for a patient who has become incompetent.

Duty: An action or observation that is expected to occur once a relationship has been established between two people, such as healthcare provider and patient.

Economic Damages: Compensation to the plaintiff for objectively verifiable monetary losses, such as past and future medical expenses and loss of past and future earnings. Also referred to as special damages.

Economist: A type of damages expert who calculates the value of future medical expenses and lost wages over time.

Eggshell Plaintiff: A "fragile" plaintiff with significant pre-existing conditions that affect the risk of, as well as the recovery from, injury. The defendant "takes the plaintiff as found."

Eighth Amendment: The constitutional amendment, ratified as part of the Bill of Rights in 1791, prohibiting excessive bail, excessive fines, and cruel and unusual punishment.

Elder Abuse: An intentional act or failure to act by a caregiver, thereby creating a risk of harm to an older or dependent adult.

Electronic Health Record (EHR): A digital patient chart. EHRs are real-time records, making information instantly available and secure to authorized users.

Electronic Medical Record (EMR): A digital version of the paper chart in a clinician's office.

Electronic Patient Portal: A secure healthcare provider website giving patients with an Internet connection access to their protected health information. It is also a means for patients to send and receive secure communications with the healthcare provider who maintains the patient portal.

Electronic Protected Health Information (ePHI): Any electronic information about health status, provision of healthcare, or payment for healthcare that is created or collected by a covered entity (or its business associate) that can be linked to a specific individual. It is legally protected and, to preserve privacy, cannot be divulged.

Elements of Proof: The constituent parts of a claim that must be proven for the claim to succeed. In a civil tort negligence claim, they are duty, breach of duty, causation, and damages.

Eligibility: With regard to Medicare, meeting the legal requirements for benefits. One must still file an application to become entitled.

Emancipated Minors: Persons under the age of majority who are independent of parental control and assume most adult responsibilities.

Emergency Medical Treatment and Active Labor Act of 1986 (EMTALA): A federal law requiring hospital emergency departments to medically screen every patient who seeks emergency care and to stabilize those with medical emergencies prior to transfer to another facility, regardless of health insurance status or ability to pay.

Employee Retirement Income Security Act of 1974 (ERISA): A law designed to protect the rights of employees who receive employer-provided benefits such as pensions, deferred retirement income, and healthcare benefits.

Entitled: With regard to Medicare, an individual who has satisfied the requisite contributions during employment and attained the age requirement or certain disabilities to be eligible for benefits.

Entity: A person, partnership, organization, or business that has a legal and separately identifiable existence.

Environmental Protection Agency (EPA): An independent federal agency in the executive branch that is responsible for setting pollution-control standards in the areas of air, water, solid waste, pesticides, radiation, and toxic materials.

Epidemiology: A scientific discipline which, among other things, describes disease over time in specific populations, searches for hazardous factors affecting and influencing health in populations, and quantitatively estimates risks of specific diseases of exposed persons.

Errors and Omissions (E&O) Insurance: A type of professional liability insurance that protects companies and their workers or individuals against claims made by clients for inadequate work or negligent actions.

Essential Functions: The duties considered crucial to the job the worker has or wants. One must have the physical and mental qualifications to fulfill the job's essential functions.

Ethical Codes: See Code of Ethics.

Evaluation: As a legal nurse consultant standard, the process of determining the progress toward attainment of expected case outcomes, including the solicitation of feedback regarding the effectiveness of work product materials.

Evidence: Any matter of fact that a party to a lawsuit offers to prove or defend against an issue in the case.

Evidentiary Burden: The obligation to produce evidence to properly raise an issue at trial and to show the existence or non-existence of a fact in issue.

Evidentiary Hearing: A legal proceeding conducted for the presentation or determination of evidence.

Examination Before Trial (EBT): See Deposition.

Exception-Based Documentation: A method of medical record documentation in which only exceptions (significant findings) to normal body system assessments are documented.

Usual and normal assessment findings are not documented. Also known as variance charting or charting by exception.

Excess Carrier: An insurance carrier that provides excess coverage to an insured.

Excess (Insurance) Coverage: Liability insurance that provides coverage above (in excess of) an underlying or primary insurance policy. It protects the insured against judgments in excess of the primary policy's limits and may involve an additional insurance carrier.

Exclusions: Noted services, conditions, or liabilities that an insurance policy will not cover.

Exclusive Provider Organization (EPO): A managed care organization in which the providers are exclusive to the plan and its membership.

Exclusive Remedy Doctrine: In Workers' Compensation (WC), the principle that the benefits received under the WC program are the exclusive remedy for work-related injuries. It bars employees from suing employers or co-employees.

Executor/Executrix of an Estate: A person appointed through a decedent's will to administer the estate of the decedent.

Exemplary Damages: Compensation to a plaintiff when oppressive, malicious, or fraudulent conduct is involved. It is intended to punish the defendant, set an example, and deter future behavior considered outrageous. Also called punitive damages.

Exhaustion: When Medicare Set-Aside funds have been completely spent on injury-related medical items, services, and expenses.

Exhibit: A document or object produced and identified in court as evidence.

Expert: A person possessing the knowledge, skills, and expertise concerning a particular subject who can render an opinion.

Expert Fact Witness: A witness who, by virtue of special knowledge, skill, training, or experience, is qualified to provide testimony to aid the fact-finder in matters that exceed the common knowledge of ordinary people but does not offer opinions on the standard of care.

Expert Witness: A witness who, by virtue of special knowledge, skill, training, or experience, is qualified to provide testimony to aid the fact-finder in matters that exceed the common knowledge of ordinary people. The testimony may focus on standard of care, causation, and/or damages.

Explanation of Benefits (EOB): A statement sent by health insurance companies to covered individuals explaining what medical treatments and services were paid for on their behalf.

Exposure: In insurance, the maximum amount of money that an insurer could spend on one claim (often coincides with the policy limit).

Exposure Records: Documentation of environmental workplace (1) monitoring or measuring of a toxic substance or a harmful agent or (2) biological monitoring, which directly assesses the absorption of a toxic substance or a harmful physical agent.

External Standards: Expectations for professional practice that stem from sources such as state nurse practice acts, state boards of nursing, federal organizations, independent not-for-profit organizations (such as The Joint Commission), professional nursing organizations, nursing literature, and continuing education programs. May contribute to defining the standard of care.

Fact-Finder: The person or persons who decide the facts of a case upon hearing the evidence (e.g., jury, judge, mediator, arbitrator, etc.).

Fact Witness: A witness who is not named as a defendant in a lawsuit but has knowledge of events that have occurred.

Factual Cause: A cause or factor without which the harm would not have occurred. Also referred to as "legal cause," "cause-in-fact," "actual cause," or "but for cause." The latter refers to the *but for* test used to determine factual causation: factual causation exists when the outcome would not have occurred *but for* the negligent conduct.

Failure to Warn: A failure to comply with a duty to warn others of a risk or danger.

Family Educational Rights and Privacy Act of 1974 (FERPA): A federal law that protects the privacy of a student's education records.

Federal Employers Liability Act (FELA): Provides that a railroad employee injured in the course of employment may file suit and seek the full amount of the employee's damages.

Federal Question Jurisdiction: A term used in the United States law of civil procedure to refer to the situation in which a U.S. federal court has subject matter jurisdiction to hear a civil case, because the plaintiff has alleged a violation of the Constitution, laws, or treaties of the United States.

Federal Rules of Civil Procedure: The body of procedural rules which govern all civil actions in U.S. District Courts (federal court) and after which most of the states have modeled their own rules of procedure.

Federal Rules of Evidence: The rules governing the introduction of evidence in civil and criminal proceedings in federal courts and after which many state courts have closely modeled their own evidentiary rules.

Fee Schedule: Regarding Workers' Compensation, the fees for medical care rendered allowable; healthcare providers must write-off any adjustments required by the state. Regarding expert witnesses, a document containing the expert's expectations for compensation.

Felony: A criminal offense for which a sentence is longer than a year.

Fiduciary Responsibility: A legal and ethical obligation of one person to act in the best interest of another.

Field Case Management: Case management services provided face-to-face through visits with the client at home, in an inpatient setting, and at provider's offices.

First-Degree Murder: A killing which is deliberate and premeditated.

First-Party Claim: An injury, loss, or accident claim made directly against the insurance carrier by an insured, policyholder, or beneficiary.

Focus Group: A group of individuals with diverse demographics whose thoughts, opinions, and reactions to information are solicited and studied.

Food and Drug Administration Adverse Event Reporting System (FAERS): A database that contains adverse event reports, medication error reports, and product quality complaints resulting in adverse events that were submitted to the Food and Drug Administration.

Forensic Science: Science applied to answering legal questions by the examination, evaluation, and exploration of evidence.

Foreseeability: A factor in considering whether a defendant exercised reasonable care. In assessing whether a defendant exercised reasonable care, the fact-finder considers if the defendant knew, or should have foreseen, at the time of the incident, the risk and severity of harm that could result from the defendant's conduct.

Fraud: Misrepresentation of a material fact intended to result in financial or personal gain.

Fraudulent Concealment: Deliberate hiding or suppression with the intention to deceive or defraud.

Freedom of Information Act (FOIA): A federal law that allows for the full or partial disclosure of previously unreleased information and documents controlled by the United States government.

Frye Standard: A test used by a few states to determine the admissibility of scientific evidence. It provides that expert opinion based on a scientific technique is admissible only where the techniques are generally accepted as reliable in the relevant scientific community.

Functional Capacity Evaluation: An assessment typically done by an occupational or physical therapist to determine whether an individual can meet the physical or cognitive demands of a job.

Functional Limitations: The impact of pathology and impairment on the physical or psychological function of a person as a whole.

Functional Status: A person's ability to perform normal daily activities required to meet basic needs, fulfill usual roles, and maintain health and well-being.

G (Force of Gravity): The unit of measurement of a load caused by acceleration or deceleration. The Gs in a motor vehicle collision are calculated by the accident reconstructionist.

General Acceptance Test: A standard for the admissibility of expert testimony. Expert testimony based on a scientific technique is inadmissible unless the technique has been accepted as reliable by the relevant scientific community. See Frye and Daubert Standards.

General Damages: Compensation to the plaintiff for injuries that cannot be readily valued, such as past and future pain and suffering, mental or emotional distress, loss of chance, loss of enjoyment of life, and loss of consortium. Also called non-economic damages.

Grand Jury: A body of people randomly selected in a manner like trial jurors whose purpose is to investigate and inform on crimes committed within its jurisdiction and to accuse (indict) persons of crimes when it has discovered enough evidence to warrant holding a person for trial.

Grievance: An injury, injustice, or wrong that potentially gives the injured or wronged person grounds for a formal complaint against the wrongdoer.

Guardian: A person appointed by the legal system with the power, and charged with the duty, of taking care of and managing the property and rights of another person, who, for defect of age, understanding, or self-control, is considered incapable of administering one's own affairs.

Hazard Communication Standard: One of the standards developed by the Occupational Safety and Health Administration to prevent workplace illness and injury to workers who are exposed to hazardous chemicals by providing information to employees about chemical hazards.

Healthcare Common Procedure Coding System (HCPCS): A standardized coding system describing specific medical services, supplies, and equipment. Often pronounced "hick-picks."

Healthcare Fraud: Knowingly and willfully executing a scheme to defraud a healthcare benefit program or obtaining, by means of false or fraudulent pretenses, representations, or promises, any of the money or property owned by any healthcare benefit program.

Healthcare Provider Board: A group of healthcare providers in the same profession and other appointed individuals who are responsible for interpreting and enforcing the laws and statutes governing that profession, hearing and deciding matters concerning suspension or revocation of licensure within that profession, adjudicating complaints against healthcare providers within that profession, and imposing sanctions where appropriate.

Health Care Quality Improvement Act (HCQIA): A federal act that extends immunities for state peer review committee members on a federal level.

Health Information Technology for Economic and Clinical Health Act (HITECH): An act signed into law to promote the adoption and meaningful use of health information technology.

Health Insurance Portability and Accountability Act (HIPAA): An act signed into law that established privacy and security standards to protect patients' healthcare information.

Health Maintenance Organization (HMO): A group of participating healthcare providers (e.g., physicians, hospitals, clinics) that provides medical services to enrolled members of the group health insurance plan for a fixed annual fee.

Health Plan Employer Data and Information Set (HEDIS): A comprehensive set of standardized performance measures designed to provide purchasers and consumers with the information they need for reliable comparison of health plan performance.

Hearsay: Evidence based not on a witness's personal knowledge but on another's statement not made under oath. It is usually inadmissible at trial.

Hired Gun: An expert who, for a price, will say whatever the attorney wants the expert to say to support the attorney's case.

Impairment Rating (IR): A percentage of loss of use of a body part or function compared to normal. In Workers' Compensation, the percentage is used in a mathematical calculation to determine the worker's permanent partial disability benefit.

Impeachment of a Witness: The process of calling into question the credibility of a witness.

Implementation: As a legal nurse consultant standard, the execution of the plan of action.

***In forma pauperis*:** Latin for "in the character or manner of a pauper." This designation is given to an indigent who cannot afford the normal costs of a lawsuit. The individual is permitted to disregard filing fees and court costs.

Inadmissible Evidence: Evidence that cannot be presented to the fact-finder for any of a variety of reasons.

Incompetent Individual: A person deemed by a court to be incapable of making rational decisions or giving consent on one's own behalf.

Indemnity: A sum of money paid as compensation for a loss.

Independent Contractor: A person who contracts to do work for another person according to one's own processes and methods. Legal nurse consultants who work independently (not as employees) are independent contractors, as are testifying experts.

Independent Medical Examination (IME): An examination performed by a non-treating healthcare provider to offer an opinion regarding the nature, cause, and extent of a claimant's injury and to determine appropriateness of treatment, degree of disability, and ability to work.

Indictment: A formal accusation from a grand jury against a person for a criminal offense.

Individualized Education Program (IEP): A document developed for special needs children by the parents and educators who work with them. It is tailored to the student's specific needs and guides the delivery of education to that student. It is required in all public and private schools receiving public funds for the education of children with disabilities and is required before a child can receive special education.

Informed Consent: The process of disclosing the risks, benefits, and alternatives of a proposed treatment, procedure, clinical trial, etc. and obtaining the person's permission/agreement to proceed.

Inherent Risk: A known danger, complication, condition, or potential injury that is existent in and inseparable from the activity.

Institutional Review Board (IRB): An appropriately constituted group of individuals that approves, monitors, and reviews biomedical and behavioral research involving human subjects. It provides regulatory and ethical oversight.

Intensity of Service/Severity of Illness (IS/SI): A description of how sick a patient is and the level of healthcare services that patient requires.

Intentional Tort: A civil wrong that involves an intentional act, such as assault, battery, defamation, or false imprisonment.

Internal Standards: Expectations for professional practice that stem from internal, institutional sources such as policies and procedures, professional job descriptions, or internal educational materials. May contribute to defining the standard of care.

International Classification of Diseases (ICD): An international standard diagnostic tool for epidemiological, health management, and clinical purposes that is published by the World Health Organization. It is used to code and classify morbidity data.

Interrogatories: A set or series of written questions about a case submitted by one party to another party. Interrogatories answers are usually given under oath, i.e., the person answering the questions signs a sworn statement that the answers are true.

Involuntary Manslaughter: A death occurring during the commission of a non-felony, such as a death that occurs during reckless driving.

Issue Identification: As a legal nurse consultant standard, the process of identifying the matters, problems, or subjects that are relevant to the legal claim.

Item Writer: An individual with known expertise in a specialty practice who writes items (questions) to be considered for a certification examination in that specialty.

Jail: A correctional facility maintained and run by a local municipality (city or town) or a county.

Joint Petition for Final Settlement: In Workers' Compensation, a type of settlement in which the claimant and carrier both agree to the settlement of a case in which a claim was denied or there is a dispute over the benefits.

Judgment: A decision by a court or other tribunal that fully resolves a controversy and determines the rights and obligations of the parties.

Judgment as a Matter of Law: See Directed Verdict.

Junk Science: Untested or unproven theories that are presented as scientific fact.

Jurisdiction: The practical authority granted to a legal body to administer justice within a defined field of responsibility.

Jury: A body of people sworn to give a verdict in a legal case based on evidence submitted to them in court.

Jury Ballot: A ballot or verdict form given to a jury to document its conclusions and verdict.

Jury Consultant: A consultant working with a legal team during jury selection, during trial, and, sometimes, post-trial to aid in the selection of jurors and to maximize the effectiveness of the case presentation.

Jury Focus Group: A focus group gathered in preparation for trial to help a legal team determine case value, develop case themes, identify information to emphasize or avoid, learn which arguments are accepted and persuasive, understand "public" attitudes, etc.

Jury Instructions: The set of rules given by a trial judge to the jury about the relevant laws that should guide its deliberations. Also referred to as the judge's charge to the jury.

Jury Interviews: Post-trial interviews with individual jurors that are conducted to learn how and why the verdict was reached.

Jury Trial: A trial in which a case is presented to a jury, who determines the factual questions and renders a decision.

Kennedy-Kassebaum Act: Another name for the Health Insurance Portability and Accountability Act.

Kinematics: The branch of mechanical engineering that analyzes motion.

Laser Log: A log of information (such as date, time, patient, laser operator, and name of person monitoring and setting the laser mode) maintained for each laser machine in a medical facility.

Latency: The interval between exposure to a carcinogen and the appearance of disease signs and symptoms.

Lay Witness: Any witness who does not testify as an expert witness.

Legal Guardian: See Guardian.

Legal Nurse Consultant (LNC): A registered nurse who specializes in analyzing clinically related issues in legal matters.

Legal Nurse Consultant Certified (LNCC®): A board-certified legal nurse consultant. The credential bestowed upon a legal nurse consultant by the American Legal Nurse Consultant Certification Board upon (1) meeting the eligibility criteria to sit for the certification examination and (2) passing the certification examination.

Legal Nurse Consulting: Involves (1) the application of knowledge acquired during the course of professional nursing education, training, and clinical experience to the evaluation of standard of care, causation, damages and other clinically related issues in cases or claims; (2) the application of additional knowledge acquired through education and experience regarding applicable legal standards and/or strategy to the evaluation of cases or claims; (3) critical analysis of healthcare records and medical literature, as well as relevant legal documents and other information pertinent to the evaluation and resolution of cases or claims; and (4) the development of case-specific work products and opinions for use by legal professionals or agencies handling cases or claims.

Legal Team: A group of individuals employed or hired by an attorney to support a legal matter.

Liability: Any legally enforceable obligation or responsibility.

Liability Medicare Set-Aside Arrangement (LMSA): A Medicare Set-Aside arrangement prepared in conjunction with the settlement, judgment, award or other insurance payment in a manner appropriate for liability-based insurances.

Lien: A right or claim against an asset.

Life Care Plan: A dynamic document based upon published standards of practice, comprehensive assessment, data, analysis, and research that provides an organized, concise plan for current and future needs with associated costs for individuals who have experienced catastrophic illnesses/injuries or have chronic healthcare needs.

Life Care Planner: A registered nurse or other qualified professional, such as an occupational therapist or vocational rehabilitation specialist, who provides opinions regarding future needs and associated costs for individuals with major chronic conditions and or catastrophic injuries.

Life Expectancy Expert: A type of damages expert who may be used in wrongful death cases to calculate and opine on future lost wages based upon how long the decedent likely would have lived and worked. They may also be used in cases involving brain-damaged children to opine on the child's likely life expectancy, which is then used to calculate future medical expenses.

Litigation: The process of taking legal action in court to enforce a right or seek a remedy.

Living Will: A document, signed with formalities statutorily required for a will, by which a person directs that one's life not be artificially prolonged by extraordinary measures when there is no reasonable expectation of recovery from extreme physical or mental disability.

Loss: In insurance, an injury or damage sustained by the insured as a result of an incident that is covered under the insurance policy.

Loss of Chance: A theory of recovery in medical malpractice cases for a patient's loss of chance of survival or loss of chance of a better recovery.

Loss of Consortium: A claim brought by the spouse of an injured party for the loss of the benefits of companionship caused by the injuries suffered in the accident.

Loss of Future Earnings: Permanent loss of one's ability to earn wages.

Lost Wages: Economic loss due to the inability to be gainfully employed as the result of physical or mental injury.

Lump-sum Commutation Settlement: A Workers' Compensation settlement in which the beneficiary accepts a lump-sum payment in compensation for all future medical expenses and disability benefits stemming from a work-related injury or disease.

Lump-sum Compromise Settlement: A Workers' Compensation settlement, entered when compensability is contested, that provides less in total compensation than the full claim value.

Malicious Prosecution: An intentional tort in which a plaintiff knowingly, wrongfully, and with malicious intent instituted and pursued a criminal or civil proceeding for an improper purpose and without probable cause.

Malpractice: Misconduct, negligence, or failure to properly perform duties according to professional standards of care.

Managed Care: A healthcare delivery system designed to manage costs, utilization, and quality.

Mandatory Insurer Reporting: Pursuant to Section 111 of the Medicare, Medicaid, and State Children's Health Insurance Program Extension Act of 2007, the mandatory requirement that all group health plans, liability insurance plans, self-insureds, no-fault insurance plans, and worker's compensation insurance carriers report any settlements, judgments, awards, or other payments made to Medicare beneficiaries.

Manufacturer and User Facility Device Experience (MAUDE) database: A database that houses medical device reports submitted to the Food and Drug Administration by mandatory reporters (manufacturers, importers and device user facilities) and voluntary reporters (healthcare professionals, patients, and consumers).

Manufacturer Defect: In the law of products liability, a defect in a product that was not intended.

Market Analysis: A phase of marketing research conducted to determine the characteristics and extent of a market.

Mass Tort: A civil wrong that injures many people. Examples include toxic emissions from a factory and the crash of a commercial airliner.

Material Risk: A significant potential for harm that a reasonable person would want to consider when making a decision about undergoing a medical or surgical treatment.

Material Safety Data Sheet (MSDS): See Safety Data Sheet.

Maximum Medical Improvement (MMI): A state in which an injured person reaches a treatment plateau or a point at which the medical condition cannot be improved any further.

Mechanism of Injury (MOI): The way in which an injury was sustained.

Mediation: An alternative dispute resolution process involving a neutral third party who facilitates the parties in trying to reach a resolution but lacks authority to render a decision.

Medical Device Reporting (MDR): A postmarket surveillance tool used by the Food and Drug Administration to monitor medical device performance, detect potential device-related safety issues, and contribute to benefit-risk assessments of these products. The information comes from mandatory reporters (manufacturers, device user facilities, and importers) and voluntary reporters (e.g., healthcare professionals, patients, caregivers, and consumers).

Medical Malpractice: The failure of a healthcare professional to act as a reasonably prudent similar healthcare professional would have under similar circumstances. This umbrella term is often used to refer to the malpractice of any healthcare professional, including nurses.

Medical Parole: A parole granted on humanitarian or medical grounds to an inmate who has a terminal medical condition from which the person is not expected to survive.

Medical Power of Attorney: A legal document established by a competent individual who identifies another person to make decisions regarding the individual's health care, should the individual become unable to make one's own decisions.

Medical Review Panel: A panel of healthcare professionals that reviews the merits of a claim.

Medicare, Medicaid, and State Children's Health Insurance Program Extension Act of 2007 (MMSEA): A law that mandates insurers to identify and report claims that involve Medicare beneficiaries.

Medicare Part C (Medicare Advantage Plan): A healthcare benefits plan that is an alternative to Medicare Parts A and B and is provided by private sector health insurance companies under contract with the Centers for Medicare & Medicaid Services.

Medicare Recovery: The process by which Medicare recovers (gets repaid) for any conditional payments.

Medicare Secondary Payer Act (MSP): Legislation that requires Medicare to be the secondary payer to any healthcare plan, insurance policy, Workers' Compensation plan, or liability settlement and provides for reimbursement mechanisms should payments be made conditionally.

Medicare Set-Aside: An account funded by settlement proceeds for future medical care and expenses that would otherwise be covered by Medicare.

Med Watch: The Food and Drug Administration's safety and adverse event reporting program.

Memorandum of Understanding (MOU): A document of agreement between parties with a shared commitment. Depending on the wording, it may have the binding power of a contract.

Mens Rea: See Criminal Intent.

Mentally Incompetent Person: See Incompetent Individual.

Meta-Analysis: The analysis of data from many comparable research or epidemiological studies to arrive at a single figure to represent all of them.

Metadata: Data that provides information about other data.

Mini-Mental State Examination: A widely used written assessment that measures and evaluates cognitive function and mental impairment. Often given serially to gauge the effect of time on a patient's condition.

Mini-trial: A process in which parties present highly summarized versions of their respective cases to a neutral third party and representatives from each side who have the authority to settle the dispute. After the presentations, the representatives attempt to settle the dispute. If unsuccessful, the neutral third party may serve as a mediator or may issue a nonbinding opinion as to the likely outcome of the case in court.

Minimum Data Set (MDS): A national tool used in the long-term care setting to assess a resident's needs. It is also used to determine reimbursement from Medicare and other payers.

Minnesota Multiphasic Personality Inventory: A commonly used psychological test that includes over 500 statements for interpretation by the subject. It is used clinically for evaluating personality traits and detecting various mental health disorders in adults.

Misdemeanor: A crime that is less serious than a felony and is usually punishable by fine, penalty, forfeiture, or confinement (for less than one year) in a place other than prison.

Mitigating Factor: In criminal law, any information or evidence presented to the court regarding the defendant or the circumstances that might result in reduced charges or a lesser sentence. Also known as extenuating circumstances.

Mitigation of Damages: The process of taking actions or steps to avoid, reduce, or limit the damages resulting from an event.

Motion: A written or oral request to a court or judge to obtain a ruling or order directing some act be done in favor of the requesting party.

Motion in Limine: A pre-trial motion seeking a court order that prevents another party from introducing or referring to potentially irrelevant, prejudicial, or otherwise inadmissible evidence.

National Correct Coding Initiative (NCCI): A program of the Centers for Medicare & Medicaid Services designed to promote national correct coding methodologies and reduce improper coding.

National Institute for Occupational Safety and Health (NIOSH): One of three separate bodies created by the Occupational Safety and Health Act to administer the major requirements of the Act. The role of this agency is to conduct research, education, and training.

National Institutes of Health (NIH): The U.S. federal agency for medical research.

National Library of Medicine (NLM): The largest biomedical library in the world.

National Patient Safety Goals: One of the major methods by which The Joint Commission establishes standards for ensuring patient safety in all healthcare settings. They are reviewed and published annually.

Negligence: The failure to act as an ordinary prudent or reasonable person would do under similar circumstances.

Networking: The process of meeting and establishing a network of other like professionals to enhance information exchange and business relationships.

Never Events: Preventable, serious, and concerning events of such devastating consequences that they should never happen. Also known as Serious Reportable Events.

New Drug Application (NDA): The application submitted by the sponsor of a new drug when it believes that enough evidence on the drug's safety and effectiveness has been obtained to meet the Food and Drug Administration's requirements for marketing approval. The application is assigned a six-digit number.

No-Fault Insurance: An auto insurance system in which each party's own insurance covers the damages in a motor vehicle accident (up to the policy limits) regardless of which party is at fault.

Non-binding Arbitration: An arbitration in which the arbitrator issues a decision that is not binding upon the parties. No enforceable arbitration award is issued.

Noncompliance: Failure or refusal to comply with something such as a rule, regulation, plan of care, etc.

Non-economic Damages: See General Damages.

Non-party Witness: A witness who is not a party (plaintiff or defendant) to the lawsuit.

Notice of Election (NOE): A statement signed by an individual or representative expressing one's desire for end-of-life care.

Nursing Malpractice: See Medical Malpractice.

Nursing Practice Act: State laws governing nursing practice and, in some cases, nursing education.

Occupational Disease: A disease that is gradually contracted in the usual and ordinary course of employment and caused by employment.

Occupational Noise Exposure Standard: One of the standards developed by the Occupational Safety and Health Administration in order to protect workers from hearing impairment when there is significant noise exposure.

Occupational Safety and Health Act (OSH Act): Federal legislation enacted in 1970 requiring employers to provide safe and healthy working conditions for employees.

Occupational Safety and Health Administration (OSHA): One of three separate bodies created by the Occupational Safety and Health Act to administer the major requirements of the Act. The role of this agency is to set and enforce safety and health standards, provide training outreach and education, establish partnerships, and encourage continual process improvement in workplace safety and health.

Of Counsel: Attorneys who are associated with a firm but are not partners or firm employees.

Office for Civil Rights (OCR): A sub-agency of the U.S. Department of Education that is primarily focused on enforcing civil rights laws.

Ongoing Professional Practice Evaluation (OPPE): A term originated by The Joint Commission which describes its recommendations for peer review activities and strategies.

Open Records Act: State laws that provide public access to government documents.

Opening Statement: The statement made by the attorneys for each party at the start of the trial.

Optical Character Recognition (OCR): The method of converting scanned, typed documents into searchable text.

Outcome and Assessment Information Set (OASIS): Quality information collected from Medicare home healthcare patients and submitted regularly to fiscal intermediaries who analyze the data in order to implement quality initiatives and calculate Medicare payments for services.

Pain and Suffering Expert: A type of damages expert who is typically retained by the plaintiff and offers testimony to establish the presence of pain and suffering.

Paralegal: A person qualified by education, training, or work experience who is employed by an attorney to perform specifically delegated substantive legal work for which an attorney is responsible.

Partial Autopsy: An autopsy that evaluates only a specific area or part of the body.

Partners: Attorneys in a law firm who are more experienced in the practice of law. They may have voting rights regarding firm administration matters.

Party: In legal proceedings, one of the participants in the legal matter who has an interest in the outcome. In civil proceedings, the parties are the plaintiff(s) and defendant(s). In criminal proceedings, they are the state and defendant. In administrative proceedings, they are typically called the petitioner and respondent.

Patient Self-Determination Act (PSDA): Legislation that encourages individuals to decide now about the types and extent of medical care they want to accept or refuse if they become unable to make those decisions due to illness. The PSDA requires all healthcare agencies to provide information on advance directives and to recognize and abide by an individual's living will or durable power of attorney for health care.

Peer-review: A process used by professions for monitoring and regulating member practice.

Performance Evaluation: Evaluation of an individual's practice in relation to professional standards, relevant statutes and regulation, contractual agreement, or job description.

Permanent Partial Disability (PPD): A disability in which an injured worker is permanently prevented from working at full physical capability because of injury or illness and for which a monetary benefit is awarded.

Personal Health Information: See Protected Health Information.

Personal Injury (PI) Claims: Torts that involve negligent actions resulting in physical, psychological, or economic harm to the injured party.

Personal Injury Protection (PIP): Coverage by the insured's own auto insurance carrier for medical expenses. Coverage is dictated by state auto law and the amount of coverage purchased.

Personal Protective Equipment Standard: One of the standards developed by the Occupational Safety and Health Administration to provide information on the types of protection available for employees where engineering and administrative controls are not available.

Petition: A formal written application requesting a right or benefit from an individual or group in authority; or seeking a court's intervention and action on a matter.

Petitioner: The person who filed a petition (complaint) with a professional licensing board against a healthcare provider or facility.

Physical Evidence: See Real Evidence.

Plaintiff: A person or entity who brings a legal action against another.

Pleading: A legal document that has four functions: (1) to give notice of the claim or defense; (2) to reveal the facts of the case; (3) to formulate the issues that must be resolved; and (4) to screen the flow of cases into a court.

Point of Service (POS): An insurance plan that has some of the qualities of Health Maintenance Organization and Preferred Provider Organization plans with benefit levels varying depending on whether care is received in or out of the health insurance company's network of providers.

Portability: The ability to be easily carried or moved; or the ability of software to be transferred from one machine system to another.

Position Statement: Consensus statements providing the generally accepted opinions of a group.

Power of Attorney (POA): An written instrument whereby one person (the principal) appoints and confers authority to another (the agent) to perform certain specified acts or kinds of acts on behalf of the principal.

Practice Acts: The laws that govern the practice of a regulated healthcare profession in each state.

Practice Analysis: A study and analysis of the critical skills and concepts needed to be proficient in a specialty practice. It is a critical early step in creating a certification exam that accurately reflects the specialty practice and is used to create the exam blueprint.

Practice Development: In a law firm, the networking and advertising activities used to bring in new business and maintain current client relations.

Pre-empt: To act in order to prevent an anticipated event from happening.

Pre-emption: The rule of law that, if the federal government (through Congress) has enacted legislation on a subject matter, it shall be controlling over state laws and preclude the state from enacting laws on the same subject if Congress has specifically declared it has "occupied the field."

Pre-emptory Challenge: The right of the parties, during jury selection, to reject a prospective juror without stating a reason.

Preferred Provider Organization (PPO): A type of health plan in which members receive benefits at a discounted rate if they utilize only the providers who have a contract with the plan.

Prejudicial: Tending to favor a preconceived opinion.

Preliminary Hearing: In criminal cases, a hearing in court to determine whether there is enough evidence to require a trial.

Premises Liability: A legal concept in which an injury was caused by an unsafe or defective condition on someone's property.

Premium: The amount of money paid to an insurer in return for insurance coverage.

Preponderance of the Evidence: A standard of proof in civil cases that the weight of the evidence is more probable than not (i.e., just over 50% of the evidence favors the party).

Prescription Drug Monitoring Program (PDMP): An electronic database that tracks controlled substance prescriptions in a state.

Pre-trial Detainee: A defendant who is held prior to trial on criminal charges because no bail is posted or pre-trial release was denied.

Primary Payer: Any entity required or responsible to pay first for a medical item or service under a primary plan, including but not limited to insurers, self-insurers, and group health plans.

Prison: Correctional facilities maintained and run by a state or federal government to house those offenders who have been convicted of a crime and sentenced to a period of incarceration that generally exceeds one year.

Prison Litigation Reform Act (PLRA): A U.S. federal law designed to decrease litigation brought by prisoners to the court system.

Privacy Rule: Legislation that established federal standards for the protection of health information by healthcare providers and other entities. It applies to all medical records and patient-identifying information.

***Pro Se*:** A party who represents oneself in a court proceeding without the assistance of an attorney.

Probable Cause: The standard used to determine if a crime has been committed and if there is enough evidence to believe a specific individual committed it.

Product Liability: A legal concept holding a manufacturer responsible for the article placed on the market.

Professional Licensing Board: See Healthcare Provider Board.

Professional Negligence: The failure of a professional to act as a reasonably prudent similar professional would have under similar circumstances.

Prosector: An individual (in addition to the coroner or pathologist) involved in the dissection of corpses for examination or anatomical demonstration.

Protected Health Information (PHI): Any information about health status, provision of health care, or payment for health care that is created or collected by a covered entity (or its business associate) that can be linked to a specific individual. It is legally protected and, to preserve privacy, cannot be divulged.

Proximate Cause: The primary cause of an injury as determined by the foreseeability of the probability and severity of the harm; an action that produced foreseeable consequences.

Psychological Damages: Injury or damage to the psyche resulting in impairment.

Punitive Damages: See Exemplary Damages.

Qualified Individual with a Disability: A person who, with reasonable accommodation for a disability, can perform the essential functions of a job.

Quality Assurance: Ongoing program that objectively and systematically monitors and evaluates quality and resolves identified problems.

Quality Improvement: A systematic, formal approach to the analysis of practice performance and efforts to improve quality.

Rated Age: Estimated age representing an individual's diminished health.

Real Evidence: Physical, tangible evidence that consists of material items involved in a case. Also called physical evidence.

Reasonable Accommodation: The requirement under The Rehabilitation Act of 1973 that employers take reasonable steps to accommodate an individual with a disability unless it causes the employer undue hardship.

Reasonable Care: The degree of care that an ordinarily prudent and reasonable person would exercise under similar circumstances.

Rebuttal Witness: A witness who is called to testify to rebut testimony that has already been presented.

Recording and Reporting of Occupational Injuries and Illness Standard: One of the standards developed by the Occupational Safety and Health Administration in order to identify high hazard industries and permit employees to be aware of their employer's safety record.

Re-Cross-examination: The further examination of a witness by the opposing party after re-direct examination.

Re-Direct Examination: The further examination of a witness by the party who first called and questioned the witness. It follows cross-examination.

Regulatory Compliance: The process undertaken by organizations to conform with relevant federal and state laws, policies, and regulations.

Reinsurance Carrier: An insurance company that provides insurance for other insurance companies. It is a way by which a primary insurance company transfers or cedes some of the financial risk the company assumes to another insurance company, the reinsurer.

Relative Risk: In toxic tort, the incidence rate of a certain disease in the exposed group divided by the incidence rate in the unexposed group.

Reliable: In research, the ability to produce consistent results.

Reliance Materials: The information (e.g., medical records, medical literature, expert disclosures, testimony transcripts, etc.) upon which defendant healthcare professionals or expert witnesses depend upon in their decision-making or in the formation of their opinions, respectively.

Request for Production (RFP): A formal written request compelling a party to produce materials subject to discovery rules.

Res Ipsa Loquitur: Latin for "the thing speaks for itself"; a legal doctrine that permits an inference of negligence based on the very nature of the accident of injury.

Research-Based: Founded upon evidence gleaned from and supported by scientific research that is typically published in peer-reviewed journals.

Reserves: See Claim Reserves.

Resident Assessment Instrument (RAI): A process pathway mandated by the Centers for Medicare & Medicaid Services to strengthen the interdisciplinary nature of the long-term care/skilled nursing facility.

Resource-Based Relative Value Scale (RBRVS): A healthcare provider payment system that measures three aspects of a provider's service (work, practice, and malpractice expense).

Respondeat Superior: Latin for "let the superior make answer"; an employer's liability for an employee's wrongful actions within the scope of employment.

Respondent: The healthcare professional or facility against whom a petition (complaint) has been filed with a professional licensing board or other appropriate administrative agency.

Retainer: Money that is paid in advance of work to be completed. It ensures the commitment of the receiver.

Right to Refuse: The doctrine that a person, even if involuntarily committed to a hospital, cannot be forced to submit to any treatment against the person's free will unless a life-and-death emergency exists.

Risk: A chance of loss.

Risk Management: A process that identifies, evaluates, and takes corrective action against potential or actual risks to patients, visitors, employees, or property.

Risk-Utility Test: A test used in product liability cases to determine whether a manufacturer is liable for injury to a consumer because the risk of danger created by the product's design outweighs the benefits of the design.

Role Delineation Study: A document that describes those tasks critical for competent job performance by identifying the minimum amount of knowledge and skills required to perform job-related functions. Study results are used to develop certification examinations.

Root Cause Analysis (RCA): A structured investigation that aims to identify the true cause of an unanticipated problem or event and the actions necessary to prevent a recurrence.

Rules of Civil Procedure: See Federal Rules of Civil Procedure.

Rules of Evidence: See Federal Rules of Evidence.

Safe Harbor: A legal provision that specifies that certain conduct will be deemed not to violate a given rule. It serves to reduce or eliminate liability in certain situations if certain conditions are met.

Safety Data Sheet (SDS): Documentation provided by the manufacturer that provides valuable information about a chemical, including a brief summary about the hazards and personal protective equipment that must be used when working with the chemical. Formerly Material Safety Data Sheet.

Sanctions: The penalty for non-compliance with a law or legal order.

Scheduling Order: A court order giving all parties deadlines by which specific discovery (e.g., written discovery, party depositions, expert witness disclosure, expert witness depositions) must be completed.

Scope of Practice: Describes the services qualified health professionals are competent to perform and permitted to undertake, in keeping with the terms of their professional license.

Seat Belt Defense: A form of comparative negligence that seeks to limit or reduce damages based upon plaintiff's failure to use a seat belt.

Second-Degree Murder: Murder that is not aggravated by any of the circumstances of first-degree murder.

Secondary Payer: An insurance policy or plan, such as Medicare and Medicaid, that pays after any available primary payers.

Self-Insured: An employer that chooses to provide health, disability, and/or workers' compensation benefits to employees itself or an organization that chooses to fund its own liabilities/losses (in lieu of purchasing insurance from a private carrier).

Sentinel event: Any unanticipated event in a healthcare setting resulting in death or serious physical or psychological injury to a patient or patients, not related to the natural course of the patient's illness.

Serious Medical Need: One that has been diagnosed by a healthcare provider as requiring treatment or one so obvious that even a layperson would easily recognize the necessity of a healthcare provider's attention.

Settlement: The act of adjusting or determining the dealings or disputes between persons without pursing the matter through trial.

Settlement Brochures: Confidential submissions by each party to the mediator that emphasize that party's strengths and the opponent's weaknesses in the case.

Settlement Conference: A meeting between opposing sides of a lawsuit at which the parties attempt to reach a mutually agreeable resolution of their dispute without having to proceed to a trial.

Settlement Date: The date on which a final settlement amount is agreed on by all parties associated with a case.

Sick Building Syndrome: The term used to describe the cluster of symptoms found to occur in office environments, particularly in sealed buildings with centrally controlled mechanical ventilation.

Smoking Gun: A fact not previously noticed by counsel that serves as conclusive evidence that may or may not be in the client's favor.

Special Damages: See Economic Damages.

Spoliation of Evidence: The intentional withholding, hiding, altering, fabricating, or destroying evidence.

Standard of Care: The degree of care that a reasonably prudent person would exercise under the same or similar circumstances. In the case of a professional (e.g., nurse, doctor, attorney, realtor, accountant), it is the degree of care that a reasonably prudent person in that profession should exercise under the same or similar circumstances.

Standard of Care Expert: In medical malpractice cases, an expert witness who is typically a similar healthcare provider to the defendant who, upon review of the relevant records and information, offers an informed opinion on whether the defendant complied with or deviated from the standard of care.

Standards of Practice: Guidelines that provide the framework or parameters and expectations around the professional responsibilities required to practice in a given field.

Statement of Charges: A document that identifies the allegations against a healthcare provider or facility in an administrative action that constitute the grounds for disciplinary action. It is akin to a complaint in a civil lawsuit.

Statute: A written law passed by a legislative body, whether federal, state, county or city.

Statute of Limitations: The time period within which a prospective plaintiff may bring a cause of action following the event giving rise to a potential claim.

Statutory Law: The body of law derived from statutes rather than from constitutions or judicial decisions.

Statutory or Constitutional Claim: A person's assertion of a right or interest established by state statutes or the Constitution.

Strict Tort Liability: Liability based on the fact a defect existed at the time the product left the manufacturer, wholesaler, or retailer and the defect caused the injury.

Sua Sponte: Latin for "on one's own accord." For example, it may be used to describe when a court acts on its own, rather than at the request of one of the parties.

Subcontractor: One who has entered into a contract, express or implied, for the performance of an act with the person who has already contracted for its performance.

Subject Matter Expert: An individual with knowledge, experience, and training in an area of practice, giving that individual the ability to provide expertise in a certain subject/practice area.

Subpoena: A discovery tool that requires a witness or non-party to appear or produce documents. It has the force and effect of a court order. There are two types of subpoenas: subpoena *ad testificandum* and subpoena *duces tecum*.

Subpoena *ad testificandum*: A subpoena that requires a person to testify before a court or other legal authority.

Subpoena *duces tecum*: A subpoena that requires a person to produce documents, materials, or other tangible evidence.

Substantive: Relating to the essential legal principles administered by the courts, as opposed to practice and procedure.

Substantive Evidence: Evidence that will prove a fact in a dispute.

Summary Judgment: A decision by the court, based on evidence presented by the defendant, that there is no genuine issue of material fact for a jury to consider. Therefore, the court dismisses the claim against the defendant as a matter of law.

Summons: A document that identifies the parties named in the suit, the court in which the case is venued, the type of suit (e.g., medical malpractice, product liability, etc.), and (depending on the jurisdiction) a date that triggers certain deadlines for the defendants, such as by when they must file an appearance and a pleading responsive to the complaint (e.g., an answer).

Sunshine Laws: Statutes that mandate that meetings of governmental agencies and departments be open to the public at large.

Supplemental Uninsured and Underinsured Motorist (SUM) Coverage: Automobile insurance one purchases to protect oneself if another driver causes an accident and does not have any insurance or enough insurance to compensate someone for their injuries.

Surrogate: A substitute; especially a person appointed to act in the place of another.

Surrogate Analysis: In biomechanics, the use of "crash dummies" to investigate mechanism of injury.

Temporary Total Disability (TTD): A disability in which an injured worker is temporarily prevented from working because of injury or illness and for which a monetary benefit is awarded.

Testifying Expert Witness: See Expert Witness.

Testimony: Spoken or written evidence by a competent witness under oath.

The Beck Anxiety Inventory: A commonly used psychological test that includes over 500 statements for interpretation by the subject, used clinically for evaluating personality and detecting various disorders in adults.

The Beck Depression Inventory: Standardized psychiatric questionnaire in which the subject rates statements on a sliding scale; used in the diagnosis of depression.

The Career Ability Placement Survey: An individualized norm-referenced measure of abilities related to various vocational fields.

The Halstead Category Test: A comprehensive suite of neuropsychological tests used to assess the condition and functioning of the brain, including etiology, type, localization and lateralization of brain injury.

The Joint Commission (TJC): An independent, not-for-profit organization, whose mission is to continuously improve the safety and quality of care provided to the public through the provision of healthcare accreditation and related services that support performance improvement in healthcare organizations.

The Supremacy Clause: A clause within Article VI of the U.S. Constitution which dictates that federal law is the "supreme law of the land." This means that judges in every state must follow the Constitution, laws, and treaties of the federal government in matters which are directly or indirectly within the government's control.

Third Party: A person or group besides the two primarily involved in a situation.

Third-party Administrator (TPA): A person or company hired to oversee and resolve claims and actions. Third-party administrators, known as TPAs, are often utilized by large self-insured companies, such as health maintenance organizations or large healthcare conglomerates, to handle claims against the company.

Third-party Claim: A claim made by someone who is not the policyholder (first party) or the insurance company (second party). The most common type of third-party insurance claim is a liability claim.

Third-party Counterclaim: A separate cause of action which a defendant asserts against a third person or party.

Tickler System: A computerized reminder system used to monitor deadlines and follow-up on tasks (such as medical record requests).

Timeline: A display of a list of events in chronological order.

Time-Weighted Average (TWA): Averages the levels and duration of exposure over a work shift to give an equivalent eight-hour exposure.

Tort: A civil wrong or injury other than breach of contract.

Tort of Negligence: A tort committed by failure to act as a reasonable person to someone to whom a duty is owed, as required by law under the circumstances. Negligent torts are not deliberate, and there must be an injury resulting from the breach of the duty. The plaintiff must establish all four elements of proof (duty, breach of duty, causation, damages) to prevail in the negligence claim.

Toxic Tort: A civil wrong arising from exposure to a toxic substance, such as asbestos, radiation, or hazardous waste. A toxic tort can be remedied by a civil lawsuit (usually a class action) or by administrative action.

Trial Consultant: A consultant employed or hired to assist with trial preparation, typically through the preparation of witnesses and parties for testifying at trial. Trial consultants may also assist in jury selection through the creation of a profile of desirable jurors.

Trial Simulations: An imitation trial, such as a mock trial.

Trier of Fact: See Fact-Finder.

Umbrella (Insurance) Coverage: A type of Excess (Insurance) Coverage that broadens coverage for liabilities the underlying policy might not cover.

Unbundling: Breaking a single service into its multiple components to increase total billing charges.

Uniform Commercial Code: A set of laws that provide legal rules and regulations governing commercial or business dealings and transactions.

Unintentional Tort: An unintended event or accident that results in injury or loss.

Universal Protocol: The critical component of every operation or procedure; the purpose is to promote patient safety by preventing wrong site, wrong procedure, and wrong person surgery.

Upcoding: The process of assigning a code that represents a more complex or involved service than provided and thus receives a higher reimbursement.

Usual, Customary, and Reasonable (UCR): The charges for medical services that are typical for that provider, similar to those of like providers in the same area, and justifiable given the specifics of the patient or circumstance. These UCR charges are used by payers in the health insurance industry to define the specific allowance for a particular healthcare service.

Utilization Guidelines: Companion guidelines to the Resident Assessment Instrument in a long-term care facility or skilled nursing facility.

Utilization Management: A method employed by the insurance and managed care industry to track and manage the use of medical benefits by covered beneficiaries.

Utilization Review: A process of evaluation of health care based on medical necessity and appropriateness. Utilization Review can include pre-admission review, concurrent review, discharge planning, and retrospective review.

Validity: In research, the ability to accurately measure results.

Venue: Denotes the county in which an action or prosecution is brought for trial, and which is to furnish the panel of jurors.

Verdict: A decision on a disputed issue in a civil or criminal case. The decision is rendered by the jury in a jury trial or by a judge in a bench trial.

Vicarious Liability: Tort doctrine that imposes responsibility upon one person for the failure of another, with whom the person has a special relationship (such as parent and child, employer and employee, or owner of vehicle and driver), to exercise such care as a reasonably prudent person would use under similar circumstances.

Violation of Civil Rights: Cause of action in a case claiming that personal rights guaranteed and protected by the U.S. Constitution and federal laws were violated by the defendant leading to injury or harm to the plaintiff.

Violation of Disability Rights: Cause of action in a case claiming the defendant's failure to comply with the provisions of the American with Disabilities Act of 1990 led to discrimination and injury to the plaintiff with a disability.

Violation of Resident Rights: Cause of action in nursing home/long-term care cases claiming the resident's rights and protections under state and federal were violated by the defendant leading to abuse, neglect, and injury of the plaintiff.

Vocational Benefits: The benefits under the Workers' Compensation program that assist eligible individuals with disabilities to prepare for, obtain, and/or maintain employment.

Vocational Expert: A type of damages expert who offers opinions on vocational rehabilitation, earning capacity, lost earnings, and cost of replacement labor.

Vocational Rehabilitation Specialist: A professional that provides guidance and counseling regarding assessment of work capabilities, aptitudes, and job placement, particularly for individuals with disabilities and impairments.

***Voir Dire*:** The questioning of prospective jurors by a judge, the parties, and/or attorneys in court. *Voir dire* is a tool used to achieve the constitutional right to an impartial jury, but it is not a constitutional right in itself.

Volatile Organic Compound (VOC): Any number of compounds based on the benzene ring, associated with increased risk of leukemia and lymphoma.

Voluntary Manslaughter: A criminal act that occurs when a person kills without premeditation and after serious provocation. The act takes place when there has been adequate action that causes an ordinarily reasonable person to lose control and commit the crime in passion.

Waiting Period: In Workers' Compensation, the time period immediately following an injury during which compensation is not allowed.

Watch Dog Groups: Usually non-profit groups that view their role as critically monitoring the activities of governments, industry, or other organizations and alerting the public when they detect actions that go against the public interest.

Weight of the Evidence Analysis: In toxic tort, analysis of data from different scientific fields, primarily animal tests and epidemiological studies, to assess carcinogenic risks.

Whistleblower: An employee who reports an employer wrongdoing to a government or law enforcement agency.

White Collar Crime: Non-violent crimes involving antitrust violations, computer/Internet fraud, credit card fraud, phone/telemarketing fraud, bankruptcy fraud, healthcare fraud, environmental law violations, insurance fraud, mail fraud, government fraud, tax evasion, financial fraud, securities fraud, insider trading, bribery, kickbacks, counterfeiting, public corruption, money laundering, embezzlement, economic espionage, and trade secret theft, and other forms of dishonest business schemes.

Witness: One who is called on to be present at a transaction to be able to testify to its occurrence.

Work Product: The writings (e.g., notes; memoranda; reports on conversations with a client, witness, or expert; research; and confidential materials) which an attorney or individual at the request of the attorney has developed during a case.

Workers' Compensation: A federal and state mandated insurance program that provides medical care and wage loss replacement for workers injured on the job.

Workers' Compensation Carrier: An insurance carrier authorized to write workers' compensation insurance under state or federal law.

Workers' Compensation Medicare Set-Aside Arrangement (WCMSA): A financial agreement that allocates a portion of a worker's compensation settlement to pay for future medical services related to the worker's injury, illness, or disease. These funds must be depleted before Medicare will pay for treatment related to the worker's injury, illness, or disease.

Wrongful Birth: A legal action in which someone is sued by the parents or guardian of a severely disabled child, alleging that negligent treatment or advice deprived them of the opportunity to avoid conception or terminate the pregnancy.

Wrongful Death: A legal theory argued on behalf of a deceased person's beneficiaries that alleges the person's death was attributable to the willful or negligent act of another.

Wrongful Termination: A situation in which an employee has been terminated from a job, and the termination breaches terms of the employment contract or is otherwise not in accordance with state or federal employment laws.

Acronyms, Abbreviations, and Commonly Used Legal Symbols

Noreen Sisko, PhD, RN

AAA	American Arbitration Association
AALNC	American Association of Legal Nurse Consultants
AANLCP	American Association of Nurse Life Care Planners
AAPLCP	American Academy of Physician Life Care Planners
AAR	Association of American Railroads
AARN	American Association of Rehabilitation Nurses
ABA	American Bar Association
ABMS	American Board of Medical Specialties
ABNS	American Board of Nursing Specialties
ABOHN	American Board for Occupational Health Nurses
ABSNC	Accreditation Board of Specialty Nursing Certification
ACA	Affordable Care Act
ACA	American Chiropractic Association
ADR	Alternative Dispute Resolution
AERA	American Educational Research Association
AHIMA	American Health Information Management Association
AHRQ	Agency for Healthcare Research and Quality
ALF	Assisted Living Facility
ALJ	Administrative Law Judge
ALNCCB®	American Legal Nurse Consultant Certification Board
AME	Agreed Medical Exam
ANCC	American Nurses Credentialing Center
AOB	Alcohol on breath
AOM	Affidavit of Merit
APA	American Psychological Association
APS	Adult Protective Services
ASHRM	American Society for Healthcare Risk Management
ATD	Anthropomorphic Test Devices

ATSDR	Agency for Toxic Substances and Disease Registry
AWP	Average Wholesale Price
BAA	Business Associate Agreement
BAI	Beck Anxiety Inventory
BAP1	BRCA Associated Protein 1
BCRC	Benefits Coordination and Recovery Center
BDI	Beck Depression Inventory
BLS	Bureau of Labor Statistics
BRCA	Breast cancer susceptibility gene
CAA	Care Area Assessment
CAC	Children's Advocacy Center
CACI	California Civil Jury Instructions
CAH	Critical Assess Hospital
CCM	Certified Case Manager
CDC	Centers for Disease Control and Prevention
CDRH	Center for Devices and Radiological Health
CFR	Code of Federal Regulations
CHDR	Center for Health Dispute Resolution
CLCP	Certified Life Care Planner
CME	Compulsory Medical Examination
CMS	Centers for Medicare & Medicaid Services
CMSA	Case Management Society of America
CNLCP®	Certified Nurse Life Care Planner
CO	Corrections Officer
CODIS	Combined DNA Indexing System
COHN or	
COHN-S	Certified Occupational Health Nurse (Specialist)
COM	Certificate of Merit
CoPs	Conditions of Participation
CPG	Clinical Practice Guidelines
CPLCP	Certified Physician Life Care Planner
CPT	Current Procedural Terminology
CRC	Certified Rehabilitation Counselor
CTI	Certification of Terminal Illness
DART	Days Away, Restricted or Transferred (OSHA metric)
DHHS	Department of Health and Human Services
DICOM	Digital Imaging and Communications in Medicine
DIRLINE	Directory of Information Resources Online
DMC	Decision-making capacity
DME	Durable Medical Equipment
DME	Defense Medical Examination
DOC	Department of Corrections
DOJ	Department of Justice
DOL	Department of Labor
DOT	Department of Transportation
DPH	Department of Public Health
DPOA	Durable Power of Attorney

DPOAHC	Durable Power of Attorney for Health Care
DRG	Diagnosis-Related Group
DRI	Defense Research Institute
DUI-E	Driving Under the Influence of Electronics
DUR	Drug Utilization Review
DV	Domestic Violence
DVERT	Domestic Violence Emergency Response Team
EBP	Evidence-Based Practice
EBT	Examination Before Trial
e-DUI	Driving Under the Influence of Electronics
EEOC	Equal Employment Opportunity Commission
e-filing	Electronic filing
EFM	Electronic Fetal Monitoring
EHR	Electronic Health Record
EIN	Equipment Identification Number
EME	Expert Medical Examination
EMTALA	Emergency Medical Treatment and Active Labor Act
e-PHI	Electronic Protected Health Information
EPO	Exclusive Provider Organization
ERISA	Employee Retirement Income Security Act
ESI	Emergency Severity Index
ESI	Electronically stored information
FAA	Federal Arbitration Act
FCA	False Claims Act
FCE	Functional Capacity Evaluation
FELA	Federal Employer's Liability Act
FERPA	Family Educational Rights and Privacy Act
FOIA	Freedom of Information Act
FRA	Federal Railroad Administration
FRCP	Federal Rules of Civil Procedure
FRE	Federal Rules of Evidence
GSW	Gunshot wound
HHS	Health and Human Services
HICN	Health Insurance Claim Number
HIM	Health Information Management
HIPAA	Health Insurance Portability and Accountability Act
HITECH	Health Information Technology for Economic and Clinical Health
IAFN	International Association of Forensic Nurses
IALCP	International Academy of Life Care Planners
IARP	International Association of Rehabilitation Professionals
ICD	International Classification of Diseases
ICDR	International Centre for Dispute Resolution
IDEA	Individuals with Disabilities Education Act
IEP	Individualized Education Program
IME	Independent Medical Examination
IMR	Independent Medical Review
IOM	Institute of Medicine

IRB	Institutional Review Board
ISMP	Institute for Safe Medication Practices
JLNC	Journal of Legal Nurse Consulting
JMOL	Judgment as a Matter of Law
KOP	Keep on person
LCP	Life Care Plan
LE	Life Expectancy
LNCC®	Legal Nurse Consultant Certified
LTAC	Long-Term Acute Care
LTC	Long-Term Care
LW	Living Will
MA	Medicare Advantage
MAA	Maximum Allowable Amount
MAUDE	Manufacturer and User Facility Device Experience
MBI	Minimum Background Investigation
MCO	Managed Care Organization
MDR	Medical Device Reporting
MDS	Minimum Data Set
MEC	Medical Executive Committee
MEDLARS	Medical Literature Analysis and Retrieval System
MedPAC	Medicare Payment Advisory Commission
MeSH	Medical Subject Headings
MMI	Maximum Medical Improvement
MMPI	Minnesota Multiphasic Personality Inventory
MMSE	Mini-Mental State Examination
MOI	Mechanism of Injury
MOU	Memorandum of Understanding
MPOA	Medical Power of Attorney
MSA	Medicare Set-Asides
MSDS	Material Safety Data Sheets
MSJ	Motion for Summary Judgment
MSP	Medicare Secondary Payer
MUE	Medically Unlikely Edits
NACOSH	National Advisory Committee on Occupational Safety and Health
NCBI	National Center for Biotechnology Information
NCCHC	National Commission on Correctional Health Care
NCLB	No Child Left Behind (Act)
NCQA	National Committee for Quality Assurance
NDC	National Drug Code
NIOSH	National Institute for Occupational Safety and Health
NLM	National Library of Medicine
NNLM	National Network of Libraries of Medicine
NOA	Nursing Organizations Alliance
NOE	Notice of Election
NORA	National Occupational Research Agenda
NORS	National Ombudsman Reporting System
NPA	Nurse Practice Act

NPDB	National Practitioner Data Bank
NPI	National Provider Identifier
NPSG	National Patient Safety Goals
NPUAP	National Pressure Ulcer Advisory Panel
OASIS	Outcome and Assessment Information Set
OBRA	Omnibus Budget Reconciliation Act
OCR	Office for Civil Rights
OCR	Optical Character Recognition
OEHN	Occupational and Environmental Health Nursing
OIG-HHS	Office of Inspector General—U.S. Department of Health and Human Services
OIR	Office of In Vitro Diagnostics and Radiological Health
ONC	Office of the National Coordinator for Health Information Technology
OPIM	Other potentially infectious materials
OPPE	Ongoing Professional Practice Evaluation
ORM	Ongoing Responsibility for Medicals
OSHA	Occupational Safety and Health Administration
OSHRC	Occupational Safety and Health Review Commission
P and P	Policies and procedures
PAH	Polycyclic Aromatic Hydrocarbons
PCF	Patient Compensation Fund
PDF	Portable Document Format
PDMP	Prescription Drug Monitoring Program
PEL	Permissible Exposure Limit
PHI	Protected Health Information
PHMSA	Pipeline and Hazardous Materials Safety Administration
PI	Personal Injury
PIP	Personal Injury Protection
PL	Product Liability
PLRA	Prison Litigation Reform Act
PMA	Pre-market Approval
PME	Plaintiff Medical Exam
PMID	PubMed Identifier
POA	Power of Attorney
POD	Physician-Owned Distributorships
POS	Point of Service Plan
PPACA	Patient Protection and Affordable Care Act
PPO	Preferred Provider Organization
PSDA	Patient Self-Determination Act
PSES	Patient Safety Evaluation Systems
PSO	Patient Safety Organizations
QA	Quality Assurance
QI	Quality Improvement
QIS	Quality Indicator Survey
QME	Qualified Medical Evaluators
RAI	Resident Assessment Instrument
RCA	Root Cause Analysis
RFA	Request for Admission

RFP	Request for Production
RM	Risk Management
RTS	Revised Trauma Scale
RUG	Resource Utilization Group
RUP	Restricted use pesticides
SAFE	Sexual Assault Forensic Examiner
SANE	Sexual Assault Nurse Examiner
SART	Sexual Assault Response Team
SBA	Small Business Administration
SCHIP	State Children's Health Insurance Program
SCORE	Service Corps of Retired Executives
SDS	Safety Data Sheet
SLC	Safety Labeling Changes
SOC	Standard of Care
SOL	Statute of Limitations
SOM	State Operations Manual
SSA	Social Security Administration
SUM	Supplementary Uninsured/Underinsured Motorist Coverage
TAANA	The American Association of Nurse Attorneys
TAR	Treatment Administration Record
TCE	Trichloroethylene
TE	Testifying Expert
TJC	The Joint Commission
TPA	Third-Party Administrator
TPOC	Total Payment Obligation to Claimant
TWA	Time-Weighted Average
UCC	Uniform Commercial Code
UCR	Usual, Customary, and Reasonable
ULC	Uniform Law Commission
UM	Uninsured Motorist (coverage)
USDOJ	United States Department of Justice
USP	United States Pharmacopeia
VBOP	Verified Bill of Particulars
VIS	Vaccine Information Statement
VOC	Volatile Organic Compound
WC	Workers' Compensation
WCMSA	Workers' Compensation Medicare Set-Aside
WCMSAP	Workers' Compensation Medicare Set-Aside Portal
WCRC	Workers' Compensation Review Contractor
WPS	Worker Protection Standard

Commonly Used Legal Symbols

Defendant	Δ (delta)
Paragraph	¶ (pilcrow)
Plaintiff	π or Π (pi)
Section or Sections	§ or §§

Index

Page numbers in **bold** refer to tables and those in *italic* denote figures

American Society for Health Care Risk Management (ASHRM) 535
Americans with Disabilities Act (ADA) 1990 445–6
animals 269
Anti-Kickback Statute 632
apology laws 911–12
apparent agency 79
arbitration *see* alternative dispute resolution
attorneys 692, 697, 698; communication with expert witnesses 753–4
audit trails 219–20

B

Balanced Budget Act 1997 (BBA '97) 281
bill review 677–86; abusive or fraudulent bill practices, identification of 681–3; appropriateness of procedural codes 680–1; communication 679; health care claims analysis 678–9; medically unlikely edits (MUE) 681; methodology 679–83; resources 684; test questions 686; usual, customary, and reasonable charges (UCR) 680
Burden of proof 65, 77, 257, 923–4

C

case law: *Aetna Health, Inc. v. Davila 542*, 505–6; *Avret v. McCormick* 849; *Ayers v. Jackson Township* 323; *Baer v. Connecticut Board of Examiners in Podiatry* 616; *Barclay v. Campbell* 471; *Belin v. Dingle* 478; *Bell v. Wolfish* 405; *Buckman Co. v. Plaintiffs' Legal Comm.* 300; *Canterbury v. Spence* 477; *Daubert v. Merrell Dow Pharmaceuticals, Inc.* 555, 638, 739, 825–6, 851, 852, 875, 928; *Estelle v. Gamble* 404, 406; *Farmer v. Brennan* 407; *Fosmire v. Nicoleau* 472; *Frye v. United States* 739, 825–6, 851, 928; *Geier v. American Honda Motor, Inc.* 300; *General Electric Co. v. Joiner* 555, 852; *Hickman v. Taylor* 107; *Jones v. CSX Transp., Inc.* 325; *Kindred Nursing Centers L.P. v. Clark* 913; *Kumho Tire Co. v. Carmichael* 555, 638, 852, 875; *Liu v. Boehringer Ingelheim Pharmaceuticals, Inc.* 305–6; *Majorana v. Crown Cent. Petroleum Corp.* 80; *Maloney v. Wake Hospital Systems* 849; *Marmet Health Care Center, Inc. v. Brown* 913; *Martinez v. Pinard* 144; *McCourt v. Abernathy* 234–5; *Miller v. Holtz House of Vehicles* 144; *Monell v. Department of Social Services* 409; *Norfolk & Western R. Co.* 325; *Parham v. J.R.* 472; *Plowman v. Fort Madison Community Hospital* 78; *Potter v. Firestone and Rubber Company* 323–4; *Qintero v. Encarnacion* 475; *Riegel v. Medtronic, Inc.* 299; *Santana v. Johnson* 144; *Schloendorff v. New York Hospital* 475; *Sullivan v. Edward Hospital* 740, 849; *Upjohn Co. v. U.S.* 107; *Wilson v. Seiter* 407
causation 93–6, 243–4; causation experts 265, 852–3; in personal injury 260; in toxic tort 326–8; in workers' compensation 351, 352
certificate of merit *see* affidavit of merit
certification 5, 10, 18–28, 823; ABNS Value of Certification Study 27–8; certification versus certificate programs 17, **17**; determining what to test 23–4, **23**, **25**; developing test items 24; eligibility requirements and recertification 26; and expert witnesses 855–6; future trends 28; history of the LNCC® 19; initial accreditation of the LNCC® exam 19; Legal Nurse Consultant Certified (LNCC®) credential 5, 8, 17, 33, 35–7; life care planning 556–7; LNCC® exam 22–6; LNCC® practice test 22; medical records 204; in a nursing speciality 18; overview of the LNCC® program 18–19; protecting the value of LNCC® 26–7; reaccreditation 22; research 26–7; setting the LNCC® apart through accreditation 19; standards 19, **20–1**; test questions 31; validating test items 24; working with the testing company 22–3
Certification in Legal Nurse Consulting (ALNCCB®) 10, 22, 35–7
children 380–1, 449, 473, 476; medical treatment decisions 493–6
Civil False Claims Act 631
Civil Monetary Penalties Law 632–3
civil rights *see* correctional healthcare and civil rights
Civil Rights Act 1964 435, 444
Code of Ethics and Conduct with Interpretive Discussion (AALNC) 9, 41, 43, 44, 49–50, 715
Code of Federal Regulations (CFR) 281, 465, 474, 586, 616
collateral estoppel 82
communication 15, 54, 238; with attorneys' clients in medical malpractice 799–807; barriers to 800–1; body language 801; defendant interview 803–4; definition of 800; discovery 805; with expert witnesses 861–4; initial interview 802–3; in the legal arena 801–2; legal issues 804–6; LNC-client communication process 836–7; mediation 805; plaintiff interview 803; test questions 807; trial 805–6
comparative and contributory negligence 81, 244–5, 258–9, 923–4
compensation *see* damages; workers' compensation case evaluation
confidentiality 44, 49, 66–7, 107, 733; adolescents' rights 495; business associates and the Security Rule 223–4; electronic medical records (EMR) 222–5; employment law and health and safety